CANADIAN
POLITICS

CRITICAL APPROACHES

EIGHTH EDITION

C A N A D I A N
POLITICS

CRITICAL APPROACHES

CHRISTOPHER COCHRANE
UNIVERSITY OF TORONTO

KELLY BLIDOOK
MEMORIAL UNIVERSITY

RAND DYCK
CARLETON UNIVERSITY

NELSON
EDUCATION

NELSON
EDUCATION

Canadian Politics: Critical Approaches, Eighth Edition

by Christopher Cochrane, Kelly Blidook, and Rand Dyck

VP, Product and Partnership Solutions:
Anne Williams

Managing Editor, Content Development, and Acquisitions Editor:
Mark Grzeskowiak

Marketing Manager:
Terry Fedorkiw

Content Development Manager:
Jessica Freedman

Photo and Permissions Researcher:
Natalie Barrington

Production Project Managers:
Lila Campbell and Christine Gilbert

Production Service:
Cenveo Publisher Services

Copy Editor:
Jessie Coffey

Proofreader:
Manikandan. N

Indexer:
BIM Creatives, LLC

Design Director:
Ken Phipps

Managing Designer:
Franca Amore

Interior Design:
Trinh Truong

Cover Design:
Trinh Truong

Cover Image:
Naibank/Getty Images

Compositor:
Cenveo Publisher Services

Library and Archives Canada Cataloguing in Publication

Dyck, Rand, 1943–, author

Canadian politics: critical approaches/ Christopher Cochrane (University of Toronto), Kelly Blidook (Memorial University), Rand Dyck. — Eighth edition.

Revision of: Dyck, Rand, 1943–. Canadian politics. Includes bibliographical references and index. ISBN 978-0-17-658295-1 (paperback)

1. Canada—Politics and government—Textbooks. I. Cochrane, Christopher, author II. Blidook, Kelly, 1975–, author III. Title.

JL75.D93 2016   320.971
C2016-900362-0

ISBN-13: 978-0-17-658295-1
ISBN-10: 0-17-658295-9

To
Christine Cochrane, Christine Knott,
and Joan Hildebrandt

BRIEF CONTENTS

CONTENTS

PREFACE

This book now enters its third decade of introducing readers to the fascinating field of Canadian politics. The year in which the first edition of this book appeared marked a turning point in Canadian politics. Nearly a decade of Conservative government came to an end with the ascension of Jean Chrétien and the Liberal party in the election of 1993. Now, 22 years later, a new Liberal government takes office after nearly a decade of government by Prime Minister Stephen Harper and the Conservative party. "It's like déjà vu all over again."

The country has changed a great deal over the past couple of decades; however, Canada's political institutions have not. The relative stability of political institutions in the face of rapidly changing social, economic, and international environments is an enduring theme of Canadian politics and of this book. Prime Minister Justin Trudeau and his new Liberal government have laid out an ambitious agenda of political reform. Among other changes, the new government has pledged to reform the House of Commons, the Senate, and the way votes are counted and seats are allocated in elections. We hope to provide our readers with tools and background knowledge to help them think seriously about these and many other questions that Canada now faces.

This eighth edition of *Canadian Politics: Critical Approaches* seeks to preserve the merits of its predecessor editions. It continues to present the reality of Canadian government and politics in a comprehensive yet lean and readable manner. Although it is principally designed as a textbook, we hope it is also useful and enjoyable for general readers.

This text is divided almost equally between the two parts of the Canadian political system: its "environment" and its institutions. It can thus be used for courses in either half of the subject or for full courses that cover both parts. In the former case, the book gives much emphasis to the societal setting of the political system, with discussions of regionalism, Aboriginal peoples, the French–English cleavage, ethnocultural groups, gender, class, age, religion, urban/rural location, and the global environment. Student interest in the subject is therefore stimulated by observing the clash of interests from which political activity stems. In the latter case, it includes chapters on all the institutions of Canadian government, including the Constitution, federalism, the Charter of Rights and Freedoms, the executive, bureaucracy, Parliament, and the judiciary—institutions which also feature exciting daily happenings. Part 3, which deals with equally fascinating topics—political culture, the mass media, public opinion polls, elections, parties, and advocacy groups—can be fit into either half of the subject.

In this edition, we concentrate on the following critical approaches: Institutionalism, including historical-institutionalism; State-based analysis, including policy communities, elite accommodation, and political economy; Political Sociology, including pluralism and class analysis; Political Behaviour and Political Psychology; and Rational Choice. Rather than list these critical approaches at the end of each chapter, we have integrated the approaches in each chapter alongside discussions of relevant research problems.

Although the Canadian political system functions better than most others around the world, it is far from perfect and embodies a huge "democratic deficit" such that no account could be completely satisfied with the status quo. This book therefore points out the many aspects of political and governmental operations of the country that are not working as well as they might, and suggests possible reforms and alternative arrangements. Without being ideological, the book is a critical account and seeks to make informed critics of its readers.

For those familiar with previous editions of the book, let us briefly outline what is different about this new edition:

1. Updated data and graphs to the end of 2015;

2. The 2015 federal election campaign and results;

3. A focus on "path dependence" and the increasing calls for institutional reform, especially to the House of Commons, Senate, and the electoral system;

4. A revised chapter on Aboriginal peoples which embeds non-Aboriginal peoples in the New World within the timescales of Aboriginal people, rather than the reverse;

5. A discussion of the debates surrounding "religious accommodation," including the debates in the 2015 election about the wearing of the niqab during citizenship ceremonies;

6. Explications of data and statistics that foster an intuitive grasp of what they reveal;

7. The redistribution of seats in the House of Commons;

8. The volatile nature of public opinion in Quebec regarding nationalism, federalism, party preference, and religious tolerance, as well as the re-election of a Liberal majority government;

9. References to various controversial bills passed in Parliament, and their potential consequences;

10. Updated information on media ownership, with the new addition of community newspapers;

11. The evolving relations and notable tensions between provinces and the federal government;

12. The new Charter decisions of the Supreme Court, including those on religious freedoms, prostitution, and doctor-assisted suicide;

13. The Harper government's approach to reforming the Senate, and the alternative proposed by Justin Trudeau as Liberal leader.

INSTRUCTOR RESOURCES

 The Nelson Education Teaching Advantage (NETA) program delivers research-based instructor resources that promote student engagement and higher-order thinking to enable the success of Canadian students and educators. Visit Nelson Education's Inspired Instruction website at http://www.nelson.com/inspired/ to find out more about NETA.

The following instructor resources have been created for *Canadian Politics: Critical Approaches*, Eighth Edition. Access these ultimate tools for customizing lectures and presentations at www.nelson.com/instructor.

NETA Test Bank

This resource was written by Nanita Mohan of University of Guelph. It includes 240 multiple-choice questions written according to NETA guidelines for effective construction and development of higher-order questions. Also included are 240 true/false and 120 essay questions.

NETA PowerPoint

Microsoft® PowerPoint® lecture slides for every chapter have been created by Jordan Taft of Carlton University. There is an average of 15 slides per chapter, many featuring key figures, tables, and photographs from *Canadian Politics*. NETA principles of clear design and engaging content have been incorporated throughout, making it simple for instructors to customize the deck for their courses.

Image Library

This resource consists of digital copies of figures, short tables, and photographs used in the book. Instructors may use these jpegs to customize the NETA PowerPoint or create their own PowerPoint presentations.

MindTap

MindTap® Offering personalized paths of dynamic assignments and applications, **MindTap** is a digital learning solution that turns cookie-cutter into cutting-edge, apathy into engagement, and memorizers into higher-level thinkers. MindTap enables students to analyze and apply chapter concepts within relevant assignments, and allows instructors to measure skills and promote better outcomes with ease. A fully online learning solution, MindTap combines all student learning tools—readings, multimedia, activities, and assessments—into a single Learning Path that guides the student through the curriculum. Instructors personalize the experience by customizing the presentation of these learning tools to their students, even seamlessly introducing their own content into the Learning Path. The MindTap content for *Canadian Politics: Critical Approaches*, Eighth Edition, was prepared by Rand Dyck, Carleton University, and Logan Masilamani, Simon Fraser University.

STUDENT ANCILLARIES

MindTap

MindTap® Stay organized and efficient with **MindTap**—a single destination with all the course material and study aids you need to succeed. Built-in apps leverage social media and the latest learning technology. For example:

- ReadSpeaker will read the text to you.
- Flashcards are pre-populated to provide you with a jump-start for review—or you can create your own.

- You can highlight text and make notes in your MindTap Reader. Your notes will flow into Evernote, the electronic notebook app that you can access anywhere when it's time to study for the exam.
- Self-quizzing allows you to assess your understanding.

Visit http://www.nelson.com/student to start using **MindTap**. Enter the Online Access Code from the card included with your text. If a code card is *not* provided, you can purchase instant access at NELSONbrain.com.

The preparation of this eighth edition gave us the opportunity to peruse a great deal of scholarly writing on various aspects of Canadian government and politics and to communicate with a large number of people "on the Hill" who provided us with valuable information on the workings of different parts of the political system. We also relied on the impressive, informative, and accessible websites now maintained by federal government departments and agencies and most other political actors.

The book is immensely better for having been reviewed in various editions, by a large number of helpful academics recruited by the publisher. For this edition, we particularly thank Christopher Anderson at Wilfrid Laurier University. We would also like to thank the following reviewers for their invaluable input: Tina Beaudry-Mellor, University of Regina; Mark Blythe, University of Alberta; Greg Flynn, McMaster University; Mikael Hellstrom, University of Alberta; Paul Nesbitt-Larking, Huron University College; John Soroski, MacEwan University; and others who did not wish to be acknowledged. The book is made more readable, too, for being punctuated with the work of some of Canada's leading editorial cartoonists and political photographers. We would be happy to receive further feedback—even questions—via e-mail at christopher.cochrane@utoronto.ca or kblidook@mun.ca.

The people at Nelson Education Ltd. have become an important part of our lives. Their ability to transform a nondescript manuscript into a beautiful book never fails to astound us. This edition was guided to publication by the talents and dedication of Publisher, Mark Grzeskowiak; Content Development Manager, Jessica Freedman; Marketing Manager, Terry Fedorkiw; and Production Project Managers, Lila Campbell and Christine Gilbert, along with Jessie Coffey and Ezhilsolai Periasamy.

We earnestly hope that the book contributes to a better informed and more involved and critical Canadian citizenry.

Christopher Cochrane
Kelly Blidook
Rand Dyck

ABOUT THE AUTHORS

CHRISTOPHER COCHRANE

Christopher Cochrane is Associate Professor in the Department of Political Science at the University of Toronto. He studies political disagreement in Canada and other democratic countries. He is the author of *Left and Right: The Small World of Political Ideas* (MQUP, 2015). He received his BA from St. Thomas University in Fredericton, NB, his MA from McGill, and his PhD from the University of Toronto.

KELLY BLIDOOK

Kelly Blidook is Associate Professor in the Department of Political Science at Memorial University. He received his PhD from McGill University. His research focuses mostly upon the various behaviours of Canadian members of Parliament. His book *Constituency Influence in Parliament: Countering the Centre* (UBC Press) was published in 2012.

RAND DYCK

Rand Dyck was born and raised in Calgary. After graduating from the University of Alberta with his BA in Political Science, he found the political culture of Ontario more to his liking, and took his MA at Carleton University and his PhD at Queen's. Between his graduate degrees, he experienced the life of a public servant in Ottawa, but opted instead for an academic career. He taught at Laurentian University in Sudbury for 34 years, holding all sorts of administrative positions including department chair and vice dean, and took early retirement in 2005, upon which he was titled Professor Emeritus. Among his many accomplishments and awards, Rand received both the Laurentian University Teaching Excellence Award and the Ontario Confederation of University Faculty Associations Teaching Award in 2002. He was cited for his engaging teaching style and for his extraordinary commitment to his students, many of whom became life-long friends. One particular claim to fame was his organization of the annual Laurentian University Model Parliament held in the House of Commons chamber in Ottawa. As a Political Science professor, he has a long list of published articles, chapters, public speeches, and book reviews, and continues to be asked by the media for comments on current political developments.

INTRODUCTION

Part 1 of *Canadian Politics: Critical Approaches* consists of two chapters. The first provides a general framework on which the rest of the book is built and outlines a number of different approaches to the study of politics. These approaches reveal that the subject matter of political science is not all cut-and-dried factual material and that the same topic can be viewed from different perspectives. The second chapter explores the historical context of Canadian politics and sketches its institutional foundations. These governmental institutions are examined in more depth in Parts 4 and 5, but a general knowledge of them is advisable before embarking on Parts 2 and 3. In particular, Chapter 2 deals with the aspects of the British and U.S. models that Canada chose as the basis for its own, and establishes the institutional differences between the Canadian and U.S. systems of government.

INTRODUCTION

CHAPTER 1

Approaching the Study of Politics

If you wrote a list of 10 things that are important in your life, what would be on that list? Would you include your family, friends, work, and school? Perhaps you might mention economic considerations, like supporting yourself through university or finding a job after you graduate. You might also mention travelling, a favourite pastime, or some other activity. If you are like the vast majority of Canadians, however, politics is not on your list. For most people, most of the time, "politics" is but a background conversation in the hubbub of the world around us. We hear politics in parts and pieces, and outbursts draw our attention. Yet, we often struggle to make sense of what we hear. We need the context of the conversation. This book is about the context in which Canadian politics plays out. It is about the dense web of interconnections that bind politics to so many facets of life in this country, including those things we care deeply about.

THE POLITICAL SYSTEM

Politics is the practice of attempting to influence the decisions of a collective to act, or not to act, in a particular manner. Virtually every issue is at least partly political, even if the political element is not so obvious at first glance. To say that an issue is a private issue is to claim that it should be resolved in the **private** or **voluntary sectors**, also known as **civil society**, those parts of society and the economy that function separately from government control, otherwise referred to as the **public sector**. To label an issue as a *public issue*, by contrast, is to express the opinion that some government action be taken. Which spheres of human activity should the government service and control, and which areas should it not? Whether and where we draw the line between a public issue and a private issue is a foundational assumption in thinking about politics.

Deeply ingrained and often unconscious *empirical* beliefs about the way things *are*, and *normative* beliefs about the way things *should be*, influence our views about how best to study politics and to solve real-world problems. Should the Canadian government limit greenhouse gas emissions or should regulations be minimized to attract investment and job growth in the petroleum industry? Should the government restrict Canadians' access to pornography on the Internet or should Canadians be allowed to decide for themselves what they watch online? Should the government use tax dollars to pay a portion of the costs of a university education for Canadian students or should students be forced to find scholarships, loans, employment, family supporters, and other sources of money to pay the full cost of their own education? Should the government permit wealthy people to buy higher quality healthcare or should all citizens have equal access to medical services regardless of their ability to pay? Answering each of these questions involves making numerous judgments about evidence, priorities, and values. How would you answer these questions, and why?

This list of questions barely scratches the surface of the kinds of political issues with which Canadian governments have to deal. Resolving political issues invites a discussion of a key concept in political science: power. **Power** is often defined in this discipline as the ability of one actor to impose its will on another, to get its own way, to do or get what it wants. The German political sociologist Max Weber famously defined power as "… the probability that one actor within a social relationship will be in a position to carry out his own will despite resistance. …"[1] We would say that people are powerless when they have no probability of being able to impose their will. Political science usually identifies three different kinds of power. The first is **coercion**, which means that the agent (i.e., person, group, or organization) is able to impose its will on others by using, or threatening, physical force and other forms of punishments. People obey an agent in this circumstance because they are fearful of the consequences of disobedience. Another type of power is **authority**, that is, power based on *legitimacy*. In this case, the agent can impose its will on another because the subject regards the decision-maker as having a right to make such a decision. It is a kind of power that we have agreed to be bound by because it comes from a respected source; it stems from the acceptance of an obligation to obey. In practice, authority and coercion are often connected, and the use of coercion by political figures may also be based on a widespread belief that it is legitimate in certain circumstances. Finally, *influence* is the imposition of one's will on another through persuasion and voluntary compliance—without either accompanying threats or deference to authority.

Graham Hughes/THE CANADIAN PRESS IMAGES

Students opposing tuition hikes in Montreal demonstrate in the spring of 2012, contesting the authority of government. Some of the demonstrations moved from civil disobedience to become violent.

Government refers to the set of organizations that make, enforce, and administer collective, public decisions for a society. To some extent, we obey the government because of the threat or expectation of penalties if we do not (coercion), but we also obey because we accept government decisions to be binding on us and necessary for the general good (authority). Think of stopping at a red light as an example. The majority of Canadians regard their governments as legitimate, so that government power is generally exercised as authority rather than coercion. As we shall see, however, this has not always been the case in Canada, and there are important contemporary exceptions that we will consider later in some detail.

Those who control the government can make appointments, spend money, extract taxes, enact regulations, and generally impose their will on society. In other words, they have power. In Canada and many other countries it is helpful to think of three kinds of government power: **legislative power**, or the power to *create* laws and public policies; **executive power**, or the power to *enforce* laws and *administer* public policies; and **judicial power**, or the power to *interpret* the law. These three kinds of power are usually exercised by different branches of government: the legislature or Parliament, the executive or Prime Minister and Cabinet, and the courts, respectively. Sometimes two or more branches must work together, such as in the formulation, passage, and implementation of a new law.

Governments do not exist in a vacuum; they are enmeshed in the broader society of which they are a part. How government power is exercised shapes, and is at once shaped by, conditions and pressures in the broader social environment that surrounds it. Imagine that a group wanted the government to enact a particular law or policy that was in its own financial interest. The group's capacity to influence the legislative power of government would be contingent on a wide range of factors, including the financial resources that it already had at its disposal. But the outcome of this government decision would shape the social environment in affecting the financial resources of the group in the future. As we shall see, there are many other ways in which society affects the use of government power, and vice versa. Money is not the only thing that matters in politics, but it is often an important factor.

The connections between the government and society are numerous and complex. A common way of simplifying these connections is based on the work of political scientist David Easton.[2] This approach is summarized in Figure 1.1. The core of the "political system" is a box including the legislature, the executive, and the judiciary, as well as a number of other important components such as the bureaucracy and the electoral system. This box is situated within a broader environment from which come demands or "inputs" that the political system filters and reacts to by enacting laws and policies ("outputs"). These laws and policies, in turn, shape the environment and therefore the

FIGURE 1.1 A MODEL OF THE POLITICAL SYSTEM

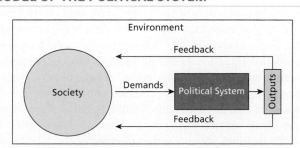

future inputs on the political system ("feedback effects"). This loop of demands–outputs–feedback locks the political system and the environment into a dynamic, circular, never-ending process in which the authorities, in addition to imposing their own priorities, react to demands, seek out public sentiment, convert some of the demands into outputs, and then respond in whatever changes in the pattern of inputs have resulted from the feedback from such outputs.

A good example of this process was the demand in the province of Quebec, especially by women's and labour groups, for universal government subsidized childcare. When the Government of Quebec acceded to these pressures and introduced five-dollar-per-day child-care in 1997 it created brand new constituencies in the province. These new constituencies included the parents and prospective parents of children in these daycares, as well as the teachers, administrators, and other workers that implemented the program. These groups, in turn, have lobbied the government on a range of issues, including the wages and working conditions of childcare workers. In this way, the voices of these parents and employees represent some of the "feedback effects" of Quebec's childcare policy. These effects prod and constrain future government actions in this area. These types of feedback effects are ubiquitous in political systems. Indeed, it may be impossible for politicians to change one and only one thing. Each change affects others things as well, often in unforeseen and unintended ways.

The authorities are bombarded by demands, no matter what means are used to transmit them. What is more striking than the vast quantity of demands, however, is that intense conflict usually exists among them. The essence of government, therefore, lies not only in making and executing decisions for society, but in having to choose among competing demands, in trying to resolve conflict, or in making social choices in the midst of social conflict. Here, let us say that in the context of government, **politics** is an activity in which conflicting interests struggle for advantage or dominance in the making and execution of public policies. It should also be added that the authorities can make their own demands, which may well carry more weight than those arising from the wider society; indeed, an important feature of governing involves the authorities attempting to convince the population to follow their own agenda.

As we shall see, Canada is a **democracy**, which means that Canada has a system of government designed to integrate the expressed wishes of the governed. The act of voting in elections is one way in which individual Canadians are able to inject their own inputs into the political process, but there are many other ways as well. These inputs can be generated on a personal basis, by means of a letter, fax, telephone call, email, tweet, or face-to-face encounter with a government official or politician. Today's governments put increasing effort into seeking out the views of the public for a variety of reasons. One is that advances in technology, such as polling and communications, make it possible for government to solicit such views; a second is that after a decade or more of downsizing government, the authorities were left with fewer policy analysis resources of their own; and a third is that more think tanks and policy advocacy organizations exist than ever before. As a result, government organizations such as the Canadian Radio-television and Telecommunications Commission (CRTC) and the National Energy Board (NEB) hold public hearings on controversial issues, in which regular citizens and other interested stakeholders are able to present their opinions and concerns to policy-makers. In 2008, for example, the CRTC held public hearings about whether Internet Service Providers (ISPs) in Canada should be allowed to slow or "throttle" the Internet traffic of Canadians connected to peer-to-peer file sharing sites. Likewise, in 2012–13, the NEB held public hearings about whether to approve the Northern Gateway pipeline

First Nations Chiefs address the National Energy Board hearings on the Northern Gateway pipeline project in January 2012.

across British Columbia from the Alberta oil sands. Virtually anyone is able to make a submission to these processes.

Sometimes such directly transmitted demands will achieve their desired results, and sometimes they will not. If not, it may be time to consider some kind of group action because, as a general rule, government authorities are more likely to respond to a demand coming from a group than from a single individual. Canadian society is replete with groups that exist to articulate political concerns. An **interest group** is an organization that exists to pursue the common interest(s) of its members. An **advocacy group** or **pressure group** is an interest group that aims to accomplish its objectives by trying to influence directly how government power is used. Such groups constitute an important part of Canadian political activity. The National Citizens Coalition (NCC) and the Women's Legal Education and Action Fund (LEAF) are two prominent examples of Canadian advocacy groups. The NCC promotes its agenda by pressuring politicians to cut taxes and reduce government spending, while LEAF pursues its objectives by providing funding for litigants advancing feminist causes through the courts. Student advocacy groups have no shortage of political issues of their own.

A **political party** is yet another type of group through which people are able to influence government. A political party is a formal organization that seeks to achieve its objectives through government by contesting elections and winning power. Thus, while it has certain similarities to an advocacy group, a political party is different in its attempt to win votes in elections. People join a political party or support it financially and often try to get it to recognize their concerns in its platform or policies. If the party forms the government, it can incorporate the demand into its decisions and government policy; if the party is in opposition, it may be able to bring the problem to national attention through mass media coverage of parliamentary proceedings.

Returning to the environment of the political system, society is characterized by much diversity, including many internal divisions. When deep and persistent divisions in society, such as those involving region, ethnicity, language, and religion, become politicized, they are often known as **cleavages**. As mentioned, while such cleavages are part of the environment of the political system, they can also be seen as the source of many of the demands expressed in day-to-day political activity.

Political science also emphasizes the concept of **identities**. Each of us has many identities—male or female, Newfoundlander or Albertan, Roman Catholic or Muslim, francophone or Aboriginal, young or old, rich or poor. Our identities evolve from those characteristics and experiences that are most important to us as individuals and groups. Canada is replete with regional identities, ethnic and linguistic identities, religious identities, class identities, and gender and sexual identities, to mention only a few. Whether a person articulates a demand in the political system based on any such identities will depend on whether he or she is conscious of such characteristics and experiences and considers them salient—to be an important part of their being.

The interconnection between government and society means that deeply ingrained assumptions, values, and interests within society as a whole are very likely to pervade the government as well. **Cultural hegemony** is the process through which dominant beliefs and assumptions about the world reinforce existing patterns of power in a society by taking alternative courses of action off the table. Before being able to change the way that government acts on an issue, therefore, it is sometimes necessary to change the way that society thinks. To a large extent, this is the domain of social movement politics.

A **social movement** is an informal alliance of individuals and interest groups who aim to achieve their objectives by changing the dominant beliefs of a society. The feminist movement, for example, challenged a number of once-widely held cultural beliefs, including the assumption that how husbands treated their wives in the home was a private matter and thus none of the public's business. The civil rights movement, particularly in the United States but also in Canada, challenged beliefs that discriminated on the basis of the colour of a person's skin. And the gay rights movement challenged many negative assumptions and attitudes about gays, lesbians, and transgendered people. The repertoire of social movement politics is broad, employing petition-signing, protests, political parties, and litigation as efforts to influence government policy. But it also includes public awareness campaigns and other activities, such as gay pride parades, which are designed to foster group identities and challenge certain hegemonic cultural beliefs of the wider society.

When it comes to the deep-seated beliefs of the public, the mass media may play a particularly important role in politics, one of which is called **agenda-setting**. The agenda-setting hypothesis was summarized by Bernard Cohen when he argued that "the press may not be successful much of the time in telling people what to think, but it is stunningly successful in telling its readers what to think about."[3] By choosing to focus on some issues rather than others, the media may set the public agenda by bringing some issues into public discourse and leaving other issues out. Whatever the direct effects of the mass media on political discourse, however, there may well be important cultural effects that are more difficult to measure and test. Consider the concept of "infotainment," which is the practice of using television shows, movies, and songs to communicate points of view to the public. Many movies aim not just to entertain us, but to make social and political statements in the process. Our exposure to the mass media, including the new social media—Facebook, Twitter, etc.—is so extensive that it may sometimes reinforce, create, or challenge our underlying assumptions about the way the world is, the way the world works, and the way the world should be; it may do so, perhaps, without our even knowing it.

Finally, we must add that the Canadian political system also possesses an external or global environment. The external environment consists of a huge number of international, multi-national, and supranational influences, such as other states, international organizations, international agreements, transnational corporations, and nongovernmental organizations (NGOs). In fact, in this age of globalization, such actors in the external environment increasingly serve as the source of demands on national systems and as constraints on domestic policymaking. Not a day goes by without the government of Canada having to factor such external influences into its decisions. The North American Free Trade Agreement (NAFTA) among Canada, the United States, and Mexico is perhaps of greatest impact, but almost every contemporary political issue has external implications, such as pipelines, the economy, and the environment.

APPROACHES TO THE STUDY OF POLITICS

As Greg Pyrcz noted, there is "a lot to be said in political studies for careful description, for simply getting the facts right and complete."[4] Facts and evidence are important in political science. As we shall see, however, political science is more than a straightforward collection of facts. Indeed, "facts do not organize themselves into concepts and theories just by being looked at," Gunnar Myrdal (1953, vii) argued. "Except within the framework of concepts and theories, there are no scientific facts but only chaos. There is an inescapably a priori element in all scientific work."[5] Political scientists employ a wide range of approaches in their trade, which in the first instance provide a guide in selecting significant and relevant facts, as well as in putting the facts together in a meaningful way. These approaches direct our attention to different aspects of social reality and emphasize different relationships within the same population and territory. Before getting into the substance of our subject, therefore, we will outline a number of such approaches that political scientists have found useful in illuminating aspects of the Canadian political system. They focus on such crucial questions as how widely power and influence are shared, which political actors in society are most important, which government institutions are most powerful, how politicians seek and maintain power, and how much government actions are affected by external factors. It is not possible to list all of these approaches here, and unfortunately for undergraduate students, political scientists even disagree about how to name, define, and categorize them. But we can outline some of the principal approaches, always remembering that they often overlap and can be linked to each other in different ways. We will start by dividing them into two broad categories: those that are oriented toward the state (institutional and state-based approaches), and those that are more society-centred (political sociology, political behaviour, political psychology, and rational choice approaches), although even this division has its critics and complications.

Institutional Approaches

Among the oldest approaches to the study of politics is the **institutional approach**. It "sees constitutions and law as the main substance of politics and government and as the proper object of political analysis; ... government is understood to be essentially constituted by a set of rules, and rules governed by overarching constitutions, written and unwritten."[6] Not only does institutionalism argue that institutions are the principal objects of study in the discipline, but it also finds that they determine much of what happens in the broader political system.

Two of the classic texts to employ the institutional approach to the study of Canadian politics were R. MacGregor Dawson's *The Government of Canada* and J.R. Mallory's *The Structure of Canadian Government*. These renowned political scientists outlined the characteristics and historical development of rules which structure the way that power is used by the Canadian government. A rule which is enforceable in court is known as a *law*, and a rule which is widely perceived as binding, but which is not enforceable in court, is known as a *convention*. As we shall see, these laws and conventions shape everything from the role of the prime minister in Canadian government to the rights of a resident or citizen of Canada. In fact, this is a country in which constitutional issues continue to attract a great deal of attention, such as that of Senate reform.

Other institutional approaches examine the effects of comparative institutional design on policy outcomes. One explanation for why Canadians have universal publicly funded healthcare and Americans do not, for example, is that the institutions of parliamentary government concentrate power in such a way that makes these kinds of bold initiatives possible. In the American system, by contrast, power is institutionally diffuse, making it easier for small groups of concerted interests to block government legislation. We would say that there are more veto points in American government than in Canadian government because there are more institutional opportunities for small groups to prevent legislation from passing.[7] Concentrated power in Canada facilitates government getting things done—both good and bad—and diffuse power in the United States makes it possible for groups to prevent the government from taking action.

According to the institutional approach, if we want to know how an organization works, we are well served by understanding the rules that govern the relationships between the people who work in that organization. Who makes decisions? How are the decision-makers chosen? How are their decisions made? And who is held accountable to whom if things go wrong?

The institutional approach is closely allied to the **historical approach** or combined with it as the **historical-institutional approach**. To discuss many aspects of the political system, it is logical to see how they evolved historically, of course, but the historical approach goes one step further. A key concept in this approach is that of "path dependence." The phenomenon of path dependence applies in many domains, and politics is no exception. "Once a country or a region has started down a track," Margaret Levi observes, "the costs of reversal are very high. There will be other choice points, but the entrenchment of certain institutional arrangements obstructs an easy reversal of the initial choice."[8] Political institutions carry decisions from the past into the future, even in cases where the reasons for those earlier decisions no longer apply. Many decisions that were made in 1867 in Canada have had lasting effects on the nature of the country. Not the least of these was the constitutional division of powers between the federal and provincial governments, a decision which committed future generations of Canadians to a political landscape characterized by federal–provincial wrangling and negotiation. Other examples include the establishment of an unelected Senate and a first-past-the-post electoral system for the House of Commons, to all of which we will return in later chapters. Understanding the ways in which institutional decisions in the past constrain actors and policy options in the future is an important goal of political science research.

For a generation or two after the Second World War, political science paid less attention to institutions and focused primarily on society and the political behaviour of individuals. But in recent years, institutionalism has been revived in the form of the *neo-institutional* approach. It is clear that the design of institutions influences political outcomes.[9] Consider, for example, that with the same proportion of votes for each party as in the recent federal election, but with a different kind of electoral system, the partisan composition of the House of Commons would be quite different. Institutions are central to the study of politics.

State-Based Approaches

It may be tempting to think of politics, particularly in democratic countries, as being shaped almost exclusively by the demands of social actors like voters, businesses, and interest groups. Yet, this bottom-up view of politics belies the capacity of state actors to use the powers of the state to shape the economic and social circumstances of their country. **State-based approaches** emphasize the autonomy of state actors. Eric Nordlinger, for example, wrote in his book on the *Autonomy of the Democratic State* that "the preferences of the state are at least as important as those of civil society in accounting for what the democratic state does and does not do."[10] By the "state" Nordlinger meant the collection of "individuals who occupy offices that authorize them, and them alone, to make and apply decisions that are binding upon any and all segments of society."[11] State actors have their own policy preferences, and they pursue these preferences, just as social actors do, by working to shape the direction and application of state power. The state authorities seek to enhance their autonomy by the internal generation of information and by maximizing their discretion, jurisdiction, and financial resources. The state acts autonomously, according to Norlinger, when state actors are able to translate their preferences into public policy, whether by leveraging support from like-minded social actors, changing the preferences of opposing social actors, or imposing their will without regard for social actors.

Still, as implied above, the state is not always able to operate with complete autonomy. Indeed, to maximize their influence and protect themselves, state forces are often wiser to develop functional links with certain private or voluntary sector interests, especially advocacy groups, than to try to act in total isolation. Thus, the concept of **policy communities** is often helpful in this discussion.[12] The state is composed of a conglomeration of specialized policy processes, each of which nurtures support from the most relevant interest in society. Policy communities are related to the notion of the **embedded state**.[13] This is the idea that although the political and bureaucratic authorities can sometimes function quite independently of societal forces, the state is so embedded in society that it cannot operate with total autonomy. Instead, a web of state–society interdependence means that the authorities interact with the leaders or elites of the groups that are most relevant to their operations. Close interaction occurs between specialized governmental elites and those of the advocacy

The Parliament Buildings, Ottawa—the seat of the Government of Canada.

groups that constitute their principal clienteles. A variation on this approach is **elite accommodation**, the idea that the political and bureaucratic leaders of the state interact with elites in society—the leaders of different ethnic, regional, or economic groups—to arrive at decisions that are in their mutual interest.[14]

Political economy is another approach that brings together the state and society; it is the study of the interaction between the state and the economy. In some variants of political economy, the state is seen as a largely autonomous entity that directs the development of the economy. The developmental state literature, for example, paints a portrait of a what is sometimes called the "*dirigiste* state"—i.e., states that steer the economic development of their countries in directions favoured and coordinated by state actors.[15] In Canada, as we shall see, considerable effort was undertaken by the Canadian state in the early years of Confederation to construct a national economy on an East–West trading axis rather than in a North–South direction that was more in line with the natural economic geography of North America. Indeed, the political economy of Canadian development often begins with the observation that Canada is rich in natural resources, also known as "staples," and that the country is situated beside a manufacturing and commercial superpower, the United States. Much of Canada's historical economic development has been centred on understanding the economic policies of the Canadian state under these circumstances.

Political Sociology Approaches

A broad set of alternatives to institutional approaches are the political sociology approaches. Political sociologists study government in the context of the broader social and economic environments of which it is a part. Whereas institutional approaches focus on rules, political sociology approaches centre on groups and societal forces. One variation is the **social cleavages approach**. A social cleavage approach emphasizes such deep-seated divisions in society as regions, ethnic background, language, religion, and economic classes. S.M. Lipset, for example, studied the social and economic conditions that favour the development of stable democracies by examining the patterns of cleavages in society. He argued that peaceful democratic politics were more likely to emerge when the cleavages in a given society cut across rather than reinforce each other. If the members of one ethnic group are very poor and the members of some other ethnic group are very rich, then we would say that the ethnic and economic cleavages are overlapping or reinforcing. On the other hand, if there are about equal numbers of poor and rich people from both ethnic groups, then the ethnic and economic cleavages would cut across each other. According to Lipset, cross-cutting cleavages are amenable to moderate and peaceful democratic politics, whereas reinforcing cleavages only deepen the divisions, promoting extreme and revolutionary politics.[16] It is very relevant to ask the question: to what extent do ethnic, linguistic, religious, territorial, and economic cleavages cut across or reinforce each other in Canada?

The focus on cleavages is closely related to the **pluralist approach**. Those who subscribe to the pluralist approach postulate that the resources to influence power are widely dispersed among many interests in society, rather than tightly controlled by one particular group of elites. From this perspective, resources include money, legitimacy, and public support. Pluralism is the analytical framework closest to the democratic ideal.[17] Thus, this approach suggests that individuals can make use of many different resources in their political participation, that those sharing a demand are free to join together to seek a governmental response, that such group action is the norm of political activity, and that authorities are open to pressure from a wide variety of such interests. Pluralism assumes that group action is more common and more effective than individual political activity, and it puts particular stress on the role of advocacy groups in the making of public policy. The term "brokerage politics" is commonly used in this connection, especially in Canada, because in a pluralist system the authorities engage in wheeling and dealing with the various groups in an effort to keep them all content. A pioneer of the pluralist approach was political scientist Robert Dahl, who wrote *Pluralist Democracy in the United States*. Paul Pross has explicitly emphasized the group approach in his work on Canadian politics, such as *Group Politics and Public Policy*. As a practical example, we could ask: would tuition fees be lower in Canadian provinces if postsecondary students were more strongly organized? It should be added, however, that even if a society can be labelled "pluralistic," the pluralist approach may not necessarily apply: the pluralist approach assumes a basic equality among the different interests in the system.

Another important variant of the political sociology approach is founded on the work of Karl Marx. Rather than groups in general, the **Marxist approach** emphasizes the role that economic groups—in particular, classes—play in shaping the nature of politics and government. For this reason, this approach is sometimes called the **class approach**.[18] In a capitalist system, Marx predicted an inevitable conflict between the two main classes: the "bourgeoisie," those who own

Songquan Deng/Shutterstock

The Toronto skyline is dominated by the head offices of Canadian banks, the heart of the capitalist system.

the means of production, such as businesses and industries, and the "proletariat," the working class. Moreover, according to Marx, the political elite normally take orders from the capitalist elite, and the state is therefore an instrument of bourgeois domination. From this perspective, politics is first and foremost about class conflict, and about how patterns of power between groups in the economy are transferred into patterns of power in government.

Political Psychology and Political Behaviour Approaches

The political psychology and political behaviour approaches examine politically related attitudes, opinions, beliefs, perceptions, expectations, motivations, and behaviours. At the core of both approaches is the notion that politics is about people, and the individual actor should therefore be better understood. These approaches became prominent in the discipline after the Second World War, and were part of the "behavioural revolution" in political science. Besides broadening the discipline, these approaches also expanded the research methods used by political scientists to include quantitative techniques—survey research and statistical analyses. Many of these approaches seek to apply methods from the natural sciences, such as systematic observation, mathematical models, and experiments, to the study of political phenomena.[19]

The **political psychology approach** adapts concepts and theories from psychology in seeking to understand why people think the way they do about politics. The role of personality in politics, for example, has been used to explain differences among people in their openness to new ideas and in their deference to authority. Early approaches in political psychology emphasized the political consequences of different "personalities" such as the "authoritarian personality." The "Big-5 Personality traits" is one classic characterization of personality differences. Many such tests can be found on the Internet, allowing you to see where your own personality fits.

The **political behaviour approach** is closely related. Many Canadian political scientists study the behaviour of individual political actors, whether as citizens, voters, or members of groups such as political parties, interest groups, and social movements. Many scholars in this field focus on the question of voter turnout. They are trying to understand why young Canadians, in particular, seem to be turning away from the electoral process. The behaviour of individual politicians is also of interest: rather than focus on the rules of the House of Commons as might be done by the institutional approach, for example, MPs' actual behaviour is scrutinized.

The Rational Choice Approach

Yet another approach to the study of politics is the **rational choice approach**. At its core, rational choice theorists assume that individuals seek to maximize their utility as efficiently as possible.[20] Utility, from this perspective, is simply the end to which action is aimed—if people seek money, then their utility is financial well-being; if they seek to alleviate the poverty of others, then their utility is poverty reduction. Rational choice theorists are not typically concerned with the origins of human motivation. Rather, they focus on how individuals and groups pursue their motivations, or "preferences," in particular situations. The goal of rational choice theorists is to provide parsimonious theories that generate reasonably accurate predictions about the world.

All rational choice theories are characterized by the assumption that behaviour is "goal-oriented" or, in other words, "instrumental." People are involved in politics, for example, because they want to get something out of it, either for themselves or for other people. Another assumption is that people pursue their goals as efficiently as they know how. When confronted with two options to achieve the exact same benefit(s), individuals will choose the option that they believe to be less costly for them in terms of money, time, and effort. And finally, individuals order their preferences rationally.

Rational choice theorists study a wide range of political phenomena, but they have been particularly adept at drawing attention to the ways in which "what is good for the individual" may be very different from "what is good for the group." The "Tragedy of the Commons" refers to a situation where there is a common collective resource that is depleted by the rational behaviour of each individual, such as the example of fish stocks. While a common group interest exists in maintaining a healthy fish stock, each fisher has an individual incentive to catch as many fish as possible. They each profit more by catching as many fish as possible rather than by voluntarily restricting their catch to preserve the resource. In other words, no matter what everyone else does, each individual often has an incentive to engage in behaviour that is detrimental to the group. Political scientist Elinor Ostrom highlighted the important role that governments can play in overcoming these problems, and for that she was awarded the Nobel Prize in Economics in 2009.

In short, political scientists have developed a large number of approaches in their study of political phenomena, far more than an undergraduate student is likely to need or appreciate. Here we have tried to select some of the most common, useful, and easily understood approaches, those that can be applied to the material in this text. These approaches should enhance your understanding of the basic material in each chapter.

CONCLUSION

Canada is not a perfect country, but it is widely and rightly seen as a model for how people with different cultures, languages, ethnicities, spiritual beliefs, and identities can live together peacefully. It is easy to take all of these things for granted, and to forget that a signature characteristic of the Canadian identity is that it is a "limited identity." The survival of Canada as a country has always depended on the willingness of Canadians to accept the basic fact that there are people who think, live, and act very differently from themselves—and who even see the country in a very different light—and yet who are just as Canadian as anybody else. The unwillingness of people on different sides to accept the diversity of the country has often created tensions, and Canada's continued survival requires the capacity and the willingness of leaders and citizens alike to make the right decisions at pivotal times. One thing is certain, however: there will be more critical times in the future.

This book aims to prepare you for these times. The politics of a country cannot be divorced from the society of which it is a part. You are part of this society, and ultimately, your country's politics are your responsibility. The following pages describe a political heritage that belongs equally to all Canadians, from the descendants of Aboriginal peoples, to the heirs of early French and British settlers, to the most recent immigrant. We live in a time of worldwide political turmoil, pressing environmental challenges, and spectacular inequality, while the advance of science and technology has changed altogether our conception of what is possible. You confront many vital responsibilities, and few easy answers.

DISCUSSION QUESTIONS

1. Do you think that concentrating on history, institutions, and the state is more or less important in the study of Canadian politics than focusing on political sociology, psychology, and behaviour? Why?

2. Generally speaking, do you think that governments do what they want to do or do they listen to the public?

3. What advocacy groups are you aware of or do you belong to?

4. Do you agree that business groups have more influence than other groups? Why or why not?

5. What can postsecondary students do to increase their influence on the Canadian political system?

MindTap® FOR MORE INFO GO TO http://www.nelson.com/student

NOTES

1. Max Weber, *The Theory of Social and Economic Organization* (New York: Free Press, 1947), p. 152.
2. David Easton, *A Systems Analysis of Political Life* (New York: John Wiley & Sons, 1965).
3. Bernard C. Cohen, *The Press and Foreign Policy* (Princeton, N.J.: Princeton University Press, 1963).
4. Greg Pyrcz, *The Study of Politics: A Short Survey of Core Approaches* (Toronto: University of Toronto Press, 2011), p. 18.
5. Gunnar Myrdal, 1953. *The Political Element in the Development of Economic Theory* (London, UK: Routledge and Kegan Paul), p. vii.
6. Greg Pyrcz, *The Study of Politics: A Short Survey of Core Approaches* (Toronto: University of Toronto Press, 2011), p. 58.
7. George Tsebelis, *Veto Players: How Political Institutions Work* (Princeton, N.J.: Princeton University Press), 2002.
8. Margaret Levi, "A Model, a Method and a Map: Rational Choice in Comparative and Historical Analysis," in M.I. Lichbach and A.S. Zuckerman, eds., *Comparative Politics: Rationality, Culture and Structure* (Cambridge: Cambridge University Press, 1997); Pyrcz, *The Study of Politics*, p. 58.
9. James G. March and Johan P. Olsen, *Rediscovering Institutions: The Organizational Basis of Politics* (New York: Free Press, 1989); B. Guy Peters, *Institutional Theory in Political Science: The New Institutionalism*, 3rd ed. (New York: The Continuum International Publishing Group, 2012).
10. Eric Nordlinger, *On the Anatomy of the Democratic State* (Cambridge, Mass.: Harvard University Press, 1981), p. 1.

11. Ibid., p. 11.
12. William Coleman and Grace Skogstad, eds., *Policy Communities and Public Policy in Canada* (Mississauga: Copp Clark Pitman, 1991); Rachel Laforest, *Voluntary Sector Organizations and the State: Building New Relations* (Vancouver: UBC Press, 2011).
13. Alan C. Cairns, "The Embedded State: State-Society Relations in Canada," in Alan C. Cairns, *Reconfigurations: Canadian Citizenship and Constitutional Change* (Toronto: McClelland and Stewart, 1995).
14. Robert A. Presthus, *Elite Accommodation in Canada* (Toronto: Macmillan, 1971).
15. Chalmers Johnson, *MITI and the Japanese Miracle* (Stanford, CA: Stanford University Press, 1982).
16. Seymour Martin Lipset, *Political Man: the Social Bases of Politics* (Garden City, NY: Doubleday, 1960).
17. Pyrcz, *The Study of Politics*, p. 68.
18. Leo Panitch, "Elites, Classes, and Power in Canada," in Michael S. Whittington and Glen Williams, eds., *Canadian Politics in the 1990s*, 4th ed. (Scarborough: Nelson Canada, 1995).
19. Richard L. Cole, *Introduction to Political Inquiry* (New York, Macmillan, 1980).
20. Anthony Downs, *An Economic Theory of Democracy* (New York: Addison Wesley, 1997).

FURTHER READING

Charlton, Mark, and Paul Barker, eds. *Crosscurrents: Contemporary Political Issues*, 7th ed. Toronto: Nelson Education, 2013.

Clarkson, Stephen. *Uncle Sam and Us: Globalization, Neoconservatism, and the Canadian State*. Toronto: University of Toronto Press, 2002.

Coleman, William, and Grace Skogstad. *Policy Communities and Public Policy in Canada*. Mississauga: Copp Clark Pitman, 1991.

Laforest, Rachel. *Voluntary Sector Organizations and the State: Building New Relations*. Vancouver: UBC Press, 2011.

MacIvor, Heather. *Parameters of Power: Canada's Political Institutions*, 5th ed. Toronto: Nelson Education, 2010.

McMenemy, John. *The Language of Canadian Politics: A Guide to Important Terms and Concepts*, 4th ed. Waterloo: University of Waterloo Press, 2006.

Pyrcz, Greg. *The Study of Politics: A Short Survey of Core Approaches*. Toronto: University of Toronto Press, 2011.

Whittington, Michael, and Glen Williams, eds. *Canadian Politics in the 21st Century*, 7th ed. Toronto: Thomson Nelson, 2008.

CHAPTER 2

Institutional Foundations and the Evolution of the State

Canada, like the United States, Australia, and much of South America, is a colonial country. This means that it was originally founded by people who moved to this part of the world from somewhere else, and that sovereignty over the territory was declared by foreign powers. Although Aboriginal peoples settled in the Americas many thousands of years ago—likely over a land bridge that opened up across the Bering Strait during the last ice age—the term "settler" in the Canadian context is generally reserved for the European settlers who arrived in more recent times, and "colonial powers" refers to the countries, particularly European powers, that laid claims to territory in the Americas. Other than Norse Vikings who briefly visited Newfoundland in the 11th century, the first Europeans to arrive to what is now Canada were the Italian and French explorers in the 1500s, and later the settlers who arrived from France in the 1600s and settled in New France, the area that is now Quebec.

Life for the new settlers was tough, and many early attempts to colonize Canada failed. Some settlements were wiped out altogether in colonial battles for territory and their inhabitants were never heard from again. Unaccustomed to the rugged wilderness and the cold winters, many of the early settlers died from a range of illnesses associated with the harsh conditions. Although, as we shall see in Chapter 4, colonial thought would soon come to be dominated by the view that the Aboriginal inhabitants were inferior to Europeans, the early settlers learned a great deal from Aboriginal peoples about survival in the Americas. As trade and social relationships between Aboriginal peoples and Europeans increased, so too did the integration of European settlers into the New World environment. The Métis people, the descendants of marriages between European traders and Aboriginal women, are an enduring legacy of that important relationship. But these early relations were not without drawbacks and conflicts; indeed, Europeans brought with them many diseases to which Aboriginal peoples had not been previously exposed, and to which they had not developed prior immunity. These diseases would come to have devastating effects on the number of Aboriginal peoples in the New World. Even so, the relations between early European settlers and Aboriginal peoples were not as exploitative and one-sided as they would later become.

Not long after the arrival of the first successful French settlers, British colonists arrived. The British Hudson's Bay Company—now familiarly known as The Bay—took possession of Rupert's Land around Hudson Bay in 1670, and Britain later gained control of Nova Scotia and Newfoundland by the 1713 Treaty of Utrecht, a treaty which ended the War of the Spanish Succession. Britain later conquered New France in the Battle of the Plains of Abraham in 1759. British colonists had, by this time, established a foothold in the United States and many were drawn to Canada by promises of land grants for farming. The British government was keen to populate its newly acquired territories with colonists who were loyal to the British crown.

As we shall see, the legacy of early settlement patterns persists in many locations across Canada, and in many aspects of Canadian society and government, including in the French language and traditions of French Canadians, such as the Acadians and the Québécois. Britain's conquest of Quebec profoundly changed the history of the colony and led to Quebec's continuing struggle to retain its distinctive character. That battle was part of the Seven Years' War between France and Britain, two traditional European rivals at the time. In addition to Quebec, Britain gained Prince Edward Island, Cape Breton, and New Brunswick by the 1763 Treaty of Paris. This reduced France's North American holdings to the small islands of Saint-Pierre and Miquelon.

EARLY INSTITUTIONAL DEVELOPMENTS

Four years after the conquest, Britain issued the **Royal Proclamation of 1763**, which created the British colony of Quebec from what was then called New France. It was the first distinctively Canadian constitutional document, a document that laid down the rules for governing the British North American colonies that comprised the territory of what would later become Canada.[1] As far as ex-Europeans were concerned, Quebec was largely made up of French-speaking farmers, clergy, and seigneurs, but the British-appointed government was English speaking, and the non-agricultural economy increasingly came under British control. The Royal Proclamation of 1763 included the stipulation that laws in the new colony should be as close as possible to those of Britain, which at the time contained many penalties and prohibitions aimed at Catholics. However, early governors of the colony saw the dangers of such a course of action and chose a more tolerant approach, one eventually codified in the 1774 Quebec Act.

An equally important aspect of the Royal Proclamation was in laying down legal rules about how future settlers in the British North American colonies were to acquire land from Aboriginals—namely, via formal treaties. Up until this time, colonists were simply setting up settlements in the New World, typically without consulting the Aboriginal groups who had occupied and used these lands for centuries. To be sure, Aboriginals did not have private property rights as they were conceptualized in much of Europe at this time, but the Royal Proclamation was nonetheless an acknowledgment by the British crown that the old colonialist doctrine of *terra nullius*—which contends that land could be claimed by a colonial power provided that it was not occupied when the colonial power discovered it—did not apply in the

CRITICAL APPROACHES

The *historical-institutional* approach is particularly relevant in this chapter. This approach emphasizes the importance of political history and the study of institutions. Historical-institutionalism argues that institutions are the principal objects of study in the discipline and that they determine much of what happens in the broader political system. Recall that "path dependence" makes it difficult to change institutional arrangements once they are established.

Thus, many decisions that were made in 1867 in Canada have had lasting effects of the nature of the country. Indeed, as this chapter outlines, relatively few major constitutional changes have been made in nearly 150 years. Even though Senate reform has been on the agenda of constitutional change throughout that period, for example, that institution continues to exist much as it started. On the other hand, the evolution of

Canadian federalism, with much stronger provinces than originally intended, indicates that certain basic changes can occur. These changes, however, are often unintended consequences of institutional design. In 1867, the most important powers of government, along with the greatest taxation powers, were assigned to the federal level. Provincial powers like education and health care were not very important in 1867, but given changes in public expectations in these fields, the institutional structure of the country set it out on a path toward increased provincial responsibilities. The taxation powers have not changed, however. As a result, provincial governments have more responsibility to spend money, but the federal government retains more power to raise money. This leads to the phenomenon of "fiscal federalism," which we discuss in detail in Chapter 18.

Canadian setting. Aboriginal groups did occupy the land, and so acquiring this land for European settlements meant that the British Crown would have to negotiate with Aboriginal peoples. These negotiations led to contracts, known as treaties, which guaranteed rights in perpetuity to Aboriginal peoples in exchange for allowing settlements on their traditional territories. These legal agreements are still in force today, and are the origins of what are called "treaty rights" for Aboriginals.

The accompanying time line highlights constitutional developments between 1759 and 1867.

The governments that were set up in the British North American colonies were not democratic. Initially, in each colony power was concentrated in the office of a governor, who was a British citizen appointed by the British monarch, and responsible primarily for protecting the interests of the mother country. Gradually, as they grew in population size and economic clout,

BOX 2.1   TIME LINE

Constitutional Developments, 1758–1867

"Canada"	*"Maritimes"*
	1758 Nova Scotia assembly
1759 British conquest of Quebec	
1763 Royal Proclamation	
	1773 Prince Edward Island assembly
1774 Quebec Act	
	1784 New Brunswick assembly
1791 Constitutional Act	
1837 Rebellions	
1840 Act of Union	
1848 Responsible government	1848 Responsible government (NS and NB)

1867 British North America Act (Constitution Act, 1867)

the interests of the colonies were taken into account in the structure of local governments. The 1774 **Quebec Act**, for example, established a council to advise the governor in the colony of Quebec. This council was initially appointed rather than elected, but, importantly for the time, the governor was able to choose French-speakers as well as English-speakers, and Catholics as well as Protestants. In deference to the local population, the colonial government also combined the British system of criminal law with the existing French system of civil law. The first elected assembly in the "Canadian" part of British North America was summoned in Nova Scotia in 1758, followed by Prince Edward Island in 1773.

In 1776, the residents of the 13 "American" colonies declared their independence from British rule. French Canadians essentially remained neutral in this dispute, and because little anti-British sentiment existed in the "Canadian" colonies, thousands of ex-Americans loyal to Britain—the United Empire Loyalists—migrated to "Canada." Many settled in modern-day New Brunswick, leading to the severing of that colony from Nova Scotia in 1784, together with the creation of its own assembly. Then, in response to pressure from those Loyalists who moved into what is now Ontario, and who were already accustomed to operating with an elected assembly, Britain passed the 1791 **Constitutional Act**. This gesture also served to reward the loyalty of the French for not joining the American Revolution. The act divided the colony in two—Upper and Lower Canada—each with a governor, an executive council, an appointed legislative council, and a locally elected assembly. In the case of Lower Canada, the appointed councils were primarily composed of Anglophones, and the assembly, of franco-phones. In Upper Canada, which was almost exclusively English, the Constitutional Act provided for British, rather than French, civil law. The executive council gradually evolved into the Cabinet, while the legislative council was the forerunner of the Senate. Thus, by 1791, all the colonies had achieved **representative government**—that is, a set of political institutions that included an elected legislative assembly. (See Figure 2.1 to trace the evolution of the political institutions.)

Although these governments were representative in the sense of having elected assemblies, they were not democratic because the government—where real power lay—was not obligated to follow the demands of the elected assembly. That assembly represented and articulated the views of the people, but had no real power over the governor and appointed councils. This situation was complicated by the cultural division in Lower Canada, where Lord Durham found "two nations warring in the bosom of a single state."[2] Reformers demanded **responsible government**, in which advisers to the governor would both be chosen from and reflect the views of the elected assembly. This presented a problem in the colonies, however, because on many subjects Britain wanted the governor to do its will, not that of the local assembly. As a result, rebellions erupted in 1837 in both Upper and Lower Canada, led by William Lyon Mackenzie and Louis-Joseph Papineau respectively, and forced the British government to appoint Lord Durham to investigate the situation.

The 1839 **Durham Report** provided a blueprint for solving the problems of assembly—executive relations, recommending that the principle of responsible government be implemented with respect to local affairs so that the executive branch would govern only as long as it retained the confidence of the elected assembly. Durham outlined a division of powers between local and imperial authorities such that in local matters the governor would follow the advice of colonial authorities, but in matters of imperial concern he would act as an agent of the British government. Responsible government came to Nova Scotia, New Brunswick, and the colony of Canada in 1848, and three years later to Prince Edward Island. In other words, all these pre-Confederation British colonies now operated on the basis that the governor chose the Cabinet or executive council from the assembly and it had to resign if it lost the confidence of the elected members. British Columbia acquired responsible government when it joined Confederation, as did the other provinces as they were created. Responsible government remains a sacred principle of Canadian government and is usually expressed as follows: a form of government in which the political executive must retain the confidence of the elected legislature and must resign or call an election if and when it is defeated on a vote of nonconfidence. At this period of time, of course, the government

FIGURE 2.1   EVOLUTION OF CANADIAN PRE-CONFEDERATION POLITICAL INSTITUTIONS

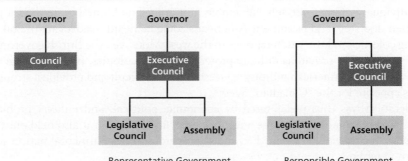

remained otherwise undemocratic in the sense that the vote for the assembly was limited to privileged white men.

Durham also recommended that Upper and Lower Canada be united into a single colony of Canada, partly in one last attempt to submerge and assimilate the French. Thus, to this day, Durham is reviled by many French Canadians. The colonies were amalgamated by the 1840 **Act of Union** (which came into effect in 1841), but English did not remain the sole language of government operations for long. When it became clear that assimilation of French Canadians would not be achieved, French was also recognized as an official language of the legislature. Moreover, most governments of the period were headed by a combination of English and French leaders.

THE ROAD TO CONFEDERATION

Shortly after achieving responsible government, the individual British North American colonies began to think of uniting. The colonies were driven to consider such a union because of economic, political, and military factors.[3] Since Britain had discontinued colonial trading preferences, and because a reciprocity treaty with the United States had expired, the colonies hoped to establish a new free trade area among themselves. This large internal market would be enhanced by a railway link between the Maritimes and central Canada, which in turn would provide the latter with a winter Atlantic port. The future prospect of annexing and developing the West was also seen as a source of economic prosperity.

Meanwhile, the colony of Canada had experienced political deadlock between its two parts, then called Canada East (Quebec) and Canada West (Ontario), as well as between the French and English component groups. Public decisions had to be made in one large, combined set of governmental institutions, yet the needs and demands of the two parts were often quite different. This led to the practice of requiring a "double majority" (a majority of members from each part of the colony) for the passage of bills. Confederation would allow greater autonomy to the two parts because while a central government would deal with problems that all the colonies had in common, provincial governments would handle distinctive internal matters on their own. Such a two-tier structure also appealed to the Maritime provinces, which did not feel like turning all decisions over to a distant central government.

The individual colonies also felt vulnerable militarily. The United States had a powerful army on their doorstep, and prominent Americans could be heard to advocate the takeover of the existing colonies and the vast territories to the west. Moreover, the British government was no longer interested in providing military protection to the colonies. By joining together, the colonies would make American military aggression more difficult and provide a stronger force to resist its appetite for the "Canadian" West.

Confederation was thus precipitated by economic, political, and military problems and seemed to most colonial leaders to be a means of solving them. But it also held out the hope that the new country would one day become a prosperous, transcontinental nation similar to its southern neighbour.

In the 1860s, Nova Scotia, New Brunswick, and Prince Edward Island began to consider forming a Maritime union, and they called the Charlottetown Conference for this purpose in 1864. When the self-invited delegates from the colony of Canada arrived, however, the idea of a larger union was put up for debate. Discussions continued at the Quebec Conference later that year, where the essentials of the Confederation scheme were agreed on. The London Conference of 1866 fine-tuned the agreement, leaving Prince Edward Island (and Newfoundland) temporarily on the sidelines. Nova Scotia, New Brunswick, and the colony of Canada—now divided between Ontario and Quebec—were officially united on July 1, 1867, by the **British North America Act**, later renamed the **Constitution Act, 1867**. Figure 2.2 is a map of Canada in 1867.

It did not take long for the country to grow. Inspired by Louis Riel, Canada acquired Rupert's Land from the Hudson's Bay Company, and Manitoba was added as a fifth province in 1870, to be followed by British Columbia in 1871 and Prince Edward Island in 1873. In 1905, Alberta and Saskatchewan were carved out of the Northwest Territories, and Newfoundland was added in 1949. Besides these 10 provinces, Canada now consists of three semi-autonomous territories: Yukon, Northwest Territories, and Nunavut. Figure 2.3 shows the map of Canada today, and changes over this period can be found at http://atlas.nrcan.gc.ca/site/english/maps/historical/territorialevolution.

FIGURE 2.2 CANADA AT CONFEDERATION, 1867

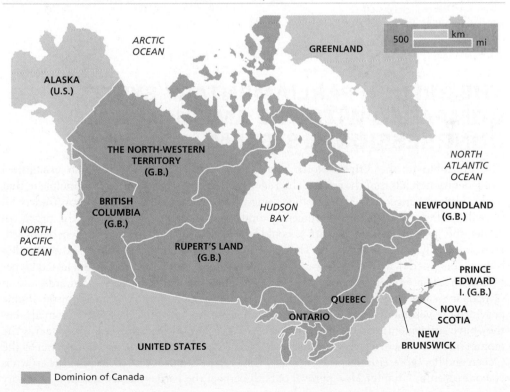

FIGURE 2.3   DATE OF ENTRY OR CREATION OF PROVINCES AND TERRITORIES

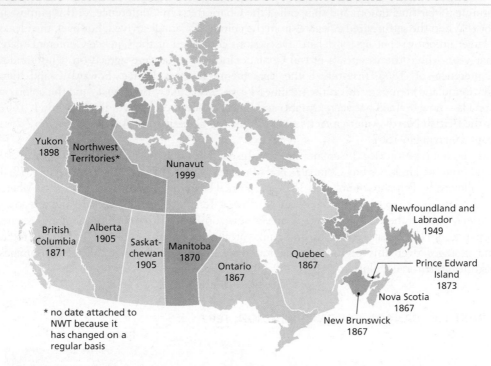

* no date attached to
NWT because it
has changed on a
regular basis

THE BRITISH PARLIAMENTARY SYSTEM COMPARED WITH THE AMERICAN CONGRESSIONAL SYSTEM

The Preamble to the British North America Act of 1867, the act which established Confederation, reads that the colonies had adopted a "Constitution similar in principle to that of the United Kingdom." Among other things, this meant that the central government in Canada (called the "federal government"), and the governments in each of the provinces (called the "provincial governments"), would be based on the parliamentary system of government, to which there are two parts. The legislative part in Canada, Britain, and other jurisdictions is composed of an elected lower house, the House of Commons, and an unelected Upper House. In Great Britain, this unelected upper house is known as the House of Lords, and in Canada it is called the Senate, with its members being appointed by the prime minister. (Some provincial governments in Canada initially had upper houses called legislative councils, but they have subsequently abolished them.) The second part of the parliamentary system is the monarch or the crown, a position which is embodied by the Queen in Great Britain and by the Queen and her representative, the Governor General, in Canada. The concept of the crown is elaborated on in Chapter 21. Approval of both parts of the parliamentary system is necessary for the passage of legislation and certain other authoritative decisions. In order to become law, as we shall see in Chapter 23, a bill in the parliamentary system must pass through both houses of the legislature and also receive the approval of the crown.

In the Constitution Act, 1867, the most important powers in Canadian parliamentary government appear to be vested in the governor general, acting by and with the advice of his or her "advisors." By convention, however, these advisors are to be chosen principally from among the members of the legislature, and, most important, they are to retain their positions as advisors only so long as they maintain the confidence of the House of Commons. In other words, the governor general can only act on most matters "by and with the advice" of his or her "advisors," and these advisors can only advise provided that they maintain majority support from among the elected members in the House of Commons. Such is the manner in which the principle of responsible government operates today.

Although the British system is called parliamentary government, and although it is said to operate on the principle of the **supremacy of Parliament**, such labels and descriptions are somewhat misleading. In practice, the most important powers in the parliamentary system of government reside with the advisors of the crown who hold the confidence of the House of Commons. These advisors are individually known as "ministers," and they are collectively known as "cabinet." The most important of these ministers, and the *first minister* appointed to cabinet, is the prime minister. The core of the parliamentary system, even in 1867, was the prime minister and the Cabinet. Although they must be members of Parliament, they are such an important part of Parliament that they often relegate both the monarch and the other members of the House of Commons and Senate to a position of insignificance. To the prime minister and Cabinet are conferred the powers to lead the country and make the most important decisions in the political system. But, as mentioned, the principle of responsible government holds that they retain their position and their powers only as long as they are supported by a majority in Parliament. If the House of Commons declares a lack of confidence in the prime minister and Cabinet, they must either resign and make way for another group to take their place, or call an election, the latter option being the most common. Because the prime minister and Cabinet ministers have seats in the legislative branch, mostly the House of Commons, and because they are the source of most legislation, the system is often termed a "fusion of powers"—that is, it involves a combination of legislative and executive powers. This is because the cabinet is normally able to get its way with the formal executive—the Governor General and the Queen—as well as with the legislature—the House of Commons and the Senate.

In the British parliamentary system, then, the prime minister and Cabinet ministers, who have seats in Parliament, are given the power to introduce most legislation and the right to control most of the time of the legislature. They also have the exclusive power to introduce legislation of a financial nature—laws either to raise or spend money. They have wide powers to make appointments, to draft subordinate legislation under the authority of laws, to conduct international affairs, and essentially all the powers necessary to provide effective political leadership for the country. The parliamentary system is executive dominated, and because the British Parliament operates in the Palace of Westminster, this system is sometimes called the **Westminster model**. Other members of Parliament (MPs) may criticize and propose amendments, the monarch (or governor general) may advise and warn, but the prime minister and Cabinet almost always get their way. This is because a majority of the members of Parliament normally belong to the same political party as the prime minister and Cabinet, and together they constitute a **majority government**. Even more in Canada than in contemporary Britain, the prime minister and Cabinet impose rigid party discipline on their MPs to support their every move. The prime minister and Cabinet have less control in a **minority government** situation, where their supporters are outnumbered by opposition MPs. The 2015 election returned a majority Liberal government, but Prime Minister Trudeau has pledged to give Cabinet ministers and backbench MPs more influence over government decision-making. Figure 2.4 outlines the Canadian political institutions.

The significance of the Senate has declined since Confederation because its appointed, rather than elected, base diminishes its members' legitimacy in a democratic age. While the formal powers of the Senate have remained virtually equal to those of the House of Commons (unlike those of the British House of Lords, whose powers have been curtailed), senators have rarely felt it proper to exercise them. Moreover, independent behaviour has usually been discouraged by the fact that the party with a majority in the Senate has usually been the same one as had a majority in the Commons. If for any reason the Senate should ultimately defeat a government bill, it does not affect the constitutional standing of the prime minister and Cabinet. In other words, the principle of responsible government in the Westminster model, whether in Britain or Canada, does not apply to upper chambers. The model outlined above is also operational in each of the provinces, except that they now all possess one-chamber, or unicameral, legislatures.

The British parliamentary system also incorporates the principle of **judicial independence**. Although courts are established by acts of Parliament and judges are appointed by the prime minister and Cabinet or attorney general, the whole judicial system is then expected to operate independently of the executive and legislative branches of government. In the case of Britain itself, the judges have considerable discretion in interpreting laws but lack the power of **judicial review**—that is, the power to declare laws invalid. The Canadian judiciary soon appropriated to itself the power to invalidate laws that violated the federal–provincial division of powers but were otherwise quite restrained.

The British parliamentary system is distinct in many ways from the U.S. presidential—congressional system. There, the president and the two houses of the legislature (Congress) are independently elected, and no one is permitted to sit in more than one branch of government. The "separation of powers" means that executive, legislative, and judicial powers are

FIGURE 2.4   AN OUTLINE OF CANADIAN POLITICAL INSTITUTIONS

EXECUTIVE

Governor General

advised by the

Prime Minister and Cabinet

advised by the

Bureaucracy

LEGISLATURE

PM and Cabinet sit in and are responsible to the

House of Commons

Senate

JUDICIARY

Courts

Judges appointed by Executive interpret laws and can overturn certain executive actions and laws passed by Parliament.

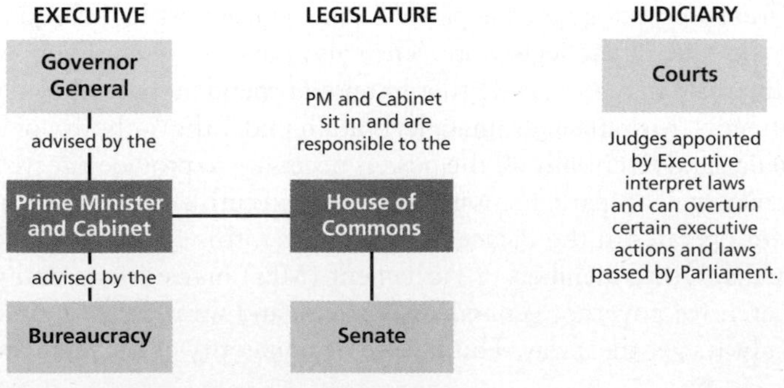

FIGURE 2.5   U.S. SYSTEM OF SEPARATION OF POWERS AND CHECKS AND BALANCES

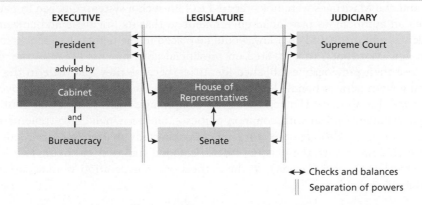

distributed to three separate branches of government: the president, Congress, and the courts, respectively. Moreover, the U.S. system is also characterized by "checks and balances" designed to ensure that the actions of any one branch of government are subject to veto by another.

Individual members of the House of Representatives and the Senate have much more legislative power than their counterparts in the British parliamentary system both in terms of initiating bills and amending or vetoing those emanating from the executive. Party discipline is also much looser, so that even if a majority of the members of Congress belong to the same party as the president, there is no guarantee that the president's initiatives will be passed. The Supreme Court also has the power of judicial review and can overturn any legislation that it feels is in violation of the Constitution. Apart from the name of the upper chamber—the Senate—the Fathers of Canadian Confederation adopted virtually nothing from the U.S. system with respect to the internal operation of the federal and provincial governments. Figure 2.5 outlines the relationships among the American political institutions.

CANADIAN AND AMERICAN FEDERALISM

Canadian Confederation was the first attempt to fuse the principles of the British parliamentary system with those of federalism, although Australia would make a similar move shortly afterward. Since the United States was the leading federal state of the day, and the one closest to Canada, the federal aspects of the new constitution were directly related to those next door.

The Fathers of Confederation were dealing with a large piece of territory, one they hoped would soon become larger, someday equalling or exceeding that of the United States. They came from colonies that had separate identities and a previous semi-autonomous existence. In this respect, the model of American federalism could not help but influence the design of the new country. It would have to be a federation of some kind, with a division of powers between the central and provincial governments.

Confederation was, to a large extent, the work of John A. Macdonald, who went on to become the first prime minister of Canada. Macdonald preferred a unitary state or legislative union in which the new central government would have almost all the powers, and the provinces would be little more than municipalities, as Box 2.2 indicates. But Quebec and the Maritimes were not prepared to join such a system. Quebec in particular demanded an autonomous provincial government so that its linguistic and cultural concerns, such as education and civil law, would be placed in the hands of a French-speaking majority. The Maritimes, too, insisted on provincial governments because they did not want to lose their previously established identities, because they had little in the way of municipal government to handle local problems, and because they were far removed from the new capital in Ottawa. Hence, the logical compromise was a system that contained a central government to deal with common purposes, and provincial governments to look after local concerns. Although this principle was essentially that of American federalism, it was also consistent with the existing British colonial tradition of having two levels of government (Britain and Canada), so the Fathers of Confederation were accustomed to such divided jurisdiction.

BOX 2.2 VOICES

Hon. John A. Macdonald: "Now, as regards the comparative advantages of a legislative and a federal union, I have never hesitated to state my own opinions. I have again and again stated in the House, that, if practicable, I thought a legislative union would be preferable. I have always contended that if we could agree to have one government and one parliament, legislating for the whole of these peoples, it would be the best, the cheapest, the most vigorous, and the strongest system of government we could adopt. But … we found that such a system was impracticable. In the first place, it would not meet the assent of the people of Lower Canada because they felt that in their peculiar position—being in a minority, with a different language, nationality and religion from the majority—in case of a junction with the other provinces, their institutions and their laws might be assailed, and their ancestral associations, on which they prided themselves, attacked and prejudiced; it was found that any proposition which involved the absorption of the individuality of Lower Canada … would not be received with favour by her people. We found, too, that though their people speak the same language and enjoy the same system of law as the people of Upper Canada … there was a great disinclination on the part of the various Maritime Provinces to lose their individuality, as separate political organizations, as we observed in the case of Lower Canada herself. Therefore, we were forced to the conclusion that we must either abandon the idea of union altogether, or devise a system of union in which the separate provincial organizations would be in some degree preserved."

Source: Confederation Debates, February 6, 1865, quoted in Ajzenstat, et al., eds. *Canada's Founding Debates* (Toronto: Stoddart Publishing, University of Toronto Press, 1999), pp. 279–80, © William D. Gairdner. Reprinted with permission of the publisher.

Macdonald accepted a federal form of government, then, to allow the former colonies to retain some of their political and economic independence, but he intended the new country to be a highly centralized federation. He felt that its economic and defensive objectives required a strong central government, a conviction shared by most of the other participants because they believed that the American Civil War (which had just ended as they began their deliberations) had been the result of too much power at the state level. Some historians have added that most of the Fathers of Confederation had links to banks, railways, and manufacturing companies, all of which looked on the Confederation project primarily as a source of profit. By controlling the development of the country at the centre, these politicians would be free to exploit the hinterland.[4]

Federalism can be defined as a **division of powers** between central and regional governments such that neither is subordinate to the other. It can be contrasted, on the one hand, with a *unitary government* or a *legislative union*, where all final authority resides with a central government, and, on the other hand, with a *confederal government*, where all final authority resides with the constituent governments. The Confederation settlement was not entirely consistent with the definition of federalism, however, because in certain respects the provinces were made subordinate to the central government. Some observers thus prefer to label the arrangement at its creation as "quasi-federal."[5] "Quasi" means "sort of, but not wholly." As we shall see in Chapter 18, Canada had a quasi-federal system in 1867 because the federal government was empowered to disallow any provincial legislation, although it could not legislate in all areas of provincial jurisdiction.

It was ironic that the Fathers of Confederation used the word "confederation," which in political science terms indicates a loose, decentralized federation, the opposite of what Macdonald intended. In the U.S. federal system, for example, the central government was given only certain delegated powers, while the residual powers remained at the level of the states. Macdonald was determined to reverse this pattern; he essentially gave the provinces 16 enumerated powers and left the residual powers at the centre. He was also careful to give Ottawa unlimited powers of taxation, broad powers to regulate trade and commerce, and power over such other important fields as defence and the criminal law.

Besides dividing powers between the two levels of government, constitutional architects in both Canada and the United States had to decide how the provinces or states would be represented at the national level. In both cases, the degree of democracy of the day required that the lower house of the legislature be based on the principle of representation by population, so that the most populous provinces or states would have the largest number of members in that chamber. To counterbalance this, and to protect the interests of the smaller states, the U.S. decided that each state, regardless of population, would have two senators at the national level. Some Fathers of Confederation preferred this idea, but others wanted representation by population in both houses of Parliament. The Canadian compromise was to base the Senate on the principle of equal *regional* representation rather than equal *provincial* representation.

Because Canadian politicians were already familiar with divided authority, it might seem that a fusion of the British parliamentary system and American federalism was not such a constitutional innovation. The colonial division of powers was of a somewhat different kind, however, and, more importantly, the whole ethos underlying the Canadian and U.S. systems was different. In the British parliamentary system, everything is designed to *facilitate* government action by concentrating power in the hands of the executive, whether in terms of its relationship with other institutions of government, such as Parliament and the courts, or with territorial units, such as local governments. In the American system, everything is designed to *inhibit* government action by preventing the concentration of power in the hands of any authority. Institutions of the national government—president, House of Representatives, Senate, and Supreme Court—should be able to veto each other, and they should collectively be kept in line by a division of powers that gives most authority to the states. It is largely because the British system is designed to facilitate government action and because the American system is designed to inhibit it that the fusion of the two systems in Canadian Confederation was such a distinctive phenomenon. John A. Macdonald saw the contradiction and tried to establish a federal system that was much more centralized than that next door.

One of the great ironies of Canadian constitutional development is that the country is now one of the most decentralized federations in the world. The evolution of Canadian federalism from a highly centralized to a highly decentralized state is discussed in Chapter 18. The reasons for this development include the enormous size of the country, strong regional sentiments, Quebec's endless quest for greater autonomy, and judicial decisions related to the division of powers that went against John A. Macdonald's intentions.

The only major change since the central institutional structure was established in Canada in 1867 was the adoption of the **Charter of Rights and Freedoms** in 1982. It added to the scope of judicial review with respect to the federal–provincial division of powers by importing American-style judicial authority in the area of protecting individual rights and freedoms. Henceforth, the courts could disallow federal or provincial legislation and other government actions that violated the Constitution either in terms of the division of powers or of the Charter of Rights.

THE ROAD TO CANADIAN SOVEREIGNTY

Having outlined the development of the basic institutions of the Canadian political system, let us trace the evolution of Canada from British colony to sovereign state. Contrary to popular belief, the British North America (BNA) Act of 1867 (that is, the Constitution Act, 1867) did not directly advance the cause of Canadian independence. It simply divided the powers that were already being exercised in Canada between a new central government and the provincial governments. British control still existed in many forms:

- British appointment of the governor general
- The power of the governor general to reserve Canadian legislation for the approval of the British Cabinet
- The power of the British government to disallow Canadian legislation
- The power of the British Parliament to amend the BNA Act
- The arbitrary extension to Canada of imperial legislation
- The paramountcy of any British legislation in conflict with Canadian statutes
- Canadian incapacity to pass legislation with extraterritorial effect
- The authority of the British Judicial Committee of the Privy Council as Canada's final court of appeal
- British control of Canadian foreign and trade policy

The act of Confederation made Canada a more respectable and viable entity and ultimately strengthened its case for greater autonomy, but it did not fundamentally alter the British–Canadian relationship.

Canada had succeeded in claiming the right to control its own tariffs even before Confederation, however, and between 1867 and 1914 it became increasingly autonomous in making commercial treaties with other countries. The same was true in terms of political treaties, although progress in this area came more slowly. One modest advance was the inclusion of Prime Minister Macdonald as a member of the British team that negotiated the 1871 Treaty of Washington. Relations with Britain were handled through the governor general, the Colonial Office, the Canadian High Commissioner in London after 1879, and in periodic Imperial Conferences after 1887.

By the end of the 19th century Canadian autonomy had progressed to the point that when Prime Minister Wilfrid Laurier sent an official contingent to the South African (Boer) War, it was done more in response to Canadian public opinion than to British pressure. In the Alaska Boundary dispute of 1903, however, the British representative on the Anglo-Canadian half of the judicial tribunal voted with the three American representatives to award the United States a long strip of the northern British Columbia coastline. In defending Canadian interests, Britain was apparently not prepared to jeopardize its relations with the United States.

The ultimate independence of Canada and of several other British colonies is usually attributed to developments connected to the First World War. Although Canada was automatically at war in 1914 as a result of British action, the Canadian government determined the extent of its own commitments, and Canada made a major contribution to the war effort. A series of conferences of Dominion prime ministers called the Imperial War Cabinet began in 1917, as Canada and the other dominions—Australia, New Zealand, and South Africa—demanded a policymaking role in return for their wartime efforts. Prime Minister Robert Borden and his counterparts took part in the Paris Peace Conference and signed the peace treaties, and the dominions became individual members of the League of Nations. Thus, by 1919, Canada had gained new international

Jonathan Hayward/The Canadian Press

The Vimy Ridge Monument commemorates the great battle in 1917. Some 3600 Canadian soldiers were killed and another 5000 injured, but it contributed to victory in the war and to Canada's independence.

status as a result of both accomplishments on the battlefield and subsequent demands for recognition at the conference table.

Postwar attempts to forge a unified Empire foreign policy broke down as various dominions sought to flex their fledgling muscles, and Prime Minister Mackenzie King insisted that Britain not co-sign the 1923 Halibut Treaty between Canada and the United States. Based on the Balfour Report, the Imperial Conference of 1926 ended with a proclamation of the complete equality in status of the United Kingdom and the dominions in internal, international, and imperial affairs. They were described in the proclamation as "autonomous Communities within the British Empire, equal in status, in no way subordinate one to another in any aspect of their domestic or external affairs, though united by a common allegiance to the Crown, and freely associated as members of the British Commonwealth of Nations."

Besides giving Canada complete autonomy in all policy fields, the 1926 declaration had implications for the position of the governor general. This official would no longer be an agent of the British government, but rather only a personal representative of the Crown. Disallowance of Canadian legislation by the British Cabinet and reservation of Canadian legislation by the governor general would now be obsolete. These arrangements were refined at another conference in 1930 and then constitutionalized in the **Statute of Westminster** of 1931. That statute provided that the Colonial Laws Validity Act (under which Dominion statutes were void if they conflicted with statutes of the Imperial Parliament) would no longer apply to the dominions, that in the future no Dominion statute was to be declared void because it was repugnant to the law of the United Kingdom, and that no act of the Imperial Parliament was to extend to a Dominion unless the latter had requested and consented to its enactment. The Statute also declared that a Dominion Parliament had the power to enact laws having extraterritorial operation.[6] The accompanying time line illustrates constitutional developments between 1867 and 1982.

BOX 2.3 TIME LINE

Constitutional Developments, 1867–1982

1919	Member of the League of Nations
1926	Balfour Declaration—Imperial Conference confers autonomy on Dominions
1931	Statute of Westminster confirms independence from Britain
1949	Supreme Court of Canada becomes final court of appeal
1982	Made-in-Canada constitutional amending formula

The drive to loosen links with Britain was thus largely engineered by prime ministers Laurier, Borden, and King, without much apparent public pressure. Reducing British control would automatically increase the power of the Canadian state that these politicians controlled. O.D. Skelton, the trusted adviser of Liberal prime ministers in the early years of the 20th century, has also been identified as a leading advocate of breaking the British bonds.

After 1931, therefore, Canada was completely independent of Britain, but a number of anomalies somewhat disguised this fact. First, Canada continued to share a head of state with

Britain, although from the Canadian perspective, that person was King or Queen of Canada. Even though the Canadian government now had the power to select the governor general, prime ministers continued to appoint British aristocrats, diplomats, and war heroes until 1952. Of more importance, because Canada had not been able to decide how to amend the BNA Act within Canada, such amendments still had to be passed by the British Parliament, albeit only at Canadian request. Also of great significance, the **Judicial Committee of the Privy Council (JCPC)** remained Canada's final court of appeal in criminal cases until 1933 and in all other cases, notably constitutional, until 1949.

Once Canada made an autonomous decision to take part, the Second World War saw the Canadian armed forces integrated with the Allied powers. Afterward, however, British–Canadian ties declined as Canada's population became more diversified in its ethnic origins, as Britain occupied a diminished role in world affairs, and as both Britain and Canada drew closer to the United States.[7] Although the definitive break occurred between 1914 and 1940, perhaps the final realization did not dawn until the Suez Crisis of 1956. The British and French bombardment of Egypt in defence of the Suez Canal in that year represented the first major international incident in which Canada found itself at odds with Britain.[8]

Other forms of disengagement occurred in the post-war period. In 1947, a new Canadian Citizenship Act recognized Canadian citizenship as a separate category from British subject. In 1949, a procedure was developed to enact constitutional amendments in Canada if they affected only the federal level of government, the same year that the Supreme Court of Canada became our final court of appeal. In 1965, Canada adopted its new flag in place of the Union Jack and Red Ensign, and in centennial year 1967, the government recognized "O Canada" rather than "God Save the Queen" as the Canadian national anthem, although it was not until 1980 that the former was designated officially. Finally, in 1982, a comprehensive domestic formula for making constitutional amendments was agreed to and enshrined in the **Constitution Act, 1982**.

Thus, in the 21st century, Canada continues to share the Queen with Britain and several other countries and is part of the Commonwealth; nationals of both Canada and Britain have invested in each other's economies; the Canadian parliamentary and legal systems are based on those of Britain; a majority of Canadians speak a variant of the English language; and many are still linked to Britain by family ties. Otherwise, however, both Canada and Britain see each other as just another friendly, foreign country, with minimal influence and no control.

PRINCIPLES OF THE CANADIAN CONSTITUTION

Apart from the **colonialism** that formally ceased in 1931, the preceding discussion has identified four basic principles of the Canadian **Constitution**.[9] First, in terms of its head of state, Canada is a **constitutional monarchy**. This is not a principle that attracts much attention, largely because the monarch herself lives in another country and because her actual power, as well as that of her Canadian representative, the governor general, is not extensive. Nevertheless, as outlined in Chapter 21, the monarchical system underlies a great deal of the operation of government in Canada, largely in the form of the Crown.[10] The **Crown** can be defined as the sum total of residual or discretionary powers still left in the hands of the monarch. The term "constitutional monarchy" basically means that the monarch reigns according to the Constitution, and one that has put most of the powers of government into someone else's hands. Almost all of the powers once exercised by the monarch have been whittled away either by legislation or by constitutional convention, although the Crown retains an important symbolic presence in the claims of Aboriginal people.

PRINCIPLES OF THE CANADIAN CONSTITUTION

- Constitutional monarchy
- Responsible government
- Federalism
- Judicial review
- Rule of law
- Democracy

The principle of responsible government, acquired in the 1840s, continues its essential role in the relationship between and executive and legislative branches of government. In fact, governments have fallen on motions of nonconfidence as recently as 2005 and 2011. But given strong party discipline in the House of Commons and the usual existence of a majority government, such ultimate control of the executive by the legislature is exercised on rare occasions; indeed, legislative control of the executive has almost been reversed on a day-to-day basis, as this chapter earlier indicated.

Federalism, based on the constitutional division of powers between the two levels of government such that neither level is subordinate to the other, has become more genuine than originally set out in the BNA Act. Not only are the provinces more important, but over the years, the division of powers became increasingly blurred as both levels of government expanded their operations and engaged in a large degree of "cooperative federalism." The Harper government, however, sought to return to a clearer separation of the two levels of government, as noted in Chapter 18.

Judicial review is the power of the courts to overturn certain executive and legislative decisions. As mentioned, judicial review originally applied primarily to the federal–provincial division of powers, but has since been extended to the courts' active protection of rights and freedoms.

At least two other fundamental principles are also embedded in the Canadian Constitution: the rule of law and democracy. The **rule of law** is another constitutional principle inherited from Great Britain that rests largely on convention and judicial precedent. In essence, it means that all government action must be based on law and that governments and government officials must obey the law. In other words, the law is supreme, and no one, including the lawmakers, is above it.[11] Courts in Canada as well as Britain have had occasion to overturn government decisions and actions that were not based on law.[12]

Finally, Canada is a **democracy**. This term, which is related to responsible government, constitutional monarchy, and the rule of law, will be analyzed more fully in Chapter 11. Four components are often associated with the word democracy: popular sovereignty, meaning that the people ultimately rule, primarily through periodic elections; political equality, meaning that everyone has one vote on election day; political freedom, meaning that during and between elections people are free to organize and advocate for political purposes; and majority rule, meaning that except in defined situations designed to protect minority rights, the will of the majority prevails. Canada was hardly a democracy in 1867, however, and political equality in terms of universal suffrage was only achieved long afterward.

CONCLUSION

This chapter has shown how Canada developed from a British colony to a sovereign state. It also traced the evolution of government institutions along the way, focusing primarily on the foundations established in 1867. Those foundations consisted of the grafting of the British parliamentary and American federal systems, although certain aspects of the latter were deliberately avoided. The discussion has also revealed the fact that the question of French–English relations has been integral to Canadian constitutional development from the very beginning. Most of the subjects of this chapter are considered in greater depth later in the text, especially in Part 4, the constitution, federalism, and the Charter of Rights, and in Part 5, the executive, bureaucracy, Parliament, and judiciary.

DISCUSSION QUESTIONS

1. How would you characterize the British treatment of French Canadians after the Conquest?

2. How did the United Empire Loyalists change the face of Canada?

3. What aspects of the French–English political relationship were established before or at Confederation?

4. What is meant by the "Westminster model," and how does it differ from the U.S. system of government?

5. What aspects of American federalism did Canada adopt, and what aspects did it reject?

6. Is there an inherent contradiction between the British parliamentary system and the American federal system? Explain.

7. What is an example of path dependence and why?

MindTap® FOR MORE INFO GO TO **http://www.nelson.com/student**

NOTES

1. Some of the key sources on Canada's constitutional evolution are W.P.M. Kennedy, ed., *Documents of the Canadian Constitution, 1759–1915* (Toronto: Oxford University Press, 1918); R. MacGregor Dawson, *The Government of Canada*, 5th ed., revised by Norman Ward (Toronto: University of Toronto Press, 1970); and Bayard Reesor, *The Canadian Constitution in Historical Perspective* (Scarborough:

Prentice Hall Canada, 1992). The following website is also useful: http://www.canadiana.org/citm/primary/primary_e.html.

2. Lord Durham, *Report of the Affairs of British North America*, Gerald M. Craig, ed. (Toronto: McClelland and Stewart, 1963).

3. P.B. Waite, *The Confederation Debates in the Province of Canada/1865* (Toronto: McClelland and Stewart, 1963); P.B. Waite, *The Life and Times of Confederation, 1864–1867*, 2nd ed. (Toronto: University of Toronto Press, 1962); Donald Creighton, *The Road to Confederation* (Toronto: Macmillan, 1964); and Richard Gwyn, *John A: The Man Who Made Us: The Life and Times of John A. Macdonald* (Toronto: Vintage Canada, 2007).

4. Stanley B. Ryerson, *Unequal Union: Confederation and the Roots of Conflict in the Canadas, 1815–1873*, 2nd ed. (Toronto: Progress Books, 1973).

5. K.C. Wheare, *Federal Government*, 4th ed. (London: Oxford University Press, 1963).

6. Dawson, *The Government of Canada*, p. 54.

7. Many historians blame the King and St. Laurent governments for the Americanization of Canada after the Second World War, but J.L. Granatstein argues that British weakness was of greater significance than any deliberate Canadian government objective. See Donald Creighton, *Canada's First Century* (Toronto: Macmillan, 1970); George Grant, *Lament for a Nation: The Defeat of Canadian Nationalism* (Toronto: McClelland and Stewart, 1965); and J.L. Granatstein, *How Britain's Weakness Forced Canada into the Arms of the United States* (Toronto: University of Toronto Press, 1989).

8. John Hilliker, *Canada's Department of External Affairs: The Early Years, 1909–1926* (Montreal: McGill-Queen's University Press, 1990).

9. Reesor, *The Canadian Constitution in Historical Perspective*, ch. 4.

10. David E. Smith, *The Invisible Crown* (Toronto: University of Toronto Press, 1996).

11. Reesor, *The Canadian Constitution in Historical Perspective*, pp. 66–71.

12. For example, Quebec premier Maurice Duplessis had no legal basis to cancel a restaurant liquor licence just because the proprietor provided bail for Jehovah Witnesses. See *Roncarelli v. Duplessis*, [1959] S.C.R. 121.

FURTHER READING

Ajzenstat, Janet, Paul Romney, Ian Gentles, and William D. Gairdner, eds. *Canada's Founding Debates*. Toronto: Stoddart Publishing, 1999.

Creighton, Donald. *The Road to Confederation*. Toronto: Macmillan, 1964.

———. *Canada's First Century*. Toronto: Macmillan, 1970.

Gwyn, Richard. *John A: The Man Who Made Us: The Life and Times of John A. Macdonald*. Toronto: Vintage Canada, 2007.

———. *Nation Maker: Sir John A. Macdonald: His Life, Our Times*. Toronto: Random House Canada, 2011.

Hilliker, John. *Canada's Department of External Affairs: The Early Years, 1909–1926*. Montreal: McGill-Queen's University Press, 1990.

Reesor, Bayard. *The Canadian Constitution in Historical Perspective*. Scarborough: Prentice Hall Canada, 1992.

Ryerson, Stanley B. *Unequal Union: Confederation and the Roots of Conflict in the Canadas, 1815–1873*, 2nd ed. Toronto: Progress Books, 1973.

Waite. P.B. *The Life and Times of Confederation, 1864–1867*, 2nd ed. Toronto: University of Toronto Press, 1962.

Chase Clausen/Shutterstock

THE SOCIETAL CONTEXT: CLEAVAGES AND IDENTITIES

The next eight chapters deal with the main elements of the societal or socioeconomic context of the Canadian political system: principally regionalism, ethnicity, class, and gender. Political scientists generally believe that these aspects of Canadian society are the most relevant to politics because they represent deep, persistent divisions in society called **cleavages**, as mentioned in Chapter 1. Each chapter examines the statistical and historical base of the relevant societal characteristic, the demands that each cleavage generates, and the current issues involved.

Another way to look at these characteristics of Canadian society is in terms of **identities**. Indeed, issues relating to ethnicity, gender, and sexual orientation are commonly referred to today as the "politics of identity" or the "politics of recognition" and some observers argue that such identities have become more important than traditional cleavages. People must be conscious of a particular characteristic—it must be part of their identity—in order to act on it politically. Many of the demands with which the authorities have to contend, and many of the interests that the authorities themselves represent, originate from such cleavages and identities.

Conflicting regional economic claims and distinctive regional identities have been constants of Canadian politics since the beginning and continue to be animating agents. In fact, the shift of population, employment, and political and economic power from central Canada to the West has become a stark reality in recent years. The French–English question and the role of Quebec traditionally overshadowed other ethnic, linguistic, and cultural identities and cleavages, but ongoing political developments justify a robust discussion of Aboriginal peoples as well as Canada's minority ethnocultural groups. The claims of various identifiable communities have been legitimated in policy, law, and the Constitution, such as in the recognition of Aboriginal rights, official bilingualism, and multiculturalism, but the achievement of such recognition did not end conflict or discrimination. That is partly because of the contrasting perceptions that each group has of its own history and evolving understandings of each group's status. Class cleavages are generally weaker in Canada than some of the other divisions mentioned. Chapter 8 will show, however, that class is an important factor in Canadian politics even if it is often overlooked. It is now also common to point to the increasing importance of sex and gender in Canadian politics, especially with respect to women, sexual orientation, and gender identity and expression. Here too, established rights do not always equate with equitable practice.

Three other cleavages and identities are considered together in Chapter 9: religion, age, and urban/rural location. These three cleavages do not always receive the same attention as the others identified above, but they are of notable importance. Although they have always been on the political agenda, they seem to have gained a new lease on life in recent years.

For the sake of clarity, these identities and cleavages are discussed in separate chapters, but in real life they interact and overlap. Sometimes these factors reinforce each other (poor immigrant women; rich Anglo businessmen), but at other times they cut across one another, as outlined in Chapter 1. In any case, the different socioeconomic groups all compete for the attention of governments.

Chase Clausen/Shutterstock

CHAPTER 3

Regionalism

Regions have always played a defining role in Canadian politics. Beginning in the country's infancy, with debates over railway construction and trade policies that favoured different parts of the geographically vast country, regional identities and economic interests have often led to lasting cleavages. While there remains debate about what exactly regions are, as we will see, some conflicts have involved larger geographic regions (i.e., western Canada) while others have tended toward provinces. Oil interests fuelled Alberta's rejection of the 1980 National Energy Program, as they do differences across the country on economic and environmental policies today, including recent fights by both Newfoundland and Labrador and Nova Scotia to remove petroleum revenues from the calculation of equalization payments. The Atlantic groundfish industry collapsed in the 1990s, and the softwood lumber dispute with the United States almost crippled British Columbia's forestry industry. Ontario argued that its residents paid billions more in federal taxes every year than they got back from Ottawa, and a widespread sentiment exists in other regions that the federal government favours Quebec because of the threat of separation.

This chapter will begin by outlining some theoretical considerations regarding the concept of regionalism and point to some of the conflicts that have arisen due to it. Questions of geography and economy are important dimensions of regionalism, and an examination of these two aspects of Canada seems to be an appropriate foundation. But since people tend to develop affective attachments to the areas of the world that surround them—their neighbourhood, city, province, and region—the discussion also includes key demands that regional cleavages and identities have generated unrelated to the economy, and some of the policies that have been made in response.

THEORETICAL CONSIDERATIONS

Although there is no doubt that the Canadian political system is characterized by regionalism, no consensus exists on exactly what those regions are or on how that concept should be defined. One way of treating regionalism in Canada would be to equate regions with provinces and territories. Of course, the political-legal-constitutional basis of provinces and territories is not synonymous with the natural, physiographic (or even socio-psychological) basis of regions, and the fit between regionalism and provinces/territories is imperfect. Nevertheless, the connection is a compelling one, and in discussing the question of regionalism, the 1979 Task Force on Canadian Unity had this to say:

> Regional communities require an institutional framework if they are to become viable units which can express themselves and organize their collective life in an effective manner. For that reason, it seems to us that the provinces and the northern territories are the basic building blocks of Canadian society and the logical units on which to focus a discussion of Canadian regionalism, even though they may not be the most "natural" regions from an economic point of view.[1]

To define regionalism in terms of such formal political-institutional boundaries would link it very closely to federalism. Provinces and territories have two primary effects as far as regional demands are concerned. On the one hand, regional demands articulated by a provincial or territorial premier are harder to ignore than those that come from less authoritative sources. In fact, to politicize such regional demands in this way may well serve to magnify them because premiers and bureaucrats can use such distinctiveness to justify an increase in their power. On the other hand, provinces and territories may be able to facilitate the decision-making process by handling local problems that are not controversial at the provincial/territorial level but that would cause great difficulty in Ottawa. The basic quest in the establishment of a federal system of government is to find the most appropriate division of powers and responsibilities between the national and provincial levels. This issue, the degree of centralization and decentralization in Canada, has never been settled to everyone's satisfaction, and Canadians still raise demands about the design of the federal system as well as about policies within it. The peculiarities of the special case of Quebec are discussed more thoroughly in Chapter 5.

A second manner of defining regionalism would be to take a geographic approach. Regions would be defined in terms of their similarity of physical features and separated from other regions by prominent topographical barriers—or even simply their general location, such as Canada's "west" or "north." To conceive of regions in this way is a fairly straightforward and useful enterprise, but it suffers from a rather static, rigid conceptualization that does not allow for change over time and that underplays the human element. It also implies, rather questionably, that geography leads to common political, social, and cultural characteristics.[2]

Some analysts prefer a third conception of regionalism which is somewhat more abstract. Regions are not fixed in political or geographic terms, but instead are fluid social creations that may change over time. They are "imagined communities" in which people feel that they have much in common with others. According to Richard Simeon, "regions are simply containers.... And how we draw the boundaries around them depends entirely on what our purposes are...."[3] In this sense, regions are primarily a state of mind—a psychological phenomenon.

A fourth approach to regionalism comes from dependency theory. It emphasizes the relations between different spatial entities, some dependent on others. In the Canadian case, this primarily relates to the dominance of central Canada over the outlying regions, and is often referred to in terms of the core and the hinterland or periphery, or the "metropolitan–hinterland" thesis. This approach focuses on the relations between the political and economic power of the centre and the underdeveloped periphery.[4] Almost all approaches to regionalism entail a significant discussion of the economy.

GEOGRAPHY

Physiographic Regions

By land mass, Canada is the second-largest country in the world. Prime Minister Mackenzie King once remarked that if some countries had too much history, Canada had too much geography.[5] Indeed, St. John's, Newfoundland is closer to London, England than to Victoria, British Columbia and many Canadians live and feel closer to adjacent U.S. states than to other Canadian regions. Such tremendous distances have always had a crucial influence on the Canadian political system, especially in generating feelings of regionalism, alienation, and economic demands. Most importantly, such distances had much to do with the creation of the provinces and territories in the first place.

The distance problem is immensely complicated by divisions caused by physical barriers. Canada is usually divided into seven physiographic regions, five with significant population, as shown in Figure 3.1. In other words, the vast territory is divided into five main regions by natural barriers running in a north–south direction. It is often simpler to travel southward to the United States than to cross the barriers into another part of Canada. The main aspect of Canadian geography that counterbalances these north–south forces is the river and lake

FIGURE 3.1 CANADA'S PHYSIOGRAPHIC REGIONS

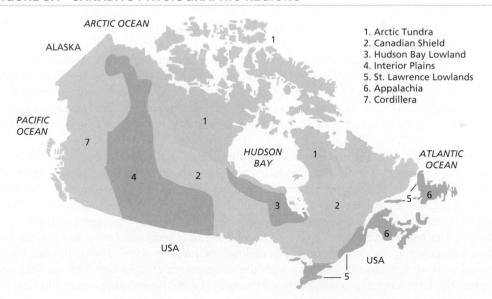

1. Arctic Tundra
2. Canadian Shield
3. Hudson Bay Lowland
4. Interior Plains
5. St. Lawrence Lowlands
6. Appalachia
7. Cordillera

CHAPTER 3 **Regionalism**

system. In this respect, the central historical role of the St. Lawrence River and the Great Lakes has often been noted.[6] After this natural east–west flow was enhanced by the construction of the St. Lawrence Seaway, ships were able to go halfway across the country, a fact that improved Canada's capacity to engage in international trade.

Transportation and Communications Systems

Apart from the Great Lakes–St. Lawrence water route, transportation and communications systems in Canada had to be constructed across the natural barriers. The establishment of each of these great transportation and communications projects dominated successive eras in Canadian politics.

Railways were the stuff of Canadian politics throughout the 19th and early 20th centuries. In particular, they formed a crucial part of the Confederation Settlement of the 1860s and 1870s. The Maritimes agreed to enter Confederation only if they were linked to central Canada by the Intercolonial Railway, and British Columbia was persuaded to join in 1871 with the promise of a transcontinental rail link within 10 years.[7] John A. Macdonald brought the Canadian Pacific Railway (CPR) project to completion in 1885, only four years behind schedule, and it became one of his lasting monuments. Although it was a private company, the CPR received enormous government assistance in the form of cash and land grants that later became prime real estate in the centre of many Canadian cities. Thus, while the building of the CPR was one of the great heroic events in Canadian history, it was also a classic example of the use of the state for the advantage of business and industry.[8]

Its original contract allowed the CPR to charge high prices, and freight rates have been a constant complaint of Western Canadians since the day the CPR was completed. Other railways were eventually built, but even with government assistance many went into receivership, and in the 1919–23 period, they were bailed out by the federal government in the creation of the Canadian National (CN) system. Thus, the establishment of CN as a Crown corporation could be seen not only as a service to isolated parts of the country but also as a benefit to bankrupt capitalist interests.

Because both CP and CN wanted out of the passenger side of the business, a separate Crown corporation, VIA Rail, was created in 1977–78. When the Mulroney government discontinued half its routes in 1990, train enthusiasts howled in protest and argued that the extent of government subsidization of highway, marine, and air transport should be taken into consideration when railway deficits were discussed. The Chrétien government then privatized CN by selling shares to the public.

The early 20th century saw automobiles replace much of the importance of rail. Because roads are primarily a provincial responsibility, however, their political significance is primarily seen at that level. The federal government was mainly called on to ensure that a highway extended across the whole country for commercial, recreational, and symbolic purposes. Thus, in 1949, the federal government signed the Trans-Canada Highway agreement with the provinces, under which Ottawa paid half the cost of bringing a transcontinental highway up to a national standard, and was eventually completed in 1962. In 1997, Prince Edward Island gained a "fixed link" to the mainland with the construction of the Confederation Bridge to replace the ferry service, an early and major example of a **public–private partnership (P3)**.

Given the distances involved, it is not surprising that demands also arose for a coordinated nationwide airline service carrying both passengers and cargo. The transport minister of the day, C.D. Howe, created Trans-Canada Airlines (now Air Canada) in 1937 as a Crown corporation. By the late 1980s, the Mulroney government argued the airline no longer served a **public policy purpose** as the country was now well served by private carriers, and privatized Air Canada. The Canadian Transportation Agency retained some regulatory powers, but with general deregulation and the transfer of major airport ownership to local nonprofit authorities in the 1990s, the federal government no longer had significant participation in the transportation industry.

MAJOR TRANSPORTATION AND COMMUNICATIONS LINKS AND AGENCIES INVOLVING GOVERNMENT

- Canadian Pacific
- Canadian National
- VIA Rail
- Trans-Canada Highway
- Trans-Canada Airlines/Air Canada
- Trans-Canada Pipeline
- Canadian Radio-television and Telecommunications Commission (CRTC)
- Canadian Broadcasting Corporation (CBC)
- Canada Post
- Telesat
- Teleglobe

Oil and natural gas pipelines, a newer means of transportation, have figured prominently in Canadian politics over the past 50 years. Although they are privately owned, the building of pipelines requires government approval. The construction of the main natural gas line to Eastern Canada, the Trans-Canada Pipeline, was probably the most controversial issue on the Canadian political agenda in the mid-1950s. The haste of C.D. Howe in ramming legislation through Parliament played a major role in the defeat of the St. Laurent government in 1957. More recently, the Keystone XL Pipeline project has generated controversy. It would have sent crude oil from Northern Alberta to refineries in Texas. However, despite various overtures from the Canadian government, US President Barack Obama vetoed a bill passed by the US Congress that would have approved the pipeline and finally announced a full rejection of the project in late 2015. The possibility of American reluctance to import oil from Canada heightened the sense of Prime Minister Stephen Harper as well as former Alberta premiers Alison Redford and Jim Prentice that Canada needed to find alternative markets for its oil reserves. The proposed Enbridge Northern Gateway Pipeline would carry oil over the Rocky Mountains to a Pacific shipping port in Kitimat, British Columbia. The oil could then be shipped by oil tankers to energy markets in Asia, particularly China. This proposal led to bitter conflict because of environmental concerns such as the potential of pipeline leaks on Aboriginal land and the increased presence of oil tankers in the hazardous waterways on the BC coast. Another alternative would be to extend or adapt existing pipelines to Eastern Canada or build new ones to replace the imported oil used in Quebec and the Maritime provinces.

Transportation presents special challenges in the North. Roads and railways were virtually nonexistent there until the Diefenbaker government sponsored its "Roads to Resources" program, and the Yellowknife region of the Northwest Territories became linked to Edmonton. The Alaska Highway, which passes through Yukon on its way from British Columbia, has been a crucial part of that territory's development. Various pipeline proposals have also been significant to the North, especially the proposed Mackenzie Valley Gas Pipeline of the 1970s. That no such pipelines have yet been constructed in the North is more a matter of economics than of concern about Aboriginal peoples or the environment, but the issue is high on the political agenda again.

As far as communications are concerned, the Canadian postal service was always a government responsibility, while telegraph, telephone, radio, and television usually developed first in the private sector. They soon led to government regulation, however, because some of these systems were natural monopolies or because of the limited number of frequencies available. That is now primarily the responsibility of the **Canadian Radio-television and Telecommunications Commission (CRTC)**. In most of these sectors demands also arose for public ownership, such as in the Prairie provinces' telephone systems. The **Canadian Broadcasting Corporation (CBC)** was created in 1932 in response to pressure for more Canadian content and more enlightened radio programming than was usually provided on local private stations, many of which relied on U.S. programs. The CBC became operational in English and French with its own stations, as well as affiliated private stations, in 1936, and CBC television began in 1952. To supplement the country's terrestrial microwave system, the government took the initiative in 1969 to launch Telesat, a joint public–private supplier of domestic communications satellite services. Intercontinental communications via submarine cables and satellites are handled by Teleglobe Canada, originally a Crown corporation that was privatized in 1987.

As we will see in Chapter 12, developments in communications technologies—particularly the Internet, smartphones, and increasingly satellite—are making it easier to communicate across the country, but they are complicating the Canadian regulatory regime. The original rationale for broadcasting regulation in Canada was related to the limited range of the electromagnetic spectrum over which it was possible to send radio and television signals. Even though spectrum scarcity is no longer relevant in light of modern communications technology, the Canadian government continues to regulate television and radio broadcasting by attaching conditions to licenses that require broadcasters to air a certain amount of Canadian content during peak viewing or listening times. The increasing ability of Canadians to access broadcasting feeds that stream live from other countries on the Internet, however, is raising questions about the effectiveness of the traditional regulatory mechanisms of government.

In short, in the field of transportation and communications, demands to overcome distances and divisions have been dominant features of Canadian politics. Governments have primarily responded with assistance to private corporations, the establishment of Crown corporations, and the creation of regulatory agencies. To create and hold together a nation, Canadians built east–west institutions that ran counter to the natural north–south geographic features of the continent and the perpetual pull of the United States. Since the late 1980s, however, governments have privatized a number of government operations and generally deregulated the transportation industry while decreasing support for communications, such as the CBC. Besides starting to dismantle these east–west links, governments began to sign north–south trade deals, leading many observers to question the continued existence of Canada as an independent nation-state. Symbolically, both CP Rail and the newly privatized CN Rail sold off track in Canada and laid off hundreds of employees while simultaneously becoming major players in the United States, and CN now calls itself "North America's Railroad." Pipeline construction and the increasing difficulty of regulating communications continue to be key issues in the Canadian political system.

Population Distribution

Physical barriers are only one complication of the distances that characterize Canada; the distribution of population is another because people are not spread uniformly throughout this gigantic territory. It is commonly emphasized that the overall density of the Canadian population is one of the lowest in the world, some 3.0 people per km^2. But it is really more significant that no permanent settlement exists in nearly 90 percent of the country and that over 70 percent of the population is huddled within 150 km of the U.S. border.[9] Provincial and territorial population disparities affect the allocation of seats in the House of Commons—indeed the whole power structure in Ottawa—and the calculation of federal transfer payments. Table 3.1 shows the population of the provinces and territories as of October 1, 2014.

TABLE 3.1   POPULATION OF PROVINCES AND TERRITORIES, OCTOBER 2014

ONTARIO	13 730 187	38.5%
QUEBEC	8 236 310	23.1%
BRITISH COLUMBIA	4 657 947	13.1%
ALBERTA	4 145 992	11.6%
MANITOBA	1 286 323	3.6%
SASKATCHEWAN	1 129 899	3.2%
NOVA SCOTIA	943 932	2.6%
NEW BRUNSWICK	754 643	2.1%
NEWFOUNDLAND/LABRADOR	526 837	1.5%
PRINCE EDWARD ISLAND	146 524	0.4%
NORTHWEST TERRITORIES	43 795	0.1%
YUKON	36 758	0.1%
NUNAVUT	36 687	0.1%
CANADA	35 675 834	

Source: Statistics Canada, Quarterly Demographic Estimates, Catalogue ¿No. 91-002-X, Table 1-1, 2014. http:// www.statcan.gc.ca/pub/91-002-x/2014003/t002-eng.htm. Reproduced and distributed on an "as is" basis with the permission of Statistics Canada.

Geographers frequently speak of the "core," "heartland," or "metropolis" on the one hand, and the "periphery" or "hinterland" on the other, and **core–periphery analysis** can be usefully applied to political science. The Toronto–Ottawa–Montreal triangle obviously constitutes the core of Canada, and Ontario and Quebec combined contain 62 percent of its people. Besides being the political core of the country, central Canada is also the economic heartland, with the largest concentration of corporate head offices, especially in the Toronto area. Moreover, it is the communications and cultural core, containing the headquarters of French and English CBC, CTV, Global, and private French television, many other Canadian cultural institutions, and most of the Canadian computer industry. However, this is changing. The population of Ontario and the West has grown more quickly than that of Quebec and the Atlantic provinces. At Confederation, there were 20 times as many Canadians living to the east of Ontario than to the west. That pattern reversed in 2010, and there are now more Canadians living to the west of Ontario than to the east of the province. Moreover, the population of Alberta and BC combined exceeds that of Quebec, and central Canada will likely soon fall below 60 percent of the total. These demographic trends are related to the increasing economic strength of western Canada resource development and the declining importance of manufacturing in the centre. As we will see in Chapter 23, some Canadian political institutions have not adapted to these changing demographic realities. In the Senate, for example, there are more representatives of the Atlantic Provinces (30) than there are of all of the Western Provinces combined (24), leading some Westerners to advocate a reformed Senate. Quebec, meanwhile, is extremely sensitive to its declining proportion of the total Canadian population, which by 1995 had fallen below a symbolic 25 percent, and since to 23 percent.[10]

ECONOMY

Having explored regionalism in geographic terms, we may now proceed to examine the Canadian economy. Such a discussion reveals striking regional economic differences that serve to reinforce geographic distinctions and create another pattern of demands on the Canadian political system.

Regional economic differences begin with primary industries—that is, the natural resource and energy base of the various provinces and territories. The importance of natural resources to the national economy has been a central tenet of the Canadian **political economy** tradition for generations, as mentioned in Chapter 1; it is usually termed the **staples theory** and is identified with the famous economic historian Harold Innis.[11] It postulates that Canadian economic development has relied on a succession of resource exports (staples)—furs, fish, timber, wheat, minerals, and energy—rather than on manufacturing; Canadians are mere "hewers of wood and drawers of water." The staples theory also includes the notions of dependence, such as of interregional exploitation, especially in the relationship between inner and outer Canada. It involves an economy that remains underdeveloped and subject to the rise and fall of international markets, a second kind of dependence. In international trade, Canada continues to this day to rely primarily on exports of natural resources, now particularly concentrated on solid and liquid minerals.

To economists, secondary industry consists of manufacturing, construction, and utilities, including electricity. Manufacturing includes the initial processing and refining of primary products as well as the making of finished goods, and generally produces more revenue and more jobs than primary industry, is less seasonal, and commands higher wages. Many observers have criticized the economic policy of almost all Canadian governments for having fostered the exploitation and exportation of raw natural resources rather than having developed an industrial policy that would give priority to manufacturing. The decline in manufacturing in Ontario in particular has many causes, including **globalization** (especially the rise of economic power in China) and the high value of the Canadian dollar, which makes it more difficult for this country to compete. Furthermore, the fact that both governments and corporations in Canada spend so little money on research and development (R&D) hinders the level of productivity in Canadian industry.

Economists then put transportation and communications, trade, finance, insurance and real estate, private services, and public administration into the tertiary or services category. Although the Canadian economy was never strong on manufacturing, much political attention in this "post-industrial" era is focused on the services sector. In outlining the trends in the Canadian labour force among the three divisions of the economy, Figure 3.2 demonstrates the contemporary importance of the tertiary sector.

The Atlantic Region

The Atlantic region historically relied on fishing, which has rarely been a very prosperous industry. In the 1990s, however, the Atlantic fishery fell into deeper trouble than ever before, primarily because of a dramatic reduction in groundfish stocks, especially cod, and an oversupply of fishers, plant workers, and trawlers. The three Maritime provinces (New Brunswick,

FIGURE 3.2 EMPLOYMENT IN CANADA BY SECTOR

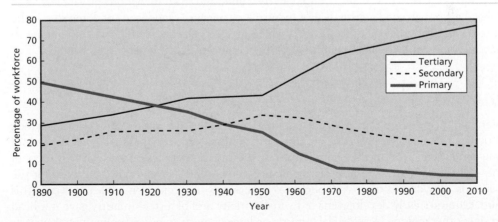

Sources: Stephen Brooks and Andrew Stritch, Business and Government in Canada (Scarborough: Prentice-Hall Canada, 1991), pg. 96; Statistics Canada, Employment by Industry, http://www.statcan.gc.ca/tables-tableaux/ sum-som/101/cst01/econ40-eng.htm, calculations by authors.

Nova Scotia, and PEI) have a substantial agricultural base, which has provided prosperity for a few large firms but generally poor returns for most farmers. New Brunswick, Newfoundland and Labrador, and Nova Scotia also engage in forestry and mining, while Labrador possesses great quantities of hydroelectric power. None of these resources led to much general prosperity in the Atlantic region, however, which is marked by considerable seasonal unemployment. Some processing and refining of natural resources takes place in the region, but among other factors, the small local market and the distance from major population centres have left the region in a state of underdevelopment. Led by New Brunswick, a new emphasis on communications technology has transformed Atlantic Canada's economy to some extent, because in the modern technological world physical distance is not the hindrance it was in the past. Newfoundland's offshore petroleum revenues have given the province a major boost, and natural gas from the Sable Island Offshore Energy Project benefits Nova Scotia. With the temporary exception of Newfoundland and Labrador, however, the Atlantic region is considerably below the national average in terms of per capita income or fiscal capacity.

Quebec

The Quebec economy is more diversified than that of the Atlantic region and somewhat more prosperous. Quebec's primary industries include farming in the St. Lawrence Lowlands, along with mining and forestry in the Canadian Shield. The shield is also traversed by numerous powerful rivers, on which huge dams have been built, making hydroelectricity Quebec's most valuable resource. Electricity is the basis of Quebec's aluminum industry, for example, as well as of much other secondary industry such as pulp and paper and newsprint. In addition, Quebec has more sophisticated manufacturing than the Atlantic region, including metals, electronics, pharmaceuticals, and aeronautics and other transportation equipment. It also houses a large financial sector. The fact that economic power in Quebec used to rest largely in English-Canadian and foreign hands fuelled the nationalist debate in that province. But since 1960 a major transformation has occurred, and both the public and the francophone private sectors in Quebec have repatriated a great deal of industrial ownership. One means of doing so was the Caisse de dépôt et placement du Québec, which invested Quebec Pension Plan premiums in domestic firms. Still, Quebec remains below the national average in per capita income.

Ontario

Ontario has had the most diversified economy of any region and until 2008 was always among the richest provinces. It has an abundance of natural resources, including a great expanse of prime agricultural land in the Great Lakes Lowlands, vast stretches of trees, and a variety of minerals in the Canadian Shield. The province also contains several powerful rivers for the production of hydroelectricity, although it is increasingly dependent on nuclear power in this regard. Ontario's early development of hydroelectricity and of a steel industry gave it a head start over other regions. A skilled labour force, a large domestic market, proximity to key parts of the United States, and the advantage of federal tariff and banking policies also helped to make it the manufacturing heartland of the country. The province now produces over half of the Canadian total, with automobiles and auto parts being most important, along with machinery, publishing, steel, food and beverages, smelting and refining, metal fabrication, and pulp and paper. Moreover, Ontario leads the country in the tertiary sector, such as finance, trade, and services, and the seats of the two largest governments in the country, in Ottawa and Toronto, also provide considerable employment. On the other hand, the forestry and manufacturing sectors have been ailing for some time, and the worldwide economic meltdown at the end of 2008 combined with the mineral wealth of western Canada forced Ontario into unprecedented have-not status.

The Prairie Region

The Prairie region is historically associated with agriculture, especially wheat, other grain, and livestock, and while that industry ebbs and flows, it continues to be important. The high value of primary industry in the Prairies in recent years, however, has largely been a result of Alberta's petroleum production, and that province has become the richest part of the country by any measure. As conventional supplies of crude petroleum declined, Alberta witnessed an enormous expansion of the oil sands as a source of synthetic oil, although by 2013 it was constrained by limited pipeline capacity. Petroleum is also of increasing significance in Saskatchewan, in concert with that province's other mineral resources, potash and uranium.

Significant declines in oil prices that began in late 2014 hit many provinces' economies hard, especially those of Alberta and Newfoundland and Labrador that depend heavily upon oil revenues.

In addition, Alberta possesses large amounts of coal, and Manitoba has nickel, copper, and zinc. Forestry has been an important industry in Manitoba and Alberta, while Manitoba's supply of hydroelectricity complements the petroleum of the other two Prairie provinces. Thus, while the Prairies also depend heavily on primary industry, their resource extraction is a more profitable venture than that of the Atlantic provinces. The Prairies are also engaged in manufacturing, including food and beverages, transportation equipment, chemicals, petrochemicals, and fertilizer. With the new wealth of the Western provinces, especially since the 1960s, the finance, trade, and service industries have expanded rapidly, and the Prairies are less dependent on Ontario in this respect than they used to be. In fact, in addition to the growing population, much corporate power has moved westward, especially to Calgary.

THE CANADIAN PRESS/Bayne Stanley

An aerial view of the Syncrude oil sands upgrader in Fort McMurray, Alberta.

British Columbia

Mountainous British Columbia is the leading forestry province and also specializes in mining, including natural gas, copper, and coal. Several fertile river and lake valleys provide for farming, and, being a coastal province, BC also possesses a significant fishing industry. The mountains are the source of several large rivers that have been dammed for the production of hydroelectricity, and, as in Quebec, the abundant electricity is used to produce aluminum. Manufacturing is primarily related to the forestry, mining, and agricultural bases of the BC economy. Immigration from Asia has expanded the services sector, especially finance, but British Columbia's heavy dependence on resource exports entails periodic economic downturns, especially for the forest industry in recent years. Fortunately for BC, as well as Alberta and Saskatchewan, China is taking a keen interest in their resource exports, while massive Chinese imports have necessitated an expansion of BC ports.

The North

The North—Yukon, Northwest Territories, and Nunavut—comprises almost 40 percent of Canada's landmass and is inhabited by a fraction of a percent of its national population. There are more people living in Prince Edward Island than in all of the northern territories combined. Mining has inspired many southerners to venture north over the years, especially in the gold rushes of the 1890s in Dawson City and the 1930s in Yellowknife. Other isolated mineral deposits have been found, but many have since been abandoned. The prospects of oil and natural gas are more promising, especially in the Mackenzie River delta and the Beaufort Sea. The unstable world price, the uncertain supply in southern Canada and the United States, the outstanding Aboriginal land claims, and the cost and difficulty of transporting the petroleum southward have all combined to limit such a flow, although the United States has recently exhibited renewed interest in northern petroleum resources. Northern Aboriginals used to be self-sufficient in hunting, fishing, and trapping, activities that continue to occupy them to some extent, while carving has become an important economic pursuit and the tourist industry is booming. Although the cold climate and poor transportation facilities conspire to retard economic development of the region, recent positive signs include the settlement of many Aboriginal land claims, the discovery of diamonds, iron, and other minerals, and the creation of the eastern territory of **Nunavut** in 1999. Increased autonomy from Ottawa should better allow the territories to respond to local needs, and the ability to retain their own resource revenues would decrease their heavy financial dependence on the federal government.

CRITICAL APPROACHES

Of the approaches outlined in Chapter 1, *social cleavages* and *pluralism* immediately come to mind in the consideration of regionalism. The geographic and economic diversities in Canada are obvious, and national policies must allow for regional variations. Power has been dispersed to the provincial and territorial political units to accommodate diversity, but in the interplay of many such forces at the national level, government policies have stemmed from vociferously articulated regional economic demands or aimed at compromises among competing regional interests.

The *political economy* approach is also relevant, given that regionalism often involves relations between state and economy. The staples theory with its reliance on natural resource exploitation, early railway policy, national tariff and banking policies, government approval of private pipelines, and corporate grants under regional development programs were all regionally oriented policies for economic development. One can see how this approach overlaps with *class analysis*, which argues that such policies were designed to benefit capitalist interests, most of which were headquartered in central Canada. One aspect of Canadian regionalism is that political parties have encouraged voters to think of Canadian politics in terms of conflict that "revolves around the allocation of power and resources across geographic units rather than, for example, among social classes."[12]

HISTORIC REGIONAL CONFLICTS

Despite most natural resources falling within provincial jurisdiction, every primary industry has at one time sought federal government support, and most other regional economic demands are primarily directed to Ottawa. As a result of regional economic differences, the national government regularly faces demands to assist a single industry or the economy of a single province or region. Many such demands have elicited a positive response, especially when the case was desperate, popular, or articulated by the right interest. Such outputs do not necessarily involve conflict between one region and another, and they sometimes benefit them all.

Oftentimes, however, demands from one region do result in conflict with those from another. Consider the ongoing debates about Canada's efforts to reduce its greenhouse gas emissions. Alberta's oil and gas sectors account for a third of Canada's greenhouse gas emissions—more than any other province. Because of geographic and economic differences between Canadian regions, efforts to reduce these emissions are likely to impose a heavier cost on Alberta as well as those provinces that depend on the oil and gas sectors than on those that do not. Economic and environmental policies that are popular among political leaders in some parts of the country are often rejected by their counterparts in others. The most pervasive historical expression of regional economic conflict has undoubtedly been between Ontario and the Prairie region.

Ownership of Natural Resources

The problem of natural resource ownership began in 1870 with the creation of the province of Manitoba. Although the Eastern provinces always had jurisdiction over their own natural resources, Ottawa decided to retain such control when the Western provinces were established. The logic of Prime Ministers John A. Macdonald and Wilfrid Laurier was that the federal government (i.e., central Canada) should control such resources in the national interest, allowing Ottawa to guide the development of the West. The Prairie provinces fought vehemently against this discrimination and were finally successful in gaining control of their natural resources in 1930.

Tariffs

The West also complained for generations that Canadian **tariff** policy was designed in the interest of central Canada at the expense of the Prairies. This was because as early as the 1879 **National Policy** Macdonald saw the tariff as a means of promoting and protecting the industrial heartland of Ontario. Adding a tariff (an import tax) to the price of imported manufactured goods would raise their price above that of goods manufactured in Canada, even if foreign production costs were lower, so that domestic goods would cost less than imports to buy. In practice, foreign firms established themselves in central Canada behind this tariff wall, but the tariff had the beneficial effect of creating jobs in Canada rather than in Britain or the United States. Ontario thus gained employment in producing tractors for Western Canada, for example, but Western Canadians felt that this was contrary to their interests because, in the absence of such a tariff, they would have been able to buy cheaper tractors from the United States. The West demanded lower tariffs at every opportunity, especially in the 1920s, when it sent its own farmer representatives to the House of Commons to fight on this front. Tariffs among all countries have gradually come down since 1945, but the issue took on a new life in the 1980s with the Western demand for free trade between Canada and the United States. Thus, the controversial Free Trade Agreement between the two countries, which took effect in 1989, can be seen in part as a response to 110 years of Western discontent with the tariff aspect of the National Policy.[13]

Transportation

Another aspect of Macdonald's National Policy that displeased the West was transportation, especially railways. In choosing to live so far from the central core of the country, some Westerners expected to pay additional transportation costs, but many demanded that railway freight rates be subsidized by Ottawa. Indeed, the Crow's Nest Pass Act (or **Crow rate**) of 1897 was an attempt to do just that, providing a low rate for transporting Prairie grain to eastern ports. After successfully fighting to retain the Crow rate in the 1920s, many Westerners were greatly upset by the Trudeau government's increase in these rates, as well as by the Chrétien government's decision in 1995 to abolish the Crow rate entirely. Another complaint was about peculiar inequities within the freight rate structure, including higher rates for finished goods than for raw materials (which discouraged manufacturing in the West), discrimination against short hauls, and deviations from the principle of distance determining price. The Fair Rail for Grain Farmers Act, passed in 2015, is yet another step in what has been a long history of government regulating the transportation of grain. The new law allows government to set a minimum amount of grain that railways must transport, regulate contracts, and arbitrate conflicts between grain producers and railways.

Banking

The West also protested against national banking policy. In contrast to community-based unit banks as in the United States, Canada deliberately developed a centralized branch banking system. This policy was in part an attempt to construct a sound, stable banking community that would avoid frequent local collapses, but the lack of competition was also favoured by the established banking interests themselves and provided more evidence of corporate pressure on government policy. The result was a handful of large national banks, usually with headquarters in Montreal or Toronto and with local branches spread across the country. From a hinterland perspective, money deposited in the local branch of a national bank would not remain in the community to be lent out for local purposes, but instead was sent to headquarters in central Canada to be used in the economic development of Ontario or Quebec. Moreover, decisions to make large loans were centralized at the head office, so that Western entrepreneurs would have to travel east if they wanted to borrow substantial sums. The operation of the banking system was another reason for the farmers' revolt of the 1920s, and such displeasure had much to do with the rise of the Social Credit Party in Alberta in the 1930s. In the 1970s, when the West became stronger in spite of this policy, Ottawa finally eased restrictions on chartering regional banks, and several new Western banks were established. At the same time, the existing national banks also saw the merit of decentralizing decision making within their own operations, so that larger decisions could be made on location. Unfortunately, several of these new Western financial institutions faltered in the 1980s, largely because of a downturn in the region's economy that Westerners blamed on Trudeau's National Energy Program.[14]

These four policy areas—resources, tariffs, transportation, and banking—represent the most serious regional economic conflicts in Canadian history, but they can be seen in a broader context. The metropolitan–hinterland thesis suggests that the West was created as a colony of central Canada and was intended to be held in a subordinate and dependent relationship.[15] Western feeling about its situation was captured in a famous cartoon in the *Grain Growers' Guide* in 1915, and although it is depicted in agricultural terms, the image is still appropriate 100 years later.

NA-3055-24/Glenbow Archives

The Atlantic Provinces

Many of the Western economic conflicts with central Canada have been echoed by the Atlantic provinces. This was especially true of the post-Confederation tariff policy, which also appeared to do the Maritimes more harm than good. Nova Scotia and New Brunswick entered Confederation in 1867 as proud and prosperous provinces, and although changes in marine technology (from wooden sailing ships to steel steamships) were probably the principal factor responsible, their economies quickly declined. Whatever the reason, Maritimers preferred to blame federal economic policy for much of their difficulty. The Atlantic provinces also shared the West's concerns about federal freight rates, although they received subsidization in this area, too. In the late 20th century, Atlantic Canadians have blamed federal fisheries management for the collapse of the groundfish stocks and for insufficient protection from foreign territorial encroachment and overfishing.

RECENT REGIONAL CONFLICTS

Against the background of historic regional conflicts, let us proceed to discuss more recent issues. Some of these are extensions of historic conflicts, while others are genuinely new, and some may be mitigated by regional cooperation.

Taxation and Regulation of Natural Resources

In the 1970s the original conflict over natural resources re-emerged, especially with respect to petroleum pricing. National energy policy in the 1950s and 1960s gave preference to the West because Alberta was guaranteed a market for its oil and natural gas as far east as Ontario. But the West overlooked that fact after the Organization of Petroleum Exporting Countries (OPEC) cartel agreed on an artificial rise in the international price of oil in 1973. At this point, federal policy began to favour the consumer/manufacturing interest of central Canada at the expense of the producer interest of the West. The height of the regional economic conflict occurred in 1980 with the Trudeau government's **National Energy Program (NEP)**, which imposed new federal taxes, retained a larger share of petroleum revenues for Ottawa, kept the national price below the world level, encouraged frontier—largely offshore—development, and promoted Canadianization of the industry, all objectives opposed by most Westerners. Eventually a partial compromise between central and Western interests was reached in 1981, and the Mulroney government later scrapped the NEP entirely. Nevertheless, the NEP had a profound effect on the Western Canadian psyche, especially when combined with the West's simultaneous opposition to Ottawa's constitutional initiatives and official bilingualism policy. The Atlantic provinces also opposed federal resource policy in the 1980s, prompting them to fight for provincial ownership of offshore petroleum.

Other Regional Economic Conflicts

Although the economic complaints of the two outlying regions have often coincided, such as that the federal government does most of its purchasing or procuring in central Canada, they have often been distinctive and occasionally at odds. In general, the East differed from the West to some extent on the Canada–U.S. Free Trade Agreement, fearing that it would eliminate many of their subsidy programs.

Another regional issue is the environment, where the Kyoto Accord was favoured by Quebec, but condemned by the Alberta government. Even though the Harper Conservatives abandoned Kyoto, Alberta is subject to increasing pressure to take action to reduce the environmental devastation caused by the oil sands—to land, water, and air. Thus, besides dividing the political parties in their proposed solutions, climate change and other aspects of environmental degradation have generated a regional cleavage primarily between the petroleum and coal producers of Alberta and Saskatchewan and the rest of the provinces. NDP leader Thomas Mulcair argued that the environmental costs of greenhouse gas emissions should be incorporated into the price of petroleum, which would reduce the profits of the industry and the value of the Canadian dollar, making central Canadian manufactured goods cheaper to export. Others urged Ontario to take advantage of Alberta's prosperity and manufacture more goods for the oil sands industry. Environmental issues have dimensions beyond regionalism, of course, and are revisited in Chapters 8 and 20.

Smaller-scale regional economic disputes have also been a routine, if not daily, occurrence in Canadian politics. Awarding the CF-18 maintenance contract to Canadair of Montreal infuriated supporters of Bristol Aerospace of Winnipeg, which had submitted a superior bid, and further reinforced Western alienation.[16] Indeed, this Mulroney government decision had much to do with the creation of the Reform Party in western Canada. Extending drug patent protection for multinational pharmaceutical firms in Quebec offended Canadian generic drug producers primarily located in Ontario; and promoting frontier petroleum exploration (including federal assistance to Newfoundland's Hibernia project) upset conventional oil and gas producers in the west. In 2011, Nova Scotia, Quebec, and BC were rival competitors for gigantic federal ship-building contracts.

Besides these regional economic conflicts that may or may not have engaged the attention of Ottawa, conflicts sometimes develop between provinces and territories. The most serious of these was probably the fight between Quebec and Newfoundland over the Churchill Falls hydroelectric project in Labrador, in which Quebec would not allow power produced in Labrador to pass through Quebec, but rather required that it be sold to Quebec (at a very favourable rate). Indeed, these types of conflictual negotiations may be revisited in the future with plans for new trans-provincial oil pipelines. Another was Ontario's insistence that its residents be allowed to work in the construction industry in Quebec, the subject of a prolonged inter-provincial battle. In the North, Yukon and Northwest Territories promoted competing natural gas pipeline proposals—the Alaska Highway and the Mackenzie River routes, respectively. Recently Alberta and BC have argued over the revenues and potential environmental costs of the proposed Northern Gateway pipeline, with BC remaining opposed to the project in 2014.

Another issue, this time *within* the prairie region, concerned whether or not the **Canadian Wheat Board** should retain its monopoly power to market western wheat and barley. The Harper government sided with those farmers who wanted to sell their grain on the open market, and in December 2011, passed legislation to end the Canadian Wheat Board monopoly.

REGIONAL ECONOMIC DISPARITIES

Conflicts between regions are exacerbated in Canada because of regional economic inequalities or disparities. As mentioned, some have-not regions blame federal economic policies for their fate. Even if this charge has some truth to it, no observer can overlook other factors: Canada's primary resources are not evenly distributed and the regions have different sizes of territory and population and are at variable distances from key export markets. In fact, regional economic disparities appear to be increasing, based primarily on the possession or lack of petroleum resources.

Among the available measures of regional economic disparity are per capita provincial gross domestic product (GDP) (the total value of all goods and services produced divided by the population of the province), per capita income, and provincial unemployment rates. These measures are shown in Table 3.2.

Traditionally, Canada had three categories of provinces: three rich ones (Ontario, Alberta, and British Columbia); four poor ones (the Atlantic provinces); and three intermediate provinces (Quebec, Manitoba, and Saskatchewan). Some shifting has occurred in recent years,

TABLE 3.2   PROVINCIAL GROSS DOMESTIC PRODUCT PER CAPITA, PER CAPITA
            INCOME, AND UNEMPLOYMENT RATE, 2013

	GDP PER CAPITA	AVERAGE ANNUAL EMPLOYMENT EARNINGS	UNEMPLOYMENT RATE (PERCENTAGE)*
NEWFOUNDLAND AND LABRADOR	67 838	49 498	11.9
PRINCE EDWARD ISLAND	39 780	39 292	10.6
NOVA SCOTIA	41 516	41 618	9.0
NEW BRUNSWICK	42 218	42 124	9.9
QUEBEC	44 499	43 299	7.7
ONTARIO	51 340	47 975	7.3
MANITOBA	48 461	43 440	5.4
SASKATCHEWAN	75 232	49 298	3.8
ALBERTA	84 390	57 772	4.7
BRITISH COLUMBIA	50 121	45 526	6.1

*2014

Source: Adapted from Statistics Canada, Gross domestic product, expenditure-based, by province and territory, CANSIM, table 384-0038 http://www.statcan.gc.ca/tables-tableaux/sum-som/l01/cst01/econ15-eng.htm; Statistics Canada, Population by year, by province and territory, CANSIM, table 051-0001, http://www.statcan.gc.ca/tables-tableaux/sum-som/l01/cst01/demo02a-eng.htm; Statistics Canada, Earnings average weekly, by province and territory, CANSIM, table 281-0027, http://www.statcan.gc.ca/tables-tableaux/sum-som/l01/cst01/labr79-eng.htm; and Newfoundland & Labrador Statistics Agency, Annual Average Unemployment Rate, http://www.stats.gov.nl.ca/statistics/Labour/PDF/UnempRate.pdf.

however, and since 2009 Ontario and Newfoundland and Labrador have exchanged places. Quebec has a larger economy than any province other than Ontario, of course, but this figure is not so impressive when expressed on a per capita basis. Alberta has typically had the lowest unemployment rate (though recently Saskatchewan's has been lower), and the average Alberta worker typically receives about $18 000 a year more than the average worker in Prince Edward Island. Saskatchewan has also moved into the "have" category in more recent times, and its premier, Brad Wall, has recently suggested that equalization payments are too high and should be scaled back. Typically, the provinces with the highest unemployment rates also have the highest provincial taxes, while Alberta's petroleum revenues allow it to get by with low income taxes and without a provincial sales tax at all.

In addition to developing national social programs and assisting various industries in a uniform national policy, successive governments have focused on two principal means to deal with the specific question of regional economic disparities.[17] One is to give federal funding to have-not provincial and territorial governments in the form of **equalization payments**, and the other is to engage in regional economic development programs.

The first of these, equalization payments, began in 1957 as a response to repeated provincial demands.[18] These annual cash grants to the have-not provinces are designed to allow them to raise their services to an acceptable national level but can be spent for any purpose. In other words, they are unconditional grants, with no strings attached. The formula according to which provincial eligibility is calculated is extremely complex and designed to equalize the per capita yield of such provincial revenues across the country, that is, the fiscal capacity of the various provinces. Provinces then fall on either the contributing to equalization (have) side or the receiving equalization (have-not) side. The equalization formula used to be renegotiated every five years at federal–provincial conferences, but Ottawa sometimes altered the formula unilaterally. Equalization payments were entrenched in the Constitution in 1982 so that although the federal government may change the formula, it cannot withdraw from its responsibility in this regard. Section 36 reads as follows:

> Parliament and the government of Canada are committed to the principle of making equalization payments to ensure that provincial governments have sufficient revenues to provide reasonably comparable levels of public services at reasonably comparable levels of taxation.

Equalization payments have become a leading regional issue in recent years. In 2002, Stephen Harper, then leader of the opposition Canadian Alliance party, referred to Atlantic Canada as espousing a "culture of defeat" due to its financial dependence upon the rest of Canada.[19] A few years later, equalization funding formulas pitted petroleum-producing provinces against the federal government. Newfoundland and Labrador and Nova Scotia claimed that for every dollar they took in from offshore petroleum revenue, 70 cents was clawed back by Ottawa by reducing their equalization payments. After aggressive protest, especially by former Newfoundland Premier Danny Williams, Prime Minister Paul Martin signed a deal with the two provinces in 2005 under which their equalization payments would not be reduced over the following eight years. The Harper government then imposed a new formula in the 2007 federal budget—a more generous formula for most provinces, especially Quebec. But the new formula included one-half of a province's non-renewable resources, which Harper had originally promised to exclude, and it also had a cap that would kick in if a have-not province developed a higher fiscal capacity than a province that did not receive such payments. Williams opposed this new formula and promoted an "Anything But Conservative" campaign during the 2008 federal election in an effort to see Harper's government defeated. In 2011–12 Alberta, Newfoundland and Labrador, Saskatchewan, and British Columbia did not qualify for equalization payments, a pattern that will likely endure for some time. The three northern territories are far from being economically self-sufficient, and depend heavily on financial resources from the federal government. The principal federal transfer to the North is the Territorial Formula Financing (TFF), an annual unconditional transfer exceeding $3 billion. Nunavut and the NWT contend, however, that if they could retain their natural resource revenues, they would not need such large annual transfers from Ottawa.

The Employment Insurance system is also relied upon to a greater extent by residents of have-not provinces, and therefore also plays an equalizing role in distributing money, although the Harper government imposed stricter rules that were widely criticized, mostly in Atlantic Canada.

The second means of reducing regional economic disparities is to establish federal **regional economic development programs**.[20] These programs started in 1935 and have undergone many changes of organization and emphasis since. The basic thrust of these programs was to designate those parts of the country that needed economic assistance, essentially the whole country except southern Ontario, and then to provide grants to firms that would locate or expand existing operations in such areas. Some grants also went to provinces or municipalities to provide the basic infrastructure that might attract industry, such as highways, water and sewage systems, and industrial parks.

Since 1987, the separate regional economic development agencies have consisted of the **Atlantic Canada Opportunities Agency (ACOA)**, Federal Economic Development Initiative in Northern Ontario (FedNor), Western Economic Diversification Canada (WD), and Canada Economic Development for Quebec Regions (CED). Some of these agencies are attached to the Industry Canada department. In 2009, a new agency was added for beleaguered southern Ontario (now FedDev Ontario), as well as the Canadian Northern Economic Development Agency, so that the whole country is now covered by federal regional development agencies.

One way that provinces seek to strengthen their economies is to cooperate with their neighbours. The Atlantic provinces have signed a number of interprovincial agreements, and in recent years the three western provinces have developed "free trade" deals among themselves.

CRITICAL APPROACHES

The *state-based approach* concentrates on the predominance of people from central Canada in authoritative positions such as the prime minister, Cabinet, House of Commons, and bureaucracy, and the ability of these authorities to operate autonomously, without public pressure. If the majority of these decision makers come from Ontario and Quebec, it is only to be expected that many federal policies will benefit the central part of the country. The nature of this centralization of power, in part, fuelled frustration in other regions of the country. Somewhat similarly, *rational choice* theory emphasizes why the voting power of central Canada swayed most government policies in this field. During the Pearson and Trudeau eras, when Quebec voted predominantly Liberal and the West voted predominantly Conservative, elections were essentially fought out in Ontario. This partly explains the thrust of Trudeau's constitutional and energy policies—especially the National Energy Program—which were supported in Ontario but strongly opposed in the West.

As we will see, *political psychology* and *behaviour approaches* can also be applied to regionalism. The natural tendency for people to feel attached to their local community and to develop regional identities has often been enhanced by provincial politicians in their attacks on federal government policies. In other words, to some extent such regional identities have been socially and politically constructed.

REGIONAL IDENTITIES

Turning to non-economic aspects of regionalism, many explanations have been proposed to account for feelings of regional identification in Canada. According to the "composition effects," regional differences emerge by virtue of different proportions of people from various groups who live in each region. If French Canadians see language issues differently from English Canadians, for example, then a regional divide on the language issue may emerge between Quebec and the rest of the country by virtue of the different proportions of French and English Canadians in these regions.

Another possible source of regional identities stems from "contextual effects." These occur when people are influenced by the environment that surrounds them. Residents of northern communities, for example, may take a particular view of the world by virtue of being influenced by the characteristics of their region such as the climate, economy, and culture. People tend to develop emotional or affective attachments to the regions in which they live and to the people who live around them, sometimes acquiring intense affinities for things as trivial as the nearest sports team.

One interesting aspect of regional identities is whether individual Canadians feel an equal attachment to their province and to the country as a whole. Figure 3.3 shows the percentage of respondents in four regions who identified more as a citizen of their province than of Canada in 2012. In Quebec, the subject of Chapter 5, this figure was almost 60 percent, whereas it hovered closer to 40 percent in the Atlantic and Western provinces, and while just over 25 percent of Ontario residents felt this way.

FIGURE 3.3 PERCENTAGE OF CANADIANS WHO CLAIM TO FEEL MORE A CITIZEN OF THEIR PROVINCE THAN OF CANADA, 2012

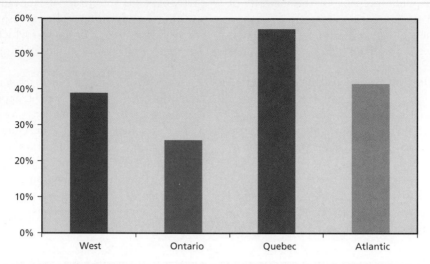

Source: Adapted from Canadian Opinion Research Archive, The Environics Institute for Survey Research, Focus Canada 2012.

The view that one's region is being unfairly treated vis-à-vis other regions of the country may generate what is called "regional alienation," a feeling of detachment from the rest of the country. In 1980, Roger Gibbins defined regional alienation in Western Canada as:

A regionally distinct political culture through and within which are expressed economic discontent, the rejection of a semi-colonial status within the Canadian state, antipathy towards Quebec and French-Canadian influence within the national government, the irritation of the West's partisan weakness within a succession of Liberal national governments, and the demand from provincial political elites for greater jurisdictional autonomy.[21]

Dissatisfaction with both the Liberal and the Conservative parties' focus on Quebec issues in the 1980s and early 1990s led to deep feelings of **Western alienation**, and was largely responsible for the formation of the Reform Party, whose initial slogan was "The West Wants In." In the 1993 federal election, the Reform Party won the majority of seats west of Ontario, and almost all the seats in British Columbia and Alberta, and then repeated this feat in 1997. After that, the party changed its leader and its name (to the Canadian Alliance) in an effort to become more appealing to the rest of the country, but without notable success. In 2003, the Canadian Alliance merged with the Progressive Conservative Party, and the leader of the newly formed Conservative Party was the Alliance's former Alberta-based leader, Stephen Harper. While he never lost sight of the regional base of the party, Harper strove to expand it, and by 2011, he managed to win enough seats in the rest of the country to form a majority government. At last, the West was "in," and in some of its policies, such as oil sands development, the Harper government took a clear-cut Western perspective. Although he faced no opposition from other parts of the country on the issue, Harper also succumbed to Saskatchewan pressure to disallow the foreign takeover of the Potash Corporation. The West can hardly claim that Ontario rules the roost any longer!

It must also be acknowledged that Western alienation also has a conservative ideological hue, especially in its most extreme dimension in Alberta. With the notable exception that Albertans elected a NDP government in 2015, ending decades of Progressive Conservative rule in that province, the collectivist strain in the Canadian political culture has traditionally been weakest in that province. Albertans have generally favoured individualist, nongovernmental solutions to public problems. To some extent, this preference for individual self-reliance is based on the relative prosperity of the region. Thus, in addition to opposition to the government regulation reflected in the Kyoto Accord, there was hostility to the long-gun registry and to the requirement in the Canada Health Act that publicly funded health services be provided in the public sector. Many Albertans are also opposed to the liberal interpretations of the Charter of Rights and Freedoms on such issues as sexual orientation and same-sex marriage. As noted in Gibbins' definition, a related theme is antagonism to official bilingualism and to constitutional reforms designed to appease Quebec.

Westerners have felt that they are regularly out-voted in the House of Commons by MPs from central Canada. It is not that Western provinces are unfairly represented in the Commons, based as it is on the principle of representation by population; however governments have often been composed mostly of MPs who are not from Canada's West. One possible solution to this problem advocated by many Westerners is to strengthen the capacity of the Senate to protect regional interests against the voting power of central Canada in the House of Commons. Alberta in particular has long advocated an elected Senate with more effective powers and with equal representation for each province regardless of population. In 2004, a number of prominent Albertans including Stephen Harper advocated building a firewall around the province, as seen in Box 3.1. Interestingly enough, in the 2012 Alberta provincial election, the Wild Rose party was defeated on a somewhat similar platform.

BOX 3.1   VOICES

In the letter, Harper and colleagues argued that Alberta had been under attack by the federal government and that a variety of federal policies had been disadvantageous to the province. It was therefore time for the province to take control of a number of policy fields that Ottawa had been allowed to occupy at the province's expense. These included pensions, personal income tax, and health care, and at the same time, Alberta should establish its own provincial police force. In short, "use of these powers will help Alberta build a prosperous future in spite of a misguided and increasingly hostile government in Ottawa … It is imperative to … build firewalls around Alberta, to limit the extent to which an aggressive and hostile federal government can encroach upon legitimate provincial jurisdiction.…" Readers are encouraged to consult the full letter published in the *National Post* on January 24, 2001, found at: http://www.cbc.ca/canadavotes2004/leadersparties/leaders/pdf/firewall.pdf. (Accessed March 6, 2012).

Source: A letter published in the *National Post* on January 24, 2001 signed by Stephen Harper, Tom Flanagan, Ted Morton, Rainer Knopff, Andrew Crooks, and Ken Boessenkool, labelled the "Alberta Firewall Letter," www.cbc.ca/canadavotes2004/leadersparties/leaders/pdf/firewall.pdf.

TABLE 3.3 REGIONAL SUPPORT FOR MAIN PARTIES IN 2015 FEDERAL ELECTION

	ATLANTIC	QUEBEC	ONTARIO	WEST	NORTH
CONSERVATIVE	19.0%	16.7%	35.0%	43.2%	22.0%
GREEN	3.5%	2.3%	2.9%	5.0%	2.5%
LIBERAL	58.7%	35.7%	44.8%	31.3%	50.1%
NDP	18.0%	25.3%	16.6%	19.4%	25.3%
BQ	—	19.3%	—	—	—

*Source: Elections Canada, Provinces and Territories (October 30, 2015), http://enr.elections.ca/Provinces
.aspx?lang=e, calculations by authors.*

A striking aspect of regionalism in Canada is the party system, as evidenced by the differential success of various parties in various regions of the country.[22] The Liberal party has been weak in Western Canada ever since John Diefenbaker's Conservatives swept the region in the 1950s. Meanwhile, Quebec traditionally voted overwhelmingly for the Liberals, although that province's peculiar regional election results favoured the Conservatives in the 1980s, the Bloc Québécois after 1993, and, in 2011, the NDP. The main parties' popular vote in different regions in the 2015 federal election can be seen in Table 3.3.

With the population of western provinces becoming an increasing proportion of the national total, it is less important than in the past for a political party to have concentrated strength in central Canada, and one lesson of the 2011 federal election was that a party could win a majority without many seats in Quebec. Prior to the election of the Liberal government in 2015, some observers had expected the NDP to become the dominant party in the declining east and the Conservatives to command the ascending west, a prospect that would not be conducive to national unity.

CONCLUSION

The Canadian physical and political environment is characterized by regional differences, and many demands stemming from these differences can be identified. Some demands seek improved transportation and communications links to bind the country more closely together. Others desire increased provincial or territorial autonomy in order to deal locally with their distinctive problems. A third set of demands relates to the specific interests of one province, territory, region, or industry under the label of regional economic cleavages and disparities. Since not all regional demands are economic in nature, however, the discussion of regionalism must also include questions of regional identities and regional alienation.

Regionalism is such a pervasive force in Canadian society that it figures in almost every chapter that follows. Given the close connection between the concepts of regions and provinces, issues that concern provinces as such are mainly dealt with in Chapter 5 (Quebec as a region), Chapter 17 (the constitution), and Chapter 18 (federalism). Regional identities and attitudinal differences are revisited in Chapter 11 (political culture), Chapter 19 (the Charter of Rights), and Part 5 (political institutions). The environment issue is mentioned again in Chapter 8, dealing with class and corporate power, and regional voting patterns and the regionalized party system are addressed again in Chapters 13, 14, and 15 (elections, parties, and election campaigns).

DISCUSSION QUESTIONS

1. Which of the traditional regional demands and complaints in Canadian federal politics do you think are unjustified?

2. To what extent do you feel a regional identity?

3. Do you think decentralization of the federal system is an answer to conflicting regional demands?

4. Are there better ways to reduce regional economic disparities than through equalization payments and regional development programs?

MindTap® FOR MORE INFO GO TO http://www.nelson.com/student

NOTES

1. Task Force on Canadian Unity, *A Future Together* (Ottawa: Supply and Services, 1979), pp. 26–27.
2. Janine Brodie, "The Concept of Region in Canadian Politics," in David Shugarman and Reg Whitaker, eds., *Federalism and Political Community* (Peterborough: Broadview Press, 1989).
3. Richard Simeon, "Regionalism and Canadian Political Institutions," in J. Peter Meekison, ed., *Canadian Federalism: Myth or Reality*, 3rd ed. (Toronto: Methuen, 1977), p. 293; Benedict Anderson, *Imagined Communities: Reflections on the Origins and Spread of Nationalism*, rev. ed. (London and New York: Verso, 1991).
4. Brodie, "The Concept of Region in Canadian Politics."
5. House of Commons, *Debates*, June 19, 1936.
6. Donald Creighton, *The Empire of the St. Lawrence* (Toronto: Macmillan, 1956). Harold Innis emphasizes the significance of the beaver fur trade, which utilized such river systems.
7. The whole romantic story is told in Pierre Berton's books *The National Dream and The Last Spike* (Toronto: McClelland and Stewart, 1970 and 1971).
8. For an analysis along these lines, see Robert Chodos, *The CPR: A Century of Corporate Welfare* (Toronto: Lorimer, 1973).
9. Statistics Canada, *Canada's Population from Ocean to Ocean* (Catalogue No. 98-120, January 1989), p. 16.
10. For a specifically geographic point of view on this question, see Scott Reid, *Canada Remapped* (Vancouver: Pulp Press, 1992).
11. Wallace Clement and Daniel Drache, *A Practical Guide to Canadian Political Economy* (Toronto: Lorimer, 1978), pp. 9–14; Wallace Clement and Daniel Drache, *New Practical Guide to Canadian Political Economy* (Toronto: Lorimer, 1985); Michael Howlett and Keith Brownsey, *Canada's Resource Economy in Transition: The Past, Present, and Future of Canadian Staples Industries* (Toronto: Emond Montgomery, 2008).
12. Brodie, "The Concept of Region in Canadian Politics," p. 36.
13. By this time many large central Canadian corporations also saw advantages for themselves in such a policy.
14. James L. Darroch and Charles J. McMillan, "Entry barriers and evolution of banking systems: Lessons from the 1980s Canadian western bank failures," *Canadian Public Administration* (June 2007).
15. Donald Smiley, *The Federal Condition in Canada* (Toronto: McGraw-Hill Ryerson, 1987), p. 159.

16. Robert Campbell and Leslie Pal, *The Real Worlds of Canadian Politics* (Peterborough: Broadview Press, 1989).
17. James A. McAllister, "Redistributive Federalism: Redistributing Wealth and Income in the Canadian Federation," *Canadian Public Administration* (December 2011).
18. Robin W. Boadway and Paul A.R. Hobson, *Equalization* (Montreal: McGill-Queen's University Press, 1998); and Harvey Lazar, ed., *Canadian Fiscal Arrangements: What Works, What Might Work Better* (Kingston: McGill-Queen's University Press, 2005).
19. Brian Laghi, "Premiers tell Harper his attack was wrong," *The Globe and Mail*, May 30, 2002, p. 8.
20. Among the early versions of such policy were the Prairie Farm Rehabilitation Administration (PFRA) of 1935, the Maritime Farm Rehabilitation Act of 1948, and the Agricultural Rehabilitation and Development Act of 1961. See also Donald J. Savoie, *Visiting Grandchildren: Economic Development in the Maritimes* (Toronto: University of Toronto Press, 2006).
21. Roger Gibbins, *Prairie Politics and Society* (Toronto: Butterworths, 1980), p. 191; Roger Gibbins and Sonia Arrison, *Western Visions: Perspectives on the West in Canada* (Peterborough: Broadview Press, 1995).
22. Lisa Young and Keith Archer, eds., *Regionalism and Party Politics in Canada* (Toronto: Oxford University Press, 2002).

FURTHER READING

Brodie, Janine. *The Political Economy of Canadian Regionalism*. Toronto: Harcourt, Brace, Jovanovich, 1990.

Canada. Task Force on Canadian Unity. *A Future Together*. Ottawa: Supply and Services, 1979.

Dyck, Rand. *Provincial Politics in Canada*, 3rd ed. Scarborough: Prentice Hall Canada, 1996.

Gibbins, Roger, and Loleen Berdahl. *Western Visions, Western Futures*. Peterborough: Broadview Press, 2003.

Howlett, Michael and Keith Brownsey, *Canada's Resource Economy in Transition: The Past, Present, and Future of Canadian Staples Industries*. Toronto: Emond Montgomery, 2008.

McAllister, James A. "Redistributive Federalism: Redistributing Wealth and Income in the Canadian Federation," *Canadian Public Administration* (December 2011).

Savoie, Donald J. *Visiting Grandchildren: Economic Development in the Maritimes*. Toronto: University of Toronto Press, 2006.

Tomblin, Stephen. *Ottawa and the Outer Provinces*. Halifax: Lorimer, 1995.

Tomblin, Stephen G., and Charles Colgan, eds. *Regionalism in a Global Society: Persistence and Change in Atlantic Canada and New England*. Peterborough: Broadview Press, 2004.

Young, Lisa, and Keith Archer, eds. *Regionalism and Party Politics in Canada*. Toronto: Oxford University Press, 2002.

Chase Clausen/Shutterstock

CHAPTER 4

Aboriginal Peoples

Canada's Aboriginal peoples are the descendants of an early human migration to North America from Northeast Asia when a land bridge opened across the Bering Strait during the last Ice Age. Although the precise timing of the first successful settlements is still debated, most archaeological and genetic analyses seem to agree that 20 000 years ago is a reasonable estimate for the first permanent settlements in North America. This puts Canadian history on a trajectory that can be difficult to fathom. One way to gain perspective on such a long time-horizon is to imagine a calendar year that encompasses 20 000 years instead of just one year.[1] Imagine, for example, that the current time in this imaginary year is 11:59 pm on December 31st, and that the preceding New Year's day, on January 1st, was 20 000 years ago instead of one year ago. One minute in this imaginary year is about 14 days in the real world. An hour lasts more than two years in the real world. And each day takes up nearly 55 years in the real world. On this imaginary calendar Canada's Aboriginal peoples would have arrived in North America nearly 365 days ago, on January 1st. By comparison, the first European settlers did not arrive until just last week; Canada was not created until two-and-a-half days ago; and the Second World War finished yesterday evening. This is all to say that Aboriginal peoples have been here for a very long time. There is more human history in the New World than in the histories of Hinduism, Judaism, Buddhism, Christianity, and Islam combined. For all intents and purposes, Aboriginal peoples have been here since "time immemorial."

This chapter begins by detailing the demographic profile of Canada's Aboriginal peoples. It then examines the historical evolution of indigenous peoples and outlines the principal political issues that Aboriginal peoples have raised since 1970, especially with respect to land and governance. The chapter concludes by outlining some of the proposed solutions to these challenges.

ABORIGINAL DEMOGRAPHIC PROFILE TODAY

The Canadian census distinguishes between Aboriginal ancestry and Aboriginal identity, with the former comprising a larger number of people. In the 2011 National Household Survey, Statistics Canada reported 1.4 million Aboriginals based on identity—that is, those who *felt* themselves to be Aboriginal—and about 1.8 million Aboriginals based on ancestry or ethnic origin. These figures, respectively, represent 4.2 percent and 5.5 percent of the Canadian population.[2] There are three official categories of Aboriginal peoples in Canada: First Nations, Métis, and Inuit. First Nations are divided into status and non-status categories, and the former are subdivided between those living on- and off-reserve. Table 4.1 shows the breakdowns for Aboriginal origins and identity.

Aboriginal Canadians are not spread uniformly across the country. The largest absolute numbers live in Ontario, but First Nations and Métis have higher proportional concentrations in the western part of the country. On the other hand, about half of the Inuit live in Nunavut, and another 30 percent in parts of adjacent provinces (Nunavik in northern Quebec, Nunatsiavut in northern Labrador) and the Northwest Territories. The areas with the highest proportions of Aboriginal peoples are Nunavut, NWT, Yukon, Manitoba, and Saskatchewan. Table 4.2 illustrates this distribution in terms of Aboriginal identity in 2011.

Turning from identities and ancestry to official, legal numbers, Aboriginal Affairs and Northern Development Canada reports some 825 000 status or registered Indians, of whom about half live on reserves.[3] There are about 2700 reserves, with an average size of about 1150 hectares, and some 616 bands or First Nations with an average population of 1300. On the other hand, Statistics Canada found that about 54 percent of all Aboriginals live in urban areas; Winnipeg, Saskatoon, Regina, and Edmonton have the highest concentrations of urban Aboriginals, although large numbers also reside in Vancouver, Toronto, and Calgary.

Regardless of the legal and identity distinctions mentioned, there are 12 major Aboriginal linguistic families, the largest being Cree, Inuktitut (the language of the Inuit), and Ojibway, but more than 60 Aboriginal languages exist. Between 15 and 20 percent of the Aboriginal population have an Aboriginal language as mother tongue, largely confined to the Inuit and those who live on reserves, and about the same number speak an Aboriginal language at home. This decreasing number leads to much concern about the disappearance of such languages.

All three categories—First Nations, Métis, and Inuit—are increasing in numbers because of high birth rates, because fewer are missed in the Census than in the past, and because more individuals are identifying themselves as Aboriginal. The latter is especially true of the Métis. Almost half of the Aboriginal population is aged 24 and under, and overall, it is growing twice as fast as its non-Aboriginal counterpart.

TABLE 4.1 ABORIGINAL ORIGINS AND IDENTITY, 2011 NATIONAL HOUSEHOLD SURVEY

	ORIGINS	IDENTITY
(FIRST NATIONS)	1 369 120 (74.6%)	851 560 (60.8%)
MÉTIS	447 665 (24.4%)	451 795 (32.2%)
INUIT	72 615 (4.0%)	59 445 (4.2%)
OTHER AND MULTIPLE		37 890 (2.7%)
TOTAL	1 836 035 (100%)	1 400 685 (100%)

Sources: Statistics Canada, 2011 National Household Survey, Statistics Canada Catalogue no. 99-011-X2011029 http://www12.statcan.gc.ca/nhs-enm/2011/dp-pd/dt-td/Rp-eng.cfm?LANG=E&APATH=3&DETAIL=0&DIM=0& FL=A&FREE=0&GC=0&GID=0&GK=0&GRP=1&PID=105402&PRID=0&PTYPE=105277&S=0&SHOWALL=0& SUB=0&Temporal=2013&THEME=94& VID=0&VNAMEE=&VNAMEF= (retrieved April 13, 2015); Statistics Canada, National Household Survey, 2011. Table: Aboriginal Identity Population, Canada, 2011. http://www12 .statcan.gc.ca/nhs-enm/2011/as-sa/99-011-x/2011001/tbl/tbl01-eng.cfm.

TABLE 4.2   DISTRIBUTION OF ABORIGINAL CANADIANS BY IDENTITY, 2011 NATIONAL HOUSEHOLD SURVEY

	NORTH AMERICAN INDIAN	MÉTIS	INUIT	TOTAL	PERCENTAGE OF PROVINCIAL/ TERRITORIAL POPULATION
ATLANTIC PROVINCES	58 845	23 000	5 255*	94 490	4.0
QUEBEC	82 425	41 000	10 950*	141 915	1.8
ONTARIO	201 100	86 015	2 035*	301 425	2.4
MANITOBA	114 225	78 830	565*	195 900	16.7
SASKATCHEWAN	103 210	52 450	215*	157 740	15.6
ALBERTA	116 670	96 865	1 610*	220 695	6.2
BRITISH COLUMBIA	155 020	69 475	795*	232 290	5.4
YUKON	6 585	800*	255*	7 705	23.1
NORTHWEST TERRITORIES	13 350	3 580*	4 160*	21 160	51.9
NUNAVUT	125	130*	27 070	27 360	86.3
TOTAL	851 560	451 795	59 445	1 400 685	4.3

NOTE: THE TOTAL FIGURE INCLUDES MULTIPLE AND OTHER RESPONSES. SOME CALCULATIONS BY AUTHORS. ASTERISKS INDICATE 2006 DATA.

Sources: Statistics Canada, Aboriginal Peoples in Canada: First Nations People, Métis and Inuit, 2011 National Household Survey, Catalogue no. 99-011-X, http://www12.statcan.gc.ca/nhs-enm/2011/as-sa/99-011-x/99-011 -x2011001-eng.cfm; Statistics Canada. Aboriginal Peoples Highlight Tables, 2006 Census, Catalogue no 97-558- XWE2006002, http://www12.statcan.ca/english/census06/data/highlights/aboriginal/index.cfm?Lang=E.

HISTORICAL EVOLUTION

As mentioned, Aboriginal peoples have inhabited North America for at least 20 000 years, with most experts linking their origins to Asia. This means that somewhere in the vicinity of 95 percent of Aboriginal history in the Americas played out in the absence of European settlers. How did Aboriginal peoples live their lives? What values and teachings did they pass from generation to generation? How did different groups interact with one another? These and many other questions are preserved in archaeological records and in the oral traditions that Aboriginal elders pass down from across the millennia. By the time of European contact, Aboriginal peoples had ways of life that had developed from thousands of years of adaptation to life in North America.

For this reason, any discussion of Aboriginal peoples in the context of Canadian government has to begin with the concept of colonialism. **Colonialism** refers to establishing, acquiring, and maintaining colonies. A colony is a human settlement in one area of the world whose

CRITICAL APPROACHES

If any chapter of this book is amenable to the *historical approach*, it would certainly be this one on Aboriginal peoples. Conflict and negotiations between Aboriginal groups and government, for example, led to the reserve system, whereupon the indigenous peoples were reduced to living on small tracts of land, often in isolated areas, instead of the large swaths of territory to which they had been accustomed. Many Aboriginal elders today were sent to residential schools as children, where abuses and indignities against Aboriginal children were rampant. The reserve and residential schools systems have had an enduring impact on all facets of Aboriginal politics.

settlers are under the control of a government in some other part of the globe. The colonial powers in Canada were the British and the French, whose governments declared sovereignty over what they considered to be their newly discovered territories. How could they claim sovereignty over territory that was already occupied by Aboriginal peoples? One of the reasons used to justify European colonialism was the principle of *terra nullius*, meaning that the territory was not previously subject to control by any other power. In the early days of settlement, many European officials did not consider Aboriginal peoples to really own or control the land that they occupied. But even though Aboriginal people did not use European systems, they nonetheless had their own systems of government and alliances to maintain control over and protect their territory. In other words, the land *was* occupied when the European powers made claims to it. It was an encouraging sign that this fact seemed to be recognized by the United Kingdom when King George III issued the **Royal Proclamation of 1763**, which divided up the territory acquired by Britain after the Seven Years War with France, and which committed the Crown to enter into negotiations over territory with the Aboriginal peoples. These negotiations often led to the signing of **treaties**, which are binding legal agreements under Canadian and international law, and which are still in effect today.

Aboriginal rights to the land were acknowledged in the Royal Proclamation of 1763, however much they have since been ignored.[4] In a large area called Indian Territory, the purchase or settlement of land was forbidden without Crown approval—that is, without a treaty between the Crown and the Aboriginal people concerned. This is sometimes called the principle of "voluntary cession." Such treaty negotiations reflect an important transition in the way that Aboriginal peoples were viewed by Europeans. They suggest that Aboriginals were now seen as occupants of the territory, a position which had previously been disregarded when the *terra nullius* rationale was invoked to justify the colonial claims of European powers. The Crown began to conclude land-cession agreements with Aboriginals in what is now southern Ontario in order to provide land for the United Empire Loyalists moving in from the United States. In these agreements, Aboriginal peoples originally received a lump-sum payment and, later, annuities. From about 1830 onward the system changed, and the Crown set aside reserves in exchange for the cession of Indian land, in addition to providing benefits, such as the right to hunt and fish on unoccupied Crown land. The first major treaties of this kind were the Robinson Treaties of 1850 in northern Ontario and the Douglas Treaties on Vancouver Island.

After Confederation, the treaty-making process continued apace, with treaties numbered 1 to 11 covering most of northern Ontario and the Prairie provinces, and parts of British Columbia, Yukon, and the Mackenzie Valley of the Northwest Territories. These treaties were primarily designed to clear Aboriginal title so that the transcontinental railway could be built and Western immigrant settlement could begin. Such treaties contained an extinguishment clause, under which pre-contact Aboriginal rights were given up in exchange for treaty rights. In return for surrendering title to the lands involved, Aboriginal peoples received tracts of land for reserves as well as other benefits, such as small annuities, schools, hunting and fishing rights, agricultural implements, cattle, and ammunition. Figure 4.1 is a map of the historic Indian treaties.

Whether or not the treaties are regarded as a positive development in the protection of Aboriginal *land*, by the time of Confederation, a dramatic change occurred in how the government handled other aspects of Aboriginal affairs; indeed Canada began to witness the most

FIGURE 4.1 HISTORIC INDIAN TREATIES

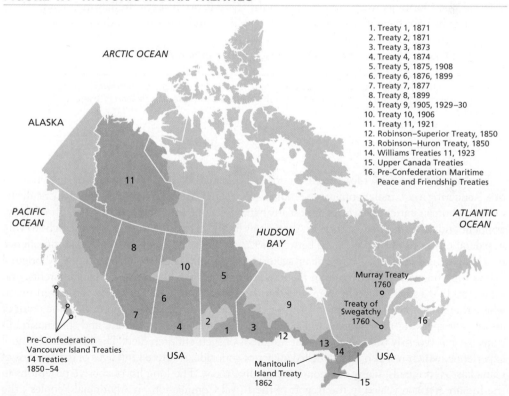

1. Treaty 1, 1871
2. Treaty 2, 1871
3. Treaty 3, 1873
4. Treaty 4, 1874
5. Treaty 5, 1875, 1908
6. Treaty 6, 1876, 1899
7. Treaty 7, 1877
8. Treaty 8, 1899
9. Treaty 9, 1905, 1929–30
10. Treaty 10, 1906
11. Treaty 11, 1921
12. Robinson–Superior Treaty, 1850
13. Robinson–Huron Treaty, 1850
14. Williams Treaties 11, 1923
15. Upper Canada Treaties
16. Pre-Confederation Maritime Peace and Friendship Treaties

Source: Historical Treaties of Canada. Indian and Northern Affairs. *Aboriginal Affairs and Northern Development Canada. Reproduced with the permission of Aboriginal Affairs and Northern Development Canada, 2015.*

negative dimension of colonialism—the exploitation, domination, and subjugation of a people by an imperial power.[5] Aboriginals were ignored in the creation of Canada except that the 1867 Constitution Act gave jurisdiction over Indians and lands reserved for the Indians to the federal government.

Parliament soon used its power to pass laws in this field which were consolidated in the **Indian Act** of 1876. The basic aim of the act was the assimilation of Aboriginals into the new white majority, such that some critics even use the word "genocide."[6] The Act provided for federal government control of almost every aspect of Indian life. In addition, one of the provisions of the Indian Act allowed for "enfranchisement," which encouraged Indians to give up their Indian status. Thus began the distinction between **Status Indians**, those registered with the federal government according to the terms of the Indian Act, and non-status Indians, those no longer registered.

BOX 4.1   VOICES

"I want to get rid of the Indian problem. I do not think as a matter of fact, that the country ought to continuously protect a class of people who are unable to stand alone. Our objective is to continue until there is not a single Indian in Canada that has not been absorbed into the body politic and there is no Indian question, and no Indian Department...."

Duncan Campbell Scott, Deputy Minister of Indian Affairs, 1920

Source: John Leslie, *The Historical Development of the Indian Act*, 2nd ed. (Ottawa: Department of Indian Affairs and Northern Development, Treaties and Historical Research Branch, 1978), p. 114.

Under the Act and its enforcement, Aboriginal Canadians suffered discrimination and indignities. Reflecting a colonial mentality, the Indian Act treated Aboriginal peoples paternalistically by requiring bureaucratic approval for almost any band decision. Traditional Aboriginal forms of government and medicine were outlawed. Aboriginals living on reserves were denied the right to vote in federal elections until 1960. And between 1927 and 1951, the Indian Act made it an offence for a band to hire a lawyer to bring a claim against Canada without government consent. Aboriginal babies were frequently removed from the reserves to be adopted by non-Aboriginal parents, and some 150 000 Indian children were forced into residential schools set up by the government, where they were forced to renounce their identities and were punished, sometimes to the point of assault, for speaking their mother tongue or engaging in their own cultural and spiritual traditions.[7] It has recently been revealed that hundreds of such children died. The residential school experience, which has also been labelled an act of genocide, shattered the lives of generations of Canadian Aboriginals, many of whom are still alive today. The long list of abusive provisions in the Indian Act is revealed in the Report of the Royal Commission on Aboriginal Peoples[8], the Truth and Reconciliation Commission, and other sources.

The second category of Aboriginals, the Métis, is composed of the descendants of French and Scottish fur traders and Indian women. The Métis, who live for the most part in the Prairie provinces, were not covered by the Indian Act or by treaties that the Crown signed with First Nations. As a result, they were often displaced from traditional lands by new settlers. Louis Riel took up their cause in two rebellions, a rebellion in 1869 in Manitoba, and a second rebellion in 1885 in Saskatchewan. The first Riel rebellion was triggered when surveyors were sent the Canadian government to divide up the lands in Canada's vast Northwest Territory. In the earliest years of Confederation, this territory encompassed all of what is now northern Ontario and the Prairie provinces. The surveyors divided the lands in Manitoba without consulting the Métis people who occupied them. If the Métis people wanted to complain, moreover, they would have to travel all the way to Ottawa where decisions about surveying were ultimately made. This was a long and perilous adventure in the period before paved roads and railways. Métis leaders demanded local and accountable control over land surveying. When this was refused by the government, the Métis rebelled. This rebellion was ultimately successful and led to the creation of the province of Manitoba. The second rebellion, in 1885, attempted to achieve the same objectives for the region that is now Saskatchewan; the rebellion was crushed by the government and Louis Riel was hanged. This left the Métis people in an even weaker position to fend for themselves. It is only in recent years that Métis people have been recognized in public policies.

One group of Aboriginals that were relatively untouched by government, although not by fur traders, missionaries, and other European explorers, was Inuit people who occupied the northernmost parts of the Northwest Territories. This territory now encompasses the Yukon, Nunavut, the Northwest Territories, northern Quebec, and parts of Labrador. A 1939 Supreme Court ruling declared that the Inuit came within the meaning of "Indians" in the 1867 Constitution Act (although not under the Indian Act), but it was not until the 1950s that the federal government began to deliver health and educational services to the Inuit. The government later relocated and consolidated Inuit communities into about 50 permanent settlements, largely on the coast of the Arctic mainland, Hudson Bay, and northern Quebec.[9] This disruption of traditional the Inuit lifestyle based on hunting and trapping caused them to depend increasingly on the government for social assistance and intermittent wages.

The legacy of the disruptions caused by colonialism and attempts at forced assimilation continues to this day.[10]

THE CANADIAN PRESS/Adrian Wyld

In late 2011 Canadians became aware of the desperate Aboriginal housing conditions in Attawapiskat, Ontario.

Many Aboriginal families have incomes far below the poverty line. Related to this level of poverty are alarming rates of Aboriginal alcoholism, violence, mortality, low educational attainment, and high unemployment. The suicide rate among Aboriginal youth is at least five times the national average, and Aboriginal Canadians are much more likely to be murdered or to die from accidents, fire, drowning, poisoning, or violence. The incidence of tuberculosis among residents of reserves is seven times that of other Canadians, while cardiovascular disease, diabetes, pneumonia and other respiratory diseases, gastroenteritis, rheumatic fever, ear infections, meningitis, hepatitis, intestinal infections, skin diseases, and disorders of the nervous system are all common. In 2009, several communities were badly hit by an outbreak of the H1N1 (swine flu) virus. The overall life expectancy of Aboriginal Canadians is about 6.6 years shorter than that of non-Aboriginals. Housing on some reserves is deficient, being severely overcrowded and in need of repair, and contaminated drinking water is a common problem.

Although the Canadian government is anxious to point out that considerable improvement has been recorded in on-reserve living conditions since 1960, it acknowledges that about 50 percent of dwellings on First Nations reserves still require renovation or replacement, as revealed in Attawapiskat, Ontario in 2011. According to one study,[11] on-reserve Aboriginal communities would have ranked 68th among 174 nations on the UN Human Development Index—alongside Venezuela and Lebanon, and well-beneath Canada as a whole, which ranked 3rd overall. The UN Human Rights Commission criticized Canada for the high rates of poverty, infant mortality, unemployment, suicide, and abuse within Aboriginal communities.

SETTING THE STAGE FOR CHANGE

However much they were abused and ignored over the previous century, Canada's Aboriginal peoples and their problems have become a major concern of Canadian politics over the past 40 years. The 1963 Royal Commission on Bilingualism and Biculturalism spoke of the English and French as being Canada's two "founding races," but attitudes seemed to be starting to change. In 1966, the Hawthorn Report, *Survey of the Contemporary Indians of Canada*, took the position that Aboriginal Canadians needed a greater degree of local autonomy and deserved a higher level of government services to compensate for everything that had happened in the past. Because non-Aboriginals had built a prosperous society on the lands and resources originally owned by Aboriginal peoples, the latter should be considered "citizens plus." Unfortunately, nothing much came of this report at the time.

Indeed, the next initiative, the 1969 **White Paper on Indians**, took the opposite approach—that Aboriginal Canadians should be treated exactly the same as other Canadians and that reserves should be dismantled and treaties and the Indian Act should be repealed. In other words, it called for their complete integration into the wider Canadian society. Many Aboriginal people were infuriated by this policy, and more than any other single factor, the White Paper was the spark that ignited the Aboriginal movement in Canada and the beginning of changes in the issue of Aboriginal governance.

Because they could hardly be expected to support the apparatus that created their existing problems, Aboriginal Canadians began to argue that they should be able to choose their own decision-making processes, at least on reserves. Before the passage of the Indian Act, they had sophisticated and distinctive forms of government and many wanted to return to such traditional ways. Going well beyond changes in the decision-making machinery, however, they demanded **Aboriginal self-government**.[12] Many Aboriginal people argued for more control over their own affairs, but the specific structures of such proposed self-government were not clear cut: they felt that an array of self-government arrangements and institutional models could be developed. In general, most of the desired responsibilities were within provincial—not federal—jurisdiction, which meant that provinces needed to be involved in the complex self-government negotiations. At the same time, it is widely acknowledged that most Aboriginal communities are not self-sufficient economically, and like have-not provinces and territories, they will require continued financial transfers from other levels of government.[13]

Many Aboriginal people were encouraged by the sympathetic 1977 Berger Inquiry into the proposed Mackenzie Valley gas pipeline,[14] as well as the increased awareness of Aboriginal issues worldwide. Now that most European colonies around the world had been liberated, partly through the efforts of the United Nations, many observers came to see that indigenous peoples in the new world had also been victims of colonialism. In some places, such as South Africa, they could pursue self-determination through majority control of an independent country, but if that was unrealistic in Canada, Aboriginal people would at least insist on reclaiming their identities, ensuring their survival and development as distinct nations, and restructuring the Canadian political system so that they would have control over their own affairs.[15] Aboriginal people organized and began to fight back, learning from the civil rights movement and the New Left of the 1960s and from anti-colonial Third World liberation movements. The incidence of sit-ins, roadblocks and other blockades, rallies, court cases, hunger strikes, and international protests increased.

FROM THE WHITE PAPER TO THE CHARLOTTETOWN ACCORD

Making progress on Aboriginal issues after 1970 has taken many forms. Some of the most common are land claims, self-government agreements, court cases, constitutional amendments, legislation, delegation of power, and formal apologies.

Early Land Claims

In much of the country North American Indians signed treaties with the Crown under which they ceded the land to the government in return for protected reserves. Especially in British Columbia and the North, however, few such treaties were signed, leaving North American Indians and Inuit in these regions without a recognized land base. Adding in the Métis, the result is that only about one-third of Aboriginal peoples have a land base on which to rely. This gives rise to the issue of **Aboriginal title**; that is, a claim to land on the basis of traditional occupancy and use rather than treaty.

When Aboriginal peoples began making such land claims in 1885, governments did not take them seriously. Indeed, as mentioned, between 1927 and 1951, the Indian Act made it an offence to raise funds or hire a lawyer to advance a land claim without the government's permission. In the wake of the reaction to the 1969 White Paper, however, the existence of such Aboriginal title was finally recognized in the *Calder* case in 1973 in connection with the Nisga'a band in British Columbia. While the Supreme Court of Canada was split on the question of whether such title had been subsequently extinguished, the Trudeau government soon announced its intention to begin to negotiate Aboriginal title. A great variety of Aboriginal land claims have, therefore, been launched in the past 40 years. They fall into two categories: **comprehensive claims** based on Aboriginal title (that is, traditional use and occupancy of land) that have not been dealt with by treaty or other legal means, and **specific claims** arising from alleged non-fulfillment of Indian treaties and other lawful obligations.

North of the 60th parallel the federal government is in charge of the land. As a result, many comprehensive claims have been settled in Yukon and the Northwest Territories. Besides providing land and money, such comprehensive claims clarify Native hunting, fishing, and trapping rights and clear obstacles to future economic development.[16] It should be noted that, as in other land claims settlements, the rights of current non-Aboriginal property owners have been protected.

In the south, where Ottawa has responsibility for "Indians and lands reserved for the Indians" but where the provinces have jurisdiction over public ("Crown") lands, land claims have moved more slowly. In general, provincial governments are probably even less sympathetic than Ottawa to the concerns of Aboriginal people, and conflict often develops between First Nations and natural resource companies as well as with non-Aboriginals who now live on the land in question. Ottawa insists that provinces be party to such settlements and contribute to their costs, arguing that it is in the provinces' interest to establish certainty of title to lands and resources.

The first provincial comprehensive land claim settlement was the 1975 **James Bay and Northern Quebec Agreement** between the Cree and Inuit and the government of Quebec, supplemented by several subsequent agreements. In return for allowing Quebec to construct a giant hydro development project in the area, the James Bay Agreement gave the Aboriginal peoples exclusive use of 13 700 km^2 of land and additional territory where they had exclusive hunting, fishing, and trapping rights, along with $225 million in cash. Although the deal was unprecedented and widely heralded in many quarters, one terrible side effect was the mercury poisoning of fish and of the people who ate them, resulting from an unanticipated chemical reaction between water and rock in the flooded land. This problem, the disruption of the caribou migration patterns, and the growing perception that the deal may have been less generous to the Aboriginal community than originally thought, led to the Crees' refusal to sign the second "Great Whale" phase of the James Bay project.

Specific land claims result from alleged breaches of the government's legal obligations and dissatisfaction with treaties—especially the fact that bands did not receive the full amount of land that the treaties promised. Since 1973, Canada has settled hundreds of specific claims, although not always to First Nations' satisfaction.

The Constitution Act, 1982 and the Meech Lake Accord

The first advance in the constitutional recognition of Aboriginal rights occurred after widespread protests in connection with the federal–provincial constitutional negotiations in 1981–82. The Constitution Act, 1982 ultimately contained two clauses of interest here. Section 25 guaranteed that the Charter of Rights and Freedoms would not be construed so as to abrogate or derogate from any Aboriginal, treaty, or other rights or freedoms pertaining to the Aboriginal peoples of Canada, including any rights recognized by the Royal Proclamation of 1763, and any rights or freedoms "that now exist by way of land claims agreements or may be so acquired." Section 35 recognized and affirmed the existing Aboriginal and treaty rights of the Aboriginal peoples of Canada, including the Indian, Inuit, and Métis peoples. Partly to conform with the equality rights clause in the Charter and partly to respond to a ruling of the United Nations Human Rights Committee in the Sandra Lovelace case, the Indian Act was amended to remove the clause that had previously taken Indian status away from Aboriginal women who married white men but granted

Manitoba MLA Elijah Harper withheld assent for the Meech Lake Accord because it did nothing for Aboriginal peoples.

such status to white women who married Indian men. Bill C-31 (1985) led to the reinstatement of nearly 100 000 Aboriginal women and their children, but since bands were allowed to control their own membership, a high proportion of those reinstated in status had difficulty in returning to the reserve. In 2005 Paul Martin named Sandra Lovelace Nicholas to the Senate.

Partly because the first ministers did not feel that Aboriginal issues had been sufficiently addressed in 1982 and partly based on the recommendations of the 1983 Penner Report (Report of the Special Committee of the House of Commons on Indian Self-Government), a series of federal–provincial first ministers' conferences on Aboriginal rights was held between 1983 and 1987. Prime ministers Trudeau and Mulroney in turn tried unsuccessfully to get provincial premiers and Aboriginal leaders to agree to the terms of a constitutional amendment recognizing the principle of Aboriginal self-government. Several premiers insisted that the concept be clarified before they would agree even in principle, while Aboriginal leaders wanted the principle recognized as an *inherent* right. At the 1987 conference, Georges Erasmus, national Chief of the Assembly of First Nations, spoke as follows:

> Nothing short of Aboriginal self-government will achieve our aspirations for survival as distinct peoples. Attempts by governments at integration and assimilation over the years have failed and we have rejected them. We must be able to control our lives on our own lands and using our own resources.[17]

Although the constitutional talks broke down, two pieces of legislation were passed to provide for self-government in specific localities. The 1984 Cree-Naskapi (of Quebec) Act set in

CP PICTURE ARCHIVE/Winnipeg Free Press/Wayne Glowacki

place self-government arrangements for the Indians of Quebec who were parties to the James Bay land claim agreement, and the 1986 Sechelt Indian Band Self-Government Act allowed the Sechelt band in British Columbia to assume control over their lands, resources, health and social services, education, and local taxation in what is usually called the "municipal model."

Because the government of Quebec had rejected the Constitution Act, 1982, Prime Minister Mulroney attempted to bring that province back into the constitutional fold with the Meech Lake Accord in 1987. However, given the absence of constitutional advance on their issues many Aboriginal groups were understandably opposed to the Accord, which addressed Quebec's constitutional demands but completely overlooked their own. Even supporters of the Accord found it hard to blame Elijah Harper for withholding unanimous consent when it came before the Manitoba legislature for final approval in 1990.

Land Issues in 1990

While some land claims were being settled after 1975, another aspect of the land question arose in the conflict at Oka, Quebec in the summer of 1990. It was the most serious conflict between Aboriginal people and authorities of modern times.[18] The municipal council's decision to expand a golf course on land claimed by resident Mohawks as sacred ground (a claim of traditional occupancy but not guaranteed by treaty) led to an armed standoff between Mohawk warriors and the Quebec provincial police in which one police officer was killed. The Mohawks were supported by the nearby Kahnawake reserve, which also set up barriers and blockaded the Mercier Bridge to Montreal. The Canadian Armed Forces were later brought in, and Aboriginal demonstrations took place across the country. Although some local non-Aboriginal residents stoned vehicles carrying Mohawk families, most Canadians hoped that the incident would speed up the process of settling hundreds of outstanding Aboriginal land claims before any worse violence occurred.

CP PHOTO/str-Shaney Komulainen

A Canadian solider and an Aboriginal protester come face-to-face in a tense standoff in Oka, Quebec, in September 1990.

Meanwhile, Aboriginal peoples were making some headway in the courts, especially in two Supreme Court of Canada decisions in 1990. In the *Sioui* case, the Court ruled that a 1760 Huron treaty was valid, and its provision that Indians be allowed "the free exercise of their Religion [and] their Customs" prevented Quebec from prosecuting Hurons for practising Native customs and fishing in provincial parks. The Court also gave Indians new hope in the *Sparrow* decision which stated that section 35(1) of the Constitution Act, 1982, affords Aboriginal people constitutional protection against provincial legislative power and that the clause should be given a generous, liberal interpretation. In this case the Court said that the Aboriginal peoples' right to fish could override provincial regulations regarding the size of a net.[19]

The Charlottetown Accord, 1992

Elijah Harper's stand on Meech Lake together with the Oka affair, both in mid-1990, precipitated a dramatic breakthrough of constitutional concern with Aboriginal issues and full participation of Aboriginal leaders in post-Meech constitutional negotiations. For the first time, Aboriginal leaders were given the same status as premiers in the talks leading up to the 1992 **Charlottetown Accord**, and that document addressed Aboriginal concerns in a more extensive and satisfactory way than it did the demands of Quebec.

The Charlottetown Accord would have recognized the inherent right of Aboriginal peoples to self-government and acknowledged that such First Nations governments constituted a third order of government in Canada, analogous to provinces. The document provided for self-government agreements to be negotiated among the three levels of government. Federal and provincial laws would remain in place until superseded by Aboriginal laws, but the latter would have to be consistent with the preservation of peace, order, and good government in Canada. In addition to provisions for Aboriginal self-government, Aboriginal peoples were to have a new role of one kind or another in the House of Commons, Senate, Supreme Court, first ministers' conferences, and the constitutional amending formula. Despite the enormous leap in official thinking that this section of the Accord represented, a majority of Aboriginal voters opposed it in the subsequent referendum. Some found the provisions lacking in detail, and many Aboriginal women worried that their individual (Charter) rights might be sacrificed for new group rights.

Although few non-Aboriginals voted against the Charlottetown Accord because of its provisions regarding Aboriginal self-government, it should be noted that there was and is a cleavage between those who are sympathetic to Aboriginal demands and those who oppose them. Provincial premiers' reluctance to constitutionalize Aboriginal self-government was previously mentioned, and some elements of the electorate contend that Aboriginal peoples already receive preferential treatment. They cite, for example, the large annual budget of Indigenous and Northern Affairs Canada with its high per capita federal spending on Aboriginal Canadians, certain tax exemptions, extensive subsidization of post-secondary education, and affirmative action programs.

ABORIGINAL ISSUES IN THE CHRÉTIEN ERA, 1993–2003

Aboriginal issues were even more dominant on the Canadian political agenda in the following decade. Although the issues were difficult, and sometimes even violent, some slow progress was recorded.

Aboriginal Self-Government

After 1992, activity in the area of Aboriginal governance focused on legislative and adminis-trative changes, such as experiments in delegating federal or provincial government powers to First Nations communities, and new self-government agreements.[20] In mid-1995, the Minister of Indian Affairs announced that Ottawa was launching new negotiations to give Aboriginal people in all provinces much wider powers, and outlined how the government would imple-ment the inherent right of Aboriginal self-government in practical, workable agreements. Not expecting to be able to achieve a formal constitutional amendment to this effect, the Chrétien government claimed that the principle was *already* contained in section 35 of the Constitution Act, 1982, and therefore *already* constitutionalized. According to the August 1995 ministerial statement, the principles of Aboriginal self-government are as follows:

- The inherent right is an existing Aboriginal right recognized and affirmed under the Canadian Constitution.
- Self-government will be exercised within the existing Canadian Constitution. It does not mean sovereignty in the international sense. Aboriginal peoples will continue to be citi-zens of Canada and the province or territory where they live.
- The Canadian Charter of Rights and Freedoms will apply fully to Aboriginal govern-ments. The current provisions of the Charter that respect the unique Aboriginal and treaty rights of Aboriginal peoples will continue to apply.
- All federal funding for self-government will come from the reallocation of existing resources.
- Where all parties agree, rights in self-government agreements may be protected in new treaties under section 35 of the Constitution Act, 1982. They may also be protected through additions to existing treaties, or as part of comprehensive land claims agreements.
- Federal, provincial, territorial, and Aboriginal laws must work in harmony. Certain laws of overriding federal and provincial importance, such as the Criminal Code, will prevail.
- The interests of all Canadians will be taken into account as agreements are negotiated.

In its report a year later the **Royal Commission on Aboriginal Peoples** identified four "touch-stones" as a framework for its recommendations. These were (1) a new relationship between Aboriginal and non-Aboriginal people based on equality, respect, and reconciliation; (2) self-determination for Aboriginal peoples within Canada through self-government—that is, the right to control their collective futures; (3) economic self-sufficiency for Aboriginal peoples, including breaking the cycle of poverty and dependency on government transfers and creating meaningful employment opportunities; and (4) personal and collective healing for Aboriginal peoples and communities, to remedy the effects of decades of mistreatment and neglect. The commission endorsed Aboriginal self-government in its widest sense and the basic separation of Aboriginal and non-Aboriginal societies. Among other things, it proposed a division between "core" areas, where Aboriginal governments would be free to exercise authority and legislate on their own initiative, and "peripheral" areas, which would require self-government treaties or agreements with other governments. It also proposed an Aboriginal Parliament, dual Canadian–Aboriginal citizenship, an independent lands and treaties tribunal, an Aboriginal development bank, an action plan on health and social conditions, and an Aboriginal-controlled education system.[21]

The Chrétien government was reluctant to rush into the implementation of the royal commission's more exotic recommendations, preferring the course on which it had previously embarked. In 1997, the government issued a general response called *Gathering Strength—Canada's Aboriginal Action Plan*. It began with a Statement of Reconciliation, apologizing for past wrongs, especially the horrors of the residential school system. Next, in a Statement of Renewal, the document adapted the royal commission's four touchstones to the following basic principles: renewing the partnerships; strengthening Aboriginal governance; developing a new fiscal relationship; and supporting strong communities, people, and economies.

Whether or not the 1995 and 1997 federal declarations amounted to anything close to "inherent Aboriginal self-government," considerable progress continued to be made at the community level. Aboriginal people now control over 80 percent of Aboriginal Affairs departmental program funding, and Aboriginal authorities increasingly deliver such services as education, language and culture, police services, health care and social services, housing, property rights, and adoption and child welfare. In this vein, Ottawa signed an agreement in 1997 with the Mi'kmaq chiefs in Nova Scotia, transferring education authority to First Nations' control. Many more First Nations were negotiating self-government agreements, whether dealing with a comprehensive range of jurisdictions, a single jurisdiction (for example, education), or combined self-government and land claims negotiations.

In the 1999 *Corbiere* case, the Supreme Court gave band members living off-reserve the right to vote in First Nations' elections.[22] Then, in 2002, Indian Affairs Minister Robert Nault introduced a new First Nations Governance Act (Bill C-61). His objective was to take quick action to ensure greater democracy and financial accountability on reserves, but most First Nations' leaders had other, longer-term priorities, notably more money, more power, and solutions to social problems. Because of such opposition, the bill was not passed by the time Paul Martin succeeded Jean Chrétien as prime minister, and the new government abandoned it.

Ipperwash, Caledonia, and Aboriginal Injustice

While such progress was made on Aboriginal issues in the Chrétien era, violence erupted again in a peaceful and legitimate land dispute in 1995 at Ipperwash, Ontario. In this case, a police officer killed an unarmed demonstrator, Dudley George. Another incendiary dispute began in 2006 in Caledonia, Ontario, over the development of a residential subdivision on what the Six Nations reserve near Hamilton claimed as their land. Roadblocks, barricades, angry confrontations, acts of violence, and unhelpful judicial rulings prompted the provincial government to try to solve the problem by buying the property from the developer.

A specific aspect of Aboriginal governance relates to the high proportion of Aboriginal peoples in Canadian jails. Indeed, some troubling criminal cases raised the question of whether they are treated fairly in the justice system: in the case of Donald Marshall, a Nova Scotia Mi'kmaq who was imprisoned for more than 10 years for a crime he did not commit; in the rape and murder of Helen Betty Osborne, a First Nations girl in The Pas, by four white men; in the shooting of an Aboriginal leader, J.J. Harper, by a Winnipeg police officer; and in the Stonechild case, where an inebriated Aboriginal youth was left by the police to freeze to death outside the city limits of Saskatoon.[23] Inquiries into these tragedies have documented the discrimination against and brutalization of Aboriginal people by every aspect of the criminal justice system.

A 2006 report from the federal ombudsman for prisons admitted that Aboriginal people are still subject to systemic discrimination once incarcerated.

It is sometimes proposed that an autonomous or parallel Aboriginal justice system be established in which Aboriginal cases would be diverted from the regular judicial process to allow convictions and sentences to be based on Aboriginal values and community traditions. So far, several provinces have allowed experimental judicial processes involving Aboriginal input; more Aboriginals people have been hired as police officers; some reserves have their own Aboriginal police forces and justices of the peace; and a few even maintain their own correctional facilities. Increasingly, judges dealing with Aboriginal defendants follow Native traditions (or consult with elders) in imposing their sentences, such as restitution, restorative justice, and banishment. With the high rate of Aboriginal incarceration in mind, the federal Parliament amended the Criminal Code in 1995 to read: "All available sanctions other than imprisonment that are reasonable in the circumstances should be considered for all offenders, with particular attention to the circumstances of Aboriginal offenders." The Supreme Court brought this clause to the attention of other judges in the 1999 *Gladue* case and reinforced its decision in 2012 in the *Ipeelee* case. It told judges that they must search out lenient or creative sentences for Aboriginal offenders that recognize the oppressive cultural conditions many have endured.[24] To some extent, however, this directive contradicted the government's new mandatory minimum sentences law.

Donald Marshall returned to court in 1999 after being charged with fishing for eels out of season. In the *Donald Marshall* cases, the Supreme Court ruled that the treaty rights of the Mi'kmaq in Atlantic Canada allowed them to make a "moderate livelihood." Subject to government regulations with respect to conservation, they could catch lobster or eels during the period when the fishing season was closed to non-Aboriginals. In the 2005 *Bernard* case, however, the Court decided that insufficient historical evidence existed to give Aboriginal peoples in Nova Scotia and New Brunswick the same right to cut trees.[25] In several provinces, landmark court decisions have held that even the Métis have hunting and fishing rights under the Constitution, no different from the rights of status Indians.

Nunavut and the Nisga'a Treaty

In the Northwest Territories, a 1992 plebiscite ratified a boundary division that led to the creation, in 1999, of a new territory called **Nunavut**. It has a public government, elected by Aboriginal and non-Aboriginal residents alike, with all the institutions associated with a province or territory. But Nunavut can be characterized as a form of Aboriginal self-government because the Inuit make up 85 percent of the population. In addition, several Yukon First Nations have signed final land claim and self-government agreements with the federal and territorial governments. They require that each First Nation have a constitution and a citizenship code; they recognize the rights of non-Aboriginals; and they outline how First Nations powers relate to territorial and federal powers.[26]

Because the province of British Columbia contains a large proportion of North American Indians and few treaties, the land claims issue has been particularly significant there. Unfortunately, the provincial government was reluctant to engage in such negotiations, and the BC Supreme Court was not much help. When the *Delgamuukw* case came to the Supreme Court of Canada in 1997, however, that court was more sympathetic. It ordered that in such cases, various kinds of oral history evidence be admissible and also provided its first comprehensive statement on Aboriginal title: a group must establish its exclusive occupation of the land in question before the time the Crown asserted sovereignty. Although the Supreme Court of Canada allowed for Crown infringement on Aboriginal title for valid legislative objectives, it specified that the groups with Aboriginal title need to be involved in the decision-making process around such a proposed infringement.[27]

As mentioned, the neighbouring Nisga'a tribe in northwest BC, which had been seeking recognition of their Aboriginal title for more than 100 years, took their claim to court in the 1973 *Calder case*. It was not until the 1990s, however, when governments of Canada and British Columbia signed the BC Treaty Commission Agreement with the First Nations of that province that serious negotiations began. The Nisga'a served as pioneers again when they finally signed the first modern-day treaty with Ottawa and the BC government in 1998. In this combined land and self-governance treaty, the Nisga'a gained 1930 km^2 of land, $190 million in cash, and self-government powers beyond those of municipal governments in return for giving up the right to future land claims and tax-exempt status. It was a complex document including sections on forestry, mining, wildlife and the environment, public access, the administration of justice, finance, taxation, and many more. Two years later, the treaty was ratified by the Nisga'a people in a referendum, as well as by the federal and BC legislatures. Although opposed by a minority of Nisga'a, some surrounding Aboriginal groups, and some in other provinces who felt that they had given up too much, the treaty's most vociferous opposition arose among non-Aboriginals in the BC legislature, where a demand for a provincial referendum was loudly voiced. Nevertheless, the Nisga'a treaty may well serve as a model for treaties with other Aboriginal groups,[28] and British Columbia is currently the site of a distinctive, busy, complex, and innovative land claims tribunal process.[29]

CONTEMPORARY ABORIGINAL ISSUES

Political Activity

One of the traditional weaknesses of the Aboriginal cause has been a general attitude of passivity and a lack of effective organization of Native groups. At the electoral level, Aboriginal peoples are dispersed across the country in such a way that they constitute a majority or plurality in only three or four constituencies. Moreover, for a variety of historical, socio-economic, and other reasons, their voter turnout rate has generally been low and they have not gravitated to a particular political party.[30] Only 35 MPs with Aboriginal origins have been elected since 1970, divided among all the major parties. The Royal Commission on Electoral Reform and Party Financing urged the establishment of separate Aboriginal seats in the House of Commons, but this idea has never been seriously debated.

While the level of electoral participation has therefore been weak, recent years have witnessed the emergence of strong and vocal advocacy groups, such as the **Assembly of First Nations** (status Indians), the Congress of Aboriginal Peoples (non-status Indians), the Métis National Council, the Inuit Tapiriit Kanatami, the Native Women's Association of Canada,

AFN National Chief Perry Bellegarde speaks at the Assembly of First Nations Special Chiefs Assembly in Gatineau, Tuesday December 8, 2015.

and the Pauktuutit Inuit Women's Association. While such organizations strengthen the Aboriginal voice in the policymaking process, the fact that they represent different groups within the Aboriginal community means that their demands sometimes conflict with each other. Many other Aboriginal groups exist at the provincial or territorial level.

Non-electoral means of pursuing Aboriginal interests have also included taking cases to court, encouraging the media to expose government abuse, and appearing before the **National Energy Board**. Aboriginal people have occasionally resorted to demonstrations or civil disobedience, such as road or train blockades, and in modern times, the Oka standoff was one of the few times that Aboriginal peoples actually took up arms.

"On-Reserve" and "Off-Reserve" Aboriginal Peoples

In the case of Aboriginal people living on reserves, former Auditor General Sheila Fraser regularly raised concerns in her reports. In 2003, for example, she noted that the promises made in modern treaties were not being fully implemented. Aboriginal leaders cited a number of causes for this problem: the ignorance in key federal agencies about land-claims agreements, the "we don't take action until forced to do so" approach enforced by the federal Department of Justice, and the technical and minimalist interpretations of the agreements by those charged with their implementation. In 2005, the auditor general continued to report that the Indian affairs department had not been helpful in assisting First Nations to expand the size of reserves through transfers of Crown land or the purchase of land in urban areas.

Moreover, land claim settlements and Aboriginal self-government are not likely to affect the fate of the many Aboriginal people who have left the reserve to live in urban centres. The rates of poverty, unemployment, violence, and substance abuse among urban Aboriginal people are almost as high as those among Indians living on reserves. Aboriginal women in particular are concerned about issues of day-to-day survival in a harsh urban environment, such as housing, education, and the future of their children. Aboriginal people are disproportionately represented among the inner-city poor all across the country, and this aspect of Aboriginal politics is likely to assume increasing importance in the future.[31] Another tragic issue is the number of Aboriginal women who have gone missing in certain large cities, some of them having been involved in the sex trade.

The Kelowna Accord and Court Cases

The Liberal government of Paul Martin convened a number of major meetings with Aboriginal leaders, culminating in the first ministers' and national Aboriginal leaders meeting in Kelowna in November 2005.[32] It was attended by the premiers, territorial leaders, and the major Aboriginal associations mentioned above. Prime Minister Martin announced that Ottawa would contribute some $5 billion over five years toward a 10-year dedicated effort to closing the gap in the quality of life between Aboriginal peoples and other Canadians, with particular reference to health, education, housing, and economic development. The House of Commons later passed a private member's bill from the former prime minister to implement the Kelowna Accord, but the Harper government ignored it.

A number of significant court decisions affecting Aboriginal peoples were made over the 2002–06 period. The Supreme Court of Canada ruled in 2002 that Aboriginal people who can prove their forebears honestly believed that government authorities had created a reserve for them may have a case even if no specific order in council verified its creation. A year later, the Supreme Court ruled that the Métis people are a distinct Aboriginal group, with a constitutional right to hunt for food. The full implications of the ruling are not yet clear, but the decision strengthened the bargaining position of this previously ambiguous group. The Court also found that Aboriginal peoples must be consulted on the development of logging, mining, or other resource projects on lands to which the title is still in dispute, although they have no veto over such projects. In a setback to Aboriginal interests, the Court ruled in 2005 that Mi'kmaq did not possess a right to cut logs on Crown land in Nova Scotia and New Brunswick without authorization, but in 2006 made a distinction between logging for commercial and domestic purposes.[33] Chapter 19 includes discussion of such Charter cases.

The Harper Government

Many developments on the Aboriginal front occurred while the Harper government was in office from 2006–15, and many others remain on the Canadian political agenda. One is the question of apologies for the abuse that Aboriginal children endured in residential schools. Most of the churches involved issued full and formal apologies for their part, and the previous Liberal government began the process of providing financial compensation. Prime Minister Martin asked former Supreme Court judge Frank Iacobucci to work with the individuals and groups involved to come up with a general solution, which was announced in the early days of the Harper government. Then, in a moving ceremony in the House of Commons in June 2008, Stephen Harper issued a full official and historic apology for the residential school policy, an excerpt from which is presented in Box 4.2, and a Truth and Reconciliation Commission was established as part of the overall settlement of this problem.

As mentioned, the Harper government distanced itself from Martin's Kelowna agreement, much to the annoyance of premiers and many Aboriginal groups. The new administration also opposed a separate Aboriginal commercial fishery on the Fraser River, put more emphasis on accountability in reserve governance, and tried to promote individual rather than collective ownership of Aboriginal land. Most Aboriginal peoples in BC were also at odds with the government in its haste to have the Northern Gateway pipeline built across their lands. But a Supreme Court decision in June 2008 countered the Harper fishing policy and upheld an

BOX 4.2   VOICES

"Two primary objectives of the Residential Schools system were to remove and isolate children from the influence of their homes, families, traditions and cultures, and to assimilate them into the dominant culture. These objectives were based on the assumption Aboriginal cultures and spiritual beliefs were inferior and unequal. Indeed, some sought, as it was infamously said, "to kill the Indian in the child." Today, we recognize that this policy of assimilation was wrong, has caused great harm, and has no place in our country...."

Prime Minister Stephen Harper's Statement of Apology on Indian Residential Schools, June 11, 2008, found at: http://www.pm.gc.ca/eng/media.asp?id=2149

Source: Excerpt from "Prime Minister Harper offers full apology on behalf of Canadians for the Indian Residential Schools system," 2008. http://www.pm.gc.ca/eng/media.asp?id=2149. Reproduced with the permission of the Office of the Prime Minister of Canada.

Aboriginal jump-start on salmon fishing in the Fraser River, based on the affirmative action provisions of the Charter of Rights.[34]

In view of the serious backlog of specific land claims, a new system was adopted in 2008. The Specific Claims Tribunal Act provided for an independent tribunal composed of superior court judges to make binding decisions on specific claims that the Minister rejected or did not approve within a three-year time period. Whether approved by the Minister or the Tribunal, a successful claim usually results in a cash settlement that can be used to purchase land to compensate for what was lost.

Although the process of signing comprehensive and specific land claims agreements seems to be exceedingly slow, the first modern urban treaty, the Tsawwassen First Nation Final Agreement in British Columbia was approved, and many more can be anticipated over the next few years. For the most recent developments in land claims and self-government agreements, see the Indigenous and Northern Affairs Canada website.[35]

In response to the *Sharon McIvor* case before the BC Court of Appeal in 2009, the government agreed to amend the Indian Act to remove a continuing discrimination against Indian women who married non-Indian men. In 2011, the deplorable living conditions on the Attawapiskat First Nation drew attention to the plight of Aboriginal people on remote reserves in Canada. Many Canadians have a hard time understanding how, in one of the wealthiest countries in the world, there are people living without access to running water, indoor bathrooms, electricity, or insulated housing. Attawapiskat was hardly an exception, however, and the revelation prompted increased speculation about the economic viability of many reserves. Such attention forced the Harper government to supply additional housing in Attawapiskat, but by the end of 2012, the perception of government neglect of accumulated Aboriginal problems generated protests across the country, including a hunger strike by the Chief of the Attawapiskat First Nation.

Aboriginal peoples are far more likely than non-Aboriginal peoples to be victims of violent crime. The homicide rate among Aboriginal peoples is nearly seven times higher than it is among non-Aboriginal Canadians.[36] These numbers have led to calls for the government to commission a national inquiry on missing and murdered Aboriginal women. The Harper government resisted these calls and argued instead that solving the problem is a matter for police investigations. In contrast, the current Liberal government launched an inquiry immediately upon being elected.

THEORETICAL CONSIDERATIONS

In theory, there are probably three main governance options that could be chosen to address the condition of Aboriginal life in Canada.[37]

- Integration and assimilation into the non-Aboriginal society. This was the route historically favoured by the Government of Canada, and one chosen by many Aboriginal people themselves. Integration and assimilation would presumably involve repeal of the Indian Act and treaties, abandonment of reserves, and denial of any kind of Aboriginal status, more or less as the 1969 Trudeau-Chrétien White Paper proposed. The migration of increasing numbers of Aboriginal people to urban areas is a variation on this option, mostly involving people who have left reserves because of the inadequacies of such an environment, but also including Métis who never had a land base.

- Given the fact that in the pre-contact period, Aboriginal peoples governed themselves, the second option would be a return to Aboriginal self-government, focused on reserves. For some, this means making reserves more autonomous of the federal department of Indigenous and Northern Affairs Canada; indeed, First Nations communities increasingly operate without detailed departmental bureaucratic supervision. This option would also include the example of the Nisga'a Treaty, where the powers of the First Nation exceed those of a municipality, including jurisdiction over natural resources and the environment. One step further would be to incorporate the concept of Aboriginal self-government as a third order of government, akin to federal and provincial levels, as proposed in the Charlottetown Accord. In this model, federal and provincial laws would still apply to Aboriginal people in certain areas of jurisdiction. Aboriginal self-government is at least theoretically feasible with a territorial base such as a reserve, but it is a much more questionable concept in situations where Aboriginal people are intermingled with others, especially in an urban setting.

- Some advocates go further and speak of Aboriginal sovereignty. This third option would involve being independent of the Canadian state. This is the ideal of those who feel that the second option would leave Aboriginal people in a "post-colonial," but still internal colonial relationship with the dominant non-Aboriginal authorities. They see all the trappings of self-government processes, land claims agreements, and Aboriginal rights court cases as basically determined by the white society's ways and needs.

CONCLUSION

Aboriginals and non-Aboriginal peoples must learn to live together. While eschewing assimilation, many argue that a certain amount of Aboriginal integration into the Canadian society may be advisable; this is what Alan C. Cairns calls "citizens plus." He and other thoughtful observers want to improve existing government programs; enlarge and strengthen reserves, attempting to make them more economically viable for those who choose to remain there; respect treaty rights; settle land claims; give Aboriginal peoples more control over their daily lives; and treat them more fairly in the justice system. Although progress so far has been slight, a new generation Aboriginal leaders has arrived on the scene. Cairns reminds us that we are all in this together:

> Aboriginal nations, given their size and resources, cannot and will not opt for an independence that exceeds their governing capacity. Non-Aboriginal Canadians cannot wipe out Aboriginal difference in pursuit of an idealized homogeneity that would make governance easier. So the choices we have to make for territorially based nations are the nature and extent of Aboriginal self-government and how we organize our common life in the areas beyond the reach of self-government.[38]

Aboriginal issues are revisited in several other points in this text. Questions relating to Aboriginal peoples in Quebec are mentioned in the next chapter, and we also return to these issues in Chapters 7 (Gender) and 8 (Class). At the same time, the place of Aboriginal people in the party and electoral systems is gaining increasing attention, and is included in Chapters 13 and 14. Aboriginal advocacy groups are discussed again in Chapter 16, as are the territories in Chapter 18 (Federalism); and Chapter 19 includes analysis of relevant Charter cases.

DISCUSSION QUESTIONS

1. How have Aboriginal identities changed in recent years?

2. What are the causes of the generally poor condition of Aboriginal life in Canada?

3. What are the principal Aboriginal demands on the political agenda, and how far can or should the government go to address them?

4. What can be done to make First Nations reserves more economically viable?

5. What is meant by Aboriginal self-government? How far should it go?

6. How would an Aboriginal justice system interact with Canada's traditional justice system?

7. What can be done to improve the living conditions of urban Aboriginals?

MindTap®   FOR MORE INFO GO TO http://www.nelson.com/student

NOTES

1. In his book *Dragons of Eden* (New York: Random House, 1977), the late Carl Sagan pioneered a similar approach for conceptualizing astronomical timescales.
2. Statistics Canada, "Aboriginal Peoples in Canada in 2006: Inuit, Métis and First Nations, 2006 Census," Catalogue no. 97-558, available at http://www12.statcan.ca/English/census06/analysis/aboriginals. This report notes that Canada has the second-largest proportion of indigenous peoples of any country; New Zealand's proportion is 15 percent, while the United States has two percent. The 2011 census did not measure Aboriginal origin or identity.
3. Aboriginal Affairs and Northern Development Canada, *Registered Indian Population by Sex and Residence 2010,* accessed February 13, 2012.
4. The Royal Proclamation was a strong statement on Indian rights, and today's Aboriginal Canadians point to the significance of its inclusion in the 1982 Charter of Rights. It can be found, among other places, in Michael Asch, *Home and Native Land: Aboriginal Rights and the Canadian Constitution* (Toronto: Methuen, 1984) and available at http://www.canadiana.org/citm/primary/primary_e.html. See Darlene Johnston, *The Taking of Indian Lands: Consent or Coercion?* (Saskatoon: University of Saskatchewan Native Law Centre, 1989).
5. Thomas R. Berger, *A Long and Terrible Shadow: White Values, Native Rights in the Americas* (Vancouver: Douglas & McIntyre, 1991); Kathleen Mahoney, "Evolving Citizenship: What Difference has 400 Years Made?" *Policy Options* (July–August 2008).
6. For example, Taiaiake Alfred, *Peace, Power, Righteousness: An Indigenous Manifesto* (Toronto: Oxford University Press, 1999), p. xv.
7. John Milloy, "A *National Crime*": The Canadian Government and the Residential School System, 1879 to 1986 (Winnipeg: University of Manitoba Press, 1998).
8. *Report of the Royal Commission on Aboriginal Peoples, Vol. 1*, Chapter 9.
9. A subsequent and controversial relocation occurred in 1953–55. See Royal Commission on Aboriginal Peoples, *The High Arctic Relocation* (Ottawa: Supply and Services Canada, 1994, Catalogue No. Z1-1991/1-41-3-1E).
10. Peter R. Oberle, *The Incidence of Family Poverty on Canadian Indian Reserves* (Ottawa: Indian and Northern Affairs Canada, 1993); Geoffrey York, *The Dispossessed: Life and Death in Native Canada* (Toronto: Lester & Orpen Dennys, 1989); and Jeremy P. White, et al, *Aboriginal Conditions: Research as a Foundation for Public Policy* (Vancouver: UBC Press, 2004).
11. Martin Cooke, Daniel Beavon, and Mindy McHardy. "Measuring the Well-Being of Aboriginal People: An Application of the United Nations Human Development Index to Registered Indians in Canada, 1981–2001," in Jerry P. White, Paul Maxim, and Dan Beavon, eds., *Aboriginal Policy Research: Setting the Agenda for Change*, Vol. 1 (Toronto: Nelson, 2004).
12. Bruce Clark, *Native Liberty, Crown Sovereignty: The Existing Aboriginal Right to Self-Government in Canada* (Montreal: McGill-Queen's University Press, 1990), argues that this right already exists and that what Aboriginals need is money, land, and cooperation to be able to exercise this right.
13. Michael S. Whittington, "Aboriginal Self-Government," in Michael Whittington and Glen Williams, eds., *Canadian Politics in the 21st Century*, 6th ed. (Toronto: Nelson, 2004).
14. Thomas Berger, *Northern Frontier, Northern Homeland: The Report of the Mackenzie Valley Inquiry* (Ottawa: Supply and Services Canada, 1977), republished by Douglas & McIntyre, Vancouver, 1988.
15. Asch, *Home and Native Land*, pp. 32–37, and Michael Asch, ed., *Aboriginal and Treaty Rights in Canada: Essays on Law, Equality and Respect for Difference* (Vancouver: UBC Press, 1997).
16. Michael S. Whittington, "Aboriginal Self-Government."
17. Georges Erasmus, "Opening Remarks," First Ministers' Conference on Aboriginal Constitutional Affairs, Ottawa, March 26, 1987. See also Frank Cassidy, ed., *Aboriginal Self-Government* (Halifax: Institute for Research on Public Policy, 1991).
18. Geoffrey York and Loreen Pindera, *People of the Pines: The Warriors and the Legacy of Oka* (Toronto: Little Brown, 1991); Craig MacLaine and Michael Baxendale, *This Land Is Our Land* (Toronto: Optimum, 1990); and Robert Campbell and Leslie Pal, *The Real Worlds of Canadian Politics*, 2nd ed. (Peterborough: Broadview Press, 1991), Ch.4.

19. *R. v. Sioui,* [1990] 1 S.C.R. 1025; *R. v. Sparrow,* [1990] 1 S.C.R. 1075. See also Kiera Ladner, "Up the Creek: Fishing for a New Constitutional Order," *Canadian Journal of Political Science* (December 2005).

20. Whittington, "Aboriginal Self-Government"; and Audrey Doerr, "Building New Orders of Government—The Future of Aboriginal Self-Government," *Canadian Public Administration* (Summer 1997); Frances Abele and Michael J. Prince, "A Little Imagination Required: How Ottawa Funds Territorial and Northern Aboriginal Governments," in Allan M. Maslove, ed., *How Ottawa Spends 2008–2009* (Montreal: McGill-Queen's University Press, 2008).

21. Royal Commission on Aboriginal Peoples, *Report of the Royal Commission on Aboriginal Peoples* (Ottawa: Supply and Services, 1996, Catalogue No. Z1-1991/1-1E), available at http://www.collectionscanada. gc.ca/webarchives/ 20071115053257 and http://www.ainc-inac.gc.ca/ch/rcap/sg/sgmm_e.html.

22. *Corbiere v. Canada (Minister of Indian and Northern Affairs)* [1999] 2 S.C.R. 203.

23. Suzanne Reber and Robert Renaud, *Starlight Tour: The Last, Lonely Night of Neil Stonechild* (Toronto: Random House Canada, 2005); Joyce Green, "From Stonechild to Social Cohesion: Anti-Racist Challenges for Saskatchewan, *Canadian Journal of Political Science* (September 2006).

24. *R. v. Gladue,* [1999] 1 S.C.R. 688; *R. v. Armbruster,* [1999] BCCA 448; *R. v. Ipeelee* (March 23, 2012).

25. *R. v. Marshall,* [1999] 3 S.C.R. 456 and *R. v. Marshall,* [1999] 3 S.C.R. 533; Ken Coates, *The Marshall Decision and Native Rights* (Montreal: McGill-Queen's University Press, 2000); *R. v. Marshall; R. v. Bernard* [2005] 2 S.C.R. 220; and Kiera L. Ladner, "Up the Creek: Fishing for a New Constitutional Order."

26. Whittington, "Aboriginal Self-Government"; and Gurston Dacks, "Implementing First Nations Self-Government in Yukon: Lessons for Canada," *Canadian Journal of Political Science* (September 2004).

27. *Delgamuukw v. British Columbia,* [1997] 3 S.C.R. 1010; *Calder v. Attorney General of B.C.,* [1973] S.C.R. 313; *Guerin v. The Queen,* [1984] 2 S.C.R. 335; and *Ontario (Attorney General) v. Bear Island Foundation,* [1991] 2 S.C.R. 570; and Stan Persky, *Delgamuukw: The Supreme Court of Canada Decision on Aboriginal Title* (Vancouver: Douglas and McIntyre, 1998).

28. Karen E. Lochead, "Whose Land Is It Anyway? The Long Road to the Nisga'a Treaty," in Robert M. Campbell, Leslie A. Pal, and Michael Howlett, eds., *The Real Worlds of Canadian Politics,* 4th ed. (Peterborough: Broadview Press, 2004).

29. Christopher McKee, *Treaty Talks in British Columbia: Building a New Relationship,* 3rd ed. (Vancouver: UBC Press, 2009).

30. Elections Canada Online, *2009 Aboriginal Policy Research Conference* available at http://www.elections .ca/content.aspx?section=med&dir=eve/ APRC& document=index&1ang=e; Kiera L. Ladner and Michael McCrossan, *The Electoral Participation of Aboriginal People, Elections Canada,* 2007, available at http://www.elections.ca/res/rec/part/paper/aboriginal/aboriginal_e.pdf, accessed March 12, 2012.

31. Law Commission of Canada, *Urban Aboriginal Governance in Canada: Re-fashioning the Dialogue* (Ottawa, 1999, Catalogue No. JL 2-5-/1999E); David Newhouse and Evelyn Peters, eds., *Not Strangers in These Parts: Urban Aboriginal Peoples* (Ottawa: Policy Research Initiative, 2003).

32. Frances Abele, Russell LaPointe, and Michael Prince, "Symbolism, Surfacing, Succession, and Substance: Martin's Aboriginal Policy Style," in G. Bruce Doern, ed., *How Ottawa Spends 2005–2006* (Montreal: McGill-Queen's University Press, 2005).

33. *Ross River Dena Council Band v. Canada,* [2002] 2 S.C.R. 816; *R. v. Powley,* [2003] 2 S.C.R. 207; *Haida Nation v. British Columbia (Minister of Forests),* [2004] 3 S.C.R. 511; *Taku River Tlingit First Nation v. British Columbia (Project Assessment Director),* [2004] 3 S.C.R. 550; *R. v. Sappier; R. v. Gray,* [2006] 2 S.C.R. 686.

34. *R. v. Kapp,* [2008] 2 S.C.R. 483.

35. Aboriginal Affairs and Northern Development Canada, *General Briefing Note on Canada's Self-Government and Land Claims Policies and the Status of Negotiations—January 2012,* available at http://www.aadnc-aandc.gc.ca/ eng/1100100031774.

36. Jodi-Anne Brzozowski, Andrea Taylor-Butts, and Sara Johnson. "Victimization and Offending among the Aboriginal Population in Canada," *Juristat: Canadian Centre for Justice Statistics* 26(3): 1–31.

37. See the contrasting views on this subject in Alan C. Cairns, *Citizens Plus: Aboriginal Peoples and the Canadian State* (Vancouver: UBC Press, 2000); Cairns, *First Nations and the Canadian State: In Search of Coexistence* (Montreal: McGill-Queen's University Press, 2005); Thomas Flanagan, *First Nations?*

Second Thoughts (Montreal: McGill-Queen's University Press, 2000); Tim Shouls, *Shifting Boundaries: Aboriginal Identity, Pluralist Theory, and the Politics of Self-Government* (Vancouver: UBC Press, 2003); Heidi Libesman, "In Search of a Postcolonial Theory of Normative Integration: Reflections on A.C. Cairns' Theory of Citizens Plus," *Canadian Journal of Political Science* (December 2005); and Mark Charlton and Paul Barker, eds., Crosscurrents: *Contemporary Political Issues*, 7th ed. (Toronto: Nelson Education, 2013), Ch.2.

38. Cairns, *Citizen Plus*, p. 212; and Heidi Libesman, "In Search of a Postcolonial Theory of Normative Integration: Reflections on A.C. Cairns' Theory of Citizens Plus."

FURTHER READING

Alfred, Taiaiake. *Wasase: Indigenous Pathways of Action and Freedom.* Peterborough: Broadview Press, 2005.

Cairns, Alan C. *Citizens Plus: Aboriginal Peoples and the Canadian State.* Vancouver: UBC Press, 2000.

———. *First Nations and the Canadian State: In Search of Coexistence.* Montreal: McGill-Queen's University Press, 2005.

Frideres, James S. and René Gadacz. *Aboriginal Peoples in Canada*, 8th ed. Toronto: Pearson Education Canada, 2008.

Green, Joyce, ed. *Making Space for Indigenous Feminism.* Black Point, NS: Fernwood Books, 2007.

McKee, Christopher. *Treaty Talks in British Columbia: Building a New Relationship*, 3rd ed. Vancouver: UBC Press, 2009.

Milloy, John. "*A National Crime*": *The Canadian Government and the Residential School System, 1879 to 1986.* Winnipeg: University of Manitoba Press, 1998.

Morrison, Andrea. *Justice for Natives: Searching for Common Ground.* Montreal: McGill-Queen's University Press, 1997.

Murphy, Michael, ed. *Canada: The State of the Federation 2003: Reconfiguring Aboriginal–State Relations.* Montreal: McGill-Queen's University Press, 2005.

Shouls, Tim. *Shifting Boundaries: Aboriginal Identity, Pluralist Theory, and the Politics of Self-Government.* Vancouver: UBC Press, 2003.

Warry, Wayne. *Ending Denial: Understanding Aboriginal Issues.* Toronto: University of Toronto Press, 2007.

Whittington, Michael S. "Aboriginal Self-Government," in Michael Whittington and Glen Williams, eds., *Canadian Politics in the 21st Century*, 6th ed. Toronto: Nelson, 2004.

Woolford, Andrew. *Between Justice and Certainty: Treaty Making in British Columbia.* Vancouver: UBC Press, 2005.

Chase Clausen/Shutterstock

CHAPTER 5

French Canada and the Quebec Question

Although French-speaking residents now make up less than one-quarter of the Canadian population, they constituted a majority of the European population in the area that is now Canada until the 1800s. Even though French colonies came under British control, the continuation of the French fact in "Canada" is no accident. It reflects centuries of government policies and political struggles both inside and outside Quebec to preserve and promote, oftentimes in the face of resistance, the French language and culture on a continent that became, year after year, increasingly English. French–English tensions are an enduring feature of Canadian political history, often reflecting rival conceptions of Canadian identity. While some sought to impose a single Anglo-Canadian identity, others aimed to preserve the cultural and linguistic distinctiveness of French Canada. Supporters of the French fact in Canada were also divided between those who saw it centred in Quebec, where most French-speakers reside, and those defending its existence throughout the whole country. The effort to reconcile these divergent objectives has been a driving force of Canadian politics.

Among all the ethnic, linguistic, and cultural issues in Canada, the French question has always had the greatest significance. This reflects the fact that it is the largest such minority, that it has been here longer than any other group besides the Aboriginals, and that it has a territorial base in Quebec. This chapter begins with a numerical profile of the French–English linguistic picture in Canada today,[1] and a brief survey of theoretical considerations regarding French Canada and Quebec. It then examines the history of French–English relations up to 1960, followed by a discussion of the Quiet Revolution in Quebec. The chapter traces developments in French–English relations at the federal level, in Quebec, and in the other provinces since 1970, and concludes with a review of contemporary issues.

THE FRENCH–ENGLISH DEMOGRAPHIC PROFILE TODAY

The distribution of French and English communities within and outside Quebec today is shown in Table 5.1. Although Statistics Canada gathers figures on ethnic origin, mother tongue, and language spoken at home, it is difficult to use statistics on ethnic origin because so many Canadians are now an ethnic mixture and because an increasing number prefer to call themselves simply "Canadians." It is more reliable to use figures for mother tongue, even though this is a measure of linguistics rather than ethnicity. Employing mother-tongue figures, then, we label the groups anglophone, francophone, and allophone, the last being those with a mother tongue other than English or French.

According to the 2011 census, the number of people in Canada as a whole having English as their mother tongue was 18 055 685 or 57.8 percent of the population, while those with French as their mother tongue numbered 7 172 560, or 21.7 percent. Because of the high immigration levels of those having other linguistic backgrounds, the number of Canadians with another mother tongue rose to 6 811 095 or 20.6 percent. While this total is almost equal to the proportion of francophones, no single "immigrant language" came close to the number of French: Punjabi led with 1.4 percent and all Chinese languages combined were 3.4 percent.

TABLE 5.1   MOTHER TONGUE IN QUEBEC, THE OTHER PROVINCES, CANADA OUTSIDE QUEBEC, AND CANADA AS A WHOLE (PERCENTAGES), 2011 CENSUS

	ENGLISH	FRENCH	OTHER		ENGLISH	FRENCH	OTHER
QUEBEC	8.3	78.9	12.8	SASKATCHEWAN	85.1	1.7	13.2
NEW BRUNSWICK	65.4	32.0	2.6	BRITISH COLUMBIA	71.2	1.5	27.3
ONTARIO	69.3	4.1	26.6	NEWFOUNDLAND/ LABRADOR	97.7	0.5	1.8
PRINCE EDWARD ISLAND	92.5	3.9	3.6	YUKON	84.1	4.6	11.3
MANITOBA	73.9	3.8	22.2	NORTHWEST TERRITORIES	77.1	2.7	20.2
NOVA SCOTIA	92.1	3.6	4.3	NUNAVUT	28.6	1.4	70.0
ALBERTA	77.8	2.1	20.1	CANADA OUTSIDE QUEBEC	73.1	4.0	23.0
				CANADA AS A WHOLE	57.8	21.7	20.6

Source: Statistics Canada, 2011 Census, Population by mother tongue and age groups (total), 2011 counts, for Canada, provinces and territories, http://www12.statcan.gc.ca/census-recensement/2011/dp-pd/hlt-fst/lang/ Pages/highlight.cfm?TabID=1&Lang=E&Asc=1&PRCode=01&OrderBy=999&View=1&tableID=401& queryID=1&Age=1. Reproduced and distributed on an "as is" basis with the permission of Statistics Canada.

TABLE 5.2   POPULATION BY REPORTED MOTHER TONGUES, CANADA, 2011

REGION	FRENCH*		ENGLISH		OTHER		TOTAL	
	NUMBER	PERCENTAGE	NUMBER	PERCENTAGE	NUMBER	PERCENTAGE	NUMBER	PERCENTAGE
CANADA	7 172 560	21.7	19 137 520	57.8	6 811 095	20.6	33 121 175	100.0
QUEBEC	6 164 745	78.9	647 655	8.3	1 003 545	12.8	7 815 955	100.0
CANADA OUTSIDE QUEBEC	1 007 815	4.0	18 489 860	73.1	5 807 550	23.0	25 305 220	100.0

* MULTIPLE RESPONSES TO THE QUESTION ON "FIRST LANGUAGE LEARNED AT HOME IN CHILDHOOD AND STILL UNDERSTOOD AT THE TIME OF THE CENSUS" (MOTHER TONGUE) WERE ALLOCATED EQUALLY AMONG THE FRENCH, ENGLISH, AND OTHER CATEGORIES. FOR MORE INFORMATION ON THIS SUBJECT, SEE THE *2011 CENSUS DICTIONARY*, CATALOGUE NO. 98-301-X.

Source: Statistics Canada, Linguistic Characteristics of Canadians, Table 3, Catalogue no. 98-314-X2011001, http://www12.statcan.gc.ca/census-recensement/2011/as-sa/98-314-x/98-314-x2011001-eng.pdf. Reproduced and distributed on an "as is" basis with the permission of Statistics Canada.

The Quebec population is made up of over six million francophones, 650 000 anglophones, and over one million allophones, or 78.9 percent, 8.3 percent, and 12.8 percent respectively. Although 86 percent of all Canadian francophones live in Quebec, over one million francophones live outside that province. Thus, while Quebec is predominantly French, and Canada outside Quebec is predominantly English, an important distinction should be made between French Canada and Quebec, as seen in Table 5.2. Outside Quebec, francophones are primarily located in Ontario and New Brunswick. The census also reported that 17.5 percent of the population could carry on a conversation in both English and French. While this is a slight drop from 17.7 percent in the 2001 census, the proportion has generally risen from a low of 12.1 percent in 1961.

DIFFERENT CONCEPTIONS OF FRENCH CANADA

The fact that most, but not all, francophones live in Quebec has given rise to two basic models with which to address the question of how to deal with the distinctiveness of French Canada. The first—the territorial principle—would recognize Quebec as the homeland of French Canada and give that province powers and resources to protect and promote its linguistic and cultural distinctiveness. Quebec would be granted some kind of special status, distinct from other provinces, and essentially be "French," while the rest of Canada would primarily be "English."[2] The second option—the personality principle—would treat Quebec as "une province comme les autres," recognize the existence of French Canada across the country, and promote bilingualism at the federal level and in the other provinces and territories.

The CANADIAN PRESS PHOTO/Francis Vachon

The Quebec flag flies over the Quebec National Assembly—the seat of the government of Quebec.

Historically, most francophones in Quebec have wanted protection or autonomy from the federal government, but until 1960 they did not demand much else from the province. This all changed in the 1960s with the Quiet Revolution in Quebec and a wholesale reversal of values. During this period, a majority of francophone Quebeckers aggressively sought more control over all aspects of Quebec life—including the economy and language policy—and began to call themselves "Québécois." They increasingly saw themselves as a majority in Quebec rather than a minority within Canada, as they had in the past. The desire of most Quebec francophones for an activist provincial government led them to demand more autonomy from Ottawa than ever before: in many aspects of social and economic policy, they wanted to do things their own way. While most francophones in Quebec sought more provincial autonomy, a small proportion identified with a French Canada that extended across the country. Energized by the Québécois, francophone minorities in the other provinces developed more positive identities over the past 50 years, sometimes associating themselves with their brethren in Quebec, but often linking themselves to each other, as non-Québéois French Canadians. Their demands were mainly in the realm of language and culture, education, and the provision of provincial services in French.

HISTORICAL OVERVIEW OF FRENCH–ENGLISH RELATIONS

Pre-Confederation Developments

As Britain gained dominance over the French colonies in North America, it did not always treat its new subjects very well. The most severe example was probably the expulsion of the Acadians in the mid-1750s. In order to thwart what it perceived as a military threat, the British military forcibly removed thousands of French-speaking Acadians from their homes in the present-day Maritime provinces and deported them to Europe and to other English colonies in North America. After the British defeated the French on the Plains of Abraham in 1759, the conquerors took control of the government and economy of Quebec and at first assumed that the population would soon become "English." Except for the clergy and the seigneurs, the French elite retreated to France, but the people continued to speak French and attend the Roman Catholic Church, which became a highly influential and autonomous organization. It would probably have been impossible to transform Quebec into an Anglo-Protestant colony—at least without a great deal of coercion and immigration—and the British soon exhibited a policy of tolerance and accommodation. By the time of the **Quebec Act** of 1774, the British recognized the inevitable, and guaranteed the French their religious rights and their own system of civil law.

As "English" immigrants moved into what is now Ontario in the 1780s, especially the United Empire Loyalists from the new United States, it became logical to divide the colony into two: Lower Canada (Quebec) would be essentially French-Catholic, and Upper Canada (Ontario) would be Anglo-Protestant. This separation was recognized in the **Constitutional Act** of 1791.

Difficulties between the popularly elected assembly and the appointed executive and legislative councils became increasingly serious after 1800, culminating in armed revolts in both colonies in 1837. The battle for more popular control in Lower Canada was complicated by the ethnic factor, as French Canadians were predominant in the assembly alone. Lord Durham felt that the ethnic problem could only be solved by another attempt to assimilate the French. Hence, he recommended that the two colonies be reunited into the colony of Canada, in which English would be the official language and the anglophone population of the rapidly expanding western portion (Ontario) would soon outnumber the French.

This final attempt at assimilation, incorporated in the **Act of Union**, was to no avail. In recognition of its failure, the French language was increasingly used along with English in the government, cabinets were usually alliances between English and French leaders, and the legislature operated on the informal principle of the double majority—legislation had to have the approval of a majority of representatives from both sections of the colony.

Given this historical evolution, the logic of Confederation and the cultural guarantees of section 133 of the **Constitution Act, 1867** are perfectly understandable. Both French and English could be used in all aspects of the new federal Parliament, and laws were passed in both languages. Both languages could also be used in whatever federal courts were later established. The francophone minorities in Ontario, Nova Scotia, and New Brunswick were inarticulate and ignored, even though the Acadian minority in New Brunswick constituted 16 percent of the provincial population. However, the Montreal-centred anglophone minority in Quebec, at 20 percent, was well organized and in control of the economy of the province. This fact ensured that English could be used along with French in the legislature and courts of Quebec. None of these constitutional provisions was particularly controversial in 1867, and protection of the Protestant school system in Quebec and the Roman Catholic system in Ontario attracted greater interest. With religious rights seen in educational terms and language rights applying only to legislatures and courts, no constitutional rights were granted to minority-language schools.

OFFICIAL BILINGUALISM IN THE CONSTITUTION ACT, 1867

- Federal Parliament, proceedings, and laws
- Federal courts
- Quebec parliament, proceedings, and laws
- Quebec courts

Ethnic/Linguistic Conflicts, 1867–1960

The Riel Rebellions

Although the two language groups have been regularly accommodated in government circles since 1867, six serious linguistic conflicts erupted from the time of Confederation to 1960. The first Riel Rebellion precipitated the creation of the province of Manitoba in 1870, as Louis Riel, a French-Catholic Métis, led the fight for provincial status. During that uprising, and in a situation of uncertain government authority, an Ontario Orangeman was executed by a Métis court-martial. Riel maintained a fairly low profile afterward, but in 1885 he re-emerged in what is now Saskatchewan to lead the second Riel Rebellion on behalf of western Aboriginals who had been mistreated by the government. After quelling the rebellion, the federal government charged Riel with treason and he was found guilty in a famous trial in Regina. Ethnic and religious tensions across the country rose to a fever pitch, for while English Protestants regarded Riel as a murderer, traitor, and madman, French Catholics believed he was a patriot and a saint. To Prime Minister John A. Macdonald fell the unenviable decision of whether to let Riel hang or to use the executive power of mercy to spare him. Caught in the middle of this heated confrontation, Macdonald followed the will of the majority and had Riel hanged. This exacerbated the level of French-Catholic outrage across the country, especially in Quebec, and the close attachment of the people of Quebec to Macdonald's Conservative Party was permanently damaged. Moreover, many argued that the Riel affair had demonstrated the lack of French-Canadian influence in Ottawa, leading to demands for greater autonomy for the province of Quebec.

Bilingualism in Manitoba

The third linguistic conflict occurred in Manitoba in 1890. Because the small settlement was about equally divided between French and English, Riel had insisted that the 1870 Manitoba Act follow the Quebec precedent of giving the two languages official status in the new province's legislature and courts. After its creation, however, Manitoba attracted thousands of English-speaking immigrants and others who chose to identify with the anglophone community. Hence, in 1890, the anglophone majority passed the Official Language Act which removed the official status of French in the province's legislature and courts, upsetting French Canadians well beyond Manitoba.[3] The Roman Catholic separate school system was abolished at the same time.

BOX 5.1   TIME LINE

Major French–English Conflicts, 1867–1945

1870	First Riel Rebellion
1885	Second Riel Rebellion
1890	Manitoba's Official Language Act
1913	Ontario's Regulation 17
1917	First conscription crisis
1944	Second conscription crisis

French Schools in Ontario: Regulation 17

The fourth main linguistic conflict concerned minority French-language education rights in Ontario. Although minority-language schools had not been constitutionally guaranteed, the Protestant schools in Quebec, mostly in Montreal, naturally operated in English, and it was only logical that French-language schools be established in francophone parts of New Brunswick and Ontario. In 1913 the Whitney government issued Regulation 17, which virtually abolished the use of French in the Ontario school system; English was to become the sole language of instruction after the third year, and the study of French as a subject was limited to one hour a day. Whitney claimed that he was doing Franco-Ontarian citizens a favour by forcing them to learn English in an English-speaking province, but those affected denounced the regulation and challenged it in court.[4]

The First Conscription Crisis

The Regulation 17 incident in Ontario had its greatest implications in Quebec during the **conscription crisis** of the First World War. As a British colony, Canada was automatically at war, but could determine its own degree of involvement. Despite small standing armed forces, the Conservative government of Robert Borden made major commitments. While English Canadians were generally keen to take up the British cause in its time of need, many in French Canada were less enthusiastic about Canada's connection to the British Empire, preferring a less imperial conception of Canadian nationhood. As the war dragged on and reinforcements were needed, few recruits came forward, so the government decided to resort to conscription—compulsory military service—in 1917. Borden knew that conscription would divide the country along ethnic lines, and having few French Canadians in his Cabinet to start with, he appealed to Liberal leader Wilfrid Laurier to join him in a coalition government. Laurier refused the offer, although most of the anglophone Liberal MPs did join in a **Union Government** in 1917. The subsequent enforcement of conscription entailed considerable violence. A riot in Quebec City in the spring of 1918, which the federal government sought to quell by sending in the army, left four people dead and many others injured. This confrontation destroyed what little French-Canadian support remained for the Conservative Party after the execution of Louis Riel.

The Second Conscription Crisis

Ontario repealed Regulation 17 in 1927 and French–English tensions returned to a normal, controllable level until they were inflamed by another conscription crisis during the Second World War. In 1939 the Liberal Prime Minister Mackenzie King was in power with a strong contingent of ministers and MPs from Quebec. Although still closely allied with Britain, Canada entered the war as an independent country, and its leader was extremely cautious in determining its degree of involvement. King knew that conscription would be resisted in French Canada, so he was even more reluctant than Borden to adopt it. After first promising not to impose conscription, King held a national plebiscite to let himself off the hook. Although 80 percent of voters outside Quebec agreed to release King from his promise, Quebeckers voted 73 percent against. On the basis of the slogan "conscription if necessary but not necessarily conscription," King managed to postpone the adoption of compulsory military service until almost the end of the war. Given the sensitivity with which conscription was imposed on this occasion, King is credited by most observers with having skillfully kept the country together in the circumstances.

CRITICAL APPROACHES

The question of French Canada and Quebec can only be understood by beginning with the *historical approach*. Given that much of present-day Canada was originally colonized by France, the accommodations made to the francophone population after the British conquest remain of crucial importance to this day. French Canada and Quebec always had some kind of distinct place in the country. The *institutional approach* emphasizes that this distinctiveness was incorporated in many of the political institutions established, including the creation of Quebec as a province in the structure of Canadian federalism and of rules regarding language rights in the constitution. In fact, constitutional arrangements regarding French Canada and Quebec continue to preoccupy the Canadian political system.

Pre-1960 Quebec Nationalism

Quebec nationalism was a strong force throughout this historical development in both provincial and federal politics. It is usually defined as a feeling of primary loyalty to Quebec, emanating from the widely held notion that it is home to a distinctive French-Canadian nation, centred on language, ethnicity, culture, history, territory, and religion. Embraced by almost all francophone Quebeckers, it usually stood for a substantial degree of political autonomy or self-determination. Francophone Quebeckers valued autonomy because Quebec was different and because they felt that such autonomy had been guaranteed in 1867. Most considered that Confederation had been a pact between two ethnic groups, English and French, and many held to the "compact theory of Confederation" that no changes could be made to the constitution without the approval of both groups, or at least the consent of the province of Quebec.

Before 1960, Quebec nationalism was largely inward-looking and defensive, primarily concerned with ensuring that the federal government kept out of that province's affairs. It was a nationalism of "survival," and was closely tied to the Roman Catholic Church. The province's identity, as extolled by such historians as Lionel Groulx, promoted the superiority of a rural, religious, family-oriented, isolated, defensive, simple, and unsophisticated French way of life. Dominated by the authoritarian Premier Maurice Duplessis (whose Union Nationale government held office 1936–39 and 1944–60), the population was taught that only he could protect them from evil external influences, such as Ottawa. Duplessis governed with three main allies: the Church, which he empowered to oversee social policy; the farmers, who were overrepresented in the legislature; and American capital, which was encouraged to enter the province and create jobs for those who were no longer needed on the farm. Duplessis was unconcerned about working conditions in these new resource and manufacturing operations or about the fact that, because the companies were foreign owned, employees had to master English to be promoted.

THE QUIET REVOLUTION: QUEBEC IN THE 1960S

The forces of modernization, urbanization, secularization, and democratization had become explosive by the time Duplessis died in 1959, and the Quebec of the past 50 years is quite a different province and society from the one that existed before 1960. In the 1960s, the province underwent a **Quiet Revolution**, consisting of a dramatic change in the values, attitudes, and behaviour of French-Canadian Quebeckers, a new collective self-confidence, and an enormous expansion of the role of the provincial state. Rather than having an inward-looking obsession with survival, it became outward-looking and aggressive, and focused on expansion and growth. Post-1960 Quebec nationalism sought to protect and promote the French language and culture, to increase the powers of the provincial government, and to reverse the dominance of Anglo and external economic power in the province. As before, most francophone Quebeckers retained a primary loyalty to their province, but not one that necessarily interfered with their allegiance to the wider country of Canada, and a large proportion of the population turned their backs on the Roman Catholic Church. These features of the new Quebec had many implications for French–English relations in both the Quebec and the Canadian political systems.

The Liberal government of Jean Lesage (1960–66) took over many of the functions previously administered by the Church.[5] The most important of these was education, which was radically modernized at all levels. Quebec suddenly began producing graduates in science, engineering, technology, commerce, political science, economics, and public administration. Health and welfare programs were also greatly expanded under public rather than charitable auspices. With the nationalization of private power companies, Hydro-Québec became a huge Crown corporation supplying all the electricity in the province. As a public institution, the company provided the government with an important tool of economic planning and development. It also constituted a symbolic breakthrough: this key aspect of economic activity would be controlled by French-Canadians, a striking confirmation of their economic emancipation. Lesage also reformed almost every piece of legislation on the books, especially labour and electoral laws; added reams of new ones; and created many government agencies.

BOX 5.2   TIME LINE

French–English Relations, 1945–1970

1949–59	Opposition to Maurice Duplessis grows
1960–66	Quebec Quiet Revolution
1963–68	Royal Commission on Bilingualism and Biculturalism
1968	Pierre Trudeau becomes Prime Minister
1968–69	Official Languages Act
1970	FLQ crisis

All these new and expanded public responsibilities required substantial additional revenues, and Lesage put immense pressure on Ottawa to increase federal–provincial grants, to allow Quebec to opt out of the conditions attached to them, and to give the province a greater share of joint taxation. In areas of provincial jurisdiction, Quebec began to move toward distinctive programs, such as designing its own pension plan, which was then used as a model for the Canada Pension Plan. The new Caisse de Dépôt accumulated a huge fund of money which was invested in provincial companies, strengthening the Quebec economy and enhancing francophone control. As time went on, the province demanded changes to the **division of powers**, including international francophone links, which led to perpetual federal–provincial discord. In the Quebec private sector francophones had lower incomes and lower-status jobs than anglophones, but the Lesage government did little of substance to rectify this situation, probably for fear of driving out Anglo-Canadian and foreign investment.

Much of the analysis of the Quiet Revolution centres on the concept of the **new middle class**—civil servants, teachers, professors, and other salaried professionals. Since upward mobility was still difficult in the English-dominated private sector, this new class used Quebec nationalism to further its own aspirations in the expansion of the Quebec state.[6] This new middle class sponsored an enormous increase in provincial government programs and agencies. But the changes incorporated in the Quiet Revolution went far beyond the role of government, including the emancipation of women and the increasing francophone control of the economy. They touched virtually every aspect of life in Quebec, and can hardly be over-emphasized.

During the early 1960s, the federal government grappled somewhat haphazardly with Quebec's new demands. John Diefenbaker (Prime Minister 1957–63) espoused an "unhyphenated" view of Canadian identity—that Canadians were all equally a part of one single nation. This rhetoric reinforced the perception among many in Quebec that the province, rather than the federal government, was ultimately responsible for the preservation of the French language and culture in Canada.

Nevertheless, the Diefenbaker government did introduce simultaneous English/French interpretation into Parliament, began printing all federal government cheques in a bilingual format, and appointed a French-Canadian governor general. Immediately after taking office, the Pearson government (1963–68) established the **Royal Commission on Bilingualism and Biculturalism** "to inquire into and report upon the existing state of bilingualism and biculturalism in Canada and to recommend what steps should be taken to develop the Canadian Confederation on the basis of an equal partnership between the two founding races." Even before the commission reported, however, Lester Pearson felt obliged to act on Quebec's demands. He gave Quebec and the other provinces more federal funds and taxation powers, removed the conditions from many shared-cost programs, and permitted Quebec to make international arrangements with France.

At the same time, and partly due to the influence of his new Justice Minister, Pierre Elliott Trudeau, Pearson sought to strengthen the position of French Canadians at the federal level. One of their priorities was that French be used as a language equal to English in the corridors of power in Ottawa. Such federally oriented Quebec francophones were also concerned about the fate of francophone minorities in the other provinces. The new self-confidence of the Québécois inspired these dwindling minorities to greater self-assertiveness.

Although the British North America Act of 1867 provided that either English or French could be used in the federal Parliament and courts, the extent of official bilingualism in Ottawa

BOX 5.3   VOICES

"All we have seen and heard has led us to the conviction that Canada is in the most critical period of its history since Confederation. We believe that there is a crisis, in the sense that Canada has come to a time when decisions must be taken and developments must occur leading either to its breakup, or to a new set of conditions for its future existence. We do not know whether the crisis will be short or long. We are convinced that it is here. The signs of danger are many and serious."

Source: Royal Commission on Bilingualism and Biculturalism, Preliminary Report (Ottawa: Queen's Printer, 1965), p. 133.

before 1960 was minimal in the executive branch, where English was the working language of the public service, at least at policymaking levels.[7] In response to the demands of francophones who did not focus on Quebec, Pearson and Trudeau introduced an Official Languages bill so that the Canadian public service would operate on a bilingual basis, much to the consternation of those unilingual public servants who were now pressured to learn French. Parliament passed the **Official Languages Act** in 1969, and since that time Canada has been officially and effectively bilingual in its federal institutions. Ottawa also began to support French immersion educational programs as well as to assist francophone minorities in other provinces.

PRINCIPAL PROVISIONS OF THE OFFICIAL LANGUAGES ACT, 1969

- Canada is a country with two official languages, English and French, and both languages have equal status, rights, and privileges in federal government institutions.
- Canadians have the right to full and equal access to Parliament and to the laws and courts and the right to be served by and communicate with the institutions of the federal government in either English or French in any office across the country or abroad where significant demand exists.
- Canadians employed by the federal government have the right to work in the official language of their choice wherever practicable, and both English- and French-speaking Canadians are ensured of equitable opportunities for employment and advancement in federal institutions.
- The Canadian government is committed to supporting the vitality of English- and French-speaking minority communities, especially by encouraging and assisting the provinces and territories in providing minority-language and second-language education.

Trudeau succeeded Pearson as prime minister in 1968, and the question of French–English relations, or "national unity," was the principal political issue throughout the 16 years that he was in power. Trudeau fought against recognition of Quebec as the homeland of French Canada and opposed giving that province special recognition or power. He argued that any kind of special status would be the first step toward separation; he feared that a nationalistic French Quebec would go back to being inward-looking and intolerant; and he felt that francophone Quebeckers would have more opportunity if they followed his example, became

The invocation of the War Measures Act in 1970 in connection with the FLQ crisis included the visible presence of armed soldiers on the streets of Montreal and Ottawa.

bilingual, and participated in the life of a larger country. Part of Trudeau's popularity in English Canada stemmed from the perception that he was "anti-Quebec," but he was passionately "pro-French" in promoting bilingualism in Ottawa and across the country.

During the 1960s, advocates of a third option had also emerged: Quebec separatism. Those who advocated that Quebec become a separate, sovereign state took their nationalistic feelings to the extreme and argued that Quebec would be better off without its connection to Canada. Most such separatists, or sovereignists, were democratic by nature and proceeded to use persuasion to advance their cause, but a small wing of the movement, the **Front de libération du Québec (FLQ)**, resorted to violence. Periodic bombings killed several people and injured at least 27 others during the 1960s. Then, in October 1970, two small cells of the FLQ kidnapped a British diplomat and abducted and murdered Quebec cabinet minister Pierre Laporte. Trudeau invoked the coercive **War Measures Act**, giving the police and armed forces special powers to quell the violence, but more than 400 innocent, peaceful separatist supporters were arrested in the process. By crushing the FLQ, by giving French Canadians more clout in Ottawa, and by constitutionalizing pan-Canadian bilingualism, Trudeau hoped to undercut any Quebec demand for special status or separation.

QUEBEC AND FRENCH CANADA SINCE 1970

The 1970s

Despite the fact that a centralist Trudeau government was in power, the first Robert Bourassa Liberal government in Quebec (1970–76) gained a degree of autonomy from Ottawa in the fields of family allowances and immigration. It also passed **Bill 22** to give primacy to the

French language in many spheres in the province, such as in the operations and documents of public and para-public authorities. As far as education was concerned, immigrant children who did not already have a "sufficient knowledge" of English were obliged to go to French-language schools. This was an attempt to have such children join the majority French linguistic group in the province rather than become "English," as so many previous immigrants had done. Relying on immigration to bolster the francophone segment of the population became a vital issue when the French-Canadian birth rate plummeted after 1960. Bill 22 also aimed at the francization of the private sector by pressuring companies to use French as the language of internal corporate operations. The more Quebec moved in the direction of French unilingualism, of course, the more English Canada resisted Trudeau's policy of national bilingualism and the larger grew the number of anglophones who left Quebec. The Bourassa government also passed the Quebec Charter of Human Rights and Freedoms (*Charte des droits et libertés de la personne*) in 1975. It bears many similarities to the Canadian Charter adopted in 1982, and as a quasi-constitutional document, has precedence over other provincial legislation.

The Parti Québécois (PQ) was elected to office in 1976 under René Lévesque with an even more nationalistic program.[8] Faced with a hostile Trudeau government in Ottawa, the PQ made few gains in provincial autonomy. But it did pass **Bill 101**, the Charter of the French Language (*Charte de la langue française*), which extended Bill 22 by making French the predominant language in the province. Bill 101 generally turned the persuasive and optional aspects of Bill 22 into coercive and mandatory ones, raising strong opposition from English-speaking Quebeckers and anglo-Canadians generally. It made French the only official language of the legislature (although laws continued to be translated unofficially into English); only individuals (not corporations) could use English in Quebec courts; the only children who could go to English schools in the province were those whose parents had done so; and all commercial signs had to be in French only.[9] All four of these clauses were subsequently ruled unconstitutional by the courts, but in other ways Bill 101 still stands: large companies must operate in French, and French continues to be the official language of the province.

CRITICAL APPROACHES

The *social cleavages* and *pluralist approaches* are very relevant to the discussion of the French–English relations. Indeed, the French–English relationship in Canadian society is the very essence of pluralism: it is a basic fact of Canadian political life and animates much of the political activity in the country. The fundamental co-existence of two dominant ethnic groups establishes an underlying pluralism and also provides the foundation for most of the other pluralistic aspects of Canadian government and society. The pluralist approach is also evident since Canada's origins in the regular bargaining between groups in the policymaking process.

continued

French–English relations and the position of Quebec in the federation then became perhaps the most prominent issues after the Quiet Revolution of the 1960s.

Class analysts are particularly interested in the relationship between class and ethnicity in Quebec.[10] During the Quiet Revolution, a new middle class of francophone Quebeckers made itself felt in the province's public sector and passed laws and initiated programs to reduce the Anglo domination of the private sector as well, such that the economic elite in Quebec today is francophone in character.

The 1980s

In 1980 the PQ government held a **referendum** on the question of pursuing a more independent relationship with Canada called **sovereignty-association**. Sovereignty with continuing links to Canada could be considered as a fourth option for dealing with the French Canada situation, somewhere between "distinct status" and complete independence. Many federal politicians, including Trudeau, Justice Minister Jean Chrétien, and several provincial premiers encouraged Quebeckers to defeat the PQ proposal, promising them "renewed federalism" if they did so.[11] When sovereignty-association was turned down by a vote of 60 percent to 40 percent, new federal–provincial constitutional negotiations began, culminating in the **Constitution Act, 1982**.

Ironically, even though the whole effort was supposed to appeal to the residents of that province, the Quebec government alone objected to the act. That was because it reflected the Trudeau vision of a centralized, symmetrical, bilingual Canada rather than recognizing the distinctive French character of Quebec. Nevertheless, it became law in all parts of the country. As far as language was concerned, the **Charter of Rights and Freedoms** incorporated in the act reinforced official bilingualism at the federal level and in New Brunswick, and guaranteed **minority-language education rights** in the provinces wherever numbers warranted. Many Quebeckers never forgave Trudeau and Chrétien for adopting such a significant constitutional document against the opposition of their provincial government.

When Brian Mulroney became prime minister in 1984 with a strategy of accommodating the views of the Quebec majority, even René Lévesque was willing to give Confederation another chance. Such a change of heart split the PQ, however, and the government collapsed. The second Bourassa government, elected in 1985, was first able to convince the Mulroney government to allow Quebec to play a fuller part in the **Francophonie**, the international French-speaking community. Then, in 1988, the Supreme Court of Canada declared the sign provision of Bill 101 to be unconstitutional as a violation of freedom of expression.[12] Bourassa responded by using the **notwithstanding clause** in the federal and Quebec charters of rights to pass Bill 178, which provided for French-only outdoor signs but allowed bilingual signs indoors. Violating what the Court had determined to be a constitutional right and giving preference to French collective rights over (English) individual rights produced a vehement reaction among English Quebeckers and an anti-Quebec, anti-French response in the rest of the country. It should be noted, however, that in 1983 some aspects of Bill 101 were voluntarily relaxed, and in 1986 Quebec ensured the provision of social and health services in English to its anglophone minority. Moreover, when the five-year limit on Bill 178 ran out in 1993, Bourassa replaced it with Bill 86, which allowed bilingual signs outside as well as inside stores, as long as the French lettering was predominant.

BOX 5.4   TIME LINE

Quebec–Canada Relations, 1970–2000

1976	Election of Parti Québécois
1980	First Quebec Referendum
1982	Constitution Act, 1982
1987–90	Meech Lake Accord
1992	Charlottetown Accord and national referendum
1995	Second Quebec referendum
1998	Supreme Court Reference on Quebec independence
2000	Clarity Act

The main item on the Bourassa–Mulroney agenda was the **Meech Lake Accord**. Designed to bring Quebec back into the Canadian constitutional fold, the accord provided for the recognition of Quebec as a **distinct society** within Canada, provincial nomination of senators and Supreme Court judges, a provincial veto on a wider range of constitutional amendments, constitutionalization of Quebec's rights in immigration, and provincial opting-out, with compensation, of federal programs set up within their jurisdiction. In many respects Meech Lake reflected the approach of the 1979 Task Force on Canadian Unity, which had been promptly shelved when its recommendations were contrary to Trudeau's vision of Canada. The Accord is discussed in more detail in Chapter 17.

The new model of French–English relations had strong support until Trudeau himself condemned it and until negative English-Canadian reaction emerged against Quebec's Bill 178. In the end, the Newfoundland and Manitoba legislatures failed to approve it before the 1990 deadline. Many Quebeckers felt betrayed again, Quebec began a much more aggressive campaign to wrest powers from Ottawa, and several Quebec members of Parliament quit their parties to sit as Quebec *indépendantistes* in the Bloc Québécois created by Lucien Bouchard. Meanwhile, Quebeckers were generally more supportive than other Canadians of Mulroney's free trade deal with the United States. Their economic self-confidence was such that they felt they could make inroads into the American market.

The 1990s

After intense post-Meech Lake discussions, the Quebec legislature decided that the province would have a referendum on **sovereignty** in 1992. Those opposed to independence hoped that the rest of Canada would offer Quebec a model of a new relationship before that time so that the voters would have an acceptable federalist option. Such a vision was embodied in the **Charlottetown Accord**. If ratified, Quebec would essentially have achieved fulfillment of its Meech Lake demands, including recognition as a distinct society within Canada based on its French-language majority, unique culture, and civil law tradition. All provinces would have received increased power over immigration, an enlarged veto over constitutional amendments, and compensation when opting out of national programs. Quebec and the other provinces would have secured some nine legislative powers in addition to immigration if they chose to use them. In the end, however, 56.7 percent of Quebeckers voted against the accord, presumably because it did not offer Quebec sufficient additional powers. Canadians outside Quebec did not like it much better.

After the disheartening and traumatic experience of the Charlottetown Accord all federal parties, especially the Chrétien Liberals elected in 1993, decided to put constitutional issues on the back burner. However, the inadequacies and rejection of the Charlottetown Accord ignited a new surge of nationalism in Quebec, and in 1994 the Parti Québécois was re-elected under Jacques Parizeau. As in 1976, the PQ argued that it was "safe" to elect it to government, because sovereignty would be decided in a separate, subsequent referendum. The Parizeau government kept adjusting its concept of sovereignty and delaying the date of the vote until it thought it had a version that would be accepted by the Quebec public.

The Quebec referendum was held in October 1995. Although the PQ government ultimately proposed a kind of sovereignty that retained significant links to the rest of Canada (such as Canadian passports and citizenship and use of the Canadian dollar), its proposal was turned down by a vote of 50.6 percent to 49.4 percent. Such a close result was not particularly comforting to those who wanted to keep the country together, especially when the charismatic Bouchard succeeded Parizeau as Quebec premier immediately afterward. Nevertheless, Bouchard resigned in 2000 without having called another referendum and, as support for Quebec sovereignty continued to fall, his successor, Bernard Landry, was also forced to abandon any such plans. Meanwhile, as noted in Chapter 17, Chrétien had asked the Supreme Court whether Quebec had a constitutional right to declare independence unilaterally, and he followed that up with the **Clarity Act**, which required any such referendum question to be approved by the federal House of Commons. Under that Act, the federal government would also decide if the size of the vote in favour of sovereignty was sufficient to trigger formal constitutional negotiations. It is discussed in more detail in Chapter 17.

The "national unity" front was more peaceful after 2000, at least in terms of demands for constitutional change. In 2003, for example, a federalist Quebec government was elected—the Liberals under Jean Charest. He was the engineer of the Council of the Federation, bringing together all provinces for interactions with Ottawa and signalling a new era of Quebec's participation in Canadian federalism. Charest also welcomed a Supreme Court decision upholding Quebec law forcing francophone parents to send their children to French-language schools. But noting the need for graduates to be increasingly bilingual, Charest did introduce English as a second language in French schools in grade 1 instead of grade 3. About this time it was revealed that the Chrétien government had awarded a number of large advertising contracts promoting national unity to Quebec communications firms that had, in turn, made financial contributions to the Liberal party. Not only was the effectiveness of such advertising debatable, but this "sponsorship scandal" sometimes reached criminal proportions. The scandal caused the federal Liberals to lose considerable support in Quebec, and in 2004, new Prime Minister Paul Martin appointed Judge John Gomery to conduct a judicial inquiry into the whole operation. Partly because of opposition attacks based on revelations before the **Gomery Inquiry**, the Martin government was defeated on a nonconfidence motion in November 2005, setting the stage for the January 2006 election won by the Conservatives under Stephen Harper.

Party Support in Quebec

Although some constituencies in Quebec can be labelled "Anglophone," most have francophone majorities, and historically both kinds of ridings tended to vote Liberal. Thus, Quebec was typically a Liberal stronghold until the election of a majority of Conservative MPs in Quebec in the 1984 and 1988 federal elections, under the leadership of the bilingual (but non-francophone) Quebecker, Brian Mulroney. Many francophones felt alienated by the Trudeau government's imposition of the Constitution Act, 1982 and its strong stance against any version of distinct status for Quebec. When Mulroney's constitutional efforts foundered, however, the separatist Bloc Québécois won a majority of seats (although never a majority of the popular vote) in the province in all federal elections between 1993 and 2008. Suddenly in 2011, under its popular leader Jack Layton, the NDP scored an unprecedented upset in the province. The 2015 election saw a slight resurgence of the Bloc in Quebec, though the Liberal Party got the biggest boost by taking 40 of the province's 78 seats. The party preferences of francophone Quebeckers have thus been highly volatile since 1982, and Table 5.3 shows the results of federal elections in Quebec from 1993 onward. Over this period, francophone minorities in other provinces, such as New Brunswick, Ontario, and Manitoba, remained more faithful in their traditional support of the Liberal party.

TABLE 5.3   SEATS AND VOTES WON BY PARTIES IN QUEBEC, 1993–2015 FEDERAL ELECTIONS

	LIBERAL		CONSERVATIVE		BLOC QUÉBÉCOIS		NDP	
	SEATS	% VOTES	SEATS	% VOTES	SEATS	% VOTES	SEATS	% VOTES
1993	19	25	1	14	54	49	0	2
1997	26	37	5	22	44	38	0	2
2000	36	44	1	6	38	40	0	2
2004	21	34	0	9	54	49	0	5
2006	13	21	10	25	51	42	0	8
2008	14	24	10	22	49	38	1	12
2011	7	14	5	17	4	23	59	43
2015	40	51.3	12	15.4	10	12.8	16	20.5

Source: Reports of the Chief Electoral Officer on 1993, 1997, 2000, 2004, 2006, 2008, 2011 and 2015 elections. 2015 source data: Elections Canada, Provinces & Territories (October 30, 2015), http://enr.elections.ca/Provinces .aspx?lang=e"

Developments in Other Provinces and Territories

The Quiet Revolution also led francophones outside Quebec to regain their French identities and to seek to preserve their language and culture. Often under pressure from Prime Minister Trudeau, some provincial premiers hoped that by extending rights or services to their francophone minorities, they would help to forestall separatism in Quebec. Thus, considerable improvement was made in minority francophone rights in many provinces after 1965.[13] Amendments to the Criminal Code in 1978 and 1988 forced all provinces and territories to provide for criminal trials in French, if demanded by the accused.[14]

Probably most important, as mentioned, all provinces and territories were bound by the Trudeau's Constitution Act, 1982, to provide education in the minority official language where numbers warranted. In addition, the Supreme Court ruled that francophone parents must have some control over their children's French-language education.[15] Moreover, Ottawa helped to create the demand for French-language schools in the nine anglophone provinces by assisting in the creation and financing of advocacy organizations that would promote its own agenda.[16] All this was designed to undercut Quebec's claim that it was the homeland of French Canada.

New Brunswick implemented its own Official Languages Act in 1969 to improve the Acadian educational system at all levels and to provide provincial government services in both languages. New Brunswick then became the only officially bilingual province in the Constitution Act, 1982.[17] Richard Hatfield's Progressive Conservative government embarked on a policy of cultural equality beyond individual or institutional bilingualism (Bill 88), and some years later, after an anti-bilingualism party elected several members to the provincial legislature, New Brunswick constitutionalized Bill 88 in 1993 to further protect the right of English and French linguistic communities in the province to distinct cultural and educational institutions.[18] Finally, in 2002, Premier Bernard Lord strengthened the Official Languages Act, especially at the municipal level of government and in the health care field.

Ontario began to provide public French-language secondary schools in 1968 and later established the right of every Franco-Ontarian to go to a French-language school. Ontario then guaranteed French trials in the provincial courts and gradually extended French-language provincial services. Premier David Peterson passed Bill 8, which became effective in 1989 and provided for the translation of laws, simultaneous French–English interpretation in the legislature, and provincial government services in French in 22 designated regions of the province. The courts also granted Franco-Ontarians the right to have French-language schools run by trustees elected by the francophone population. As in New Brunswick, the considerable voting power of the Franco-Ontarian community encouraged all parties to support such initiatives, but the combination of Quebec's Bill 178 and Ontario's Bill 8 was too much for many Ontarians to bear. In 1989–90, some 70 municipalities symbolically declared themselves officially unilingual, although such animosity subsided by the turn of the 21st century.

Manitoba moved very slowly on French-language initiatives but was pushed by a series of Supreme Court of Canada decisions beginning in 1979. The 1890 Official Language Act was declared unconstitutional (a violation of the 1870 Manitoba Act); all laws had to be passed in both languages; trials had to be available in French; and most government documents had to be published in a bilingual format.[19] Since then, governments have also expanded French-language services where required.

Given their small francophone minorities, Saskatchewan and Alberta took very little action on French-language issues. Indeed, even asking a question in French in the Alberta legislature originally created quite a controversy. In the 1988 *Mercure* case, however, the Supreme Court of Canada ruled that Saskatchewan (and, by implication, Alberta) was bound by an 1886 territorial statute to pass laws in both French and English.[20] The Court allowed the province to opt out of this requirement, however, by repealing the territorial law by means of a single, bilingual provincial statute. Both provinces proceeded to do so, but did allow French to be spoken in their legislatures and courts. With federal arm-twisting and financial incentives, Saskatchewan also began to translate some of its English-only laws into French. Meanwhile, under federal government pressure, the northern territories granted French official status, but advances for francophone minorities in other provinces have been minimal.[21]

Linguistic minorities at the provincial and territorial level find it necessary to organize in order to pursue their objectives. Such groups include the Assemblée de la francophonie de l'Ontario (AFO), the Société franco-manitobaine, and the Société des acadiens et acadiennes du Nouveau-Brunswick. These French groups have also joined others in the Fédération des communautés francophones et acadienne du Canada. Meanwhile, the English minority in Quebec has also formed its own militant pressure group, Alliance Quebec. As noted, both minority groups sought redress in the courts when they were unsuccessful in dealing with unsympathetic politicians.

CONTEMPORARY ISSUES

Aside from being home to the vast majority of Canada's francophones, Kenneth McRoberts points to other Quebec distinctions.[22] First, Quebec's political institutions are distinctive in many ways: the civil law system, the downplaying of symbols of the Crown, and the plethora of state enterprises, many of them protecting or regulating language and cultural activities. Second, Quebec has pursued many policy differences from other provinces and territories, often with a social democratic flavour: laws that are more labour friendly; distinctive childcare and pharmaceutical plans; multifunctional public clinics that combine health and social services; a more important role for the provincial government in immigration; and a distinctive form of collaboration among the state, capital, and labour. Third, Quebec is distinct in the separateness of its sources of news and entertainment and in many of the institutions of its civil society, such as advocacy groups and political parties. McRoberts concludes that "for most Quebec francophones, anything less than distinct society would not do justice to the reality of contemporary Quebec as they understand it."[23] They see Quebec as the heartland of French Canada; a province that needs special constitutional recognition and has the responsibility to protect itself in the North American English linguistic environment. The Quebec corporate elite is now a francophone group, and, along with the new middle class in the Quebec public sector, sees itself benefiting from increased provincial autonomy.

Recalling the fate of the Meech Lake and Charlottetown Accords, recognition of Quebec as a distinct society is not likely to be supported by enough other provinces (and their publics) to be constitutionally entrenched, although such recognition would be a bare minimum for most Quebeckers today. In the short-term, however, more asymmetrical arrangements were developed with Quebec—treating it differently from other provinces in an informal way—and redressing what Quebec saw as a fiscal imbalance between the two levels of government. Paul Martin, Stephen Harper, and Jean Charest all seemed prepared to pick up on the work of Lester Pearson, Brian Mulroney, and Robert Bourassa in this respect. Many observers feel that the only hope of keeping the country intact in a recognizable form is to find a formula along these lines that would be supported by a majority of Canadians both inside and outside Quebec.[24]

As prime ministers, Paul Martin and Stephen Harper both treated Quebec in a slightly different fashion from other provinces, which is usually referred to as **asymmetrical federalism**. Harper appealed to Quebec with the promise of (decentralized) "open federalism," of fixing the "fiscal imbalance" between the two levels of government, and of giving Quebec a role in the Canadian delegation to UNESCO. He was also the author of a House of Commons resolution that recognized the Québécois as a nation within a united Canada.[25] This resolution was more symbolic than substantive, falling short of the special constitutional recognition that many Quebec politicians have demanded in the past. Nevertheless, without opening up the Pandora's box of constitutional reform, it was appreciated by Quebeckers, at least until they developed many specific policy differences with the Harper government—generally supporting government promotion of the arts, the gun registry, same-sex marriage, and the environment, while disliking Canadian involvement in Afghanistan, and its strong pro-Israel position in the Middle East. While Quebeckers did not seem to support Harper's "tough on crime" agenda, this appeared to shift in 2015 toward support for new criminal and security measures brought in by the Conservative government.

Within Quebec, new forms of nationalism can be identified. The nationalism of the 1960s and 1970s was closely related to the expansion of the provincial state, but as francophones repatriated the private sector in Quebec in the 1980s, especially in the era of globalization and neoliberalism, the concept of "market nationalism" emerged. The distinctiveness of Quebec was no longer threatened by market forces; indeed, controlled by francophones, such forces could be bulwarks in its defence.

About the same time, analysts began to distinguish between "civic" and "ethnic" nationalism in Quebec. As the proportion of allophones increased, a provincial policy of "interculturalism" appeared. New immigrants were told that they could retain their distinctive practices and cultures as long as they entered into the use of French as the common language of Quebec public life. Quebec nationalism would no longer be based on ethnicity and restricted to "pure laine" francophones. The new civic nationalism would welcome non-francophones who felt loyal to Quebec and recognized that the use of French was the essential condition for the cohesion of Quebec society. This distinction has left the concept of "Québécois" rather ambiguous—does it refer only to those of French ethnicity or to this wider, more varied group?

Related to that issue was the increasing concern among some residents about the number of immigrants in the province as well as about certain minority religious and ethnic group practices. Most observers felt that the future of the French language was secure, but others noted that the bulk of new immigrants settled in City of Montreal, where the proportion of residents with French mother tongue had fallen in the 2006 census to just over 50 percent. Then, in response to complaints about Islamic and other religious dress and symbols, Premier Charest appointed a two-person commission (Bouchard-Taylor) to hold public hearings and make recommendations with respect to the "reasonable accommodation" of such differences.

Contrary to the media uproar, the commissioners believed that newcomers were not a threat to the Quebec way of life. They recommended that the government of Quebec should be totally secular, treating all religions alike but not denying them individual expression, and that people of all cultures and faiths should share in a common inclusive state defined by the French language.[26] Nevertheless, with the niqab in mind, Charest thought it necessary to pass a law requiring citizens receiving public services to have their faces uncovered to promote identification and communication.

Meanwhile, post-secondary students staged the massive "Maple Spring" protests in 2012 over proposed tuition increases, even though Quebec's fees were among the lowest in the country. Along with the election of so many NDP MPs in 2011, this protest was a sign of the continuing volatility and restlessness of public opinion in Quebec, exacerbated by the judicial inquiry into corruption in the construction industry.

In the September 2012 provincial election, the Charest government was defeated and the Parti Québécois, under Pauline Marois, came to power with 31.9 percent of the popular vote and 54 of 125 seats in the National Assembly. While viewed by some as the end of constitutional peace in the country, the limited

Christian accused of inflicting religious beliefs on Quebec immigrant.

Vance Rodewalt/Artizans

support for the PQ and for its referendum proposal probably guaranteed that no major confrontations with the federal government were imminent. In 2013, the PQ government introduced a controversial "secular charter" which would have, among other things, prohibited public service employees from wearing overt religious symbols. While the government viewed the policy as "reasonable accommodation" of religions, critics saw it as a means of limiting religious freedoms among minority groups in the province.

Marois chose to fight an election on the issue in 2014, hoping support for the proposal would carry the PQ to a majority government. However, well-known businessperson Pierre Karl Paladeau joined the PQ as a candidate and spoke about his goal of achieving sovereignty, which appeared to soften support for the PQ, and may have aided Phillippe Couillard's Liberal party—which opposed the secular charter—to win a majority of seats.

Although Quebec gained three seats in the House of Commons in 2015, its population continues to decline as a proportion of the national total, and the 2011 election proved that a majority government could be elected with few seats from that province. In fact, after a promising start, the Harper government seemed less and less interested in Quebec, being more concerned with the expanding western half of the country. For the first time in decades, Quebec was not central to the national policymaking process.

CONCLUSION

The ethnic cleavages that are such a prominent feature of the Canadian political system are based in part on the number and variety of groups involved and on their contrasting identities—the perceptions that each group has of its own history and current status. The French are acutely conscious of their current minority position in the country as a whole, as opposed to constituting a majority within Quebec. French Canadians desperately want to preserve their language and culture against the pervasive forces of Anglo-American television and other media. Most Quebec francophones want to enlarge their capacity to govern themselves, and those outside Quebec want to maximize opportunities to use their own language. English-speaking Canadians, however, remain the largest single group and some resent the number of jobs, mostly in the public sector, that now require fluency in French. They also tend to support the principle of provincial equality and are skeptical about distinct status for Quebec. Yet, as McRoberts says, "the majority of Quebec francophones remain just as determined as ever that their distinctiveness be recognized and accommodated."[27]

The political significance of Quebec and French Canada ensures that they are featured in almost every chapter of this text. Readers have already encountered many of the issues relating to them in Chapter 2 (the institutional foundations of Canada), Chapter 3 (Quebec as a region), and Chapter 4 (Aboriginals issues in Quebec). The fact that northern Quebec is populated almost exclusively by Aboriginals, for example, has constituted a problem for sovereignists; this is discussed more fully in Chapter 17 on constitutional reform. That chapter also reiterates how Pierre Trudeau designed the Constitution Act, 1982 in order to promote his vision of the relationship between Quebec and French Canada. Before that, Chapter 9 again notes the significant historic role of religion in Quebec, Chapter 11 picks up on this chapter to discuss a Quebec or French-Canadian subculture, and Chapters 13–15 emphasize the important part that that province plays in electoral and party politics in Canada. Of course, Quebec is central to the discussion of Canadian federalism (Chapter 18), and several Charter cases have emerged from that province (Chapter 19). The four main institutions of government detailed in Part 5 also have to give considerable attention to the place of Quebec and language questions.

DISCUSSION QUESTIONS

1. How would you characterize the interaction between the English majority and the French minority in Canadian history?

2. What are their respective visions of their place in Confederation?

3. Should the French minorities outside Quebec have the same rights and services as the English minority in Quebec?

4. Is the territorial or the personality principle a more realistic basis for language policy in Canada?

5. Why do most Quebeckers insist on the constitutional recognition of Quebec as a distinct society within Canada? What additional powers do they seek?

6. What is likely to happen to official bilingualism if Quebec ever separates?

MindTap®   FOR MORE INFO GO TO **http://www.nelson.com/student**

NOTES

1. Although the label "English" is sometimes used in this chapter to refer to language, as opposed to ethnic origin, special mention should be made of the Scots in Canada, who historically controlled the fur trade, the banks and other financial institutions, the major universities, and much of the government. Many prime ministers, for example, were of Scottish background. See Pierre Berton, *Why We Act Like Canadians* (Toronto: McClelland and Stewart, 1982), pp. 77–78.
2. Kenneth McRoberts, "Making Canada Bilingual: Illusions and Delusions of Federal Language Policy," in David Shugarman and Reg Whitaker, eds., *Federalism and Political Community* (Peterborough: Broadview Press, 1989); and McRoberts, *Misconceiving Canada: The Struggle for National Unity* (Toronto: Oxford University Press, 1997). See also Guy Laforest, *Trudeau and the End of a Canadian Dream* (Montreal: McGill-Queen's University Press, 1995).
3. But see A.G. *Manitoba v. Forest*, [1979] 2 S.C.R. 1032. Canada's involvement in the British Boer War also irritated French–English relations to a limited extent.
4. In the *Ontario Roman Catholic Separate School Trustees v. Mackell*, [1917] A.C. 62 case, the Supreme Court confirmed that constitutional protection in educational matters applied only to religious minorities, not linguistic ones.
5. Dale Thomson, *Jean Lesage and the Quiet Revolution* (Toronto: Macmillan, 1984).

6. Kenneth McRoberts, *Quebec: Social Change and Political Crisis*, 3rd ed. (Toronto: McClelland and Stewart, 1993); and Kenneth McRoberts, "Quebec: Province, Nation, or Distinct Society?" in Michael S. Whittington and Glen Williams, eds., *Canadian Politics in the 21st Century*, 7th ed. (Toronto: Thomson Nelson, 2008).

7. It was not until 1927 that postage stamps became bilingual; in 1934 bilingual bank notes were introduced; and in 1945 bilingual federal family allowance cheques were provided in Quebec. See Office of the Commissioner of Official Languages, *Our Two Official Languages Over Time*, rev. and updated ed. (Ottawa, 1996); and Graham Fraser, *Sorry, I Don't Speak French: Confronting the Canadian Crisis That Won't Go Away* (Toronto: McClelland and Stewart, 2006).

8. Graham Fraser, *René Lévesque and the Parti Québécois in Power* (Toronto: Macmillan, 1984). For France's role in the whole saga, see J.F. Bosher, *The Gaullist Attack on Canada, 1967–1997* (Montreal: McGill-Queen's University Press, 1998).

9. William Coleman, "From Bill 22 to Bill 101: The Politics of Language under the Parti Québécois," *Canadian Journal of Political Science* (September 1981).

10. Janine Brodie and Jane Jenson, *Challenge, Crisis and Change: Politics and Class in Canada Revisited*, 2nd ed. (Ottawa: Carleton University Press, 1990).

11. McRoberts, *Misconceiving Canada*.

12. *Ford v. Quebec (Attorney General)*, [1988] 2 S.C.R. 712.

13. C. Michael MacMillan, *The Practice of Language Rights in Canada* (Toronto: University of Toronto Press, 1998).

14. See *R. v. Beaulac*, [1999] 1 S.C.R. 768, a case in which the Supreme Court reaffirmed the right of an accused person to be tried in his or her mother tongue.

15. *Mahe v. Alberta*, [1990] 1 S.C.R. 342; Troy Q. Riddell, "Official Minority-Language Policy outside Quebec: The Impact of Section 23 of the Charter and Judicial Decisions," *Canadian Public Administration* (Spring 2003); and Michael D. Behiels, *Canada's Francophone Minority Communities: Constitutional Renewal and the Winning of School Governance* (Montreal: McGill-Queen's University Press, 2004).

16. Leslie Pal, *Interests of State: The Politics of Language, Multiculturalism, and Feminism in Canada* (Montreal: McGill-Queen's University Press, 1993).

17. New Brunswick court cases include *Jones v. A.G. New Brunswick*, [1975] 2 S.C.R. 182; *Société des Acadiens v. Association of Parents*, [1986] 1 S.C.R. 549; and *Société des Acadiens et acadiennes du Nouveau-Brunswick Inc. v. Canada*, [2008] 1 S.C.R. 383.

18. James Ross Hurley, *Amending Canada's Constitution: History, Processes, Problems and Prospects* (Ottawa: Supply and Services, 1996).

19. Manitoba cases include *A.G. Manitoba v. Forest, [1979] 2 S.C.R. 1032; Reference re Manitoba Language Rights*, [1985] 1 S.C.R. 721; *Order re Manitoba Language Rights*, [1985] 2 S.C.R. 347; *Bilodeau v. Attorney General Manitoba*, [1986] 1 S.C.R. 449; and *Reference re Manitoba Language Rights*, [1992] 1 S.C.R. 212. Parallel Quebec cases include *Attorney General of Quebec v. Blaikie*, [1979] 2 S.C.R. 1016; and *MacDonald v. City of Montreal*, [1986] 1 S.C.R. 460.

20. *R. v. Mercure*, [1988] 1 S.C.R. 234.

21. French minority educational rights were strengthened by a decision of the Supreme Court in the PEI case *Arsenault-Cameron v. Prince Edward Island*, [2000] 1 S.C.R. 3.

22. McRoberts, "Quebec: Province, Nation, or Distinct Society?"

23. Ibid.

24. Kenneth McRoberts, *Misconceiving Canada*; and R.A. Young, *The Struggle for Quebec* (Montreal: McGill-Queen's University Press, 1999); see articles in *Policy Options*, December 2004/January 2005, April 2007, and July/August 2008.

25. Chantal Hébert, *French Kiss: Stephen Harper's Blind Date with Quebec* (Toronto: Knopf Canada, 2007).

26. The Bouchard-Taylor Report can be found at http://www.accommodements.qc.ca/documentation/rapports/rapport-final-integral-en.pdf; see also articles in *Policy Options*, September 2007.

27. McRoberts, "Quebec: Province, Nation, or Distinct Society?"

FURTHER READING

Behiels, Michael D. *Canada's Francophone Minority Communities: Constitutional Renewal and the Winning of School Governance*. Montreal: McGill-Queen's University Press, 2004.

Bothwell, Robert. *Canada and Quebec: One Country, Two Histories*, rev. ed. Vancouver: University of British Columbia Press, 1998.

Cook, Ramsay. *Canada, Quebec and the Uses of Nationalism*. Toronto: McClelland and Stewart, 1995.

Fraser, Graham. *Sorry, I Don't Speak French: Confronting the Canadian Crisis That Won't Go Away*. Toronto: McClelland and Stewart, 2006.

Gagnon, Alain-G., and Raffaele Iacovino. *Federalism, Citizenship and Quebec: Debating Multinationalism*. Toronto: University of Toronto Press, 2006.

Hébert, Chantal. *French Kiss: Stephen Harper's Blind Date with Quebec*. Toronto: Knopf Canada, 2007.

Laforest, Guy. *Trudeau and the End of a Canadian Dream*. Montreal: McGill-Queen's University Press, 1995.

Maclure, Jocelyn. *Quebec Identity: The Challenge of Pluralism*. Montreal: McGill-Queen's University Press, 2003.

MacMillan, C. Michael. *The Practice of Language Rights in Canada*. Toronto: University of Toronto Press, 1998.

Martel, Marcel, and Martin Pâquet. Speaking Up: A History of Language and Politics in Canada and Quebec. Toronto: Between the Lines, 2012.

McRoberts, Kenneth. *Misconceiving Canada: The Struggle for National Unity*. Toronto: Oxford University Press, 1997.

———. "Quebec: Province, Nation, or Distinct Society?" In Michael S. Whittington and Glen Williams, eds., *Canadian Politics in the 21st Century*, 7th ed. Toronto: Thomson Nelson, 2008.

Salée, Daniel, and Michael Murphy. *Canada: the State of the Federation: 2005: Quebec*. Montreal: McGill-Queen's University Press, 2005.

Young, Robert A. *The Struggle for Quebec*. Montreal: McGill-Queen's University Press, 1999.

Chase Clausen/Shutterstock

CHAPTER 6

Ethnocultural Minorities

Canada is often called an "immigrant society," reflecting the fact that it has long had a large number of immigrants arriving every year. Today, nearly one in five Canadians was born in a foreign state, placing us among the countries with the highest proportion of its population born elsewhere. Immigration has always been an important feature of Canadian society, but changing worldwide demographic patterns mean that immigration has long served to bring new cultural diversity to Canada. The areas of the world from which immigrants to Canada have arrived has changed over time. Nowadays, immigrants to Canada tend to come from Asia, the Middle East, and Africa.

This chapter begins with a profile of immigration and ethnocultural minorities in Canada and puts that portrait into historical context. It then raises some theoretical considerations regarding racism, racialization, and ethnic identities, before discussing the historic pattern of discrimination that new Canadians experienced. The next part deals with demands for equality and inclusion and with responses to such demands in the period after 1970, especially the success in achieving the policy of multiculturalism. The chapter ends with an account of the many current issues in this field.

A PROFILE OF ETHNOCULTURAL MINORITIES TODAY

Statistics Canada's 2011 National Household Survey records 264 different ethnic identities in Canada. Table 6.1 provides statistics on the largest ethnic groups in Canada, and reveals the continuing European character of the overall population.

On the other hand, in showing a typical recent year of immigration statistics, Table 6.2 reveals the changing nature of ethnocultural minorities in Canada. These immigration patterns give rise to the concept of **visible minorities**, defined in the Employment Equity Act as "persons, other than Aboriginal peoples, who are non-Caucasian in race or non-white in colour." The 2011 National Household Survey reported that visible minorities numbered over six million Canadians, or 19.1 percent of the population.

TABLE 6.1 LARGEST ETHNIC GROUPS IN CANADA, 2011

CANADIAN	10 563 805	CHINESE	1 487 580
ENGLISH	6 509 500	NORTH AMERICAN INDIAN	1 369 035
FRENCH	5 065 690	UKRAINIAN	1 251 170
SCOTTISH	4 714 970	EAST INDIAN	1 165 145
IRISH	4 544 870	DUTCH	1 067 245
GERMAN	3 203 330	POLISH	1 010 705
ITALIAN	1 488 425	RUSSIAN	550 550

Source: Statistics Canada, 2011 National Household Survey, Ethnic Origins, Catalogue no. 99-010-X2011028, https://www12.statcan.gc.ca/nhs-enm/2011/dp-pd/dt-td/Rp-eng.cfm?LANG=E&APATH=3&DETAIL=0&DIM=0 &FL=A&FREE=0&GC=0&GID=0&GK=0&GRP=0&PID=105396&PRID=0&PTYPE=105277&S=0&SHOWALL=0&S UB=0&Temporal=2013&THEME=95&VID=0&VNAMEE=&VNAMEF=. Reproduced and distributed on an "as is" basis with the permission of Statistics Canada.

TABLE 6.2 TOP 10 SOURCE COUNTRIES 2013*

RANK	SOURCE COUNTRY	NUMBER OF IMMIGRANTS
1	CHINA	34 126
2	INDIA	33 085
3	PHILIPPINES	29 539
4	PAKISTAN	12 602
5	IRAN	11 291
6	UNITED STATES	8 495
7	UNITED KINGDOM	5 826
8	FRANCE	5 624
9	IRAQ	4 918
10	REPUBLIC OF KOREA	4 509

* SOURCE COUNTRY BASED ON COUNTRY OF CITIZENSHIP.

Source: Citizenship and Immigration Canada. Facts and Figures 2013. Permanent Residents by source country. http://www.cic.gc.ca/english/resources/statistics/facts2013/permanent/10.asp. Reproduced with permission of Citizenship and Immigration Canada, 2015.

Nearly 90 percent of visible minorities in Canada live in the seven biggest cities in the countries. Indeed, 41 percent of Canada's visible minorities live in Toronto alone, and 71 percent live in Toronto, Vancouver, and Montreal combined. In both Toronto and Vancouver visible minorities make-up nearly half of the urban populations (47 percent and 45 percent, respectively). For Calgary, Edmonton, Montreal, and Winnipeg, the share of these cities populations that are visible minorities are 28.1 percent, 22.4 percent, 20.3 percent, and 19.7 percent, respectively.

THEORETICAL CONSIDERATIONS

Canada is not alone in containing a variety of ethnocultural groups; indeed, most modern states are characterized by cultural pluralism. Such ethnic collectivities normally share ancestry, language, religious beliefs, and cultural traditions, leading to a sense of identity, although such identities are socially constructed to a large extent, as suggested in Chapter 1.[1] Such heterogeneity may give rise to discussions of race and racism. Social and natural scientists today generally take the position that, despite appearances, there are no significant biological differences between such groups and they avoid the word "race" in this connection. Nevertheless, people may behave as if such differences are profound; they may demonstrate attitudes of "racism" despite what scientists say; and governments may resort to "racial profiling," as in collecting statistics on crime. Such attitudes and policies could refer to the people of any group, but are more likely to relate to "visible minorities." That term, which has official status in the Canadian lexicon, has sometimes been criticized for being racist in itself.

Although there are no inherent biological differences among varied ethnicities, people often have feelings of identification with their own ethnic group. A change in immigrant identities occurred in the 1960s when the country was consumed with debates about upgrading the official status of the francophone component, and other ethnocultural groups began to ask about their place in Canadian society. The "politics of identity" was said to characterize members of minority groups who began to feel strong ethnocultural identities and demand "recognition" of those identities by the Canadian government.

This development raised the theoretical question, also noted in the previous chapters, about how the political system should treat ethnocultural differences. Prior to 1970, in the absence of an official policy, the general approach was to encourage assimilation into the dominant anglo-conformity of English Canada, and unequal treatment of non-British or non-French newcomers was not of much concern. Still, the U.S. ideal of the "melting pot"—of melting away ethnic differences and treating everyone alike—was never entrenched in Canada. Rather, the government declared in 1971 an official policy of "multiculturalism." This policy commits the Government of Canada to promoting and preserving Canada's multicultural heritage; it includes a greater commitment to the principle of equality, and perhaps veers toward a kind of collective group identity as opposed to a feeling of individualism.[2]

HISTORY OF CANADIAN IMMIGRATION

Let us put the ethnocultural portrait into historical context. Aboriginal peoples settled in what is now Canada too long ago to be considered immigrants. The British and French might be labelled as immigrants, but they were almost the only other ethnocultural groups in Canada before 1867. Those three groups are sometimes considered the "founding peoples" of the country, although, ironically, Aboriginals had to fight to be included in the definition. Following the Aboriginals, the French, and the British, people from many other lands began to immigrate to Canada. By 1867, a sizable German contingent had arrived, and, shortly afterward, the wide-open spaces of northern Ontario, the Prairies, and British Columbia attracted large numbers of immigrants from continental Europe as well as from Britain and the United States. Railway construction and Western settlement were two key objectives of the Macdonald government's 1879 **National Policy**, and the first dramatic surge of immigrants arrived during the 1880s, many of them homesteaders in the prairies. These included Danes, Dutch, Icelanders, Poles, Ukrainians, Finns, Norwegians, and Swedes. In addition, between 1881 and 1884, nearly 16 000 Chinese labourers were brought into British Columbia to work on the construction of the CPR. A substantial number of Blacks came to Canada among the Loyalists and/or to escape from slavery in the United States.[3]

Between 1910 and 1913, the largest number of immigrants in the country's history arrived in Canada—1.4 million over four years. The prosperous 1920s were another active decade, but immigration declined significantly during the Depression and the Second World War. After the war, another huge wave of immigrants came to Canada, largely from southern Europe. They were supplemented by postwar refugees from around the world. Figure 6.1 indicates the fluctuations in the number of new immigrants in Canada since 1860.

FIGURE 6.1   IMMIGRATION: A HISTORICAL PERSPECTIVE, 1860–2013

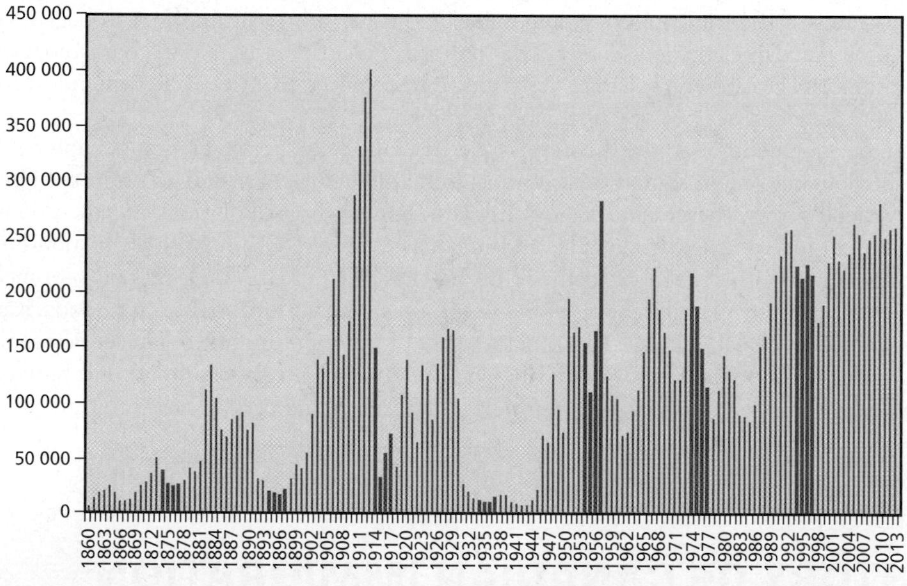

Source: Citizenship and Immigration Canada, Facts and Figures 2013, http://www.cic.gc.ca/english/resources/statistics/facts2013/permanent/index.asp#figure1. Reproduced with permission of Citizenship and Immigration Canada, 2015.

Overall, Britain was the leading source of immigrants between 1900 and 1965. During that time, immigration policy favoured British, American, and European newcomers; they were considered to be well educated, skilled, and better able to assimilate. Most people of British/Celtic background saw Canada as a "British," "English," or Caucasian country, and immigrants in the post-Confederation period generally tried to fit into that mould. Nevertheless, even without official sanction, many retained their original languages and cultures, and developed hyphenated identities, such as an Italian-Canadian identity or a German-Canadian one. Their ethnocultural identity was essentially a low-profile private matter, however, and they rarely made political demands on this basis.

The **Immigration Act** was significantly amended over the 1960s to remove its most discriminatory features, and Canadian immigration patterns changed radically over the following 50 years, as Figure 6.2 demonstrates. In 1957, more than 90 percent of the immigrants were from Britain or continental Europe, a figure that has fallen to about 16 percent. In contrast, Asian immigrants accounted for less than two percent of total immigrants in 1957 but now constitute about 50 percent annually.

Those immigrants to Canada who come to stay—permanent residents—are divided into three main categories: family class, economic class, and refugees. Temporary residents mainly

FIGURE 6.2 PRINCIPAL SOURCES OF PERMANENT RESIDENTS IN CANADA, 2004–2013

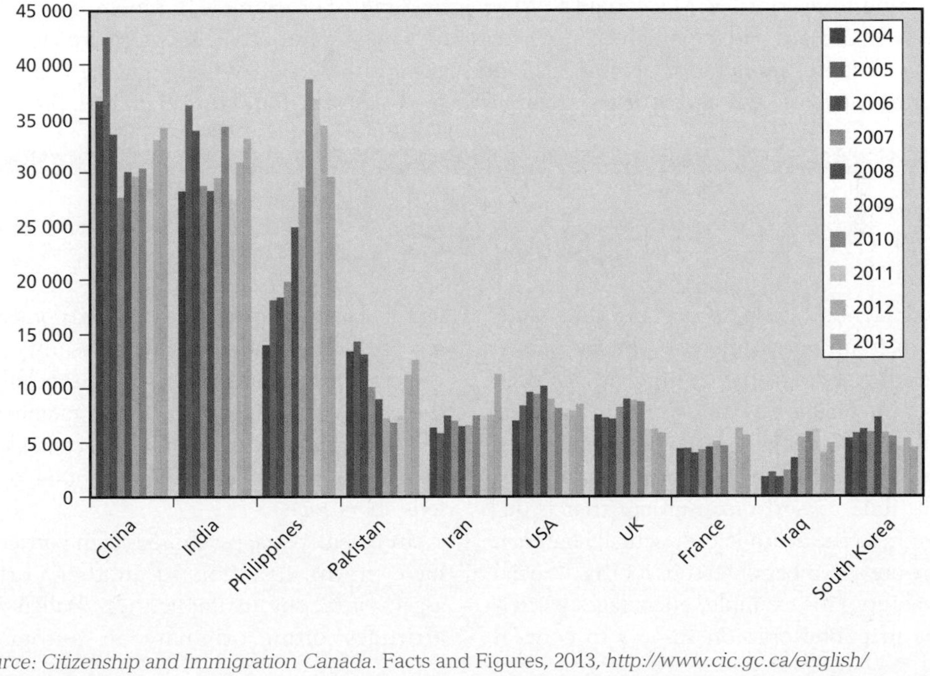

Source: Citizenship and Immigration Canada. Facts and Figures, 2013, http://www.cic.gc.ca/english/resources/statistics/facts2013/permanent/10.asp. Reproduced with permission of Citizenship and Immigration Canada, 2016.

include foreign workers, and foreign students. In 2013 the number in each of these categories was as follows:

Family Class	79 684
Economic Class	148 181
Refugees	24 049
Foreign Workers:	
Temporary Foreign Workers	118 024
International Mobility Program	161 541
Intl. Students	194 075

Source: Citizenship and Immigration Canada. Facts and Figures, 2013. http://www.cic.gc.ca/english/resources/statistics/facts2013/permanent/10.asp. Reproduced with permission of Citizenship and Immigration Canada, 2016.

RACIAL DISCRIMINATION

Canadian history was pervaded by racial or ethnic discrimination, which can be defined as unfavourable treatment based on prejudice regarding ancestry. Discrimination arose in the first place from the immigration process itself. Most Canadians of the 21st century would cringe at some of the racist comments made and racist immigration policies pursued by prime ministers stretching from John A. Macdonald to Mackenzie King.[4] For example, Chinese immigrants from 1885 onward had to pay a head tax to enter the country, prior to being prohibited entirely by the Chinese Immigration Act of 1923, and during the Second World War the Canadian government refused to accept Jewish refugees trying to escape from Hitler's Europe. As noted

CRITICAL APPROACHES

Social scientists study issues of race and immigration from many different vantage points. When it comes to studying racism, however, one of the challenges facing researchers using Political Psychology and Political Behaviour approaches is the tendency of people to report an attitude toward racial groups that is different from the attitude they actually harbour. There are a number of reasons for this. "Social desirability," for example, encourages participants in public opinion surveys to conceal unpopular or offensive ideas for fear of social reproach. Respondents may deny antipathy toward a particular racial group, especially if the person interviewing them is a member of that group. Social desirability effects make it difficult for researchers to elicit genuine opinions about race.

In recent years, psychologists in particular have drawn attention to another critical aspect of racism: its implicitness. Beliefs and attitudes often originate in automatic cognitive processes that are unknown even to the people who harbour them. People may hold negative attitudes about a racial group and yet be unaware that they hold these kinds of attitudes. Racism may originate, for example, as a tinge of discomfort in the presence of certain groups. This discomfort may bias a person's assessment in a particular setting, even as the ultimate source of that discomfort remains hidden from the person who experiences it. In other words, people may harbour negative attitudes about racial groups and be genuinely unaware that they hold these attitudes. Psychologists have developed tests for measuring these kinds of implicit racial attitudes. You can learn about and take some of these tests at https://implicit .harvard.edu/implicit/education.html.

above, for 100 years Canadian immigration policy gave preference to Caucasians, but as time went on, Canada moved further and further away from its British origins. Moreover, with an increasing realization of the bias in the country's immigration policy, international and domestic pressure forced the Diefenbaker and Pearson governments to revise the Immigration Act to remove its preference for anglo-Europeans.

Those immigrants who managed to meet the official criteria often settled in minority ethnic communities and started their own social and cultural organizations, such as clubs, choirs, folk dance troupes, and newspapers. Many families spoke the "old country" language at home, but the children generally became proficient in English at school, and the second generation often assimilated into the anglo-Canadian way of life, as intended. Whatever their hyphenated identities, members of such ethnic minorities maintained a low public profile and made few demands. Once arrived, they were largely ignored by federal and provincial governments, although the occasional privilege was granted, such as promises to Mennonites and Hutterites of exemption from military service. In Manitoba between 1896 and 1916 it was even legal to establish bilingual English and other-language schools in areas of concentrated ethnic minority settlement.

BOX 6.1 VOICES

"There will, I am sure, be general agreement with the view that the people of Canada do not wish, as a result of mass immigration, to make a fundamental alternation on the character of our population. Large-scale immigration from the Orient would change the fundamental composition of the Canadian population."

Source: Prime Minister Mackenzie King, *House of Commons Debates* (May 1, 1947), p. 2645.

Immigrants were more likely to be discriminated against on the basis of their ethnic origin and were often subject to blatant racism. This discrimination was written into laws beyond the Immigration Act, such as detention, electoral, and employment legislation. During the First and Second World Wars, some who had come from countries with which Canada was at war were treated harshly. In the first contest, Canada interned immigrants from the Ukraine, and because the federal franchise was sometimes based on provincial franchises, the bias against Asians in British Columbia carried over to federal elections. At the federal level itself, Canadian citizens who came from countries with which Canada was at war (principally Germany and Austria) had their vote taken away in the 1917 election.

Untold cases of discrimination against both visible and invisible ethnic minorities in the area of employment have occurred throughout Canadian history. In the early part of the last century, for example, British Columbia labour laws prohibited the hiring of Asians in order to preserve jobs for whites; in Saskatchewan, Chinese Canadians were not allowed to employ white women; and Black Canadians faced legalized discrimination in Ontario and Quebec, including segregated schools.

The worst case of federal government mistreatment of visible minorities was that of Japanese Canadians in the Second World War. When Japan entered the war, Canadian citizens of Japanese origin were automatically suspected of being loyal to Japan, a suspicion without any foundation. Canadian citizens of Japanese background were uprooted from the west coast, interned in "relocation centres," and had their property confiscated. At the end of the war, about 4000 people were deported.[5] Moreover, until after the Second World War, Canadians of Chinese, Japanese, and East Indian descent had no vote unless they had served in the armed forces. Conversely, until 1975, British subjects resident in Canada could vote in federal elections even without becoming Canadian citizens.

Immigrants have also faced a number of extra-legal barriers that made it difficult for them to play an active part in politics, government, and society in general. One such barrier was discrimination within political parties. People of minority ethnocultural origins were generally not welcomed into mainstream parties, and when they did find entry, were usually given only subordinate roles. They had a hard time winning party nominations, unless it was in a clear-cut "ethnic" constituency. It was not until the Diefenbaker era, around 1960, that Canadians of Ukrainian background started to make inroads into the Conservative Party, and only two MPs before 1964 were from visible minorities.[6]

Most people who belong to visible minorities faced racial animosity, at least including abusive comments, on a regular basis.[7] After laws were passed to prohibit discrimination in the labour market, visible minority immigrants still often found it difficult to secure employment because their education and experience were frequently discounted and their skills underutilized. Even if they were successful in getting hired, they were often victims of pay inequities or promotion blockages.[8] The end result was a racialized hierarchy in all aspects of society.[9]

OVERCOMING DISCRIMINATION: MULTICULTURALISM, EQUITY, AND INCLUSIVENESS

It has already been noted that changes to the Immigration Act in the 1960s began to alter the ethnic composition of the Canadian population and with it, Canadians' traditional perceptions of themselves. This increase in the numbers of people of different ethnocultural origins gave them more leverage to demand improvements in their status as citizens. Changes in the 1970s and 1980s were largely positive for such groups and started with the adoption of the policy of multiculturalism.

The original mandate of the 1963 Royal Commission on Bilingualism and Biculturalism was to concentrate on the English and French languages and cultures and to make recommendations in the wake of the Quiet Revolution in Quebec. By that time, however, the number of people in the country belonging to other ethnocultural groups was sufficient to force a change in the commission's terms of reference. Largely because of pressure from Ukrainian Canadians, the Royal Commission was also asked to examine "the contribution made by other ethnic groups to the cultural enrichment of Canada and the measures which should be taken to safeguard that contribution." The term "multiculturalism" came into use at about this time, and the commission recommended that increased government attention be given to other ethnic groups, including public funding in certain areas. With this encouragement, these groups began to demand changes in public policies as well as verbal and moral support.

In 1971, partly because of the Royal Commission recommendations, group pressure, and politicians hoping to win votes, the Trudeau government announced a new official policy of multiculturalism within a bilingual framework.[10] **Multiculturalism** is the official recognition of the diverse cultures in a plural society; it involves encouraging immigrants to retain their linguistic heritages and ethnic cultures instead of abandoning them and assimilating with the dominant group. The government felt that it was "overdue for the people of Canada to become more aware of the rich tradition of the many cultures"[11] in the country. It argued that the Canadian identity would not be undermined by multiculturalism; indeed, cultural pluralism was the very essence of the Canadian identity. Such diversity makes Canada a more interesting place to live in terms of foods, restaurants, languages, entertainment, sports, and cultures. In providing links to virtually every other country in the world, this array of ethnic groups also enhances Canada's international image and influence.[12] At the same time as retaining their individual cultures, members of such minorities were encouraged to integrate linguistically by becoming fluent in English or French; in other words, they were expected to learn at least one of the official languages. Ottawa established a number of new programs to implement the multiculturalism policy and a government department to administer them.

BASIC OBJECTIVES OF MULTICULTURALISM POLICY

- To assist cultural groups in retaining and fostering their identity
- To assist cultural groups in overcoming barriers to their full participation in Canadian society
- To promote creative exchanges among all Canadian cultural groups
- To assist immigrants in acquiring at least one official language

To some people of such ethnic origins, however, multiculturalism did not provide for complete equality because it seemed to be subordinate to the policy of official bilingualism which preserved the historic dominance of the British and French. Others saw multiculturalism as more symbolic than substantive, a policy that was primarily aimed at preserving ethnic folklore. Some Quebeckers viewed multiculturalism as an attempt to diminish their claim of being a distinct society within Canada, as "French" culture was treated as just one of many others in the country.

Once in place, however, the policy of multiculturalism legitimized demands for many other changes in terms of promoting ethnocultural identities and removing barriers to equity and inclusiveness. The next stage was the government's creation of the Canadian Human Rights Commission in 1978. Most provinces already had such bodies to deal with complaints of discrimination in the private sector and to promote anti-discrimination educational programs, but the new commission closed certain loopholes within the federal government's jurisdiction.

Another advance was the **Charter of Rights and Freedoms** in 1982 which provided constitutional protection against discrimination by federal and provincial governments in the equality rights clause, section 15. The Charter also endorsed affirmative action programs to overcome past discrimination. After intense pressure from various ethnocultural minorities, section 27 was added to the Charter to the effect that it would be interpreted "in a manner consistent with the preservation and enhancement of the multicultural heritage of Canadians."

In 1988, a new Canadian Multiculturalism Act was passed that gave multiculturalism a stronger legal base by consolidating existing policies and practices into legislation. In 1991 the Mulroney government created a new Department of Multiculturalism and Citizenship, but it has undergone a number of organizational changes since.

In 1986 the federal **Employment Equity Act** designated visible minorities, women, people with disabilities, and Aboriginals as groups that could benefit from employment equity programs with respect to hiring in the public service and in large companies dealing with the government. Although those not included in these categories complained about reverse discrimination, some minority ethnic leaders criticized the lack of specific goals and timetables in the legislation.[13] The Act was strengthened in 1995.

The treatment of Japanese Canadians during the Second World War nagged at the Canadian conscience for nearly 45 years until the Mulroney government announced a settlement package in the 1988 **Japanese Redress Agreement**, which provided, among other things, $21 000 for each of the surviving internees. This led to demands from other ethnic minorities that they be similarly compensated for wartime or other collective discrimination in Canada.

Colin McConnell/GetStock.com

Kindergarten children in Toronto represent the changing face of urban Canadian schools.

Some provinces also demonstrated support for the concept of multiculturalism. Ontario, for example, instituted a heritage languages policy in its school system and in 1993, passed the strongest employment equity legislation in the country. In Quebec, French-speaking immigrants were welcomed in order to bolster the francophone population, while others were required to attend the French-language school system. Quebec adopted a policy of "interculturalism" which allowed immigrants to retain certain cultural distinctions while integrating into the French-speaking community by accepting that French was the common language of public life. In this respect, groups such as the Haitian community managed to hang on to their own culture.

Taking their cue from Aboriginal, francophone, and anglophone minority groups, nearly every other ethnic group established a national organization to promote its culture and to function as an advocacy group from time to time. Examples include the National Congress of Italian Canadians, the German Canadian Congress, and the National Association of Japanese Canadians. The government itself actively encouraged many such groups to organize, and they were to find common ground in the Canadian Ethnocultural Council, which also received considerable government funding.[14]

CURRENT ETHNOCULTURAL ISSUES

Immigration and diversity are perennial issues in Canadian politics. The 1990 decision of the RCMP to allow Sikh Mounties to wear turbans as a religious symbol produced considerable opposition. So did the rule prohibiting the wearing of turbans in the halls of the Royal Canadian Legion. On the other hand, the House of Commons lost no time in waiving a similar rule when the first turbaned Sikh MP was elected in 1993. Because most newcomers to Canada settle in Toronto, Montreal, and Vancouver, tensions also sometimes rise to the fore of local politics. Relations between the African-Canadian community and the Montreal and Toronto police forces were strained, and because some police forces believed that people of certain ethnic groups were disproportionately involved in crime, they engaged in the practice of racial profiling.

In recent years, immigration and ethnocultural issues have figured prominently on the current Canadian political agenda.[15] There are concerns in some parts of Canada surrounding issues of religious accommodation, especially but not exclusively with respect to Muslims. As a result of changing immigration patterns, Muslims represent one of the fastest growing demographic groups in Canada and certainly the fastest growing religion. The percentage of Muslims in Canada has doubled over the past 15 years, and it is expected to double again over the next 15. Concerns about the hair and face coverings worn by Muslim women, for example, have recently arisen in Canadian politics. For some, these issues represent a fundamental clash between secular and religious visions of society. For others, these issues are little more than pretexts for antipathy toward a maligned minority group.

THE CANADIAN PRESS IMAGES/Adrian Wyld

Conservative MP Tim Uppal.

CHAPTER 6 **Ethnocultural Minorities**

In response to these pressures, the Government of Quebec appointed a special commission in 2008 to make recommendations on "reasonable accommodation" of religions minorities. The Bouchard-Taylor Commission argued that it was possible to impose reasonable restrictions on religious minorities in the interests of preserving a secular state, while also accommodating religious diversity. This report did not end the debate. The Quebec government passed a law in 2010 that required Muslim women to bare their face (remove their niqab) when dealing with provincial government authorities. When the federal government heard in 2011 that some women were swearing their oath of citizenship with a face covering such as a niqab or burka, Immigration Minister Kenney issued an immediate ban. The government ban was eventually struck down by the courts as a violation of the Citizenship Act's provisions for religious accommodation. Although the Conservative Government of Stephen Harper intended to appeal this decision to the Supreme Court of Canada, the newly-elected Justin Trudeau announced that his government would not appeal these lower court rulings. As a result, it is now possible to swear the oath of citizenship while wearing a niqab or burqa.

The Temporary Foreign Worker program is another political issue related to immigration. Canada now takes in a huge number of temporary foreign workers each year. These are people from other countries that come to Canada to work, but who do not necessarily become citizens or permanent residents. In addition to the 180 000 who entered in 2010, for example, some 250 000 others were already here. Many of these "temporary" workers stay for years, and many re-enter Canada regularly. Although such temporary workers can apply to become permanent residents, few do so, leaving their status precarious and ineligible for normal immigration services. For example, Maria Venancio, a young Pilipino woman who moved to Canada to work at a McDonald's restaurant under the Temporary Foreign Worker program, was struck by a car on her way to work and became a quadriplegic. Because she could no longer work, and because she was not a citizen or permanent resident, she faced deportation back to the Philippines. Although the labour of these temporary workers is heavily relied on in certain industries, especially agriculture and as domestic caregivers, many observers are concerned about their quality of life. Some also wonder why unemployed Canadians could not do such work, or why companies should not pay higher salaries if they cannot attract the workers that they need from among the Canadian population.[16] Indeed, in employment insurance (EI) reforms introduced in 2012, the government said that employers must give preference to an unemployed Canadian rather than a foreign worker, although they were allowed to pay the latter 15 percent less.

While changing the EI rules in 2012, the Harper government also introduced significant reforms to the immigration system. It sought to eliminate the existing backlog of nearly one million applicants and start anew, emphasizing higher levels of English or French fluency and younger applicants; giving more power to employers to hand-pick immigrants based on their skills, along with creating a new stream for tradespeople; and assessing professionals' credentials before they immigrate.

The role of the provinces in the immigration process is significantly increasing. Although immigration is a concurrent constitutional responsibility of both levels of government, Quebec was the only province to take much interest in it until fairly recently. Over the years, Ottawa gradually widened Quebec's authority to choose its own immigrants, as that province preferred those who spoke French. As a result of other provinces seeking similar involvement and flexibility, they are all now able to nominate immigrants under the Provincial Nominee Program, and Western provinces in particular want to nominate more. Because this devolution has been agreeable to both sides, it has not been particularly controversial, but it leads to the question of how much uniformity of standards remains.

Immigration cases constitute a large part of the workload of the Federal Court of Canada, as seen in Chapter 24. Sometimes ethnocultural cases also get to the Supreme Court of Canada. In a number of communities, for example, the issue of Sikh children wearing their kirpan (a dull, blunted ceremonial dagger) to school has been raised, and a Supreme Court decision in 2006 which permitted

TOUGH NEW REFUGEE LAWS

Sue Dewar/Artizans

such a practice did not silence those who felt that it constituted a danger in the schoolyard.[17]

Studies of recent immigrants have concluded that they do not do as well financially as either earlier immigrants or Canadian-born counterparts, and in fact many live below the poverty line. One factor in this scenario is that recent immigrants have trouble entering the work force because their professional credentials are often not recognized by provincial or territorial accreditation bodies, although this problem is often due to inadequate knowledge of English or French. Immigrant women especially find it difficult to stay in one job long enough to qualify for employment insurance benefits, so that they often fall back on social assistance. The attributes of ethnicity, gender, and class often reinforce each other.[18]

Many ethnocultural minorities continue to experience discrimination. Blacks, South Asians, and Chinese were the leading groups to report discrimination in a 2002 study, especially in the workplace and in retail settings.[19] After the events of September 11, 2001, it was often Canadian Muslims and Arabs who were victims of a backlash, being subjected to greater scrutiny by law enforcement and immigration officials and airport security personnel.[20] Besides being subjects of suspicion within Canada, many Muslims and Arabs found it difficult to enter the United States, and a few who did, such as Maher Arar, found themselves unjustly targeted as terrorists.

Most Canadians believe that immigrants should be expected to conform to the values of their new country. An Environics survey in 2011 sponsored by the Trudeau Foundation produced the following results on Canadians' expectations which were endorsed by Minister Kenney at the time. New immigrants

- should be required to adopt Canadian values of tolerance of others and gender equity (97 percent)*

---

* Pierre Elliott Trudeau Foundation, Canadian public perspectives on immigration: A national opinion survey, http://www.trudeaufoundation.ca/sites/default/files/environics_-_trudeau_foundation_2011_conference _presentation_on_immigration_-_nov_19-2011.pdf.

- should be required to accept the pre-eminence of Canadian law over any religious laws (89 percent)
- should become familiar with Canadian history and culture (88 percent)
- should raise their children as Canadians (79 percent)
- should be fluent in either English or French (78 percent)
- should make an effort to create ties with non-immigrants outside their own ethnic group (77 percent).[21]

According to the 2001 census, about 700 000 Canadians are also citizens of another country. Some observers see the concept of dual citizenship as a problem, while others feel that it is a benefit to Canada. In any case, on her appointment as governor general, Michaëlle Jean felt it appropriate to renounce the French part of her dual citizenship. Party leaders Stéphane Dion and Thomas Mulcair, on the other hand, did not deem such a decision necessary in their respective cases.[22]

Related to this issue is the charge that some immigrants are too engaged in homeland politics and that they bring internal ethnic conflicts to their new land. Some immigrants undoubtedly see themselves as "diaspora"—displaced from the homeland for various reasons, but hoping to return. The Sikh and Sri Lankan communities are sometimes singled out in this connection, but they are not alone. It is also said that involvement in politics abroad tends to deflect energies away from political participation in Canada. Stasiulis and Abu-Laban admit that homeland politics is a common occurrence among many ethnic minorities, but answer the criticism in these terms: "There is little evidence that an ethnic community highly politicized on homeland issues cannot simultaneously participate in Canadian politics."[23]

Although members of ethnic minorities are involved in all aspects of public policies, one particular area of interest to many of them is Canadian foreign policy. In fact, this is not a recent phenomenon: Canadians have always been concerned about the relationship between Canada and their country of origin. But in recent years, for example, the Harper government was often criticized by Arab-Canadian groups for its staunch support of Israel in the politics of the Middle East. This criticism was reinforced by what many regarded as a government hard line on questionable terrorist suspects, such as Omar Khadr, and the general Arab-Muslim focus of anti-terrorism policies. Beyond that issue, the Harper government has been accused of pursuing electoral support by pandering to various diasporas in its foreign policy when it is not in the national interest.

In terms of political representation, the number of candidates and MPs from ethnic minority groups continues to increase, but still remains considerably below their proportion of the overall population.[24] Stasiulis and Abu-Laban explain this as follows:

[T]he statistical underrepresentation of ethnic and visible minorities within the major parties can be explained in terms of a variety of structural, cultural, and organizational obstacles. For recent immigrants lacking official-language skills, linguistic barriers intersect with lack of familiarity with the Canadian political culture and system. Racial minorities confront discrimination practiced at the highest levels of party structures.... [F]or all marginalized groups, there is a legacy of exclusion that is reinforced by the hegemonic bicultural discourse of party politics, by patterns of recruitment through networks, and by party traditions such as the incumbency factor within the electoral process.[25]

Historically, the Liberal party had a virtual stranglehold on the minority ethnic vote, but both the Conservatives and NDP later made inroads in these communities. In fact, from 2006 to 2015, the Harper government vigorously wooed ethnocultural minorities through mailings and appearances at important celebrations, especially by Minister Jason Kenney. The Conservative majority in the 2011 election can be largely attributed to an increase in the party's seats in suburban Toronto and Vancouver in which visible minorities constituted a large proportion of the population, and the number of visible minority MPs increased to 9.4 percent.[26] In 2015, however, the Liberals elected 39 visible minority MPs, out of a record total of 47. This number constituted 14 percent of all MPs,[27] nearly equal to the proportion of visible minorities in the overall population.

CONCLUSION

Various waves of immigration have changed the traditional conception of what it is to be Canadian. Given the current low birthrate and an aging society, immigration is necessary for any expansion of the Canadian economy, and immigrants now come primarily from developing countries. On the other hand, despite official multiculturalism and employment equity policies, many immigrants to Canada continue to experience considerable discrimination at an everyday level. Even if the discrimination is not explicit, such practices may nonetheless have harmful effects on new immigrants' well-being. Canada may well be a world leader in the way a variety of ethnocultural communities live together peacefully, and although most Canadians value the policy of multiculturalism, they would also prefer to see immigrants integrate themselves more fully into the wider Canadian society.

Issues related to ethnocultural minorities are readdressed in Chapters 7 (gender) and 8 (class). They are mentioned again in Chapters 13, 14, and 15 in connection with parties and elections. Ethnocultural issues are revisited in Chapter 19 (Charter of Rights and Freedoms), and immigration cases constitute a large part of the workload of the Federal Court, as seen in Chapter 24.

DISCUSSION QUESTIONS

1. What annual levels of immigration do you think are appropriate? What kinds of immigrants should Canada seek?

2. How has massive recent immigration affected the Canadian identity?

3. To what extent should immigrants be encouraged to retain their languages, cultures, and customs? Should such retention be supported by the public purse?

4. To what extent should established Canadian practices and customs be modified to accommodate recent immigrants?

5. How does racism operate in Canadian society? From where does it originate? What do you think of the psychological tests for measuring the potentially latent sources of racism (https://implicit.harvard.edu/implicit/education.html)?

NOTES

1. Daiva Stasiulis and Yasmeen Abu-Laban, "Unequal Relations and the Struggle for Equality: Race and Ethnicity in Canadian Politics," in Michael Whittington and Glen Williams, eds., *Canadian Politics in the 21st Century*, 7th ed. (Toronto: Nelson Education, 2008), p. 288. Much of the following discussion relies on this source. See also Maria A. Wallis, Lina Sunseri, and Grace-Edward Galabuzi, *Colonialism and Racism in Canada: Historical Traces and Contemporary Issues* (Toronto: Nelson Education, 2010).
2. Stasiulis and Abu-Laban, "Unequal Relations," p. 304; the entire June 2010 issue of the *Canadian Journal of Political Science* deals with the issues covered in this chapter.
3. Anne Milan and Kelly Tran, "Blacks in Canada: A Long History," *Canadian Social Trends* (Statistics Canada, Catalogue No. 11-008, Spring 2004).
4. Stasiulis and Abu-Laban, "Unequal Relations," 7th ed., pp. 290–91, is one account of this bigotry.
5. Ann Gomer Sunahara, *The Politics of Racism: The Uprooting of Japanese Canadians during the Second World War* (Toronto: Lorimer, 1981).
6. Alain Pelletier, "Politics and Ethnicity: Representation of Ethnic and Visible Minority Groups in the House of Commons," in K. Megyery, ed., *Ethnocultural Groups and Visible Minorities in Canadian Politics: The Question of Access* (Toronto: Dundurn Press, 1991), p. 127.
7. Constance Backhouse, *Colour-Coded: A Legal History of Racism in Canada, 1900–1950* (Toronto: University of Toronto Press, 1999); John Marlyn, *Under the Ribs of Death* (Toronto: McClelland and Stewart, 1957, 1964). Debra Thompson asks why racism has received so little academic examination in Canadian political science in "Is Race Political?" *Canadian Journal of Political Science* (September 2008).
8. Kelly Tran, "Visible Minorities in the Labour Force: 20 Years of Change," *Canadian Social Trends* (Statistics Canada, Catalogue No. 11-008, Summer 2004); and Boris Palameta, "Low Income among Immigrants and Visible Minorities," *Perspectives on Labour and Income* (Statistics Canada, Catalogue No. 75-001-XPE, Summer 2004).
9. Wallis, et al., *Colonialism and Racism in Canada: Historical Traces and Contemporary Issues*, p. 1.
10. Many observers also feel that the policy of multiculturalism was a means of undercutting any recognition of Quebec's distinct culture or distinct status.
11. Prime Minister's Statement in the House of Commons, October 8, 1971; and Andrew Cardozo and Louis Musto, eds., *The Battle over Multiculturalism: Does It Help or Hinder Canadian Unity?* (Ottawa: PSI Publishing, 1997).
12. The most philosophical (but still very readable) discussion of multiculturalism in Canada can be found in the writings of Will Kymlicka, such as *Finding Our Way: Rethinking Ethnocultural Relations in Canada* (Don Mills: Oxford University Press, 1998).
13. Daiva Stasiulis, "Deep Diversity: Race and Ethnicity in Canadian Politics," in M.S. Whittington and G. Williams, eds., *Canadian Politics in the 1990s*, 4th ed. (Scarborough: Nelson Canada, 1995), p. 209.
14. Leslie Pal, *Interests of State: The Politics of Language, Multiculturalism, and Feminism in Canada* (Montreal: McGill-Queen's University Press, 1993).
15. Wallis, et al., *Colonialism and Racism in Canada: Historical Traces and Contemporary Issues*, Part Four.
16. Delphine Nakache and Paula J. Kinoshita, *The Canadian Temporary Foreign Worker Program: Do Short-Term Economic Needs Prevail over Human Rights Concerns?* (Montreal: Institute for Research on Public Policy, 2010).
17. *Multani v. Commission scolaire Marguerite-Bourgeoys*, [2006] 1 S.C.R. 256.
18. Garnett Picot and Arthur Sweetman, *Making It in Canada: Immigration Outcomes and Policies* (Montreal: Institute for Research on Public Policy, 2012).

19. Mohammed Al-Waqfi and Harish C. Jain, "Racial inequality in employment in Canada: Empirical analysis and emerging trends," *Canadian Public Administration* (September 2008).
20. Stasiulis and Abu-Laban, "Unequal Relations," 6th ed., p. 371.
21. Trudeau Foundation, "The Making of Citizens: A National Survey of Canadians," available at http://www.trudeaufounation.ca/resource/public/conferen/2011-the-making-of-citizens-beyond-the-canadian-co/opinion-poll, accessed on April 29, 2012.
22. Audrey Macklin and Francois Crépeau, *Multiple Citizenship, Identity and Entitlement in Canada* (Montreal: Institute for Research on Public Policy, 2010).
23. Stasiulis and Abu-Laban, "Unequal Relations," 7th ed., p. 299.
24. Jerome H. Black and Lynda Erickson, "Ethno-Racial Origins of Candidates and Electoral Performance: Evidence from Canada," *Party Politics* 12, 4 (2006): 541–61.
25. Stasiulis and Abu-Laban, "Unequal Relations and the Struggle for Equality," 7th ed., p. 298.
26. Public Policy Forum, *Edging Toward Diversity: A Statistical Breakdown of Canada's 41st Parliament, with Comparisons to the 40th Parliament*, June 2011, available at http://www.ppforum.ca/sites/default/files/edging_towards_diversity_final.pdf.
27. Andrew Griffith, "Big Shift or Big Return? Visible Minority Representation in the 2015 Election." https://multiculturalmeanderings.wordpress.com/2016/03/05/big-shift-or-big-return-visible-minority-representation-in-the-2015-election/.

FURTHER READING

Abu-Laban, Yasmeen, and Christina Gabriel. *Selling Diversity: Immigration, Multiculturalism, Employment Equity, and Globalization.* Peterborough: Broadview Press, 2002.

Backhouse, Constance. *Colour-Coded: A Legal History of Racism in Canada, 1900–1950.* Toronto: University of Toronto Press, 1999.

Bissoondath, Neil. *Selling Illusions: The Cult of Multiculturalism in Canada.* Toronto: Penguin, 1994.

Black, Jerome H., and Lynda Erickson. "Ethno-Racial Origins of Candidates and Electoral Performance: Evidence from Canada," *Party Politics* 12, 4 (2006): 541–61.

Cardozo, Andrew, and Louis Musto, eds. *The Battle over Multiculturalism: Does It Help or Hinder Canadian Unity?* Ottawa: PSI Publishing, 1997.

Citizenship and Immigration Canada. *Discover Canada: The Rights and Responsibilities of Citizenship: Study Guide*, 2011, available at http://www.cic.gc.ca/english/resources/publications/discover/index.asp.

Day, Richard J.F. *Multiculturalism and the History of Canadian Diversity.* Toronto: University of Toronto Press, 2000.

James, Carl, ed. *Possibilities and Limitations: Multicultural Policies and Programs in Canada.* Black Point, NS: Fernwood Publishing, 2005.

Kelley, Ninette, and Michael Trebilcock. *The Making of the Mosaic: A History of Canadian Immigration Policy.* Toronto: University of Toronto Press, 1998.

Kernerman, Gerald. *Multicultural Nationalism: Civilizing Difference, Constituting Community.* Vancouver: UBC Press, 2005.

Kymlicka, Will. *Finding Our Way: Rethinking Ethnocultural Relations in Canada.* Don Mills: Oxford University Press, 1998.

Pal, Leslie. *Interests of State: The Politics of Language, Multiculturalism, and Feminism in Canada.* Montreal: McGill-Queen's University Press, 1993.

Pratt, Anna. *Securing Borders: Detention and Deportation in Canada.* Vancouver: UBC Press, 2005.

Stasiulis, Daiva. "Unequal Relations and the Struggle for Equality: Race and Ethnicity in Canadian Politics." In Michael Whittington and Glen Williams, eds., *Canadian Politics in the 21st Century*, 7th ed. Toronto: Nelson Education, 2008.

Stoffman, Daniel. *Who Gets In: What's Wrong with Canada's Immigration Program—and How to Fix It.* Toronto: Macfarlane Walter Ross, 2002.

Sunahara, Ann Gomer. *The Politics of Racism: The Uprooting of Japanese Canadians during the Second World War.* Toronto: Lorimer, 1981.

Troper, Harold, and Morton Weinfeld. *Ethnicity, Politics and Public Policy.* Toronto: University of Toronto Press, 1999.

Wallis, Maria A., Lina Sunseri, and Grace-Edward Galabuzi. *Colonialism and Racism in Canada: Historical Traces and Contemporary Issues.* Toronto: Nelson Education, 2010.

CHAPTER 7

Gender

Feminists seek gender equality—employment equity, pay equity, equity in law, equity in the various institutions of government, and equity in the family setting. Not all women agree on all these demands, however, and a large proportion of men support these goals. Gender issues have created considerable political controversy and are of increasing significance. Women are taking an increasing role in the economic and political systems, though despite the significant step of Prime Minister Justin Trudeau naming a cabinet with 50 percent females, the proportion of women prominent in Canadian politics and government remains far below this figure. Abortion, divorce, child care, labour, reproduction issues, sexual harassment, and sexual assault are major societal concerns. Beyond the equality of women are other gender and sexual-orientation issues concerning the LGBT (Lesbian, Gay, Bisexual, Transgender) community.

This chapter begins by looking at certain theoretical considerations regarding gender, before outlining the historical evolution of women's rights in Canada. It then examines issues relating to the women's movement today, which has brought a new set of demands onto the political agenda. After discussing the contemporary manifestations of such issues, the chapter concludes with some of the issues that continue to face the gay, lesbian, and transgender communities.

THEORETICAL CONSIDERATIONS

Gender is more than meets the eye. Although the concepts of gender and sex are closely related, the distinction that is usually made between them is that sex refers to biological differences, while gender refers to the behavioural, cultural, or psychological traits associated with one's sex; it is socially and politically constructed.[1] Social structures—traditions, customs, practices, and institutions—are important in determining how individual members of society see themselves and behave. Such structures help form our identities, and the concept of gender is based in that identity.

We all have multiple identities, and those most important to us can change over time. Because other identities overshadowed gender for much of the first 100 years after

Confederation, "farm women, working women, French-Canadian women, Protestant women, western women, [and] city women had quite different collective identities following from the ways in which class, religion, and place entwined in Canadian politics. There was no single identity, nor was there a single women's politics."[2] One of the main forces behind the whole discussion of identity politics in the past 40 years or so, however, has been the women's movement, as women increasingly put a priority on gender in determining their identity. As women became conscious of their differences from men in the political system—as well as their exclusion from it—they began to emphasize gender politics and the politics of recognition. Of course, women were not all agreed on their interests—ideological differences among them remained—but they did share a new consciousness that their gender was important. This movement also broadened the idea of what is "political." The feminist movement argued that traditional male definitions of politics are too narrow; for example, men had overlooked aspects of the political system in which women had been significant participants: community groups, charities, and other informal local networks.[3]

This focus upon achieving gender equality in turn alerted us to different conceptions of equality. Policies that provide for formal gender equality usually seem desirable, but they may result in outcomes that do not achieve substantive equality. Feminists point out that in certain situations, women may have to be treated differently from men in order to achieve true equality.

EVOLUTION OF WOMEN'S RIGHTS TO 1970

Men and male-oriented issues virtually monopolized Canadian politics pre-1900. In those early years, women had to fight for educational and occupational rights, such as admission to universities and to the medical and legal professions.[4] This battle was led by the first prominent feminist, Dr. Emily Stowe, who in 1880 was the first female to practice medicine in Canada. The first female lawyer was admitted to the bar in 1897. Women later demanded the right to make contracts and to own property, and increasingly began to work in factories and offices, to become teachers and nurses, and to make major contributions on the farm. At the turn of the century, farm women in particular became active in reform organizations of many kinds, pressing for the prohibition of alcohol, the establishment of new public health facilities, better housing, and improved working conditions for women and children.

As influential as they were in promoting these causes, women still lacked a key form of power—the vote. Thus, in what is sometimes called the "first wave" of a transnational women's movement, women demanded the franchise. This issue aroused great conflict between those who saw women primarily as wives and mothers, whose influence could be best exercised within the home, and those who felt that women should be treated as equals of men in the wider society.

After the outbreak of the First World War, proponents of female suffrage argued that women should be rewarded for their contribution to the war effort. Thus, after the vociferous efforts of some of the most articulate women of the day, Manitoba, Alberta, and Saskatchewan extended the right to vote in provincial elections to women in 1916; Ontario and British Columbia followed suit a year later; and all the jurisdictions except Quebec and the Northwest Territories shortly afterward. The first women legislators in the British Commonwealth, Louise McKinney and Roberta MacAdams, were elected in Alberta in 1917, and were replaced in 1921 by Nellie McClung and Irene Parlby. Mary Ellen Smith was elected to the British Columbia legislature in 1918 and became the first Canadian female cabinet minister in 1921.

At the federal level, the Borden government deliberately manipulated the franchise for the 1917 election, in part by giving the vote to women in the armed services (mostly nurses) and to close relatives of soldiers fighting abroad—women who would likely support the war effort. With no adverse effects, the vote was extended a year later to all women, and they had their first chance to exercise this new right in the 1921 election.

Many reforms in social legislation took place immediately after the enfranchisement of women. These included mothers' allowances, child welfare acts, the prohibition of child labour, and an increase in the age for compulsory schooling and at which marriage could be solemnized within a province. At the federal level, the divorce law was amended to establish "equality of cause" between wife and husband, and the Old Age Pensions Act was passed.[5] These reforms and other advances were achieved only after constant pressure: organizing women's groups; writing leaflets, plays, and letters to the editor; engaging in demonstrations and debates; and lobbying politicians. Yet, although the right to vote entailed the right to hold office (except in New Brunswick until 1934), very few women were actually elected.

In 1921 Agnes Macphail was the first woman elected to the House of Commons. But it was not until 1935 that a second woman, Martha Black, was elected. Macphail stayed on until 1940 and then became one of the first two women elected to the Ontario legislature in 1943. A vigorous and articulate legislator, Macphail promoted radical and progressive causes of many kinds, but she could only do so much by herself to advance women's issues in such an entrenched male bastion.[6]

The five most eastern provinces were slower to elect women, as Table 7.1 indicates. It was not until 1940 that Quebec women were enfranchised in provincial elections, largely as a result of the determined leadership of Thérèse Casgrain and after 13 previous bills to this effect were defeated. Even worse, the legal status of married women under the Quebec Civil Code was such that until 1955 a woman could not seek a separation on the grounds

Agnes Macphail, the first female Member of Parliament in Canada.

CHAPTER 7 **Gender** **139**

TABLE 7.1   WOMEN'S FRANCHISE AND FIRST WOMAN ELECTED

	FRANCHISE	FIRST WOMAN ELECTED
CANADA	1917–18	1921
MANITOBA	1916	1920
ALBERTA	1916	1917
SASKATCHEWAN	1916	1919
BRITISH COLUMBIA	1917	1918
ONTARIO	1917	1943
NOVA SCOTIA	1918	1960
NEW BRUNSWICK	1919	1967
YUKON	1919	1967
NEWFOUNDLAND	1925	1975
QUEBEC	1940	1961
NORTHWEST TERRITORIES	1951	1970

Sources: Penney Kome, Women of Influence: Canadian Women and Politics *(Toronto: University of Toronto Press, 1985); Terence H. Qualter,* The Electoral Process in Canada *(Toronto: McGraw-Hill Ryerson, 1970).*

of her husband's adultery, and until 1964 had no right to carry on a trade without her husband's consent.[7]

The number of women who won seats in the House of Commons before 1970 was minuscule: usually only one per election and never more than four. Indeed, many of the pre-1970 female MPs were the widows or daughters of male members of Parliament. Female participation at the candidate level was inhibited by many factors. First, both sexes were traditionally socialized into the view that politics was a masculine pursuit and that women should remain in the home. Second, most women were constrained by the responsibilities of homemaking and child-rearing. Such roles had little prestige and prevented women from accumulating the money, contacts, and experience that political careers usually require. The long hours and unpredictable schedules of politicians conflicted with most women's family commitments, which prevented them from being away from home for any length of time, and at least delayed a woman's entry into active politics. Third, political parties discouraged female candidacies, however much they needed women at the constituency level to raise money and stuff envelopes. Most parties set up a separate women's auxiliary organization rather than encourage their participation in the mainstream of the party, and generally felt that it was safer to nominate a male as their candidate. Figure 7.1 shows how few women were elected to the House of Commons before 1970.

FIGURE 7.1 PERCENTAGE OF WOMEN ELECTED TO THE HOUSE OF COMMONS, 1921–2015

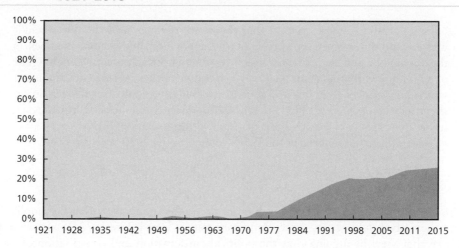

Sources: Prepared by authors based on Andrew Heard, Women Candidates, Canadian Federal Elections, 1921–2011, http://www.sfu.ca/~aheard/elections/women-elected.html; 2015 data from CBC News, The new House of Commons: More women and aboriginal MPs (Oct 21, 2015), http://www.cbc.ca/news/politics/multimedia/the-new-house-of-commons-more-women-and-aboriginal-mps-1.3280256.

Until the late 1920s, no women had been appointed to the other house of Parliament—the Senate. When an enterprising group of Western women took this issue to court, the Supreme Court of Canada ruled in 1928 that women were not eligible for such appointment. In 1929 this decision was appealed to the Judicial Committee of the Privy Council, which in the **Persons case** overruled the Supreme Court and declared women to be "qualified persons" within the meaning of section 24 of the 1867 Constitution Act and eligible to sit in the Senate. The women's movement continues to celebrate this decision in the form of the "Persons Day Breakfast." Prime Minister Mackenzie King immediately appointed Cairine Wilson to the Senate, but even here progress was slow. The second woman was not appointed until 1935, and 18 years would pass before three more received the call.

It was not until 1957 that the first woman, Ellen Fairclough, was appointed to the federal Cabinet, by John Diefenbaker; she was followed by Judy LaMarsh in 1963. The advance of women to the cabinet at the provincial level was also very slow. However, women were frequently elected to mayoralty posts and were often the backbone of quasi-political community organizations.[8]

Nevertheless, gradual improvements continued to be made in federal and provincial programs and legislation. The federal Family Allowances Act of 1944, for example, provided a small monthly payment to each Canadian mother to help care for her children and often represented the only independent income the woman possessed. In 1952 Ontario passed the first equal pay legislation, to be followed by federal legislation two years later. The invention of the birth control pill in 1960 led to profound changes in many women's lives; amendments to the Criminal Code in 1969 allowed the advertisement of birth control devices in Canada; and a new Divorce Act in the same year made it easier for people to end a marriage.

BOX 7.1   VOICES

"Their Lordships are of opinion that the word 'persons' in s. 24 does include women, and that women are eligible to be summoned to and become members of the Senate of Canada. ... The exclusion of women from all public offices is a relic of days more barbarous than ours. ... Customs are apt to develop into traditions which are stronger than law and remain unchallenged long after the reason for them has disappeared. ... The British North America Act planted in Canada a living tree capable of growth and expansion within its natural limits."

The Judicial Committee of the Privy Council in the 1930 "Persons Case"

This discussion of the advance of women in the formal political system has implied that women themselves did not play a very significant role, at least before 1970. Modern feminists challenge that view by arguing that the political participation and contribution of women should be seen in a broader light. They may have been scarce in the corridors of power, but they were active and important in "small-p" politics, often called "civil society" or organizations distinct from the family, state, and economy. This includes charities, nongovernmental organizations, community groups, women's groups, faith-based organizations, professional associations, unions, self-help groups, social movements, business associations, coalitions, and advocacy groups. As Jaquetta Newman argues, "we need to recognize these groups as *political*, not just social, actors. Their social networks and activism do not just 'lead to' politics, but expand its definition."[9]

CRITICAL APPROACHES

Although *feminist approaches* were not mentioned in Chapter 1, they certainly exist in the discipline of political science and are most relevant here. Such approaches question many underlying assumptions about and misrepresentations of women, and point out how the construction of gender results from traditional practices in families, schools, and churches, and are reinforced by the mass media.[10] Men were the main players in the early political system, as well as the analysts and interpreters of that system; men made the decisions, and they defined what politics was all about. Beyond the concern about the basic inequality of women in society, however, feminist approaches take many different forms.

The *historical-institutional* and *state-based* approaches explain the lack of action on women's issues before 1970 by the fact that women were largely excluded from the whole formal political system by the construction of governmental institutions, societal norms, and composition of the Cabinet and bureaucracy. The Judicial Committee of the Privy Council decision on whether women were "persons" is an illustration of an overdue and dramatic change. These approaches draw attention to the fact that women were traditionally excluded from political power because they bore a disproportionate share of the responsibility for housework and childcare. It is worth noting in this context that the countries with the highest proportion of women in elected office tend to have the most generous government childcare programs.

THE WOMEN'S MOVEMENT AFTER 1970

By 1970 attitudes toward women and their role in society had changed sufficiently that it was now possible to speak of the **women's movement**, and the word **feminist** came into common usage. Such terms describe those who seek to establish complete gender equality, to free all people from restrictive gender roles, and to end the subordination of certain genders. However, within the women's movement a variety of perspectives exist, and feminism can take various forms. As mentioned, there was even a call to "reinvent" the discipline of political science along feminist lines and to examine women's political participation in nontraditional forums. Moreover, it was shown that in such settings as the televised leaders' debate, the presence of a woman leader can make a difference.[11]

This "second wave" of the women's movement coincided with similar developments in other Western countries and the **Royal Commission on the Status of Women**, which had been appointed in 1967 and reported in 1970. That report "provided a solid statistical base and a framework for most of the feminist action that followed during the 1970s."[12] The Royal Commission made 167 recommendations, not all of which have been implemented. Since that time, though, gender issues have become an important and regular factor in politics, and most governments now designate a minister responsible for women's issues, beginning at the federal level in 1971. In 1972 the federal government established the Office of Employment Opportunity, followed by the Canadian Advisory Council on the Status of Women in 1973; the first federal–provincial conference on women's issues was convened in 1982, and in 1995 Ottawa issued the Federal Plan for Gender Equality. This plan committed the government to applying gender-based analysis in the development of all new legislation, policies, and programs. A major part of Status of Women Canada, a government agency, was the Women's Program, which supported the work of organizations promoting women's full participation in Canadian society, though funding cuts since 2006 have limited those organizations' work and forced some to close.

Representation in Politics and Government

In the post-1970 era, women's participation in politics and government increased substantially. Table 7.2 shows the increase in the number and proportion of women in the House of Commons in this period. Many of the factors that inhibited women from becoming politicians before

TABLE 7.2   REPRESENTATION OF WOMEN IN THE HOUSE OF COMMONS, 1972–2015

ELECTION	NUMBER ELECTED	PERCENTAGE OF MPs
1972	4	2
1974	9	3
1979	11	4
1980	14	5
1984	27	10
1988	39	13
1993	53	18
1997	62	21
2000	62	21
2004	65	21
2006	64	21
2008	69	22
2011	76	25
2015	88	26

Sources: Prepared by authors based on Andrew Heard, Women Candidates, Canadian Federal Elections, *1921–2011, https://www.sfu.ca/~aheard/elections/women-elected.html; 2015 data from CBC News,* The new House of Commons: More women and aboriginal MPs, *http://www.cbc.ca/news/politics/multimedia/the-new-house-of-commons-more-women-and-aboriginal-mps-1.3280256.*

1970 are still present, although in recent years some parties have created mandates and special funds to support female candidates. It is now accepted knowledge that while women may face additional barriers to party nominations, they do not face a vote disadvantage in elections themselves.

Given the decision-making powers of the Cabinet, it is probably more important for women to be included in that institution rather than in parliament alone, and by the 1980s one or two token female ministers were clearly insufficient. Brian Mulroney usually had six women in his cabinets after 1984, and the rest of the provinces and territories eventually appointed women ministers. Bob Rae came close to gender equality in his 1990 Ontario NDP cabinet, as did Jean Charest later in Quebec, and Justin Trudeau appointed a cabinet with an equal number males and females, though the proportion of women cabinet ministers has otherwise rarely exceeded that in the legislature.

In the post-1970 period Canada finally saw women elected as political party leaders. Alexa McDonough (NDP) led the way in Nova Scotia in 1980, and many women have been leaders of provincial parties since. After Rosemary Brown made a serious stab at the NDP national leadership in 1975 and Flora MacDonald for the PCs in 1976, it remained for Audrey

McLaughlin to make history when she was elected leader of the federal New Democratic Party in 1989, the first woman to lead a major national party. Alexa McDonough succeeded her in 1995, and Elizabeth May became the national Green Party leader in 2006.

In the 1990s, Canada finally had a female prime minister and two provincial premiers. Rita Johnston inherited the BC premiership from her predecessor, Bill Vander Zalm, in 1991, while Catherine Callbeck in Prince Edward Island was the first woman to be elected to premiership in 1993. Similarly to Johnston, Kim Campbell took over the federal PC leadership and prime ministership in 1993, only to lose the subsequent election to Jean Chrétien, at least partly because of the faults of her male predecessor.

Jeanne Sauvé pioneered women's political participation in several fields: she was the third federal woman Cabinet minister, the first woman Speaker of the House of Commons, and the first woman governor general (1984), followed by Adrienne Clarkson in 1999 and Michaëlle Jean in 2005. Meanwhile, Bertha Wilson became the first woman to sit on the Supreme Court of Canada in 1982. After 1989, the Supreme Court had either two or three women out of nine, until it increased to four as a result of Paul Martin's 2004 appointments. Women judges have also been appointed at an ever-increasing rate in other courts, and constitute about one-quarter of those appointed by the federal government.

Within the federal bureaucracy, the first women joined the RCMP in 1974, and the first woman deputy minister (Sylvia Ostry) was appointed in 1975; in the 1980s, women became eligible for full combat roles in the armed forces, and the first woman general was named in 1988. In 1993, Jocelyn Bourgon became the first woman to hold the top public service position in Ottawa, Clerk of the Privy Council and Secretary to the Cabinet. Women have also increased their participation in provincial and territorial government and politics beyond the positions mentioned above; many have become successful ministers of finance.[13] Despite these breakthroughs at the provincial, territorial, and federal levels in absolute numbers, however, many observers still raise the question of how much influence women actually have in the policymaking process.

Employment Issues

Since women constitute about 48 percent of the labour force, one major feminist concern is employment. Overall, some 58 percent of those over 15 years of age are part of the paid workforce, but this rate rises to 77 percent of women between the ages of 25 and 54.[14] Women have traditionally been paid less than men, underrepresented in managerial positions, and discouraged from undertaking nontraditional occupations. Demands for "equal pay for work of equal value" or **pay equity** have led to legislation at the federal level and in many provinces. By 1997 women's full-time earnings had risen to an average of about 70 percent of men's, where it plateaued, just like their political representation, and a federal task force report on pay equity in 2003 called for more vigorous legislation.

The federal government got itself embroiled in a mammoth and protracted pay equity dispute with its own clerical staff, most of whom were female, which it finally settled in late 1999 for $3.6 billion. The federal Crown corporation Canada Post was ordered to pay $150 million in a similar case, and companies within federal jurisdiction, such as Bell Canada, refused to respond to pay equity demands of their employees until ordered to do so by the courts. On the other hand, in 2004 the Supreme Court of Canada ruled that

Linamar Corporation Chief Executive Officer Linda Hasenfratz speaks during the annual general meeting of shareholders in 2010.

when the Province of Newfoundland was facing an "exceptional financial crisis" in 1991, it was justified in backtracking on a pay-equity commitment despite the equality rights provision in the Charter.[15]

Beyond pay equity is the broader subject of **employment equity**—that is, the elimination of discrimination in hiring and promotion, which is sometimes combined with **affirmative action** programs to give preference to women and other groups in order to make up for past systemic inequities. In 1980 the federal bureaucracy established a pilot project with respect to affirmative action in the hiring of women, and in 1983 affirmative action was made mandatory in all federal government departments. The 1984 *Report of the Royal Commission on Equality in Employment*, written by Rosalie Abella, became the foundation of the 1986 Employment Equity Act. This law extended employment equity requirements to all Crown corporations, all federally regulated companies with more than 100 employees, and other large companies in receipt of major government contracts. Ottawa strengthened the federal Employment Equity Act in 1995.

The area in which women are most severely underrepresented is at the top of private sector corporations, a leading cause of overall pay differentials. According to recent figures, of Canada's Top 500 companies, only 30 are led by women, three prominent current CEOs being Heather Reisman at Indigo Books and Music, Inc., Monique Leroux at the Desjardins Group, and Linda Hasenfratz at Linamar. In 2012, women held only 15.9 percent of board director positions (up from 9.8 in 2001), and in 2012, women held 18.1 percent of senior officer positions (up from 14 percent in 2002).[16] The shortage of women in senior executive positions means that the pool of female candidates for board directorships is limited. At the same time that women were generally gaining greater equality in the workplace, the predominant neoliberal ideology after 1985, along with its counterpart, globalization, often weakened government attempts to promote employment equity,[17] but Crown corporations ranked much above the private sector in having women in senior officer roles.

In 2009, 67 percent of all employed women worked in teaching, nursing and related health occupations, clerical and other administrative positions, and sales and service occupations, and constituted a majority in each field. In many of these areas, pay is relatively low and opportunities to advance are often limited. However, it should not be overlooked that women have made gains in several professional occupations: for example, women constituted 58 percent of all doctors and dentists in Canada, 53 percent of business and financial professionals, and 36 percent of the self-employed.[18] About 27 percent of women work part-time (constituting 67.5 percent of the part-time work force), sometimes by choice but often by necessity. Part-time workers generally have few benefits and little job security, and in this era of global restructuring, with companies turning even more to part-time contract workers, women usually suffer the most.

The value of work performed by women without pay is of concern to many observers but has been difficult to estimate. Economists point out that although women who work for pay contribute to government revenues by paying income taxes, women who work in the home without remuneration generally carry out a variety of functions, such as caring for the young and seniors, which reduce the demand for public services. Unpaid work in the home makes a major contribution to the economy that does not show up in traditional statistics, but according to one 1992 estimate, its value was nearly $300 billion, or 41 percent of the gross domestic product.[19] The reduction in social programs after the advent of neoliberalism only increased the burden of unpaid caregiving roles performed primarily by women.

The 1992 study found that women performed two-thirds of unpaid work, such as household maintenance, caregiving, and volunteer work (which was worth some $16 580 per year on an individual basis), and, on average, women spent almost twice as much time on housework as men. But by 2010, with the dual-income family becoming the norm, men were sharing this burden a bit more equitably.

Constitutional, Legal, and Aboriginal Women's Issues

A third category of post-1970 women's issues is related to constitutional and legal issues. The first of these was the question of equality rights in the 1982 **Charter of Rights and Freedoms**. This was especially important because the courts had made a mockery of the gender equality provision in the 1960 Bill of Rights. As the Charter emerged from federal–provincial negotiations, gender equality was to be lumped into section 15 with such other factors as race, religion, and age, which governments would be allowed to override with the notwithstanding clause. Such treatment at the hands of 11 male first ministers galvanized the women's movement as never before; as a result of pressure from women's groups, section 28 was added to the final document to give gender equality a place of its own and protection from the **notwithstanding clause**.[20]

Women thus became part of the coalition that included other Charter-based rights-bearers who used the Charter of Rights and Freedoms to advance their causes.[21] There followed a series of feminist challenges to laws that women felt discriminated against them. For example, women achieved the right to maternity leave under the Unemployment Insurance Act. Although they had mixed success in the so-called "rape-shield" cases (hoping to restrict questions about past sexual history put to defendants in a case of sexual assault), the courts agreed that "no means no" with respect to a woman's consent to sexual relations. Battered wives have been excused for murdering their offending husbands; gender discrimination in private employers' disability plans has been removed; and physical requirements that discriminate against women must be proven to be necessary for a job. The government itself encouraged such legal activity with the **Court Challenges Program** under which it subsidized the Legal Education and Action Fund (LEAF) in making such challenges. This was a continuation of Pierre Trudeau's attempt to strengthen the women's movement by funding advocacy groups.[22] Women protested when the Mulroney government cancelled the Court Challenges Program in 1992, and it was reinstated by the Chrétien administration, only to be eliminated a second time (except with respect to official language cases) by the Harper government.

On the constitutional front, in the 1987–90 period the **National Action Committee on the Status of Women (NAC)** and certain subsidiary groups actively opposed the Meech Lake Accord. Having become part of the constitutional policy community in 1982, they demanded participation in any subsequent constitutional decisions and were concerned that the accord, drawn up by 11 men, had nothing to say about women's rights. NAC was also unhappy with the Charlottetown Accord because even though the equality of men and women was reiterated in the Canada clause, it was articulated in weaker language than that of other rights. Like Aboriginals, official francophone minorities, people with disabilities, and other groups that had achieved constitutional standing in 1982, women's groups were not satisfied with subsequent constitutional documents unless their status was further reinforced.[23]

Another long-standing legal issue was that of the equality of Aboriginal women relative to Aboriginal men. A provision in the Indian Act denied Indian status to Native women who married white men, but no such loss was involved when an Indian man married a white woman. After the *Lavell* case in 1974 upheld this clause in the Indian Act, much pressure was brought to bear, including a critical decision by the Human Rights Committee of the United Nations involving Sandra Lovelace. In 1985, Bill C-31 repealed this provision, and the Indian Act was amended to restore Indian status and the right to be considered for band membership to Indian women (and their children) who had lost such status through intermarriage. A year before, the Constitution itself was amended to recognize and affirm that Aboriginal and treaty rights were guaranteed equally to male and female persons.

Reproduction, Sexuality, Health, and Violence Issues

One of the main feminist rallying cries of the post-1970 period was that women must be able to control what happens to their own bodies. Many women's organizations supported Dr. Henry Morgentaler in his long fight (including several court cases, clinic raids, and jail terms) to reform the Criminal Code's provisions on abortion. Although amendments were made in 1968, feminists did not regard these as sufficient, and the Supreme Court of Canada threw out the abortion law in the famous 1988 *Morgentaler* case.[24] The prospect of having no law at all restricting abortion was appealing to most feminists, but a sizable proportion of public opinion disagreed; in 1990 the Mulroney government introduced a compromise abortion law, which was defeated in the Senate. The Mulroney government also appointed a Royal Commission on New Reproductive Technologies, whose 1993 report endorsed a cautious approach to this controversial subject and was not turned into legislation until a decade later.

Prostitution, pornography, sexual harassment, and sexual assault are other major areas of concern to women's groups. While they universally oppose practices that exploit or demean women, some women defend the "freedom of expression" argument in discussions of pornography, and some, the "right to work" in defence of prostitution. The courts have also become engaged in these issues and ruled in 1990, for example, that the existing law against soliciting was valid as a "reasonable limit" on freedom of speech.

Also of concern are the courts' treatment of sexual assault cases, sexual harassment in the workplace, and violence against women. In one study, 50 percent of all Canadian women reported that they had experienced at least one incident of violence by a male since the age of 16, and nearly 40 percent, one incident of sexual assault.[25] Women were usually the victims in cases of spousal assault, so the federal government embarked on an initiative to combat family violence after 1988 that, among other things, contributed to the creation of shelters for battered women. By 2006, however, due to cuts by both Liberal and Conservative governments, federal funding for women's shelters had almost disappeared.[26] The "Montreal massacre" of December 1989, in which 14 female students were killed at the École Polytechnique, gave the issue of gun control a particularly feminist and Québécois perspective.

In 2014, the issues of sexual harassment and assault were thrust into the national spotlight when a CBC personality was charged with sexual assault and two sitting MPs were accused of harassment and assault by another MP. The issue exposed parliament's lack of policies for dealing with complaints by MPs, and led to committee recommendations for a new sexual harassment code.

The Feminization of Poverty and Child Care

Chapter 8 will reveal the large extent to which Canada has experienced the **feminization of poverty**. Of sole-support mothers in 1989, for example, over 50 percent lived below the poverty line. With or without a partner, large numbers of women with preschool children find it necessary to work outside the home to support themselves and their families. The Canada Child Tax Credit is designed to help poorer families with children, but provincial governments often reduce their own social assistance payments by the amount of the federal benefit so that the recipients are no further ahead. Pay equity, employment equity, higher minimum wages, increased unionization, and improved job training and literacy programs will also help decrease the incidence of women living in poverty.

One of the major unresolved "women's issues" is that of daycare for children. Many women qualify for up to a year of maternity benefits under the Employment Insurance program, but then face the difficulty of finding, let alone financing, daycare for their children. The Mulroney government introduced legislation for a national daycare program in 1988, but it fell victim to the budgetary restraints of 1989–92. A Liberal electoral promise throughout the 1990s also went unfulfilled until the Martin government negotiated individualized childcare agreements with each province and territory to provide significant funding in this field. But it was not a true national daycare program, and only Quebec's $5-a-day childcare (later raised to $7.00, then $7.30, and now includes higher rates based on income) approached a standard that daycare advocates would find adequate. Even in Quebec, however, there are more children that need daycare than the number of subsidized spaces available for them. Nearly 65 percent of mothers with children under the age of three are currently in the workforce, and nearly 70 percent with children between three and five years of age,[27] yet only a fraction of these mothers are able to find licensed full-time daycare spaces. Rather than work toward a national system of childcare spaces, the Harper Conservatives cancelled the Liberals' federal–provincial deals and began to pay families $1200 annually per child and let them find their own solutions.

Women's Centres and Women's Groups

Many women's centres were established in the 1980s, financed by federal and/or provincial governments. Although such centres primarily served as support and referral agencies for battered wives and others seeking help, they also promoted a variety of other women's causes, such as abortion law reform. The Mulroney government cut the budget for such centres in 1989 and 1990, but then restored some of the funding after a vehement protest. With the demise of the Canada Assistance Plan under the Liberals in 1996, funding for women's centres and many other services for women were cancelled, while others were discontinued by the Harper government.

In 1973, the federal government set up the Canadian Advisory Council on the Status of Women in response to the Royal Commission on the Status of Women. But a year before, it was the inaction of the government that led to the establishment of the foremost women's advocacy group in Canada, the National Action Committee on the Status of Women (NAC). At its height, NAC functioned as an umbrella lobbying group for more than 700 local and national member groups representing more than three million women. An indication of its importance and of politicians' consciousness of the female vote was the separate televised leaders' debate held on women's issues in 1984 and sponsored by NAC.[30]

Michael Maslin/The New Yorker Collection/ The Cartoon Bank

"The problem? The problem is that, for every rock I earn doing the same work as you, you earn two rocks."

Because it was less sympathetic to NAC and affiliated groups than the Trudeau regime had been, and because it anticipated criticism of its cutbacks, the Mulroney government refused to attend NAC's annual meetings in 1989 and 1990. It even began to fund the rival organization, REAL (Realistic, Equal, Active for Life) Women, which was founded in 1984 and opposed all feminist demands. When Ottawa changed the method of distributing grant money to women's groups to a project-by-project basis in 1998–99, NAC complained that the Chrétien government was treating it even more disrespectfully than the Conservatives had done. The organization has ceased to play any significant role, and while it attempted a renewal in the mid-2000s, it appears to have since disappeared.

CONTEMPORARY ISSUES

Few of the issues discussed above have been fully resolved, either in Canada or other countries, and most remain on the political agenda. But once progress was made on some of these questions, a third wave of the feminist movement was detected from about 1995 onward. While still concerned about "second-wave" problems, that "third wave" widened the feminist agenda to some extent and emphasized new and different issues, such that its focus is not as clear-cut as previously. While not all women agreed with all of the items on the "second-wave" agenda, it would be unreasonable to expect any greater unanimity on a more diffuse approach.

As suggested above, some critics of second-wave feminism argued that the women's movement of that era was mostly centred on white, middle-class women. As in the example of NAC, less affluent and visible minority women sought to refocus the debate on issues of their own. In other cases, third-wave feminism was concerned with celebrating sexuality in general, as well as in non-heterosexual forms, and had an increased global concern—problems of sexism, racism, and poverty around the world. The Internet was a valuable tool with which to combat such widespread problems.

Still, the old issues continued to resurface. For example, while abortion remains a prominent political problem in the United States, Canada is one of the few countries in the world without legal restrictions on the procedure, and the federal government tends to avoid the issue. Nevertheless, when the Harper government emphasized child and maternal health abroad, its exclusion of abortion from such programs raised much controversy. Further, access to abortion is highly limited in some regions, especially in Atlantic Canada, and PEI has no abortion providers at all.

In 2013 the Supreme Court of Canada deemed parts of Canada's law regarding prostitution unconstitutional. While prostitution itself was legal, various behaviours surrounding it remain illegal in the new law passed in 2014; there is some confusion as to how it can be legally practiced, and critics argue the new laws do not make work safer for those who engage in it.

On the issue of remuneration, the Harper government slipped a provision into the 2009 budget that took pay equity away from the jurisdiction of the Canadian Human Rights Commission and put it into the collective bargaining process, a move most women regarded as regressive. Moreover, the Harper government's cancellation of the mandatory long-form Census for 2011 and its replacement with a voluntary survey meant that the quantity and quality of data about women would be significantly reduced. On the other hand, the percentage of sole-support mothers who live below the low-income cut-off, commonly accepted as the poverty line, declined to about 21 percent.[31]

In the new century, somewhat encouraging signs also emerged of increased representation of women in government. For example, by 2011 women occupied 45 percent of executive jobs and constituted nearly 55 percent of the federal government work force.[32] In fact, it has been seriously suggested that because women are doing so well in the federal public service in both numbers and influence, they no longer need to be included as a category in the Employment Equity Act.

Since 2008, Canada has seen females as premier of five provinces and one territory, including premiers Christy Clark of British Columbia, Kathleen Wynne of Ontario, and most recently Rachel Notley of Alberta. Meanwhile, Table 7.3 reveals the number and percent of women candidates and women MPs in the 2015 federal election. The figures show marginal improvements in both areas, with a particular jump in the number of women candidates and women elected by the NDP—in both cases over 40 percent.

Beyond the question of candidates, political scientists are particularly interested in the behaviour of women voters. As mentioned in Chapter 15, women have traditionally been slightly more likely than men to prefer the Liberals and NDP to the Conservative party. Studies have shown that compared to men, women are less supportive of individualism and market forces, more supportive of social programs to help those in need, more resistant to the use of force, and more tolerant of new lifestyles and changing values.

During the 2015 election, some surveys found notable differences in the party preferences of women and men, in contrast to a less pronounced difference in 2011. It is possible this was due to variation in attention on certain issues, or in part due to stronger efforts by the NDP and Liberals to field female candidates and a Liberal pledge to have a gender-balanced Cabinet. Whatever the case, Elisabeth Gidengil's research has previously suggested that greater variation exists among women voters in terms of race and class than in general between women and men, though it is possible this depends in part on the positions taken by parties at election time.[33]

TABLE 7.3   WOMEN CANDIDATES AND MPs IN THE 2015 FEDERAL ELECTION

PARTY	WOMEN CANDIDATES	%	WOMEN MPs	%
NDP	145	43	18	42
LIBERAL	105	31	50	27
CONSERVATIVE	68	20	17	17
BQ	22	28	2	20
GREEN	131	39	1	100
TOTAL	471	33	88	26

Sources: Equal Voice, "Despite Dramatic Results, No Meaningful Change in the Percentage of Women Elected to Parliament," http://us7.campaign-archive2.com/?u=edc96b30d97838f2d42e39fdf&id=cb1402fbdb&e= 57aa973747; Equal Voice, Percentage of Women Candidates, http://www.equalvoice.ca/speaks.cfm; and Huffington Post, Canada Election 2015: Number Of Female Candidates Goes Up Since 2011, http://www .huffingtonpost.ca/2015/09/30/almost-1-800-candidates-from-23-parties-on-ballot-only-one-third-are -women_n_8224034.html.

GAY, LESBIAN, AND TRANSGENDER ISSUES AND IDENTITIES

Perhaps on no other issue has Canadian public opinion changed more drastically over the past 30 years than on the question of sexual orientation. Canadian public opinion about homosexuality has been transformed from the early 1980s—where hostile attitudes were the norm—to today, where gays and lesbians have access to the same legal rights to marry as all other Canadians. Even so, a number of concerns still confront the gay, lesbian, and transgender communities, not the least of which is the bullying toward, and lack of acceptance for, these groups.

The change in public opinion towards gays and lesbians has happened in a wide range of countries across the world, but nowhere as much as in Canada. Figure 7.2 tracks these changes across time. In 1981, fully 51 percent of Canadians felt that homosexuality was "never justifiable," a figure that fell by more than half, to 20 percent, in 2005. This change is larger than any other opinion shift recorded by the World Values Survey over this timeframe.

As demands began to be made by the gay and lesbian communities, politicians occasionally responded—and a few even admitted to being gay—but recognition was primarily reached through the courts.[34] One of the first demands in this area was for protection from individual discrimination in human rights codes; that is, to prevent discrimination in the private sector, such as in hiring or accommodation. Quebec was the first province to enact legislation prohibiting discrimination on the grounds of **sexual orientation**. The federal government was among the laggards in this area, not adding such a clause to the federal Human Rights Act until 1996.

When the Charter of Rights was adopted in 1982, section 15 on equality rights prohibited discrimination by government or in law on the basis of sex. Although sexual orientation was not explicitly included, the Supreme Court of Canada decided unanimously in the 1995 *Egan* case that the section did indeed include sexual orientation. In 1998, the Supreme Court reaffirmed that the Charter included sexual orientation, ruling in the *Vriend* case that

FIGURE 7.2 PERCENT OF CANADIANS EXPRESSING STRONG OPPOSITION TO HOMOSEXUALITY ("NEVER JUSTIFIABLE"), 1981–2005

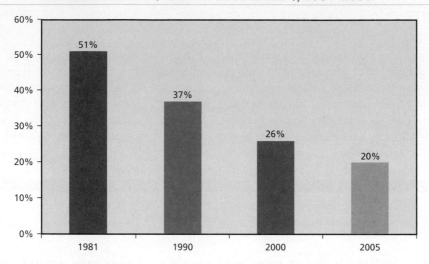

Source: World Values Survey (Canada), 1981, 1990, 2000, 2005, http://www.worldvaluessurvey.org.

this be added to the Alberta Individual Rights Protection Act.[35] Thus, by the late 1990s, whether by legislation or court decision, sexual orientation had been added to all the human rights codes in Canada. Meanwhile, it was only with difficulty in 1995 that Justice Minister Allan Rock was able to increase sentences for those convicted of committing hate crimes, including crimes against homosexuals.

The next phase of the battle for equality in this area centred on gay and lesbian couples. In 1998 the Ontario Court of Appeal recognized same-sex survivor pension benefits in the *Rosenberg* case, and many employers in both the public and the private sectors extended employee benefits (health, dental, and retirement plans, and so on) to same-sex couples. In the *M. v. H* case in 1999, the Supreme Court outlawed the clause in the Ontario Family Law Act that restricted financial support to opposite-sex spouses after separation from their partner.[36] Henceforth a same-sex spouse could apply for such support just as in any common-law relationship. About the same time, the federal government passed pension legislation that granted survivor benefits to the gay and lesbian partners of its own employees and also withdrew objections to gays and lesbians receiving survivor benefits under the Canada Pension Plan.

Based on this case and subsequent pressure, the federal and most provincial governments introduced omnibus legislation in the 1999–2002 period to remove discrimination against same-sex unions. Thus, in a giant leap forward, same-sex couples are now treated equally with heterosexual couples in most aspects of the law. The 2001 census included a question on same-sex partners for the first time, and the 2002 changes to the Immigration Act included a gender-neutral clause.[37]

The most recent issue that arises in the gay and lesbian communities relates to same-sex marriage. In 1999, parliament voted to uphold the traditional definition of marriage as a union between a man and a woman, though an Angus Reid poll indicated that more than 50 percent of Canadians were supportive of same-sex marriage. Meanwhile, Quebec passed pioneering legislation in 2002 to extend full parental rights to same-sex couples in the province. Under a "civil union," they would have the same status and obligations, including adoption rights, as heterosexual couples. Then, in 2003, in the case of *Halpern v. Canada (Attorney General)*, the Ontario Court of Appeal ruled that the ban on same-sex marriage was discriminatory and unconstitutional as a violation of **equality rights**, and ordered the immediate recognition of such marriages. Between 2004 and 2005, virtually all provincial and territorial appeal courts made decisions similar to that of Ontario. When Prime Minister Chrétien referred the issue to the Supreme Court in the *Reference re Same-Sex Marriage*, the judges generally agreed with these lower court decisions and upheld the proposed legislation.[38] Despite the Supreme Court ruling, Parliamentary debate was bitterly divided. A slightly amended law (Bill C-38) was passed in July 2005, and a large majority in 2006 voted against reopening the issue. Then, in 2011, the Canadian citizenship guide was revised to include the following statement: "Canada's diversity includes gay and lesbian Canadians, who enjoy the full protection of and equal treatment under the law, including access to civil marriage."[39]

Transgender issues also remain prominent in Canada, with bullying, discrimination, and police treatment of trans persons often making national headlines. A private members' bill introduced by NDP MP Randall Garrison that would have prohibited discrimination based on gender identity or gender expression was passed by the House of Commons in 2013. However, amendments made by the Senate held up the bill, and it did not pass into law before the 2015 election.

CONCLUSION

Although women's issues have been on the political agenda at least since the turn of the 20th century, today's politicians must pay much more attention to gender questions than ever before. Increased participation by women in the work force and in society in general has created dramatic changes in the political system. This chapter has shown that, although the record is mixed in the post-1970 period, women have made immense progress overall. By the start of the 21st century, the movement broadened out, and one of the main obstacles to further progress included the fiscal restraint practised by all governments. "Dismantling the state" was not generally good for the furthering of women's equality, which often depended on deliberate government intervention. The increasing number and proportion of women in influential positions, however, should guarantee that advances will be made in the future. At the same time, the gay and lesbian communities have recently experienced many victories in their struggle for equality, although most of their successes have so far been achieved in the courts.

Concerns about women's political involvement and representation reappear in Chapters 15 (election campaigns) and 23 (Parliament). The general feminization of poverty is discussed in Chapter 8 (class). The representation of women in the bureaucracy and judiciary are revisited in Chapters 22 (bureaucracy) and 24 (judiciary). There has been little improvement in other areas of concern to the feminist movement, and that movement continues to suffer from weakened advocacy groups as noted in Chapter 16. Legal issues relating to both women and the gay and lesbian communities primarily resurface in Chapter 19, which discusses the Charter of Rights and Freedoms.

DISCUSSION QUESTIONS

1. Are you personally affected by the gender cleavages and identities discussed in this chapter? If so, how?

2. How do you explain the increase in women's collective self-consciousness over the past 40 years?

3. To what extent should the private sector adopt employment equity programs?

4. Should government take responsibility for public daycare programs?

5. How far should governments go in ensuring equal treatment for "non-traditional" sexual orientation and gender identities?

MindTap®   FOR MORE INFO GO TO http://www.nelson.com/student

NOTES

1. Jacquetta Newman and Linda White, *Women, Politics, and Public Policy: The Political Struggles of Canadian Women* (Don Mills, ON: Oxford University Press, 2012), p. 12.
2. Jane Jenson, "Wearing Your Adjectives Proudly: Citizenship and Gender in Turn-of-the Century Canada," *Canadian Political Science Association* (May 1990), p. 12.
   For more information go to http://www.canadianpolitics7e.nelson.com
3. Jacquetta Newman, "Small-p Politics: Women Working Outside Formal Political Structures," in Mark Charlton and Paul Barker, *Crosscurrents: Contemporary Political Issues,* 7th ed. (Toronto: Nelson Education, 2013). On the related subject of social capital, see Elisabeth Gidengil and Brenda O'Neill, eds., *Gender and Social Capital* (New York: Routledge, 2006).
4. Status of Women Canada, *Toward Equality for Women—A Canadian Chronology,* 1993; Jean Cochrane, *Women in Canadian Politics* (Toronto: Fitzhenry & Whiteside, 1977); Penney Kome, *Women of Influence* (Toronto: University of Toronto Press, 1985); Janine Brodie, *Women and Politics in Canada* (Toronto: McGraw-Hill Ryerson, 1985); Linda Kealey and Joan Sangster, eds., *Beyond the Vote: Canadian Women and Politics* (Toronto: University of Toronto Press, 1989); and Sandra Burt, Lorraine Code, and Lindsay Dorney, eds., *Changing Patterns: Women in Canada* (Toronto: McClelland and Stewart, 1988).
5. Royal Commission on the Status of Women, *Report* (Ottawa: 1970), p. 338.
6. Doris Pennington, *Agnes Macphail, Reformer: Canada's First Female M.P.* (Toronto: Simon & Pierre, 1989); and Terry Crowley, *Agnes Macphail and the Politics of Equality* (Toronto: Lorimer, 1990).
7. Micheline D. Johnson, *History of the Status of Women in the Province of Quebec,* Background study for the Royal Commission on the Status of Women (Ottawa, 1968), p. 49.
8. Janine Brodie, *Women and Politics in Canada* (Toronto: McGraw-Hill Ryerson, 1985), and "Women and Political Leadership: A Case for Affirmative Action," in Maureen Mancuso, Richard Price, and Ronald Wagenberg, eds., *Leaders and Leadership in Canada* (Toronto: Oxford University Press, 1994); and Heather MacIvor, *Women and Politics in Canada* (Peterborough: Broadview Press, 1996).
9. Newman, "Small-p Politics: Women Working Outside Formal Political Structures," p. 257.
10. Greg Pyrcz, *The Study of Politics: A Short Survey of Core Approaches* (Toronto: University of Toronto Press, 2011).
11. Jill Vickers, *Reinventing Political Science: A Feminist Approach* (Halifax: Fernwood Publishing, 1997); Sandra Burt, "Looking Backward and Thinking Ahead: Toward a Gendered Analysis of Canadian Politics," in Michael Whittington and Glen Williams, eds., *Canadian Politics in the 21st Century,*

5th ed. (Scarborough: Nelson, 2000); and Elisabeth Gidengil and Joanna Everitt, "Conventional Coverage/Unconventional Politicians: Gender and Media Coverage of Canadian Leaders' Debates, 1993, 1997, 2000," *Canadian Journal of Political Science* (July/August 2003).

12. Kome, *Women of Influence*, p. 86.
13. Jane Arscott and Linda Trimble, eds., *In the Presence of Women: Representation in Canadian Governments* (Toronto: Harcourt Brace, 1997).
14. Statistics Canada, *Women in Canada: A Gender-Based Statistical Report* (Catalogue No. 89-503-X, 2010), available at http://www.statcan.gc.ca/pub/89-503-x/89-503-x2010001-eng.htm; Melissa Cooke-Reynolds and Nancy Zukewich, "The Feminization of Work," *Canadian Social Trends* (Statistics Canada, Catalogue No. 11-008, Spring 2004).
15. See *Newfoundland (Treasury Board) v. N.A.P.E.*, [2004] 3 S.C.R. 381.
16. Catalyst, "Statistical Overview of Women in the Work Place," March 3, 2014, http://www.catalyst.org/knowledge/statistical-overview-women-workplace.
17. Yasmeen Abu-Laban and Christina Gabriel, *Selling Diversity: Immigration, Multiculturalism, Employment Equity, and Globalization* (Peterborough: Broadview Press, 2000).
18. Statistics Canada, *Women in Canada: A Gender-based Statistics Report*, 2011.
19. William Chandler, "The Value of Household Work in Canada, 1992," *National Income and Expenditure Accounts, Fourth Quarter 1993*, 41, no. 4 (Catalogue No. 13-001), based on the 1992 General Social Survey.
20. See Penney Kome, *The Taking of Twenty-Eight* (Toronto: Women's Educational Press, 1983), and *Women of Influence*, Ch. 10.
21. Alan Cairns, *Disruptions: Constitutional Struggles, from the Charter to Meech Lake* (Toronto: McClelland and Stewart, 1991); and Rainer Knopff and F.L. Morton, *Charter Politics* (Toronto: Nelson Canada, 1992).
22. Leslie Pal, *Interests of State: The Politics of Language, Multiculturalism and Feminism in Canada* (Montreal: McGill-Queen's University Press, 1993); Christopher P. Manfredi, *Feminist Activism in the Supreme Court: Legal Mobilization and the Women's Legal Education and Action Fund* (Vancouver: UBC Press, 2004); and *R. v. Lavallee*, [1990] 1 S.C.R. 852.
23. Cairns, *Disruptions*.
24. Robert Campbell and Leslie Pal, *The Real Worlds of Canadian Politics*, 2nd ed. (Peterborough: Broadview Press, 1991); Janine Brodie, Shelley A.M. Gavigan, and Jane Jenson, *The Politics of Abortion* (Toronto: Oxford University Press, 1992); *R. v. Morgentaler,* [1988] 1 S.C.R. 30; *Borowski v. Canada (Attorney General)*, [1989] 1 S.C.R. 342; and *Tremblay v. Daigle*, [1989] 2 S.C.R. 530.
25. Holly Johnson, *Dangerous Domains: Violence Against Women in Canada* (Scarborough: Nelson Canada, 1996), based on Statistics Canada, *The Violence Against Women Survey*, 1993.
26. Sandra Burt, "Moving Forward or Stepping Back? Taking Stock of Current Policies on Women's Status in Canada," in Michael Whittington and Glen Williams, eds. *Canadian Politics in the 21st Century*, 7th ed. Toronto (Nelson Education, 2008), p. 273.
27. Statistics Canada, *Women in Canada: A Gender-based Statistics Report*, 2010.
28. Burt, "Looking Backward and Thinking Ahead: Toward a Gendered Analysis of Canadian Politics," in Whittington and Williams, *Canadian Politics in the 21st Century*, 5th ed., p. 308.
29. Abu-Laban and Gabriel, *Selling Diversity*, p. 158.
30. Jill Vickers, Pauline Rankin, and Christine Appelle, *Politics as If Women Mattered: A Political Analysis of the National Action Committee on the Status of Women* (Toronto: University of Toronto Press, 1993); Alexandra Dobrowolsky, "The Women's Movement in Flux: Feminism and Framing, Passion, and Politics," in Miriam Smith, ed., *Group Politics and Social Movements in Canada* (Peterborough: Broadview Press, 2008).
31. Statistics Canada, *Income in Canada—2009*, Catalogue no. 75-202-X, available at http://www.statcan.gc.ca/pub/75-202-x/75-2020x2009000-eng.htm.
32. Treasury Board Secretariat, Employment Equity in the Public Service of Canada, 2010–11, available at http://www.tbs.sct.gc.ca/reports-rapports/ee/2010-2011/eetb-eng.asp.
33. Elisabeth Gidengil, "Beyond the Gender Gap," *Canadian Journal of Political Science* (December 2007); Sylvia Bashevkin, *Women, Power, Politics: The Hidden Story of Canada's Unfinished Democracy* (Toronto: Oxford University Press, 2009); Elizabeth Goodyear-Grant, "Who Votes for Women Candidates and Why? Evidence from Recent Canadian Elections," in Cameron D. Anderson and Laura B. Stephenson, eds., *Voting Behaviour in Canada* (Vancouver: UBC Press, 2010); Melissa Haussman and L. Pauline Rankin, "Framing the Harper Government: "Gender-Neutral" Electoral Appeals while Being

Gender-Negative in Caucus," in Allan M. Maslove, ed., *How Ottawa Spends 2009–2010* (Montreal: McGill-Queen's University Press, 2009); and Jon H. Pammett and Christopher Dornan, eds., *The Canadian Federal Election of 2011* (Toronto: Dundurn, 2011).

34. Didi Herman, *Rights of Passage: Struggles for Lesbian and Gay Legal Equality* (Toronto: University of Toronto Press, 1994); Miriam Smith, *Lesbian and Gay Rights in Canada: Social Movements and Equality-Seeking, 1971–1995* (Toronto: University of Toronto Press, 1999); David Rayside, *Queer Inclusions, Continental Divisions: Public Recognition of Sexual Diversity in Canada and the United States* (Toronto: University of Toronto Press, 2008); and Miriam Smith, "Identity and Opportunity: The Lesbian and Gay Rights Movement," in Smith, *Group Politics and Social Movements in Canada*.

35. *Egan v. Canada*, [1995] 2 S.C.R. 513; and *Vriend v. Alberta*, [1998] 1 S.C.R. 493.

36. *M. v. H.*, [1999] 2 S.C.R. 3.

37. Website of EGALE (Equality for Gays and Lesbians) available at http://www.egale.ca.

38. J. Scott Matthews, "The Political Foundations of Support for Same-Sex Marriage in Canada," *Canadian Journal of Political Science* (December 2005); David Rayside and Clyde Wilcox, eds., *Faith, Politics, and Sexual Diversity in Canada and the United States* (Vancouver: UBC Press, 2011).

39. Citizenship and Immigration Canada, *Discover Canada: The Rights and Responsibilities of Citizenship*, 2011.

FURTHER READING

Abu-Laban, Yasmeen, and Christina Gabriel. *Selling Diversity: Immigration, Multiculturalism, Employment Equity, and Globalization.* Peterborough: Broadview Press, 2000.

Bashevkin, Sylvia. *Welfare Hot Buttons: Women, Work and Social Policy Reform.* Toronto: University of Toronto Press, 2002.

———. *Women, Power, Politics: The Hidden Story of Canada's Unfinished Democracy.* Toronto: Oxford University Press, 2009.

Brodie, Janine, Shelley A.M. Gavigan, and Jane Jenson. *The Politics of Abortion.* Toronto: Oxford University Press, 1992.

Burt, Sandra. "Moving Forward or Stepping Back? Taking Stock of Current Policies on Women's Status in Canada," in Michael Whittington and Glen Williams, eds., *Canadian Politics in the 21st Century*, 7th ed. Toronto: Thomson Nelson, 2008.

Dobrowolsky, Alexandra. *The Politics of Pragmatism: Women, Representation, and Constitutionalism in Canada.* Toronto: Oxford University Press, 1999.

Herman, Didi. *Rights of Passage: Struggles for Lesbian and Gay Legal Equality.* Toronto: University of Toronto Press, 1994.

Manfredi, Christopher P. *Feminist Activism in the Supreme Court: Legal Mobilization and the Women's Legal Education and Action Fund.* Vancouver: UBC Press, 2004.

Newman, Jacquetta. "Small-p Politics: Women Working Outside Formal Political Structures," in Mark Charlton and Paul Barker, eds., *Crosscurrents: Contemporary Political Issues*, 7th ed. Toronto: Nelson Education, 2013.

———, and Linda White. *Women, Politics, and Public Policy: The Political Struggles of Canadian Women*, 2nd ed. Don Mills: Oxford University Press, 2012.

Pal, Leslie. *Interests of State: The Politics of Language, Multiculturalism and Feminism in Canada.* Montreal: McGill-Queen's University Press, 1993.

Rayside, David. *Queer Inclusions, Continental Divisions: Public Recognition of Sexual Diversity in Canada and the United States.* Toronto: University of Toronto Press, 2008.

Smith, Miriam. *Lesbian and Gay Rights in Canada: Social Movements and Equality-Seeking, 1971–1995.* Toronto: University of Toronto Press, 1999.

Statistics Canada, *Women in Canada: A Gender-Based Statistical Report* (Catalogue No. 89-503-X, 2010), available at http://www.statcan.gc.ca/pub/89-503-x/89-503-x2010001-eng.htm.

Vickers, Jill. *Reinventing Political Science: A Feminist Approach.* Halifax: Fernwood Publishing, 1997.

Young, Lisa. *Feminists and Party Politics.* Vancouver: UBC Press, 2000.

Chase Clausen/Shutterstock

CHAPTER 8

Class

A few Canadian families are among the richest people in the world, while a large number of others line up at soup kitchens and food banks because they cannot afford to buy food. Hundreds of thousands of Canadians lost their jobs in the worldwide economic meltdown at the end of 2008 and many others lost a huge proportion of their pension plans and savings. All of these examples are related to class and class cleavages. The concept of class is not as clear-cut as that of region, ethnicity, or gender, and Canadians are generally more conscious of regional and ethnic divisions. Nevertheless, class is an important generator of political activity in most countries, and Canada has its deep-seated class cleavages as well. A discussion of class in Canada must therefore not only clarify the concept, but also explain why it is not a more significant factor in Canadian politics. This chapter will begin by discussing various theoretical considerations involving class, present a statistical profile of class in Canada, and then examine the political role of the upper, middle, and working classes, and of those below the poverty line. It concludes with a discussion of the social safety net.

THEORETICAL CONSIDERATIONS

When dealing with the concept of class, it is customary to start with Karl Marx, who predicted that every capitalist economy would produce a class system consisting primarily of the **bourgeoisie**, the owners of the means of production—factories, mines, etc.—and the **proletariat**, the workers. The bourgeoisie would seek to accumulate as much wealth (and power) as it could, while the proletariat would sell their labour for a price; the former would pay the latter as little as possible (and less than they were worth), thereby accumulating profit or surplus value. The state would take orders from the capitalist elite, becoming an instrument of bourgeois domination, and respond to any resistance with **coercion**. Although religion and the prospect of a pleasant afterlife might keep them content for a while, the workers would eventually come to resent their low wages and exploitation, and finally engage in a violent revolt.

Many modern observers see much truth in what Marx wrote more than 100 years ago, but most would modify his analysis to some extent in the light of subsequent developments, which is why the term "class analysis" is a preferable label. While Marx did provide for a small **petite bourgeoisie** of farmers, small-business people, and self-employed professionals, this class has become more significant than he expected. Furthermore, the **new middle class** of civil servants, teachers, nurses, and other salaried professionals was almost unforeseen in the mid-1800s, and it has become another large and important force. Thus, those who analyze politics in terms of class today speak of the bourgeoisie (the economic or corporate elite), the petite bourgeoisie (the old or upper middle class), the new middle class (salaried professionals), and the proletariat (the "working class"). As well, they often identify "fractions" within each class.[1] Class analysts refer to the use of the state to benefit the middle or working classes as "legitimation." Given today's universal franchise, most modern democratic governments find it politically advantageous to disguise its activity on behalf of capital, but class analysts still emphasize that by humanizing and legitimizing the capitalist system and by disguising support for it, the authorities continue to enable the bourgeoisie to pursue the basic accumulation function. They do contend, however, that other classes can influence events if they act as a class.

Those social scientists who are interested in class but do not approach it from the neo-Marxist tradition commonly divide individuals and families into the upper, middle, and working classes, based on such interrelated factors as income, wealth, occupation, and education. With these measures, the divisions between the classes are less clear-cut. Although such inequalities both produce and result from inequalities in other characteristics, such as education and occupation, income is the simplest measure to use in this discussion.

Regardless of approach, there is an obvious division in Canada between the rich and poor, and even between more nuanced income and occupational groups. On the other hand, these cleavages are neither as pronounced as most others discussed in this section of the book nor as prominent in Canadian politics as in many other countries. Indeed, the contemporary emphasis in political science on the politics of identity is rarely focused on the characteristic of class. In some political systems, ethnicity or gender identities may be replacing class as a basis of political participation, but Canadian politics has rarely revolved around this fundamental characteristic of society. Because consciousness must precede identity, the principal explanation must be that the working and poorer classes in Canada have a low level of **class-consciousness**. Why?

Those who defend the lack of such consciousness argue that other social divisions take precedence in Canada, that the system permits social mobility, that most people feel they are middle class, that material benefits are widely shared, and that the political system has accommodated working-class interests along with those of other groups. Those who decry the lack of working-class class-consciousness argue that the political elite has defined what is politically relevant in society in regional, ethnic, and religious terms instead of in terms of class or ideology.[2]

In discussing the "myth of classlessness," Allahar and Côté pin the blame for this self-delusion on the predominant liberal ideology, which explains social inequalities as stemming from varied individual effort and not from structured class relations.[3] Moreover, the poor, lacking in resources and often having given up, could hardly be expected to mount the kind of political organization that could challenge the defenders of the status quo.

Janine Brodie and Jane Jenson make the point that class-consciousness requires prior ideological and organizational activity by groups, such as unions, farmers, cooperatives, and other reformers. They demonstrate that classes as active and self-conscious social actors have to be created, and that class-based organizations must precede the expectation of class-based voting.[4]

The attempts by farmers and unions to redefine Canadian politics in class terms were repelled by the traditional parties; their leaders were co-opted by the Liberal Party; and both organizations were internally divided. Moreover, many Canadian affiliates of American unions were encouraged to remain aloof from partisan politics. Despite such discouragement, a much stronger left-wing political presence developed in Canada than in the United States, especially in the form of the CCF/NDP,

"WHAT'S HAPPENED to US, HARLOW? WE USED to BE IN FAVOR OF TAXING THE RICH to HELP THE POOR."

Harley Schwadron/Artizans

and the existence of a discourse of class and democratic socialism that those parties provided contributed to a stronger sense of class-consciousness in this country.

Another problem in analyzing social class is the distinction between "objective" and "subjective" class. Objective class refers to the class into which analysts place a person, according to criteria such as type of work or level of income, while subjective class means the class to which people think or feel they belong, even if it contradicts objective standards. Many people who consider themselves to be middle class would be categorized as working class by social scientists, and Marx himself foresaw the phenomenon of "false consciousness." Somewhat similarly, many people who do see themselves as working class adopt a deferential attitude toward their "betters."

A qualification that should also be added relates to the changing nature of class. Some analysts contend that those born after 1945 have distinctive "post-materialist" orientations that are less concerned with traditional class polarization than with "quality of life" and "lifestyle" questions, such as environmental, women's, identity, and minority group issues.[5] Others point out that class often overlaps with gender (women) and ethnicity (Aboriginal, ethnocultural minorities, and immigrants), putting many people at a double or triple disadvantage.

A PROFILE OF CLASS DIVISIONS IN CANADA TODAY

A common means of measuring income inequality is to divide the population into five groups of equal numbers, or quintiles, ranging from highest to lowest income, and to indicate the share of total income received by each group. Figure 8.1 presents such proportions for the year 2009 and shows that in terms of "market income" (before government transfers and taxes), the highest quintile held over 52 percent of the income and the lowest quintile had only 1.1 percent. Government transfers provide much of the income of the lowest quintile, and taxes take a little away from the rich to redistribute to the poor. Even after taxes and transfers, however, the highest-earning 20 percent of the population still gained about 44 percent of the total income, while the lowest quintile received only 4.9 percent.

FIGURE 8.1   SHARE OF TOTAL NATIONAL INCOME, BY INCOME QUINTILE, 1976–2011

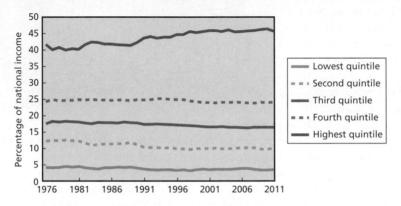

Source: Statistics Canada, Table 202-0701 - Market, total and after-tax income, by economic family type and income quintiles, 2011 constant dollars, annual, CANSIM Table 202-0701, http://www5.statcan.gc.ca/cansim/a26?lang=eng&retrLang=eng&id=2020701&&pattern=&stByVal=1&p1=1&p2=-1&tabMode=dataTable&csid=, Reproduced and distributed on an "as is" basis with the permission of Statistics Canada.

CRITICAL APPROACHES

This whole chapter revolves around *class analysis*. Scholars adopting this approach in Canada often maintain that the corporate elite is always the most powerful force in the political system and that in the post-1985 era of neoliberalism such influence was only exacerbated. The corporate elite adopted a very effective strategy of placing on the national agenda, and making dominant, certain overarching themes: first, free trade; then the deficit and debt; and, more recently, tax cuts. Each of these has as its inevitable product the reduction of the size and role of the state.

THE UPPER CLASS

Identifying the Corporate Elite

It is not difficult to identify those who compose the upper class or **corporate elite**. Canada possesses many fabulously rich entrepreneurs and some of the wealthiest families in the world. In December 2011 *Canadian Business* magazine counted 59 Canadian billionaires, and estimated the wealth of the 10 richest Canadians as shown in Table 8.1.

Another category of wealthy Canadians is the corporate chief executive officers (CEOs) who do not necessarily own their own firms. The total average compensation of the top 100 CEOs in Canada for one year alone—2014—was over $9 million, which includes the value of salary, bonus, incentives, shares, and other benefits. Over half of this compensation came from the net proceeds of cashing in stock options, which, as capital gains, were taxed at half the regular income tax rates. This figure compared to $47 358 for the full year earnings of a person working at the average wage and salary in Canada, and $21 216 for the full year earnings at the minimum wage and salary.[6] To put these numbers in perspective, somebody with the Thomson family's wealth could spend $47 358 every hour of their life for 62 years, and still be worth over $350 million.

The individuals and families of great wealth or income identified above, and others of slightly inferior stature, own or control many of the large corporations operating in Canada. Some individuals and families own hundreds of firms, and the extent of intercorporate connections is high.[7] In recent years, many have been more concerned with taking over competitors (often reducing the labour force in the process) rather than creating any new wealth or jobs or investing in increased productivity in the country.

TABLE 8.1   10 RICHEST CANADIANS, 2014

RANK	NAME	NET WORTH (BILLIONS)	COMPANIES
1	THOMSON FAMILY	$26.1	THOMSON REUTERS, *GLOBE AND MAIL*
2	GALEN WESTON	$10.4	LOBLAWS, HOLT RENFREW
3	IRVING FAMILY	$7.9	OIL, FORESTRY, GAS STATIONS, MEDIA
4	ROGERS FAMILY	$7.6	ROGERS COMMUNICATIONS
5	JIMMY PATTISON	$7.4	AUTO SALES, FOOD, MEDIA, FORESTRY
6	SAPUTO FAMILY	$5.2	FOOD, REAL ESTATE, TRANSPORTATION
7	PAUL DESMARAIS	$4.9	FINANCIAL SERVICES, MEDIA
8	JEFF SKOLL	$4.9	EBAY
9	RICHARDSON FAMILY	$4.4	AGRICULTURE
10	CARLO FIDANI	$4.1	REAL ESTATE

Source: Canadian Business, "Rich 100, 2014 full list," (Jan 9, 2014), http://www.canadianbusiness.com/lists-and -rankings/rich-100-the-full-2014-ranking/. Used with permission.

A final point here concerns the vital part that Canadian banks play in the operations of the corporate elite. They do so because much corporate activity is financed by large bank loans. Thus, many of the individuals named above sit on the boards of directors of major Canadian banks, where their presence assures their company or companies of preferential banking treatment.[8] Indeed, a whole theory has been advanced regarding the manner in which the banks have directed the development of the Canadian economy. They have contributed to the widespread foreign ownership in Canada because of their preference for financing foreign branch plants in Canada rather than domestic manufacturers; they have exacerbated regional disparities in their preference for central Canadian clients; and they have encouraged a resource-based economy by preferring export-oriented resource companies to manufacturing.[9]

Most members of the corporate elite inherited a good deal of their wealth, such a transfer being facilitated by the lack of a wealth or inheritance tax in Canada. As far as the other aspects of their social background are concerned, the near Anglo-Protestant monopoly of earlier years is beginning to change. Although Toronto remains the financial capital of the country, the economic elite is also increasingly diverse in terms of geography, with a new Western flavour.

Demands of the Corporate Elite and Results

Members of the economic elite have diverse political preferences and many contribute generously to philanthropic causes. To a large extent, however, political advocates for elite interests tend to advocate for minimal government intervention: they want to cut government spending on social programs, to balance the annual budget, and to reduce the accumulated national debt. They advocate avoiding estate or wealth taxes as well as corporate and progressive individual taxes, while providing generous loopholes, write-offs, and tax shelters.[10] These interests also seek to minimize government regulation, labour standards, and environmental protection, as well as anti-combines laws and other restrictions on corporate takeovers. As Peter Newman says, "what unites [the capitalist elite] is common resentment of the multiplying intrusions of politicians and bureaucrats into the once-sacrosanct ground of Canadian capitalism."[11]

Governments have normally responded positively to such demands. Under the Mulroney government, for example, the progressive nature of the personal income tax was reduced when 10 tax brackets were reduced to three. The Chrétien Liberals allowed the Bronfman family to transfer $2 billion in Seagram shares to the United States, averting about $700 million in capital gains taxation in the process. The Paul Martin budgets in the mid-1990s managed to balance the budget by slashing transfers to the provinces, mostly for social programs. And when the executive branch of government was not forthcoming, the corporate elite sometimes found comfort in actions of the Senate or the courts; for example, the Supreme Court has extended to corporations aspects of the Charter of Rights and Freedoms that were intended to protect individuals.

In fact, the business community played an important role in setting the entire government agenda, especially after 1985 or so, in the movement to neoliberalism in Canada. Big business was the principal advocate of free trade agreements, balancing the budget, reducing the debt, and then reducing taxes, and it emerged as a much "freer" and more powerful force in relation to the state. Nevertheless, the spate of corporate collapses, especially of companies involved in fraudulent accounting practices at the expense of shareholders and employees, has produced much anger.

Conrad Black was imprisoned for committing a variety of corporate crimes and the Canadian Democracy and Corporate Accountability Commission reiterated the call for internal corporate accountability.[12] A great deal of the worldwide financial crisis of 2008–09 can be attributed to the greed of certain corporate executives.

Three principal exceptions to big business's pressure to minimize the role of government must be noted. First, although the economic elite demands that governments minimize spending on others, it often expects sizable chunks of public funds for itself. The new "acquisitors," for example, have "exploited to [the] utmost the Canadian tradition of government subsidies in everything from offshore oil to horror films."[13] This tradition goes back as far as the end of the 19th century, when railway companies were given generous amounts of public funds and public lands. It has continued in a wide range of fields at the federal level ever since, especially in terms of regional economic development, and is carried on in giveaways to resource companies at the provincial and territorial level. Advocates for corporate interests defend such requests on the basis of creating jobs and generally promoting the trickling down of benefits from the top of the economic ladder to the bottom.

A second exception to the general pattern of corporate demands is the occasion on which the economic elite actually favour new social programs. Its motives here included increasing the purchasing power of the poor and working class, reducing the amounts that companies themselves had to pay in employee benefits, improving their corporate image, and ensuring the basic stability of society so that the upper classes did not have to worry about violent protests from the poor or unemployed. For example, companies operating in Canada gain a huge competitive advantage because they do not have to take much responsibility for the health insurance of their employees due to the universal public health program. Alvin Finkel writes of the reform measures adopted in the Depression of the 1930s: "The actions taken were those that businessmen-politicians and other pro-capitalist politicians believed would placate working-class and farmer demands while being assured at the same time that business power within the overall system would be preserved."[14]

In the third place, business leaders sometimes favour an expansion of government activity, usually in the provision of basic utilities or infrastructure, which will decrease their costs or increase their profits. For example, businessmen in Ontario shortly after 1900 encouraged the provincial government to create a Crown corporation to provide a cheap, reliable supply of electricity, and resource companies have often demanded that governments build roads and railways to save them the trouble.

The Canadian state gives priority to big-business demands because it depends on the private sector, to a large extent, to create jobs. Many of the tax cuts and government handouts to corporations are predicated on job maintenance or job creation, although they do not always have this result. Beyond that, there are several reasons that politicians respond to the demands of the economic elite. First, corporate executives and politicians often come from the same ranks, including prime ministers and ministers of finance. Brian Mulroney, John Turner, and Paul Martin are good examples. Second, companies have many avenues of influence available: making a direct, personal pitch to governments; using professional lobby firms to help them contact public decision makers for a fee; and taking advantage of their membership in pressure groups. Among the hundreds of business pressure groups in existence, the **Canadian Council of Chief Executives** (formerly the BCNI, and now known as the Business Council of Canada (BCC)) is probably the most powerful, representing as it does the chief executive officers of the

150 largest firms in the country.[15] Third, throughout their history both the Conservative and Liberal parties have largely been financed by large corporate contributions, and a link between such donations and general public policy, if not to specific corporate favours, was not difficult to establish. In addition, in the 1988 election, Canadians witnessed an unprecedented parallel campaign in which the country's major corporations spent millions of dollars on top of their party donations to persuade Canadian voters of the merits of free trade.

Environmental protection has become one of the leading political issues in Canada and elsewhere, and to some extent can be framed as an issue pitting polluting corporations against ordinary citizens. Of course, the latter can also be encouraged or forced to change their behaviour in ways that would benefit the environment, but any serious reduction in greenhouse gases or other degradation of the environment will require curbs on the pollution emitted by large corporations. They were, in fact, the leading lobbyists against the Kyoto Accord or any effective post-Kyoto plan, whether it be regulation, a carbon tax, a "cap and trade" system, or simply a concrete limit on emissions.[16] It is probably true that the Harper government's pro-business stance was nowhere so obvious as in its lack of action in this field, although as noted in Chapter 3, this issue also possesses a strong regional dimension.

Occasionally corporations do not get everything they demand; for example, the large banks lobbied for authority to engage in mergers for some time without success.[17] The Harper government annoyed the corporate community (and many retirees) when it removed the tax advantages of corporate income trusts. And sometimes the most heinous corporate behaviour is punished, as when the federal and provincial governments demanded $10 billion from one of Canada's largest tobacco companies for having smuggled cigarettes into the country in the early 1990s. Eventually, two Canadian tobacco companies were indeed fined over $1 billion in 2008 after pleading guilty to orchestrating such a smuggling scheme. Although these were the largest fines ever levied in Canada, some observers noted that they were much smaller than originally proposed, that the companies had many years to pay them, and that the company executives who devised the scheme were not punished. Tobacco companies face continuing multi-billion dollar lawsuits claiming that they contributed to the death of people who smoked their products.

THE MIDDLE CLASS

As outlined earlier, the traditional middle class, or "petite bourgeoisie," consists of affluent farmers, small-business people, and self-employed professionals, including doctors and lawyers. This group could also be called the old or upper-middle class. The "new middle class" consists of civil servants, teachers, and other salaried professionals, such as nurses, social workers, librarians, engineers, accountants, and the like. Neo-Marxists generally emphasize the importance of the ownership of the means of production, but as Leo Panitch observes, the 20th century saw the development of a stratum of employees without such ownership or control but who "nevertheless dispose of labour in terms of managing, supervising, and controlling the labour of others."[18]

To some extent, these two fractions of the middle class have considerably different economic interests and therefore different identities and political demands. First, the members of the petite bourgeoisie are usually much wealthier than those of the new middle class and have

average payments, a shorter maximum duration of benefits, and a dramatic reduction in the percentage of the unemployed qualifying for benefits.[23] The decline hit women much harder than men. With thousands of unemployed workers eliminated from the EI program, it is no wonder that the fund accumulated an annual surplus of some $6 or $7 billion, which both the Chrétien and the Martin governments lumped into general revenues, helping them to balance the budget. On the other hand, improvements have been made in recent years in the areas of maternity, parental, and adoption leave. In 1989, 74 percent of those unemployed qualified for benefits, whereas since 1996, it remained in the 40 percent range. This was particularly tragic after 2008, when the collapse of the economy produced a large increase in the unemployment numbers and fewer than half received employment insurance benefits. In addition, the regional variations in the program were harshly criticized. Some of the problems with EI, of course, relate to the changing nature of work itself. Stable, permanent jobs are increasingly being replaced with temporary, contingent, part-time, contract work with accompanying anxiety and few benefits, including pensions.

The Harper government was concerned with the contradiction of labour shortages in many fields and many parts of the country coinciding with high unemployment rates, so it revamped the EI system in its 2012 budget to try to bridge this gap. It divided the unemployed into three categories: frequent claimants, occasional claimants, and long-tenured workers—and the more frequent the claim, the less likely that the claimant will be allowed to remain on EI when a "suitable" job becomes available. The government gave itself the power to define suitability in terms of pay, qualifications, and location, targeting seasonal workers and others who repeatedly depended on EI. Not surprisingly, this change was attacked by those in regions of high unemployment and by working class advocates who feared that claimants would be forced to take poorly paid, demeaning, and distant jobs.

Organized labour has many other concerns, many of them at the provincial level: laws that make it difficult to form a union and inadequacies in child care, health care, education and training, pay equity, workers' rights, occupational health and safety, and pension and wage protection in the case of corporate bankruptcies. Labour works in conjunction with many allied groups in advancing these issues with the government. The trade union movement did not initially have much luck in taking its issues to the courts, but the Supreme Court made several recent decisions that were more sympathetic to organized labour. Most importantly, the Court overturned its own earlier ruling and decided that collective bargaining was indeed protected by the freedom of association clause in the Charter of Rights and Freedoms.[24] On the other hand, in its limited sphere of jurisdiction, the Harper government became impatient with the collective bargaining process and passed back-to-work legislation involving Canada Post, Air Canada, and CP Rail.

The **Canadian Labour Congress (CLC)** is the lobbying body for more than three million workers. The CLC has the largest actual membership of any advocacy group in the country and therefore represents the greatest number of voters. Its influence is diminished, however, by its divergent values and its outsider status, as well as by the fact that not all unions belong to it. Whether it increased or decreased its influence by affiliating with the NDP in 1961 is still an open question. Many unions have not joined any central organization, and others have formed such rival groups as the Confédération des syndicats nationaux. The historic factionalism within the Canadian union movement has not helped the cause of the working class.[25]

THE POOR

Serious poverty in Canada is undeniable, and the poor can be defined as those living below the **poverty line**.[26] Among the many contested issues in this area, however, is how to define poverty in the first place. Different organizations use varied definitions of poverty, which are sometimes highly ideological. Statistics Canada traditionally used a bureaucratic term, "Low-Income Cut-Off" (LICO), but even its before- and after-tax figures are considerably different, and the agency now employs a variety of measuring instruments. Using its "before tax and transfer" statistics, the population living in poverty declined from 25 percent in 1969 to 15.3 percent in 2005 to 13.5 percent in 2009, or 4.4 million people. These figures present a much bleaker picture than "after tax and transfer" statistics, which for 2009 was 9.6 percent or 3.2 million.[27] The justification for using the former figure here is that the poverty line is arbitrary and low, that a large group of near-poor exists just above it, and that many below it are *far* below it.

The aspect of poverty that is probably most heartbreaking is that over 20 percent of the poor people in Canada are children; nearly 10 percent of children live in poverty. This average rate increases for children with disabilities, children of Aboriginal and visible minorities, and children of recent immigrants. In 2003, the high-school dropout rate among children from poor families was 3.3 times the rate of others. This link between low income and low education is self-perpetuating, and ways must be found to encourage the children of poor families to pursue their education.[28] The *Canadian Poverty Fact Book* asserts that "the educational opportunities of children, whether at the primary, secondary or postsecondary level, must not be limited by the economic circumstances of their parents."[29] It also documents how children from low-income families stand out from their better-off peers: "They are less healthy, have less access to skill-building activities, have more destructive habits and behaviours, live more stressful lives, and are subject to more humiliation. In short, they have less stable and less secure existences and as a result they are likely to be less secure as adults."[30]

Although the House of Commons passed a resolution in 1989 to eliminate child poverty in Canada by the year 2000, the number of children living in poverty actually increased by 50 percent during the 1990s. Because of the improved economy, this figure dropped by 2009, but even so, nearly 21 percent of families headed by a lone-parent mother were below the poverty line.[31] In terms of depth of poverty, lone-parent mothers with children are also further below the poverty line than other groups; hence the expression, the **feminization of poverty**. Much could be said about each of the other categories of people living in poverty, such as women, Aboriginals, people with disabilities, recent immigrants, and seniors. In other words, class, gender, and ethnicity are often mutually reinforcing.[32]

A major dimension of poverty is the issue of housing, especially since all levels of government have virtually abandoned the field of social, public, or co-op housing. The high cost of housing as a proportion of income is forcing the poor to reduce their spending on other necessities, such as food, which puts an unbearable strain on a charitable food banks. Even worse, an increasing number of poor people are now actually homeless.

Many poor people work full-time, and others part-time, such that the poor can be about equally divided between those who work and those who are unemployed or unemployable.

The working poor try to scrape by on the minimum wage or have more than one low-paying job. Because the minimum wage is even lower than welfare benefits (both being below the poverty line), many working poor choose to go on welfare because they are often better off that way. Rather than raise the minimum wage, however, some provincial governments reduced welfare benefits in the 1990s. Even the combined incomes of two family members earning the minimum wage would not raise them above the poverty line. As with the working class above the poverty line, employment insurance is of vital importance to the working poor.[33] In the sweeping changes brought to the program by the Mulroney, Chrétien, and Harper

Couple living in car hope to use home renovation tax.

governments discussed above, the lowest-income groups were the biggest losers.

When their EI runs out, the working poor become the welfare poor. Welfare benefits vary considerably across provinces and territories, but they are not generous anywhere. One must sell off most of one's possessions in order to qualify, and earned income is usually deducted from welfare benefits, so that it is often not worth the effort to find a job. Moreover, leaving the social assistance rolls usually means giving up free prescription drug and dental benefits and incurring new work-related expenses.[34]

Although the poor do try to fight back, they are generally unorganized and collectively inarticulate in the political system. They lack the skills to function effectively as advocacy groups, primarily because they do not have the education, money, or time. However, a number of groups attempt to include the voice of the poor in the political process. One is the Canadian Council on Social Development (CCSD), which represents middle-class, bureaucratic, and even some corporate concern with the state of social policy in the country. It has often provided the blueprint for social reform and is an important source of data on social programs. Because the CCSD does not actually represent the poor, as such, the Trudeau government created the National Council of Welfare (NCW) in 1969 as an advisory group to speak on behalf of welfare clients themselves. Its members included welfare recipients, public housing tenants, and other low-income citizens as well as those involved in providing services to the poor. It also produced studies of the poverty problem and other social issues. Perhaps it is not surprising that the NCW was disbanded by the Harper government. A third group, the National Anti-Poverty Organization (NAPO), was formed in 1971. It is an umbrella organization of some 700 local, provincial, and territorial anti-poverty groups and individuals across the country, representing Canadians living below the poverty line. Considering its lack of resources, it is surprisingly articulate. NAPO has since changed its name to Canada Without Poverty.

CRITICAL APPROACHES

State-based theorists argue that because of the divisions within the working class and their low level of class-consciousness, politicians and bureaucrats can ignore their demands more easily than in the case of regional economic and ethnic demands. Moreover, since very few working-class politicians have ever been elected in Canada and most bureaucrats are of middle-class background, policies have been designed in the interests of those in power. Rodney Haddow has gone further to synthesize the class-based and state-centred approaches in his study of poverty reform in Canada. He shows that the bureaucrats in the influential finance department look at every issue through the eyes of big business, acting as an agent of capitalist class interests in the halls of power.[35] It should also be noted, however, that some bureaucrats take a wider view of the national interest. Those public servants in departments oriented toward lower classes, such as health, welfare, labour, and human resources development, along with their provincial counterparts, have been known to join organizations like the CCSD and do what they can to persuade the politicians to adopt their recommendations.[36]

THE RISE AND DECLINE OF THE SOCIAL SAFETY NET

The Rise

Reflecting the influence of the affluent economic elite, the North American predilection to abide by private market forces, and the assumption that jurisdiction over such matters rested primarily with the provinces, the federal government was slow to get involved in the provision of health and social service programs.[37] By the early 1980s, however, Canada had become a **welfare state** in which federal, provincial, and municipal governments were engaged in a wide range of programs that contributed to a **social safety net** that protected the weakest members of society, especially those unable or not expected to earn a living on their own. The principal federal measures can be divided into five basic fields—those relating to the young, seniors, people with disabilities, the unemployed, and public health care.

Almost all of these measures faced much upper-class and corporate opposition before being implemented. As time went on, however, the economic elite needed to legitimate its rule once the vote was extended to the working class, and Keynesian economics stressed the importance of the working class having purchasing power to keep the economy moving. The

Liberal Party adopted a wide-ranging program in 1919 which included a guarded promise of insurance against unemployment, sickness, old age, and other disability. But it was not until 1927 that Canada's first old age pension act was passed. At that point, the minority Mackenzie King government made a bargain with the two Labour MPs to pass it in return for their general support. Nothing much else happened in this policy area until the Depression of the 1930s, one of whose products was the creation of the Cooperative Commonwealth Federation or CCF Party. In its *Regina Manifesto* of 1933, the party proposed "employment insurance and social insurance to protect workers and their families against the hazards of sickness, death, industrial accident and old age," and "publicly organized health, hospital and medical services." The Conservative government of

As CCF premier of Saskatchewan, Tommy Douglas pioneered public health insurance in Canada and was named "the greatest Canadian" in a CBC contest in 2005.

R.B. Bennett then enacted an Employment and Social Insurance Act in the middle of the Depression, but it was later declared unconstitutional by the courts. After a constitutional amendment transferred unemployment insurance to federal jurisdiction, the Liberal government introduced the Unemployment Act in 1940.

In 1944, the King government passed the Family Allowances Act, and a year later published a comprehensive recommendation for post-war economic and social policies called the Green Book proposals based on **Keynesian economics**. Meanwhile, the CCF party took office in Saskatchewan under Premier Tommy Douglas. In a dramatic breakthrough in North American public policy, it introduced a public hospital insurance program, which was soon emulated in several other provinces and then adopted as a national federal–provincial scheme in the mid-1950s.[38] With Ottawa paying half the cost of hospital insurance, the Saskatchewan CCF went a step further with a public medicare program, covering doctors' fees. The subsequent national medicare plan was brought in by the Pearson Liberals in the 1960s when it was in a minority position in Parliament depending on NDP support. The Pearson government introduced the Canada Assistance Plan in similar circumstances to pay half the cost of provincial and municipal social assistance programs.[39]

The trade union movement, churches, many other progressive groups and organizations, scholarly reports, and foreign models were all part of advocating and developing such social programs and pressing the government to implement them. But it is generally understood that the Liberal party, which introduced many of these programs at the federal level, did so in part on the basis of CCF experiments in Saskatchewan as well as to undercut the growing support for that party and its successor, the NDP.

BOX 8.1   VOICES

When he was a boy, Tommy Douglas suffered from a bone disease in his knee and was put in the public ward of a Winnipeg hospital as a charity patient. The young house doctor said that his leg must be cut off, but by accident, a brilliant orthopaedic surgeon selected Douglas for a teaching demonstration and saved his leg. "I shall always be grateful to the medical profession …, but the experience of being a charity patient remains with me. Had I been a rich man's son the services of the finest surgeons would have been available. As an iron moulder's boy, I almost had my leg amputated before chance intervened and a specialist cured me without thought of a fee. All my adult life I have dreamed of the day when an experience like mine would be impossible and we would have in Canada a program of complete medical care without a price tag. That is what we aim to achieve in Saskatchewan—the finest health service available to everyone in the province regardless of ability to pay."

Source: Tommy Douglas, as Premier of Saskatchewan, quoted in Robin F. Badgley and Samuel Wolfe, *Doctors' Strike: Medical Care and Conflict in Saskatchewan* (Toronto: Macmillan, 1967), p. 20.

In fact, while the question of class-based voting has been widely explored in Canadian political science, Chapter 15 will show that not much evidence has been found. One might expect that the working class would tend to vote CCF/NDP, and probably does so more than other classes, but it is not a strong relationship. This suggests that the working class has a weak consciousness of its class position as well as that the Liberal party in particular often undermined such consciousness with seductive promises and policies.

The Decline

The social safety net peaked in Canada in the early 1980s, after which both federal and provincial governments became obsessed with their accumulated debts and current budgetary deficits, which they, along with business interests and conservative think tanks, largely blamed on overspending on social programs. Although such expenditures continue to loom large in federal, provincial, and territorial government budgets, Canada actually stands near the bottom of OECD countries in the proportion of gross domestic product spent on social programs, as seen in Table 8.4. It is possible, therefore, that debts and deficits have been caused by under-taxation rather than by overspending; indeed, on a comparative basis, Canada derives less tax revenue from corporations than most of its major allies do. As noted earlier, Canada is also one of the few major Western industrialized countries without a tax on inheritance or wealth.[40]

Many observers saw the Mulroney government's package of economic policies (1984–93)— the Canada–U.S. Free Trade Agreement, privatization, deregulation, tax reform, reductions in transfers to the provinces and territories, and cutbacks in social programs—as an integrated

TABLE 8.4   TOTAL SOCIAL EXPENDITURE AS A PERCENTAGE OF GROSS DOMESTIC PRODUCT, 2014, AGGREGATED DATA (OECD COUNTRIES)

FRANCE	31.9	UNITED KINGDOM	21.7
FINLAND	31.0	IRELAND	21.0
BELGIUM	30.7	NEW ZEALAND	20.8[2013]
DENMARK	30.1	POLAND	20.6
ITALY	28.6	CZECH REPUBLIC	20.6
AUSTRIA	28.4	SWITZERLAND	19.4
SWEDEN	28.1	UNITED STATES	18.6
SPAIN	26.8	AUSTRALIA	19.0
GERMANY	25.8	SLOVAK REPUBLIC	18.4
PORTUGAL	25.2	CANADA	17.0
NETHERLANDS	24.7	ICELAND	16.5
GREECE	24.0	ESTONIA	16.3
SLOVENIA	23.7	ISRAEL	15.5[2013]
LUXEMBOURG	23.5	TURKEY	12.5[2013]
JAPAN	23.1[2010]	KOREA	10.4
HUNGARY	22.1	CHILE	10.0[2013]
NORWAY	22.0	MEXICO	7.9[2012]

Source: Based on data from OECD, "Social Expenditures: Aggregated Data" (2014), http://www.oecd-ilibrary .org/social-issues-migration-health/data/social-expenditure/aggregated-data_data-00166-en.

strategy. Although the government claimed that these measures were introduced either to improve the economy or to cut the deficit (and the benefits might "trickle down" to the poor), they had the collective effect of reducing the standard of living of the poor and the working class. Several provinces, led by Alberta and Ontario, made their own massive cuts in social spending and would have done so regardless of reductions in federal transfers.[41] Then, under the Chrétien Liberals (1993–2003), Paul Martin's budgets cut transfers to the provinces and territories even further, especially in health, postsecondary education, and welfare: a decrease of $7 billion between 1996 and 1998. Besides lumping the three programs together under the label **Canada Health and Social Transfer (CHST)**, Ottawa repealed the Canada Assistance Plan and removed the conditions under which provinces received such funding. This meant that welfare would now have to fight it out with health and postsecondary education within provincial budgetary processes, and provincial governments could restrict social assistance eligibility and promote "workfare" schemes at will. In other words, although less was heard about it, the welfare sector bore the brunt of federal cutbacks even more than the health and education sectors.

All of these government cuts to social programs and the resulting deterioration in the way of life of millions of Canadians led to increasing protests around the turn of the 21st century. This was particularly true of the Ontario Coalition Against Poverty, whose leader, John Clarke, was arrested for a variety of offences and jailed for 25 days without trial. Even the United Nations scolded Canadian governments for what had transpired. Its Committee on Economic, Social and Cultural Rights criticized Canada in 1998 for its departure from the UN Covenant on these matters, especially given its obvious capacity to achieve a high level of respect for all UN Covenant rights. It slammed Ottawa and the provinces for having adopted the policies "which exacerbated poverty and homelessness among vulnerable groups during a time of strong economic growth and increasing affluence."[42]

When the economy picked up around the turn of the new century and the enthusiasm for neoliberalism declined to some extent, federal and provincial governments began to make marginal improvements in their social programs. The Martin government (2003–06), for example, established the Early Learning and Child Care Initiative, a flexible distribution of $5 billion over five years to support provincial and territorial programs in these fields on a bilateral basis. Another move was to divide the Canada Health and Social Transfer into two constituent parts, health programs and social programs, so that the former would not absorb the entire fund. Martin provided a major long-term boost to health care funding, with special emphasis on reducing waiting times and made a deal with the NDP in the minority government situation in 2005 that put $4.5 billion into additional spending on the environment, social housing, foreign aid, and tuition reduction. The improvement in the economy resulted in a decrease in the proportion of people living below the poverty line, but came to an abrupt end with the worldwide economic meltdown at the end of 2008.

Partly because of that situation and partly because of more general conditions, a movement called "Occupy Canada" arose in mid-October 2011. Related to a collective protest that started in the United States (Occupy Wall Street), the movement targeted social and economic inequality and corporate influence on government. The protesters claimed to be speaking for the 99 percent against the one percent, and at least 20 Canadian cities witnessed rallies and non-violent demonstrations, often involving encampments in downtown parks that were eventually evicted a month or more later, with a handful of arrests. The original protests attracted considerable sympathy, and may have inspired the Quebec student protest in 2012. At about the same time, the United Nations Right-to-Food Envoy criticized the widespread poverty and hunger he discovered on his visit to Canada.

CONCLUSION

Whatever conception of class is employed, the existence of different classes in Canadian society cannot be denied. In this chapter, it was useful to divide the population into four classes: upper, middle, working, and the poor. If such class cleavages do not usually result in much political activity at the lower levels, it must be that many Canadians are unaware of them, consider them acceptable, or feel powerless to change them. Nevertheless, income disparities continue to increase, the union movement shows signs of decline, and the Harper government's pursuit of a balanced budget hits disadvantaged Canadians most.

Even though class in Canada is rarely given the attention that it receives in other political systems, the subject is connected to many other chapters of this book. Class has already been linked to preceding chapters in terms of the socioeconomic position of Aboriginal peoples, francophones, recent immigrants, ethnocultural minorities, and women, and class subcultures are mentioned in Chapter 11 (political culture). The role of multinational corporations is considered in Chapter 10 (the global environment), and of domestic corporations in Chapter 12 (media ownership) and Chapter 13 (financing political parties). Advocacy groups representing different classes are included in Chapter 16, and various class interests in the courts are raised in Chapter 19 (the Charter of Rights). Finally, the dominance of middle-and upper-class individuals and interests is emphasized in Part 5 on the institutions of government.

DISCUSSION QUESTIONS

1. To what class do you and your family belong? Assess your family's class-consciousness.

2. What is the best way to define and distinguish among social classes?

3. Why do so many Canadians conceive of Canada as a middle-class nation?

4. Do you feel that the economic elite owe their wealth and power primarily to their own honest, individual efforts or to inheritance, exploitative forms of profit-making, and manipulation of the political system?

5. Given that unions are generally the best way of improving the lot of the working class, why are they not more popular among members of that class?

6. How do you explain the existence of the social safety net, given the lack of political power of the poor and working class?

7. What would you do to eliminate child poverty?

MindTap®   FOR MORE INFO GO TO **http://www.nelson.com/student**

NOTES

1. Some readers will find this to be a great oversimplification of Karl Marx. Others will want to read modern variations, such as the Goldthorpe-Ericson class scheme which divides occupations into seven categories. See Gordon Marshall, et al., *Against the Odds? Social Class and Social Justice in Industrial Societies* (Oxford: Clarendon Press, 1997).
2. Janine Brodie and Jane Jenson, *Crisis, Challenge and Change: Party and Class in Canada Revisited* (Ottawa: Carleton University Press, 1988).
3. Anton L. Allahar and James E. Côté, *Richer and Poorer: The Structure of Inequality in Canada* (Toronto: Lorimer, 1998), pp. 24–26.
4. Brodie and Jenson, *Crisis, Challenge and Change.*
5. Neil Nevitte, Herman Bakvis, and Roger Gibbins, "The Ideological Contours of 'New Politics' in Canada: Policy, Mobilization and Partisan Support," *Canadian Journal of Political Science* (September 1989); and Neil Nevitte, *The Decline of Deference: Canadian Value Change in Cross-National Perspective* (Peterborough: Broadview Press, 1996).

6. Hugh Mackenzie, *Glory Days: CEO Pay in Canada Soaring to Pre-Recession Hights* (Ottawa: Canadian Centre for Policy Alternatives, 2015); *Canadian Business* (Jan. 20, 2014), http://www.canadianbusiness.com/lists-and-rankings/richest-people/top-100-highest-paid-ceos-2015/ (accessed April 27, 2015).

7. Tony Clarke, *Silent Coup: Confronting the Big Business Takeover of Canada* (Toronto: Lorimer, 1997); Allahar and Côté, *Richer and Poorer*; Jamie Brownlee, *Ruling Canada: Corporate Cohesion and Democracy* (Black Point, NS: Fernwood Publishing, 2005); and Diane Francis, *Who Owns Canada Now?* (Toronto: HarperCollins, 2008).

8. Stephen Brooks and Andrew Stritch, *Business and Government in Canada* (Scarborough: Prentice Hall Canada, 1991), pp. 143–53.

9. R.T. Naylor, *The History of Canadian Business* (Toronto: Lorimer, 1975).

10. Linda McQuaig details "how the rich won control of Canada's tax system … and ended up richer" in *Behind Closed Doors* (Toronto: Penguin, 1987). See also her *The Quick and the Dead* (Toronto: Penguin, 1991) and other writings.

11. Peter C. Newman, *The Canadian Establishment*, vol. 2: *The Acquisitors* (Toronto: McClelland and Stewart, 1990), p. 569.

12. Havina S. Dashwood, "Canadian Mining Companies and Corporate Social Responsibility: Weighing the Impact of Global Norms," *Canadian Journal of Political Science* (March 2007) finds some evidence of corporate social responsibility.

13. Newman, *The Acquisitors*, p. 13.

14. Alvin Finkel, *Business and Social Reform in the Thirties* (Toronto: Lorimer, 1979), p. 176.

15. See Peter C. Newman, *Titans: How the New Canadian Establishment Seized Power* (Toronto: Penguin Books, 1998), in which Tom d'Aquino boasts of determining the government's entire agenda; Peter Clancy, "Business Interests and Civil Society in Canada," in Miriam Smith, ed., *Group Politics and Social Movements in Canada* (Peterborough: Broadview Press, 2008).

16. Douglas MacDonald, *Business and Environmental Politics in Canada* (Peterborough: Broadview Press, 2007).

17. Russell Alan Williams, "Mergers If Necessary, but Not Necessarily Mergers: Competition and Consolidation at Canada's 'Big Banks,'" in Robert M. Campbell, Leslie A. Pal, and Michael Howlett, eds., *The Real Worlds of Canadian Politics*, 4th ed. (Peterborough: Broadview Press, 2004).

18. Leo Panitch, "Elites, Classes, and Power," in Michael S. Whittington and Glen Williams, eds., *Canadian Politics in the 1990s*, 4th ed. (Scarborough: Nelson Canada, 1995), p. 168.

19. I owe this observation (as well as many other improvements to the book) to Prof. Jim Silver of the University of Winnipeg.

20. McQuaig, *Behind Closed Doors*.

21. Abella, *On Strike*; and Walter Stewart, *Strike!* (Toronto: McClelland and Stewart, 1977), Ch. 4.

22. See the annual account in Statistics Canada, such as: http://www.labour.gc.ca/eng/resources/info/publications/union_coverage/union_coverage.shtml

23. Z. Lin, "Employment Insurance in Canada: Recent Trends and Policy Changes," *Canadian Economic Observer* (July 1998).

24. *R.W.D.S.U., Local 558 v. Pepsi Cola Canada Beverages (West) Ltd.*, [2002] 1 S.C.R. 156; *Dunmore v. Ontario (Attorney General)*, [2001] 3 S.C.R. 1016; *Reference re Employment Insurance Act (Can.)*, ss. 22 and 23, [2005] S.C.R. 669; and *Health Services and Support—Facilities Subsector Bargaining Assn. v. B.C.*, [2007] 2 S.C.R. 391, which overturned the earlier 1987 *Labour Trilogy* case. The Court continued its erratic pattern of decisions in this area with *Ontario (Attorney General) v. Fraser*, [2011] 2 S.C.R. 3.

25. Gad Horowitz, *Canadian Labour in Politics* (Toronto: University of Toronto Press, 1968). See also David Camfield, "The Working-Class Movement in Canada: An Overview," and Charlotte Yates, "Organized Labour in Canadian Politics: Hugging the Middle or Pushing the Margins?" in Smith, *Group Politics and Social Movements in Canada*.

26. The field of social policy analysis is now blessed with a multitude of organizations that provide data relevant here. These include the Canadian Council on Social Development, the National Council of Welfare, the Caledon Institute of Social Policy, Canada Without Poverty, the Centre for Social Justice, the Ontario Coalition for Social Justice, the Canadian Labour Congress, and the Canadian Centre for Policy Alternatives.

27. Statistics Canada, CANSIM Table 202-0701, "Market, total and after-tax income, by economic family type and income quintiles," available at http://www5.statcan.gc.ca/cansim/a26, accessed March 15, 2012.
28. National Council of Welfare, *Poverty Profile, 2001* and *Welfare Incomes, 2004*; and Campaign 2000, *Putting Children First: 2005 Report Card on Child Poverty in Ontario*; Statistics Canada. 2012. "A First Look at Provincial Differences in Educational Pathways from High School to College and University," available at http://www.statcan.gc.ca/pub/81-004-x/2007002/9989-eng.htm.
29. Canadian Council on Social Development, *The Canadian Poverty Fact Book—1989*, p. 93; and *The Progress of Canada's Children*, 1997.
30. *The Canadian Poverty Fact Book, 1994*, p. 2.
31. Statistics Canada, "Percentage of persons in low-income after tax, by economic family type, 1976–2008," available at http://www.statcan.gc.ca/pub/89-503-x/2010001/article/11388/tb1013-eng.htm, accessed March 11, 2012; Monica Townson, *Women's Poverty and the Recession* (Ottawa: Canadian Centre for Policy Alternatives, 2009).
32. National Council of Welfare, "A Snapshot of Racialized Poverty in Canada—Statistical Tables (2012)," available at http://www.ncw.gc.ca/1.3bd.2t.1ils@eng.jsp?1id=391.
33. It was implemented shortly after the Depression, when unemployed men were placed in labour camps. When they began a trek from BC to Ottawa, they were blocked by police in the Regina Riot of July 1, 1935.
34. TD Economics, *From Welfare to Work in Ontario: Still the Road Less Travelled* (Toronto: TD Bank Financial Group, 2005).
35. Rodney Haddow, *Poverty Reform in Canada 1958–1978: State and Class Influences on Policy Making* (Montreal: McGill-Queen's University Press, 1993); and Rianne Mahon, "Canadian Public Policy: The Unequal Structure of Representation," in Leo Panitch, ed., *The Canadian State: Political Economy and Political Power* (Toronto: University of Toronto Press, 1977).
36. Richard Splane, "Social Policy-Making in the Government of Canada: Reflections of a Reformist Bureaucrat," in S.A. Yelaja, ed., *Canadian Social Policy* (Waterloo: Wilfrid Laurier University Press, 1978); and Rand Dyck, "The Canada Assistance Plan: The Ultimate in Cooperative Federalism," *Canadian Public Administration* (Winter 1976). Carl Cuneo and Leslie Pal engaged in an interesting intellectual dialogue on the question of the significance of class in the bureaucracy in the March 1986 issue of the *Canadian Journal of Political Science*.
37. Denis Guest, *The Emergence of Social Security in Canada*, 3rd ed. (Vancouver: UBC Press, 1998); Jacqueline S. Ismael, ed., *Canadian Social Welfare Policy: Federal and Provincial Dimensions* (Montreal: McGill-Queen's University Press, 1985).
38. Among many sources on the subject, A.W. Johnson, *Dream No Little Dreams: A Biography of the Douglas Government of Saskatchewan, 1944–1961* (Toronto: University of Toronto Press, 2004).
39. P.E. Bryden, *Planners and Politicians: Liberal Politics and Social Policy 1957–1968* (Montreal: McGill-Queen's University Press, 1997).
40. Roger S. Smith, *Personal Wealth Taxation* (Toronto: Canadian Tax Foundation, 1993), p. iii; and Conference Board of Canada, "Canada's Record on Poverty Among the Worst of Developed Countries—And Slipping," September 17, 2009, available at http://www.conferenceboard.ca/press/newsrelease/10-21.aspx.
41. Walter Stewart, *Dismantling the State* (Toronto: Stoddart, 1998); Don Waterfall, *Dismantling Leviathan: Cutting Government Down to Size* (Toronto: Dundurn Press, 1995); and Stephen McBride and John Shields, *Dismantling a Nation* (Halifax: Fernwood Publishing, 1993, 1997).
42. UN Committee on Economic, Social and Cultural Rights, "Concluding Observations on Canada's 3rd Periodic Report," (E/C. 12/1/Add. 31, 10 December 1998).

FURTHER READING

Allahar, Anton L., and James E. Côté. *Richer and Poorer: The Structure of Inequality in Canada*. Toronto: Lorimer, 1998.

Brodie, Janine, and Jane Jenson. *Crisis, Challenge and Change: Party and Class in Canada Revisited*. Ottawa: Carleton University Press, 1988.

Brownlee, Jamie. *Ruling Canada: Corporate Cohesion and Democracy.* Black Point, NS: Fernwood Publishing, 2005.

Canadian Centre for Policy Alternatives. *The CCPA Monitor.* Ottawa: monthly, and other assorted publications.

Clarke, Tony. *Silent Coup: Confronting the Big Business Takeover of Canada.* Toronto: Lorimer, 1997.

Guest, Denis. *The Emergence of Social Security in Canada*, 3rd ed. Vancouver: University of British Columbia Press, 1998.

Hale, Geoffrey. *The Uneasy Partnership: Politics of Business and Government in Canada.* Peterborough: Broadview Press, 2006.

Johnson, A.W. *Dream No Little Dreams: A Biography of the Douglas Government of Saskatchewan, 1944–1961.* Toronto: University of Toronto Press, 2004.

MacDonald, Douglas. *Business and Environmental Politics in Canada.* Peterborough: Broadview Press, 2007.

McBride, Stephen, and John Shields. *Dismantling a Nation: The Transition to Corporate Rule in Canada*, 2nd ed. Halifax: Fernwood Publishing, 1997.

McQuaig, Linda. *Behind Closed Doors.* Toronto: Penguin, 1987.

National Council of Welfare. Various publications.

Ornstein, Michael, and H. Michael Stevenson, *Politics and Ideology in Canada: Elite and Public Opinion in the Transformation of a Welfare State.* Montreal: McGill University Press, 1999.

Osberg, Lars. *A Quarter Century of Economic Inequality in Canada: 1981–2006.* Ottawa: Canadian Centre for Policy Alternatives, April 2008, available at www.GrowingGap.ca.

Panitch, Leo, ed., *The Canadian State: Political Economy and Political Power.* Toronto: University of Toronto Press, 1977.

Stewart, Walter. *Dismantling the State.* Toronto: Stoddart, 1998.

Studies in Political Economy: A Socialist Review. Ottawa: Carleton University.

Treff, Karin, and Deborah Ort. *Finances of the Nation 2011.* Toronto: Canadian Tax Foundation, 2012.

Chase Clausen/Shutterstock

CHAPTER 9

Urban/Rural Location, Religion, and Age

Is there a greater need to possess a rifle in rural than in urban communities? Is discourse in the House of Commons dominated by big-city issues? Is December 25 still Christmas or just a generic "holiday"? Which group is in greater need of government support: seniors or children? Will the aging population soon bankrupt the public health care system? Is a good pension no longer a realistic expectation?

Beyond the regional, ethnic, gender, and class cleavages and identities discussed above, the urban/rural split, religion, and age constitute three social factors that have considerable potential for political controversy. Of the three, religion has been prominent in Canada's past, especially at the provincial level, but today's religious issues are of a somewhat different complexion. As the population grows older and as rural areas decline in numbers, at least relative to urban areas, the claims of seniors and of urban communities are increasing in political significance. At the same time, Canadians living in rural areas complain of neglect.

THEORETICAL CONSIDERATIONS

As with other social characteristics, those of rural/urban religion and age can be measured in numerical terms, and differences and divisions can be labelled as **cleavages**. But also in common with characteristics addressed in earlier chapters, numbers alone do not do full justice to their political implications. To be of political significance, such characteristics must have salience to the individuals involved, and that gives rise to the concept of **identities**. As mentioned in Chapter 1, such identities tend to be socially constructed, at least to a large extent. The number and proportion of Canadians approaching and surpassing the age of retirement is increasing rapidly, and they are likely to view their age, and not to mention their retirement status, as part of their identity. Religion is another important source of identity. Indeed, 44 percent of Canadians place a high degree of importance on religion in their life.[1] While "rural" and "urban" might seem straightforward enough at first sight, the distinction between them is not necessarily clear-cut: some people have a foot in both camps or live in and identify with an ambiguous suburban, small town, or rural area adjacent to a big city. Moreover, some observers even regard "rural" and "urban" as social constructions based on "perceptions, identity, power, and symbols."[2] All of these identities are felt to be important by large proportions of the population.

URBAN/RURAL LOCATION

Statistics Canada categorized 81 percent of the population as urban and 19 percent as rural in the 2011 census, the basic definition of "urban" being centres of at least 1000 people and a population density over 400 people per square kilometre. In these terms, the majority of Canadians have been designated as urban-dwellers since 1931, and the percentage has gradually increased in every decade since 1974. Figure 9.1 shows the corresponding proportion of the population living in rural areas since 1851. In 2011, the total urban population exceeded 27 million while the rural population plateaued at just over six million. Some observers regard this definition of rural as too narrow, however, and would add in small towns with more than 1000 residents, which have many of the same concerns as rural populations.[3] Because of such definitional difficulties, Statistics Canada also uses such categorizations as "census metropolitan influenced zones."

Chapter 3 observed that 62 percent of the population lives in Ontario and Quebec, and that the Toronto–Montreal–Ottawa triangle constituted the political and economic core of the country. But the distribution of the Canadian population is even more complicated.

FIGURE 9.1 PROPORTION OF THE CANADIAN POPULATION LIVING IN RURAL AREAS SINCE 1851

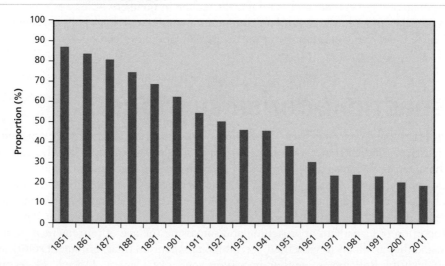

Source: Statistics Canada, 2011 Census, http://www12.statcan.gc.ca/census-recensement/2011/as-sa/98 -310-x/2011003/fig/fig3_2-1-eng.cfm. Reproduced and distributed on an "as is" basis with the permission of Statistics Canada.

In addition to this national **core–periphery system**, a series of regional core–periphery systems exists across the country. Several metropolitan centres dominate their own regional hinterlands: Vancouver in British Columbia; Edmonton and Calgary in Alberta; Regina and Saskatoon in Saskatchewan; Winnipeg in Manitoba; Toronto in Ontario; Montreal in Quebec; and Halifax and St. John's in Atlantic Canada. The same could be said of Whitehorse in Yukon, Yellowknife in the Northwest Territories, and possibly Iqaluit in Nunavut. The interior of British Columbia and northern Ontario are two examples of regions within a province that feel isolated from and exploited by their own economic cores, Vancouver and Toronto, respectively.

Such regional cores are heavily urbanized and are termed "census metropolitan areas" (CMAs) by Statistics Canada. As seen in Table 9.1, the 33 largest metropolitan centres in Canada, those with over 100 000 residents each, constituted 69 percent of the total population

TABLE 9.1   POPULATION OF CENSUS METROPOLITAN AREAS, 2011 CENSUS

TORONTO	5 583 064	REGINA	210 556
MONTREAL	3 824 221	SHERBROOKE	201 556
VANCOUVER	2 313 328	ST. JOHN'S	196 966
CALGARY	1 214 839	BARRIE	187 013
EDMONTON	1 159 869	KELOWNA	179 839
OTTAWA*	921 823	ABBOTSFORD/MISSION	170 191
QUEBEC	765 706	SUDBURY	160 770
WINNIPEG	730 018	KINGSTON	159 561
HAMILTON	721 053	SAGUENAY	157 790
KITCHENER/CAMBRIDGE/WATERLOO	477 160	TROIS-RIVIÈRES	151 773
LONDON	474 786	GUELPH	141 097
ST. CATHARINES/NIAGARA	392 184	MONCTON	138 644
HALIFAX	390 328	BRANTFORD	135 501
OSHAWA	356 177	SAINT JOHN	127 761
VICTORIA	344 615	THUNDER BAY	121 596
WINDSOR	319 246	PETERBOROUGH	118 975
GATINEAU*	314 501		
SASKATOON	260 600	TOTAL	23 100 000

*THE AUTHORS HAVE SEPARATED OTTAWA-GATINEAU INTO TWO PARTS.

Source: Statistics Canada, 2011 Census, Population and dwelling counts, for census metropolitan areas, 2011 and 2006 censuses, http://www12.statcan.ca/census-recensement/2011/dp-pd/hlt-fst/pd-pl/Table-Tableau .cfm?Lang=Eng&T=205&S=3&RPP=50. Reproduced and distributed on an "as is" basis with the permission of Statistics Canada.

in 2011, and 35 percent of the population lived in the three largest cities alone. More than one politician has calculated that the support of only these highly urbanized areas would be enough to form a government.

Although there has always been some tension between urban and rural interests in Canadian politics, it has no doubt been exacerbated by such a pattern of steady urbanization. Many observers talk of a new cleavage in Canadian politics, and ironically enough, both rural and urban interests feel that they are not getting the attention they deserve from Ottawa. Just as they are hard to differentiate by definition, it is difficult to generalize about either sector—each is diverse, and each is in a state of change.

The demands of urban Canada are often complicated by the combination of downtown and suburban areas that have been amalgamated into one administrative unit. As they grow larger and encounter more complex problems, major urban centres increasingly ask Ottawa for help in dealing with such issues as poverty, housing, transportation, immigration, and crime. Periodically since about 1970, the federal government has established agencies concerned with urban problems, such as secretariats for urban issues. The Martin government revived such interest with an "Agenda for Cities," but when smaller communities wanted a piece of the action, it became the New Deal for Cities and Communities, and the Cities Secretariat in the Privy Council Office became the Ministry of State for Infrastructure and Communities. One of Martin's main promises in this regard was to help support urban public transportation systems by sharing the proceeds of the federal gas tax with municipalities. The Harper government was less interested in a direct federal–municipal relationship.

On the other hand, a brief list of key aspects of rural Canada today would include the following:[4]

- Rural Canada is characterized by low-density as opposed to high-density living, with greater distances separating people and settlements, and a narrower range of services available to them.
- Rural communities provide transportation links between large urban centres and many of the recreation areas used by urban Canadians.
- Rural Canada is partly agricultural, but the number of people engaged in agriculture has been declining for decades.
- The rural agricultural population is no longer primarily defined in terms of family farms; the number of farms has decreased, the size has increased,[5] and farms are increasingly owned by corporations.
- The remaining farm families usually have to supplement their incomes with off-farm and nonfarm work such that they now receive only 26.5 percent of their income from farming activities.
- Rural Canada is also the location of other primary industries: mining, forestry, petroleum, fishing, and hydroelectricity. Some of these industries are marked by significant seasonal unemployment and are heavily reliant on Employment Insurance.
- Government concern with balancing budgets over the period since 1995 resulted in a substantial reduction in the number of schools, hospitals, post offices, and other government offices in rural areas and small towns.
- Rural Canada is characterized by an exodus of young people, often leaving for educational advancement and not returning.

Many of these factors have led to an angry sentiment of **rural alienation** in recent years, primarily reflecting a loss of power to the benefit of urban Canada. Until 30 years ago, the interests of rural Canada were more forcefully represented than their numbers deserved. Rural Canada is still somewhat overrepresented in the House of Commons, but the number of rural politicians has declined, leading to the realization that, politically speaking, rural Canada does not matter much in electoral terms. Moreover, governments, academics, and other "experts" view cities as the economic engines of the country and pay less attention to rural areas.

Rural Canada thus exhibits a growing belief that it is not in control of its own destiny, politically or economically, and that those in power do not understand its issues or take them seriously. Gun control, tax assessments, land use regulations, and environmental issues are often cited as examples, while the Charter of Rights and Freedoms protects minority rights but not those of property owners. Somewhat similar to the phenomenon of Western alienation, rural Canada finds an institutional structure stacked against it, but does not have the comfort of provincial governments to defend its interests. Rural Canadians do have organized advocacy groups, including the Canadian Federation of Agriculture, the National Farmers Union, and the more militant Rural Revolution, but sometimes find it necessary to take to the streets to protest the low level of farm incomes or to blockade the food distribution system.

Almost all aspects of agriculture have sought federal government assistance at one time or another.[6] Persistent demands are made for agricultural credit and subsidies, often to match those given farmers in other countries, and to ensure that international trade agreements do not disadvantage Canadian farmers. They remind us that they cannot continue to provide food for urban dwellers unless they derive an adequate financial return, and that they in turn purchase goods and services from those who depend on such food. Conflict often arises among producers of different commodities, and producers of the same commodity are sometimes divided among themselves, such as about the value of marketing boards, including the **Canadian Wheat Board**, whose monopoly on grain marketing in the prairie provinces came to an end in 2012.[7] A more specialized case had to do with the discovery of mad cow disease in one Alberta cow in 2003, in response to which more than 30 countries restricted the import of Canadian beef and cattle. The U.S. and Japanese restrictions devastated the Canadian beef industry; farmers fought desperately for compensation and felt strongly that their concerns were not taken seriously by the government.[8]

Each of the other primary industries has its own demands, too numerous to mention here. But more general rural demands include guaranteed Internet access and more adequate health services.[9] Internet availability and reliability remain a major concern in rural Canada, and the CRTC pressures Internet providers to improve the situation. Indeed, broadband Internet service can provide electronic delivery of health, education, and government services, such as telemedicine and tele-health innovations, in the absence of actual health care personnel and facilities. Rural residents fight for the restoration of postal and other government services, as well as private services, such as banks. The lack of public transportation is often a serious rural issue, while rural and urban communities have a shared concern with a safe environment. For example, the contamination of the public water system at Walkerton, Ontario, which killed seven people and made more than 2000 ill, was caused by *E. coli* bacteria contained in run-off from area farms that developed partly because of inadequate regulation. Another shared concern is the disappearance of prime agricultural land because of urban development and sprawl— subdivisions and shopping centres. Although everyone decries this situation from the point of

Sue Dewar/Artizans

Ontario farmer criticizes budget money going to public transportation.

view of having less land for the production of food, some farmers are happy to sell their land because it was not providing a good living for their families.

Whether urban or rural, the country is divided into municipalities, and in the first instance, local issues are addressed at this level. But since municipalities constitute a constitutionally subordinate level of government with limited financial resources, local concerns often find their way onto the agenda of upper-level governments as well. Generally speaking, provinces discourage official contact between municipalities and the federal government. The **Federation of Canadian Municipalities** is the collective national voice for all types of municipalities in the country, and regularly interacts with the federal was well as provincial governments.[10]

Besides dealing with the municipal level of government on distinct local issues, the federal government often faces different demands with respect to national policies from rural, urban, and suburban parts of the electorate, reflecting certain differences in values or needs. Perhaps the leading case was that of registering guns.[11] The "gun control" law of the 1990s was widely supported by urban voters and vehemently opposed by a majority of rural voters who claimed that hunting was part of their lifestyle, if not essential to their well-being. Of course, the law did not prohibit the ownership of hunting rifles, only requiring their registration, but many opponents argued that confiscation would follow. The Harper government initially announced a legal amnesty for long-gun owners who had not yet registered their guns, and when it achieved a majority, it passed legislation to disband the long-gun registry.

Large urban centres have younger, more diversified populations in ethnocultural terms, more recent immigrants, higher average levels of education and incomes, and lower levels of religious attendance. As a result, other federal policies have had a differential appeal to urban and rural voters. One study based on early 1990s data emphasized two broad differences related to moral conservatism: homosexuality and feminism. People living in small places were more opposed to same-sex marriage than were those in larger centres, and were more likely to object to women working outside the home. Indeed, rural Canada rarely elects any female members of Parliament. There were also small differences on questions related to Quebec, such as the designation of that province as a distinct society.[12] It is usually thought that rural and urban areas also differ to some extent on such issues as immigration, multiculturalism, and abortion. In other words, urban Canadians are more open to diversity, change, new technology, and globalization; rural Canadians are more wary of social change, they value family bonds, and they may be more community minded.[13]

Not surprisingly, Canada has experienced a certain rural–urban split in terms of party preference. The Liberal Party has essentially been an urban party for generations, as has the NDP, while the Conservative Party did not make many inroads into metropolitan centres except for Calgary. In the 2006 and 2008 federal elections, the Harper Conservatives were shut out of central Toronto, Montreal, and Vancouver, the three largest cities in Canada. Claiming that the lack of representation of these three centres around the Cabinet table would be dysfunctional for the government and the country, Prime Minister Harper appointed a senator to represent Montreal and lured David Emerson across the floor from the Liberals to speak for Vancouver. That Harper was prepared to face great controversy over these two moves indicates how important he felt such large-city representation to be. The party put much emphasis on attracting urban ethnocultural minorities after 2008, and the Conservatives made major urban gains in the 2011 election, especially in Toronto. In 2015, however, the Liberals regained most of these seats.

RELIGION

Historically, religious cleavages and identities in Canada coincided to a considerable extent with those of language and ethnicity, so that the interests of French Catholics were often at odds with those of Anglo-Protestants. Especially in the earlier years, the religious conflict even overshadowed the ethnic one, usually being a problem between Protestants and Roman Catholics within the Christian church. As this issue has diminished to some extent in recent years, other religious issues have gained more prominence.

Separate Schools

The first main religious demand in Canada came from Roman Catholic and Protestant minorities who wanted their own separate school systems. The Protestant minority in Quebec and the Roman Catholic minority in Ontario were successful in having this right established in law at the elementary level before Confederation. Thus, in the **Constitution Act, 1867**, these two minority school systems were given constitutional protection in section 93:

> Nothing in any [provincial] Law shall prejudicially affect any Right or Privilege with respect to Denominational Schools which any Class of Persons have by Law in the Province at the Union....

The section goes on to say that if either provincial legislature ever tried to abolish such separate school systems, the aggrieved minority could appeal to the federal Cabinet, which was empowered to introduce remedial legislation to restore them. Manitoba was created on the same basis, and the issue first came to a head in that province in 1890 when the Anglo-Protestant majority passed legislation abolishing the Roman Catholic separate school system. On appeal to the courts, the Judicial Committee of the Privy Council ruled that the legislation was valid: Catholics were not *prohibited* from establishing their own school system—they would merely have to help pay for the public system as well! They then appealed to the federal Cabinet under the terms of section 93. The Bowell government introduced remedial legislation, but it did not pass before the 1896 election, and the new prime minister, Wilfrid Laurier, proceeded to negotiate a compromise on the issue with the province rather than use the remedial power. When the Laurier government created Alberta and Saskatchewan in 1905, those provinces were required to provide full-fledged parallel public and Catholic systems.

In Ontario, section 93 was considered to guarantee public funding of the existing separate school system up to grade 8. When an increasing number of students went further in school, Roman Catholic pressure resulted in partial funding being extended to grades 9 and 10. Then, in 1984, after having previously opposed any change in the situation, Progressive Conservative Premier Bill Davis suddenly announced an extension of full public funding to the end of high school. This was no doubt related to the fact that the Catholic proportion of the provincial population had reached a strategic 35.6 percent. Table 9.2 indicates the proportion of Canadians belonging to major religious denominations in the 2011 National Household Survey.

A Roman Catholic demand for greater public funding usually provokes a backlash among supporters of the public system. In the case of Ontario, the extension of funding in 1984 was challenged in the courts, but the Supreme Court upheld the new law. Although it was an apparent breach of the new Charter of Rights and Freedoms (adopted in 1982), this discrimination in favour of the Roman Catholic faith had been given constitutional protection in 1867 (and 1982), and the Supreme Court declined to change it.

In the case of Quebec, however, the outcome was different. After the Quiet Revolution, language superseded religion as the key to the identity of the great majority of Quebeckers. A consensus developed among all religious and linguistic groups that the provincial school system should be transformed into one based on language rather than religion. The constitutional amendment required to override section 93 passed the Quebec legislature easily, but it barely

TABLE 9.2 RELIGION IN CANADA, 2011 NATIONAL HOUSEHOLD SURVEY

DENOMINATION	NUMBER	PERCENTAGE
ROMAN CATHOLIC	12 810 705	39.0
PROTESTANT	8 741 350	26.7
NO RELIGION	7 850 605	23.9
MUSLIM	1 053 945	3.2
CHRISTIAN ORTHODOX	550 690	1.7
HINDU	497 965	1.5
SIKH	454 965	1.4
BUDDHIST	366 830	1.1
JEWISH	329 495	1.0
TOTAL	32 852 320	

Source: Adapted from Statistics Canada. 2013. National Household Survey (NHS) Profile. 2011 National Household Survey. Catalogue no. 99-004-XWE, (September 11, 2013), http://www12.statcan. gc.ca/nhs -enm/2011/dp-pd/prof/index.cfm?Lang=Eproducts/analytic/companion/rel/canada.cfm. Reproduced and distributed on an "as is" basis with the permission of Statistics Canada.

got through the House of Commons because many Catholic MPs worried that it might have a domino effect on separate school systems in other provinces.

In a sense, it did. When Newfoundland and Labrador entered Confederation in 1949, several different religious groups were guaranteed their own separate school systems. A shortage of finances and a spirit of ecumenicalism saw the three main Protestant groups voluntarily amalgamate their schools in 1968; however, the Roman Catholics and Pentecostals were determined to maintain their own. By the 1990s, especially at a time of serious recession, the provincial government of Clyde Wells decided to establish one public school system in the province. A referendum on the issue held in 1995 approved the government plan, which would have left the churches with a limited role in the system. When the Roman Catholics and Pentecostals refused to cooperate, new Premier Brian Tobin called for a second referendum in 1997 that cut out the churches entirely, and his bill passed by a larger margin, eventually also being approved by the federal Parliament. This leaves only Ontario, Saskatchewan, and Alberta with fully funded Roman Catholic separate school systems. Meanwhile, after Quebec introduced its secularized school system in 2008, it brought in a mandatory ethics and religious instruction program that discussed a variety of religious traditions. This program was challenged in the Supreme Court in 2012 but upheld because it did not violate anyone's specific freedom of religion.[14] In the same year, Ontario premier Dalton McGuinty ignored Catholic protests when he promoted gay–straight student alliances in all of the province's schools.

CRITICAL APPROACHES

The *historical-institutional approach* to religion in Canada would emphasize the rights granted to Roman Catholics in the Constitution Act, 1867, especially the provision for separate religious schools. Although the Catholic–Protestant divide is not as important today as it was in Canadian politics at the time of Confederation and for the next half century or so afterward, most of the constitutional rights that Catholics managed to obtain during that period persist to the present day. Three provinces maintain a constitutionally protected and publicly funded Catholic school system. It is certainly reasonable to assume, for a number of reasons, that no current provincial government would create a publicly funded Catholic school system. Yet, decisions that were made in 1867 became entrenched as large organizations and interested social groups resisted subsequent efforts to abolish these separate school boards. As a result, separate Catholic school boards persist in Ontario, Alberta, and Saskatchewan.

Other Religious Issues

As mentioned in Chapter 5, the Roman Catholic Church was a formidable force in Quebec politics, both federal and provincial, until the Quiet Revolution of the 1960s. In that earlier era, religious cleavages regularly surfaced in terms of the proper proportion of people appointed as cabinet ministers and other public officeholders. Other federal issues with a Protestant–Catholic religious overtone included relations with the Vatican, immigration, birth control, divorce, and abortion. Whatever the official position of the Church, it was only after many Roman Catholics were quite obviously taking the birth control pill that the sale of contraceptive devices was legalized in 1968. By then, too, thousands of Roman Catholics were seeking divorces or annulments, so the Divorce Act was amended to permit divorce on grounds other than adultery, and to force Quebec and Newfoundland to handle divorces in their own courts, as in other provinces. Justice Minister Pierre Trudeau also amended the abortion laws, but it fell to Dr. Henry Morgentaler to challenge the still rigid provision in the Criminal Code, which the Supreme Court removed in 1988. Even after it was legalized, abortion continued to be opposed by many religious groups, including the Catholic Church and evangelical Christians. Morgentaler's abortion clinic in Toronto was bombed in 1992, and his installation in the Order of Canada in 2008 ignited considerable protest.

Canadians of Jewish ethnicity and faith have faced both governmental and private sector discrimination until recent times. Canada did not permit Jewish immigration from Europe in the 1930s, for example; the Christian elitism of Canadian politics of the time would not allow Mackenzie King to name David Croll to the federal Cabinet (later settling for an appointment to the Senate); and anti-Semitism pervaded society. Nowadays, however, it is conventional to find a place in the federal Cabinet for at least one person of Jewish background, and in an appeal for Jewish votes, Conservative leader Joe Clark made an unfulfilled election promise in 1979 to move the Canadian embassy in Israel from Tel Aviv to Jerusalem. It was largely because of pressure by Jewish groups that the government began to prosecute Canadians accused of killing Jews in Nazi concentration camps in Europe in the Second World War. Cases have also gone to court involving anti-Semitic denials of the Holocaust.

As early as the 1980s, court decisions outlawed the recital of the Lord's Prayer in Ontario public schools unless it was accompanied by readings from other religious groups. About the same time, the courts struck down the Lord's Day Act, which restricted commercial activity on Sunday for religious reasons. The Supreme Court did allow similar legislation to be passed if its limitations on Sunday activity were based on the desirability of a common day of rest, for which purpose Sunday just happened to be chosen, but most provinces have since removed any such restrictions.

One issue that was prominent in the 1990s was the question of Sikh members of the RCMP and other police forces being allowed to wear their turbans as part of religious tradition. Related to this was the issue of Sikh children wearing their ceremonial kirpan daggers while attending public schools.

In some provinces, minority religions have persuaded the authorities to provide partial funding for religious schools other than Roman Catholic, but this has been quite controversial in Ontario. The Harris government rejected such calls from Jews, Muslims, and evangelical Christians, even after they won support from the United Nations, although it enacted a tax credit scheme for parents whose children attended any kind of private school. The McGuinty government cancelled this initiative on obtaining office. When Ontario PC leader John Tory proposed to provide public funding for all religious schools in 2007, however, a backlash developed which guaranteed his loss in the election.

Meanwhile, earlier governments in Ontario had allowed the practice of settling certain family disputes in a Jewish court (a *beit din*) instead of using the regular courts, as long as all parties to the dispute were agreed. But when a Muslim organization signalled its intention to employ sharia law in the arbitration of internal family conflicts in 2005, the McGuinty government cancelled the practice for all religious groups.[15] At the federal level, faith-based groups have won CRTC approval for their own individual or ecumenical radio and television stations. A few provincial civil servants, citing their own freedom of religion, refused to perform same-sex marriages, and one demand so far untouched by the politicians is the question of polygamy, an issue that has gone to court.

Current Religious Issues

In general, the traditional religious cleavage in Canadian society between Protestants and Roman Catholics is not one that is likely to engender much political conflict, especially at the federal level, in the 21st century. Figure 9.2 indicates that the proportion of the Canadian-born with no religious affiliation increased significantly over the 1985–2004 period, as did the group that had a religious affiliation but did not attend religious services. In 2004, their combined figures were close to 50 percent. On the other hand, those who immigrated to Canada over the past 20 years were more stable in these two respects, with about 65 percent taking their religion seriously.

As religious identity becomes less salient to many Canadians of longstanding residence, other religions denominations have grown in size and have developed a heightened sense that their identities should be reflected in public policies. These groups include Muslims and evangelical Christians, and the conflict is often between Christians collectively and non-Christians, or between the nonreligious and the strong adherents in a variety of religions. The Harper

FIGURE 9.2 CANADIAN-BORN LOSING FAITH MORE THAN IMMIGRANTS

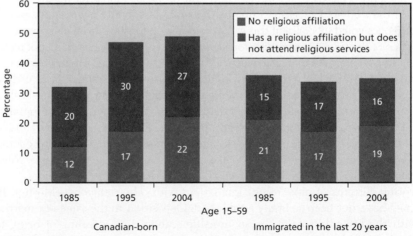

Sources: Statistics Canada, Warren Clark and Grant Schellenberg, "Who's Religious?" Canadian Social Trends, (Summer 2008), p. 4, Catalogue No.11-008, http://www.statcan.gc.ca/pub/11-008-x/11-008-x2006001-eng.pdf. Reproduced and distributed on an "as is" basis with the permission of Statistics Canada.

government proposed to allow the Heritage Minister to deny tax credits to film or television projects that it deemed offensive or not in the public interest, and prominent evangelical activist Charles McVety, president of the Canada Family Action Coalition, took some credit for pushing the government in this direction. Under fire for cultural policies in general, however, Harper later abandoned this proposal.

The main new religious issues in recent years involve Muslims, as their proportion of the population increases and as their issues become more prominent around the world. As mentioned in Chapter 6, after the terrorist attacks of 9/11, Canadian Muslims and Arabs were often victims of a backlash.[16] While a handful of home-grown Islamic terrorists have been charged and convicted, others remain in custody as mere suspects. Some who had been suspects, either in Canada or the United States, such as Maher Arar, have been cleared of any such connections. Omar Khadr, a Canadian citizen who was fighting as a 15-year-old alongside the Taliban in Afghanistan, was captured after he was wounded in a battle against coalition soldiers. Khadr was sent to the U.S. prison camp in Guantanamo Bay, Cuba, where he was charged and eventually pleaded guilty to killing an American soldier. Khadr was repatriated to Canada where he was expected to serve out his sentence in a Canadian prison. Khadr was parolled in 2015, against the wishes of the Harper government. Meanwhile, the Harper government reversed the balanced Canadian foreign policy between Israel and Arabs in the Middle East, becoming the strongest overseas supporter of the Jewish state.

The integration of newcomers into Quebec society, perhaps especially visible Muslim immigrants, is a particular problem for those whose sense of nationalism is based on French ethnicity rather than a more inclusive Quebec. When opposition to certain distinctive new practices flared up in the province, Premier Charest appointed a commission to make recommendations on "reasonable accommodation." As mentioned in Chapter 6, that commission basically argued that immigrants were not a threat to the French character of Quebec, but this conclusion did not end the debate, and a law was passed to require Muslim women to bare their face when dealing with public authorities.

Political scientists are especially interested in how people of various religions vote. One of the constants in the study of Canadian voting behaviour, at least until very recently, was that most Roman Catholics voted Liberal, and this was a major reason for the Liberal party being in government so much of the time. Despite this strong correlation, political science could not really explain it,[17] but this link has been weakening in recent elections. Despite its appeal to those with no religious affiliation, the CCF/NDP had a connection to the Social Gospel movement in its early years and even later attracted many United Church ministers to its ranks. Meanwhile, evangelical Christians took an active part in the Reform Party and the Canadian Alliance and were strong supporters of Stockwell Day when he won the leadership of the party. After the new Conservative Party of Canada was established, people belonging to this creed were sometimes accused of capturing control of local party associations in order to choose a like-minded Conservative candidate. Nevertheless, **evangelicalism** is a much less significant force in Canadian than in American politics.[18]

The voting patterns of more recent immigrants with other religions—Muslim, Buddhist, and Hindu—have not been so firmly established. Opposition to the same-sex marriage issue, disgust with the Liberals' role in the sponsorship scandal, and a feeling of being taken for granted by the Liberals may have lured many of them to support Stephen Harper's Conservative Party in 2006 and 2008. The Harper government certainly tried to woo Muslim and other such voters with some of its more conservative domestic policies, but its strong support for Israel in foreign policy and its rigid approach to "anti-terrorism," such as in its protracted refusal to bring Omar Khadr home from Guantanamo Bay, were not conducive to this purpose.

The Canadian Islamic Congress repeatedly felt snubbed by that government. In any case, the Conservative majority in the 2011 election was largely attributable to its newly won seats in suburban Toronto which were heavily populated by visible and "new" religious minorities. These ridings returned to the Liberals in 2015.

AGE

Because society generally feels that neither the young nor seniors should be expected to work for a living, and since most people pass through various age categories, few actually oppose in principle the demands from these two sectors of the population. While the young and middle-aged may complain about the costs of supporting the elderly, and those in higher age brackets may object to paying taxes to finance education and other public programs for the young, intergenerational conflict should not be exaggerated. Still, as seniors make up an increasing proportion of the electorate, their concerns have greater impact on the political system than ever before. Policies relating to children and young adults are mostly provincial and territorial in nature and were mentioned earlier in the chapters on class and gender, while the issue of the lack of political engagement on the part of young people is addressed in Chapter 15, which includes a graph on estimated voter turnout rate by age. This section will therefore concentrate on seniors.

CRITICAL APPROACHES

Why are there often differences between the young and the old when it comes to a wide range of political behaviours and attitudes? Scholars working in the field of political behaviour often distinguish two broad kinds of age-related differences: "life-cycle effects" and "generational effects." Life-cycle effects refer to age-related differences that stem from the different kinds of interests and experiences that people have at different stages of their life. People may be more concerned about investments in postsecondary education when they are younger because it affects them more directly. As people get older, however, they may buy a house, start to earn a better income, and thus become more concerned with issues surrounding taxation and less preoccupied with postsecondary education. These life-cycle differences refer to attitudes

that change as people get older. But when it comes to generational effects, people's attitudes are relatively stable. Generational effects refer to age-related differences that persist throughout the life cycle. These age differences may stem from the shared experiences of an age group at some period in time. The Great Depression, for example, left a mark on the attitudes of those who lived through these experiences that persisted throughout their lives. Those who came of age during the more prosperous post-War era acquired different attitudes than their parents and grandparents. As a result, the older Canadians who lived through the Great Depression tended to harbour attitudes about spending and thrift that differed markedly from the attitudes of younger Canadians who did not experience the Depression.

Earlier Struggles

Seniors were one of the first groups in society to be identified for public support by the federal government. This occurred in 1926 with the passage of the Old Age Pensions Act, which provided a tiny monthly payment, based on a means test, to those aged 70 and over, jointly financed by Ottawa and the provinces. In 1951, such pensions were transformed into a universal, federal Old Age Security (OAS) program; since then the monthly payment increased regularly, and the age of eligibility dropped to 65. Ottawa brought in the contributory Canada Pension Plan (CPP) in 1964, and in 1966 the Guaranteed Income Supplement (GIS) was added for those who had little or no other income. Finally, the Spouses' Allowance, introduced in 1975, provides a monthly payment to those between 60 and 65 who are spouses, widows, or widowers of a pensioner with little or no income. Several provinces and territories also provide supplementary old age benefits of one kind or another, and many of those in the labour force have workplace pensions to which both they and their employers contribute. But given the limitations of all these programs, many Canadians set aside money before they retire in Registered Retirement Savings Plans (RRSPs) and deduct the amount from their income tax.

The Mulroney government was the first to try to reduce its support of seniors by partially de-indexing the OAS from cost-of-living increases in 1985. This led to a spontaneous national protest of "grey power" that forced the government to change its mind. The seniors demonstrated an enviable vitality in mobilizing the National Pensioners and Senior Citizens Federation and other groups on this issue, which provided a rare example of applying sufficient pressure to change a provision in a national budget. However, seniors have not been as well organized since and have lost some ground. In the 1989 budget, the government reduced its commitment by eliminating OAS payments from those whose with high incomes (now $110 000) and partially clawing back the pension from those earning over $50 000 (now $68 000) annually. A somewhat similar conflict occurred when Paul Martin engaged in massive cutbacks as finance minister in the 1995 budget. In this case, Martin and Prime Minister Chrétien came to an unprecedented brink of conflict, with the PM carrying the day before the budget was delivered.[19] In other words, even in the absence of an adversarial interest (except for those who wanted to balance the budget), seniors have had to fight to maintain existing programs.

More positive responses were the creation of a National Advisory Council on Aging in 1980 and the designation by a number of governments of a cabinet minister to be in charge of seniors' affairs. Thus, like women, Aboriginals, immigrants, and ethnocultural minorities, seniors usually have a minister and a bureaucratic agency to speak for them within the political elite.

Population Projections

How is the population divided by age, and what does the future portend in this respect? Statistics Canada estimated the 2011 Canadian population at 34.5 million, divided into the following age groups: 5 645 000 people under age 15 (16.4 percent); 23 864 500 people between the ages of 15 and 64 (69.2 percent); and 4 973 400 people over 65 years of age (14.4 percent).[20] The average age of the population has been increasing and will increase more as time goes on, as shown in Figure 9.3. In projecting future population figures, it is necessary to make assumptions about fertility rates, life expectancy, immigration, and emigration.[21]

FIGURE 9.3 PROPORTION OF PERSONS AGED 65 YEARS AND OVER IN CANADA, 1956 TO 2006, AND ESTIMATED PROPORTION OF PERSONS AGED 65 YEARS AND OVER, 2011 TO 2036

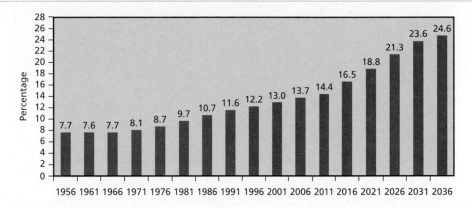

Sources: Statistics Canada, 2006 Census. Fig. 2, http://www12.statcan.ca/census-recensement/2006/as-sa/ 97-551/figures/c2-eng.cfm; Statistics Canada, Population Projections for Canada, Provinces and Territories: Table 10-1 – Population by age group and sex, low-growth scenario (L), July 1st – Canada, 2010 to 2036, http://www.statcan.gc.ca/pub/91-520-x/2010001/t334-eng.htm (April 6, 2012). Reproduced and distributed on an "as is" basis with the permission of Statistics Canada.

The current Canadian fertility rate is about 1.5; that is, there is an average of 1.5 births per woman. Although a fertility rate of 2.1 is required to replace the existing population, the current rate should continue to increase the population until about 2025 because of the high proportion of women of childbearing age. After that, deaths will exceed births, so that any increase in population will depend entirely on immigration.

After 2011, as the postwar "baby boom" generation (those born between 1946 and 1966) reaches retirement age, the number of people aged 65 and over will rise dramatically to nearly 10 million by 2036, including more than 500 000 over the age of 90! In short, the proportion of seniors will increase from 14.4 percent to nearly 25 percent over the 2011–36 period. While the group over 65 is increasing, the proportion under 15 will decrease from 16.4 percent in 2011 to 14.3 percent in 2036. Taking the two groups together, they increase from about 30 percent in 2011 to 39 percent by 2036. According to Statistics Canada's 2006 "medium growth" projections, the number of seniors will begin to exceed the number of children in about 2016, as indicated in Figure 9.4.

Statistics Canada refers to those between the ages of 15 and 64 as the "working-age population." Assuming that they are in the labour force and financially self-sufficient and that those under 15 and over 65 are not, sociologists talk of the **dependency ratio**—the proportion of the population that is financially dependent on others for the financing of pensions, social security, education, medical services, and other government programs. The dependency ratio is expressed as the number of people of dependent ages per 100 persons of working age. The dependency ratio was 44 in 2011 (i.e., for every 100 people between 15 and 65, there were 44 in the dependent age ranges) and will increase to about 64 by the year 2036.[22]

Two main public policy implications flow from the increasing dependency ratio and transformation of the dependent group from young to old. First, the financial burden of children is

FIGURE 9.4 PROPORTION OF PERSONS AGED 65 YEARS AND OVER AND CHILDREN AGED 14 AND UNDER, CANADA, 1971-2031

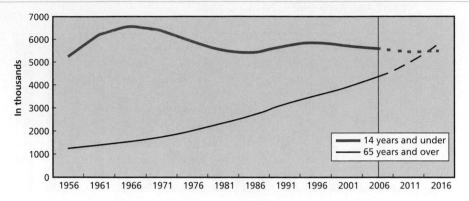

Sources: Statistics Canada, 2006 Census: Portrait of the Canadian Population in 2006, by Age and Sex, Figure 1, Number of persons aged 65 years and over and number of children aged less than 15 years in the Canadian population, 1956 to 2016, http://www12.statcan.ca/census-recensement/2006/as-sa/97-551/figures/c1-eng.cfm. Reproduced and distributed on an "as is" basis with the permission of Statistics Canada.

usually borne by the immediate family, but seniors make a larger claim on public resources—according to some estimates, 2.5 times as much. Second, the senior group itself will also grow older, with those over 80 being more dependent than those between 65 and 79, and therefore even more expensive in support programs.

Future Issues

This changing age structure, especially the increase in the proportion of seniors, is likely to have profound effects on the pattern of demands in the political system. Although many seniors are self-sufficient, the Parliamentary Budget Officer reported that governments are not engaged in sufficient planning for the massive aging of the population, as the work force shrinks in proportion to the growing pool of retirees with demands for health spending and elderly benefits. Let us examine some of these concerns.[23]

Given the increasing number of seniors and the declining fertility rate, most observers see the need for large-scale immigration to bolster the number of contributors to public pension plans. Because public pensions provide barely enough for many people to live on, it is regrettable that fewer than half of seniors have registered pension and savings plans with which to supplement public programs. Employer pension plans often leave much to be desired, and most lost a substantial amount of their value in the worldwide economic meltdown of 2008–09. Even employers that remained standing had trouble meeting their pension obligations, and this continues to be a crucial issue for both provincial and federal governments to address. Contrary to these perceived needs, and generating much controversy, the Harper government announced in its 2012 budget that the minimum age of eligibility for the OAS would be raised from 65 to 67.

The question of mandatory retirement has also arisen in recent years, although this issue does not necessarily divide people on the basis of age. Some older people want to work beyond age 65, either for financial or psychological reasons, but many retire early. However, mandatory retirement is usually supported by the trade union movement as a means applying pressure for better pensions. The Supreme Court ruled that mandatory retirement policies or laws are discriminatory on the basis of age but justifiable as a "reasonable limit." Nevertheless, one jurisdiction after another has abolished mandatory retirement, either on the basis that it is discriminatory or because it is increasingly felt that the economy needs more people to work beyond 65 years of age.

Of utmost importance in the future will be the increased demand for health services. Ottawa provides huge annual grants to the provinces and territories for health care, but it is at the provincial and territorial level that demands for improved health care are generally articulated. Many seniors worry that in any future rationing of such services, they will be considered expendable. Not only do they battle against any retraction of the health care system, but they also advocate an expansion—to include a national pharmacare program, home care, and long-term care in the Canada Health Act, for example. Given the difficulty most governments have had in balancing their budgets, however, there is little sign of improving the public health care system.

The public purse will only be able to afford adequate medical care for seniors if a change is made from the emphasis on hospitalization to caring for them as much as possible in their own homes, partly by means of home support programs. This in turn raises the question of housing. The federal government reduced the role of Canada Mortgage and Housing Corporation in social and cooperative housing that was of interest to seniors, although some funding for home renovations has been added, and some provinces and/or municipalities provide seniors with a shelter allowance to reduce their burden of property taxes. Many localities are experiencing a crisis in long-term care: those in need of nursing home care often have to do without, needlessly occupy acute-care beds in hospitals, or end up in facilities far from where they and family members live. A related problem concerns the "sandwich generation," family members caught between the demands of caring simultaneously for both their children and related seniors. This stressful situation sometimes calls out for tax breaks, compensation, or at least information on long-term illnesses and disabilities.[24]

Seniors have not been particularly well organized over the years, but because they have no real adversaries, several programs of benefit to them have been adopted after pressure from other quarters. The success of the National Pensioners and Senior Citizens Federation, which

Brian Gable/The Globe and Mail/Canadian Press

CHAPTER 9 **Urban/Rural Location, Religion, and Age**   **199** suddenly sprang into action in connection with the 1985 budget de-indexation affair, convinced Canadian seniors that they would have to fight their own battles. That organization continues to function, as does Canadian Pensioners Concerned and the Canadian Association of Retired Persons.

On the other hand, the growing numbers of seniors has been noticed by political parties, especially because they constitute the age cohort that is most likely to vote. As we shall see in Chapter 15, there is a dramatic increase in turnout as the age of voters rises.

CONCLUSION

This chapter has demonstrated the increasing chasm between rural and urban Canada, in which both interests compete for government attention. It also showed certain value differences between rural and urban Canadians. As for religion, although church attendance continues to fall, traditional issues, such as funding for separate schools, still surface periodically. A variety of new religious concerns have emerged in recent years, largely traceable to the arrival of diverse religious groups in Canada. In terms of age, the extent to which the Canadian population is growing older is quite dramatic, and the political system will have to devote more resources to the needs of this cohort of society.

Several of the issues raised in this chapter have links to previous ones, such as the connection between religion and ethnicity, whether French or ethnocultural minorities (Chapters 5 and 6). Urban and rural locations are linked to geography (Chapter 3), and age may be connected to class (Chapter 8). More importantly, the three concerns of this chapter reappear in terms of political parties and voting behaviour (Chapters 14 and 15) as well as of advocacy groups (Chapter 16). Geographic location is related to the electoral system and representation in Parliament (Chapters 13 and 23), and religion is revisited in Chapter 19 (the Charter of Rights and Freedoms).

DISCUSSION QUESTIONS

1. To what extent are the concerns of urban and rural Canadians at odds with each other?

2. Does a declining share of the population mean rural concerns are destined to be increasingly ignored?

3. What historic demands of a religious nature continue to have political relevance today?

4. What are the more recent religious issues on the Canadian political agenda?

5. How much will the Canadian political agenda change as a result of the aging of the population?

MindTap®   FOR MORE INFO GO TO http://www.nelson.com/student

NOTES

1. Warren Clark and Grant Schellenberg, "Who's Religious?" Statistics Canada, *Canadian Social Trends* (Summer 2006).
2. V. du Plessis, R. Beshiri, R. Bollman, and H. Clemenson, "Definition of Rural," Rural and Small Town Analysis Bulletin 3, no. 3, pp. 1–17, as quoted in Bill Reimer, "Rural and Urban: Differences and Common Ground," in Harry H. Hiller, ed., *Urban Canada: Sociological Perspectives* (Oxford University Press, 2005), p. 73; Federation of Canadian Municipalities website.
3. Reimer, "Rural and Urban: Differences and Common Ground," p. 71.
4. Reimer, "Rural and Urban: Differences and Common Ground."
5. Statistics Canada, *2011 Census of Agriculture.* "Snapshot of Canadian Agriculture," available at http://www.statcan.gc.ca/pub/95-640-x/2012002/00-eng.htm.
6. A good source of such demands is the Canadian Federation of Agriculture.
7. Grace Skogstad, "The Dynamics of Institutional Transformation: The Case of the Canadian Wheat Board," *Canadian Journal of Political Science* (September 2005).
8. CBC News, "Mad Cow Disease in Canada: The Science and The Story," April 24, 2006, available at http://www.cbc.ca/news/background/madcow.
9. For a practical look at non-agricultural rural issues, see Roger Fitzgerald, "Challenges Facing Rural Communities: A Newfoundland and Labrador Perspective," *Canadian Parliamentary Review* (Autumn 2005).
10. Federation of Canadian Municipalities, *Policy Statement,* "2005 Policy Statement on Rural Issues"; cited on January 15, 2006, available at http://www.fcm.ca/english/policy/rural.html.
11. Samuel A. Bottomley, "Locked and Loaded: Gun Control Policy in Canada," in Robert M. Campbell, Leslie A. Pal, and Michael Howlett, eds., *The Real Worlds of Canadian Politics: Cases in Process and Policy,* 4th ed. (Peterborough: Broadview Press, 2004).
12. Fred Cutler and Richard W. Jenkins, "Where One Lives and What One Thinks: Implications of Rural–Urban Opinion Cleavages for Canadian Federalism," in Hamish Telford and Harvey Lazar, eds., *Canada: The State of the Federation 2001* (Kingston: Institute of Intergovernmental Relations, 2002).
13. Michael Adams, "The Seeds of Electoral Realignment: The Urban–Rural Divide is Overtaking Region as a Predictor of How Canadians Will Vote," *The Globe and Mail,* March 26, 2008.
14. *S.L. v. Commission scolaire des Chênes,* [2012] 1 S.C.R. 235.
15. Marion Boyd, "Religion-Based Alternative Dispute Resolution: A Challenge to Multiculturalism," available at http://www.irpp.org/books/archive/AOTS3/Boyd.pdf.
16. Daiva Stasiulis and Yasmeen Abu-Laban, "Unequal Relations and the Struggle for Equality: Race and Ethnicity in Canadian Politics," in Michael Whittington and Glen Williams, eds., *Canadian Politics in the 21st Century,* 7th ed. (Toronto: Nelson Education, 2008).
17. André Blais, "Accounting for the Electoral Success of the Liberal Party in Canada," *Canadian Journal of Political Science,* 38 (2005): 821–40; André Blais, Elisabeth Gidengil, Richard Nadeau, and Neil Nevitte, *Anatomy of a Liberal Victory: Making Sense of the Vote in the 2000 Canadian Election* (Peterborough: Broadview Press, 2002).
18. Jonathan Malloy, "The Politics of Canadian and American Evangelical Christians: Comparing Big Apples and Small Oranges?" in *American Review of Canadian Studies* (Fall 2009); "Christian Activists Capturing Tory Races," *The Globe and Mail,* May 27, 2005; Trevor W. Harrison, "Populist and Conservative Christian Evangelical Movements: A Comparison of Canada and the United States," in Miriam Smith, ed., *Group Politics and Social Movements in Canada* (Peterborough: Broadview Press, 2008).
19. Edward Greenspon and Anthony Wilson-Smith, *Double Vision: The Inside Story of the Liberals in Power* (Toronto: Doubleday Canada, 1996), Ch. 16; Lawrence Martin, *Iron Man: The Defiant Reign of Jean Chrétien* (Toronto: Viking Canada, 2003), pp. 101–05.
20. Statistics Canada, *Population by sex and age group, 2011,* accessed on June 13, 2012. See also the 2011 Census figures, which are very similar.
21. In the projection shown, Statistics Canada assumes a continuing fertility rate of about 1.5, that life expectancy will rise by about four years by 2031, and that immigration will continue at between 250 000 and 300 000 newcomers per year.

22. Statistics Canada, *Population Projections for Canada, Provinces and Territories: Table 10-1—Population by age group and sex, low-growth scenario (L), July 1st—Canada, 2010 to 2036*, available at http://www .statcan.gc.ca/pub/91-520-x/2010001/t334-eng.htm.
23. Neena L. Chappell, *Population Aging and the Evolving Care Needs of Older Canadians: An Overview of the Policy Challenges* (Montreal: Institute for Research on Public Policy, 2011).
24. Cara Williams, "The Sandwich Generation," *Canadian Social Trends* (Statistics Canada, Catalogue No. 11-008, Summer 2005).

FURTHER READING

Blais, André, Elisabeth Gidengil, Richard Nadeau, and Neil Nevitte. *Anatomy of a Liberal Victory: Making Sense of the Vote in the 2000 Canadian Election*. Peterborough: Broadview Press, 2002.

Bottomley, Samuel A. "Locked and Loaded: Gun Control Policy in Canada," in Robert M. Campbell, Leslie A. Pal, and Michael Howlett, eds., *The Real Worlds of Canadian Politics: Cases in Process and Policy*, 4th ed. Peterborough: Broadview Press, 2000.

Chappell, Neena L. *Population Aging and the Evolving Care Needs of Older Canadians: An Overview of the Policy Challenges*. Montreal: Institute for Research on Public Policy, 2011.

Cutler, Fred, and Richard W. Jenkins. "Where One Lives and What One Thinks: Implications of Rural–Urban Opinion Cleavages for Canadian Federalism," in Hamish Telford and Harvey Lazar, eds. *Canada: The State of the Federation 2001*. Kingston: Institute of Intergovernmental Relations, 2002.

Harrison, Trevor W. "Populist and Conservative Christian Evangelical Movements: A Comparison of Canada and the United States," in Miriam Smith, ed. *Group Politics and Social Movements in Canada*. Peterborough: Broadview Press, 2008.

Hiller, Harry H., ed. *Urban Canada: Sociological Perspectives*. Oxford University Press, 2005.

Malloy, Jonathan. "The Politics of Canadian and American Evangelical Christians: Comparing Big Apples and Small Oranges?" in *American Review of Canadian Studies* (Fall 2009).

Skogstad, Grace. "The Dynamics of Institutional Transformation: The Case of the Canadian Wheat Board." *Canadian Journal of Political Science* (September 2005).

Chase Clausen/Shutterstock

CHAPTER 10

Canada's External Environment: The United States and the World

The Canadian armed forces have participated in many United Nations peacekeeping operations, but in recent years took a more aggressive part in conflicts in Afghanistan and Libya. Thirty percent of Canada's Gross Domestic Product (GDP) comes from exports to other countries, and 70 percent of those exports go to one country: the United States. Anglophones in Canada watch far more American TV shows than Canadian ones. And Canadian policy-makers are bound by myriad international rules and commitments relating to the economy, the environment, politics, and the military. Canada does not exist in a vacuum; instead, it is linked to the rest of the world by all sorts of political, economic, defensive, technological, cultural, demographic, and individual ties. These links constitute the global environment of the Canadian political system. They have an ever-increasing impact on it, causing Canadian governments more and more difficulty in pursuing their own policy preferences.

Canada started out as a combination of French and British colonies, with all of its basic decisions being made by colonial powers abroad. As Canada emerged into a sovereign state, the world was becoming increasingly interdependent so that even though the country gained the legal powers to make decisions for itself, it faced a multitude of external influences. Given its location, Canada is particularly susceptible to influence from the United States, which is perhaps the most dominant political, economic, cultural, and military force in human history. This chapter thus details Canada's slow but steady absorption into the U.S. sphere of influence. It discusses the demands that the United States makes on the Canadian political system, the effects of the U.S. presence on Canadian values and opinions, and the policies that have been adopted to both foster and resist such absorption. But at the same time, the Canadian political system is increasingly subject to a wider variety of international, multinational, and supranational pressures, many of which can be subsumed under the heading of **globalization**.

The chapter begins with a discussion of this wider context and later emphasizes the continuing importance of the United States, which affects Canada both in bilateral and multilateral dimensions.[1]

THE GLOBAL SETTING
Foreign Governments

Foreign governments make decisions every day in both foreign and domestic policy that can have an effect on Canada. Sometimes this impact is deliberate, but often it is unintentional. Of course, it is the responsibility of our foreign affairs officials (and, in really crucial situations, the minister of foreign affairs, the minister of finance, or even the prime minister) to put pressure on such governments so that their decisions are not harmful to Canada. Policies of the United States are far more likely than those of other foreign governments to have an impact on Canada, and these will be detailed later in the chapter.

Included in the long list of other countries' policies that affect Canada are European Union bans on the import of Canadian seal products and furs from animals caught by using leg-hold traps, restrictions on certain lumber exports, and disagreements over the labelling of champagne and scallops. Given the integration of the Canadian and American economies, so-called "Buy American" provisions, which the United States government sometimes institutes in order to prevent government funds from flowing to foreign companies, are often perceived as threatening to Canada's economic wellbeing. On the other hand, Canada has long complained that a number of European countries overfished within Canadian territorial waters and had a major role in the destruction of the groundfish industry. China is an increasingly important player on the international scene and in Canada's own policymaking process, related to massive imports of manufactured goods; exports of Canadian raw materials; investment in each other's economy; immigration to Canada; and environmental, human rights, and foreign policy issues. Another realm of recent interaction and potential conflict between Canada and other governments is the Arctic, especially as global warming allows for substantial sea traffic and mineral exploration in the region.

AP Photo/Susan Walsh/Canadian Press Images

U.S. President Barack Obama, right, listens as Canada's Prime Minister Justin Trudeau, left, speaks during a bilateral meeting at the Asia-Pacific Economic Cooperation summit in Manila, Philippines, Thursday, Nov. 19, 2015.

International Organizations

Canada has joined a multitude of international organizations with the aim of taking advantage of opportunities to influence other countries' policies, to expand external trade, and to promote joint objectives with other states. Nevertheless, such membership often entails obligations and responsibilities that influence Canadian domestic or foreign policies. A list of the principal international organizations to which Canada belongs is provided below, but a few examples of how such organizations have an impact on Canadian policies should be mentioned. Belonging to the United Nations gives a middle-ranking country a platform to promote its altruistic and its self-interested objectives. The UN has always been central to Canadian foreign policy: Canada has preferred to base its actions on **multilateralism** in this and other international organizations. But the UN also makes claims on Canada, such as to pay our regular share of its budget and to answer the call (and pay the bill) whenever it decides to set up a peacekeeping force in far-flung trouble spots around the world. The United Nations has also criticized several domestic Canadian policies, including Quebec's language legislation; federal and provincial laws on labour, Aboriginals, and women; and the deterioration of social programs leading to widespread problems of poverty and hunger. Although the United Nations has few coercive resources to apply to governments that break their commitments to its covenants, the organization wields considerable prestige, and its moral suasion is sometimes enough to make governments change their domestic policies.

LEADING INTERNATIONAL ORGANIZATIONS TO WHICH CANADA BELONGS

- United Nations (UN)
- World Trade Organization (WTO)
- North Atlantic Treaty Association (NATO)
- North American Aerospace Defense Command (NORAD)
- International Monetary Fund (IMF) and the World Bank
- Organisation for Economic Co-operation and Development (OECD)
- Commonwealth
- La Francophonie
- Organization of American States
- G7 and G20
- Asia-Pacific Economic Cooperation Council (APEC)

The **World Trade Organization (WTO)** can actually require its members to change their trading practices. For example, in response to American complaints, the WTO ordered Canada to discontinue a federal excise tax and postal subsidies to protect domestic magazines. It has also ruled on such issues as the EU ban on Canadian beef, Canadian and Brazilian subsidies to their aerospace industries, export subsidies to Canadian dairy products, drug patent policy, Australia's ban on imports of Canadian salmon, and the Canada–U.S. Auto Pact. The WTO has thus become a huge impediment to the pursuit of Canadian government policies in a wide range of sensitive fields.

The WTO is not alone. The International Monetary Fund (IMF) puts pressure on member countries with respect to the size of national deficits, advising the Canadian government in 1991 not to raise public servants' salaries and, in 1999, to cut income taxes and the debt. International organizations to which Canada does not belong can also make decisions that have a major influence on domestic policies. The Organization of Petroleum Exporting Countries (OPEC) raised the international price of oil in the early 1970s with dramatic implications for Canadian petroleum policies as well as federal–provincial relations.

The G7 and G20 were two principal forums in which Canada and other members sought to deal with the global financial meltdown after 2008. In this situation, Canada actually tried to influence other countries' policies more than the reverse.[2] As part of this crisis, Canada hosted the G7 (then G8) and G20 meetings in June 2010, but the meetings agreed to only the most general policy objectives. A principal controversy was Canada's refusal to fund abortion in its initiative to improve the health of mothers in poor countries. Moreover, the G20 in Toronto was overshadowed by somewhat violent protests and the controversial police response. Some observers predict that the G20 will emerge as a more important body than the G8, diluting Canada's international influence.

International Agreements

Beyond the obligations and covenants of such international organizations as mentioned above, Canada often signs international agreements with one or more foreign governments. Once again, such agreements usually present both opportunities and obligations, and provide a certain amount of constraint on subsequent domestic policymaking. Of all such agreements signed by Canada over the years, the Canada–U.S. Free Trade Agreement and the North American Free Trade Agreement stand out. They will be discussed in detail below. Individual provinces have also signed agreements with other countries or with adjacent U.S. states in a kind of transborder regional integration.

Transnational Corporations and Globalization

The pressures exerted by a foreign government are regularly made on behalf of corporations with head offices in that country, and, as mentioned, international agreements are often about removing government controls on corporate behaviour. This sometimes makes it difficult to distinguish between demands made by foreign governments and those by **transnational corporations**. Such corporations have always tried to influence domestic political systems wherever they established themselves, but traditionally these demands did not differ in kind from those of companies headquartered in that country. Globalization is changing the nature of corporate behaviour, however, in both the economic and the political spheres. It is commonly characterized by the lowering of tariffs, the creation of larger free trading areas, and the increasing mobility of capital and worldwide corporate competition. Such "economic forces have pushed the issue of market liberalization to the forefront" and capital's perception "that there is too much government hindering the globalization process … had led to an assault on the powers of the nation-state."[3] The world is increasingly one integrated global economic unit in which national boundaries are much less significant than in the past. The principal characteristics of globalization are listed below.

PRINCIPAL CHARACTERISTICS OF GLOBALIZATION

- Comprehensive free trade agreements
- Removal of state controls on corporate behaviour
- Cross-border capital flows
- Worldwide corporate competition
- Mega-mergers of the largest transnational corporations
- Massive diffusion of technological change, including the Internet
- Closure of transnational plants in developed countries and migration to the developing world

- Widespread movement of people through immigration, permeability of borders, and transnationalism
- Increasing cultural interaction and harmonization

Globalization has had many implications for the Canadian economy, mostly on the closing of transnational corporations' manufacturing plants in this country, especially in Ontario. As noted in Chapter 8, however, Canada has a number of transnational corporations of its own. The main political implication of globalization is that it is increasingly difficult for national, provincial, and territorial governments to maintain distinctive labour, tax, or environmental laws because such companies regularly threaten to move to other jurisdictions that they find more congenial. On the other hand, successful and divergent banking policies in recent years are proof that it is still possible to pursue the Canadian national interest.

International Terrorism

Although the term is difficult to define, let us say that **terrorism** is any act intended to cause death or serious bodily harm to civilians "…with the purpose of intimidating a population or compelling a government or an international organization to do or abstain from doing any act."[4] This activity can be committed by domestic or external groups, but after the bombing of the World Trade Center in New York City and the Pentagon in Washington, DC, on September 11, 2001 (often called "9/11" for short), the concern with international terrorism greatly increased. These suicide missions by al-Qaeda terrorists caused some 3000 casualties and represented a significant addition to the global context within which individual states operate. The attacks led to dramatic changes in American policies at home and abroad; most other states, including Canada, also took actions in response, some of their own volition and some at the insistence of the United States. Canada passed a comprehensive piece of anti-terrorism legislation that gave sweeping powers to the government and threatened individual freedoms. Canada was also persuaded to become part of the military operations in Afghanistan, the headquarters of al-Qaeda.

Along with an increased integration of the two countries' armed forces, the American government has been adamant about beefing up security measures along the Canada–U.S. border. Considering that the United States has made the fight against terrorism its primary global mission, international terrorism has become a new constant in the Canadian policymaking process. Indeed, two terrorist attacks on Canadian soil have resulted in calls for

Uncle Sam in control of Northern Command.

still more counter-terrorism measures and security. A Canadian-citizen who was known to security officials for his radical political and religious beliefs attacked and killed a Canadian soldier in Quebec in October 2014. A few days later, a Canadian solider on ceremonial guard at the National War Memorial in Ottawa was killed when a gunman who sympathized with a foreign terrorist group attacked the Canadian parliament. These attacks led the government to propose and adopt Bill-C51, a controversial anti-terrorism act that seeks to expand information sharing across government agencies and make it easier for the police and the courts to imprison people who are suspected of undermining Canadian security. Supporters of the bill claim that these measures are necessary in order to keep Canadians safe from terrorist attacks. Critics object that the proposed legislation undermines privacy, free expression, and legal rights of Canadian citizens. As we shall see in later chapters, this line of debate is a recurring theme in Canadian politics, especially since the advent of the Charter of Rights in 1982.

U.S. INFLUENCES IN DEFENCE, FOREIGN, AND BORDER POLICIES

Canadian Defence Policy

Shortly after Confederation, Britain withdrew its garrisons from Canada and left the colony to fend for itself militarily. Britain expected Canadian assistance in the Boer War around the turn of the 20th century, however, and much greater military support in the First World War, regardless of whether these wars were relevant to Canada.

Canada's first military engagement after achieving full autonomy in 1931 was the Second World War, which began in 1939. A year later, Canada and the United States signed the Ogdensburg Agreement, which set up the Canada–United States Permanent Joint Board on Defence to study the common defence problems of the two countries. In 1941, the year the United States entered the war, the Hyde Park Declaration extended the planning of continental defence to cover the production of war materials.

After the war, in 1949, the United States, Canada and most Western European countries formed a new military alliance, the North Atlantic Treaty Organization (NATO), in order to contain the Soviet Union. Commitments to NATO required a great increase in the size of the Canadian permanent armed forces. In 1950, Canada made a significant military contribution to the U.S.-led and UN-mandated military intervention in Korea, where Canada lost 1500 lives.

The next phase of the North Americanization of Canadian defence was a series of radar lines built across northern Canada in the 1950s to intercept anticipated Soviet bombers. These arrangements led to the North American Aerospace Defense Command (NORAD) of 1958. This agreement provided for a joint Canada–U.S. air defence system with headquarters in Colorado and with an American as commander-in-chief and a Canadian as second-in-command. A Defence Production Sharing Program was established in 1959, the same year in which the Diefenbaker government cancelled the legendary Canadian fighter jet, the Avro Arrow. The advisability of this cancellation continues to be debated, and it has resulted in the continued reliance on foreign-produced aircraft for Canadian air defence.

Prime Minister John Diefenbaker also encountered two serious missile crises in the 1957–63 period. When U.S. President John Kennedy announced a naval blockade of Cuba because of the establishment of Soviet missile bases in that country, the Canadian Cabinet waited three days before putting its armed forces in a state of highest alert. The Cuban missile crisis thus soured relations between the two leaders, a state of affairs compounded by American annoyance at Canada's stand with respect to Bomarc missiles. These had been established by the U.S. at two bases in Canada as part of the NORAD Agreement and were intended to be armed with nuclear warheads. Some Cabinet ministers wanted to take possession of the warheads as planned, but others argued that to place the warheads on Canadian soil would appear to foster the nuclear arms race. This Canadian–American defence relationship became a prominent issue in the 1962 and 1963 election campaigns. The Diefenbaker government eventually fell apart over the issue in 1963; it was defeated on a nonconfidence motion and the Liberals won the resulting election under Lester Pearson. The new prime minister had the warheads installed as part of Canada's international commitments, but they were ultimately removed in 1971.

Pearson's successor, Pierre Trudeau, cut defence spending and, in a new emphasis on protecting domestic sovereignty, halved Canada's NATO contingent in 1969. The most prominent new issue had to do with the U.S. request to test the Cruise missile over Canadian territory because of the resemblance of our terrain to that of the Soviet Union. Despite considerable popular protest, the Trudeau government allowed the tests to take place, as did succeeding governments.

The Mulroney government promised to make defence a much higher priority than it was during the Trudeau years and published a hawkish White Paper on the subject in 1987. Partly because of public opposition, and partly because of budgetary considerations, the Paper was not implemented, a decision that was vindicated when the Cold War effectively ended a year or so later. However, when Iraq invaded Kuwait in 1990, Canada readily agreed to participate in the U.S.-led Gulf War coalition, which was, like the Korean affair, theoretically a United Nations operation. Canada then participated in the various phases of the Balkan war in the former Yugoslavia.

When U.S. President George W. Bush attacked the Saddam Hussein regime in Iraq, he expected Canadian participation. But Prime Minister Chrétien decided that the situation neither represented an imminent security threat nor had sufficient authority from the United Nations, and he declined to join the U.S.–U.K. coalition. Bush also added considerable pressure on other countries to endorse the Ballistic Missile Defence (BMD) system, but Canada demurred. Nevertheless, an increasing "interoperability" between the armed forces of the two countries occurred, and they did sign an accord to jointly deploy military forces and emergency services in the event of a terrorist attack or other disaster. At the same time, Canada more or less withdrew from its traditional peacekeeping contributions to the United Nations, where a need continues to exist, but became increasingly engaged in a fighting role in Afghanistan.

Independent of, but consistent with, U.S. pressure, both the Martin and Harper governments strengthened the Canadian military, which had been largely neglected during the Chrétien regime. Canada has been increasingly concerned about defending its sovereignty in the Arctic, and both governments announced that Canadian forces would be more active and visible in the North. The U.S. proceeded to establish a unified command within its armed forces (Northcom) to supplement NORAD with responsibility for coordinating activities of U.S. forces throughout North America, and the two countries renewed the NORAD agreement.[5]

A Canadian soldier stands by a CF-18 jet fighter.

The Canadian military mission in Afghanistan soon became the most significant aspect of Canadian defence policy.[6] The mission was extended to mid-2011, even as Canadian casualties continued to mount (some 158 dead and hundreds of serious injuries), and a small Canadian continent remained in Afghanistan in a non-combat, training role. One of the many controversial aspects of that mission was what Canadian troops did with the enemy Afghan fighters they captured, called detainees. These prisoners were turned over to Afghan authorities but with concerns that they might be or had been tortured, contrary to the Geneva Convention on the conduct of war. Just as the Afghan mission was winding down, Canada joined with several other NATO countries to use force in toppling the Gadhafi regime in Libya. As of 2015, Canada began contributing aircraft and training personnel to the U.S.-led Middle East Stabilization Force in Iraq and Syria.

Canadian Foreign Policy

To the extent that foreign policy can be distinguished from defence policy, the degree of U.S. influence in this field has also been controversial.[7] Canada sees itself as a "middle power" that emphasizes multilateral approaches in global affairs. It prefers to work with many other states simultaneously to achieve its foreign policy objectives, whether through ad hoc arrangements or international organizations. Its most famous hour probably occurred when foreign minister Lester Pearson was responsible for the creation of the first UN peacekeeping force in 1956. At the same time, Canada is always under pressure to agree with the United States. Although we did not become directly involved in the Vietnam War, many Canadians would have preferred a foreign policy more critical of many U.S. military or diplomatic initiatives around the world. Because they were ostensibly established in the name of the United Nations, the Canadian government was quick to respond to U.S. demands to contribute to its military efforts in the Gulf War and its peacekeeping mission in Somalia. In response to broader international pressure, Canada made a major contribution in the Bosnian civil war, as well as in trying to end the tribal warfare in Rwanda. As mentioned, Canada has an impressive record as an international peacekeeper, having participated in 63 such exercises.

In the 1990s, Canada undertook a number of new foreign policy initiatives that had wide support around the world but not as much next door. Canada was a leader in the campaign to ban anti-personnel landmines, which culminated in an anti-landmines treaty signed in Ottawa in 1997. This country was also at the forefront of the effort to establish an International Criminal Court, building on its active participation in prosecuting former Yugoslavian war criminals before the UN International Criminal Tribunal. Former Foreign Affairs Minister Lloyd Axworthy put these and other initiatives (cross-border problems with illicit drugs, weapons, terrorism, refugees, and the environment) in the context of a move from concentrating on "state security" to "human security" and from "peacekeeping" to "peacebuilding." During his last two years in office, Jean Chrétien made aiding Africa one of Canada's top foreign policy priorities.[8] Nevertheless, despite expressed concerns about the third world, Canada remains far below the international standard of contributing 0.7 percent of GNP to foreign aid. The Harper government's foreign policy was undistinguished and more oriented toward the Americas; in fact, a 2007 Strategic Counsel public opinion poll indicated that Canadians generally felt it was too heavily influenced by the United States. Harper also aimed to become a more important international player, partly based on Canada's strong economy, energy production, and its military power, and insisted on being Israel's greatest supporter. This change of policy was probably one reason why Canada lost its bid for a UN Security Council seat in 2010. On certain issues, the provinces are also increasingly interested in Canada's foreign policy, such as energy producers regarding exports and Quebec on cultural policy, while Elections Canada tries to promote democracy abroad, such as in monitoring foreign elections.

Canadian Border Policy

Although Canadian and American authorities had always worked cooperatively along the "greatest undefended border in the world," the events of September 11, 2001 led to increased concern and collaboration.[9] Three months later, the two countries signed the Smart Border Declaration and launched a joint 30-point action plan. Canada and the U.S. also pledged to relieve congestion at key crossing points by investing in border infrastructure, and promised to share information and intelligence and coordinate the work of enforcement agencies in addressing common threats. This initiative was undertaken primarily at the behest of the United States and has not been without problems. For example, the United States tends to engage in racial profiling at the border, hassles Canadian citizens or landed immigrants who are of Muslim or Arab origin, and both countries began to arm their border guards. In 2003, Canada consolidated its border personnel into the Canada Border Services Agency and, in 2005, the United States announced that Americans and Canadians would need a passport to enter the U.S. rather than a more widely held document like a driver's licence. Federal and provincial governments opposed this proposal on the grounds that it would be a major impediment to cross-border movement, especially trade, but were not capable of changing it. Because nothing much came of the "Smart Border" declaration and because movement across the "thickening" Canada–U.S. border was only becoming more difficult, U.S. President Obama and Prime Minister Harper met in 2011 to kick-start progress on a perimeter security deal regarding cross-border trade. Meanwhile, Canada had a difficult time persuading the U.S. to build a second bridge between Windsor and Detroit—Canada's main bilateral trade connection.

U.S. ECONOMIC INFLUENCES ON CANADA

The economic influence of the United States on Canada is probably even more pervasive than is its impact on defence, foreign, and border policy. This influence is felt in almost every aspect of Canadian life, including investment, trade, the environment, energy, and labour unions.

Much of this pressure predated the Canada–U.S. Free Trade and the North American Free Trade agreements, whose effects go far beyond trade, but was only exacerbated by those two treaties. In many ways, Canada constitutes a zone within the American economy rather than a distinctive national economy,[10] although in other ways Canada is increasingly under a broader range of external economic influences.

Foreign Investment

In the "British period" of Canadian history, a great deal of investment in Canada came from Britain. Some of this foreign capital was in the form of British companies operating in Canada, such as the Hudson's Bay Co., but to a large extent it consisted of Canadian borrowing in the London bond market in what is called "portfolio investment" or "debt securities." Interest had to be paid on such loans, but ownership remained largely in Canadian hands.

When Canada entered the "American period" of its history, the source of foreign investment largely shifted from Britain to the United States and the form of investment switched from loans to "direct" or "equity" investment—that is, control through the ownership of shares. Thus, to a large extent the Canadian economy has come to consist of branch plants of U.S. parent corporations. These companies typically operate in many other countries, too, and therefore gain the label of multinational or transnational corporations. Figure 10.1 indicates the shift from British to U.S. investment in Canada between 1900 and 1967.

FIGURE 10.1 PERCENTAGE OF BRITISH, U.S., AND OTHER FOREIGN INVESTMENTS IN CANADA, 1900–1967

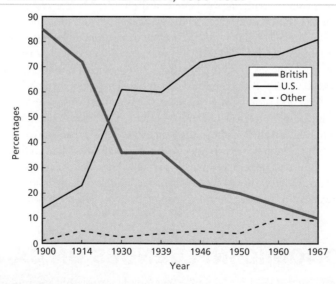

Source: Foreign Direct Investments in Canada 1972, *p. 15. Reproduced with the permission of the Privy Council Office.*

"Free market" economists are enthusiastic boosters of unlimited foreign investment. They claim that maximum efficiency results from capital being able to flow to wherever it will yield the greatest returns. They argue that Canada needs foreign capital and that such investment creates jobs, which in turn raise the Canadian standard of living. They also say that Canadians are too timid to take advantage of risky investment opportunities in their own country and that efficiency is enhanced when multinationals transfer "state-of-the-art" technology and well-trained managers and management techniques to their branch plants.

Others take the view that these advantages are short-term or short-sighted.[11] First, more capital may eventually flow out of the country in interest and dividends than was originally brought in. Second, multinationals are likely to purchase supplies and component parts from the parent company or parent country rather than buying them and creating employment in Canada. Third, such plants usually remain small and inefficient ("truncated") because they are designed to serve only the Canadian market rather than encouraged to compete in export markets with the parent plant or branches set up in other countries. Finally, critics also claim that a branch plant economy suffers because most of its research and development (R&D) is done in the parent plant. This limits the number of interesting and challenging jobs in science, engineering, and technology located in Canada. As convenient as it is to import such technology, this process hinders Canadian innovative efforts to develop distinctive export products and to increase productivity.

This pattern of economic development was fostered in the first instance by the **National Policy** of 1879, which put a tariff on imported manufactured goods. Rather than export to Canada from the United States and pay the tariff, American companies set up branch plants within Canada behind the tariff wall. This was advantageous for the creation of employment in Canada and contributed to the general prosperity of the country, especially Ontario.

Other foreign companies moved in to exploit Canadian natural resources. "A large proportion of the investment in resource exploitation reflected the needs of the United States investors for raw materials for their processing and manufacturing plants in the United States." This integration often had the practical impact "of reducing the likelihood of further processing activity of Canadian natural resources in Canada."[12] Thus, along with many aspects of manufacturing, the mining, forestry, and petroleum industries came to be characterized by a high degree of foreign, mostly U.S., ownership. In fact, the **Gray Report** of 1972 (*Foreign Direct Investment in Canada*) began with these words: "The degree of foreign ownership and control of economic activity is already substantially higher in Canada than in any other industrialized country and is continuing to increase."[13] Some of the largest multinationals operating in Canada are identified in Table 10.1.

Critics of the situation also worry that if layoffs or shutdowns are necessary, these are usually slated for branch plants first, and such a high degree of U.S. ownership perpetuates the resource-export orientation of the Canadian economy. The ultimate symbolic disadvantage of foreign-owned companies is that they may occasionally choose or be required to conform to the laws of the country in which their parent is located rather than those of Canada. The extension of U.S. laws to branch plants located in Canada, typically under the Trading with the Enemy Act, is called **extraterritoriality**. On several occasions when such branch plants in Canada tried to do business with countries on the U.S. "enemy list," they were told that they had to follow U.S. law, thus reducing production and job opportunities in Canada.

TABLE 10.1   LARGE FOREIGN-OWNED COMPANIES IN CANADA

BEST BUY CANADA (U.S.)	NEXEN/CNOOC (CHINA)
CARGILL (U.S.)	NOVELIS (UNITED STATES)
COSTCO WHOLESALE CANADA (U.S.)	PRATT & WHITNEY CANADA (U.S.)
DIRECT ENERGY MARKETING (U.K.)	SEARS CANADA (U.S.)
FORD MOTOR CO. OF CANADA (U.S.)	STAPLES BUSINESS DEPOT (U.S.)
GENERAL MOTORS CANADA (U.S.)	SYSCO FOOD SERVICES (U.S.)
HEWLITT-PACKARD (CANADA) (U.S.)	TOYOTA CANADA (JAPAN)
HOME DEPOT CANADA (U.S.)	ULTRAMAR (U.S.)
HONDA CANADA (JAPAN)	WAL-MART CANADA (U.S.)
HSBC BANK (U.K.)	WESTCOAST ENERGY (U.S.)
IBM CANADA (U.S.)	APPLE CANADA (US)

Statistics for 2009 on the state of foreign investment in various Canadian industries are shown in Figure 10.2. In general, the proportion of foreign control declined between 1971 and 1984 but has increased since—to 19.6 percent of the total economy. Not surprisingly, the United States is the parental home to over half of the foreign ownership in Canada (owning about 10.1 percent of the Canadian economy). The Canadian manufacturing industry is characterized by greater foreign ownership than any other sector.

The policies that Canadian governments have adopted to counter this threat of U.S. or other foreign ownership and control of the Canadian economy can be divided into four main categories. First, Crown corporations have been established, partly to ensure that the company involved remains in Canadian hands. Atomic Energy of Canada Ltd. and Petro-Canada were federal creations developed in response to demands that a Canadian presence in strategic industries be retained.

Second, while leaving other corporations to function privately, the federal government often established regulatory agencies. The principal government response to the Gray Report was the creation of the **Foreign Investment Review Agency (FIRA)**. FIRA "screened" foreign takeovers of large Canadian companies and new ventures by foreign firms in Canada, approving the deal if it involved "significant benefit to Canada." Although the Cabinet rarely disallowed any such initiatives and imposed minimal conditions, the proportion of foreign ownership of Canadian industry declined while it was in place, and FIRA became a major irritant to the United States. The first act of the less nationalistic Mulroney government in 1984 was to replace FIRA with Investment Canada. In its recast form, the agency had the opposite objective of attracting *increased* foreign investment to Canada. Then, in the Canada–U.S. Free Trade Agreement, Investment Canada was restricted to screening acquisitions of firms with a value over $150 million and could not impose any performance requirements. The National Energy Board, the Canadian Nuclear Safety Commission, and the Canadian Transportation

FIGURE 10.2 ASSETS UNDER FOREIGN CONTROL BY SELECTED INDUSTRIES, 2011 (PERCENTAGES)

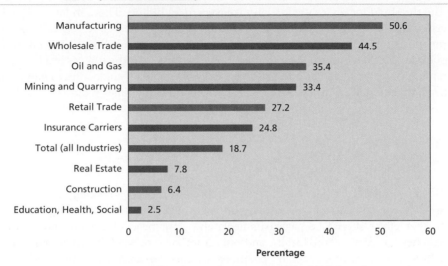

Source: Statistics Canada, Corporations Returns Act, Catalogue 61-220-x (2011), http://www.statcan.gc.ca/pub/61-220-x/2011000/t141-eng.htm. Reproduced and distributed on an "as is" basis with the permission of Statistics Canada.

Agency are other regulatory agencies designed to protect the Canadian national interest in important respects.

Third, ownership restrictions and tax incentives were introduced. Maximum foreign ownership limits exist in certain fields, such as broadcasting, financial institutions, newspapers, and publishing. Incentives to Canadian ownership were exemplified by the National Energy Program of 1980. The fourth category of protectionist measures consisted of funding agencies such as the Business Development Bank of Canada, whose mandate is to encourage Canadian entrepreneurship when the commercial banks are not interested.

Many of these policies were half-hearted and others were later diluted under U.S. pressure. Many were weakened or withdrawn by the Mulroney government, both to increase foreign investment and to remove irritants in the Canada–U.S. relationship. Although the degree of foreign investment increased considerably after the mid-1980s, this was widely seen as a natural ingredient of globalization and the source of badly needed jobs. But the foreign take-overs of the Hudson's Bay Company, Molson, Labatt, Domtar, Inco, Falconbridge, Dofasco, and Fairmont Hotels in 2005–06 raised increased concern among economic nationalists. Other recent foreign takeovers include Alcan, Four Seasons' Hotels, Algoma Steel, Ipsco, LionOre Mining, North American Oil Sands, Stelco, and AbitibiBowater.

A variety of cases have recently resurrected the issue of whether foreign investment in Canada is always desirable. For the first time since 1985, the Canadian government blocked a foreign takeover of a Canadian company in 2008, feeling that the Alliant Techsystems purchase of MacDonald-Dettwiler, a Canadian aerospace firm, would not be of net benefit to Canada. After a groundswell of opposition from Saskatchewan, the Harper government rejected a second foreign takeover—the bid for the Potash Corporation of Saskatchewan by an Australian firm in 2011. On the other hand, Chinese companies continued to invest heavily in Canadian natural resources, the government eased foreign ownership restrictions in the telecom sector, allowed Amazon.com to set up its own book distribution centre in Canada, and raised the threshold for reviewing foreign takeovers to $1 billion. Then, in late 2012, Harper approved the purchase of Nexen Inc. by the Chinese state-owned CNOOC Ltd., but at the same time issued new rules on foreign takeovers of Canadian firms. Box 10.1 is taken from a column in the *National Post* when large grain handler Viterra was the subject of a foreign takeover in mid-2012. A related concern is the tendency of Canadian companies to move some of their head-office functions to the United States, which is sometimes referred to as the "hollowing out" of corporate Canada.

BOX 10.1   VOICES

"[T]he question [of what is in the national interest] is easily answered. Losing any sizable head office to a foreigner is never in the national interest. And legislation to that effect should be passed immediately.... [I]f head offices are moved to another jurisdiction, the loyalty, and respect for laws, moves with them. Foreign CEOs ... can move Canadian operations, patents, research, employees and tax expenditures around the world to suit their purpose and to suit the purpose of the jurisdiction in which they operate. They have no allegiance. They usually offer only lower- or middle-management jobs. They support no ballet companies, clinics for kids, theatre troupes, work support programs for disabled Canadians, hospital wings for the cities in which they operate.... Ottawa should stop playing Boy Scout to the world's corporate predators.... And a moratorium should be imposed on all buyouts, in any industry, until this government and the people of Canada fully understand the implications of losing big head offices."

Source: Material reprinted with the express permission of *National Post,* a division of Postmedia Network Inc.

Trade

External trade has always been a crucial component of the Canadian economy. At the same time as they tried to maximize their exports, countries used to seek to protect their domestic industry from foreign competition through the imposition of tariffs, quotas, and customs duties. Then, in 1911, Prime Minister Laurier negotiated a reciprocity treaty with the United States, only to go down to defeat on the issue, after which the treaty was cancelled. After the Second World War, however, major states began to abandon trade protection for trade liberalization and, in 1947, Canada signed the General Agreement on Tariffs and Trade (GATT), under which signatories pledged to remove such trade restrictions on a multinational basis. GATT has since been transformed into the much more powerful World Trade Organization (WTO) which allows its members to go even further with bilateral agreements, as Canada and the United States did in defence production arrangements.

TABLE 10.2 LEADING BUYERS OF CANADIAN EXPORTS AND SUPPLIERS OF IMPORTS, 2014

	EXPORTS (%)		IMPORTS (%)
UNITED STATES	75.6	UNITED STATES	66.9
CHINA	3.9	CHINA	6.8
UNITED KINGDOM	3.0	MEXICO	3.3
JAPAN	2.1	GERMANY	2.5
MEXICO	1.3	JAPAN	1.8

Source: Statistics Canada, Imports, Exports and Trade Balance-of-Payments, by Country or Country Grouping, *CANSIM Table 228-0069, http://www.statcan.gc.ca/tables-tableaux/sum-som/l01/cst01/gblec02a-eng.htm. Calculations by Authors. Reproduced and distributed on an "as is" basis with the permission of Statistics Canada.*

Canadian exports to the United States exceeded those to the United Kingdom after 1921 and rose to record highs by 2001. Table 10.2 indicates Canada's five leading trading partners on both the import and export sides in 2014. Because of geographic proximity, it is only logical that Canada and the United States be closely linked by trade. It is even more natural because of their complementary resources and industries—the abundance of primary resources in Canada and the amount of manufacturing in the United States. Indeed, provinces trade more with neighbouring states than with one another, although much of this trade is of an intrafirm character rather than truly international.

Given the degree to which Canadian prosperity depends on export trade, it is advantageous to have ready access to the U.S. market; it is also convenient to have such a close supply of goods that are not produced in Canada. However, to have put so many eggs in one basket means that in times of a U.S. recession the demand for Canadian goods falls off and the Canadian economy takes a nosedive too, as was particularly evident after 2008. Furthermore, protectionist pressure in the United States for new or increased tariffs or quotas against Canadian exports can have a devastating effect on certain industries, such as softwood lumber.

Canadian policymakers had been concerned for some time that the country was dangerously dependent on the U.S. economy while being left out of the various regional trading blocs being formed, especially the European Union. The Diefenbaker and Trudeau governments tried unsuccessfully to diversify the Canadian export market to Britain and Europe, respectively, while the Pearson government signed the sectoral **Auto Pact** with the United States to guarantee a balanced exchange of automobiles and parts.

THE CANADA-U.S. FREE TRADE AGREEMENT

Modern pressure for a free trade agreement with the United States came largely from the corporate sector, led by the Business Council on National Issues and western Canadian resource producers. Brian Mulroney was converted to the idea when U.S. protectionist measures began to be felt in Canada and when the Macdonald Royal Commission on the Economic Union and Development Prospects for Canada recommended that the country take such a "leap of faith." Mulroney found an advocate of free trade in the White House, and the Canada–U.S. Free Trade Agreement took effect on January 1, 1989.

The 1989 **Canada–U.S. Free Trade Agreement (FTA)** was probably the most significant agreement that this country ever signed. It is a wide-ranging pact that covers virtually every aspect of the bilateral relationship.[14] The agreement essentially removed almost all barriers to the cross-border flow of goods and services between the two countries. Each could henceforth send its products to the other without tariffs, quotas, or other impediments, but each continued to apply its own tariffs to imports from other countries. For any subsequent conflicts in trade between the two countries, a complex **dispute-settlement mechanism** involving binational panels and binding arbitration was set up. If either country refused to abide by the final decision of the arbitrators, however, the other could retaliate ("countervail"), as before.

Sending goods and services "across the border without impediment" means that neither government could regulate, restrict, or tax such goods and services as they crossed the border. This is because for most purposes the two countries were to be seen as a single market in which corporations based in either were to be treated equally. Both countries committed to give "national treatment" to each other's companies—to treat them the same way as their own. In other words, free trade deals are primarily about reducing the role of government and turning more powers over to corporations in the marketplace. It is a tremendous concession to corporations for governments to voluntarily abandon their powers in this way.

Those Canadians who favoured the agreement argued that in the absence of the deal the United States would have continued to apply a series of protectionist measures, threatening more jobs. Canadian firms would now have access to the huge unprotected U.S. market, allowing them to expand and create employment. Supporters of the FTA admitted that many Canadian firms would go under and thousands of Canadian jobs would be lost because of the competition from larger American companies. But they claimed that such competition would force Canadian corporations to become stronger, more specialized and efficient, and more capable of functioning in the global economy. Defenders also hailed the likelihood of increased U.S. investment in Canada, as well as higher levels of investment from other countries wanting to take advantage of Canadian access to the U.S. market. Many asked whether any practical alternative existed.

Opponents of free trade argued that the deal would lead to a loss of jobs rather than an increase, because the Canadian market would be inundated by U.S. exports and small Canadian firms would not be able to compete. Massive layoffs and shutdowns were predicted, especially in industries where the labour force was largely female. Jobs would also be lost because U.S. branch plants would close, supplying the Canadian market instead from the parent plant south of the border, and some Canadian firms would move to the U.S. to take advantage of backward labour and environmental laws in certain states. It was, they argued, clearly designed to enshrine neoliberal values and corporate rights and prevent the recurrence of such economic nationalistic measures as FIRA and the National Energy Program.[15] Opponents felt that for reasons outlined throughout this chapter, the existing degree of integration of the two countries' economies was already detrimental to Canadian interests.

Many opponents worried that the deal would endanger agricultural marketing boards, regional development programs, and the Canadian social safety net, and they expected pressure for policy harmonization in every field: taxation, pollution control, product standards, and social programs. They also saw threats to basic Canadian values, in which there would be pressure for less government, less caring and equality, and more social Darwinism ("survival of the fittest"). Finally, they felt that the Free Trade Agreement would reduce Canadian flexibility of action on the world stage and limit its ability to pursue an independent Canadian foreign policy.

NORTH AMERICAN FREE TRADE AGREEMENT

The ink was hardly dry on the Canada–U.S. Free Trade Agreement when the Mulroney government began talks with the United States and Mexico about a **North American Free Trade Agreement (NAFTA)**. This 1994 agreement essentially extended the FTA to Mexico, and most provisions in the two agreements were identical. (Thus, the expression "NAFTA" is now commonly used to include both agreements.) Canada entered the agreement mainly to prevent the other partners from endangering its position, although some corporations pressured it to do so, seeing it as a means of enhancing the efficiency of their operations.[16]

Opponents feared that companies would move from Canada to Mexico because of the low wages and less stringent environmental standards in that country; they also complained that Mexico was able to negotiate stronger clauses on energy and culture than had Canada under the FTA. Although the Canadian government claimed that certain domestic services and industries were either protected or not affected by NAFTA (culture, water, environmental, health, safety and labour standards, and social programs), critics noted that the protective wording in these fields was weak. NAFTA includes Chapter 11, under which a foreign company can sue a country on the grounds that a government policy reduced its profits. Canada lost at least two multimillion dollar lawsuits in this connection, the most infamous involving the gasoline additive MMT. Ethyl Corporation of Virginia used NAFTA rules to force Canada to roll back its ban on this ingredient, which is widely regarded as a hazard to health.[17]

After 20 years or so, the results of the trade agreements have been mixed. On the one hand, trade between Canada and the United States has boomed in both directions; on the other, thousands of Canadian manufacturing jobs have disappeared. Some of the broader fears may have been overblown, and where they have been realized, it is sometimes impossible to separate the effects of the free trade agreements from those of technological change, globalization, the value of the Canadian dollar, worldwide neoliberal forces, and the early 1990s recession. The number of conflicts has been large, however, and some of the same issues that precipitated the Free Trade Agreement have continued to be problematic, especially Canadian exports of softwood lumber, the agricultural sector, and cultural industries.[18] In fact, when the softwood lumber dispute was "resolved" in 2006, it was outside the parameters of the trade agreements, whose tribunals had usually ruled in Canada's favour. Other specific areas of dispute have included uranium, beer, magnesium, steel, swine, wheat, sugar, peanut butter, tobacco, milk, meat, paper, salmon and herring, poultry products, magazine publishing, patents, dairy products, and country-music television.[19] As for NAFTA, many observers agreed that it failed all three signatories: it has not ended

Canada–U.S. trade disputes, it has not brought prosperity to Mexico, and it has not stopped the flow of illegal immigrants from Mexico into the United States. While some Canadians try to persuade themselves that a new North American identity has emerged, many other observers disagree.[20] Some Canadians would prefer to cut Mexico out of NAFTA, because its relationship with the U.S. is so different from our own.

The American administration repeatedly refused to recognize NAFTA rulings that U.S. restrictions on softwood lumber violated the agreement, leading many Canadians to advocate withdrawing from the agreements. They argued that the U.S. was taking the same bullying approach to trade arrangements with Canada as it was in its foreign policy around the world. Another issue—the "Buy American" program—surfaced during the Great Recession of 2009: it was only when individual states and municipalities in the U.S. cancelled contracts with Canadian suppliers that people realized the free trade agreements applied exclusively to the two countries' national level of government.

OTHER TRADE ISSUES

Critics of NAFTA were generally more willing to trust the WTO on trade matters, since that organization seemed to make fairer decisions and had teeth to enforce them. They also pointed out that Canada could take advantage of increased markets in other parts of the world, such as China, India, and Brazil. It is true that Canada–China trade is increasing rapidly, and Canada has subsequently signed free trade agreements with Costa Rica, Israel, the European Free Trade Association (Norway, Switzerland, Iceland, and Liechtenstein), Peru, Jordan, Chile, Colombia, and Panama. Canada recently signed a free trade agreement with Ukraine and the European Union (CETA) and the Trans-Pacific Partnership (TPP).[21]

CRITICAL APPROACHES

An *institutional approach* would emphasize the effects of Canada's membership in international institutions on domestic politics in the country. For example, as a member of NAFTA, Canada is not allowed to implement policies which serve as trade barriers to disadvantage American and Mexican companies or to subsidize Canadian companies to give them a competitive advantage. Such institutions and their rules also affect the whole nature of the Canadian economy. Once based on an East–West trading axis, the Canadian economy has been reoriented on a North–South basis as a result of free trade agreements. It would now be far costlier for Canada to withdraw from NAFTA than it would have been immediately following the signing of the agreement, demonstrating that a decision made in the past has implications for options in the future.

The Environment

Environmental problems often transcend national borders and require transnational solutions. In 1987, concerns about the rapid depletion of the ozone layer motivated 47 countries to sign the Montreal Protocol, which committed these countries to phasing out the use of chlorofluorocarbons (CFC). In 1991, Canada and the United States signed an Air Quality Agreement in an effort to reduce the level of acid rain falling on both side of the border. Both of these agreements are generally considered to have been successful in addressing the key environmental challenges of this era.

The pollution of the Great Lakes is another serious bilateral environmental problem between Canada and the United States. Here again, most of the responsibility rests with the chemicals discharged from the larger proportion of factories and waste dumps situated on the U.S. shores of the lakes. Phosphorus levels were reduced in the 1970s, but the Great Lakes are still in a critical state because of toxic pollution.

Fishing on Canada's east and west coasts has been another environmental problem. Because of the peculiarities of the boundary between British Columbia and Alaska, Canada and the United States have had continuing differences over west coast salmon. A boundary dispute was settled in 1984, but then a conflict erupted over conservation. Canadian salmon fishers voluntarily reduced their catch because of dwindling stocks, but neither U.S. fishers nor the U.S. government was prepared to follow suit. On the east coast, fishing constituted a long-standing environmental issue but primarily with European countries. A number of them historically hauled huge quantities of fish from the Grand Banks just outside Canadian territorial waters. They even defied multinational agreements to abide by annual quotas until, at least in the case of cod, too few fish were left for either Europeans or Canadians to catch.

In recent years, the most prominent environmental problem has been global warming and climate change, almost universally believed to be caused by greenhouse gas emissions. In 1997, Canada signed the Kyoto Protocol, a multilateral agreement in which countries committed to reducing greenhouse gases. Many Canadians did not resent this particular external pressure, although there were differences of opinion within the country, as noted in Chapter 3. A principal problem, however, was that U.S. President George W. Bush refused to ratify the treaty. Among other implications, this would probably have forced Canadian corporations into a position of comparative disadvantage when they had to adhere to new restrictions that were not equally

Protesters gather on Parliament Hill in Ottawa over the Keystone XL pipeline.

THE CANADIAN PRESS/Sean Kilpatrick

contingent on U.S. competitors. The Harper government abandoned Kyoto and opted for the much less stringent Copenhagen Accord in 2009. While it also promised to match whatever environmental policies were adopted south of the border,[22] the 2012 budget significantly weakened Canadian environmental laws. In recent years, the U.S. has pushed for more stringent restrictions on greenhouse gases, with Canada often pushing in the opposite direction. What many see as federal inaction in Canada and the United States has motivated some provincial and state governments to work together in an effort to reduce global warming.

Energy

In the energy sector, the voracious U.S. industrial complex usually wants to import Canadian electric power and petroleum. Governments in Quebec, New Brunswick, Manitoba, and British Columbia have been eager to export electricity, and those of Alberta, Saskatchewan, British Columbia, and Nova Scotia to supply oil or natural gas. The federal government has normally approved these sales with little hesitation, although the **National Energy Board** is charged with ensuring that long-term Canadian needs not be compromised in the process. Aboriginal and environmental groups in some provinces have not been so favourably disposed to the hydro or nuclear plants necessary to produce the electricity, however, and Canadian nationalists worry about the future supply of petroleum for domestic purposes. Environmentalists on both sides of the border are concerned about the greenhouse gases, water pollution, and the desecration of land involved in the massive operation of the Alberta oil sands, the source of much of the oil exports to the U.S.[23] Petroleum producers and the Canadian and Alberta governments are anxious that the U.S. may turn its back on such oil imports for environmental reasons or eventually become self-sufficient. Thus, while continuing to press the U.S. to agree to the Keystone XL pipeline between Alberta and Texas, Canada also pursued the Northern Gateway pipeline from Alberta to the BC coast, to export oil to Asia, and began to consider more pipelines to the eastern provinces.

The degree of U.S. ownership of the Canadian petroleum industry also caused considerable conflict between the two countries. The **National Energy Program (NEP)** of 1980 set a target of 50 percent Canadian ownership of the oil and gas industry by 1990 and gave certain preferences to Petro-Canada and private Canadian firms. U.S. petroleum companies in Canada protested, and their government pressured Canada to remove these incentives to Canadianization. The Trudeau government made minor concessions, while the Mulroney Cabinet dismantled the NEP entirely and began to privatize Petro-Canada. The Canada–U.S. Free Trade Agreement created a North American energy pool in which prices could not be discriminatory (that is, Canada had to sell oil, gas, or electricity to the United States at the Canadian domestic price), and if cutbacks were ever necessary, domestic sales had to be reduced by the same proportion as exports. One implication was that New Brunswick could not claim preferential treatment over New England states when it came to the distribution of Sable Island natural gas via the Maritimes and Northeast Pipeline.

Trade Unions

Historically, Canadian trade unions were closely allied with those in the United States. Many unions in Canada, such as the United Steelworkers of America and the United Auto Workers, were part of "international unions" that had their headquarters in the United States.

without it.[31] An assortment of tax credits is also available, while heritage ministers have repeatedly tried to reform the film distribution system so that theatres would screen more Canadian feature films.

Publishing

The Canadian publishing industry consists of Canadian companies and branches of foreign firms. Both kinds of companies also sell foreign titles in Canada, and estimates of imported books as a proportion of total book sales range from 45 percent to 70 percent. Canadian firms, such as Nelson Education, the publisher of this book, and McClelland and Stewart produce a much larger number of new titles in Canada than branch-plant firms that put greater efforts into distributing their foreign titles. Books are like television shows: they are cheaper to import than to make domestically. The problem is aggravated by the lack of effort to sell Canadian books at Canadian bookstores. Paperback books at newsstands, drug stores, and supermarkets come almost entirely from the United States because the publishers and distributors who control the supply are U.S.-owned companies.

The Canadian government supports the production, distribution, and promotion of Canadian books in a variety of ways, including financial assistance.[32] As for foreign investment in the industry, when the parent publisher of a Canadian subsidiary is taken over by another foreign firm, the Canadian branch is supposed to be sold to a Canadian buyer, although this has not always happened. For example, a British firm, Pearson Education, was allowed to buy Prentice Hall Canada, an American company.

Newspapers, Radio, and Sound Recordings

The Canadian newspaper and radio industries are much more autonomous than the industries discussed above. Firms in these industries are required by law to remain in Canadian hands, and several aggressive Canadian chains are alive and well in both industries. Today, the publicly owned CBC radio is commercial free, has virtually 100 percent Canadian content, and can be heard in almost every part of the country. Programs like *The Current*, *As It Happens*, *Q*, and *Cross-Country Checkup* are widely regarded as crucial links in keeping the country together.

Nevertheless, the influence of the United States can be detected in these industries, too: the ready availability in some centres of such U.S. papers as *USA Today* and of U.S. radio stations; the reliance on U.S. newsgathering agencies abroad, such as American Press reports; the dependence on U.S. sources for comics, crossword puzzles, commentators, and personal-advice programs and columns; and the tendency to include a large proportion of news coverage of U.S. events.

The CRTC requires that AM and FM radio stations play 35 percent Canadian music, and this regulation has generally been seen as the catalyst for the explosion of the Canadian music industry over the past 30 years. In addition, the Canada Music Fund is designed to strengthen the Canadian sound recording industry by offering financial assistance for the production, distribution, and marketing of Canadian music products.[33] In 2005, the CRTC authorized satellite radio, which many observers did not feel included sufficient Canadian-content restrictions.

Other Cultural Industries

Other cultural fields could also be mentioned, but the basic situation there is much the same: most aspects of Canadian culture are heavily influenced by U.S. institutions and values, and most Canadians accept this state of affairs without complaint. The concern for protection from U.S. domination and for promotion of Canadian content was first given official expression in the **Massey Royal Commission** Report on National Development in the Arts, Letters, and Sciences in 1951. That commission recommended that public financial assistance be provided to the arts, and, in response, the Canada Council (now the **Canada Council for the Arts**) was set up in 1957. It gives life-maintaining grants to hundreds of individual writers, artists, musicians, and playwrights as well as to almost every orchestra, theatre centre, art gallery, ballet, and opera company in the country. The Social Sciences and Humanities Research Council of Canada (SSHRCC) somewhat similarly subsidizes academic research and writing. Other than the measures mentioned above, Canada has imposed ownership restrictions in several areas of the cultural field, and Canadian immigration regulations require that before hiring a non-Canadian, employers must demonstrate that no qualified Canadian is available.

Canadian Cultural Industries in an Age of Globalization

Some observers believe that the technological changes and convergence characteristic of globalization have made it almost impossible to regulate the inflow and transmission of electronic content. Moreover, in another aspect of globalization, some of the measures that Canada has chosen in the past to promote and protect Canadian culture have fallen afoul of the rules of international trade organizations and agreements. One means that has been selected in the past to avoid the latter restrictions is to negotiate a broad exemption for cultural industries, but as examples cited above indicate, this has not always been successful. An alternative is to develop a new international instrument on cultural policies and trade that would allow Canada and other like-minded countries to maintain policies that promote their own cultural industries. Such an instrument would have to state explicitly when domestic protectionist cultural measures would be permitted and would not be subject to trade retaliation. Many other countries share Canada's concerns about cultural sovereignty, but it would not be easy to counter the forces of globalization in order to treat trade in cultural goods and services differently from trade in other areas.

U.S. INFLUENCES ON OTHER ASPECTS OF CANADIAN LIFE

Defence, foreign, and border policies, economics, and culture may stand out, but even before the free trade agreements, American influence was also established in practically every other aspect of Canadian life. Many of these influences have been or will be noted in other chapters of this book, but a brief catalogue can be included here. In areas sometimes far removed from politics are the cross-border links of many religious organizations and fraternal groups, like the Kiwanis and Masons, which have their headquarters in the United States. No one can deny the integration of Canadian and American professional sport, including the loss of some of the Canadian orientation of the National Hockey League.[34] A major area of scientific activity in Canada has been the development and refinement of the "Canadarm," this country's contribution to the U.S. space program. How predictable that the division of Spar Aerospace that produced this symbol of Canadian expertise was sold to U.S. interests in 1999!

In the semi-political realm, many social and political protest movements, including farmer and women's movements, anti-poverty and Aboriginal groups, and the Occupy movement of 2011, have spilled over the border to some extent, although in some cases the external influences go well beyond the United States. In the political system, American influences (as well as those from other countries) can be seen in the changing nature of Canadian political values (less deference, demands for more popular participation) and in party ideologies (the shift to the right). Party leadership conventions have long been considered to be an adaptation of those in the United States, and many would regard the whole Reform Party/Canadian Alliance phenomenon as a U.S. transplant. Certainly its proposed Triple-E Senate was based precisely on the equivalent American chamber. The Canadian lobbying industry increasingly resembles that across the border, and the adoption of the Charter of Rights and Freedoms has had the tendency to legalize, and therefore Americanize, the operation of the whole political system.[35]

CONCLUSION

Canada follows U.S. examples because of tradition, adoration, convenience, or economics; because the U.S. presence makes it necessary; and because of explicit U.S. government or corporate pressure. Most observers expected that, directly or indirectly, the free trade agreements would increase such U.S. influence on almost all aspects of Canadian policy. Thus, during the 20th century, Canada went from being a British colony to a colony of the United States, or from colony to nation to colony.[36] Furthermore, as political, economic, and environmental developments become common global problems, Canada must increasingly respond to transnational and supranational demands. As insistent as demands may be from forces in the domestic Canadian society, Canadian politicians must also pay greater attention to their global surroundings. Indeed, the government may already have signed away many of the powers that would be useful in attending to domestic problems.

Just as globalization in general and the influence of the United States in particular affect almost every aspect of Canadian life, they also come into virtually every chapter of this book. But they are especially central to the following two chapters, which deal with the Canadian political culture and the mass media. They are also an important part of the context of Part 4, the section on the constitution, federalism, and the Charter of Rights and Freedoms.

DISCUSSION QUESTIONS

1. Is globalization just another name for giving multinational corporations free rein to maximize their profits?

2. How much scope does globalization leave to nation-states to make distinctive domestic policies?

3. How much scope does Canada have to develop an independent foreign policy?

4. What are the advantages and disadvantages of foreign investment in Canada? What are the advantages and disadvantages of the other economic relationships between the Canada and the United States?

5. What are the advantages and disadvantages of NAFTA? What alternatives were available in the increasing regionalization of world trading patterns?

6. What are the advantages and disadvantages of the close cultural relationship between Canada and the United States?

7. Does North America exist?

MindTap® FOR MORE INFO GO TO **http://www.nelson.com/student**

NOTES

1. Recent books on Canadian–U.S. relations include Brian Bow, *The Politics of Linkage: Power, Interdependence, and Ideas in Canada–US Relations* (Vancouver: UBC Press, 2009) and Geoffrey Hale, *So Near Yet So Far: The Public and Hidden Worlds of Canada–US Relations* (Vancouver: UBC Press, 2012).
2. Stephen L. Harris, "The Global Financial Meltdown and Financial Regulation: Shirking and Learning—Canada in an International Context," in G. Bruce Doern and Christopher Stoney, eds., *How Ottawa Spends 2010–2011* (Montreal: McGill-Queen's University Press, 2010).
3. Stephen McBride and John Shields, *Dismantling a Nation: Canada and the New World Order* (Halifax: Fernwood Publishing, 1993), p. 20; Linda McQuaig, *The Cult of Impotence: Selling the Myth of Powerlessness in the Global Economy* (Toronto: Viking, 1998); and Stephen Clarkson, *Uncle Sam and Us: Globalization, Neoconservatism, and the Canadian State* (Toronto: University of Toronto Press, 2002).
4. Defined by a UN panel on March 17, 2005; David A. Charters, *The (Un)Peaceable Kingdom? Terrorism and Canada before 9/11* (Montreal: Institute for Research on Public Policy, October 2008).
5. Danford Middlemiss and Denis Stairs, *The Canadian Forces and the Doctrine of Interoperability: The Issues* (Montreal: Institute for Research on Public Policy, 2002); and J.L. Granatstein, *A Friendly Agreement in Advance: Canada–US Relations, Past, Present, and Future* (Toronto: C.D. Howe Institute, 2002); see also articles in *Policy Options* (May 2005).
6. Janice Gross Stein and Eugene Lang, *The Unexpected War: Canada in Kandahar* (Toronto: Viking Canada, 2007).
7. K.R. Nossal, *The Politics of Canadian Foreign Policy*, 3rd ed. (Scarborough: Prentice-Hall Allyn Bacon Canada, 1997); Tom Keating, *Canada and World Order: The Multilateralist Tradition in Canadian Foreign Policy*, 2nd ed. (Oxford University Press, 2002); and the annual series *Canada among Nations* produced by the Norman Paterson School of International Affairs at Carleton University and published by McGill-Queen's University Press.
8. Lloyd Axworthy, *Navigating a New World: Canada's Global Future* (Toronto: Knopf Canada, 2004); and Jennifer Welsh, *At Home in the World: Canada's Global Vision for the 21st Century* (Toronto: HarperCollins, 2004); see also articles in *Policy Options* (February 2005).
9. See Foreign Affairs and International Trade Canada, "Border Action Plan," cited on June 5, 2012, available at http://www.actionplan.gc.ca/eng/feature.asp?mode=preview&pageId=337; Institute for Research on Public Policy, *Policy Options*, July/August 2006.

10. Glen Williams, "Regions within Region: Canada in the Continent," in Whittington and Williams.

11. Kari Levitt, *Silent Surrender: The Multinational Corporation in Canada* (Toronto: Macmillan, 1970).

12. Government of Canada, *Foreign Direct Investment in Canada*, (Ottawa: Supply and Services, 1972), p. 14.

13. Ibid., p. 5.

14. Bruce Doern and Brian Tomlin, *Faith and Fear: The Free Trade Story* (Toronto: Stoddart, 1991); Robert Campbell and Leslie Pal, *The Real Worlds of Canadian Politics*, 2nd ed. (Peterborough: Broadview Press, 1991); and Clarkson, *Uncle Sam and Us*.

15. John W. Warnock, *Free Trade and the New Right Agenda* (Vancouver: New Star Books, 1988), pp. 116–17.

16. Government of Canada, *The North American Free Trade Agreement at a Glance* (1993, Catalogue No. E74-56/1-1993E); Jeffrey M. Ayres, *Defying Conventional Wisdom: Political Movements and Popular Contention against North American Free Trade* (Toronto: University of Toronto Press, 1998).

17. For a list of Chapter 11 disputes, see Foreign Affairs and International Trade Canada, Dispute Settlement, "NAFTA—Chapter 11—Investment," available at http://www.international.gc.ca/trade-agreements-accords-commerciaux/disp-diff/gov.aspx. Canada actually won a Chapter 11 case with the rejection of the claim of United Parcel Service that Canada Post, as a Crown corporation, was competing unfairly against it.

18. Foreign Affairs and International Trade Canada, Trade Negotiations and Agreements, "Dispute Settlement"; cited March 19, 2012; available at http://www.international.gc.ca/trade-agreements-accords-commerciaux/disp-diff/index.aspx?lang=en.

19. For a list of other NAFTA disputes, including softwood lumber, see NAFTA Secretariat, Decisions and Reports, available at http://www.nafta-sec-alena.org/en/DecisionsandReports.asp?x=312; for an assessment after 20 years, see Institute for Research on Public Policy, *Policy Options*, October 2007.

20. Stephen Clarkson, *Does North America Exist? Governing the Continent after NAFTA and 9/11* (Toronto: University of Toronto Press, 2008).

21. Patrick Georges and Marcel Mérette, *Canada's Strategic Trade Policy Options: Deeper Continental Integration or Diversification?* (Montreal: Institute for Research on Public Policy, 2010).

22. Geoffrey E. Hale, "Canada–US Relations in the Obama Era: Warming or Greening?" in Doern and Stoney, eds. *How Ottawa Spends 2010–2011*.

23. Andrew Nikiforuk, *Tar Sands: Dirty Oil and the Future of a Continent* (Vancouver: Greystone Books, 2008).

24. Human Resources and Skills Development Canada, *Union Membership in Canada—2010*, available at http://www.hrsdc.gc.ca/eng/labour/labour_relations/info_analysis/union_membership/2010.shtml, accessed March 19, 2012.

25. Joseph F. Fletcher, Heather Bastedo, and Jennifer Hove, "Losing Heart: Declining Support and the Political Marketing of the Afghanistan Mission," *Canadian Journal of Political Science* (December 2009); Joseph F. Fletcher and Jennifer Hove, "Emotional Determinants of Support for the Canadian Mission in Afghanistan: A View from the Bridge, *CJPS* (March 2012).

26. David V.J. Bell, "Political Culture in Canada," in Michael Whittington and Glen Williams, eds., *Canadian Politics in the 21st Century*, 7th ed. (Toronto: Thomson Nelson, 2008), p. 244.

27. Michael Dorland, ed., *The Cultural Industries in Canada* (Toronto: Lorimer, 1996); Foreign Affairs and International Trade Canada, "Canadian Culture in a Global World" (1999); cited on March 25, 2009; available at http://www.international.gc.ca/trade-agreements-accords-commerciaux/fo/canculture.aspx?lang=en#tphp; and Clarkson, *Uncle Sam and Us*.

28. Wallace Clement, *Continental Corporate Power* (Toronto: McClelland and Stewart, 1977); Gordon Laxer, *Open for Business: The Roots of Foreign Ownership in Canada* (Don Mills: Oxford University Press, 1989).

29. Statistics Canada, "Television Viewing," Catalogue no. 87F0006XIE, March 2006. Statscan has apparently discontinued measuring television viewing.

30. Department of Communications, *Report of the Task Force on the Economic Status of Canadian Television* (Ottawa, 1991), p. 9.

31. Herschel Hardin, *Closed Circuits* (Vancouver: Douglas & McIntyre, 1985); and Marc Raboy, *Missed Opportunities: The Story of Canada's Broadcasting Policy* (Montreal: McGill-Queen's University Press, 1990).

32. Canadian Heritage, Arts and Cultural Industries, cited on March 19, 2012; available at http://www
.pch.gc.ca/eng/1266244047506/1266200598020.
33. Ibid.
34. Ibid.
35. Jim Silver, *Thin Ice: Politics and the Demise of an NHL Franchise* (Halifax: Fernwood Publishing, 1996).
Fortunately, the Winnipeg Jets have returned to Winnipeg!
36. Donald Creighton, *Canada's First Century* (Toronto: Macmillan, 1970); and George Grant, *Lament for
a Nation: The Defeat of Canadian Nationalism* (Toronto: McClelland and Stewart, 1965.) Northrop Frye
notes that Canada passed from a pre-national to a post-national phase without ever having become a
nation, in his Conclusion to Carl F. Klinck, ed., *The Literary History of Canada: Canadian Literature in
English* (Toronto: University of Toronto Press, 1976).

FURTHER READING

Axworthy, Lloyd. *Navigating a New World: Canada's Global Future*. Toronto: Knopf Canada, 2004.

Bow, Brian. *The Politics of Linkage: Power, Interdependence, and Ideas in Canada–US Relations*. Vancouver: UBC Press, 2009.

Canada Among Nations. Annual. Montreal: McGill-Queen's University Press.

Clarkson, Stephen. *Uncle Sam and Us: Globalization, Neoconservatism, and the Canadian State*. Toronto: University of Toronto Press, 2002.

———. *Does North America Exist? Governing the Continent after NAFTA and 9/11*. Toronto: University of Toronto Press, 2008.

Cohen, Andrew. *While Canada Slept: How We Lost Our Place in the World*. Toronto: McClelland and Stewart, 2003.

Hale, Geoffrey. *So Near Yet So Far: The Public and Hidden Worlds of Canada–US Relations*. Vancouver: UBC Press, 2012.

Hart, Michael. *A Trading Nation: Canadian Trade Policy from Colonization to Globalization*. Vancouver: University of British Columbia Press, 2002.

Holloway, Steven. *Canadian Foreign Policy: Defining the Canadian National Interest*. Peterborough: Broadview Press, 2006.

McBride, Stephen. *Paradigm Shift: Globalization and the Canadian State*, 2nd ed. Black Point, NS: Fernwood Publishing, 2005.

McDonough, David S., ed. *Canada's National Security in the Post-9/11 World: Strategy, Interests, and Threats*. Toronto: University of Toronto Press, 2012.

McDougall, John. *Drifting Together: The Political Economy of Canada–US Integration*. Peterborough: Broadview Press, 2006.

McQuaig, Linda. *The Cult of Impotence: Selling the Myth of Powerlessness in the Global Economy*. Toronto: Viking, 1998.

Stein, Janice Gross, and Eugene Lang. *The Unexpected War: Canada in Kandahar*. Toronto: Viking Canada, 2007.

Urmetzer, Peter. *Globalization Unplugged: Sovereignty and the Canadian State in the Twenty-First Century*. Toronto: University of Toronto Press, 2005.

Welsh, Jennifer. *At Home in the World: Canada's Global Vision for the 21st Century*. Toronto: HarperCollins, 2004.

Sadeugra/iStock

3

LINKING PEOPLE TO GOVERNMENT

Having examined the societal and external environments of the Canadian political system, we are ready to explore Canadian politics, as such. The three traditional elements of Canadian politics are the electoral system, political parties, and pressure groups, all of which, along with political participation, voting, and the election campaign, are discussed in separate chapters in this part. But the context of values, attitudes, identities, and opinions in which these three familiar institutions operate must also be examined. Moreover, no one can deny the ubiquitous importance of the mass media and public opinion polls as links between people and government today. Thus, we begin with chapters on the Canadian political culture and political socialization, the mass media, and public opinion polls.

CHAPTER 11

The Canadian Political Culture

Most Canadians think they live in the best country on earth, but they do not get overly excited by national symbols like the flag or "O Canada." Others would prefer to live in an independent Quebec and some would not object to becoming part of the United States. Canadians have historically looked on the state as a benevolent force, although recent surveys indicate widespread disrespect for all institutions in society, including government. But Canadians still take much satisfaction in their public health care system and in the Charter of Rights and Freedoms. All these phenomena and countless others are encompassed in the concept of **political culture**, which can be defined as the sum total of the politically relevant values, beliefs, attitudes, identities, and orientations in a society. Vague and elusive as these values and attitudes may be, they influence what is done within a political system and therefore demand investigation.

Political culture includes feelings people have toward the overall political community of Canada—reactions to national symbols (the flag, the national anthem, the Constitution) and feelings of patriotism, nationalism, and pride, including the question of how people feel toward their province or territory as opposed to the whole country. A second aspect of political culture involves beliefs regarding the role of the state—how large a part do Canadians want government to play in their lives and what kinds of policies should it adopt? Another variable consists of orientations to the decision-making apparatus. How do Canadians feel, in general, about the police, the bureaucracy, the courts, and the politicians? Do citizens trust them? Alternatively, do people feel that their participation in the political system can make any difference?

This chapter will focus on the Canadian commitment to democracy, distinguish between the political values of Canadians and Americans, and in the process, attempt to compile a list of basic Canadian values. Although political culture is usually considered to be fairly stable, it will also be necessary to sketch how, in the Canadian case, it seems to be changing. It will also discuss the concept of subcultures or "limited identities."

CRITICAL APPROACHES

Political culture is a core concept in the *political psychology* and *political behaviour approaches* as well. They ask, for example, what is it that makes people in one country or area different from those in another? The term "culture" is often loosely defined, but the evidence of systematic differences between people in different areas and in different eras is very strong. One of the most influential theories of cultural change is the postmaterialism thesis that will be briefly discussed later in this chapter. In a nutshell, it suggests that people socialized during periods of economic and physical insecurity are more likely to concern themselves with materialistic priorities like economic growth, while those who are products of periods of affluence and security, by contrast, are more likely concerned with postmaterial needs like self-expression and self-fulfillment.[1]

THEORETICAL CONSIDERATIONS

Given the abstract nature of the concept of political culture, let us first try to elaborate on its definition. David Bell provides this clarification: "Political culture consists of the ideas, assumptions, values, and beliefs that shape our understanding and behaviour as citizens in the world of politics. It affects the ways we use politics, the kinds of social problems we address, and the solutions we attempt."[2] Jane Jenson adds that political culture sets boundaries to political action and limits the range of actors that are accorded the status of legitimate participants, the range of issues considered to be included in the realm of meaningful political debate, and the policy alternatives feasible for implementation.

Political culture thus determines what is normal and acceptable and what is not, and consists of the dominant values and expectations in the political system. These values and expectations lead to the kinds of political decisions and behaviour that the various elites in society have deemed to be legitimate.

Bell points out that political scientists use two principal methods of identifying the ingredients of political culture.[3] One is to survey individual Canadians and ask them about their attitudes and values. If and when such values and attitudes are widely shared, they can be said to constitute the collective political culture. A second approach is to develop an understanding of the political culture from observing the operation of the political system and society more generally. This can be achieved, for example, from a reading of history and literature and from a study of government decisions and political institutions.

Emphasizing history, two influential contributions to the debate about the Canadian political culture are those of American academics Louis Hartz and Seymour Martin Lipset. Hartz enunciated the "fragment theory" according to which the dominant values established in different parts of North America were those held by the Europeans who first arrived on this continent and reflected the political culture of the country from which they came.

Hartz argued that the dominant political value in France when Quebec was first settled was feudalism, with hierarchical and communitarian characteristics, and the political culture of Quebec and French Canadians has been distinctive ever since. On the other hand, the political culture that English-speaking settlers brought to North America favoured liberalism, individual freedom, and equality—the prevailing values of Britain at the time.[4] Canadian political scientist Gad Horowitz picks up the discussion to differentiate English Canada from the United States. He argues that those who objected to the dominant values in the United States, the United Empire Loyalists, came to Canada and, along with their liberal views, they brought other elements to the ideological mix, including a "Tory touch," which incorporated collectivism, paternalism, elitism, and a strong state. This legitimation of ideological diversity in Canada had the effect of allowing socialism to become part of the political culture as well, reinforced by waves of a later fragment—British working class immigrants. Thus, according to Horowitz, the Canadian political culture is dominated by liberalism, but it is accompanied by significant touches of conservatism and socialism.[5]

In Lipset's analysis, sometimes called the "formative events" theory, the dominant values of any society have their foundation in great historical events. That would be the American revolution, as far as the U.S. political culture goes, and the "counter-revolution," the reaction against that revolution, that was a formative event in Canadian history.[6] Although Hartz and Lipset begin from completely different premises, they end up complementing each other's approach, and both give considerable emphasis to the United Empire Loyalists as the principal founders of the Canadian political culture. Interestingly enough, John Ralston Saul has challenged these theories with the argument that it is the Aboriginal values with which the Loyalists and other European settlers came into contact that were actually more important.[7]

He calls Canada a Métis civilization, and is not the only commentator to disagree with Hartz and Lipset. They continue to have much influence in this discussion, however, raising the distinction between anglophone and francophone values in Canada as well as the difference between the dominant values of Canada as a whole and those of the United States. Of course, more recent waves of immigrants and more recent formative events have also had an impact on the Canadian political culture.

DEMOCRACY

In the past, many features of the Canadian political system were undemocratic. At the time of Confederation, few even had that aspiration, but the "official thinking" soon purported to claim that Canada was a democracy. That commonly accepted view of things was far from true, but Canada has become increasingly democratic over time. It could still be much improved in this respect, but the first conclusion that emerges from a quest for Canadian political values today is that almost all Canadians believe in democracy. The preamble to the 1982 Canadian Charter of Rights and Freedoms acknowledges democracy to be a foremost value in the country when it speaks of Canada as a "free and democratic society," but the Charter is not particularly enlightening about what this means. **Democracy** is defined in hundreds of ways, some of them quite contradictory, but in the modern Western world it usually includes the elements of popular sovereignty, political equality, political freedom, and majority rule.[8]

Popular Sovereignty

Canadian students learn about democracy by viewing rowdy Question Period.

Michael de Adder/Artizans

Popular sovereignty means that the people have the final say, which in large, modern political systems usually takes the form of elections at certain specified intervals. At the federal, provincial, and territorial levels in Canada, the Constitution requires that elections be held at least every five years, and tradition usually reduces this interval to four. For most Canadians, this is a sufficient opportunity for the exercise of popular sovereignty, although few would be content with anything less. Some states have a tradition of consulting the public more often or more specifically by means of plebiscites or referendums, but these devices are largely foreign to the Canadian mentality. Although their incidence is slightly higher at the provincial and municipal levels, only three national plebiscites or referendums have occurred since 1867: in 1898, on the prohibition of liquor sales; in 1942, on conscription; and in 1992, on the Charlottetown Accord. At least in the past, Canadians cherished "representative democracy," in which elected officials and appointed authorities made decisions on their behalf.

Popular sovereignty is thus normally exercised in periodic elections, which are, more than anything, mere opportunities to select those who will be responsible for making the big political decisions over the next four years or so on behalf of the whole population. As pointed out in Chapter 15, specific policy mandates in election campaigns are not as common as we might expect. Needless to say, it is an element of the law-abiding nature of most Canadians that everyone recognizes the legitimacy of the election results and accepts this expression of the popular will, whatever the defects in the electoral system. Although Canadians allow public officials such as judges to be appointed, many observers think it is time to make the Senate an elected body.

Political Equality

Given the significance of elections as the means of implementing the principle of popular sovereignty, a second aspect of democracy is that everyone is equal on election day. In essence, this means that every person has one vote and no more than one vote, as provided by the Canada Elections Act and the Charter of Rights and Freedoms. It is only in relatively recent times, however, that Canada has met this ideal, and at one time or another in the past several groups were excluded: women, those without property, Aboriginal Canadians, and various minority ethnocultural groups.

The principle of one person–one vote is a minimal expression of **political equality**. A major deviation from the ideal occurs if members of Parliament are not distributed among provinces on the basis of "representation by population." Chapter 13 reveals significant deviations in this respect. Another discrepancy occurs if electoral districts are not of equal population size within a province, which is also a considerable problem because of Canada's huge uninhabited spaces. These are issues that concern political scientists more than the general public but are of increasing interest to the courts as well.

It should also be said that even if every vote carried exactly equal weight, considerable room for inequality remains in the electoral system. Political parties in Canada have, to a large extent, been privately financed and it may well be that those who contributed money to a party or candidate expected to get something in return. Thus, those who have the resources to help finance elections are likely to have more influence than those who merely vote. Beyond election day itself, tremendous inequalities in political influence begin to emerge, such as in advocacy group and lobbying activity. Such disparities may lie outside the scope of political equality as a bare ingredient of the definition of democracy, but they are of concern to many observers.

Political Freedom

Just as the 1982 Charter of Rights and Freedoms enhanced protection of aspects of popular sovereignty and political equality, it also provided an explicit constitutional statement of **political freedom** in Canada, as discussed in detail in Chapter 19. According to section 2 of the Charter,

Everyone has the following fundamental freedoms:

(a)   freedom of conscience and religion;

(b)   freedom of thought, belief, opinion and expression, including freedom of the press and other media of communication;

(c)   freedom of peaceful assembly; and

(d)   freedom of association.

While the Charter may have clarified, strengthened, or expanded these political freedoms, it is a mistake to think that it created them. What the Charter basically provided was a new means of enforcing rights and freedoms—using the courts to invalidate legislation that infringed on them rather than having to persuade politicians to do so. It is therefore interesting to note the extent to which these freedoms were respected or violated before the adoption of the Charter.

Leaving aside government mistreatment of Aboriginals, which went far beyond denial of political freedom, government authorities, as well as the public, generally supported political freedoms as a long-standing part of the Canadian political culture. As in the case of political equality, however, there were many breaches of this principle—and one might ask: political freedom for whom? Three of the most striking cases where political freedoms were seriously infringed upon occurred at the federal level.[9] The first interference with freedom of

Japanese Canadians relocated to internment camps during the Second World War.

speech or assembly had to do with section 98 of the Criminal Code prohibiting "unlawful associations." Introduced after the 1919 Winnipeg General Strike and not repealed until 1936, the language of section 98 was sufficiently wide "to encompass the extravagant rhetoric of a trade-union meeting." It was used by the police to spy on unions, socialist and social democratic organizations, and minority ethnic groups; the Communist Party was a particular target, and many party members were imprisoned or deported. The second major case involved the incarceration or deportation of Canadians of Japanese extraction during the Second World War, depriving this group of personal liberty, property, and livelihood. The third example, the invocation of the War Measures Act in 1970, outlawed support for the FLQ but was used to imprison more than 400 nonviolent Quebec separatists who had no connection to that organization. Some observers saw a fourth, post-Charter case of government infringement of political freedom in the anti-terrorism legislation after 2001.

The use of such measures on even three or four occasions raises the question of how committed the political authorities were to the principle of political freedom. Furthermore, the overwhelming popular support given to the implementation of such restrictive measures indicates a rather superficial commitment to political freedom on the part of the population at large.[10] Such indifference relates to the strong Canadian feeling of deference to authority, which is discussed below. Although Canadians normally believe in political freedom, they seem prepared to let the authorities restrain such individual or group liberty at the least suggestion of violence.

Violations of political freedom have been more common at the provincial level, especially during the authoritarian regime of Maurice Duplessis in Quebec and with the peculiarities of the William Aberhart Social Credit government in Alberta. Some observers questioned the commitment to political freedom of more recent provincial authorities when, in 1981–82, certain premiers insisted that the "notwithstanding" clause be inserted into the Charter of Rights and Freedoms. Federal and provincial governments are thereby both allowed to override the political freedoms guaranteed in the Charter merely by admitting that intention. In the first 30 years after adoption of the Charter, however, the notwithstanding clause was hardly ever used, as noted in Chapter 19. On the other hand, security concerns have trumped certain legal rights in the post-9/11 era, and the mass arrests of protesters at the G20 summit in Toronto in 2010 were evidence of excessive police power.

Majority Rule and Minority Rights

The Canadian conception of democracy also incorporates the notion of **majority rule**—that is, in case of dispute, the larger number takes precedence over the smaller number. This principle is generally accepted in elections and in legislatures that result from elections. At the same time, however, it is felt necessary to protect certain minorities from the actions of the majority, so that specific minority rights are given constitutional protection. The Constitution Act, 1867 recognized existing Roman Catholic and Protestant minority education rights in the provinces, as well as French and English minority language rights in the federal and Quebec legislatures and courts. Extension of these rights to Manitoba and their subsequent removal and resurrection were discussed in Chapter 5.

Over the past generation, Canada has extended minority rights in the Constitution to a considerable degree. The 1982 Charter of Rights and Freedoms guaranteed French and English language rights in the operation of the federal and New Brunswick governments, as well as French and English minority-language education rights in parts of all provinces and territories where numbers warrant. The Charter also guaranteed equality rights for women (who are not actually a minority), and prohibited federal, provincial, and territorial discrimination against various types of minorities. The fact that the notwithstanding clause can be used to override minority rights other than those dealing with language or gender indicates that certain rights were considered more sacred than others, and that majority rule still applies in certain cases. But women and Charter-based minorities—official language, ethnocultural, Aboriginal, and others—have all used their new constitutional status to protect and promote their own interests.

Thus it is safe to say that almost every Canadian would claim democracy to be a fundamental political value of the country today and would support the four main ingredients identified. Despite many gaps, Canadian governments, both before and after 1982, have probably had as respectable records in refraining from the violation of democratic principles as any in the world. Nevertheless, given the fact that popular sovereignty is exercised only every four years or so, as well as the limited scope of political equality, the apparent ease with which governments can violate fundamental freedoms, and the tension between majority rule and minority rights, the extent to which democracy is indeed a fundamental Canadian value should not be overstated. Moreover, even if Canadians believe in democracy, they are troubled by the "democratic deficit" they witness in the operation of the political system. Almost every chapter of this book reveals aspects of the system that could function more democratically.[11]

DISTINGUISHING BETWEEN CANADIAN AND AMERICAN VALUES

Beyond the consensus on democracy, it is difficult to find widespread agreement on other values that constitute the Canadian political culture. One approach that bears promise, however, is to contrast widely held Canadian values with those of the United States. Canadian and American values are very much alike, of course, but a focus on the differences can be quite revealing. A rich academic literature exists on this subject, the key proponent of this approach being the American sociologist Seymour Martin Lipset in his book *Continental Divide.*

As mentioned above, Lipset's analysis ties in well with another prominent interpretation of Canadian values, often called the Hartz-Horowitz or fragment theory.

Many observers have made the point that while the American Declaration of Independence lists the objectives of "life, liberty and the pursuit of happiness," Canada's 1867 Constitution Act talks about "peace, order and good government." Lipset goes on from this point to outline his basic distinction as follows: "Canada has been and is a more class-aware, elitist, law-abiding, statist, collectivity-oriented, and particularistic (group-oriented) society than the United States."[12] Among Canadian commentators on the subject, Pierre Berton noted that Canadians are law abiding peaceful, orderly, deferential toward authority, cautious, elitist, moralistic, tolerant, diffident, and unemotional.[13] Canada is often considered to be a "kinder, gentler" society than that next door. This approach leads us to identify five basic categories of Canadian values that can be distinguished from those in the United States. They are a balance between individualism and collectivism; particularism, diversity, and tolerance; deference to authority; egalitarianism; and caution, diffidence, dependence, idealism, and nonviolence.

Balance Between Individualism and Collectivism

If there is a value other than democracy to which most Canadians adhere, it is probably that of **individualism**, liberalism, or capitalism, often expressed as the sanctity of private enterprise or individual economic freedom. The general principle is widely shared that everyone should be free to go about their business as they choose and that those with the greatest talent or who work the hardest should reap the benefits of their abilities and labour. In Paul Sniderman's survey, for example, 65 percent of Canadians believed that people who have made a lot of money were "willing to work and take advantage of the opportunities all of us have,"[14] while 13 percent felt that they have usually done so at the expense of others. The extent of commitment to individualism can be best gauged, however, in comparison with the United States.

Although both countries have "mixed economies" today—that is, a combination of private enterprise and government involvement—the United States remains the world's last stronghold of liberalism or individualism with a relatively smaller public sector than other modern states. This is only to be expected, given its revolutionary origins—revolting against an oppressive foreign government—and its self-proclaimed role since 1945 as the leader of the "free world" and capitalist forces. Canada, however, has been less hostile toward public intervention and more inclined to rely on government. This is partly because of the geographic environment of the Canadian political system and the U.S. threat, as seen in Chapters 3 and 10, but it also stems from the basic Canadian value of collectivism or community, a value derived from the French feudal system and the arrival of the United Empire Loyalists. Both founding groups, to say nothing of a similar value shared by Aboriginal Canadians, saw society not as a mass of grasping, ambitious individuals, but as an organic community in which all people—high and low—had their place and did their respective part to contribute to the welfare of the whole. In Sniderman's survey, 58 percent of Canadians agreed with the statement "I am glad that I have a government that looks after me in so many ways," while 32 percent disagreed; 50 percent of Canadians agreed that "the government should see to it that everyone has a job and a standard of living" compared to only 25 percent of Americans.[15]

The balance between capitalism and **collectivism** in Canada can be seen in Table 11.1, which shows, in terms of the total value of the economy, the percentage of revenue taken by

TABLE 11.1 TOTAL GOVERNMENT REVENUE, EXPENDITURES, AND DEBT, AS PERCENTAGE OF GDP, OECD COUNTRIES, 2012–2014

GENERAL GOVERNMENT REVENUE (2013–14)		GENERAL GOVERNMENT SPENDING (2013–14)		GENERAL GOVERNMENT DEBT (2012–14)	
MEXICO	24.5	MEXICO	24.4	LUXEMBOURG	29.1
KOREA	33.2	KOREA	31.8	NORWAY	32.2
U.S.	33.2	SWITZERLAND	33.5	SWITZERLAND	45.7
SWITZERLAND	33.6	AUSTRALIA	36.6	KOREA	53.5
JAPAN	33.9	U.S.	38.7	CZECH REP.	57.1
AUSTRALIA	34.0	CANADA	39.6	SLOVAK REP.	60.3
IRELAND	34.9	IRELAND	39.9	DENMARK	60.7
CANADA	37.8	NEW ZEALAND	40.1	POLAND	62.3
SPAIN	37.8	SLOVAK REP.	41.8	SWEDEN	62.4
POLAND	38.7	CZECH REP.	42.0	AUSTRALIA	63.6
SLOVAK REP.	38.9	ICELAND	42.3	FINLAND	71.0
NEW ZEALAND	39.7	JAPAN	42.3	NETHERLANDS	76.0
UK	39.8	POLAND	42.3	GERMANY	81.5
CZECH REP.	40.1	LUXEMBOURG	42.6	AUSTRIA	98.1
LUXEMBOURG	42.6	GERMANY	43.3	HUNGARY	100.2
NETHERLANDS	43.9	SPAIN	43.9	CANADA	105.7
PORTUGAL	44.5	UK	44.9	FRANCE	110.4
GERMANY	44.6	NETHERLANDS	46.1	ICELAND	112.0
ICELAND	45.3	NORWAY	47.3	UK	114.1
GREECE	45.8	PORTUGAL	49.2	SPAIN	115.8
HUNGARY	47.6	GREECE	49.7	U.S.	122.6
ITALY	48.1	HUNGARY	50.9	BELGIUM	129.7
AUSTRIA	49.8	ITALY	51.4	IRELAND	136.7
SWEDEN	51.0	AUSTRIA	51.6	ITALY	143.0
BELGIUM	51.1	SWEDEN	53.8	PORTUGAL	149.6
FRANCE	53.5	BELGIUM	54.2	GREECE	178.2
NORWAY	54.8	FRANCE	56.2	JAPAN	239.3
FINLAND	55.2	DENMARK	57.0	NEW ZEALAND	N/A
DENMARK	58.8	FINLAND	59.0	MEXICO	N/A

Source: OECD Data, Economy and Government, https://data.oecd.org/gga/general-government-revenue .htm#indicator-chart. [General Government Spending/GDP calculations by authors]. Most recent available yearly data for each country.

government, the percentage of expenditure made by government, and the national debt of government. In all three measures of the size of the public sector, Canada is in an intermediate position relative to other Western democracies, although slightly on the low side. This complements an observation made in Table 8.4 in Chapter 8 with respect to government social expenditures as a percentage of gross domestic product.

Thus, although Canadians might instinctively claim a commitment to capitalism and might still be less reliant on the state than many other countries, it would be more accurate to say that the accumulation of public demands has given Canada an economy almost equally divided between private and public sectors. Further proof of this balance can be seen in the surveys of the 2000 Canada Election Study, where Canadians were found to be evenly divided in their faith in free enterprise as opposed to the role of government.[16]

Canada is generally less collectivist than Western Europe, and although the difference between the two North American countries should not be overstated, much concrete evidence of a significant variation exists. The extent of federal and provincial Crown corporations, including broadcasting, transportation, and electricity and other resources, is greater in Canada than in the United States; the Canadian public health insurance system stands out in contrast to that of the United States; the Canadian social security system is considered more adequate; and taxes are generally higher in order to finance such collective activity. In just about every policy field, in fact, the extent of government intervention is greater in Canada than in the United States. Two other differences between the two countries are that individual property rights, so valued in the United States, are not guaranteed in the Canadian Constitution, and that while many private American individuals and corporations are generous philanthropists, Canadians are more likely to have charitable causes funded by the government.[17]

Particularism, Diversity, and Tolerance

A second difference in the basic values of the two countries has to do with the distinction between "universalism" and "particularism," leading many to argue that pluralism is a more appropriate description of Canada than of the United States. This distinction is commonly expressed in terms of the melting pot and the mosaic: immigrants to the United States are urged to become "unhyphenated" Americans, whereas Canada encourages the retention of cultural particularisms; Canada is officially a "tossed salad" rather than a "blender." Sometimes this Canadian diversity or heterogeneity is simply called tolerance, and sometimes it is linked to the recognition of group rights as opposed to individual rights. The distinctiveness of the French-Canadian Roman Catholic community in Quebec was the original basis of this value, but it has now spread to policies of multiculturalism and recognition of other group rights, even in the Constitution.

As noted in Chapter 6, multiculturalism means encouraging the retention of minority ethnic cultures rather than trying to assimilate all newcomers into some kind of homogeneous Canadianism. This official policy is seen as a means of enriching and enlivening the country, encouraging new Canadians to feel at home, promoting tolerance and minimizing discrimination, and perhaps enhancing Canada's contribution to world harmony. In his writings, Will Kymlicka makes the point that Canada was a world leader in constitutionalizing multiculturalism, in accommodating national minorities through territorial autonomy (Quebec), and in constitutionalizing Aboriginal rights, treaties, self-government, and land claims. The federal government has recognized both National Multiculturalism Day (June 27) and National Aboriginal Day (June 21).[18]

Even if there are limits to Canadian support for multiculturalism, as noted in Chapter 6, and even if an ethnic revival has occurred in many countries, including the United States, particularism in Canada has other dimensions. It can be extended to women in the sense that they, like minority groups, generally benefit from more advanced legislation than in the U.S. It could also relate to the greater secularism in Canada that permits a commitment to minority rights, such as same-sex marriage,[19] as well as being seen in terms of acknowledging the existence of social classes. Americans are even less class-conscious than Canadians, being imbued with the belief that through hard work anyone can make it to the top, and more Americans than Canadians feel that they belong to the middle class. All of this affects the tolerance for trade unions, which is greater in Canada because middle-class America sees no need for them. Particularism has a territorial dimension, too—Canadian provinces have greater powers than American states. Decentralization in Canada is accompanied by stronger regional or provincial loyalties and identities, again because of the example set by Quebec. Finally, American universalism can also be seen in its foreign policy, which would brook no compromise with "evil empires" (Ronald Reagan) and the "axis of evil" (George W. Bush), whereas Canada has often played a useful negotiating role on the international scene because of the lessons of compromise and tolerance learned at home.[20]

Deference to Authority

Another fundamental difference between Canadian and American values is the higher level of **deference to authority** in Canadian society.[21] Canadians demonstrate greater respect toward the law, judges, police, religious leaders, and many others with "legitimate power." Peace, order, and good government rather than individual liberty is the Canadian ideal, and many observers have noted that Canada is probably the only country where a police officer, the Mountie, is a national symbol—certainly a contrast to the U.S. hero Horatio Alger, the self-made man. Unlike Americans, Canadians are not instinctively suspicious of the state; indeed, Canadians have seen the government not in terms of an alien imposition but rather as the authorized agent to respond to their individual and collective demands. Such respect for authority and trust in government goes so far as to permit much greater government secrecy in Canada than in the United States, to be less concerned about the admissibility of evidence obtained illegally by the Crown,[22] and even to allow the RCMP to engage in a wide range of illegal activities, such as opening mail.[23] Surveys seem to indicate that Canadians opt for security over civil liberty, having no concern with video cameras in public places, for example,[24] although the American obsession with terrorism since September 2001 might have changed many attitudes in that country on these issues.

Deference is related to other values already mentioned. Americans are the epitome of the "Protestant ethic"—that is, members of Protestant sects that emphasize hard work in this life as the key to entering the next. But in their frenzy to get ahead at all costs, individualistic, competitive, and achievement-oriented Americans may find it necessary to bend or break the law. Canadians, slightly less obsessed with material success, are more likely to obey a law even if they do not like it. Crime rates are considerably lower in Canada, gun control laws are stronger, and the drug problem is less severe.[25] Furthermore, the United States has many more lawyers per capita, and Americans are more litigious by nature, having a much greater propensity to take disputes to court.

Deference to authority comes in part from the monarchical and feudal traditions, which contain the idea of an organic community made up of people of different status. These values were reinforced by the two dominant churches in Canadian history, Roman Catholic and Anglican, which recognize priests, bishops, archbishops (as well as cardinals and popes, in the former case) in a great hierarchy between ordinary mortals and God. Americans, exalting the sovereignty of "We, the People," revolted against the monarchical system and, when it came to religion, turned to anti-elitist, Protestant sects in which power resided in the local congregation. Respect for authority and the law is also related to the settlement of the Western frontier. In the Canadian West and in the North, the law and enforcement of the law by the RCMP preceded settlement, whereas in the violent American frontier, settlers arrived ahead of the law. This state of affairs not only provided Canada with a more peaceful settlement of its frontier (and, believe it or not, better treatment of its Aboriginals) but also reinforced the previously established respect for law and order.

Egalitarianism

One striking example of the claim that Canada is more egalitarian than the United States is in the constitutional equality of women. In the United States, a proposed Equal Rights Amendment to the constitution failed to pass, whereas about the same time, Canada adopted a strong guarantee of gender equality (including affirmative action) in the 1982 Charter of Rights and Freedoms. The Charter also aims to guarantee equality and prevent discrimination on many other grounds such as ethnicity, religion, age, and sexual orientation. Somewhat similarly, the health and welfare programs that flow from Canadian collectivism ensure a greater degree of equality for the poor and working classes.[26] One Statistics Canada study showed that the poorest 25 percent of Canadian families have more purchasing power than their U.S. counterparts, while the opposite was the case at the top of the income scale, and another study confirmed that Canada ranks higher on intergenerational social mobility.[27] Canada extends this redistributive egalitarianism to have-not regions as well as have-not individuals through equalization payments. The subtle differences in the public's commitment to equality in the two countries are revealed in the fact that 47 percent of Americans agreed that "we have gone too far in pushing equal rights in this country," compared with only 31 percent of Canadians.[28]

Canadian **egalitarianism** is connected to the comparative strength of class-consciousness, trade unions, and social democratic parties in the two countries. For example, the CCF and New Democratic Parties, which are based on that very principle, have no real equivalents in the United States. Egalitarianism in Canada can also be seen in a strong cooperative movement, stretching from Prairie grain elevators to Quebec's caisses populaires to the Antigonish movement in the Maritimes. Perhaps it also results from the feeling of *noblesse oblige* among those in the upper echelons of the hierarchy, the feudal concept that the lord was responsible for the well-being of his serfs. In any case, Lipset argues that Canadians are more committed to "redistributive egalitarianism, while Americans place more emphasis on meritocratic competition and equality of opportunity." He also admits that the United States has a greater hierarchy of educational institutions than is found in Canada.

however, they suddenly became more self-confident, wanting to influence public policies and demanding their place as candidates or participants in constitutional negotiations. Aboriginals have a distinct conception of their place in Canadian society and many seek to govern themselves, while the ethnocultural minorities want to be full participants in the overall political system.

Class Subcultures

Within the general Canadian political culture, different classes exhibit somewhat distinctive values, attitudes, and orientations, even where the individuals involved are lacking in class-consciousness. Attitudes of trust in government and feelings of political efficacy naturally decline from upper-to middle-to working-class groups and are lowest among the poor. It is also likely that the upper classes are less committed to communitarian and egalitarian values than the working classes and are more attached to elitism and hierarchy. In short, the upper classes have a political subculture distinguished by feelings of self-confidence, trust, and participation, and by demands for the retention of the status quo; the working classes have a political subculture characterized by alienation, lack of participation, and demands for substantial economic reform. Most of the poor have dropped out of the political system entirely, evidence of a truly distinctive subculture.[42]

CRITICAL APPROACHES

The *pluralist approach* centres on the "limited identities" that characterize Canadian society and the many subcultures that exist in the country, each one providing a shading to the national values identified. It also focuses on the values of particularism and tolerance. Rather than emphasize the elite interaction that emanates from such subcultures, however, pluralists note that most of these interests are organized into advocacy groups and that public policies are the outcome of a broader interplay among such groups.

Class analysts attach themselves to the collectivist values identified in this chapter, but are otherwise generally critical of the Canadian values and attitudes identified.

In particular, they emphasize the narrow conception of democracy held by most Canadians, deriding the notion of one person–one vote as a genuine measure of political equality and the view that political freedom is meaningful in the absence of economic and social freedom. They also contend that the capitalist ethic is still predominant among the political and economic elite and that much of the government intervention that has occurred has been welcomed rather than opposed by the bourgeoisie. They put little stock in such "tory" ideas as trusting a concerned and paternalistic political or economic elite to advance the position of the working class.

CONCLUSION

Although the values and attitudes that constitute the political culture of any society are difficult to establish, certain Canadian political values can be identified, the foremost being a rudimentary belief in democracy. In many cases, it helps to see Canadian values in contrast to those of the United States. Canada has a more even balance between individualism and collectivism; it gives greater weight to particularism, tolerance, and deference to authority; it is also more egalitarian, cautious, diffident, and dependent. To some extent, however, these differences between Canadian and American values may be in decline. Efforts to define pan-Canadian values, attitudes, and identities are also complicated by the existence of regional, ethnic, and other political subcultures and identities.

Because the political culture provides the value context within which the Canadian political system operates, the contents of this chapter are relevant to virtually everything else in the text. Previous chapters have already had connections to the values, attitudes, identities, and subcultures mentioned here. The global and especially the U.S. influences on Canada's political culture were also addressed earlier. The next chapter on political socialization, the mass media, and public opinion polls is closely linked to political culture, especially in terms of how the basic values and attitudes are transmitted and how they can be measured, while the following four chapters—elections, political parties, voting, and advocacy groups—examine how political values impact on political behaviour. Part 4, the Constitutional Context, revisits such questions as amending the constitution to better reflect the contemporary political culture, how that political culture affects federal–provincial relations, and how the Charter has strengthened certain basic values. Finally, Part 5 examines the operation of the institutions of government in the context of the limits imposed by the political culture.

DISCUSSION QUESTIONS

1. Do you believe that periodic elections are a sufficient means of exercising the principle of popular sovereignty, and that the principle of one person–one vote is a sufficient mark of political equality?

2. How deep is the Canadian commitment to political freedom? What situations do you think justify government restriction of such freedom?

3. What kinds of minority rights should be protected in the Constitution, and in what circumstances should Canada follow the principle of majority rule?

4. To what extent has the traditional Canadian political culture been transformed in recent years?

5. Is the Canadian political culture more than a collection of limited identities?

MindTap®   FOR MORE INFO GO TO http://www.nelson.com/student

NOTES

1. Ronald Inglehart, "The Silent Revolution in Europe: Intergenerational Change in Post-Industrial Societies," *American Political Science Review* (December 1971).
2. David V.J. Bell, "Political Culture in Canada," in Michael Whittington and Glen Williams, eds., *Canadian Politics in the 21st Century*, 7th ed. (Toronto: Thomson Nelson, 2008), p. 228; Jane Jenson, "Changing Discourse, Changing Agenda," quoted in Bell, p. 231.
3. Bell, "Political Culture in Canada," pp. 236–40.
4. Louis Hartz, *The Founding of New Societies* (New York: Harcourt, Brace and World, 1964).
5. Gad Horowitz, "Conservatism, Liberalism and Socialism in Canada: An Interpretation," *Canadian Journal of Economics and Political Science* (May 1966).
6. Seymour Martin Lipset, *Continental Divide* (New York: Routledge, 1990).
7. John Ralston Saul, *A Fair Country: Telling Truths about Canada* (Toronto: Viking Canada, 2008). Another recent treatment of the Canadian political culture is Andrew Cohen, *The Unfinished Canadian: The People We Are* (Toronto: McClelland and Stewart, 2007).
8. Henry B. Mayo, *An Introduction to Democratic Theory* (New York: Oxford University Press, 1960), Ch. 4; Patrick Dunleavy and Brendan O'Leary, *Theories of the State: The Politics of Liberal Democracy* (London: Macmillan, 1987); and David Held, *Models of Democracy*, 2nd ed. (Stanford: Stanford University Press, 1996).
9. Thomas R. Berger, *Fragile Freedoms* (Toronto: Clarke, Irwin & Co., rev. and updated, 1982).
10. Paul M. Sniderman, Joseph F. Fletcher, Peter Russell, and Philip E. Tetlock, *The Clash of Rights: Liberty, Equality, and Legitimacy in Pluralist Democracy* (New Haven, CT: Yale University Press, 1996).
11. Patti Tamara Lenard and Richard Simeon, eds., *Imperfect Democracies: The Democratic Deficit in Canada and the United States* (Vancouver: UBC Press, 2012); Peter Aucoin, Mark D. Jarvis, and Lori Turnbull, *Democratizing the Constitution: Reforming Responsible Government* (Toronto: Emond Montgomery, 2011).
12. Lipset, *Continental Divide*.
13. Pierre Berton, *Why We Act Like Canadians* (Toronto: McClelland and Stewart, 1982).
14. Sniderman et al., *The Clash of Rights*, p. 91.
15. Ibid., pp. 99 and 123.
16. André Blais, Elisabeth Gidengil, Richard Nadeau, and Neil Nevitte, *Anatomy of a Liberal Victory: Making Sense of the Vote in the 2000 Canadian Election* (Peterborough: Broadview Press, 2002), p. 102.
17. Allan Gregg and Michael Posner, *The Big Picture: What Canadians Think About Almost Everything* (Toronto: Macfarlane Walter & Ross, 1990), pp. 11–13, 29.
18. Will Kymlicka, *Finding Our Way: Rethinking Ethnocultural Relations in Canada* (Don Mills: Oxford University Press, 1998), among many other works. In his book, *Utopia: The Surprising Triumph of Canadian Pluralism* (Toronto: Viking Canada, 2007), Michael Adams argues that support for the Canadian mosaic is holding fast.
19. Michael Adams and others emphasize the secularism of Canada in contrast to the religiosity of the United States. One survey found 27 percent of Canadians opposed to same-sex marriages compared with 47 percent opposed in the U.S.
20. Given evidence of intolerance at home, this self-defined Canadian international image may be a touch moralistic.
21. Edgar Friedenberg, *Deference to Authority* (White Plains, NY: M.E. Sharpe, 1980); and Judy M. Torrance, *Public Violence in Canada* (Montreal: McGill-Queen's University Press, 1986).
22. Section 24(2) of the Charter allows the admissibility of tainted evidence if it does not detract from the "repute" of the Court!
23. Sniderman, *The Clash of Rights*, p. 27.
24. Centre for Research and Information on Canada, *Portraits of Canada 2005* (January 2006), p. 10.
25. Statistics Canada, *Crime Comparisons between Canada and the United States* (Catalogue No. 85-002-XPE 2001, December 18, 2001); and Statistics Canada, "Homicides," *The Daily*, September 29, 2004. On a per capita basis, three times as many murders and twice as many aggravated assaults are committed in the United States as in Canada. Despite the law and order orientation of the Harper government, the crime rate has generally been in decline for some time.

26. For a recent perspective on the differences between Canadian and U.S. health care systems, see Statistics Canada, *Joint Canada/United States Survey of Health: Findings and Public-Use Microdata File*, available at http://www.statcan.ca/english/freepub/82M0022XIE/free.htm.

27. W. Wolfson and B. Murphy, "Income Inequality in North America: Does the 49th Parallel Still Matter?" *Canadian Economic Observer* (Catalogue No. 11-010-XPB, August 2000). See Miles Corak, "Equality of Opportunity and Inequality across the Generations: Challenges Ahead," *Policy Options* (March–April 2005), and Educational Policy Institute, Global Higher Education Rankings 2005, available at http://www.educationalpolicy.org/pdf/Global2005.pdf.

28. Sniderman et al., *The Clash of Rights*, Ch. 4.

29. Margaret Atwood, *Survival* (Toronto: Anansi, 1972); W.L. Morton, *The Canadian Identity* (Toronto: University of Toronto Press, 1961); and Dominique Clift, *The Secret Kingdom: Interpretations of the Canadian Character* (Toronto, McClelland and Stewart, 1989), p. 227.

30. Lipset, *Continental Divide*, Ch. 4; *Maclean's*, July 1, 1995, p. 15; Michael Adams says that Canadians fear "committing an unforgivable act of hubris" if they praise their country, *Sex in the Snow: Canadian Social Values at the End of the Millennium* (Toronto: Penguin Books, 1998), p. xxi. Perhaps we become immodest in constantly proclaiming our modesty!

31. According to Walter Stefaniuk, *You Asked Us … About Canada* (Toronto: Doubleday Canada, 1996), the Canadian habit of frequently adding "eh?" to a spoken sentence is a "politeness marker," designed to include the listener in the conversation, p. 1.

32. Citizenship and Immigration Canada, *Discover Canada: The Rights and Responsibilities of Citizenship: Study Guide* does not provide a succinct list, but is not inconsistent with our discussion. As revised by the Harper government, it puts greater emphasis on Canada's military traditions and the monarchy, and as mentioned in Chapter 7, adds that "Canada's diversity includes gay and lesbian Canadians, who enjoy the full protection of and equal treatment under the law, including access to civil marriage" (http://www.cic.gc.ca/english/resources/publications/discover/index.asp).

33. *Maclean's*, July 1, 1995, p. 15.

34. Neil Nevitte, *The Decline of Deference: Canadian Value Change in Cross-National Perspective* (Peterborough: Broadview Press, 1996), argues that the change in Canadian values is consistent with changes in other advanced industrial states and is not the result of American influence.

35. Environics Research Group, *Environics/CBC 2006 Federal Election Survey*, January 2006, at http://erg.environics.net/news/default.asp?aID=598.

36. J.M.S. Careless, "Limited Identities," *Canadian Historical Review* (March 1969), pp. 1–10.

37. Nelson Wiseman, *In Search of Canadian Political Culture* (Vancouver: UBC Press, 2007).

38. Telford and Lazar, *Canada: The State of the Federation 2001*; Ailsa Henderson, "Regional Political Cultures in Canada," *Canadian Journal of Political Science* (September 2004).

39. Nelson Wiseman, "The Pattern of Prairie Politics," *Queen's Quarterly* (Summer 1981); Jarod J. Wesley, *Code Politics: Campaigns and Cultures on the Canadian Prairies* (Vancouver: UBC Press, 2011).

40. Pierre Elliott Trudeau, "Some Obstacles to Democracy in Quebec," in *Federalism and the French Canadians* (Toronto: Macmillan, 1968).

41. David McGrane, "Political Marketing and the NDP's Historic Breakthrough," in Jon H. Pammett and Christopher Dornan, eds., *The Canadian Federal Election of 2011* (Toronto: Dundurn, 2011).

42. Michael Ornstein, Michael Stevenson, and Paul Williams, "Region, Class and Political Culture in Canada: Is There an English-Canadian Subculture?" *Canadian Journal of Political Science* (June 1980).

FURTHER READING

Adams, Michael. *Fire and Ice: The United States, Canada and the Myth of Converging Values*. Toronto: Penguin Canada, 2003.

Ajzenstat, Janet, and Peter J. Smith, eds. *Canada's Origins: Liberal, Tory or Republican?* Montreal: McGill-Queen's University Press, 1995.

Bell, David. "Political Culture in Canada," in Michael Whittington and Glen Williams, eds., *Canadian Politics in the 21st Century*, 7th ed. Toronto: Thomson Nelson, 2008.

Cohen, Andrew. *The Unfinished Canadian: The People We Are*. Toronto: McClelland and Stewart, 2007.

Gidengil, Elisabeth, André Blais, Neil Nevitte, and Richard Nadeau. *Citizens*. Vancouver: UBC Press, 2004.

Gregg, Allan, and Michael Posner. *The Big Picture: What Canadians Think About Almost Everything*. Toronto: Macfarlane Walter & Ross, 1990.

Kymlicka, Will. *Finding Our Way: Rethinking Ethnocultural Relations in Canada*. Don Mills: Oxford University Press, 1998.

Lipset, Seymour Martin. *Continental Divide*. New York: Routledge, 1990.

Nevitte, Neil. *The Decline of Deference: Canadian Value Change in Cross-National Perspective*. Peterborough: Broadview Press, 1996.

Telford, Hamish, and Harvey Lazar, eds. *Canada: The State of the Federation 2001: Canadian Political Culture(s) in Transition*. Kingston: Institute of Intergovernmental Affairs, 2002.

Thomas, David, and Barbara Boyle Torrey, eds. *Canada and the United States: Differences That Count*, 3rd ed. Peterborough: Broadview Press, 2008.

Wiseman, Nelson. *In Search of Canadian Political Culture*. Vancouver: UBC Press, 2007.

CHAPTER 12

Political Socialization, the Mass Media, and Public Opinion Polls

Levels of political knowledge among the general public fall short of the democratic ideal: people care less, think less, and know less about politics than is commonly expected. This is understandable to some extent because most people have school, jobs, family, and friends to attend to, as well as other obligations that seem more immediately important. Nonetheless, people in democratic countries are asked periodically to make judgments about those who lead them, and sometimes to decide between different policies. Thus, people have to know at least something about the politicians, the political parties, and the packages of policy options from which they must choose in an election.

It is now commonly observed that the mass media and public opinion polls are two of the most important elements in the political system. The mass media—principally television, newspapers, radio, and the Internet—are the primary source of most Canadians' knowledge and opinion about topical political issues and current personalities. Another important link between people and government is the public opinion poll, as parties, advocacy groups, governments, and the media themselves seek to discover Canadians' opinions on every conceivable matter.

This chapter begins by outlining the various agents of political socialization—the sources of public values and information. It then surveys the state of the media in Canada, and concludes with a discussion of the proliferation of public opinion polls.

THEORETICAL CONSIDERATIONS

Chapter 11 defined political culture as the collection of basic values, ideas, assumptions, and beliefs that shape our understanding and behaviour as citizens in the world of politics. This chapter is largely about the acquisition or transmission of such political values, attitudes, and information. Those who hold the dominant values in society would only be expected, consciously or unconsciously, to transmit them to the rest of the population, including new immigrant arrivals and the younger generation. Sometimes these influential actors—these elites—will deliberately seek to own the mass media, one of the most important agents of political socialization; at other times, they will exert their influence through their control of other parts of the economy, the educational system, the bureaucracy, or religious or cultural organizations. Such a process of defining what is normal—often called **cultural hegemony**— underlies much of the material in this chapter.

These elites are not a homogenous group that set out in concert to manipulate the public. First, disagreement exists at the elite level, and second, people's minds are not blank screens on which members of the elite are able to inscribe their opinions. Nevertheless, it is difficult to counter the values that become dominant at the elite level and that are transmitted to the rest of society via agents of political socialization.[1]

POLITICAL SOCIALIZATION

Political socialization is the process by which individuals acquire their basic political values and attitudes as well as their political information and opinions. Looked at in another way, it is the process by which society passes on its basic values or political culture from one generation to another. Political socialization is sometimes called political learning or education. The process of political socialization consists in part of direct, individual observation of political phenomena, but is mostly performed by intermediaries or agents of socialization. It is relatively easy to identify the main agents of political socialization in Canada but much more difficult to evaluate their relative impact. We begin with the family, school, and peers, and then examine other such influences.

The Family

The portrait of a "family" is more varied today than in the past, but it remains the basic cell of Canadian society. Despite many modern pressures, parents, grandparents, or other guardians, are the first major influence on a child's attitudes and values. At the very least, families provide children with certain circumstances of birth, especially their regional and ethnic origins and their social class, all of which are bound to have some effect on children's political attitudes and behaviour.[2] Second, most children absorb attitudes and values, some of which are of political significance, in a kind of osmosis from their family's behaviour. Parents' casual comments about politics, politicians, and police are good examples. Third, some parents deliberately try to indoctrinate their children with certain political values, such as supporting a particular political party or developing a sense of civic obligation.[3] On the other hand, the political impact of the family in modern times should not be overestimated, for political socialization is a process that continues throughout life.

The School

The school is the second main agent of political socialization. Although Canada has distinctive provincial and territorial educational systems, the decline of the family's influence and the greater use of child-care centres and kindergarten have probably increased the importance of the "school." Like the family, it is an early enough influence that it is likely to shape basic lifelong values. All school systems in Canada and elsewhere deliberately attempt to inculcate certain basic values and attitudes, including some of a political nature, such as a feeling of affection or support for the country, the governmental apparatus, the head of state, the police, the flag, and

Vance Rodewalt/Artizans

the national anthem. Some, even in Canada, go beyond this to dwell on the virtues of other ideological, moral, religious, or political values.

Given the diversity of Canadian society, many questions arise about the role of the school in the political socialization process. Since the provinces and territories have jurisdiction over education, they may contribute to distinctive regional political cultures and identities at the expense of the overall country. The radically different accounts of certain historical events found in French and English textbooks, such as whether Louis Riel was a traitor or a hero, are often cited as examples of the biased role of formal education in this process.[4] One point is clear: the forces of dualism, regionalism, and continentalism in Canadian society make it difficult for the school system to develop a pan-Canadian sense of national identity.[5]

Most observers feel that the current state of Canadian political education is deficient and that students are not exposed to enough direct teaching about politics. When it comes to current events, for example, high-school students usually demonstrate a deplorable lack of knowledge, and a recent study of 18- to 24-year-olds by the Dominion Institute found that only 46 percent could name Canada's first prime minister and only 26 percent knew the year of Confederation.[6] Only Ontario, Manitoba, Nova Scotia, and Quebec require high school students to take a dedicated Canadian history course to graduate.

Peers

Peers are the third main agent of political socialization. Peers are simply those around us who are part of our lives or have influence, such as friends, acquaintances, or co-workers. While "peer pressure" is generally thought of as affecting younger people, we are all susceptible to peer influence throughout our lives. Wherever and whenever two or more people communicate, political issues of one kind or another may arise, and one person can influence the other. In peer-group discussions "around the water-cooler," one person often becomes dominant, because of that person's knowledge, position, or strength of character.

Ironically, people may actually gain more information about politics from their networks of loose acquaintances than from their families and close friends. The reason for this, as sociologist Marc Granovetter explained, is that our relationships with family and friends tend to be "closed networks"—that is, the people are likely to be closely connected.[7] Political information, therefore, circulates within the network and usually reinforces what we already believe. In our wider group of acquaintances, by contrast, each person is likely to have *different* friends, family, and acquaintances. This "open network" includes many potential sources of new information and ideas.

Other Agents of Political Socialization

Families, schools, and peer networks are important sources of political socialization in Canada but certainly not the only ones. The mass media—the main subject of this chapter—will be examined below, but political parties, religious faiths, groups of various kinds, corporations, think tanks, and the government itself are also influences on political attitudes, values, and opinions.

Political parties practice the art of persuasion and seek to influence opinions and party preferences on a daily basis. Those who identify with a particular party often find that the simplest means of forming an opinion on an issue is to take their cue from the party leader. The more a person identifies with a party or leader, the greater the propensity to defer to the partisan perspective expressed.

Like political parties, individual corporations are in the business of persuasion, trying to sell their own goods and services. Sometimes, however, companies will also try to influence political attitudes and opinions, an effort that is called **advocacy advertising**. Many such corporations were involved in the free trade debate, especially during the 1988 election campaign, expressing their support through "speeches, debates, letters, advertisements, information sessions with employees, and inserts in newspapers."[8] Others have used the media to try to influence Canadians' opinions on tax changes, environmentalism, drug patents, and nuclear energy. Petroleum companies, as an example, have responded to criticisms from environmentalists by distributing advertisements that present their corporations in a positive light.

Churches have often influenced the political values, attitudes, and opinions of their members. The classic case was the Roman Catholic Church in Quebec before 1960, when it had a close relationship with political authorities and often told its members how to behave politically. While that church continues to take stances on political issues, some positions—such as those on the LGBT community—appear to have softened. Other religious denominations may also articulate positions on political issues, with two religious groups that appear to be taking an increased interest in politics in Canada being evangelical Christians and Muslims. As such, religion may be becoming a more important factor in political socialization. However, as noted in Chapter 11, Canada is a more secular society than the United States, and religion plays a lesser role in political socialization here than it does there.[9]

More than half of the Canadian population belongs to an organized group of some kind, and although most groups are non-political, all have the potential to influence members' political views. Such interest groups as the Canadian Labour Congress, the Catholic Women's League, and the Canadian Medical Association also try to extend their influence beyond their own members to the public at large.

Many interest groups are sources of useful information about public policy, and it is sometimes difficult to separate them from "think tanks," whose main purpose is to provide analyses of such policies. Some think tanks are considered on the "right" side of the political spectrum—for example, the Fraser Institute, the C.D. Howe Institute, the Canada West Foundation, and the Macdonald-Laurier Institute. Some are considered to be in the "centre," such as the Institute for Research on Public Policy, the Caledon Institute, and the Canadian International Council. Those on the "left" that specialize in social policy include the Canadian Centre for Policy Alternatives, the Broadbent Institute and the Council of Canadians.[10]

Finally, the government itself is often engaged in efforts to influence public views and behaviour. Sometimes this is done for what are widely recognized as legitimate purposes, such as encouraging physical fitness and discouraging smoking, impaired driving, racial discrimination, violence against women, and the use of drugs. Sometimes it is done for broadly acceptable political purposes, such as promoting tourism in Canada, the purchase of Canadian-made goods, or national unity. Governments are also expected to inform the public about new laws, regulations, and programs, but there is a fine line between providing simple information and extolling the virtues of such initiatives for partisan purposes. Following the 1995 Quebec referendum, Jean Chrétien's government spent hundreds of millions of dollars in a pro-Canada advertising campaign in that province. This led to the "sponsorship scandal," where some went back into party members' pockets and campaigns. More recently, the Harper government was criticized for its aggressive promotion of the Alberta oil sands and for what some saw as Conservative Party promotion in communicating new government policies.

How Canadians individually and collectively acquire their political values, attitudes, and opinions is a complicated question. Moreover, many Canadians are only semi-socialized: they simply do not have many political values, attitudes, and opinions or much political information. The leading study of this subject concluded that not only is *lack* of information a serious problem, but even worse is the large degree of *misinformation* among the electorate. Many Canadians are misinformed about basic policy-relevant facts, such as underestimating the gap between the rich and poor and the generally dismal condition of Canada's Aboriginal peoples, and overestimating the extent of crime.[11]

THE MASS MEDIA

The mass media—television, newspapers, magazines, radio, and the Internet—are an important mechanism of political socialization and source of information about politics. While families, schools, and peer networks are likely to influence lifelong values and attitudes, the media primarily transmit opinions on topical issues and personalities. Such short-term stimuli are important, however, in determining how people vote.

In surveying the state of the mass media industries in Canada today, we should first note that the privately owned media exist primarily to make a profit, and that whatever political functions they serve are incidental.[12] Such profits may be threatened by the significant costs involved in delivering comprehensive political information. Second, as in so many other aspects of Canadian life, the mass media are divided along linguistic lines, largely English and French, with an increasing number operating in other languages. Third, while the mass media are the source of most Canadians' political *information*, they also have "considerable influence on the beliefs and perspectives presented to Canadians. These choices help to determine available role models, images of reality, definitions of what is political, concepts of community, and other elements of our political culture."[13]

On the other hand, the impact of the media should not be overstated. In the first place, the media have competition from other agents of political socialization. Second, a diversity of viewpoints is expressed in the media, and people choose their media sources deliberately. A Bay Street banker is more likely to pick up a copy of a conservative newspaper like the *Wall Street Journal*, for example, than a copy of the *Socialist Worker*. In this way, media exposure does not shape a person's political opinions; rather, people choose to expose themselves to media sources that accord with their pre-existing political views. From this perspective, the media are more effective at reinforcing people's opinions than at shaping or changing them. And, in the third place, many people are sophisticated enough to resist a biased or one-sided story.[14] Nevertheless, two of the principal ways in which the media have an impact are in terms of "agenda-setting" and "framing."

In its **agenda-setting** function, the media tell people what to think about, what the important issues are, and which political personalities are significant; indeed, the media help to define what is political.[15] The stories that lead a news broadcast, for example, draw more attention than those that appear at the end, and issues that are not at all discussed in the media, by contrast, are likely to fall off the radar of public opinion altogether. Setting the agenda of public opinion is an important form of media influence.

A closely related form of media influence is *framing*. Framing deals with the *manner* in which information about an issue is presented. It occurs when, in the process of covering an issue, the media draw attention to some considerations rather than to others. A general election may be framed by journalists as a horserace among party leaders, as a contest among ideologies and principles, or several other ways.[16]

Media Ownership and Control in Canada

Because of the perceived influence of the media on public opinion, concerns have arisen in many quarters about concentrated media ownership as well as about the extent of exposure to foreign media in Canada. Although the Canadian media are domestically owned, corporate ownership in this field is concentrated in a relatively small number of firms. Moreover, Canadians are susceptible to much media influence from the United States.

Newspapers

There are more than 100 daily newspapers and over 1000 community newspapers in Canada, and a majority of Canadians access this news (though some do so on the Internet). Rather than being based on independently owned operations, the Canadian newspaper industry has been characterized by concentrated chain ownership for decades, although the names and faces have changed. In 2015, the Postmedia chain owned 45 dailies—35 coming in a deal with Quebecor/Sun Media. Table 12.1 shows the number of dailies owned by chains in Canada. It is worth noting that while the Postmedia purchases changed the landscape of ownership, many of the wealthiest families in the country continue to control portions of the daily newspaper industry, such as the Péladeau family (Quebecor), and in some cases one owner has a monopoly in a single province (Irving in New Brunswick) or metropolitan area (Postmedia in Vancouver).

TABLE 12.1 CHAIN OWNERSHIP OF CANADIAN DAILY NEWSPAPERS

OWNER	NUMBER	EXAMPLES
POSTMEDIA NETWORK/SUN MEDIA	45	*NATIONAL POST, OTTAWA CITIZEN, CALGARY HERALD, VANCOUVER SUN*
TC TRANSCONTINENTAL	11	*ST. JOHN'S TELEGRAM, CAPE BRETON POST, MOOSE JAW TIMES-HERALD, METRO (HALIFAX, MONTREAL)*
TORSTAR	9	*TORONTO STAR, HAMILTON SPECTATOR, METRO (VARIOUS CITIES)*
GROUPE CAPITALES MÉDIAS	6	*LA TRIBUNE (SHERBROOKE), LE SOLEIL (QUÉBEC)*
BLACK PRESS	4	*RED DEER ADVOCATE, KIMBERLEY DAILY BULLETIN*
QUEBECOR	3	*LE JOURNAL DE MONTRÉAL, LE JOURNAL DE QUÉBEC*
GLACIER MEDIA	3	*VICTORIA TIMES COLONIST, PRINCE GEORGE CITIZEN*
BRUNSWICK NEWS	3	*SAINT JOHN TELEGRAPH JOURNAL, MONCTON TIMES & TRANSCRIPT*
CONTINENTAL NEWSPAPERS	3	*KELOWNA DAILY COURIER, THUNDER BAY CHRONICLE HERALD*
ALTA NEWSPAPER GROUP	3	*LETHBRIDGE HERALD, MEDICINE HAT NEWS*
FP CANADIAN NEWSPAPERS	2	*WINNIPEG FREE PRESS, BRANDON SUN*
SMALLER CHAINS & INDEPENDENTS	10	*THE GLOBE AND MAIL, LE DEVOIR (MONTRÉAL), LA PRESSE (MONTRÉAL), HALIFAX CHRONICLE-HERALD, SING TAO DAILY*

Source: Newspapers Canada, "Canadian Daily Newspaper Ownership (September 2015), http://www
.newspaperscanada.ca/about-newspapers/ownership/ownership-daily-newspapers/.

Concentrated ownership of Canadian newspapers has always caused considerable concern in many quarters, fearing that the owner will gain an unhealthy degree of influence over public opinion by establishing a common point of view for all papers in the chain. This anxiety deepened when there appeared to be collusion *between* the Southam and Thomson chains in 1980. These actions prompted an investigation under the Combines Act, and charges of collusion were laid. Nothing demonstrates the weakness of Canadian competition laws as much as the acquittal of Thomson and Southam chains of these charges,[17] although an earlier case against Irving's monopoly in New Brunswick met the same fate in the courts.

The incident led the Trudeau government to appoint the **Kent Royal Commission on Newspapers**, which called for some divestment of existing ownership as well as rigid control of future concentrations. Tom Kent also expressed concern with the degree to which newspapers were involved in the ownership of radio and television stations, cable TV, and magazines, and recommended restrictions on multimedia holdings. Moreover, he sought to ensure that individual newspaper editors had complete autonomy so that they could not be told how to do their job by a common corporate owner. Under strong corporate pressure, however, the government took no action.[18] The Canadian media landscape has continued to change in ways that some argue is anti-competitive. In 2016 Postmedia slashed 90 jobs and merged newsrooms in cities where it owned two newspapers, combining formerly competing news organizations.

When Conrad Black was a dominant force in the industry, he created considerable alarm because of his strong ideological perspective.[19] The Asper family, however, turned out to be even more insistent than Black that their newspapers speak with one voice, namely their own. They prepared national editorials that had to be carried by every newspaper in the chain; they regularly spiked (that is, denied publication of) items, including editorial cartoons, to which they objected; and they fired columnists, editors, or publishers who did not share their point of view. Following the lead of the *National Post*, which they had bought from Black, they transferred their support from the Liberals to the Conservatives, and in the 2006 election campaign, owner David Asper publicly endorsed Stephen Harper at a party rally. These initiatives confirmed the worst fears of what can happen when a large number of media outlets have a single owner who is determined to mould Canadians' thinking on public issues.

The newspaper industry is under financial pressure largely because of the rise of the Internet, and many newspapers can now be read in whole or in part online. Another feature of the industry is free dailies. Four main ownership groups now publish free daily newspapers in most of Canada's largest cities, with an estimated daily circulation of 1.6 million copies. These include Postmedia (*24 Hours*, Toronto and Vancouver), Torstar/Metro International (*Metro*, various cities) and Quebecor (*24 Hours*, Montreal).

Broadcasting

The radio and television industries are distinct from newspapers in two respects: the degree of government regulation involved—primarily through the **Canadian Radio-television and Telecommunications Commission**—and the public ownership of the English CBC and French Radio-Canada networks.

Canadians' radio listening has declined to about 18 hours per week on average.[20] The publicly owned **Canadian Broadcasting Corporation (CBC)** accounted for more than 12 percent of total listening in 2007, with the CBC being the favourite of university graduates, those in professional occupations, and seniors. Through hundreds of transmitter stations, coverage is almost nationwide. In addition, CBC operates northern services and Radio-Canada International. CBC radio has a sophisticated audience and plays a major role in transmitting information and opinion among Canadians in its extended newscasts and public affairs programs.

Apart from CBC/Radio-Canada, the Canadian radio industry consists of nearly 650 local, mostly private, stations, with FM now vastly exceeding AM in listeners. These stations put varying degrees of effort into newsgathering and public affairs programming. Stations used to be independently owned, but are increasingly characterized by chain ownership, just as in the newspaper industry. Ownership changes frequently, and the majority of the radio market in Canada is controlled by a handful of firms; BCE, for example, bought CHUM stations in 2007 and the Astral empire in 2012. Like newspapers, radio stations must be Canadian owned, but the limited Canadian content on private radio stations became a problem. Since they mainly transmit music, the CRTC issued Canadian-content rules—at least 35 percent of music played on a radio station between 6 a.m. and midnight must qualify as Canadian content, as noted in Chapter 10. In 2005, the CRTC authorized satellite radio with what many observers felt were inadequate Canadian-content guarantees.

The average Canadian also watches about 15 hours of television per week and depends on that medium for most of his or her political information.[21] The publicly owned CBC/Radio-Canada has stations across the country, with English production centred in Toronto and French production in Montreal. These are supplemented by agreements with several privately owned affiliated stations, which telecast a certain amount of CBC programming.

The CBC also established its Newsworld channel in 1989 (now renamed CBC News Network) and its French equivalent, RDI, in 1995. These all-news channels cover many political events live and more extensively than the regular CBC, and provide much regional coverage, documentaries, and in-depth interview programming. Although their audience is small, most members of the political elite tune in regularly. Keen observers of Canadian politics also watch the national parliamentary channel, now called the Cable Public Affairs Channel (CPAC). In some provinces another channel carries provincial legislative proceedings, and several provinces have educational television channels.

CBC television has a strong commitment to Canadian programming but suffers from a chronic shortage of funds. After severe bloodletting under the Mulroney government and the appointment of hostile members to its board of directors, the CBC had reason to expect better treatment under the Chrétien regime. Instead, that government slashed the CBC budget even further, precipitating the resignation of the corporation's president. Repeated cuts also occurred on the Harper watch.

On the private side of television, the CTV network, acquired by BCE in 2011, consists of more than 24 stations centred in CFTO in Toronto; it also operates a 24-hours news channel and other specialty channels. The Toronto-based Global system, previously owned by the Asper family of Winnipeg, was purchased by Shaw Communications of Calgary. It now considers itself to be the third national English-language network, along with its own specialty channels. Several major cities also

CBC anchor Peter Mansbridge interviews Prime Minister Stephen Harper.

have one or more independent private English stations. Pierre Péladeau established a right-wing television version of his Sun newspapers (Sun News Network) in 2011, though the station was closed down in 2015. On the French side, Péladeau's TVA network is centred in Télé-Métropole in Montreal.

At least 85 percent of Canadian homes subscribe to cable or satellite television, more than in any other country. To some extent the CRTC regulates which channels they carry, but in general, they are designed to bring the major U.S. networks into almost every Canadian home. This gives most Canadians two chances to view popular U.S. shows—either on the originating network or on CTV or Global, which bid ferociously for such programs. The Canadian cable industry is dominated by the giants of Canadian television and radio—Rogers Communications, Shaw Cablesystems, Cogeco, and Péladeau's Vidéotron—and satellite, by BCE.

It is also notable that concerns about corporate ownership and its effect on content have been present in broadcasting as they have been with newspapers. In 2015, it was found that David Crull, President of Bell Media, tried to limit news coverage of CRTC chairman Jean-Pierre Blais after the CRTC made a decision that was not favourable to Bell. Crull stepped down after it was determined he had interfered with journalistic decisions within Bell-owned CTV and BNN.

The initial rationale for government regulation of broadcasting in Canada was "spectrum scarcity." Broadcasters required exclusive access to certain bandwidths of the electromagnetic spectrum in order to transmit their messages without interference, and the number of such frequencies was limited. The government felt that the available spectrum should be allocated to companies that were Canadian owned and that were prepared to broadcast Canadian content. As technology has evolved, however, spectrum scarcity is no longer a problem, and cable and satellite customers now have hundreds of channels. This enormous increase in the number of available channels has served to seriously dilute the audience of the conventional Canadian television stations.

Requiring Canadian television stations to be domestically owned or to telecast 50 percent or more Canadian content is virtually meaningless when almost all residents are within reach of a large assortment of U.S. television channels. On this point, Fred Fletcher talks of "American images crowding out Canadian ones,"[22] and Ed Black writes of the problem of trying to serve a small population in two language groups "who live in tempting, embarrassing, and almost smothering proximity to [ten times as many] Americans who speak the language of Canada's majority…. They also have the world's most penetrating and effective system for transmitting ideas en masse."[23] Peter Trueman adds:

> I have felt for years that the greatest threat to Canada's integrity as a nation is not the crisis in Quebec … but American television…. Think of the overwhelming preponderance of American programming, which in an unobtrusive way pumps us full of American values, American hopes, American history, even American patterns of speech.[24]

Although the CBC-TV has recently gone to an almost all-Canadian format in prime-time hours, the private stations and networks realize that profits can generally be maximized by telecasting as much U.S. programming as the CRTC will allow. The production of Canadian programs on CTV and Global, apart from newscasts, is minimal. In 2013, 8 of the 10 most-watched regular-programming TV shows on Canadian television were produced in the United States—*Amazing Race Canada* and *Hockey Night in Canada* were the only exceptions. Nevertheless, we should not underestimate the devoted audience of Canadian national newscasts, with about one million viewers per night, and programs such as *This Hour Has 22 Minutes*, *Canada AM*, *The Morning News*, *the fifth estate*, *Marketplace*, *Téléjournal*, *Le Point*, and W5.

The Changing Media World

David Taras has summarized the changes in the media world as a convergence of technologies, of news and entertainment, of cultures, and of corporations.[25] The first involves the merging of television, telephone, satellite, cable, and Internet technologies. Wireless carriers now offer television service on cellphones via the Internet and telephone companies offer TV and Internet services. This convergence of telecommunications technologies has been accompanied by increasing convergence of corporations that operate in the once-upon-a-time separate areas of television and telephone industries. The convergence of these corporations is tracked in Table 12.2, illustrating the fact that the four mega-media corporations in Canada continue to expand. For example, in 2012, BCE pursued Astral Media which owned a portfolio of English- and French-language pay-TV and specialty cable TV channels as well as a large

TABLE 12.2   LARGEST MEDIA CONGLOMERATES IN CANADA, 2015

ROGERS	QUEBECOR	BCE (BELL MEDIA)	SHAW	COGECO
OMNI, CITY-TV	TVA	CTV, CTV2	GLOBAL TV NETWORK	COMMUNITY CHANNELS
SPECIALTY CHANNELS	SPECIALTY CHANNELS	SPECIALTY CHANNELS	SPECIALTY CHANNELS	
INTERNET	INTERNET	INTERNET	INTERNET	INTERNET
CABLE	CABLE	SATELLITE	CABLE	CABLE
RADIO	NEWSPAPERS	RADIO		RADIO
TELEPHONES	TELEPHONES	TELEPHONES	TELEPHONES	TELEPHONE (VOIP)
MAGAZINES	MAGAZINES	OUT-OF-HOME ADVERTISING		OUT-OF-HOME ADVERTISING
	BOOK PUBLISHING VIDEO STORES MUSIC			

Sources: CRTC. 2014. Communications Monitoring Report 2014: Broadcasting System, http://www.crtc.gc.ca/eng/publications/reports/policymonitoring/2014/cmr4.htm; Rogers. 2015. About Us, http://www.rogersmedia.com/about-us/; Quebecor, n.d., "Canadian Leader in Telecommunications, Entertainment, News Media and Culture," http://www.quebecor.com/en/content/communications-giant; Bell Media. 2015. About Us, http://www.bellmedia.ca/about-bellmedia/; Shaw. 2015. About Us, http://www.shaw.ca/Corporate/About-Shaw/Shaw-Companies/; Cogeco. 2015. Company Overview, http://corpo.cogeco.com/cgo/en/company-overview.

network of radio stations, and increasingly rivals Quebecor's media holdings in Quebec. The convergence of news and entertainment relates primarily to making television news more entertaining while reducing its serious content, and the convergence of cultures refers to the expansion of American popular culture around the world.

Few if any of these changes are positive for the vital place of the media in the Canadian political system. Television, with its convergence of news and entertainment, provides a more superficial understanding of political developments than newspapers. Since reliance on television in English Canada usually means exposure to American television, this tendency detracts from public knowledge in a second way (the convergence of cultures). The increased concentration of ownership of newspapers, radio, and television (the convergence of corporations) is not a healthy development in any democracy that values the maximum diversity of opinions. Such ownership only enhances the predominance of the right-wing opinion already amply supplied by radio talk-show hosts, think tanks, columnists, and pundits. However, the opposite trend toward a fragmentation of audiences allows individuals to ignore broader public questions as they expose themselves to media coverage of only a few personal interests.

Many parts of the media industry have recently cut corners in order to stay in business, such that political news is often sacrificed in the process. Besides the general deterioration of political coverage, there has been a serious decline in local coverage—fewer local television and newspaper voices.

The Internet

Probably even more significant than changes in the existing media industry is the impact of the Internet. It now rivals television as a medium of mass communications, in addition to its other functions.[26] Looked at another way, the three traditional media increasingly rely on the Internet to supplement their offerings, and regularly refer their audiences to their websites. In 2014, Canada ranked second among G8 countries (behind the UK), and sixteenth in the world, with 87 percent of Canadian households having internet access—up from 79 percent in 2010.[27] As television viewing continues to decline in Canada, especially among the younger demographic, Internet usage (including watching shows online) increases.[28] Prime Minister Stephen Harper's office began a weekly web-video entitled *24 Seven* in 2014 that detailed the Prime Minister's life and activities.

Aside from providing access to newspapers, television and radio networks, Parliament, the courts, government departments and agencies, political parties, advocacy groups, and other actors in the political system, the Internet is now an integrated part of parties' and candidates' election campaigns. It often allows for direct and instantaneous feedback between the sender and receiver, brings together print and electronic communication methods into a single medium, and permits the targeting of small segments of the population.

Although the Internet is a liberating force that permits people to gain information, connect with others who have similar concerns, and provide direct feedback to government, it does have a negative side. There remains a "digital divide" in computer ownership and Internet use between lower- and upper-income Canadians. Whereas 95 percent of the top income quartile have Internet access, only 62 percent of the bottom income quartile have it.[29] A lesser divide on Internet access exists between different educational levels, age groups, and locations. Notably, the Internet is threatening the whole future of the newspaper industry, which has been such an important source of political information in the past. Many newspapers have folded in recent years, citing new technology and competition, and many more have scaled back distribution and employees.

Another feature of the Internet is the blog, that is, a web-based, self-published opinion piece (though many large media websites include blogs by staff writers). Micro blogging sites such as Twitter have become increasingly important in politics and political campaigns, not just in Canada but also in countries that do not permit open expressions of dissent. Some blogs are quite scholarly in nature, some are used by party insiders to express unauthorized opinions, and some media personalities employ them to supplement their more orthodox output. Stephen Harper expelled Garth Turner from the Conservative party caucus in part because of the critical comments he made on his personal blog.

Much is made today of social media—Facebook, Twitter, YouTube, etc., and there is much to suggest the Internet is playing a big role in terms of reach. The Internet is now accessed weekly by 81 percent of adults in Canada, which surpasses the proportion that access newspapers (66 percent) or magazines (54 percent)—though clearly some content would be digital forms of these same print media. Among those aged 18–24 years, weekly Internet usage (98 percent) slightly exceeds television access (97 percent) and radio (78 percent). Further, among both those aged 18–24 years and 24–34 years, total weekly time spent on the Internet exceeds that of any other media form. All this suggests that the Internet as a media form is approximately as important as television, and possibly more important than other media forms, at least in terms of reach.[30]

The Media and the Public

Public Perceptions of the Media

As noted above, most of the information Canadians receive about the political process comes from television, newspapers, radio, or the Internet. When asked about their use of various media for political information, respondents to the 2011 Canadian Election Survey indicated a preference for viewing news on television, with 51 percent stating that they generally view television news seven days per week, compared to 41 percent for radio, 28 percent for newspapers, and 20 percent for Internet. Rather than having a direct impact on virtually every individual, though, it is likely that the media primarily influence such peer-group leaders—those people who pay close attention to political developments—who then, in turn, transmit this information and opinion to those around them.

The Reality of Different Media Coverage

Public perceptions of the merits of the different media, especially that television is superior to newspapers, are somewhat distressing to those who know their real advantages and disadvantages. Newspapers generally offer more comprehensive coverage of political events, presenting both greater factual information and a wider range of interpretation. Because of cost and time constraints, television is restricted in the number of items it can cover in any newscast and must present a shorter and more superficial account of political events than newspapers. In a 60- to 90-second news clip with a 10-second sound bite of the actual voice of political leaders, how something is said is sometimes more important than what is said. Research indicates that the length of the sound bite is even decreasing, and "Canadians are rarely exposed to their leaders for anything longer than the time it takes for them to blurt out 8 or 10 words."[31] The transcript of a 30-minute newscast would make up about one-third of a single newspaper page.[32]

Moreover, because it is a visual medium, television must aim to show colourful, dramatic, emotional, conflictual, or entertaining pictures. Riots, demonstrations, and political conventions usually make good television, but the daily routine of politics does not lend itself as well to compelling visual coverage. Witness the efforts taken by politicians and the media to find contrived and engaging settings in which to stage political happenings, make announcements, or tape interviews. From Question Period to election campaigns, political events are now designed to appeal to television's definition of the news. Television portrays images and impressions and is therefore much better at dealing with political leaders and personalities than with issues.

These characteristics make television more open to distortion and exploitation, with the result that it may well be the least believable and most biased of the three media.[33] This situation is exacerbated by the increasing tendency of political parties and politicians to gear their activities to the demands of television. Press conferences are now dominated by television lights and cameras; leaders' tours during election campaigns are "photo opportunities"; and party conventions and leaders' debates are scheduled for maximum airtime. In addition, in preparing for elections, parties put greater effort into designing television commercials and trying them out before focus groups than in devising solutions to the country's problems. The televised leaders' debate has become the single most important event in an election campaign, and elections may turn more on leaders' images than issues, policies, local candidates, or other leading figures in the party. The appearance, style, and general image of the party leader, including his or her ability to perform on television, have become of crucial importance.[34] This was apparent in the 2015 Alberta election, in which the New Democratic Party replaced the governing Progressive Conservative Party that had ruled the province for 44 years. While many factors likely play a role, the election was seen to have turned on a strong debate performance by the NDP leader, Rachel Notley, and a weak performance by the sitting premier, Jim Prentice.

Unfortunately, Canada has one of the lowest rates of daily newspaper circulation and one of the highest rates of television-viewing among Western industrialized states; in other words, it suffers from a condition known as "television-dependency."[35] Distinct from newscasts, however, all-news channels like CBC News Network, CPAC, and public affairs programs on other channels have the time to delve into political issues in more depth.

On the other hand, the broadcast media and opposition parties still tend to take their cues from newspapers. Although television is the most important channel for the distribution of news, daily newspapers remain the major news-gathering institutions in the media system.[36] Thus, while the "average" Canadian relies on television for political information, those with political influence—whether in government, parties, advocacy groups, or peer-group situations—depend on newspapers. Those who prefer newspapers over television tend to have higher educations, higher incomes, and are better informed, and the degree of political participation increases sharply with a person's level of newspaper consumption. In other words, those who make the effort to increase their political information by reading a newspaper are not only better informed but are also most likely to go on to engage in some form of political participation.[37]

Among newspapers, *The Globe and Mail* is read by nearly three-quarters of Canada's top-level decision makers across the country and more than 90 percent of media executives; it thus tends to set the agenda for other news organizations.[38] The independent *Le Devoir* occupies a somewhat similar position in French Canada. It is likely that few beyond the political elite read or are influenced by the editorials in such newspapers, however, and there is little evidence that editorial endorsement has much impact on the outcome of elections.[39]

The Media and the Politicians

Politicians need publicity and therefore have a great interest in how the media cover their behaviour. Even though they and their bureaucratic advisers have their own direct sources, these authorities also depend on the media to provide information they need about what is happening at home and abroad. The media, in turn, rely on the authorities for much of their information. A number of issues arise from this mutually dependent relationship.

Politicians and Media Owners

In the newspaper era, when papers were individually owned by their editor, newspaper owners were generally on friendly terms with politicians, and regular confidential consultations took place. Several editors, including Joseph Howe and George Brown, were politicians themselves, and one politician, Henri Bourassa, founded a newspaper, *Le Devoir*. Most papers had a partisan perspective that was evident in both their news columns and editorials. However, such factors as chain ownership, the quest for a mass audience, and the public expectation that partisanship be restricted to the editorial page have changed the relationship between politicians and media owners. Indeed, to a large extent, the "party press" has been replaced by the "critical press."[40] On the other hand, some newspapers retain partisan views; for example, the *Toronto Star* is consistently Liberal, and the *National Post*, Conservative.

Politicians and Journalists

A second issue is the relationship between working journalists—usually members of the **parliamentary press gallery**—and the politicians. Both groups are essentially engaged in the same business, the one needing publicity and the other, information. In principle, reporters should maintain enough distance from politicians to cover them objectively; however, it is often necessary to cultivate close relations to get the kind of information the media seek. Journalists also worry that a critical account of a politician on one occasion may jeopardize a good story the next time around.

Another issue relates to the complex legal question of libel, often defined as "a false statement about a person that is to his or her discredit."[41] In general, the media in Canada are cautious in what they write or broadcast, and the politicians are fairly thick-skinned, so that court cases involving libel are relatively rare. Less serious instances of media bias or error are supposed to be handled by the CRTC, individual companies' "ombudsmen," or voluntary press councils.

News Management

"News leaks" are yet another issue in the relations between media and politicians. When governments do not know what course to follow, they sometimes leak a proposal to the media

confirm them; at the very least, they "seek out information that conforms to their predispositions … and avoid or reinterpret any contrary and non-supportive messages."[46]

Given this great conglomeration of viewpoints, public opinion is very difficult to gauge. Haphazard methods, such as reading editorials or letters to the editor or listening to open-line programs, are obviously unreliable, but so are many amateur public opinion surveys. However, professional agencies engaged in scientific polling claim to be able to select a small sample of people and report with a high degree of accuracy the opinions of the whole population. Such polls have assumed an immense importance in contemporary Canadian politics: "No political party plans campaign strategy without them, no government is prepared to risk major policy initiatives without gauging public opinion, and for major news organizations they are an indispensable reporting tool, both between and during elections."[47]

Who are these professional pollsters? Although the Canadian branch of the Gallup Poll has operated in Canada since 1941, political and governmental polling did not begin in earnest until about 1960. The Liberal and Conservative parties originally hired U.S. polling companies but then designated official Canadian party pollsters who also had corporate clients and did lucrative work for government departments when their respective parties were in power. Canada now possesses many successful public opinion polling companies that are regularly hired by media outlets, political parties, advocacy groups, governments, or government departments, and some of them are listed below. All of them also do much non-political polling, and many have become Canadian multinationals. A number of lobbying firms, especially Earnscliffe Strategy Group and Hill and Knowlton, also do polling as part of their comprehensive consulting work.

LEADING PUBLIC OPINION POLLING FIRMS

- Angus Reid
- Compas Public Opinion and Customer Research
- Ekos Research Associates
- Environics Research Group
- Harris-Decima
- Ipsos Canada
- Leger Marketing
- Nanos Research
- Pollara
- Strategic Counsel

These professional polling companies have slightly different methodologies within the broad framework of selecting a random sample of people, asking their opinion, and reporting the results within a certain confidence range—typically that the results are accurate within plus or minus four percent 19 times out of 20. The "random" sample means that each person in the target population has an equal probability of being selected, and the larger the sample, the greater the confidence of the result. Increasingly, however, public opinion companies are turning to other, less costly, forms of polling, such as online polls of standing panels of respondents, which raise questions about the representativeness of such polls.

One way that a survey's accuracy can be tested is through a comparison of its results immediately before an election with the electoral outcome itself. The immediate pre-election findings of most professional agencies have usually been within the range of accuracy that the survey claimed, but exceptional inaccurate predictions do occur. When two or more firms are seeking the same information but produce different results, doubts naturally arise about their methodology. The randomness of the sample, the way a question is worded, the optional responses available, the sequence of the questions, the degree to which respondents are telling the truth, and many other variables can influence the result and account for such differences. Timing is also an important consideration because results can sometimes be out of date by the time they are tabulated and reported. In the 2004 federal election, almost all of the polls under-estimated the Liberal vote, which pollsters explained on a large shift in voter preference in the last two days of the campaign. They rejected the frequently heard argument that telephone polling had become less accurate because so many people now possess cell (mobile) phones with numbers that are not listed in a directory. In January 2006, the pollsters were much closer, as they were in 2008. Many questioned the polls in 2011 when the NDP, which had never elected more than 43 MPs, began to make large and sustained gains in the polls. On election day, predictions were generally accurate when the NDP became Official Opposition for the first time, though slight under-estimations in the Conservative vote had many questioning if there would be a minority or a majority government. While some provincial elections have seen large differences between poll results and actual election results, such as the 2013 British Columbia Election and the 2014 Ontario Election, the 2015 federal election again saw similarities between polls and vote totals, with actual vote proportions within about two percent of the average predictions. However, most seat predictions by pollsters were inaccurate because of significant swings in the geographic concentrations of votes. In Quebec for example, the Liberal Party, which had not been as competitive in recent elections, took a majority of seats with under 36 percent of the vote and won many ridings it was not previously considered to be competitive in. Thus, the result of a Liberal majority government was not foreseen by many despite reasonably accurate national polls.

The Importance of Polls in Elections

Public opinion polls are closely connected to elections. One main issue that arises in this connection is whether the pre-election predictions of such polls influence the actual election results. This question cannot be answered categorically, but it is unlikely that their direct effect is that great. First, most voters do not pay much attention to the poll results; second, not everyone believes them; and third, it is not important to everyone to vote for the winning side. Although some voters may want to jump on the victorious bandwagon—the **bandwagon effect**—at least a few are likely to switch to the predicted loser—"the underdog effect"—either out of sympathy or to try to prevent a majority victory for the prospective winner.[48]

However, polls may have a significant indirect effect on the election results. The media are as obsessed with the polls as the politicians are, and the survey results may well cause the media to concentrate on those parties and politicians who are in the lead, or ignore those who are trailing. Furthermore, polls have a considerable effect on party morale. A positive poll usually generates greater enthusiasm and effort, better candidates, and larger financial contributions, while a negative poll saps the spirit of leaders, candidates, and foot soldiers alike. Both of these results undoubtedly affect the subtle "momentum" of the campaign.

Another issue can be addressed more categorically: polls definitely detract from the discussion of real issues in the election campaign.[49] The media are fascinated by polls primarily because they are good for business, and, given the media's ability to influence the political agenda even during election campaigns, they emphasize the **horse-race effect** of the contest. The media tend to spend more time on trying to determine who is ahead than on comparative analysis of party platforms, asking leaders to comment on the latest poll results, for example, rather than on how the party would deal with a particular public problem. Now that the media actually hire polling firms, survey results are becoming major news items in themselves.[50] To avoid this criticism, the CBC has a policy of not conducting public opinion surveys during an election campaign; however, it is not above reporting on polls done by others. Although it has not been proven, one concern is that polls may affect the voter turnout rate by generating feelings of complacency or hopelessness.

Many political losers have blamed their fate on negative public opinion polls and some have called for the prohibition of polls during part or all of the campaign. Such bans do exist in many countries.[51] Whatever their faults, however, polls enliven the campaign and increase the information available, and many argue that to prohibit their publication in the media would not prevent parties, candidates, and others from conducting their own surveys. While ignorance of each party's support might increase intrigue in the campaign and necessitate more focus on issues, some argue the main effect of a publication ban would be to give crucial information to those who could afford to conduct a survey and to deny it to the general public, a highly undemocratic suggestion.[52] Matthews et al. (2012) also suggest that much political learning can come from poll coverage as journalists extend coverage beyond the numbers themselves and begin to give potential explanations for why the number are what they are.[53]

One of the amendments to the Canada Elections Act made in the wake of the Royal Commission on Electoral Reform was to prohibit the broadcast, publication, or dissemination of the poll results in the last three days of the campaign. This restriction was soon challenged by the Thomson and Southam newspaper chains as a violation of freedom of the press, and their challenge was upheld by the Supreme Court of Canada.[54] A ban on the publication of polls on election day itself was subsequently enacted, and the law requires polling organizations to provide a full account of their methodology.

CRITICAL APPROACHES

Political psychology and *political behaviour approaches* are highly relevant on the issue of polls. Political psychologist John Zaller, for example, has written about the "vagaries" of public opinion polling, not the least of which is the possibility that many of the respondents are simply answering a question rather than revealing a preference.[55] It is likely that many of the people asked a question in a public opinion poll have not really thought much about it and are therefore giving an answer "off the top of their head" that may well change after further reflection. If, however, there is something about the survey that is priming people to think about the question from one perspective rather than another, then the poll itself may produce biased results. Rival groups may present opposing poll results because they can manipulate questions to achieve the results they desire.

Impact of Polls on the Authorities

Perhaps an even more significant question in the study of public opinion is the relationship between polls and the actions of the authorities.[56] For nearly 100 years after Confederation, governments had to act in the absence of a reliable survey, but governments nowadays spend huge sums of public funds on surveying public attitudes on various issues. A typical example was the polling done by the Liberal government before the 2000 pre-election budget. By using both traditional polls and focus groups, the Earnscliffe pollsters revealed that a majority of Canadians preferred a cut in the progressive income tax to a flat tax, as espoused by the Canadian Alliance, even among those who would personally benefit more from a flat tax. Such preferences were implemented in the budget, and Finance Minister Paul Martin's budget speech confidently ridiculed the flat tax approach. After criticizing the Liberal government for an excessive expenditure on public opinion polling, the Harper government was shown to have spent even more: it commissioned an average of two polls every working day in 2006–07 at a cost to taxpayers of $31 million.[57]

Since opinion is likely to be considerably divided, however, polls do not always provide clear-cut policy guidance, and even when public opinion is clearly in favour of a certain course of government action, the authorities may decide otherwise. This may be the consequence of the politicians' own convictions, the recommendations of the public service, the pressure of advocacy groups and lobbyists, or the rigidity of party discipline. Indeed, some hold the view that even in a democracy, politicians are not obliged to *follow* public opinion; they may also *lead* it.[58] This is especially the case now that we realize how uninformed, superficial, and changeable most voters' opinions really are. If politicians and bureaucrats do not follow a clear-cut preference among the public, they may actually be relying on a deeper understanding of the issue, the greater information at their disposal, a more sophisticated analysis of its implications, a concern for minority groups' rights, or a less prejudicial attitude. Capital punishment has been an issue on which public opinion was quite clear, for example, but one on which the authorities repeatedly went their own way. Should Parliament reinstate capital punishment in response to majority popular opinion based on a mistaken impression about rising crime rates, a desire for retribution, and an assumption of deterrence? Most political issues are even more complicated than capital punishment, and, on most, public opinion is much more divided; thus, the correlation between public opinion and public policy is not as strong as might be expected.

Christopher Page's study of this subject reinforces many of the observations made above.[59] In connection with the Trudeau initiative on constitutional reform in the early 1980s, Page observes that polls had little effect on the content of the Charter, but were useful in maintaining the government's resolve to go through with the reform as well as in designing the way to sell it to the public. Somewhat similarly, the Mulroney government had decided on the GST proposal before it did much polling; indeed, the policy was adopted in defiance of the polls. Nevertheless, government polling helped to decide the details of the policy (e.g., to exempt groceries) and how to reduce its unpopularity as it was communicated to the public. On gun control, the Chrétien government also made the decision to act before it polled the public on the subject. But Liberal polls which indicated a generally favourable public reaction were used to keep dissident MPs and provinces in line, and in the communications campaign with respect to implementation.

Thus, Page argues that on these three key issues, at least, the government policy was decided before it engaged in polling. Except perhaps on the GST, polling encouraged the government to pursue the policy upon which it had previously embarked, but it mostly affected government communications operations about a policy rather than the substance of the policy itself.[60] He also points out that in addition to their own polling, governments examine polls done by interest groups, the media, and other sources. Polls are used in every aspect of the policymaking process, and are more often sponsored by the bureaucracy than ministers' offices or the Prime Minister's Office. Governments appreciate the security of a supportive poll, but they realize the superficiality of many peoples' opinions, and they actually lead public opinion as much as they follow it.[61]

It should be added that the proliferation of public opinion polls severely undercuts the argument in favour of **referendums**. Public opinion polls already provide a quick, cheap, frequent, and accurate picture of the public's views, so there is little danger that the government will not know how the population feels about an issue.

CONCLUSION

Students of political science and other readers of this book may well belong to the small proportion of the population for whom politics is a central concern and who are well informed. Such readers must be careful not to assume that the rest of the population is so well socialized into politics. In any case, this chapter has demonstrated the significance of the media, especially television, daily newspapers, and increasingly the Internet, and documented the abundant use of public opinion polls and polling firms. Individually and combined, the electronic media and public opinion polls have completely transformed Canadian politics in the past 50 years.

The media are central to Canada's political system and are revisited in several other chapters. That particularly includes elections, political parties, and government. Indeed, both the government and opposition parties are in a daily contest for favourable media coverage all aimed at improving their fortunes in the next election. The media also constitute a vital link to Canada's external political environment, especially the United States. Public opinion polls are equally important for parties and in elections, but are also of daily significance in the policymaking process—by the party in power, the bureaucracy, and those whose responsibility it is to criticize their proposals. Political socialization is closely linked to the previous chapter on political culture.

DISCUSSION QUESTIONS

1. Think about the relative importance of the agents of political socialization in your own life. Can you decipher your own socialization process?

2. Does the fact that media companies have an impact on public opinion mean that ownership should be more regulated than in other industries?

3. What are the advantages and disadvantages of obtaining information from each of television, radio, newspapers, and the Internet?

4. Should the publication of public opinion polls be prohibited at some stage of an election campaign?

5. How seriously should the authorities take the results of public opinion polls? Is the government justified in taking so many public opinion polls at public expense? Explain.

MindTap®   FOR MORE INFO GO TO **http://www.nelson.com/student**

NOTES

1. John Zaller, *The Nature and Origins of Mass Opinion* (New York, NY: Cambridge University Press, 1992).
2. Ronald Landes, "Political Education and Political Socialization," in Jon Pammett and Jean-Luc Pépin, eds., *Political Education in Canada* (Halifax: Institute for Research on Public Policy, 1988), p. 17.
3. Jon Pammett, "The Development of Political Orientations in Canadian School Children," *Canadian Journal of Political Science* (March 1971).
4. Marcel Trudel and Genevieve Jain, *Canadian History Textbooks: A Comparative Study* (Ottawa: Royal Commission on Bilingualism and Biculturalism, 1970).
5. Landes, "Political Education and Political Socialization," p. 17.
6. John Ricker and Alan Skeoch, "The Contribution of Ontario's Schools to Political Education," in Pammett and Pépin, *Political Education in Canada*, p. 70; the Dominion Institute, available at http://www.dominion.ca.
7. Mark S. Granovetter, "The Strength of Weak Ties," *The American Journal of Sociology* 78, no. 6 (1973): 1360–80.
8. Alan Frizzell, Jon H. Pammett, and Anthony Westell, *The Canadian General Election of 1988* (Ottawa: Carleton University Press, 1989), p. 69.
9. Michael Adams, *Fire and Ice: The United States, Canada and the Myth of Converging Values* (Toronto: Penguin Canada, 2003).
10. Hillary Clark, "Mapping Canadian Think Tanks". (Accessed on May 20, 2015 at: http://theagenda.tvo.org/blog/agenda-blogs/mapping-canadian-think-tanks)
11. Elisabeth Gidengil, André Blais, Richard Nadeau, and Neil Nevitte, *Citizens* (Vancouver: UBC Press, 2004).
12. Peter Trueman, *Smoke and Mirrors: The Inside Story of Television News in Canada* (Toronto: McClelland and Stewart, 1980); Paul Nesbitt-Larking, *Politics, Society, and the Media: Canadian Perspectives* (Peterborough: Broadview Press, 2001).
13. Frederick J. Fletcher and Robert Everett, "The Media and Canadian Politics in an Era of Globalization," in Michael Whittington and Glen Williams, eds., *Canadian Politics in the 21st Century*, 6th ed. (Toronto: Thomson Nelson, 2004), p. 428.
14. Zaller, *The Nature and Origins of Mass Opinion*.
15. Bernard C. Cohen, *The Press and Foreign Policy* (Princeton, N.J.: Princeton University Press, 1963), p. 13.
16. Heather McIvor, *Parameters of Power*, 5th ed. (Toronto: Nelson Education, 2010), p. 522; Linda Trimble and Shannon Sampert, "Who's in the Game? The Framing of the Canadian Election 2000 by *The Globe and Mail* and the *National Post*," *Canadian Journal of Political Science* (March 2004); Faron Ellis and Peter Woostencroft, "The Conservative Campaign: Becoming the New Natural Governing Party? In Jon H. Pammett and Christopher Dornan, eds., *The Canadian Federal Election of 2011* (Toronto: Dundurn, 2011), p. 29.
17. Stephen Brooks and Andrew Stritch, *Business and Government in Canada* (Scarborough: Prentice Hall Canada, 1991); Nesbitt-Larking, *Politics, Society and the Media*, chs. 2 and 5. The mutually

advantageous simultaneous closings were deemed by the courts to be a coincidence and a normal part of doing business.

18. David Taras, *The Newsmakers* (Scarborough: Nelson Canada, 1990), pp. 8–17.

19. James Winter, *Democracy's Oxygen: How Corporations Control the News* (Montreal: Black Rose, 1997); Maude Barlow and James Winter, *The Big Black Book: The Essential Views of Conrad and Barbara Amiel Black* (Toronto: Stoddart, 1997); and John Miller, *Yesterday's News: Why Canada's Daily Newspapers Are Failing Us* (Halifax: Fernwood Publishing, 1998).

20. Statistics Canada, "Radio Listening, 2007," *The Daily*, September 18, 2008. The agency has apparently stopped collecting data on this question.

21. Statistics Canada, "Survey of Household Spending," 2009, available at http://www.statcan.gc.ca/daily-quotidien/091218/dq091218b-eng.htm, accessed on April 17, 2012. The agency apparently no longer collects data on this specific question.

22. Frederick J. Fletcher and Daphne Gottlieb Taras, "Images and Issues: The Mass Media and Politics in Canada," in Michael S. Whittington and Glen Williams, eds., *Canadian Politics in the 1990s*, 3rd ed. (Scarborough: Nelson Canada, 1990), p. 229.

23. Edwin R. Black, *Politics and the News: The Political Functions of the Mass Media* (Toronto: Butterworths, 1982), p. 80.

24. Trueman, *Smoke and Mirrors*, p. 161.

25. Taras, *Power and Betrayal*; and Russell Mills, "Reflections on the State of Canadian Media," *Canadian Parliamentary Review* (Winter 2003–04).

26. Tamara A. Small, "parties@canada: The Internet and the 2004 Cyber-Campaign," in Pammett and Dornan, *The Canadian General Election of 2004*; Darin Barney, *Communications Technology* (Vancouver: UBC Press, 2005); and Ann Dale and Ted Naylor, "Dialogue and Public Space: An Exploration of Radio and Information Communications Technologies," *Canadian Journal of Political Science* (March 2005).

27. CIRA Factbook 2014, available at http://cira.ca/factbook/2014/the-canadian-internet.html, accessed on April 1, 2015.

28. Canada, "CRTC issues 2014 report on state of Canadian broadcasting industry," available at http://news.gc.ca/web/article-en.do?nid=881199.

29. Ibid.

30. IAB Canada. "2014: Internet in the Media Garden," available at http://iabcanada.com/wp-content/uploads/2014/12/V2-Total-Canada-2014-CMUST-Exec-Summary-Nov-18-2014.pdf, accessed on April 2, 2015.

31. Taras, *Power and Betrayal*, p. 208.

32. Taras, *The Newsmakers*, p. 102.

33. Ibid., Ch. 4.

34. Ibid., Ch. 5; Howard K. Penniman, ed., *Canada at the Polls, 1984* (Durham, NC: Duke University Press, 1988), pp. 184 and 201; and Levine, *Scrum Wars*.

35. Henry Milner, "Civic Literacy in Comparative Context," *Policy Matters* (July 2001) (Montreal: Institute for Research on Public Policy), pp. 16–18.

36. Fletcher and Everett, "The Media and Canadian Politics in an Era of Globalization," p. 433.

37. William Misher, *Political Participation in Canada: Prospects for Democratic Citizenship* (Toronto: Macmillan, 1979), p. 73; and Gidengil et al., *Citizens*, pp. 25–35.

38. Fletcher, *The Newspaper and Public Affairs*, p. 30; and Taras, *The Newsmakers*, pp. 87–89.

39. Fletcher, *The Newspaper and Public Affairs*, p. 11.

40. Dornan and Pyman, "Facts and Arguments," pp. 192–94; and Nesbitt-Larking, *Politics, Society, and the Media*, chs. 2 and 5.

41. Siegel, *Politics and the Media in Canada*, p. 80.

42. Black, *Politics and the News*, p. 12; and Taras, *The Newsmakers*, p. 234.

43. Kristen Kozolanka, "Communication by Stealth: The New Common Sense in Government Communication," in Allan M. Maslove, ed., *How Ottawa Spends, 2009–2010* (Montreal: McGill-Queen's University Press, 2009); see also books by such press secretaries as Patrick Gossage, *Close to the Charisma: My Years between the Press and Pierre Elliott Trudeau* (Toronto: McClelland and Stewart, 1986), and Michel Gratton, *So, What Are the Boys Saying?* (Toronto: McGraw-Hill Ryerson, 1987) as well as Taras, *The Newsmakers*, pp. 125–30, 158, 172.

44. Fletcher and Everett, "The Media and Canadian Politics in an Era of Globalization," p. 432. See also Taras, *Power and Betrayal*, p. 52; and Craig Forcese and Aaron Freeman, *The Laws of Government: The Legal Foundations of Canadian Democracy* (Toronto: Irwin Law, 2005).

45. Fletcher and Taras, "Images and Issues," pp. 233–34.

46. Black, *Politics and the News*, p. 168. In his definitive book, Christopher Page writes: "many people have opinions which are inconsistent, weakly held, and subject to change." *The Roles of Public Opinion Research in Canadian Government* (Toronto: University of Toronto Press, 2006), p. 168.

47. Frizzell et al., *The Canadian Federal Election of 1988*, p. 91. See also Nesbitt-Larking, *Politics, Society, and the Media*, Ch. 12; and Michael Marzolini, "Public Opinion and the 2006 Election," in Pammett and Dornan, eds., *The Canadian General Election of 2006*, Ch. 10.

48. André Turcotte supports the bandwagon effect in "Polls: Seeing Through the Class Darkly," in Pammett and Dornan, *The Canadian Federal Election of 2011*.

49. Taras, *The Newsmakers*, pp. 187, 192–94; Peter Desbarats, *Guide to Canadian News Media* (Toronto: Harcourt Brace Jovanovich, 1990), p. 138; and Waddell and Dornan, "The Media and the Campaign," pp. 239–42.

50. Gidengil et al., *Citizens*, p. 65; and Trimble and Sampert, "Who's in the Game? The Framing of the Canadian Election 2000 by *The Globe and Mail* and the *National Post*."

51. Claire Hoy, *Margin of Error* (Toronto: Key Porter Books, 1989), pp. 219–20; and Taras, *The Newsmakers*, p. 193.

52. Hoy, *Margin of Error*, p. 228. Hoy discusses the government's first poll on the conscription issue in 1942, which it wanted to keep secret (p. 14).

53. J. Scott Matthews, Mark Pickup, and Fred Cutler, "The Mediated Horserace: Campaign Polls and Poll Reporting," *Canadian Journal of Political Science* 45 no. 2 (2012): 261–87.

54. *Thomson Newspaper Co. v. Canada (Attorney General)*, [1998] 1 S.C.R. 877.

55. Zaller, *The Nature and Origins of Mass Opinion*, p. 36.

56. Richard Johnston, *Public Opinion and Public Policy in Canada* (Toronto: University of Toronto Press, 1986); and François Petry and Matthew Mendelsohn, "Public Opinion and Policy Making in Canada, 1994–2001," *Canadian Journal of Political Science* (September 2004).

57. Andrea D. Rounce, "Ottawa's Spending on Public Opinion Research: Implications for Democratic Governance," in G. Bruce Doern, ed., *How Ottawa Spends 2006–2007* (Montreal: McGill-Queen's University Press, 2006).

58. Hoy writes that in one view "the essence of parliamentary democracy is that we elect politicians to lead, to take risks, to stand for something more than the latest popular sentiment or the collective public wisdom, which may be based more on short-term emotion or outright ignorance than on anything else," *Margin of Error*, p. 7.

59. Page, *The Role of Public Opinion Research in Canadian Government*.

60. Ibid., p. 184.

61. Ibid., Conclusion. For future issues that polls have revealed, see David Herle, "Poll-driven Politics—The Role of Public Opinion in Canada," Institute for Research on Public Policy, *Policy Options* (May 2007).

FURTHER READING

Barney, Darin. *Communications Technology*. Vancouver: UBC Press, 2005.

Butler, Peter M. *Polling and Public Opinion: A Canadian Perspective*. Toronto: University of Toronto Press, 2007.

Everitt, Joanna, and Brenda O'Neil, eds. *Citizen Politics: Research and Theory in Canadian Political Behaviour*. Toronto: Oxford University Press, 2002.

Fletcher, Frederick J., and Robert Everett. "The Media and Canadian Politics in an Era of Globalization," in Michael Whittington and Glen Williams, eds., *Canadian Politics in the 21st Century*, 7th ed. Toronto: Thomson Nelson, 2008.

Gidengil, Elisabeth, André Blais, Richard Nadeau, and Neil Nevitte. *Citizens*. Vancouver: UBC Press, 2004.

Miller, John. *Yesterday's News: How Canada's Daily Newspapers Are Failing Us*. Halifax: Fernwood Publishing, 1998.

Nesbitt-Larking, Paul. *Politics, Society, and the Media: Canadian Perspectives*. Peterborough: Broadview Press, 2001.

Page, Christopher. *The Roles of Public Opinion Research in Canadian Government*. Toronto: University of Toronto Press, 2006.

Pammett, Jon H., and Christopher Dornan, eds. *The Canadian General Election of 2011*. Toronto: Dundurn, 2011.

Taras, David. *Power and Betrayal in the Canadian Media*, updated ed. Peterborough: Broadview Press, 2001.

Winter, James. *Democracy's Oxygen: How Corporations Control the News*. Montreal: Black Rose, 1997.

Sadeugra/iStock

CHAPTER 13

Elections and the Electoral System

If elections are a crucial component in the definition of a democracy, it is important that they be conducted in the most "free and fair" way possible. Anyone should be able to contest the election, everyone should be able to vote, every vote should be equal on election day, and every province and territory should be fairly represented in the House of Commons. In most technical respects, the Canadian electoral system meets such standards, but it does not fare so well in terms of proportionality. It does not award seats in proportion to a party's popular vote, and many critics advocate a more proportional system. Historically, too, much controversy surrounded the question of party and election finance, as contributions often came with strings attached, and some parties grossly outspent others.

This chapter examines the formal, legal, and official aspects of the electoral system, and has four parts: redistribution or redrawing the electoral map, the official organization of elections, an evaluation of the lack of proportionality in the electoral system and suggestions for reform, and party and election finance. The actual electoral contest between political parties and candidates raises controversies of its own, but these and questions of electoral behaviour and party support are discussed in Chapter 15.

THEORETICAL CONSIDERATIONS

The primary function of elections is to allow the mass of citizens to choose their parliamentary representatives and, indirectly, their governmental leaders.[1] Besides recruiting political leaders, elections serve to inform the public, which is part of the political socialization function. Moreover, both political parties and advocacy groups take advantage of elections to articulate certain interests, and most parties try to aggregate interests in putting forward a comprehensive, attractive election platform. Elections also serve a legitimation function. That is, by exercising their franchise, voters legitimize the power of those elected by agreeing to be bound by their decisions. This activity presumably also generates popular support for the political system as a whole.

Elections similarly help to integrate the country by putting everyone in it through a common national experience. To the extent that policy concerns are central to the campaign, elections may also provide policy guidelines for the authorities and a feeling of political efficacy for the voters. Even if such policy mandates are somewhat lacking, the electorate can at least remove a government whose policies or performance were judged to be inadequate.

The question of whether elections are free and fair arises in political systems that claim to be democratic.[2] Canadian elections are "free" in the sense that almost anyone or any party can enter the race, although there are built-in advantages for existing parties and disadvantages for smaller, newer entrants. These advantages and disadvantages relate primarily to media coverage and election finance. Another aspect of fairness is the question of proportionality, that is, the extent to which representation in the House of Commons reflects the wishes of the voters. A close relationship between the popular vote a party receives and its electoral representation is not a major objective of Canada's electoral system. Thus, Canada has seen much recent interest in electoral reform.[3]

DRAWING THE ELECTORAL MAP

In a House of Commons where each MP represents a geographic constituency, the electoral process begins by dividing the country into single-member electoral districts.[4] This process, called **redistribution**, involves two stages: first, deciding how many seats in the Commons to allot to each province and territory; and second, actually drawing constituency boundaries within the provinces.

Distribution of Seats among Provinces

The Constitution Act, 1867 requires that the readjustment process be repeated after each decennial census—for example, 2001 and 2011. Given the federal character of Canada, with its strong provincial and territorial loyalties, the search for a fair means of distributing seats in the House of Commons among the provinces and territories has been a long and unsatisfactory one. Different formulas have been used over the years, but none has ever commanded unanimous support. The formula used following the 2011 census was altered slightly from the one that resulted in the 308 seats in the House of Commons after the 2004, 2006, and 2008, and 2011 elections. The new system actually represented a constitutional amendment because it not only added seats to the Commons, but also changed the formula involved. The 308-seat formula has been placed on this text's website, and Table 13.1 illustrates how the calculations were made for the 338-seat Commons that took effect for the 2015 federal election.[5]

The three territories are each given one seat automatically, while the population of each province is divided by the "electoral quotient" to provide the initial allocation of seats. That quotient was set at 111 166 for the post-2011 redistribution. The "senatorial clause" and the "grandfather clause" are then applied, so that no province can have fewer MPs than it has senators, and no province can have fewer MPs than it had in 1985. After that, an adjustment was made for Quebec because it would otherwise have been underrepresented in the Commons in proportion to its share of the population.

TABLE 13.1 ALLOCATION OF SEATS IN THE HOUSE OF COMMONS FOR THE 2015 FEDERAL ELECTION

PROVINCE/ TERRITORY	POPULATION ESTIMATE	÷ ELECTORAL QUOTIENT	= INITIAL SEAT ALLOCATION	+ SENA- TORIAL CLAUSE	+ GRAND- FATHER CLAUSE	+ REPRE- SENTATION RULE	= TOTAL SEATS
BRITISH COLUMBIA	4 573 321	111 166	42	—	—	—	42
ALBERTA	3 779 353	111 166	34	—	—	—	34
SASKATCHEWAN	1 057 884	111 166	10	—	4	—	14
MANITOBA	1 250 574	111 166	12	—	2	—	14
ONTARIO	13 372 996	111 166	121	—	—	—	121
QUEBEC	7 979 663	111 166	72	—	3	3	78
NEW BRUNSWICK	755 455	111 166	7	3	—	—	10
NOVA SCOTIA	945 437	111 166	9	1	1	—	11
PRINCE EDWARD ISLAND	145 855	111 166	2	2	—	—	4
NEWFOUNDLAND AND LABRADOR	510 578	111 166	5	1	1	—	7
YUKON	34 666	N/A					1
NORTHWEST TERRITORIES	43 675	N/A					1
NUNAVUT	33 322	N/A					1
TOTAL	34 482 779						338

Source: House of Commons Seat Allocation by Province (table), Elections Canada, 2011. This reproduction is a copy of the version available at www.elections.ca. Reproduced with the permission of Elections Canada, but adaptation rests with the author.

Drawing Constituency Boundaries

The second phase of the redistribution process, drawing constituency boundaries within each province, was historically the prerogative of the politicians. They regularly engaged in the process of **gerrymandering**—or manipulating constituency boundaries to increase the re-election probability of the members of the government party.[6] In the absence of any written rules, some constituencies had huge populations while others were extremely small. The Electoral Boundaries Readjustment Act of 1964 established a new system, however, so that beginning with the post-1961 redistribution, this task has been performed by independent commissions. An electoral boundaries commission is appointed for each province, chaired by a judge designated by the chief justice of the province. The other two members of each commission are appointed by the Speaker of the House of Commons and are often chosen from the political science community. All commissions depend extensively on the support and assistance of Elections Canada staff, and digital computerized technology now simplifies the task of drawing electoral maps.

The commissions swing into action as soon as the provincial population figures are available from the census. Theirs is a very delicate task of trying to arrive at a design that results in constituencies of approximately equal population size throughout the province while also accounting for geographic characteristics, communities of interest, and other peculiarities. The most difficult problem is in dealing with sparsely populated rural or northern regions at the same time as concentrated urban centres. In recognition of this problem, constituencies are allowed to deviate from the average population figure to a maximum tolerance of plus or minus 25 percent, and even to exceed this limit "in circumstances viewed by the commission as being extraordinary" in order to arrive at a manageable geographic size for all districts. The commissions must also consider the "community of interest or community of identity in or the historical pattern of an electoral district." Thus, rural and northern constituencies tend to be under the provincial quotient, and southern, urban ones tend to be slightly over it. The Royal Commission on Electoral Reform and Party Financing recommended a tolerance of 15 percent, but court decisions have been satisfied with plus or minus 25 percent.[7] In the 2003 operation, only two constituencies out of 308 exceeded the 25 percent limit (Labrador and Kenora), and only 19 exceeded plus or minus 15 percent of the provincial quotient.[8]

The publication of the map of proposed electoral boundaries in local newspapers and on the commission's website is followed by a period of public hearings, which are normally held at several different locations in the province. During these hearings interested individuals, municipalities, groups, and MPs appear to express their views on the proposals. Then, within 10 months of the availability of the population data, the commissions must complete their reports. They are sent to the Speaker of the House of Commons, who refers them to the appropriate Commons committee, which has 30 days while the House is sitting to discuss and raise objections to the report. The committee's proceedings are sent back to the electoral boundaries commissions, which have the authority to alter their report or leave it as is. Thus, it is the independent commissions and not the politicians who have the final say. Because of the time needed by the chief electoral officer, returning officers, and political parties to make adjustments in their operations, the new boundaries cannot be used at an election until at least seven months after the date that the representation order encompassing the new boundaries is proclaimed.

It takes fewer votes in smaller provinces and in rural parts of all provinces to elect a member of Parliament. As a result, such votes are worth more than those in large provinces or in urban areas. These deviations serve to undermine to some extent the basic democratic principle of political equality or "one person, one vote." In general, however, Canadians accept this deviation from the principle of representation by population or political equality out of ignorance or recognition of the fact that the Canadian population is peculiarly distributed. However, the democratic rights provision of the Charter of Rights and Freedoms opens up the possibility of a legal challenge on this subject, and as mentioned in Chapter 19, several provincial redistribution schemes have been taken to court.

THE OFFICIAL ELECTION MACHINERY

Setting the Date

Until 2007, the prime minister had the prerogative to set the date of the election within a five-year period from the previous electoral contest. Largely based on the government party's standings in the public opinion polls, the election was typically called about four years after the previous campaign. The average time between elections since 1867 has been about 41 months, reflecting the shorter tenure of minority governments. Going into the fifth year, especially to the five-year limit, was usually seen as a sign of political weakness, and most governments waiting that long have been defeated. The governor general had to approve the prime minister's request to **dissolve Parliament** in order to call an election, but this was normally automatic. Only once in Canadian history, in rather peculiar circumstances in 1926, did a governor general refuse such a request, as discussed in Chapter 21. The defeat of a government in a nonconfidence vote in the House of Commons is the alternative way in which an election is precipitated, in which case the prime minister's leeway is limited to choosing the exact date. Such a defeat of the Paul Martin government led to the election of January 2006, as did the defeat of the Stephen Harper government to the May 2011 election, although the government was re-elected.

Public opinion polls can be wrong, of course, or public opinion can change between the calling of the election and the actual voting day, so that the apparent advantage for the party in power in choosing the election date is not absolute. Indeed, Chapter 15 emphasizes the highly volatile nature of Canadian party preferences. Nevertheless, because of the potential unfairness of the system and because the uncertainty of the date caused inconvenience to many of those involved, some observers advocated the establishment of fixed election dates, an innovation now adopted by most of the provinces.

At the federal level, the Harper government passed legislation in 2007 which set fixed election dates, with the subsequent one supposed to be October 19, 2009. The law left a loophole for the prime minister to advise the governor general to call an election before that date, but this was intended to be used only in the case of a nonconfidence vote, as might have occurred in the minority government situation. Breaking the spirit of the new law, however, Harper employed the escape clause to call the October 14, 2008 election without the government being defeated. The prime minister was thus still able to take advantage of calling an election when it suited his purposes. Criticism of this move in 2008 may mean that such an abuse will not be repeated,[9] and the Harper majority government waited for the fixed election date in 2015.

Election Officials

The **chief electoral officer** is responsible for the overall administration of the election and must function with absolute impartiality.[10] This post is therefore filled by a resolution of the whole House of Commons, rather than by a regular public servant hired by the government. However, returning officers, who organize the election in each of the electoral districts (also called constituencies or ridings), used to be chosen by the Cabinet, and were usually partisan

Harley Schwadron/Artizans

artizans.com

"I'M LOOKING FOR VOTER FEEDBACK. TELL ME WHAT I NEED to SAY to GET RE-ELECTED, AND I'LL SAY IT!"

appointees. Ironically, once appointed, returning officers were expected to function in a completely nonpartisan fashion. Before the election call, each returning officer will have divided the constituency into polling divisions (or polls) of about 350 voters each, and a typical urban constituency will have about 225 polls. Because such preparations must be made beforehand, returning officers work part-time between elections and full-time during the campaign. They usually served until a different party came to power and replaced them with its own supporters. Many observers argued that this peculiar and paradoxical situation should be changed, and it finally was, in the Harper government's 2006 **Federal Accountability Act**.[11] Since then, Elections Canada chooses returning officers on a nonpartisan basis.

The Voters' List

In Canadian federal elections, the **voters' list** was historically compiled from scratch after the election writ was issued. This was done by means of a door-to-door enumeration in which the returning officer appointed two enumerators to collect the names of eligible voters in each polling division. It was largely because of this lengthy process that Canadian election campaigns used to last at least 47 days.

Reforms introduced in 1996 provided for a National Register of Electors, the base of which was compiled in one last door-to-door enumeration in April 1997 (except in Alberta and Prince Edward Island, which used the most recent provincial voters' list). Henceforth, that register is automatically revised from such sources as income tax, Canada Post, citizenship and immigration, driver's licence, and vital statistics files, although with such a modern mobile population, it is a struggle to keep it up-to-date. A major advantage of a permanent voters' list is that the length of the election period could be reduced to 36 days. The main difficulty is in getting all new eligible voters onto the list. While they may be added automatically from sources such as the Canada Revenue Agency and provincial and territorial motor vehicle registrars, they may have to take personal initiative, and Elections Canada welcomes their approach at any time.

In fact, those eligible voters not on the preliminary list have ample opportunity to be added during the campaign, and a ballot can even be issued on election day itself to a qualified person whose name is not on the list, though controversial changes made by the Harper government in 2014 made this process somewhat more difficult in what it claimed was an effort to decrease voter fraud. Voters on the list must present one piece of government-issued photo ID such as a driver's licence, or in the absence of a photo, two pieces of authorized identification—at least one of which must have a current address. A person who has identification without a current address may have another voter with full identification vouch for her/him.

Nomination

About 95 percent of candidates are nominated at a meeting of a political party, but they must then submit formal **nomination** papers, endorsed by 100 people on the local voters' list, and a $1000 deposit. Candidates receive this deposit back if and when they file their financial statement. Up to and including the 2015 election, official candidates of registered parties had to obtain the party leader's endorsement to use the party name on the ballot. This requirement was mainly adopted to pre-empt the possibility of local conflicts over who was the legitimate standard-bearer of the party, but it effectively gave the leader a veto over nominations—with many implications.[12] In 1974, for example, Robert Stanfield denied the party label to Leonard Jones, who was nominated as the Conservative candidate in Moncton, because of his outspoken opposition to official bilingualism. Similarly, Brian Mulroney refused to endorse discredited ex-Cabinet minister Sinclair Stevens in 1988. When a number of Liberal backbenchers voted against government bills in mid-1995, Jean Chrétien warned them that he might not sign their nomination papers in the next election, although only John Nunziata ultimately met this fate, and then ran successfully as an Independent. Following the 2015 election, parties will be able to choose a signatory who is not the party leader for candidate nominations, although it is not yet clear what process each party will choose.

Election Day

Once the election is called, the returning officer arranges for the ballots to be printed and allows people to vote in advance polls or by special ballot. Recent reforms made voting much more convenient for those not at home on election day, including members of the armed forces, government officials posted abroad, and others temporarily out of the country. By this time, the returning officer is also busy hiring and training deputy returning officers and poll clerks to look after each polling station on election day and finding appropriate polling stations, typically in schools, church basements, or community centres.

Canadian federal elections are held on Mondays, and the polls used to be open from 9 a.m. to 8 p.m. local time. Because voters in the western part of the country complained that the winning party was often determined before their votes had even been counted, the Royal Commission on Electoral Reform and Party Financing proposed a system of staggered hours for different time zones. This recommendation was implemented for the 1997 and subsequent elections and meant that the polls close at approximately the same real time all across the country. Thus, the ballots are counted and results announced more or less simultaneously. The dissemination of results from one region where the polls have closed to another where they are still open was historically disallowed; however, this law was changed by the Harper government, allowing the communication of results as they occur. Voters are entitled to three consecutive hours off work in which to cast their ballot, and the sale of liquor is no longer prohibited during polling hours. Other recommendations of the Royal Commission that made the system more user-friendly include the provision for level access polling stations, the establishment of mobile polls for seniors and those with disabilities, the appointment of interpreters, and the use of a template for those with vision impairments.

Voters mark their X in private on the ballot provided, and when the polls close the deputy returning officer and poll clerk count them, usually in the company of scrutineers from the various candidates who are allowed to challenge unorthodox markings on ballots and generally keep the whole process honest. Results are announced an hour or so after the polls close and the candidate with the most votes is declared elected. This **single-member-plurality** (SMP) system (sometimes referred to as *first-past-the-post*) means that the winner usually does not have a majority of the votes cast, only a plurality.

The Ballot

The secret ballot was introduced into federal elections in 1874. In the first two elections after Confederation, people voted orally and were subject to bribery or intimidation, including the threat of physical assault if they voted the wrong way! The candidates are listed in alphabetical order on the ballot, which contains their party affiliation, if any. The chief electoral officer keeps a registry of political parties, and a party need only have a single candidate to be registered and to use the party label on the ballot.[13] Such parties must also register their national and constituency official agents and auditors for the purposes of keeping track of the party's and candidates' finances. Twelve parties were registered for the 1988 election, 14 for 1993, 10 for 1997, 11 for 2000, 13 for 2004, 15 for 2006, 19 for 2008, 18 for 2011, and 23 for 2015.[14]

The Franchise

The extension of the **franchise (or vote)** beyond males with substantial property was mentioned in passing in Chapters 4 to 8.[15] This evolution in Canada was complicated by the use of different provincial franchises in federal elections between 1867 and 1885 and between 1898 and 1917. The federal franchise between 1885 and 1898 required that males be property owners, but this qualification was gradually eliminated in most provinces about 1900. By this time, women had won the vote in certain municipal elections, and they gained the provincial franchise in Manitoba, Saskatchewan, and Alberta in 1916. In 1917 the federal franchise was manipulated so as to maximize support for the incumbent government. The vote was extended to women serving in the war, and female relatives of men serving overseas, but Canadian citizens who had come from "enemy alien" countries were denied the vote. In 1918 all women were granted the vote, and after 1920 a uniform federal franchise existed that included all Canadian citizens with the exception of Aboriginals and those of Asian ancestry (especially those from Japan, China, and India). The latter were not allowed to vote in British Columbia provincial elections, and the federal law disqualified anyone who for reasons of race was denied the vote under provincial electoral statutes. Such restrictions were removed by 1948, and the vote was extended to the Inuit in 1950 and to Registered Indians in 1960. The voting age was reduced from 21 to 18 in 1970, and British subjects who were not Canadian citizens lost their vote in 1975.

DATES OF EXTENSION OF THE FRANCHISE IN FEDERAL ELECTIONS

- 1918: Women
- 1948: Asian Canadians
- 1950: Inuit
- 1960: Registered Indians
- 1970: Persons 18 years of age
- 1988: Judges and people with mental disabilities
- 1999: Returning officers
- 2002: All prisoners

By 1975, the **Canada Elections Act** disqualified only the following individuals from voting: the chief and assistant chief electoral officers, returning officers (except in the case of a tie), federally appointed judges, prison inmates, those deprived of their liberty by reason of mental disabilities, and those convicted of corrupt or illegal electoral practices. During the 1988 campaign, however, three of these disqualifications were challenged in the courts in terms of the Charter of Rights and Freedoms, which guarantees the vote to every Canadian citizen. In the case of judges and those with mental disabilities, the provisions of the act were declared unconstitutional and the disqualifications removed. The courts made a number of contradictory decisions on whether prison inmates should be able to vote, and the 1993 amendments gave the vote in federal elections to inmates serving sentences of less than two years. In 1996, however, long-term prisoners were successful in persuading the courts to remove the two-year restriction, a decision confirmed by the Supreme Court of Canada in 2002.[16] In 1999, returning officers received the right to vote, and in the case of a tie in a constituency, a by-election will be held rather than have the returning officer cast a deciding vote.

Controversies during the 2011 and 2015 Elections

Following the 2011 election, investigations confirmed that fraudulent phone calls—made largely to Liberal supporters and designed to suppress the vote by misinforming them of their polling station location—had come from Conservative party sources, precipitating the "robocall" scandal. The Council of Canadians went to court to challenge the results in various ridings, and the Federal Court found that fraud had occurred, though no results were annulled. The only person charged criminally, Michael Sona—who had acted as director of communications for the Conservative candidate in Guelph, Ontario—was found guilty and sentenced to nine months in prison and 12 months of probation.

In an unrelated court case, the defeated Liberal candidate in Etobicoke Centre persuaded a judge to nullify the results in that constituency which the Conservative candidate won by 26 votes when the court found that 79 votes should be set aside as invalid. This *Opitz-Wrzesnewskyj* decision was reversed by a divided Supreme Court, the majority feeling that without any allegation of fraud, imperfections in the conduct of elections are inevitable.

Despite concerns leading into the following election, 2015 did not see similar claims of fraud or invalidated ballots, though there were reports of pre-marked ballots in both advance polls and on election day. Elections Canada claimed that the ballots in question were simply the result of printing errors, and no evidence has arisen that these affected the election outcome.

THE PROPORTIONALITY OF THE ELECTORAL SYSTEM

In each constituency, the candidate with the most votes wins, even if this is less than a majority. Among the advantages of this single-member-plurality electoral system are its simplicity for the voter, its quick calculation of results, and its provision of a clear-cut representative for each constituency. SMP has usually provided a majority government in Canada—that is, the winning party obtains over 50 percent of the seats, which some observers also take as an advantage. However, others refer to it as a "false majority" because the winning party rarely wins at least 50 percent of the popular vote.[17] Indeed, when all the local results are accumulated nationally, the proportion of seats a party wins does not necessarily bear much relationship to its overall share of the **popular vote**.

Take as an extreme, hypothetical example a two-person race in each constituency in which the Liberal candidate beat the Conservative candidate by one vote in every case: the Liberal Party would then win 100 percent of the seats from just more than 50 percent of the vote, and the Conservative Party would have zero percent of the seats from just less than 50 percent of the vote. In fact, this example is not so hypothetical: in the New Brunswick election of 1987, the Liberals won 100 percent of the seats with about 60 percent of the popular vote. Many political scientists and other observers look beyond the results in each electoral district and argue that party representation in the House of Commons should be more proportional to overall popular support.

Discrepancies between Seats and Votes: National Level

The actual disparities can be analyzed for both the national and the provincial levels.[18] Overall, in 29 elections since 1921, the party with the largest popular vote almost always won more seats than its proportion of the vote, while the second party was usually underrepresented. When it comes to minor parties, those with concentrated regional support, like the Bloc Québécois, were often overrepresented, while those with broad national ("diffuse") support usually lost out. The CCF/NDP, for example, regularly received only about half as many seats as its popular vote merited. With concentrated support in Quebec in 2011, however, the NDP took one-third of the total seats, which slightly exceeded its vote proportion.

On 15 occasions out of 30, this electoral system manufactured a majority government in terms of seats, even though the leading party did not win a majority of the vote. In fact, in only three federal elections after 1921 (1940, 1958, and 1984) did the winning party obtain at least 50 percent of the vote, and this produced a majority government. Despite this tendency to produce a majority government, with four or five major parties in the race, a minority government is likely even in an SMP system, and on 11 other occasions, a minority government resulted. Perhaps the most objectionable aspect of SMP is that on three occasions (1957, 1962, and 1979) the party with the second-largest popular vote ended up with more seats than the party that came first, and went on to form the government, as sometimes happens in the provinces as well.[19]

In the 1993 context, the Liberals and Bloc were overrepresented, but Reform, the NDP, and especially the PCs, deserved more seats in terms of their popular vote. Reform should have been the official opposition in the sense that it received more votes than the Bloc; the NDP deserved party status because seven percent of the vote would theoretically produce about 20 seats; and the Conservatives ran a close third to Reform in the popular vote and more than doubled the vote of the NDP but suffered from ridicule of its two-member caucus. The 1997 election also gave the Liberals a majority of seats that their popular support did not justify, awarded the regionally concentrated Bloc more seats than it merited, and continued to underrepresent the more nationally based PCs and NDP. The Liberals won another underserved majority in the 2000 election, which was still unkind to the Conservatives and NDP. Then, in 2004, 2006, and 2008, no party won a majority of seats, but the NDP (and Greens) were seriously disadvantaged, while the Harper Conservatives and Trudeau Liberals won artificial majorities in 2011 and 2015 respectively. Table 13.2 presents these figures for the 1993–2015 period.

TABLE 13.2   PERCENTAGE OF THE POPULAR VOTE AND PERCENTAGE OF SEATS BY PARTY FOR FEDERAL ELECTIONS, 1993–2015

		LIBERAL	PC	NDP	REFORM/ALLIANCE	BQ
1993	% VOTE	41.3	16.0	6.9	18.7	13.5
	% SEATS	60.0	0.7	3.1	17.6	18.3
1997	% VOTE	38.5	18.8	11.0	19.4	10.7
	% SEATS	51.5	6.6	7.0	19.9	14.6
2000	% VOTE	40.8	12.2	8.5	25.5	10.7
	% SEATS	57.1	4.0	4.3	21.9	12.6
		LIBERAL	CONSERVATIVE	NDP		BQ
2004	% VOTE	36.7	29.6	15.7		12.4
	% SEATS	43.8	32.1	6.2		17.5
2006	% VOTE	30.2	36.3	17.5		10.5
	% SEATS	33.4	40.3	9.4		16.6
2008	% VOTE	26.3	37.7	18.2		10.0
	% SEATS	25.0	46.4	12.0		15.9
2011*	% VOTE	18.9	39.6	30.6		6.1
	% SEATS	11.0	53.9	33.4		1.3
2015*	% VOTE	39.5	29.3	19.7		4.7
	% SEATS	54.4	31.9	13.0		3.0

*IN 2011 AND 2015, THE GREEN PARTY WON ONE SEAT (0.3%) WITH 3.9% AND 3.4% OF THE VOTE RESPECTIVELY; IN 2008, IT WON NO SEATS BUT RECEIVED 6.8% OF THE VOTE.

Source: Reports of the Chief Electoral Officer, adapted by the author; Elections Canada, Preliminary Results, http://enr.elections.ca/National.aspx?lang=e.

Discrepancies between Seats and Votes: By Province

Another set of disparities between popular vote and seat figures in federal elections exists on a province-by-province basis. In this case, Alan Cairns was particularly struck by the disparity between the Conservative vote and seats in Quebec (1896–1984) and between the Liberal vote and seats in Western Canada (since 1957).

Cairns observed that such disparities affect parties in three principal ways: image, strategy, and policy. Each party's image is largely derived from the attention given to its number of elected members in the House of Commons rather than from its popular vote. Thus, when the Conservatives had virtually no members from Quebec before 1984, they gained a non-French or anti-French image, even though they usually obtained at least 13 percent of the popular vote in that province. Similarly, the Liberals acquired an image of an anti-Western party after 1957 because they elected few members west of Ontario, even though they normally received more than 20 percent of the Western vote. In 2000, the Canadian Alliance took nearly 24 percent of the vote in Ontario, but in winning only two seats in the province, it was thought to have been confined to the West.

As far as strategy is concerned, when Conservatives despaired of electing members from Quebec and felt they could form a government without much representation from that province, they ignored it, especially in 1957.[20] The Liberals often felt that campaigning in the West was a waste of time and money and therefore concentrated their effort elsewhere. These strategies are not good for keeping the country together, one of the functions that political parties and elections are supposed to perform.

Finally, since the elected members of the party have a major role to play in the development of party policy, Conservative policy did not reflect the concerns of French Canada when the party lacked francophone and Quebec MPs, just as Liberal policy tended to ignore Western concerns because so few Liberals were elected from Western Canada. This is especially serious for the party that forms the government, when it has few or no MPs from a province or region to put into the Cabinet. Between 1962 and 1984, either Quebec or the West was effectively left out of national decision-making at the Cabinet level. Residents of such provinces or regions understandably feel that national policy does not reflect their interests and either turn to provincial governments to defend these interests or start to think in separatist terms. Such a dynamic appeared evident in Quebec in 2011, when the surging Conservatives won only five seats on their way to a majority government, and the same situation has typically been evident in many western provinces that shunned the Liberal Party during its majorities from 1993–2004. Nevertheless, while Alberta and Saskatchewan remain Conservative bases, Quebec turned back significantly to the Liberals during that party's surge in 2015. Table 13.3 shows the distribution of seats won per province and territory and the breakdown of the seats–votes ratio for the 2015 election.

Beyond the problems identified by Cairns, SMP is criticized in other ways. It is said to promote the overrepresentation of white males because each party can only nominate a single candidate in each constituency and may be tempted to choose the "lowest common denominator." It may discourage voter turnout because those who support candidates who are not likely to win will not bother to vote when their effort will be "wasted." And it may encourage voters to opt for their second-choice candidate ("strategic voting") because their first choice has no chance of winning.

	CONSERVATIVES			LIBERALS			NDP			BQ		
	SEATS	%S	%V	SEATS	%S	%V	SEATS	%S	%V	SEATS	%S	%V
NEWFOUNDLAND AND LABRADOR	0	0	10.3	7	100	64.5	0	0	21	0	0	0
PRINCE EDWARD ISLAND	0	0	19.3	4	100	58.3	0	0	16	0	0	0
NOVA SCOTIA	0	0	17.9	11	100	61.9	0	0	16.4	0	0	0
NEW BRUNSWICK	0	0	25.3	10	100	51.6	0	0	18.3	0	0	0
QUEBEC	12	15.4	16.7	40	51.3	35.7	16	20.5	25.4	10	12.8	19.3
ONTARIO	33	27.3	35	80	66.1	44.8	8	6.6	16.6	0	0	0
MANITOBA	5	35.7	37.3	7	50	44.6	2	14.3	13.8	0	0	0
SASKATCHEWAN	10	71.4	48.5	1	7.1	23.9	3	21.4	25.1	0	0	0
ALBERTA	29	85.3	59.5	4	11.8	24.6	1	2.9	11.6	0	0	0
BC*	10	23.8	30	17	40.5	35.2	14	33.3	25.9	0	0	0
NWT	0	0	18	1	100	48.3	0	0	30.8	0	0	0
NUNAVUT	0	0	24.8	1	100	47.2	0	0	26.5	0	0	0
YUKON	0	0	24	1	100	53.6	0	0	19.5	0	0	0
TOTAL	99	29.3	31.9	184	54.4	39.5	44	13	19.7	10	3	4.7

* ONE GREEN SEAT IN BRITISH COLUMBIA.

Source: Elections Canada, *Preliminary Results, November 4, 2015, http://enr.elections.ca/Provinces.aspx?lang=e. Elections Canada. This reproduction is a copy of the version available at www.elections.ca. Reproduced with the permission of Elections Canada.*

Remedies

Given these problems, reform of the electoral system is increasingly urged. The most extreme remedy would be a system of "proportional representation" in which constituencies would be eliminated and each party would receive as many seats in each province as its popular vote dictated. Although such a system has its advocates, most observers feel that Canadians do not want to part with local constituency representation. William Irvine first proposed a system somewhat akin to that in Germany—usually called "mixed member proportional"—in which about half of the MPs would be elected from constituencies, as they are now. The others, called "provincial MPs," would be designated on the basis of popular vote by party in each province to bring each party's proportion of popular vote and percentage of seats into line, both in individual provinces and across the country as a whole. Irvine hoped to overcome the lack of representation of important segments of opinion in party caucuses and the Cabinet, as well as to avoid the sense of regional–ethnic alienation that stems from the current situation.[21] Individual parties would probably have the prerogative of drawing up a list of candidates from which these "provincial MPs" would be selected. In such a case, women and minority ethnocultural candidates could be placed at the top of the list and obtain increased representation as a result. It would also mean that fewer votes would be "wasted," because even if a person's vote did not help elect a constituency MP, it would likely contribute to the election of those MPs based on popular vote.

Sensing that such a reform might be too radical for Canadian taste, several authorities have suggested a more modest "top-up" system in which the SMP system would be supplemented by a smaller number of proportional MPs, say 50 or 60, who would overcome the worst problems of the existing system but still theoretically make majority government possible. This system would start with the regularly elected constituency MPs who are necessary to ensure the representation of all parts of Canada. But some 50 supplementary MPs would be added, to be distributed on the basis of popular vote by party by province. They would correct the greatest discrepancies between the proportion of seats and votes.

For the party in power, such supplementary MPs could provide provincial representation in the Cabinet; for opposition parties, they would speak up for their provinces in the caucus and in Parliament, improving the party's image and policies. Representing an entire province, it is not likely that such provincial MPs would be underemployed, and they would probably soon shed the status of "second-class" representatives. Alternatively, they could concentrate on committee and other legislative work in the Commons. To avoid the negative connotations of being chosen by party officials in back rooms, and giving them more democratic legitimacy, they could be drawn from the party's candidates in each province who were most narrowly defeated in the general election and would seek re-election in a specific constituency the next time around.

Reform along more proportional lines was first officially endorsed by the Pépin–Robarts Task Force on Canadian Unity in 1979, and the idea appealed to both Pierre Trudeau and Ed Broadbent as party leaders at the time. It would favour all federalist parties in some ways, and perhaps the unity of the nation as a whole. On the other hand, many are worried about the prevalence of minority or coalition governments; some feel it would give party organizers too much power in choosing and ranking candidates, and others argue that parties should have to fight for victory solely in individual constituencies.

In 2015, the Trudeau Liberals were elected on a platform that included changing Canada's SMP electoral system, but there has been much interest in electoral reform in recent years at the provincial level. In British Columbia, a Citizens' Assembly recommended that the province adopt a single transferable vote (STV) system consisting of multi-member constituencies in which voters ranked candidates on their ballot. More proportional representation would be achieved with the election of a wider array of candidates in the local areas. In a referendum in 2005, the proposal received 57 percent support, but the government had previously set the threshold for change at 60 percent, so the proposal was abandoned until the election of 2009. In Prince Edward Island, a recommendation for a "top-up" system (17 constituency seats and 10 proportional members) was more decisively defeated in a referendum in the same year.

Ontario held a referendum on October 10, 2007 on whether to adopt a mixed-member proportional electoral system in which the legislature would have 90 electoral districts and an additional 39 MPPs based on popular vote from party lists. Voters would have two ballots, one for their local representative and one for their party preference. The proposal was soundly defeated: 37 percent voted for MMP and 63 percent voted to retain SMP.

When British Columbia staged its second referendum on electoral reform in 2009, the results were almost opposite to those of 2005: only 39 percent supported the STV system. Still, serious advocates of electoral reform like Fair Vote Canada are not likely to let the problem die.[22]

CRITICAL APPROACHES

The kind of electoral system used can make a significant difference in the election outcome. The *institutionalist approach* emphasizes how the rules and mechanics of the electoral system can affect the results; for example, the choice of SMP rather than a more proportional system tends to influence which party many people choose to support, how political parties campaign, and which people are elected. Similarly, the rules surrounding party finance—as we will see below—shape how political parties go about the business of raising money.

Political psychology and *political behaviour approaches* are particularly interested in voting behaviour, which is also discussed in more detail in Chapter 15. For example, to what extent do people choose *not* to vote for their most favoured candidate in order to vote for a lesser choice that has the greatest chance of defeating their least favoured option? This practice, called strategic voting, is probably most common in SMP electoral systems and has often been expected among some NDP supporters who voted for the Liberal party in order to try to defeat the Conservative candidate. Although strategic voting certainly happens to some extent, it has probably not been a decisive factor in a national election.

FINANCING ELECTIONS

Pre-1974

Before 1974, Canada had no effective laws with respect to party and election finance, and numerous irregularities and outright scandals occurred. The Liberal and Conservative parties relied almost completely on contributions from big business at the national level, which usually produced a surplus to be distributed to candidates' campaigns as well, and candidates were otherwise dependent on donations from small local firms. Both parties had fundraisers (sometimes called "bagmen")—often senators who could exploit their corporate connections and make use of their abundant spare time—assisted by corporate volunteers. Businesses also made contributions in kind, such as various skilled human resources. Corporate contributions were supplemented by fundraising dinners, but party leaders themselves occasionally had to come to the party's rescue. This was especially the case in the Depression elections of 1930 and 1935, when the Conservatives were led by a multimillionaire, R.B. Bennett. The CCF/NDP depended primarily on individual membership fees, supplemented by union contributions, but in this case the flow of funds was reversed, and the local candidates had to help finance the central campaign. Overall, the Liberals and Conservatives raised and spent far more than the CCF/NDP, at both the national and the local levels.[23]

The secrecy surrounding party and election finance before 1974 makes it difficult to know how many irregularities and scandals actually took place. The first to come to light was the **Pacific scandal** of 1872, in which a group of businessmen eager to obtain the contract to build the CPR donated some $350 000 to John A. Macdonald's election campaign. When the scandal was revealed, Macdonald's government was defeated in the House of Commons, precipitating another election, which he lost. The second major scandal that came to public attention was the Beauharnois scandal of 1930, in which a similar group gave $600 000 to the Liberal Party in hopes of obtaining the contract to build the Beauharnois Dam on the St. Lawrence River. By the time the deal was publicly exposed, the Liberal Party was in Opposition, and its leader, Mackenzie King, rather incredulously denied any knowledge of such a large contribution.[24] In the 1960s, the Rivard scandal involved drug trafficker Lucien Rivard, who had been a regular contributor to the Liberal Party. He apparently felt that such donations, in addition to his attempted bribery of a government lawyer in a bail proceeding, should get him out of jail. These schemes did not work for him, but another—throwing a hose over the prison wall and escaping—turned out quite well!

The Rivard and other small-scale scandals in the 1960s, together with increasing public expectations of political morality, caused the Pearson government to appoint a commission on the subject of party and election finance in 1964. But when its recommendations were published two years later, no action was taken. It required the heightened sense of public outrage at political immorality in the United States (the Watergate scandal), along with Opposition pressure in the minority government period of 1972–74, to produce legislation more or less as recommended in 1966. Amendments to the Canada Elections Act were passed in 1974 but did not take effect until the election of 1979.

Federal Election Finance Law and Its Results, 1974–2003

The Federal Election Finance Law had four basic provisions.[25] First, although no limit was placed on the size of contributions, a ceiling was imposed on both national party spending and on candidate expenditures. Second, the disclosure provision required that the names of those contributing more than $100 be filed with the chief electoral officer and that such records be open to public inspection. Third, a tax credit provision was added so that contributors would receive a 75 percent income tax credit for contributions up to $100 and declining afterward, to a maximum tax credit of $500. Finally, candidates who received at least 15 percent of the vote would have a portion of their expenses subsidized by the public purse, the original formula being replaced by a flat 50 percent rate in amendments made in 1983. Parties that received a certain minimum percentage of the vote were also subsidized for a portion of their central campaign expenditures.

The objectives of the legislation were thus to increase the equity, transparency, and participatory nature of the electoral system. Equity would be enhanced in limiting candidate and national party spending, as well as by the public subsidy provision; the disclosure clause would make it difficult in the future for large, secret contributions to be made in return for some favourable government decision; and the tax credit would encourage individual contributions and reduce Liberal and Conservative dependence on corporations.

How did political parties obtain such funds? Liberal, PC, and later, Alliance parties tended to use well-connected corporate supporters who volunteered their time in soliciting funds from other members of the corporate elite. The largest corporations in the country often gave annual contributions of $100 000 or more to both Liberal and Conservative parties. All parties also used direct-mail techniques: after obtaining lists of individual names from magazines, professional organizations, or any other likely source, they mailed out hundreds or thousands of computer-generated letters soliciting contributions, highlighting the tax credit available. Sometimes parties conferred special benefits on those giving more than a certain sum, such as being invited to a reception with the leader. The Liberals and Conservatives especially also raised huge amounts of money at dinners ($100/plate, $500/plate, etc.) at which the party leader or other luminaries spoke. The NDP sometimes received a small number of large union donations.

Federal Election Finance Law after 2003

In the light of financial disparities among parties, compounded by the constant scent of scandal surrounding corporate contributions, it became increasingly common to propose the prohibition of corporate (and trade union) contributions, allowing only individual citizens to contribute to political parties. Quebec pioneered this system over 30 years ago in its provincial elections, and Manitoba and Nova Scotia followed suit under NDP governments. The Chrétien government ran into an abundance of ethical problems in its third term, and as part of a package to clean up the way political parties and government operated, a new regime for election finance came into effect in January 2004.[26]

The most significant part of the reform was to severely restrict corporate and trade union contributions and to limit individual donations to $1000 per year. To compensate for such losses, parties were entitled to an annual public allowance or reimbursement of $1.75 for each vote they received in the preceding election. All the major political parties seemed satisfied that the loss of corporate (or union) contributions was more than made up for by the new taxpayer-funded **per-vote subsidy**, and even the seat-less Green party started to receive about $1 million a year based on its popular vote.

The Harper government made additional reforms of party and election finance in its Federal Accountability Act, such that corporations and trade unions can no longer contribute at all to elections, nominations, or leadership candidates. This reform had a significant effect on the many facets of the relationship between unions and the NDP, as mentioned in Chapter 14.[27] All parties were expected to put great effort into raising contributions from individuals, but the Conservatives had far more success in this regard than any of the others, aggressively soliciting funds by means of the Responsive Marketing Group (RMG) call centre in Ottawa. The results can be seen from the various party returns for the year 2013 in Table 13.4.

Thus, as a result of the Chrétien and Harper reforms, corporate and union contributions are prohibited, and the current provisions concerning contributions and subsidies are as follows: in 2015 individuals are limited to an annual contribution of $1500 (increasing by $25 each year) to a party, constituency association, and candidate; such contributions are eligible for a 75 percent tax credit for contributions up to $400, with the percentage declining thereafter with the maximum credit being $650; the identity of contributors of more than $200 must be disclosed; a candidate who receives at least 10 percent of the votes is reimbursed for 60 percent of his or her election expenses; and national parties are eligible to receive a public rebate of 50 percent of their election expenses.

When the Harper Conservatives gained a majority government in 2011, they passed legislation to reduce the annual per-vote public subsidy incrementally over the 2012–15 period, after which they would no longer be paid. Such a change represented a serious challenge to all the other parties, especially the Liberals, BQ, and Greens. In fact, an initial attempt to cut the subsidy by the minority Conservative government in 2008 resulted in an attempted BQ-Liberal-NDP coalition. Harper, however, argued that several other kinds of public subsidy of parties remained.

The Harper Conservatives also engaged in other controversial election practices. First, since there is no restriction on spending outside the election period, a party with a large war chest and which knows when the election will be held can gain a significant advantage over its opponents by advertising in the unrestricted pre-election period. In the case of Stephen

TABLE 13.4 NATIONAL PARTY CONTRIBUTIONS, 2013

PARTY	CONTRIBUTIONS	INDIVIDUAL CONTRIBUTORS
CONSERVATIVES	$18 100 956	80 135
LIBERALS	$11 292 846	71 655
NDP	$8 162 309	39 218
GREEN	$2 211 956	14 500
BQ	$417 030	4 146

Source: National Party Contributions, 2013 (submitted), Elections Canada. http://www.elections.ca/WPAPPS/ WPF/EN/PP/. This reproduction is a copy of the version available at www.elections.ca. Reproduced with the permission of Elections Canada.

Harper's party, such advertising frequently took the form of attack ads on other party leaders. Second, the Conservatives were accused of transferring funds between federal and constituency levels in the 2006 election in order to evade the legal spending limits by over $1 million, in what was called the "In and Out" scandal. The four party officials charged ultimately issued an agreed statement with Elections Canada in which they admitted guilt to exceeding the party's election expense limit and providing an incomplete election expenses return. The party fund was fined a total of $2000 and the party itself was fined a total of $50 000.[28]

Following the 2011 election, 2 MPs left office due to overspending in elections. Conservative MP and cabinet minister Peter Penashue was found by Elections Canada to have accepted ineligible donations and to have exceeded the spending limit during the 2011 campaign. Penashue ran unsuccessfully as a Conservative in a byelection in 2013 to regain his seat. In 2014, Conservative MP Dean Del Mastro left office after being convicted of crimes including overspending, over-contributing to his own campaign, and knowingly submitting false information during the 2008 election.

CRITICAL APPROACHES

Class analysts see a link between political parties that hold power and accommodation of elite or business interests. Of course this has changed with recent party finance changes to a large degree, yet historically governing parties received much of their contributions from corporations, and corporations in turn received tax concessions, loans, grants, and contracts; preferential legislation and regulations; and free trade agreements. Now that corporate contributions have been eliminated, the corporate elite must find other ways to apply its influence.

Rational choice scholars contend that established parties and politicians seek to shape the rules in their own interest. Richard Katz and Peter Mair, for example, argue that competing political parties collude with each other to enact policies that protect their share of the electoral market, and which keep new political parties out of the game.[29] The rules in question relate to the electoral system itself, party finance, and the distribution of broadcast time, all of which have been rigged at one time or another to favour themselves, as mentioned in Chapter 15. Such rules have often had the effect of making it difficult for new political parties to get into the game.

Third-Party Advertising and the Royal Commission on Electoral Reform and Party Financing

Another problem in the realm of election finance is **third-party advertising**—that is, spending by groups other than candidates and political parties. The 1974 act prohibited advocacy group spending during an election campaign that favoured or opposed a party or candidate. It was argued that the only way party and candidate spending ceilings could be effective was if any spending on their behalf by advocacy groups was included in the parties' budgets. But in the 1980s more and more groups began to advertise for or against various parties or candidates without having these expenses included in the parties' budgets. Although such advertising was clearly a violation of the spirit of the act as well as its specific terms, the **National Citizens Coalition (NCC)** went to court to challenge the act in 1984. The Alberta court ruled the restrictions unconstitutional as a violation of the freedom-of-expression provisions of the Charter of Rights and Freedoms.

Third-party advertising increased enormously in the 1988 election campaign, especially in the case of the pro-free trade group, the Canadian Alliance for Trade and Job Opportunities.[30] With only one political party in favour of free trade, namely the Conservatives, any advertising that supported the Free Trade Agreement also promoted the Conservative Party. Thus the Conservatives benefited from some $5 million in advertising by advocacy groups on top of their own national budget of nearly $8 million, with the same large corporations contributing to both causes. Such third-party advertising made a mockery of party spending ceilings and is widely thought to have helped the Conservatives achieve re-election by turning the momentum of the campaign back in their favour during the last two weeks, especially in Ontario.

Shortly after the 1988 election, the Mulroney government appointed a **Royal Commission on Electoral Reform and Party Financing**. Headed by Pierre Lortie, that commission identified several other concerns, held public hearings across the country, and commissioned extensive academic research. On the question of third-party advertising, the royal commission recommended that spending during the election period by individuals or organizations other than candidates and political parties be restricted to $1000. This limit was legislated before the 1997 election, in a diluted form, but it was immediately challenged by the Stephen Harper–led NCC, and Alberta courts once again found that it violated the Charter.

The new Canada Elections Act passed before the November 2000 election imposed an overall ceiling on third-party advertising during the campaign of $150 000, of which no more than $3000 could be spent in each electoral district on advertising for or against candidates. The NCC challenged these new spending limits once again, but the new law was upheld by the Supreme Court of Canada in 2004.[31] These amounts were adjusted for inflation annually, and in 2015 sat at $205 800, with a local limit of $4116, pro-rated for a 37-day campaign.[32] The National Citizens Coalition continued its tradition in this regard, but many of the other third parties were on the left of the spectrum, such as the Council of Canadians, Make Poverty History, Friends of Canadian Broadcasting, and many unions. Since the Canadian Labour Congress and individual unions are no longer allowed to make financial contributions to the NDP, one of their alternative means of support now takes the form of third-party advertising.[33]

CONCLUSION

Because elections are central to the operation of Canadian democracy, it remains crucial that we consider which election system would best serve Canadians' needs. Although the actual operation of the SMP system on election day is largely satisfactory, and many problems of party and election finance have been eliminated, the principle of representation by population is widely breached, and parties are not awarded seats (and therefore power) in proportion to their popular support.

This chapter is closely related to the following two on political parties and the election campaign. It also has links to some of the demographic chapters earlier in the book as well as the Charter of Rights, especially in terms of the extension of the right to vote. Moreover, elections constitute the basis of the House of Commons, and therefore, as well, the Executive branch of government in Part 5 of the book.

DISCUSSION QUESTIONS

1. Given the peculiar distribution of the Canadian population, to what extent should we adhere to the principle of "representation by population"?

2. Should the party leader have a veto on local nominations? Why or why not?

3. Should the electoral system be reformed in a more proportional direction? If so, how?

4. Should further changes be made to the law governing party and election finance?

5. What are the arguments on each side of the debate over third-party advertising?

MindTap® FOR MORE INFO GO TO **http://www.nelson.com/student**

NOTES

1. Jon H. Pammett, "Elections," in Michael Whittington and Glen Williams, eds. *Canadian Politics in the 21st Century*, 7th ed. (Toronto: Thomson Nelson, 2008); Heather MacIvor, ed. *Election* (Toronto: Emond Montgomery, 2009).
2. See, for example, Richard Rose, ed., *The International Encyclopedia of Elections* (Washington: CQ Press, 2000); and David Butler, Howard Penniman, and Austin Ranney, eds., *Democracy at the Polls: A Comparative Study of Competitive National Elections* (Washington: American Enterprise Institute, 1981).
3. See, for example, Ontario Citizens' Assembly Secretariat, *From Votes to Seats: Four Families of Electoral Systems*; and Denis Pilon, *The Politics of Voting: Reforming Canada's Electoral System* (Toronto: Emond Montgomery, 2007).
4. John Courtney, *Elections* (Vancouver: UBC Press, 2004), Ch. 3.
5. A more detailed outline of this process is provided on the Elections Canada website. The distribution of seats per province is based on Statistics Canada's population projections, while the design of each provincial electoral map is based on the 2011 Census.
6. For Sir John A. Macdonald's efforts, see R.M. Dawson, "The Gerrymander of 1881," *Canadian Journal of Economics and Political Science* (May 1935).
7. See Chapter 19; John C. Courtney, Peter MacKinnon, and David E. Smith, eds., *Drawing Boundaries: Legislatures, Courts and Electoral Values* (Saskatoon: Fifth House Publishers, 1992); and John Courtney, *Commissioned Ridings* (Montreal: McGill-Queen's University Press, 2001); *Reference re Provincial Electoral Boundaries (Sask.)*, [1991] 2 S.C.R. 158.
8. Elections Canada, "Federal Electoral Districts—Representation Order of 2003." For 1995, see Louis Massicotte, "Electoral Reform in the Charter Era," in Alan Frizzell and Jon H. Pammett, eds., *The Canadian General Election of 1997* (Toronto: Dundurn Press, 1997), p. 178.

9. Peter H. Russell, "Learning to Live with Minority Parliaments," in Russell and Lorne Sossin, eds., *Parliamentary Democracy in Crisis* (Toronto: University of Toronto Press, 2009), p. 139.

10. Courtney, *Elections*; Louis Massicotte, "The Chief Electoral Officer of Canada," *Canadian Parliamentary Review* (Autumn 2003).

11. *Completing the Cycle of Electoral Reforms: Recommendations from the Chief Electoral Officer of Canada following the 38th General Election* (Chief Electoral Officer of Canada, 2005), p. 14.

12. William Cross, *Political Parties* (Vancouver: UBC Press, 2004), Ch. 4.

13. MacIvor, *Canadian Politics and Government in the Charter Era*, Ch. 9. An amendment was made to the Canada Elections Act in 2001 that allowed a party with a minimum of 12 candidates—rather than the previous requirement of 50 candidates—to place the party label on the ballot, but in 2003 the Supreme Court overruled this decision as discriminatory: one candidate was enough. This case, centred on the Communist Party of Canada, also allowed smaller parties to issue tax receipts to donors and to retain unspent election contributions. See *Figueroa v. Canada (Attorney General)*, [2003] 1 S.C.R. 912.

14. In 2015: Conservative, Liberal, NDP, Green, Bloc Québécois, Alliance of the North, Animal Alliance Environment Voters, Canada, Canadian Action, Christian Heritage, Communist, Democratic Advancement, Forces et Démocratie, Libertarian, Marijuana, Marxist-Leninist, Accountability Competency and Transparency, Pirate, Progressive Canadian, Rhinoceros, Seniors, Bridge, and United parties.

15. Elections Canada, *A History of the Vote in Canada*, 2nd ed. (Ottawa: Chief Electoral Officer of Canada, 2007); and Courtney, *Elections*, Ch. 2.

16. Chief Electoral Officer, *Towards the 35th General Election* (Ottawa: 1994, Catalogue. No. SE 1-5/1993); Massicotte, "Electoral Reform in the Charter Era"; *Sauvé v. Canada (A.G.)*, [1993] 2 S.C.R. 438; *Sauvé v. Canada (Chief Electoral Officer)*, [1996] 1 F.C. 857; and *Sauvé v. Canada (Chief Electoral Officer)*, [2002] 3 S.C.R. 519.

17. Peter H. Russell, *Two Cheers for Minority Government: The Evolution of Canadian Parliamentary Democracy* (Toronto: Emond Montgomery, 2008).

18. Alan C. Cairns, "The Electoral System and the Party System in Canada," *Canadian Journal of Political Science* (March 1968).

19. The most prominent provincial examples are Quebec, 1944, 1966, and 1998; Saskatchewan, 1986 and 1999; BC, 1941 and 1996; and New Brunswick, 2006.

20. John Meisel, *The Canadian General Election of 1957* (Toronto: University of Toronto Press, 1962).

21. William Irvine, *Does Canada Need a New Electoral System?* (Kingston: Institute of Intergovernmental Relations, Queen's University, 1979).

22. Henry Milner, ed., *Making Every Vote Count: Reassessing Canada's Electoral System* (Peterborough: Broadview Press, 1999); Milner, ed., *Steps Toward Making Every Vote Count: Electoral System Reform in Canada and Its Provinces* (Peterborough: Broadview Press, 2004); Law Commission of Canada, *Voting Counts: Electoral Reform for Canada* (Ottawa, 2004); Fair Vote Canada, available at http://www.fairvotecanada.org/fvc.php; and Pilon, *The Politics of Voting: Reforming Canada's Electoral System*.

23. K.Z. Paltiel, *Political Party Financing in Canada* (Toronto: McGraw-Hill Ryerson, 1970).

24. Richard Gwyn, *Nation Maker: Sir John A. Macdonald: His Life, Our Times*, Volume II (Toronto: Random House Canada, 2011); T.D. Regehr, *The Beauharnois Scandal* (Toronto: University of Toronto Press, 1990).

25. W.T. Stanbury, "Regulating Federal Party and Candidate Finances in a Dynamic Environment," in H.G. Thorburn and Alan Whitehorn, eds., *Party Politics in Canada*, 8th ed. (Toronto: Prentice Hall, 2001); Cross, *Political Parties*, Ch. 7.

26. Cross, *Political Parties*, Ch. 7; Craig Forcese and Aaron Freeman, *The Laws of Government: The Legal Foundations of Canadian Democracy* (Toronto: Irwin Law, 2005), pp. 100–132; and W. Scott Thurlow, "Financing Canadian Elections," *Canadian Parliamentary Review* (Winter 2008–09).

27. Harold Jansen and Lisa Young, "Solidarity Forever? The NDP, Organized Labour, and the Changing Face of Party Finance in Canada," *Canadian Journal of Political Science* (September 2009); David Coletto, Harold J. Jansen, and Lisa Young, "Stratarchical Party Organization and Party Finance in Canada," *Canadian Journal of Political Science* (March 2011).

28. Public Prosecution Service of Canada, "Agreed Statement of Facts—2011-11-10," available at http://www.ppsc-sppc.gc.ca/eng/nws-nvs/comm/2011/10_11_11b.html.

29. Richard Katz and Peter Mair, "Party Democracy: The Emergence of the Cartel Party," *Party Politics* (January 1995).
30. *Toronto Star*, December 9, 1989, p. C1.
31. Massicotte, "Election Reform in the Charter Era"; *National Citizens' Coalition Inc. v. A.G. Canada*, [1984] 11 D.L.R. (4th) 481; *Somerville v. Canada (A.G.)*, [1996] 136 D.L.R. (4th) 205 (Alta C.A.); *Libman v. Quebec (Attorney General)*, [1997] 3 S.C.R. 569; and *Harper v. Canada (Attorney General)*, [2004] 1 S.C.R. 827.
32. Elections Canada, Third Party Election Advertising Expenses Limits, available at http://www .elections.ca/content.aspx?section=pol&document=index&dir=thi/limits&lang=e.
33. Jansen and Young, "Solidarity Forever? The NDP, Organized Labour, and the Changing Face of Party Finance in Canada"; David McGrane, "Political Marketing and the NDP's Historical Breakthrough," in Jon H. Pammett and Christopher Dornan, eds., *The Canadian Federal Election of 2011* (Toronto: Dundurn, 2011).

FURTHER READING

Cairns, Alan C. "The Electoral System and the Party System in Canada," *Canadian Journal of Political Science* (March 1968).

Courtney, John. *Elections*. Vancouver: UBC Press, 2004.

Cross, William. *Political Parties*. Vancouver: UBC Press, 2004.

Forcese, Craig, and Aaron Freeman. *The Laws of Government: The Legal Foundations of Canadian Democracy*. Toronto: Irwin Law, 2005.

Jansen, Harold, and Lisa Young. "Solidarity Forever? The NDP, Organized Labour, and the Changing Face of Party Finance in Canada," *Canadian Journal of Political Science* (September 2009).

Law Commission of Canada. *Voting Counts: Electoral Reform for Canada*. Ottawa, 2004.

Lawlor, Andrea, and Erin Crandall. "Understanding Third-Party Advertising: An Analysis of the 2004, 2006 and 2008 Canadian Elections," *Canadian Public Administration* (December 2011).

MacIvor, Heather, ed. *Election*. Toronto: Emond Montgomery, 2009.

Marland, Alex, and Thierry Giasson, eds. *Canadian Election Analysis: Communication, Strategy, and Democracy*. Vancouver: University of British Columbia Press, 2015.

Milner, Henry, ed. *Steps Toward Making Every Vote Count: Electoral System Reform in Canada and Its Provinces*. Peterborough: Broadview Press, 2004.

Pammett, Jon H. "Elections," in Michael Whittington and Glen Williams, eds., *Canadian Politics in the 21st Century*, 7th ed. Toronto: Thomson Nelson, 2008.

———, and Christopher Dornan, eds. *The Canadian Federal Election of 2011*. Toronto: Dundurn, 2011.

Pilon, Denis. *The Politics of Voting: Reforming Canada's Electoral System*. Toronto: Emond Montgomery, 2007.

CHAPTER 14

Political Parties and the Party System

Political parties are integral to the operation of almost every aspect of a modern political system, but Canadians are generally more attuned to their faults than their virtues. Parties are widely criticized for their patronage appointments, for their vicious attacks on each other and each other's leaders, and for their loud and often obnoxious behaviour during Question Period in the House of Commons. It is often difficult to appreciate the value of political parties, but they should not be known by their defects alone.

For most of the post-1867 period, the Liberal and (Progressive) Conservative parties dominated the Canadian political scene. The New Democratic Party became a stable contender after 1961, while various smaller parties have come and gone, some of them forming governments at the provincial level. When the Conservatives self-destructed in 1993 and two new parties joined the fray, the Reform Party (later, the Canadian Alliance) and the Bloc Québécois, the Liberals gained a new lease on life. But they began to decline after 2000 and the two "right-wing" parties reunited in 2003. This new Conservative Party of Canada formed minority governments after the 2006 and 2008 elections and won a majority in the 2011 election, while the NDP displaced the Liberals as the official opposition. The Liberal Party returned from their historic lows in 2008 and 2011 to win a majority government in the 2015 election. The Conservative Party, meanwhile, formed the opposition, and the NDP was relegated to third place.

This chapter is divided into four main sections: the historical evolution of Canadian political parties, interpretations of the Canadian party system, party ideology, and party organization. Party and electoral finance were examined in Chapter 13, and the role of parties in the electoral campaign, including electoral behaviour and party support, is discussed in Chapter 15.

THEORETICAL CONSIDERATIONS

A **political party** can be defined as an organized group that nominates candidates and contests elections in order to influence the personnel and policy of government. Parties are distinct from other groups in society in two main ways. First, whereas interest groups generally possess a fairly narrow focus and articulate a single interest, political parties are usually broader in scope and seek to aggregate, combine, consolidate, or appeal to many different interests or demands. In the process, parties reduce these demands to a manageable quantity called "issues." In this way, political parties play a central role in structuring political disagreement and in drawing attention to some issues rather than to others—functions of political socialization, citizen education, and **agenda-setting**.

Second, while other groups provide "functional" representation—economic, occupational, cultural, religious, etc.—political parties are closely tied to the formal institutions of government, including the electoral system and Parliament, all of which are based on territorial representation.

Another function of political parties is to recruit decision makers, primarily by means of the electoral system. As their candidates, they usually choose people who have been party members for some time and who have been "groomed" or trained. The government party also appoints certain political officeholders, often from the ranks of its own supporters, a practice referred to as **political patronage**.

Parties are also integrally involved in the legislative and executive operations of government. The formal and informal procedures of the House of Commons and Senate are completely imbued with partisan considerations, especially in the party discipline they display, while the Canadian Cabinet tradition is that all ministers are drawn from a single party, even in a minority government situation, so that they will be able to come to agreement more easily on government policy.

Beyond this list of functions, parties may be engaged in formulating public policy. In theory, at least, each party develops a distinctive election platform; the successful party then proceeds to implement it, while the opposition parties continue to provide clear-cut policy alternatives. In reality, the policymaking role of political parties is often minimal: parties do not always provide policy alternatives to the electorate; governments frequently ignore their election platforms in office; and they often obtain policy ideas from other sources.[1]

Theoretical considerations about political parties also centre on different kinds of parties. One way to categorize them is in terms of appeal. "Broker" or brokerage parties generally try to appeal to a wide range of interests in society in order to form a majority government based on a coalition of groups, but in the process relinquish any claim to a focused ideological approach. Ideological or "missionary" parties, on the other hand, try to cut through such divisions by emphasizing a central message, usually based on social class or a right- or left-wing ideology.

Parties can also be categorized in terms of organization. Run by a small group of notables, "cadre" parties are not particularly democratic in structure or operation. "Mass" parties, on the other hand, tend to promote a large membership with significant influence in the functioning of the party. It is often the case that broker and cadre categories overlap, as do the missionary and mass designations. Heather McIvor deems most of this terminology obsolete, at least in the Canadian case, and that our three main parties can all be called "electoralist," being essentially focused on winning elections. Even so, she distinguishes between "catch-all" parties (Liberals and Conservatives) that mainly want to maximize their votes, and "programmatic" parties (NDP and Bloc Québécois) that retain a somewhat ideological agenda.[2] Such issues of ideology and organization will be examined later in the chapter.

HISTORICAL EVOLUTION OF CANADIAN PARTIES

At this point, a brief discussion of the historical evolution of the Canadian political party system may be useful. Ken Carty suggests dividing this evolution into four parts, or four party systems; these can be distinguished by the number of parties in contention and their different approaches to seeking election, and can be structured around a list of prime ministers, their parties, and their dates of office.[3]

The First Party System, 1867–1921

From 1867 to 1921, the Conservative and Liberal parties virtually monopolized Canadian politics. David Smith points out that successful party leaders, such as John A. Macdonald and Wilfrid Laurier, sponsored great national projects on the one hand while being masters of detailed constituency and patronage politics on the other.[4]

PRIME MINISTERS, 1867–1921

JOHN A. MACDONALD	CONSERVATIVE	1867–73
ALEXANDER MACKENZIE	LIBERAL	1873–78
JOHN A. MACDONALD	CONSERVATIVE	1878–91
JOHN ABBOTT	CONSERVATIVE	1891–92
JOHN THOMPSON	CONSERVATIVE	1892–94
MACKENZIE BOWELL	CONSERVATIVE	1894–96
CHARLES TUPPER	CONSERVATIVE	1896
WILFRID LAURIER	LIBERAL	1896–1911
ROBERT BORDEN	CONSERVATIVE	1911–20
ARTHUR MEIGHEN	CONSERVATIVE	1920–21

The Conservative Party is usually said to have had its beginnings in 1854 when John A. Macdonald formed a coalition of four pre-Confederation groupings: Tories and Moderates from Upper Canada (Ontario), along with English businessmen and French Conservatives from Lower Canada (Quebec). Party lines for individual politicians were quite flexible in those days, and many MPs were called "ministerialists" because of their promise to support the ministry of the day in return for government favours. Alliances among groups were also unstable, but Macdonald's coalition gradually melded into an organized political party. The two main groups left out of this coalition—the French radicals in Quebec and the Clear Grits from Upper Canada—later became the nucleus around which the Liberal party took form.

After Macdonald was disgraced by the Pacific scandal, the Liberals took office between 1873 and 1878 under Alexander Mackenzie, but his government reflected this early lack of

Wilfrid Laurier, Canada's first French-Canadian prime minister.

cohesion. Macdonald returned to power in 1878 and the Conservatives demonstrated increasing party unity as time went on. After the execution of Louis Riel, however, French-Canadian support started to fall away from the Conservative Party, helped by the fact that an attractive francophone, Wilfrid Laurier, soon became leader of the Liberal Party. Macdonald died in 1891, and his party experienced a period of great instability as it went through four leaders in the subsequent five years. Thus, with the government party in decline and the Liberals finally showing the marks of a well-organized national party, it is not surprising that Laurier won the watershed election of 1896.[5] At that time Canada moved from Conservative **one-party dominance** to a classic **two-party system** in which Liberals and Conservatives competed on equal terms. Thus, the "first party system" can be subdivided into two parts, before and after 1896.

Laurier governed quite successfully until he was beaten in 1911, when the two main issues were reciprocity (free trade with the United States) and the naval question (whether Canada should establish its own navy or contribute to that of Britain). Robert Borden's Conservatives took over and were soon confronted with the monumental task of managing Canada's war effort. After three years of war, Borden concluded that conscription would have to be adopted, but, conscious of French-Canadian opposition, he proposed a coalition government with Laurier, who still led the Opposition Liberals. Most English-speaking Liberal MPs agreed to join the Conservatives in a **Union Government** in 1917, but Laurier and the French-Canadian Liberals remained in opposition, leaving that party badly split. With conscription, the Conservatives almost totally alienated French Canada, at the same time as the policies of both Conservative and Liberal parties upset the farming community in English Canada, notably the West. Thus, while Mackenzie King succeeded Laurier as Liberal leader in 1919 and skillfully pursued party reconciliation, Arthur Meighen inherited an unpopular Conservative Party in 1920 when he took over from Borden.

The Second Party System, 1921–1957

The 1921 election marked the end of the two-party system in Canada; from that point onward, there were always other parties in contention, leading to the label **two-plus** or **two-and-a-half party system**, at least until 1980. Moreover, in this period dominated by Mackenzie King and Louis St. Laurent, the Liberal government was characterized by decentralized ministerial accommodation in which strong regional Cabinet ministers exercised a great deal of individual power and then spoke for their regions in the development of a national consensus.

PRIME MINISTERS, 1921–1957

MACKENZIE KING	LIBERAL	1921–26
ARTHUR MEIGHEN	CONSERVATIVE	1926
MACKENZIE KING	LIBERAL	1926–30
R.B. BENNETT	CONSERVATIVE	1930–35
MACKENZIE KING	LIBERAL	1935–48
LOUIS ST. LAURENT	LIBERAL	1948–57

In 1921, farmers entered the contest with their own Progressive candidates and elected more members than the Conservatives,[6] while two Labour members were also successful. Farmers were particularly unhappy with conscription, tariff, agricultural, and transportation policies, as well as prevailing political practices, such as party patronage and rigid party discipline in the House of Commons. Nevertheless, Mackenzie King led his Liberals to victory in 1921, in 1925, and again in 1926 (after a brief Conservative interruption caused by the King–Byng dispute discussed in Chapter 21), and by the late 1920s most of the Progressive MPs either had become Liberals or had been defeated. A few of the more radical farmers joined with the Labour members to form the Ginger Group in Parliament, while the Liberals were defeated in 1930, primarily because of the onset of the Great Depression.

By this time the Conservatives were led by R.B. Bennett. Although he exercised vigorous leadership and even departed from orthodox Conservative policy to some extent, Bennett could not cope with the unemployment, poverty, and general devastation wrought by the Depression. Along with almost every other government in office during this period, Bennett's Conservatives were defeated in 1935, and Mackenzie King's Liberals returned to power.

Besides contributing to this change of government, the Depression was the catalyst for the creation of several new political parties, and marks the division between two parts of the "second party system." The Co-operative Commonwealth Federation (CCF) was formed in Calgary in 1932, an amalgam of the parliamentary Ginger Group, the intellectual League for Social Reconstruction (largely centred in Toronto and Montreal), and various farmer and labour groups and scattered socialist and farmer–labour parties, primarily from the West. In 1933 the party adopted its radical platform, the Regina Manifesto, at its meeting in that city, and chose Labour MP J.S. Woodsworth as its leader. The party elected several MPs in 1935 and took office in Saskatchewan in 1944 under T.C. (Tommy) Douglas.[7]

The Social Credit Party was born in Alberta in 1935 around the charismatic evangelist William Aberhart. The party was originally concerned with the reform of the banking system as a means of dealing with the Depression but abandoned this platform when it proved to be both unworkable and unconstitutional. After Alberta became prosperous with the discovery of oil in the 1940s, Social Credit transformed itself into an orthodox conservative party under E.C. Manning. The party remained in power in Alberta for 36 years, came to power in British Columbia in 1952, and elected several Western MPs.[8]

In Quebec, a group of disgruntled progressive Liberals defected from their provincial party in 1935 to join forces with the chronically unsuccessful provincial Conservative Party in the formation of the new Union Nationale. The leader, Maurice Duplessis, quickly discarded the comprehensive reform program on which the party was elected a year later and became ultra-conservative. Despite this shift in emphasis, the Union Nationale remained in power in Quebec until 1960 with only a four-year interruption between 1940 and 1944.[9]

None of these developments impeded the Liberal Party at the federal level; it continued to elect majority governments from 1935 to 1948 under Mackenzie King and then, until 1957, under his successor, Louis St. Laurent. King's conciliatory skills were severely tested during the Second World War (1939–45), but his government avoided a serious second **conscription crisis**. He also presided over the initiation of the Canadian welfare state. The St. Laurent period was one of great prosperity, largely financed by a tremendous inflow of American investment.[10]

The Conservative Party floundered for 20 years after 1935, having previously alienated French Canada and having been blamed, however unfairly, for the Depression. It changed leaders repeatedly, changed party policy to some extent, and changed the party name to Progressive Conservative in 1942, all to no avail.

The Third Party System, 1957–1993

The Liberal dominance was at least temporarily halted in the 1957 election. The next 35 years was a period of alternating minority and majority governments, Progressive Conservative and Liberal. David Smith contends that the Diefenbaker and Trudeau eras were marked by a more pan-Canadian approach, as each leader had a vision of the national interest that he sought to impose. In this period as well, television linked individual voters to these leaders without the need for regional intermediaries. Some of these characteristics might also be applied to the Mulroney era. From 1957 to 1980, the system was marked by two major parties and two minor parties.

PRIME MINISTERS, 1957–1993

JOHN DIEFENBAKER	PROGRESSIVE CONSERVATIVE	1957–63
LESTER B. PEARSON	LIBERAL	1963–68
PIERRE ELLIOTT TRUDEAU	LIBERAL	1968–79
JOE CLARK	PROGRESSIVE CONSERVATIVE	1979–80
PIERRE ELLIOTT TRUDEAU	LIBERAL	1980–84
JOHN TURNER	LIBERAL	1984
BRIAN MULRONEY	PROGRESSIVE CONSERVATIVE	1984–93
KIM CAMPBELL	PROGRESSIVE CONSERVATIVE	1993

John Diefenbaker became Conservative Party leader in 1956 and led the party to a surprising minority government victory a year later and then to a record majority in 1958. This was partly due to the public's increasing resentment of Liberal complacency and arrogance, as demonstrated in the infamous **pipeline debate**. Diefenbaker's decline was almost as rapid as his ascent, however, as his government fell apart over defence policy. The party was reduced to a minority government position again in 1962, and defeated a year later, after which it engaged in a long period of bitter in-fighting over the leadership question.[11]

During the Diefenbaker period, significant developments in two minor parties took place. The CCF, which had seen its fortunes decline throughout the 1950s, decided to combine its efforts with those of the new national labour organization, the Canadian Labour Congress. The result was the creation of the New Democratic Party (NDP) in 1961. T.C. Douglas was persuaded to leave the premiership of Saskatchewan to become the first national NDP leader.[12] Then, out of the blue, a group of Social Credit or Créditiste MPs was elected from Quebec in 1962, just when the western wing of the party was starting to decline.[13]

Lester Pearson's Liberals were elected in 1963 and re-elected in 1965, but were never able to win a majority government. Nonetheless, in spite of his minority status, Pearson tackled many controversial issues, particularly the new nationalism in Quebec, the Canada Pension Plan, medicare, and a new flag. One opposition party or another supported each of Pearson's measures so that he was able to continue in office until he retired.[14]

In 1968, the Liberals gained a majority government under their new leader, Pierre Elliott Trudeau, but just narrowly defeated Robert Stanfield's Conservatives in 1972. In the resulting minority government, the Liberals worked closely with the NDP, but this support was withdrawn two years later. With Trudeau ridiculing Stanfield's proposal for wage and price controls, the Liberals were returned with a majority in 1974, only to turn around and implement such a policy themselves. By 1979, the Liberals had apparently accumulated other faults as well, for they were defeated by the Conservatives, now led by Joe Clark. Nine months later, the Clark government fell with parliamentary rejection of its budget, and Trudeau led his party back to power in early 1980.[15]

The 1980s can be considered the second part of the third party system and even labelled a **three-party system** because, at least between elections, the NDP became entrenched as a national party. At the same time, the separatist Parti Québécois formed the government of Quebec between 1976 and 1985 under René Lévesque. After persuading Quebeckers to give Canada one last chance in their 1980 referendum, Trudeau patriated the Constitution, together with a **Charter of Rights and Freedoms**, and enacted the controversial **National Energy Program**.[16] He resigned in 1984, turning the reins over to John Turner, who was pitted against the new Conservative leader, Brian Mulroney. In the 1984 election, the Conservatives won a landslide victory, including a startling majority of the seats in Mulroney's home province of Quebec.[17] After the negotiation of the **Canada–U.S. Free Trade Agreement** and the **Meech Lake Accord**, Mulroney led his party to a second successive majority government in 1988, only to see Meech Lake fail to acquire the unanimous approval of new provincial governments in 1990. A second attempt at comprehensive constitutional reform, the **Charlottetown Accord**, failed in a national referendum in 1992.

The Fourth Party System, 1993–2015

The Liberal Party's obsession with Quebec was the main reason that the West preferred the Conservatives after 1957. When Westerners perceived that the Mulroney Conservatives were likewise concerned primarily with holding on to their unprecedented Quebec support after 1984, however, many residents turned to support the new Reform Party headed by Preston

Manning, son of the former Social Credit premier of Alberta. Then, with the collapse of the Meech Lake Accord, sovereignist sentiment increased in Quebec, and several Conservative and Liberal MPs defected to form a new federal separatist party, the Bloc Québécois. Thus, five parties of considerable strength contested the 1993 federal election, and produced a highly unusual result: the Liberals did well across the country, the Bloc Québécois displaced the Conservatives in Quebec, and the Reform Party routed the Conservatives in the West. The PCs held on to 16 percent of the popular vote but retained only two seats, and the NDP did badly everywhere. Given that a minimum of 12 seats is required for official party standing in the House of Commons, only three parties came back as recognized parties, two of them new, and it seemed that a real and regionalized **multi-party system** had developed.[18] In the 1997 election, the PCs and NDP regained some ground and the House of Commons found itself with five official parties.

PRIME MINISTERS, 1993–

JEAN CHRÉTIEN	LIBERAL	1993–2003
PAUL MARTIN	LIBERAL	2003–06
STEPHEN HARPER	CONSERVATIVE	2006–2015
JUSTIN TRUDEAU	LIBERAL	2015–

Given the fact that the Reform Party did not substantially increase its support in Ontario or the five easternmost provinces in the 1997 federal election, Manning began to promote the idea of a "United Alternative." He primarily hoped to attract the remaining supporters of the PC Party to join in a new right-wing party. In January 2000, the Reform Party transformed itself into the Canadian Reform Conservative Alliance, known as the Canadian Alliance, but most Progressive Conservatives steadfastly refused to join. Former Alberta provincial treasurer Stockwell Day then beat Manning for the leadership of the new party in July 2000.[19] The 2000 election also returned five official parties, all with regionalized support; the Liberals won another majority government and the Canadian Alliance formed the official Opposition. But after much internal criticism of Alliance leader Stockwell Day, he was replaced by Stephen Harper in 2002, while Joe Clark became leader of the Progressive Conservatives for the second time.

Paul Martin became Liberal leader in 2003, while Peter MacKay replaced Clark as leader of the PCs. MacKay then agreed to a merger of the PC and Alliance parties to "unite the right" in the new Conservative Party of Canada. The MacKay–Harper pact was promptly supported by a majority of the members of each party in hastily arranged votes, although many PC members, including Clark, refused to join, and the new combined party chose Harper as its leader in March 2004.

Between 1993 and 2011, the Bloc Québécois held more than 40 percent of the voter support in Quebec, significantly reducing the traditional Liberal dominance of the province. Indeed, when some 50 Quebec seats were automatically siphoned off by the Bloc, it was difficult for any party to win a majority in the rest of Canada. Thus Canada witnessed only minority governments between 2004 and 2011. The Liberals and Conservatives were clearly the major parties, while the Bloc and NDP were significant minor players. It was Harper's Conservatives,

BOX 14.1   EVOLUTION OF CANADIAN PARTY SYSTEM BY ERA

Era	Major Parties	Minor Parties	Label
1867–96	Conservative	Liberal	One-party dominance
1896–1921	Liberal, Conservative		Two-party system
1921–35	Liberal, Conservative	Progressives	Two-plus party system
1935–57	Liberal	Conservative, CCF Social Credit	One-party dominance
1957–80	Liberal, Conservative	CCF/NDP, Social Credit	Two-plus-two party system
1980–93	Liberal, Conservative, NDP		Three-party system
1993–2003	Liberal	Reform (Canadian Alliance), NDP, Conservative, Bloc Québécois	Multi-party system
2003–2015	Liberal, Conservative	Bloc Québécois, NDP	Two-plus-two party system

however, that formed a minority government after the 2006 election.[20] The 2008 election gave the Conservatives another minority, but in 2011, they gained a majority, with 166 seats. Jack Layton led the NDP to second place with 103 seats, having made a major breakthrough in Quebec primarily at the expense of the BQ, while the Liberals fell to a record low of only 34 seats. In 2015, however, the Liberals surged back to power, winning 184 of the now 338 seats in the House. The Conservative party, with 99 seats, formed the official opposition. The NDP, with just 48 seats, was reduced once again to third-party status.

The whole evolution of the Canadian party system, together with sub-eras, can be summarized as in Box 14.1. A recent analysis of this same evolution has been made in terms of "dynasties" and "interludes." The five principal dynasties were the long periods of dominance by Mackenzie King and Louis St. Laurent, Lester Pearson and Pierre Trudeau, John A. Macdonald, Wilfrid Laurier, and Jean Chrétien and Paul Martin. Most of the other sub-eras were mere interludes. The longstanding dynasties were marked by three keys to victory: public trust in their management of the economy, the national unity file, and the welfare state.[21]

INTERPRETATIONS OF THE CANADIAN PARTY SYSTEM

Faced with the rather unusual party system—or succession of party systems—just outlined, several political scientists have proposed theories or interpretations in order to explain them. Some of these theoretical considerations were mentioned at the beginning of the chapter, especially the distinction between broker and ideological parties.

Library and Archives Canada/C-027645

Mackenzie King, the longest-serving prime minister, thwarted class politics with his successful pursuit of brokerage politics.

The Broker System

The most traditional explanation of Canadian political parties is the **broker or brokerage** theory.[22] The essence of this interpretation is that, given the multiple cleavages in Canadian society and the function of parties to aggregate interests, political parties in Canada should be conciliators, mediators, or brokers among the cleavages already identified—that is, regions, ethnic and linguistic groups, genders, classes, religions, ages, and urban and rural locations. The theory suggests that maximizing their appeal to all such groups is not only the best way for parties to gain power, but, in the fragmented Canadian society, is also necessary in order to keep the country together. Thus, in their search for power, parties should act as agents of national integration and attempt to reconcile as many divergent interests as possible.

The interests to which parties give most attention are presumably those of greatest concern to the voters, reflecting their personal identities. In the past, religion was often prominent, while gender and age are emerging as increasingly important in the future. Throughout most of Canadian history, however, the two overriding cleavages or identities that have concerned people as well as parties were those of region and ethnicity. Although the class cleavage is the central focus of politics elsewhere, it has usually attracted little attention in Canada, and the broker theory emphasizes the middle-class consciousness of most Canadians. The broker theory can thus be seen to argue that the Liberal and Conservative parties have no basic ideological orientation and merely promise to satisfy the most important concerns felt by the voters at any point in time. Alternatively, they can be said to disguise their real ideological interests—protecting the capitalist system—by emphasizing ethnic and regional identities instead of class interests. In any case, ideological differences between these two parties are not profound. Defenders of the broker system argue that parties should not foment artificial class conflicts and ideological differences in a country that is already seriously divided: they should bring people together rather than drive them apart.

However appealing the broker system may appear, its negative implications should not be overlooked. By concentrating on regional and ethnic cleavages, parties minimize the role of ideology in Canadian politics. Parties are opportunistic and pragmatic rather than offering the electorate a choice of principled, distinctive programs. Parties do not generate innovative policy approaches but are content instead to respond to public opinion polls and advocacy group demands. What parties offer to the electorate in the place of a choice of solutions to national problems are alternative slogans and leaders, the latter especially important in a television age.

Ideological or Class-Based Parties

A second perspective on the Canadian party system, and a reaction to the broker approach, is the concept of **ideological or class-based parties**.[23] Like the broker model, this theory is partly an explanation of the existing system, but when it comes to prescribing an ideal situation it rejects the national status quo. Class-based analysts expect that in the pre-democratic period, two parties will develop, both of which defend the capitalist system. When the vote is extended to the working class, however, a new left-wing, working-class party will emerge that displaces one of the existing parties, generally forcing politics to take on an ideological and class-based character. This evolution clearly occurred in Britain, for example, and can also be seen to some extent in the United States.

When the vote was extended to the working class in Canada at the turn of the 20th century, some isolated labour, socialist, and communist political activity occurred, and by 1920 new class-based, ideological farmer and labour parties existed. But the newly enfranchised working class did not manage to create a successful class-based party, as the Liberals and Conservatives did everything in their power to discourage such a development, by using both seductive and coercive techniques.

Mackenzie King introduced policy innovations to attract farmer and labour voters and co-opted leaders of both farmer and labour movements into the Liberal Cabinet, while the Conservatives used force to quell the 1919 Winnipeg General Strike and the 1935 On-to-Ottawa Trek of the unemployed.[24] Eventually, the farmers' intense interest in politics declined, and the working class continued to support the two old-line parties on ethnic/religious and regional grounds, rendered content by the occasional piece of social legislation.

The Depression represented the collapse of the capitalist system and, as might have been expected, gave rise to new ideological parties. Of these, the CCF became the most sustained working-class party, but most members of that class continued to support the two traditional parties. Although unionization expanded significantly in the 1940s, the CCF's success was impeded by the Liberal Party's exploitation of divisions within the working class,[25] and by extremist anti-CCF propaganda sponsored by the business community. The CCF achieved its highest popular standing in the 1943–45 period, after which Liberal welfare initiatives helped to draw off working-class support. As mentioned, this decline led to the creation of the NDP in 1961 as a marriage of the CCF and the CLC, but even with the NDP's organic link to the labour movement, most working-class Canadians continued to vote Liberal or Conservative.

Explanations for the lack of class-consciousness among the Canadian working class were noted in Chapter 8.[26] As mentioned there, the Liberals and Conservatives were well established when the vote was extended to the working class, and they continued to define politics in non-class terms, either appealing to ethnic/religious and regional groups or else developing pan-Canadian appeals that diverted attention from class-based issues. These parties persuaded most voters that they belonged to the middle class and gave them the impression of inclusion

Why the Green and Marijuana Parties remain minor parties.

and social mobility. At the same time, the upper and middle classes were always conscious of their own class position and voted accordingly.

Advocates of a class-based party system claim that it would provide ideological alternatives in elections that would make them more meaningful. Moreover, the broker system, with its emphasis on multiple cleavages, is dangerously destabilizing. If the Liberals and Conservatives are unsuccessful as brokers, an ethnic–regional unit can threaten to separate. In such circumstances, class could be the integrating ingredient: "A nation like Canada, which is in danger of falling apart on ethnic-regional lines, may be held together by a politics which unites the people of various regions and ethnic groups around the two poles of left and right."[27] Canadians would ideally be united by their common class position into two national class-based, somewhat ideologically polarized parties. Moreover, it is said that class-based politics and parties are already the norm in Western Canadian provincial politics, so that this theory is quite a realistic proposition after all. Many observers see an increasing left/right ideological divide between the main parties, while more brokerage-oriented politics falters.

PARTY IDEOLOGY

Some observers have concluded that no basic ideological differences exist between the Liberal and Conservative parties:[28] either they are both pure broker parties with no ideology, responding pragmatically and opportunistically to public opinion polls in the pursuit of power, or else they are equally committed to the capitalist system but prepared to remedy its worst faults to maintain popular support. An alternative, more comprehensive and theoretical perspective that includes the NDP in the analysis, is that genuine ideological differences do exist in Canada and that such ideologies as **liberalism**, **conservatism**, and **social democracy** can be found to differentiate Canadian parties. The ideological continuum can be sketched in diagrammatic form, as in Figure 14.1. This perspective is sometimes called the fragment theory, as mentioned in Chapter 11.[29] It suggests that the basic ideology in Canada is liberalism, but that traces of

FIGURE 14.1   THE IDEOLOGICAL CONTINUUM IN CANADA

	LEFT	CENTRE	RIGHT	
Collectivism				Individualism
	NDP	Liberal Party	Conservative Party	
Egalitarianism				Inequality

socialism and conservatism also exist, and that each of the ideologies is more or less represented by a corresponding party. Such liberalism seeks to liberate the individual and maximize each individual's freedom and potential, something that almost all Canadians would support. Differences emerge, however, about who should be liberated, about what the inhibiting agent is, and about how to go about such liberation, primarily focusing on the role of the state.

Conservatism seeks to liberate the individual from the restrictions of the state. Reducing the role of the state to a minimum and allowing private market forces to determine the distribution of power and wealth is often labelled **individualism**. Minimizing the tax burden on individuals is a key priority, but conservatism also advocates little government regulation and ownership, and leaving people to fend for themselves instead of being supported by public social programs. Conservatives do not cherish inequality, but if such policies result in inequalities or elitism, they are generally unconcerned; inequalities are both natural and deserved—some people are better and some work harder than others. These attitudes are labelled as being on the **right**. Historically, those who took this position were found primarily in the Conservative Party, and an even more extreme faction became the core of the Reform Party, and later the Canadian Alliance.

Social democracy, conversely, seeks to liberate the individual from the inequalities and exploitation of the capitalist system. It believes in **egalitarianism**, and it prescribes a large element of state action or **collectivism** in order to achieve such liberation and equality. These views are generally referred to as being on the **left**. In particular, this ideology emphasizes government planning, regulation, ownership of some of the major industries of the country, progressive taxation, and redistribution of income through social programs. Adherents are sometimes subdivided between "democratic socialists" and "social democrats," depending on the extent to which they want the state to intervene and the extent of equality they want to effect. The early CCF was certainly more socialistic than the current New Democratic Party, with the latter's majority being of the social democratic persuasion. The CCF/NDP take credit for introducing public health insurance when they formed the government of Saskatchewan, pressing for other social welfare programs, advocating a more progressive taxation system, creating a variety of Crown corporations in the provinces where they held power, and supporting the creation of several such government bodies in Ottawa.

Liberalism, almost by default, falls between the other two ideologies. In fact, it has a dual personality and can be subdivided into "welfare" and "business" variants. Business liberals believe that the state inhibits individual self-fulfillment and that its role should be minimized so that individualism can prevail. Welfare liberals, conversely, take the view that the state can be a positive agent in liberating individuals from the constraints of other forces including the private-enterprise economy. Liberals therefore stand for a combination of individualism and collectivism and a combination of equality and inequality, which they usually label "equality of opportunity." Being composed of business and welfare liberals, the Liberal party is located in the centre of the Canadian ideological continuum. Although Liberals obviously hold private market forces in greater esteem than does the NDP, Liberal governments introduced old age pensions, family allowances, and many other social welfare programs over the years. Under bureaucratic influence, the Liberals brought **Keynesian economics** to Canada, and the CCF/NDP and Liberals both claim credit for the development of the Canadian **welfare state**. Historians generally point out that the Liberal Party made an ideological shift about 1919 from a business-liberal to a welfare-liberal orientation, although some observers saw a shift backward after 1993.

To complicate the picture to some extent, a second wing of the former Progressive Conservative Party was the "progressive" element, people who were sometimes called **Red Tories**. These conservatives combined beliefs in privilege and collectivism, seeing society as an organic whole, emphasizing community values as well as individualism, and standing for order, tradition, stability, and noblesse oblige. They believed in hierarchy, in which everyone should occupy his or her place, but they also had a paternalistic concern with the condition of all the people. This aspect of conservatism is not unique to Canada, being found quite commonly in Britain and the rest of Europe; it stands out only in contrast to a lack of such sentiment within American conservatism. Thus, the ideology of the Progressive Conservative Party was not clear-cut; it was somewhat divided, just as in the case of the other two parties. Pre-Mulroney Conservatives sometimes exhibited a strong red tory touch, such as in the creation of the RCMP, **CBC**, CNR, the **Canadian Wheat Board**, and the **National Energy Board**, in the Bennett New Deal, and in the Stanfield proposal for **wage and price controls**. It was sometimes difficult to distinguish among social democrats, welfare liberals, and Red Tories, and some New Democrats felt closer to Red Tories than to certain Liberals.[30]

Historically, there was so much overlap in the ideological orientation of the Liberal and Conservative parties in particular that it is sometimes difficult to detect the distinctions made above, and political scientists often asked the question: "Does party matter?"[31] Indeed, from about 1945 to 1980 the Liberal and Conservative parties shared a basic ideological approach that emphasized economic growth based on foreign investment, expansion of the welfare state, and engagement in a certain amount of macroeconomic government regulation.[32] As time went on, however, this consensus broke down. Thus, especially after the Conservatives took office in 1984, policy and ideological differences between the two parties were more obvious, with the Mulroney government pursuing a business-liberal agenda in which renewed reliance was placed on market forces—privatization, deregulation, deficit reduction, and cutting social programs—and the extent of government intervention was actually reduced. In other words, conservatism up to this point had upheld the status quo and simply opposed further change, but the new brand of conservatism wanted to turn the clock back and "dismantle the state" to some degree.[33]

Indeed, after 1985, the whole ideological spectrum shifted to the right. For the first time in Canadian history, social programs were cut back rather than expanded; Crown corporations were privatized rather than created; taxes were cut rather than raised; regulations were repealed rather than promulgated; public debts and deficits were reduced rather than increased; and public servants were fired rather than hired. The phenomenon went beyond one or two parties; it happened around the world, and in Canada it affected governing parties of all ideological persuasions in the 1990s: the NDP, especially in Saskatchewan; the Parti Québécois; and Liberal governments in several provinces and in Ottawa.

The Reform Party was very much part of this shift to the right; it exerted great influence at both federal and provincial levels; and Reform-minded Conservative parties were elected in Alberta and Ontario. Their actions were all consistent with a belief in individualism and lacked the collectivist value,[34] representing a new philosophy of government often called **neoliberalism** or **neoconservatism**. Although the two terms are often used to mean the same thing, a distinction can be made between them. Both advocate that government withdraw from economic policy, but sometimes neoconservatism is taken to mean a belief in a strong state that can promote certain traditional social values and regulate social behaviour. Neoconservatives were "social conservatives" who opposed abortion, public child care, gay rights, same-sex marriage, and employment equity. The Reform Party and the Canadian Alliance contained both neoliberals and neoconservatives, and were a particular magnet for social conservatives.[35]

It should be added that the Reform Party/Alliance had two other main concerns. First, it believed in populism—that is, it was against elitism and professed to value the wisdom of ordinary people. To some extent this is also an Americanism as opposed to the traditional Canadian belief in British parliamentary democracy. The second was a territorial focus—that the West was getting short-changed within Confederation.

It seemed logical to Reform party leader Preston Manning to engineer some kind of merger of right-wing forces in the country, but many observers believed that there was more of an ideological divide between the two parties than met the eye. Tory leader Joe Clark declined the invitation, and PC conventions in 1999 and 2002 supported his position. As mentioned, it was left to two new leaders—Stephen Harper of the Alliance and Peter MacKay of the PCs—to engineer a "reuniting of the right" in December 2003, to be called the Conservative Party of Canada with Harper as its new leader. Although Joe Clark and many other "progressive" Conservatives were offended by the new party's right-wing tendencies, its policies were generally more moderate than those of the Reform/Alliance. In April 2005, for example, Harper repudiated a proposal from Preston Manning and Mike Harris that Ottawa should repeal the Canada Health Act. Few observers believed that Harper had truly changed his values, but he and others at least realized that they had been out of touch with a majority of Canadians. Alexandra Dobrowolsky emphasizes the policy convergence of Canadian parties in recent years, which reflects a new centrist consensus. Many signs indicated that while Harper was moving to the centre from the right, Jack Layton's NDP was also moderating from the left.[36]

At a policy convention in November 2008, Stephen Harper urged the delegates to take a pragmatic, less ideological approach to the issues under discussion, although many right-wing resolutions were adopted. Then, as the economic situation became a crisis, the government introduced a budget in January 2009 that provided for a deficit of some $64 billion over the next two years. Although virtually all countries were engaged in the same massive deficit-stimulus policy, many Canadian Conservatives were alarmed at this sudden change in ideological direction, and *Maclean's* magazine proclaimed "the end of Canadian Conservatism." The 2012 budget—the first under a Harper majority government—proposed to cut program spending by $5.2 billion a year for three years, and to raise the retirement age from 65 to 67. These were conservative policies to be sure, but the cuts were not as severe as in the 1995 federal budget which was introduced by a Liberal government. On the other hand, the government slipped many other right-wing measures into the omnibus budget implementation bill, a sign that with his majority, Harper was willing to become increasingly conservative.

Protecting the environment has now become one of the leading issues on the political agenda. While all parties have outlined approaches to dealing with this problem, the Green, Bloc, NDP, and Liberal plans all involve greater government intervention, including the taxation of carbon, placing ceilings on emissions, and ensuring effective environmental assessments of new projects. Thus, to a large extent, environmental protection falls on the left side of the ideological spectrum.[38] The Conservatives, especially with their majority, significantly reduced the federal government's role in environmental protection, partly by minimizing assessment processes and partly by delegating much of the policy field to the provinces.

PARTY ORGANIZATION

A political party has been defined as an organized group, but the structure of such a group requires clarification. One main component of the party is the **parliamentary party** or **party caucus**—that is, the party's elected representatives in Parliament. Here we are more concerned with the **extra-parliamentary party** organization made up of party activists and executive members, the party headquarters or staff, and ordinary party members. The principal aspects of party organization that bear examination are party membership, party leadership selection and review, party policymaking, and general structures and operations. Party and election finance were discussed in Chapter 13.

Party Membership

While large segments of the Canadian population identify with a political party, much as people identify with sports teams, all accounts of formal party membership in Canada find that it represents a very small proportion of the population—probably in the range of under two percent.[39] Within each party people join for a variety of reasons,[40] having different ideas about how the party should operate and what kinds of policies it should pursue. Some people, "office-seekers," join because they want the prestige and benefits associated with obtaining elected office. Others join because they want to influence party policies or help the party to pursue them. These people are known as "benefits-seekers" or "policy-seekers." Finally, some people join parties for the fun of it, because they like associating with other people, or because their friends belong to the party. They are drawn to political party for its "solidary benefits."[41]

Political parties depend enormously on this small group of rank-and-file members to donate their time and money for the operation of the party. Party members volunteer to canvass door-to-door during election campaigns; they run local constituency organizations; they attend policy and leadership conventions; and sometimes they even become party candidates. In the 2011 federal election, for example, rank-and-file members of the NDP were asked to stand for office in some Quebec constituencies where the party was having a hard time finding a local candidate. The NDP did not plan to win in these constituencies, but wanted to have candidates in every riding, even if they knew they were going to lose. After the NDP's unprecedented success in Quebec, however, many of these volunteers—some of whom had never visited their constituency—found themselves elected to Ottawa! Political scientists and others who see the need for strong political parties in a democracy regret the weakness of party membership in Canada. Parties should be more than electoral machines, but even in that function, technology cannot do everything; a party can only be successful if it has a substantial membership base.

Party Leadership

Since the leader is such a dominant presence in any political party, it is important to examine how parties choose such leaders. The Liberals relied on the parliamentary party to select its leaders before 1919 and the Conservatives did so until 1927, but both parties then moved to choose their leaders at national delegate conventions.[42] The years and winners of party leadership contests are contained in Table 14.1.

An even more democratic procedure than the leadership convention has been used in recent years—sometimes every card-carrying member of the party has been allowed to cast a vote for the leadership, called "one member-one vote" or OMOV. Such a procedure avoids much of the cost of holding a national convention, eliminates the unholy fight among various candidates for delegates at the constituency level, ensures that the decision is not left to the more affluent members of the party who can afford the travel costs, and removes the circus atmosphere of the convention. The Parti Québécois was the first party to move to such an OMOV leadership selection process, and many other provincial party leaders have now been elected on this basis. Party members can vote by phone, by mail, online, or by casting their ballot at the local level. Such procedures have potential problems of their own, however, including technological breakdowns, an unrepresentative electorate, and the involvement of voters who have no knowledge of the candidates or who actually support other parties. Many partisans also feel that the loss of the publicity value of a nationally televised convention is too high a cost, and suggest that by imposing spending limits on candidates and subsidizing delegates' expenses some of the worst features of conventions can be avoided.

Despite the advantages of a full-fledged convention, all parties have been influenced by the pressure for more popular participation in the leadership selection process. The Liberal Party

TABLE 14.1 DATES OF ELECTION OF MAJOR PARTY LEADERS

LIBERAL	CONSERVATIVE	CCF/NDP
1919 MACKENZIE KING	1927 R.B. BENNETT	1932 J.S. WOODSWORTH
1948 LOUIS ST. LAURENT	1938 ROBERT MANION	1942 M.J. COLDWELL
1958 LESTER B. PEARSON	1942 JOHN BRACKEN	1960 HAZEN ARGUE
1968 PIERRE E. TRUDEAU	1948 GEORGE DREW	1961 T.C. DOUGLAS
1984 JOHN TURNER	1956 JOHN DIEFENBAKER	1971 DAVID LEWIS
1990 JEAN CHRÉTIEN	1967 ROBERT STANFIELD	1975 ED BROADBENT
2003 PAUL MARTIN	1976 JOE CLARK	1989 AUDREYMCLAUGHLIN
2006 STÉPHANE DION	1983 BRIAN MULRONEY	1995 ALEXA MCDONOUGH
2008 MICHAEL IGNATIEFF	1993 KIM CAMPBELL	2003 JACK LAYTON
2013 JUSTIN TRUDEAU	1995 JEAN CHAREST	2012 THOMAS MULCAIR
	1998 JOE CLARK	
	2003 PETER MACKAY	
	2004 STEPHEN HARPER	
REFORM/CANADIAN ALLIANCE		**BLOC QUÉBÉCOIS**
1991 PRESTON MANNING		1990 LUCIEN BOUCHARD
2000 STOCKWELL DAY		1997 GILLES DUCEPPE
2002 STEPHEN HARPER		2011 DANIEL PAILLÉ

adopted a new system in 1992 which combined giving every party member a vote with having a leadership convention. Each member voted on the leadership candidates, as well as for delegates, and the latter were elected in proportion to the popular vote received by each leadership candidate at the local level. Once they got beyond the first ballot at the convention, however, such delegates could use their own judgment. In 2006, Stéphane Dion was in third place on the first ballot and then engineered alliances to win on the fourth.[43] After the "emergency" selection of Michael Ignatieff in late 2008, the Liberals adopted the OMOV system in May 2009 for the choice of leaders in the future. For the 2013 contest, they also allowed party "supporters" who were not actual members to vote.

The PC Party put its new leadership selection process into play in 1998. It gave each member of the party a vote but weighted these votes so that each constituency had equal power, regardless of the size of its membership, and in choosing Stephen Harper in 2004, the new Conservative Party employed the same system. In 2003, the NDP allowed all members to vote for leader and had a small convention to celebrate the occasion. When Jack Layton died, the party conducted a long leadership campaign which culminated in a convention attended by about 4000 members, while thousands of other party members voted by mail or online.

CRITICAL APPROACHES

Political parties play a pivotal role in *political psychology* and *behaviour approaches*. Parties serve as a reference point to which individuals in the electorate orient themselves politically. People develop psychological attachments to parties—they come to cheer for their party's leaders and support their party's policies, much as one might support a local sports team. The concept of partisanship—a cognitive and affective attachment to a political party—is perhaps the central concept in the study of political behaviour.

In its 2013 leadership race, the Liberal party expanded voting privileges to a class of non-members, which they called "party supporters." This reflected the party's effort to stem its declining membership numbers and to reach out, in particular, to young people. Unlike members, who have to pay a small fee in order to acquire and maintain their membership status, this new class of party supporters merely had to pledge that they supported the party and were not members of any other party. The Liberals used a preferential ballot and single transferable voting system whereby party members and supporters ranked the candidates in order of preference. If no candidate was ranked first by a sufficiently large number of voters, the candidate with the fewest votes was dropped from the list and the second preferences of the lowest candidate's supporters were then reallocated among the remaining candidates. This process would continue until one candidate passed the threshold required for victory. Justin Trudeau won handily on the first ballot.

Most parties also have **leadership review** mechanisms in their constitutions, although these vary in detail. The NDP used to open nominations for the position of leader at each national convention, so the leader could be immediately replaced. Nowadays, however, the party only has a vote on whether it should hold a leadership convention.

As a result of the civil war within the party over John Diefenbaker's leadership between 1962 and 1967, the PC party added a

THE CANADIAN PRESS/Frank Gunn

Thomas Mulcair wins the NDP leadership on March 24, 2012.

leadership review provision to their constitution in 1974. It consisted of a vote at a convention on the question "Are you in favour of holding a leadership convention?" It was first invoked after the defeat of Joe Clark's government in 1981. Two years later, an almost identical 67 percent opposed a leadership convention, but Clark decided this degree of support was insufficient, so he resigned. Although he ran to succeed himself in the subsequent leadership race, he was defeated by Brian Mulroney. At the same time, the leadership review mechanism was changed: the question was put only at the first convention following an election that the party lost, a provision included in the constitution of the new Conservative Party.

The Liberals added a leadership review clause in 1966 to the effect that at the first convention after each election (win or lose), delegates vote on whether they want to have a leadership convention. When it appeared that Jean Chrétien would lose the vote scheduled for February 2003, he announced his retirement in advance and was spared such a leadership review. Paul Martin declared his intention to step down immediately after the electoral defeat of January 2006, and when Stéphane Dion led the Liberal party to defeat in 2008, he was forced to resign almost immediately—even before a leadership review. The party executive opted to consult only the caucus, defeated candidates, and party officials in choosing Michael Ignatieff to replace him until his leadership was merely confirmed by the party convention. When Ignatieff did poorly in the 2011 election, he resigned; the party elite chose Bob Rae as interim leader, pending a convention in 2013.

Party Policymaking

All political parties have difficulty designing their policymaking processes. On the one hand, some people join a party with the aim of contributing to party policy, but on the other, politicians do not want to be saddled with unrealistic policy commitments. Thus, all parties struggle to combine these two forces—policy-seeking and office-seeking—in the most appropriate way, and membership input is usually the loser. Even more striking is that most parties put very little effort at all into policy research.

Liberal and Conservative national conventions or general meetings usually include a policy session and sometimes focus primarily on policy. But even if specific resolutions are debated and passed, which is not always the case, party leaders retain the right to determine official party policy. Although parliamentary leaders may be influenced by such discussions to some extent, they are in no way bound by the policy resolutions of the party organization.

The Liberal Party did not even hold a national convention between 1919 and 1948, and instead mainly relied on the public service for policy advice. When the Liberals found themselves in opposition after 1957, and cut off from the public service, Lester Pearson was forced to turn to the party organization to help develop new policy proposals. He convened a famous thinkers' conference in Kingston in 1960, followed by a party conference that debated the ideas brought forward. Once in power after 1963, the Pearson government quickly implemented most of the policies that the party had adopted. Under Pierre Trudeau, the party held several more party policy conferences, but did not pay much attention to the results.[44] Jean Chrétien tried to replicate the successful early 1960s experience with a policy conference in 1991, followed by a party convention a year later. The Red Book used as the party platform in the 1993 election drew substantially on these two party meetings. The Liberals did not have another serious discussion of policy within the party until after Paul Martin's defeat in 2006, but the ensuing leadership instability eclipsed any serious discussion of party policy.

The Conservatives discussed policy to some extent at their many leadership conventions. But after the 1956 convention, John Diefenbaker attempted to destroy all evidence of its policy proposals. When Robert Stanfield became leader, he was anxious to develop a stronger policy orientation and encouraged policy discussions within the party. As prime minister, Brian Mulroney relied primarily on the public service, royal commissions, backroom advisers, and public opinion polls for policy guidance. The new Conservative Party held a policy convention in March 2005, and after several heated debates, adopted a 50-page Policy Declaration which generally reflected a compromise between the previous Canadian Alliance and PC positions. This document was helpful in designing the party's 2006 election platform, but thereafter, the leader felt little constraint from policy resolutions adopted by party conventions.

The NDP has always claimed to be particularly distinctive in the realm of party policy-making. It has regular policy sessions every two years, which are indeed the predominant item on the convention agenda. Constituency associations are invited to submit resolutions in advance, and resolutions passed by the convention are considered to be official and binding on the leader and the parliamentary party. The party's executive and council are allowed to submit resolutions of their own, however, and the council, which is subject to greater leadership manipulation than the convention, has the authority to "flesh out" the meaning of policies adopted. If the NDP policymaking process is now less distinctive from other parties, this party still gives greater priority to policy debate and takes more seriously the resolutions passed.

Given that the generation of policy is one of the weakest aspects of party operations in Canada, many recommendations have been made for reform. The Royal Commission on Electoral Reform and Party Financing, for example, strongly urged parties to establish foundations that would engage in serious policy research, whether or not their ideas were subject to approval of grassroots party members. Bill Cross comes to the same conclusion:

> Parliamentary parties in both government and opposition would benefit from serious study undertaken by their extraparliamentary parties toward providing policy alternatives and guidance to the parliamentary parties. Such activity would serve to encourage those Canadians with policy concerns to participate in party activity rather than looking to interest groups as a way to influence public policy. A beneficial side effect might also be a weakening of the growing concentration of government-party decision making within the prime minister's office.[45]

General Structures and Operations

Conventions

All parties have constitutions that outline their objectives, structures, and procedures. In theory, at least, the ultimate authority in each party is the party convention, which all parties now hold quite regularly at an average of about two-year intervals. The convention agenda normally includes the election of the party executive, constitutional amendments, policy discussions, and instruction in local election organization, but such conventions also serve important social and morale-building purposes. In the Liberal and Conservative parties, each constituency association is entitled to an equal number of delegates, while in the NDP representation is based on the size of the local membership. All parties include certain ex-officio delegates, such as MPs, and, in some cases MPPs, MLAs, and nominated or recently defeated candidates. Both the Liberals and the NDP have tried to become more inclusive and representative with an array of women's, youth, campus, Aboriginal, ethnocultural, and other associated groups. The NDP has maintained an organic link to trade unions since it was formed in 1961, giving them a distinct position in many aspects of party organization. But this connection has weakened in recent years, partly because of the reforms to party and finance legislation, as mentioned in Chapter 13.[46]

Party Executive

Each party has a national executive, including a president, vice-presidents, treasurer, and so on, and each establishes a number of executive committees. These officials usually perform such duties on a part-time basis, although it is helpful for the president to be close to Ottawa and readily available for meetings, campaign organization, and other functions. Both the Liberals and the Conservatives have sometimes elected a senator as party president, since such a person has considerable free time and is on the public payroll, saving the party the cost of a presidential salary. The party president usually has the confidence of the leader, and the contest for the presidency is sometimes a surrogate vote on the leadership.

Party Headquarters

The three main national parties maintain a headquarters office in Ottawa, which is staffed by permanent party employees and headed by the national director. These chief executive officers maintain close relations with the leader and caucus, and, in the case of the party in power, the Prime Minister's Office (PMO). In each case, the size of the party staff varies considerably, depending on the state of party finances and the imminence of an election, and the PC and NDP offices were temporarily but dramatically scaled down after the 1993 election. The role of party headquarters during election campaigns is outlined in Chapter 15. Between elections, headquarters perform a variety of functions, such as collecting money, ensuring local organizations are alive and well, arranging for speakers at local annual meetings, planning conventions, publishing newsletters, maintaining a website, conducting surveys, and researching policy.

The Iron Law of Oligarchy

To complete the analysis of party organization, the relationships among the party membership, the executive, the parliamentary caucus, and the party leadership should be examined. Robert Michels claimed that a tendency toward elitism is inevitable within all organizations, including political parties, giving rise to his famous **iron law of oligarchy**.[47] Even in parties that seek or profess to operate democratically, a small elite invariably develops such that rank-and-file party members have little real power. As organizations grow and attract more members, according to Michels, they become so complicated that the only people capable of understanding them are the people who work full time within them. The rank-and-file "amateur" members become dependent on full-time officials for information about the party, thus enhancing the officials' power. Similarly, a small group of executive members often seek re-election for many terms, and use their experience, access to party information, connections, control of party funds, and influence over party policy to do so. Member apathy is also a factor, for the great bulk of party members are inactive and quite happy to have a handful of activists take charge.

Moreover, whether or not in government, party leaders have a tendency to create a small coterie of advisers who cut the leader off from party influence. This was particularly so in the Liberal Party during the tenure of Pierre Elliott Trudeau. As party leader, Trudeau virtually ignored the party organization, paying little attention to its policy-generation efforts, its increasing debt, and its cynical electoral strategies. In fact, he left almost all party and electoral matters in the hands of people who held no official position in the Liberal Party. Beyond Trudeau, a great deal of control generally comes to reside with the leader and the surrounding personal advisers, professional consultants, pollsters, political strategists, and media and advertising experts.

Another common development is that the parliamentary wing of the party claims precedence over the extra-parliamentary party organization. In terms of policy, for example, when a party has official status in the House of Commons, it is entitled to hire a substantial number of researchers. Even in Opposition, the complement of publicly paid staff supporting the leader, caucus, and individual MPs clearly outnumbers the staff at party headquarters and may prescribe different policy approaches than come out of party policy discussions. Moreover, when a party forms the government, it has the entire public service to advise it, and may find that the world looks somewhat different from the position of public responsibility than from the Opposition benches. Caucus members are usually more concerned about getting re-elected than are policy-oriented party members, and may thus seek to tone down certain ideas emanating from the grassroots of the party.

The Law of Cuvilinear Disparity

A related influential law of political party organization was proposed by political scientist John May.[48] According to May, the members of political parties can be divided into three groups; the high-status party elite, including government executives, legislators, and candidates for office; the intermediate-status "sub-leaders" comprised of convention delegates, members of constituency associations, local organizers, and hardcore partisans in the electorate; and the low-status non-elite—that is, party supporters in the electorate.

May argues that the vast majority of the population is not ideologically motivated and is relatively indifferent toward politics. Such people are unlikely to get involved in a political party; they are therefore members of the electorate, but not of a party. Other people, however, are very ideological, and join political parties in order to follow their ideological convictions. Ideologues are not only more likely to join parties, but, because they do, they are also likely to surround themselves with other people who think the same way, thus reinforcing their original ideological commitment. Finally, the people at the very top of political party organizations are professionals that have been recruited from the upper echelons of society, and who are primarily concerned with keeping their jobs. Unlike party activists, party leaders also interact on a daily basis with leaders from other parties, people who are likely to have different points of view about politics. These people are likely to say and do what is necessary in order to win elections.

As a result of these characteristics of organizational membership, a pattern emerges whereby the lowest and highest echelons of political parties advocate moderate and non-ideological positions—the lowest echelons because they are largely non-ideological, and the upper echelons because they want to win elections and need the support of regular voters in order to do so. The middle echelon, however—the sub-leaders—are composed of activists committed to certain core ideological principles. In left-wing parties these activists are likely to be strongly left-wing, and in right-wing parties they are likely to be strongly right-wing. Hence the law of curvilinear disparity: according to May, mid-level party activists tend to be ideological policy-seekers, whereas the party's professional elite and the haphazard non-elites in the electorate tend to be more moderate and pragmatic.

Federal–Provincial Party Links

The federal nature of Canada creates two levels of government at which political parties seek to influence policy and personnel, raising the question of the relationship between national and provincial party organizations.[49] To oversimplify the situation, the Conservative Party could be said to have a "confederal" character—that is, the federal and provincial Conservative parties are essentially independent of each other and always have been. There is virtually no formal organizational or financial link between the two wings of the party, and the provincial wing is nonexistent in British Columbia, Saskatchewan, and Quebec. Thus, federal and provincial party memberships are separate, and a complete set of federal riding associations and executives coexists with provincial party organizations at the grassroots level. Now, of course, the federal party has a different name (Conservative Party of Canada) from the Progressive Conservative parties at the provincial level.

By contrast, the NDP could be called an "integrated" party except in Quebec. Most people join the NDP at the provincial level and automatically become members of the national party, but similarly, those who initially join the federal party become instantaneous members of the provincial party. Provincial offices of the party theoretically serve the needs of both wings of the party, and a provincial convention may also deal with federal matters from its own perspective. In addition, federal organizers work out of provincial offices in the pre-election period and the provincial party headquarters devotes its full attention to the federal election campaign once it is called. The two levels of the party are also integrated financially. The 1995 Renewal Convention sought to give the federal party a more stand-alone presence, such that revenue sharing is less important, and 75 percent of the federal council is elected at the federal convention of the party rather than at provincial conventions.

The Liberal Party is characterized by two different federal–provincial relationships. In Quebec and the four western provinces, the party is split into federal and provincial wings, each of which has separate finances, memberships, constituency associations, executives, conventions, and offices. The Liberal party also has separate wings in Ontario, although the membership and constituency associations tend to overlap considerably, largely because provincial and federal electoral districts coincide, making it easy for the two levels of the party to coordinate their efforts.[50] The other provinces have a joint Liberal Party, although such an integrated relationship probably gives the party a provincial orientation. In these provinces, it is possible to join the federal party directly, but it is more common to join the provincial party and become an automatic member of the federal organization. The Liberals made constitutional changes in 2006 to strengthen the federal wing of the party, but the lack of a national membership list continued to hamper their fundraising efforts.

The Yukon legislature operates with political parties, and the territorial Liberals and NDP are each connected to their respective national parties. The Northwest Territories and Nunavut are characterized by nonpartisan, consensus government and do not have parties at the territorial level. Nevertheless, all three national parties have small organizations in each of the territories for federal political purposes.

Federal–Local Party Links: The Franchise Model

Besides the federal–provincial links within a political party, the relationship between the federal party and its local constituency associations should be mentioned, especially the "franchise model" pioneered by Ken Carty. It is based on the idea that Canadian parties are large national competitive organizations that have local branches or franchises that respond to the distinctiveness of their immediate environments, somewhat akin to Canadian Tire or McDonald's. As in the case of the private sector models, each organizational element of the party has its respective functions and not all local constituency associations operate exactly alike:

> Their central organizations are typically responsible for providing the basic product line—policy and leadership; for devising and directing the major communication line and appeal—the national campaign; and for establishing standard organizational management, training, and financing functions.… Local units … provide the basic organizational home for most individual members, and are normally charged with delivering the product by creating organizations that can find and support candidates, as well as mounting campaigns to mobilize the vote on election day.[51]

This model has implications for all of the organizational questions considered above, including party membership, leadership, and policymaking, as well as for candidate selection and electoral effort as discussed in Chapter 15.

CONCLUSION

However much Canadians tire of their endless bickering and lack of inspiration, political parties perform several crucial functions in the political system. In particular, they sort out the political issues and, in trying to bridge some of the many Canadian cleavages, make the political system more manageable. Many political observers are concerned about the danger of major political parties being outflanked by single-issue groups, whether as advocacy groups during and between election campaigns or as single-interest parties, in the representation of political interests and as the focus of political activity. Such scholars argue that steps must be taken to strengthen mainline parties so that they can overcome their current lack of organizational depth and their weak membership base, and enhance their capacity to perform their representational and policymaking functions. Perhaps Canadians expect too much of their parties and place on them too much of the burden of keeping the country together. Perhaps parties do not perform their functions well and are also dysfunctional in some respects. Perhaps their functions and methods of operation are in a state of change. But they must not be allowed to deteriorate further.

While parties are mentioned with enormous frequency throughout the book, they figure most prominently in the preceding and following chapters on elections and election campaigns. They are also the essential determinant for the operation of the House of Commons.

DISCUSSION QUESTIONS

1. Why are political parties so prominent at the federal and provincial levels of government in Canada and so insignificant at the municipal level in most cases?

2. What historical events, political personalities, or other factors have been determining influences in the evolution of the Canadian party system?

3. Given the negative implications of the broker system, do you feel it would be advantageous to move to a class-based, ideological system? Why or why not?

4. Is there a distinctive ideological base for the major parties in Canada? Is the new Conservative Party a broker or an ideological party?

5. What is the best method of choosing party leaders and the best approach to leadership accountability?

6. Is it possible in this complex, technological, information-driven age for ordinary party members to make useful policy suggestions for national policies, or is it inevitable that the policymaking function be turned over to party leaders and their advisers, bureaucrats, and advocacy groups? Would party foundations help?

MindTap® FOR MORE INFO GO TO **http://www.nelson.com/student**

NOTES

1. William Cross, *Political Parties* (Vancouver: UBC Press, 2004).
2. Heather MacIvor, *Parameters of Power: Canada's Political Institutions*, 5th ed. (Toronto: Nelson Education, 2010), pp. 367–78; David McGrange, "Political Marketing and the NDP's Historic Breakthrough," in Jon H. Pammett and Christopher Dornan, eds., *The Canadian Federal Election of 2011* (Toronto: Dundurn, 2011), pp. 79 and 93.
3. R.K. Carty, "Three Party Systems: An Interpretation of the Development of National Politics," in Hugh G. Thorburn and Alan Whitehorn, eds., *Party Politics in Canada*, 8th ed. (Scarborough: Prentice Hall Canada, 2001).
4. David E. Smith, "Canadian Political Parties and National Integration," in Alain Gagnon and Brian Tanguay, eds., *Canadian Parties in Transition*, 2nd ed. (Scarborough: Nelson Canada, 1996). Carty and Smith divide the periods in the same way but use different criteria. See also Gagnon and Tanguay, *Canadian Parties in Transition*, 3rd ed. (Peterborough: Broadview Press, 2007).
5. J. Murray Beck, *Pendulum of Power* (Scarborough: Prentice Hall Canada, 1968); and John Duffy, *Fights of Our Lives: Elections, Leadership and the Making of Canada* (Toronto: HarperCollins, 2002).
6. W.L. Morton, *The Progressive Party in Canada* (Toronto: University of Toronto Press, 1950).
7. Walter Young, *Anatomy of a Party: The National CCF 1932–1961* (Toronto: University of Toronto Press, 1969); Walter Young, *Democracy and Discontent* (Toronto: Ryerson Press, 1969); and S.M. Lipset, *Agrarian Socialism: The Cooperative Commonwealth Federation in Saskatchewan* (Los Angeles: University of California Press, 1950).
8. Alvin Finkel, *The Social Credit Phenomenon in Alberta* (Toronto: University of Toronto Press, 1989).
9. H.F. Quinn, *The Union Nationale* (Toronto: University of Toronto Press, 1963).
10. Reginald Whitaker, *The Government Party: Organizing and Financing the Liberal Party of Canada 1930–58* (Toronto: University of Toronto Press, 1977).

11. J.L. Granatstein, *The Politics of Survival: The Conservative Party of Canada, 1939–1945* (Toronto: University of Toronto Press, 1967); and George Perlin, *The Tory Syndrome: Leadership Politics in the Progressive Conservative Party* (Montreal: McGill-Queen's University Press, 1980).

12. Maurice Pinard, *The Rise of a Third Party: A Study in Crisis Politics* (Scarborough: Prentice Hall Canada, 1971); and Michael Stein, *The Dynamics of Right-Wing Protest: A Political Analysis of Social Credit in Quebec* (Toronto: University of Toronto Press, 1973).

13. Peter C. Newman, *The Distemper of Our Times* (Toronto: McClelland and Stewart, 1968); and Andrew Cohen, *Lester B. Pearson* (Toronto: Penguin Canada, 2008).

14. Jeffrey Simpson, *Discipline of Power: The Conservative Interlude and the Liberal Restoration* (Toronto: Personal Library, 1980).

15. Christina McCall-Newman, *Grits: An Intimate Portrait of the Liberal Party* (Toronto: Macmillan, 1982); and Stephen Clarkson and Christina McCall, *Trudeau and Our Times*, 2 vols. (Toronto: McClelland and Stewart, 1990 and 1994).

16. Alan Frizzell and Anthony Westell, eds. *The Canadian General Election of 1984* (Ottawa: Carleton University Press, 1985); and Graham Fraser, *Playing for Keeps* (Toronto: McClelland and Stewart, 1989).

17. R. Kenneth Carty, William Cross, and Lisa Young, "Building a Fourth Canadian Party System," in Thorburn and Whitehorn, eds., *Party Politics in Canada*; Alan Cairns, "An Election to Be Remembered: Canada 1993," *Canadian Public Policy* (September, 1994); Alan Frizzell, Jon H. Pammett, and Anthony Westell, *The Canadian General Election of 1993* (Ottawa: Carleton University Press, 1994); and R. Kenneth Carty, William Cross, and Lisa Young, *Rebuilding Canadian Party Politics* (Vancouver: UBC Press, 2000).

18. Faron Ellis, "The More Things Change … The Alliance Campaign," in Jon H. Pammett and Christopher Dornan, eds., *The Canadian General Election of 2000* (Toronto: Dundurn, 2001).

19. Tom Flanagan, *Harper's Team: Behind the Scenes in the Conservative Rise to Power* (Montreal: McGill-Queen's University Press, 2007).

20. Lawrence LeDuc, Jon H. Pammett, Judith I. McKenzie, and André Turcotte, *Dynasties and Interludes: Past and Present in Canadian Electoral Politics* (Toronto: Dundurn, 2010); Elisabeth Gidengil, et al., *Dominance and Decline: Making Sense of Recent Canadian Elections* (Toronto: University of Toronto Press, 2012).

21. H.G. Thorburn, "Interpretations of the Canadian Party System," in H.G. Thorburn, ed., *Party Politics in Canada*, 6th ed. (Scarborough: Prentice Hall Canada, 1991); Matthew Mendelsohn, "Four Dimensions of Political Culture in Canada Outside Quebec: The Changing Nature of Brokerage and the Definition of the Canadian Nation," in Hamish Telford and Harvey Lazar, eds., *Canada: The State of the Federation 2001* (Kingston: Institute of Intergovernmental Relations, 2002); and Anthony Sayers, "The End of Brokerage? The Canadian Party System in the 21st Century," in Michael Whittington and Glen Williams, eds., *Canadian Politics in the 21st Century*, 7th ed. (Toronto: Thomson Nelson, 2008).

22. Janine Brodie and Jane Jenson, *Crisis, Challenge and Change: Party and Class in Canada Revisited* (Ottawa: Carleton University Press, 1988); Charles Taylor, *The Pattern of Politics* (Toronto: McClelland and Stewart, 1970); and Gad Horowitz, "Toward the Democratic Class Struggle," in Trevor Lloyd and Jack McLeod, eds., *Agenda 1970* (Toronto: University of Toronto Press, 1968).

23. On seduction, see Whitaker, *The Government Party*, for example, the co-opting of Saskatchewan farm leader C.A. Dunning and Humphrey Mitchell from the labour movement; on coercion, see Judy Torrance, *Public Violence in Canada* (Montreal: McGill-Queen's University Press, 1986).

24. The Liberals actually welcomed communist support if such working-class divisions would weaken the CCF. Gad Horowitz, *Canadian Labour in Politics* (Toronto: University of Toronto Press, 1968).

25. Jon Pammett, "Class Voting and Class Consciousness in Canada," *Canadian Review of Sociology and Anthropology* 24, no. 2 (1987); Keith Archer, "The Failure of the New Democratic Party: Unions, Unionists, and Politics in Canada," *Canadian Journal of Political Science* (June 1985); Michael Ornstein, H. Michael Stevenson; A. Paul Williams, "Region, Class and Political Culture in Canada," *Canadian Journal of Political Science* (June 1980); and Elisabeth Gidengil, "Class and Region in Canadian Voting: A Dependency Interpretation," *Canadian Journal of Political Science* (September 1989).

26. Horowitz, "Toward the Democratic Class Struggle," p. 254.

27. Conrad Winn and John McMenemy, *Political Parties in Canada* (Toronto: McGraw-Hill Ryerson, 1976), pp. 4–5.

28. Louis Hartz, *The Founding of New Societies* (New York: Harcourt, Brace and World, 1964); Gad Horowitz, "Conservatism, Liberalism and Socialism in Canada: An Interpretation," *Canadian Journal of Economics and Political Science* (May 1966); Gad Horowitz, "Notes on 'Conservatism, Liberalism and Socialism in Canada,'" *Canadian Journal of Political Science* (June 1978); William Christian and Colin Campbell, *Political Parties and Ideologies in Canada*, 3rd ed. (Toronto: McGraw-Hill Ryerson, 1990); and William Christian and Colin Campbell, *Parties, Leaders, and Ideologies in Canada* (Toronto: McGraw-Hill Ryerson, 1996).

29. Neil Nevitte, Herman Bakvis, and Roger Gibbins, "The Ideological Contours of 'New Politics' in Canada: Policy, Mobilization and Partisan Support," *Canadian Journal of Political Science* (September 1989).

30. James McAllister, "Do Parties Make a Difference?" in Gagnon and Tanguay, eds., *Canadian Parties in Transition*; Winn and McMenemy, *Political Parties in Canada*.

31. Duncan Cameron, "Political Discourse in the Eighties," in Gagnon and Tanguay, eds., *Canadian Parties in Transition*; and Michael Ornstein and H. Michael Stevenson, *Politics and Ideology in Canada* (Montreal: McGill-Queen's University Press, 1999).

32. Walter Stewart, *Dismantling the State* (Toronto: Stoddart, 1998); and Stephen McBride and John Shields, *Dismantling a Nation: The Transition to Corporate Rule in Canada* (Halifax: Fernwood Publishing, 1997).

33. Brooke Jeffrey, *Hard Right Turn: The New Face of Neo-Conservatism in Canada* (Toronto: HarperCollins, 1999); and Trevor Harrison, *Of Passionate Intensity: Right-Wing Populism and the Reform Party of Canada* (Toronto: University of Toronto Press, 1995).

34. Trevor W. Harrison, "Populist and Conservative Christian Evangelical Movements: A Comparison of Canada and the United States," in Miriam Smith, ed., *Group Politics and Social Movements in Canada* (Peterborough: Broadview Press, 2008).

35. Alexandra Dobrowolsky, "Political Parties: Teletubby Politics, The Third Way, and Democratic Challenge(r)s," in Michael Whittington and Glen Williams, eds., *Canadian Politics in the 21st Century*, 6th ed. (Toronto: Thomson Nelson, 2004); G. Bruce Doern, "The Harper Conservative Agenda: True Blue or Liberal-Lite?" in his *How Ottawa Spends 2006–2007* (Montreal: McGill-Queen's University Press, 2006). Conservative ideology in the 2011 election is discussed in Pammett and Dornan, *The Canadian Federal Election of 2011*, pp. 16 and 100, and especially in the chapter by Jim Farney and Jonathan Malloy, "Ideology and Discipline in the Conservative Party of Canada," while NDP ideology is addressed in David McGrane's chapter, pp. 78–82.

36. Cameron D. Anderson and Laura B. Stephenson, "Environmentalism and Party Support in Canada: Recent Trends outside Quebec," *Canadian Journal of Political Science* (June 2011).

37. Cross, *Political Parties*, Ch. 2; R. Kenneth Carty and Munroe Eagles, *Politics Is Local: National Politics at the Grassroots* (Toronto: Oxford University Press, 2005).

38. Anthony Downs, *An Economic Theory of Democracy* (New York: HarperCollins, 1957); Joseph A. Schlesinger, "On the Theory of Party Organization," *Journal of Politics* (May 1984); Peter C. Ordeshook, *A Political Theory Primer* (New York: Routledge, 1992).

39. James Q. Wilson, *Political Organizations* (New York, N.Y.: Basic Books, 1974); Donald Wittman, "Candidate Motivation: A Synthesis of Alternative Theories," *The American Political Science Review* 77, no. 1 (1983): 142–57.

40. William Cross and Lisa Young asked Canadian political party members about what they thought was the "best thing" about being a member of a political party. Of their 3 520 respondents, 42 percent answered that it was a way to support or influence the party's policies, but seven percent cited social reasons and another seven percent said that they wanted to be involved in party decision making. "Policy Attitudes of Party Members in Canada: Evidence of Ideological Politics," *Canadian Journal of Political Science* (December 2002).

41. John C. Courtney, *The Selection of National Party Leaders* (Toronto: Macmillan, 1973); John C. Courtney, *Do Conventions Matter? Choosing National Party Leaders in Canada* (Montreal: McGill-Queen's University Press, 1995); Cross, *Political Parties*, Ch. 5.

42. The 2006 Liberal convention is covered in articles in Institute for Research on Public Policy, *Policy Options* (February 2007).

43. Joseph Wearing, "Can an Old Dog Teach Itself New Tricks? The Liberal Party Attempts Reform," in Gagnon and Tanguay, eds., *Canadian Parties in Transition*.

44. Cross, *Political Parties*, p. 46; Irvin Studin, "Revisiting the Democratic Deficit: The Case of Political Party Think Tanks," Institute for Research on Public Policy, *Policy Options*, February 2008; Greg Flynn, "Rethinking Policy Capacity in Canada: The Role of Parties and Election Platforms in Government Policy-Making," *Canadian Public Administration* (June 2011).

45. Harold Jansen and Lisa Young, "Solidarity Forever? The NDP, Organized Labour, and the Changing Face of Party Finance in Canada," *Canadian Journal of Political Science* (September 2009).

46. Robert Michels, *Political Parties* (New York: Free Press, 1966).

47. John D. May, "Opinion Structure of Political Parties: The Special Law of Curvilinear Disparity," *Political Studies* 21, no. 2 (1972): 135–51.

48. Donald Smiley, *Canada in Question: Federalism in the Eighties*, 3rd ed. (Toronto: McGraw-Hill Ryerson, 1980); and Rand Dyck, "Relations between Federal and Provincial Parties," in Gagnon and Tanguay, eds., *Canadian Parties in Transition*, 2nd ed.

49. Royce Koop, *Grassroots Liberals: Organizing for Local and National Politics* (Vancouver: UBC Press, 2011).

50. Roland Kenneth Carty, "The Politics of Tecumseh Corners: Canadian Political Parties as Franchise Organizations," *Canadian Journal of Political Science* (December 2002).

51. Maurice Duverger, *Political Parties: Their Organization and Activity in the Modern State* (London: Methuen, 1964), p. 217.

FURTHER READING

Anderson, Cameron D., and Laura B. Stephenson. "Environmentalism and Party Support in Canada: Recent Trends outside Quebec," *Canadian Journal of Political Science* (June 2011).

Carty, R. Kenneth. *Canadian Political Party Systems*. Peterborough: Broadview Press, 1992.

———, William Cross, and Lisa Young. *Rebuilding Canadian Party Politics*. Vancouver: UBC Press, 2000.

Cross, William. *Political Parties*. Vancouver: UBC Press, 2004.

Flanagan, Tom. *Harper's Team: Behind the Scenes in the Conservative Rise to Power*. Montreal: McGill-Queen's University Press, 2007.

Gagnon, Alain-G. and A. Brian Tanguay, eds. *Canadian Parties in Transition*, 3rd ed. Peterborough: Broadview Press, 2007.

Gidengil, Elisabeth, et al. *Dominance and Decline: Making Sense of Recent Canadian Elections*. Toronto: University of Toronto Press, 2012.

Horowitz, Gad. "Conservatism, Liberalism and Socialism in Canada: An Interpretation," *Canadian Journal of Political Science* (May 1966).

Jansen, Harold, and Lisa Young, "Solidarity Forever? The NDP, Organized Labour, and the Changing Face of Party Finance in Canada," *Canadian Journal of Political Science* (September 2009).

Jeffrey, Brooke. *Hard Right Turn: The New Face of Neo-Conservatism in Canada*. Toronto: HarperCollins, 1999.

LeDuc Lawrence, Jon H. Pammett, Judith I. McKenzie, and André Turcotte. *Dynasties and Interludes: Past and Present in Canadian Electoral Politics*. Toronto: Dundurn, 2010.

Pammett, Jon H. and Christopher Dornan, eds., *The Canadian Federal Election of 2011*. Toronto: Dundurn, 2011.

Sayers, Anthony Sayers. "The End of Brokerage? The Canadian Party System in the 21st Century," in Michael Whittington and Glen Williams, eds., *Canadian Politics in the 21st Century*, 7th ed. Toronto: Thomson Nelson, 2008.

Thorburn, H.G., and Alan Whitehorn, eds. *Party Politics in Canada*, 8th ed. Toronto: Prentice Hall, 2001.

Sadeugra/iStock

CHAPTER 15

The Election Campaign, Voting, and Political Participation

Following 12 years of Liberal government, why were Stephen Harper's Conservatives elected in 2006? How did the Conservatives build support to form a majority in 2011, and how did the Liberals return from third party status to form their own majority in 2015? What are the components of a national election campaign? To what extent do the media coverage of the campaign and the leaders' debate influence the results? How are the campaigns of local candidates organized? What determines why and how people vote? What other kinds of political participation do Canadians engage in?

Elections are not only the most colourful and exciting element of the Canadian political system, but they are also in many ways the most important. Certain elections are great landmarks in a country's history and often change its course. Almost all the daily efforts of parties and politicians are ultimately geared toward maximizing their support in the next electoral contest. The election campaign constitutes the arena in which political parties, the mass media, public opinion polls, and political participation all come together to play their most extensive and interconnected role.

The official side of the electoral system was examined in Chapter 13. This chapter explores the more lively side of the campaign—that dominated by political parties, party leaders, candidates, the media, and public opinion polls. The chapter has four main parts: the national party campaign, the local candidate campaign, voting, and other forms of political participation.[1]

THE NATIONAL PARTY CAMPAIGN

Party Headquarters and Pre-Writ Preparations

At the national level, political parties begin thinking about the next election almost as soon as the last one is over. During the minority government period from 2004 to 2011, parties had to be election ready at all times and thus engaged in a "permanent campaign," but even though they had the luxury of a four-year gap after 2011, election planning never ceased. This planning entails setting up a national campaign committee, which ponders such matters as strategy, policy, image, and budget. Most federal parties also have campaign committees in each province, with varying degrees of centralization or decentralization of authority. Parties usually hire extra organizers in the pre-election period and deploy them to reactivate local associations. Funds permitting, party headquarters also conducts public opinion polls throughout the interelection period to see how the voters perceive the various leaders, parties, and issues. For the party in power, especially in a majority position, such polls used to be central to deciding when to call the election in the first place. In a minority government situation, the polls may be of even greater benefit to the opposition parties in deciding when to defeat the government.

Another party activity that begins before the calling of the election is the search for good candidates. This is essentially a task of the local party organizations, and the party headquarters rarely imposes a candidate on an unwilling constituency association. However, the leader, regional lieutenants, and party organizers are always on the lookout for new blood, and head office may try to parachute a few "star" candidates into safe seats. The Liberals, Conservatives, and NDP all run a full slate of candidates, so where local organizations are weak, the national party sometimes has to take the initiative to find a candidate for them, and in most cases engages in a serious vetting of local aspirants.[2]

National fundraising is another activity that goes on between elections, although it intensifies immediately before and during the election period. Chapter 13 noted that, since 2007, election financing laws ban donations from corporations and unions and now restrict individual donations to political parties to $1500 per year. The public **per-vote subsidy** for parties was phased out entirely by 2015.

Once the election is called, party headquarters continues to perform such activities as polling, fundraising, and candidate recruitment. Either before or immediately after the election call, headquarters also holds campaign colleges, schools, and seminars for candidates, campaign managers, and other local campaign officials. In addition, headquarters will design logos, other artwork, and leaflets that candidates can order or adapt for their own local purposes. Another headquarters activity is the preparation of draft issue letters and fact sheets for candidates to use, either in promoting their own party's platform or in attacking that of others. During the campaign, headquarters communicates with candidate campaigns on a daily basis to ensure uniformity of presentation, and to alert candidates to a change in course. As the campaign approaches, party headquarters is actually converted into a "war room," in which the expanded team of political strategists works around the clock, organizing the leader's tour and the media advertising, telephoning thousands of voters, helping local candidates with every imaginable kind of problem, generating as many political problems as they can for their opponents, and preparing responses to any negative media coverage that their party or leader receives.

The Conservative party put much effort in developing the Constituency Information Management System (CIMS), which is a massive database of millions of Canadian voters. Based on names and addresses from Elections Canada voters' lists and telephone numbers from phone directories, it includes information collected from phone calls and door-to-door canvassing by local volunteers, including each individual's degree of support for the party and policy issues of interest. The telemarketing company Responsive Marketing Group (RMG) is the key to collecting such voter-contact information, which, when matched with census data, could also show much about the voter's whole neighbourhood. The CIMS is important in the election campaign to seek out volunteers, identify potential supporters, deliver election messages, and get out the vote on election day. Between elections, it is also vital in fundraising efforts. Some critics believe that the system was also used in the robocall scandal in 2011 to dissuade Liberal supporters from voting. Other parties were slower in developing their databases.[3]

Election Strategy

Election strategy involves deciding which groups within the electorate are to be targeted; whether to emphasize the leader or issues, and, if the latter, which issues; and whether to mount an offensive or defensive campaign. To some extent, all parties divide the constituencies into three groups—safe, marginal, and unwinnable—and put their primary effort in the middle category. That includes designing the itinerary of the leader's tour and deciding where extra organizational efforts and financial contributions will be concentrated. Once the election is called, the national campaign committee discusses such things as "modification to the leader's tour, daily tracking of polling results, and focus group findings, carries out ongoing testing of campaign slogans and phrasing, determines the final changes of the ads and when to replace one round of ads with subsequent ones, and makes preparations for the leaders' debates."[4]

The Election Platform

In each election, political parties produce a document called a platform or a manifesto that features prominently the list of policies, promises, and priorities that they intend to implement if elected. One of the Liberals' great assets in the 1993 campaign, for example, was their "Red Book," *Creating Opportunity: The Liberal Plan for Canada*. To some extent the Red Book was based on a thinkers' conference in 1991 and policy debates at a party convention in 1992. Jean Chrétien claimed that, if elected, he would adhere to every word, and the book provided a tremendous prop for a leader who was otherwise not policy oriented in his public appearances.[5] The Liberals claimed by 1996 that they had implemented 78 percent of their promises, although conspicuously unfulfilled was their promise that was widely understood to mean they would get rid of the GST. By 2006, it was the Conservative platform that was most comprehensive and that attracted the most attention, and Stephen Harper chose to emphasize five major promises from the

Prime Minister Justin Trudeau celebrates the Liberal party victory in the 2015 federal election campaign.

NICHOLAS KAMM/AFP/Getty Images

platform in his campaign.[6] Confirming the observation that opposition parties often offer a more comprehensive electoral manifesto than the government, Stéphane Dion insisted that the Liberals focus on the Green Shift idea in 2008.

In the 2015 election, the Liberal Party released its platform entitled *A New Plan for a Strong Middle Class*, which laid out promises to cut middle class taxes, spend more on infrastructure and public transport (requiring budget deficits), and make Parliament more accountable. The Conservatives' *Protect Our Economy* focused heavily upon balanced budgets, tax cuts, and freer trade. The NDP's platform, entitled *Building the Country of Our Dreams* promised a universal childcare system and prescription drug program, alongside greater environmental protection and balanced budgets. The Green Party's *Building a Canada that Works. Together.* focused upon building an environmentally sustainable economy, abolishing post-secondary tuition, and strengthening food security and health care.

The Leader's Tour

The leader's tour consists of each party leader crisscrossing the country many times over the campaign period. Similar to a royal tour, party officials go ahead of the leader to make sure that every detail is in place. The leader is then accompanied by a horde of strategists and support staff, as well as by reporters who pay to travel aboard the party-chartered plane or bus. All this effort is expended not only to attract attention in the areas visited but also to generate national media coverage. Because this kind of coverage is free, in contrast to paid advertising, and because television news is very important in reaching voters, parties spare no trouble or expense to obtain it. To generate a successful leader's tour, according to Frizzell and Westell, parties

> should arrange events every day so that the TV crews, pressed by deadlines and demands from home stations for footage, will have little option but to picture the leader in a favourable setting … [and] ensure that in every speech or statement there is a phrase that sums up the message in a couple of seconds.[7]

An innovation began in 1997 where, instead of each network placing a complete crew of its own on each of the leader's tours, the five major television networks—CBC, CTV, Global, Radio-Canada, and TVA—pooled their resources and personnel on the party leaders' campaign planes and buses. Thanks to new communications technologies, from the 2000 election onwards, the team on each leader's tour has been more closely connected to the party's war room back in Ottawa. This allows each leader to react instantaneously to developments in the others' campaigns and publicize messages through various party-run communication outlets.

Media Coverage

As mentioned, parties hope that the leader's tour will garner them one positive story every day on the national television news and in daily newspapers; after all, Canadian television newscasts typically attract up to one million viewers nightly. While such coverage of the leader's tour is mutually advantageous to the parties and the television networks, some observers question how much value it provides to voters to see, newscast after newscast, the leaders repeating the same message to rousing applause at the designated stop of the day.[8]

Although Canada does not have the same 24-hour live television news cycle as the United States, political parties in this country have increasingly been drawn into this frenetic phenomenon. Unlike the old days, when reporters would prepare a story for the evening news and solicit the opinions from different sides, giving the parties involved an opportunity to influence the story, the rise of non-stop news coverage, especially on the Internet, means that political parties may not even hear about a story until they see it or read about it in the news. Time is of the essence. Letting one side of the story linger unchallenged for too long may result in it becoming the accepted wisdom about an issue. The war room must provide an instantaneous response, but sometimes the immediacy of the responses means that they are not always well thought out or vetted by the higher-ups on the campaign team. While it is difficult to know how big a difference it made in the election result, an image of a dead young Syrian refugee, Alan Kurdi, during the 2015 campaign created a media frenzy around Canada's policy on refugees, and many perceived the Conservative response on the issue as inadequate or even uncaring.

National Media Advertising

Each party turns its national paid media advertising over to one or more advertising agencies, along with at least some indication of the party's campaign strategy. As noted in Chapter 12, the most important part of the media campaign is television, and most parties spend huge amounts of money on the production of television commercials alone (increasingly these are circulated online and receive even larger audiences as a result, compared to print or radio advertising). Each party's advertisements vary across languages and from region to region, so great differences often exist in the messages voters receive. Nowadays, of course, parties increasingly also advertise on the Internet, and parties develop elaborate online strategies.

The purchase of broadcast time in the campaign period is regulated by the Elections Act. Representatives of registered parties meet with the Broadcasting Arbitrator before the election to try to agree on an allocation of commercial broadcasting time. If they cannot agree, the arbitrator decides on the allocation within the guidelines of the act. It requires each broadcaster to make available six and one-half hours of prime time for purchase during the campaign. Such an allocation among parties is primarily based on the number of seats held in the House of Commons and on popular vote received in the previous election. No party can receive more than one-half of the total time, but *candidates* are allowed to purchase time for their own use outside what is allotted to *parties*. Having been awarded more than twice as much time as the Liberals and three times as much as the NDP in 1988, the Conservatives were allowed to saturate the airwaves in the last week of the campaign. In addition to purchasable time, parties are awarded free radio and television time in the same proportions.

Many observers, including supporters of minor parties, considered the earlier distribution of paid and free broadcasting time to be extremely unfair, and in 1992, the Reform Party successfully challenged its original allotment for the forthcoming election in the courts. Since then, the Broadcasting Arbitrator uses discretion to increase the time of smaller parties. The results during the 2015 election for the larger parties are shown in Table 15.1.

TABLE 15.1 ALLOCATION OF BROADCASTING TIME, MAJOR PARTIES, 2015 ELECTION

POLITICAL PARTY	MINUTES:SECONDS
CONSERVATIVE PARTY OF CANADA	107:00
NEW DEMOCRATIC PARTY	78:30
LIBERAL PARTY OF CANADA	45:30
GREEN PARTY OF CANADA	20:30
BLOC QUÉBÉCOIS	16:30
MARXIST-LENINIST PARTY OF CANADA	9:30
CHRISTIAN HERITAGE PARTY OF CANADA	8:30
LIBERTARIAN PARTY OF CANADA	8:00
COMMUNIST PARTY OF CANADA	7:30
RHINOCEROS PARTY	7:30
CANADIAN ACTION PARTY	7:30
PIRATE PARTY OF CANADA	7:30
PROGRESSIVE CANADIAN PARTY	7:30
ANIMAL ALLIANCE ENVIRONMENT VOTERS PARTY OF CANADA	7:30
MARIJUANA PARTY	7:00
UNITED PARTY OF CANADA	7:00
PARTY FOR ACCOUNTABILITY, COMPETENCY AND TRANSPARENCY	7:00
SENIORS PARTY OF CANADA	6:00
DEMOCRATIC ADVANCEMENT PARTY OF CANADA	6:00
FORCES ET DÉMOCRATIE	6:00
CANADA PARTY	6:00
BRIDGE PARTY OF CANADA	6:00
TOTAL	**390:00**

Source: Elections Canada, 2015. "2015 Allocation of Paid Time," available at http://www.elections.ca/content .aspx?section=abo&dir=bra/all/2015&document=index&lang=e. Used with permission.

When the Reform Party case went to the Alberta Court of Appeal again in 1995, that court struck down the clause that prevented a party from purchasing more than its allocated time on any station. Thus, from 1997 onward, parties were allowed to purchase more time than allocated to them under the act, providing stations were willing to sell them such time and subject to the overall limits on each party's election expenses. The official allocation therefore became most significant as the basis for the distribution of free time for each party. Another court case effectively removed the blackout rules that prohibited *candidate* advertising on election day and the day before, although the decision left intact the prohibition on *party* advertising during the last 48 hours.[9]

Political campaign advertisements seek to make one's own party or leader look good; in this endeavour, however, one of the biggest obstacles that the party strategists confront is the strategists from the other parties. Elections are competitive enterprises; thus, the best efforts of a party to portray its agenda or its leader in a positive light are often accompanied by the concerted attempt of the other parties to do the opposite. Political advertisements that draw attention to the supposed flaws of another candidate or party are called "attack ads."

One of the most memorable negative commercials was run by the Progressive Conservatives in 1993. It featured Jean Chrétien's face (the left side slightly paralyzed from a childhood disease) with such voice-over comments as "I personally would be very embarrassed if he were to become prime minister of Canada." After an instantaneous public uproar, leader Kim Campbell had the commercial removed.[10] In the 2000, 2004, and 2006 elections Liberal Party advertisements portrayed Stockwell Day and then Stephen Harper as right-wing ideologues with a "hidden agenda" that they would implement if they were elected. In the 2008 election, the Conservative Party launched a series of viciously personal negative ads about Liberal leader Stéphane Dion, and in 2011, about Michael Ignatieff, including the "Just Visiting" ads which questioned the Liberal leader's loyalty to Canada.

Although negative ads are designed to suppress support for the candidate and party being attacked, the evidence is mixed about whether they actually accomplish this end.[11] Indeed, parties in Canada may have to be careful that they do not go too far and generate derision or ridicule for the party doing the attacking. However, it is possible, as Jonathan Rose argues, that negative advertising can have some benefits, if it (a) focuses upon policy issues, (b) provides evidence, (c) makes a distinction between party positions, and (d) is relevant to governing.[12]

Party advertising outside the campaign period is not regulated, and a party can purchase as many television advertisements as it can afford. Once regarded as wasted spending so far from the date of an actual election, such advertising is increasingly common. The Conservative party has engaged in massive attack ads in the inter-election period to pummel new Liberal leaders before they had a chance to define themselves.[13]

Political Marketing

In recent years, party advertising has morphed into the more general concept of "political marketing." It can be defined as

> a constant process involving gathering market intelligence through formal and informal means, developing party policies and a party brand, mobilizing party members, building relationships with stakeholders, positioning in relation to competing parties, targeting certain segments of voters, allocating scarce resources, and communicating a party's policy offerings through paid advertising and the management of news media.[14]

Although the Conservative party was the first in Canada to embrace this wider concept, the NDP under Jack Layton was close behind. As noted, political marketing is focused on developing a party brand and analyzing existing and potential markets for that brand, in much the same manner as marketing conducted for consumer products and services. Such branding often focuses upon people's emotions rather than reasoned thoughts about politics, and develops "niche" markets rather than aiming for a national policy consensus.[15]

Susan Delacourt demonstrates the new emphasis that political parties put on targeting specific segments of voters. With its massive collection of information on the identity of individual voters, the Conservative party is particularly well placed to engage in the practice of dividing the electorate into tiny slices or groups of customers, finding out what they want, and promising it to them. All of this is at the expense of offering broad policies in the public interest. She distinguishes between advertising and political marketing—the former consisting of promoting the party's own policies, while the latter seeks to discover what prospective supporters want and then shaping party policies around voter demand.

The Leaders' Debates

The televised leaders' debates are another main aspect of the national campaign.[16] These debates have been held in every election since 1968 except 1972, 1974, and 1980. Debates tend to benefit the opposition party leaders who might otherwise have difficulty obtaining coverage, but it would be virtually impossible for the incumbent prime minister to refuse such a debate anymore. Originally a byproduct of the influence of American presidential politics, the debates have become a crucial aspect of the campaign because of the combined importance of leaders and television (something Canadians also see instituted in parliamentary Question Period, as noted in Chapter 23).

The leaders' debates are not mentioned in either the Canada Elections Act or the television broadcasting regulations, and the consortium of television stations that carry them essentially set the rules. The recommendation of the **Royal Commission on Electoral Reform and Party Financing** that the debates become obligatory and regulated has not been implemented. In 1993, with a large number of parties in the race, the consortium agreed that only five parties would take part: those that were represented in Parliament and that had had a consistent impact in public debates and public opinion. The 1997 and 2000 debates also consisted of the leaders of the five largest parties, and those in 2004 and 2006 of only four. In 2008, Green Party leader Elizabeth May managed to get herself admitted to the leaders' debates at the last minute, but was not permitted to participate in the 2011 debate because her party had no seats in the House of Commons before the election.

In 2015, the Conservatives refused to participate in the consortium debates (though they later agreed to attend the consortium's French debate) and Canadians instead saw a greater variety of debates than had been the case in previous years. The first, which included the Conservatives, Liberals, NDP, and Green leaders, was hosted by *Maclean's* (Rogers Media). Another debate focusing on the economy was hosted by *The Globe and Mail*, and one focusing upon foreign policy was hosted by the Aurea Foundation (Munk Debates), but neither of these included the Green party. On top of the consortium, another French debate was hosted by TVA. The BQ attended each of the French debates, though the Green party was only invited to the consortium debate.

Although they are carefully coached and briefed (speechwriters prepare opening and closing statements and one-liners), the leaders are placed in a much less controlled setting than they are used to. The debates are thus one of the few opportunities for the public to see them functioning on their own. The 1984 and 1988 debates each featured a dramatic one-on-one exchange between Brian Mulroney and John Turner that was also endlessly replayed afterward. Since 1984 there have been separate French and English debates (and two in each language in 2006), making it virtually imperative for a party leader to be bilingual.

As noted, each party immediately sends forth its **spin doctors** to persuade reporters that its leader won,

THE CANADIAN PRESS/Frank Gunn

One of the televised leaders' debates during the 2015 election.

but whether the public makes up its own mind on the winner or awaits the verdict of media commentators is not entirely certain. Each leader's performance is judged in relation to the others, as well as relative to the media's expectations. Studies show that approximately half of the voters watch the debates.[17] Those who do so tend to be well-informed, peer-group opinion leaders who may well influence others who failed to tune in. Partly because of the large size of the audience and partly because sound bites may be replayed afterward, the debates "dominate journalistic commentary for at least several days." However, the debates should not be overemphasized, especially if there is no clear-cut winner, because "they can also be rapidly overtaken by other campaign events."[18] In 2011, the most remarkable aspect of the debates was Jack Layton's putdown of Michael Ignatieff in the English debate and his impressive performance in the French debate, which acted as a springboard to the increasing NDP support in Quebec.[19]

The 2015 Election Campaign

The October 19, 2015 election was the first held under Canada's fixed-date election law. The prime minister asked the governor general to dissolve parliament on August 4, and the 78-day campaign was the longest since 1872. The Conservatives, Liberals, and NDP all started the campaign with similar levels of support, though the NDP had the highest polled support until about mid-September, with polls showing average support of about 31 percent NDP, 29 percent Conservative, and 27 percent Liberal up to that time.

One high profile controversy early in the campaign was the court case of Senator Mike Duffy, whose inappropriate expenses of approximately $90 000 had been covered by a personal cheque form Harper's then chief of staff Nigel Wright. The case saw testimony suggesting that Harper's current chief, Ray Novak, was also told and emailed details of the transaction at the time it occurred, though he claimed he never knew of the transaction until media broke the story.

The second was a photo of a drowned Syrian refugee boy named Alan Kurdi, which set off a debate about Canada's response to the refugee crisis. There were reports that Kurdi's father had recently been denied entry to Canada, and a particular exchange between the CBC's Rosemary Barton and Immigration Minister Chris Alexander—in which Barton claimed Alexander was avoiding answering questions—gave the impression the governing Conservatives were on their heels on the issue. Nevertheless, neither issue saw significant changes occur in opinion polls.

The loss of a court case in which the Harper government was fighting to have the wearing of religious face covering banned during citizenship ceremonies brought much attention to the issue. As noted in Chapter 5, there is considerable enthusiasm for banning religious symbols in Quebec, and the NDP's position of allowing face coverings began to eat into its voter support in that province. It has been argued that, because many voters on the centre-left simply wanted to see the Conservatives lose government, this drop in support began to build Liberal momentum as many voters chose the opposition party most likely to succeed.[20]

Each party also had various controversies with candidates throughout the campaign, with many from all parties quitting due to embarrassing events or communications (many via social media) during the campaign or, in some cases, years prior. As was the case in 2011,[21] social media appeared to play a significant role in the campaign both in terms of promoting parties and political gaffes, although it remains unclear that this medium has surpassed other media or traditional campaign tactics in terms of overall impact.

As noted above, the party leaders also took part in debates and while expectations were that Justin Trudeau, the least experienced of the three main leaders, would do poorly, all leaders performed reasonably well in each case. Indeed, by the end of the campaign, there were many suggestions that Trudeau had been a very effective campaigner, even if he was less experienced.

The Liberals ultimately won a majority with 184 seats, taking every seat in Atlantic Canada and 39.5 percent of the popular vote. The Conservatives won 99 seats, and the NDP won 44 seats. Bloc Québécois leader, Gilles Duceppe, who returned from retirement to help build the party back after winning only four seats in 2011, saw his party win 10 seats. Duceppe, however, failed to secure his own riding and he resigned once the election results were reported. Stephen Harper also resigned as party leader.

THE LOCAL CANDIDATE CAMPAIGN

The other part of the election campaign takes place at the local level, where individual candidates compete for office. First, they must be officially nominated, and then, they try to get themselves elected.

Nomination

At the local level, each party's first priority is the **nomination** of its candidate. In the case of incumbents, ambitious newcomers, and those who anticipate the date of the next election, the nomination meeting is often held before the election is called. This allows many preparations, such as the production of lawn signs, to be made ahead of time so that the campaign can get off to a strong and early start.

Nominating candidates is one of the most important functions of political parties.[22] Unfortunately, it is another of their functions that leaves much to be desired. Although it is generally a wide-open opportunity for ordinary people to participate and influence the direction of the political system, the nomination process does not usually generate much interest. First, many party nominations are uncontested. Leaders sometimes decree that incumbents should be re-nominated without competition, which is a serious constraint on democracy. But even without that edict, sitting MPs are rarely challenged for the nomination, though a small few even lose nomination contests to run again. Second, discussion of policy is usually discouraged in the nomination process, although an aspiring candidate will sometimes be the standard-bearer for a particular interest. Third, those seeking the party nomination often recruit hundreds of new members who turn out to vote for them, overwhelming long-standing party members. Although such a process allows for the integration of new Canadians and voters into the political process, these "instant members" rarely stay around to become useful participants, especially if their favourite loses the nomination.

There are conflicting opinions about the intervention of the central party in the nomination process. In some ways, it is more democratic to allow the local constituency association to select the candidate on its own. But central office guidance can sometimes produce a better candidate or lead to a more representative set of candidates across the country. Jean Chrétien acquired the right as Liberal leader to name local candidates without a nomination meeting, and used the power to recruit "star" candidates, women, and visible minorities, and occasionally to veto a candidate with objectionable views. The NDP once hoped to achieve gender parity among its candidates but was later content with having nearly 50 percent women or members of minority groups. This effort often entails difficult negotiation between headquarters and riding associations, but the NDP normally ends up with the most representative roster of candidates. Stéphane Dion promoted the nomination of women in 2008, and in advance of the election, the central Conservative party stripped the party nomination from several candidates chosen at the constituency level. Recent changes to the Elections Act may soften this power to choose candidates, as party leaders will no longer necessarily have the power to veto candidates in future elections.

Given the explicit recruitment function of elections, it turns out that parties have nominated a set of candidates quite unrepresentative of the general population. In particular, nominated candidates underrepresent women, the working class, ethnocultural minorities, and Aboriginals. The number of women candidates increased significantly in 1993 to 476, before falling off in 1997 and 2000. Starting in 2004, a candidate could deduct daycare expenses when seeking the party nomination, but still only 391 women were nominated in that campaign. In 2006, 23.3 percent of the total candidates were women; in 2008 and 2011, the figure rose to 28 percent, and in 2015 it rose again to 33 percent.[23] However, as Bill Cross points out, "[t]here is no evidence that voters are less likely to support a female or minority candidate either in a nomination contest or in a general election. In fact, when women seek party nominations they succeed in numbers equal to men, and when women are nominated in competitive ridings, they are elected at rates similar to men."[24],* This conclusion was bolstered by the election of a record number of women MPs in 2011 and 2015.

---

* Cross, Political Parties, p. 74. See also Jerome H. Black and Bruce M. Hicks, "Visible Minority Candidates in the 2004 Federal Election," Canadian Parlimentary Review (Summer 2006); and Jerome H. Black, "The 2006 Federal Election and Visible Minority Candidates: More of the Same?" Canadian Parliamentary Review (Autumn 2008).

The Local Campaign[25]

Once the nomination has taken place, a campaign committee headed by the campaign manager is established (see Figure 15.1). In most campaigns the other key official is the canvass organizer, who sets up the door-to-door "foot canvass" to distribute literature or the telephone canvass. Whether canvassers contact voters on the doorstep or on the phone, the object is only secondarily to spread the party's message. Canvassers primarily hope to discover the party or candidate preferences of prospective voters and to seek out their own supporters. Armed with a voters' list, they will put a positive, negative, or other distinguishing mark beside the names of all voters contacted. To cover an entire constituency in this fashion, especially if it is done two or three times, as is often attempted by the NDP, requires a veritable army of volunteers and an elaborate hierarchical organization.[26] Because the campaign will need volunteers for many other tasks as well, and because few people relish door-to-door canvassing, the canvass organizer will probably not have enough workers and will therefore have to concentrate efforts in priority polls. If money is more plentiful than personnel, the local campaign may rely instead on media advertising but, as at the national level, the increasing fragmentation of the television audience raises doubts about whether this is a good investment.

In recent elections, some constituency associations have done their own local polling, and because a permanent voters list makes it easier to find voters' phone numbers and addresses, parties are employing even more sophisticated techniques. Rather than just identifying supporters and opponents, for example, parties use massive phone banks to find out which issues concern individual voters, especially marginal ones, and to follow up with a customized letter or even candidate visit to address such issues. The Conservatives were the first party to become expert at computer-assisted mail and telephone campaigning directed at members of key groups in targeted constituencies.[27] Most local campaigns now require the services of a webmaster to oversee the candidate's website and other Internet operations. Major parties develop a voter database containing information on individual voters, combining data from Elections Canada, telephone and email addresses, and details collected by door-to-door and telephone canvassers. Of these, the Conservative party's Constituent Information Management System (CIMS) is the most sophisticated, as mentioned.

FIGURE 15.1 STRUCTURE OF A TYPICAL LOCAL CAMPAIGN COMMITTEE

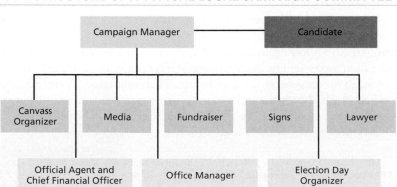

In the past, much of this work was voluntary, but campaigns increasingly engage paid staff. The local campaign is thus a complex operation requiring more and more sophistication, staffing, and funding. Parties will no doubt continue to find further innovative ways to contact voters involving new technologies.[28] The candidate, meanwhile, is extremely busy knocking on doors, attending community events, possibly participating in all-candidates' debates, telephoning known and potential supporters, doing media interviews, and in some cases, engaging in new social media.

This book's authors are happy to encourage all forms of political participation, and note that political parties are always willing to accept volunteers with open arms. Various skills may be used in initially volunteering for a party, and will likely lead to more interesting and rewarding work with more experience.

All this activity culminates on election day, when the organization tries to have party scrutineers placed in all the polls. Ideally, an inside scrutineer in each poll keeps track of which people on the list have cast their ballot, while an outside scrutineer periodically collects this information and then heads out to encourage all those previously identified as party supporters to get out to vote.

The fact that a number of NDP candidates in Quebec were elected in 2011 without any evidence of a local campaign raises the question of whether all this effort is necessary. Even earlier studies showed that the local candidate had less effect on the voter's decision than the party he or she represented or the party leader. But in 2011, the sudden wave of NDP support in Quebec based on the national campaign was so overwhelming that in many cases it seems little more was needed.

THE VOTER CHOICE

Canadians who decide to vote in an election have to make a choice among the candidates that are presented to them. How do they decide? This decision is complicated and the factors that determine it vary from person to person. However, there are certain systematic patterns to these voting decisions that enable political scientists to sketch out rough maps of how voters make decisions. One such multi-stage analytical framework focusing on the factors that seem to have the greatest impact on the greatest number of voters is presented out in Figure 15.2. This comprehensive model considers almost every possible factor that could be involved.[29]

Sociodemographic Bases of Party Support

The first factor that may influence the voters' choice is their sociodemographic characteristics, such as their geographic region, the type of setting they live in (rural or urban), ethnic background, religion, and gender. These relate to the cleavages and identities discussed in Chapters 3 to 9 and were heavily emphasized in the early research on voting behaviour.[30]

First, there are wide variations in regional support for different parties, some of which have been constant for generations and others that are of more recent origin. Between 1957 and 1993, the Progressive Conservatives were dominant in the West, for example, and before 1984 the Liberals almost always had Quebec to themselves. In 1993, the Reform party challenged

FIGURE 15.2 EXPLAINING THE VOTING DECISION

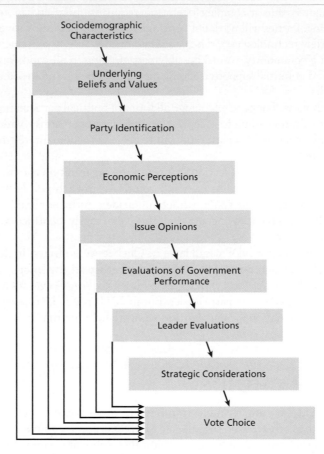

the PCs in the West, and between that election and 2011, the Bloc Québécois attracted the most support in Quebec.

Table 3.3 (in Chapter 3) showed a breakdown of party support by region in the 2015 election. What has been most surprising in recent elections is probably the collapse of the Bloc in Quebec, and the rise of the NDP to first place in that province, followed by the Liberal Party once again establishing itself as the strongest party in Quebec. This means that Quebec has voted successively for four different parties since 1980 and returned to where it began: Liberals, Progressive Conservatives, the Bloc, and the NDP, followed yet again by a return to the Liberals.

A third marked pattern in Canadian voting behaviour emerges on the basis of religion.[31] Roman Catholics have been strongly inclined to vote Liberal, whether they were French, English, or of other ethnic background and regardless of where they lived in the country. Political scientists have always found it difficult to explain this historic Liberal–Catholic connection,[32] although it has recently declined. A similar historic tendency existed for those with no formal religion to vote NDP, with the Conservatives picking up a disproportionate amount of the Protestant vote. The Reform Party and Canadian Alliance seemed particularly attractive to evangelical Christians, who then cast their lot with the new Conservative party after 2004.

Turning to ethnicity, the Liberal Party has traditionally appealed to French-Canadian voters, both outside and inside Quebec. Within francophone Quebec, the Conservatives did well only in the Mulroney era; after 1993, the BQ always had a stronger appeal than the Liberals to Quebeckers of French origin; but the Liberals gained the support of almost all those of non-French ethnicity. The Liberal Party was severely damaged among Quebec francophones by the "sponsorship scandal" in 2004 and 2006, however, leaving room for the Conservatives to capture a significant federalist vote in that province in the latter campaign. In 2011, the francophone vote in Quebec went predominantly to the NDP.

For decades, the Liberal party attracted the support of most post-Second World War immigrants, including new Canadians of non-European origin (increasingly members of visible minorities) who apparently reacted with gratitude to the fact that the Liberal Party was in office when they arrived. The Conservatives' efforts before and after the 2006 election at courting ethnocultural minorities are often said to have paid considerable dividends in the 2008 and 2011 elections by further reducing Liberal support in these communities. After intense solicitation, the Conservatives did much better, especially in Toronto and suburbs, in 2011, though they lost many of these seats in 2015.

The accusation is also sometimes made that Canadian foreign policy is designed in the interests of domestic political support for the party in power. Canada's aggressive verbal attack against the Russian invasion of Ukraine in 2014 is cited as an example, given that there are over 1.2 million Canadians of Ukrainian descent, many living in strategically located constituencies.

It is mostly in Quebec that age is a significant factor, as younger voters in that province prefer the Bloc but, generally speaking, older voters across the country find the Conservatives most appealing. A certain amount of gender gap has sometimes been detected—that men tend to be slightly more attracted to conservative parties, and women to the Liberals or NDP. Recent studies of the significance of gender have found this to be a complicated issue, and it appeared to decline in 2011.[33]

A final demographic factor is social class, with the expectation being that upper-class citizens would vote Conservative, the middle class would support the Liberals, and the working and poorer classes would vote NDP. In most Western democracies such a pattern is quite significant, but it is not borne out well in Canada, which generally lacks strong **class-consciousness**. As indicated in Chapter 8, only a small proportion of the working class has ever voted for working-class parties, and what distinctive support the NDP once received from those who belonged to unions or those with lower incomes now seems to have disappeared.[34] In 2006, one prominent labour leader, Buzz Hargrove, urged working-class Canadians to vote strategically, either Liberal or NDP, to keep the Conservatives out. Hargrove was then expelled from the NDP, and Stephen Harper aimed to corral a segment of the working class vote for himself. NDP ties to the labour movement are probably weaker than ever, and Jack Layton subtly pushed the party toward the ideological centre.[35]

Of all the socioeconomic factors, Roman Catholics and ethnocultural minorities were the bedrock of Liberal support for decades. But the support of both groups dwindled considerably over the past decade, and that in itself explains much of the fact that the Liberals dropped to a record low in the 2008 election and even lower in 2011.[36]

Core Values and Beliefs

A second major factor influencing how Canadians vote is their core values and beliefs; the 2000 election study showed that values and beliefs have a substantial impact on voter choice.[37] Within Quebec, the electorate was split down the middle on one question: Quebec sovereignty. Those in favour of this concept voted for the Bloc Québécois, and those against it voted Liberal. Outside Quebec, there was a more traditional ideological division between left and right connected to faith in the free market system as opposed to the desirability of government intervention. Those more inclined to government intervention tended to choose the Liberals or the NDP. In other words, although little or no class voting is now apparent, ideological voting is still significant, perhaps more than otherwise thought.[38] This is presumably why the Liberals tried to focus on the differences in "values" in both 2004 and 2006, claiming to be more collectivist and compassionate.

The role of core values is further complicated by the question of social values. Many Canadian Alliance supporters, for example, had a distinctive view of the role of the family and religion, and to some extent Alliance and PC voters parted company on whether a strong state should intervene to enforce traditional social values, such as on questions of censorship, homosexuality, or abortion. The new Conservative Party continued to attract social conservatives but tried to avoid mention of most of their issues.

Party Identification

Ever since they began studying electoral behaviour, Canadian political scientists have been wrestling with the question of **party identification**—that is, whether voters have a feeling of closeness or psychological attachment to a particular political party.[39] It has generally been thought that the degree of party identification was considerably lower in Canada than in most other countries, resulting in the fact that we had few **safe seats**. But a study of the 2000 election found that Canadians had a stronger feeling of attachment to a party than previously thought. Between 50 percent and 60 percent of voters demonstrated a consistent party preference and a full 25 percent of the electorate considered themselves to be Liberals. The other parties followed far behind.

At that time two significant implications seemed to follow from the Liberal Party having about one-quarter of the electorate on its side before the election was even called. First, because about half of the electorate had made up its mind before the campaign started, the campaign was primarily a struggle to win over the other half.[40] Second, the Liberals would lose the election only if all the short-term factors that influence the noncommitted voters—leadership, candidates, issues, and so on—were slanted in favour of some other party. By 2008, however, the Liberals had lost their head start of greater numbers of core supporters; in fact, by then, more voters identified with the Conservative party, and this trend continued to 2011.[41]

The Issues, the Economy, and the Government's Performance

The next three factors that are expected to influence voters are the issues raised in the campaign, the state of the economy, and the voters' assessment of the incumbent government's performance.[42]

Political scientists have given the question of issues a great deal of study. On the one hand, it would be logical for voters to make their choice on the basis of party positions relating to current political issues, that being the general understanding of what elections are all about and that being what voters often claim to do. On the other hand, many voters prove to have only the most simplistic understanding of public issues and often have difficulty articulating their thoughts on the issues that supposedly influenced them.

Moreover, voters have to choose among a number of parties contesting the election, each of which "packages" a number of issues in a certain way. Voters do not normally share the same packages of issue positions, making it impossible for many to project their issue opinions in their choice. Electors get only one vote, and they may agree with one party on some issues, a different party on other issues, and yet a third party on still other issues. Occasionally, of course, an election will be dominated by one particular issue, such as the "free trade" election of 1988, but even then, many voters have their idiosyncratic reasons for making their choice.

The preceding analysis casts doubt on the question of whether elections provide a policy mandate for the successful party—hence the concept of the **absent mandate**. Even when Canadian parties present a comprehensive election platform, they do not seem to feel bound by the specific policies they proposed in the campaign, such as the Liberal opposition to wage and price controls in 1974 and to the GST in 1993. Moreover, the limited role that issues play in the campaign seriously detracts from the claim of any government that it has a mandate to pursue a particular policy. For example, free trade was never mentioned in the 1984 campaign and the GST was almost totally overlooked in 1988. And on the rare occasion that a single issue figures prominently, the winning party almost never obtains a majority of the total votes cast and certainly not a majority in all regions of the country, "so a national mandate is absent."[43] The free trade issue in 1988 provided the closest thing to a policy mandate for any

THE RED WAVE

artizans.com

Bado/Artizans

Justin Trudeau rides the red wave.

Canadian government in recent times, yet the Conservatives received only 43 percent of the overall popular vote and less than 40 percent in six provinces and territories.[44]

It is often speculated that voters will reward an incumbent government in favourable economic circumstances and punish the government party if the economy is faltering.[45] Several election studies have reinforced observation of this *economic voting*, especially in terms of the unemployment rate. Between 2000 and 2008, however, the state of the economy was relatively strong, such that it was taken for granted and did not have much impact on the voting decision. By 2011, the economy was slowly emerging from recession, but the Conservatives were generally thought to be the best stewards in difficult financial circumstances.[46]

Somewhat related to the performance of the economy is the general performance of the incumbent government. In theory, a voter satisfied with the current government's performance would support it and one dissatisfied would vote for an opposition party. In 2004 and 2006, it was not so much the Liberal government's policies that voters disputed, but rather, their behaviour—their "culture of entitlement." Liberal arrogance in general, and several actions of questionable integrity, primarily the sponsorship scandal, led many in the electorate to vote for a "change."

Leadership

In many election surveys, respondents are asked whether their vote was based primarily on party leader, candidate, issues, or the party generally, a distinction not always easy for voters to make.[47] The role of the local candidate has rarely elicited much attention, and as mentioned above, issues did not count for much in most recent elections, while general party preference did. But what about the party leader? For a time, political scientists thought that the importance of party leader in the voting decision was on the increase as a result of the enormous power of the prime minister's position, the growing importance of television as a source of electoral stimulation and information, the fact that television primarily focused on party leaders, and the belief that party identification was weak in Canada.[48] But since the days of Pierre Elliott Trudeau, the significance of the party leader has been downplayed in most election analysis. As Pammett puts it, "despite the fact that popular commentary is fond of debating the effects of the leaders' appearance, dress, hairstyles or speaking styles on the public, the bulk of the population does not rate these things highly when it comes to making up their minds."[49] On the other hand, as revealed in the cases of Dion and Ignatieff, a leader who is deemed by the public to be weak will drag the party down. Moreover, the 2011 election also witnessed positive leadership: "managerial leadership" from Stephen Harper, and "charismatic leadership" from Jack Layton, whose personal popularity is usually credited for much of the NDP breakthrough in Quebec.[50]

Strategic Voting

Strategic voting is defined as voting for one's second-favourite party when it is perceived to have a better chance than one's first choice of defeating the party disliked most.[51] Such a practice reverses the decision that the voter had come to at the end of the long sequence of influences and is an attempt to make a vote count when it might otherwise be "wasted."

Although strategic voting is increasingly common in the vocabulary of election analysis, it requires a sophisticated voter to appreciate it. The 2000 election study revealed that it was nonexistent in Quebec and practised by only three percent of voters outside that province— mostly by people who would otherwise have voted PC or NDP but wanted to ensure the defeat of a Liberal or Alliance candidate. There was much talk of strategic voting in 2006, especially by Buzz Hargrove and both of the party leaders he endorsed, though past study has suggested the total strategic vote in Canada is between two and five percent (and some votes may even work at cross-purposes).[52] It likely has had little effect on the overall election results.

CRITICAL APPROACHES

The *rational choice* model is among the most relevant to elections. Extensive public opinion polling by political parties confirms the claims of this approach that parties make calculated promises to get elected, concentrating on strategically located groups. Parties tend to ignore their committed supporters as well as those who are hostile, and then, within a certain ideological range, promise whatever the polls tell them will maximize their electoral success. Nevertheless, the preceding account of voting behaviour puts into question some of the other claims of the rational choice approach, at least with respect to its assumption of rational and well-informed voters and of the successful party emerging with a specific policy mandate.

Rational choice theory has also struggled with the question of why people actually turn out to vote. In a classic rational choice formulation of the calculus of voting, William Riker and Peter Ordeshook formalize the decision as Reward = Benefit of Preferred Party Winning + Probability of Casting the Decisive Vote – Costs of Voting.[53] Since the probability of casting the decisive ballot is so low—far less than winning the lottery—it makes little sense from this perspective for people to undertake the costs of voting. Whereas many scholars have wrestled with the question of why people do not vote, rational choice theorists have typically had to contend with the problem of why anyone bothers to vote in the first place.

The *pluralist* and *social cleavages approaches* emphasize the necessity of designing a party's election platform so that it appeals to many groups in society—all major ethnocultural categories, industries, regions, genders, and classes. Such platforms are usually classic brokerage documents. Election manifestoes are increasingly based on what public opinion polls indicate the public wants or is willing to accept. Pluralists also point to the socioeconomic group preferences that have been evident in elections and emphasize the extent to which each party appeals to a coalition of certain groups.

POLITICAL PARTICIPATION

The act of voting is a manifestation of a broader category of behaviours known as **political participation**. Political participation consists of "those voluntary activities by citizens that are intended to influence the selection of government leaders or the decisions they make."[54] Numerous avenues of political participation exist, but actual participation takes effort, which not everyone is willing to exert, and is partly related to the possession of **political efficacy**—a sense of political competence and a feeling that one can have some impact on the system. Participation also depends on the possession of such resources as time, money, and information. In the Canadian case, the opportunities for participation far exceed actual levels of involvement.

Electoral Participation

Voting on election day is a crucial aspect of democracy, as previously defined, and is the most common form of political participation in Canada. The voter turnout rate is also one of the few forms of participation that can be regularly and reliably measured. Figure 15.3 tracks voter turnout in every Canadian election since 1867. The bottom line indicates the percentage of the Canadian population voting in each election, whereas the top line shows the percentage of eligible voters voting in each election. The top line is the normal and official measure of voter turnout. For a variety of reasons, however, including laws which have prevented certain groups from voting, such as women and Aboriginals, the proportion of the population that is eligible to vote has varied over time. Thus, it is helpful to look as well as the proportion of the total Canadian population that has cast a ballot in these elections.

FIGURE 15.3   PERCENTAGE VOTER TURNOUT IN FEDERAL ELECTIONS, 1867–2015

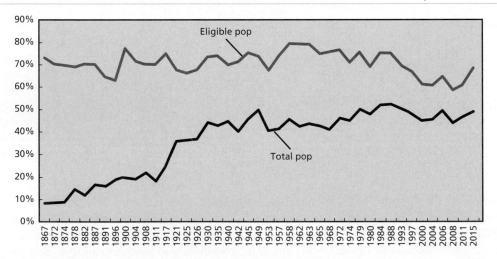

Source: Adapted from Elections Canada, Voter Turnout at Federal Elections and Referendums, http://www .elections.ca/content.aspx?section=ele&dir=turn&document=index&lang=e; "Preliminary Results", Elections Canada, http://enr.elections.ca/National.aspx?lang=e. Calculations completed by authors.

The overall average national turnout rate between 1900 and 1988 was about 72 percent, or nearly three-quarters of those eligible to vote. Since the 1988 election, however, the turnout rate has dipped more than 14 percentage points, from 75.3 percent to 60.9 percent, though it rebounded significantly in 2015 to 68.5 percent. The explanation for this decreasing turnout rate in Canadian federal elections is undoubtedly complex. Indeed, explaining the declining turnout rates is one of the central goals of the voting behaviour researchers. Whatever its precise causes, one thing is clear: voter turnout is not just declining in Canada; the same phenomenon is occurring in many other advanced industrial countries as well.

There has been much concern in Canada in recent years about the low turnout rate among people under the age of 30; it is estimated that only 25 percent of this cohort voted in the 2000 federal election. The three most common reasons for not voting given by those in this group were as follows: lack of interest (28 percent); lack of time (23 percent); and lack of appeal on the part of, or lack of faith in, parties, leaders, and candidates (20 percent). Most such young people lack a sense of civic duty and do not feel that voting is important for its own sake or that it is an essential obligation of living in a democracy. Most are neither cynical nor alienated; they are just not interested and do not see politics as relevant to their lives.[55] Elections Canada conducted a survey after the 2011 election in which it found that young people who discussed politics with their family and friends or who took a civics course in high school reported higher voting rates than others, and thus endorses strengthening civic education in the country's schools and positive family discussions about the political system. Elections Canada also put much effort into a campaign to raise youth voter turnout rates and calculates that it rose in subsequent elections.

Within the group that does vote, we can distinguish among degrees of knowledge and involvement. The level of information of the typical voter should not be overestimated, and many who vote pay little or no attention to the campaign. Although 80 percent claim to expose themselves to television or newspaper coverage of the election campaign, only 20 percent follow politics closely on a daily basis between elections. The level of factual and conceptual knowledge increases with level of education and reading about politics in newspapers; significant regional variations are also evident, but viewing political programs on television was of negligible impact.[56]

A study of the 1984 election found that as a national average, voters could name 3.3 provincial premiers (out of 10) and 36 percent could define the concepts of left and right and place the NDP as the furthest left of the three main parties. A 2000 study revealed that only 26 percent could name the current prime minister, the minister of finance, and the Leader of the Opposition. In 2002, a poll showed that only 47 percent knew that the Canadian Alliance party was to the right of the New Democrats, while 18 percent said it was to the political left. And in various international studies of political knowledge, Canada usually ranks in the middle or lower range.[57] The leading study of the subject recently concluded as follows:

> The Canadian public contains deep pockets of political ignorance and political illiteracy. Over 40 percent of Canadians were unable to name the leaders of the federal political parties, even though they were being interviewed right after an election in which those leaders had figured prominently. As for the parties' issue positions, 30 percent of Canadians could not identify one single promise with the party making it. And most Canadians were unable to identify which party was on the left and which was on the right.[58]

Beyond those who cast an "informed vote," a smaller proportion of the electorate becomes actively involved in the election campaign. A small number attend all-candidates meetings; some join a political party and vote at its local nomination meeting; some contribute money to political parties; some contribute time to a local candidate to do mailing, telephoning, or door-to-door canvassing; and a small number in each constituency become totally preoccupied with the local campaign. Members of this last group, including candidates themselves, are sometimes called "gladiators," as distinct from the great bulk of the population, who are primarily "spectators."[59]

According to party reports to Elections Canada, 212 000 Canadians made financial contributions to political parties in (non-election year) 2013. Even so, these figures represent less than one percent of the entire electorate, although an undetermined number donated smaller amounts.[60]

Non-electoral Participation

The political participation of most Canadians peaks at election time, but many avenues are open between elections in which to make demands, demonstrate support, or otherwise become involved in the political process. Party membership lists are not disclosed by parties, yet numbers are known to fluctuate widely and the total number of members is expected to be less than two percent of the population.[61] It is known that many people sign up before or during the campaign and then let their membership lapse afterward.

Another means of political participation is to join a voluntary group, an action that at least 60 percent of Canadians claim to do.[62] As seen in Chapter 16, any group, whatever its primary orientation, can become an advocacy group so that membership in any group is potentially political. In the unlikely event that the group does take a political turn, however, passive members rarely do more than send the occasional preprinted postcard or email to their MP or the prime minister. However, active executive and staff members of such groups may become highly involved in political campaigns. Even more initiative is required to form such a group, usually to protest against some political decision or lack of action at the municipal, provincial, territorial, or federal level.

Such group participation usually involves communicating with the authorities in routine ways, but occasionally it takes the form of peaceful demonstrations (locally or on Parliament Hill), sit-ins and other types of civil disobedience, and the rare case of violent protest. As noted above, Canadians are generally a peaceful lot, and instances of political violence are uncommon. The main historical incidents of violence were the two Riel Rebellions of 1869–70 and 1885, the conscription riots in Quebec City in 1918, the Winnipeg General Strike of 1919, the Regina Riot (of the unemployed) of 1935, various FLQ incidents of the 1960s culminating in the FLQ crisis of 1970, and the Mohawks' armed standoff at Oka in 1990.[63]

Canadians can also participate politically between elections as individuals—sending letters to MPs or the prime minister; writing letters to the editors of newspapers; calling radio or television phone-in shows; signing petitions; joining Facebook groups, tweeting, or engaging in chats or other online communities. As with so many other aspects of political participation, however, it is difficult to obtain solid data on the degree of this category of individual involvement. Figure 15.4 reveals the percentage of Canadians who engaged in selected political activities in 2012.

FIGURE 15.4   PARTICIPATION IN POLITICAL ACTIVITIES BESIDES VOTING

ONLINE DISCUSSION:	%
I CIRCULATED OR REPOSTED POLITICAL INFORMATION ON SOCIAL NETWORKING SITES SUCH AS FACEBOOK AND TWITTER.	17
I USED EMAIL OR INSTANT MESSAGING TO DISCUSS SOCIETAL/ POLITICAL ISSUES.	30
I BLOGGED ABOUT A POLITICAL ISSUE.	15
I PARTICIPATED IN AN ONLINE GROUP ABOUT A SOCIETAL/POLITICAL ISSUE.	25
OFF-LINE DISCUSSION:	
I DISCUSSED A SOCIETAL/POLITICAL ISSUE FACE TO FACE OR ON THE PHONE.	40
I WROTE A LETTER TO THE EDITOR ABOUT A POLITICAL ISSUE.	17
I MADE A PUBLIC SPEECH ON A POLITICAL ISSUE.	15
I ORGANIZED A PUBLIC EVENT OR MEETING ABOUT POLITICS.	12
ACTIVISM:	
I SIGNED A PETITION.	51
I BOYCOTTED/"BUYCOTTED" A PRODUCT.	49
I WAS PART OF A PROTEST.	14
CIVIC ENGAGEMENT:	
I WORKED WITH OTHERS ON AN ISSUE IN MY COMMUNITY.	30
I WAS ACTIVE IN A GROUP OR ORGANIZATION.	58
I DONATED TO A POLITICAL/SOCIETAL CAUSE.	26
I DID VOLUNTARY WORK.	55
FORMAL ENGAGEMENT:	
I CONTACTED AN ELECTED OFFICIAL ABOUT AN ISSUE THAT CONCERNS ME.	31
I ATTENDED A POLITICAL MEETING.	20
I VOLUNTEERED IN AN ELECTION.	10
I DONATED TO A POLITICAL PARTY OR CANDIDATE.	10
I AM OR HAVE BEEN A MEMBER OF A POLITICAL PARTY.	10

Samara Canada, Samara Democracy Report #6, "Lightweights? Political Participation beyond the Ballot Box," (2013) p.3, www.samaracanada.com.

CONCLUSION

Although public opinion polls are increasingly common, elections remain the definitive measure of the public will. As such, elections leave much to be desired, because they rarely produce a victorious party with a specific policy mandate. Parties may offer only vague slogans like "national unity" or "time for a change"; elections frequently turn on leader or party images; successful parties often renege on their policy promises once in office; and a large proportion of voters pay little attention to the campaign. Attack ads in recent years have also made Canadian election campaigns less agreeable than in the past, although no less exciting.

This chapter is closely related to the preceding two on the formal electoral system and political parties. It also has links to the chapters on political culture and the mass media and public opinion polls and, in dealing with the kinds of candidates who are elected, it has connections to Chapter 23 on the House of Commons.

DISCUSSION QUESTIONS

1. How might the substance of each party's campaign (policy platform) be enhanced compared to its symbols (personality, image, and advertising)?

2. Is the distribution of media time during election campaigns fair? If not, how could it be improved?

3. Is it fair to exclude minor party leaders from the leaders' debates?

4. How rational and well informed is the average voter?

5. If you voted recently, explain how you came to your decision.

MindTap®   FOR MORE INFO GO TO **http://www.nelson.com/student**

NOTES

1. Carleton University professors have edited excellent studies of each Canadian federal election since 1984. The editors involved were Alan Frizzell, Anthony Westell, and since 2000, Jon H. Pammett and Christopher Dornan, including their *The Canadian General Election of 2011* (Toronto: Dundurn, 2011).
2. Pammett and Dornan, eds., *The Canadian General Election of 2011*, pp. 95 and 171.
3. Tom Flanagan, *Harper's Team: Behind the Scenes in the Conservative Rise to Power* (Montreal: McGill-Queen's University Press, 2007, pp. 85–87; *Globe and Mail*, March 1, 2012, p. A4.
4. Alan Whitehorn, "Alexa McDonough and the Atlantic Breakthrough for the New Democratic Party," in Frizzell and Pammett, *1997*, p. 94; each party's election strategy in 2011 is discussed in Pammett and Dornan, *2011*.
5. Stephen Clarkson, "Yesterday's Man and His Blue Grits: Backward into the Future," in Frizzell, *1993*, p. 33.

6. More comprehensive election manifestoes are a characteristic of the "Fourth Party System," according to R.K. Carty, William Cross, and Lisa Young, *Rebuilding Canadian Party Politics* (Vancouver: UBC Press, 2000). See also Greg Flynn, "Rethinking Policy Capacity in Canada: the Role of Parties and Election Platforms in Government Policy-Making," *Canadian Public Administration* (June 2011); Stephen Clarkson in "The Liberal Threepeat," in Pammett and Dornan, *2000*, and Faron Ellis and Peter Woolstencroft. "A Change of Government, Not a Change of Country: The Conservatives in the 2006 Election," in Pammett and Dornan, *2006*.

7. Frizzell, Pammett, and Westell, *1988*, p. 75; and David Taras, *The Newsmakers* (Scarborough: Nelson Canada, 1990), pp. 154–67.

8. Mary Francoli, Josh Greenberg, and Christopher Waddell, "The Campaign in the Digital Media," in Pammett and Dornan, *2011*, Ch. 9.

9. *Reform Party of Canada et al. v. Canada (Attorney General)*, Alberta Court of Appeal, March 10, 1995; and *Somerville v. Canada (Attorney General)*, Alberta Court of Appeal, June 5, 1996.

10. Peter Woolstencroft, "'Doing Politics Differently': The Conservative Party and the Campaign of 1993," in Frizzell, *1993*, p. 20; Lionel Lumb, "The Television of Inclusion," in Frizzell, *1993*, p. 122; and Walter I. Romanow, Michel de Repentigny, Stanley B. Cunningham, Walter C. Soderlund, and Kai Hildebrandt, *Television Advertising in Canadian Elections: The Attack Mode, 1993* (Waterloo: Wilfrid Laurier University Press, 1999).

11. Bryce Corrigan and Ted Brader. "Campaign Advertising: Reassessing the Impact of Campaign Ads on Political Behavior," in Stephen K. Medvic, ed. *New Directions in Campaigns and Elections*. (New York: Routledge, 2011).

12. Jonathan Rose. "Are Negative Ads Positive? Political Advertising and the Permanent Campaign." In David Taras and Christopher Waddell (eds) *How Canadians Communicate IV: Media and Politics*. (Athabasca University Press, 2012).

13. Pammett and Dornan, *2011*, pp. 17, 31, and 226.

14. David McGrane, "Political Marketing and the NDP's Historic Breakthrough," in Pammett and Dornan, *2011*, pp. 77–79; Alex Marland, Thierry Giasson, and Jennifer Lees-Marshment, eds., *Political Marketing in Canada* (Vancouver: UBC Press, 2012).

15. Susan Delacourt, *Shopping for Votes: How Politicians Choose Us and We Choose Them*. (Douglas and McIntyre, 2013).

16. Lawrence LeDuc, "The Leaders' Debates: (… And the Winner Is …)," in Frizzell and Pammett, *1997*; Lawrence LeDuc and Richard Price, "Great Debates: The Televised Leadership Debates of 1979," *Canadian Journal of Political Science* (March 1985); and David Lanoue, "Debates That Mattered: Voters' Reaction to the 1984 Canadian Leadership Debates," *Canadian Journal of Political Science* (March 1991).

17. LeDuc, "The Leaders' Debates," in Frizzell and Pammett, *1997*, p. 212; and Attallah and Burton, "Television"; Pammett and Dornan, *2001*, p. 288.

18. LeDuc, "The Leaders' Debates," pp. 207–8

19. Harold D. Clarke, et al., "Winners and Losers: Voters in the 2001 Federal Election," in Pammett and Dornan, *2011*, p. 291.

20. Bill Curry, "NDP faces reversal of fortune in Quebec as Liberal support surges," *The Globe and Mail*, Oct. 20, 2015, available at http://www.theglobeandmail.com/news/politics/ndp-faces-reversal-of-fortune-in-quebec-as-liberal-support-surges/article26882447/.

21. Francoli, Greenberg, and Waddell, "The Campaign in the Digital Media," in Pammett and Dornan, *The Canadian Federal Election of 2011*.

22. William Cross, *Political Parties* (Vancouver: UBC Press, 2004), Ch. 4; William Cross, "Grassroots Participation in Candidate Nominations," in Joanna Everitt and Brenda O'Neill, eds., *Citizen Politics: Research and Theory in Canadian Political Behaviour* (Toronto: Oxford University Press, 2002); R.K. Carty, "The Politics of Tecumseh Corners: Canadian Political Parties as Franchise Organizations," *Canadian Journal of Political Science* (December 2002); and William Cross, "Candidate Nomination in Canada's Political Parties," in Pammett and Dornan, eds., *2006*, Ch. 7. Anthony Sayers has categorized candidates as high profile, local notable, party insider, or stop gap in his *Parties, Candidates, and Constituency Campaigns in Canadian Elections* (Vancouver: UBC Press, 1999).

23. Andrew Heard, *Elections*, available at http://www.sfu.ca/~aheard/elections/women-elected.html. Equal Voice, EV Tallies the Total, http://us7.campaign-archive1.com/?u=edc96b30d97838f2d42e39fdf&id=e795e16d1c&e=32b204b4f7

24. Cross, *Political Parties*, p. 74. See also Jerome H. Black and Bruce M. Hicks, "Visible Minority Candidates in the 2004 Federal Election," *Canadian Parliamentary Review* (Summer 2006); and Jerome H. Black, "The 2006 Federal Election and Visible Minority Candidates: More of the Same?" *Canadian Parliamentary Review* (Autumn 2008).

25. William Cross and Lisa Young, "Explaining Local Campaign Intensity: The Canadian General Election of 2008," *Canadian Journal of Political Science* (September 2011); Alex Marland, "Constituency Campaigning in the 2011 Canadian Federal Election," in Pammett and Dornan, *2011*; Royce Koop, *Grassroots Liberals: Organizing for Local and National Politics* (Vancouver: UBC Press, 2011).

26. Jerome H. Black, "Revisiting the Effects of Canvassing on Voting Behaviour," *Canadian Journal of Political Science* (June 1984); Lynda Erickson and R.K. Carty, "Parties and Candidate Selection in the 1988 Canadian General Election," *Canadian Journal of Political Science* (June 1991); and Pammett and Dornan, *2011*, p. 175.

27. George Perlin, "Opportunity Regained: The Tory Victory in 1984," in Howard R. Penniman, ed., *Canada at the Polls, 1984* (Durham, NC: Duke University Press, 1988), p. 85; and Attallah and Burton, "Television."

28. Munroe Eagles, "The Effectiveness of Local Campaign Spending in the 1993 and 1997 Federal Elections in Canada," in *Canadian Journal of Political Science* (March 2004).

29. Blais et al., *Anatomy of a Liberal Victory*, Ch. 5; Cameron D. Anderson and Laura B. Stephenson, eds., *Voting Behaviour in Canada* (Vancouver: UBC Press, 2010); Mebs Kanji, Antoine Bilodeau, and Thomas J. Sotto, eds., *The Canadian Election Studies: Assessing Four Decades of Influence* (Vancouver: UBC Press, 2012); Elisabeth Gidengil, et al., *Dominance and Decline: Making Sense of Recent Canadian Elections* (Toronto: University of Toronto Press, 2012).

30. Amanda Bittner, "The Effects of Information and Social Cleavages: Explaining Issue Attitudes and Vote Choice in Canada," *Canadian Journal of Political Science* (December 2007) is one researcher who gives more emphasis to other factors in more recent times.

31. Blais et al., *Anatomy of a Liberal Victory*, p. 93.

32. André Blais, "Accounting for the Electoral Success of the Liberal Party in Canada," *Canadian Journal of Political Science* (December 2005).

33. Blais et al., *Anatomy of a Liberal Victory*, Ch. 6; Elisabeth Gidengil, "Beyond the Gender Gap," *Canadian Journal of Political Science* (December 2007); Marie Rekkas, "Gender and Elections: An Examination of the 2006 Canadian Federal Election," *Canadian Journal of Political Science* (December 2008); Pammett and Dornan, *2011*, pp. 327–29.

34. Blais et al., *Anatomy of a Liberal Victory*, p. 94.

35. Pammett and Dornan, *2011*, p. 91.

36. Elisabeth Gidengil, Joanna Everitt, Patrick Fournier, and Neil Nevitte, "Anatomy of a Liberal Defeat," paper presented at the 2009 Canadian Political Science Association.

37. Blais et al., *Anatomy of a Liberal Victory*, Ch. 7.

38. Ibid., p. 112.

39. Ibid., p. 115.

40. Jon H. Pammett, "The People's Verdict," in Pammett and Dornan, eds., *2000*, p. 306.

41. Gidengil et al., "Anatomy of a Liberal Defeat"; Pammett and Dornan, *2011*, pp. 282 and 300; Pammett, "Elections," in Michael Whittington and Glen Williams, eds., *Canadian Politics in the 21st Century*, 7th ed. (Toronto: Thomson Nelson Canada, 2008), pp. 158–60.

42. Blais et al., *Anatomy of a Liberal Victory*, chs. 9, 10, and 11.

43. Harold D. Clarke, Jane Jenson, Lawrence LeDuc, and Jon H. Pammett, *Absent Mandate* (Toronto: Gage, 1984), p. 182.

44. Surveys indicated that only about one-half of the voters claimed to make up their mind primarily on the basis of the free trade issue, some on each side. Frizzell, *1988*, p. 124; and Richard Johnston, André Blais, Henry E. Brady, and Jean Crête, "Free Trade and the Dynamics of the 1988 Canadian Election," in Joseph Wearing, ed., *The Ballot and Its Message* (Toronto: Copp Clark Pitman, 1991).

45. As pointed out by Fred Cutler, many voters have a hard time distinguishing between the effects of federal and provincial government economic policies, "Whodunnit? Voters and Responsibility in Canadian Federalism," *Canadian Journal of Political Science* (September 2008).

46. Faron Ellis and Peter Woolstencroft, "The Conservative Campaign: becoming the new Natural Governing Party?" in Pammett and Dornan, *2011.*

47. Pammett, "The People's Verdict," p. 298; and André Blais, Elisabeth Gidengil, Agnieszka Dobrzynska, Neil Nevitte, and Richard Nadeau, "Does the Local Candidate Matter? Candidate Effects in the Canadian Election of 2000," *Canadian Journal of Political Science* (July/August 2003).

48. Blais et al., *Anatomy of a Liberal Victory*, p. 165.

49. Pammett, "The Voters Decide," in Frizzell and Pammett, *1997,* p. 234; see also Pammett, "The People's Verdict," pp. 298–99.

50. Pammett and Dornan, *2011,* pp. 8, 85, and 294.

51. Blais et al., *Anatomy of a Liberal Victory*, p. 181.

52. André Blais , Eugénie Dostie-Goulet , and Marc André Bodet. "Voting Strategically in Canada and Britain". In Bernard Grofman, André Blais and Shawn Bowler (eds), *Duverger's Law of Plurality Voting* (New York: Springer, 2009)

53. William Riker and Peter Ordeshook, "A Theory of the Calculus of Voting," *American Political Science Review* (March 1968).

54. William Mishler and Harold D. Clarke, "Political Participation in Canada," in Michael S. Whittington and Glen Williams, eds., *Canadian Politics in the 1990s*, 4th ed. (Scarborough: Nelson, 1995), p. 130.

55. Jon H. Pammett and Lawrence LeDuc, "Explaining the Turnout Decline in Canadian Federal Elections: A New Survey of Non-Voters" (March 2003), available at http://www.elections.ca/loi/tur/tud/TurnoutDecline.pdf; Anne Milan, "Willing to Participate: Political Engagement of Young Adults," *Canadian Social Trends* (Statistics Canada, Catalogue No. 11-008, Winter 2005); and Lawrence LeDuc and Jon H. Pammett, "Voter Turnout in 2006: More than Just the Weather," in Jon H. Pammett and Christopher Dornan, eds., *The Canadian General Election of 2006* (Toronto: Dundurn, 2006).

56. Ronald D. Lambert, James, E. Curtis, Steven D. Brown, and Barry J. Kay, "The Social Sources of Political Knowledge," *Canadian Journal of Political Science* 21, no. 2 (June 1988), pp. 359–74. See also Henry Milner, *Civic Literacy in Comparative Context* (Montreal: Institute for Research on Public Policy, 2001).

57. Paul Howe and David Northrup, "Strengthening Canadian Democracy: The Views of Canadians," *Policy Matters* (Montreal: Institute for Research on Public Policy) 1, no. 5 (July 2000), p. 40; Milner, *Civic Literacy in Comparative Context*, pp. 8–11; and Compas poll, April 29, 2002.

58. Elisabeth Gidengil, André Blais, Neil Nevitte, and Richard Nadeau, *Citizens* (Vancouver: UBC Press, 2004), p. 69.

59. Ibid., pp. 124–26.

60. Elections Canada, *Financial Reports: Registered Party Financial Returns, 2010.*

61. R. Kenneth Carty, William Cross, and Lisa Young, *Rebuilding Canadian Party Politics* (Vancouver: UBC Press, 2000).

62. Statistics Canada, General Social Survey on Social Engagement, 2003.

63. Torrance, *Public Violence in Canada.*

FURTHER READING

Anderson, Cameron D., and Laura B. Stephenson, eds. *Voting Behaviour in Canada.* Vancouver: UBC Press, 2010.

Blais, André, Elisabeth Gidengil, Richard Nadeau, and Neil Nevitte. *Anatomy of a Liberal Victory: Making Sense of the Vote in the 2000 Canadian Election.* Peterborough: Broadview Press, 2002.

Brodie, Janine, and Jane Jenson. *Crisis, Challenge and Change: Party and Class in Canada Revisited.* Ottawa: Carleton University Press, 1988.

Cross, William. *Political Parties.* Vancouver: UBC Press, 2004.

————, ed. *Political Parties, Representation, and Electoral Democracy in Canada.* Toronto: Oxford University Press, 2002.

Gidengil, Elisabeth, André Blais, Richard Nadeau, and Neil Nevitte. *Citizens.* Vancouver: UBC Press, 2004.

Gidengil, Elisabeth, et al. *Dominance and Decline: Making Sense of Recent Canadian Elections.* Toronto: University of Toronto Press, 2012.

Kanji, Mebs, Antoine Bilodeau, and Thomas J. Scotto, eds. *The Canadian Election Studies: Assessing Four Decades of Influence.* Vancouver: UBC Press, 2012.

Marland, Alex, Thierry Glasson, and Jennifer Lees-Marchment, eds., *Political Marketing in Canada.* Vancouver: UBC Press, 2012.

Pammett, Jon. "Class Voting and Class Consciousness in Canada," *Canadian Review of Sociology and Anthropology* 24, no. 2 (1987).

————. "Elections," In Michael Whittington and Glen Williams, eds., *Canadian Politics in the 21st Century,* 7th ed. Toronto: Thomson Nelson Canada, 2008.

————, and Christopher Dornan, eds. *The Canadian General Election of 2011.* Toronto: Dundurn, 2011.

Thorburn, H.G., and Alan Whitehorn, eds. *Party Politics in Canada,* 8th ed. Toronto: Prentice Hall, 2000.

Wells, Paul. *Right Side Up: The Fall of Paul Martin and the Rise of Stephen Harper's New Conservatism.* Toronto: McClelland & Stewart, 2006.

Young, Lisa, and Keith Archer, eds. *Regionalism and Party Politics in Canada.* Toronto: Oxford University Press, 2002.

CHAPTER 16

Advocacy Groups, Social Movements, and Lobbying

Over the years, the **Canadian Federation of Students (CFS)**, representing half a million members, and the Canadian Association of University Teachers, speaking for 65 000 professors, librarians, and researchers, have both tried to persuade federal and provincial governments to restore or increase public funding to postsecondary education and freeze tuition fees. The **Canadian Council of Chief Executives** (now known as the **Business Council of Canada**), conversely, applauded the governments' balanced-budget doctrine, with its increased reliance on market forces. While environmentalist groups advocated the immediate implementation of the Kyoto Protocol, the Canadian Association of Petroleum Producers tried to convince the public that the environmental record of oil companies in northern Alberta was not as disastrous as often portrayed.

Such groups as these develop in almost every political system when individuals or companies with common concerns band together to strengthen their cause. They are often called **interest groups** or **pressure groups** and can be defined as any group that seeks to influence government policy without contesting elections—that is, without putting forward its own candidates. Alternatively, they have been defined as "organizations whose members act together to influence public policy in order to promote their common interest."[1] Although the terms are basically interchangeable, it could be said that an interest group *becomes* a pressure group when it actively pursues an objective with government, while **advocacy group** is a more generic term.[2] This discussion must also include **social movements**, which generally possess a less formal structure and bring new values into the political system. The term "civil society" is used to refer to such groups, and it is often argued that widespread participation in such groups is a prerequisite to a strong democratic political system.

The term **lobbying** is used to refer to any organized attempt to influence the authorities, an activity that is most commonly undertaken by pressure groups but could of course be done by individuals, companies, or other political actors. Increasingly, however, pressure groups have been joined by professional lobbying firms in this activity.

Once having established their functions and discussed certain other theoretical considerations, this chapter proceeds to identify some of the leading Canadian advocacy groups and social movements, to outline their targets and methods of operation, and then to examine the activity of professional lobbying firms.

THEORETICAL CONSIDERATIONS

In the traditional discussion of functions performed in the political system, advocacy groups are assigned the primary task of "interest articulation." They normally have a narrow focus and are organized around a single, central interest which they try to impress on those in authority. In the process of articulating such interests, advocacy groups may well be part of the **agenda-setting** process that was mentioned in Chapter 12. They may introduce items to the political agenda as well as help structure public debate surrounding those issues that are already there. In fact, the media's role in setting the agenda may well focus on demands raised by such groups. National advocacy groups often experience internal regional, provincial/territorial, ethnic, linguistic, or class tensions that must be bridged in constructing the message that they want to articulate, so that such groups also play a limited part in the aggregation of interests. Paul Pross thus prefers to speak of the "interest promotion" function of such groups.[3]

Advocacy groups aim to influence the policymaking process and are benefited in this respect by the enhanced complexity of society. Public issues now require information that is so technical and voluminous that politicians and parties actually seek out advocacy groups' expertise. Consequently, they regularly interact with the bureaucracy to work out technical arrangements to their mutual satisfaction and present these proposals to the politicians and parties as a fait accompli. This fundamental transformation of the policymaking process will be emphasized in Chapter 20.

Pross adds that such groups are also engaged in the function of legitimation. When groups participate peacefully and cooperatively, they demonstrate support for the political system and confer legitimacy on both it and those with whom they are interacting. Governments encourage groups to lend them such legitimacy and support by "drawing them into a privileged advisory position," and sometimes by helping to create them. By keeping the authorities abreast of current demands and societal changes, advocacy groups promote "general political stability."[4]

While advocacy groups are never entirely satisfied with their lot in the political system, most of them are an integral part of that system. In other words, they operate within and support the context of the dominant values and expectations of society, perhaps without even realizing it.[5] But however difficult it is to think beyond the status quo, one of the challenges to the traditional way of doing things comes from social movements, which engage in a struggle to expand the boundaries of the existing system.

THE ARRAY OF CANADIAN ADVOCACY GROUPS

The number of advocacy groups operating in Canada is in the thousands, so not all can be identified here. Instead, only some of the largest, most influential, or more interesting will be mentioned. Such a selective list can be seen in Table 16.1.

TABLE 16.1 LEADING NATIONAL CANADIAN ADVOCACY GROUPS

BUSINESS	ETHNIC
BUSINESS COUNCIL OF CANADA	FÉDÉRATION DES COMMUNAUTÉS FRANCOPHONES ET ACADIENNE DU CANADA
CANADIAN CHAMBER OF COMMERCE	ASSEMBLY OF FIRST NATIONS
CANADIAN MANUFACTURERS & EXPORTERS	CANADIAN ETHNOCULTURAL COUNCIL
CANADIAN FEDERATION OF INDEPENDENT BUSINESS	NATIONAL CONGRESS OF ITALIAN CANADIANS
RETAIL COUNCIL OF CANADA	NATIONAL ASSOCIATION OF JAPANESE CANADIANS
CANADIAN BANKERS ASSOCIATION	**RELIGIOUS**
CANADIAN ASSOCIATION OF BROADCASTERS	CANADIAN COUNCIL OF CHURCHES
CANADIAN CONSTRUCTION ASSOCIATION	CANADIAN CONFERENCE OF CATHOLIC BISHOPS
CANADIAN ASSOCIATION OF PETROLEUM PRODUCERS	NATIONAL COUNCIL OF CANADIAN MUSLIMS
CANADIAN LIFE AND HEALTH INSURANCE ASSOCIATION	CANADIAN JEWISH CONGRESS
MINING ASSOCIATION OF CANADA	**PUBLIC INTEREST GROUPS**
CANADA'S RESEARCH-BASED PHARMACEUTICAL COMPANIES	COUNCIL OF CANADIANS
CANADIAN GENERIC PHARMACEUTICAL ASSOCIATION	JOHN HOWARD SOCIETY
FOREST PRODUCTS ASSOCIATION OF CANADA	CANADIAN CIVIL LIBERTIES ASSOCIATION
CANADIAN HOME BUILDERS' ASSOCIATION	CANADIAN COUNCIL ON SOCIAL DEVELOPMENT
AGRICULTURE	NATIONAL COUNCIL OF WELFARE
CANADIAN FEDERATION OF AGRICULTURE	GREENPEACE CANADA
NATIONAL FARMERS UNION	MOTHERS AGAINST DRUNK DRIVING (MADD CANADA)
LABOUR	NON-SMOKERS' RIGHTS ASSOCIATION
CANADIAN LABOUR CONGRESS	CANADA WITHOUT POVERTY (FORMERLY NAPO)
PROFESSIONS	SIERRA CLUB OF CANADA
CANADIAN BAR ASSOCIATION	**OTHER**
CANADIAN MEDICAL ASSOCIATION	CANADIAN TAXPAYERS FEDERATION
CANADIAN NURSES ASSOCIATION	ROYAL CANADIAN LEGION
CANADIAN ASSOCIATION OF UNIVERSITY TEACHERS	CONSUMERS' ASSOCIATION OF CANADA
CANADIAN ASSOCIATION OF CHIEFS OF POLICE	EGALE CANADA
CANADIAN TEACHERS' FEDERATION	FEDERATION OF CANADIAN MUNICIPALITIES
CANADIAN FEDERATION OF STUDENTS	

Business Groups

In the case of business, nothing prevents individual companies from lobbying on their own behalf for grants, subsidies, tariff changes, loan guarantees, tax write-offs, government contracts, or policy changes, and many firms do so on a regular basis. In addition, it is evident from Table 16.1 that the private firms within almost every industry have organized a common pressure group to promote the interests of the industry as a whole.[6] Thus, to a large extent, the "system of business interest associations in Canada is highly fragmented, consisting of many small, narrowly focused organizations."[7] William Coleman counted about 600 business groups that were active in Canadian federal politics, about 40 percent of which were in the manufacturing sector. In summarizing the business pressure group scene, he noted

> a relatively small number of associations with members that are generally large firms, operating in large oligopolistic sectors. These associations spend in excess of $1 million annually, employ a minimum of 10 to 15 people, are institutionally bilingual, and have an officer, if not their head office, in Ottawa. Associations in this category are visible to the attentive public; their leaders are quoted frequently in the business press and move freely in government circles.... The several roles they play gives them a system of comprehensive political contacts, ranging from lower and middle technical levels of the bureaucracy to senior officials, MPs, and Cabinet ministers.[8]

Superimposed on these industrial groupings are such "peak" organizations as the Business Council of Canada (BCC), the Canadian Manufacturers and Exporters (CME), the Canadian Chamber of Commerce (CCC), and the Canadian Federation of Independent Business (CFIB). The Business Council of Canada, formerly known as the Canadian Council of Chief Executives, represents the chief executive officers of the 150 largest firms in the country. The CCCE sees itself as Canada's "premier business association," and was particularly influential with the Mulroney Conservative government. It fought hard for the Canada–U.S. Free Trade Agreement, after which it then sought "to broaden

THE CANADIAN PRESS/Pawel Dwulit

The heads of the Canadian Federation of Independent Business, the Business Council of Canada, and the Canadian Chamber of Commerce talk to Prime Minister Harper at an economic round table meeting in Ottawa in 2010.

public understanding of the need for more responsible fiscal policies." Those policies included balancing the budget and reducing taxes, all of which meant reducing the role of government. Although Canada thus lacks a single peak voice for the business community as a whole, that community may be even more influential for being represented by at least four national organizations.

On the agricultural side of business, about 100 active associations vie for influence.[9] The broadest is the Canadian Federation of Agriculture (CFA), which represents 200 000 farm families as well as some 20 provincial farm and commodity organizations. The National Farmers Union (NFU) is a more radical group, and many other specific commodity groups exist independently, such as the Canadian Cattlemen's Association.

Nonbusiness Groups

The **Canadian Labour Congress (CLC)** functions as a common voice for organized labour, but only 69 percent of Canadian union members actually belong to unions affiliated with the CLC. It maintains a link to the New Democratic Party, as do many of its individual unions, and is unique among Canadian advocacy groups in demonstrating such an overt partisan preference.

Many of the minority ethnocultural communities in Canada have their own organizations, such as the National Congress of Italian Canadians, the German Canadian Congress, the National Association of Japanese Canadians, and the National Association of Canadians of Origins in India. Some 30 such groups have been brought together, with government support, in the peak organization the Canadian Ethnocultural Council. The largest of several Aboriginal groups is the **Assembly of First Nations**. The English and French are organized only where they are minorities—the anglophone Alliance Quebec and the Fédération des communautés francophones et acadienne du Canada, which incorporates provincial units, such as the Assemblée de la francophonie de l'Ontario. Most of the religious denominations in Canada function as advocacy groups from time to time, with the Canadian Conference of Catholic Bishops, the United Church of Canada, the Canadian Council of Churches, and the Canadian Jewish Congress probably being most influential.

Most professions have organizations that speak for their members on relevant issues, the Canadian Medical Association and the Canadian Bar Association being two of the oldest and most important. In addition to serving the needs of its own members, the CMA advises the government on other health matters in the broader public interest. Besides representing the interests of lawyers, judges, notaries, law teachers, and law students, the CBA is uniquely involved in the legislative process, since it has expertise in every aspect of the law.

The Royal Canadian Legion is by far the largest veterans' organization, going back to 1926 and representing those who served in Canada's armed forces or who are associated with them. Besides working for better pensions and other benefits for its own members and a strong military establishment, the Legion is prominently involved in public service and charitable work.

Other Categorizations of Advocacy Groups

However much any of the above-mentioned groups claim to be pursuing the public interest, they can be generally categorized as "self-interested" groups because their principal concern is to improve their own position, usually economic. The true "public interest" group exists to promote causes that it sees as beneficial to society as a whole and that do not directly benefit its own members: the John Howard Society (improving prison conditions and the lot of ex-inmates), the Canadian Council on Social Development (promoting better social policy), the Canadian Civil Liberties Association (protecting civil liberties from government infringement), and a variety of environmental groups, among others.

Most of the groups named above and many others are called **institutionalized groups** because they are permanent, well-established, formal organizations. Almost all maintain a head office in Ottawa with a full-time staff, a sizable budget, and a reasonably stable membership. Most have developed continuous links with the authorities and represent their members' interests on a daily basis, year after year.

These characteristics are not possessed by all advocacy groups, however, and other labels have been attached to them. Some groups spring up spontaneously around a specific issue, and once it is resolved, they fade away. Such **issue-oriented groups** lack the institutionalized groups' permanence, office, staff, budget, membership, and access to the authorities. Instead, they more likely resort to attracting public attention to their cause through media coverage of actions like demonstrations. Because issue-oriented groups usually disappear when the issue has been resolved, they are not as familiar as institutionalized groups, but several famous examples can be cited. In the early 1970s the Stop Spadina group opposed extension of the Spadina Expressway in Toronto and the People or Planes group fought against building the proposed Pickering airport east of that city; later, "Bread Not Circuses" opposed Toronto's bids to host the Olympic Games.[10] Other recent cases include Rural Dignity, a spontaneous national group that sprang up to fight against the deterioration of rural and small-town life in general, and of its mail service in particular, and the Foundation for Equal Families, which fought for same-sex amendments to federal statutes. If their issue is not resolved, or if they anticipate further challenges, such groups may become a more permanent fixture, gradually evolving from an issue-oriented group to the institutionalized category.

Other categorizations are sometimes useful in discussing advocacy groups. Most groups are "autonomous" in the sense that they develop without government initiative, although they may later seek government financial support. However, politicians or bureaucrats may actually be involved in the creation of such groups, whether for personal gain or in the hope of promoting a certain public policy objective. In the late 1960s, for example, the federal government began to fund anti-poverty, women's, minority official language, Aboriginal, and other ethnic groups.[11] The Mulroney government cut back on grants to many such groups, however, both for fiscal and for ideological reasons, something Pierre Trudeau's government had also done on occasion when a particular group became too critical of the hand that fed it. Such grant reductions demonstrate a lack of political sincerity as well as the dangers involved in becoming too critical and too dependent.[12]

CRITICAL APPROACHES

The *pluralist approach* would seem, at first sight, most relevant to the subject of advocacy groups. It argues that public policy emerges from the competition and accommodation among organized groups, claiming that all interests in society are free to organize and participate, as the array of advocacy groups listed in this chapter at least partially confirms. But Miriam Smith argues that the contentions of pluralism are seriously flawed and that it is impossible not to recognize the persistent social inequality that creates barriers to the formation of advocacy groups that represent the permanently marginalized interests in society.[13] Her observation would suggest that the *class approach* is actually more appropriate. Class analysts refute the pluralist claim that with a little effort any interest can organize itself into a group, and decry the disparity in resources and consequent influence between affluent business groups and hard-pressed labour, farmer, consumer, Aboriginal, women's, and anti-poverty groups. Class analysts contend that the predominance of business groups flows naturally from the marriage of a capitalist economy with a democracy. Leo Panitch writes that "it is not that political and bureaucratic officials decide to favour capitalist interests in case after case; it is rather that it rarely even occurs to them that they might do other than favour such interests."[14] As mentioned in Chapter 8, this is partly because the state is dependent on businesses for the performance of the economy.

SOCIAL MOVEMENTS

Political scientists often find it useful to distinguish between advocacy groups and social movements. Many of the issue-oriented groups referred to are, in fact, part of larger, unstructured social movements, of which the environmental, women's, peace, human rights, and consumers' movements have been most prominent. Other examples include the Aboriginal, gay liberation, and animal rights movements. A social movement has been defined as an informal network of organizations and individuals who, on the basis of a collective identity and shared values, engage in political or cultural struggle intended to expand the boundaries of the existing system and undertake collective action designed to affect both state and society.[15] Social movements begin at the margins of the political system and possess an alternative set of values and expectations. Although they rarely have much immediate impact, many have managed to change society's way of thinking over time. They bring new issues into the system, but are forced to try to alter social values before they can succeed in changing specific government policies. Social movements usually consist of coalitions of small, local groups that have not (yet) hardened into a cohesive national pressure group.[16]

Movements such as those relating to women or the environment run into much bureaucratic and political party resistance and often do not achieve immediate success.[17] In the long run, however,

THE CANADIAN PRESS/Adrian Wyld

they widen the scope of public discourse, and parties and other mainstream political institutions eventually respond. Take recent improvements in legislation with respect to women and the environment, for example, and changes in public attitudes toward war, Aboriginals, gays and lesbians, and the treatment of animals. As mentioned above, social movements are one of the most effective means, over time, of changing basic societal values.

The Council of Canadians is a citizens' movement of about 100 000 members that provides a critical voice on key national issues, such as safeguarding social programs, promoting economic justice, renewing democracy, asserting Canadian sovereignty, preserving the environment, and promoting alternatives to corporate-style free trade. It has been active on such issues as trade agreements, public pensions, bank mergers, media ownership, genetically modified foods, health care, and the sale of Canadian water. The Internet facilitates both national and international grassroots political campaigns, and such international social movements and networks are often seen

Officials from Amnesty International present boxes of petitions concerning the repatriation of Omar Khadr during a news conference on Parliament Hill in February 2009.

as one of the few counterweights to corporate globalization in the modern world.[18] The Council of Canadians is indeed part of an international network called the Blue Planet Project, which seeks to protect the world's fresh water from the threats of trade and privatization. The Council also works closely with other groups, such as the CLC, the CFS, the Sierra Club, and the Canadian Centre for Policy Alternatives. The CCPA produces regular reports, including the annual *Alternative Federal Budget*, a detailed, sophisticated document that is meant to show that despite globalization and fiscal pressures, there *are* alternatives, contrary to what governments have said.

CRITICAL APPROACHES

An important purpose of social movement politics is to raise awareness about issues and oftentimes to change the way people think. A *political psychology approach* to social movements might examine the ways in which such movements couch their appeals in the language of existing principles held by a population. For example, social movement politics in Canada has succeeded in generating a sea change in attitudes toward gays and lesbians, in part by reframing homosexuality into the domains of human freedom and equality.

ADVOCACY GROUP STRUCTURES

A word should be added about the structure of advocacy groups. Issue-oriented groups may burst forth anywhere an issue arises—at the federal, provincial, territorial, or municipal level. Institutionalized groups, conversely, tend to be organized wherever government decisions regularly affect them. The federal nature of the country means that authoritative decisions are made at two (or even three) levels of government, and most institutionalized groups parallel the federal structure of government. They find it advantageous to be organized at both levels because, as discussed in Chapter 18, the division of powers between the federal and the provincial governments is so blurred. While the Canadian Medical Association comprises autonomous provincial and territorial divisions (such as the Manitoba Medical Association), the Canadian Chamber of Commerce (CCC) and the Canadian Labour Congress (CLC) have strong provincial branches (such as the Ontario Chamber of Commerce and the Nova Scotia Federation of Labour, respectively). The CCC and CLC in particular also maintain municipal organizations—local chambers of commerce or boards of trade in every sizable community and local labour councils across the country.

Many groups, including teachers, nurses, and professors, are actually more strongly organized at the provincial level than in Ottawa. This is because they are more affected by decisions of provincial governments than by federal ones. Some, such as the medical and legal professions, are even delegated powers by provincial and territorial governments to regulate themselves.

By increasing the number of decision-making centres in the political system, federalism generally makes it easier for groups to block government action but harder to initiate new programs. Postsecondary student groups, for example, find their resources stretched as they try to influence both levels of government. Sometimes the national organization requests assistance from the provincial wings in dealing with an issue in Ottawa, while at other times a provincial unit seeks support from the national organization. The insurance industry and the medical profession first fought against medicare in Saskatchewan when it was introduced, then transferred the fight to Ottawa to oppose a national program, and finally went back to individual provinces to try to persuade them to stay out of the national scheme.[19] At other times, certain groups use their closer relations with provincial governments to transform the provinces into allies in the group's attempt to pressure Ottawa, such as the petroleum industry's campaign against the National Energy Program and the Kyoto Accord or the Assembly of First Nations' efforts to gain the federal government's attention.[20]

Many national groups are beset by regional and linguistic problems, and the Quebec wing of many national organizations has a distinct status of one kind or another. Other groups seem to handle the cleavages fairly well, having a regular provincial branch in Quebec, attempting to operate on a bilingual basis at the national level, and striving to reconcile regional–ethnic differences within the organization.[21]

TARGETS AND METHODS OF ADVOCACY GROUP ACTIVITY

Besides being affected by the federal system, Canadian interest groups are very much influenced in their operations by the fact that they exist in a parliamentary system. This, despite the name, places most of the decision-making power in the hands of the bureaucracy, the prime minister, the Cabinet, and individual ministers. Advocacy groups that understand this basic truth direct most of their attention to these parts of the executive branch of government.

Policy Communities and Policy Networks

In discussing advocacy groups, the concepts of **policy communities** and **policy networks** should be mentioned.[22] These concepts are based on the premise that each field of public policy is discrete and specialized, with its own constellation of participants. Each policy *community* consists of a set of government agencies, advocacy groups, corporations, institutions, media people, and individuals, including academics, who have an interest in that particular policy field and attempt to influence it. Paul Pross argues that every policy community is divided into two parts. The first, the "sub-government," includes a "lead government agency," other policymaking agencies, and a small group of interests with the right to be consulted on a daily basis; the second, the "attentive public," is composed of the other actors mentioned. In either case, these actors initially attempt to establish their legitimacy with the lead agency, and if they achieve such recognition and status, they may be appointed to advisory committees and be made part of the agency's information flow. Pross cites the examples of the Canadian Bankers Association and the Canadian Tax Foundation as groups that have achieved such legitimacy, as opposed to the National Farmers Union, which has not. Once such groups are given the privilege of consultation and access to strategic information, they normally behave quite cooperatively, and the whole policy community becomes cohesive and mutually supportive. Figure 16.1 illustrates this conception of the policy community.

Policy *networks* are sometimes seen as a narrower set of actors within the policy community with a higher level of interest in the policy field and with a more formal and frequent kind of interaction.[23] The literature on policy networks emphasizes that government consultation with outside groups is far more important than ever before and is just as often initiated by public policymakers as by the external interests that want to influence them. A major contributing cause of this development was the downsizing of government departments in the 1990s, which cost them crucial analytical capacities. While becoming more dependent on outside sources, however, governments began to pay them millions of dollars to produce such knowledge. Thus, policy networks emphasize the role of information and expertise rather than only the articulation of interests. Beyond the *need* for expertise, the new emphasis on policy networks is based on the widespread feeling that governments *should* seek the contribution and cooperation of the third, nonprofit, or **voluntary sector** of individuals, public interest groups, policy-oriented organizations, think tanks, and the like—in order to produce and execute better policy.[24] There is an increasing sentiment among authorities that civic engagement can lessen widespread public cynicism about government, and more will be said about such policy communities and policy networks in Chapter 20.

The Bureaucracy

As will be discussed in Chapter 22, the bureaucracy advises the prime minister, the Cabinet, and the ministers on almost all of their decisions; it drafts legislation and regulations according

FIGURE 16.1 THE POLICY COMMUNITY

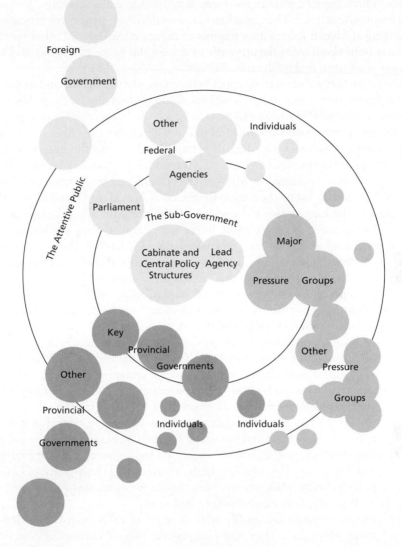

Source: A. Paul Pross, "Pressure Groups: Talking Chameleons," Michael S. Whittington and Glen Williams, eds. Canadian Politics in the 1980s, 2nd ed. 1984. Methuen. (1984), p. 304. Used with permission of the authors.

to the Cabinet's general instructions; it proposes budgets and spends government money; and it implements policies and programs once they have been given Cabinet or legislative approval. All of these areas hold considerable scope for bureaucratic discretion.[25] It is for this reason that institutionalized groups in particular direct their messages at the bureaucratic target more than at any other institution of government. Many group demands involve technical matters that only the bureaucracy understands and that it may be able to satisfy without reference to the politicians. Such groups try to cultivate close relationships with senior public servants so that they feel comfortable in contacting these officials on an informal, direct, day-to-day basis. This contact can take the form of telephone calls, meetings, letters, e-mails, faxes, and business lunches.[26] The Canadian Construction Association, for example, holds an annual meeting at Meech Lake with a number of deputy ministers and other senior government officials from about eight departments to discuss the issues of the day and ensure the continuation of an open and productive dialogue.

The close relationship that often develops between an advocacy group and its most relevant government department is increasingly a reciprocal one, as desirable for the public service as it is for the group. In return for the various ways in which the bureaucracy can respond to group demands, the group may possess information that the department needs or desires in order to understand certain situations with which it is trying to deal, and the executive directors of many such groups are accustomed to regular calls for advice. Moreover, as issues become too complex for politicians—ministers or MPs—to understand, and larger numbers of issues, constituents, and obligations eat up their time, legislation is drafted in skeletal form with the specifics delegated to the bureaucracy to be added later in the form of regulations or "delegated legislation." Bureaucrats regularly consult interested groups as they draft such legislation, design new programs, and draw up regulations. As president of the Canadian Tobacco Manufacturers' Council, for example, Bill Neville managed to dilute the original regulations dealing with the anti-smoking message that the Health Department imposed on packages of cigarettes.[27] A group may also be a valuable ally in persuading other bureaucratic agencies or Cabinet to do what the department wants and in various "output" functions described below.

Thus, what is called a **clientele relationship** sometimes develops between such groups as the Royal Canadian Legion and Veterans Affairs Canada, between the Canadian Federation of Agriculture and Agriculture and Agri-Food Canada, between the Canadian Medical Association and Health Canada, between the petroleum and mining associations and Natural Resources Canada, and between business organizations and the Department of Finance and Innovation, Science and Economic Development Canada. The relations between such an agency or department and its allied advocacy groups may become so close that it is difficult to tell them apart. The agency or department almost becomes an extension of the group, making policy in the interest of the group and promoting within the higher councils of government the interests they both represent. The minister, deputy minister, and Department of Finance speak for the business community, while the minister, deputy minister, and Agriculture and Agri-Food Canada speak for the farming community, and so on.

Although advocacy groups are usually seen in terms of their "input" function—making demands or "policy advocacy"—they may also perform various implementation or "output" functions. A group may be better equipped to inform its specialized membership or audience about new laws, regulations, or programs than a department that is restricted to the conventional media or other regular channels of communication. Minority ethnocultural groups, for example, can help Immigration, Refugees and Citizenship Canada in the dissemination of information about policy changes to a specialized audience. In some cases, as noted, certain groups are even delegated powers of self-regulation, especially the medical and legal professions at the provincial and territorial level. As governments coped with decreasing funds in the 1990s, they often sought private-sector partnerships as a way of offloading services, improving service delivery, and encouraging civic engagement.[28]

Besides such direct, personal, informal contact, interest groups interact with the bureaucracy through numerous permanent and ad hoc advisory committees. Most departments set up several advisory committees and offer representation on them to the advocacy groups most affected. The National Council of Welfare is a classic case of a group that was not only created by government to serve as an advisory committee directly representing poor people but was even given a home and staff within the building housing the Welfare Department (now Employment and Social Development Canada).

In addition, public servants themselves may be members of interest groups. For example, bureaucrats in social services departments often belong to the Canadian Council on Social Development, a situation that naturally assists the group in maximizing its influence; medical bureaucrats may belong to the Canadian Medical Association; and legal bureaucrats, to the Canadian Bar Association. In fact, considerable movement of personnel takes place between interest groups and the higher levels of the public service: officials often move from advocacy group jobs to the bureaucracy or vice versa.

The Prime Minister, the Cabinet, and Ministers

The prime minister, the Cabinet, and ministers form the second branch of government that advocacy groups frequently try to influence. This is because they make the major governmental decisions in a parliamentary system, as discussed in Chapter 21. Since many decisions are made by single ministers or Cabinet committees, it is probably most productive to submit single-issue representations to individual ministers, who actually spend much of their time in meetings with such groups.[29] If a minister stays in one position long enough, an advocacy group may be able to construct a more personal, informal relationship, as did the Canadian Federation of Agriculture with Jimmy Gardiner, who served as minister of agriculture from 1935 to 1957. Unfortunately for such groups, the practice of shuffling ministers from one department to another every couple of years decreases the likelihood of developing such intimacy. The social scene in Ottawa should also be mentioned because parties and receptions provide excellent opportunities for Cabinet ministers, deputy ministers, and established group representatives (especially corporate representatives) to meet and mingle. Occasionally, ministers are themselves members of the interest group, in which case this interlocking membership is probably an advantage to the group. Less institutionalized groups, however, may have to forgo such close relationships with Cabinet ministers in favour of letters, faxes, or other means of more formal or mass communication.

The concept of **elite accommodation** is particularly relevant to this process. It claims that most public decisions in Canada emerge from the interaction of three agents: the Cabinet, the senior public service, and pressure groups, especially in the business field. The individuals who occupy the top positions in these sectors are elites both in the sense of being small numbers of people with disproportionate amounts of power (compared with ordinary citizens) and in terms of their exclusive socioeconomic backgrounds, coming from families of higher social class, higher incomes, and higher educations. Robert Presthus thus postulates that the common backgrounds and values of political, bureaucratic, and corporate leaders help to facilitate agreement among them.[30] Commanding the heights of these sectors of society, they easily accommodate each other in the working out of public policies. Lobbyists from professional lobbying firms also fit perfectly into this arrangement.

Parliament

The third main branch of the government is the legislature or Parliament, but, as is discussed in Chapter 23, it largely legitimizes decisions previously taken by the executive. That being the case, the House of Commons is not as often the target of advocacy group activity, but it does remain the object of considerable attention. One of the main reasons that a bill is usually sent to a legislative committee during its passage is to allow interest groups to make representations on it, and such committee scrutiny of bills involving group submissions may carry on for weeks. Especially in a majority government situation, however, ministers have traditionally been reluctant to accept amendments proposed at the legislative stage, so that groups were better advised to make their case at the executive level before the bill was made public. It has even been said that the sight of a pressure group at the legislative level in Canada is a sign that the group has already failed at the level of the bureaucracy and the Cabinet. Nevertheless, many group-inspired amendments to legislation have been accepted in recent years, perhaps most notably the changes made to the Charter of Rights before its final adoption in the early 1980s as a result of pressure from such groups as women, Aboriginals, people with disabilities, and ethnocultural minorities. The Standing Committee on Finance, with its pre-budget hearings, is integrated into the expenditure management system and listens to established groups on an annual basis. Groups also converge on MPs in their offices or inundate them with letters, e-mails, or postcards from group members. For example, while not diminishing its influence at the levels of Cabinet and bureaucracy, the Canadian Chamber of Commerce is particularly adept at applying pressure on MPs through its base in almost every constituency across the country. Groups also meet with chairs of Commons standing committees, individual party caucuses, or caucus committees. Certain MPs may already belong to the interest group or may be persuaded to join, in which case they can be expected to speak on behalf of the group on a committee or in the Commons, in another aspect of interlocking membership between groups and authorities. Many groups hold receptions on Parliament Hill to develop a positive image with its hungry, thirsty denizens, and MPs are often happy to attend celebrations and dinners held by various groups as part of their broader electoral strategies.

The upper chamber of Parliament, the Senate, can also be lobbied by groups, but it may be involved in a somewhat different dimension. At least in the past, many senators had close corporate connections and functioned regularly as lobbyists for big business, such that the Senate was called a "lobby from within."[31] During passage in that chamber, much legislation was considered by the Senate Committee on Banking, Trade and Commerce, many of whose members held directorships in Canadian banks and other large corporations. Such connections did not deter committee members from active consideration of questions relating to financial institutions in what appears to be a classic case of conflict of interest. Today's senators are not so closely tied to the corporate sector.

Other Targets

Advocacy groups have many targets beyond these three main branches of government. If they can find a legal or constitutional angle to their demand, for example, such groups may take cases to the courts. Corporations have sometimes challenged federal or provincial legislation in the courts as a violation of the division of powers. Francophone groups have used the courts to uphold constitutionally guaranteed minority group language rights when politicians were reluctant to do so, and Aboriginal groups are increasingly using the courts to recognize or broaden the meaning of treaty and Aboriginal rights. The Charter of Rights and Freedoms provides added potential for targeting the courts by actually inviting individuals and groups to challenge federal or provincial legislation they consider to be discriminatory. Women's groups have been involved in many such cases, and same-sex groups made major advances in the courts at the end of the 20th century.[32] Earlier in the post-1982 period, the government actually encouraged disadvantaged groups to use the courts as part of their struggle with financial support from the **Court Challenges Program**. As shown in Chapter 19, however, it was corporate interests that most often challenged laws against the Charter.

As mentioned, only the Canadian Labour Congress has seen fit to attach itself formally to a political party. This strategy may have reduced the group's impact on Liberal and Conservative governments as it awaited an NDP victory. Chapter 13 discussed reforms to party and election finance laws that have forced the CLC and its member unions to find new ways of supporting the party.[33] Other groups remain scrupulously nonpartisan so that they can exert equal influence on whichever party is in power.

Another target of group activity is the **royal commission**. Although not so common any more, these elaborate investigations of public problems normally invite interest groups and experts to submit briefs in public hearings to supplement whatever original research the commission itself undertakes, as well as to generate support for its recommendations. Sometimes an interest group is actually represented on the commission itself, as in the case of the Canadian Medical Association and the Hall Royal Commission on Medical Services in the 1960s.

Besides their direct representations to government, advocacy groups increasingly try to influence public opinion in the hope that the authorities will respond to a clear message from the public. In what is called **advocacy advertising**, corporations and groups also use paid media advertising in an attempt to sway public opinion to their point of view.[34] For example, both Canada's Research-Based Pharmaceutical Companies and the rival Canadian Generic Pharmaceutical Association have taken out media advertisements to make their case on the question of patent protection for new pharmaceuticals. In 2002, there was massive advertising on both sides of the Kyoto Protocol, and in 2005, by the Canadian Nuclear Association. The Internet has allowed groups to mobilize both domestically (through such social networks as Facebook) and internationally.

Many advocacy groups increase their public profile once an election has been called.[35] This phenomenon, discussed in Chapter 13, is usually called **third-party advertising**. Groups on both sides of the abortion debate and the **National Citizens Coalition** are regular examples, while the Canadian Alliance for Jobs and Trade Prospects and its anti-free-trade counterpart, the Pro-Canada Network, were particularly visible in 1988. National or local groups sometimes target particular politicians, especially ministers, for defeat. The Canada Elections Act places strict limits on third party advertising during election campaigns, but no such limits exist outside of an election campaign. Prime Minister Stephen Harper used this law to his advantage by doubling the length of the 2015 Canadian election campaign period. This reduced the amount of anti-Conservative messaging that unions and other groups were able to broadcast.

Groups may also employ demonstrations, protest marches, tractor parades, sit-ins, and road and bridge blockades.[36] Some of these are peaceful and legal, such as the orderly demonstrations that are an almost daily occurrence on Parliament Hill and that frequently greet prime ministers on their travels. The Canadian Federation of Students organized the pan-Canadian Days of Action in October 1998, featuring protest marches, rallies, sit-ins, and informational pickets, and opponents of gun control participated in a demonstration to burn their firearm registration forms. But the frustration of Aboriginal, environmentalist, and groups increasingly sometimes the form of civil disobedience, such as the "Occupy movement" in 2011.

There is always the danger that a demonstration intended to be peaceful may degenerate into violence, such as the protests of postsecondary students in Quebec in the spring of 2012. Or, in the case of the G8/G20 demonstrations in 2010, the protest may be infiltrated by violence-prone individuals or groups. The armed Aboriginal standoff at Oka, Quebec, in 1990 was one of the rare occasions in which a group deliberately resorted to violence, but this occurred only after governments failed to respond to the Mohawks' verbal protests.

As political issues increasingly cross national borders, advocacy group action now often takes a transnational form. Miriam Smith demonstrates three ways in which this happens: groups appeal to international organizations to pressure the Canadian state, they form alliances with other groups outside Canada to pursue common objectives, and they mobilize to influence politics elsewhere in the world.[37] Aboriginal and women's groups in Canada are good examples of using the United Nations to further their domestic causes. Both have also developed links with similar groups in other countries, as have those opposed to comprehensive trade agreements and those aiming to protect the environment. Groups in Canada are also active in protesting certain policies of other states.

GROUP RESOURCES AND DETERMINANTS OF SUCCESS

Why are groups sometimes successful and sometimes not? A variety of factors are involved in accounting for such success and failure, including the following:

- sympathy of and access to the government
- information
- financial position of the government
- members and cohesion
- money
- popularity of the cause
- absence of opposition

The sympathy of the government and access to policymakers are usually very important.[38] If a basic correspondence exists between the demands of the group and the government's stated objectives—if they share basic values—the advocacy group will have greater success than if there is a vast gap in ideological perspective. For example, the Mulroney and Harper Conservative governments were obviously more receptive to business than labour representations.[39] The Harper government was determined to promote development of the petroleum and coal industries, regardless of environmental considerations; it responded to coal companies to defer enforcement of regulations, and worked closely with the Canadian Association of Petroleum Producers on several fronts.

Information is a second crucial resource in advocacy group politics.[40] Especially at the bureaucratic level, where much of this politics takes place, any vital information that is lacking as the public service designs programs will be eagerly accepted. The Canadian Bar Association, for example, is often asked for advice in both the substance of many issues and the drafting of legislation.

Many group demands relate to the spending of public money, and as a result the financial position of the government will often influence a group's success. In the free-spending 1960s and 1970s, for example, groups such as the Canadian Federation of Students felt more fulfilled than during the last 30 years which were generally marked by government restraint.

The size of the group may also be important because membership numbers represent votes. In this respect, the Canadian Labour Congress should be regularly successful in having the authorities respond to its demands because it is the largest advocacy group in the country. But the lack of cohesiveness among its three million members limits its impact.[41] Not all union members belong to the CLC and even amongst those that do, unity, commitment, and militancy are seriously lacking. Postsecondary students could also benefit from greater cohesion in the world of advocacy politics. In contrast, the Royal Canadian Legion and the Canadian Chamber of Commerce are able to mobilize their local members to inundate the authorities with demands for concerted action.[42]

Money, of course, can be used by advocacy groups to buy staff, offices, organization, expertise, publicity, and other useful weapons. The four peak business groups are very well-endowed financially, giving them the capacity to generate information and to transmit it effectively. Except for business groups or highly paid professions, however, most groups struggle with their finances.[43]

It will also help if the cause is supported by public opinion—if it is consistent with the prevailing values of society in general. For example, although Canadian banks are used to getting their way with government, it was largely because of the negativity of public opinion that various governments have rejected bank mergers over the past 15 years.[44]

Finally, a group will be more influential if it has no organized opposition. One of the reasons for the success of the Canadian Medical Association over the years, for example, was that it had medical politics almost all to itself.[45]

Taking all these resources into account, as claimed in Chapter 8, business groups are the most likely to get their way. In his book, *Titans*, Peter C. Newman argued that the agenda of the Mulroney and Chrétien governments was set by the Business Council of Canada. First, it was free trade, then deficit reduction, and then tax cuts. He claims that these two governments came to agree that what was good for that group was good for Canada, and its president emerged as "the most powerful influence on public policy formation in Canadian history."[46]

LOBBYING IN CANADA

The tendency of the rich and powerful, including big business, to benefit from pressure group politics and elite accommodation can only be enhanced by recent developments in the practice of lobbying in Canada. If lobbying is the activity of trying to influence the authorities, it is, of course, a perfectly legitimate activity for anyone to undertake in a democracy. Traditionally, individuals, companies, unions, and advocacy groups of all kinds have done their own lobbying, but in recent years Canada has seen the mushrooming of professional lobbying—consultant lobbyists or government relations firms that lobby on behalf of an individual, company, advocacy group, or other organization in return for payment of a fee.

Emergence of Modern Lobbying

Those engaged in the new lobbying industry justify their existence largely in terms of the increasing size and complexity of government. The federal government grew enormously in the 1960s and 1970s, and the policymaking process was restructured so that corporations and advocacy groups could no longer find their way around Ottawa.[47] That the hostile budgets of 1980 (National Energy Program) and 1981 (corporate tax reform) caught the business community by surprise also contributed to the development of new means through which the corporate sector could make its voice heard more effectively.

The early 1980s was thus a period in which new avenues of influence were being sought, and an expansion of lobbying firms appeared to take place about the time the Mulroney government was elected in 1984. Many of the leading figures in the initial establishment of professional lobby firms were cronies of the prime minister.[48] Certain leading legal firms also set up lobbying operations. Given that the bureaucracy can satisfy many of the corporations' needs, several bureaucrats left government employment to join or form lobbying firms in order to capitalize on their inside knowledge and connections. Conflict-of-interest guidelines were supposed to preclude senior government ex-employees from dealing with their former departments for a certain time after their departure from public employment but these rules were sometimes broken.

Legalizing Lobbying: The Registration System

After the emergence of such professional lobbying firms, a consensus developed among politicians that legislation, registration, and regulation were necessary. The registration idea was part of the Mulroney Conservatives' ethics package unveiled after its early troubled record of Cabinet resignations due to conflicts of interest and numerous legal charges against Tory backbenchers.[49]

According to the 1985 Lobbying Act, a lobbyist is an individual who, " … for payment, on behalf of any person or organization …

a) undertakes to communicate with a public office holder in respect of

    i)   the development of any legislative proposal …

    ii) the introduction, passage, defeat or amendment of any bill or resolution …

    iii) the making or amendment of any regulation …

    iv) the development or amendment of any policy or program …

    v) the awarding of any grant or contribution or other financial benefit … or

    vi) the awarding of any contract.

b) arrange a meeting between a public office holder and any other person."[50]

The legislation acknowledged that lobbying public officeholders was a legitimate activity, but it required lobbyists to register because it was desirable that officials and the public knew who was attempting to influence government and because paid lobbyists should not impede free and open access to government. It excluded representations made to parliamentary committees or other cases where the representations were a matter of public record and submissions made in direct response to a written request for advice or comment from a public officeholder.

The law divided lobbyists into two categories: those who worked for a client for a fee were classified as "Tier I" lobbyists, while "Tier II" lobbyists included those who engaged in traditional pressure group or corporate lobbying—that is, "in-house" employees whose duties involved communicating with public officeholders on behalf of the organization that employed them. Both types of lobbyists had to register their activities in the Registry of Lobbyists.

Many critics felt that the legislation was very weak and contrasted it with the U.S. law on this subject, which was adopted in 1946.[51] Some lobbyists did not register, and even when they did, the disclosure provisions in the Canadian law were quite minimal. The law did not require revelation of the specific object of the representations and was almost totally lacking in an effective enforcement mechanism.

The Lobbyists Registration Act was strengthened in 1995, primarily to require the inclusion of following additional information:

- if the client is a corporation, the name and business address of the parent corporation and those subsidiaries that directly benefit from the lobbying activity;
- if the client is a coalition, the name and business address of each corporation or organization that is a member of the coalition;
- subject matters, including the specific legislative proposal, bill, resolution, regulation, policy, program, grant, contribution, financial benefit, or contract sought;
- name of each department or other governmental institution lobbied;
- source and amount of any government funding provided to the client;
- whether payment is contingent on the success of the lobbying; and
- communication techniques used, including grassroots lobbying; that is, appeals to the public through the mass media or direct communications that seek to persuade members of the public to communicate directly with and apply pressure on the public officeholder.[52]

Coalitions and grassroots lobbying efforts had to be registered for the first time, and if contingency fees were involved, this had to be disclosed. As for enforcement, the six-month limitation of proceedings on contraventions was extended to two years. The ethics counsellor previously appointed by the Liberal government to administer the Conflict of Interest Code for ministers was required to work with interested parties to develop a code of conduct for lobbyists, which took effect in March 1997.[53]

Lobbying under the Chrétien, Martin, and Harper Governments

In the Chrétien government, ministers were forced to get by with a small number of partisan assistants, and the bureaucracy was allowed to operate with greater independence. Hence, the

"Let the politicians fight. The lobbyists and bureaucrats will continue to run the government."

Chris Wildt/Artizans

focus of lobbyists' efforts switched to some extent from ministers' offices to the level of the senior bureaucracy.

Lobbying became more sophisticated over time. Instead of (or in addition to) promising access to ministers, lobbyists now had to be able to tell their clients what the government was thinking and where it was going and to provide strategic advice on how and whom to lobby. But while the revised law was a slight improvement, it remained highly defective. "By leaving vague the definitions of lobbying, and by excluding any lobbying associated with a consultative exercise, the government … left much room for those sincerely wishing to avoid disclosing their activities or their aims to do so."[54] Moreover, the enforcement of the law left much to be desired. It was not until 1999 that the RCMP looked into its first potential violation of the act in connection with a Liberal activist, René Fugère, a man close to the prime minister, who did not register as a lobbyist but met civil servants on behalf of a Shawinigan hotel owner who received a $100 000 government cheque to expand his operations. After the RCMP investigation into the affair, the prosecutors decided not to file a criminal charge, even though Fugère clearly engaged in lobbying without registering. Two later cases were reviewed by the registrar of the Lobbyists Registration Branch but were not even referred to the RCMP for further investigation.

There were other serious problems with lobbying during the Chrétien regime, especially the increasing dependence of government departments themselves on lobbying firms. In particular, because such firms often include polling in their repertoire of services, departments started hiring them for advice that involved gauging the state of public opinion. Paul Martin employed the lobbying firm Earnscliffe to do pre-budget polling in 2000, and Ottawa observers noted that Earnscliffe was closely tied to virtually everything done by Martin and the Department of Finance while he was there. Many claim that there was a blatant conflict of interest when Earnscliffe both lobbied the Department on behalf of clients on the one hand and did communications and polling for the department on the other. Many at Earnscliffe were later at the heart of Martin's campaign to seek the Liberal leadership. Indeed, many lobbyists worked part-time for the Liberal Party or for individual Liberal leadership contenders.

The **Gomery Report** on the Quebec sponsorship scandal supported further revisions to the lobbying registration scheme, incorporating some, but not all, of the recommendations made by the organization Democracy Watch.[55] The Harper government's **Federal Accountability Act** renamed the LR Act the **Lobbying Act** and made significant changes. It banned contingency fees; provided for the appointment of a commissioner of lobbying as an independent agent of Parliament with additional investigatory powers; prohibited ministerial staffers, ministers, and senior public servants from registering as lobbyists for five years after leaving office; required that lobbyists record telephone calls and in-person meetings (but not e-mails) with senior public officeholders; and extended the period during which infractions could be investigated to 10 years.[56] Nevertheless, most of its provisions did not come into effect until July 2008 and others were watered down in the regulations issued under the Act. Thus, most lobbying firms in Ottawa were happy to take on new Conservative partners who would undoubtedly prove to be positive additions. The Office of the Commissioner of Lobbying in Canada provides documentation on this subject, available at http://ocl-cal.gc.ca/app/secure/orl/lrrs/do/slctRprt?action=lobbyistReport. In August 2015, some 765 consultant lobbyists had 2041 active registrations; these were supplemented by 1658 in-house Corporation lobbyists and 2639 in-house Organization lobbyists.[57] Table 16.2 lists some of the largest such firms and their principal clients in 2015.

Because of the fees involved, big corporations and business pressure groups make the greatest use of consultant lobbyists; many corporations are clients of more than one professional lobbying firm, and many employ their own in-house lobbyists as well. Traditional pressure groups sometimes engage professional lobbyists to supplement their supplications to government because consultant lobbyists tend to be better strategists and can be used to build coalitions and share expenses on matters in which such cooperation is advantageous. Only a small number of trade unions, First Nations, and other nonprofit organizations have employed lobbyists, and that partisan ties continue to play a significant part in the lobbying process makes the system doubly objectionable. Moreover, companies can deduct lobbyist fees (or the fees of belonging to an advocacy group) from their corporate income tax. Young and Everitt would like to level the playing field a bit by allowing tax credits for contributions to genuine public interest groups.[58]

Statistics from the Commissioner of Lobbying in mid-2012 show that the six government institutions most actively lobbied were the House of Commons, Industry Canada, the Prime Minister's Office, Finance Canada, Foreign Affairs and International Trade, and the Privy

TABLE 16.2 SELECTED CONSULTANT LOBBYING FIRMS AND PRINCIPAL CLIENTS, 2015

FIRM	CLIENTS
GLOBAL PUBLIC AFFAIRS	SHELL CANADA, CANADIAN ASSOCIATION OF PETROLEUM PRODUCERS, BAYER, AMEX CANADA
HILL & KNOWLTON	BELL CANADA, MERCK FROSST, RX&D—CANADA'S RESEARCH-BASED PHARMACEUTICAL COMPANIES
EARNSCLIFFE STRATEGY GROUP	MICROSOFT, GENERAL MOTORS, SHAW COMMUNICATIONS, CIBC, MCDONALD'S CANADA

Source: Created by authors using data from Office of the Commissioner of Lobbying of Canada. http://ocl-cal.gc.ca/eic/site/012.nsf/eng/home.

Council Office. The most common subject matter of active registrations at that time were industry, environment, taxation and finance, and international trade.[59] These two sets of figures reveal two unsurprising developments: most of the lobbying is done with respect to economic issues (that is to say, by business interests), and given the centralized operation of the Harper government, the PCO and PMO became two of the agencies most heavily subject to lobbying efforts. Because the official registration reports are still not particularly forthcoming, it is fortunate that a private company, Advocacy Research Centre (ARC), fills the gap with a biweekly edition of the *Lobby Monitor*. This publication details the major lobbying efforts currently in progress, the techniques being used, and the people involved. A more critical account comes from periodic revelations of Democracy Watch, which reminds us of the continuing secrecy over lobbyists' fees and the cost of a lobbying campaign, subjects that are transparent in the corresponding U.S. law.

CONCLUSION

This chapter confirms the contention that advocacy groups and lobbying are becoming increasingly important in the Canadian political system. The number and activity of such groups have grown over time, and however much they are an unintended appendage to the system, modern government could simply not do without them. More and more, government is actually seeking their involvement in the policymaking process. As for lobbying, the Harper government's Federal Accountability Act made some improvements, although this murky underside of Canadian politics could still use additional regulation and transparency. One main issue is the continuing unlevel playing field among business and professional interests on the one hand and social movements and unorganized interests on the other. The lobbying industry in particular has given corporate interests a powerful new means of influence at the very time that corporate contributions to political parties were prohibited on the ground that they increased the "democratic deficit."

This chapter is thus primarily linked to Chapter 8 (class) and the various branches of government, discussed in Chapters 20 to 24, especially the bureaucracy. But advocacy groups based on ethnicity, gender, class, religion, age, and location were also encountered in Chapters 4 through 9, and Chapter 13 included "third-party" engagement in election campaigns.

DISCUSSION QUESTIONS

1. Are you a member of any groups that at least occasionally try to influence government policy? Are you familiar with any local issue-oriented groups or social movements?

2. Why do business groups have more influence than other kinds of groups? Do they have too much?

3. How could the unorganized be helped to organize and how could weak groups be strengthened in order to offset the influence of business?

4. What factors led to the growth in the professional lobbying industry in Canada in recent years?

5. Even after the Harper government's Federal Accountability Act, how could the Lobbying Act be strengthened?

MindTap®   FOR MORE INFO GO TO http://www.nelson.com/student

NOTES

1. Paul Pross, *Group Politics and Public Policy* (Toronto: Oxford University Press, 1986).
2. Lisa Young and Joanna Everitt, *Advocacy Groups* (Vancouver: UBC Press, 2004).
3. Ibid., pp. 21–22; and Miriam Smith, "Interest Groups and Social Movements," in Michael Whittington and Glen Williams, eds., *Canadian Politics in the 21st Century*, 7th ed. (Toronto: Nelson Education, 2008).
4. Pross, *Group Politics and Public Policy*, pp. 92–93.
5. Miriam Smith, "Interest Groups and Social Movements," 7th ed., p. 171; Miriam Smith, *Group Politics and Social Movements in Canada*, Ch. 1.
6. William D. Coleman, *Business and Politics: A Study of Collective Action* (Montreal: McGill-Queen's University Press, 1988); Stephen Brooks and Andrew Stritch, *Business and Government in Canada* (Scarborough: Prentice Hall Canada, 1991), Ch. 7; W.T. Stanbury, *Business–Government Relations in Canada* (Toronto: Methuen, 1986), esp. Ch. 7; Geoffrey Hale, *The Uneasy Partnership: Politics of Business and Government in Canada* (Peterborough: Broadview Press, 2006); Peter Clancy, "Business Interests and Civil Society in Canada," in Smith, *Group Politics and Social Movements in Canada*; and group websites.
7. Coleman, *Business and Politics*, p. 6.
8. Ibid., p. 45. In 1994 he counted more than 600 in "One Step Ahead: Business in the Policy Process in Canada," in Mark Charlton and Paul Barker, eds., *Crosscurrents: Contemporary Political Issues*, 2nd ed. (Scarborough: Nelson Canada, 1994).
9. Grace Skogstad, *The Politics of Agricultural Policy-Making in Canada* (Toronto: University of Toronto Press, 1987).
10. Jim Silver, *Thin Ice: Money, Politics and the Demise of an NHL Franchise* (Halifax: Fernwood Publishing, 1996).
11. Leslie Pal, *Interests of State: The Politics of Language, Multiculturalism, and Feminism in Canada* (Montreal: McGill-Queen's University Press, 1993).
12. See William Coleman and Grace Skogstad, eds., *Policy Communities and Public Policy in Canada* (Mississauga: Copp Clark Pitman, 1990); and Young and Everitt, *Advocacy Groups*, pp. 76–82.
13. Smith, "Interest Groups and Social Movements," 7th edition, pp. 170–71.
14. Leo Panitch, ed., *The Canadian State: Political Economy and Political Power* (Toronto: University of Toronto Press, 1977), p. 14.
15. Susan D. Phillips, "New Social Movements in Canadian Politics: Past Their Apex?" in J.P. Bickerton and A.G. Gagnon, eds., *Canadian Politics*, 3rd ed. Peterborough: Broadview Press, 1999; William K. Carroll, ed., *Organizing Dissent: Contemporary Social Movements in Theory and Practice*, 2nd ed. (Toronto: Garamond Press, 1997); Smith, "Interest Groups and Social Movements"; Jill Vickers, *Reinventing Political Science: A Feminist Approach* (Halifax: Fernwood Publishing, 1997); and Matt James, *Misrecognized Materialists: Social Movements in Canadian Constitutional Politics* (Vancouver: UBC Press, 2006).
16. Claude Galipeau, "Political Parties, Interest Groups, and New Social Movements," in Alain Gagnon and Brian Tanguay, eds., *Canadian Parties in Transition* (Scarborough: Nelson Canada, 1989).

17. Alexandra Dobrowolsky, "The Women's Movement in Flux: Feminism and Framing, Passion, and Politics," and Judith I. McKenzie, "The Environmental Movement in Canada: Retreat or Resurgence?" in Smith, *Group Politics and Social Movements in Canada*.

18. Jeffrey M. Ayres, *Defying Conventional Wisdom: Political Movements and Popular Contention against North American Free Trade* (Toronto: University of Toronto Press, 1998); and R.S. Ratner, "Many Davids, One Goliath," in Carroll, ed., *Organizing Dissent*.

19. Malcolm Taylor, *Health Insurance and Canadian Public Policy* (Montreal: McGill-Queen's University Press, 1978).

20. M.W. Bucovetsky, "The Mining Industry and the Great Tax Reform Debate," in Paul Pross, ed., *Pressure Group Behaviour in Canadian Politics* (Toronto: McGraw-Hill Ryerson, 1975); Glyn Berry, "The Oil Lobby and the Energy Crisis," *Canadian Public Administration* (Winter 1974); and Glen Toner and Bruce Doern, "The Two Energy Crises and Canadian Oil and Gas Interest Groups," *Canadian Journal of Political Science* (September 1986).

21. William D. Coleman and Tim A. Mau, "French–English Relations in Business-Interest Associations: 1965–2002," *Canadian Public Administration* (Winter 2002); David Cameron and Richard Simeon, *Language Matters: How Canadian Voluntary Associations Manage French and English* (Vancouver: UBC Press, 2010).

22. Pross, *Group Politics and Public Policy*, Ch. 6; Coleman, *Business and Politics*, Ch. 4; Leslie A. Pal, *Beyond Policy Analysis: Public Issue Management in Turbulent Times*, 3rd ed. (Toronto: Thomson Nelson, 2006), Ch. 6; and Smith, "Interest Groups," p. 223.

23. Pal, *Beyond Policy Analysis*, Ch. 6; Young and Everitt, *Advocacy Groups*, p. 7; Donald J. Savoie, *Breaking The Bargain: Public Servants, Ministers, and Parliament* (Toronto: University of Toronto Press, 2003), Ch. 6; Steve Patten, "Democratizing the Institutions of Policy-Making: Democratic Consultation and Participatory Administration," *Journal of Canadian Studies* (Winter 2001); and Eric Montpetit, "Public Consultations in Policy Network Environments: The Case of Assisted Reproductive Technology Policy in Canada," *Canadian Public Policy* (2003).

24. Pal, *Beyond Policy Analysis*, p. 261; Rachel Laforest, *Voluntary Sector Organization and the State: Building New Relations* (Vancouver: UBC Press, 2011).

25. Paul Pross, "Parliamentary Influence and the Diffusion of Power," *Canadian Journal of Political Science* (June 1985).

26. Pross, Group Politics and Public Policy; Brooks and Stritch, *Business and Government in Canada*, Ch. 7; Coleman, *Business and Politics*; and Stanbury, *Business-Government Relations in Canada*, Ch. 7.

27. Brooks and Stritch, *Business and Government in Canada*, pp. 237–38.

28. Leslie Seidel, *Rethinking the Delivery of Public Services to Citizens* (Montreal: Institute for Research on Public Policy, 1995); and Coleman, *Business and Politics*, Ch. 3.

29. Pross, "Parliamentary Influence and the Diffusion of Power."

30. Robert Presthus, *Elite Accommodation in Canada* (Toronto: Macmillan, 1973). On corporatism, see Stephen McBride, "Public Policy as a Determinant of Interest Group Behaviour: The Canadian Labour Congress' Corporatist Initiative, 1976–1978," *Canadian Journal of Political Science* (September 1983).

31. Colin Campbell, *The Canadian Senate: A Lobby from Within* (Toronto: Methuen, 1983), and John McMenemy, "The Senate as an Instrument of Business and McGraw-Hill Ryerson, 1991). See also David McInnes, *Taking It to the Hill: The Complete Guide to Appearing before Parliamentary Committees*, 2nd ed. (Ottawa: University of Ottawa Press, 2006).

32. Miriam Smith, *Lesbian and Gay Rights in Canada: Social Movements and Equality-Seeking, 1971–1995* (Toronto: University of Toronto Press, 1999); Young and Everitt, *Advocacy Groups*, pp. 112–15; and Smith, "Interest Groups," p. 225.

33. Harold Jansen and Lisa Young, "Solidarity Forever? The NDP, Organized Labour, and the Changing Face of Party Finance in Canada," *Canadian Journal of Political Science* (September 2009).

34. Brooks and Stritch, *Business and Government in Canada*, pp. 260–64; Stanbury, *Business-Government Relations in Canada*, Ch. 12; and Smith, "Interest Groups," p. 226.

35. Young and Everitt, *Advocacy Groups*, pp. 195–11; and Smith, "Interest Groups," p. 222.

36. Young and Everitt, *Advocacy Groups*, pp. 115–21; and Smith, "Interest Groups," p. 220.

37. Smith, "Interest Groups," pp. 226–28.

38. Young and Everitt, *Advocacy Groups*, pp. 131–32.

39. Peter C. Newman, *Titans: How the New Canadian Establishment Seized Power* (Toronto: Penguin, 1998), pp. 154–62.

40. Young and Everitt, *Advocacy Groups*, pp. 133–34.

41. David Camfield, "The Working-Class Movement in Canada: An Overview," and Charlotte Yates, "Organized Labour in Canadian Politics: Hugging the Middle or Pushing the Margins?" in Smith, *Group Politics and Social Movements in Canada.*

42. The Canadian Chamber of Commerce, "Action Call," 1990.

43. Young and Everitt, *Advocacy Groups*, pp. 47–51.

44. John A. Chenier and Scott R. Duncan, eds., *The Federal Lobbyists, 1999* (Ottawa: ARC Publications, 1999), pp. 225–29; and Russell Alan Williams, "Mergers If Necessary, but Not Necessarily Mergers: Competition and Consolidation at Canada's 'Big Banks,'" in Robert M. Campbell, Leslie A. Pal, and Michael Howlett, eds., *The Real Worlds of Canadian Politics*, 4th ed. (Peterborough: Broadview Press, 2004).

45. Malcolm Taylor, "The Role of the Medical Profession in the Formulation of Public Policy," *Canadian Journal of Economics and Political Science* (February, 1960).

46. Newman, *Titans*, pp. 154–62; Young and Everitt, *Advocacy Groups*, pp. 135–136; and Hale, *The Uneasy Partnership: Politics of Business and Government in Canada.*

47. Peter Aucoin, "Organizational Change in the Machinery of Canadian Government: From Rational Management to Brokerage Politics," *Canadian Journal of Political Science* (March 1986).

48. Brooks and Stritch, *Business and Government in Canada*, Ch. 4; and Craig Forcese and Aaron Freeman, *The Laws of Government: The Legal Foundations of Canadian Democracy* (Toronto: Irwin Law, 2005), Ch. 8.

49. Ian Greene, "Conflict of Interest and the Canadian Constitution: An Analysis of Conflict of Interest Rules for Canadian Cabinet Ministers," *Canadian Journal of Political Science* (June 1990).

50. Lobbying Act, R.S.C., 1985, c.44(4th Supp.).

51. Brooks and Stritch, *Business and Government in Canada*, p. 240; and John Sawatsky, *The Insiders: Government, Business, and the Lobbyists* (Toronto: McClelland and Stewart, 1987), Epilogue.

52. Office of the Commissioner of Lobbying of Canada, available at http://www.ocl-cal.gc.ca/eic/site/ 012 .nsf/Intro.

53. Ibid.

54. John A. Chenier, ed., *The Federal Lobbyists, 1995* (Ottawa: ARC Publications, 1995), p. ii; and Forcese and Freeman, *The Laws of Government*, p. 465.

55. Democracy Watch, "The System is the Scandal," press release issued on April 14, 2005, as well as press releases of November 22, 2004 and August 18, 2005, available at http://www.dwatch.ca; Forcese and Freeman, *The Laws of Government*, Ch. 8.

56. Robert Shepherd, "Evaluating the Rationale of the New Federal *Lobbying Act*: Making Lobbying Transparent or Regulating the Industry?" in Allan M. Maslove, ed., *How Ottawa Spends 2009–2010* (Montreal: McGill-Queen's University Press, 2009).

57. Office of the Commissioner of Lobbying of Canada, available at http://ocl-cal.gc.ca/app/secure/orl.lrss/ do/slctRprt?action=lobbyistReport.

58. Young and Everitt, *Advocacy Groups*, pp. 82–86.

59. Office of the Commissioner of Lobbying of Canada.

FURTHER READING

Ayers, Jeffrey M. *Defying Conventional Wisdom: Political Movements and Popular Contention against North American Free Trade.* Toronto: University of Toronto Press, 1998.

Brock, Kathy, ed. *Delicate Dances: Government and the Nonprofit Sector in Canada.* Montreal: McGill-Queen's University Press, 2003.

Carroll, William K., ed. *Organizing Dissent: Contemporary Social Movements in Theory and Practice*, 2nd ed. Toronto: Garamond Press, 1997.

Coleman, William, and Grace Skogstad. *Policy Communities and Public Policy in Canada*. Mississauga: Copp Clark Pitman, 1990.

Democracy Watch. Periodic press releases.

Hale, Geoffrey. *The Uneasy Partnership: Politics of Business and Government in Canada*. Peterborough: Broadview Press, 2006.

Howlett, Michael, and M. Ramesh. *The Political Economy of Canada: An Introduction*. Toronto: McClelland and Stewart, 1992.

James, Matt. *Misrecognized Materialists: Social Movements in Canadian Constitutional Politics*. Vancouver: UBC Press, 2006.

Jansen, Harold, and Lisa Young. "Solidarity Forever? The NDP, Organized Labour, and the Changing Face of Party Finance in Canada," *Canadian Journal of Political Science* (September 2009).

Laforest, Rachel. *Voluntary Sector Organization and the State: Building New Relations*. Vancouver: UBC Press, 2011.

———. *The Lobby Monitor*. Ottawa: ARC Publications, biweekly.

McInnes, David. *Taking It to the Hill: The Complete Guide to Appearing before Parliamentary Committees*, 2nd ed. Ottawa: University of Ottawa Press, 2006.

Newman, Peter C. *Titans: How the New Canadian Establishment Seized Power*. Toronto: Penguin, 1998.

Pal, Leslie A. *Interests of State: The Politics of Language, Multiculturalism, and Feminism in Canada*. Montreal: McGill-Queen's University Press, 1993.

———. *Beyond Policy Analysis: Public Issue Management in Turbulent Times*, 4th ed. Toronto: Nelson Education, 2010.

Phillips, Susan D. "Interest Groups, Social Movements, and the Voluntary Sector: En Route to Reducing the Democratic Deficit," in James Bickerton and Alain-G. Gagnon, eds., *Canadian Politics*, 4th ed. Peterborough: Broadview Press, 2004.

Sawatsky, John. *The Insiders: Power, Money and Secrets in Ottawa*. Toronto: McClelland and Stewart, 1987.

Smith, Miriam, ed. *Group Politics and Social Movements in Canada*. Peterborough: Broadview Press, 2008.

———. "Interest Groups and Social Movements," in Michael Whittington and Glen Williams, eds., *Canadian Politics in the 21st Century*, 7th ed. Toronto: Nelson Education, 2008.

Young, Lisa, and Joanna Everitt. *Advocacy Groups*. Vancouver: UBC Press, 2004.

CANADIAN CHARTER OF RIGHTS AND FREEDOMS

THE CONSTITUTIONAL CONTEXT

The constitutional context of Canadian government and politics forms the framework of the "government" part of the political system. In this analysis, Part 4 picks up from Chapter 2 but goes into much greater depth. Chapter 17 discusses the Canadian Constitution in general and the succession of attempts to make major changes to it. One of the most important parts of the Constitution is the relationship between the different levels of government, and Chapter 18 examines all aspects of Canadian federalism. The other central feature of the Constitution since 1982 is the Charter of Rights and Freedoms. Chapter 19 reveals how it has been interpreted and how it has affected the operation of the whole Canadian political system.

CHAPTER 17

The Canadian Constitution and Constitutional Change

What is the Canadian Constitution? Is it written or unwritten? What are its principal parts? What process should be used to amend it? Should the division of powers between Ottawa and the provinces be altered? Where do Aboriginal peoples fit? Should Quebec be granted constitutional recognition as a distinct society? Should the Constitution be given a new, inspiring preamble? These and related constitutional questions have obsessed Canadian policymakers and scholars for years, yet many remain unresolved. Canada went through several attempts at constitutional review after 1960, but most of the issues involved spilled over into the 21st century.

The Canadian Constitution would be easier to comprehend if it consisted of a single piece of paper by that name. In the absence of such a document, we can define a **constitution** as the whole body of fundamental rules and principles according to which a state is governed. To be more specific, the Constitution provides for the basic institutions of government and the relations among them, the relations between national and provincial governments, and the relations between governments and citizens.[1] In other words, the constitution provides the basic framework for the operation of the whole political system. Such a comprehensive definition suggests that the final product will not be neat and tidy and that some of its ingredients may not be written down at all.

This chapter begins by examining the ingredients of the Canadian Constitution and then considers successive attempts at constitutional change. The latter include the search for a domestic amending formula, the quest for a constitutional Charter of Rights, and the pressures for constitutional change arising from the Quiet Revolution in Quebec, especially the Constitution Act, 1982, the 1987 Meech Lake Accord, the 1992 Charlottetown Accord, and post-Charlottetown developments, each attempting to resolve the "Quebec problem." Not all constitutional issues since 1960 revolve around Quebec, however; some relate to other institutional changes, and many concern the place of Aboriginal peoples.

COMPONENTS OF THE CANADIAN CONSTITUTION

In the search for the components that fit the definition of a constitution provided above, it will be seen that the Canadian Constitution is a great hodgepodge. Unlike the United States and many other countries, Canada does not have a single document called "the Constitution." Instead, some parts of it are written and other parts are unwritten. The principal components of the Canadian Constitution are as follows:

- the Constitution Act, 1867
- formal amendments to the Constitution Act, 1867
- British statutes and orders in council
- organic Canadian statutes
- the Constitution Act, 1982
- judicial decisions
- constitutional conventions

The Constitution Act, 1867

We start with the formal, legal documents, the most important of which is the **British North America (BNA) Act, 1867**, which, in 1982, was officially renamed the **Constitution Act, 1867**.[2] The whole idea of Confederation was the subject of exciting and eloquent debate in the 1860s, and the philosophical roots of Canada's foundation have prompted much recent scholarly discussion, some of which is captured in Chapter 18. The Constitution Act, 1867, was the law passed by the British Parliament that joined Nova Scotia, New Brunswick, Ontario, and Quebec together as the new Dominion of Canada, as mentioned in Chapter 2. The act contained many of the components that would be expected in a constitution, providing for much of the basic machinery and institutions of government and establishing a federal system. The most significant of these provisions will be examined in detail in subsequent chapters. Among other locations, the act can be found on this book's website.

The act lacks an inspirational introduction, and its preamble is seriously out of date. It merely states that the four original provinces have expressed their desire "to be federally united with a constitution similar in principle to that of the United Kingdom." Many of the subsequent 147 clauses are also obsolete, and several have actually been repealed. Box 17.1 illustrates its main provisions.

While the Constitution Act, 1867, continues to function as the foundational document of the Canadian constitution, it does not contain much detail about the executive and judicial branches of government, and it included virtually nothing about limiting the powers of government in relation to the people. It said little about provincial constitutions, and Aboriginal peoples were merely mentioned as a subject of the authority of the federal government. The act also lacked any mention of how it could be amended, but since it was a statute of the British Parliament, most formal changes have been made by the British Parliament at Canadian request.

BOX 17.1   MAIN PROVISIONS OF THE CONSTITUTION ACT, 1867

Part III: Executive Power: Queen, Governor General, and Canadian Privy Council (Note that the Prime Minister and Cabinet are not explicitly mentioned.)

Part IV: Legislative Power: Senate and House of Commons

Part V: Provincial Constitutions: Lieutenant Governor; Ontario and Quebec legislatures

Part VI: Distribution of Legislative Powers: s. 91, federal powers; s. 92, provincial powers; s. 93, education; s. 95, concurrent powers

Part VII: Judicature: s. 96, federal appointment of superior court judges; Parliament may set up a general court of appeal, but note that the Supreme Court of Canada is not explicitly established

Part VIII: Revenues, debts, assets, and taxation, including provincial possession of their own public lands.

Part IX: Miscellaneous: s. 132, treaty power; s. 133, official languages

Part X: Admission of other colonies

Amendments to the Constitution Act, 1867

Formal amendments to the 1867 act are indeed the second ingredient of the Canadian Constitution. Schedule I to the Constitution Act, 1982, lists 17 amendments to the 1867 act made by the British Parliament and another eight made by the Canadian Parliament. The former were often termed "British North America Acts" of whatever year in which they were passed, but in 1982, most were renamed "Constitution Act" of the appropriate year. The most important of the 17 British amendments to the 1867 Act are as follows:

- Constitution Act, 1907: established a new regime of federal–provincial grants
- Constitution Act, 1915: established a new distribution of Senate seats
- Constitution Act, 1930: transferred ownership of natural resources to Western provinces
- Constitution Act, 1940: added unemployment insurance to the list of federal powers
- Newfoundland Act, 1949: joined that province to Canada
- Constitution Act, 1951: allowed Ottawa to legislate with respect to old age pensions
- Constitution Act, 1960: set a mandatory retirement age of 75 for provincial superior court judges
- Constitution Act, 1964: extended federal power in the concurrent field of old age pensions

British Statutes and Orders in Council

The third major component of the Canadian Constitution is a collection of British statutes and orders in council. Chief among these is the **Statute of Westminster**, 1931, which declared Canada to be totally independent of Britain. There were four main British orders in council— that is, decisions of the British Cabinet. Along with the 1949 amendment that incorporated

Newfoundland and Labrador, these orders in council completed the territorial dimensions of what we now know as Canada and are included in the Constitution for that reason. They are as follows:

- Rupert's Land and North-Western Territory Order, 1870: transferred Hudson's Bay Company lands to Canada
- British Columbia Terms of Union, 1871: joined that province to Canada
- Prince Edward Island Terms of Union, 1873: joined that province to Canada
- Adjacent Territories Order, 1880: added Arctic Islands to Canada

Organic Canadian Statutes

"Organic" Canadian statutes are laws passed by the Parliament of Canada that are of special or quasi-constitutional status. To start with, these include the three Canadian statutes that carved provinces out of the Northwest Territories: the Manitoba Act of 1870 and the Saskatchewan and Alberta Acts of 1905. But most observers argue that many other Canadian laws are of constitutional significance, such as the **Supreme Court Act**, an ordinary law that fleshes out the provisions of the 1867 act with respect to the judicial branch of government. Other key statutes that establish or modify essential institutions or the way they operate include the Federal Court Act, the Parliament of Canada Act, the Bill of Rights, the Canada Elections Act, the Indian Act, the Citizenship Act, the Emergencies Act, the Canadian Human Rights Act, the Yukon Act, the Nunavut Act, and the Constitutional Amendments Act.

Constitution Act, 1982

The **Constitution Act, 1982** was, in a sense, the last amendment to the 1867 Constitution Act to be passed by the British Parliament, but it is worthy of separate mention. The Constitution Act, 1982, was appendixed to the **Canada Act**, passed by the British Parliament, that finally terminated all British authority over Canada.[3] This process is referred to as the "patriation" of the Canadian constitution. As noted in Chapter 21, however, the constitutional documents of 1982 did not alter the position of the monarchy in Canada. The same person continues to be recognized as Queen of Canada as is claimed by several other countries, including Britain.

Ron Poling/The Canadian Press

Queen Elizabeth signs Canada's constitutional proclamation in Ottawa on April 17, 1982, as Prime Minister Pierre Trudeau looks on.

Although Canada was completely self-governing after 1931, many amendments to the 1867 act still had to be made by the British Parliament because no formula had been developed to do so in Canada. Along with patriation, therefore, the Constitution Act, 1982, contained a domestic constitution-amending formula, which is examined below.

The second main aspect of the Constitution Act, 1982 was the **Charter of Rights and Freedoms**. The Charter guaranteed fundamental, democratic, legal, egalitarian, and linguistic rights and freedoms against government intrusion. In other words, the Charter of Rights and Freedoms imposed formal new limitations on the government in interaction with its citizens. In addition, it changed the manner in which such civil liberties were protected, now relying more on judicial interpretation than parliamentary restraint. The Charter is examined in depth in Chapter 19.

The 1982 act also contained provisions on equalization payments to have-not provinces and on Aboriginal rights, and included a slight change to the division of powers between federal and provincial governments. Equalization payments previously rested on a statutory basis, but would henceforth be constitutionally guaranteed, although the actual formula involved in their calculation could change over time. As mentioned in Chapter 4, section 25 of the document (part of the Charter) provided that it would not diminish Aboriginal rights, while section 35, though not part of the Charter, was designed to enhance Aboriginal and treaty rights. As far as the division of powers was concerned, a new section, 92A, was added that clarified and extended provincial powers over natural resources.

According to the Constitution Act, 1982, the Constitution of Canada consists of the British statutes and orders in council and some of the Canadian statutes mentioned above. These formal, legal documents make up the Constitution in the narrow sense of being subject to the constitutional amending formula adopted in 1982. Important as they are, these documents are silent on so many vital aspects of the fundamental rules and principles according to which Canada is governed that they cannot possibly constitute the entirety of the Canadian Constitution. Most authorities would therefore cast a much wider net in selecting the ingredients of the Constitution in its broader sense.

Judicial Decisions

The definition of the Canadian constitution must also include judicial decisions that have clarified or altered provisions of the 1867 act or other parts of the Constitution. The largest body of such decisions consists of the judgments of the British **Judicial Committee of the Privy Council (JCPC)**, Canada's final court of appeal until 1949, which significantly affected the division of powers between the federal and provincial governments. As mentioned in Chapter 18 on Canadian federalism, it was John A. Macdonald's intention to create a strong central government, but the Judicial Committee interpreted the 1867 act in such a way as to minimize federal powers and maximize those of the provinces. The court decisions that effected such a wholesale transformation of the federal nature of the country have to be considered part of the Constitution alongside the actual provisions of the original act.

A few early court decisions also imposed restrictions on government power vis-à-vis its citizens—that is, in the area of rights and freedoms—and many such decisions have been made since the Charter of Rights was adopted in 1982. These "rights and freedoms" decisions are also part of the Constitution, along with the "division of powers" decisions mentioned.

Constitutional Conventions

Thus far, each of the ingredients listed can actually be found in written form, however difficult it would be to collect them all together. The final component of the Constitution, however, has never been confined to writing. It consists of **constitutional conventions**, defined as unwritten rules of constitutional behaviour that are considered to be binding by and on those who operate the Constitution but that are not enforceable by the courts.[4] Conventions develop from traditions and through constant recognition and observance become as established, rigid, and sacrosanct as if they were written down. Many of these informal rules have been inherited from Britain, some have been modified in the Canadian environment, and others are unique to Canada. Although such conventions cannot be enforced by the courts, they are sometimes recognized by judges, giving them added authority over the actions of politicians. But, as in Britain, conventions are no less real for remaining in an unwritten form, and many are among the most important parts of the Canadian constitution. As Peter Hogg writes, "[w]hat conventions do is prescribe the way in which legal powers shall be exercised. Some conventions have the effect of transferring effective power from the legal holder to another official or institution. Other conventions limit an apparently broad legal power, or even prescribe that a legal power shall not be exercised at all."[5] Many constitutional conventions, for example, relate to the executive branch of government, which is given slight attention in the 1867 act. These include the very position of prime minister and Cabinet, the dominant role of these offices even when the written words give formal powers to the governor general, and the principle of responsible government—that the Cabinet must resign or call an election if it loses the confidence of the House of Commons. Others will be discussed at relevant points in subject chapters.

It should be added that some actions that are *legal* according to the formal written words of the constitution may actually be *unconstitutional* if they violate a convention that has superseded a written power. An example would be the power of the governor general to withhold assent from a piece of legislation. But if the courts cannot enforce conventions, why are they consistently obeyed? Hogg replies that breach of a convention would result in "serious political repercussions"—dismissal, defeat, disgrace—and eventually to changes in the law so that it would not happen again.

The Constitution of Canada, therefore, is a rather complex phenomenon. It has two central documents—the Constitution Act, 1867 with its amendments, and the Constitution Act, 1982—and it contains other written documents, including other British statutes and orders in council, organic Canadian statutes, and British and Canadian court decisions. In its unwritten part, it incorporates a whole series of constitutional conventions that fill in gaps or alter the way in which written provisions are implemented. For better or worse, the widest definition of a constitution requires the inclusion of all these components. Many observers would prefer a neater Constitution, some want it to be updated, and others would like it to be more inspirational so that it could function more satisfactorily as a symbol of unity. Thus far, however, attempts to recast the Canadian Constitution in any of these ways have foundered.

THE PRE-1960 QUEST FOR CONSTITUTIONAL CHANGE

Constitutional change has almost always been on the Canadian political agenda. In the early years of Confederation, one principal concern involved completing the territorial integrity of Canada with the eventual creation of 10 provinces and now three territories. Another early constitutional issue was achieving autonomy from Britain by means of the Statute of Westminster (1931), along with the abolition of court appeals to the Judicial Committee of the Privy Council (1949). Two other persistent constitutional questions also arose before 1960: the search for a formula by which the 1867 act and the Constitution generally could be formally amended in Canada, and the proposal that rights and freedoms or civil liberties be given constitutional protection. These two issues then became enmeshed in constitutional demands inspired by the **Quiet Revolution** in Quebec. The simultaneous consideration of many large constitutional issues—amending formula, charter of rights, division of powers, institutional change, status of Quebec, and later Aboriginals—has acquired the label of "mega-constitutional change." The four key packages of such mega-constitutional changes were the 1970 Victoria Charter, the Constitution Act, 1982, the 1987 Meech Lake Accord, and the 1992 Charlottetown Accord. Of these four documents, only one was ultimately adopted, and many constitutional issues remain unresolved. Some of these developments were previously raised in Chapter 5 on French Canada and Quebec.

A Domestic Constitutional Amending Formula

As the final thrust toward full Canadian independence took place after the Balfour Declaration of 1926, it became clear that Canadians would have to find a way to amend the 1867 act in Canada. For the next 55 years, federal and provincial governments wrestled with the problem without being able to agree on an acceptable balance between rigidity and flexibility: a constitution should not be too easy to amend, but neither should it be impossible.

Attempts to find a domestic **constitutional amending formula** began in 1927, but since no success was achieved before 1931, the Statute of Westminster contained a clause allowing the British Parliament to amend the 1867 act at Canadian request. Further attempts were made in 1935–36, and in 1949 a partial domestic amending formula was adopted that became the BNA Act Amendment (#1) of 1949. That act added a clause to section 91 to the effect that in matters of concern to the national government alone, the federal Parliament could make constitutional amendments in Canada, without reference either to the provinces or to Britain. However, five exceptions remained, the most important being that any amendment affecting the provinces would still have to be made by the British Parliament. The basic question regarding such amendments was whether they should require the unanimous approval of the provincial governments before being sent to London. This was the position taken by virtually every government of Quebec in order to protect its rights and powers and is referred to as the "compact theory" of Confederation. In this view, Confederation was a compact among the provincial signatories, such that no part of it could be changed without unanimous provincial consent. Many other provinces also came to support this theory, even though it was of dubious legal standing and was ultimately rejected by the Supreme Court of Canada.

In the absence of a resolution of this problem, a constitutional convention developed such that the federal government would not request an amendment to the federal–provincial division of powers without the unanimous consent of the provinces. Thus, in the case of the amendments in 1940, 1951, 1960, and 1964, Ottawa did not ask Britain to act until it had obtained the agreement of all the provinces.[6]

Further attempts to find a complete domestic formula were made around 1950 and 1960, and federal–provincial agreement was reached on the Fulton–Favreau formula in 1964. After having agreed to this formula, however, the Jean Lesage government of Quebec rescinded its approval—ironically now fearing that the unanimity requirement would prevent Quebec from making certain changes that it wanted—and the formula died.

As discussed above, a domestic constitutional amending formula was finally adopted as part of the Constitution Act, 1982. Part V of the act actually provided for five such formulas, depending on the subject matter of the amendment:

1. unanimous consent of federal and provincial legislatures
2. consent of Parliament and seven provincial legislatures representing at least 50 percent of the population
3. consent of Parliament and one or more provinces affected
4. consent of Parliament alone
5. consent of a provincial legislature alone

The essence of these five formulas is presented in Box 17.2.

BOX 17.2 CANADA'S CONSTITUTIONAL AMENDING FORMULAS, 1982

1. Section 41 requires unanimous federal and provincial consent to amend any of the following items:
   (a) the office of the Queen, the Governor General and the Lieutenant Governor of a province;
   (b) the right of a province to a number of members in the House of Commons not less than its number of Senators;
   (c) the use of the English or the French language at the federal level;
   (d) the composition of the Supreme Court of Canada; and
   (e) changes to this list of subjects requiring unanimous consent.

2. Section 38, dealing with other matters affecting both levels of government, requires the approval of the federal Parliament and the legislatures of two-thirds of the provinces representing at least 50 percent of the Canadian population. However, no amendment that reduces provincial powers, rights, or privileges can affect a province that does not agree to it. Section 39 provides that if such an amendment relates to education or culture, Canada must provide compensation to any province to which the amendment does not apply. Thus, if nine provinces and the federal government agreed to transfer education from provincial to federal jurisdiction, Ottawa would have to pay compensation to the province that continued to operate its own education system.

For greater clarity, section 42 lists certain subjects to which the two-thirds and 50 percent formula applies, including:

(a) the principle of proportionate representation of the provinces in the House of Commons;

(b) the powers of the Senate and the method of selecting Senators;

(c) the number of members by which a province is entitled to be represented in the Senate and the residence qualifications of Senators;

(d) the Supreme Court of Canada, other than its composition;

(e) the extension of existing provinces into the territories; and

(f) the establishment of new provinces.

3. Section 43 stipulates that constitutional matters applying to one or more but not all provinces, including boundary alterations and changes to the use of the English or French languages within a province, can be amended with the approval of the federal Parliament and the legislative assembly of each province to which the amendment applies.

4. Section 44 provides that constitutional provisions relating to the executive government of Canada or the Senate and House of Commons can be amended by the federal Parliament alone. This was previously the situation according to the partial amending formula adopted in 1949 and allowed that clause to be repealed.

5. Section 45 states that each province can amend its own constitution in matters not affecting any other jurisdiction (or the position of lieutenant governor), as had previously been the case.

In general, the rigidity and opting-out provisions of the 1982 amending formula were considered a victory for the provinces and a trade-off for accepting the federal government's Charter of Rights.[7] The formula required that the federal Parliament and provincial *legislatures* approve such amendments, not just *cabinets*, as had often sufficed in the past. This innovation had later implications for the Meech Lake Accord, for although it was initially adopted by all 10 provincial *premiers*, it ran into trouble when it came before certain provincial *legislatures*. The formula also allows constitutional amendments to be made without the consent of the Senate if they are adopted a second time by the House of Commons after 180 days. Thus, the 1982 amending formula was not a simple one and was not designed to approve amendments easily. It did, however, put an end to requests to the British Parliament to make Canadian constitutional amendments on our behalf.

A Constitutional Charter of Rights

Given the lack of a constitutional charter of rights in Britain and that country's generally respectable record of protecting civil liberties, based on parliamentary restraint, the common law, public opinion, and political culture, Canadians were not originally concerned about the absence of a bill of rights in their Constitution. Some began to advocate such an addition to the constitution, however, after witnessing federal mistreatment of Japanese Canadians in the Second World War; provincial discrimination against Asians, especially in British Columbia, and Jehovah's Witnesses and political dissidents in Quebec; and violations of freedom of the press in Alberta. One person who felt very strongly about this question was John Diefenbaker, and after he became prime minister he had Parliament pass a Bill of Rights in 1960. But the bill had major structural weaknesses that led many observers to recommend constitutionalizing it. That was part of the rationale for the adoption of the Charter of Rights and Freedoms, as part of the Constitution Act, 1982, which is discussed in detail in Chapter 19.

MEGA-CONSTITUTIONAL CHANGE, 1960–2000

The unresolved issues of a domestic amending formula and a constitutional charter of rights then became part of the third main thrust of change, which emanated from the Quiet Revolution in Quebec. This was primarily related to Quebec's place in the Canadian federation as well as to the general division of powers between the two levels of government. Such demands for mega-constitutional change dominated Canadian politics for the next 40 years,[8] and to some extent, they still threaten the existence of the country as we know it. The timeline in Box 17.3 lists the significant constitutional developments over the period 1960–2000.

BOX 17.3   MEGA-CONSTITUTIONAL DEVELOPMENTS, 1960–2000

1. Quiet Revolution in Quebec, 1960–66
2. Confederation of Tomorrow Conference, 1967
3. Federal–provincial constitutional conferences, 1968–71
4. Victoria Charter, June 1971
5. Trudeau's proposal for patriation and amending formula, 1975–76
6. Election of Parti Québécois, 1976
7. Trudeau's Bill C-60, 1978
8. Task Force on Canadian Unity, January 1979
9. René Lévesque's sovereignty-association proposal, November 1979
10. Quebec referendum, May 1980
11. Federal–provincial constitutional conferences, June and September 1980
12. Federal unilateral package, October 1980
13. Supreme Court decision on unilateral package, September 1981
14. Federal–provincial conference, November 1981
15. Proclamation of Constitution Act, 1982, April 17, 1982
16. Bourassa government's five demands, 1985
17. Meech Lake conferences, April and June 1987

18. Legislative ratification of Meech Lake Accord, 1987–90
19. Federal–Provincial Conference on Meech Lake Accord, May 1990
20. Death of Meech Lake Accord, June 1990
21. Allaire and Bélanger–Campeau Reports, 1991
22. Citizens' Forum, November 1990–June 1991
23. New federal constitutional reform package, September 1991
24. Federal–provincial–territorial–Aboriginal negotiations, April–August 1992
25. Charlottetown Accord, August 1992
26. National referendum, October 26, 1992
27. Election of PQ government in Quebec, 1994
28. Quebec referendum on sovereignty, October 30, 1995
29. Supreme Court decision on unilateral declaration of independence, August 1998
30. Clarity Act, 2000

The Victoria Charter

As noted in Chapters 5 and 18, many of Quebec's demands could be and were addressed by bureaucratic, legislative, financial, and judicial decisions at the federal level, in Quebec, or in other provinces, and did not require formal constitutional changes. By the end of the 1960s, however, the government of Quebec was demanding changes of a constitutional nature, demands often echoed by certain other provinces. Following the Confederation of Tomorrow Conference in 1967, a series of federal–provincial conferences over the 1968–71 period led to agreement on the Victoria Charter in June 1971.

The **Victoria Charter** contained a constitutional amending formula and a constitutionalized bill of rights, provided for provincial consultation on Supreme Court appointments, guaranteed equalization payments to redress regional disparities, and represented progress on changes to language rights and to the federal–provincial division of powers. But after endorsing the document in Victoria, Quebec's Bourassa government changed its mind; in responding to nationalist public opinion in the province, it vetoed the package because Quebec had not received sufficient additional powers in the field of social policy.

The Constitution Act, 1982

The 1970s and early 1980s thus saw a constitutional tug-of-war between Ottawa and Quebec, with the other provinces arrayed in between, over the amending formula, the Charter of Rights, the Supreme Court, the Senate, language rights, and the division of powers. As noted in Chapter 5, the Trudeau strategy continued to be based on the constitutionalization of the Official Languages Act and the extension of French-language rights and services from coast to coast to coast in order to undermine Quebec's claim to be linguistically distinctive and therefore to require additional powers.[9] Increasingly, Trudeau had to fight the other provinces, too, as most of them also demanded greater decentralization.

After the collapse of the Victoria Charter, Trudeau tried a number of devices to pre-empt the election of a separatist government in Quebec and, after its success in 1976, to convince Quebeckers to follow his lead instead. The Pépin–Robarts Task Force on Canadian Unity might have been a fruitful basis on which to approach the problem, but because its recommendations differed from Trudeau's own principles of centralization, symmetrical federalism, and national bilingualism, he immediately dismissed them. In May 1980, four years after its election, the Parti Québécois government asked the people of Quebec for a mandate to negotiate **sovereignty-association** with the federal government—that is, Quebec would be a sovereign state but with continued economic links to the rest of Canada. Trudeau and other federal ministers entered the referendum campaign, promising that if Quebeckers turned down the PQ plan, Ottawa would initiate a process of constitutional renewal. When Quebec rejected Lévesque's proposal by a margin of 60 percent to 40 percent, Trudeau immediately embarked on a new round of federal–provincial constitutional discussions.

By October 1980, however, Trudeau abruptly gave up trying to reach federal–provincial agreement and issued his own package of constitutional reform proposals, which he intended to have adopted by the British Parliament without provincial consent. This package was par-ticularly provocative to the Quebec government and a large proportion of Quebeckers because it reflected Trudeau's vision rather than the kind of constitutional reform—a distinct status and increased powers for Quebec—that they assumed he had promised in the referendum debate. Many observers feel that Trudeau misled Quebeckers in the speeches he made in the 1980 referendum campaign.[10]

Upset at both the substantive and the procedural aspects of the Trudeau initiative, sev-eral other provinces also challenged it in the courts. In one of its most famous decisions, the Supreme Court of Canada ruled in the *Patriation Reference* case that nothing in *law* pre-vented the federal government from unilaterally requesting that such an amendment be made by Britain. However, it agreed with the dissenting provinces that unilateral federal action would violate the constitutional *convention* that provincial consent should be secured beforehand. In a rare example of judicial recognition of conventions, the Court went on to interpret the convention as requiring a "substantial degree of provincial consent" but not necessarily unanimity. A majority of the Court argued that the federal nature of Canada would be greatly changed if Ottawa could unilaterally alter the powers of the provincial governments in this way.[11]

Meanwhile, Trudeau's package had been subject to Parliamentary hearings in which a multitude of interest groups presented briefs to support and/or strengthen the document, as the Charter of Rights section became particularly popular. The governments of Ontario and New Brunswick had always supported the initiative, and the addition of s. 92A giving the provinces enhanced jurisdiction over natural resources brought the federal NDP onside. The Supreme Court decision prompted Trudeau to sit down with the premiers again and they engaged in three days and nights of tough negotiations in November 1981. The constitutional amending formula was a major stumbling block (with an alternative referendum proposal discussed), and Quebec insisted that it receive financial compensation if it opted out of any federal programs. Several provinces, principally Alberta, Saskatchewan, and Manitoba, disliked the Charter, especially in that it would give additional powers to the courts.

This impasse was broken with the addition of the innovative **notwithstanding clause**, which allowed governments to pass a law in violation of certain Charter rights for a maximum five-year period, although disagreement continued over which parts of the Charter would be subject to it. Although other provinces had sided with Quebec's objections on various issues throughout the week, when René Lévesque went to

André-Philippe Côté (Le Soleil). Reproduced with permission.

sleep on November 4, the other nine provinces continued negotiations with the federal government during "the night of the long knives." Lévesque arose to find that the others had come up with compromises on all sides to reach a consensus. As mentioned, according to the Supreme Court, unanimous consent was not required. Lévesque was outraged, expressed his dissent, and stormed back home, the great irony being that Quebec had been the inspiration behind the whole exercise in the first place. The amended package was passed by Parliament, approved by the British Parliament as an appendix to the Canada Act (1982), and signed by the Queen on April 17, 1982 on Parliament Hill.[12]

The act itself has already been extensively discussed. It contained a domestic constitutional amending formula and a Charter of Rights. It also included the constitutional entrenchment of equalization payments to have-not provinces, a section on Aboriginal rights, and an amendment to the division of powers that enhanced provincial control over natural resources. The Charter essentially constitutionalized the federal and New Brunswick Official Languages Acts to guarantee the rights of official-language minorities to government services, trials, and so on. It also established the rights of official-language minorities to schools in their own language wherever numbers warranted. The clear objective of these provisions was to entrench official bilingualism across the country to the extent that Prime Minister Trudeau could persuade provincial premiers to do so. However, the Constitution Act, 1982, did not respond to any of the demands for constitutional change emanating from Quebec. It is not surprising that Quebec Premier René Lévesque refused to sign it, but it is doubtful that a federalist premier of that province would have reacted much differently.

The Quebec government then sent a reference to the Supreme Court asking it to recognize that, by convention, Quebec had a veto on constitutional amendments, but this contention was denied. Thus, the province was legally bound by the document in almost all respects.[13] This imposition created much hostility within Quebec toward Trudeau, Justice Minister Jean Chrétien, the other provinces, and the Charter itself. Until the PQ government was defeated in 1985, it symbolically invoked the notwithstanding clause on every piece of legislation passed by the Quebec legislature.

The Meech Lake Accord

Although the 1982 act was operative in Quebec, newly elected Prime Minister Brian Mulroney was determined that Quebec should symbolically re-join the Canadian constitutional family "with honour and enthusiasm." He therefore asked the new federalist Quebec premier, Robert Bourassa, to outline his conditions for such a reunion. The Quebec government proceeded to make five demands:

1. constitutional recognition of Quebec as a "distinct society" within Canada
2. a veto on constitutional amendments affecting Quebec
3. increased jurisdiction over immigration
4. participation in Supreme Court appointments
5. financial compensation when Quebec opted out of national programs set up by Ottawa within provincial jurisdiction

After considerable preparation, Mulroney called the premiers together at Meech Lake in April 1987 and with surprising speed they agreed to a document that addressed Quebec's demands and became known as the **Meech Lake Accord**. The prime minister secured unanimous provincial consent by extending to the other provinces most of the same rights as were demanded by Quebec. The document also contained clauses that constitutionalized the Supreme Court of Canada, provided for provincial participation in Senate appointments, and guaranteed annual first ministers' conferences on the Constitution and on the economy.[14]

Despite the relative ease with which it was drafted, the Meech Lake Accord generated much controversy. The leading opponent of Meech Lake was former Prime Minister Pierre Trudeau, whose vision of a centralized, symmetrical, bilingual federation was at odds with the document. He was alarmed that it would give the provinces more power and recognize Quebec as a distinct society, acknowledging that French-speaking Canadians are centred in Quebec. He was not alone in opposing the designation of Quebec as a distinct society within Canada and especially the phrase that it was the role of the government and legislature of Quebec to "preserve and promote" that distinctiveness. No one was sure what implications the **distinct society** clause would have for the federal–provincial division of powers, leaving it for judicial clarification on an issue-by-issue basis. Trudeau argued that in a federation all provinces had to have exactly equal status, and that, armed with the distinct society clause, Quebec would immediately begin to challenge federal powers in a variety of fields. Others worried about the status of the anglophone and Aboriginal minorities within Quebec, as well as the francophone minorities in other provinces and territories. A second objection to the accord was that it enlarged the list of subjects that required unanimous provincial consent in the constitutional amending formula, especially the list contained in section 42, such as changes to most aspects of the Senate and the creation of new provinces. Many critics felt that Senate reform and the transformation of the northern territories into provinces would be virtually impossible if such amendments required agreement of all 10 provinces instead of only seven.

Objections to Quebec's expanded role in immigration and to provincial involvement in the nomination of judges to the Supreme Court of Canada were also raised by those opposed to increased provincial power. But concerns expressed more vehemently related to the provision allowing provinces to opt out of national programs within provincial jurisdiction and be compensated by Ottawa. Fears were expressed that satisfactory new national social programs (such as a national daycare program) would never materialize because provinces would be compensated for programs that merely met national *objectives*, not national *standards*.

Others condemned the process through which the accord had emerged—a behind-the-scenes gathering of (male) first ministers. In the post-Charter era, Alan Cairns argues that the constitution was no longer the exclusive preserve of governments; individual Canadians insisted on being part of the constitutional amendment process. Thus, the primacy of Quebec's concerns was rejected by those given constitutional standing by the Charter—women, Aboriginals, and members of multicultural and other minority groups.[15] On the other hand, many political scientists and other constitutional authorities believe to this day that the adoption of the Meech Lake Accord, to complement the Constitution Act, 1982, might have spared the country much of its constitutional anguish ever since. Each of the document's components can be justified in a true federation where the federal government should not be able to impose its will on the provinces and in a country where one province that stands out in linguistic and cultural terms.

According to the constitutional amending formula adopted in 1982, the accord then had to be approved by the federal and all provincial *legislatures* within three years—that is, before June 23, 1990.[16] In most cases such legislative approval came rather easily, but governments changed in New Brunswick and Manitoba before the accord could be ratified by the legislatures of those two provinces, and their new governments had reservations about the accord. On the other hand, the new Clyde Wells government in Newfoundland, seeing the issue in the same way as Trudeau, rescinded the approval that that province's legislature had previously given to the accord.

Thus, with three provinces left to ratify the accord, Prime Minister Mulroney convened a first ministers' conference in Ottawa in May 1990. After a week of protracted, behind-the-scenes negotiations, the participants emerged with a modest companion resolution that had been adopted to the satisfaction of Manitoba and New Brunswick. Still with his substantive and procedural reservations, Wells would only agree to put it before the Newfoundland legislature, not to endorse it. Amid a bitter public exchange between Wells and the federal government, the Newfoundland legislature did not vote on the accord a second time before the deadline. Meanwhile, the accord ran into new difficulty in the Manitoba legislature, where Aboriginal MLA Elijah Harper delayed passage beyond the deadline because of the absence of any advance for Aboriginal peoples.

Chuck Mitchell/The Canadian Press

Prime Minister Brian Mulroney makes a pitch for the Meech Lake Accord in the House of Commons in June 1990.

The Charlottetown Accord

With the death of the Meech Lake Accord, most Quebeckers felt betrayed for a second time in 10 years. Nationalist and separatist sentiment mushroomed over the next year or so as the Quebec Liberals and Parti Québécois issued new constitutional proposals. The Liberal position first appeared as the Allaire Report, which called for a highly decentralized federation in which Quebec and the other provinces would have almost all powers, including 22 new ones. According to the report, Quebec would insist on exercising its full sovereignty in the areas of jurisdiction already exclusive to it according to the present Constitution, notably social affairs, urban affairs, culture, education, housing, recreation, family policy, manpower policy, natural resources, health, and tourism. It would do the same in other fields that it somewhat dubiously claimed were currently either shared with Ottawa or not mentioned in the Constitution, such as agriculture, unemployment insurance, communications, regional development, energy, environment, language, research and development, and public security. Ottawa and Quebec would share jurisdiction over Aboriginal affairs, revenue and taxation, immigration, financial institutions, justice, fisheries, foreign policy, the post office, telecommunications, and transportation, and the federal government would have exclusive power over only defence, customs and excise, and management of the national debt.

Representing both major parties as well as other interests in the province, Quebec's Bélanger–Campeau Committee report argued that unless a satisfactory proposal for a new constitutional arrangement was forthcoming from the rest of Canada, Quebec should separate. It therefore recommended that a referendum on Quebec sovereignty be held in 1992. Bélanger–Campeau anticipated that in the interim, the rest of Canada would offer Quebec some kind of new partnership, perhaps along the lines of the Allaire Report, so that Quebeckers would essentially have two alternatives before them when they cast their vote.

Responding to the criticism that the public had been shut out of the Meech Lake negotiations, the Mulroney government appointed the Citizens' Forum on Canada's Future in 1990. Headed by Keith Spicer, it encouraged ordinary Canadians to discuss constitutional issues in a variety of settings and transmit their views to the committee. A large proportion of Canadians engaged in angry exchanges, the Constitution becoming a lightning rod for every conceivable grievance in the country. After listening to some 400 000 Canadians over an eight-month period, Spicer's 1991 report supported recognition of Quebec's distinctiveness, Aboriginal self-government, and settlement of Aboriginal land claims. However, the forum suggested that official bilingualism was a divisive issue and government funding for multiculturalism should be cut.

In these circumstances, the prime minister appointed Joe Clark as the minister responsible for constitutional affairs and set up a special Cabinet committee on Canadian unity and constitutional negotiations. The committee agreed on a 28-point package of constitutional proposals in September 1991 called *Shaping Canada's Future Together*. Clark was persuaded to try to develop a collective federal–provincial–territorial–Aboriginal response to offer to Quebec before the looming referendum. After several rounds of negotiations, Clark, the nine premiers, the territorial first ministers, and the Aboriginal leaders all agreed on a comprehensive constitutional proposal in July. Quebec Premier Bourassa considered that it was promising enough to return to the bargaining table for the first time since the demise of the Meech Lake Accord, and a full-fledged constitutional conference took place in Ottawa in mid-August. After nearly a week of hard bargaining, the leaders unanimously

BOX 17.4   MAIN PROVISIONS OF THE CHARLOTTETOWN ACCORD

Canada Clause: retained recognition of Quebec as a distinct society within Canada, as well as enumerating other fundamental values and characteristics of the country.

Triple-E Senate: each province would have six Senators (equal) and each territory, one. They would be elected, except in Quebec. Some Senate powers would be reduced, but others strengthened (effective). To compensate Ontario and Quebec for their loss of 18 senators each, these two provinces would be given 18 additional seats in the House of Commons, and Quebec was guaranteed a minimum of 25 percent of Commons seats in perpetuity.

Aboriginal Self-Government: the inherent right to Aboriginal self-government would be enshrined in the constitution, and Aboriginal governments would constitute a third order of government, analogous to federal and provincial governments.

Division of Powers: retained the provisions of the Meech Lake Accord, but Ottawa offered to withdraw from many other fields.

Other: retained the provisions of the Meech Lake Accord with respect to the Supreme Court; changed the constitutional amending formula somewhat; added a social charter to guarantee rights to health care, social services, education, and collective bargaining, and protection for the environment.

signed a new constitutional accord on which they put the final touches in Charlottetown a week later.[17] **The Charlottetown Accord** had four main parts: the Canada clause, a Triple-E Senate, Aboriginal self-government, and changes to the division of powers, as indicated in Box 17.4.

The 1992 Referendum

Although supported by all those around the table, the accord would be of no effect until ratified by Parliament and the 10 provincial legislatures. Before ratification, however, the federal government announced that a national **referendum** would be held on the new constitutional deal on October 26, 1992, the same date selected by Quebec for its constitutional referendum, now to be held on the Charlottetown Accord rather than on sovereignty. The decision to hold such a referendum was based on three main considerations: Alberta and British Columbia laws required a referendum on constitutional amendments, so the people in three provinces would be voting on the accord in any case; Meech Lake had been criticized for lack of public input; and public approval would lend legitimacy to the agreement and spur the 11 legislatures into speedy affirmative action.

On a national basis the referendum result was 55 percent "No" and 45 percent "Yes." As shown in Table 17.1, majorities voted no in Quebec, Nova Scotia, the four Western provinces, and Yukon. Even though the referendum was not legally binding, there was no point in bringing the constitutional package before legislatures for ratification: the Charlottetown Accord was dead.

TABLE 17.1   RESULTS OF THE NATIONAL REFERENDUM ON THE CHARLOTTETOWN ACCORD (PERCENTAGES)

	YES	NO
NEWFOUNDLAND AND LABRADOR	63.2	36.8
PRINCE EDWARD ISLAND	73.9	26.1
NOVA SCOTIA	48.8	51.2
NEW BRUNSWICK	61.8	38.2
QUEBEC	43.3	56.7
ONTARIO	50.1	49.9
MANITOBA	38.4	61.6
SASKATCHEWAN	44.7	55.3
ALBERTA	39.8	60.2
BRITISH COLUMBIA	31.7	68.3
NORTHWEST TERRITORIES	61.3	38.7
YUKON	43.7	56.3
TOTAL	45.0	55.0

Source: Elections Canada. Chief Electoral Officer of Canada, Referendum 92: Official Voting Results *(Ottawa, 1992), pg. 4; Directeur general des elections du Quebec. Rapport des resultants officials du scrutiny – Referendum du 26 October 1992 (Sainte-Foy, 1992), pg. 49.*

Public opinion polls showed that few Canadians understood either the rationale for or the specific contents of the accord; instead, many people who voted "No" did so to vent their anger and frustration with Prime Minister Mulroney, the premiers, politicians, and governments in general.[18] Such was the problem of holding the vote during a period of severe recession and at a time when respect for incumbent politicians was at an all-time low. Voters were not in a generous frame of mind, and rather than seeing the accord as a multi-sided compromise, they generally felt that it gave too much to others and not enough to themselves. Thus, the negative vote in Quebec was largely based on the view that the accord was a dilution of Meech Lake and did not give Quebec sufficient new powers, but many outside Quebec argued that that province got too much. Many Westerners did not see the proposed reforms to the Senate as sufficient protection of their interests in Ottawa, and many Aboriginal Canadians were dissatisfied with the provisions on self-government. Indeed, although the accord was primarily designed to address the constitutional insecurity of Quebec, Aboriginal Canadians, and Western and smaller provinces, a majority in all three groups believed that their elites had not bargained hard enough on their behalf. Pierre Trudeau and Reform Party leader Preston Manning were two of the leading opponents.

CRITICAL APPROACHES

The *historical-institutional approach* is highly relevant to the Constitution and constitutional change. Canada's constitutional evolution can only be understood in historical terms, and primarily involves the basic institutions established and the fundamental rules they adopted. Once certain constitutional rules were put in place, they profoundly affected the future development of the country. As a result of these rules, some policy options in the future were effectively taken off the table.

For most of our history, constitutional questions have primarily been the preserve of federal and provincial political and bureaucratic elites, suggesting a *state-based* approach to understanding them. Before 1982, constitutional accommodations could be made among first ministers and their advisers at federal–provincial conferences and only needed to be ratified by federal and provincial cabinets. After 1982, legislative approval was also required, but it took time and innovation before the wider society became involved.

On the other hand, while the public's interest in such matters in recent years is quite obvious and lends itself to the *pluralist approach*, Matt James argues that social movements have actually been involved in Canadian constitutional politics for a long period of time.[19] Pluralists also emphasize that several elite-designed proposals have foundered once exposed to public opinion: the Fulton–Favreau formula and the Victoria Charter in Quebec, and Meech Lake in other parts of the country. The public demanded more meaningful participation in the process since 1982, and incrementally gained it. When three provinces decided to hold referenda on the Charlottetown Accord, the prime minister chose to have a national referendum, and it is commonly thought that if the issue of mega-constitutional reform is ever revisited, a referendum will be held again, even though it is not necessary according to the constitutional amending formula.

Post-Charlottetown Constitutional Developments

One year later, in 1993, the Chrétien Liberals were elected on the promise that they would concentrate on improving the economy and put constitutional issues aside. However, the Parti Québécois returned to power in Quebec in 1994 on the exact opposite platform—that it would move quickly to take Quebec out of Confederation. When polls showed that Premier Jacques Parizeau could not persuade a majority of Quebec voters on the question of his choice—complete independence—he succumbed to the pressure of public opinion and from Bloc leader Lucien Bouchard and agreed to an extensive list of continuing links to Canada.[20] This seriously watered-down proposal was ratified in an agreement between the PQ, the BQ, and Mario Dumont, leader of the small party Action Démocratique du Québec (ADQ). The legislature passed a bill setting the referendum date for October 30, 1995. The convoluted question put to the people of Quebec was as follows: "Do you agree that Quebec should become sovereign, after having made a formal offer to Canada for a new economic and political partnership, within the scope of the bill respecting the future of Quebec and of the agreement signed on June 12, 1995?"

The bill in question would allow a sovereign Quebec to use the Canadian dollar as its currency and its residents to retain concurrent citizenship and carry Canadian passports. It anticipated the adoption of a new Quebec constitution and retention of Quebec's existing boundaries. The government of Quebec was then to propose a treaty of economic and political partnership with the rest of Canada. The treaty would set up a joint Council (executive), Secretariat (bureaucracy), Assembly (legislature), and Tribunal (court); establish rules for the division of assets and debt; and provide for the free movement of goods, individuals, services, and capital. If agreement with the rest of Canada on such a treaty was not achieved within a year, Quebec would unilaterally declare its sovereignty and expect recognition by other states, later claiming to have had secret support from France. It also anticipated continued membership in the North American Free Trade Agreement. Premier Parizeau virtually vacated the leadership of the "Yes" campaign when it became obvious that the cause had a chance only if the much more popular Bouchard became its effective leader.

The federal government stuck to its position that if Quebeckers could be persuaded that "Yes" meant actual separation, a majority would vote "No." Even when the question was toned down, Ottawa made no counter-offers until polls showed that its strategy was seriously flawed and could lead to defeat. In the final week of the campaign, Prime Minister Chrétien made several promises if Quebeckers voted "No." The three principal changes he alluded to were some kind of recognition of Quebec as a distinct society, some kind of veto over constitutional amendments, and some kind of decentralization of powers from Ottawa. The other dramatic development of the last few days was a gigantic "No" rally held in downtown Montreal, made up primarily of Canadians from coast to coast who "invaded" the city to tell Quebeckers how much the rest of Canada wanted them to stay.

A large Canadian flag is passed through a crowd as thousands streamed into Montreal from all over Canada to rally for national unity three days before the Quebec referendum.

The result of the 1995 referendum could not have been closer: 50.6 percent voted "No," while 49.4 percent voted "Yes." The turnout rate was a record 92 percent. Considerable controversy surrounded the high number of rejected ballots (most of them favouring the "No" side), but it was clear that nearly 60 percent of the francophones in the province had voted "Yes." Close but still defeated, Parizeau promptly resigned the premiership in favour of Bouchard.

After the suspenseful Quebec referendum results, Prime Minister Chrétien kept his promises, but was unable to actually entrench them as constitutional amendments. For example, he had Parliament pass a resolution recognizing Quebec as a distinct society within Canada. In order to give Quebec a veto on constitutional amendments that affected that province, Parliament passed a law to the effect that regardless of the official constitutional amending formula, Ottawa would not agree to such an amendment without the approval of each region of the country (including Quebec). In addition, labour-market training would be informally transferred from federal to provincial jurisdiction wherever desired. Such measures were part of "Plan A" or the "carrot" approach of being "nice" to Quebec.[21] The government also pursued the "stick" approach or "Plan B," the principal part of which was to refer a hypothetical question to the Supreme Court of Canada, asking it to rule on the legality of a unilateral declaration of independence by Quebec.

As a result of these actions, the constitutional amending formula provided for in the Constitution Act, 1982 has been informally amended and now rests on the 1996 Constitutional Amendments Act instead. In the case of any proposed amendment that requires the approval of at least seven provinces representing at least 50 percent of the population, the federal government will henceforth not act until the change has acquired the approval of each of the following:

- Ontario
- Quebec
- British Columbia
- two or more of the Prairie provinces representing a majority of the Prairie provinces' population (which would have to include Alberta)
- two or more of the Atlantic provinces representing at least 50 percent of the region's population.[22]

In August 1998, the Supreme Court delivered its decision on the legality of Quebec separation.[23] It answered the specific questions in the negative: "secession of a province 'under the Constitution' could not be achieved unilaterally"; furthermore, international law did not give Quebec the right to unilateral secession from Canada because "Quebec does not meet the threshold of a colonial people or an oppressed people, nor can it be suggested that Quebecers have been denied meaningful access to government to pursue their political, economic, cultural and social development."

Although that part of the judgment pleased federalists, the Court did not stop there. It went on to say that "the continued existence and operation of the Canadian constitutional order could not be indifferent to a clear expression of a clear majority of Quebecers that they no longer wish to remain in Canada." In other words, "a clear majority vote in Quebec on a clear question in favour of secession would confer democratic legitimacy on the secession initiative which all of the other participants in Confederation would have to recognize."

The Court added that "although there is no right, under the Constitution or at international law, to unilateral secession, the possibility of an unconstitutional declaration of secession leading to a *de facto* secession is not ruled out. The ultimate success of such a secession would be dependent on recognition by the international community."

Fred Chartrand/The Canadian Press

Intergovernmental Affairs Minister Stéphane Dion defends the Clarity Act in the House of Commons, December 1999.

Bouchard then called an election for November 30, 1998. Although he won the largest number of seats, Jean Charest's Liberals actually collected a greater number of votes. This lukewarm public endorsement forced Bouchard to postpone plans for yet another referendum on some variation of Quebec sovereignty. As mentioned in Chapter 5, Prime Minister Chrétien then introduced the **Clarity Act**, drafted by federal–provincial affairs minister Stéphane Dion. It essentially translated into law the Supreme Court decision denying Quebec's right to a unilateral declaration of independence. Although the bill stopped short of articulating what a "clear majority" would be in numerical terms, it did specify that the federal government would not recognize a Quebec referendum result that did not involve a clear expression of the will of the population that the province *should cease to be part of Canada*. The federal government would not tolerate a question that involved continuing economic or political arrangements with Canada, nor engage in negotiations that did not address the division of assets and liabilities; border changes; the rights, interests, and territorial claims of Aboriginal peoples; and the protection of minority rights.

Chrétien believed such legislation was required because the questions asked in the Quebec referendums of 1980 and 1995 were deliberately vague. The new act did not incite the inflammatory backlash in that province that some observers had expected, and the Liberals actually improved their position in Quebec in the November 2000 federal election. Nevertheless, one month later, Quebec passed an "Act respecting the exercise of the fundamental rights and prerogatives of the Quebec people and the Quebec state." It declared that Quebec would determine its own referendum question without intervention from Ottawa. At least for the time being, this ended the quest for mega-constitutional change.

CRITICAL APPROACHES

A *rational choice approach* might draw attention to the strategic reasons for which political actors adopt certain constitutional amendments at a given point in time—including avoiding the constitution itself and simply passing legislation instead. In one variant of this argument, constitutional developments stem from the interaction among representatives of the political, economic and/or cultural elites, as they aim to put certain rules over and above the regular day-to-day powers of subsequent legislatures, thereby reducing uncertainty about the rules in the future and, likely, perpetuating rules that are advantageous to these actors.

SINGLE-ISSUE CONSTITUTIONAL CHANGE

Post-1982 Formal Constitutional Amendments

On another constitutional front, some 11 constitutional amendments of a less comprehensive nature have been passed since 1982. They are listed in Box 17.5. The 1983 amendment was adopted under section 38 of the Constitution Act, 1982—that is, it required the approval of seven provinces representing at least 50 percent of the population (in fact, all but Quebec approved it) —while seven were adopted under section 43, the part of the amending formula involving the federal Parliament and the single province affected. The amendments of 1985, 1999, and 2011, adopted under section 44, affected the federal government alone.[24]

BOX 17.5 SINGLE-ISSUE CONSTITUTIONAL AMENDMENTS SINCE 1982

1983: Constitution Amendment Proclamation, 1983: Added a new section 25(b), new sections 35(3) and (4), a new section 35.1, and a new section 37, all relating to Aboriginal peoples

1985: House of Commons: Changed the formula for representation therein

1987: Newfoundland: Added Pentecostals to the list of religious denominations that had a right to operate their own schools

1993: New Brunswick: Strengthened the principle of French–English dualism in the province's public institutions

1993: Prince Edward Island: Provided that the Confederation Bridge would replace the federal government's obligation of a steamship service to the province

1997: Newfoundland: Reduced the role of the churches in the province's school system

1997: Quebec: Permitted a change in the structure of the school boards in the province from a religious to a linguistic basis

1998: Newfoundland: Made the school system completely secular

1999: Nunavut: Provided representation in the House of Commons and Senate separate from the Northwest Territories

2001: Newfoundland and Labrador: Changed the name of the province

2011: House of Commons: Changed the formula for representation therein

Constitutional Change relating to Aboriginal Canadians

Chapter 4 and earlier parts of this chapter demonstrated that Aboriginal Canadians were not well served by the constitution historically. The Constitution Act, 1982, made some advance in this respect, containing two clauses that had the potential to protect and enhance their position. As mentioned, section 25 ensured that Aboriginal and treaty rights were not diminished by the Charter, while section 35 guaranteed new Aboriginal and treaty rights. Section 35 was itself amended in 1983, and has played a part in a variety of ways in which the constitutional position of Aboriginal Canadians has been strengthened. First, several judicial decisions advancing Aboriginal interests have been based on section 35; second, Prime Minister Chrétien decreed that the section actually included the inherent right to Aboriginal self-government; and third, it has been a catalyst for new treaties, land claims, and self-government agreements. Such treaties and agreements based on section 35 are therefore themselves now part of the constitution. The Royal Commission on Aboriginal Peoples concluded that even older treaties constitute "social contracts that have enduring significance and that as a result form part of the fundamental law of the land. In this sense they are like the terms of union whereby former British colonies entered Confederation as provinces."[25]

Instruments of Constitutional Change other than Formal Amendments

Most observers contend that large-scale constitutional negotiations are not likely to succeed because in the foreseeable future too many conflicting interests are in question. Given the rigidity of the formal amending formula, to say nothing of the notion that a national referendum would be required to ratify the results, mega-constitutional failure is almost guaranteed. It might be better to live with the current dissatisfaction than the trauma that inevitably results from the failure of intense efforts at constitutional change. Perhaps the system can carry on with further reforms short of formal constitutional amendments.[26] Box 17.6 lists some of the instruments that have been used since 1982 to address unsolvable constitutional issues by circumventing formal constitutional amendments as well as possible uses of such instruments in the future. Many of these measures are addressed in the two chapters that follow, falling as they do within the realms of federalism and the Charter of Rights and Freedoms.

As explained in greater detail in Chapter 23, the Harper government attempted to use organic statutes to reform Canada's Senate, but met much criticism, and was ultimately informed through a reference to the Supreme Court in 2014 that such reforms require constitutional amendments. Similarly, as explained in Chapter 24, when the Harper government tried to amend the Supreme Court Act (to change rules regarding judicial appointments) with a clause in the omnibus budget implementation bill in the spring of 2014, the Supreme Court again ruled that such a change required unanimous provincial consent.

Canada also joined other countries that recognize Elizabeth II as head of state in changing the line of succession (making it gender-neutral) in 2013. The Harper government did so with the *Succession to the Throne Act*, a simple act of Parliament. But some constitutional

BOX 17.6   INSTRUMENTS TO CIRCUMVENT FORMAL CONSTITUTIONAL CHANGES

1. Parliamentary resolutions and declarations
   - recognizing Quebec as a distinct society within Canada (1995)
   - recognizing the Québécois as a nation within a united Canada (2006)
   - recognizing that the principle of the inherent right to Aboriginal self-government was already incorporated in section 35 (1995)
2. Organic statutes
   - Constitutional Amendments Act (1995)
3. Federal–provincial agreements
   - delegation of powers, e.g., labour market training
   - on initiating new federal programs (e.g., Social Union Framework Agreement)
   - on inter-provincial trade (e.g., Agreement on Internal Trade)
   - international role for provinces (e.g., Quebec and UNESCO)
4. Federal–provincial finance
   - solving the "fiscal imbalance" with increased transfers
   - health care agreements
   - curtailing the federal "spending power"
5. Aboriginal treaties, land claims, self-government, and other agreements
   - Nunavut
   - Nisga'a Treaty
   - delegation of responsibility for programs
6. Judicial decisions
   - place of private health care insurance
   - same-sex marriage
   - Aboriginal cases
7. Constitutional conventions
   - inviting territorial leaders to first ministers' meetings
   - creation of the Council of the Federation
   - Parliamentary involvement in Supreme Court appointments

scholars claim that a formal constitutional amendment is required under Section 41 of the Constitution Act, 1982, which would necessitate unanimous provincial consent. The issue is now before the courts.

CONCLUSION

Canada has one of the oldest constitutions in the world. Although it has been altered incrementally over its long existence by formal amendments, judicial interpretation, and constitutional conventions, its basic provisions remain intact. For 40 years after the start of Quebec's Quiet Revolution, the issue of mega-constitutional change was never far from the top of the Canadian political agenda. The incomplete success of 1982 led to the dismal failures of 1990 and 1992, and an abandonment of the effort after 2000. For the time being, therefore, we have resorted to less formal means of achieving some of the stated objectives.

This chapter is linked in particular to Chapter 5 on French Canada and Quebec and to the following chapters on federalism and the Charter of Rights and Freedoms.

DISCUSSION QUESTIONS

1. Is the 1982 constitutional amending formula appropriate? If not, how should it be changed? Did the informal change in 1996 help?

2. What is your assessment of the key provisions of the Meech Lake and Charlottetown Accords? Would we have been better off if one or the other had been adopted?

3. To what extent should politicians be guided by popular referendums on constitutional matters?

4. What are the advantages and disadvantages of "mega-constitutional change"— Canadians attempting to address all their constitutional problems simultaneously?

5. To what extent can Canadians resolve their "constitutional" problems in extra-constitutional ways?

MindTap®   FOR MORE INFO GO TO **http://www.nelson.com/student**

NOTES

1. Alan C. Cairns has defined the Constitution in similar terms as follows: "[It] is the body of understandings defining the basic institutions of government and the relations between them, plus the relationships between governments in the federal system, and between the citizens and those governments," in *Constitution, Government, and Society in Canada* (Toronto: McClelland and Stewart, 1988), p. 31.
2. The act can be found at http://www.canlii.org/en/ca/const/const1867.html or http://www.solon.org/Constitutions/Canada/English/ca_1867.html. See Bernard Funston and Eugene Meehan, eds., *Canadian Constitutional Documents Consolidated* (Scarborough: Carswell, 1994).
3. The Constitution Act, 1982 is a Canadian statute that is an appendix to the Canada Act, a British statute, and the Charter of Rights and Freedoms is part of the Constitution Act, 1982.
4. Many definitions of conventions exist and are discussed by Andrew Heard in *Canadian Constitutional Conventions* (Toronto: Oxford University Press, 1991). See also Heard, "Constitutional Conventions and Parliament," *Canadian Parliamentary Review* (Summer 2005).
5. Peter Hogg, *Constitutional Law of Canada*, 2nd ed. (Toronto: Carswell, 1985), p. 12; Craig Forcese and Aaron Freeman, *The Laws of Government: The Legal Foundations of Canadian Democracy* (Toronto: Irwin Law, 2005). The question of judicial recognition of such conventions is addressed below.
6. On about 10 other occasions constitutional amendments were made without prior consultation with the provinces because Ottawa considered that they were of exclusive federal concern. These included repeated redistributions of seats in the House of Commons and the entry of Newfoundland and Labrador into Confederation. See Guy Favreau, *The Amendment of the Constitution of Canada* (Ottawa: Queen's Printer, 1965); and Paul Gérin-Lajoie, *Constitutional Amendment in Canada* (Toronto: University of Toronto Press, 1950).

7. Cairns, *Constitution, Government, and Society in Canada*.

8. Edward McWhinney, *Quebec and the Constitution 1960–1978* (University of Toronto Press, 1979); Edward McWhinney, *Canada and the Constitution 1979–1982* (University of Toronto Press, 1982); and Peter Russell, *Constitutional Odyssey*, 3rd ed. (Toronto: University of Toronto Press, 2004).

9. Kenneth McRoberts, *Misconceiving Canada: The Struggle for National Unity* (Toronto: Oxford University Press, 1997); and Michael Mandel, *The Charter of Rights and the Legalization of Politics in Canada* (Toronto: Wall and Thompson, 1989; rev. ed. 1994), pp. 17, 20, 22, and 111.

10. See, for example, Gordon Robertson, *Memoirs of a Very Civil Servant: Mackenzie King to Pierre Trudeau* (Toronto: University of Toronto Press, 2000). Robertson is even more appalled at Trudeau's intervention in the debate over the Meech Lake and Charlottetown Accords.

11. *Reference re Amendment of the Constitution of Canada*, [1981] 125 D.L.R. (3rd) 1. See Heard, *Canadian Constitutional Conventions*, and Mandel, *The Charter of Rights*, pp. 22, 24–34, 111.

12. Keith Banting and Richard Simeon, eds., *And No One Cheered: Federalism, Democracy and the Constitution Act* (Toronto: Methuen, 1983); and Roy Romanow, J. Whyte, and H. Leeson, Canada ... Notwithstanding: The Making of the Constitution 1976–1982 (Toronto: Methuen, 1984).

13. *Re: Objection to a Resolution to Amend the Constitution*, [1982] 2 S.C.R. 793. See Marc Gold, "The Mask of Objectivity: Politics and Rhetoric in the Supreme Court of Canada," *The Supreme Court Law Review* 7 (1985).

14. Michael Behiels, ed., *The Meech Lake Primer: Conflicting Views of the 1987 Constitutional Accord* (Ottawa: University of Ottawa Press, 1989); *Canadian Public Policy* (September 1988); Roger Gibbins, ed., *Meech Lake and Canada: Perspectives from the West* (Edmonton: Academic Printing and Publishing, 1988); Peter Hogg, *Meech Lake Constitutional Accord Annotated* (Toronto: Carswell, 1988); and K.E. Swinton and C.J. Rogerson, *Competing Constitutional Visions: The Meech Lake Accord* (Toronto: Carswell, 1988).

15. Cairns, *Constitution, Government, and Society in Canada*; and Alan C. Cairns, *Disruptions: Constitutional Struggles, from the Charter to Meech Lake* (Toronto: McClelland and Stewart, 1991).

16. The former Cabinet secretary and clerk of the Privy Council, Gordon Robertson, argued strenuously that no such deadline existed but to no avail.

17. Alan C. Cairns, *Reconfigurations: Canadian Citizenship and Constitutional Change* (Toronto: McClelland and Stewart, 1995); Curtis Cook, ed., *Constitutional Predicament: Canada after the Referendum of 1992* (Montreal: McGill-Queen's University Press, 1994); Kenneth McRoberts and Patrick Monahan, eds., *The Charlottetown Accord, the Referendum and the Future of Canada* (Toronto: University of Toronto Press, 1993); Peter H. Russell, *Constitutional Odyssey*, 3rd ed.; Patrick C. Fafard and Douglas M. Brown, Canada: The State of the Federation 1996 (Kingston: Institute of Intergovernmental Affairs, 1996); and F. Leslie Seidel, *Seeking a New Canadian Partnership: Asymmetrical and Confederal Options* (Montreal: Institute for Research on Public Policy, 1994).

18. Richard Johnston, André Blais, Elisabeth Gidengil, and Neil Nevitte, *The Challenge of Direct Democracy: The 1992 Canadian Referendum* (Montreal: McGill-Queen's University Press, 1996).

19. Matt James, *Misrecognized Materialists: Social Movements in Canadian Constitutional Politics* (Vancouver: UBC Press, 2006).

20. Réjean Pelletier, "From Jacques Parizeau to Lucien Bouchard: A New Vision? Yes, But ..." in Lazar, *Canada: The State of the Federation 1997*.

21. Robert Howse, "Searching for Plan A: National Unity and the Chrétien Government's New Federalism," in Lazar, *Canada: The State of the Federation 1997*; and Gordon Gibson, *Plan B: The Future of the Rest of Canada* (Vancouver: Fraser Institute, 1994).

22. Jennifer Smith, "Informal Constitutional Development: Change by Other Means," in Herman Bakvis and Grace Skogstad, eds., *Canadian Federalism: Performance, Effectiveness, and Legitimacy* (Toronto: Oxford University Press, 2002).

23. *Reference re Secession of Quebec*, [1998] 2 S.C.R. 217; David Schneiderman, ed., *The Quebec Decision: The Supreme Court Case and Commentary* (Toronto: Lorimer, 1999).

24. J.R. Hurley, *Amending Canada's Constitution: History, Processes, Problems and Prospects* (Ottawa: Minister of Supply and Services Canada, 1996).

25. *Report of the Royal Commission on Aboriginal Peoples*, Vol. 2, Ch. 2, 1.3 (Ottawa, 1996).

26. Harvey Lazar, ed., *Canada: The State of the Federation 1997: Non-constitutional Renewal* (Kingston: Institute of Intergovernmental Relations, 1997); and Fafard and Brown, *Canada: The State of the Federation 1996*.

FURTHER READING

Cairns, Alan C. *Constitution, Government and Society in Canada*. Toronto: McClelland and Stewart, 1988.

———. *Disruptions: Constitutional Struggles, from the Charter to Meech Lake*. Toronto: McClelland and Stewart, 1991.

———. *Reconfigurations: Canadian Citizenship and Constitutional Change*. Toronto: McClelland and Stewart, 1995.

Funston, Bernard, and Eugene Meehan, eds. *Canadian Constitutional Documents Consolidated*. Scarborough: Carswell, 1994.

Heard, Andrew. *Canadian Constitutional Conventions*. Toronto: Oxford University Press, 1991.

Hogg, Peter. *Canada Act Annotated*. Toronto: Carswell, 1982.

———. *Meech Lake Constitutional Accord Annotated*. Toronto: Carswell, 1988.

Hurley, J.R. *Amending Canada's Constitution: History, Processes, Problems and Prospects*. Ottawa: Minister of Supply and Services Canada, 1996.

James, Matt. *Misrecognized Materialists: Social Movements in Canadian Constitutional Politics*. Vancouver: UBC Press, 2006.

Lazar, Harvey, ed. *Canada: The State of the Federation 1997: Non-constitutional Renewal*. Kingston: Institute of Intergovernmental Relations, 1997.

McRoberts, Kenneth. *Misconceiving Canada: The Struggle for National Unity*. Toronto: Oxford University Press, 1997.

———, and Patrick Monahan, eds. *The Charlottetown Accord, the Referendum and the Future of Canada*. Toronto: University of Toronto Press, 1993.

McWhinney, Edward. *Quebec and the Constitution 1960–1978*. Toronto: University of Toronto Press, 1979.

———. *Canada and the Constitution 1979–82: Patriation and the Charter of Rights*. Toronto: University of Toronto Press, 1982.

Romanow, Roy, J. Whyte, and H. Leeson. *Canada ... Notwithstanding: The Making of the Constitution 1976–1982*. Toronto: Methuen, 1984.

Russell, Peter. *Constitutional Odyssey*, 3rd ed. Toronto: University of Toronto Press, 2004.

Seidel, F. Leslie. *Seeking a New Canadian Partnership: Asymmetrical and Confederal Options*. Montreal: Institute for Research on Public Policy, 1994.

Young, Robert A. *The Struggle for Quebec: From Referendum to Referendum?* Montreal: McGill-Queen's University Press, 1999.

The Federal System

Canada comprises 10 provinces and three territories; the provinces are autonomous within the powers given them by the Constitution, but the territories are constitutionally subordinate to the federal government. Although the territories increasingly function as provinces, exercising similar powers, these powers could theoretically be revoked. A discussion of the provinces as separate political systems has been placed on the website of this book, while this chapter focuses on federal–provincial relations. Figure 18.1 shows the division of Canada into provinces and territories, together with their capitals.

Liberal Prime Minister Mackenzie King once said that he would not give "one red cent" to a Tory provincial government. Federal–provincial squabbles are a daily occurrence in Canadian political life, but less visible than the conflict are the immense cooperation and collaboration between the two levels of government. In the 1930s, the courts threw out federal legislation aimed at alleviating the Depression, ruling that only the provinces could pass such laws. In the postwar period, though, Ottawa introduced a multitude of national programs within provincial jurisdiction and through financial inducements persuaded the provinces to join them. Later, throughout the 1990s, the federal government cut back on such transfers, to considerable provincial and public complaint. Early in the 21st century, health care, the environment, finance, and justice constituted some of the most fertile grounds for further federal–provincial interaction, involving both conflict and cooperation.

The federal character of Canada is designated in the Canadian Constitution and can be seen in almost every aspect of governance and society. The federal system is closely related to regional economic cleavages and regional identities; it is important for ethnic cleavages and identities; it influences the Canadian political culture; and it affects the operation of the electoral system, political parties, and advocacy groups. Federalism also has a major impact on the institutions of the national government.

In a formal sense, **federalism** can be defined as a division of powers between central and regional governments such that neither is subordinate to the other. This definition distinguishes the relationship between national and provincial governments from that between provincial and municipal governments; in the latter case the municipalities are clearly subordinate entities while in the former, provinces are "coordinate" or equal in status to the central government. This equality of status is provided for in the constitutional division of powers between

FIGURE 18.1   MAP OF THE PROVINCES AND TERRITORIES AND THEIR CAPITALS

the two levels of government, which is found primarily in sections 91 and 92 of the Constitution Act, 1867. Other aspects of federalism are also important, such as federal–provincial financial relations (taxing and spending) and joint policymaking mechanisms. Moreover, the institutions of federalism are embedded in a very diverse "federal society" that supports such a two-tier structure of government. As the Supreme Court said in the *Quebec Secession* case, "federalism is a legal response to the underlying political and cultural realties that existed at Confederation and continue to exist today."[1]

When the provinces are all treated alike by the constitution and by the federal government, the system is called "symmetrical federalism," and when they are singled out for distinctive treatment, the term **asymmetrical federalism** is used. The Constitution Act, 1867 has several clauses that refer to a specific province, and Ottawa has occasionally treated one province (usually Quebec) differently from others. Nevertheless, asymmetrical federalism remains exceptional and controversial in many quarters, especially to the Pierre Trudeau vision of Canada.

Municipal governments may be subordinate to their provincial masters, but they are also important components of the overall government structure in Canada, even if they are not part of the official "federal" system. Indeed, actions of the federal government often have implications for municipalities and vice versa. More and more observers are recommending that large cities, at least, be somehow brought into the ambit of Canadian federalism. Table 18.1 shows the relative significance of the three levels of government in terms of employment, which total more than 10 percent of Canada's total population.

TABLE 18.1   FEDERAL, PROVINCIAL/TERRITORIAL, AND MUNICIPAL EMPLOYMENT, 2012

FEDERAL	521 829
PROVINCIAL/TERRITORIAL	1 760 081
MUNICIPAL	1 405 072

Source: Adapted from Statistics Canada, Table 183-0002 - Public sector employment, wages and salaries, seasonally unadjusted and adjusted, monthly, CANSIM, http://www5.statcan.gc.ca/cansim/a26?lang=eng&retrLang=eng&id=1830002&paSer=&pattern=&stByVal=1&p1=1&p2=-1&tabMode=dataTable&csid=. Calculations by authors. Reproduced and distributed on an "as is" basis with the permission of Statistics Canada.

This chapter begins by outlining the federal system in Canada at its creation; it then traces the evolution of the federal system, especially through changes in the division of powers and federal–provincial financial relationships. In the following section this evolution is depicted in chronological phases, as the federal system veered between centralization and decentralization. The chapter concludes with a discussion of Canadian federalism today.

THE CONFEDERATION SETTLEMENT

The fundamentals of Canadian federalism, often called the **Confederation Settlement**,[2] were incorporated into the **British North America Act, 1867**, which in 1982 was renamed the **Constitution Act, 1867**. As noted in Chapter 2, the principal architect of Confederation was Sir John A. Macdonald, who intended the new country to be a highly centralized federation. In many ways, in fact, the Confederation Settlement was not consistent with the modern definition of federalism because in certain respects the provinces were made subordinate to the central government.[3] The Confederation Settlement consisted of five principal components:

- the division of powers between the central and provincial governments
- the division of financial resources
- federal controls imposed on the provinces
- provincial representation in the central institutions
- certain cultural guarantees

As far as the **division of powers** between the central and provincial governments was concerned, the Fathers of Confederation gave the provinces 16 specific **enumerated powers** in section 92 (e.g., hospitals and municipal institutions) and then left everything else—the **residual powers**—to Ottawa, in section 91. For greater certainty, however, section 91 also included a list of 29 federal powers, such as trade and commerce and national defence. Two **concurrent powers**—agriculture and immigration—were listed in section 95, and section 132 provided the federal government with the power to implement Empire treaties, regardless of their subject matter (see Box 18.1).

BOX 18.1 THE CORE OF THE FEDERAL–PROVINCIAL DIVISION OF POWERS

Federal Powers	Provincial Powers	Concurrent Powers
Trade and commerce	Direct taxation within the province	Agriculture
Any form of taxation	Public lands	Immigration
National defence	Hospitals and health care	Old age pensions
Banking	Municipal institutions	
Aboriginals	Education	
Criminal law	Property and civil rights	
Interprovincial	Administration of justice	
Transportation and communication		

In the division of financial resources, federal dominance was even more clear-cut. The Fathers gave Ottawa the power to levy any mode or system of taxation, which included both **direct** and **indirect taxes.** Since the only tax widely used at the time was the customs duty (an indirect tax), provincial power over direct taxation was not considered to be very significant. Instead, the provinces were expected to raise their revenues from the sale of shop, saloon, tavern, and auctioneer licences, as well as to rely on federal subsidies. The federal government was to pay each province an annual per capita grant of 80 cents plus a small subsidy to support its government and legislature. The federal government also assisted the provinces by assuming their pre-Confederation debts. It should be added that the provinces were authorized to raise revenues from their natural resources, but this source was not taken very seriously because few such resources (except trees) had yet been discovered.

In a clear departure from what is now regarded as the federal principle, Ottawa was given several means of controlling the provinces. The federally appointed lieutenant governors had an alternative to giving royal assent to a provincial law—the power of **reservation.**

Library and Archives Canada/C-006388

Sir John A. Macdonald, the architect of a strong federal government.

They could *reserve* provincial legislation for the consideration of the federal Cabinet, which could then approve or reject it. Even if the lieutenant governor gave assent to a piece of provincial legislation, however, the federal Cabinet could subsequently *disallow* it—the power of **disallowance**. Then, under section 92(10)(c), the **declaratory power**, the federal government could *declare* any local work or undertaking to be for the general advantage of Canada and thus place it within federal jurisdiction.

Given the highly centralized nature of the division of powers, the limited financial resources of the provinces, and the federal controls, it is clear that the Confederation Settlement of 1867 placed the provinces in a subordinate position, somewhat akin to municipalities, rather than giving them the equal or coordinate status provided for in the modern definition of federalism.

In the light of the federal government's dominant position, it is not surprising that the provinces were concerned with their representation in the national policymaking system. The fourth aspect of the Confederation Settlement, therefore, was agreement on provincial representation in the House of Commons and the Senate, a question of much greater concern at the time than the division of powers. The great compromise that allowed Confederation to go forward was that the provinces would be represented according to population in the Commons but that *regional* equality would prevail in the Senate. Thus, each of the three original regions—the Maritimes, Quebec, and Ontario—was to receive 24 senators, appeasing smaller provinces that could be easily out-voted in the lower chamber.

Such concern about provincial representation *within* the institutions of the national government has come to be called "intrastate federalism," as opposed to an emphasis on relations *between* federal and provincial governments, which is sometimes termed "interstate federalism."[4] Beyond the House of Commons and the Senate, interests of the various provinces can be represented within the Cabinet and, perhaps less explicitly, within the bureaucracy and Supreme Court, an issue that arises in the discussion of these institutions in the next part of the book. To some extent, federal–provincial (or interstate) tensions can be reduced if intrastate mechanisms are working effectively so that the people of all provinces feel adequately represented within the national policymaking process. But rigid party discipline, representation by population in the House of Commons, and unilateral federal appointment of senators and Supreme Court judges may diminish such confidence, and, as a result, provincial premiers often come to be the principal articulators of provincial interests.

Confederation was more than just a union of provinces: it was also the uniting of a French culture with an English population. (Nobody gave Aboriginals much thought at the time.) Thus, the fifth aspect of the Confederation Settlement might be called cultural guarantees. Considering the anxiety of French Canadians about the preservation of their language and culture, these guarantees were surprisingly minor. Section 133 of the 1867 act made French and English official languages in the federal Parliament and federal courts as well as in the Quebec legislature and Quebec courts—but nowhere else. At the time, religion was probably of greater concern than language, so existing separate school systems in the provinces (especially Ontario and Quebec) were guaranteed by allowing the federal government to step in to restore them, if necessary, according to section 93. French Canada was also protected by giving power over property and civil rights to the provinces so that Quebec could maintain certain cultural particularisms, including its civil law system.

Because the evolution of French-language rights is discussed in Chapter 5 and since the question of representation is addressed in Chapter 23, this chapter will proceed to track the development of the Confederation Settlement in its other three aspects—the division of powers, financial resources, and federal controls.

EVOLUTION OF CANADIAN FEDERALISM TO 2000

In discussing the evolution of Canadian federalism, a key concern will be to explain how the very centralized federation created in 1867 became the highly decentralized Canada of today. This trend can be documented in all three areas—the division of powers, financial resources, and federal controls.

Division of Powers

The evolution of the division of powers between federal and provincial governments can be examined in two respects: formal constitutional amendments that altered the division of powers, and judicial decisions that interpreted sections 91, 92, and 132 of the Constitution Act, 1867. It will be seen that the latter development was by far the more important.

Constitutional Amendments

Since 1867, only five formal constitutional amendments have been adopted that directly affected the division of powers. First, in 1940, unemployment insurance was added to the list of federal powers in section 91 after the courts had earlier declared it to belong to the provinces. Second, in 1951, old age pensions were made a concurrent power, allowing the federal government into this area as well. Third, in 1964, federal jurisdiction in the pensions field was enlarged to include widows' and survivors' benefits and disability pensions. Fourth, in 1949, the federal Parliament was allowed to amend the Constitution unilaterally in areas of purely federal concern, a power previously held by Britain. (This amendment was repealed in 1982 with the adoption of a more general amending formula.) Finally, in the **Constitution Act, 1982**, the new section 92A increased provincial jurisdiction over natural resources, while the Charter of Rights and Freedoms generally reduced the powers of both levels of government. Thus, in the first three cases, the net result was a slight increase in federal powers, but, as pointed out in Chapter 17, this increase was accomplished with the unanimous consent of the provinces. The 1982 natural resources amendment was the only formal constitutional amendment that in any way increased provincial powers at the expense of Ottawa.

Judicial Interpretation

Judicial interpretation of the federal and provincial powers in the 1867 act is a much more complicated subject. Before 1949, the **Judicial Committee of the Privy Council** (JCPC) in London was Canada's final court of appeal, and most constitutional decisions were rendered by that body. There is no doubt that its decisions had a major impact in transforming the nature of Canadian federalism from a centralized to a decentralized system, whether it acted out of ignorance or by deliberate design. The JCPC decisions can be examined primarily in terms of the Peace, Order and Good Government clause, the Trade and Commerce power, and the Treaty power.

Section 91 of the 1867 act has two parts. First, the **Peace, Order and Good Government clause** says that all powers not given to the provinces in section 92 are left with the federal government. This is also known as "POGG" or the residual clause, and reads as follows:

> It shall be lawful for the Queen, by and with the Advice and Consent of the Senate and House of Commons, to make laws for the Peace, Order and good Government of Canada, in relation to all matters not coming within the Classes of Subjects by this Act assigned exclusively to the Legislatures of the Provinces; and for greater Certainty, but not so as to restrict the Generality of the foregoing Terms of this Section, it is hereby declared that (notwithstanding anything in this Act) the exclusive Legislative Authority of the Parliament of Canada extends to all Matters coming within the Classes of Subjects next hereinafter enumerated.

Then, for greater certainty, a list of 29 examples of federal powers is included, a clause that was logically unnecessary and eventually became counterproductive. In a nutshell, in the course of its judgments the Judicial Committee drove a wedge between these two parts of section 91; it decided that the list of 29 examples constituted the *real* federal powers; and it ignored the Peace, Order and Good Government clause except in time of national emergency. How it managed to transform the residual clause into an emergency clause, the so-called **emergency doctrine**, is very difficult to fathom, and is the subject of much scholarly discussion and whole books and courses on Canadian constitutional law. However, the JCPC gave an extremely broad interpretation to section 92(13), property and civil rights in the province, finding that almost any matter that was the subject of a federal–provincial constitutional dispute could be incorporated within this provincial power. That is why so little was left over for the federal residual clause. A brief summary of the leading POGG cases is included in Box 18.2.

BOX 18.2   A BRIEF SUMMARY OF THE LEADING POGG CASES[5]

In *Russell v. the Queen*, 1882, the federal Temperance Act was challenged. This law provided the means by which the people of a local community could vote to outlaw the sale of alcohol. The JCPC ruled that the regulation of liquor was not mentioned explicitly in sections 91 and 92, and that although it affected property and civil rights (Mr. Russell's tavern and his right to operate it), the main purpose of the act was the promotion of public order and safety throughout the Dominion. Thus, the federal act was a valid exercise of the Peace, Order and Good Government power.

However, in an 1883 case, *Hodge v. the Queen*, the Judicial Committee ruled that there was a "double aspect" to the regulation of liquor—"subjects which in one aspect and for one purpose fall within s. 92, may in another aspect and for another purpose fall within s. 91." This decision opened the door for provincial action in the liquor field as well. In 1892, in the *Maritime Bank* case, provincial lieutenant governors were given equality of status to the Governor General, an equality that generally applied to the two levels of government as a whole. Then, in the Local Prohibition case of 1896, the JCPC said that the Peace, Order and Good Government clause was merely "supplementary" to the powers listed in section 91, and that POGG would come into play only if a subject could not be found in the list of powers in either section 91 or 92, and if the subject had

continued

"attained such dimensions as to affect the body politic of the country as a whole." From this point, at which the POGG clause was divorced from the rest of section 91 and the examples effectively became *the* federal powers, matters in dispute were increasingly found to fit into property and civil rights in the provinces.

POGG was then transformed into an emergency clause in a series of cases in the 1920s. In the 1922 *Board of Commerce* case, the Privy Council said that the regulation of prices and profiteering would normally fall within section 92(13), and only in special circumstances, such as war or famine, could such matters become of national importance. In the 1924 *Fort Frances* case, federal regulation of the price and supply of newsprint was upheld because it had been done in wartime, an emergency that justified federal action in a field that would ordinarily be provincial. Finally, in the 1925 *Toronto Electric Commissioners v. Snider* case, federal legislation to deal with serious strikes was ruled unconstitutional since labour–management relations were normally matters of property and civil rights in the province and could only become the subject of federal action in an emergency. Faced with the disparity between this line of interpretation (that POGG was only an emergency clause) and that used in the *Russell* case (that POGG was a simple residual clause), the JCPC resorted to a reinterpretation of the earlier case: the evil of drunkenness at the time of the *Russell* case must have amounted to a national emergency!

A series of "New Deal" cases followed in the 1930s in which federal laws in the fields of unemployment insurance, labour standards, and the marketing of farm products were ruled invalid because they dealt with property and civil rights in the provinces and because the legislation was intended to be permanent rather than deal only with the temporary emergency of the Depression. In other words, federal actions based on the emergency doctrine had to be temporary measures. These highly controversial decisions rendered Ottawa impotent in dealing with the human devastation wrought by the Depression. Strangely enough, however, when the *Russell* case was duplicated in the 1946 *Canada Temperance Federation* case, the JCPC disavowed the emergency doctrine and reverted to the simple residual basis of POGG.

When appeals to the Privy Council were abolished in 1949, all eyes were on the Supreme Court to see which line of interpretation it would take with respect to POGG—emergency power or residual clause? The record has been unclear, but in general the federal level has won more cases than it did before 1949. Perhaps this reflects the Supreme Court's better understanding of the Canadian situation or its reaction to the excessive provincial orientation of the JCPC. Some of these federal victories have been based on POGG as a simple residual clause (with an issue having national but not emergency dimensions), such as the *Johannesson* case, which reaffirmed federal control over aviation and airports; the BC and Newfoundland off-shore minerals cases, which gave Ottawa jurisdiction over the area beyond the BC and Newfoundland coasts; and *Munro v. National Capital Commission*, which permitted federal regulation of property in the National Capital Region. But in the leading decision, the *Anti-Inflation Act reference* of 1976, the Court was badly split. The majority of judges who upheld the federal law in question did so for different reasons: some adhered to the emergency doctrine, while others were prepared to accept a broader interpretation of POGG.

More recent cases, such as *Crown Zellerbach* in 1988 and *Oldman River* in 1992, strengthened federal jurisdiction over pollution control with extra-provincial implications. The Court seems to have concluded that POGG can be used in nonemergency cases to cover single, distinctive, indivisible subjects that have reached national dimensions and that a province would be unable to deal with properly on its own (the "provincial inability test"). Some such cases involved the federal criminal law power, which was also used by the Supreme Court to uphold the federal government's gun registration law in the *Firearms Act Reference*. Later, in March 2015, the Supreme Court ruled in a split decision that Quebec had no legal right to the data collected under the federal long-gun registry that was abolished in 2012. Based on the federal criminal law power, the majority said that Parliament had a right to abolish the data rather than provide it to Quebec because the division of powers overrode the principle of cooperative federalism.

Ottawa's control over telephones and telecommunications has also been enhanced; federal maternity benefits have been upheld as part of the Employment Insurance Act; and in a case involving LEGO®, the federal power over trade marks prevailed.[6] Even if a recent pro-Ottawa stance can be detected, however, now often relying on the **criminal law** power, the net effect of judicial interpretation of the Peace, Order and Good Government clause since 1867 was a great increase of provincial powers at federal expense.

A similar fate awaited the federal **Trade and Commerce clause**, section 91(2). The Fathers of Confederation deliberately expressed this clause in wide, general, unlimited terms (the regulation of trade and commerce) but as early as the *Parsons* case in 1881 the JCPC basically restricted federal power to international and interprovincial trade. In addition to drawing a rigid line between interprovincial trade (federal) and intraprovincial trade (provincial), the courts created a no-man's land wherever the two kinds of trade were unavoidably combined. The general result of this interpretation was to enhance the provincial power over property and civil rights, and to downgrade the federal commerce power. Since 1949, the Supreme Court has rendered more realistic judgments in this area, recognizing the complexity of the situation and often favouring the federal side. But, in 2011, the Supreme Court ruled that a federal proposal for a regulator of national securities (stocks and bonds) could not be sustained by the Trade and Commerce power—a victory for the provinces.[7]

The **Treaty power**, section 132, effectively says that in cases of Empire treaties, the division of powers becomes inoperative and the federal government can implement them regardless of subject matter. Such was the decision of the *Aeronautics* case of 1932, and the *Radio* case of the same year applied this rule to non-Empire treaties as well. However, in the 1937 *Labour Conventions* case, the JCPC reversed itself and said that Ottawa could only implement treaties the subject matter of which was within federal jurisdiction. In this particular case, the subject matter fell instead into property and civil rights.

The combined effect of the judicial interpretation of the Peace, Order and Good Government clause, the Trade and Commerce clause, and the Treaty power has been to reduce significantly the intended dominance of the federal government and to increase substantially the scope of provincial powers, especially with the broad interpretation given to property and civil rights. This influence has been controversial in political, judicial, and academic circles because it was clearly contrary to John A. Macdonald's conception of Canadian federalism and because it did not permit Ottawa to take many initiatives desired by centralist advocates.[8] The JCPC could deal only with the cases brought before it, of course, so that the decentralized results of its interpretation depended on a greater number of challenges to federal than to provincial laws. Several such cases were initiated by corporations that expected to be given a freer hand in their pursuit of profits if power remained at the provincial level. Other cases were started by provincial premiers with the support of their cabinets and advisers, which followed naturally from the legitimation in a federal constitution of subnational elites.

However, many observers contend that the Judicial Committee's line of interpretation was consistent with the increasing size and distances that characterized the country as time went on, as well as with societal forces and public orientations, at least outside Ontario. They argue that Canada has a federal, decentralized, diversified *society*, and the provincial bias pervading so many of the JCPC's decisions was "in fundamental harmony with the regional pluralism" of that society. However desirable centralization may have seemed at the outset, it was inappropriate in the long run "for the regional diversities of a land of vast extent and a large, geographically concentrated, minority culture."[9] Most French-Canadian observers, for example, were quite happy with the work of the JCPC. Thus, Alan Cairns finds it impossible "to believe that a few elderly men in London deciding two or three constitutional cases a year precipitated, sustained, and caused the development of Canada in a federalist direction the country would otherwise not have taken."[10] Moreover, he observes,

> the discovery and amplification of an emergency power in Section 91 may have done an injustice to the intentions of Macdonald for the residual power, but it did allow Canada to conduct herself virtually as a unitary state in the two world wars in which centralized government authority was both required and supported.[11]

Federal–Provincial Finance

In the Confederation Settlement, the federal government was given the power to levy any kind of tax, while the provinces were restricted to direct taxation.[12] Ottawa assumed provincial debts (also paying debt allowances to those provinces with smaller debts) and paid unconditional grants to the provinces based on 80 cents per capita and in support of governments and legislatures. Although the intention was thus to create a highly centralized federation, the financial factor also ultimately contributed to the increased power of the provinces. This situation came about because the provinces successfully lobbied for larger federal grants, mostly unconditional in nature, than were set out in 1867; because the provinces levied direct taxes, such as income taxes, which they were not expected to use; and because some provincial revenues, such as those from natural resources, turned out to be more significant than anticipated.

Provincial revenues proved to be inadequate from the beginning, and special grants and arrangements had to be made immediately. A wholesale change in the grant system followed in 1907. By this time, too, the provinces had begun to levy their own direct personal and corporate income taxes, a situation complicated by the federal entry into the same fields during the First World War.[13] About the same time, the **conditional grant** made its appearance. This was a grant paid by the federal government to the provinces in an area of provincial jurisdiction but for which provincial revenues were deemed to be inadequate. The provinces usually had to match the federal share of 50 percent, as well as adhere to whatever conditions or standards Ottawa imposed. The most important conditional grant in the early years was the old age pension, which started in 1927.

With both levels of government taxing the same personal and corporate incomes, but in a totally uncoordinated fashion, and with the two levels starting to become intertwined in conditional grant programs, the federal–provincial financial situation became increasingly complicated. This muddied state of affairs worsened with the advent of the Depression, when even fewer funds were available to go around. The result was the appointment of the **Rowell–Sirois Commission**, officially the Royal Commission on Dominion–Provincial Relations, in 1937. One of the recommendations of its 1940 report—that the costly responsibility for unemployment insurance be transferred to the federal government—was quickly implemented by means of a constitutional amendment.

Before 1940, therefore, the two levels of government operated with relative independence on both the taxation and the expenditure sides of public finance. Since the Second World War, however, they have become intimately intertwined, and Ottawa has taken the lead (sometimes with provincial encouragement) in coordinating the various ingredients of the federal–provincial financial relationship. The complicated federal–provincial financial situation since 1940 might be simplified somewhat by taking three aspects separately: taxation agreements, conditional and block grants, and equalization payments.

Federal–Provincial Taxation Agreements

After 1942, the taxation side was characterized by a series of five-year federal–provincial agreements. The name and terms of the **taxation agreements** changed over the years, but the basic objective was the same: to effect a degree of coordination in the field of federal–provincial taxation. The main taxes in question were personal and corporate income taxes. Between 1962 and 2000, for example, the provincial portion of an individual's personal income tax was calculated as a percentage of the federal income tax ("tax on tax"), so that while the federal tax was standard across the country, except for Quebec, the provincial portion was allowed to vary.

Conditional and Block Grants

The Rowell–Sirois Report frowned on shared-cost programs, preferring that each level of government operate independently. Nevertheless, joint programs expanded considerably after 1940, as pressure from the CCF, industrial unions, and other newly articulated interests on the left forced federal and provincial

PREMIERS DISCUSS HEALTH CARE

Sue Dewar/Artizans

governments into the joint development of a **welfare state**. The most important shared-cost social programs were postsecondary education (1952), hospital insurance (1957), the Canada Assistance Plan (CAP) (1966), and medical insurance (1968). Hospital and medical insurance were later combined as health insurance.

Federal grants for postsecondary education have always been of a **block grant** variety— that is, a sum of money given to each province for part of the operating costs of post-secondary educational institutions, without any detailed conditions or strings attached. Between 1967 and 1977 these grants were based on a formula of providing 50 percent of such expenditures.

The other major **shared-cost programs** originally fell into the conditional grant category. The usual pattern here was that after it had laid down certain conditions, the federal government paid approximately 50 percent of the cost of each program. In the case of hospital insurance, for example, Ottawa would pay half the cost of provincial programs that provided their residents with basic hospital care without charge. The provinces could finance their half of the program costs from premiums or general tax revenues. Medical insurance was an extension of the prior program to cover basic doctors' services. Under the Canada Assistance Plan, Ottawa similarly funded half the costs of almost any provincial or municipal program that provided social assistance and welfare services based on need.

Most of these programs fell constitutionally within provincial jurisdiction, but Ottawa maintained that its **spending power** allowed it to make payments to individuals, institutions, and other governments in fields over which Parliament did not necessarily have the power to regulate. Moreover, the federal government was often responding to provincial demands. It even claimed that it could attach conditions to such spending and often did so. The constitutional status of this argument was addressed by the courts in several cases.[14]

Although a combination of provincial pressure and federal political and bureaucratic expansionism inspired most of these programs, the provinces often criticized the federal conditions attached as being out of place in areas of provincial jurisdiction. Quebec in particular took this point of view in the early 1960s. The Pearson government responded to this demand by allowing provinces to "opt out" of certain conditional grant programs and continue to receive federal funding as long as they maintained an equivalent program. Then, in the 1970s, Ottawa became upset at the rapidly escalating costs of many of these programs, along with its commitment to finance 50 percent of whatever the provinces spent on them.

In 1977 the federal government therefore transferred health insurance from the conditional to the block grant category, under the Established Programs Financing Act. Ottawa removed the detailed conditions attached to the health insurance programs, as many provinces wanted, but in return, it no longer felt obliged to pay 50 percent of the provincial program costs. The federal grants now took the form of tax transfers as well as cash, and henceforth, Ottawa would increase its funding of such programs by only a certain annual percentage, which would no longer cover one-half of their overall costs. The tax transfers represent federal tax revenue forgone as a result of a coordinated reduction of federal taxes and an increase in provincial taxes such that the position of the taxpayer is left unchanged.

Removing the conditions from health insurance grants, however, led to problems with hospital user fees, doctors' double-billing, and the provinces' use of health care funds for other purposes. Federal and public displeasure at these developments led Ottawa to pass the **Canada Health Act** in 1984, to much provincial chagrin. This law allows the federal government to penalize provinces that do not meet its five conditions in the provision of public health insurance:

1. *Comprehensive*: covering all necessary health services provided by hospitals and medical practitioners

2. *Universal*: covering the whole population

3. *Portable*: covering the costs of provincial residents while temporarily absent from the province

4. *Accessible*: not impeding or precluding reasonable access to services by extra charges

5. *Publicly administered*

The Canada Assistance Plan remained a conditional grant program, with Ottawa continuing its 50 percent contribution, until the Mulroney government put a ceiling on its CAP contributions to the three richest provinces.

The 1995 federal budget brought in by Finance Minister Paul Martin inaugurated a major transformation of federal–provincial transfer payments. Beginning in 1996–97, postsecondary education, health insurance, and the Canada Assistance Plan were combined into one block grant called the **Canada Health and Social Transfer (CHST)**. It was a combination of cash payments and tax points, but represented a significant reduction in previous amounts, and Ottawa's expenditures were no longer driven by provincial costs. As a block grant, the CHST would not contain the previous conditions of CAP; the only condition on welfare transfers was that provinces not impose a minimum residency requirement. Ottawa felt that it could not retain previous conditions when it was reducing its contributions and was particularly loath to provoke the PQ government of Quebec immediately before the 1995 referendum.

All the federal off-loading, including the CHST and the shift to tax points, had serious consequences for many social programs, especially in have-not provinces. Because the latter do not have a strong tax base, they benefit more from the transfer of dollars than of tax points. These and other developments in fiscal federalism thus constituted some of the ways in which the "redistributive state" was eroded. Moreover, few social reformers trusted provincial governments to spend the smaller transfers on social programs. The federal Liberal government announced that it would continue to enforce the principles of the Canada Health Act, however, and fought with Alberta over the funding of private health clinics that charged "facility fees."

After the turn of the century, federal transfers began to increase again. Table 18.2 shows how much each province and territory received in 2015–16 in major federal transfers, by which time the CHST had been replaced by the Canada Health Transfer (CHT) in support of health care and the Canada Social Transfer (CST) in support of other social programs including postsecondary education. Table 18.2 includes Equalization Payments, discussed below, for a grand total of over $68 billion.

TABLE 18.2 MAJOR FEDERAL TRANSFERS TO THE PROVINCES AND TERRITORIES, 2015–2016 ($ MILLIONS)

	HEALTH TRANSFER	SOCIAL TRANSFER	EQUALIZATION PAYMENTS	OTHER	TOTAL
NEWFOUNDLAND/ LABRADOR	501	191	—	—	692
PRINCE EDWARD ISLAND	140	53	361	—	554
NOVA SCOTIA	897	342	1 690	116	3 044
NEW BRUNSWICK	718	273	1 669	—	2 660
QUEBEC	7 852	2 990	9 521	—	20 363
ONTARIO	13 091	4 986	2 363	—	20 440
MANITOBA	1 230	468	1 738	—	3 436
SASKATCHEWAN	1 081	412	—	—	1 493
ALBERTA	3 966	1 511	—	—	5 477
BRITISH COLUMBIA	4 439	1 690	—	—	6 129
YUKON	35	13	874*	—	923
NORTHWEST TERRITORIES	42	16	1 233*	—	1 290
NUNAVUT	35	13	1 454*	—	1 503
TOTAL	34 026	12 959	20 902	116	68 004

*TERRITORIAL FORMULA FINANCING (CONSTITUTING $3 561 OF THE $20 902 EQUALIZATION TOTAL).

Source: Department of Finance Canada, Federal Support to Provinces and Territories, http://www.fin.gc.ca/ fedprov/mtp-eng.asp. Contains information licensed under the Open Government Licence – Canada. Calculations by authors. Reproduced with the permission of the Department of Finance, 2015.

Equalization Payments

The third aspect of federal–provincial finance consists of **equalization payments**.[15] In 1957 the federal government began to pay unconditional grants to have-not provinces based on provincial need, so that all provinces could offer a relatively equal standard of services. At first only three provincial taxes were considered in the equalization formula, but the number later increased to 33—including almost every conceivable source of provincial revenue. Typically, Ontario, British Columbia, and Alberta were above the national average and did not receive equalization payments, but Alberta petroleum revenues raised the national average so high that Ontario began to qualify in 1980, and an adjustment to the formula had to be made. Any province whose total per capita revenue is below the average receives a payment based on the per capita shortfall multiplied by the province's population. Equalization payments were not touched by the federal reforms of 1995, but became very controversial after 2000, as will be discussed below.

Other Provincial and Territorial Revenues

The provinces and territories have discovered and levied more than 30 forms of direct taxation that were unanticipated in 1867.[16] The enormous natural resource revenues that some provinces receive on top of direct taxation and federal contributions are also significant. Over and above the revenue that is collected in the form of corporate income taxes, provinces obtain specific natural resource revenues from forests, including taxes on logging operations; leases and rentals of Crown lands; and royalties, rentals, and stumpage fees from timber and forest management. They also get revenues from mines, including taxes on mining operations, acreage taxes, licence and permit fees, rentals and lease payments, and royalties on mineral production. In addition, the petroleum-producing provinces collect revenue from oil and gas, including proceeds from the sale of Crown oil and gas leases, taxes on oil and gas production, royalties, freehold taxes, lease rentals, and fees and permits.[17] Given such petroleum revenues, Alberta in particular sometimes took in more revenue than it knew what to do with, and typically receives nearly one-third of its revenues from this source.

Thus, the combination of unanticipated federal grants, direct taxes, and natural resource revenues has contributed significantly to the enhanced status of the provinces in the Canadian federal system. It should be added that pressure for decentralization and for turning taxation power over to the provinces comes from those provinces that have substantial personal and corporate incomes to tax. The Atlantic provinces and Manitoba sometimes fight against decentralization because they would not benefit if their taxation powers were expanded. They want to keep the federal government strong so that it can redistribute revenues at least by means of equalization payments.[18] It should also be repeated that the two levels of government began by operating more or less independently of each other, taxing and spending in different areas, with federal grants being unconditional in nature. As time went on, the federal and provincial governments became closely intertwined by taxation agreements on the revenue side and by conditional and block grant programs in terms of expenditures.

Federal Controls

As mentioned, the 1867 Constitution Act contained three specific federal controls over the provinces: reservation, disallowance, and the declaratory power. The decline in the use of these powers has also enhanced the stature of the provinces. In the first 30 years after Confederation all three controls were actively employed, and this had the effect of keeping the provinces subordinate to Ottawa.[19] Their use gradually decreased after that, the two major exceptions being the combating of anti-Asian legislation in BC around 1900 and the outlawing of Social Credit legislation in Alberta in the 1930s. Overall, reservation was used 70 times, but on 14 of these occasions the federal government assented to the provincial legislation that the lieutenant governor had reserved, and it was last exercised in 1961. The federal Cabinet used its disallowance power 112 times, most recently in 1943. The declaratory power was resorted to on 470 occasions, mostly to put local railroads into federal jurisdiction in the early years, but not since 1961. It is now a convention of the Constitution, superseding the written words of the 1867 act, that Ottawa not use these federal controls.[20] As these were the federal powers that originally precluded Canada from being classified as a true federation, their disuse has meant that the provinces have shrugged off their subordinate status. Canada is now a genuine federation and a highly decentralized one at that.

Of the five parts of the Confederation Settlement, then, three have contributed to the decentralization of Canadian federalism: the division of powers, federal–provincial finance, and federal controls. But some of the societal forces underlying this decentralizing evolution should be identified explicitly. They include geography—the distances, divisions, and some very large provinces; the development of strong, distinctive provincial and regional identities and political cultures; and Quebec nationalism, characterized by demands for more powers, which were often echoed by other provinces.[21] As Cairns reminds us, institutional developments were consistent with the basic evolution of the "federal" Canadian society.

PHASES OF CANADIAN FEDERALISM

Canadian federalism can also be examined by dividing the years since 1867 into a number of eras.[22] These divisions demonstrate pendulum-like swings between centralization and decentralization and show that the evolution from a centralized to a decentralized federal system has not been a unilinear process.

Canadian Federalism, 1867–1945

The period 1867–96 can be classified as one of *quasi-federalism*, in which the provinces were subordinate to Ottawa. The courts gave the intended broad interpretation to federal powers, especially the Peace, Order and Good Government clause; the federal level was still predominant in finance; and John A. Macdonald made widespread use of the federal controls of reservation, disallowance, and the declaratory power.

The period 1896–1914 can be termed one of *classical federalism*. During these years the two levels were equal in status and independent. By now, the courts generally favoured the provinces, the latter had more money to spend, and the federal government made little use of its controls, so that the provinces were no longer subordinate. This was also the period before taxation agreements and conditional grants—that is, federal and provincial governments functioned independently of each other.

Classical federalism was displaced by *emergency federalism* during the war years, 1914–20. In this era the courts permitted the federal government virtually unlimited powers under the emergency doctrine and the War Measures Act. The federal government also increased its financial resources in this period with the imposition of personal and corporate income taxes. Ironically, in this most centralized phase of Canadian federalism—more centralized even than in the first 30 years—the use of the federal controls was unnecessary because of the courts' emergency interpretation of the Peace, Order and Good Government clause.

Between the wars, from 1920 to 1939, Canada reverted to another period of *classical federalism*. In these years, again, the two levels of government were equal in status (neither subordinate to the other) and operated more or less independently. Only a few conditional grants, for example, were developed during this time.

During the Second World War, from 1939 to 1945, Canada entered another period of *emergency federalism*. Once again, the courts allowed Ottawa to operate almost like a unitary government under the emergency interpretation of POGG and the War Measures Act. Public finance was also highly centralized with the development of the Wartime Taxation Agreements, under which the federal government took complete control over personal and corporate income taxes and succession duties. As in the First World War, any additional use of the federal controls was unnecessary.

Canadian Federalism, 1945–2000

The postwar world brought with it a completely new phase: **cooperative federalism**. The essence of this concept is that although neither level is subordinate to the other (the same as in classical federalism) they are closely intertwined, rather than operating independently. Here the crucial variable is financial relations. As noted in that connection earlier, the post-1945 period was marked by federal–provincial taxation agreements on the revenue side and a host of shared-cost programs in terms of expenditures.

Cooperative federalism results from several developments.[23] First, federal and provincial objectives often must be harmonized if public policy is to be effective, such as in the case of countercyclical fiscal policy. Second, public pressure forces the federal government to establish minimum standards throughout the country in the provision of certain public services within provincial jurisdiction, such as health care. Third, the two levels of government compete for tax revenues and end up needing to coordinate these efforts to some extent, at least for the convenience of taxpayers. Fourth, given a generally vague division of powers, federal and provincial ministers and bureaucrats usually seek to maximize their jurisdiction and eventually overlap with the other level of government. Federal and provincial government operations are no longer confined to separate "watertight compartments."

Cooperative federalism is made operational by a great deal of federal–provincial inter-action at all levels—first ministers, departmental ministers, deputy ministers, and even lesser officials, who engage in almost continuous consultation, coordination, and cooperation. Since the ministers and bureaucrats involved are all part of the executive branch of government, post-1945 Canadian federalism was sometimes labelled **executive federalism**. Two main implications of executive federalism are that legislatures, political parties, and the public at large are not given much role to play in decisions that emerge from the secrecy of meetings of executive officials, and that federal–provincial conflicts are worked out in conferences rather than referred to the courts.

At the highest level is the **first ministers' conference**, that is, a **federal–provincial conference** of premiers and the prime minister (to which territorial premiers were usually invited after 1992). This institution is not provided for in the written Constitution and rests on a conventional base.[24] Nevertheless, after 1945 many significant Canadian policy decisions were made in this forum, especially with respect to constitutional issues, shared-cost programs, and taxation and fiscal arrangements.[25] Some of these had to be ratified later by federal and provincial legislatures, but legislative approval was usually a formality. Such agreements could rarely be altered in any legislature because they would then have to be changed in all 11.

Conducted at the level of departmental ministers and leading bureaucrats, this type of federalism is sometimes labelled "functional" or "bureaucratic" federalism. Bureaucratic federalism is frequently more successful than first ministers' conferences, partly because the officials involved often share certain professional norms, and once they reach a consensus, these experts may be able to "sell" it to their departmental ministers. Such federalism works best with cabinets in which individual federal and provincial ministers and deputy ministers have considerable autonomy so that they can interact productively with their counterparts at the other level of government.[26]

Canadian federalism between 1945 and 1960 may have been "cooperative" in the sense that the two levels of government were closely intertwined, but it continued to be highly centralized in the immediate postwar period. The ministers and bureaucrats in Ottawa who had almost single-handedly run the country during the Second World War were reluctant to shed their enormous power. Moreover, they had discovered **Keynesian economics**, which prescribed a leading role for the central government in guiding the economy. The Diefenbaker government after 1957 was more sensitive to provincial demands, and the whole picture was increasingly complicated from about 1960 onward by the **Quiet Revolution** in Quebec. For the first time since 1890 or so, language and culture became important again in a constitutional sense. An extension of official bilingualism and the concept of provincial opting-out were hallmarks of this phase of Canadian federalism, which saw a significant degree of decentralization take place, especially under Lester Pearson.

With his diplomatic skills, Lester Pearson personified the operation of cooperative federalism.

By the time Pearson handed power over to Pierre Trudeau in 1968, Quebec and the other provinces were more aggressive than ever. But because the Trudeau government was not prepared for any further decentralization, the period is often called "competitive federalism."[27] Thus, block funding replaced conditional grants in important areas, leaving the two levels less intertwined than before. Moreover, first ministers' conferences frequently failed to come to any agreement, and Ottawa often chose to act unilaterally. Besides politicians displacing bureaucrats in this phase, federal–provincial conflicts were more frequently referred to the courts, resulting in a renewed emphasis on the division of powers.

The Trudeau era was characterized by years of federal–provincial discord over resource and energy policies, especially the **National Energy Program**, federal–Newfoundland conflict over offshore oil, and federal–Saskatchewan conflict over the regulation and taxation of that province's oil and potash industries. When these disputes coincided with Trudeau's unilateral attempt to amend the Constitution and to entrench official bilingualism as a national policy, many Western Canadians began to re-examine their place in the federation. Some of the heat was reduced when Trudeau conceded the new section 92A, which recognized enhanced provincial jurisdiction over natural resources, in order to secure federal NDP support for the 1982 constitutional package and as a peace offering to the West. Trudeau refused to budge on most of the demands made by Quebec, and that province consequently refused to support the **Constitution Act, 1982**. As mentioned in the previous chapter, Trudeau was committed to a centralized, officially bilingual, and symmetrical federation; he opposed stronger provinces in general, and refused to recognize Quebec as any different from the others.

When Brian Mulroney came to power in 1984, he was determined to improve federal–provincial relations and embark on another period of decentralized, Pearsonian cooperative federalism. During his first term many would say he succeeded, for much of the federal–provincial animosity of the Trudeau years seemed to dissipate. Western and Eastern concerns about energy resources were resolved to a large extent in the 1985 Western and Atlantic Accords. But federal–provincial relations in this period were often raised to the level of constitutional issues, such that the period from 1984–2000 is sometimes labelled "constitutional federalism."[28] The hallmark of the Mulroney approach, of course, was the 1987 **Meech Lake Accord**, which was designed to bring Quebec symbolically into the new constitutional framework and which would have generally increased provincial powers at Ottawa's expense.[29] Trudeau was the leading dissenter, feeling that Mulroney had given too much away. When that failed, Mulroney had a second round of mega-constitutional negotiations leading to the 1992 **Charlottetown Accord**, as mentioned in Chapter 17, but that package of constitutional reforms was defeated in a national referendum.

On non-constitutional issues, the Mulroney government increasingly aroused provincial anger, especially as it became obsessed with deficit reduction and cut back on grants to the provinces. The Mulroney government also enforced the Liberals' Canada Health Act, which imposed penalties on provinces that allowed doctors to extra-bill or permitted hospitals to charge user fees. Ontario, Alberta, and British Columbia objected to the 1990 policy of reducing their grants under the Canada Assistance Plan, and several provinces were opposed to the Canada–U.S. and North American Free Trade Agreements. Mostly by designing the trade agreements to minimize their interference in provincial jurisdiction, Mulroney succeeded in getting them adopted.[30] The Goods and Services Tax (GST) was another major federal–provincial issue during the Mulroney era, when only Quebec agreed to partial integration of its sales taxes with the new federal tax, even though many mutual advantages would have accrued to other provinces had they done so. Mulroney's decision to give the CF-18 maintenance contract to Quebec rather than Manitoba aroused such ire in western Canada that Reform soon replaced the Conservatives as the region's favoured party.

The Chrétien decade (1993–2003) could also be placed in the "constitutional federalism" era, partly because that government had to contend with issues left over from the previous regime. For example, it was successful in negotiating a reduction in barriers that provinces imposed to the free movement of people, goods, services, and capital across the country. This quasi-constitutional accord was called the **Agreement on Internal Trade** and came into effect in July 1995.[31] The Chrétien government had no initial success in implementing their promise to replace the GST, however, only managing to persuade three Atlantic provinces to harmonize their retail sales taxes with the federal tax. Moreover, Ottawa made the provinces angry with reductions in their transfers from 1995 to 1999. The principal complaints included severe reductions in health, postsecondary education, and welfare transfers, although seven provinces were pleased that Ottawa did not cut equalization payments.[32]

In the wake of the 1995 Quebec referendum on sovereignty, Ottawa decided to cede Quebec's foremost demand—provincial control over labour-market training. Rather than risk embarking on a form of asymmetrical federalism, however, the Chrétien government offered to transfer this responsibility to all provinces via bilateral and slightly different federal–provincial deals.[33] As noted in the previous chapter, the Quebec referendum also led to the Clarity Act of 2000. Another quasi-constitutional development was the **Social Union Framework Agreement (SUFA)**, finalized among the premiers and Prime Minister Chrétien (with Quebec dissenting) in February 1999. The two most significant points were that the federal government agreed not to introduce new social programs involving transfers of money to the *provinces* without the support of a majority of provinces, and that Ottawa retained the right to use its spending power to make transfers directly to *people*. An example of such federal–provincial cooperation was the 1997 Child Tax Benefit with a new integrated National Child Benefit system. Whether or not this new system had much effect on reducing child poverty, it was a model of how the two levels of government could work together.[34]

CRITICAL APPROACHES

As in the case of the Constitution, the *historical-institutional* and *state-based* approaches are most relevant to the Canadian federal system. The convoluted historical evolution of Canadian federalism centres around the institutions involved—especially the constitution, federal and provincial governments, and the judiciary. The subject cannot be understood except in the historical interaction among such institutions.

The state-based approach supplements the historical-institutional approach because those federal and provincial governments usually act in their own interests or in accordance with their own conception of the public interest, without much concern for the wishes of the general public.[35] The overarching concern of the national

political elite—prime ministers, federal cabinets, and leading bureaucrats—has usually been to construct a strong central government. But the creation of provinces produced counterbalancing provincial political elites—premiers, provincial cabinets, and bureaucrats—who were more interested in building strong provinces. The centralist and decentralist swings identified in this chapter are sometimes analyzed in terms of the concepts of "nation-building" as opposed to **province-building**. Federal authorities argue for greater jurisdiction, revenue, conditions, standards, and controls, while provincial authorities fight for maximum provincial revenue, flexibility, and freedom. State-based theorists contend that much of the federal–provincial discord is an artificial competition among federal and provincial politicians and bureaucrats, rather than a real fight reflecting public interests.

Class analysts also have something to say about Canadian federalism.[36] They argue that broad provincial jurisdiction has precluded stronger national social programs and labour and environmental standards. They claim that the corporate elite has often used its influence with provincial governments to frustrate national initiatives and challenge the federal government in court in order to enhance provincial jurisdiction.[37] More generally, business wants a relatively weak, non-redistributive federal government, and to some extent class analysts argue that constitutional debates and seemingly obscure skirmishes over the details of fiscal federalism have been a veil behind which a struggle has been waged over the size and character of the central state.

Canadian Federalism in the 21st Century

Since the year 2000, as mentioned in Chapter 17, the country has avoided formal constitutional changes of any kind, and Canadian federalism in the first decade of the 21st century is probably best described as a "collaborative federalism."[38] Despite the fact that the formal Constitution lists only three concurrent powers, despite the reduction in the role of all governments from about 1985 to 2000, and despite the attempt to disengage over the previous 15 years or so, federal and provincial governments continue to be intertwined in programs in almost every policy field. Canada is characterized by a large amount of *de facto*, unofficial, concurrent jurisdiction,[39] and even though first ministers rarely meet collectively in formal conferences any more, there is probably as much federal–provincial interaction as ever at the ministerial and bureaucratic levels. Given the enormous degree of federal–provincial interaction that will be required in the future and an extremely rigid constitutional amending formula, the two or three levels of government have no choice but to work together in non-constitutional channels.

Moreover, the whole structure of Canadian federalism since 2000 has been somewhat transformed by new players and new relationships, including Aboriginal self-government, direct contact between the federal government and cities, and relations between provincial governments and foreign states. Meanwhile, at the initiative of Quebec Premier Jean Charest, the annual premiers' conference was transformed into the **Council of the Federation**. Its objective was to speak with a strong, united voice for the provinces and territories in their relations with the federal government, and considerable progress was made on institutionalizing the Council. Provinces have also signed regional agreements, such as the Council of Atlantic Premiers, the New West Partnership Trade Agreement between Alberta, BC and Saskatchewan, and the electricity agreement Newfoundland and Labrador signed with Nova Scotia.

In 2003, Prime Minister Paul Martin promised the premiers a closer relationship than that of his predecessor, while Stephen Harper came to power in 2006 with a policy of **open federalism**, signalling the adoption of an even more decentralist approach.[40] While the two regimes were both quite collaborative and generous, Martin's government was active in initiating new programs, usually with provincial consent, whereas Harper discontinued many such programs and, especially from 2012 onward, adopted an approach to the provinces more akin to classical federalism—keeping each level of government in a separate compartment.[41] In fact, Harper did not hold first-ministers conferences during his final six years in office. Justin Trudeau, however, pledged upon becoming prime minister to work more closely with provinces and met with premiers one month after winning the 2015 election. Let us examine a few key federal–provincial policy developments.

Taxation Agreements

Apart from Quebec, Alberta was the first province to withdraw from the 40-year-old integrated federal–provincial income tax system. This was because it wanted to adopt a "flat tax" that was incompatible with the base of the federal system. The other provinces soon disengaged as well because with federal tax cuts, a provincial "tax on tax" would have led to decreased revenues. All the provinces have now separated their provincial income tax rates from the federal income tax scheme and apply the provincial tax directly to residents' income— a "tax on income" instead of a "tax on tax." All provinces except Quebec still allow the federal Canada Revenue Agency to collect their taxes for them,[42] but Ottawa reminds them that they are free to raise their own taxes rather than always seeking larger federal transfers. Ontario decided to join the list of provinces that agreed to harmonize their retail sales taxes with the federal GST, but BC rejected the proposal in a referendum.

Health Care[43]

Even before the publication of the Romanow report on the future of health care, which recommended larger federal health grants, the provinces persuaded Ottawa to increase its transfers in this field (and it has continued to do so as seen in Figure 18.2). This was primarily because the federal government had reduced its contributions when it brought in the Canada Health and Social Transfer and because it began running a budget surplus. The 2003 federal budget provided a set, five-year payment of $16 billion (the Health Reform Transfer) for primary health care. In 2004, as noted above, the CHST was split into the CHT and CST. That same year Paul Martin famously signed a 10-year $41 billion health care agreement with the provinces that increased transfers in this field by six percent per year, and the 2003 Reform Transfer payment was included in the CHT. The asymmetrical dimension of the deal aroused controversy, with Quebec being treated somewhat differently from the other provinces.[44] Although this money was intended to solve the health care problem for a generation, it did not take long for the provinces to ask for more.

As time went on, Ottawa was increasingly reluctant to penalize provinces that violated the Canada Health Act in one way or another, as it had a legal right to do.[45] But on the basis of the Romanow report, the Health Council of Canada was established as an independent body to advise Canadians on the performance of their health system, although Alberta and Quebec chose not to join.

The reluctance of the federal government to penalize provinces for violations of the Canada Health Act was reinforced when the Supreme Court of Canada ruled in the June 2005 *Chaoulli* case that Quebec's ban on private insurance in the provision of core health services was unconstitutional. Using the Charter of Rights and Freedoms rather than the division of powers to interfere with the operation of the Canada Health Act, the Court gave Quebec a year in which

FIGURE 18.2 GROWTH IN HEALTH AND SOCIAL TRANSFERS TO PROVINCES 1996–2015

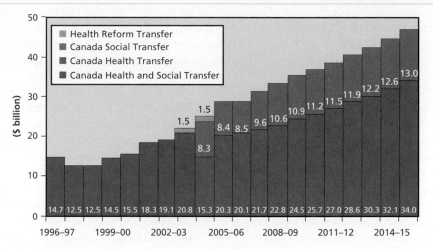

Source: Department of Finance Canada, History of Health and Social Transfers (2014), http://www.fin.gc.ca/fedprov/his-eng.asp. Contains information licensed under the Open Government Licence – Canada. Reproduced with the permission of the Department of Finance, 2015.

to ensure that the public system provided timely treatment.[46] Several other provinces announced plans to rely more heavily on private health care facilities in order to reduce wait times, arguing that such an addition of profit-oriented services would not violate the Canada Health Act as long as those who were forced to use them had their costs covered by the public program.

The Harper government increased federal transfers to the provinces in the health care field, specifically to reduce wait times, which was one of its first five election priorities. Then, as the Martin Health Care Accords neared their end, Harper unilaterally announced a new federal–provincial health transfer plan for the post-2014 period. The annual six percent increases would continue until the 2016–17 fiscal year, after which they would be tied to the rise in GDP, with a floor of at least three percent. Although it was presented without consultation, Harper thought the provinces would appreciate this offer because Ottawa would no longer attach any conditions about how the provinces had to spend the money. As part of its partial withdrawal from the health sector, the Harper government also announced in 2013 that it would no longer help fund the Health Council of Canada. The new policies were an example of Harper's compartmentalized view of federalism, and were not welcomed by many health policy analysts. In fact, the provinces immediately set up a working group on health-care innovation to provide some uniformity of action in this field.

Equalization Payments and Other Federal–Provincial Transfers

As prime minister, Paul Martin agreed to revise the equalization formula in another first ministers' conference in 2005. Besides the demand for a general increase in the amount of such payments, Nova Scotia and Newfoundland and Labrador had a specific complaint with respect to their offshore petroleum industries. They claimed to be losing 70 cents in equalization payments for every new dollar of petroleum revenue they took in. Martin later negotiated side deals with those two provinces that allowed them to retain offshore petroleum revenues with no reduction of equalization payments.[47] At this point, Ontario complained about an annual $23 billion gap between what it sent to Ottawa and what it received back. In compensation, it ended up receiving several billion dollars over five years for immigration services, labour-market training, international border infrastructure, and meeting Kyoto requirements.

Stephen Harper promised to redress the so-called **fiscal imbalance** between the two levels of government, a constant refrain from Quebec in particular.[48] The 2007 federal budget did indeed seek to "fix" it with a boost in long-term funding support for training, post-secondary education, and infrastructure projects. As for equalization, as mentioned in Chapter 3, a new formula considerably increased the total amount of the transfer, especially for Quebec. Inspired by the O'Brien Report, the formula is now based on only five taxes: personal income tax, business income tax, consumption tax, property tax, and one-half of a province's non-renewable resource revenues. It uses a 10-province average, but imposed a cap on the payments a province would receive if it exceeded the fiscal capacity of a non-recipient province. Newfoundland and Labrador and Nova Scotia were permitted to stay with the Atlantic Accord if they wished, but the new formula would be more generous in the short-term, at least. Newfoundland's Progressive Conservative premier Danny Williams was alarmed at Harper's change of heart with respect to not completely exempting resource revenues as well as the imposition of the cap, and campaigned against him—"Anything But Conservative"—in the 2008 federal election. The new formula may have been somewhat simplified, but many observers argued that it continued to contain inequities, such as in not recognizing the higher costs that some provinces incurred in the provision of services.

At the meeting of the Council of the Federation in July 2013, provincial premiers were particularly critical of the proposed federal Canada Jobs Grant program, which cut federal transfers to the provinces for skills training. This conflict proceeded until March 2014, when federal Employment Minister Jason Kenney came to an agreement with the Council under which he would negotiate bilateral arrangements with the provinces. In the case of Quebec, then on the eve of an election call, the province signed a separate (asymmetrical) agreement. At their meetings in 2013, the premiers also sought more federal funding for disaster mitigation after devastating floods in Alberta and Ontario, generally supported a new west-to-east national oil pipeline, objected to federal infrastructure transfers on a project-by-project basis, and remained opposed to the Employment Insurance changes introduced in 2012. In addition, they were concerned about such issues as reform of the Canada Pension Plan, uncertainties in foreign investment rules, and the general state of federal-provincial relations. At the 2014 meeting in Charlottetown, the premiers singled out the increased burden of financing health care (especially for seniors) and the need for greater federal funding for infrastructure projects.

In her 2014 budget, Ontario premier Kathleen Wynne complained that the Harper government had imposed over 100 cuts on that province, and much of her following election campaign was centred on federal–provincial relations. The Parliamentary Budget Officer confirmed that the federal government is shortchanging Ontario by some $1.2 billion under the equalization payments formula alone. Finance Minister Joe Oliver later announced in December 2014 that Ontario would receive an extra $1.25 billion in 2015–16.

The Environment

Never before has an environmental issue caused so much federal–provincial discord as the Kyoto Protocol. As with other treaties, Ottawa had the constitutional power to sign and ratify the treaty, but not necessarily the complete jurisdiction to implement it. In 2002, Prime Minister Chrétien suddenly announced the ratification of Kyoto before any interprovincial agreement was in place. In Alberta's eyes, in particular, Kyoto appeared as a reincarnation of the NEP,

Provinces seek fewer emissions and more transfer payments from Alberta.

although when it became clear that neither the Chrétien nor the Martin governments had any specific plan for implementation, the provinces stopped complaining.[49]

While the environment remains prominent on the political agenda, constitutional jurisdiction in this field is somewhat ambiguous. "Environmental protection" is such a vast subject that aspects of it fall into bailiwick of both levels of government, but the Harper government was more concerned to promote petroleum production and the mining industry in general. It abandoned the Kyoto Protocol, politicized the environmental assessment process, and delegated much of its environment regulatory power to the provinces. In some cases, such as coal, provinces could manage their own emission regulations in an equivalency arrangement, and provinces could generally do their own environmental assessments of smaller economic projects—further examples of separating federal and provincial operations. The federal plan, announced shortly before the summer break and upcoming 2015 election, targets a 30 percent cut below 2005 levels by 2030; however, it depends heavily upon provinces to meet their own set targets. Trudeau met with premiers to discuss climate change in November 2015 and signalled that Canada's plan for climate change would be strengthened under his government.

Aborginals

Although Aboriginals are theoretically under federal jurisdiction, their issues increasingly assume a federal–provincial dimension. This is partly because land claims often involve Crown land owned by the province. Aboriginal peoples have usually fallen into a constitutional void, with the result that services to them, federal or provincial, are woefully inadequate. Moreover, there are different levels of government responsibility for different categories of Aboriginal people—status Indians, non-status Indians, Métis, and so on. "The system is complex and involves many changing sites of initiative":[50] first ministers' conferences, the Supreme Court, comprehensive land claims, specific land claims, self-government agreements, program transfers and devolution, and relations between Aboriginal governments and urban-based Aboriginals on the one hand and provincial, territorial, and municipal governments on the other. As difficult as it is for Aboriginal peoples to achieve agreement from Ottawa, negotiation with most provincial governments is even more troublesome. On the positive side, federalism provides a model for Aboriginal self-government to be raised, ultimately, to a third order of government in Canada, but much work needs to be done on a practical level to provide Aboriginals with the services they should be able to expect as Canadian citizens.

Aboriginal issues were a priority for the Paul Martin government. As mentioned in Chapter 4, he convened a meeting between first ministers and national Aboriginal leaders in Kelowna in 2005. Martin announced that the federal government would commit $5 billion over five years toward a 10-year effort to close the gap in the quality of life between Aboriginal peoples and other Canadians. The premiers were enthusiastic participants and pledged to make significant contributions of their own.

Stephen Harper did not honour the full Kelowna commitment with respect to additional funding for Aboriginal problems. He held an important meeting with the National Chief of the Assembly of First Nations, Shawn Atleo, in 2012 to discuss a more effective way to improve the level of reserve services. However, First Nations chiefs rejected a proposed education bill in 2013, and Atleo quit in 2014 when chiefs disapproved of his work on the bill.

Child Care and Early Childhood Development

After earlier increases in federal transfers, the Martin government brought in "the first new national social program in a generation." As mentioned in Chapter 8, agreements were signed with each province, with few strings attached, in which they would share some $5 billion over five years for child care purposes. Action in this field as well as in health can be seen as "targeted" federal funding (rather than conditional or block grants, as such): federal transfers that are specified for certain areas of policy but that may not require provinces to meet specific conditions. This new type of transfer still allows the federal government to direct the shape of provincial programs.[51] The Harper government came to office with a promise to scrap these new early childhood and child care agreements; instead, families were given an annual payment of $1200 (increasing to $1920 in 2015) for each child under six and allowed to use the money in whichever way they chose.

Bringing in the Cities

For the most part, Canadian federalism has ignored municipal governments in the past. "This is primarily because of the way in which provinces have generally resisted ... any direct involvement by the federal government in helping local governments deal with persistent urban problems."[52] But large metropolitan centres were now demanding more powers, as well as the right to be directly involved in federal–provincial discussions dealing with their needs. They asked for more taxation powers and more federal funding for such problems as mass urban transit, other infrastructure, housing, health, the environment, and public education for immigrant children. They would also like to see the re-creation of a federal department of urban affairs and to carve out a non-subordinate niche within the Constitution.

As noted in Chapter 9, Paul Martin provided considerable opportunity for cities to contribute to federal policy, eventually creating a Ministry of State for Infrastructure and Communities, and exempted municipalities from paying the GST on their purchases. But his government's major contribution to cities (and other communities) was to share the revenues from the federal gasoline excise tax: Ottawa would transfer the equivalent of five cents per litre to a total of $5 billion over five years. Tailored bilateral agreements with the provinces would provide that these transfers be passed on to municipalities to help finance environmentally friendly infrastructure projects. While Harper distanced himself from the Martin approach of "bringing in the cities," he continued the excise tax agreement and, after the 2008 economic meltdown, local infrastructure projects became a much higher priority of the government.[53] By means of the Building Canada Fund, which was renewed in 2014 with $10 billion over 10 years for provinces, regions, and municipalities, Ottawa not only helped provincial and municipal governments, but also ensured that their infrastructure spending was aligned with federal thinking.

Provinces and External Relations

Canadian federalism is being challenged by provincial demands to be involved in the country's external relations.[54] A certain amount of interaction between provinces and foreign states has taken place for many years, highlighted by Quebec's participation in the Francophonie. Quebec wants to play an even more prominent role on the world stage, while other provinces, especially Alberta, demand a say in Canadian foreign and trade policies that affect them, such as petroleum exports. With its enormous daily cross-border trade with the United States, Ontario is also concerned with maintaining an open border in the post-9/11 era. The extent of provincial cooperation with neighbouring states has increased in recent years, such as in the Annual Conference of New England Governors and Eastern Canadian Premiers, Ontario and Quebec cooperation with the Council of Great Lakes Governors, and the Western Climate Initiative, a cap and trade agreement among provinces and states most concerned about the environment.

Justice

A tight connection exists between federal and provincial responsibilities in the field of the administration of justice. Ottawa has jurisdiction over the criminal law, but the provinces generally enforce it. Adult offenders receiving a prison sentence of two years or more go to federal penitentiaries while those receiving lesser prison sentences are committed to provincial correctional facilities. The "tough-on-crime" agenda of the Harper government included mandatory minimum prison sentences for many "crimes" that previously were dealt penalties of "conditional sentences" short of going to prison. Thus, the number of people being sent to provincial jails was expected to increase dramatically, and besides being opposed to the whole thrust of the agenda, especially when it was not supported by data that demonstrated any increase in crime, the provinces were up in arms that their correctional costs would increase. They had not been consulted about the issue and had not been promised any financial compensation.

Quebec

When he first came to power, Harper was particularly solicitous of Quebec. Besides the federal–provincial financial generosity mentioned above, he fulfilled that province's demand to have a seat in the Canadian delegation to UNESCO, sponsored a resolution in the House of Commons that recognized the Québécois as a nation within a united Canada, and allowed Quebec to sign a labour-mobility agreement with France. As time went on, however, Harper paid decreasing attention to Quebec in this and other respects. As mentioned, one of his few national initiatives was the attempt to establish some kind of overall system of regulating the securities industry, which was vigorously opposed by Quebec and Alberta. When this effort failed at the Supreme Court, Harper began to pursue a less activist approach, happy to confine each level of government to its own jurisdiction. The new, activist Justin Trudeau government was much more interested in interacting with the provinces, and began to hold regular first ministers' meetings.

CONCLUSION

Federalism in Canada is both based on and reinforces regional, economic, and ethnic cleavages. In the beginning, the Canadian federal system was highly centralized, but this original design soon proved to be inappropriate for the society in which it operated. When the cleavages became difficult to overcome, and as "province-builders" competed with "nation-builders," Canada was gradually transformed into a very decentralized federation. Both in the courts and in negotiations with Ottawa, the provinces successfully fought for more powers and more financial resources. Although federalism often seems to be an unending source of intergovernmental discord, as well as a convenient excuse at both levels of government for not responding to demands, the importance of the continuing maze of cooperative federal–provincial interaction cannot be overestimated. In this respect, the original division of powers between the two levels of government has almost become irrelevant, although in his preference for more limited state intervention, Stephen Harper appeared to take it more seriously, and we will continue to see how the federal relationship with the provinces develops under Justin Trudeau.

This chapter is closely linked to the preceding one on the Constitution. Chapter 3 on regionalism is also connected to federalism, but almost every chapter of the book reveals the effects of this central principle of the Canadian political system.

DISCUSSION QUESTIONS

1. Are you a centralist or a decentralist? Why? What are the advantages and disadvantages of centralization and decentralization in Canadian federalism?

2. Is it possible to have a clear-cut division of powers between federal and provincial governments in a modern era of such extensive government activity?

3. Should the federal government be able to spend money for any purpose, even within provincial jurisdiction? Should it be able to set conditions on provincial health care programs?

4. What are the advantages and disadvantages of executive federalism?

5. How have the weaknesses of intrastate federalism contributed to the importance of interstate federalism?

NOTES

1. Reference re *The Secession of Quebec*, [1998] 2 S.C.R., p. 244.
2. Donald Smiley, *The Canadian Political Nationality* (Toronto: Methuen, 1967).
3. K.C. Wheare, *Federal Government*, 4th ed. (London: Oxford University Press, 1963).
4. D.V. Smiley and R.L. Watts, *Intrastate Federalism in Canada* (Toronto: University of Toronto Press, 1985).
5. Peter Russell, Rainer Knopff, and Ted Morton, *Federalism and the Charter* (Ottawa: Carleton University Press, 1989); Peter Russell, et al., *The Court and the Constitution: Leading Cases* (Toronto: Emond Montgomery, 2008); Peter Hogg, *Constitutional Law of Canada* (Toronto: Carswell, Student Edition, 2006); Patrick J. Monahan, *Constitutional Law* (Toronto: Irwin Law, 1998); and Bernard Funston and Eugene Meehan, *Canada's Constitutional Law in a Nutshell*, 2nd ed. (Toronto: Carswell, 1998).
6. *R. v. Crown Zellerbach Canada Ltd.*, [1988] 1 S.C.R. 401; *Alberta Government Telephones v. Canada (Canadian Radio-television and Telecommunications Commission)*, [1989] 2 S.C.R. 225; *Friends of the Oldman River Society v. Canada (Minister of Transport)*, [1992] 1 S.C.R. 3; *Ontario Hydro v. Ontario (Labour Relations Board)*, [1993] 3 S.C.R. 327; *Téléphone Guèvremont Inc. v. Quebec (Régis des télécommunications)*, [1994] 1 S.C.R. 878; *R. v. Hydro-Quebec*, [1997] 3 S.C.R. 213; *Reference Re: Firearms Act (Can.)*, [2000] 1 S.C.R. 783; *Reference re Employment Insurance Act*, [2005] 2 S.C.R. 669; and *Kirkbi AG v. Ritvik Holdings Inc.*, [2005] 3 S.C.R. 302. See also *Reference Re: Canada Assistance Plan (B.C.)*, [1991] 2 S.C.R. 525; and Gerald Baier, "The Courts, the Constitution, and Dispute Resolution," in Herman Bakvis and Grace Skogstad, eds., *Canadian Federalism: Performance, Effectiveness, and Legitimacy*, 3rd ed. (Toronto: Oxford University Press, 2012).
7. *Reference re: Securities Act*, [2011] 3 S.C.R. 837.
8. V.C. MacDonald, "Judicial Interpretation of the Canadian Constitution," *University of Toronto Law Journal* 1 (1935–36); and the O'Connor Report, Senate of Canada, 1939. It is ironic that judicial interpretation contributed to decentralizing a centralized Canadian federation but centralized a decentralized federation in the United States. See Roger Gibbins, *Regionalism* (Toronto: Butterworths, 1982), Ch. 4.
9. Alan C. Cairns, "The Governments and Societies of Canadian Federalism," *Canadian Journal of Political Science* (December 1977).
10. Alan C. Cairns, "The Judicial Committee and Its Critics," *Canadian Journal of Political Science* (September 1971), and reprinted in Cairns, *Constitution, Government and Society in Canada* (Toronto: McClelland and Stewart, 1988). See also John T. Saywell, *The Lawmakers: Judicial Power and the Shaping of Canadian Federalism* (Toronto: University of Toronto Press, 2003).
11. Cairns, Constitution, Government, and Society in Canada, p. 63.
12. Canadian Tax Foundation, *Finances of the Nation* (Toronto: Annual); David B. Perry, *Financing the Canadian Federation, 1867–1995: Setting the Stage for Change* (Toronto: Canadian Tax Foundation, 1997); James A. McAllister, "Redistributive Federalism: Redistributing Wealth and Income in the Canadian Federation," *Canadian Public Administration* (December 2011); and Robin W. Boadway and Paul A.R. Hobson, *Intergovernmental Fiscal Relations in Canada* (Toronto: Canadian Tax Foundation, 1993).
13. Direct taxes are derived from the very people who are intended to pay them, while indirect taxes are extracted from one person or company in the expectation that they will be passed on to someone else.
14. Not only does Ottawa have the power to spend; it can also abruptly stop spending! *Reference re Canada Assistance Plan (B.C.)*, [1991] 2 S.C.R. 525; *Finlay v. Canada (Minister of Finance)*, [1993] 1 S.C.R. 1080; Keith Banting, *The Welfare State and Canadian Federalism* (Kingston: McGill-Queen's University Press, 1982), pp. 52–54; Andrew Petter, "Federalism and the Myth of the Federal Spending Power,"

Canadian Bar Review (September 1989); and Christopher Dunn, "The Federal Spending Power," in Dunn, ed., *The Handbook of Canadian Public Administration*, 2nd ed. (Toronto: Oxford University Press, 2010).

15. T.J. Courchene, *Equalization Payments: Past, Present and Future* (Toronto: Ontario Economic Council, 1984); and Robin W. Boadway and Paul A.R. Hobson, *Equalization* (Kingston: McGill-Queen's University Press, 1998).

16. G.V. La Forest, *The Allocation of Taxing Powers under the Canadian Constitution*, 2nd ed. (Toronto: Canadian Tax Foundation, 1981).

17. Canadian Tax Foundation, *Provincial and Municipal Finances, 1989*, p. 12:1.

18. Jim Silver, "Constitutional Change, Ideological Conflict and the Redistributive State," in James McCrorie and Martha MacDonald, eds., *The Constitutional Future of the Prairie and Atlantic Regions of Canada* (Regina: Canadian Plains Research Center, 1992).

19. G.V. La Forest, *Disallowance and Reservation of Provincial Legislation* (Ottawa: Queen's Printer, 1965).

20. Andrew Heard, *Canadian Constitutional Conventions* (Toronto: Oxford University Press, 1991).

21. Garth Stevenson, "Federalism and Intergovernmental Relations," in Michael Whittington and Glen Williams, eds., *Canadian Politics in the 21st Century*, 7th ed. (Toronto: Thomson Nelson, 2008).

22. This discussion is loosely based on J.R. Mallory, "The Five Faces of Canadian Federalism," in P.-A. Crépeau and C.B. Macpherson, eds., *The Future of Canadian Federalism* (Toronto: University of Toronto Press, 1965).

23. Donald Smiley, *Canada in Question: Federalism in the Seventies* (Toronto: McGraw-Hill Ryerson, 1972), p. 56.

24. Heard, *Canadian Constitutional Conventions*, pp. 110–16.

25. Richard Simeon, *Federal–Provincial Diplomacy* (Toronto: University of Toronto Press, 1972).

26. J. Stefan Dupré, "Reflections on the Workability of Executive Federalism," in Richard Simeon, ed., *Intergovernmental Relations* (Toronto: University of Toronto Press, 1985); D.V. Smiley, *The Federal Condition in Canada* (Toronto: McGraw-Hill Ryerson, 1987), pp. 87–89; and Carolyn M. Johns, et al., "Formal and Informal Dimensions of Intergovernmental Administrative Relations in Canada," *Canadian Public Administration* (March 2007).

27. Richard Simeon and Ian Robinson, "The Dynamics of Canadian Federalism," in James Bickerton and Alain G. Gagnon, eds. *Canadian Politics* (Toronto: University of Toronto Press, 5th ed., 2009).

28. Ibid.

29. The Meech Lake Accord is discussed in Chapter 17.

30. Grace Skogstad, "International Trade and the Evolution of Canadian Federalism" in Bakvis and Skogstad, *Canadian Federalism*, 3rd ed., Ch. 11.

31. Robert H. Knox, "Economic Integration in Canada through the Agreement on Internal Trade," in Harvey Lazar, ed., *Canada: The State of the Federation 1997: Non-Constitutional Renewal* (Kingston: Institute of Intergovernmental Relations, Queen's University, 1997); and Mark R. MacDonald, "The Agreement on Internal Trade: Trade-Offs for Economic Union and Federalism," in Bakvis and Skogstad, *Canadian Federalism*, Ch. 11.

32. Among the best sources on this subject are the reviews published annually since 1980 by the Queen's University Institute of Intergovernmental Relations.

33. Herman Bakvis, "Checkerboard Federalism? Labour Market Development Policy in Canada," in Bakvis and Skogstad, *Canadian Federalism*, Ch. 11.

34. Ken Battle, "The 1997 Budget and the Child Benefits Package," in Thomas J. Courchene and Thomas A. Wilson, *The 1997 Federal Budget: Retrospect and Prospect* (Kingston: John Deutsch Institute for the Study of Economic Policy, 1997); and Linda A. White, "The Child Care Agenda and the Social Union," in Bakvis and Skogstad, *Canadian Federalism*, Ch. 6.

35. Richard Simeon and David Cameron, "Intergovernmental Relations and Democracy: An Oxymoron If There Ever Was One?" in Bakvis and Skogstad, *Canadian Federalism*, Ch. 15, write that any notion that democracy and federalism coincide is an oxymoron!

36. See, for example, John Porter, *The Vertical Mosaic* (Toronto: University of Toronto Press, 1965).

37. J.R. Mallory, *Social Credit and the Federal Power in Canada* (Toronto: University of Toronto Press, 1954); and Silver, "Constitutional Change, Ideological Conflict and the Redistributive State."

38. Simeon and Robinson, "The Dynamics of Canadian Federalism."

39. Keith G. Banting, "Remaking Immigration: Asymmetric Decentralization and Canadian Federalism," and Bakvis and Skogstad, "Performance, Effectiveness, and Legitimacy," in Bakvis and Skogstad, *Canadian Federalism*, 3rd ed.

40. Adam Harmes, "The Political Economy of Open Federalism," *Canadian Journal of Political Science* (June 2007), emphasizes the neoliberal component of the policy.

41. Keith Banting, et al., *Open Federalism: Interpretations, Significance* (Kingston: Institute of Intergovernmental Relations), 2006; Allan M. Maslove, ed., *How Ottawa Spends 2008-2009* (Montreal: McGill-Queen's University Press, 2008).

42. Douglas M. Brown, "Fiscal Federalism: Maintaining a Balance," in Bakvis and Skogstad, *Canadian Federalism*, 3rd ed.; Stevenson, "Federalism and Intergovernmental Relations," (2008), p. 90.

43. Antonia Maioni, "Health Care," in Bakvis and Skogstad, *Canadian Federalism*, 3rd ed; Allan M. Maslove, "Health and Federal–Provincial Fiscal Arrangements: Lost Opportunity," and Gerald W. Boychuk, "How Ottawa Gambles: Rolling the Dice in Health Care Reform," in G. Bruce Doern, ed., *How Ottawa Spends 2005–2006* (Montreal: McGill-Queen's University Press, 2005).

44. Tom McIntosh, "Intergovernmental Relations, Social Policy and Federal Transfers after Romanow," *Canadian Public Administration* (Spring 2004).

45. See *The Globe and Mail*, December 13, 2002, for a list of such violations up to that time.

46. *Chaoulli v. Quebec (Attorney General)*, [2005] 1 S.C.R. 791.

47. *Achieving A National Purpose: Putting Equalization Back on Track* (Ottawa: Department of Finance Canada, May 2006); Stevenson, "Federalism and Intergovernmental Relations," (2008), p. 91; publications of the Mowat Centre for Policy Innovation, available at http://mowatcentre.ca/.

48. Sujit Choudhury, et al., *Dilemmas of Solidarity: Rethinking Redistribution in the Canadian Federation* (Toronto: University of Toronto Press, 2006); André Plourde, "Offshore Energy Revenues and Equalization: Having Your Cake and Eating it Too?" in G. Bruce Doern, ed., *How Ottawa Spends 2006–2007* (Montreal: McGill-Queen's University Press, 2006); Institute for Research on Public Policy, *Policy Options*, September 2006 and March and April 2007 issues; and McAllister, "Redistributive Federalism: Redistributing Wealth and Income in the Canadian Federation."

49. Mark Winfield and Douglas Macdonald, "Federalism and Climate Change Policy," in Bakvis and Skogstad, 3rd ed., *Canadian Federalism*, Ch. 13; Thomas J. Courchene and John R. Allan, eds., *Canada: The State of the Federation 2009: Carbon Pricing and Environmental Federalism* (Kingston: Institute of Intergovernmental Relations, 2010).

50. Martin Papillon, "Canadian Federalism and the Emerging Mosaic of Aboriginal Multi-Level Governance," in Bakvis and Skogstad, *Canadian Federalism*, 3rd ed., Ch. 15.

51. Gérard Boismenu and Peter Graefe, "The New Federal Toolbelt: Attempts to Rebuild Social Policy Leadership," *Canadian Public Policy* 30: 1 (2004); Cheryl Collier and Rianne Mahon, "One Step Forward, Two Steps Back: Child Care Policy from Martin to Harper," in Allan M. Maslove, ed., *How Ottawa Spends 2008–2009* (Montreal: McGill-Queen's University Press, 2008).

52. Andrew Sancton, "The Urban Agenda," in Bakvis and Skogstad, *Canadian Federalism*, 3rd ed., Ch. 16; Robert Young and Christian Leuprecht, *Canada and the State of the Federation 2004: Municipal–Federal–Provincial Relations* (Kingston: Institute of Intergovernmental Relations, 2005); and Tindal and Tindal, *Local Government in Canada*.

53. Enid Slack and Richard M. Bird, "Cities in Canadian Federalism," *Institute for Research on Public Policy, Policy Options* (December 2007/January 2008); Robert Hilton and Christopher Stoney, "Federal Gas Tax Transfers: Politics and Perverse Policy," in Allan M. Maslove, ed., *How Ottawa Spends 2009–2010* (Montreal: McGill-Queen's University Press, 2009); and the entire September 2009 issue of *Canadian Public Administration*.

54. Christopher J. Kukucha, "From Kyoto to the WTO: Evaluating the Constitutional Legitimacy of the Provinces in Canadian Foreign Trade and Environmental Policy," *Canadian Journal of Political Science* (March 2005); Heather MacIvor, *Parameters of Power*, 5th ed. (Toronto: Nelson Education, 2010), pp. 112–16.

FURTHER READING

Bakvis, Herman, and Grace Skogstad, eds. *Canadian Federalism: Performance, Effectiveness, and Legitimacy*, 3rd ed. Toronto: Oxford University Press, 2012.

Banting, Keith, et al. *Open Federalism: Interpretations, Significance*. Kingston: Institute of Intergovernmental Relations, 2006.

Canadian Tax Foundation. *Finances of the Nation*. Toronto, annual (under various authors).

Courchene, Thomas J., et al. *The Federal Idea: Essays in Honour of Ronald L. Watts*. Kingston: Queen's Policy Studies Series, 2011.

Harrison, Kathryn, ed. *Racing to the Bottom? Provincial Interdependence in the Canadian Federation*. Vancouver: UBC Press, 2005.

Hogg, Peter. *Constitutional Law of Canada*, student ed. Toronto: Carswell, 2006.

Institute of Intergovernmental Relations, Queen's University. *Canada: The State of the Federation*, annual (under the name of various editors).

LaSelva, Samuel. *The Moral Foundations of Canadian Federalism: Paradoxes, Achievements, and Tragedies of Nationhood*. Montreal: McGill-Queen's University Press, 1997.

Maslove, Allan M., ed. *How Ottawa Spends 2008–2009*. Montreal: McGill-Queen's University Press, 2008.

McAllister, James A. "Redistributive Federalism: Redistributing Wealth and Income in the Canadian Federation," *Canadian Public Administration* (December 2011).

Monahan, Patrick. *Constitutional Law*, 2nd ed. Toronto: Irwin Law, 2002.

Russell, Peter, et al. *The Court and the Constitution: Leading Cases*. Toronto Emond Montgomery, 2008.

Saywell, John T. *The Lawmakers: Judicial Power and the Shaping of Canadian Federalism*. Toronto: University of Toronto Press, 2003.

Stevenson, Garth. "Federalism and Intergovernmental Relations," in Michael Whittington and Glen Williams, eds., *Canadian Politics in the 21st Century*, 7th ed. Toronto: Thomson Nelson, 2008.

Tindal, C. Richard, and Susan Nobes Tindal. *Local Government in Canada*, 7th ed. Toronto: Nelson Education, 2009.

Treff, Karin, and Deborah Ort. *Finances of the Nation 2011*. Toronto: Canadian Tax Foundation, 2012.

CHAPTER 19

The Charter of Rights and Freedoms

Does the right to freedom of expression permit unrestricted access to pornography? Does a person have the right to call a lawyer when stopped by a police officer and asked to take a breath test? Does freedom of association guarantee the right to strike? Does a person who has a terminal illness have a right to assisted suicide? Should tobacco companies be allowed to advertise cigarettes? Should police officers be able to enter dwellings without a search warrant? Does the state have a right to outlaw private health insurance? And in any of these cases, who should have the last say—legislatures or judges?

Civil liberties consist of rights and freedoms that individuals enjoy beyond the reach of the government or the state. Such rights and freedoms are an integral part of a democratic political system and represent territory into which the government is not allowed to enter as it makes and enforces public policy for a society. Chapter 16 pointed out that a constitution typically provides fundamental rules regarding the relationship between government and citizens, but that the Constitution Act, 1867, did not have much to say in this regard. Although many such civil liberties have always existed in Canada, they were constitutionalized and enlarged upon in 1982 in the form of the Charter of Rights and Freedoms, and it is increasingly the task of the judiciary to determine if and when governments have encroached on those rights. The Charter has had a profound influence on the Canadian political system in protecting such rights and freedoms, but it has also affected the operation of many other aspects of the system.

This chapter begins by defining such rights and freedoms and discussing the means of protecting them in Canada before 1982. The central part of the chapter examines the provisions of the Charter of Rights and Freedoms and some of the principal court cases that interpreted each clause in its first 30 years of existence. It concludes by discussing the implications of the Charter for the overall political system.

DEFINING AND PROTECTING RIGHTS AND FREEDOMS

Rights and freedoms are commonly classified into four categories.[1] The first relates to political liberties, including the fundamental freedoms of speech, press, assembly, and religion. The second, legal rights, includes the procedural rights of a person suspected or accused of committing a crime, a liberty encompassing that person's right to legal counsel, a presumption of innocence, bail, and a fair trial. The third aspect of such rights and freedoms involves equality rights—that is, freedom from discrimination on such bases as gender, race, religion, or age. Canadians almost universally support these three categories of rights and freedoms, and they are therefore embedded in the Charter. The fourth category, economic rights, is more controversial. Although the right to own property, for example, is recognized in law as well as in the Canadian Bill of Rights, it was not enshrined in the Charter.[2]

Political systems that value such rights and freedoms have adopted two principal methods to protect them. The British approach is to make Parliament supreme but on the presumption that neither the legislature nor the executive would infringe civil liberties, because both are held in check by public opinion, tradition, the political culture, and self-restraint. Such rights and freedoms are so deeply ingrained in the values of the people and politicians alike that the latter would never think of infringing them, even though, in theory, Parliament could do so. Although the courts cannot overturn legislation in Britain—that is, they do not have the power of **judicial review**—they do have wide **judicial discretion** in the interpretation of laws, and many civil libertarian values have been introduced into the law as canons of interpretation.[3] Thus, even in the British system, judicial precedents accumulated into the common law offer protection against arbitrary government action. So does the basic constitutional principle, the **rule of law**, which requires that every official act be based on law. In typical British manner, then, the fact that they were not written down did not mean that civil liberties did not exist.

The American approach, derived in reaction to an imperial government that *did* encroach on colonial liberties, is to provide for a written statement of civil liberties (usually called "civil rights") in a constitutional Bill of Rights. Then, if legislation is passed or the executive takes action that is felt to violate a person's rights, such acts can be challenged in the courts. It is up to the courts to determine whether the government has infringed civil rights as defined in the Constitution. The courts thus have the power of judicial review and can overturn offensive legislation or executive acts.

Neither the British nor the American system remotely approaches perfection, and both are designed only to restrict the actions of *governments*. In most cases, that is, bills and charters of rights do not extend to *private*, interpersonal relationships. Prohibitions against private discrimination, such as in employment and accommodation, are instead generally covered by human rights codes. Each province and territory in Canada has such a code, as does the federal government, and they are enforced by human rights commissions through investigation, conciliation, and, if necessary, adjudication of disputes.

EN ROUTE TO THE CHARTER

A discussion of protecting rights and freedoms in Canada can be divided into three eras.[4] In the first, Canada inherited the British system based on parliamentary restraint within **parliamentary supremacy**. For the most part, therefore, Canadians' civil liberties depended on politicians voluntarily respecting them or protecting them in legislation. Although many abuses can be enumerated, the Canadian record reflected the tenor of the times, and was probably as good as that of any other contemporary state—certainly no worse than the U.S. system where such rights were embedded in the constitution.

Unlike the United Kingdom, the Canadian situation was complicated by the adoption of federalism. Hence, Canada possessed two supreme legislatures, one in Ottawa and another in the provinces, each operating within its own constitutional jurisdiction. Federalism allowed the courts to engage in judicial review in the sense of invalidating federal or provincial legislation that violated the division of powers. In doing so, federalism also opened the door to judicial review in the protection of rights and freedoms. That is, if the courts could show that either level of government infringed civil liberties in the process of exceeding its jurisdiction in terms of the division of powers, then the courts could strike down the law.

Thus, even before the adoption of a constitutional bill or charter of rights, the Canadian courts were able to intervene to a limited extent to overturn legislation that violated such rights. The simultaneous violation of the division of powers and civil liberties most often took place at the provincial level, where the courts found provincial legislation infringing federal power in the realm of criminal law.

The courts sometimes supplemented this ground for their decisions by citing the preamble to the 1867 Constitution Act. It speaks of Canada's desire to have "a constitution similar in principle to that of the United Kingdom." Because civil liberties were generally recognized in Britain (albeit without judicial review) they should also be applicable to Canadians. This interpretation, sometimes called an **implied bill of rights**, would have allowed the courts to go beyond the division of powers in striking down legislation that violated rights and freedoms, but it was rarely and inconsistently applied.[5]

Many abuses of rights and freedoms were never taken to court, and of those that were, most were dismissed. But three principal cases of judicial protection of such rights and freedoms in the period before 1960 can be cited. First, freedom of the press was at issue in the 1938 *Alberta Press Bill* case. The Alberta legislation allowed the government to order newspapers to reveal the sources of unfavourable comment and gave it the right to respond to criticism. The courts found this legislation invalid because it was an infringement of the federal criminal law power.[6] In the 1950s the freedom of religion of Jehovah's Witnesses in Quebec was at stake, such as in requiring them to obtain permission from the chief of police before they could distribute their literature on the sidewalk. Once again the federal criminal law power and the preamble proved to be useful in overturning a provincial law.[7] In 1957 the Supreme Court disposed of Premier Maurice Duplessis's **Padlock Law** on the same grounds. This law had given the premier and attorney general the power to padlock any building that Duplessis considered was being used for the propagation of communism and bolshevism, but having left these terms undefined, it was used against opposition groups of any kind.[8]

Fred Chartrand/The Canadian Press

John Diefenbaker, the architect of the Canadian Bill of Rights, 1960.

Another means of protecting rights and freedoms even in the pre-1960 period was to find executive actions to be contrary to the rule of law. This ground was used successfully on three occasions with respect to police and government treatment of Jehovah's Witnesses in the Duplessis period in Quebec. In the most famous case, the court found the premier himself had acted contrary to the rule of law. That is, he took action based not on law but on his dislike of Jehovah's Witnesses when he personally cancelled a tavern owner's liquor licence.[9]

Violations of civil liberties that did not also offend the division of powers or rule of law gave the courts little discretion. For example, in a 1903 case that concerned denial of the vote to Asians in British Columbia provincial elections, the courts ruled that such electoral matters were entirely within the jurisdiction of provincial politicians.[10] Neither did Canadian Blacks find any satisfaction in the courts when they challenged discriminatory practices.[11] Although the federal government was generally more sensitive to rights and freedoms than the provinces were, its record left much to be desired, especially in the case of Aboriginals, women, radical speech, and minorities of various kinds, including its treatment of citizens of certain ethnocultural origins during the two world wars. Ottawa's internment of Canadian citizens of Japanese extraction during the Second World War proved both that the federal government was not above reproach and that the courts could do nothing about it.[12]

Thus, before 1960, both federal and provincial politicians were occasionally guilty of violating civil liberties. This fact and the realization that the courts could rarely be counted on to invalidate such actions persuaded John Diefenbaker to enact the **Canadian Bill of Rights** in 1960.[13] He was also influenced, as were many other states about the same time, by the United Nations' adoption of the Universal Declaration on Human Rights; indeed, the province of Saskatchewan had pioneered such a bill on Canadian soil. The Bill of Rights therefore inaugurated the second era in the protection of rights and freedoms in Canada.

The document's apparent aim was to allow the courts to invalidate legislation that they found to conflict with the Bill of Rights, but if so, this aim was not clearly articulated. The courts were never completely certain whether they had been given this power or not. Other serious gaps in the bill were that it applied only to the federal government, not to the provinces; that it allowed legislation to be passed that overrode the bill, as long as this was acknowledged (a notwithstanding clause); that as an ordinary piece of legislation, the bill could be amended in the routine way; and that it was superseded by the War Measures Act, at the very time that it might be needed most.

Not surprisingly, the courts made limited use of the Bill of Rights. Only once, in the *Drybones* case of 1970, did they decide that a clause of an act violated the Bill of Rights and was therefore inoperative.[14] The Bill was more useful in clarifying legal rights and was referred to in several cases to fill in gaps in such definitions as what was meant by the "right to counsel," the "right to an interpreter," and the "right to a fair hearing." Several other cases arose regarding violations of rights and freedoms within federal jurisdiction, but in each case the Court found a way around applying the Bill of Rights. Provinces occasionally violated civil liberties in the post-1960 period, too, but the Bill of Rights was of even less assistance in such cases.[15]

THE CHARTER OF RIGHTS AND FREEDOMS

Recognizing the limitations and ambiguities of the Canadian Bill of Rights, and wanting to incorporate new kinds of rights into the Constitution, several politicians, most notably Pierre Trudeau, attempted to improve it. Ironically, in the midst of this quest, Trudeau invoked the War Measures Act in 1970 and used it not only to fight the terrorist FLQ but also to encroach on the freedom of speech of innocent, nonviolent Quebec separatists. Finally, in 1982, with the adoption of the **Charter of Rights and Freedoms**, part of the **Constitution Act, 1982,** he accomplished his objective. The Charter essentially replaced the Bill of Rights, using much of its language in the sections on fundamental freedoms and legal rights, but going beyond it to include democratic, linguistic, mobility, egalitarian, and limited Aboriginal rights.

Trudeau wanted to remedy the deficiencies in the Bill of Rights. But he was also determined to entrench official bilingualism, as well as official minority-language education rights across the country, in an effort to undercut Quebec's claim that it represented French Canada. In other words, the individual rights of Canadians would be strengthened at the expense of group rights, such as those of Quebec. Moreover, Trudeau hoped to counter centrifugal forces throughout the land and pressures for general decentralization to the provinces by creating an instrument that the courts could use to cut down self-serving provincial laws. As a new national symbol, the Charter would also serve to increase the allegiance of all citizens to the national government.[16]

The Charter is generally a much stronger document than its predecessor. Besides being broader in scope, the Charter applies equally to both federal and provincial governments, and, being entrenched into the Constitution, it is difficult to amend. It states very clearly that the courts are to invalidate any government actions or legislation that they feel are in conflict with the provisions of the Charter.

On the other hand, the rights articulated in the Charter are not absolute. In the first place, section 1 indicates that such rights are subject to "such reasonable limits, defined by law, as can be demonstrably justified in a free and democratic society." The courts are thus allowed to find that although a piece of legislation does violate certain rights, it is still acceptable according to their definition of reasonable limits. Second, in the areas of fundamental freedoms, legal rights, and equality rights, either level of government is allowed to pass legislation contrary to the Charter by means of the notwithstanding clause, section 33. Governments were not expected to acknowledge in advance that legislation was contrary to the Charter, so the notwithstanding clause would normally come into play when legislation was introduced to override a judicial decision regarding a Charter right. Such a bill can be exempted from the provisions of the Charter only for a five-year period, after which it becomes inoperative if not re-passed for another five years.

The Charter of Rights and Freedoms has profoundly affected the operation of the Canadian political system. Let us now examine the provisions of the Charter and see how they have been interpreted by the courts, especially the Supreme Court of Canada. The following discussion only sketches the broad lines of Charter interpretation during its first 30 years of operation and is not intended to be a definitive statement of the law.[17] Significant new cases will be posted on this book's website.

The Reasonable Limits Clause

Section 1 is often called the **reasonable limits clause** and reads as follows:

> The Canadian Charter of Rights and Freedoms guarantees the rights and freedoms set out in it subject only to such reasonable limits prescribed by law as can be demonstrably justified in a free and democratic society.

In interpreting the limits that can be "demonstrably justified in a free and democratic society," the Supreme Court developed guidelines in the *Oakes* case, which have come to be called the **Oakes test**. First, the objective of the government in limiting a right must be pressing and substantial; second, the means must be proportional to that objective. Three criteria are attached to this second point: the limit must be rationally connected to the government objective; it should impair the right as little as is necessary in order to achieve the objective; and the costs of the impairment to the right must be proportional to their benefits. The Supreme Court has made extensive use of section 1, upholding many laws considered violations though still reasonable limits upon Charter rights.[18]

The 2001 *Sharpe* case on child pornography presents a useful example of how the Court applies the reasonable limits clause. Although the judges ruled that the law prohibiting the possession of child pornography infringed Mr. Sharpe's freedom of expression, it was upheld as a reasonable limit on that Charter right because

- the *objective* of the law that criminalized the possession of child pornography (eradicating the sexual exploitation of children) was "pressing and substantial"
- the *means* chosen by Parliament (prohibiting the possession of child pornography) were "rationally connected" to the objective
- the law represented a "minimal impairment" of the Charter right by allowing minor and reasonable exceptions (e.g., innocent photographs of a baby in the bath)
- the "benefits" of prohibiting such materials outweighed any "costs" or deleterious effects to the right to freedom of expression since the law does not interfere significantly with speech possessing social value.[19]

Fundamental Freedoms

Section 2 lists the following **fundamental freedoms**:

a) freedom of conscience and religion;

b) freedom of thought, belief, opinion and expression, including freedom of the press and other media of communication;

c) freedom of peaceful assembly; and

d) freedom of association.

Freedom of Religion

With respect to freedom of religion, the Supreme Court invalidated the Lord's Day Act as an infringement of freedom of religion because its restrictions on Sunday activities were clearly related to the Christian Sabbath and discriminated against other religions. The Court did, however, uphold the Ontario Retail Business Holidays Act, designed to preserve Sunday as a day of rest on a secular rather than a religious foundation, a ruling that has been widely ignored. A number of cases have taken the view that a child welfare authority may approve a blood transfusion for a child despite the parents' religious beliefs to the contrary. Public schools may no longer hold an exclusively Christian school prayer or religious studies classes, but Ontario's publicly funded Roman Catholic separate school system was upheld as a pre-Charter constitutional right even though its existence discriminated against other religions. In 2006 the Supreme Court ruled that Sikh students could carry their (sheathed) ceremonial daggers called kirpans to school based on freedom of religion and backed up by the Canadian commitment to multiculturalism. And, in 2012, Quebec's new non-denominational religion and ethics course was upheld against a claim that it violated freedom of religion. In 2015 a ruling recognized "collective aspects of religious freedom" and allowed for exemptions from the Quebec course.[20]

In April 2015, the Supreme Court ruled that the town council of Saguenay, Quebec could not recite a prayer before its council meetings because this offended the religious neutrality that the state must demonstrate in its operations. Many municipal councils across the country immediately ceased a similar practice.

Freedom of Expression

With respect to freedom of expression, a wide range of issues has been brought before the courts. Perhaps most controversial was the Supreme Court's rejection of the French-only sign provision of Quebec's **Bill 101**, which was held to be a violation of Quebec's own Charter of Rights as well. The Court decided that freedom of expression included not only the freedom to express ideas but also the freedom to choose the language in which to express them. Moreover, the concept of freedom of expression incorporated "commercial expression." In this case, the Court hinted that it would be a reasonable limit if the law provided for the *predominant* rather than the *exclusive* use of French on commercial signs. Freedom of commercial expression was also involved in Quebec's successful effort to restrict advertising aimed at children. But the Supreme Court disallowed the federal prohibition of cigarette advertising: the Court ruled that a *partial* ban would be more acceptable, and the government amended the legislation accordingly. The weak new Tobacco Act was upheld by the Supreme Court in 2007 against another tobacco industry challenge.[21]

In cases involving anti-Semitic denials of the Holocaust, a majority of the Court concluded that the section of the Criminal Code prohibiting the dissemination of hate literature was a reasonable limit on freedom of expression.[22] In cases involving the labour movement, the Court ruled that freedom of expression includes the freedom of trade unions to engage in picketing, even secondary picketing, and that the right to distribute leaflets regarding a labour dispute is even more extensive.[23]

Other cases have arisen in connection with election campaigns. Attaching posters on public property, including utility poles, was protected by freedom of expression, and paying a portion of the campaign expenses of candidates and parties from the public purse does not infringe a taxpayer's right to freedom of expression. After limits on third-party advertising during election campaigns were invalidated several times in the Alberta courts, the Supreme Court of Canada finally upheld them, as noted in Chapter 13. However, the provision in the Canada Elections Act prohibiting the publication of public opinion polls during the final three days of a federal election campaign was overturned and later limited by law to election day itself. Federal legislation prohibiting public servants from engaging in electoral work for a political party or candidate was found to be invalid, but the more balanced Ontario legislation on the subject was upheld.[24]

Freedom of expression encompasses freedom of the press and the media, and several cases have dealt with this issue. The Court has usually sided with the media, such as in allowing the CBC to show the movie *The Boys of St. Vincent* even if it might have prejudiced upcoming sexual abuse trials. The Court upheld the right of the media to expose police tactics used to entice confessions from murder suspects and said that police search warrants should be open to media scrutiny unless their exposure would cause genuine harm. But the judges found it a reasonable limit that the Criminal Code prohibits the publication of the name of the victim of sexual assault if the victim so requests, and to clear the court in the case where public knowledge would further victimize the victim of sexual assault. The Nova Scotia legislature was even allowed to limit media access to its proceedings.[25]

Obscenity also falls into this category, where one main case stands out, *R. v. Butler*.[26] The Court divided pornography into different categories, saying that portrayals of sex with violence and sex that is degrading or dehumanizing can be restricted by the authorities, but that a portrayal of explicit sex that is neither violent nor degrading is generally acceptable unless it depicts children. Parliament strengthened the provisions dealing with child pornography, which were upheld in the *Sharpe* case, as mentioned. Whether pornographic fiction or art sometimes has artistic merit has been another difficult issue.

Regarding prostitution, following from an Ontario court decision in 2012, in 2013 the Supreme Court struck down criminal laws prohibiting brothels, living off the avails of prostitution, and communication in public with clients. While selling sex in Canada is not illegal, the government's response—in a bill passed in 2014—maintains the buying of "sexual services" as illegal. The new bill also restricts communications in some locations, advertising aside from doing it oneself, and profiting from proceeds of someone else's sex work.

Freedom of Peaceful Assembly and Association

Freedom of association has often been involved in labour union cases. In 2001, for example, the Supreme Court invalidated an Ontario law that prohibited the unionization of agricultural workers and upheld a Quebec law that forced construction workers to join one of five unions in the industry. In other words, freedom of association carries with it the right, or in some cases the obligation, to join a union. However, in an earlier set of less labour-friendly decisions, the Court ruled that freedom of association does not guarantee the right of trade unions to strike. Thus, freedom of association did not prevent federal or provincial legislatures from passing back-to-work legislation or otherwise interfere in the collective bargaining process. Labour was happier with the ultimate disposition of the *Lavigne* case, in which the Court rejected Mr. Lavigne's objection to part of his union dues going to support causes with which he did not agree. Then, in 2007, the Supreme Court reversed itself on the question of whether collective bargaining was protected by the Charter right of freedom of association. In siding with the BC

Hospital Employees' Union, the Court struck down a provincial law that had ripped up their contracts and privatized thousands of health-care jobs. Still, the sanctity of collective bargaining must be determined on a case-by-case basis.[27]

In January 2015, the Supreme Court ruled that the prohibition on collective bargaining by the RCMP was a violation of freedom of association. Then, two weeks later, the Court went beyond the BC Hospital Employees' case to clarify that the right to strike is an essential part of a meaningful collective bargaining process, overturning a Saskatchewan law that denied such a right.

Democratic Rights

Under **democratic rights** in sections 3 to 5, the Charter guarantees that every citizen of Canada has the right to vote in federal and provincial elections; that no Parliament can continue for more than five years from the previous election, except in time of real or apprehended war, invasion, or insurrection; and that each Parliament must sit at least once every year. A number of cases regarding elections were already mentioned in terms of freedom of expression, while section 3 has been cited in several cases dealing with federal and provincial electoral laws that deny the vote to certain categories of people. At the national level, it was used in the 1988 election to invalidate provisions in the Canada Elections Act that withheld the vote from federally appointed judges and people with mental disabilities. Many similar cases have arisen in connection with provincial electoral laws, especially relating to prisoners, persons on parole, and those remanded but not yet charged. In 1993 the Supreme Court agreed with the Federal Court of Canada that denying prisoners the right to vote violated section 3, but in the meantime, the law had been amended to allow those serving less than two years to vote. When the amended law was challenged in turn, all prisoners were awarded the vote in federal elections.[28]

Another interesting application of section 3 arose in cases involving the drawing of provincial electoral maps, especially in British Columbia and Saskatchewan. Indeed, the courts surprised many observers by ruling that such a matter came within the scope of section 3 at all. In the 1989 *Dixon* case in British Columbia, the map was disallowed because electoral boundaries did not approach "equality of voting power." Similarly, in Saskatchewan, the Court of Appeal invalidated that province's electoral map in 1991 primarily because of disparities between the size of urban and rural ridings, but a quick appeal to a divided Supreme Court of Canada re-established it. Even though the electoral map systematically

Inmate at Montreal Detention Centre casts his ballot in the 2004 federal election after all inmates won the right to vote.

Ryan Remiorz/The Canadian Press

overrepresented rural voters, a majority of the Court decided that they would not insist on greater equality in the size of constituencies because "effective representation" had been achieved.[29]

The democratic rights section was also used to invalidate sections of the Canada Elections Act that required a political party to run at least 50 candidates before it could be registered. These provisions meant that an unregistered party could not use its label under the candidate's name on the ballot, issue tax receipts for contributions, or retain unspent election contributions. The Supreme Court argued that smaller parties serve a purpose in the electoral process, even if they are unlikely to win, and the law was eventually amended to allow the registration of a party with only a single candidate.[30]

Mobility Rights

Under section 6, **mobility rights**, every citizen of Canada has the right to enter, remain in, and leave Canada, and every citizen or permanent resident has the right to take up residence and pursue the gaining of a livelihood in any province. However, laws providing for reasonable residency requirements for receiving public services are acceptable, as are laws that give preference to local residents if the unemployment rate in that province is higher than the national rate. Mobility rights were included in the Charter because of Pierre Trudeau's concern that some provinces were restricting the entry of residents of other provinces, as in the case of cross-border employment, but such rights have not featured frequently in judicial interpretation. When professionals tried to use this clause to gain access to seek to work in another province, the Court upheld the right of each province to establish its own professional qualifications. It also ruled that PEI legislation taxing non-residents at a higher level than residents did not violate section 6.[31]

Legal Rights

Legal rights are contained in sections 7 to 14. In section 7, everyone has the right to life, liberty, and security of the person and the right not to be deprived thereof except in accordance with the principles of fundamental justice. "Security of the person" was used as the main basis for throwing out the abortion provision of the Criminal Code in the famous *Morgentaler* case in 1988. A majority of the Court ruled that that law, with all its arbitrary and bureaucratic procedures, violated the security of the person of the woman concerned and constituted a "profound interference with a woman's body." Having invalidated the abortion law in the *Morgentaler* case, the Court found no fetal right to life in the Quebec Charter of Rights, the Canadian Criminal Code, or the common law, and ruled that the "father" had no right to prevent an abortion. In the 1999 *Dobson* case, the Court ruled that a woman could not be sued for having harmed her fetus during pregnancy.[32]

Canada has had three high-profile assisted suicide (or mercy killing) cases. In the first, Sue Rodriguez tried to persuade the Court that since she was dying of Lou Gehrig's disease, security of the person should provide her with the right to an assisted suicide. The judges were divided, but the majority ruled against her. Then, when Robert Latimer took the life of his severely disabled daughter because he could not bear to see her in such pain, the Supreme Court unanimously upheld the provisions of the Criminal Code with respect to murder and refused to recognize this as a special case.[33] More recently, however, in early 2015 the Court unanimously decided in *Carter v. Canada* that doctor-assisted death should be permitted. The Court allowed one year for Parliament to make adjustments to the Criminal Code. During this time the decision was stayed, though the government tabled no legislation prior to the 2015 election, and the Trudeau government received an additional 4-month extension. It is possible the most meaningful response will come within provinces, which could regulate the provision of health services, though the federal government will still adjust the Criminal Code.

Security of the person was also involved in the *Operation Dismantle* case dealing with the attempt to halt the testing of the American Cruise missile in Canada. The Supreme Court ruled that the causal link between missile testing and the threat to the security of the person because of the potential escalation of the international arms race was uncertain, speculative, and hypothetical.[34]

Perhaps the most controversial decision with respect to section 7 concerned the public health care system in the 2005 *Chaoulli* case. The question raised was whether excessive waiting times jeopardized the life, health, and psychological well-being of Canadians. The Court was evenly divided on whether the provincial law that banned the purchase of private health insurance for core medical services was unconstitutional according "life, liberty, and security of the person," but Madam Justice Deschamps tipped the balance against the law by referring only to the Quebec Charter. Thus, although the decision was limited in the first instance to Quebec, a number of provinces used the case to justify allowing an expansion of private health care facilities to which people capable of paying the fee could shorten their wait times for treatment. Somewhat similarly, the operation of the controversial Insite supervised drug injection clinic in Vancouver was upheld; to close it would endanger the life, health, and security of the person of those who used its services.[35]

"Security of the person" and "fundamental justice" combined in the *Singh* case to require the Immigration Department to provide an oral hearing for refugee claimants when their life could be in danger if deported. Fundamental justice necessitated giving such claimants an opportunity to state their case and to know the case against them, a decision that caused much of the subsequent backlog in the immigration department.[36]

Fundamental justice is often linked to the presumption of innocence in section 11(d). For example, in the *Daviault* case, the Supreme Court allowed an extreme state of drunkenness to be used as a rare defence in a rape case; otherwise, it ruled, the accused's right to fundamental justice and presumption of innocence would have been violated. The government quickly amended the law to prevent a recurrence of this interpretation. In the *Stinchcombe* case, the Court said that section 7 strengthened the obligation of police and prosecutors to hand over all relevant evidence to the accused well before trial. In 2004, in connection with two people implicated in the Air India explosion, the Court upheld provisions of the Anti-Terrorism Act that allowed for investigative hearings in which judges could compel witnesses to speak.

In a major blow to the women's movement, the *Seaboyer* decision invalidated the rape-shield law that had prohibited the use of evidence of the complainant's previous sexual activity. But Parliament responded by amending the Criminal Code, primarily by tightening up the concept of consent—"no means no." Then, in another case that attracted much public attention, the Supreme Court overturned the acquittal of an Alberta man who had sexually assaulted a young woman during a job interview in a trailer. Although the woman said "no" three times to his sexual advances, the Alberta courts considered his actions "less criminal than hormonal," and were roundly criticized by the Supreme Court for dealing in "inappropriate myths and stereotypes."[37]

Section 8 establishes the right to be secure against unreasonable search and seizure. In dismissing the charge of collusion between the Southam and Thomson newspaper chains, the Court extended this right to corporations. A police officer's demand to see a person's driver's licence and insurance card during a spot check is not an unreasonable search, and male prisoners can be frisked by female guards. But taking blood samples without legal authorization and strip searches at Canadian border points without the opportunity to contact counsel were declared to be Charter violations.[38] In 2014 the Supreme Court ruled that police cannot obtain basic information about customers from Internet providers without a judge-issued search warrant.

Section 9 grants the right not to be arbitrarily detained or imprisoned, and section 10 reads that, on arrest or detention, everyone has the right to be informed promptly of the reasons, the right to contact a lawyer without delay, and the right to be informed of that right. A huge number of Charter cases have arisen in this connection: for example, the Court has ruled that random police spot checks are a reasonable limit on the right not to be arbitrarily detained, and that roadside breath tests do not include the right to retain counsel. However, if a person fails that test and is asked to accompany the officer to a police station, the individual has a right to retain counsel before taking the police station breathalyzer test. The Court has insisted that a person has the right to be told of his or her right to a lawyer as well as to legal aid, and must have a reasonable opportunity to exercise these rights. In 2014, the Court told police officers that they need to be prompt and proactive in helping suspects find a telephone to call their lawyer.

Section 11 includes a variety of rights available to a person charged with an offence. "To be tried within a reasonable time" has been controversial after the *Askov* decision, which found that a delay of almost two years between a preliminary hearing and a trial had been excessive.[39] The lower courts took this to mean that everyone had a right to a trial within six to eight months of being charged, and some 34 500 cases were stayed, dismissed, or withdrawn in Ontario alone. The Supreme Court then took the unprecedented initiative to point out in a speech by one of its members that this was not what the *Askov* decision intended.

Persons charged cannot be compelled to testify against themselves, cannot be denied reasonable bail without just cause, and are presumed innocent until proven guilty according to law in a fair and public hearing by an independent and impartial tribunal. Persons charged are guaranteed trial by jury where the maximum punishment for the offence is imprisonment for five years or more and, whether finally acquitted of the offence or found guilty and punished, cannot be tried for it again.[40]

Everyone has the right not to be subjected to any cruel and unusual treatment or punishment. Indeterminate sentences for dangerous offenders have been upheld, and in the Robert Latimer case, mentioned above, the Court ruled that the minimum mandatory sentence of 10 years in jail was not grossly disproportionate, given the gravity of the offence. In the *Burns* case, the Supreme Court refused to extradite two men to the United States without assurances that they would not face the death penalty. In 2004, however, the Court upheld the Criminal Code provision that allowed parents and teachers to use reasonable force in spanking a child or pupil for correctional purposes.[41] The Court has struck down various minimum mandatory prison sentences brought in by the Harper government as being excessive.

The Court has struck down various minimum prison sentences brought in by the Harper government on these grounds.

Section 14 provides that a party or witness in any proceedings who does not understand or speak the language in which the proceedings are conducted or who is deaf has the right to the assistance of an interpreter. In the *Tran* case, the Supreme Court ruled that an accused must receive a continuous, precise, impartial, competent, and contemporaneous interpretation of what is said, reinforcing section 14 with section 27 on the multicultural heritage of Canada.[42]

Equality Rights

Equality rights are contained in section 15, which reads as follows:

1. Every individual is equal before and under the law and has the right to the equal protection and equal benefit of the law without discrimination and, in particular, without discrimination based on race, national or ethnic origin, colour, religion, sex, age or mental or physical disability.

2. Subsection (1) does not preclude any law, program or activity that has as its object the amelioration of conditions of disadvantaged individuals or groups including those that are disadvantaged because of race, national or ethnic origin, colour, religion, sex, age or mental or physical disability.

BOX 19.1 TERRORISM AND THE CHARTER

Increasing concern about **terrorism** since 9/11 has raised serious questions about the balance between national security and many legal rights, including life, liberty, security of the person, and right to counsel, as well as several fundamental freedoms.

Sometimes these issues are related to the Anti-Terrorism Act and sometimes to the Immigration and Refugee Protection Act. In a 2002 deportation case dealing with a "Tamil Tiger" deemed to be a terrorist, for example, the Supreme Court ruled that a new deportation hearing was in order because the person in question could be subject to torture once back in Sri Lanka. In other cases, security certificates permit the government to detain suspected terrorists for several years without trial and without revealing the evidence against them, after which they can be deported, still ignorant of their alleged crime.

As terrorist charges worked their way up the judicial hierarchy, the *Charkaoui* case challenged the provisions of the Immigration and Refugee Protection Act that allowed the government to imprison security suspects for an indefinite period without even knowing the case against them. In a 2007 decision, the Supreme Court ruled that the use of secret testimony to imprison and deport foreigners as possible terrorist suspects violates the Charter's guarantee of fundamental justice and a fair hearing. The Court

continued

suspended its ruling for a year, allowing parliament to draft a new law compatible with the Charter.

Then, in June 2008, Charkaoui won a second Supreme Court decision when it ordered CSIS to stop systematically destroying interview notes and other evidence gathered during national security probes. In the fall of 2009, most of the surveillance restrictions on Charkaoui and some of the others involved in stalled security-certificate cases were eased when the Crown said it would rather drop the case than reveal how CSIS had obtained its information against them. Mohamed Harkat has also been before the Federal Court on numerous occasions regarding his security certificate after CSIS destroyed the recordings of taped conversations.

Meanwhile, in May 2008 the Supreme Court ruled that Omar Khadr, detained by the U.S. at Guantanamo Bay, was entitled to see the documents relevant to the charges against him, including the records of CSIS interviews in the possession of the Canadian Crown. In another case, the Federal Court ruled in April 2009 that the government must demand that U.S. authorities return Khadr to Canada on the basis of fundamental justice, but the Harper government appealed. In 2010 the Supreme Court agreed that the 15-year-old's Charter rights had been violated, but then backtracked to say that it was not appropriate for the Court to give direction as to the diplomatic steps necessary to address the breaches of his rights. In short, his right to life, liberty, and security of the person was subject to the federal government's prerogative powers over foreign affairs. Meanwhile, Momin Khawaja was convicted on seven terrorist charges and acquitted of two others, while several of the suspects in the "Toronto 18" terrorism case were found guilty. Two were sentenced to life in prison (with no chance of parole for at least five years), and the sentences of a few others were increased on appeal. In September 2012, Khadr was finally repatriated, and in December, the Supreme Court upheld the new Anti-Terrorism Act.[43] Against the views of the Conservative government, Omar Khadr was released on bail in May 2015.

In January 2015, the government introduced a new Anti-Terrorism Act to strengthen the powers of CSIS, create new criminal offences related to encouraging terrorism, make it easier for authorities to restrict the movement of suspected terrorists, and remove restrictions on information-sharing among 17 federal departments and agencies. Opposition parties, the Privacy Commissioner, and a large number of experts in the field criticized aspects of the new law, which they claimed violated Charter rights.

In the *Andrews* case the Supreme Court laid down a two-step process for interpreting equality rights. The Court first determines if the case in question involves an inequality in law or treatment in terms of the personal characteristics listed in section 15 (or of others analogous to them), and then whether there has been a discrimination—that is, a harmful or prejudicial effect. In other words, inequalities and distinctions are permitted if no negative discrimination or disadvantage—social, political, or legal—is involved. According to Ian Greene, the Court made it clear that "it intends to interpret section 15 to help clearly disadvantaged groups in society."[44] Still, the Court has had some difficulty in pursuing a consistent line of interpretation, although it tried to do so in the 1999 *Law* case, in which it denied Canada Pension Plan survivor benefits to a widow under 35 years of age.

To cite only some examples, the Supreme Court overturned the 1978 Bill of Rights decision that allowed the Unemployment Insurance Commission to discriminate against pregnant women. In addition, it agreed that provincial human rights codes must not prevent girls from playing on boys'

The Canadian Supreme Court agrees to gay marriage.

athletic teams. In the *Corbiere* case, it ruled that band members living off-reserve have the right to vote in First Nations elections, and in the *Eldridge* case, that the equality rights of deaf people are violated if those involved are not provided with sign language interpreters in a hospital. In a somewhat similar case, the Supreme Court ruled in 2012 that a North Vancouver school board had discriminated against a dyslexic child who was not given adequate help to obtain literacy.

In the case of mandatory retirement, the Court said that, however discriminatory, it was reasonable for laws to require retirement at age 65. On the other hand, such discrimination has been eliminated in various provincial human rights codes. The government of Newfoundland and Labrador was allowed to back away from pay equity because of the severe fiscal situation of the time; Quebec was allowed to pay lower welfare allowances to people under 30 years of age, and the BC health system was not required to fund specialized programs for autistic children.[45]

Many section 15 cases have dealt with **sexual orientation**; in fact, judicial interpretation of equality rights made Canada one of the most progressive countries in the world regarding such issues as same-sex marriage. In the 1995 *Egan* case, the Supreme Court ruled unanimously that the Charter prohibited discrimination on the basis of sexual orientation, even though this ground was not explicitly listed in section 15. (The Court has recognized citizenship and marital status as other analogous grounds to the rights enumerated in section 15 but has so far rejected social condition or poverty.) Then, in the *Vriend* case, it reaffirmed this decision and ordered Alberta to add that ground to its Individual Rights Protection Act. Same-sex benefits received a major boost in the 1999 M. *v.* H. case, in which the Ontario Family Law Act was found to be a violation of section 15 when it provided post-separation support only for an opposite-sex spouse. And, as mentioned in Chapter 7, the Ontario Court of Appeal ruled in 2002 that the definition of marriage between a male and a female discriminated against same-sex couples. After similar decisions in most other provinces, the Chrétien government sent a reference case to the Supreme Court of Canada, which generally agreed with lower appeal court decisions, and Parliament passed a law confirming the change. It also ruled that unlike legally married couples, common-law partners (of any gender) cannot claim an equal division of matrimonial property if their relationship breaks down.[46]

Subsection (2) of section 15 permits **affirmative action** programs that give preference to those who have been discriminated against in the past. This clause has rarely been involved in Charter decisions, although the Kapp case allowed Aboriginals to get a one-day jump-start on fishing for salmon in the Fraser River.[47]

Box 19.2 lists 15 of the most important Charter decisions to date, at least from a political science point of view. This list does not include significant Supreme Court decisions based on non-Charter grounds.

BOX 19.2 15 OF THE MOST IMPORTANT CHARTER DECISIONS

1. *Big M Drug Mart* [1985]: Strikes down Lord's Day Act restriction on Sunday shopping as a violation of freedom of religion
2. *Oakes* [1986]: Establishes guidelines for interpreting section 1, the reasonable limits clause
3. *Ford* [1988]: Disallows the Quebec sign law as an infringement of freedom of expression
4. *Morgentaler* [1988]: Outlaws Criminal Code restrictions on abortion, primarily on the basis of security of the person
5. *Keegstra* [1990]: Decides that freedom of expression does not extend to disseminating hate literature
6. *Askov* [1990]: Sets a limit for the right to be tried within a reasonable time
7. *Sparrow* [1990]: Delivers a strong statement on Aboriginal rights
8. *Butler* [1992]: Limits freedom of expression in relation to pornography
9. *Rodriguez* [1993]: Rules that security of the person does not include the right to assisted suicide
10. *Egan* [1995]: Decides that equality rights include sexual orientation
11. *Delgamuukw* [1997]: Defines Aboriginal title to land and rules that oral evidence is valid in making such a claim
12. *M v. H* [1999]: Extends sexual orientation protection to same-sex couples
13. *N.A.P.E.* [2004]: Allows Newfoundland government to defer pay equity payment in time of economic hardship.
14. *Chaoulli* [2005]: Overturns the monopoly of public health care insurance for core medical services
15. *Health Services and Support* [2007]: Overturns earlier decision (Labour Trilogy) that freedom of association did not guarantee the right to collective bargaining.

Source: Adapted by authors from Andrew Heard, "The Judiciary: The Power behind the Throne," in Rand Dyck, ed., *Studying Politics: An Introduction to Political Science*, 4th ed. (Toronto: Nelson Education, 2012), p. 262.

Official Languages of Canada

Sections 16 to 22 of the Charter constitutionalize the federal and New Brunswick official languages acts and reaffirm the limited official bilingualism of Quebec and Manitoba. These sections guarantee that certain federal and New Brunswick government agencies will operate on a bilingual basis, as discussed in Chapter 5. Although judicial interpretation of linguistic rights has been extensive, it related mostly to the original provisions of the 1867 Constitution Act as well as the 1870 Manitoba Act, rather than to the 1982 Charter. The extension of official bilingualism in the federal and New Brunswick official languages acts was ruled valid; several aspects of Quebec's Bill 101 were invalidated because they conflicted with section 133 of the 1867 act; the 1890 Official Language Act of Manitoba, which removed French as an official language in the province, was considered a violation of the Manitoba Act; and the

Pierre Trudeau promoted minority-language education rights as the central element of the Charter of Rights and Freedoms.

Supreme Court then required Manitoba to translate all its laws into French. As noted above, the unilingual sign provisions of Bill 101 were challenged in terms of freedom of expression rather than on the basis of sections 16 to 23. A new section, 16.1, was added to the Charter in 1993 to reinforce the equality of the two official languages in New Brunswick. That being the case, the Supreme Court ruled in 2008 that RCMP officers working as a provincial police force in New Brunswick had to be bilingual.[48]

Minority-Language Education Rights

Section 23 deals with **minority-language education rights**, and some would argue that they were the part of the Charter with which Pierre Trudeau was most concerned.[49] Section 23 requires provinces to provide anglophone and francophone minorities with education in their own language, where numbers warrant. Thus, the Supreme Court struck down the provision in Bill 101 that allowed only the children of parents who were themselves products of the English school system in Quebec to go to that system, essentially those who were already there (the "Quebec clause"). Indeed, section 23 (the "Canada clause") was deliberately drafted so that it would conflict with this clause, ensuring that Canadian citizens who moved to Quebec could also send their children to the English schools. In other provinces, the Supreme Court has decided not only what number of francophone students warrant a French-language school but also that it must have a "distinct physical setting" and that French-language parents must have a say in the "management and control" of it.[50]

CRITICAL APPROACHES

Of the approaches outlined in Chapter 1, *pluralism* is most relevant to the addition of the Charter of Rights in the protection of civil liberties in Canada. In emphasizing individualist values and lauding the Charter in protecting them, pluralists draw their inspiration from the ideology of liberalism as articulated by such philosophers as John Locke and John Stuart Mill. Liberalism emphasizes the basic rationality of all people and advocates equality and liberty as embodied in the fundamental freedoms—of speech, press, religion, and association—and in the rule of law. Pluralists expect that equality rights together with affirmative action programs will help remove various kinds of discrimination. They also observe that judicial decisions have been ideologically balanced, citing cases that have favoured both business and labour. Rather than be concerned that the legalization of politics has discouraged groups and popular movements from engaging in traditional political organization, pluralists welcome an additional means by which such demands can be advanced, and point to special programs to fund certain kinds of Charter challenges.

Other Provisions

Enforcement

Section 24 makes clear, where the Bill of Rights did not, that the courts have the power to interpret the Charter and to invalidate laws or government actions that conflict with it. It also moves in the American direction with regard to the admissibility of evidence. The Charter does not actually bar illegally obtained evidence, as in the United States; the admission of such evidence is acceptable as long as it does not bring the administration of justice into disrepute. The Supreme Court laid the basis for interpreting this section in the *Collins* case.[51] First, evidence should be excluded if it would prejudice the fairness of the trial, and second, the more seriously the obtaining of the evidence violates the Charter, the more compelling is the need to exclude it. Third, however, if to exclude the evidence would bring the judicial system into disrepute, the evidence should not be excluded. Such questionable evidence usually related to a violation of the right to counsel or to an unreasonable search or seizure.

General Provisions

Sections 25 through 30 relate to specific groups in society and were discussed in relevant chapters earlier in the book. Section 25 says that the rights and freedoms in the Charter should not be construed so as to abrogate or derogate from any Aboriginal, treaty, or other rights or freedoms that pertain to the Aboriginal peoples of Canada, including any rights or freedoms that have been recognized by the Royal Proclamation of October 7, 1763, and any rights or freedoms that may be acquired by the Aboriginal peoples of Canada by way of land claims settlement.

A more positive Aboriginal clause in the Constitution Act, 1982, is section 35, which is not actually part of the Charter itself. The potential of the 1982 document to advance Aboriginal rights has never been clear, but encouraging signs emerged from the *Sparrow*, *Sioui*, and the first of the *Marshall* cases. In acquitting an Aboriginal of the offence of using a bigger fishing net than authorized by law, the Supreme Court asserted that governments must bear the burden of proving that laws are necessary if they have a negative effect on any Aboriginal right. In another early case on the subject of treaty rights, the Court ruled that an ancient treaty-based fishing right took precedence over a Quebec law that prohibited fishing in provincial parks. Then, as mentioned in Chapter 4, the *Delgamuukw* case provided a comprehensive statement on Aboriginal title and opened the door to accepting oral history evidence for purposes of such land claims.[52]

In 2003, the Supreme Court ruled that the Métis people are a distinct Aboriginal group, with a constitutional right to hunt for food. The Court also decided that Aboriginals must be consulted on the development of logging, mining, or other resource projects on lands the title to which is still in dispute, but that they have no veto over such projects. The Court found in 2005 that the Mi'kmaq did not possess a right to cut logs on Crown land in Nova Scotia and New Brunswick without authorization, although a year later logging for domestic use was allowed.[53]

Section 27, which has been cited sparingly, asserts that the Charter shall be interpreted in a manner consistent with the preservation and enhancement of the multicultural heritage of Canadians, and section 28 reads that notwithstanding anything in the Charter, the rights and freedoms referred to in it are guaranteed equally to male and female persons. The women's movement considered the addition of section 28 essential so that governments would not be able to use the notwithstanding clause (section 33) to override the gender equality provision of section 15. Section 29 protects section 93 of the 1867 Constitution Act, which guaranteed existing Protestant and Roman Catholic separate schools. Although section 93 clearly discriminates against other religions, the drafters of the Charter did not want to take responsibility for altering rights established in the original Constitution.[54]

APPLICATION OF THE CHARTER

Section 32 clarifies that the Charter extends to the Parliament and government of Canada, including Yukon and the Northwest Territories (and now Nunavut), and to the legislature and government of each province. By implication, it also applies to the municipal level of government. Thus, all legislation in Canada must be consistent with the Charter, as must all actions of government executives—ministers, public servants, police officers, and so on. The private sector is not intended to come within the ambit of the Charter, but certain institutions occupy an ambiguous position. The Charter has been applied to law societies, because they have been delegated governmental powers, and to community colleges, but more autonomous semi-public institutions, such as hospitals and universities, are exempt in their internal operations. As mentioned earlier, federal and provincial human rights codes rather than the Charter regulate certain aspects of the private sector. But since such codes take the form of laws, they must also remain consistent with the Charter.[55]

The Notwithstanding Clause

Section 33 is the famous **notwithstanding clause**. Parliament or legislatures may exempt laws from three parts of the Charter—fundamental freedoms (section 2), legal rights (sections 7–14), and equality rights (section 15)—but not from democratic rights, mobility rights, or linguistic rights. This provision was a compromise between the provincial premiers, who wanted the clause to apply to the whole Charter, and Prime Minister Trudeau, who was adamant that it could not be used to circumvent the sections about which he cared most. For the sections it covers, a federal or provincial legislature merely has to expressly declare in a statute that the act or a provision thereof shall operate notwithstanding a specific provision of the Charter. If such action is taken, however, it is only valid for five years, after which it lapses or must be re-enacted.

Despite the number of times the Supreme Court has invalidated federal or provincial legislation since 1982, governments have rarely re-enacted such provisions under section 33. Over the first 20 years, it was used in only three high-profile situations.[56] The government of Grant Devine used section 33 to pass back-to-work legislation to settle a 1986 public service strike in Saskatchewan. During the first Parti Québécois period in Quebec, up to 1985, the notwithstanding clause was routinely applied, as a matter of principle, to all new legislation passed in that province. The Liberal government of Robert Bourassa discontinued that practice but used the notwithstanding clause to get around the Supreme Court decision with respect to bilingual signs in the province. As mentioned, when the Supreme Court ruled that French-only store signs violated their owners' freedom of expression, Bourassa invoked section 33 (and the equivalent clause in the Quebec Charter of Rights) and then passed what he considered to be a compromise law that allowed certain bilingual signs inside the store.

This incident, together with a general public adoration of the Charter and a distrust of politicians who sought to find ways around it, gave the notwithstanding clause a negative reception in most of English Canada. Since 1988, therefore, politicians have rarely even contemplated its use. As noted, Quebec has its own reasons to dislike the Charter, but Alberta otherwise provides the main locus of anti-Charter sentiment, and a number of incidents arose in that province that tempted the government to use section 33. One was to prevent the victims of a sterilization program (from an earlier period in the province's history) from appealing for compensation. Another was when the Supreme Court of Canada ruled that sexual orientation had to be added to the Alberta Individual Rights Protection Act, and a third occurred when the Supreme Court legalized same-sex marriage. The Alberta-based Reform Party also asked the federal government to use the notwithstanding clause to override a lower BC court decision justifying the possession of child pornography as an element of freedom of expression, but this decision was eventually overturned by the Supreme Court of Canada.[57]

Nevertheless, section 33 is often defended as a general principle: it allows democratically elected legislators to have the final say. It also takes pressure off judges to solve political crises because they know that politicians can, if necessary, override their strictly legal decisions.[58] Reflecting the fact that it was born of political compromise, the notwithstanding clause in the Charter leaves Canadians with a strange system under which the courts can overrule the legislatures and the legislatures can overrule the courts. Rank Canadian political compromise that it is, this system of protecting civil liberties may turn out to be superior to either total legislative supremacy or exclusive judicial review. Some observers advocate the abolition of the notwithstanding clause, but others, not wanting to entrust their fate entirely either to legislatures or to courts, prefer the checks and balances that they provide to each other.

CRITICAL APPROACHES

Class analysts have a less positive view of the Charter because rights have often been extended to benefit corporations rather than individuals, such as in Sunday shopping, tobacco advertising, and search and seizure cases. Moreover, the costs of taking cases to the courts are generally prohibitive except to wealthy individuals and corporations, and in 1992 the Mulroney government cancelled the Court Challenges Program that had funded many Charter cases. After the Liberals resurrected the Program, the Harper government cancelled it for a second time. Michael Mandel also stresses the Charter's preference for individualism over collectivism, adding that it "unites people against the state but the result is to leave them at the mercy of private power."[59]

Class analysts also emphasize the elitist background of judges and question whether they can make fair decisions for the ordinary mortals who appear in court. For example, Andrew Petter writes,

> there is nothing about the Canadian judiciary to suggest that they possess the experience, the training or the disposition to comprehend the social

impact of claims made to them under the Charter, let alone to resolve those claims in ways that promote, or even protect, the interests of lower income Canadians.[60]

A debate emerged in the field of Canadian *political behaviour* after 1982 about whether the Charter created interest groups centred on particular constitutional clauses. Feminists as well as gay and lesbian groups, for example, tended to mobilize around section 15 of the Charter, which guarantees equality rights. Many academics argued that the Charter fundamentally altered the nature of politics in the country, turning it toward a rights-based and legalistic focus on so-called "post-material" and identity issues such as freedom of speech, women's equality, and gay rights. Others challenged this kind of institutional explanation, arguing instead that the Charter was the product rather than the cause of broader currents in public opinion.[61] Indeed, many countries that did not adopt a constitutionally entrenched Bill of Rights also experienced the same kind of changes in public opinion that Canada witnessed throughout the 1980s and 90s.

IMPLICATIONS OF CONSTITUTIONALIZING THE CHARTER OF RIGHTS

After more than 30 years of experience, the Charter of Rights and Freedoms continues to attract both lively support and opposition. Supporters and opponents alike agree, however, that the Charter has significantly changed the operation of the Canadian political system. The courts have become involved in most of the difficult political issues that have arisen over the past quarter-century: Aboriginal rights, abortion, assisted suicide, Cruise missile testing, doctor-assisted death, French-only signs, gender equality, health care, impaired driving, mandatory retirement, minority-language schools, official bilingualism, political rights of public servants, pornography, prostitution, redistribution of constituency boundaries, religious accommodation, the right to strike, same-sex marriage, separate schools, sexual assault, sexual orientation, Sunday shopping, terrorism, and tobacco advertising. Such cases have enmeshed the courts in considerable political controversy and, as Russell says, the Charter has "judicialized politics and politicized the judiciary."[62]

The first major implication of constitutionalizing the Charter, therefore, was to increase the role of the courts in the political process at the expense of elected politicians. Adopted at a time when politicians were generally regarded with considerable cynicism and disrespect, the Charter was embraced by the Canadian public as a welcome addition to the Constitution. In fact, it became a hallowed national symbol in just the way Prime Minister Trudeau hoped it would. Many Canadians, especially young people, were oblivious to the fact that most of these rights existed before 1982, but in any case, the vast majority had more faith in judges than in parliamentarians and believed that their rights would be better protected that way, as indicated in Table 19.1.

Ian Greene finds disturbing the fact that in a democracy so many citizens would prefer to have issues decided by courts rather than by elected legislatures:

> There would be many benefits to having these kinds of issues debated and resolved more frequently through the political process, and public debate that surrounds it, than through the courts. Public debate can have an educative effect, allowing misinformation created by such factors as stereotyping to be challenged.[63]

Nevertheless, most Canadians seem to have agreed with most of the Supreme Court's decisions and have been impressed by the conduct of the judges in their approach to this difficult work. For example, the Court has aimed for unanimity in its decisions and to a large extent avoided ideological and partisan divisions. It has written eloquent and often ground-breaking judgments, delivering a balance between upholding current laws and government decisions and overturning them.

In general terms, the three groups that benefited most from the first 30 years of Charter litigation were probably official-language minorities, those in trouble with the law, and the gay and lesbian communities. While not everyone would agree with all the decisions made in favour of individuals belonging to such categories, it is seems clear that politicians would not have advanced such causes so quickly, and were led by the Court in their law-making functions

TABLE 19.1 COURTS VERSUS LEGISLATURES: WHO SHOULD HAVE THE FINAL SAY

	PERCENTAGE OF RESPONDENTS
COURTS	59.6
LEGISLATURE/GOVERNMENT	26.5
DON'T KNOW/REFUSED	13.9

Source: Paul Howe and David Northrup, "Strengthening Canadian Democracy: The Views of Canadians," Policy Matters (Montreal: Institute for Public Policy) 1, No. 5 (July 2000), p. 100. Reproduced by permission of Institute for Public Policy (IRPP, Montreal).

in many fields. Official-language rights are stronger, miscarriages of justice are rarer, and Canada has become one of the most progressive countries in the world in dealing with questions of sexual orientation. Other groups that expected giant strides from the Charter—women, ethnocultural minorities, Aboriginals, persons with disabilities, etc.—have benefited from some decisions but are somewhat disappointed overall.

A second, related implication of the adoption of the Charter is that minority groups increasingly bypass the usual political processes—legislatures, cabinets, and bureaucracies—and take their demands directly to the courts instead.[64] To some extent this has happened when such groups were unable to accomplish their goals through traditional political activity; after all, it can be argued, democracy is more than majority rule; it is also about individual and minority rights, which in some cases might be better protected by courts than by legislatures.[65] However, groups may simply believe that it is less trouble to go to court than to engage in the struggle of mobilizing popular support for their cause. Seymour Martin Lipset fears that the Charter will remove one of the last traits that distinguish Canadians from Americans by increasing the litigious character of citizen–state relations and bring about a "rights-centred" political culture.[66]

A third implication of the Charter is that public consciousness of the policymaking role of the courts has created greater interest in the quality and nature of judicial appointments. In general, at least at the level of the Supreme Court, governments have taken greater care than in the past in making such appointments.[67]

Criticism from Right and Left

Despite this generally favourable perspective on the Charter, the movement toward greater judicial power in Canada has been criticized from both the right and the left. Coming from the right, Morton and Knopff are upset that Charter decisions have benefited women and various minority groups against what they believe to be the majoritarian views of elected legislatures and the general public. They construct a kind of conspiracy theory that, contrary to the public interest, judges who sought more power for themselves have been aided and abetted by the very groups in society that are mentioned in the Charter and that stood to benefit from judicial rather than political decisions.[68] Indeed, they coined the term "court party" to describe the link between "Charter groups," such as official-language minority groups, feminists, civil libertarians, Aboriginals, visible minority groups, people with disabilities, and gays and lesbians, and the ascendancy of judicial power in Canadian politics. They also argue that the Charter has had an effect on the federal–provincial relationship: "Ottawa has been able to forge a strategic alliance with select, non-territorial-based interest groups and with sympathetic federally-appointed judges" at the expense of the provinces.[69] If this is true, the Charter has been working even more to his liking than Trudeau anticipated!

Taking the opposite perspective, Michael Mandel has made the most scathing attack from the left on the "legalization of politics" in Canada. He argues that although the Charter has been sold as enhancing democracy and the power of the people, it has really reduced the degree of popular control over government by transferring power from representative, accountable legislatures and politicians to unrepresentative, unaccountable, and unrestrained judges, courts, and an elitist legal profession. He adds: "It is both simpler and cheaper to get to see your MP than to get to see a judge."[70]

Mandel also asserts that legalized politics enhances individual and corporate rights against the collective welfare of the community, as in the tobacco advertising and health care decisions. The adoption of individualistic American values in the Charter, as opposed to traditional Canadian collectivism, is strengthened by the tendency of the courts to cite American precedents when making their decisions.[71] Radha Jhappan reminds us that the Charter deals primarily with individual rights; Trudeau was not much interested in collective rights (such as of the province of Quebec), and the few collective rights included in the Charter relate to francophone minority groups and Aboriginals.[72]

Mandel's third point is that legalized politics is conservative, class-based politics that defends existing social arrangements and undermines popular movements. For a variety of reasons, including the cost of litigation, the background and attitudes of judges, and the biases in the law and the Charter, the socially disadvantaged and labour unions were better off without the document. He says: "The Charter is capable of opposing every kind of discrimination but class discrimination." Joel Bakan adds that the Charter is "Just Words" and that its principles have failed to promote social justice because it is interpreted by such a conservative institution and because it cannot force government into taking action—it can only strike down initiatives already undertaken.[73] Jhappan adds that most of the rights and freedoms are of a negative variety, with the guarantee of minority-language education rights being the best example of positive rights.[74]

The left consequently argues that corporations have been some of the biggest winners in Charter litigation. Concentrating on "users," Gregory Hein shows that corporations, not women or minority groups, are the single biggest interest in taking Charter cases to the courts, as seen in Figure 19.1. But Mandel and Hein are not the only ones to hold that business has also been a major beneficiary. The editors of *Charting the Consequences: The Impact of Charter Rights on Canadian Law and Politics* remind us that many Charter rights have been extended to corporations and that businesses have used the Charter "to challenge all variety of legislative measures."[75]

FIGURE 19.1   ORGANIZED INTERESTS IN COURT, 1988–1998

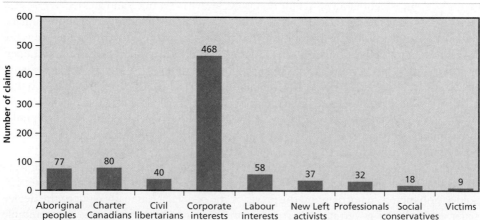

Source: Greg Hein, "Interest Group Litigation and Canadian Democracy," Choices (Montreal: Institute for Research on Public Policy) Vol. 6, No. 2 (March 2000), p. 9. Reproduced by permission of Institute for Research on Public Policy (IRPP, Montreal).

Liberal governments brought in the **Court Challenges Program** to level the playing field for disadvantaged interests, and Conservative governments abolished it. Moreover, the Charter has often caused internal divisions within such groups over whether to pursue a legal or political strategy, and these groups' agendas "have had to conform to a more liberal, individualistic path than they might otherwise have chosen to follow."[76]

Although there is a grain of truth in the arguments of both left and right, the consequences of adding the Charter to the Canadian constitution are probably not as drastic as either contends. Despite all the criticism of its decisions, the Court found that most of the challenged laws were *not* violations of the Charter; in a high proportion of other cases, it invoked the reasonable limits clause to allow laws to stand even though they violated one Charter right or another. When governments chose to defend existing laws, they were usually successful, and much effort is now put into "Charter-proofing" new laws so that they will not likely be subject to judicial challenge. James Kelly argues that the development of a rights culture *within government* and the elevation of the Department of Justice to central agency status in the drafting of new legislation have reduced the potential for judicial power; instead, he speaks of "legislative activism."[77] On the other hand, the new political role of the courts has sometimes been exploited by the politicians. The latter are "often quite relieved to have controversial and unpredictable issues transformed into 'nonpartisan' questions about rights and about the correct interpretation of the Constitution to be taken off their hands and resolved in the courts."[78]

Dialogue between Legislatures and Courts

Going beyond the left–right critiques, many scholars now talk about a "dialogue" between legislatures and courts. Such a dialogue is likely to result in incremental changes in legislation rather than judicial rejection of entire laws. Janet Hiebert and Kent Roach have provided the most comprehensive and balanced analyses of the interplay between the Supreme Court and Parliament. They both conclude that the definition of rights and freedoms should not be the prerogative of the courts alone. Parliament also has a role to play—it "shares responsibility with the judiciary for determining how the Charter should direct social conflicts."[79] Parliament and the courts look at many Charter issues from understandably different perspectives, neither of which is right or wrong. Hiebert finds that Parliament has sometimes been too deferential to the judicial definition of rights and freedoms and too inclined to revise laws so that they will meet the Court's legalistic standards rather than what legislators really feel is in the public interest. The *Chaoulli* decision in 2005 regarding waiting times in the public health care system contained a heated debate among the judges themselves regarding the issue of deferring to legislators on such an obviously political rather than legal issue. It is the clearest case yet of individual rights usurping collective values, and demonstrates that judicial activism does not always come from the left.

CONCLUSION

The protection of civil liberties in Canada historically occupied an intermediate position between the parliamentary sovereignty of Britain and the judicial review of the United States. The adoption of the Charter of Rights and Freedoms in 1982 had a profound effect on the operation of the whole Canadian political system in transferring power from politicians and legislatures to judges and courts. However, the reasonable limits and notwithstanding clauses in the Charter are unique Canadian responses and reassert the involvement of politicians in the process of defining rights and freedoms.

The significance of the Charter is such that it is linked to almost every other chapter of this book. Primarily related to Chapter 17 on the Constitution and Charter 24 on the Judiciary, it also has an impact on the institutions of government—the executive, bureaucracy, and Parliament—which are subject to Charter constraints. But Charter decisions have also affected many socio-economic issues discussed in Part 2, such as Aboriginals, official languages, gender, ethnocultural and religious minorities, corporations, unions (and labour more broadly), and age—even relations with the United States. Similarly, the mass media, elections, political parties, and advocacy groups have also been subjects of Supreme Court decisions based on the Charter.

DISCUSSION QUESTIONS

1. What are the advantages and disadvantages of the "reasonable limits" clause in the Charter?

2. What are the advantages and disadvantages of the "notwithstanding" clause in the Charter?

3. Are Canadian fundamental freedoms and other democratic values better protected since 1982? Why or why not?

4. Does legalized Charter politics inherently favour business interests and discriminate against those with social disadvantages?

5. Does the Charter discourage traditional political activity?

6. Should Parliament play a larger role in the definition of rights and freedoms in Canada?

MindTap®   FOR MORE INFO GO TO **http://www.nelson.com/student**

NOTES

1. Peter Hogg, *Constitutional Law of Canada*, student ed. (Toronto: Carswell, 2006).
2. Alexander Alvaro, "Why Property Rights Were Excluded from the Canadian Charter of Rights and Freedoms," *Canadian Journal of Political Science* (June 1991).
3. Although the British courts do not have such power, the European Court of Justice, part of the European Union, can make nonbinding decisions on whether British acts violate civil liberties. Moreover, the European Convention has now been incorporated into the British Human Rights Bill. Although the British courts do not have the explicit right to strike down public law that they deem to be in conflict with the European Convention, the Human Rights bill virtually obliges the government to rewrite statutes in response to criticism by the courts.

4. Radha Jhappan, "Charter Politics and the Judiciary," in Michael Whittington and Glen Williams, eds., *Canadian Politics in the 21st Century*, 7th ed. (Toronto: Thomson Nelson, 2008) and Heather MacIvor, *Canadian Politics and Government in the Charter Era* (Toronto: Thomson Nelson, 2006). See also Constance Backhouse, *Colour-Coded: A Legal History of Racism in Canada, 1900–1950* (Toronto: University of Toronto Press, 1999).

5. It was first articulated in the *Alberta Press Bill* case and used as a supplementary argument to criminal law in several cases but never on its own.

6. *Reference re Alberta Statutes*, [1938] S.C.R. 100.

7. *Saumur v. City of Quebec*, [1953] S.C.R. 299.

8. *Switzman v. Elbling and Attorney-General of Quebec*, [1957] S.C.R. 285.

9. *Roncarelli v. Duplessis*, [1959] S.C.R. 121. In *Chaput v. Romain*, [1955] S.C.R. 834, police had broken up a private meeting of Jehovah's Witnesses, and in *Lamb v. Benoit*, [1959] S.C.R. 321, the police arrested Jehovah's Witnesses for distributing their literature. In all three cases, action of the authorities was ruled contrary to the rule of law.

10. *Cunningham v. Tomey Homma*, [1903] A.C. 151. However, the federal power over naturalization and aliens had allowed the Court to overturn an earlier anti-Asian law in BC in *Union Colliery Co. of B.C. Ltd. v. Bryden*, [1899] A.C. 580.

11. Ian Greene, *The Charter of Rights* (Toronto: Lorimer, 1989), p. 18; Backhouse, *Colour-Coded*.

12. Thomas Berger, *Fragile Freedoms*, rev. ed. (Toronto: Clarke Irwin, 1982). Greene also refers to the secret trials held in connection with the Gouzenko spy affair in 1945, in *The Charter of Rights*, p. 21. See also Chapter 11.

13. Walter Tarnopolsky, *The Canadian Bill of Rights*, 2nd rev. ed. (Toronto: McClelland and Stewart, 1975); Christopher MacLennan, *Toward the Charter: Canadians and the Demand for a National Bill of Rights, 1929–1960* (Montreal: McGill-Queen's University Press, 2003).

14. *R. v. Drybones*, [1970] S.C.R. 282. The Indian Act created a liquor offence that had harsher penalties for Indians than the equivalent offence for non-Indians.

15. *Brownridge v. The Queen*, [1972] S.C.R. 926; *A.-G. Ont. v. Reale*, [1975] 2 S.C.R. 624; and *Lowry and Lepper v. The Queen*, [1974] 26 D.L.R. (3rd) 224; *Robertson and Rosetanni v. The Queen*, [1963] S.C.R. 651; *A.G. Can. v. Lavell and Isaac v. Bédard*, [1974] S.C.R. 1349; *Hogan v. The Queen*, [1975] 2 S.C.R. 574; *Oil, Chemical and Atomic Workers International Union v. Imperial Oil Ltd. and A.-G. B.C.*, [1963] S.C.R. 584; *Walter v. A.-G. Alta.*, [1969] S.C.R. 383; *Morgan v. A.-G. P.E.I.*, [1976] 2 S.C.R. 349; *A.-G. Can. and Dupond v. Montreal*, [1978] 2 S.C.R. 770; and *Nova Scotia Board of Censors v. McNeil*, [1978] 2 S.C.R. 662.

16. Peter Russell, "The Political Purposes of the Canadian Charter of Rights and Freedoms," *Canadian Bar Review* (March 1983).

17. For a more comprehensive account, see Heather MacIvor, *Canadian Politics and Government in the Charter Era*; Robert J. Sharpe and Kent Roach. *The Charter of Rights and Freedoms*, 3rd ed. (Toronto: Irwin Law, 2005); Thomas Bateman, et al., *The Court and the Charter: Leading Cases* (Toronto: Emond Montgomery, 2008); and James B. Kelly and Christopher P. Manfredi, eds., *Contested Constitutionalism: Reflections on the Canadian Charter of Rights and Freedoms* (Vancouver: UBC Press, 2009).

18. *R. v. Oakes*, [1986] 1 S.C.R. 103; and Janet Hiebert, *Limiting Rights: The Dilemma of Judicial Review* (Montreal: McGill-Queen's University Press, 1996).

19. *R. v. Sharpe*, [2001] 1 S.C.R. 45.

20. *R. v. Big M Drug Mart Ltd.*, [1985] 1 S.C.R. 295. Of course, Big M itself had no religion, but "worshipped only the Almighty Dollar." Michael Mandel, *The Charter of Rights and the Legalization of Politics in Canada*, rev. ed. (Toronto: Wall & Thompson, 1994), p. 316; *R. v. Edwards Books and Art Ltd.*, [1986] 2 S.C.R. 713 (Chief Justice Dickson's famous passage about a restful, recreational Sunday is located on p. 770); *Zylberberg et al. v. The Director of Education of the Sudbury Board of Education* (1988), 65 O.R. 641 (Ont. C.A.); *Alder v. Ontario*, [1996] 3 S.C.R. 609; *Re Davis* (1982), Can. Charter of Rights Ann. 9.1-1 (Alta. Prov. Ct.—Fam. Div.); *B. (R.) v. Children's Aid Society of Metropolitan Toronto*, [1995] 1 S.C.R. 315; *Jack and Charlie v. R.*, [1985] 2 S.C.R. 332; *Multani v. Commission scolaire Marguerite-Bourgeoys*, [2006] 1 S.C.R. 256; *S.L. v. Commission scolaire des Chênes*, [2012] 1 S.C.R. 235; and *Loyola High School v. Quebec (Attorney General)*, [2015] S.C.C. 12.

21. *Ford v. Quebec (Attorney General)*, [1988] 2 S.C.R. 712; *Devine v. Quebec (Attorney General)*, [1988] 2 S.C.R. 790; *Irwin Toy Ltd. v. Quebec (Attorney General)*, [1989] 1 S.C.R. 927; *RJR-MacDonald Inc. v. Canada (Attorney General)*, [1995] 3 S.C.R. 199; and *Canada (Attorney General) v. JTI-Macdonald Corp.*, [2007] 2 S.C.R. 610.

22. *R. v. Keegstra*, [1990] 3 S.C.R. 697; and *R. v. Zundel*, [1992] S.C.R. 731.

23. *RWDSU v. Dolphin Delivery Ltd.*, [1986] 2 S.C.R. 573; *B.C.G.E.U. v. British Columbia (Attorney General)*, [1988] 2 S.C.R. 214; and *RWDSU, Local 558 v. Pepsi-Cola Canada Beverages (West) Ltd.*, [2002] 1 S.C.R. 156.

24. *Ramsden v. Peterborough (City)*, [1993] 2 S.C.R. 1084; *MacKay v. Manitoba*, [1989] 2 S.C.R. 357; *Osborne v. Canada (Treasury Board)*, [1991] 2 S.C.R. 69; *Thomson Newspapers Co. v. Canada (Attorney General)*, [1998] 1 S.C.R. 877; *Libman v. Quebec (Attorney General)*, [1997] 3 S.C.R. 569; and *Harper v. Canada (Attorney General)*, [2004] 1 S.C.R. 827.

25. *Canadian Newspapers Co. v. Canada (Attorney General)*, [1988] 2 S.C.R. 122; *Canadian Broadcasting Corp. v. New Brunswick (Attorney General)*, [1996] 3 S.C.R. 480; *Dagenais v. Canadian Broadcasting Corp.*, [1994] 3 S.C.R. 835; *New Brunswick Broadcasting Co. v. Nova Scotia (Speaker of the House of Assembly)*, [1993] 1 S.C.R. 319; *R. v. Mentuck*, [2001] 3 S.C.R. 442; and *Toronto Star Newspapers Ltd. v. Ontario*, [2005] 2 S.C.R. 188.

26. *R. v. Butler*, [1992] 1 S.C.R. 452; and *R. v. Skinner*, [1990] 1 S.C.R. 1235.

27. *Reference re Public Service Employee Relations Act, Labour Relations Act, and Police Officers Collective Bargaining Act of Alberta*, [1987] 1 S.C.R. 313. Two other simultaneous cases completed the "labour trilogy": *Public Service Alliance of Canada v. The Queen*, [1987] 1 S.C.R. 424; and *Saskatchewan v. Retail, Wholesale and Department Store Union*, [1987] 1 S.C.R. 460. See also *Lavigne v. Ontario Public Service Employees Union*, [1991] 81 D.L.R. (4th) 545 (S.C.C.); Joel Bakan, *Just Words: Constitutional Rights and Social Wrong* (Toronto: University of Toronto Press, 1997); *Dunmore v. Ontario (Attorney General)*, [2001] 3 S.C.R. 1016; and *R. v. Advance Cutting and Coring Ltd.*, [2001] 3 S.C.R. 209. The reversal case was *Health Services and Support—Facilities Subsector Bargaining Assn. v. British Columbia*, [2007] 2 S.C.R. 391. But see also *Ontario (Attorney General) v. Fraser*, [2011] 2 S.C.R. 3.

28. *Canadian Disability Rights Council v. Canada*, [1988] 3 F.C. 622; *Sauvé v. Canada (Attorney General)*, [1993] 2 S.C.R. 438; and *Sauvé v. Canada (Chief Electoral Officer)*, [2002] 3 S.C.R. 519.

29. *Dixon v. British Columbia (Attorney General)*, [1989] 59 D.L.R. (4th) 247 (B.C.S.C.); and *Reference re Provincial Electoral Boundaries (Sask.)*, [1991] 2 S.C.R. 158. Other cases have not gone as far as the Supreme Court of Canada, but the PEI electoral map was disallowed by the courts of that province, while the Alberta map was upheld.

30. *Figueroa v. Canada (Attorney General)*, [2003] 1 S.C.R. 912.

31. *Law Society of Upper Canada v. Skapinker*, [1984] 1 S.C.R. 357; *Black v. Law Society of Alberta*, [1989] 1 S.C.R. 591; and *Basile v. Attorney-General of Nova Scotia*, [1984] 11 D.L.R. (4th) 219 (N.S.C.A.).

32. *R. v. Morgentaler*, [1988] 1 S.C.R. 30; *Borowski v. Canada (Attorney General)*, [1989] 1 S.C.R. 342; *Dobson (Litigation Guardian of) v. Dobson*, [1999] 2 S.C.R. 753; MacIvor, *Canadian Politics and Government in the Charter Era* contrasts Morgentaler's fate before and after the adoption of the Charter, pp. 77–79.

33. *Rodriguez v. British Columbia (Attorney General)*, [1993] 3 S.C.R. 519; *R. v. Latimer* [2001] 1 S.C.R. 3.

34. *Operation Dismantle Inc. v. The Queen*, [1985] 1 S.C.R. 441.

35. *Chaoulli v. Quebec (Attorney General)*, [2005] 1 S.C.R. 791; *Canada (Attorney General) v. PHS Community Services Society*, [2011] 3 S.C.R. 134.

36. *Singh v. Minister of Employment and Immigration*, [1985] 1 S.C.R. 177; *Re B.C. Motor Vehicle Act*, [1985] 2 S.C.R. 486; *R. v. Beare; R. v. Higgins*, [1988] 2 S.C.R. 387; and *R. v. Malmo-Levine; R. v. Caine*, [2003] 3 S.C.R. 571. See also *R. v. D.B.* [2008] 2 S.C.R. 3 regarding sentences under the Youth Criminal Justice Act.

37. *R. v. Daviault*, [1994] 3 S.C.R. 63; *R. v. Stinchcombe*, [1991] 3 S.C.R. 326; *R. v. Seaboyer*, [1991] 2 S.C.R. 577; *R. v. Ewanchuk*, [1999] 1 S.C.R. 330; and *Application under s. 83.28 of the Criminal Code (Re)*, [2004] 2 S.C.R. 248. Janet Hiebert discusses the sexual assault cases and the interplay between the courts and Parliament in *Charter Conflicts*, Ch. 5.

38. *Hunter v. Southam Inc.*, [1984] 2 S.C.R. 145; *R. v. Dyment*, [1988] 2 S.C.R. 417; *R. v. Beare; R. v. Simmons*, [1988] 2 S.C.R. 495; *R. v. Hufsky*, [1988] 1 S.C.R. 621; *R. v. Thomson*, [1988] 1 S.C.R. 640;

R. v. Ladouceur, [1990] 1 S.C.R. 957; *Weatherall v. Canada (Attorney General)*, [1993] 2 S.C.R. 872; and *R. v. Golden*, [2001] 3 S.C.R. 679. See also *R. v. Kang-Brown*, [2008] 1 S.C.R. 456 regarding the police use of sniffer dogs.

39. *R. v. Askov*, [1990] 2 S.C.R. 1199; and *R. v. Rahey*, [1987] 1 S.C.R. 588.

40. *R. v. Hebert*, [1990] 2 S.C.R. 151; *R. v. Broyles*, [1991] 3 S.C.R. 595; *Valente v. the Queen*, [1985] 2 S.C.R. 673; *R. v. Oakes*, [1986] 1 S.C.R. 103; *R. v. Whyte*, [1988] 2 S.C.R. 3; *R. v. Holmes*, [1988] 1 S.C.R. 914; and *R. v. Vermette*, [1988] 1 S.C.R. 985.

41. *R. v. Smith (Edward Dewey)*, [1987] 1 S.C.R. 1045; *R. v. Lyons*, [1987] 2 S.C.R. 309; *R. v. Milne*, [1987] 2 S.C.R. 512; *Kindler v. Canada (Minister of Justice)*, [1991] 2 S.C.R. 779; *R. v. Latimer*, [2001] 1 S.C.R. 3; *United States v. Burns*, [2001] 1 S.C.R. 283; and *Canadian Foundation for Children, Youth and the Law v. Canada (Attorney General)*, [2004] 1 S.C.R. 76.

42. *R. v. Tran*, [1994] 2 S.C.R. 951.

43. Greene, *The Charter of Rights*, p. 172; *Andrews v. Law Society of British Columbia*, [1989] 1 S.C.R. 143; *R. v. Turpin*, [1989] 1 S.C.R. 1296; David Schneiderman and Kate Sutherland, eds., *Charting the Consequences: The Impact of Charter Rights on Canadian Law and Politics* (Toronto: University of Toronto Press, 1997), Chs. 6, 7, 8, and 9; and Bakan, *Just Words*.

44. *Suresh v. Canada (Minister of Citizenship and Immigration)*, [2002] 1 S.C.R. 3; *Charkaoui v. Canada (Citizenship and Immigration)*, [2007] 1 S.C.R. 350; Ronald J. Daniels, Patrick Macklem, and Kent Roach, eds. *The Security of Freedom: Essays on Canada's Anti-Terrorism Bill* (Toronto: University of Toronto Press, 2002); Kent Roach, *September 11: Consequences for Canada* (Montreal: McGill-Queen's University Press, 2003); Irwin Cotler, "From Professor to Justice Minister: Charter Rights and Anti-Terrorism," Institute for Research on Public Policy, *Policy Options* (November 2007); Craig Forcese, *Catch and Release: A Role for Preventive Detention without Charge in Canadian Anti-terrorism Law* (Montreal: Institute for Research on Public Policy, 2010); *R. v. Khawaja* (December 14, 2012).

45. The Bill of Rights case was *Bliss v. A.-G. Can.*, [1979] S.C.R. 183; the Charter case that overturned it was *Brooks v. Canada Safeway Ltd.*, [1989] 1 S.C.R. 1219; the Supreme Court refused to review the Ontario Court of Appeal ruling in the *Blainey* case, which found that this was not a case of reasonable limits; and *McKinney v. University of Guelph*, [1990] 3 S.C.R. 229, where the Court said it would defer to legislatures in the area of mandatory retirement. See also *Eldridge v. British Columbia (Attorney General)*, [1997] 3 S.C.R. 624; *Corbiere v. Canada (Minister of Indian and Northern Affairs)*, [1999] 2 S.C.R. 203; *Law v. Canada (Minister of Employment and Immigration)*, [1999] 1 S.C.R. 497; *Newfoundland (Treasury Board) v. N.A.P.E.*, [2004] 3 S.C.R. 381; *Gosselin v. Quebec (Attorney General)*, [2002] 4 S.C.R. 429; *Auton (Guardian ad litem of) v. British Columbia (Attorney General)*, [2004] 3 S.C.R. 657, but see *Moore v. British Columbia (Education)* (November 9, 2012); and *New Brunswick (Human Rights Commission) v. Potash Corporation of Saskatchewan Inc.* [2008] 2 S.C.R. 604. A decision of the Federal Court of Appeal in July 2012 upheld Air Canada's mandatory retirement policy with respect to pilots. See also *Withler v. Canada (Attorney General)*, [2011] 1 S.C.R. 396.

46. *Egan v. Canada*, [1995] 2 S.C.R. 513; *Vriend v. Alberta*, [1998] 1 S.C.R. 493; *M. v. H.*, [1999] 2 S.C.R. 3; *Reference re Same-Sex Marriage*, [2004] 3 S.C.R. 698. Hiebert discusses these cases and the interplay between courts and legislatures in *Charter Conflicts*, Ch. 8.

47. *R. v. Kapp*, [2008] 2 S.C.R. 483.

48. *Jones v. A.G. New Brunswick*, [1975] 2 S.C.R. 182; *Attorney General of Quebec v. Blaikie*, [1979] 2 S.C.R. 1016; *A.G. Manitoba v. Forest*, [1979] 2 S.C.R. 1032; *Reference re Manitoba Language Rights*, [1985] 1 S.C.R. 721; *Order re Manitoba Language Rights*, [1985] 2 S.C.R. 347; *Bilodeau v. Attorney General Manitoba*, [1986] 1 S.C.R. 449; *Reference re Manitoba Language Rights*, [1992] 1 S.C.R. 272; and *Société des Acadiens et Acadiennes du Nouveau-Brunswick Inc. v. Canada* [2008] 1 S.C.R. 383.

49. Kenneth McRoberts, *Misconceiving Canada: The Struggle for National Unity* (Toronto: Oxford University Press, 1997).

50. *Attorney General of Quebec v. Quebec Association of Protestant School Boards*, [1984] 2 S.C.R. 66; *Mahe v. Alberta*, [1990] 1 S.C.R. 342; and *Arsenault-Cameron v. Prince Edward Island*, [2000] 1 S.C.R. 3. In *Doucet-Boudreau v. Nova Scotia (Minister of Education)*, [2003] 3 S.C.R. 3, the Supreme Court made an interesting decision with respect to the implementation of its decisions in ruling that a Nova Scotia judge was right to order the province to speed up the construction of French-language schools.

51. *R. v. Collins*, [1987] 1 S.C.R. 265.

52. *R. v. Sparrow*, [1990] 1 S.C.R. 1075; *R. v. Sioui*, [1990] 1 S.C.R. 1025; *Delgamuukw v. British Columbia*, [1997] 3 S.C.R. 1010; *Ontario (Attorney General) v. Bear Island Foundation*, [1991] 2 S.C.R. 570; and *R. v. Marshall*, [1999] 2 S.C.R. 456 and 533.

53. *R. v. Powley*, [2003] 2 S.C.R. 207; *Haida Nation v. British Columbia (Minister of Forests)*, [2004] 3 S.C.R. 511; *Taku River Tlingit First Nation v. British Columbia (Project Assessment Director)*, [2004] 3 S.C.R. 550; *R. v. Marshall; R. v. Bernard*, [2005] 2 S.C.R. 220, *R. v. Sappier; R.v. Gray*, [2006] 2 S.C.R. 686; and *R. v. Kapp*, [2008] 2 S.C.R. 483.

54. *Reference re Bill 30, An Act to Amend the Education Act (Ont.)*, [1987] 1 S.C.R. 1148.

55. *RWDSU v. Dolphin Delivery Ltd.*, [1986] 2 S.C.R. 573; and *McKinney v. University of Guelph; Lavigne v. Ontario Public Service Employees Union*, [1991] 2 S.C.R. 211. The *Blainey* case found that a clause in the Ontario Human Rights Code allowed discrimination against women in sports organizations, and since this was inconsistent with the Charter, it was held to be of no force or effect and was later repealed. This case demonstrates how the Charter can indirectly affect the private sector, as does the *Vriend* case.

56. It has been used on about 14 other occasions of no public significance. See Tsvi Kahana, "The Notwithstanding Mechanism and Public Discussion: Lessons from the Ignored Practice of s. 33 of the Charter," *Canadian Public Administration* 44, no. 3 (2001); and MacIvor, *Canadian Politics and Government in the Charter Era*, p. 379.

57. The distinctive Quebec and Alberta approaches to the Charter are discussed in Schneiderman and Sutherland, *Charting the Consequences*, Chs. 1 and 2; see also Rainer Knopff and F.L. Morton, *Charter Politics* (Scarborough: Nelson Canada, 1992). Alberta actually used the notwithstanding clause regarding same-sex marriage, but the subsequent Supreme Court ruling that it was within federal jurisdiction made that moot.

58. Greene, *The Charter of Rights*, p. 107; and Mandel, *The Charter of Rights*, pp. 87–96.

59. Mandel, *The Charter of Rights*, rev. ed., p. 301.

60. Quoted in Ibid., p. 43.

61. Ian Brodie and Neil Nevitte, "Evaluating the Citizens' Constitution Theory," *Canadian Journal of Political Science* (June 1993).

62. Peter Russell, "The Political Purposes of the Canadian Charter of Rights and Freedoms," Institute for Research on Public Policy, *Policy Options* (February 2007).

63. Greene, *The Courts* (Vancouver: UNC Press, 2006), p. 149.

64. Russell, "The Political Purposes of the Canadian Charter of Rights and Freedoms"; Schneiderman and Sutherland, *Charting the Consequences*, Chs. 6–9; and Miriam Smith, *Lesbian and Gay Rights in Canada: Social Movements and Equality-Seeking, 1971–1995* (Toronto: University of Toronto Press, 1999).

65. Robert Martin and Philip L. Bryden debate whether the Charter is undemocratic in Charlton and Barker, eds., *Crosscurrents*, 3rd ed.

66. Seymour Martin Lipset, *Continental Divide* (New York: Routlege, 1990).

67. Andrew Heard, "The Charter in the Supreme Court of Canada: The Importance of Which Judges Hear an Appeal," *Canadian Journal of Political Science* (June 1991). See Chapter 24.

68. F.L. Morton and Rainer Knopff, *The Charter Revolution and the Court Party* (Peterborough: Broadview Press, 2000).

69. F.L. Morton and Rainer Knopff, "The Charter Revolution and the Court Party," *Osgoode Hall Law Journal* (Fall 1992); Knopff and Morton, *Charter Politics*; MacIvor, *Canadian Politics and Government in the Charter Era*, Ch. 7; and Jeremy A. Clarke, "Beyond the Democratic Dialogue, and Towards a Federalist One: Provincial Arguments and Supreme Court Responses in Charter Litigation," *Canadian Journal of Political Science* (June 2006).

70. Mandel, *The Charter of Rights*, rev. ed., p. 69.

71. Christopher Manfredi, "The Use of United States Decisions by the Supreme Court of Canada under the Charter of Rights and Freedoms," *Canadian Journal of Political Science* (September 1990).

72. Jhappan, "Charter Politics and the Judiciary," p. 193.

73. Mandel, *The Charter of Rights*, rev. ed., p. 440; and Bakan, *Just Words*.

74. Jhappan, "Charter Politics and the Judiciary," pp. 193–95.

75. Schneiderman and Sutherland, *Charting the Consequences*, p. 346, and Chs. 3 and 4. The BC Health case may soften this assessment, but see Jhappan, "Charter Politics and the Judiciary," pp. 199–200.

76. Schneiderman and Sutherland, *Charting the Consequences*, p. 344.

77. Schneiderman and Sutherland, *Charting the Consequences*, pp. 344–45; James B. Kelly, *Governing with the Charter: Legislative and Judicial Activism and Framers' Intent* (Vancouver: UBC Press, 2005) emphasizes the "Cabinet-centred" and bureaucratic approaches in the drafting of legislation, rather than judicial activism.
78. Heard, "The Charter in the Supreme Court of Canada."
79. Hiebert, *Charter Conflicts*, p. xii; Kent Roach, *The Supreme Court on Trial: Judicial Activism or Democratic Dialogue* (Toronto: Irwin Law, 2001); MacIvor, *Canadian Politics and Government in the Charter Era*, Ch. 4; and Matthew A. Hennigar, "Expanding the 'Dialogue' Debate: Canadian Federal Government Responses to Lower Court Charter Decisions," in *Canadian Journal of Political Science* (March 2004). Kelly, on the other hand, argues that the Cabinet and Department of Justice have already ensured that legislation meets Charter standards in the drafting process.

FURTHER READING

Bakan, Joel. *Just Words: Constitutional Rights and Social Wrongs.* Toronto: University of Toronto Press, 1997.

Bateman, Thomas, et al. *The Court and the Charter: Leading Cases.* Toronto: Emond Montgomery, 2008.

Borovoy, Alan. *When Freedoms Collide: The Case for Our Civil Liberties.* Toronto: Lester & Orpen Dennys, 1988.

Daniels, Ronald J., Patrick Macklem, and Kent Roach, eds. *The Security of Freedom: Essays on Canada's Anti-Terrorism Bill.* Toronto: University of Toronto Press, 2002.

Greene, Ian. *The Charter of Rights.* Toronto: Lorimer, 1989.

Hiebert, Janet. *Limiting Rights: The Dilemma of Judicial Review.* Montreal: McGill-Queen's University Press, 1996.

———. *Charter Conflicts: What Is Parliament's Role?* Montreal: McGill-Queen's University Press, 2002.

Hogg, Peter W. *Constitutional Law of Canada*, student ed. Toronto: Carswell, 2006.

Jhappan, Radha. "Charter Politics and the Judiciary," in Michael Whittington and Glen Williams, eds., *Canadian Politics in the 21st Century*, 7th ed. Toronto: Thomson Nelson, 2008.

Kelly, James B. *Governing with the Charter: Legislative and Judicial Activism and Framers' Intent.* Vancouver: UBC Press, 2005.

———, and Christopher P. Manfredi, eds. *Contested Constitutionalism: Reflections on the Canadian Charter of Rights and Freedoms.* Vancouver: UBC Press, 2009.

Knopff, Rainer, and F.L. Morton. *Charter Politics.* Scarborough: Nelson Canada, 1992.

MacIvor, Heather. *Canadian Politics and Government in the Charter Era.* Toronto: Thomson Nelson, 2006.

Mandel, Michael. *The Charter of Rights and the Legalization of Politics in Canada*, rev. ed. Toronto: Wall and Thompson, 1994.

Morton, F.L., and Rainer Knopff. *The Charter Revolution and the Court Party.* Peterborough: Broadview Press, 2000.

Roach, Kent. *The Supreme Court on Trial: Judicial Activism or Democratic Dialogue.* Toronto: Irwin Law, 2001.

© Mark Spowart/Alamy Stock Photo

5

GOVERNING

Having considered the societal and constitutional contexts of the political system and the means of linking people to government, we now begin to focus on the authorities themselves or what might be termed "governing." This section, therefore, examines the individual institutions of government in detail. These institutions are the executive, including the Crown, the prime minister, and the Cabinet; the bureaucracy or public service; Parliament, including the House of Commons and the Senate; and the judiciary. The functions and operations of each branch of government are analyzed, as are the kinds of authoritative decisions that each can make. Initially, however, Chapter 20 briefly discusses the evolution of government in Canada and then puts these institutions into the context of the policymaking process. It thus provides an overview of how these institutions interact with one another to produce public policies. It also outlines the array of policy instruments from which the authorities choose.

© Mark Spowart/Alamy Stock Photo

CHAPTER 20

The Policymaking Process and Policy Instruments

To many citizens, "Ottawa" is one big blur; it is simply "the government" or "the prime minister." Some people with more sophistication distinguish (and disparage) "the politicians," "the bureaucrats," or "the judges" but without much knowledge of who is really responsible for the decisions about which they are complaining. Although the institutions of government interact in many and mysterious ways, it is the job of political science to distinguish one from the other and to analyze how they operate both individually and collectively.

The discussion of the individual institutions of government that follows in subsequent chapters will be more meaningful if it is first put into the context of the evolution of government since 1867 and of the policymaking process. This chapter provides an overview of that process, indicating in a general way how the various institutions interact with one another in the making of public policy. This is followed by an elaboration of the concept of policy communities and networks, which was first broached in Chapter 16. The chapter ends with an overview of policy instruments—that is, the various devices among which the authorities choose to give effect to their decisions.

THE CHANGING ROLE OF THE STATE

Government was defined in Chapter 1 as the set of institutions that make and execute collective public decisions for a society. That chapter explained how most Canadians initially try to satisfy their needs and wants without government intervention—that is, in the private or voluntary sectors—but may eventually call for some kind of collective, public sector action.

Until about 100 years ago, the role of government in society was very limited, and we often refer to the period prior to 1900 as that of the "negative state."[1] Before the 20th century, people expected the government to provide for their security, internal and external, but it was otherwise an era of individual and family self-reliance and self-sufficiency. Canada had a relatively larger state role than most other countries at the time, such as in the construction of canals and railways and in Aboriginal, immigration, and tariff policies, but the wide array of public services to which we are accustomed today, such as education, health, and social programs, were essentially left to the private sector or to charitable organizations.

Over the first 85 or so years of the 20th century, however, government operations expanded enormously and directly affected citizen's lives in various ways it had not before. Thus, the period after 1900 is often called that of the "positive state." As European and North American societies became increasingly democratic, the newly enfranchised women and working classes demanded that the government intervene to a larger extent to improve their lot. Mothers' allowances, minimum wage laws, old age pensions, and public protection of children were some of the marks of the early positive state. Other aspects of government intervention were prompted by the forces of population expansion, industrialization, and urbanization, as the excess of agricultural workers migrated to cities or found other types of employment. At the provincial level, the invention of the automobile had many implications for governments, especially the demand for the construction of roads. Wars were another common catalyst for increased government activity, and the First World War (1914–18) had precisely that effect. Canada increased the size of its armed forces, and afterward governments helped soldiers to get re-established in civilian life with pensions, housing, land, training, and other benefits. Canadians had never developed an animosity to the state that is characteristic of American society, and so they found it natural to turn to the government to solve other problems with which people could not cope on their own.

Then came the Great Depression of the 1930s, and once again people sought help from the government. It was at that point that even the United States saw the need for dramatic public intervention, primarily in the form of the "New Deal." This initiative, like its diluted versions in Canada, brought the government into agricultural and other natural product marketing, more labour legislation, social security, housing, relief measures and provision of employment by means of public works projects. In many parts of the world, the Depression was barely over before the outbreak of the Second World War (1939–45), which had the usual effect of further expanding the role of government.

In the late 1930s John Maynard Keynes, a British economist, made a powerful case for a much more interventionist government. Partly in response to the Depression, he argued that when private-sector economic activity declined and less money was being spent, the government should intervene with increased spending in order to balance out the extremes of the business cycle. The government, he argued, should even borrow money in such periods and spend it on transfers to individuals or on public works that would keep the economy moving. In contrast, when the private economy got overheated and was engaged in too much spending, the government should spend less and tax more, partly to take money out of the system and partly to repay the money it had borrowed during the previous downturn (or save for the next one).

The articulation of **Keynesian economics** coincided with the arguments made by many other social scientists that there was a moral reason for government involvement in the economy. They contended that ordinary people had a right to education, health care, housing, labour standards, and social services—ideas promoted by the growing ranks of unionized workers and increasingly popular left-wing political parties. The state should step in to promote human welfare against the ravages of unemployment, poverty, illness, disability, and old age. A complementary case could be made in Canada that the government should provide transportation and communications links across the country that could probably not be operated at a profit by the private sector. Even private business interests were in favour of government intervening to stabilize the economy.

As a result of such pressures, by 1950 or so Canada (and most Western European countries) had developed into a **welfare state** and was practising at least some degree of Keynesian economics. A wide range of social programs and government transfers to individuals had been created, including unemployment insurance, family allowances, old age pensions, housing programs, and the beginnings of public health care. But the government also was heavily involved in the private-sector economy, with the Bank of Canada regulating interest rates, and the government basing its own expenditure and taxation policies on countercyclical budgeting. Virtually all political parties were committed to this core public agenda, although governments started to diverge from the principle of balancing their budgets over the business cycle, seduced into running deficits in order to satisfy all the demands that came their way, whether through spending too much or not taxing enough.

The role of government in Canada and in most Western industrialized democracies continued to grow until the mid-1980s, at which point a profound reaction set in around the world against further government intervention. An increasing consensus emerged among politicians, bureaucrats, the media, commentators, think tanks, and many citizens that "government over the past forty years has grown too big, absorbs too many resources, and is a drag on both economic performance and civic independence."[2] We had too much government expenditure, too much taxation, too much regulation, and too much government debt; governments were spending, taxing, regulating, employing, owning, and owing too much. People wanted to keep more of their hard-earned incomes, and they expected others to become more self-reliant. After about 1985, therefore, governments of all ideological persuasions were consumed with tax reduction, balancing their budgets, and downsizing and restructuring their operations in what constituted a new relationship among governments, markets, and civil society.

The parties in power in Ottawa, including both the Mulroney and the Chrétien regimes, made massive cuts in government operations. This central shift in state policy, which coincided with increasing **globalization**, involved privatizing many Crown corporations and other public programs; removing regulations, especially in areas of corporate behaviour; signing a series of free trade agreements that prohibited governments from acting in certain previously common ways; reducing government debts; cutting taxes; and providing social services of greatly reduced quality.

When referring to this new philosophy of government, the terms **neoliberalism** or **neoconservatism** are often used. These two words actually mean much the same thing in terms of a retreat from the welfare state: the government withdraws from the economy and allows it to operate on the pre-1900 capitalist principles of *laissez-faire*. Sometimes, however, the two terms are distinguished by the preference of neoconservatives to have government withdraw from *economic* policy but not from a role of promoting certain *social* values, such as the traditional role of men, women, and the family, and orthodox sexuality. Such neo- or social conservatives oppose employment equity, affirmative action, multiculturalism, and

same-sex rights, and support activist state measures to regulate behaviour in such areas as education, abortion, marriage, and freedom of expression.

In principle, it was probably a valuable exercise for politicians and bureaucrats to re-examine everything that government was doing to see if it was really necessary or whether it could be done better in other ways. It is likely important that governments adjust spending patterns to avoid reliance on deficits during good economic times. Nevertheless, the adjustment saw the poorest segment of society bear the greatest burden of this downsizing of government. Moreover, as mentioned in Chapter 8, one school of thought argued that there was never a spending problem at all—the imbalance was caused by an unwillingness to tax and an abundance of tax loopholes. These critics assert that the concern with the deficit was just an excuse to embark on a neoliberal ideological tangent to reduce the role of government and make the world safe for market forces.

By the early years of the 21st century, however, governments could no longer ignore demands for more adequate public services, including an improved health care system. Thus, federal and provincial governments started to move beyond the neoconservative consensus of the previous 15 or 20 years: they began to take in more revenues and spend more money to compensate for earlier cutbacks. Now that governments were balancing their books on an annual basis, they operated more even-handedly than in the preceding period, reacting prudently but positively to public needs that could not be met without their intervention.

Suddenly, at the end of 2008, the world economy nearly collapsed and most countries faced an economic crisis unlike anything since the Depression of the 1930s. Companies went bankrupt or laid-off a large proportion of their employees, the banks in most states required massive bailouts in order to allow them to continue to extend credit, pension plans were threatened because their funds were invested in stocks of greatly depreciated value, and government revenues dried up. In these desperate circumstances, many governments began to borrow and spend money as they never had before. As the private sector contracted, it was generally agreed that governments should provide fiscal stimulus to promote economic growth. Thus, in the 2009–10 period, the Canadian federal and provincial governments ran up huge deficits. The fiscal stability of Canadian governments over the 2000–08 period was shattered as a federal Conservative government that believed in lower taxes, balanced budgets, and debt reduction had to dramatically shift gears, running Canada's largest deficit ever in 2009 (though those of the mid-1980s were larger if adjusting for inflation).[3] By 2012 or so, the economy seemed to have improved somewhat, so that governments again began to be concerned with balancing their budgets. Toward this objective, Ottawa announced the layoff of 20 000 public servants over the following three years. Table 20.1 shows financial projections from the 2014 federal budget.

TABLE 20.1 PROJECTION OF FEDERAL GOVERNMENT REVENUES AND EXPENDITURES 2012–2013 TO 2018–2019 ($ BILLIONS)

	2012–13	2013–14	2014–15	2015–16	2016–17	2017–18	2018–19
BUDGETARY REVENUES	256.6	264.0	276.3	293.3	306.8	317.7	332.4
TOTAL EXPENSES	275.6	280.5	279.2	286.9	298.7	309.7	322.1
BUDGETARY BALANCE	−18.9	−16.6	−2.9	6.4	8.1	8.1	10.3

Source: Department of Finance Canada, 2014 Budget, http://www.budget.gc.ca/2014/docs/plan/ch4-2-eng .html. Contains information licensed under the Open Government Licence – Canada. Reproduced with the permission of the Department of Finance, 2015.

THE POLICYMAKING PROCESS

Public policy can be defined as "a course of action or inaction chosen by public authorities to address a given problem or interrelated set of problems."[4] Leslie Pal adds that every policy has three key elements: the definition of the problem, the goals to be achieved, and the instruments or means chosen to address the problem and to achieve the goals. In Chapter 1, a model of the whole political system was presented; it included such components as demands, outputs, feedback, the authorities, and the environment. Now imagine focusing in more detail on the authorities part of that model. The result would be an enlargement of that part of the system directly involved in the policymaking process and would look something like the model shown in Figure 20.1. Here, as in the model shown in Chapter 1, it should be emphasized that the process is circular and ongoing, without a definable beginning or end, in which policies adopted at an earlier stage or in a different policy field or problems that develop in the implementation stage become the reasons behind the initiation of new demands on the state.

As the model suggests, the actual policymaking process can be divided into six phases: initiation, priority-setting, policy formulation, legitimation, implementation, and interpretation. Not all policies or decisions involve such an elaborate process including all the institutions of government; indeed, many can be made unilaterally by the prime minister, the Cabinet, a minister, the bureaucracy, or the courts. But the model shows the policymaking process in its broadest form—that is, a policy that requires the passage of a new law or an amendment to an existing law and that is later interpreted by the courts. Such a model does not necessarily imply that decision makers within each phase will function with complete rationality; they may equally well act out of expediency or habit.

Initiation

The authorities are bombarded daily with hundreds of demands. These demands emanate from many different sources: the provinces and territories, opposition parties, the media, advocacy groups, lobbyists, corporations, election promises, personal concerns of ministers or

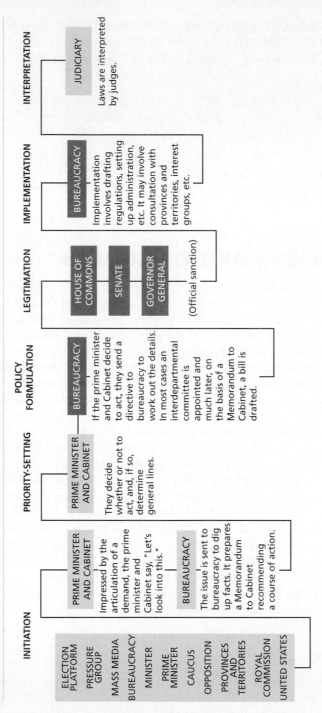

FIGURE 20.1   THE CANADIAN POLICYMAKING PROCESS

INITIATION

ELECTION PLATFORM
PRESSURE GROUP
MASS MEDIA
BUREAUCRACY
MINISTER
PRIME MINISTER
CAUCUS
OPPOSITION
PROVINCES AND TERRITORIES
ROYAL COMMISSION
UNITED STATES

PRIME MINISTER AND CABINET

Impressed by the articulation of a demand, the prime minister and Cabinet say, "Let's look into this."

BUREAUCRACY

The issue is sent to bureaucracy to dig up facts. It prepares a Memorandum to Cabinet recommending a course of action.

PRIORITY-SETTING

PRIME MINISTER AND CABINET

They decide whether or not to act, and, if so, determine general lines.

POLICY FORMULATION

BUREAUCRACY

If the prime minister and Cabinet decide to act, they send a directive to bureaucracy to work out the details. In most cases an interdepartmental committee is appointed and much later, on the basis of a Memorandum to Cabinet, a bill is drafted.

LEGITIMATION

HOUSE OF COMMONS
SENATE
GOVERNOR GENERAL

(Official sanction)

IMPLEMENTATION

BUREAUCRACY

Implementation involves drafting regulations, setting up administration, etc. It may involve consultation with provinces and territories, interest groups, etc.

INTERPRETATION

JUDICIARY

Laws are interpreted by judges.

the prime minister, the government caucus, the bureaucracy, foreign countries (usually the United States), or other forces within the internal or external environments of the political system. It is commonly observed that in many fields of policy, including economic policy and the environment, the policymaking process is increasingly internationalized.

The policymaking process is set in motion, then, when the prime minister and Cabinet, frequently termed the **government**, have been impressed with the articulation of a demand and decide to look into the matter further. On a smaller scale, a single minister may also make such a decision. Donald J. Savoie reminds us, however, not to underestimate the extent to which ministers pursue initiatives recommended to them in "mandate letters" from the prime minister.[5] If the initiative comes from the bureaucracy, it may be the result of an evaluation of existing policy ("policy evaluation") which has revealed a preferable alternative. It is at this point that a "demand" is sometimes said to become an "issue." An issue, therefore, is a demand that has made it onto the public agenda and that is under serious consideration by the authorities. In such a case, the Cabinet ordinarily sends a directive to the bureaucracy that it wants more information on the matter.

Priority Setting

The second phase of the policymaking process involves the prime minister and Cabinet again, this time in their priority-setting capacity. Responding to a course of action recommended by the public service, they decide which of the proposals they have selected for consideration are worthy of adoption. In other words, the prime minister and Cabinet (or, on lesser issues, an individual minister) must decide whether or not to take action on the issue, and, if they decide to act, they must determine the general lines of the new initiative. At this point the Cabinet may also choose which policy instrument will be most appropriate to achieve their objective. Here a major constraint is the cost of the proposal, since almost all proposals face fierce competition for scarce resources.

Policy Formulation

Once it has approved a proposal in principle, the Cabinet usually sends another directive to the bureaucracy to work out the details in what is called the policy formulation phase.

This is often a very time-consuming process that requires coordination among many federal government departments (now called "horizontal

Michael de Adder/Artizans

management"[6]) and may also involve consultation with provincial governments, interest groups, and others. Policy communities and policy networks play an increasingly important role at this stage, and questions may be referred back to the Cabinet for further direction. On major, complex policy initiatives, the Cabinet sometimes issues a "White Paper," which provides a clear indication of its intentions but still leaves room for public input with respect to details. If the proposal requires legislative action, the policy formulation stage culminates in a bill being drafted on the basis of the Memorandum to Cabinet. During this process, the minister will probably discuss the principles of the proposal with interested members of the government caucus. Once a bill has been drafted and approved by the responsible minister, it is sent to the leader of the government in the House of Commons. After reviewing its consistency with relevant Cabinet decisions, this minister reports to Cabinet and seeks authority for the introduction of the bill into the House of Commons.

Legitimation

The proposal then enters the legislative arena, that is, Parliament—the House of Commons and the Senate. The relevant minister may accept technical alterations to the bill as it proceeds through the House of Commons and the Senate, but opposition amendments often challenge the basic integrity of the original draft and are therefore not encouraged. Certainly the main intent or principle of the bill cannot be changed without going back for the Cabinet's approval. The legislative stage is referred to as legitimation because the bill is put under the scrutiny of all the democratically elected representatives of the people and made legitimate by their approval. The Cabinet and members of Parliament contribute political expertise to the process, but given the shortage of time and limited technical expertise that are characteristic of the legislative branch, most such bills are passed in "skeletal" form—that is, a statute usually contains only the general principles or objectives that the authorities want to achieve. The act then delegates authority to the relevant minister, on the advice of the bureaucracy, to issue regulations to flesh it out later in the process. The legitimation stage ends with the token approval of the governor general, which is the sign that the policy has been officially sanctioned.

Implementation

Royal assent is by no means the end of the policymaking process. Few laws attain any significance just by sitting on the statute books; they must be implemented in order to be made effective. Implementation often requires the setting up of new administrative machinery—new staff, new agencies, new field offices, and new operational manuals, among other things. It is therefore not surprising that most legislation does not automatically take effect on royal assent; it is not "proclaimed" or made operational until the government is ready to implement it.

Implementation almost always involves the drafting of detailed **regulations** by the bureaucracy, to add meat to the skeleton of the statute. These officially go by the name of "statutory instruments," but they are also called subordinate or delegated legislation and are necessary because MPs lack the time and expertise to put such technical details into the law itself. Because the regulations are not in the law, they can also be changed fairly easily and are often developed in close consultation with the outside interests affected. Even though they have the same legal standing as if they were part of the enabling statute, the regulations that a law authorizes the executive to make are given only slight scrutiny by Cabinet, ministers, or Parliament, and thus are almost the exclusive preserve of the bureaucracy. Regulations are published in the *Canada Gazette* but are not likely to be noticed except by the interests to whom they apply. Afterward, the regulations are scrutinized by the **Standing Joint Committee on the Scrutiny of Regulations**.

Interpretation

The policymaking process may well end, at least for the time being, with the implementation phase. But if new legislation is involved, it is often subject to judicial interpretation, and its constitutionality may even be challenged in the courts. Thus, it is appropriate to add a sixth phase to the policymaking process, that of judicial interpretation. Judges always impact a law by means of how they interpret it, but if a statute is actually challenged in the courts, the judiciary must decide whether its provisions are contrary to the Charter of Rights and Freedoms or to the division of powers between federal and provincial governments.

POLICY COMMUNITIES REVISITED

Although this section of the book focuses on the operation of the authoritative "governmental" policymaking institutions, they operate within a never-ending "political" environment. Indeed, if various interests know that the government has a problem under active consideration, they usually step up their attempts to influence the course of that discussion. Moreover, policymakers find it increasingly advantageous, if not necessary, to consult and even to develop partnerships with relevant organized external interests. It is in this context that the concept of **policy communities** should be mentioned again.[7]

Although Figure 20.1 provides a framework in which to understand the policymaking process and the interaction of various government institutions in general, it must be emphasized that distinctive policy communities, participants, and processes are involved in different policy fields. Power is dispersed in many directions, and different politicians, bureaucrats, advocacy groups, and individuals participate in different sectors of public policy. As seen in Figure 16.1, the prime minister, Cabinet, and central policy structures are at the core of the whole process regardless of subject matter, but each policy community has its own "lead government agency," normally a department of government: Health for health policy, Fisheries and Oceans for fisheries policy, and so on.

Each lead agency is surrounded by associated Crown corporations and regulatory agencies, such as the CBC and CRTC, which operate at arm's length from the Canadian Heritage department or the Canadian Transportation Agency and VIA Rail, which are linked to Transport Canada. Also connected are the major advocacy groups, lobbyists, think tanks, corporations, provincial governments, and parliamentary committees interested in their respective policy fields.

Interaction between government departments and advocacy groups has always been a two-way street, and bureaucrats have found it helpful to consult with affected interests as they went about making policy. For a variety of reasons, however, the reliance of policymakers on outside groups has become much heavier in recent years, a development that Donald Savoie phrases as "looking elsewhere for policy advice."[8] Governments now regularly integrate citizens, groups, clients, experts, academics, and other stakeholders as part of the policy development process.

government department. All of these, at least in the short run, are substitutes for any substantive government action. It is commonly held, for example, that a royal commission—which will study a given issue at length with independence from government departments—is appointed to take the heat off the government in connection with some problematic situation in the hope that by the time the commission reports, the problem will have evaporated.

Exhortation

The third degree of intervention is often called exhortation. This instrument goes one step further than the symbolic response because in this case the government urges the public to change its behaviour in some way. Exhortation uses persuasion in an attempt to secure voluntary compliance with government objectives without recourse to threats or rewards. Commercials to encourage physical fitness are one example, while others are pleas to restrain wage demands, to conserve the use of water or electricity (without any accompanying rate increases or regulations), or to promote the use of "blue box" programs or condoms. Because of its need to change public attitudes in order to accept major policy shifts, especially the Free Trade Agreement and GST in the 1980s, and to highlight equity and lifestyle policy concerns, the federal government became the country's largest advertiser. But in the new governance environment since then, information-based instruments have become even more important.[11]

Tax Expenditures

Tax expenditures are the fourth category of policy instrument. These consist of tax credits and tax deductions that individuals or companies can claim by spending money in certain ways: putting money into retirement plans, contributing to political parties, making certain kinds of investments, donating to charities, and so on. Some of these tax expenditures are included in Table 20.2. Tax expenditures do not actually involve taxing or spending by government; rather, they are tax-based incentives to use individual or corporate income in particular ways. Tax expenditures are widely used because they are basically invisible and do not attract much criticism; they neither *seem* to cost any money nor involve any sort of coercion. Although tax expenditures are a popular policy instrument, as corporations and individuals vigorously seek them out in order to reduce their taxes, it should be added that they do come at a cost. They result in reducing the amount of revenue that the government would otherwise receive by billions of dollars a year, funds that it could use for redistributive purposes. Those who do not qualify for such tax credits, especially lower-income individuals, end up paying higher taxes to make up the difference.

TABLE 20.2 SELECTED REVENUES FORGONE THROUGH SELECTED TAX EXEMPTIONS OR CREDITS, PROJECTIONS 2014 ($ MILLIONS)

REGISTERED PENSION PLANS	$14 475
REGISTERED RETIREMENT SAVINGS PLANS	$ 8125
PARTIAL INCLUSION OF CAPITAL GAINS	$ 4970
CHARITABLE DONATIONS	$ 2305

Source: Department of Finance Canada, Tax Expenditures and Evaluations 2014, *http://www.fin.gc.ca/taxexp-depfisc/2014/taxexp14-eng.asp.*

Public Expenditures

The fifth policy instrument, one that is much more obvious, is public expenditures. Unlike tax expenditures, public spending involves the actual disbursement of funds acquired and controlled by the state. The size of modern government budgets is an indication of how frequently the authorities have tried to solve problems by spending public money. The instrument of public expenditure has many subcategories. Governments provide transfer payments to individuals, such as in employment insurance, old age security, and social assistance programs; the federal government advances money to the provinces for health care, postsecondary education, and many other purposes; governments subsidize farmers, fishers, artists, and orchestras, and give contracts, grants, loans, and loan guarantees to corporations. The **spending power** of the federal government—that is, its right to spend money for any purpose it chooses—was discussed in Chapter 18. The government also engages in public expenditure in the provision of public services—helping the unemployed to find jobs, defending the country, or engaging in research. In an age of retrenchment, of course, governments tried to avoid this policy instrument and reduced their expenditures and services quite dramatically in the mid-1990s, only to spend much more during the recession of 2008–09, and then again reduce spending in 2012. Table 20.3 indicates some key areas of spending by the federal government during 2014.

TABLE 20.3 FEDERAL GOVERNMENT EXPENSES, 2013–2014 ($ MILLIONS)

MAJOR TRANSFERS TO PERSONS	
ELDERLY BENEFITS	$ 41 786
EMPLOYMENT INSURANCE BENEFITS	$ 17 300
CHILDREN'S BENEFITS	$ 13 136
MAJOR TRANSFERS TO OTHER LEVELS OF GOVERNMENT	
SUPPORT FOR HEALTH & SOCIAL PROGRAMS	$ 42 785
FISCAL ARRANGEMENTS	$ 15 610
GAS TAX FUND	$ 2107
DIRECT PROGRAM EXPENSES	
OTHER TRANSFER PAYMENTS	$ 36 698
CROWN CORPORATIONS	$ 7484
NATIONAL DEFENCE	$ 21 511
ALL OTHER DEPARTMENTS AND AGENCIES	$ 50 217
PUBLIC DEBT CHARGES	$ 28 220
TOTAL EXPENSES	$276 827

Source: Department of Finance Canada, Annual Financial Report of the Government of Canada Fiscal Year 2013–2014, https://www.fin.gc.ca/afr-rfa/2014/report-rapport-eng.asp. Contains information licensed under the Open Government Licence – Canada. Reproduced with the permission of the Department of Finance, 2015.

Regulation

Government becomes more intrusive still when it chooses the sixth policy instrument, regulation.[12] Almost every aspect of our lives is now regulated by government, although we may not always be aware of it. Examples, some of which are actions of provincial, territorial, or municipal governments, include minimum wage laws; highway speed limits; restaurant and elevator inspections; the grading of eggs; building codes; consumer product safety; rent controls; pollution emissions; hunting, fishing, driver, and liquor licences; store hours; seat belt laws; Canadian content on radio and television; telephone rates; and bilingual labelling.

Government regulation interferes with individual or corporate freedom more than any instrument listed previously and is therefore more frequently criticized. But such regulations were obviously considered necessary by one government or another in order to promote some greater public purpose, such as public health, safety, or order; Canadianization; bilingualism; or protection from corporate exploitation. Many of these regulatory functions have been delegated to semi-independent regulatory agencies, such as the CRTC, marketing boards, provincial rent control tribunals, or liquor licensing boards, rather than to regular government departments. Such agencies are discussed in more detail in Chapter 22. Ordinarily, the less money the government has available to spend, the more heavily it will rely on the instrument of regulation. But in the era of neoliberalism, the corporate sector, in particular, pressed for a pulling back of government in this area too, resulting in a large amount of **deregulation**. International trade agreements have also constrained the use of regulatory instruments.

Taxation

Taxation, the seventh type of policy instrument, is generally considered even more intrusive than regulation because although it also has the effect of constraining behaviour, it actually takes something tangible away from the individuals or corporations on whom it is imposed.[13] Previous chapters have provided some indication of the number and kinds of taxes levied by both federal and provincial governments. Personal and corporate income and general sales taxes are used by both levels of government, to say nothing of excise taxes; special taxes on alcohol, tobacco, amusement, and gasoline; natural resource levies; health insurance premiums; payroll taxes; and the property taxes used by municipal governments. Just as in the case of regulation, however, many people are not conscious of all the taxes they pay. Thus, the relative extent of the intrusiveness of taxation is somewhat subjective, depending on the awareness of and degree of constraint imposed by various taxes, as well as on the level of consciousness of and support for the public programs they are used to finance. The public became aroused over the very visible GST, for example, even though it largely replaced the invisible manufacturers' sales tax.

In the post-1985 environment, governments primarily balanced their budgets by reducing expenditures rather than by increasing their taxes. Indeed, as soon as a balanced budget was in sight, there were demands for tax cuts. However, various charges and fees for special benefits and services grew in use.[14] Besides user fees imposed on many social services in recent years, bridge and highway tolls are becoming more common. Table 20.4 indicates the taxes paid to the federal government in 2014.

TABLE 20.4 TAXES PAID TO FEDERAL GOVERNMENT, 2014 ($ BILLIONS)

PERSONAL INCOME TAX	$ 130.8
CORPORATE INCOME TAX	$ 36.6
NON-RESIDENT INCOME TAX	$ 6.4
OTHER TAXES (INCLUDING SALES TAX) AND DUTIES	$ 46.1
TOTAL	**$219.9**

Source: Department of Finance Canada, Annual Financial Report of the Government of Canada Fiscal Year 2013–2014, https://www.fin.gc.ca/afr-rfa/2014/report-rapport-eng.asp.

Public Ownership

The eighth policy instrument is **public ownership**, typically taking the form of a Crown corporation. Governments routinely regulate and tax private companies, but "nationalizing" them—taking them into public ownership or creating Crown corporations—represents a greater degree of government intervention. At both federal and provincial levels, the "collectivist" streak in the Canadian political culture has given rise to the existence of a large number of important state enterprises, including the Canadian Broadcasting Corporation, the Canada Mortgage and Housing Corporation, the Bank of Canada, Farm Credit Canada, Atomic Energy of Canada Ltd., Canada Post, and electric power corporations in most provinces. Governments usually resort to public enterprise only as a last resort, however, when taxation and regulation fail to meet their objectives.[15] In the wave of neoliberalism that swept the country in the late 1980s and 1990s, the Mulroney and Chrétien governments **privatized** several Crown corporations, including Air Canada and Canadian National, putting such organizations (back) into the private sector. Several provincial governments also privatized some of their Crown corporations.

State of Emergency

Baxter-Moore completes his catalogue of nine policy instruments with the **state of emergency**.[16] In a situation of natural disasters, domestic insurrection, or external military threat, governments can usually invoke emergency powers. These powers give special coercive functions to the police and military to assist the government in achieving its policy objectives. The use of the **War Measures Act** in the First and Second World Wars is the best Canadian example. Prime Minister Trudeau invoked the War Measures Act again in 1970 to deal with the FLQ crisis. Armed forces personnel suddenly appeared on the streets of Ottawa and Montreal, the police were given extraordinary powers, and certain civil liberties were suspended.[17] Acknowledgment that the War Measures Act was inappropriate in these circumstances led to the creation of a less coercive Emergencies Act in 1988. Happily, the state of emergency is used less frequently than any other policy instrument in Canada, although the armed forces have been called on to help out in natural disasters, such as severe flooding in Manitoba, the ice storm in central Canada and New Brunswick, and a heavy snowfall in Toronto.

CRITICAL APPROACHES

The *rational choice approach* argues that in the initiation and priority-setting phases the Cabinet will choose to look into and then act on those issues that are in its self-interest. In choosing policy instruments, the authorities will similarly be guided by the anticipated reaction of marginal voters who will keep them in office. Rational choice theory not only helps scholars understand why authorities enact the policies that they do, but it also provides a guide for political actors when they consider different policy options. Drawing on certain assumptions about people's motivations, governments may use rational choice theory in an effort to predict the consequences of different policy options—for example, about increasing or decreasing social welfare benefits, implementing user fees at hospitals, and so on.

The *class analysis approach* assumes that whatever the formal phases of the policy-making process, the political system ultimately responds to the demands of the bourgeoisie or corporate elite. This school of analysis emphasizes the connections between the state and corporate elites and, although discovering much evidence of such linkage, adds that "the economically powerful have not had to seek political office directly [for] their interests are usually served by those who are already there."[18] Class analysis finds that the political, bureaucratic, and corporate elites share many characteristics and values.[19]

THE ENVIRONMENT AS A CASE STUDY

The issue of the environmental protection provides a good example (oversimplified here) of how a public problem can be addressed by using different policy instruments. Historically, of course, the pollution problem was ignored, and was later given token, symbolic recognition without any substantial government action. The third stage was exhortation, which has now been common for some time. Individuals have been urged by government to "reduce, reuse, and recycle," such as in blue box campaigns, and corporations have been drawn into signing voluntary agreements to reduce their emissions of various kinds. There have also been tax expenditure programs designed to cope with environmental pollution—corporate tax credits for investing in abatement equipment, for example.

Governments have been spending increasing amounts of their budgets on environmental measures, such as air and water testing and cleaning up certain sources of toxic soil contamination. Several provinces, especially Ontario, are using public funds to promote wind power, including subsidies to corporations to create jobs in the manufacture of windmills and other technology. Government environmental monitoring and assessments should also be mentioned as a particular form of public expenditure in this policy area. Many new projects, federal and provincial, are now subject to environmental assessments before they can proceed, assessments which may lead to complete approval, total rejection, or more likely, modification to reduce their environmental impact. Interestingly enough, the global economic meltdown of 2008 led the Canadian government to exempt some emergency infrastructure projects from such environmental assessments.

The broader problem of greenhouse gas emissions and climate change has led the public to expect governments to get more serious about protecting the environment, with the oil sands in Alberta and coal-fired electricity plants in several provinces as particular targets. Federal and provincial governments are contemplating various regulatory and taxation schemes to deal with such problems. One idea is a carbon tax, pioneered in different forms in Quebec and British Columbia, and the focus of the Liberal party's Green Shift concept in the 2008 federal election.[20] A carbon tax could be imposed on heavily polluting companies or on consumers who buy carbon-based products such as coal, oil, natural gas, and gasoline. An alternative policy instrument would be the imposition of concrete caps on such polluters (regulation), or a cap and trade system in which companies that are capped could buy credits from others that operated below their regulated limit. While there remains much dispute about which of these approaches is more realistic and effective, some environmentalists advocate using both taxation and regulation simultaneously. There is probably no appetite to nationalize companies in order to force them to reduce their pollution of the environment, but some environmentalists are almost at the point of advocating the declaration of a state of emergency!

The environmental assessment of proposed petroleum pipeline routes has become one of the most important current issues in Canadian politics and reflects an increasing internationalization of the policymaking process. At one point the new concern with global warming in the United States was expected to lead that country to adopt measures that would restrict imports of petroleum from the Alberta oil sands. It was also suggested that in order to avoid this problem, Canada might simply decide to adopt President Obama's environmental standards, with matching emission targets set by Canada and the U.S. for both the Kyoto (1997) and Copenhagen (2009) conferences, though Canada has not matched the U.S. on more recent targets. On the other hand, Obama has so far rejected the construction of the Keystone XL pipeline between Alberta and oil refineries in Texas. The issue of greenhouse gas emissions in the *production* of such petroleum in Alberta was also part of the opposition to the pipeline in the United States.

At the same time, the Canadian petroleum industry and both the federal and Alberta governments were promoting the construction of the Northern Gateway pipeline linking the oil sands to the port of Kitimat, British Columbia, after which the oil would be transported to Asia. As far as the promoters of the oil sands were concerned, the temporary rejection of Keystone made it even more imperative to develop the Gateway pipeline. In this case, the primary opposition was not from importing countries, but rather from Aboriginals and other environmentalists who feared the damage from a pipeline breach or an oil tanker disaster. This issue also illustrates the necessity of federal and provincial governments working together in their choice of policy instruments.

In 2012, the federal budget was seen by some as a significant step backward by the federal government in the realm of environmental protection, reducing the role of the state in the interests of promoting economic growth, especially resource development in western Canada:[21]

- delegating environmental regulation to the provinces, especially assessment of smaller projects
- reducing the number of environmental assessments of big projects by giving the minister the power to decide which industrial projects require one

- setting a two-year limit on National Energy Board assessments and giving the cabinet the power to allow a project rejected by the NEB
- stripping requirements from the Fisheries Act that would protect fish habitat
- reducing protection for species at risk
- repealing the Kyoto Protocol Implementation Act
- scrapping the National Round Table on the Environment and the Economy, which repeatedly recommended the adoption of a carbon tax
- reducing the ability of non-governmental organizations to intervene in the environmental assessment process

While Canada has set emissions targets at 30 percent below 2005 levels by 2030, the 2015 budget seemed to maintain a low priority on environmental matters, including no mentions of climate change, emissions, or global warming. On the other hand, the new Justin Trudeau government made climate change one of its priorities and immediately began working with the provinces to address the issue.

CONCLUSION

This discussion of the policymaking process and policy instruments provides a framework on which to hang the remaining chapters of the book, which deal in greater detail with the individual institutions of government. It also introduces the range of devices available to a government in order to achieve its objectives.

This chapter is closely linked to the four which follow, dealing with each of the main institutions of government in turn. It is also related to Chapter 16, which discussed the role of advocacy groups and policy communities in the policymaking process.

DISCUSSION QUESTIONS

1. How did the environment of governance change after 1900? After 1985? After 2000? After 2015? Why?

2. Do the individual characteristics of the prime minister and Cabinet ministers affect their policy choices? Are electoral considerations dominant in their choices?

3. Do you agree with the sequence of policy instruments outlined in the continuum of degree of government intrusiveness?

MindTap® FOR MORE INFO GO TO **http://www.nelson.com/student**

NOTES

1. John C. Strick, *The Public Sector in Canada: Programs, Finance and Policy* (Toronto: Thompson Books, 1999).
2. Leslie A. Pal, *Beyond Policy Analysis: Public Issue Management in Turbulent Times*, 4th ed. (Toronto: Nelson Education, 2010), Ch. 2.

3. CBC News, Canada's Deficits and Surpluses, 1963–2014. http://www.cbc.ca/news2/interactives/ canada-deficit/ (accessed April 22, 2015).

4. Ibid., p. 2.

5. Donald J. Savoie, *Governing from the Centre: The Concentration of Power in Canadian Politics* (Toronto: University of Toronto Press, 1999), pp. 137–38, 324, 343. See also Greg Flynn, "Rethinking Policy Capacity in Canada: the Role of Parties and Election Platforms in Government Policy-Making," *Canadian Public Administration* (June 2011).

6. Herman Bakvis and Luc Juillet, *The Horizontal Challenge: Line Departments, Central Agencies and Leadership* (Ottawa: Canada School of Public Service, 2004).

7. Pal, *Beyond Policy Analysis*, Ch. 6; Paul Pross, *Group Politics and Public Policy*, 2nd ed. (Toronto: Oxford University Press, 1992), especially Ch. 6; William Coleman and Grace Skogstad, *Policy Communities and Public Policy in Canada* (Mississauga: Copp Clark Pitman, 1990); and previously discussed in this book in Chapter 16.

8. Donald Savoie, *Breaking the Bargain: Public Servants, Ministers, and Parliament* (Toronto: University of Toronto Press, 2003), Ch. 6; Pal, *Beyond Policy Analysis*; Donald E. Abelson, *Do Think Tanks Matter? Assessing the Impact of Public Policy Institutes* (Montreal: McGill-Queen's University Press, 2002); and Kathy Brock, ed., *Delicate Dances: Government and the Nonprofit Sector in Canada* (Montreal: McGill-Queen's University Press, 2002).

9. Nicolas Baxter-Moore, "Policy Implementation and the Role of the State," in Robert Jackson, Doreen Jackson, and Nicolas Baxter-Moore, eds., *Contemporary Canadian Politics: Readings and Notes* (Scarborough: Prentice Hall Canada, 1987). Other sources on the subject include Michael Howlett, M. Ramesh and Anthony Perl, *Studying Public Policy: Policy Cycles and Policy Subsystems*, 3rd ed. (Toronto: Oxford University Press, 2009); Pal, *Beyond Policy Analysis*, Ch. 4; and Privy Council Office, *Guide to Making Federal Acts and Regulations*.

10. Baxter-Moore, "Policy Implementation and the Role of the State," p. 340.

11. Pal refers to exhortation as information-based instruments.

12. John C. Strick, *The Economics of Government Regulation: Theory and Canadian Practice*, 2nd ed. (Toronto: Thompson Books, 1993).

13. There is some disagreement about these points in the literature: sometimes regulation is considered more intrusive than taxation, and at other times taxation is treated as a type of regulation.

14. Pal, *Beyond Policy Analysis*, p. 178.

15. Allan Tupper and Bruce Doern, *Public Corporations and Public Policy in Canada* (Montreal: Institute for Research on Public Policy, 1981).

16. See also Craig Forcese and Aaron Freeman, *The Laws of Government: The Legal Foundations of Canadian Democracy* (Toronto: Irwin Law, 2005), Ch. 10.

17. H.D. Munroe, "Style within the Centre: Pierre Trudeau, the War Measures Act, and the Nature of Prime Ministerial Power," *Canadian Public Administration* (December 2011).

18. Dennis Olsen, *The State Elite* (Toronto: McClelland and Stewart, 1980), p. 21; and Wallace Clement, *The Canadian Corporate Elite: An Analysis of Economic Power* (Toronto: McClelland and Stewart, Carleton Library, 1975).

19. Clement, *The Canadian Corporate Elite*, p. 258; Robert Presthus, *Elite Accommodation in Canada* (Toronto: Macmillan, 1973); and Rodney Haddow, *Poverty Reform in Canada 1958–1978: State and Class Influence on Policy Making* (Montreal: McGill-Queen's University Press, 1993).

20. Cameron D. Anderson and Laura B. Stephenson, "Environmentalism and Party Support in Canada: Recent Trends outside Quebec," *Canadian Journal of Political Science* (June 2011); Thomas J. Courchene and John R. Allan, eds., *Canada: The State of the Federation 2009: Carbon Pricing and Environmental Federalism* (Kingston: Institute of Intergovernmental Relations, 2010).

21. *Ottawa Citizen*, May 8, 2012; Douglas Macdonald, "Harper Energy and Climate Change Policy: Failing to Address the Key Challenges," and Francois Bregha, "Time to Get Serious about the Strategic Environmental Assessment of Federal Government Policies and Plans," in Christopher Stoney and G. Bruce Doern, eds., *How Ottawa Spends 2011–2012* (Montreal: McGill-Queen's University Press, 2011).

FURTHER READING

Anderson, Cameron D., and Laura B. Stephenson. "Environmentalism and Party Support in Canada: Recent Trends outside Quebec," *Canadian Journal of Political Science* (June 2011).

Bakvis, Herman, and Luc Juillet. *The Horizontal Challenge: Line Departments, Central Agencies and Leadership*. Ottawa: Canada School of Public Service, 2004.

Barker, Paul. *Public Administration in Canada*. Toronto: Thomson Nelson, 2008.

Baxter-Moore, Nicolas. "Policy Implementation and the Role of the State: A Revised Approach to the Study of Policy Instruments," in Robert Jackson, Doreen Jackson, and Nicolas Baxter-Moore, eds., *Contemporary Canadian Politics: Readings and Notes*. Scarborough: Prentice Hall Canada, 1987.

Courchene, Thomas J., and Donald Savoie, eds. *The Art of the State: Governance in a World Without Frontiers*. Montreal: Institute for Research on Public Policy, 2003.

Inwood, Gregory J. *Understanding Canadian Public Administration: An Introduction to Theory and Practice*, 3rd ed. Toronto: Pearson Education Canada, 2009.

Lecours, André, ed. *New Institutionalism: Theory and Analysis*. Toronto: University of Toronto Press, 2005.

Pal, Leslie A. *Beyond Policy Analysis: Public Issue Management in Turbulent Times*, 4th ed. Toronto: Nelson Education, 2010.

Pross, Paul. *Group Politics and Public Policy*. Toronto: Oxford University Press, 1986.

Strick, John C. *The Public Sector in Canada: Programs, Finance and Policy*. Toronto: Thompson Books, 1999.

CHAPTER 21

The Executive: Crown, Prime Minister, and Cabinet

During a royal visit, Queen Elizabeth is often mistakenly referred to as Queen of England rather than Queen of Canada. Some Canadians are very attached to the monarchy, but others cannot understand what all the fuss is about. On the political front, few events in Ottawa match the suspense and speculation of the naming of a new Cabinet or a major Cabinet shuffle. Almost every member of Parliament aspires to become a Cabinet minister someday, and many ministers hope to become prime minister. These positions offer many perks and much prestige, the possibility of influencing public policy, and the opportunity to do favours for the minister's constituency, province, and supporters.

As seen in Chapter 20, the prime minister and Cabinet are active in many phases of the Canadian policymaking process. Their decisions will sometimes be overturned by the courts, and occasionally even by Parliament, and are usually based to a considerable extent on advice from the bureaucracy. But in the end, the prime minister and Cabinet do make and are responsible for making the biggest political decisions in the country. This chapter begins with a discussion of the Crown, including the monarch and governor general, and then examines the political executive: the prime minister and Cabinet.

THE CROWN

To classify Canada as a **constitutional monarchy** means that it is a democracy headed by a king or queen. In other words, the Queen is the Canadian head of state, but she reigns according to the Constitution. Canada is also said to have "dual executive"—the formal and largely symbolic executive powers are given to the Queen or governor general, but the effective executive is made up of the prime minister and Cabinet.

The concept of the **Crown** revolves around the head of state and can be defined as the collectivity of executive powers exercised by or in the name of the monarch. Many executive decisions are made as "advice" to the Queen or governor general, even if the latter have no real control over them and must *take* the advice, whatever they think of it. But the Crown is not only the collectivity of executive powers; it also represents the entire state and embodies what belongs to the people collectively—it is a metaphor for the country. This can be seen in Crown corporations (state-owned corporations) or Crown lands (state-owned lands). The Crown is also central to the legal system: Crown attorneys, those who prosecute crimes on behalf of society; court cases initiated in the name of the Queen referred to as *R.* (for *Regina*) *v. John Doe* or court cases against the government (*Smith v. The Queen*); branches of the judiciary called the Court of Queen's Bench; and lawyers awarded the title of Queen's Counsel (QC). The term "royal" is also widely used in Canada to refer to institutions that function for the advantage of all in the name of the Queen: the Royal Canadian Mint; royal commissions, which investigate problems for the general good; the Royal Canadian Mounted Police, whose job is to capture violators of society's laws; and the Canadian navy and air force, to which the Harper government restored the Royal label. Three important aspects of Parliament also reflect the existence of the monarchical system: royal assent, the speech from the throne, and Her Majesty's Loyal Opposition. "Loyal Opposition" demonstrates that criticism of the government has been legitimized and institutionalized in the name of the Queen.

The concept of the Crown is not widely understood by Canadians, and, as David Smith writes, it is largely "invisible" to them.[1] For example, since the Queen represents the whole state and its people, oaths of allegiance to the Queen are really pledges of support for the Canadian political system, and "God Save the Queen" really means "God help us to govern ourselves."[2] The Ontario Court of Appeal reaffirmed this point in 2014 when it rejected a Charter of Rights challenge to the Citizenship Act, which requires prospective Canadian citizens to pledge their allegiance to Queen Elizabeth, her heirs, and successors. To put the Queen's picture on stamps or coins, in classrooms or courtrooms, is not to glorify her personally but to recognize her as a unifying symbol of the state. Nearly every state finds it useful to have such a decorative, ceremonial figure.

Paul Chiasson/The Canadian Press

Queen Elizabeth in Halifax on her 2010 tour of Canada.

In speaking of the powers of the Crown, it is best to see them as being in the possession of the Queen but exercised by the prime minister and Cabinet. The monarch "holds the powers on behalf of the people," as a custodian or trustee. She does not use them, but her presence keeps those who do wield them from becoming too powerful or irresponsible. As mentioned, it is an elegant fiction that the government of the day *advises* the Crown on the use of such powers. It is probably beneficial to divert favourable popular feelings to the harmless head of state because politicians might abuse such popularity. Another misconception is that the adoption of the

Constitution Act, 1982 affected Canada's relationship with the Queen. That act allowed Canada to amend its own Constitution, but it left the Queen in place as the Canadian head of state: it is a personal relationship that no longer has anything to do with the country called the United Kingdom.

The Governor General

The Queen of Canada, Elizabeth II, is also Queen of other countries, and normally resides in Britain. That means that she needs a local representative in Canada—the governor general—to carry out her work. The Queen remains the Canadian head of state, but in her absence the governor general may perform any of her functions and exercise any of her powers. Until 1926 the governor was a double agent: besides being the representative of the Queen, he was an agent of the British government, and as long as Canada was a British colony, the governor general exercised authority over Canada on behalf of the British Cabinet. Today, the governor general is only the personal representative of the Queen and has no connection whatsoever to the British government. The Canadian prime minister actually chooses the governor general, who serves a term of approximately five years. Surprisingly, even though the Canadian government has made the selection ever since 1926, it continued to appoint British governors general until 1952, when Vincent Massey became the first Canadian-born person to hold the post. Since then, as indicated in Table 21.1, Canada has alternated anglophone and francophone appointments.

Powers of the Crown

The Queen of Canada and governor general derive their powers, all of which are exercised according to firmly established constitutional conventions, from three main sources: the

TABLE 21.1   GOVERNORS GENERAL SINCE 1952

VINCENT MASSEY	1952–1959
GEORGES VANIER	1959–1967
ROLAND MICHENER	1967–1974
JULES LÉGER	1974–1979
EDWARD SCHREYER	1979–1984
JEANNE SAUVÉ	1984–1990
RAMON HNATYSHYN	1990–1995
ROMEO LEBLANC	1995–1999
ADRIENNE CLARKSON	1999–2005
MICHAËLLE JEAN	2005–2010
DAVID JOHNSTON	2010–

Constitution Act, 1867, the Letters Patent, and the royal prerogative. Section 9 of the 1867 act declared that the "Executive Government and Authority of and over Canada is … vested in the Queen," and section 15 made her commander-in-chief of Canada's military forces. Among the powers explicitly given to the Queen was the one to appoint extra senators, as was done by Brian Mulroney in 1990, although this must be done on the recommendation of the governor general. The 1867 act gave the governor general the power to appoint regular senators and judges, to appoint the Speaker of the Senate, to give royal assent to legislation, and to recommend money bills to the House of Commons. In addition, it referred to the governor general's power to summon and dissolve Parliament. The governor in council, meaning the Cabinet operating in the name of the Crown, was given the power to appoint lieutenant governors and other officers. In fact, the act was somewhat sloppy in not carefully distinguishing between the governor general and the governor in council, which suggests that even as early as 1867 the governor was normally expected to act on the advice of the Cabinet.

The Letters Patent is an obscure document that creates the office of governor general and accords it additional authority. The Letters Patent confers on the governor general all powers of the monarchy with respect to Canada, including the title of commander-in-chief; the power to appoint and remove ministers and judges; the power to summon, prorogue, and dissolve Parliament; and the power of pardon.

The royal prerogative or **prerogative powers** involve the residual authority of the Crown that remains from the days when the monarch was almost absolute. These are unwritten powers, based on custom and convention, although some of them, such as the right to summon and dissolve Parliament, are mentioned in constitutional documents. Being unwritten, the prerogative powers are vulnerable to parliamentary restriction. Many such powers have been taken away and given to the prime minister and Cabinet—such as the power to negotiate treaties, to declare war and peace, and to appoint ambassadors—and those that remain could be removed if Parliament chose to do so.

Despite the impressive theoretical list of powers possessed by the Queen and governor general, there is no doubt that in a democratic age almost all of them must be exercised on the advice of the government—the prime minister and Cabinet—of the day. It would be totally unconstitutional, for example, for the governor to refuse to give assent to any piece of legislation. The Queen retains a minimal right to decide on certain honours herself, primarily within Britain, but the governor general was stripped of this power in the early years of this century. Canada created its own set of honours in 1967, the Order of Canada, and although such honours are presented by the governor general, they are decided on by a nonpartisan committee consisting of the chief justice of Canada, the clerk of the Privy Council, the deputy minister of Canadian Heritage, the chair of the Canada Council, the president of the Royal Society of Canada, and the chair of the board of the Association of Universities and Colleges of Canada.

The most important prerogative power of the governor general is the appointment of the prime minister, but this must be performed on the basis of constitutional convention.[3] In ensuring that the office of prime minister is never vacant, the governor general normally relies on the operation of political parties and elections, and does not have far to look. On two occasions in the 1890s, however, the governor had to help find a person to be prime minister. That action was necessitated by the sudden death of John A. Macdonald in 1891 and then of John Thompson in 1894; in both cases the Conservative Party did not possess an obvious successor. Political parties are better organized today and prefer to choose their own leader. Thus, if the position should suddenly become vacant, such as through the death of the prime minister, the Cabinet or government caucus would name an acting leader pending a leadership convention.

The two most controversial acts of Canadian governors general took place in 1896 and 1926, when the governors in question acted on their own initiative in refusing the advice of the prime minister and Cabinet. The first concerned the question of making government appointments. Many appointments are officially authorized by the governor general, even though they are actually decided on by the prime minister or Cabinet. But the Charles Tupper government chose to retain office after it lost the 1896 election (awaiting defeat in the House of Commons), and during that interim period presented a list of several recommended appointments to the governor general, which he refused to make. Lord Aberdeen felt that the newly elected Wilfrid Laurier, rather than the recently defeated Tupper, had the authority to make such appointments. Aberdeen thought that he was actually upholding the Constitution by interceding.

The second famous case of refusing government advice, the **King–Byng dispute**, had to do with the **dissolution of Parliament**. The governor general normally summons and dissolves Parliament on the advice of the prime minister, but in 1926 Lord Byng refused Mackenzie King's request to dissolve Parliament and call an election. In this case, the governor general was primarily influenced by the fact that a motion of censure against the government regarding a scandal in the Customs Department was under debate in the House of Commons. The request for a dissolution appeared to be an attempt to curtail debate and avoid defeat in the Commons. In addition, the opposition Conservatives actually had more seats than the governing Liberals (who had been kept in power with the support of the Progressives), and an election had been held only eight months before. Thus, it seemed logical to Lord Byng to try to avoid an election when an alternative government might be available. As in 1896, the governor general felt that he was upholding the Constitution against unscrupulous behaviour by the government rather than subverting the democratic will.

Most authorities agree that King's advice was inappropriate and that Byng was right in not automatically acceding to the advice.[4] However, many feel that Byng should not have refused until he had assured himself that another viable government could be found. When the Meighen government fell three days later and was granted a dissolution, it appeared that the governor had acted in a partisan way. Byng's position was further weakened when the electorate returned King to office in the subsequent election. Although it should not be thought that the voters understood the subtleties of the situation or cast their ballots primarily on this issue, the impression that the election results repudiated the governor general's intervention has probably made subsequent governors wary of using their prerogative powers.

Another potential prerogative power of the governor general is to dismiss a government. Constitutional convention allows a governor to do so if the government refused to resign after an election defeat or refused to resign or call an election after a clear vote of nonconfidence. This has never happened at the federal level in Canada, and is never likely to, but the power was exercised as recently as 1975, amid great controversy, in Australia. Indeed, in the 1981–82 period in Canada, Governor General Edward Schreyer contemplated forcing an election (tantamount to dismissing a government) if the Trudeau government had not backed down from its threat to impose unilateral amendment of the Constitution and agreed to further negotiations with the provinces.

Some controversy remains among constitutional scholars about the possession and use of such reserve powers, but all agree that in normal circumstances governors general must act on the advice of the prime minister and Cabinet. One view is that in a democratic age, the governor general should leave even outrageous government behaviour to the will of the electorate, while the other is that certain rare exceptions continue to exist. But even in this scenario, before they invoke such emergency powers, "they must be sure they have reached the danger point, and that their actions will stand up to the subsequent judgment of other institutions and the people."[5]

The governor general has been called an insurance policy against the unforeseeable, or a "constitutional fire extinguisher" whose emergency powers can be used only "when normal controls cannot operate and a crisis gets out of hand."[6] Andrew Heard adds that "governors should intrude into the democratic process only to the minimum extent absolutely required for the basic functioning of Parliamentary government."[7] Since the governor general is to be seen as an impartial symbol of unity, any act that could remotely be interpreted as partisan must be avoided.

Two incidents occurred toward the end of 2008 that raised the question of the governor general's discretionary powers. The Harper government had passed legislation for fixed election dates, with the next to be held in October 2009. However, rather than wait for the parliamentary defeat of his minority government, the PM asked the governor general for an election in October 2008. Most observers felt that the loophole in the law that allowed for an earlier election was designed to come into play only upon the defeat of the government on a nonconfidence vote. Given that the previous election had been a full two years before, however, no one really expected the governor general to object, even if Harper was breaking the spirit of his own law.

Sean Kilpatrick/The Canadian Press

Governor General David Johnston presents the Medal of Bravery awarded to their father to Brandon and Riley Kelly at Rideau Hall in February, 2012.

That election returned the Harper government, but it was still short of a majority. In December, when the minister of Finance introduced economic update amidst a worldwide economic meltdown, the three opposition parties signed a coalition agreement in which they declared their readiness to form an alternative Liberal–NDP government with Bloc support to avoid an election. In order to cling to power, Harper delayed a scheduled nonconfidence vote, and then preempted it with a request to Governor General Michaëlle Jean to prorogue Parliament to avoid the vote altogether. Harper argued that he would recall Parliament at the end of January 2009 with a full-fledged budget which would reflect the real economic situation and involve ample public consultation in the interim. Expert opinion was divided as to whether the governor general should accept the PM's advice to prorogue because if this request was not a violation of the unwritten rules of the constitution (constitutional convention), it came very close. But in the end, she took his advice, perhaps believing that a cooling-off period was in order and also in part because the government had survived a confidence vote on the Throne Speech shortly before the economic update. It was the only case since 1874 in which any controversy over the prerogative power of *prorogation* was even raised, and scholars continue to debate whether the governor general still had the power to refuse a prorogation in 2008 and if she did, whether she should have used it.[8]

Upon the expiry of Michaëlle Jean's five-year term in September 2010, Harper chose David Johnston as the next Governor General. It was widely noted that Johnston's credentials included a strong legal background, including experience as a former Dean of Law.

Other Functions of the Crown

Leaving aside these very rare occasions involving the prerogative powers, the governor general primarily plays a ceremonial and symbolic role. The governor general presides over the opening of Parliament, reads the government's speech from the throne, lays a wreath at the national war memorial on Remembrance Day, and leads Canada Day celebrations. The governor general is busy entertaining at Rideau Hall: visiting dignitaries must be wined and dined, honours and awards must be presented, and receptions of every kind must be held. Foreign diplomats present their credentials to, and take their leave of, the governor general acting as the Canadian head of state. Although extremely busy in Ottawa, the governor general is also expected to maintain a hectic travel schedule, promoting national unity, demonstrating moral leadership, encouraging good works as patron of many service organizations, and performing other ceremonial functions across the country. Adrienne Clarkson and Michaëlle Jean both excelled at such functions.[9] The Stanley and Grey Cups were both donated by governors general, and the Lady Byng trophy by Lord Byng's wife.

Between the drastic intervention of the emergency powers and the glamorous ceremonial activities lies the traditional advisory role of the monarch: the right to be consulted, the right to encourage, and the right to warn the prime minister in their regular confidential meetings.[10] Prime ministers often find it helpful to confide certain problems to the governor general that cannot be discussed with anyone else, and on which the governor general might be able to offer sage advice. Because of the limited term of office, the usefulness of the governor general to a Canadian prime minister cannot compare with the Queen's 60 years of experience in advising a British prime minister in this respect, but many prime ministers have spoken warmly of these relationships.[11]

Advantages and Disadvantages of the Monarchy

The fact that the Queen's role as Canadian head of state is left over from the time that Canada was a British colony has given rise to considerable dissatisfaction with the position.[12] Some Canadians feel that it is inconsistent with their country's independent status and find that her British background and residence seriously detract from her ability to perform one of her main functions—to serve as a symbol of Canadian national unity. On the other hand, supporters of the monarchy point out that the Crown played a part in allowing French-speaking Canadians to retain rights and privileges after the Conquest,[13] and that the monarchy helps to legitimize the pluralism of society by attracting attention to groups and demands that might otherwise be overlooked. Aboriginals have a special relationship with the Crown, and their cause often benefits from the impartial prestige and media power of the monarchy. It is also argued that Canada gains from the worldwide celebrity status of the Queen and her capacity for pomp and ceremony. Moreover, apart from paying the costs of a royal visit, Canada gets all the prestige of the monarchy free of charge. The monarchy also helps to distinguish Canada from the United States, and as head of the Commonwealth, the Queen provides a link between Canada and many other countries.

Supporters of the monarchy also point out that the great advantage of dividing the head of state and head of government functions is to make the best use of the prime minister's time. The latter can concentrate on the serious business of governance, while the governor general tends to the ceremonial functions. It is difficult for a partisan prime minister to serve as a symbol of unity, but, being above the partisan fray, it is theoretically possible for a governor general or Queen to do so. Even if a consensus developed over an alternative head of state for the country, however, Canada has made it almost impossible to amend the constitution in this respect. Ironically, the prorogation controversies of 2008 and 2009, together with the Harper government's efforts to bolster the position of the Crown in various ways, have actually brought the monarchy to greater public consciousness in recent years and without any noticeable demand for change.

CRITICAL APPROACHES

People often couch debates about the formal executive in Canada in normative terms: should we have a largely symbolic and unelected head of state, should we have a powerful and elected head of state as in the United States, or should we have an elected and largely symbolic head of state as in have Germany? As we mentioned in Chapter 1, assumptions about the way things are also shape our beliefs about the way things should be, and vice versa. Indeed, one argument for preserving an unelected head of state is based on two claims about the way things are, both of which implicate the *political behaviour* and *political psychology approaches*. The first claim is that unelected heads of state will not have real power in democratic countries because they lack democratic legitimacy. Elected heads of state, on the other hand, do have democratic legitimacy, and may use that legitimacy as a basis for exercising the powers of the office as independently and vigorously as they can. The second claim is that powerful heads of state are dangerous, because the head of state is effectively the symbol of a country, and people may rally around their national symbols, particularly during periods of crisis. In such a crisis, according to this line of argument, an elected head of state, with the winds of democratic legitimacy and public opinion at their back, is difficult to stop.

THE PRIME MINISTER AND CABINET

The prime minister and Cabinet are usually referred to as the **government** of the day, as in "the Trudeau government." Although the ministers are also members of Parliament, it is in their capacity as the government that they perform the leadership function in the political system.[14] We begin by examining the powers of the political executive in Canada and then discuss the pre-eminent position of the prime minister. The composition and operation of the Cabinet, including Cabinet committees, are addressed in the following sections, after which an outline of Cabinet support agencies is provided.

Powers of the Prime Minister and Cabinet

Given the importance of the prime minister and Cabinet, it is ironic that they are not provided for in the written parts of the Constitution; instead, their functions and powers rest on custom and convention. What *is* provided for in the 1867 **Constitution Act** is a Privy Council to advise the governor general in the exercise of the powers of that office. As mentioned above, at other points the 1867 act refers to the governor in council, which essentially means the Cabinet functioning as the Privy Council. In fact, the Cabinet acts as a committee of the Privy Council, but rather than merely advising the governor general, it actually makes the decisions in question. With the rare exception of governors general intervening on their own discretion, the prime minister and Cabinet exercise whatever powers are given to the Queen or the governor general in the Constitution. It is from this source that many decisions made by the Cabinet take the form of **orders in council**.

Thus, after an election, the governor general calls on the leader of the party with the most members elected to the House of Commons (or the one mostly likely to be able to command a majority of MPs) to become prime minister and to form a government. If there is any doubt about who won the election, an incumbent prime minister has the right to remain in office until defeated in the House of Commons, but the transfer of power usually takes place within a few weeks of the election and before Parliament meets. The prime minister assumes the title "Right Honourable"[15] and selects the Cabinet ministers, all of whom are sworn into the Privy Council. This allows them to use the title "Honourable" as well as the initials "PC" (Privy Councillor) behind their name. These are lifelong appointments and titles and members of former Cabinets remain in the Privy Council, such that it contains about 400 members. But only those in the Cabinet of the day are invited to Cabinet meetings, hence the concept of the Cabinet as a committee of the Privy Council. Periodically other prominent people are appointed to the Privy Council as an honour, but they are not invited to Cabinet meetings either, and the Privy Council as a whole rarely meets. The title "president of the Privy Council" can be assumed by the prime minister, but it is often bestowed on another Cabinet minister, such as the minister of intergovernmental affairs.

In normal circumstances, then, the prime minister and Cabinet exercise the powers of the Crown. These powers include the summoning, proroguing, and dissolving of Parliament and the appointment of senators, judges, and other officials. The prime minister and Cabinet, rather than the governor general, really recommend money bills to Parliament, and all international acts and the general conduct of foreign relations are the prerogative of the Cabinet, including declaring war and peace, sending troops abroad, signing treaties, appointing ambassadors, and recognizing foreign governments. The Cabinet may feel it politically advantageous to have Parliament debate these issues and may need to submit legislation to Parliament to make treaties effective, but unlike in the U.S. system, such international acts are essentially within the purview of the executive, not the legislature. In recent years, the prime minister, Cabinet, or other ministers have made several decisions based on the prerogative powers of the Crown that have been upheld by the courts when challenged, although the Supreme Court has made somewhat contradictory rulings on the extent to which such powers are subject to the **Charter of Rights and Freedoms**.[16]

Exercising the powers of the Crown is only a small part of the reason that the prime minister and Cabinet are the centre of gravity in the Canadian political system. More important is their responsibility for providing overall political leadership and determining priorities for the country. That is, the prime minister and Cabinet decide which problems to deal with, establish the general thrust and direction of new policies, and determine the spending priorities of the government. As noted in Chapter 20, the Cabinet is bombarded by demands but chooses to look into only a few of them in the initiation phase of the policymaking process, and then gives the green light to even fewer in the priority-setting phase. In the British and Canadian systems, the responsibility for initiating legislation rests primarily with the prime minister and Cabinet. As will be seen in Chapter 23, opportunities do exist for other members of Parliament to introduce bills, but most of the time of the House of Commons is set aside for government business.

The **speech from the throne** provides the prime minister and Cabinet with an opportunity to outline their legislative program at the beginning of the session, while the Constitution requires that any bill to raise or spend money must also originate with the Cabinet. The Cabinet's virtual monopoly over the passage of legislation should ensure coordination among government policies, while its total monopoly over financial legislation is designed to guarantee a close relationship between policies adopted and the funds to make them effective. Such strong executive leadership, based on tradition, necessity, and the Constitution Act, has evolved over many centuries and has generally proven itself to be an effective way to run a country. As noted below, such leadership is based on the twin concepts of collective and individual ministerial responsibility.

Beyond the powers of the Crown and this general leadership function, Cabinet power is derived from specific acts of Parliament. Almost every law delegates to a minister or the governor in council the power to make decisions of one kind or another. These include the quasi-legislative power to issue **regulations** under a law, sometimes called delegated or subordinate legislation. That is, on the advice of their bureaucrats, ministers are given the power to flesh out the bare bones of the statute with detailed stipulations that Parliament did not have the time or expertise to discuss. The Cabinet is similarly given many quasi-judicial powers, such as hearing appeals from regulatory tribunals like the Canadian Radio-television and Telecommunications Commission (CRTC).

It is also on the basis of such acts of Parliament that individual ministers are charged with supervising the administration of their departments. They provide direction and leadership, establish priorities, and transmit the prime minister's or their personal or party perspectives, all in an effort to ensure that public servants remain accountable to democratically elected leaders and public opinion. In addition, ministers are involved in Parliament, answering questions about the department's operations, defending departmental spending proposals, and piloting bills emanating from the department. Nowadays, it is common to refer to a minister's "portfolio" as including the department along with any service agencies, administrative tribunals, and Crown corporations that are linked to the minister but operate at arm's length.

The principle of individual **ministerial responsibility**—each minister being held responsible to Parliament for everything that goes on in his or her department—was once thought to entail a minister's resignation over errors of public servants, even those that the minister knew nothing about. In an age of big government, however, the principle has lost most of its meaning. Ministers can still be criticized for departmental failures and are expected to correct them, but they rarely resign except in cases of serious personal mistakes and conflicts of interest.[17] The sanction for error rests more with the prime minister (demotion or forced resignation) than with Parliament; thus it is said that ministers are also "accountable to the prime minister."[18]

The Prime Minister

The system of government that Canada inherited from Britain has traditionally been called **Cabinet government**, because the Cabinet was a collective decision-making body. But such a label does not do justice to the modern pre-eminence of the prime minister. Most observers agree that Cabinet government has been transformed into a system of **prime ministerial government**,[19] and no one doubts that the prime minister has enormous power and should be singled out for special attention.

Prime ministers have always lent their name and style to the government, such as the "Trudeau Cabinet" or the "Mulroney government," and "the ebb and flow of the fortunes of the government are directly linked to their performance."[20] Donald J. Savoie demonstrates how this pre-eminence begins before the prime minister is even sworn into office. An elaborate transition-planning process led by the Privy Council Office and involving the entire deputy minister community is designed to give the incoming PM all he or she needs to know about forming and operating a government, and many

Stephen Harper gave new meaning to the concept of prime ministerial government.

Adrian Wyld/The Canadian Press

significant decisions are made in this transition period. This process requires such a focus on one person because at that point in time, the PM is the only known member of the incoming Cabinet.[21] Party leaders who realistically expect to defeat the incumbent government now establish a partisan transition team well before the election results show whether it will be needed. The Privy Council document *Accountable Government: A Guide for Ministers* talks of the prime minister setting the general direction of government policy, choosing the principal holders of public office, deciding on the organization and procedures of the Cabinet, determining the broad organization and structure of the government, establishing standards of conduct for ministers, and having special responsibilities for national security, federal–provincial–territorial relations, and the conduct of international affairs.[22]

The pre-eminence of the prime minister over Cabinet colleagues can consequently be seen in 10 of the PM's principal powers, rights, or responsibilities, and be enumerated as follows:

- Cabinet-maker
- Chair of Cabinet meetings
- Party leader
- Chief policymaker
- Leading player in the House of Commons
- Chief personnel manager
- Controller of government organization
- Adviser to governor general
- Chief diplomat
- Public persuader

First, the prime minister is the Cabinet-maker.[23] Prime ministers select their own ministers and, subject to certain conventions discussed below, decide which portfolios to assign them. Ministers are also issued with "mandate letters" that inform them of the PM's policy expectations in their portfolio.[24] Ministers thus owe allegiance to the prime minister, who can promote and demote them, ask for their resignation, and, if necessary, dismiss them. All of these possibilities tend to keep ministers submissive if and when there is any difference in their policy priorities. Prime ministers are usually reluctant to drop or demote ministers who have outlived their usefulness, although appointment to the Senate has sometimes provided a valuable safety valve in this connection.

The prime minister's chairing of Cabinet meetings is a second main source of power. To start with, the prime minister determines the agenda of such meetings. A former Cabinet secretary wrote, for example, that for any reason the prime minister deems sufficient, the order of business may be altered, and an agenda already settled may be set aside in favour of other subjects of greater importance and urgency. The PM may suspend meetings, summon additional meetings, dispense with or extend the normal record kept by the secretary, or modify or set aside the normal rules of procedure.[25] In addition to the usual advantages of a chair, the prime minister receives advice from the Privy Council Office on various ministers' views on each agenda item and on how to achieve the PM's own objectives in the meeting. The prime minister is also advantaged by the peculiar way in which Cabinet decisions are arrived at. Rather than by motions and votes, the decision is reached when the PM summarizes the discussion and "calls the consensus." If and when this bears little resemblance to the actual tenor of the meeting,[26] ministers who do not agree with this interpretation either keep quiet or resign. Even though many decisions are now made by Cabinet committees, the prime minister decides which committees will be struck, who will chair them, who will sit on them, and which matters will be sent to them, so that this delegation of power from the full Cabinet does not necessarily reduce the PM's control.[27]

Third, the prime minister is the leader of the party. The PM's pre-eminence has probably increased over the years as political parties have become more cohesive and as election campaigns have come to focus on party leaders.[28] In fact, many ministers may have been elected on the leader's coattails. Some prime ministers, like Pierre Trudeau, may ignore and neglect the party between elections, but others, like Brian Mulroney and Stephen Harper, seemed to be more clearly in personal control of the party machine. As leader, the prime minister can control party organization, personnel, strategy, and policy.[29] Moreover, unlike other ministers, some of whom may have specialized constituencies of support within the party, the PM has been chosen by the party as a whole and can usually count on a broad base of support. As a party leader, the prime minister's power is further enhanced by his or her authority to approve of candidate nominations.

Fourth, the prime minister could be called chief policymaker. It has already been shown how the PM has the first word on government policy, such as in deciding how seriously to take the party's election platform and in issuing mandate letters to new ministers. But he or she also has the last word, whether in personal interaction with individual ministers, within the Cabinet chamber, in Parliament, or in other forums, such as the media. Modern government, of course, is too complex for a political leader to have an active role in formulating *all* policies, but the prime minister can pursue a number of personal priorities, as well as play a critical role in defining other problems.[30] In extreme examples, R.B. Bennett delivered a startling series of radio broadcasts in 1935 that committed his Conservative Party to a wide-ranging, radical "new deal"; Pierre Trudeau returned from a meeting with West German Chancellor Helmut Schmidt in 1975 to announce a major restraint program without even consulting his minister of finance; and Jean Chrétien bulldozed ahead with his Clarity Act despite widespread opposition from Cabinet colleagues and the Liberal caucus. Two of Stephen Harper's key decisions that did not even receive Cabinet discussion included the motion to recognize the Québécois as a nation and the ill-fated economic update in late 2008 that came close to causing a constitutional crisis. Occasionally, however, the PM may retreat in order to preclude the resignation of an important minister, such as sometimes occurred in the strange relationship between Jean Chrétien and his finance minister, Paul Martin.[31]

Fifth, the prime minister is the central player in the House of Commons.[32] Even though prime ministers now delegate direction of the business of the House to a government House leader, they are still expected to be there every day for the oral Question Period (in contrast to Britain, where the prime minister appears only once a week), in which they set the tone for the government as a whole.[33] However, on a day that they expect a particularly rough reception from the Opposition, prime ministers can find an excuse to absent themselves from the House and leave their ministers to answer for some problem. As the leading parliamentarian, the PM decides how government MPs will vote on almost every matter and what kind of behaviour requires expulsion from the government caucus.[34]

A sixth source of prime ministerial pre-eminence is an enormous power of appointment. Besides ministers, this includes the appointment of senators, Supreme Court and other judges, deputy ministers, heads of a wide range of government agencies, certain diplomats, and lieutenant governors. In many cases, these order in council appointments are made on a patronage basis.[35] The appointment power can serve to keep those hopeful for appointment docile and supportive, as well as to impose the PM's ideological position on much of the government.

Given the extent and power of the bureaucracy today, the prime minister's control over government organization—the seventh power—is also significant. Subject to usually routine parliamentary approval, and on the advice of the Machinery of Government section of the Privy Council Office, the PM can decide to create new departments and set out their mandates. Prime ministers can also reorganize government departments, such as Trudeau's amalgamation of Trade and Commerce and External Affairs to give the latter a more commercial orientation. Under Mulroney and Chrétien, it became more common to abolish departments or agencies and privatize Crown corporations. Stephen Harper re-amalgamated several departments and agencies that Paul Martin had severed from each other.

Eighth, the prime minister personally advises the governor general on such matters as the prorogation and dissolution of Parliament.[36] The prorogation power was prominent in 2008 and 2009, as noted above, and the threat of dissolution is sometimes thought to be important in permitting prime ministers to get their own way in conflicts with ministers, government backbenchers, or the parliamentary Opposition because members do not want to risk their seats and the many benefits of public office. The fixed election date law was supposed to eliminate this power, but a loophole allowed the prerogative to continue.

Furthermore, in an era of globalization and summit diplomacy, the prime minister increasingly overshadows the minister of foreign affairs on the world stage.[37] The prime minister doubled as secretary of state for external affairs until 1946 and still functions as Canada's chief diplomat in annual bilateral meetings with the U.S. president, annual meetings of the Group of Eight and G20 leading industrial countries, Commonwealth conferences, meetings of the Francophonie and APEC, occasional appearances at the United Nations, and endless trips abroad.

Finally, the prime minister is also the chief "public relations officer" of the government, or "public persuader."[38] Television has become the main instrument for transmitting the prime minister's message to his or her party, the government, and the public, and survival in the "battleground" of media relations "threatens to become the key determinant of prime ministerial success."[39] Pearson, Trudeau, Mulroney, Chrétien, and Martin all made televised appeals to seek support on various issues, for example, but the PM does not need to search out publicity or national media attention—it is always there.[40] A crucial position in the Prime Minister's Office is the press secretary, who organizes the prime minister's media appearances and often speaks on the PM's behalf.[41] Stephen Harper was unusual in his rather antagonistic attitude toward the media.

To perform these 10 varied and significant functions, the prime minister must be adequately advised. It is not surprising, therefore, that both Trudeau and Mulroney substantially enlarged their two principal sources of advice, the Prime Minister's Office (PMO) and the Privy Council Office (PCO), and Chrétien, Martin, and Harper relied heavily on both. These two agencies will be examined in detail below.

Given all these powers, especially in a situation of being supported by a deferential majority in the House of Commons, the PM can usually succeed in controlling the policy and personnel of government. Richard Crossman and others trace the historical evolution of the centre of power in the British parliamentary system from monarch to Parliament, from Parliament to Cabinet, from Cabinet to public service, and from public service to prime minister.[42] In many respects, in fact, the Canadian prime minister with a **majority government** in the House of Commons is more powerful than the American president, except of course in terms of international clout, because the latter must bargain with Congress to get his agenda adopted. Indeed, the expansion of the PCO and PMO, the holding of prime ministerial news conferences, the making of televised addresses to the nation, luxurious travel arrangements, and other conspicuous trappings of power have led many observers to criticize the presidentialization of the office of prime minister.[43] Although he may overstate the situation slightly, Donald Savoie writes that within the operation of the government itself, in a majority situation, the PM has few constraints other than lack of time.[44]

Savoie's conclusions are reinforced by those of Lawrence Martin in *Harperland: The Politics of Control*.[45] Martin argues that Stephen Harper had a "ravenous hunger for control" and a "puritanical discipline," as well as the amazing capacity to absorb the details of virtually every policy area. He claims that mandate letters to ministers informing them of what was expected from their departments were virtual straitjackets, and that all public pronouncements by ministers, MPs, bureaucrats, and diplomats had to be approved by the Prime Minister's Office.

Given this general understanding of prime ministerial power, many observers were surprised at how quickly British Prime Minister Margaret Thatcher (the "Iron Lady") was dumped when her party decided to remove her. In Canada, however, even unpopular PMs have stayed on well beyond their "shelf life." The main exception was in 1896 when Mackenzie Bowell's Cabinet rebelled and forced him from office, whereas, in 1963, John Diefenbaker survived a Cabinet revolt by appealing over the heads of the Cabinet to his supporters in the government caucus.[46] Jean Chrétien was pressured to retire before he planned, and lost several battles within his own party as the leadership convention approached, such as a motion to have Commons committee chairs elected rather than appointed by the PM. However, freed from the constraints of seeking re-election, Chrétien actually adopted a more activist agenda in 2003 than in the preceding nine years, including the refusal to participate in the Iraq war.

Other observers emphasize the restraints on the power of the prime minister: he or she may be forced to compromise, especially in a minority situation, even within the *internal* operation of government. The PM is certainly subject to *external* constraints, such as limited finances, a hostile media, opposition from the provinces and strong advocacy groups, international influences, and the limits to which government policy of any kind can effect societal change. The prime minister is often at the mercy of events, and they may cause a loss of public support and in turn much of his or her overall influence. Graham White concludes that the prime minister has "formidable raw power" but falls short of being an autocrat.[47]

It is worth addressing the question of how much power a prime minister has when not backed up by a majority in the Commons. In the first place, executive decisions that do not require Parliamentary approval can be made in the same confident way, whether the government has a majority or not. These include government appointments, treaties, the summoning of Parliament, and so on. For example, the Martin government ignored the House of Commons' rejection of more than one of its executive appointments. But a **minority government** has to be more careful with respect to any decisions that need to be passed by Parliament. In a typical minority situation, the prime minister must negotiate delicate compromises with one or more opposition parties, making policy concessions in return for support. The Martin government was nearly defeated in the spring of 2005, only managing to hold on by amending its budget so that it gained the approval of the NDP. But the Martin Liberals lost a motion of nonconfidence in November of that year when even the NDP voted against them because they would not compromise on health care policy.

The main question in a minority situation, then, is whether or not opposition parties are ready for an election. Do they have enough funds, are they organizationally prepared, and would the public approve if they precipitated an early vote? The PM of a minority government can function in a bullying manner if the opposition parties are afraid of causing an election and find excuses to keep a government in office. Even though Harper came to power in 2006 with five main priorities that had scant support among any opposition parties, for example, he managed to see at least four of them adopted with some concessions, and few observers saw much difference between the degree of prime ministerial control in his minority and majority governments.

PRIME MINISTERIAL TENURE AND STYLE

Out of 22 prime ministers between 1867 and 2015, nine held the position for two years or less, while 13 served at least a four-year term of office, as shown in Table 21.2. Of the 13 longest-serving PMs, nine were lawyers, eight were anglophone Protestants, four were francophone Catholics, and Brian Mulroney was a bilingual anglophone Catholic. Robert Borden came from the Atlantic region, five hailed from Quebec, four from Ontario, and R.B. Bennett, John Diefenbaker, and Stephen Harper spent their adult lives in the West. At least two (Bennett and Trudeau) were extremely wealthy, and several others (Chrétien, St. Laurent, Mulroney,

TABLE 21.2 PRIME MINISTERS OF CANADA, RANKED BY TENURE IN OFFICE*

MACKENZIE KING	21 YR., 5 MO.	LESTER PEARSON	5 YR.
JOHN A. MACDONALD	19 YR.	ALEXANDER MACKENZIE	4 YR., 11 MO.
PIERRE ELLIOTT TRUDEAU	15 YR., 5 MO.	PAUL MARTIN	2 YR., 2 MO.
WILFRID LAURIER	15 YR., 3 MO.	JOHN THOMPSON	2 YR.
JEAN CHRÉTIEN	10 YR., 1 MO.	ARTHUR MEIGHEN	1 YR., 8 MO.
STEPHEN HARPER	9 YR., 8 MO.	JOHN ABBOTT	1 YR., 5 MO.
BRIAN MULRONEY	8 YR., 9 MO.	MACKENZIE BOWELL	1 YR., 4 MO.
ROBERT L. BORDEN	8 YR., 9 MO.	JOE CLARK	9 MO.
LOUIS ST. LAURENT	8 YR., 7 MO.	KIM CAMPBELL	133 DAYS
JOHN DIEFENBAKER	5 YR., 10 MO.	JOHN TURNER	80 DAYS
R.B. BENNETT	5 YR., 3 MO.	CHARLES TUPPER	69 DAYS

*JUSTIN TRUDEAU CAME TO POWER ON OCTOBER 19, 2015.

and King) had abundant corporate connections. Lester Pearson and Mackenzie King came from elitist academic–public-service backgrounds.

Michael Whittington provides a thumbnail sketch of the styles of recent prime ministers.[48] Mackenzie King was a broker and coalition-builder who avoided taking action as much as possible; John Diefenbaker had a charismatic appeal to the public; and Lester Pearson had a collegial style of leadership with cabinet colleagues, opposition leaders, and provincial premiers. Pierre Trudeau began with a "cool" image in public but emphasized stern rationality in making decisions; Brian Mulroney was suave and businesslike but craved popularity; and Jean Chrétien promoted the image of a backwoods "hick" behind which he used his considerable political acumen to manage affairs as he intended. After his stellar performance as finance minister, Paul Martin disappointed many observers as PM, with too many priorities and not being able to make decisions until a crisis loomed. Stephen Harper was a shrewd, self-disciplined strategist and organizer with clear priorities and the will to keep his colleagues in line.[49]

Composition of the Cabinet

In theory, all Cabinet ministers are equal, although in practice this is far from the case. Pierre Trudeau periodically designated one minister as deputy prime minister, and Stephen Harper was the first prime minister afterward not to appoint such a deputy. A forerunner to the deputy prime minister was the francophone "lieutenant" of various anglophone first ministers. Ernest Lapointe (1923–41) and Louis St. Laurent (1941–48), the Quebec lieutenants of Mackenzie King, were each given wide discretion to deal with issues from that province. Macdonald used George-Étienne Cartier in a similar role for a few years, and to some extent C.D. Howe was an anglophone lieutenant to Louis St. Laurent.[50]

Below the deputy PM, if there is one, are the regular departmental ministers, each normally in charge of a single department. An informal ranking of these departments may result in variations in influence among this group of ministers, with finance, foreign affairs, justice, trade, health, treasury board, industry, human resources, defence, and transport usually being among the key portfolios. Next, a handful of ministers may not have full-fledged departments to administer but may instead be attached to larger departments, and the list is completed with the government leaders in the House of Commons and the Senate.

PMs sometimes also appoint junior ministers, variably called ministers without portfolio, ministers of state, or secretaries of state. Unlike in Britain, the Canadian tradition was that all ministers, even these junior ones, were included in the Cabinet. However, Jean Chrétien's nine or 10 secretaries of state were in the ministry but not in the Cabinet; they came to Cabinet meetings at the invitation of the PM, and attended Cabinet committee meetings when specific items of interest to them were on the agenda. Paul Martin had many junior ministers, but they were theoretically equal in status to departmental ministers, while Stephen Harper originally established a much smaller Cabinet in which almost every minister had a department to run. In 2007, he added five junior ministers called *secretaries of state*, later called *ministers of state*, who were in the ministry but not in the Cabinet.[51]

Because the Cabinet occupies such a central position in the Canadian policymaking process, every interest in the country would like to be represented around the Cabinet table.[52]

This desire alone creates pressure to expand its size. In general, the Cabinet contained about 13 or 14 ministers before 1911, then rose to around 20 until about 1960, increased to 30 under Trudeau, and to around 40 in the Mulroney period. Chrétien reduced the size of his Cabinet to 23 in 1993, but it rose to 28 in his second and third terms. Martin had close to 40, while Harper started out with only 27, which later grew to 38. Justin Trudeau began with a cabinet of 31.

Although the prime minister decides who will sit in the Cabinet, several conventions have come to constrain the PM's prerogatives in the selection of ministers.[53] In the first place, reflecting the fact that Canada is a democracy and that ministers represent the people, all Cabinet ministers must have a seat in Parliament. As in Britain, and unlike the United States, ministers sit in the legislative branch of government at the same time as they form the executive. A seat in Parliament would theoretically include a seat in the Senate. A number of senators sat in the early post-Confederation cabinets—indeed, senators Abbott and Bowell served briefly as prime minister in the 1890s—but the modern tradition is to include only one senator in the Cabinet. This senator serves as government leader in that chamber and usually has no departmental responsibilities. The Diefenbaker Cabinet functioned between 1958 and 1962 without a single senator, however, while Brian Mulroney gave Senator Lowell Murray important responsibilities as minister of federal–provincial relations in the Meech Lake period.

It is possible for the prime minister to name someone to the Cabinet who has not won election to the Commons, but convention dictates that such a person run in a by-election as soon as possible to obtain a seat. This sometimes happens when a PM appoints someone of unusual qualifications from outside parliamentary life, rather than a sitting backbencher, a practice that does not reflect well on the party's parliamentary caucus. In at least two cases such appointees lost the by-election in which they sought entry to the House and ultimately resigned from the Cabinet, confirming the view that it is impossible to sit in the Cabinet very long without a seat in Parliament.[54] Having been selected as Liberal leader in 1984 after an absence from politics, John Turner even served briefly as prime minister without a seat, but this was only temporarily legitimate.

A prime minister will usually feel compelled to appoint veteran MPs to the Cabinet, including those who served in previous Cabinets or those who ran for the party leadership. It is often thought safer to put leadership rivals into the Cabinet, subject to all its constraints, than to leave them to continue their campaigns outside. As a result, able newcomers are often overlooked. The prime minister may also be concerned with the ideological slant of the Cabinet, seeking either to balance various ideological factions within the party or else to ensure that a particular stream predominates.

The next constraint on the prime minister is the convention that each province be represented in the Cabinet. This flows from the fact that Canada is a federation and that the Senate has never performed its intended role of representing provincial interests in Ottawa. Thus, with the occasional exception of Prince Edward Island, every province that has elected a member to the government side of the chamber has always been awarded a Cabinet position. In both the Trudeau and Clark governments, the prime minister chose to appoint more than a single senator to the Cabinet in order to represent provinces that had not elected any or enough government members. Harper's first cabinet had two senators, one the government leader, and the other to compensate for his lack of an MP from Montreal. Nunavut and PEI were both represented in Harper's later cabinets, but Nova Scotia's Peter MacKay was designated to also represent PEI from 2006 to 2008 and Newfoundland and Labrador from 2008 to 2011. The convention of provincial representation usually results in some ministers being appointed only because their province needs a Cabinet representative rather than because of their merits, leaving worthy MPs from other locations excluded because their region is already adequately served.

It is not only that residents of a province feel more secure if one of their number is in the Cabinet; it is also useful for the Cabinet itself to have such provincial representation.[55] In fact, ministers essentially wear two hats: they speak for their department as well as for their province. This arrangement is functional for patronage as well as policy purposes: those government appointments and contracts awarded on a partisan basis will be the responsibility of the relevant provincial minister, often called the "political minister" for that province.

Larger provinces are not content with a single minister, of course, and in a Cabinet of 30 or more, Ontario and Quebec have sometimes exceeded ten. In such cases the ministers can be distributed so that each region within the province gains its own representative. Before 1984 and after 2011 Quebec was underrepresented in the Cabinet when the Conservatives were in power, largely because not many members were elected from that province, while the West was inadequately represented in the Pearson and Trudeau cabinets. Table 21.3 indicates the regional distribution of federal Cabinet ministers (including the prime minister) when each new government took office.

The next convention of Canadian Cabinet-making is the need for a balance of ethnic representation. A proper balance of anglophone and francophone ministers may result almost automatically from the carefully constructed provincial representation. French Canadians were underrepresented even in Liberal governments before 1963, however, and often grossly underrepresented in Conservative cabinets. It was only in the Pearson, Trudeau, and Mulroney cabinets that francophone ministers achieved or exceeded fair numerical representation. Those of other minority ethnocultural origins were not proportionately represented in Canadian Cabinets until the Clark and Mulroney periods, but every Cabinet now has a more diversified ethnic hue, including a few members from visible minority groups.

As for other social divisions, the religion factor was much more important in the pre-1900 period than it is today. A balance between Protestants and Catholics and even of different Protestant sects was originally a concern, but ministers increasingly decline to declare a religious affiliation. To some extent, prime ministers now aim to go beyond the Christian group; the Jewish community has usually claimed one or two spots since the initial appointment of Herb Gray in 1969, and other faiths have recently been represented. Nowadays, prime ministers are more concerned with appointing women to the Cabinet. The number gradually increased from one in 1957, to 11 of 38 in 2008, and to 15 of 31 in 2015. Matheson writes of a representative Cabinet as follows:

> Adherence to the representation principle first introduced by Sir John A. Macdonald in 1867 has brought together the elites from the various subcultures and provided them with a means whereby they can work together to stabilize the Canadian political system. Thus in the Canadian context the Cabinet has filled a dual role, for in addition to exercising the usual functions of executive leadership, the Cabinet has provided an arena in which the elites may counter the dysfunctional and unstabilizing effects of cultural, regional, and religious fragmentation.[56]

TABLE 21.3 REGIONAL DISTRIBUTION OF FEDERAL CABINET MINISTERS AT THE BEGINNING OF EACH MINISTRY

	ATLANTIC	QUEBEC	ONTARIO	WEST	TOTAL
MACDONALD (1867)	4	4	5	—	13
MACKENZIE (1873)	5	3	6	—	14
MACDONALD (1878)	5	4	4	1	14
LAURIER (1896)	4	5	4	1	14
BORDEN (1911)	4	5	7	2	18
BORDEN (1917)	6	4	9	3	22
MEIGHEN (1920)	5	3	6	3	17
KING (1921)	4	6	6	3	19
BENNETT (1930)	4	5	7	3	19
KING (1935)	5	5	4	2	16
ST. LAURENT (1948)	4	6	7	3	20
DIEFENBAKER (1957)	8	3	6	4	21
PEARSON (1963)	4	7	11	4	26
TRUDEAU (1968)	6	10	10	3	29
CLARK (1979)	5	5	11	9	30
TRUDEAU (1980)	5	12	12	4	33
TURNER (1984)	5	10	12	2	29
MULRONEY (1984)	5	11	11	13	40
CHRÉTIEN (1993)	3	5	10	5	23
MARTIN (2003)	5	9	17	8	39
HARPER (2006)	3	5	9	10	27
HARPER (2011)	5	4	14	15	39
TRUDEAU (2015)	4	7	11	8	31*

Source: W.A. Matheson, The Prime Minister and the Cabinet (Toronto: Metheun, 1976), updated by authors.
* 1 from Nunavut.

Once the PM has chosen the people who will form the Cabinet, they must be assigned portfolios—that is, departmental responsibilities. Certain traditions surround this task, too, such as that finance usually goes to an anglophone in whom the business community has confidence; fisheries and oceans is normally given to someone from Atlantic Canada (or BC); and agriculture has traditionally (but not always) gone to a Westerner. Justice was historically awarded to a Quebecker, primarily because of the dual system of law in that province, and public works was also often claimed by a minister from Quebec. It was sometimes argued that francophone ministers preferred Cabinet posts that dispensed a great deal of patronage, while only anglophones were trusted with the big economic portfolios.[57] Whatever truth there might once have been in this portrait, it changed dramatically under Trudeau, as he appointed the first francophone ministers of trade and commerce and finance, and many Anglo ministers also relished the distribution of patronage.

It is not normally expected that ministers will be experts in the field to which they are appointed, partly because the electorate is not likely to furnish the prime minister with members of Parliament with such credentials. Indeed, an argument can be made that a semi-expert is more dangerous than a total amateur since the latter will have enough sense to listen to the real experts within the department, while the former might try to substitute his or her limited knowledge for theirs. Thus, apart from the minister of justice being a lawyer, there is no necessary relationship between ministers' training or pre-political occupation and their departmental assignment.

Parliamentary secretaries are not Cabinet ministers, although they are sometimes seen as "ministers-in-waiting." They have been a permanent fixture on the political scene since 1943 and have been provided for in legislation since 1959. They are MPs of the government party who "assist the minister in such manner as the minister directs," which most often takes the form of making speeches on behalf of the minister, receiving deputations, sitting in for the minister in House debates (whether of government or private members' bills or on adjournment), defending the department's Estimates, and maintaining liaison with other MPs. Paul Martin gave his parliamentary secretaries added status by swearing them into the Privy Council; they then became "honourable" for life and played a larger part in substituting for the minister. Harper discontinued the practice appointing them to the Privy Council, but did mandate parliamentary secretaries to play an active role in the government, primarily by sitting on the relevant Commons standing committee.[58]

Operation of the Cabinet

Collective Responsibility, Cabinet Solidarity, and Secrecy

The Cabinet was traditionally seen as a collective decision-making body. Significant exceptions to this notion now include decisions made single-handedly by the prime minister, decisions made by Cabinet committees, and decisions made by individual ministers. Regardless of which or how many ministers are involved in making such decisions, however, the Cabinet operates on the principle of **collective responsibility**. In other words, all members of the Cabinet are collectively responsible for carrying out the government's policies. Because of the fact that individual ministerial responsibilities often overlap or have implications for other ministers, members of the Cabinet engage in extensive formal and informal consultation with each other, part of a process called horizontal management.[59]

Collective responsibility is closely related to the principle of **Cabinet solidarity**, which means that all ministers must publicly defend all Cabinet policies or else resign. The most extreme manifestation of Cabinet solidarity can be seen in terms of the annual **budget**, the most important government policy statement of the year. Regarding the fact that only the finance minister and PM usually know much about it until the budget is delivered in Parliament, Matheson writes:

> This procedure is unfortunate, in that it prevents the experience of the Cabinet from being utilized in the preparation of the budget and makes a mockery of the idea of Cabinet responsibility, since ministers must assume responsibility for something they have had little or no voice in preparing. It also illustrates the great influence of the civil servants who advise the Minister of Finance on this matter.[60]

Ministerial resignations because of policy differences are very rare in Canada, perhaps only 30 since 1867,[61] which suggests that the thought of giving up the perks of office engenders considerable flexibility in ministers' principles. In 2007, Michael Chong resigned from the Harper government on a matter of principle: not being able to support the motion that the "Québécois represent a nation within a united Canada." Cabinet solidarity has only been suspended in some cases of conscience issues such as votes on capital punishment and abortion.

Cabinet solidarity and collective responsibility are also linked to a third principle, that of **Cabinet secrecy**, confidentiality, or "cabinet confidences." Cabinet operations are shrouded in secrecy and ministers are not supposed to disclose information about its deliberations. Such confidentiality protects state secrets, protects the Cabinet against opposition and media exploitation of ministerial discord, and protects senior civil servants from identification and public criticism. Cabinet secrecy is also justified as the only way in which ministers can engage in no-holds-barred discussion of crucial issues and in which public servants can render impartial advice. Cabinet documents are not normally made public for 20 years, and, as a result, we do not know as much about how the Cabinet operates as about decision-making bodies that meet in public.[62] However, clever ministers are conscious that information represents power and that a well-timed leak can sometimes benefit them when involved in a battle within Cabinet. A Privy Council document reveals how these three principles are related:

> Ministers are bound by their oath as Privy Councillors. This oath reflects parliamentary government's core convention of Cabinet solidarity, by which Ministers share collective responsibility for the actions of government and speak to Parliament and Canadians with a single voice. This requires frank discussion in Cabinet and confidentiality in Cabinet decision making.[63]

Departmental, Institutionalized, and Prime Minister–Centred Cabinets

As mentioned, Cabinet-level decisions can be made by the prime minister alone, by the Cabinet collectively, by a Cabinet committee, or by a single minister. In this connection, a distinction is sometimes made between a **departmental Cabinet** and an **institutionalized Cabinet**. The former was characteristic of the Canadian Cabinet before 1960 or so, perhaps especially in the Mackenzie King and St. Laurent eras, in which ministers and departments were largely autonomous. Each developed its own policies and programs with little regard for central coordination and with only minimal prime ministerial interference. Strong ministers could make many decisions and policies without consulting their colleagues, and such ministers tended to remain in charge of a single department for long periods, rather than being shuffled on a regular basis. Such autonomous departmental ministers often doubled as strong regional ministers, who were also allowed to handle regional responsibilities on their own.[64] In addition, senior appointed officials usually served their careers within a single department and became "carriers of the interests, traditions, skills and memories of these particularized bureaucratic organizations."[65] At the same time, however, prime ministers could make certain decisions unilaterally, and some interfered in the operations of various departments more than others. R.B. Bennett and John Diefenbaker gained reputations for excessive interference, for example, while Louis St. Laurent was said to give too much authority to individual ministers.[66]

Despite the assumption of collective Cabinet decision making, the institutionalized or collegial Cabinet is really a product of the period after 1960 and the enormous expansion of government activity in the next 25 or so years. As society and its problems became more complex, individual ministers and departments could no longer make decisions and policies in isolation. The policies of one department almost inevitably affected those of another, necessitating more consultation and coordination with the result that ministerial collegiality replaced departmental autonomy. To some extent the need for policy coordination coincided with the view that Cabinet ministers should have greater control over the bureaucracy, while another stimulus was the development of techniques for more rational government decision making. The Pearson era was transitional in this respect, and the institutionalized Cabinet became fully developed in the Trudeau period, coinciding with his approach of increasing the rationality of government policymaking.[67]

In the new approach, the Priorities and Planning Committee of Cabinet established the overall priorities of the government so that policymaking was no longer so ad hoc and incremental. Then, the Prime Minister's Office and the Privy Council Office were expanded and strengthened so as to provide independent policy analysis to the prime minister and Cabinet. The Department of Finance and the Treasury Board Secretariat also became more effective central agencies, advising the Cabinet on its financial decisions. This change gave the prime minister and Cabinet the resources to challenge bureaucratic initiatives that were often rubber-stamped before.

Next, to avoid Cabinet overload and to enhance specialization within it, most of the Cabinet's work was done in committees. Cabinet procedures were also rigidly adhered to, including agendas, advance notice of issues, and advance circulation of background documents. In addition, new techniques of policy analysis, especially at the bureaucratic levels, provided ministers with a more rational basis for their decisions. Moreover, the attempt to go beyond traditional departmental thinking on problems led to the setting up of new ministries of state and task forces, and public discussion of policy options was encouraged by means of publishing Green Papers and White Papers on a subject before the Cabinet had made up its mind.

All of these measures tended to render Cabinet decisions more coordinated, organized, disciplined, political, and rational, hence the term "institutionalized Cabinet." Whatever the benefits of this approach, however, it also had negative implications. First, ministers did not have the time or capacity to study all the background documents that were prepared for them. Second, departmental bureaucrats often became subordinate not to their ministers but to the new central agencies, the PCO, PMO, Treasury Board Secretariat, and Department of Finance. Third, policies were often coordinated and analyzed to the point of paralysis.[68]

Fourth, as was usually the case in previous governments, a small, informal group of trusted ministers and intimate advisers emerged as a "supergroup" who made key decisions regardless of the authorized channels.[69] Finally, since this decision-making model was generally replicated at the provincial level, it had particularly negative effects on federal–provincial relations.

John Turner and Brian Mulroney dismantled much of the "rational" policymaking machinery, both of them feeling that it was too elaborate, complex, and slow. They also argued that the responsibility of individual ministers should be restored, and, being distrustful of the bureaucracy, Mulroney relied excessively on the PMO and ministers' offices, and underutilized the PCO.[70] Jean Chrétien announced his intention to revert to the St. Laurent model of a departmental Cabinet in which individual ministers and departments were allowed to look after their own affairs, and the maze of Cabinet committees was reduced. Even in an era of government downsizing, however, the complexity of issues required more coordination and consultation than the 40-year-old model could provide. The finance department began to fill the gap, partly because the budget and the deficit were the driving forces of the day, but also because some kind of coordinating device was needed. Insiders reported that the influence of other central agencies, especially the PCO, was also stronger than ever in the Chrétien government. If such a Cabinet is neither departmental nor institutionalized, Christopher Dunn suggests that we call it a "prime minister–centred Cabinet." This is consistent with the argument that we now have prime ministerial government rather than Cabinet government and is also in keeping with Donald Savoie's theme that power is increasingly concentrated around the prime minister.[71] This would be a good label for the Harper Cabinet, too.

CRITICAL APPROACHES

The *historical-institutional* and *state-based approaches* outlined in Chapter 1 have much to say about the political executive, given that it is probably the most powerful institution in the governing of Canada. It is quite remarkable how little those institutions have changed over time, and even more surprising, perhaps, because to a large extent they rest on constitutional conventions rather than written rules. The power of the prime minister and Cabinet is obvious, but they rely heavily on another institution of government, the bureaucracy, for advice.

The affairs of an increasingly large and complex state have come to depend especially on the horizontal or control bureaucracy, such as the Privy Council Office (PCO) and the Prime Minister's Office (PMO). This dependence has eroded the influence of rank-and-file politicians and led to calls for institutional reform in Parliament. Institutional reforms that increase the power of MPs, especially at the expense of party leaders and the PMO, has been a subject of considerable debate in Canadian politics over the past two decades.

Cabinet and Cabinet Committees

When a meeting of the full Cabinet is scheduled, the Privy Council Office proposes an agenda for the prime minister, including supporting documents, which is circulated in advance. Ministers sit around the Cabinet table in order of precedence, while the clerk of the Privy Council, two deputy secretaries, and one or two note-takers sit along the wall. These officials are rarely asked to speak, but they may pass notes to the prime minister. The PCO will have prepared a scenario note suggesting issues that the PM may want to raise, including guidance in getting through the meeting successfully. The chief of staff of the PMO is also usually present. Historically, the Cabinet as a whole met for about three hours once a week.

Since the mid-1960s, more and more Cabinet work has been done by Cabinet committees rather than by the full Cabinet.[72] In the Pearson, Trudeau, and Mulroney regimes, the Priorities and Planning Committee was clearly the most important Cabinet committee. Its special functions included setting priorities, allocating budgets, reviewing other committee decisions, making many important decisions itself, and supervising federal–provincial relations. Being chaired by the prime minister and containing the most important ministers also added to its significance. However, Joe Clark pioneered the two-tier Cabinet in Canada by explicitly naming an inner Cabinet instead of a Priorities and Planning (P&P) Committee. In fact, during that brief period, the full Cabinet rarely met. Chrétien did not have a P&P Committee, while Martin's was short-lived, but the latter's Operations Committee served similar purposes. Under all recent prime ministers, committee decisions were normally annexed to the agenda of the full Cabinet meeting and did not require further discussion, while the frequency of meetings of the full Cabinet declined.

Except for a short daily meeting before Question Period to rehearse responses to anticipated questions, the full cabinet under Stephen Harper only met about once a month.[73] Instead, he had two active executive committees of Cabinet, the Priorities and Planning Committee, with its traditional functions including expenditure management, and the Operations Committee. Operations met on Mondays (and additionally as required) and is seen as a firefighting body, dealing with unforeseen events, issue management, legislation, parliamentary management, and communications, including oversight of government advertising. The Operations Committee was particularly important in the minority government period, which required management of government business on a

CP PHOTO/Winnipeg Free Press-Jeff De Boo

Joe Clark, a short-term prime minister in 1979, who pioneered the two-tier cabinet.

day-to-day, blow-by-blow basis, including relations with the opposition parties in Parliament. The Priorities and Planning Committee, chaired by the PM, met on Tuesdays, and ratified most other committee decisions, including those of Operations. Harper's other Cabinet committees—called policy committees—were treasury board, social affairs, economic prosperity and sustainable growth, foreign affairs and defence, and national security.[74]

Each Cabinet committee normally meets once a week or as required, and ministers are likely to be members of two or more committees. Each committee is supported by a secretariat within the PCO that works with the sponsoring department. Unlike Cabinet as a whole, ministers may bring advisers—usually their deputy ministers—to Cabinet committee meetings when they are sponsoring an item that is subject to consideration or they are expecting to be called to speak. It has also become common practice to invite officials from the Treasury Board Secretariat and the Department of Finance, if financial considerations may be raised, or the Department of Justice, to answer legal questions.

A **Memorandum to Cabinet (MC)** is the tool that an individual Minister uses to obtain the support of Cabinet colleagues for a proposed course of action, and becomes the main decision-making instrument on which to make a committee recommendation (CR) to Cabinet.[75] Less formal instruments can also be used where no decision is required. Under Harper's "command and control" management style, policy committees were left little room for unscripted policy deliberation.

The MC starts in an individual department, which develops a policy or legislative proposal. MCs are usually drafted in response to priorities laid out in the minister's mandate letter, the speech from the throne, or the budget, but pressures may come from other sources, including international obligations. The department and minister may also have their own priority policy or legislative proposals that are not part of the announced government priorities but which they want to pursue through the Cabinet committee system. When such a proposal involves many departments, a lead minister is designated, with other ministers being considered as co-sponsors of the proposal. Agreement between sponsoring ministers and the PCO is normally required before the proposal can proceed for consideration. A draft is prepared by the lead department, and once it is sufficiently well developed, it is presented at an interdepartmental meeting of officials to which are invited all relevant departments, including central agencies. Resolution of any differences with central agencies as well as with other departments greatly enhances the chances that the proposal will succeed. The sponsoring minister is also expected to have sounded out the views of **stakeholders**, parliamentarians, especially the government caucus, and where relevant, the provinces. Once the MC is signed by the sponsoring minister, it is sent to the PCO which must give authorization to print and distribute the document, and it is the prime minister's prerogative to determine to which Cabinet committee each MC is referred.

The PCO prepares a briefing note for the committee chair that includes the positions of the Treasury Board Secretariat and Department of Finance, and most importantly, the PCO's own recommendation. The sponsoring minister presents the item to the committee and answers questions from other ministers. The departmental deputy minister and officials from the Treasury Board Secretariat (TBS), Finance, or Justice may also be asked to clarify technical issues. The PCO has several key officials in attendance, including a note taker, and the PMO normally has one or two officials in the room as well. As in the case of Cabinet as a whole, officials may pass notes to the Chair or other ministers. The Chair summarizes the discussion and where a consensus has been achieved, the item is given approval in principle. Following the meeting, the PCO issues a committee recommendation for ratification at an upcoming meeting of the P&P Committee or Cabinet as a whole. Where consensus cannot be reached in the committee, the Chair can recommend that the sponsoring minister report back with a modified proposal in order to respond to the concerns raised.

The **Treasury Board** operates somewhat differently from other Cabinet committees. It has its own support agency, the TBS, and the Cabinet committee sits in judgment as TBS officials across the table present cases for the proposed expenditure of funds. Paul Martin expanded the Treasury Board's mandate to include the previous functions of the Special Committee of Cabinet (ratifying most orders in council and regulations), while Stephen Harper added responsibility for accountability and ethics. In other words, the Treasury Board now has a policy orientation function, being responsible for the Federal Accountability Act.

When Donald Savoie asserts that "Cabinet is no longer where the important decisions are made,"[76] he is in part stating a matter of fact—the full Cabinet does not really make decisions because they have already been made in Cabinet committees. But his theme is that ministers and Cabinet as a whole are increasingly subordinate to the prime minister, who can influence decisions of Cabinet committees as well as of individual ministers in a variety of ways. The flow of government business is often from the centre to the departments, instead of from departments to the centre, and ministers have moved from being sources of power to being mere advisers to the PM. With a few exceptions, they are not even the most influential advisers, either. In short,

> power in the federal government has shifted away from line ministers and their departments towards the centre, and also, within the centre itself, power has shifted to the prime minister and his senior advisers at both the political and public service levels and away from Cabinet and Cabinet committees.[77]

Savoie has more recently further reduced the significance of the Cabinet when he talks of "court government." By that expression, he means "that effective political power now rests with the prime minister and a small group of carefully selected courtiers. I also mean a shift from formal decision-making processes in cabinet and, as a consequence, in the civil service, to informal processes involving only a handful of key actors."[78]

Central Agencies

In addition to the regular departments that advise individual ministers and which are the subject of Chapter 22, four main agencies exist to support the prime minister and the Cabinet as a whole. These **central agencies**, already mentioned in passing, are the Privy Council Office, the Department of Finance, the Treasury Board Secretariat, and the Prime Minister's Office, although the PMO, being partisan, is not officially recognized as a central agency by the bureaucracy. Another unofficial central agency is the Department of Justice (DOJ), especially since the advent of the Charter of Rights and Freedoms. James Kelly argues that the "DOJ has emerged as a central agency because the cabinet has prioritized the importance of governing with the Charter, and this has facilitated the emergence of a rights culture within the legislative process and the machinery of government."[79]

The Prime Minister's Office

The **Prime Minister's Office (PMO)**, made up of temporary, partisan loyalists, was considerably expanded by both Trudeau and Mulroney. It deals with such matters as the prime minister's relations with ministers, caucus, and party; partisan appointments; correspondence; media relations; public appearances; travel; constituency matters; and speeches; and briefs the PM on legislative proceedings. It also organizes the PM's hectic schedule of appointments and meetings, monitors political developments, offers policy advice from a partisan point of view, and helps the PM handle crises.[80]

When Brian Mulroney first came to office, he put all of his closest advisers into the PMO and expanded its influence even beyond the level it had enjoyed under Trudeau. However, after a series of political mistakes, most of these original advisers were let go and a new chief of staff brought order to the operation. Ironically, Mulroney seconded a career public servant to transform this partisan office. Under each of Jean Chrétien, Paul Martin, and Stephen Harper, the PMO had a reputation for imposing the prime minister's will on almost everything the government did. Recent PMOs have been primarily involved in communications and media relations work, being the ultimate "spin doctors" in the government, as well as exercising strict information control, especially in the Harper regime.[81]

The Privy Council Office

To cope with increased demands because of the pressure of war, the **Privy Council Office** was recognized as the Cabinet Secretariat in 1940.[82] Ever since, the PCO has been responsible for organizing and supporting the decision-making system of Cabinet and its corresponding committees. These functions serve to ensure that government policy and programs are horizontally coordinated and that the institutions of government are well structured to respond to the needs of Canadians. Prime Minister Trudeau expanded the Privy Council Office with the objective of establishing a source of policy advice for himself as prime minister, independent of regular departments, with which he could counter bureaucratic recommendations. As with his predecessors, Harper relied heavily on PCO support in providing leadership and direction to the government. Unlike the partisans of the PMO, the Privy Council Office is composed of senior, nonpartisan public servants, and the significance of the PCO can be seen in the fact that its head, the **clerk of the Privy Council and secretary to the Cabinet,** is the highest-ranking public servant in the government. The responsibilities of the Privy Council Office radiate from the clerk's three primary functions.[83]

First, the clerk is the deputy minister to the prime minister. In this capacity, the clerk renders advice and support to the PM on all issues that may affect the government. The PCO provides non-partisan advice and information from across the public service, consultation and collaboration with sources beyond the government, and information on Canadians' priorities.

Second, the clerk is secretary to the Cabinet. In this role, the clerk supports the Prime Minister in his or her role as chair of Cabinet and supports the Cabinet as a whole in its deliberations, facilitating the smooth operation of the Cabinet decision-making system. In its policy coordination and analysis role, the PCO works closely with line departments as well as with the other principal central agencies to ensure that new proposals are consistent with the government's overall objectives and policies and that all affected interests have been consulted. The PCO schedules and provides logistical support for meetings of Cabinet and Cabinet committees, as mentioned earlier. Each Cabinet committee is attached to a policy secretariat in the PCO, whose head functions as secretary for the committee. This official is responsible for managing all aspects of the operation of a committee's meetings and provides advice to the chair of the committee on agenda items. The PCO also communicates Cabinet decisions to departments and agencies to advance the government's agenda, prepares orders in council, and submits advice on government structure and organization.

Third, the clerk is the head of the public service. The clerk works with the senior leadership of that service to ensure that the government has the policy, management, and human resources capacity it requires. This public service leadership function includes the management of the appointments process for senior positions in the federal government, setting human resources policies, and ensuring that the public service is capable of meeting its changing responsibilities. Because the clerk is responsible for the quality of expert, professional advice and service provided by the bureaucracy to the political executive, he or she advises on the machinery of government and the appointment, mandates, and promotion of deputy ministers.

Besides these three basic functions, the PCO supports several other ministers in their functions. These include the leader of the government and chief government whip in the House of Commons and the leader of the government in the Senate. The Legislation and House Planning Secretariat assists these ministers in the pre-parliamentary and parliamentary stages of legislation and in maintaining communications with the opposition parties. The PCO also provides leadership and coordination in all aspects of federal–provincial relations, and a whole section of the office serves the minister of intergovernmental affairs. The Harper and Justin Trudeau governments had another "PCO minister" in charge of democratic reform.

Besides the clerk, the senior management group within the PCO includes the associate secretary to the Cabinet and deputy minister of intergovernmental affairs, and the national security advisor to the PM. Other PCO officials are the deputy secretaries of operations; plans and consultation; legislation, house planning, and the machinery of government; foreign and defence policy; and senior personnel and public service renewal. The clerk chairs a meeting of senior PCO officials every morning to identify issues to raise with the PM. The clerk and the chief of staff of the PMO meet daily (sometimes jointly) with the prime minister to review problems and, respectively, render nonpartisan and partisan advice. Even though these two key officials provide advice from different angles, they usually (but not always) have little problem in their relationship.[84] The prime minister will be supported throughout the day with detailed strategy notes with regard to attending meetings, talking to important people in the office, or making critical telephone calls, all of which helps the PCO to obtain the kind of results it considers best.

Thus, it could be said that the clerk of the Privy Council is the lynchpin of the government of Canada. This chapter has already established that the prime minister vastly outranks individual Cabinet ministers, and the clerk, the closest adviser to the PM, has his or her "safe pair of hands" on almost everything that really counts.[85] This includes preparing transition books for a new government, drafting the speech from the throne, working with the finance department and the Treasury Board Secretariat on the budget, organizing the machinery of government, writing mandate letters for ministers and deputy ministers, appointing and evaluating deputy ministers, chairing the coordinating committee of deputy ministers, keeping an eye on Memorandums to Cabinet, helping to strategize Cabinet and Cabinet committee meetings, and keeping track of federal–provincial relations. The prime minister may be the most important player in the actual making of government decisions, but the clerk will be advising on almost every one. To quote the Gomery report, "the Prime Minister sits at the apex of the political hierarchy, while the Clerk sits at the apex of the bureaucratic hierarchy. Together, they wield a great deal of power and influence."[86]

The Department of Finance

The **Department of Finance** and the Treasury Board Secretariat primarily supply financial advice to the Cabinet and have historically exercised a cautioning, restraining influence on new program proposals.[87] The finance department is responsible for the government's overall revenue and expenditure situation (macroeconomic policy), including its accumulated debt and annual deficit (if any), and advises on allocations among departments. Under the powerful deputy minister, the department is also the chief adviser on taxation policy and on transfer payments to the provinces and territories. Although reporting directly to the minister of finance and in that sense an ordinary department of government, Finance has a special responsibility of advising the Cabinet collectively on such matters, being incorporated into the process of developing Memorandums to Cabinet as well as preparing the annual budget.

The finance department has always enjoyed considerable pre-eminence, but in an age of government restraint and retrenchment, its influence necessarily increased; especially in the first term of the Chrétien regime, the finance department really determined the government's agenda.[88] When finance said that there was no more money available, for example, Red Book promises were ignored. To some extent it was the minister of finance talking, but in large measure he was repeating what his senior officials told him to say.

The Treasury Board Secretariat

The Treasury Board is a committee of Cabinet chaired by the minister called the president of the Treasury Board, who is in turn in charge of a full-fledged government department, the **Treasury Board Secretariat (TBS)**.[89] This secretariat, under the secretary of the Treasury Board, has the overall responsibility for controlling regular departmental spending, being involved in the detailed development of departmental budgets, the Estimates, and overseeing the actual expenditure of funds. The TBS is also in charge of labour relations in the public service and issues policies on personnel, administration, and finance. Although its perspective is more detailed than that of finance, the two agencies usually see things in a similar light, and the Treasury Board Secretariat's influence also increases when a government is obsessed with its deficit. As mentioned, under Stephen Harper, the mandate of the department was broadened to include supervision of the **Federal Accountability Act** and other ethics issues.

CONCLUSION

Although it is anomalous for Canada to share its head of state with other countries, there are advantages in having a head of state separate from the head of government. On a daily basis, of course, the political executive is the most significant part of the policymaking process. MPs want to be appointed to the Cabinet, and societal interests want to feel represented there. Given its importance, the composition of the Cabinet and the manner in which the political executive makes decisions are of great interest to political science. This chapter has shown how the executive decision-making process has changed over time and how power has come to be concentrated in the hands of the prime minister and central government agencies.

This chapter is primarily linked to the two that follow. As the political executive, the prime minister and Cabinet depend very heavily on the bureaucracy, the permanent executive, in both the formulation and implementation of their policies. The PM and Cabinet also need Parliament to authorize many of their decisions, but this is a more conflictual relationship that is open to public view. Being the most powerful part of the government, where almost everything in the system comes together, the prime minister and Cabinet are also related to every other chapter of the book.

DISCUSSION QUESTIONS

1. Was Lord Byng justified in 1926 in refusing to grant Prime Minister Mackenzie King a dissolution of Parliament?

2. What are the advantages and disadvantages of recognizing the Queen as our head of state?

3. Do the prime minister and Cabinet, backed up by a majority in the House of Commons, have too much power in the Canadian system of government?

4. Do you think "Cabinet government" or "prime ministerial government" is a more accurate label for the Canadian system of government? In the absence of the American system of checks and balances between president and Congress, what constraints must the prime minister live with?

5. Do you agree with the Gomery Report that the powers of the Clerk of the Privy Council should be reduced?

MindTap®   FOR MORE INFO GO TO http://www.nelson.com/student

NOTES

1. Indeed, David E. Smith, *The Invisible Crown* (Toronto: University of Toronto Press, 1995), writes that "the Crown is the organizing force behind the executive, legislature, administration, and judiciary in both the federal and province spheres of government [and] reaches into every area of government activity," p. x.

2. Frank McKinnon, *The Crown in Canada* (Calgary: McClelland and Stewart West, 1976), p. 13. See the new book, Jennifer Smith and D. Michael Jackson, eds., *The Evolving Canadian Crown* (Montreal and Kingston: McGill-Queen's University Press), 2012.

3. Edward McWhinney, *The Governor General and the Prime Ministers: The Making and Unmaking of Governments* (Vancouver: Ronsdale Press, 2005). McWhinney offers 10 rules for a governor general to follow. See also Craig Forcese and Allan Freeman, *The Laws of Government: The Legal Foundations of Canadian Democracy* (Toronto: Irwin Law, 2005), pp. 28–31.

4. See, for example, MacKinnon, *The Crown in Canada*, pp. 127–132; J.R. Mallory, *The Structure of Canadian Government*, rev. ed. (Toronto: Gage, 1984), pp. 51–57; and Eugene A. Forsey, *The Royal Power of Dissolution of Parliament in the British Commonwealth* (Toronto: Oxford University Press, 1943; reprinted 1968).

5. MacKinnon, *The Crown in Canada*, p. 124.

6. Heard, *Canadian Constitutional Conventions*, p. 123.

7. Ibid., p. 47.

8. Peter H. Russell and Lorne Sossin, eds. *Parliamentary Democracy in Crisis* (Toronto: University of Toronto Press, 2009); Peter Aucoin, Mark D. Jarvis, and Lori Turnbull, *Democratizing the Constitution: Reforming Responsible Government* (Toronto: Emond Montgomery, 2011); and Nicholas A. MacDonald and James W.J. Bowden, "No Discretion: On Prorogation and the Governor General," *Canadian Parliamentary Review* (Summer 2011).

9. Even so, Opposition parties in the Commons cut the Estimates of the GG's budget by $400 000 as a reprimand for Clarkson overspending on her circumpolar trip. Adrienne Clarkson, *Heart Matters* (Toronto: Viking Canada, 2006).

10. Walter Bagehot, *The English Constitution* (London: Collins, 1963), first published in 1867; and McWhinney, *The Governor General and the Prime Ministers*, p. 166.

11. See, for example, MacKinnon, *The Crown in Canada*, pp. 56, 101, 103; and Vincent Massey, *What's Past Is Prologue* (Toronto: Macmillan, 1963).

12. David E. Smith, *The Republican Option in Canada, Past and Present* (Toronto: University of Toronto Press, 1999), does not find a republican spirit in either Canada's past or present.

13. W.L. Morton, *The Canadian Identity* (Toronto: University of Toronto Press, 1961); Smith, *The Invisible Crown*; Colin M. Coates, ed., *Majesty in Canada: Essays on the Role of Royalty* (Toronto: Dundurn, 2006); John Fraser, *The Secret of the Crown: Canada's Affair with Royalty* (Toronto: Anansi, 2012).

14. Michael S. Whittington, "The Prime Minister, Cabinet, and Executive Power in Canada," in Michael Whittington and Glen Williams, eds., *Canadian Politics in the 21st Century*, 7th ed. (Toronto: Thomson Nelson, 2008); Graham White, *Cabinets and First Ministers* (Vancouver: UBC Press, 2005); Andrew Heard, *Canadian Constitutional Conventions* (Toronto: Oxford University Press, 1991), Ch. 3; and various Privy Council Office documents cited below.

15. This title was originally based on appointment to the British Privy Council, but Lester Pearson created "Right Honourable" as a Canadian title, which is bestowed on the prime minister, governor general, and chief justice of the Supreme Court.

16. Forcese and Freeman, *The Laws of Government*, pp. 31–37, 337–49. In 2004, in an exercise of the royal prerogative, Foreign Affairs Minister Bill Graham refused to issue a passport on grounds of national security. In 2012, Prime Minister Harper employed the mercy prerogative to pardon violators of Canadian Wheat Board and gun registry regulations. The courts ruled that his removal of Helena Guergis from Cabinet was not susceptible to judicial review, and that the government could withdraw from the Kyoto Protocol on the basis of the treaty power. Philippe Lagassé contrasts Supreme Court decisions in the *Operation Dismantle* and *Omar Khadr* cases in "Parliamentary and Judicial Ambivalence Toward Executive Prerogative Power in Canada," *Canadian Public Administration* (March 2012).

17. Ministers who resigned or were fired or dropped recently for such reasons include Art Eggleton, Andy Scott, Lawrence MacAulay, and Maxime Bernier.

18. Privy Council Office, *Accountable Government: A Guide for Ministers and Ministers of State* (Ottawa: Government of Canada, 2011); cited on February 9, 2011, available at http://www.pco-bcp.gc.ca/index.asp?lang=eng&page=information&sub=publications&doc=ag-gr-eng.htm; and Forcese and Freeman, *The Laws of Government*, Ch. 6, pp. 384–92.

19. The concept was first popularized by Richard Crossman in Britain in his "Introduction" to Walter Bagehot's *The English Constitution* (London: Collins, 1963) and elaborated in *The Myths of Cabinet Government*

(Cambridge, MA: Harvard University Press, 1972). See also Donald J. Savoie, *Governing from the Centre: The Concentration of Power in Canadian Politics* (Toronto: University of Toronto Press, 1999); Jeffrey Simpson, *The Friendly Dictatorship* (Toronto: McClelland and Stewart, 2001), p. 4; Savoie, *Court Government and the Collapse of Accountability in Canada and the United Kingdom* (Toronto: University of Toronto Press, 2008), which substitutes "court government" for "prime ministerial"; and Christopher Dunn, "The Central Executive in the Canadian Government: Searching for the Holy Grail," in Christopher Dunn, ed., *The Handbook of Canadian Public Administration*, 2nd ed. (Toronto: Oxford University Press, 2010).

20. Savoie, *Governing from the Centre*, p. 71.

21. Ibid., pp. 81–82.

22. Privy Council Office, *Accountable Government: A Guide for Ministers and Ministers of State, 2011*, available at http://www.pco-bcp.gc.ca/docs/information/publications/ag-gr/2011/docs/ag-gr-eng.pdf; Leslie Pal and David Taras, eds., *Prime Ministers and Premiers: Political Leadership and Public Policy in Canada* (Scarborough: Prentice Hall Canada, 1988); and Peter Aucoin, "Prime Ministerial Leadership: Position, Power, and Politics," in Maureen Mancuso, Richard G. Price, and Ronald Wagenberg, eds., *Leaders and Leadership in Canada* (Toronto: Oxford University Press, 1994).

23. W.A. Matheson, *The Prime Minister and the Cabinet* (Toronto: Methuen, 1976), Ch. III; and R.M. Punnett, *The Prime Minister in Canadian Government and Politics* (Toronto: Macmillan, 1977), Ch. 4.

24. Savoie, *Governing from the Centre*, pp. 137–39, 343.

25. A.D.P. Heeney, "Cabinet Government in Canada: Developments in the Machinery of the Central Executive," *Canadian Journal of Economics and Political Science* (August 1946); and Savoie, *Governing from the Centre*, p. 125.

26. Savoie, *Governing from the Centre*, p. 328.

27. Privy Council Office, *Accountable Government*. A book by a long-time secretary to the Cabinet Gordon Robertson, *Memoirs of a Very Civil Servant: Mackenzie King to Pierre Trudeau* (Toronto: University of Toronto Press, 2000), contains much interesting material on the working style of prime ministers King, St. Laurent, Pearson, and Trudeau.

28. Leslie Pal, "Prime Ministers and Their Parties: The Cauldron of Leadership," in Pal and Taras, *Prime Ministers and Premiers*.

29. Matheson, *The Prime Minister and the Cabinet*, pp. 127–28; on Stephen Harper's role as party leader, see Faron Ellis and Peter Woolstencroft, "The Conservative Campaign: Becoming the New Natural Governing Party?" In Jon H. Pammett and Christopher Dornan, eds., *The Canadian Federal Election of 2011* (Toronto: Dundurn, 2011).

30. Leslie Pal, "Hands at the Helm? Leadership and Public Policy," in Pal and Taras, *Prime Ministers and Premiers*, p. 25; and Savoie, *Governing from the Centre*, p. 316.

31. Lawrence Martin, *Iron Man: The Defiant Reign of Jean Chrétien* (Toronto: Viking Canada, 2003), pp. 100–03; Edward Greenspon and Anthony Wilson-Smith, *Double Vision: The Inside Story of the Liberals in Power* (Toronto: Doubleday, 1996), pp. 256–66; and Eddie Goldenberg, *The Way It Works: Inside Ottawa* (Toronto: McClelland & Stewart, 2006).

32. Punnett, *The Prime Minister in Canadian Government and Politics*, Ch. 6; and Matheson, *The Prime Minister and the Cabinet*, Ch. IX.

33. Savoie, *Governing from the Centre*, p. 94.

34. According to Helena Guergis, Harper dismissed her from the Cabinet and Conservative caucus without informing her of the reasons.

35. Privy Council Office, *A Guide Book for Heads of Agencies: Operations, Structures and Responsibilities in the Federal Government* (August 1999) lists 3500 governor in council appointments: judges, diplomats, agencies, boards, commissions, Crown corporations, and government departments; see also Simpson, *The Friendly Dictatorship*, pp. 14–18; Jeffrey Simpson, *Spoils of Power* (Toronto: Collins, 1998); and Forcese and Freeman, *The Laws of Government*, pp. 238–46.

36. Simpson, *The Friendly Dictatorship*, p. 39; Russell and Sossin, *Parliamentary Democracy in Crisis*.

37. Kim Richard Nossal, "Political Leadership and Foreign Policy: Trudeau and Mulroney," in Pal and Taras, *Prime Ministers and Premiers*; and Savoie, *Governing from the Centre*, pp. 134–37.

38. Frederick Fletcher, "The Prime Minister as Public Persuader," in Hockin, *Apex of Power*. See also Punnett, *The Prime Minister in Canadian Government and Politics*, p. 22.

39. David Taras, "Prime Ministers and the Media," in Pal and Taras, *Prime Ministers and Premiers*, p. 36.

40. Savoie, *Governing from the Centre*, p. 72. In fact, an obsession with media attacks on minor points often distracts PMs from more important aspects of their work.
41. Gossage, *Close to the Charisma*; Michel Gratton, *So, What Are the Boys Saying?* (Toronto: McGraw-Hill Ryerson, 1987); and Bill Fox, *Spinwars: Politics and New Media* (Toronto: Key Porter Books, 1999).
42. Fred Schindeler, "The Prime Minister and the Cabinet: History and Development," in Hockin, *Apex of Power*, p. 22.
43. Denis Smith, "President and Parliament: The Transformation of Parliamentary Government in Canada," in Hockin, *Apex of Power*, p. 315.
44. Savoie, *Governing from the Centre*, pp. 87–97, 108.
45. Lawrence Martin, *Harperland: The Politics of Control* (Toronto: Viking Canada, 2010).
46. Peter C. Newman, *Renegade in Power* (Toronto: McClelland and Stewart, 1963).
47. White, *Cabinets and First Ministers*. On page 83, White outlines what an autocrat would be like and concludes that this is not a good description of the prime minister. But he does not challenge the basic argument put forward by Savoie and others that Canadian first ministers wield remarkable power (p. 99). For other accounts of constraints, see Paul Barker, "The Limits on the Power of the Prime Minister," in Mark Charlton and Paul Barker, eds., *Crosscurrents: Contemporary Political Issues*, 5th ed. (Toronto: Thomson Nelson, 2006).
48. Michael M. Atkinson and David C. Docherty, "Parliament and Political Success in Canada," in Michael Whittington and Glen Williams, *Canadian Politics in the 21st Century*, 6th ed. (Toronto: Thomson Nelson, 2004). See also Patrice Dutil, "Prime ministers and public administration," *Canadian Public Administration* (June 2008); and Michael Bliss, *Right Honourable Men: The Descent of Canadian Politics from Macdonald to Chrétien* (Toronto: HarperCollins, 2004). A panel of academics rated Lester Pearson as the best PM in the last 50 years. See *Policy Options*, June/July, 2003.
49. Martin, *Harperland*, emphasizes Harper's obsession with control. See also H.D. Munroe, "Style within the Centre: Pierre Trudeau, the War Measures Act, and the Nature of Prime Ministerial Power," *Canadian Public Administration* (December 2011).
50. F.W. Gibson, *Cabinet Formation and Bicultural Relations* (Ottawa: Queen's Printer, 1970), Ch. VIII; John English, "The 'French Lieutenant' in Ottawa," in R.K. Carty and W.P. Ward, eds., *National Politics and Community in Canada* (Vancouver: University of British Columbia Press, 1986); and Matheson, *The Prime Minister and the Cabinet*, pp. 34–38.
51. Privy Council Office, *Accountable Government 2011*.
52. Matheson, *The Prime Minister and the Cabinet*, chs. II and V.
53. Heard, *Canadian Constitutional Conventions*.
54. General A.G.L. McNaughton served for more than nine months as minister of defence in 1944–45, suffering a by-election loss and a general election loss before finally resigning from the Cabinet. Pierre Juneau resigned as secretary of state when he failed to win a by-election in 1975. Chrétien appointed three ministers from outside the House: Stéphane Dion, Pierre Pettigrew, and Brian Tobin. Then, despite his emphasis on doing things more democratically than his predecessors, Stephen Harper convinced one newly elected Liberal to cross the floor to continue to serve in the Cabinet and appointed an unelected Conservative to the Senate to represent Montreal in the Cabinet.
55. Herman Bakvis, *Regional Ministers* (Toronto: University of Toronto Press, 1991); Bakvis, "Cabinet Ministers: Leaders or Followers" in Mancuso et al., eds., *Leaders and Leadership in Canada*.
56. Matheson, *The Prime Minister and the Cabinet*, pp. ix, 22–23.
57. See the case studies in the study of the Royal Commission on Bilingualism and Biculturalism edited by Frederick W. Gibson, *Cabinet Formation and Bicultural Relations*. Gibson argues that francophones had no monopoly on the desire for patronage, p. 172.
58. Privy Council Office, *Accountable Government 2011*.
59. Ibid.; Forcese and Freeman, *The Laws of Government*, pp. 370–84.
60. Matheson, *The Prime Minister and the Cabinet*, pp. 90–91.
61. S.L. Sutherland, "Responsible Government and Ministerial Responsibility: Every Reform Is Its Own Problem," *Canadian Journal of Political Science* (March 1991), p. 101. In Paul Martin's government, a junior minister resigned from Cabinet over same-sex marriage.
62. In a July 2002 decision, the Supreme Court of Canada upheld the principle of Cabinet confidentiality but ruled that it is not absolute—*Babcock v. Canada (Attorney General)*, [2002] 3 S.C.R. 3; and Forcese and Freeman, *The Laws of Government*, Ch. 9.

63. Privy Council Office, *Accountable Government: A Guide for Ministers and Ministers of State, 2011*; Nicholas d'Ombrain, "Cabinet Secrecy," *Canadian Public Administration* (Fall 2004).

64. Bakvis, *Regional Ministers*.

65. Donald Smiley, *The Federal Condition in Canada* (Toronto: McGraw-Hill Ryerson, 1987), p. 88.

66. Matheson, *The Prime Minister and the Cabinet*, p. 178.

67. G. Bruce Doern and Peter Aucoin, eds., *The Structures of Policy-Making in Canada* (Toronto: Macmillan, 1971); *Public Policy in Canada* (Toronto: Macmillan, 1979); Colin Campbell and George Szablowski, *The Superbureaucrats* (Toronto: Macmillan, 1979); and Peter Aucoin, "Organizational Change in the Machinery of Canadian Government: From Rational Management to Brokerage Politics," *Canadian Journal of Political Science* (March 1986).

68. Peter Aucoin, "Organizational Change in the Machinery of Canadian Government."

69. Punnett, *The Prime Minister*, p. 110; Walter Stewart, *Shrug: Trudeau in Power* (Toronto: New Press, 1971), Ch. 11.

70. Aucoin, "Organizational Change in the Machinery of Canadian Government."

71. Savoie, *Governing from the Centre*, p. 325; Jocelyne Bourgon, *Third Annual Report to the Prime Minister on the Public Service of Canada* (Ottawa: Privy Council Office, 1995), p. 16; and Christopher Dunn, "The Central Executive in Canadian Government: Searching for the Holy Grail," in which he reminds us that a prime minister's design of government is "remarkably personalistic."

72. Earlier Cabinet committees were primarily used in the First and Second World Wars. See descriptions in Punnett, *The Prime Minister in Canadian Government and Politics*, pp. 72–74, and Matheson, *The Prime Minister and the Cabinet*, pp. 83–87.

73. This account is based on PCO documents as well as interviews with key PCO officials, for which I am extremely grateful.

74. Cabinet Committees can be found at http://www.pm.gc.ca/eng/feature.asp?pageId=53&featureId=8, retrieved February 5, 2012.

75. See http://www.pco-bcp.gc.ca/index.asp?lang=eng&page=information&sub=publications&doc=mc/mc-eng.htm. An outline of the contents of a memorandum to cabinet has been placed on this book's website.

76. Savoie, *Governing from the Centre*, p. 260.

77. Ibid., pp. 7–8, 338.

78. See Donald J. Savoie's books, *Power: Where Is It?* (Montreal: McGill-Queen's University Press, 2010) and *Court Government and the Collapse of Accountability in Canada and the United Kingdom*. This is suspiciously similar to the description of the Trudeau cabinet!

79. James B. Kelly, *Governing with the Charter: Legislative and Judicial Activism and the Framers' Intent* (Vancouver: UBC Press, 2005), p. 222.

80. Marc Lalonde, "The Changing Role of the Prime Minister's Office," *Canadian Public Administration* (Winter 1971); Jeffrey Simpson, *The Friendly Dictatorship*, p. 34; Savoie, *Governing from the Centre*, p. 99; and Thomas Axworthy, "Of Secretaries to Princes," *Canadian Public Administration* (Summer 1988).

81. Michael Whittington, "The Prime Minister, Cabinet, and the Executive Power in Canada." Harper's first Chief of Staff, Ian Brodie, was replaced after the 2008 election with Guy Giorno, who had served Ontario Premier Mike Harris in the same capacity, after which Nigel Wright was seconded from the private sector to serve in this capacity. Lawrence Martin also emphasizes information control.

82. A.D.P. Heeney, *The Things That Are Caesar's* (Toronto: University of Toronto Press, 1972), Ch. 6; and Gordon Robertson, "The Changing Role of the Privy Council Office," *Canadian Public Administration* (Winter 1971).

83. Privy Council Office, *The Role of the Clerk*, available at http://www.clerk.gc.ca/eng/feature.asp?featureId=19&pageId=88; *The Role and Structure of the Privy Council Office 2011*, available at http://www.pco-bcp.gc.ca/index.asp?land=eng&page=information&sub=publications&doc=Role/role2010-eng.htm; and *About PCO*, available at http://www.pco-bcp.gc.ca/index.asp?lang=eng&page=about-apropos, all accessed February 5, 2012; Patrice Dutil, ed., *Searching for Leadership: Secretaries to Cabinet in Canada* (Toronto: University of Toronto Press, 2008).

84. Much of the early success of the Harper government was attributed to the advice of Privy Council Clerk Kevin Lynch, who apparently had a good relationship with Harper's Chief of Staff Ian Brodie; but Lynch found the new Chief of Staff, Guy Giorno, more difficult to work with and retired in favour of new Clerk, Wayne Wouters.

85. Donald Savoie's description, *Governing from the Centre*, Ch. 5.
86. Commission of Inquiry into the Sponsorship Program and Advertising Activities, *Restoring Accountability* (Ottawa: Minister of Public Works and Government Services, 2006), p. 147.
87. Donald J. Savoie, *The Politics of Public Spending in Canada* (Toronto: University of Toronto Press, 1990), Ch. 4.
88. Edward Greenspon and Anthony Wilson-Smith, *Double Vision: The Inside Story of the Liberals in Power* (Toronto: Doubleday Canada, 1996).
89. Savoie, *The Politics of Public Spending in Canada*, Ch. 5.

FURTHER READING

Aucoin, Peter, Mark D. Jarvis, and Lori Turnbull. *Democratizing the Constitution: Reforming Responsible Government*. Toronto: Emond Montgomery, 2011.

Bliss, Michael. *Right Honourable Men: The Descent of Canadian Politics from Macdonald to Chrétien*. Toronto: HarperCollins, 2004.

Dunn, Christopher, ed. *The Handbook of Canadian Public Administration*, 2nd ed. Toronto: Oxford University Press, 2010.

Forcese, Craig, and Allan Freeman. *The Laws of Government: The Legal Foundations of Canadian Democracy*. Toronto: Irwin Law, 2005.

Goldenberg, Eddie. *The Way It Works: Inside Ottawa*. Toronto: McClelland & Stewart, 2006.

Heard, Andrew. *Canadian Constitutional Conventions*. Toronto: Oxford University Press, 1991.

Lagassé, Philippe. "Parliamentary and Judicial Ambivalence Toward Executive Prerogative Power in Canada," *Canadian Public Administration* (March 2012).

Martin, Lawrence. *Harperland: The Politics of Control*. Toronto: Viking Canada, 2010.

McWhinney, Edward. *The Governor General and the Prime Ministers: The Making and Unmaking of Governments*. Vancouver: Ronsdale Press, 2005.

Pal, Leslie A. *Beyond Policy Analysis: Public Issue Management in Turbulent Times*, 4th ed. Toronto: Thomson Nelson, 2010.

Privy Council Office. *Accountable Government: A Guide for Ministers and Ministers of State*. Ottawa: Government of Canada, 2011.

Savoie, Donald J. *Governing from the Centre: The Concentration of Power in Canadian Politics*. Toronto: University of Toronto Press, 1999.

———. *Court Government and the Collapse of Accountability in Canada and the United Kingdom*. Toronto: University of Toronto Press, 2008.

———. *Power: Where Is It?* Montreal: McGill-Queen's University Press, 2010.

Simpson, Jeffrey. *The Friendly Dictatorship*. Toronto: McClelland and Stewart, 2001.

Smith, David E. *The Invisible Crown*. Toronto: University of Toronto Press, 1995.

Smith, Jennifer, and D. Michael Jackson, eds. *The Evolving Canadian Crown*. Montreal and Kingston: McGill-Queen's University Press, 2012.

White, Graham. *Cabinets and First Ministers*. Vancouver: UBC Press, 2004.

Whittington, Michael S. "The Prime Minister, Cabinet, and Executive Power," in Michael Whittington and Glen Williams, eds., *Canadian Politics in the 21st Century*, 7th ed. Toronto: Thomson Nelson, 2008.

CHAPTER 22

The Bureaucracy

Federal public servants deliver the mail, issue old age security cheques and passports, process income tax and GST/HST forms, admit immigrants, approve new drugs and search for illicit ones, guard penitentiaries, negotiate treaties with domestic Aboriginals as well as with foreign countries, and provide myriad other services that are often taken for granted by the general public. For the most part, the federal bureaucracy performs these functions in a more than satisfactory manner, but if any hitch occurs, Canadians are quick to condemn the "red tape" and "slow-moving bureaucrats" in Ottawa. Whether such faults are more characteristic of government than of large, private-sector corporations remains an open question.

Even though the bureaucracy, or public service, is generally not as visible as the other three branches of government, it is no less important. Most citizens encounter public servants in the provision of services, but the bureaucracy is probably even more significant in its advisory role. Modern government is so pervasive and complex that the prime minister and ministers hardly ever make a move without the advice of their permanent, expert staff. Most public servants work in various government departments, but these are supplemented by a vast array of Crown corporations and administrative agencies of many kinds. In fact, the bureaucracy has become so large and indispensable that many observers wonder whether it can be kept under political control.

This chapter begins by examining the functions and powers of the bureaucracy. It then deals in turn with the three main kinds of bureaucratic organization, and concludes with a discussion of controlling the bureaucracy and recent attempts to reform it.

FUNCTIONS AND POWERS OF THE BUREAUCRACY

The traditional function of the bureaucracy is that of policy *implementation*—that is, administering policies established by the prime minister, Cabinet, and Parliament. Although this is still an important part of its work, the bureaucracy is equally involved in the function of policy *making*. Besides advising the politicians in their capacity as rule makers, the bureaucracy is delegated wide "quasi-legislative" powers to make subordinate rules on its own. And although the courts are the foremost adjudicators of disputes in society, the bureaucracy has also encroached on their territory in the adjudication function, such that many disputes are now resolved by "quasi-judicial" regulatory tribunals. Less formally, the bureaucracy engages in interest articulation, in the sense of various departments speaking up for their own concerns or helping to advance the demands of their principal clientele.

If the significance of the bureaucracy can be seen in its performance of all of these functions, it can also be demonstrated by examining the presence of the public service in the model of the policymaking process presented in Chapter 20. First, it plays a crucial part in the initiation phase. The bureaucracy may be a source of demands, since administrators of a program are likely to be among the first to recognize its inadequacies. Even if a demand reaches the prime minister and Cabinet from other sources, once the politicians decide to look into an issue further, the public service will usually be asked to provide them with additional information and advice.

If the prime minister and Cabinet decide to take action at the priority-setting stage, the bureaucracy is then centrally involved in the policy formulation phase. With its concentration of technical information and experience, the public service spends a great deal of its time in formulating policies because the details of such policies are usually beyond the grasp of the politicians.

Once the policy, program, or law has received political authorization in the legitimization phase, implementation is almost exclusively a bureaucratic responsibility. Because of the time and informational constraints on Parliament, most bills are passed in rather general or skeletal form, and the real meat or substance of the law is expressed in the **regulations** issued under it. These are published under the authority of the minister or Cabinet in the *Canada Gazette*. The implementation of a law may thus see the bureaucracy making decisions that constitute quasi-legislative outputs that involve time-consuming negotiations with the provinces or with relevant interest groups.

Eventually, it is the bureaucracy that actually provides the service, does the regulating, collects the taxes, or performs whatever other activities are necessary to apply the law. Implementation also requires disseminating information to the public about new policies or programs. Governments now spend great quantities of public funds advertising their programs on the grounds that this is essential if they are to be fully effective. A final aspect of implementation is program evaluation—that is, an assessment of the adequacies of a policy after a period of operation. Program evaluation is becoming a more sophisticated addition to the field of policy analysis.

Given its role in almost all phases of the policymaking process, reference to "bureaucratic power" in political science or contentions that the bureaucracy is more powerful than the legislature or even the prime minister and Cabinet should not be surprising. It is more conventional to say that the prime minister and Cabinet make the most important decisions in the political system and that they theoretically control the bureaucracy. The bureaucrats *advise* on almost every decision, but the prime minister and ministers actually *make* the political decisions. Donald Savoie argues that career officials "respond whenever *clear* and

Captain Stephen Harper makes civil servants walk the plank.

consistent political direction is given,"[1] but this is not to deny the extent of bureaucratic power in the modern state.

As far as the size of the bureaucracy is concerned, about 200 000 people work in the regular departments, but when all the assorted agencies are added, it grows to about 400 000 people, which includes 65 000 armed forces personnel and 25 000 in the RCMP. Then about 100 000 people work in federal business enterprises, making a grand total of about half a million people. In its attempt to balance the budget, the Harper government laid off some 20 000 public servants between 2012 and 2015.

CRITICAL APPROACHES

The bureaucracy is one of the most important institutions of government and therefore amenable to the *institutional approach*. Indeed, no institution is so imbued with written and unwritten rules that rarely change and that affect the behaviour of politicians, groups, and the public with which it interacts. Bureaucratic power is also central to the *state-based approach*, which generally contends that the bureaucracy is a world unto itself. Ministers are so busy with other responsibilities that they have little or no time left to spend in their departments. They have only the most superficial idea of what their departments are doing; for the most part, these are self-governing operations, subject only to the authority of other bureaucratic central agencies. Even the prime minister and Cabinet as a whole can do little but take the advice of the secretary to the Cabinet, the deputy minister of finance, the governor of the Bank of Canada, and a handful of other key officials.

GOVERNMENT DEPARTMENTS
Number, Structure, and Size

Government **departments** are created and reorganized by Acts of Parliament, which also set out the responsibilities of each. But the prime minister and Cabinet can determine the internal structure of the department and even have the power to transfer responsibilities from one department to another. The name and number of departments is relatively stable over time, and Table 22.1 lists the size of the principal government departments as of 2014.

The government department assumes a pyramidal shape, with the minister at its apex. Because ministers in this system (unlike in the United States) are chosen from among the politicians elected to Parliament, it is too much to hope that they will be experts in the work of the department or able managers. All that is expected is that they are individuals with intelligence, ideas, common sense, and an ability to relay government priorities and public opinion to departmental experts as well as to relate expert advice from the department to Parliament and the public. Ministers will naturally develop some expertise if they stay in one Cabinet position for any length of time, but nowadays they are often shuffled to another department just as they are getting the hang of it.

TABLE 22.1   GOVERNMENT DEPARTMENTS WITH SIZE OF WORKFORCE, 2011 AND 2014

DEPARTMENTS AND AGENCIES	2011	2014	CH(%)
ABORIGINAL AFFAIRS AND NORTHERN DEVELOPMENT	5050	4405	−12.8%
AGRICULTURE AND AGRI-FOOD	6050	4572	−24.4%
CANADIAN HERITAGE	1942	1640	−15.6%
CITIZENSHIP AND IMMIGRATION	4514	4918	8.9%
ENVIRONMENT	6608	5872	−11.1%
FINANCE	771	719	−6.7%
FISHERIES AND OCEANS	10 243	9097	−11.2%
FOREIGN AFFAIRS AND INTERNATIONAL TRADE	4624	5607	21.3%
HEALTH	9716	8761	−9.8%
EMPLOYMENT AND SOCIAL DEVELOPMENT CANADA	23 092	19 802	−14.2%
INDUSTRY	5360	4541	−15.3%

(Continued)

DEPARTMENTS AND AGENCIES	2011	2014	CH(%)
JUSTICE	4986	4410	−11.6%
NATIONAL DEFENCE	26 297	22 112	−15.9%
NATURAL RESOURCES	4570	3782	−17.2%
PRIVY COUNCIL OFFICE	825	665	−19.4%
PUBLIC SAFETY	1038	962	−7.3%
PUBLIC WORKS AND GOVERNMENT SERVICES	13 475	11 352	−15.8%
TRANSPORT	5213	4500	−13.7%
TREASURY BOARD SECRETARIAT	1989	1548	−22.2%
VETERANS AFFAIRS	3743	2939	−21.5%

Source: Treasury Board of Canada Secretariat, Employment Equity in the Public Service of Canada 2010–11, http://www.tbs-sct.gc.ca/reports-rapports/ee/2010-2011/ee04-eng.asp. Office of the Chief Human Resource Officer, Treasury Board of Canada Secretariat, 2015; Treasury Board of Canada Secretariat, Table 1: Distribution of Public Service of Canada Employees by Designated Group According to Department or Agency, http://www .tbs-sct.gc.ca/reports-rapports/ee/2013-2014/tab01-eng.asp. Office of the Chief Human Resource Officer, Treasury Board of Canada Secretariat, 2015.

Responsibility and Accountability at the Top of the Department

Ministers are responsible for their department in the sense that they are expected to provide overall direction and accept criticism for its faults. In other words, ministers take most of the credit or blame for what the department does, whether or not they know what is going on within it. As pointed out in Chapter 21, the principle of individual **ministerial responsibility** was once thought to mean that ministers had to resign over serious mistakes made by their public servants, even if unaware of the errors. No cases of such resignations can be found in Canada since 1867, and in this age of big government it is not a realistic proposition. What does ministerial responsibility mean today? First, ministers occasionally resign over their personal mistakes, but not as routinely as in Britain. Second, they must take political responsibility and answer to Parliament for all the actions of their officials. The minister must explain and defend the actions of the department in Parliament, especially during Question Period, and when a bureaucratic error is made, the minister must apologize and promise to correct the mistake. Third, although ministers may discreetly discipline the offender, they should not violate the traditions of public-service anonymity.[2]

Several serious bureaucratic errors occurred during the Chrétien regime that prompted much questioning of the notion of responsibility and accountability. One was in Human Resources Development Canada (HRDC) in the 1990s in connection with its job-creation programs. No one accepted responsibility for the fiasco, and as a result the auditor general observed that a strict notion of individual ministerial responsibility seemed unrealistic in

CHAPTER 22 **The Bureaucracy**

Canadian politics. "Canada has never modernized its doctrine to distinguish between the minister's area of public responsibility and that of his senior public servants," the Auditor General wrote. "To me, there is a certain lack of realism in holding ministers ultimately accountable for everything."[3] The question of accountability will be further addressed toward the end of the chapter.

The more permanent head of the department is the **deputy minister**. Appointed by the prime minister on the advice of the secretary to the Cabinet, "deputies" or "DMs" are usually career public servants. In other words, they are rarely patronage appointments. Deputy ministers have two principal roles: they act as the chief policy adviser to the minister and function as the manager of the department; they, not the minister, really run the department.[4] This again raises the question of whether DMs should therefore be responsible for departmental mistakes. Such officials used to spend a lifetime working their way to the top of a single department and became great experts in its subject matter. Since the 1962 Glassco Report, which recommended the adoption of private-sector managerial techniques in the public sector, emphasis in the appointment of deputy ministers has switched from expertise in the subject matter of the department to managerial skills that can be applied in any administrative setting. In recent years they, too, have been frequently shuffled from one department to another. Even so, the deputy minister is usually in the department longer than the minister and is thus likely to develop greater knowledge of its work. Deputy ministers also interact regularly with DMs in other federal departments, provincial DMs in corresponding departments, and the heads of advocacy groups particularly interested in the department's work.[5]

The relationship between the minister and the deputy minister is of great interest and concern to political science and public administration.[6] In theory, the minister sets the priorities for the department, based to some extent on the party platform, the prime minister's objectives, and the minister's own projects. Whether in determining priorities or in implementing them, the DM ideally provides a number of options among which the minister can choose. The deputy should give the minister advice that is not only based on administrative, technical, and financial considerations but that is also sensitive to the political context. Evidence exists that the reality of the relationship sometimes approaches this theoretical ideal. However, weak ministers may be mere puppets of their bureaucratic advisers, and even strong ministers may encounter bureaucratic resistance to new initiatives, such as in being denied relevant information, having it delayed, or in having new policies implemented without enthusiasm.[7] In any case, ministers are busy doing other things and do not spend much time in their departmental offices. In most cases (finance being an exception), the minister and deputy minister only see each other during a weekly briefing session.[8]

Besides their loyalty to their department, deputy ministers nowadays have strong links to "the centre" of government, especially the Privy Council Office. The clerk of the Privy Council chairs weekly deputy minister committee meetings, monthly luncheons, and semi-annual retreats. Deputy ministers have been appointed by the centre, their promotion prospects depend on the centre, and they spend a great deal of their time "managing sensitive files for the centre."[9] Through the clerk, deputy ministers have a connection to the prime minister that increasingly approaches the importance of the relationship with their own minister. The problem of deputy ministers' reconciling their loyalty to their minister and to the clerk and the PCO was singled out for considerable attention in the Gomery Report.[10]

Exempt Staff

It is not easy for a single, solitary, temporary, amateur minister to impose his or her will on the deputy minister and the hundreds or thousands of other expert, permanent public servants who have established departmental attitudes, values, policies, and procedures. In this situation, the small personal staff that ministers are allowed to appoint may be of some assistance. The "political" or **exempt staff** provides ministers with advisers and assistants who share their political commitment and who can complement the professional, expert, and nonpartisan advice and support of the public service. The exempt staff is primarily engaged in promoting the image and reputation of the minister and doing favours for supporters and friends. Although they may provide partisan policy advice, any effort to interfere in the administration of the department will be strongly resented by the deputy minister.[11] In the Mulroney regime, ministers set up large offices headed by a powerful chief of staff whose authority rivalled that of the deputy minister and who was, among other things, the target of most lobbying efforts. As in other ways, Jean Chrétien reverted to an earlier era by reducing the size and significance of ministerial offices.

Exempt staff became another issue at the **Gomery Inquiry** for two reasons. First, it was a common practice for a person to leave the minister's office to become a lobbyist, and second, those who had worked for a minister for at least three years were allowed to slip into public service positions at the same level as they previously occupied.[12] Stephen Harper agreed: his **Federal Accountability Act** prohibited ministers, staffers, and senior public servants from becoming lobbyists for five years after leaving office (with loopholes as revealed in Chapter 16), and required ministerial staffers to compete for internal job postings.

The Rest of the Department

Below the deputy minister, the department is typically divided into several branches, each headed by an assistant deputy minister (ADM); these in turn are subdivided again and again. Figure 22.1 illustrates the hierarchical structure of a hypothetical government department. Those divisions of a department that actually carry out services and interact with the public are

FIGURE 22.1   ORGANIZATIONAL CHART OF A HYPOTHETICAL GOVERNMENT DEPARTMENT

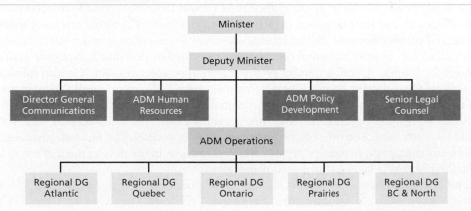

said to be performing "line" functions. Except for the top managerial posts, most of the line positions in any department will be located in the "field"—in local offices in communities across the country. But every department will also have "staff" divisions that serve such internal needs as policy development and research, personnel, financial, information, and legal services. These positions are normally located in Ottawa along with the heads of the line divisions.

The hundreds or thousands of public servants in the department are ranged in descending levels of authority under the deputy minister and share four basic characteristics: they are expert, permanent, impartial, and anonymous. First, they are chosen on their merits—ability, knowledge, training, or experience—for the duties their positions entail. Second, they are career public servants, who normally remain within the public service until retirement. Third, they are nonpartisan and expected to serve whichever party comes to power with equal loyalty and enthusiasm. Fourth, bureaucrats are not normally identified in public; instead, the minister speaks for the department and takes the public and parliamentary responsibility for its performance. Even when public servants brief the media about new policies, for example, they are only referred to as "officials of the department."

The federal public service is divided into six occupational categories, within which are a large number of more specific occupational groups:

1. Management or Executive
2. Scientific and Professional (e.g., nursing, auditing)
3. Administrative and Foreign Service (e.g., personnel administration, program administration)
4. Technical (e.g., drafting)
5. Administrative Support (e.g., clerical, regulatory, secretarial)
6. Operational (e.g., correctional officer, firefighter)

Relations with Other Departments and Central Agencies

The operation of a government department is complicated by the necessity of interacting with other departments as well as by the authority of various central agencies to intervene in its affairs. Since almost any law, policy, or program affects a variety of departments, many interdepartmental committees exist. Beyond these, whenever a new policy is under active consideration, an ad hoc interdepartmental committee is appointed to look into it. Not only must the problem be examined from a number of departmental perspectives, but it is also subject to considerable bureaucratic "politics" and "territorial claims." Ministers as well as deputy ministers constantly have to reconcile their departmental interests with the need to coordinate their activities with other departments, and they generally cannot act unilaterally if such action would have any impact on other departments' programs or policies. The increasing necessity of collaboration among a number of departments and agencies in the development of a new law, policy, or program is labelled **horizontal management**.[13]

The central agencies that complicate the life of a department include the Public Service Commission (PSC), the Treasury Board Secretariat (TBS), the Privy Council Office (PCO), the Department of Finance, and the Prime Minister's Office (PMO), most of which were mentioned in Chapter 21. The **Public Service Commission** is a three-member board that safeguards the principles of competence, nonpartisanship, and representation, and that is theoretically in charge of all hiring, promotions, and dismissals. In practice, however, the PSC delegates much of its authority to deputy ministers in individual departments. It is primarily concerned with policing the merit system—that is, preventing appointments and promotions from being made on partisan or discriminatory grounds.

The **Treasury Board Secretariat** was discussed in Chapter 21, but its role merits re-emphasis, especially in connection with human resources, financial, and expenditure management. The TBS essentially determines the terms and conditions of employment for the public service. It is in charge of the classification or reclassification of positions and represents the employer in the collective bargaining process. On the financial management side, the TBS is responsible for the preparation of the Estimates, normally cutting back on departmental spending proposals. The TBS also establishes the policy framework in such areas as information technology, contracting, and accounting; oversees the actual expenditure of public funds; and tries to improve departmental management through such devices as program evaluation.[14] Along with the TBS, the **Department of Finance** is usually an opponent of new department spending programs and an advocate of retrenchment.

Under the 2003 Public Service Modernization Act, even more flexibility was delegated from the PSC and the TBS to departmental deputy ministers in the hiring process. In fact, the definition of "merit" was changed to eliminate the necessity of competitions as long as the candidate met the "essential qualifications for the work to be performed." Rather than do their own hiring, however, departments increasingly rely on private employment agencies to furnish them with candidates.[15] In 2009, the human resources functions of the TBS were consolidated in the new Office of the Chief Human Resources Officer.

The Privy Council Office's relations with regular government departments were also referred to in Chapter 21. They primarily arise in connection with policy development and coordination, the reallocation of programs among departments, the reorganization of departments, and senior management appointments. Although the deputy minister will probably have had a hand in the mandate letter given to the new minister of the department, these letters are ultimately drafted by the PCO with the approval of the PM. The PCO will also take a great interest in any new policy proposal emanating from the department, typically in a Memorandum to Cabinet. The Prime Minister's Office, however, does not interact frequently with departments except with respect to new policy initiatives or political problems (i.e., crises) involving the prime minister.

The Merit Principle and a Representative Bureaucracy

For about 40 years after Confederation, the Canadian public service operated on the **spoils system,** under which the party that won an election could replace those holding civil service positions with its own friends and supporters. One of the main motives for entering the political arena in that era was to reward family and friends with **political patronage**—government jobs and contracts. Such partisan, amateur personnel proved to be increasingly inadequate as government operations grew more complex after the turn of the century, hence the passage of the Civil Service Amendment Act in 1908, which created the Civil Service Commission (predecessor to the Public Service Commission). It meant that public servants in Ottawa were hired on the **merit system**, and, after the adoption of the 1918 Civil Service Act, field positions were also to be based on merit. Politicians, however, were reluctant to give up their traditional right to reward their supporters with government jobs, and it is difficult to say exactly when the merit system was finally entrenched. The foundations of the modern merit system in Ottawa were laid in the 1930s at External Affairs, Finance, and the Bank of Canada.[16]

Almost as soon as the merit system was fully effective, the call began to be made that the bureaucracy should be more representative of the society it served. Given the power of the public service and the assumption that its recommendations and decisions would reflect the origins, identities, and pre-public-service values of its members, many critics argued that the public service could be responsive to all parts of society only if it included a proportional representation of various groups in the population. The senior levels of the public service had always overrepresented males, anglophones, the middle and upper classes, the well-educated, and Ontarians.[17] Thus, it was claimed that policy recommendations and implementation reflected an insensitivity to women, francophones, and other minority ethnocultural groups, to the peculiarities of hinterland regions and provinces, and to the working class and the poor.

The first main concerns in the establishment of a **representative bureaucracy** were the small number of francophones in the higher reaches of the bureaucracy and the virtual absence of the use of the French language at the policymaking levels. The passage of the **Official Languages Act** of 1969 essentially made the executive branch of government bilingual. It gave both English- and French-speaking citizens the right to deal with head offices of government departments in either official language, as well as with local offices where numbers warranted. It also expanded language-training programs started by the Pearson government in 1964, made recruitment and promotion of francophones a higher priority, and designated certain positions as bilingual. The position of commissioner of official languages was created to be responsible for assessing the implementation of the policy, dealing with complaints, and reporting back to Parliament. It was fortunate that the Quebec educational system had improved by this time so that the new policy involved little or no loss of quality in government appointments and promotions. It did, however, ignite a backlash against the preference given to French Canadians and to bilingualism.

As of 2014, 43 percent of public service positions (79 403) had been designated as bilingual, 49.6 percent (90 827) as English-essential, four percent (6 589) as French-essential, and another 3.2 percent (5 903) as requiring either official language. It has thus become increasingly indispensable for public service executives to be bilingual. In 1998, for example, new second-language proficiency requirements were imposed for those at or aspiring to the assistant deputy minister level, and in 2003–04, the official bilingualism policy across the whole public service was further strengthened. By 2014, 68 percent of public servants declared English to be their first official language and 32 percent declared French.[18] When the 2012 budget led to massive layoffs and to a general shuffling of thousands of public servants into different jobs, and the government gave them a year's grace to meet the language requirements of their new positions.

Women also began to be targeted for increased representation in the higher levels of the public service in the 1960s and 1970s.[19] In addition, the **pay equity** program of the 1980s and 1990s was primarily designed to ensure that women received equal pay for doing work that had the same value as that done by men. Many occupational groups made up largely of women have had their salaries increased as a result, but in 2009, the Harper government removed pay equity issues from the jurisdiction of the Canadian Human Rights Commission and injected them into the collective bargaining process.

The next stage of making the public service more representative of society came in 1983, when an explicit **affirmative action** program was adopted for women, Aboriginals, and people with disabilities; two years later the list was expanded to include members of visible minorities. Once again, this did not necessarily result in a decline in the quality of appointments and promotions, but it sparked opposition from those who did not fall into the designated categories. A new Employment Equity Act in 1995 required identification and elimination of employment barriers against persons in the four designated groups and the adoption of positive policies and practices that would ensure that such people achieved a degree of representation in each occupational group proportional to their numbers in the Canadian workforce. Table 22.2 indicates the percentage of people in the four designated groups in each of the six main occupational categories. In terms of workplace availability, women, Aboriginals, and people with disabilities are slightly overrepresented in the federal public service, while members of visible minorities are somewhat underrepresented. Women make up 45 percent of the Executive group and 80 percent of the Administrative Support category. The **employment equity** program extends to corporations with federal government contracts worth $200 000 or more, but it has probably had little impact on such companies.

TABLE 22.2   PUBLIC SERVICE BY EMPLOYMENT EQUITY GROUPS, 2013–2014

OCCUPATIONAL GROUP	ALL EMPLOYEES	WOMEN	ABORIGINAL PEOPLES	PERSONS WITH DISABILITIES	MEMBERS OF A VISIBLE MINORITY GROUP
	NUMBER	*PERCENT*	*PERCENT*	*PERCENT*	*PERCENT*
EXECUTIVE	5252	46.1	3.7	5.4	8.5
SCIENTIFIC AND PROFESSIONAL	31 854	51.3	3.1	4.5	17.2
ADMINISTRATIVE AND FOREIGN SERVICE	82 710	62.9	5.4	6.3	14.1
TECHNICAL	12 593	24.9	4.2	4.8	7.7
ADMINISTRATIVE SUPPORT	19 891	78.7	6.5	7.7	14.5
OPERATIONAL	28 971	29.2	6.1	4.7	8.5
TOTAL	181 356	57.6	10.6	10.0	11.8

Source: Treasury Board of Canada Secretariat, Employment Equity in the Public Service of Canada 2013–14, *http://www.tbs-sct.gc.ca/reports-rapports/ee/2013-2014/tab09-eng.asp. Office of the Chief Human Resources Officer, Treasury Board of Canada Secretariat, 2015.*

The Estimates System

As noted at several earlier points in the book, politicians and bureaucrats spend a great deal of their time discussing the expenditure of public funds. Members of Parliament want money for their constituencies, premiers and federal ministers press for financial support for their provinces, and bureaucrats seek funding for their programs and departments. In addition, much of the pressure on the authorities from advocacy groups, lobbyists, and corporations consists of demands for federal funds. In earlier eras such spending was the prerogative of individual politicians or governing parties and was carried out on a patronage basis. Nowadays, the expenditure process has been highly bureaucratized, and it is the function of the **Estimates** system to decide how such funds will be allocated in any fiscal year. The Estimates documents provide more than just the amount of money that each department and agency plans to spend in the next fiscal year: they are a valuable source of information on departmental plans and priorities and also contain departmental performance reports.

Under the current expenditure management system, the Cabinet decides, on the advice of the Department of Finance, the Treasury Board Secretariat, and the Privy Council Office, what the government's financial priorities and overall level of government revenue and expenditure will be. New policy proposals and new spending initiatives must also be specifically approved at this level. The whole budgetary process has been portrayed as a contest between "spenders" and "guardians."[20] The spenders are most of the ministers and departments in whose interest it is to increase their budgets. Spenders try to introduce new programs and expand existing ones in order to raise their prestige and enhance the support of their clientele. The guardians are essentially the Minister of Finance and the President of the Treasury Board, along with their respective departments, who are ordinarily seen as villains by almost everyone else involved.

Many government programs are automatically funded by the statutes that create them. The expenditures for these programs, called "statutory appropriations," cannot be changed without amending the relevant statutes; they are therefore more or less fixed and uncontrollable. Because these appropriations constitute about two-thirds of the total budget, they seriously limit the Cabinet's discretion in altering the level or pattern of government expenditure.

The preparation of the Estimates involves projections of the cost of new and existing programs at the departmental level within the limits and guidelines laid down by higher authorities. A great deal of interaction takes place between the managerial personnel of each department and the Treasury Board Secretariat, as deputy ministers and ministers try to maximize their departmental allocations while TBS personnel engage in cutting them back. At the end of the process, the Estimates are consolidated for Cabinet approval and introduced into Parliament by the President of the Treasury Board before the beginning of the next fiscal year. Because the Estimates are prepared so far in advance of actual spending, several sets of Supplementary Estimates are usually necessary to provide for unforeseen contingencies throughout the fiscal year.

Departmental Interaction with Provinces and the Public

As noted in Chapter 18, much of the interaction between federal and provincial governments takes place at the bureaucratic level. Because the division of powers between federal and provincial governments is often vague and because both levels usually try to maximize their jurisdiction, the two levels end up operating programs in the same fields. Limitations on provincial finances have also prompted the provinces to request federal financial assistance, to which Ottawa has usually attached conditions, making itself even more intertwined with provincial governments. At the height of cooperative federalism, federal and provincial program administrators would interact harmoniously in the design and operation of such integrated programs.[21] It is still the case that in almost every federal department, officials communicate regularly with their provincial counterparts, often by letter, fax, e-mail, or telephone, and sometimes more formally in federal–provincial conferences at the bureaucratic level.

In addition to such vertical department-to-department interaction, each level of government has set up bureaucratic agencies to supervise federal–provincial relations. Although these central agencies are necessary to keep track of the maze of such connections and although they may facilitate federal–provincial bureaucratic cooperation in some instances, they often complicate the friendly relations that individual federal departments have established with their provincial counterparts.

The close relationship between advocacy groups and the bureaucracy was already discussed in Chapter 16. Groups that want to influence either the formulation or the implementation of policies and programs are active in taking their message to the relevant government department. Sometimes public servants resist the approach of self-seeking groups, but at other times the department may actually welcome it, especially if the group has vital, reliable information that will lead to the development of a more effective program, if the group can help muster support for the departmental initiative among other key players in the policymaking process, or if it can serve as a channel of communication to that part of the public that is interested in the particular proposal.

These mutually advantageous contacts between a group and a department may become so close and congenial that a symbiotic **clientele relationship** develops. The department gives official recognition to the group, regularly consults it on policy development and implementation, and gives it representation on advisory committees. It is in this connection that Chapters 16 and 20 spoke of policy communities. Where such a congenial, supportive group does not already exist, it may even be necessary for the department to create it.[22]

As has been mentioned earlier, it is partly because the government lost much of its policy analysis capacity in the severe downsizing of the 1990s that bureaucrats depend more heavily on outside advice today. It may also be that that era had the effect of enhancing the value of public consultation (and polling). For example, 2001 produced an Accord between the Government of Canada and the voluntary sector, which committed both sides to extensive interaction. Another factor is probably that more outside information is available than ever before, whether in universities, advocacy groups, research institutes, or think tanks. Some of the latter include the Canadian Centre for Policy Alternatives, the Institute for Research on Public Policy, the Canadian Tax Foundation, the C.D. Howe Institute, and the Canada West Foundation. In any case, it is almost as normal nowadays for bureaucrats to seek out information and support from outside actors as it is for advocacy groups to impose pressure on their own initiative.[23]

CRITICAL APPROACHES

One of the most influential approaches to the study of bureaucracy, which was particularly popular in the 1990s, is the *rational choice approach*. This approach draws attention to the interests and strategies of individual actors in government institutions. In the context of bureaucracy, the individuals are the civil servants and the institutions are the rules of the organization. In one variant of the rational choice approach to bureaucracy, for example, scholars noted that "moving up the ladder" in the civil service means taking charge of large divisions with many employees and programs. This creates a perverse incentive that rewards managers in the civil service for expanding the number of programs and employees under their command. Some rational choice theorists—not to mention a good number of politicians—invoked the notion of the "budget-maximizing bureaucrat" in their explanations, and proposed solutions for the exponential and supposedly unwieldy growth of the public sector. From this vantage point, politicians would have to find a way to reward civil servants for cutting in their departments, or, at the very least, to prevent civil servants from being rewarded for the creation of expensive and ineffective programs. On the other hand, politicians may be agreeable to bureaucratic objectives as long as public servants help them stay in power by keeping them out of trouble and by pacifying electorally strategic interest groups. Donald Savoie contends, however, that the traditional bargain between the public service and the politicians has been broken.[24]

CROWN CORPORATIONS

The second most important form of bureaucratic organization is the **Crown corporation**. These are government-owned operations that assume a structure similar to a private corporation. Crown corporations may be private firms that have been nationalized by the government by buying their shares (CN and Petro-Canada), they may be transformed from regular departments (Canada Post), or, most typically in Canada, they may be created from scratch (Canada Mortgage and Housing Corporation). Canada has about 45 parent Crown corporations at the federal level, which have a total of about 60 subsidiaries. Table 22.3 lists some major federal Crown corporations and the number of people they employ. In total, Crown corporations have over 90 000 employees.

The corporate structure referred to includes a board of directors, president, vice-presidents, and general manager. The Cabinet appoints the president or CEO and the board of directors, which theoretically set the general policy of the corporation. In 2001, the auditor general pointed out that Crown corporation boards were packed with partisans lacking the basic skills needed to oversee such large businesses, and the Gomery Report called for an end to political involvement of CEOs and directors of Crown corporations.[25]

TABLE 22.3   MAJOR FEDERAL CROWN CORPORATIONS AND NUMBER OF EMPLOYEES, 2013

CANADA POST CORPORATION	53 760
CANADIAN BROADCASTING CORPORATION	8359
ATOMIC ENERGY OF CANADA LTD.	3285
VIA RAIL CANADA INC.	2716
CANADA MORTGAGE AND HOUSING CORPORATION	1900
BUSINESS DEVELOPMENT BANK OF CANADA	1989
FARM CREDIT CANADA	1634
BANK OF CANADA	1608
EXPORT DEVELOPMENT CANADA	1130

Source: Treasury Board of Canada Secretariat, Major Federal Crown Corporations and Number of Employees, 2011, http://www.tbs-sct.gc.ca/reports-rapports/cc-se/crown-etat/efp-esf-eng.asp?fiscalQuarter=2013-09-30, Government Operations Sector, Treasury Board of Canada Secretariat, 2015.

A second distinguishing feature of the Crown corporation is that it is not subject to day-to-day political direction. The statute that creates the corporation sets out its objectives to some extent and the Cabinet may issue certain general policy guidelines, but the corporation otherwise operates more or less independently. The Cabinet minister to whom the Crown corporation is attached largely acts as a channel of communication between it and Parliament, passing on answers to parliamentary inquiries but not being held responsible for the corporation in the same way as for a regular department. However, because the government created the Crown corporation, appoints its leading personnel, and usually provides some of its funds, the minister and Cabinet cannot totally avoid responsibility for its actions. Crown corporations must now submit a corporate plan to the minister as well as an annual year-end report to Parliament. In some cases the Cabinet can issue a directive to the corporation if informal persuasion to change its ways has not been effective, and a government can make deep cuts in a Crown corporation's budget, as the CBC repeatedly discovered.

Third, because many of them compete with private-sector firms, Crown corporations are expected to function without undue interference from bureaucratic administrative policies, such as those of the Public Service Commission and the Treasury Board Secretariat. The Financial Administration Act contains different categories of Crown corporations, ranged in order of increasing independence from government control; as a general rule, the greater the financial self-sufficiency of the corporation, the greater its autonomy.

The Crown corporation is a logical structure for a governmental operation of a commercial or industrial nature; it may also be used in politically sensitive areas, such as broadcasting; and the case for a Crown corporation rather than a department is always stronger if the operation has private-sector competition. Canada once had a unique blend of public and private corporations in such areas as air and rail transportation, broadcasting, and petroleum that led one observer to refer to Canada's "public enterprise" political culture.[26]

Like other government operations, then, Crown corporations have a **public policy purpose**. They are created where the private sector has not met public needs, often because no profit would be feasible in serving the widely dispersed Canadian population. The basic objective of Crown corporations is to provide a public service, not to make a profit, but because most Crown corporations need annual public subsidies, they are often criticized for being inefficient. In fact, however, they are usually just as efficient as private companies; the subsidies are necessary to finance operations that are simply unprofitable by any standard.

The 1980s witnessed a worldwide trend toward the **privatization** of public enterprises led by Margaret Thatcher in Britain. During this period, the Mulroney government privatized Air Canada and Petro-Canada. Such privatizations were largely made for ideological reasons: Conservative governments in particular had a preference for the private sector, and the proceeds from the sale of Crown corporation shares often helped to reduce the national deficit. Privatizers also argued that such Crown corporations no longer served a public policy purpose and that they would operate more efficiently as private companies.

Other changes in the operation of Crown corporations are also afoot. In recent years, for example, local port and airport corporations have become autonomous structures. The **Canadian Wheat Board** became a shared-governance corporation, with farmers electing 10 out of 15 members of the board of directors before the Harper government removed its monopoly powers over the sale of western wheat and barley and then privatized it. Recently created Crown corporations include the Canada Pension Plan Investment Board and PPP Canada, Inc., a federal agency promoting **public–private partnerships** including shared investment in infrastructure projects.

ADMINISTRATIVE AGENCIES

Administrative agencies, sometimes called administrative or regulatory tribunals, constitute a third form of bureaucratic organization. Some of the most important are listed in Table 22.4. In structure, most such agencies and tribunals bear considerable resemblance to Crown corporations. They are usually made up of a chair and board, which are appointed by the Cabinet, and advised by a permanent, expert staff. They typically receive policy guidelines from the Cabinet, but ministers are kept at arm's length from their day-to-day operations. Like Crown corporations, they are at least somewhat exempt from the Public Service Employment Act and Treasury Board Secretariat human resource policies. The incidence of partisanship in appointments to the chair and board has unfortunately been large: indeed, such agencies remain one of the last refuges of patronage in the political system. Among its many patronage appointments, the Harper government named a large number of retired police officers to the National Parole Board, expecting them to have a "get-tough" approach. Harper also fired the President of the Canadian Nuclear Safety Commission and the President of the Canadian Wheat Board, declined to renew the contracts of the head of the Canadian Firearms Registry and the Veterans' Ombudsman, contributed to the resignation of the heads of Statistics Canada, the Military Police Complaints Commission, and the RCMP Public Complaints Commission, and quarrelled with the Information Commissioner, the Chief Electoral Officer, and the Parliamentary Budget Officer.

TABLE 22.4   LEADING AGENCIES, BOARDS, COMMISSIONS, AND TRIBUNALS

ATLANTIC CANADA OPPORTUNITIES AGENCY	CANADIAN TRANSPORTATION AGENCY
CANADA BORDER SERVICES AGENCY	CORRECTIONAL SERVICE OF CANADA
CANADA REVENUE AGENCY	IMMIGRATION AND REFUGEE BOARD
CANADIAN DAIRY COMMISSION	LIBRARY AND ARCHIVES CANADA
CANADIAN FOOD INSPECTION AGENCY	NATIONAL ENERGY BOARD
CANADIAN ENVIRONMENTAL ASSESSMENT AGENCY	NATIONAL FILM BOARD
CANADIAN HUMAN RIGHTS COMMISSION	NATIONAL PAROLE BOARD
CANADIAN INTERNATIONAL DEVELOPMENT AGENCY	NATIONAL RESEARCH COUNCIL
CANADIAN NUCLEAR SAFETY COMMISSION	PARKS CANADA AGENCY
CANADIAN RADIO-TELEVISION AND TELECOMMUNICATIONS COMMISSION	PUBLIC HEALTH AGENCY OF CANADA ROYAL CANADIAN MOUNTED POLICE
CANADIAN SPACE AGENCY	STATISTICS CANADA

One specific type of agency, **regulatory tribunals**, may make **quasi-legislative** rules and regulations, such as in the case of the Canadian-content regulations of the **Canadian Radio-television and Telecommunications Commission**. A typical regulatory tribunal also makes **quasi-judicial** decisions based on the Cabinet's policy guidelines and its own regulations. They issue radio and television licences, approve long-distance telephone rates (CRTC), decide contentious immigration cases (Immigration and Refugee Board), review transportation rates (Canadian Transportation Agency), approve oil, natural gas, and electricity exports as well as new pipeline proposals (**National Energy Board**), and allow prisoners out of jail (National Parole Board).

These functions could presumably be performed by regular government departments, but they are given to semi-independent regulatory tribunals in order to divorce them from political and especially partisan considerations. Such functions are usually of an adjudicative nature and could also be performed by the courts. But these kinds of decisions demand a technical expertise not expected in judges, and it is hoped that the decisions of regulatory agencies will be made more quickly and more cheaply than those of the courts.

At the same time, however, regulatory tribunals are expected to provide an impartial, court-like hearing, and in many cases lawyers are present in the same capacity as in court. Decisions of such agencies are normally appealable to the courts on procedural grounds but not on the substance of the case. Some are appealable to the Cabinet on the merits of the case (e.g., CRTC decisions on long-distance telephone rates), but the Cabinet usually declines to overturn the agency's decision.

There is a wide variety of other administrative agencies. Such "structural heretics"[27] include royal commissions, advisory councils like the National Council of Welfare, funding bodies, agents of Parliament, and other one-of-a-kind agencies. The largest such agencies are the Canada Revenue Agency, Canada Border Services Agency, the Canadian Food Inspection

TABLE 22.5 AGENTS OF PARLIAMENT

AUDITOR GENERAL
CHIEF ELECTORAL OFFICER
COMMISSIONER OF LOBBYING
COMMISSIONER OF OFFICIAL LANGUAGES
CONFLICT OF INTEREST AND ETHICS COMMISSIONER
INFORMATION COMMISSIONER
PRIVACY COMMISSIONER
PUBLIC SECTOR INTEGRITY COMMISSIONER

Agency, Statistics Canada, and Correction Services of Canada. Some of the most popular are funding agencies, such as the National Research Council and the Social Sciences and Humanities Research Council. These agencies exhibit varying degrees of independence from the minister but generally operate at some distance.

The relationship between the government and independent agencies like the RCMP or the Canadian Security Intelligence Service (CSIS) is always somewhat problematic. In an era of anti-terrorism, the secretive activities of such security-related agencies, the rivalry between them, and their relations with U.S. agencies have caused considerable concern.

Agents of Parliament are most the independent type of structure because they are agencies attached to Parliament rather than to the executive branch of government.[28] They are divorced from the government of the day, either because they are meant to be critical or because they are supposed to serve all members impartially. The principal such agents are listed in Table 22.5. While some bureaucrats feel that these agents are too powerful, they are often the only source of information for parliamentarians on the operation of government departments, and many MPs would like the **Parliamentary Budget Officer** to become a fully independent agent as well.

Royal commissions are a traditional instrument of policy advice, with about 450 having been appointed since 1867. Generally speaking, such commissions are very formal, in-depth inquiries set up by the Cabinet to investigate some difficult problem for which the resources of the regular public service are considered inadequate. Royal commissions may be made up of from one to 10 commissioners, usually people of stature and expertise, and normally involve extensive public hearings and an elaborate research program. They are often regarded somewhat cynically because of the length of time it takes them to produce a report, and because they cost a great deal of money. The cynics also point out that governments have not had a good record of implementing royal commission recommendations and that such commissions are often appointed to take the heat off a particular issue. The government has not ordered a Royal Commission since 2006, which represents an exceptionally long period between Commissions.

Sometimes royal commissions are also seen as devices with which to educate the public to the government's way of thinking or of generating support for a policy the government already had in mind. Nevertheless, many royal commissions have served a useful purpose, and many public policies, such as equalization payments, medicare, official bilingualism, and free trade, owe their existence, at least in part, to royal commission reports. Royal commissions are often referred to by the name of their chair, such as Rowell–Sirois (Federal–Provincial Relations, 1940), Hall (Health Services, 1964–65), Macdonald (Economic Prospects, 1985), and Romanow (Future of Health Care, 2002). The Royal Commission on Aboriginal Peoples (RCAP) and the Commission on the Future of Health Care are the most significant in recent times, but the Harper government preferred to appoint smaller, short-term advisory panels or task forces.

CONTROLLING THE BUREAUCRACY

Given the enormous influence and considerable power of the bureaucracy in the modern state, democracies are understandably concerned about keeping the public service under control. Similarly, the issue of accountability is of increasing significance.

Prime Minister, Ministers, and Cabinet

In the first place, the prime minister, individual ministers, and the Cabinet as a whole are supposed to provide political control of the bureaucracy. The minister both gives direction to the public service and has the power to veto any of its proposals, at least in theory. Real ministers have provided varied accounts of what actually happens in practice: some argue that ministers can control their departments, while others feel that they were often manipulated by their public servants. Even where the minister in charge is weak or manipulated, however, the prime minister or Cabinet as a whole may step in from time to time to reject bureaucratic advice and opt for an alternative proposal whose political implications are more to their liking.

Bureaucrats Controlling Bureaucrats

In the second place, the power of some bureaucrats is controlled by other bureaucrats, such as the financial control of the Treasury Board Secretariat and the Finance department, the personnel control of the Public Service Commission and the TBS, and the policy control of the Privy Council Office. The Martin government provided the TBS with a clearer focus to scrutinize departmental plans, performance, and spending, while the comptroller general was upgraded to a distinct office within the TBS, reporting to the minister, and with close ties to comptrollers in departments and agencies. In addition, Martin's "whistle-blowing" legislation, strengthened by Harper's Accountability Act, was designed to allow bureaucrats to be safe from punishment for revealing improper activities of their colleagues or superiors.

House of Commons

The third line of defence against bureaucratic power is the House of Commons.[29] Although its operations will be examined in more detail in Chapter 23, one principle of parliamentary government is that the executive (Cabinet or bureaucracy) is not allowed either to raise or spend money without parliamentary approval. In practice, proposals for tax changes as well as spending proposals

Auditor General Michael Ferguson.

all originate with the executive, they are rarely altered in the legislative process, and the taxing and spending usually begin before Parliament has given its consent. But ultimately Parliament must pass all such financial measures. The process of examining the Estimates gives the House of Commons an opportunity to question and criticize ministers and deputy ministers about all aspects of their departmental spending, programs, and policies. Furthermore, the **Auditor General** keeps an eye on the spending process and later informs Parliament of instances where funds were spent unlawfully or unwisely. The **Public Accounts Committee** of the House goes through the auditor general's report and calls onto the carpet those ministers or deputy ministers who have committed the worst financial faults.

Four other principal means are used by the House of Commons to control the bureaucracy. The first is the daily oral Question Period. In this case, the Commons must act through the intermediary minister who is theoretically responsible for everything the department does. Although the minister is expected to take the blame for bureaucratic errors, public servants seek to avoid bringing such embarrassment or disrepute upon their minister and department. Second, members of Parliament receive requests on a daily basis from their constituents to intervene on their behalf to speed up or correct bureaucratic decisions. MPs and their staff normally handle such problems with a telephone call or a letter to the public servant or minister concerned. A third kind of parliamentary control of the bureaucracy is exercised by the standing committees of the House, which have the authority to study all matters relating to the mandate, management, organization, and operation of the departments assigned to them. This mandate includes reviewing programs, policies, expenditures, and senior appointments. Finally, the **Standing Joint Committee on the Scrutiny of Regulations** attempts to review the reams of regulations that the bureaucracy produces annually.

The Judiciary

A fourth kind of control of the bureaucracy is provided by the judiciary. The power of the courts to overturn decisions of bureaucrats in regular government departments is essentially restricted to breaches of the law or actions taken beyond the public servant's jurisdiction. Such cases are rare, but the **Charter of Rights and Freedoms** provides more scope for this kind of judicial review of bureaucratic action than in the past. In the *Singh* case, for example, the Supreme Court ruled that the immigration department had to provide an oral hearing for refugee claimants. In the *Little Sisters* case, the Supreme Court of Canada told customs officers that they must not discriminate against gay or lesbian material and that all sexually oriented material must be judged by the same criteria. The Charter's effect on the bureaucracy primarily relates to police officers, a special kind of public servant, and most often employed at the provincial or municipal level. Regulatory agencies are usually expected to operate in a court-like manner, and their decisions can be overturned by the courts for procedural abuses as well as for exceeding their jurisdiction. The **Federal Court of Canada**, to be discussed in Chapter 24, specializes in hearing appeals from such regulatory agencies.

Watchdog Agencies

Every Canadian province except Prince Edward Island has supplemented these four means of controlling the bureaucracy with the appointment of an ombudsman, an official of the legislature to whom people can complain about bureaucratic decisions, mistakes, abuse, discrimination, delays, or indecision. Ombudsmen try to correct such errors by persuasion, but, if that fails, they can resort to the power of legislative and media publicity. Canada has no overall ombudsman at the federal level, but several watchdog officials exist to deal with specialized complaints. For example, the correctional investigator looks into complaints from inmates against prison authorities, and the veterans' ombudsman deals with veterans' problems. More independent are the officers or agents of parliament listed in Table 22.5. They include the Commissioner of Official Languages who explores public or bureaucratic claims regarding infringement of the Official Languages Act, and the Privacy Commissioner, who investigates complaints from citizens who believe that their privacy rights have been invaded. For example, after being criticized by the privacy commissioner, customs officials changed their practice of routinely opening certain heavy mail and sending it to immigration officials when they suspected it might contain information on illegal immigration and fraudulent documents.

The Information Commissioner

One of the most important of these watchdog agencies is the **Information Commissioner**. Canadian governments traditionally functioned under a thick cloak of secrecy at both the Cabinet and the bureaucratic levels. This tradition prevented the opposition and the public from knowing what alternative policies were considered in the executive branch, what kind of public opinion polling was carried out, and what advice was actually offered by the bureaucracy to the Cabinet. The **Access to Information Act** was passed in 1983 and considerably improved the situation, although the many exemptions in the act meant that it was not entirely effective. When citizens, journalists, companies, or interest groups apply to a department for a piece of government information, they are supposed to receive it within 30 days. If they are denied such government information, they can appeal to the Information Commissioner, who uses moral suasion to resolve the matter but can also overrule the department, with a final to appeal to the Federal Court.

The Auditor General

Although the auditor general was mentioned above as one means of parliamentary control over the bureaucracy, the office deserves specific attention.[30] The auditor general's staff operate something like secret agents within the public service, recording any decisions or practices that are illegal, immoral, wasteful, or otherwise ill advised. These agents are not narrow financial auditors—they have no hesitation in making broad policy recommendations to the government in the periodic auditor general's reports to Parliament. Being an officer of Parliament gives the auditor almost complete independence from the government of the day.

The auditor's exposure of deficiencies in the financial management of job-creation programs of Economic and Social Development Canada were mentioned earlier in the chapter. The firearms registry was supposed to be almost financially self-sufficient, but the Department of Justice estimated in 2000 that the program would cost at least $1 billion by 2005. What troubled the auditor general even more than the cost overruns, however, was that the department and government generally tried to hide the dramatic increase from Parliament. It was also Auditor General Sheila Fraser who first discovered the abuses in the sponsorship scandal, as bureaucrats directed government advertising contracts to corporations with connections to the Liberal Party.[31]

Bureaucratic Accountability

In the wake of its near-defeat in the 1995 referendum on Quebec sovereignty, the Chrétien government got into serious ethical problems on the issue of government-financed advertising and sponsorship programs to promote Canada at sporting and cultural events in Quebec.

More than $23 million went to Groupaction Marketing, the federal government's agent in awarding such contracts, a firm that had close ties to the Liberal Party and had contributed to it financially. While the whole scheme was orchestrated in the PMO, the auditor general reported that senior bureaucrats broke nearly every rule in the book in awarding questionable contracts, while the RCMP investigated several cases. Newly elected Prime Minister Paul Martin appointed an independent ethics commissioner, who would review the actions of all MPs, including the prime minister and ministers, and report to the House of Commons. Martin also revised various codes of conduct within the bureaucracy, and appointed the Gomery Inquiry to get to the bottom of the "sponsorship scandal."

In his first report, Gomery established that there had been partisan political involvement in the administration of the sponsorship program; insufficient oversight by senior public servants; deliberate actions taken to avoid compliance with federal legislation and policies; a culture of entitlement among political officials and public servants involved; and the refusal of Ministers, senior officials in the Prime Minister's Office, and public servants to acknowledge any responsibility for the mismanagement that had occurred.[32]

In his second report, Gomery called for a rebalancing of the relationship between Parliament and government with the assignment of clearer accountability to both politicians and public servants. A key concern had to do with the principle of individual ministerial responsibility as opposed to the role of deputy ministers in running their departments. This issue had been questioned for some time, especially with respect to the problems in ESDC and the firearms registry, where serious errors were committed but the public found it hard to nail anyone with accountability. Indeed, in the earlier Al-Mashat affair in 1991, when the former Iraq ambassador to the U.S. was illegally admitted to Canada as a landed immigrant, ministers took the unusual step of blaming public servants for the errors.[33]

As noted earlier in the chapter, the minister is not expected to know everything that is going on in his or her department and yet is theoretically responsible. Meanwhile, the deputy minister, who really runs the department, is not held responsible. The official view has been that ministers are *accountable* to Parliament even for the statutory obligations of their deputies; deputy ministers are *answerable* on behalf of their ministers before Parliamentary committees but not *accountable*. Gomery recommended that to become more familiar with their departments, deputy ministers should remain in their posts for a longer period of time, at least three years and preferably five. More significantly, deputy ministers and senior public servants should be held accountable for their legal responsibilities before the Public Accounts Committee.[34]

To some extent the Conservatives owed their election in 2006 to the sponsorship scandal. Prime Minister Stephen Harper promised and delivered a wide-ranging Federal Accountability Act which was mentioned earlier in this and other chapters. It was a mammoth document that affected almost every aspect of government operations. In some respects Harper's initiative coincided with the recommendations made in the Gomery Report, but in many others it fell short, such as in failing to strengthen the information commissioner and in leaving loopholes as in the Lobbying Act.[35]

On the question of making deputy ministers somewhat more accountable for the operation of their departments, Harper did not go as far as Gomery recommended. DMs were designated as "accounting officers" and *answerable* for their departments before the Public Accounts Committee; they remained *accountable* to their ministers, however, who in turn continued to be responsible or accountable to parliament.[36] Considerable controversy and confusion continue to exist surrounding this question.

CONCLUSION

This chapter illuminates the usually invisible world of the Canadian bureaucracy, an exceedingly complex operation that is charged to undertake an incredible number of tasks. It is a challenge to organize and coordinate the nearly half a million people performing such specialized functions. A central question that arises in any discussion of the bureaucracy is whether it is out of control, an issue that primarily relates to the delicate relationship between the public service and the politicians. Several means of control were discussed above, but the question remains. Another main issue that this subject raises is ensuring that the public service is well positioned to offer the best possible advice to the government and that it provides services to the public in the most satisfactory way. The Canadian bureaucracy continues to strive to improve its performance in both respects.

This chapter is primarily linked to the preceding one on the political executive; indeed, the operations of the two parts of the executive are very closely connected. It is also tied to the policymaking discussions in Chapters 16 (advocacy groups) and 20, and less directly, to most other chapters.

DISCUSSION QUESTIONS

1. What is the ideal relationship between the minister and the deputy minister and between the deputy minister and Parliament?

2. Do central agencies interfere excessively with the deputy minister's responsibility to manage the department?

3. To what extent should Canada establish a "representative bureaucracy"?

4. Given the necessity of the bureaucracy in the modern state, are the democratic controls on its power sufficient?

5. How do you feel about downsizing the public service, privatizing Crown corporations, and deregulation? What are the costs and benefits of these reforms?

MindTap®   FOR MORE INFO GO TO **http://www.nelson.com/student**

NOTES

1. Donald J. Savoie, *Governing from the Centre: The Concentration of Power in Canadian Politics* (Toronto: University of Toronto, 1999), pp. 7–8.
2. S.L. Sutherland, "Responsible Government and Ministerial Responsibility: Every Reform Is Its Own Problem," *Canadian Journal of Political Science* (March 1991); S.L. Sutherland, "The Al-Mashat Affair: Administrative Responsibility in Parliamentary Institutions," *Canadian Public Administration* (Winter 1991); Nicholas d'Ombrain, "Ministerial responsibility and the machinery of government," *Canadian Public Administration* (June 2007); and Privy Council Office, *Accountable Government: A Guide for Ministers and Ministers of State*, 2011, cited on February 22, 2012, available at http://www.pco-bcp .gc.ca/docs/information/Publications/ag-gr/2008/docs/ag-gr-eng.pdf.
3. Auditor General's Report, *Reflections on a Decade of Serving Parliament* (February 2001), p. 57. See Donald J. Savoie, *Breaking the Bargain: Public Servants, Ministers, and Parliament* (Toronto: University of Toronto Press, 2003).
4. Savoie, *Governing from the Centre*, p. 248.
5. Privy Council Office, *Accountable Government: A Guide for Ministers and Ministers of State*, 2011, Annex E, p. 41, available at http://www.pco-bcp.gc.ca/docs/information/publications/ag-gr/2011/docs/ ag-gr-eng.pdf.
6. Gordon Osbaldeston, *Keeping Deputy Ministers Accountable* (Toronto: McGraw-Hill Ryerson, 1990); Jacques Bourgault, "The Role of Deputy Ministers in Canadian Government," in Christopher Dunn, ed., *The Handbook of Canadian Public Administration*, 2nd ed. (Toronto: Oxford University Press, 2010); and Maurice Henrie, *The Mandarin Syndrome: The Secret Life of Senior Bureaucrats* (Ottawa: University of Ottawa Press, 2006).
7. See the exchange between Flora MacDonald and Mitchell Sharp in Paul Fox and Graham White, eds., *Politics: Canada*, 7th ed. (Toronto: McGraw-Hill Ryerson, 1991); and between Flora MacDonald and Don Page in Mark Charlton and Paul Barker, eds., *Crosscurrents: Contemporary Political Issues*, 2nd ed. (Scarborough: Nelson Canada, 1994).
8. Savoie, *Governing from the Centre*, pp. 241–42.
9. Ibid., p. 10.
10. John H. Gomery, *Restoring Accountability: Phase 2 Report* (the Gomery Report), (Ottawa: Commission of Inquiry into the Sponsorship Program and Advertising Activities, 2004), Ch. 8.

11. Privy Council Office, *Accountable Government: A Guide for Ministers and Ministers of State, 2011*, Annex R, p. 45, available at http://www.pco-bcp.gc.ca/docs/information/publications/ag-gr/2011/docs/ag-gr-eng.pdf.

12. Gomery Report, Ch. 7, pp. 135–37.

13. Herman Bakvis and Luc Juillet, *The Horizontal Challenge: Line Departments, Central Agencies and Leadership* (Ottawa: Canada School of Public Administration, 2004); Leslie A. Pal, *Beyond Policy Analysis: Public Issue Management in Turbulent Times*, 4th ed. (Toronto: Nelson Education, 2010), Ch. 7; and Savoie, *Governing from the Centre*, pp. 13, 56–57, and 62.

14. Pal, *Beyond Policy Analysis*, Ch. 7; and Savoie, *Governing from the Centre*, pp. 295–96.

15. Tim J. Bartkiw, "Temporary Help Agency Employment in the Federal Government," in G. Bruce Doern and Christopher Stoney, eds., *How Ottawa Spends 2010–2011* (Montreal; McGill-Queen's University Press, 2010).

16. J.L. Granatstein, *The Ottawa Men: The Civil Service Mandarins 1935–1957* (Toronto: Oxford University Press, 1982).

17. John Porter, *The Vertical Mosaic* (Toronto: University of Toronto Press, 1965); Dennis Olsen, *The State Elite* (Toronto: McClelland and Stewart, 1980); and Bryan Evans, et al., "Profiling the Public-Service Elite: A Demographic and Career Trajectory Survey of Deputy and Assistant Deputy Ministers in Canada," *Canadian Public Administration* (Winter 2007).

18. Treasury Board of Canada Secretariat, *Annual Report on Official Languages 2013–2014*, available at http://www.tbs-sct.gc.ca/psm-fpfm/ve/ol-lo/reports-rapports/2013-2014/arol-ralo-eng.asp#app4, retrieved on Sept. 2, 2015.

19. Kathleen Archibald, *Sex and the Public Service* (Ottawa: Queen's Printer, 1970); Task Force on Barriers to Women in the Public Service, *Beneath the Veneer, vol. 1* (Ottawa: Supply and Services, 1990); Caroline Andrew, "Women and the Public Sector," in Dunn, *The Handbook of Canadian Public Administration*.

20. Donald J. Savoie, *The Politics of Public Spending in Canada* (Toronto: University of Toronto Press, 1990); David A. Good, *The Politics of Public Money: Spenders, Guardians, Priority Setters and Financial Watchdogs inside the Canadian Government* (Toronto: University of Toronto Press, 2007). Good argues that guardians and spenders have now been joined by "priority setters" (Prime Minister and PCO) and "financial watchdogs" (Auditor General), as in "Budgeting in Canada: Beyond Spenders and Guardians," in Dunn, *The Handbook of Canadian Public Administration*.

21. Rand Dyck, "The Canada Assistance Plan: The Ultimate in Cooperative Federalism," *Canadian Public Administration* (Winter 1976).

22. Paul Pross, *Group Politics and Public Policy* (Toronto: Oxford University Press, 1986); William D. Coleman and Grace Skogstad, eds., *Policy Communities and Public Policy in Canada* (Mississauga: Copp Clark Pitman, 1990).

23. Pal, *Beyond Policy Analysis*, Ch. 6; and Savoie, *Breaking the Bargain: Public Servants, Ministers, and Parliament*, Ch. 6.

24. Savoie, *Breaking the Bargain: Public Servants, Ministers, and Parliament*; Bakvis and Jarvis, *From "New Public Management" to "New Political Governance."*

25. Auditor General's Report, *Reflections on a Decade of Serving Parliament*, p. 18; Auditor General, *Status Report*, February 15, 2005, Ch. 7; and Gomery Report, *Restoring Accountability*, Ch. 10, pp. 188–90.

26. Herschel Hardin, *A Nation Unaware: The Canadian Economic Culture* (Vancouver: J.S. Douglas, 1974); Herschel Hardin, *The Privatization Putsch* (Halifax: Institute for Research on Public Policy, 1989).

27. J.E. Hodgetts, *The Canadian Public Service: A Physiology of Government, 1867–1970* (Toronto: University of Toronto Press, 1973).

28. Jeffrey Graham Bell, "Agents of Parliament: A New Branch of Government?" *Canadian Parliamentary Review* (Spring 2006); John A. Stillborn, "The Officers of Parliament: More Watchdogs, More Teeth, Better Governance?" in Doern and Stoney, eds., *How Ottawa Spends 2010–2011*.

29. Paul Thomas, "Parliament and the Public Service," in Dunn, *The Handbook of Canadian Public Administration*; David A. Good, "Parliament and Public Money: Players and Police," *Canadian Parliamentary Review* (Spring 2005).

30. S.L. Sutherland, "On the Audit Trail of the Auditor General: Parliament's Servant, 1973–80," *Canadian Public Administration* (Winter 1980); and S.L. Sutherland, "The Politics of Audit: The Federal Office of the Auditor General in Comparative Perspective," *Canadian Public Administration* (Spring 1986); and see Auditor General's reports.

31. Gomery Report, *Restoring Accountability*, Ch. 4, pp. 75–80.
32. Gomery, *Restoring Accountability*, p. 197; see also articles in *Policy Options*, June 2005 and June 2006; Ian Greene and David Shugarman, "Commission of Inquiry into the Sponsorship Program and Advertising Activities, Phase I Report and Phase II Report," *Canadian Public Administration* (Summer 2006); Savoie, *Breaking the Bargain: Public Servants, Ministers, and Parliament*.
33. S.L. Sutherland, "The Al-Mashat Affair: Administrative Responsibility in Parliamentary Institutions."
34. Gomery Report, *Restoring Accountability*, Ch. 5.
35. Despite the length and breadth of the Federal Accountability Act and the constraints it imposed on the behaviour of public servants, many observers question its effects and even the sincerity of its intentions. Apart from its provisions regarding party finance, lobbying, and prosecutions, its most significant parts included the enactment of a new conflict of interest act covering ministers, their staff and advisers, and government in council appointments; the strengthening of the power of the Auditor General and the auditing and accountability procedures within departments; and the creation of the positions of Parliamentary Budget Officer and an independent procurement auditor.
36. Alan Gilmore, "The Canadian Accounting Officer: Has it Strengthened Parliament's ability to Hold the Government to Account?" in Dunn, *The Handbook of Canadian Public Administration*, 2nd ed.; Mark D. Jarvis, "The Adoption of the Accounting Officer System in Canada: Changing Relationships?" *Canadian Public Administration* (December 2009); Jonathan Malloy and Scott Millar, "Why Ministerial Responsibility Can Still Work," in G. Bruce Doern, ed., *How Ottawa Spends, 2007–2008: The Harper Conservatives—Climate of Change* (Montreal: McGill-Queen's University Press, 2007).

FURTHER READING

Bakvis, Herman, and Mark D. Jarvis, eds. *From "New Public Management" to "New Political Governance": Essays in Honour of Peter C. Aucoin*. Montreal: McGill-Queen's University Press, 2012.

Bakvis, Herman, and Luc Juillet. *The Horizontal Challenge: Line Departments, Central Agencies and Leadership*. Ottawa: Canada School of Public Service, 2004.

Barker, Paul. *Public Administration in Canada*. Toronto: Thomson Nelson, 2008.

Dunn, Christopher, ed. *The Handbook of Canadian Public Administration*. Toronto: Oxford University Press, 2002; 2nd ed., 2010.

Inwood, Gregory J. *Understanding Canadian Public Administration: An Introduction to Theory and Practice*, 3rd ed. Toronto: Prentice Hall Canada, 2009.

Johnson, David. *Thinking Government: Public Sector Management in Canada*, 2nd ed. Peterborough: Broadview Press, 2006.

Pal, Leslie A. *Beyond Policy Analysis: Public Issue Management in Turbulent Times*, 4th ed. Toronto: Nelson Education, 2010.

Privy Council Office. *Accountable Government: A Guide for Ministers and Ministers of State, 2011*, available at http://www.pco-bcp.gc.ca/docs/information/publications/ag-gr/2011/docs/ag-gr-eng.pdf.

Savoie, Donald J. *Breaking the Bargain: Public Servants, Ministers, and Parliament*. Toronto: University of Toronto Press, 2003.

Treff, Karin, and Deborah Ort. *Finances of the Nation 2011*. Toronto: Canadian Tax Foundation, 2012.

CHAPTER 23

Parliament

The elected representatives of the Canadian people meet in open, verbal combat in Question Period in the House of Commons about 135 days a year. Members of Parliament on the opposition side of the House attack the prime minister and other ministers for acts of omission and commission, while the government responds with laudatory statements and statistics on its own performance. In these exchanges and other debates, politicians' reputations are often made and broken. The House of Commons is the central link between the public and the government in Canadian democracy, and, as such, is the furnace of national politics. Most interests in society are represented there in one way or another, and they clash on a regular basis. The Commons is the primary battleground for the hearts and minds of Canadian voters, and House debate is a "lead-up" to the subsequent election campaign. The Senate, on the other hand, is normally a much more peaceful place and is viewed by many Canadians as a group of unelected, elderly party hacks who collect generous remuneration for doing little work. This impression is not entirely correct, however, and when the Senate's majority belongs to a different party from that in the Commons, its work becomes much more interesting.

Every four or five years (or more often with minority governments), voters in each local constituency elect their representative to the House of Commons. Because they have a direct part in electing its members, because it operates publicly, and because they often see it in action on television, Canadians are generally more familiar with the House of Commons than with any other political institution. This familiarity has sometimes led such voters and viewers to think that the Commons has more power in the policymaking process than it actually does. Although it is largely to enhance that power that the proposals to reform the procedures of the House are regularly advanced, the institution has other functions that are not widely understood.

In addition to the House of Commons, the Parliament of Canada includes the Crown (currently the Queen, though represented by the governor general) and the Senate, and a bill must be approved by all three parts to become a law. Indeed, every federal statute begins with the words, "Her Majesty, by and with the Advice and Consent of the Senate and House of Commons of Canada, enacts as follows...." In this respect Canada is sometimes said to employ the **Westminster model** of government because it is based on the British system. As noted in Chapter 2, this model begins with a bicameral legislature: an elected lower house with primary legislative powers answerable to the polity through elections, and an upper house with limited legislative powers, in law or in fact. The executive is chosen based on which party leader can maintain the "confidence" (a majority of votes) of the lower house. This leader becomes the Prime Minister, who then choses the Cabinet (usually other members of the Prime Minister's party in the lower house, though upper house members can be included), which drives or "energizes" the legislative process. The government or Cabinet is in charge of and responsible for the conduct of parliamentary business, while an institutionalized opposition has the right to criticize the government and the ability to make that criticism felt. The Westminster model, therefore, promises potent government and political stability through the prime minister and Cabinet, along with political accountability through open debate.

In popular parlance, however, the word **Parliament** is often used synonymously with the Commons, which is by far its most important part. Hence members of the House of Commons are called members of Parliament or MPs. They can be largely divided into three main groups: those who also serve as Cabinet ministers (the **government**), those who support the Cabinet (government **backbenchers**), and those who oppose the government (the **opposition**).

This chapter examines the House of Commons from a number of perspectives. These include its functions and powers, its composition, the parliamentary timetable, party discipline and the party caucus, stages and kinds of legislation, the organization and officers of the House, the committee system, members' services, the roles of MPs, the government–opposition balance, minority government, and reform of the institution. The chapter later explores the role of the Senate.

FUNCTIONS AND POWERS OF THE HOUSE OF COMMONS

Historically, a basic principle of Canadian government was the sovereignty or **supremacy of Parliament**—that is, apart from interfering in provincial jurisdiction and with other minor exceptions, Parliament could pass laws of any kind that were virtually beyond review by any other organ of government, including the courts. This principle was considerably transformed in 1982, however, with the adoption of the Canadian **Charter of Rights and Freedoms**. The courts have now been given the power to review both federal and provincial legislation in terms of the Charter and to invalidate such legislation when contradiction exists. In striking down legislation however, the courts—at least in theory—suggest that legislation be redrafted to fit with the Charter, and the **notwithstanding clause** allows for the reassertion of parliamentary sovereignty on many points. As noted in Chapter 19, the courts and Parliament are engaged in a dialogue of sorts on these issues.

The principal function of the House of Commons (and Senate) is the legislative function—to pass laws, although, as the previous two chapters have shown, these are usually formulated by the executive branch. A second function is that of representation: MPs (and senators) articulate local and other interests by means of questions, statements, and petitions, and party caucuses try to bring these interests together to form one position. The third function is scrutiny—to hold the executive branch accountable through questions, debates, and committee work. The fourth is to review the financial initiatives of the government.

Another way to address the functions of the House of Commons is in its relationship to the prime minister and Cabinet. The House of Commons does not govern, but, in the first instance, through motions of confidence and nonconfidence, it decides who will form the government; second, it provides that government, on behalf of the people, with the authority, funds, and other resources necessary for governing the country; third, by acting as a constant critic and watchdog, it makes the government behave; and fourth, it provides an alternative government by enabling the opposition to present its case to the public and potentially replace the party in power.[1]

In discussing the functions of the House of Commons it is also instructive to examine its role in the chart of the policymaking process outlined in Chapter 20. In the first place, Parliament may be involved in the initiation phase by raising issues in the daily Question Period and in general debates, in criticizing existing spending programs, or by means of private members' bills. It is then virtually nonexistent in the priority-setting and policy formulation phases. Where the Commons dominates the picture is in the legitimation stage. Whether or not bills are refined in the course of their passage through the House of Commons, they are at least legitimated. This means that Cabinet proposals embodied in bills are given democratic approval and made legitimate by their passage through the formal, authorized channels of the Commons. It may not make many significant changes, but the House does subject bills to extended debate and publicizes their advantages and disadvantages before converting them into laws or statutes. C.E.S. Franks calls this process the "mobilization of consent."[2] The legislative stage serves to inform the public of the content of new policies, and out of this "prolonged warfare," acceptance is eventually obtained. This debate essentially prepares the electorate for its decision on how to vote in the next election. The House then has little say in the fifth and sixth phases, the implementation and interpretation of laws, including scant supervision of regulations issued by the executive.

The various ways of looking at the functions of the House of Commons noted above emphasize the role of the institution as a whole. In their representative role, individual members also have interest articulation and ombudsman functions, as they speak out for their constituencies and provide service to their constituents.

COMPOSITION OF THE HOUSE OF COMMONS

The basic principle in establishing the House of Commons is that each province is represented in proportion to its population. Chapter 13 outlined how the 338 seats in the Commons are distributed among the provinces and territories, with the following results: Ontario, 121; Quebec, 78; BC, 42; Alberta, 34; Manitoba, 14; Saskatchewan, 14; Nova Scotia, 11; New Brunswick, 10; Newfoundland and Labrador, 7; PEI, 4; Northwest Territories, 1; Nunavut, 1; and Yukon, 1.

Even if members of Parliament other than Cabinet ministers have only a limited role in the policymaking process, they are important enough to justify an inquiry into their social-background characteristics. Since they are elected to represent territorial units and usually live in or near their constituencies, MPs become representative of the population in a geographic sense. Although it is not inevitable that they will be representative in terms of ethnic background, this tends to be true in the case of English and French origins. The **Constitution Act, 1867,** required from the beginning that all House documents be printed in English and French, but the absence of simultaneous interpretation until 1958 and the unilingualism of most MPs served to limit the interaction between the two linguistic groups. Nowadays, they are increasingly bilingual.

However, members of Parliament do not reflect the population as well in terms of other ethnocultural groups, although the number of visible-minority MPs continues to increase. The 2015 election saw 47 visible-minority MPs (14 percent of all MPs) elected, which is the highest proportion in history, though still less than the 19 percent that make up Canada's population.[3] Then, although not as exclusive as Cabinet ministers, MPs typically have higher educational levels and higher-status occupations than the general population. Historically the legal profession furnished the largest single group in the Commons, but the number of MPs with a business background has exceeded the number of lawyers since the 1984 Conservative victory. A rough indication of the leading occupations of members of Parliament elected in 2011 is provided in Table 23.1, which shows that businesspeople, managers, and educators are most numerous, but that the working class continues to be severely underrepresented.

Members are also unrepresentative of the population with respect to gender. Relatively few women have been elected to the House of Commons, although the number is on the increase, reaching 39 out of 295 in 1988, 54 in 1993, 62 of 301 in both 1997 and 2000, 65 of 308 in 2004, 64 in 2006, 69 in 2008, 76 in 2011, and 88 in 2015. The high proportion of MPs without any previous service in elected office at the provincial level should also be mentioned. With less than 10 percent of recent MPs having previously served in a provincial legislature, it is evident that federal and provincial political careers in Canada are quite distinct, although 20 to 25 percent of MPs come with municipal government experience.

What is probably most striking about Canadian members of Parliament, especially compared with other legislatures around the world, is their rapid turnover in office. With such a small number of **safe seats**, the proportion of new members after each election is about 40 percent, and the average length of time in office is less than 10 years. This means that Canadian MPs are

TABLE 23.1 OCCUPATIONAL DISTRIBUTION OF MPs, 2011

FIELD	NUMBER OF MPs
MANAGER, DIRECTOR, EXECUTIVE	63
BUSINESS	59
EDUCATION	50
LAWYER	44
CONSULTANT	36
AGRICULTURE	20

NOTE: MANY MPs LISTED MORE THAN ONE OCCUPATION.

Source: Parliament of Canada, Top 10 Occupations in the House of Commons, 2011, *http://www.parl.gc.ca/ Parlinfo/Lists/Top10Occupations.aspx?Menu=HOC-Bio-Occ & Section=03d93c58-f843-49b3-9653 -84275c23f3fb&Chamber=03d93c58-f843-49b3-9653-84275c23f3fb&Parliament=&Name=&Party=&Province= &Gender=&CurrentParliamentarian=True (accessed April 10, 2012). Reproduced with the permission of the Library of Parliament, 2015.*

transient amateurs who engage in "avocational politics."[4] Few members remain in Parliament long enough to develop an understanding of the institution, to master their extra-parliamentary responsibilities, or to stand up to a long-serving prime minister. Because of the decimation of the Conservatives and NDP, the 1993 turnover was more than 75 percent, but even the relatively calm 1997 and 2000 elections produced a turnover of 30 percent and 15 percent, respectively. It was only about 20 percent in 2004 and 2011, but jumped to 35 percent in 2004 and 2011, and the 2015 election saw significant change again, with approximately 60 percent of MPs not returning either due to retirement or failure to be re-elected.

THE PARLIAMENTARY TIMETABLE

Perhaps the best way to get an overview of the work of the House of Commons is by examining the parliamentary timetable—the agenda of a typical session and a typical week. The Constitution requires that Parliament meet at least once a year, but it now sits for about 26 weeks, or 130 days, per year, from mid-September to mid-December, and from late-January to mid-June, incorporating a weekly break per month.

The Typical Session

A session begins with the **speech from the throne**, prepared by the prime minister (and advisers) and read by the governor general. Its function is to outline the government's legislative plans for the session, although the speech is often worded so vaguely that it is not a reliable guide. That speech introduces the throne speech debate, a six-day debate in which MPs can talk about anything that comes to mind. Party leaders and Cabinet ministers may use the occasion to articulate their priorities, while backbenchers often expound on the wonders or troubles of their constituency.

The second major event of the session is the **budget** and the budget debate, though depending on the length of the session, which is ultimately determined by the government so long as it maintains confidence, more than one budget may be presented. The budget itself is the annual financial statement of the government delivered by the minister of finance, chiefly concerned with tax changes and the broad outlines of expenditures for the forthcoming fiscal year. Among other things, the budget usually fleshes out the vague promises of the speech from the throne. So that no one can take advantage of tax changes beforehand, the budget is shrouded in secrecy until its delivery, and real or apparent "budget leaks" always generate great controversy. The budget sets the stage for a four-day freewheeling debate and provides the opposition with a second opportunity to try to defeat the government. Majority governments need not worry, but the Trudeau and Clark minority governments were defeated on their budgets in 1974 and 1979, respectively, and the Martin and Harper minority governments were forced to amend their respective 2005 and 2009 budgets. Legislation incorporating the specific tax changes mentioned in the budget comes along later, although the changes usually take effect as of budget night.

The details of the government's spending proposals for the next fiscal year are contained in the **Estimates**. Their presentation is the third major item of business in the session. Once tabled, however, the Estimates are transmitted to standing committees of the House for scrutiny, so that they actually occupy little time of the Commons as a whole. The Estimates are part of the "supply" process—granting the government a supply of funds with which to finance its activities.

A fourth element of the session consists of the 22 days when the opposition parties choose the subject of debate and the government in turn responds. These are related to granting the government supply, and therefore variously called "supply," "allotted," or **opposition days**. They are divided proportionately among the opposition parties and distributed throughout the session, at the rate of approximately one per week.

Other than these four components, the time of the House of Commons is essentially taken up with the discussion of bills, and most of that time with bills introduced by the government. Indeed, it is partly because of the volume of government legislation that sessions of Parliament often exceed a year in length, but the cycle of events just outlined is ideally repeated on an annual basis.

When the government wants to take a break within a session, it "adjourns" the House; when it wants to bring a session to an end, it "prorogues" the Commons; and an election call results in the **dissolution of Parliament**. Because government bills not passed by prorogation die and must start again from scratch in the next session, governments sometimes allow sessions to continue beyond one year until all prioritized legislation is complete. Alternatively, they may hold short sessions based on what is deemed necessary. In 1988–89, the Mulroney government held a session of only 11 sitting days to pass the Canada–U.S. Free Trade Agreement. The Harper government prorogued the House in December 2008, after only 13 sitting days, to avoid a nonconfidence motion.

The Typical Week

The weekly House of Commons schedule can be seen in Figure 23.1. The 1982 reforms eliminated the traditional evening sittings in favour of meeting in the morning, now starting at 11:00 a.m. on Monday, 10:00 a.m. on Tuesday, Thursday, and Friday, and 2:00 p.m. on Wednesday, and finishing at 7:00 p.m. from Monday to Thursday and at 2:30 on Friday. Wednesday mornings are reserved for party caucus meetings. The items on the daily agenda are statements by members, Question Period, government orders (usually government bills), private members' business (usually private members' bills), and the adjournment proceedings. "Routine proceedings" include the tabling of documents, statements by ministers, presentation of petitions and committee reports, and introduction and first reading of bills.

The highlight of the day is the 45-minute **Question Period**.[5] This period offers the opposition its best opportunity to criticize and embarrass the government as it grills the prime minister and Cabinet ministers about their deficiencies and faults. Ministers are not given notice of such questions, but before going into the chamber they are briefed by aides who try to anticipate what questions might be asked. Even greater daily effort goes into the preparation and rehearsal of questions by opposition party leaders and their staff. The **Leader of the Opposition** and the leader of any other recognized party begin the attack, and the Speaker of the House distributes the opportunity to ask questions to various opposition parties in a rough proportion to their numbers. Government backbenchers are also allowed to participate, but they usually ask "planted" questions to which ministers give prepared and self-serving replies. Because

FIGURE 23.1 WEEKLY ORDER OF BUSINESS

Hours	Monday	Tuesday	Wednesday	Thursday	Friday
10:00 – 11:00		Routine Proceedings		Routine Proceedings	Government Orders
11:00 – 11:15	Private Members' Business				Statements by Members
11:15 – 12:00					Oral Questions
12:00 – 1:00	Government Orders	Government Orders		Government Orders	Routine Proceedings
1:00 – 1:30					
1:30 – 2:00					Government Orders
2:00 – 2:15	Statements by Members	Statements by Members	Statements by Members	Statements by Members	Private Members' Business
2:15 – 2:30	Oral Questions	Oral Questions	Oral Questions	Oral Questions	
2:30 – 3:00					
3:00 – 5:30	Routine Proceedings Government Orders	Government Orders	Routine Proceedings Notices of Motions for the Production of Papers Government Orders	Government Orders	
5:30 – 6:30		Private Members' Business	Private Members' Business	Private Members' Business	
6:30 – 7:00	Adjournment Proceedings	Adjournment Proceedings	Adjournment Proceedings	Adjournment Proceedings	

Source: House of Commons, Daily Order of Business, http://www.parl.gc.ca/About/House/DOB/dob-e.htm. Reproduced with permission of the House of Commons Canada.

ministers often respond in a deliberately vague manner, supplementary questions to those initially posed are allowed, but the objective of the opposition is not so much to elicit information as to portray the government in a negative light. Such exchanges, along with corridor interviews and hallway "scrums"—a melee of reporters, microphones, and cameras—based on Question Period, find their way onto the television news and form the backbone of all media reporting on the House. Anyone who has observed Question Period is likely to be upset at the rowdy behaviour of members of Parliament, and it is true that the British chamber is more sedate. However, the rules demand a certain amount of civility, such as a prohibition on name-calling or accusations of lying, and require MPs to speak to each other through the Chair and to refer to each other by the name of their constituency, as the "Honourable Member for …."

Provision is also made for written questions from MPs who are genuinely concerned with seeking detailed information.

The 15 minutes preceding Question Period each day are set aside for members' statements, during which MPs may speak on any matter for 60 seconds, such as reminding the House that this is "Heart Month" or that a constituent has won an award, though these statements are also increasingly planned by parties to deliver partisan messages.[6] After Question Period, the regular business is the discussion of government orders, usually government bills, and debates that are the basic routine of Commons life. At this point in the day most of the MPs as well as the **parliamentary press gallery** leave the chamber in search of more pressing or more interesting activity, and the deputy speaker replaces the Speaker, completely changing the atmosphere of the House. The public and media pay little attention to these debates, as do, in many cases, MPs themselves. The few members assigned to make up quorum on any day are often communicating via email or text, reading the newspaper, or working on their laptops.

Only five hours a week are reserved for **private members' bills** and motions. These are bills and motions, introduced either by government members not in the Cabinet or by opposition members, of which very few become law. Despite having limited impact, they have attracted more attention in recent years, as noted below.

Finally, the adjournment proceeding, or "late show," is a half-hour opportunity at the end of the daily sitting (6:30 to 7:00 p.m.) four times a week to pursue issues that MPs feel were inadequately answered in the Question Period. Three members have five minutes each to restate their question, and a parliamentary secretary representing the minister has five minutes to respond.

Given the sharply adversarial nature of Question Period and the relative dullness of the rest of the parliamentary day, television coverage of the House of Commons does little to enhance the public's support of the government or politicians in general. However, "the all-consuming ritual of adversarial combat completely dominated by political parties" has its defenders. It serves the functions of keeping government conduct under constant surveillance and of providing an alternative regime,[7] and it presents a clear-cut picture to the electorate of which party is responsible for everything that has been done.[8]

PARTY DISCIPLINE

Probably the most significant aspect of the operation of the House of Commons is that everything is organized along party lines and that **party discipline** is so rigid. Almost all members belong to one party or another, and, with rare exceptions, the MPs of each party vote together. The most obvious reason that members of Parliament so consistently toe the party line, at least on the government side of the House, is the system of **responsible government**. It is generally believed, both inside and outside Parliament, that if the Cabinet is defeated on a major measure, it must resign or call an election. To ensure that Cabinet proposals are passed, therefore, government backbenchers always have to put party loyalty ahead of the consideration of their own views or those of their constituents.[9] That perception is not entirely valid, however, and the principle of responsible government could be interpreted more flexibly to apply only to the speech from the throne, the budget, the Estimates, and explicit nonconfidence motions, as discussed later. The Martin government moved in that direction, but the Harper government preferred greater discipline by considering more votes to be those of confidence.

Apart from the fact that some degree of party discipline is a corollary of the principle of responsible government, several reasons can be cited to explain why MPs of any party stick together in parliamentary votes. One is the tendency of people who belong to a political party to see things in a similar light—a natural cohesiveness common to most organized groups. Related to this cohesiveness is an equally natural deference to the leadership of the party and a desire to present an image of party unity to the public. In addition, MPs are encouraged to support the party line because of the prospects of promotion. Government backbenchers who are supportive can become committee chairs, parliamentary secretaries, or Cabinet ministers, while even in opposition parties MPs can be given more important responsibilities.[10] Members also want to participate in the distribution of perks available in parliamentary life: the best offices, the best committees, opportunities to travel at public expense, and the chance to participate in Question Period, all of which are generally controlled by party whips. Another inducement is to receive full support of the party organization in the next election, including campaign funds and a visit by the party leader. Moreover, many MPs depend on the government to provide them with employment if they suffer defeat and are not unmindful of this future dependence while serving in the House. The ultimate sanctions for disloyal behaviour are expulsion from the party caucus, involving relegation to the unpleasant status of an independent, and denial of the party label in the next election. For all these reasons, parties usually vote as blocs, and a government with a majority of seats typically feels confident that it can get parliamentary approval for its proposals. Party discipline is probably even more rigid in a minority government situation.

An executive-centred system with rigid party discipline, despite criticisms, certainly has its advantages. Forcing MPs to toe the party line has allowed the executive to pursue a collectivist public interest beyond the narrow interests of constituencies, regions, and provinces, and has permitted Canadian governments to be more activist and welfare-oriented than legislature-centred systems, such as in the United States.[11] Party discipline protects MPs individually and collectively from the threats of single-interest pressure groups and lobbyists, whose presence is increasing, and frees the prime minister from time-consuming negotiations with individual MPs. Because it makes clear that the government party is responsible for everything that is done, party discipline also promotes the accountability of that party to the electorate. This argument is related to the fact that most voters choose the party, including the leader and the platform, rather than the local candidate. That is to say, most MPs are elected based on their party label rather than their personal ability to represent their constituents, and must at least balance these two loyalties.

The British House of Commons is the model for the Canadian House in many ways, but party discipline is looser in that chamber and even in a majority situation, legislation is frequently defeated without entailing the resignation of the government.[12] Franks attributes this significant difference in the operation of the two chambers to several factors: the larger number of members in Britain means that discipline is harder to enforce; incumbent British MPs can be sure of renomination, regardless of their degree of party loyalty; and the large proportion of safe seats results in fewer members being dependent on party patronage for their post-parliamentary livelihood. Moreover, long-serving British MPs usually coexist with short-term prime ministers and are not so obsessed with promotion to the Cabinet. They are more

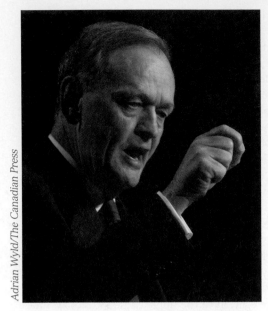

Adrian Wyld/The Canadian Press

Jean Chrétien took a hard line on party discipline.

content than their Canadian counterparts to remain on the backbenches or to act as committee chairs, combining outside interests with their parliamentary responsibilities.[13]

There are some in Canada who advocate more **free votes** and greater opportunity for MPs to represent the interests of their constituencies rather than slavishly follow the dictates of the party. The Mulroney government allowed "free votes" on capital punishment and abortion that featured a dramatic split among Tory MPs, and a "compromise" abortion bill was defeated in a free vote in the Senate. At the same time, three Conservative MPs were expelled from the party caucus and two were denied the party's candidacy.[14]

As prime minister, Jean Chrétien took a hard line on party discipline. In 1995, for example, when many Liberal backbenchers absented themselves from the vote on the government's gun registration bill and three voted against it, the PM quickly retaliated by removing the latter from their committee assignments. When Warren Allmand voted against the 1995 budget, the prime minister's attempt to remove him as a committee chair was delayed by Reform MPs, who disagreed with what he said but defended his right to dissent from the Liberal line. Chrétien even threatened not to sign the nomination papers of Liberal candidates in the next election if they voted against government measures. Such a fate befell John Nunziata, who was expelled from the Liberal caucus for his attack on the government for not removing the GST.

Soon afterward, about half of the Liberal caucus began to feel that it was time for Chrétien to resign, most of them favouring Paul Martin as his successor, and Chrétien was forced to set a retirement date. As he declined into lame-duck status in 2002, 55 Liberal backbenchers broke with the government on an opposition motion based on Martin's proposal to allow standing committees to elect their own chairs rather than have them imposed by the PMO.

Paul Martin came to power with a promise of reducing the rigidity of party discipline. He instituted a scheme involving three categories of votes: first, where Liberal MPs had to support the government; second, where the government told MPs how it wanted them to vote, but where private members were allowed to dissent; and third, a free vote even for ministers. In his regime, most bills fell into the second category, with only votes of confidence and a limited number of matters of fundamental importance to the government falling into the first. The Liberal caucus split on free votes on same-sex marriage in both the Chrétien and the Martin regimes and, during Martin's watch, on Canadian participation in the U.S. Ballistic Missile Defence system. In Martin's minority, two government bills were defeated—both connected to the division of foreign affairs and international trade into separate departments—but because the government did not consider these to be confidence votes, it ignored their defeat. Many regard the Martin reforms as a desirable compromise between excessive and insufficient party discipline, but Stephen Harper dismissed Garth Turner from the Conservative caucus in 2006 for his individualistic behaviour, and took the same strict approach to party discipline that Chrétien had done.[15]

In 2015, Parliament passed a private member's bill—The Reform Act—introduced by Conservative MP Michael Chong that could take away the party leader's power to sign nomination papers, as well as give party caucuses (discussed below) the ability to vote on procedures for expelling MPs from caucus and for removing the party leader. However, the provisions in the act allow caucuses to decide whether to enact them, and most caucuses chose not to do so when they resumed following the 2015 election.

CAUCUS MEETINGS

The other side of this public display of party discipline is that MPs are allowed to speak their mind in the secrecy of the **party caucus**.[16] Caucus consists of all the elected members of each party (and senators who choose or are allowed to attend) and meets behind closed doors on Wednesday mornings. As in the case of Cabinet secrecy, however, members occasionally "leak" caucus information for their own benefit. Provincial and regional caucus meetings of each party are held before the general caucus meeting, and caucus committees are often appointed. MPs of like mind can also form informal task forces.

Unlike the practice in Britain, the prime minister and Cabinet ministers attend the government party caucus meeting. Most prime ministers use caucus primarily to inform their backbenchers of government plans; others are reasonably receptive to backbench arguments and suggested alternatives; and some do both. Ministers may discuss the principles of a new policy with interested backbenchers in the course of its development, but it would breach the tradition of the House to show the caucus an actual bill before it is introduced in the Commons. Although no votes are taken, sufficient backbench dissatisfaction may occasionally carry the day. Many examples could be cited, even in the Chrétien era, where the caucus had a significant influence on Cabinet policy, while Martin ordered his ministers to discuss every new proposal with the relevant caucus committee. The aforementioned Mulroney compromise abortion bill was probably unique in actually being written by a committee of four ministers and eight backbenchers.[17] Whether backbench MPs argue strenuously in caucus and whether they persuade the Cabinet to change position, the whole process is shrouded in secrecy, so voters are not aware of it; all that is evident in public is MPs voting as their leader tells them.

STAGES AND KINDS OF LEGISLATION

The great bulk of legislation introduced takes the form of **public bills**. These are general bills that relate to matters of public policy and affect all Canadians, such as the Income Tax Act or the Canada Health Act. Most public bills (and virtually all that involve the raising or spending of money) are sponsored by the government and introduced by a Cabinet minister, thereby being titled **government bills**. They are numbered from C-1 to C-200 in each session. As noted earlier, most of the weekly and yearly agenda is taken up with such government business.

A certain amount of time, however, now normally five hours per week, is set aside for members who are not in the Cabinet to introduce legislation and motions of their own. Because these MPs (on whichever side of the House) are private members, their proposals are called private members' bills and are numbered from C-201 upward in each session. These bills are also of a general public policy nature, but until 1995 they could not involve the expenditure of public funds. Since then, private members' bills that entail spending can be introduced, but they require a "royal recommendation" from the government before third reading and they still cannot impose or increase taxes. Private members' bills rarely become statutes unless they are embraced by the government. Historically, the most that private members could hope for was that the Cabinet might incorporate their ideas into a government bill, which occurs occasionally.

Since 1986, however, there have been incremental changes to see more examination of private members' bills and motions. Today, members' names are listed randomly at the beginning of a Parliament. The first 30 of these may have a bill or motion considered, and the list is later replenished. Such bills and motions are now allowed two one-hour debates, and almost all are votable. In many cases, private members' bills are not "whipped"—that is, are not subject to party discipline—so MPs can exercise their own discretion. If a private member's bill passes second reading, it goes on to committee for further review. Examples of private members' bills that made it to the statute books include those upholding nonsmokers' rights; changing the names of various electoral districts; recognizing the beaver as a symbol of Canadian sovereignty, hockey as Canada's national winter sport, and lacrosse as our national summer sport; eliminating the excise tax on jewellery; and extending hate propaganda to sexual orientation.[18] Private members' bills that passed in recent minority government periods include John Godfrey's Federal Sustainable Development Act and former Prime Minister Paul Martin's bill to implement the Kelowna Accord, but they were ignored by the Harper government. On the other hand, when a private member's bill in 2012 called for clinical trials of the so-called "liberation therapy" for people with multiple sclerosis, the Minister of Health lobbied aggressively to defeat it, as did Prime Minister Harper on a Conservative private member's motion to re-examine the issue of abortion.

Private bills, on the other hand, refer to a specific person or private corporation. They originate in a petition, and require the payment of a fee. Certain divorces used to be effected by Acts of Parliament and took the form of private bills, while today this category mostly consists of bills incorporating companies and religious denominations. Other recent examples included a bill for the City of Windsor to acquire ownership of the Canadian portion of the Windsor–Detroit Tunnel, and those that allowed certain couples to marry even though they were related to each other within prohibited degrees of consanguinity. Private bills now originate in the Senate and occupy very little of the Commons' time.

Turning to the stages of the legislative process, Figure 23.2 shows the labyrinth that a bill must go through in order to become a law—essentially three readings in each chamber. Most government bills originate in the Commons, although, with the exception of money bills, they may be first introduced in the Senate. First reading simply means that a bill has been introduced—it is tabled, printed, and made public—and may be briefly explained. Some days later, the bill comes up for second reading. This stage involves a debate on the principle

FIGURE 23.2   LEGISLATIVE PROCESS IN THE CANADIAN PARLIAMENT

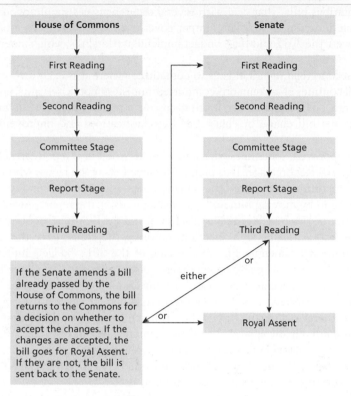

of the bill and may last several days or even weeks if it is controversial. The individual clauses of the bill are not discussed or amendable at this stage. A favourable vote at the end of the second-reading debate means that the bill has been approved in principle, although not necessarily in detail.

Even if the opposition has little hope of defeating a bill, it may expect that prolonged exposure of the flaws in the legislation will persuade the government to amend it. Failing that, public opinion can be aroused through media coverage to the extent that the electorate will remember the incident when the next election occurs. Excessive opposition debate is called a **filibuster**, but government and opposition rarely agree on what is excessive. In 1913, during protracted opposition to the government's Naval Bill, the Borden government introduced **closure**, a rule allowing a majority government to cut off debate. This device was used with discretion until the **pipeline debate** of 1956, and it is widely believed that the abusive resort to closure helped to defeat the government a year later.[19] The closure rule is still on the books and has been used more routinely in majority situations in recent years, especially by the Harper government after the 2011 election. However, it is more civilized to negotiate with the opposition parties over the time to be allocated to debating various issues. Standing Order 78 provides for three kinds of time-allocation motions depending on how much opposition party consent can be acquired. It is partly to avoid long debates that government legislation deliberately leaves wide discretion to the executive to issue regulations so that acts will not have to come back to the House for frequent amendments. Similarly, the government often introduces "omnibus bills" that deal with several different issues simultaneously rather than having multiple individual bills. The Harper government's Federal Accountability Act was such a bill, as were the 2012 and 2014 budget implementation bills, which amended numerous different acts.

Following second reading, a bill goes to committee, where it is examined in detail. In the small, informal confines of a Commons committee, ministers, public servants, advocacy groups, and other experts offer explanations or criticisms. As a result, when the committee members later scrutinize the bill clause by clause, modest clarifications and improvements are often made.

After being approved, sometimes with amendments, the bill is reported back to the House in what is called the Report stage. This phase gives members of the House who were not on the committee an opportunity to move other amendments. In 1999, the opposition discovered a new delaying tactic by moving hundreds of amendments at the report stage. The Canadian Alliance used this device to delay the Nisga'a Treaty, and the Bloc Québécois to prolong debate on the Clarity Act. After the 2000 election, however, the House gave the Speaker greater authority to limit such amendments. In the case of the 2012 budget implementation bill (C-38), the Speaker pared over 800 amendments down to about 150. Once the bill is concurred in at the Report stage, it goes to third reading for a final, overall appraisal.

Assuming the bill started in the Commons, it must then go through the same procedure in the Senate, but there it is usually disposed of in much faster order. In the rare case that the Senate amends a bill already approved by the Commons, the bill will have to go back to that house to see if it is acceptable in its amended form. If the Senate and House of Commons continue to disagree, the bill is usually abandoned, and although a provision exists for a conference between representatives of the two houses, it is rarely used.

Once a bill is passed in identical form by both houses, it is given royal assent in a special ceremony held in the Senate. The governor general or, more likely, a Supreme Court judge acting as "deputy governor general" nods in approval, and the bill becomes a law or statute, although it may not be immediately proclaimed. An alternative procedure allows royal assent to be conferred by a simple written declaration by the governor general at Rideau Hall or by the deputy governor general in the Supreme Court building.[20]

Although this may seem like an overly complicated process, each stage has a distinctive purpose and most bills must be debated for some time before the media and public begin to pay attention to them and absorb their merits and faults. Reasonably lengthy consideration of the bill helps the electorate to make up its mind about whether to re-elect the government that introduced such legislation or to opt for an opposition party that criticized it effectively.

In 1994, the House adopted rule changes that allowed a bill to go to committee after first reading, before it had been approved in principle. Such a procedure considerably widens the scope of committee influence, but it applies only to government legislation and can be used only with the minister's consent. For example, when the Harper government introduced a bill to give authorities new powers to police the Internet, it generated so much opposition that it was sent to committee for revamping before second reading. According to another new procedure, a committee can be directed to study an issue and prepare a bill. This was done in the case of the post-1991 redistribution process. These changes illustrate a slight loosening up of the Cabinet's dominance of the legislative process, but such devices are not often used.

ORGANIZATION AND OFFICERS OF THE COMMONS

The Speaker

The layout of the Commons chamber is illustrated in Figure 23.3. The leading official of the House of Commons is the presiding officer, the **Speaker**, for whom one deputy and two

FIGURE 23.3   LAYOUT OF THE HOUSE OF COMMONS CHAMBER

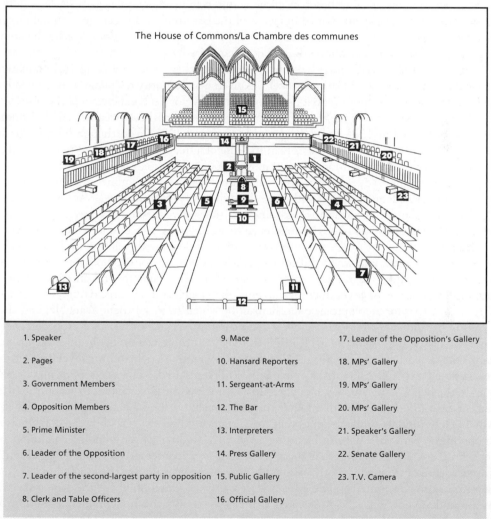

The House of Commons/La Chambre des communes

1. Speaker	9. Mace	17. Leader of the Opposition's Gallery
2. Pages	10. Hansard Reporters	18. MPs' Gallery
3. Government Members	11. Sergeant-at-Arms	19. MPs' Gallery
4. Opposition Members	12. The Bar	20. MPs' Gallery
5. Prime Minister	13. Interpreters	21. Speaker's Gallery
6. Leader of the Opposition	14. Press Gallery	22. Senate Gallery
7. Leader of the second-largest party in opposition	15. Public Gallery	23. T.V. Camera
8. Clerk and Table Officers	16. Official Gallery	

Source: House of Commons, The House of Commons Chamber, http://www.parl.gc.ca/marleaumontpetit/ DocumentViewer.aspx?Sec=Ch06&Seq=4&Language=E. Reproduced with permission of the House of Commons Canada.

acting speakers can substitute in the chair. Speakers cannot articulate the needs of their constituency or constituents in the Commons, as such, but in compensation, ministers and bureaucrats are especially sensitive to the concerns that the Speaker discusses with them outside the chamber. In addition to ceremonial and administrative functions, the Speaker interprets and enforces the written rules of the Commons, which are called the **Standing Orders,**[21] as well as unwritten traditions, practices, conventions, and usages. Given the powers of the Speakership—recognizing which member can speak and ruling on whether motions are in order, whether debate is relevant, whether questions are urgent, and whether an unruly MP should be expelled—it is important for the person selected to be competent as well as totally impartial.

Speakers were historically chosen by prime ministers from among their party's MPs and thus carried the suspicion of being biased in favour of the government. In seeking eventual reward beyond the Speakership, such as promotion to Cabinet, some also feared displeasing the prime minister, the dispenser of such rewards. A major change in the selection process in 1986 allowed MPs to choose their own Speaker by secret ballot, rather than merely ratifying the nomination of the prime minister. In 1988, the Speaker was given new authority to "name" (i.e., suspend) a member for the rest of the day and for a period of five days for a second breach of the rules.

Peter Milliken was elected Speaker of the Commons after the November 2000 election, and was re-elected in 2004 and again in both 2006 and 2008, even though he then sat in Opposition. The Speaker can vote only in the case of a tie, and Milliken was twice forced to break a tie in the Martin minority period in May 2005. The vote on a supplementary budget bill was the first time a Speaker was ever required to break a tie on a nonconfidence vote, and he followed precedent by voting with the bill so that debate on it could continue. Milliken also made two enduring decisions regarding questions of parliamentary privilege and contempt of Parliament. In 2010, Opposition parties forced through a Commons motion ordering the Harper government to release uncensored copies of documents relating to the treatment of Afghan detainees, and when the government refused to do so, the Speaker of the House had to make a ruling. He declared that Parliament has a fundamental and unlimited right to order the production of government documents. But given their sensitive nature, he urged all parties to search for a compromise mechanism by which to make them available, and after weeks of behind-the-scenes wrangling, a small committee agreed on such a procedure, with the NDP dissenting. Again in 2011, Milliken ruled that there was no doubt that the government had failed to comply with a parliamentary committee's demand for revelation of the costs related to the Conservatives' crime bills. Milliken stated: "This is a serious matter that goes to the heart of the House's undoubted role in holding the government to account." After further hearings, the committee found the government to be in contempt of Parliament, which led to a nonconfidence motion in the Commons that was passed by the combination of opposition parties: "That this House agree with the findings of the standing committee on procedure and House affairs that the government is in contempt of Parliament, which is unprecedented in Canadian parliamentary history, and consequently, the House has lost confidence in the government." The 2011 budget was to be voted on about the same time and would undoubtedly have been defeated as well, but it was the nonconfidence motion on contempt that actually precipitated the May 2011 election. Conservative MP Andrew Scheer was elected as Speaker following that election, and, at the age of 32, became the youngest person to fill that role.

House Leaders, Party Whips, and Clerk

From within their ranks, each party selects a House leader and a party whip. The government **House leader** is a Cabinet minister who manages the government's business in the Commons. This minister seeks to work out an agenda for House business with the opposition House leaders, who function as procedural strategists for their parties and often speak for their parties if their leaders are absent. Especially in a minority government situation, it is essential for the various party house leaders to work well together. **Party whips** are responsible for ensuring that their members are present for important votes and that they vote the right way.[22] Whips must therefore know the whereabouts of their MPs at all times. They also distribute members' offices, assign members to parliamentary committees, and line up the order of party speakers in Question Period and debates. It is largely through the whips, therefore, that party leaders impose discipline on their members. Members' opportunities to speak, to serve on the committee of their choice, and to travel as part of parliamentary delegations are largely influenced by their degree of party loyalty. In return, whips seek out backbench opinion on various matters and transmit it to the party leadership. Given the power of the party whips and party House leaders to organize its business, independent MPs and those MPs who belong to a party with fewer than 12 members find little opportunity to participate.

The chief permanent official of the Commons is the clerk of the House. This position is analogous to a deputy minister in a government department. As chief procedural adviser to the Speaker and manager of the support staff attached to the Commons, the clerk is also required to act in a totally nonpartisan manner. The clerk is assisted at the table by the deputy clerk and several principal clerks. Since the sergeant-at-arms rarely has to wield the mace to escort unruly MPs out of the chamber, that position also has administrative responsibilities attached.

Voting

Turning to the voting procedure in the Commons, decisions are in the first instance made orally when the Speaker invites members to say "aye" or "nay." In declaring which side won, the Speaker is guided by the numbers rather than the volume on each side, and on a routine matter in a majority situation, this will probably suffice. When either side wants a formal recorded vote it will request a **division**. In this case the division bells ring until the government and official Opposition party whips agree that all their available members have arrived, at which time a standing vote is conducted. It used to be that if either whip refused to give the go-ahead, the bells could ring indefinitely, but after the two-week "bell-ringing incident" of 1982, a 30-minute limit was adopted in 1986. A new procedure in 1994 allowed for deferred divisions with all-party consent, so that most votes are now held between late Monday and late Wednesday, when most members are there. To save time, if several votes are to take place in sequence, the result of one vote can be "applied" to subsequent votes with unanimous consent.

MPs sometimes engage in the practice of "pairing," in which two members on opposite sides make arrangements such that if one is legitimately absent for a vote, the other does not vote either. Party whips are involved in putting members' names in the registry of pairs, and paired members are listed at the end of the division list printed in *Hansard*. In general, pairing is most advantageous for the government, so that it will not be defeated on a crucial vote, and opposition parties are therefore not enthusiastic about the practice. Indeed, in slim majority and minority government situations, ministers sometimes have to cancel trips in order to be present for a vote or, to reduce the numbers on the other side, face the unappetizing alternative of taking an opposition member along with them!

Speeches

The length of speeches that MPs are allowed to make has been severely curtailed over the past 30 or so years. The 1982 reforms generally shortened them from 40 minutes to 20, but this depends on who is speaking, in what debate, and at what stage of the debate. In many cases, especially as a debate drags on, the maximum length is reduced to 10 minutes. Because each party's first speech in a debate has no limit, however, the Canadian Alliance MP who began the debate on the Kyoto Protocol in 2002 spoke for several days, as did the lead NDP speaker in the 2012 budget debate.

What is said in such speeches is also of interest here. Of all the **parliamentary privileges** and rights of MPs, individual and collective, the most important is the protection from libel action for anything said in the chamber. Occasionally MPs take advantage of their privileged position in this respect by declining to repeat outside the House certain remarks they have made within.[23] Another form of Parliamentary privilege is to find the government or some person to be in contempt of Parliament, such as for misleading MPs or for not providing adequate information.

THE COMMITTEE SYSTEM

Much of the important legislative work of the House takes place outside the Commons chamber in a variety of committees. These include standing and special committees of the Commons itself, as well as joint standing and special committees of the Commons and Senate combined. Committees allow a small number of people to develop expertise in a particular field and to examine proposals in depth; moreover, if several committees operate simultaneously, a greater volume of business can be accomplished. In an ideal situation, committees could allow private members to make constructive contributions to the governing of the country and to do so in a consensual rather than an adversarial atmosphere. In Britain, committees have always had an autonomous position, including the choice of their own chair, and many members have found career satisfaction at this level rather than yearning for appointment to the Cabinet.

Committees were not used in a systematic way for most of Canadian history, and membership was so unstable that they failed to develop expertise. Repeated reforms of the Commons committee system since 1968 have made it more significant; in fact, observers usually focus on committee work as the most promising way of making legislatures more meaningful. David Docherty reminds us that committees are usually more relaxed and less partisan than the House as a whole, committee members are more directly engaged in policy discussions, committees encourage specialization, they have significant powers of investigation, and they are staffed by nonpartisan employees of the legislature.[24]

Standing committees are set up more or less permanently in most of the substantive areas of government policy, such as international trade or natural resources. They have two principal functions: to examine the Estimates—that is, the government's spending proposals—and to analyze legislation at the committee stage.[25] The Estimates of Health Canada, for example, are scrutinized by the Standing Committee on Health. In examining bills after second reading, committees question ministers, public servants, advocacy groups, and other expert witnesses, some of whom try to convince committee members to approve the bill as introduced, and others, to make changes. The Standing Committee on Finance is perhaps most important and now engages in wide-ranging pre-budget consultations. The newest is the Standing Committee on Government Operations and Estimates which was designed to examine all public spending and federal operations not formally reviewed by any other parliamentary committee, complementing the work of the Standing Committee on Public Accounts.

As a result of the 1986 changes, standing committees have additional functions and resources. Because they largely parallel government departments, they are authorized to investigate any aspect of the departments with which they are associated, including a review of non-judicial government appointments. However, even a negative vote will not necessarily prevent the government from making such appointments or taking contrary action. Committee clerks are employees of the House of Commons who provide administrative and procedural support, while policy analysts are assigned from the staff of the Library of Parliament. Committees also have a budget for such items as travel.

Smaller, more stable, and more expert membership has served to increase the effectiveness of standing committees. Representation on all committees is proportional to party standings in the House, so that a majority government in the Commons will have a majority on each committee. Standing committees frequently set up smaller subcommittees to expedite discussion of a variety of concerns. The Standing Committees in 2015 are listed below.

Committee chairs are elected by committee members but until 2002 they were usually pre-selected by the Prime Minister's Office. At that point, as mentioned, a large group of Liberal backbenchers joined with the opposition parties to force a change in this procedure so that chairs were henceforth elected by secret ballot. The Harper PMO reverted to the earlier practice of indicating the MP it wanted as the committee chair. Except for four committees—access to information, privacy and ethics, government operations and estimates, status of women, and public accounts—chairs come from the government side. Each committee also has two vice-chairs, one from the official Opposition and the other from another opposition party. The **Standing Committee on Public Accounts** has the important function of examining the reports of the **auditor general**, the official of Parliament who audits the government's accounts.[26] Cabinet ministers do not sit on committees, but the presence of the relevant parliamentary secretary provides a link to the government and the corresponding minister and department.

Special committees are occasionally established for some specific, temporary purpose, especially if the government party has an excess of backbenchers and some issue arises that is beyond the normal jurisdiction of standing committees. Special committees usually have an investigatory function—to examine an issue before the government has made up its mind on how to deal with it. Such committees may therefore be an important part of the initiation phase of the legislative process. The House occasionally appoints a "legislative committee" to examine a specific piece of legislation.

BOX 23.1   HOUSE OF COMMONS STANDING COMMITTEES, 2015

Aboriginal Affairs and Northern Development

Access to Information, Privacy and Ethics

Agriculture and Agri-Food

Canadian Heritage

Citizenship and Immigration

Environment and Sustainable Development

Finance

Fisheries and Oceans

Foreign Affairs and International Development

Government Operations and Estimates

Health

Human Resources, Skills and Social Development and the Status of Persons with Disabilities

Industry, Science and Technology

International Trade

Justice and Human Rights

Liaison

National Defence

Natural Resources

Official Languages

Procedure and House Affairs

Public Accounts

Public Safety and National Security

Status of Women

Transport, Infrastructure and Communities

Veterans Affairs

In addition to the standing and special committees of the House of Commons alone, the Commons and Senate sometimes work together in **joint committees**. Joint committees obviously avoid duplication and involve senators earlier in the process than is usually the case. The most important is the **Standing Joint Committee on Scrutiny of Regulations**, which has the vital but unenviable responsibility of scrutinizing the mounds of **regulations** and other subordinate legislation issued by the executive branch each year. If the legal staff of the committee find something objectionable about a set of regulations, and the committee members agree, it usually is able to persuade the relevant department to make changes. If not, it has the power to recommend rescission of offensive delegated legislation. The other standing joint committee is on the Library of Parliament, while special joint committees can also be established, such as the one that was involved in the development of the Constitution Act, 1982.

Finally, there is the committee of the whole. This is simply the entire Commons membership sitting in the chamber as a committee. In such a case, the Speaker is replaced in the chair by the deputy speaker, and the rules are somewhat relaxed. This committee is only used to debate appropriation bills (once the Estimates have been approved), urgent bills (such as back-to-work legislation), and certain noncontroversial bills. Otherwise, the House prefers to use smaller committees that can meet simultaneously in committee rooms outside the Commons chamber.

It is primarily the transformation of the committee system in recent years that has enhanced the position of ordinary MPs in the legislative process. As committees became smaller, more stable in their membership, and more expert in their field, and as their members developed greater collegiality, they sometimes shed some of their partisanship. Between 1986 and 1993, for example, many of these committees developed a consensus on the issues before them that cut across party lines. Such committees became newly independent sources of power in the legislative system, and this led to the acceptance of an unprecedented number of committee amendments to government bills. Since 1993, and especially in the four- or five-party Parliaments after 1997, committees found it more difficult to achieve such a cross-party consensus. Some of the standing committees functioned well between 2006 and 2011, without a government majority, while others almost came to a standstill due to extreme animosity between Conservative and Opposition members. The Harper regime developed a manual for committee chairs explaining how to manipulate witness lists, circumvent Opposition motions, and limit criticism of the government.[27] In 2011, the Conservatives gained a majority on each committee, and sometimes moved the body "in-camera"—excluding the media and the public.

One advantage of all committees that meet outside the Commons chamber is that they can listen to representations from advocacy groups, bureaucrats, and other experts.[28] It was traditionally said that pressure groups and lobbyists did not make much use of the legislative branch of government because the crucial decisions had previously been made in the executive. Committees often make minor amendments to bills, however, and there is always a possibility that the committee recommendations can change the government's mind on larger questions; for example, substantial changes were made to the proposed Constitution Act, 1982 as a result of group representations to the parliamentary committee which studied it.

MEMBERS' SERVICES AND ETHICS

Deciding how much to pay members of Parliament is an intractable problem. Providing MPs with considerably more than the average industrial wage is a way to ensure public criticism, but the higher the level of remuneration, the better the quality of person that will likely be attracted to parliamentary life. The peculiar insecurity of political office in Canada must also be taken into account. In 2001, parliamentarians voted themselves a raise and incorporated their previous tax-free expense allowance into their overall salary. The basic pay for MPs in 2015 was $167 400, while senators received $142 400. On top of this basic income, large numbers of MPs receive additional payments for supplementary responsibilities as indicated in Table 23.2.

In addition to this basic pay, backbench MPs receive many other benefits and services at public expense or on a subsidized basis. MPs are given an annual budget of about $300 000 which is mostly used to hire staff. They are provided with an office on Parliament Hill and in the constituency, and virtually unlimited office expenses, telephone, mailing, printing, and travel privileges. Parliamentary parties receive funds for research purposes, and additional funds are provided for the operation of the offices of opposition leaders, whips, House leaders, and caucus chairs. Such funding is provided only to recognized parties in the House—that is, groups of at least 12 members—a major blow to the Conservatives and the NDP between 1993 and 1997. More controversial is the MPs' pension plan. In 1995, the Liberals removed some of the extremely generous provisions for newly elected MPs: they would have to wait to age 55 to collect; they could not "double-dip," collecting their pensions and other government salaries

TABLE 23.2   SELECTED SUPPLEMENTARY ALLOWANCES FOR ADDITIONAL RESPONSIBILITIES, 2015 ON TOP OF $167 400

PRIME MINISTER	$167 400
SPEAKER, CABINET MINISTER, LEADER OF THE OPPOSITION	$80 100
MINISTER OF STATE	$60 000
LEADERS OF OTHER PARTIES	$56 800
DEPUTY SPEAKER, OPPOSITION HOUSE LEADER	$41 500
CHIEF GOVERNMENT AND OPPOSITION WHIP	$30 000
PARLIAMENTARY SECRETARIES, HOUSE LEADERS OF OTHER PARTIES	$16 600
WHIPS OF OTHER PARTIES, COMMITTEE CHAIRS	$11 700

Source: Parliament of Canada, Indemnities, Salaries and Allowances, Members of the House of Commons, *http://www.parl.gc.ca/Parlinfo/Lists/Salaries.aspx?Menu=HOC-Politic&Section=03d93c58-f843-49b3-9653 -84275c23f3fb. Reproduced with permission of Library of Parliament, 2015.*

at the same time; and they could opt out entirely. Some Reform MPs who opted out later re-entered the plan, which the Harper government tightened up in 2012. Following the 2015 election, MPs must wait until age 60 to collect.

The lot of backbench members of Parliament is obviously much improved from earlier eras, and their every need is now provided for. Although their remuneration and services might seem excessive, the expenses of serving some 100 000 constituents and the insecurity of parliamentary life should not be underestimated. If their expenses were not completely covered, only wealthy individuals could seek federal political office.

Although Canada has had a Conflict of Interest Code for cabinet ministers for some time, such a code for ordinary MPs was only adopted in 2004 as part of the ethics package that Prime Minister Chrétien introduced when his government was facing assorted charges of unethical behaviour, including the sponsorship scandal.[29] Among other things, it required disclosure of assets held and gifts and hospitality received, and possible breaches of the Code were examined by the ethics commissioner. The system did not function well, but Harper's **Federal Accountability Act** strengthened and renamed the office: the Conflict of Interest and Ethics Commissioner.

ROLES OF MEMBERS OF PARLIAMENT

The roles that members of Parliament perform can be seen in two different lights. First, in terms of how they vote, MPs can be classified as trustees, constituency delegates, or party delegates. "Trustees" would be MPs who feel obliged to vote according to their own conscience, their own understanding of the issue in question, or their own conception of the national interest. Alternatively, "constituency delegates" would be MPs who vote the way they think a majority of their constituents would want them to vote or in their conception of the best interests of their constituency. In other words, in situations where the two did not coincide, trustees would place their own views above those of their constituents, while constituency delegates would do the reverse. However much MPs may claim to fall into either of these categories, in practice they rarely deviate from the party line. In fact, then, they could usually be labelled "party delegates." If the party caucus determines a position that conflicts with either their own views or those of their constituents, MPs almost always put the party position first. The reasons for such rigid party discipline were discussed earlier in the chapter.

The other way to examine the roles of MPs is in terms of how they spend their time or what their priorities are.[30] The first role in this respect is the lawmaker, devoting attention to the legislative process and committee work, such as introducing, amending, and debating legislation. MPs are supported in these tasks by the Research Branch of the Library of Parliament, but since this role is usually irrelevant to their constituents, this is not a priority for many members. Another role is being a propagandist for one or more causes. This involves using every opportunity available—Question Period, general debates, and even public speeches outside of Parliament—to press for certain reforms they believe in. Determined crusaders for proportional representation or freedom of information reform would be good examples. Then there is the goal of promoting their constituency and bringing back public favours, a role that could be called representational. This requires lobbying ministers and public servants for new public buildings, roads, wharves, and other facilities so that they will have something "concrete" to show for themselves by the time of the next election. Finally, all MPs perform the daily function of ombudsmen or social workers for their individual constituents, intervening with ministers or public servants to hasten administrative decisions, to correct bureaucratic errors, and to repair governmental injustices. There will always be constituents with passport, immigration, employment insurance, pension, and many other kinds of problems, and some MPs specialize in trying to resolve them. This "caseload" of MPs is now so heavy that they are provided with considerable administrative assistance in both their Ottawa and their constituency offices so that they will have some time left over for their other duties.[31] In fact, according to David Docherty, between 1988–97 MPs reported that approximately 42 percent of their time was devoted to constituency work. Meanwhile, legislative tasks took up just under 25 percent of MPs' time, and both policy development and party duties were estimated to take about 13 percent of their work time.

The life of an MP is incredibly busy. Although they do not spend much time in the Commons chamber apart from Question Period and when assigned to maintain quorum, MPs are engaged from morning till night in meetings and talking with individual and groups of constituents, interest groups, the media, bureaucrats, party officials, staff, and other parliamentarians, including committee meetings. Besides assuming heavy responsibilities in Ottawa, they are expected to be seen frequently in the constituency, both in their offices and at myriad social events, usually on weekends or when Parliament is recessed. The public sometimes assumes that MPs are not working when the Commons is not in session, but this is a badly mistaken perception. All this activity interferes with a normal family life, whether those with spouses and children move their families to Ottawa or leave them at home to be visited when time permits.

One way of looking at legislatures, which is especially important in the political behaviour approach, involves surveying or otherwise measuring the opinions and attitudes of legislative members. Surveys of candidates for office, and in-depth studies of how politicians think and behave while in office are examples of legislative research in the *political behaviour* and *psychology* traditions.[32]

The decisions that are made in parliamentary settings—which policies to support, which bills or motions to prioritize, when to speak up or oppose a proposal—are relatively minor for MPs in the Canadian context. Nevertheless, the behaviours of both parties and parliamentarians alike are often studied using the *rational choice* approach. This is because both must pursue their interests, which include gaining votes, increasing their share of influence (or power), and implementing favourable policies. When a party opposes a government bill, or when an MP chooses to vote with or against her/his party's wishes, it is usually a strategic decision.

THE GOVERNMENT–OPPOSITION BALANCE

An objective look at Parliament reveals a basic dilemma: the government wants to get legislation passed expeditiously, but the opposition must have time to articulate constituency needs as well as a chance to criticize government proposals in order to make the public aware of their defects. One manner of addressing this conflict is to summarize the ways in which the Cabinet controls the Commons, especially in a **majority government** position, and then the ways in which the Commons controls the Cabinet.

The prime minister and Cabinet, through the governor general, summon, prorogue, and dissolve Parliament, and then basically determine the agenda of parliamentary business. The Cabinet has a monopoly on the introduction of financial legislation and a virtual monopoly on the legislation that is actually passed. The prime minister and Cabinet control almost all parliamentary committee work and also have the power to introduce closure to cut off debate or time-allocation motions to curtail it. Backing up all these specific devices of Cabinet dominance are two other general powers. Through the whip, the prime minister and Cabinet enforce party discipline on their MPs in order to achieve their ends, and they have at their disposal the vast informational resources of the public service. Thus, it is sometimes said that the prime minister and Cabinet operate as a virtual dictatorship until they have to face the electorate again some four or five years down the road.

Parliamentary control over the Cabinet, on the other hand, refers mainly to opportunities to criticize and to delay, rather than any real power to alter the Cabinet's proposals or to throw the government out. MPs, especially on the opposition side, have the daily option to ask oral questions of ministers, in addition to the 15 minutes set aside for members' statements, and

30 minutes for adjournment proceedings four times per week. They can also submit written questions seeking detailed information. MPs can criticize the government generally or raise their own initiatives in the throne speech and budget debates, as well as select the topic of debate in the 22 opposition days per session. Marginal reforms were made in 2001 to strengthen the role of backbenchers: more money was allocated to registered parties for research and other caucus services; members' office budgets were increased; the housing allowance was raised; and the research capacity of the Library of Parliament was expanded. MPs can introduce legislation in the form of private members' bills, criticize specific Cabinet measures at the second-reading stage, introduce amendments at the committee and report stages, and scrutinize the government's spending proposals. Opposition MPs may at least delay the adoption of government measures by prolonging debates and by raising procedural points. But when all is said and done, the prime minister and Cabinet usually get their way.

In their scrutiny or accountability function, members of Parliament, especially on the opposition side, are assisted by a number of independent agents or officials of Parliament, the most famous of which is the auditor general. But as mentioned in Chapter 22, several other offices fall into this category, including the Information Commissioner, the Privacy Commissioner, the Commissioner of Official Languages, the Conflict of Interest and Ethics Commissioner, the Lobbying Commissioner, and the Chief Electoral Officer. A new such officer created in 2008 was the **Parliamentary Budget Officer (PBO)**, who is available to MPs to review the expenditures of any part of government and the general financial picture of the country. A dispute arose, however, over how independent the PBO, Kevin Page, was really intended to be, and he had to fight for adequate resources.[33] Page was replaced at the end of his term in 2013 by Jean Denis Frechette, who has been similarly critical of government's lack of compliance with information requests.

MINORITY GOVERNMENT

The foregoing account assumes that the government is in a majority position in the Commons. Between 2004 and 2011, however, Canada was characterized by a **minority government** situation—in which the government was outnumbered by opposition members. A minority government is less dominant; it may have to negotiate with opposition parties to some extent, such as to amend its proposals, abandon them, or even accept opposition initiatives. Many observers who deplore the normal arrogance of a majority government and who regret that so much opposition talent and so many opposition ideas ordinarily go to waste actually prefer to have a minority government in office.

Eugene Forsey reminds us that minority government is not exceptional, is not necessarily weak and indecisive, and does not have to be short-lived.[34] Between 1867 and 2011 there were 12 minority governments in Canada: 1921–25 and 1925–26 (King), 1926 (Meighen), 1957–58 and 1962–63 (Diefenbaker), 1963–65 and 1965–68 (Pearson), 1972–74 (Trudeau), 1979–80 (Clark), 2004–06 (Martin), and 2006–08 and 2008–11 (Harper). Few of these governments could have been called weak and indecisive because of their minority position; many, such as the 1957–58 Diefenbaker government, were more active and courageous than the majority governments that preceded or followed them. Some were exceptionally bold and decisive, especially the Pearson governments and the Trudeau minority which were particularly sensitive to opposition demands. Although minority governments did not last as long as majority governments, not all of them ended by being defeated against their will (1926, 1963, 1979, 2005, 2011); in several cases, the prime minister himself decided to call an election (1965, 1968, 2005) or welcomed the defeat (1958, 1974).[35]

Minority governments in Canada have usually operated on an ad hoc basis; that is, the government of the day relied on one opposition party or another to support it on key legislation or nonconfidence votes. The Trudeau minority (1972–74) had a more stable relationship with the NDP, sometimes called a "loose alliance," and regularly negotiated mutually advantageous compromises. A closer arrangement was the formal agreement between the Liberals and NDP in Ontario between 1985 and 1987. The NDP was not represented in the cabinet, but promised to support the government for two years in return for the Liberals refraining from calling an election. The most stable solution to a minority government would be a formal coalition government, where a second party actually had representatives in the cabinet. Over the years, several provinces have experienced such coalition governments. At the federal level, Canada had a formal coalition government between Conservative and English-speaking Liberal MPs during the latter part of the First World War, but since the Conservatives already had a majority, this was primarily arranged for purposes of keeping the country together. It was partly because of the rare occurrence of formal coalition governments in Canada (in contrast to their widespread existence in many other political systems) and the lack of understanding that they were a respectable alternative in a minority government situation that the possibility of a Liberal–NDP coalition in late 2008 raised so much interest and concern.

In a minority government situation, much is made of one or more opposition parties holding the balance of power. On occasion, for example, this position has allowed the CCF or NDP to force a Liberal minority to adopt some of its policies. But holding the balance of power is not normally an enviable position, especially if the opposition cannot amend or defeat a government measure without throwing out the whole government. If any such defeat were taken as a vote of nonconfidence in the government, it would probably precipitate another election. Such an opposition party may not have the finances to engage in a quick succession of election campaigns, and is sometimes thought to suffer at the hands of an electorate that blames it for the inconvenience and expense of another vote.

This leads to a discussion of the principle of responsible government—that the Cabinet must have the confidence of the Commons or else call an election or resign. It is not always clear whether the Cabinet is required to take such drastic action. In a majority situation the problem is most unlikely to arise, but does a government in a minority position have to resign or call an election over any and every defeat? Atkinson and Docherty refer to the "erroneous notion that the defeat of any government-sponsored bill requires the government's resignation. No such requirement exists, except perhaps in the minds of MPs."[36] In 1968, the Pearson government was defeated on a piece of financial legislation, but the PM argued that the defeat was a fluke and that his government should be allowed to carry on. Because there is no question about the defeat of the government on a **nonconfidence motion**, including the speech from the throne and the budget, the matter was decided when the Cabinet subsequently survived an explicit nonconfidence motion.[37] As mentioned, two of the Martin government's bills were defeated, but he carried on regardless. Such an understanding of what constitutes nonconfidence—explicit motions rather than defeat of ordinary bills—could be extended to majority situations as well. An account of some of the excitement over the fate of the minority Martin government in 2005 has been placed on this book's website.

Michael de Adder/Artizans

The Martin government was subsequently defeated on a nonconfidence motion, and the election which followed produced the Harper minority government in 2006. When the polls showed that none of the parties was likely to win a majority in the foreseeable future, they collectively found ways to ensure that the government would not be defeated on a nonconfidence vote or a vote that could be seen as one of nonconfidence. Both sides made concessions from time to time, but the most common way to avoid a government defeat was for the Liberals to abstain. Harper called an election in October 2008 before being defeated, but then came close to defeat shortly afterward, as discussed in Chapter 21. When the government introduced a superficial and partisan economic update, the three opposition parties signed a coalition agreement, in which they declared their readiness to form an alternative Liberal–NDP government with BQ support. In order to cling to power, Harper delayed a scheduled nonconfidence vote, and then pre-empted it with a successful but controversial request to the governor general to prorogue Parliament to avoid the vote altogether.

Unfortunately for the advocates of the concept of coalition government, this particular coalition had certain unique defects (most notably requiring support of the sovereignist BQ) and was vilified by the Conservatives. When Parliament returned in the new year, the Liberals were no longer interested in the coalition and supported the Conservative budget (with minor amendments), so that the Harper minority government carried on.[38] By early 2011, however, the Conservative government had annoyed opposition parties in so many ways—especially in its denial of information on various issues—that even the Speaker of the Commons agreed the government was in contempt of Parliament—a first in Canadian history. The Harper government fell on the resulting opposition nonconfidence motion, but the electorate returned it in a majority position.

REFORM OF THE HOUSE OF COMMONS

The imbalance between government and opposition is so great, at least in a majority situation, and the legislative role of ordinary MPs has been so ineffective that parliamentary reform is never far from the minds of political scientists and politicians alike. Reform proposals have primarily been designed to remedy excessive partisanship, Cabinet domination, and the lack of influence of the private member.

At the end of the 1960s, changes in the committee system, the provision for timetabling the business of the House, and the funding of parliamentary parties for research purposes "inaugurated the modern era of parliamentary government."[39] Then, in the 1970s, MPs saw considerable improvement in their services, especially in parliamentary and constituency offices and staff. In addition, the proceedings of the Commons began to be televised in 1977, with later provision being made to televise committee proceedings. One of the ways in which television changed members' behaviour was that they began to applaud instead of pound on their desks to indicate approval, something that was also appreciated by the simultaneous interpreters![40] In 1982, a severe altercation occurred between the Trudeau government and the Conservative opposition over the form and substance of the National Energy Program, such that the opposition left the division bells ringing for 15 days. The incident led all concerned to strive to improve Commons procedures, and as a result of the McGrath Committee, further reforms were made in 1986 including the election of the Speaker by secret ballot.[41]

In 1991, the Mulroney government introduced changes aimed at accomplishing the same amount of parliamentary work in less time, giving MPs more time in their constituencies, and making the committee system more effective. The temporary loosening of party discipline under Paul Martin and the creation of an independent ethics commissioner reporting to Parliament are probably the most significant reforms in modern times. Martin established a three-line whip voting system (similar to that used in the U.K.), in which the number of "lines" determines how government members must behave. On matters of confidence, all government members must vote the government position on the matter (three-line), on lesser matters but still those of government policy, only the executive must vote the government position on the matter (two-line), and on some matters all members are free to vote as they wish (one-line). Such changes enhanced the legislative role of backbenchers, though use of the three-line whip did not continue with the Conservative government that followed. Changes implemented in 2015 through Michael Chong's bill—as noted earlier—may lead to some decreases in leader power over MPs, but it is also noteworthy that Franks argues that reform should be advocated with caution and that "Parliament is more in need of understanding than change."[42]

PURPOSES AND POWERS OF THE SENATE

The ideal of democracy was still not enthusiastically accepted in the 1860s and the Fathers of Confederation felt it advisable to provide for an appointed body that would exercise "sober second thought" with respect to measures emanating from the popularly elected House of Commons. Thus, the Senate was to be the equivalent of the British House of Lords, an older, conservative influence, with a minimum age of 30, appointment for life, and a relatively high property qualification ($4000 of equity in land in the province or territory of residence and a net worth of $4000 over and above all debts). Sir John A. Macdonald argued that the Senate should protect minorities and the rich were always fewer in number than the poor![43]

Second, the smaller provinces would agree to join Confederation and accept representation by population in the House of Commons only if they were overrepresented in the Senate. The Fathers settled on a Senate that would be based on equal *regional* representation, a compromise between equal provincial representation (as in the United States) and the principle of representation by population. Such a system gave the Maritimes and Quebec a limited amount of protection against the voting power of Ontario in the Commons. It followed that senators were supposed to represent their regions and provinces within the national policymaking system.

A third function of the Senate, not explicitly provided for in 1867 but that can also be seen as part of the concept of sober second thought, is to improve legislation from a technical point of view. This function—to act as a non-ideological, routine revising chamber that picks up on flaws in legislation that have not been noticed during its passage through the busy Commons—has become one of the Senate's most important roles over the years.

As far as powers were concerned, the Senate was given a veto over all legislation, a power that was not restricted as in the case of the British House of Lords. The only point of Senate inferiority to the Commons was that "money bills"—legislation involving the raising or spending of money—had to be introduced in the lower chamber. Nothing in law prevented the Senate from delaying, amending, or vetoing any bills, whether or not they involved money, although in the latter case, amendments could not *increase* taxes or expenditures. It was only the Standing Orders of the House of Commons that claimed the Senate could not amend money bills, an assertion never accepted by the upper chamber.[44]

It was not until 1982 that the Senate's power was in any way reduced, and that had to do only with constitutional amendments, not ordinary legislation. According to the Constitution Act, 1982, the Senate can delay a constitutional amendment only for 180 days. If the upper house has not approved such an amendment by then, it can be re-passed by the Commons and bypasses the Senate in the process of ratification.

COMPOSITION OF THE SENATE

As mentioned, the basic structural principle of the Senate agreed to at the time of Confederation was equal regional representation. Thus Ontario, Quebec, and the Maritimes received 24 senators each. In the case of Quebec, the province was divided into 24 senatorial regions so that an appropriate balance of anglophone and francophone representatives would be chosen. Otherwise, senators do not officially represent a specific region of their province, although prime ministers usually give some attention to geographic balance, and on an individual, unofficial basis, senators themselves may choose to concentrate on one part of the province. When Prince Edward Island joined Confederation, it received four of the 24 Maritime senators, reducing the number for Nova Scotia and New Brunswick to ten each. In a general reform in 1915 the West was designated as a senatorial region with 24 senators, preserving the principle of equal regional representation, with six allocated to each Western province. In 1949,

IF DRAFTED – I WILL NOT RUN … IF ELECTED – I WILL NOT SERVE … IF APPOINTED TO THE SENATE – WELL, THAT'S A WHOLE DIFFERENT BALL OF WAX!

harrop ©

artizans.com

Newfoundland was awarded six senators in addition to the 96 already allotted, so as to leave the Maritime contingent intact. Finally, in 1975, Yukon and the Northwest Territories were given one senator each, as was Nunavut in 1999, so that the total became 105 ($4 \times 24 + 6 + 3$), allowing for only slight deviations from the principle of equal regional representation.

Section 24 of the 1867 Constitution Act gives the governor general the power to appoint senators, but by convention this is done on the "advice" of the prime minister. Prime ministers have usually chosen partisan supporters, such as MPs seeking a safe haven, defeated MPs or candidates, those who have served the party organization well, retired premiers or other former provincial politicians, and federal Cabinet ministers who have outlived their usefulness. Hence, almost all of those appointed could be called "party hacks," and the image of the Senate was set: a "home for the aged," a "pension scheme for retired party warriors," and a reward for businessmen's contributions to the party war chest. More positively, however, most senators could be seen as possessing valuable political experience.

In addition to rewarding faithful service to the party in the past, many appointments were made on the assumption that the new senator would continue to promote the party in the future. Such senators carried on as party presidents, fundraisers, organizers, election campaign strategists or managers, or in other partisan capacities. Most prime ministers have made the occasional nonpartisan or cross-party appointment, perhaps as a "cover" for yet more partisan nominees, and because the Senate was already overwhelmingly stacked with Liberals, Pierre Trudeau deliberately replaced a Tory with a Tory on six occasions.

In the past, senators were traditionally English or French male lawyers or businessmen, many of whom maintained active business connections after their appointment.[45] Most saw nothing wrong with carrying on as directors of various corporations or even being appointed to new ones at the same time as they held public office. They had spare time, they welcomed the supplementary income, and they could be useful links between the corporate and political worlds. Because of ideological opposition to the whole concept of an appointed chamber, left-wing groups have refused the occasional offer of appointment, leaving labour and working-class representation in the Senate virtually nonexistent.[46]

The Constitution Act, 1867 speaks of "qualified persons" being eligible for appointment to the Senate, which was originally understood to include only men. In one of the most famous court cases in Canadian history, however, an enterprising group of women challenged this interpretation, and in the 1929 **Persons case**, the Judicial Committee of the Privy Council decided that "persons" did indeed include women.[47] Henceforth women were eligible to sit in the Senate, and their number reached 39 in 2012. Such a large contingent of women has actually altered the Senate's operation to some extent, as noted below. In addition, ethnic and religious considerations have often played a part in Senate appointments. From the Diefenbaker period onward, prime ministers sought to diversify Senate membership in ethnocultural terms, and senators have been appointed as representatives of the Aboriginal, Ukrainian, Italian, Greek, Icelandic, and Black Canadian communities, among others. Indeed, the Senate appointments have been seen in some cases as opportunities to add representatives of groups that are otherwise under-represented in the House of Commons.

Senators originally served for life, and many lived to the ripe old age of 80, 90, or 100. Lester Pearson had a constitutional amendment passed in 1965 to the effect that incumbent senators could stay until death or retire at 75 with a pension, but all subsequent appointees would have to retire at 75. In normal circumstances only one senator sits in the Cabinet (the government leader in the Senate). But both Joe Clark (1979–80) and Pierre Trudeau (1980–84) had three or four senators in their Cabinets to fill in gaps in their provincial representation, and Stephen Harper started out with two, one to represent Montreal. Because Harper believed in an elected Senate, he initially left many vacancies unfilled—18 in December 2008. However, because these vacancies actually disadvantaged the Conservative party in the Senate, Harper suddenly filled them with partisan supporters before the end of the year. Continuing this practice, he achieved a Conservative plurality in the chamber in early 2010 and later an absolute majority. Liberal leader Justin Trudeau divorced the Liberals in the Senate from those in the Commons in January 2014, and ruled that senators could no longer attend meetings of the Liberal caucus. He proposed that future senators be appointed after an "open, transparent, non-partisan process."

OPERATION OF THE SENATE

In the light of its intended functions, what can be said about the actual operations of the Senate? First, as for acting as a conservative influence on legislation and representing the interests of property, two examples stand out, the first being the Senate's defeat of the first Old Age Pensions bill in 1925. But after an election in which Mackenzie King was deemed to have received a mandate for the legislation, the Senate passed the bill a year later. The other was the Senate's repeated refusal until 1936 to repeal the notorious section 98 of the Criminal Code that had been passed at the height of the Winnipeg General Strike in 1919 and clearly infringed freedom of speech.

The Senate has also been accused of being a lobby for the business community. At the time that Colin Campbell wrote *The Canadian Senate: A Lobby from Within*, many senators had corporate connections, especially those who sat on the Senate Committee on Banking, Trade and Commerce. He cited the Senate's adopted function of "business review," as its members "bargain and negotiate on business's behalf for amendments which are essential for a favourable financial and commercial climate." Campbell revealed the "one-sided review which takes place in a legislature created by a political system which bends over backwards to ensure that business has preferential access to the policy process."[48] The "new breed" of senators appointed since Campbell wrote are much less likely to come from the business community, however; more women have been selected, and most have a wider perspective.

Second, it must be concluded that the Senate has never effectively represented provincial and regional interests in the national policymaking process. This is not particularly surprising when senators owe their appointment to the federal prime minister and not to any provincial or regional constituency. Moreover, many senators settle down in the comfortable environs of Ottawa and rarely go near the region they ostensibly represent. As a result, the regional representation function was soon undertaken by the Judicial Committee of the Privy Council, regional ministers in the federal Cabinet, and provincial premiers in their interactions with the prime minister.

Of the Senate's original purposes, then, the first has been rendered archaic and the second has been assumed by other agencies. Today's senators therefore justify their existence primarily in terms of the third function mentioned—routine, technical revision of bills. R.A. MacKay argues that the nonpartisan, noncontroversial revising function of the Senate is virtually indispensable, and F.A. Kunz calls it one of great usefulness.[49] Similarly, the rules allow a bill to be introduced simultaneously in both chambers so that the Senate can engage in an unhurried "pre-study" of the bill rather than wait until it has passed three readings in the Commons. It has been normal in recent sessions of parliament for the government to introduce a few bills, including the Anti-Terrorism Act, in the Senate in this way.

Senators also seek to emphasize other important aspects of their work. One is the Senate's consideration of private bills. These concern individuals, companies, and other institutions, and are a nuisance to the busy House of Commons, which is often backlogged with public bills. Since 1934, almost all private bills have been introduced in the Senate, where the background work can be done so that the Commons can approve them routinely at a later date. For a period the Senate functioned as a divorce court for Quebec and Newfoundland, when religious opposition to divorce in those two provinces pre-empted turning this responsibility over to their courts. Divorces were a special kind of private bill, and between 1964 and 1968 (when they finally became a judicial matter in those two provinces) divorces were disposed of by the Senate without reference to the Commons.

Another kind of work not originally provided for is the study of various public problems by Senate committees in what Colin Campbell calls "social investigations." Senators often have the experience, expertise, independence of mind, and time to conduct inquiries that relieve the pressure on the House of Commons and are cheaper than royal commissions. Among the memorable reports of the Senate over the years were those on poverty, aging, unemployment, the mass media, science policy, land use, national defence, fisheries, Canadian–American relations, and the Canadian Security Intelligence Service. Senate committees now churn out reports at a dizzying pace on a wide range of subjects. Two of its most famous recent reports were on the legalization of marijuana and the Kirby Report on health care. Although the former did not achieve its objective, and marijuana has not been legalized, the Kirby Report had a major impact on health care discussions, especially regarding guaranteed maximum wait times.[50] The government also implemented the recommendation of the Carstairs Report on end-of-life care that income security and job protection be extended to family members who care for the dying. Senate committees usually have more success when the government requests them to study an issue than when they undertake their own initiatives.

Finally, the Standing Joint Committee on the Scrutiny of Regulations has the responsibility of reviewing the great quantity of subordinate legislation issued every year. Although MPs also sit on this joint committee, the senators have more time to devote to its tedious work and perhaps approach it with more independence of mind.[51]

The question still arises: worthy as all of these new-found functions are, do they collectively justify the expense of the Senate? Many mediocre appointments have been made over the years, but the chamber has always had a number of impressive occupants. Although some senators have done virtually no work for their paycheques, others have made useful contributions. Many have outside interests, so that only a few are totally focused on their senatorial responsibilities. Senator Colin Kenny, for example, led a crusade against the tobacco industry and persuaded the government to take a number of anti-smoking initiatives that helped in the dissolution of the Canadian Tobacco Manufacturers' Council. He then became a leading spokesperson on defence issues. Given its lack of a popular base, however, any good work that the Senate does will always be somewhat suspect and not given the respect it deserves.

The Senate timetable is rather lax. Attendance is taken, and most senators show up three days a week for no more than 27 weeks a year. There being no shortage of time, the rules are quite relaxed; the Speaker is chosen by the prime minister and has a vote on all matters. There is a question period, but it is a challenge for the one senator who normally sits in the Cabinet to answer for the whole range of government activity. Prime ministers and Cabinets have often been disrespectful of the institution, leaving many vacancies for long periods of time and expecting it to pass large quantities of legislation quickly at the end of a session.

The Senate's exercise of its power to amend or veto legislation must be put into the context that an appointed legislative chamber lost much of its legitimacy with the spread of democratic sentiment shortly after Confederation. Thus, the Senate did not usually feel justified in defying the will of the popularly elected House of Commons.[52] Moreover, given the partisan nature of Senate appointments, the majority in that chamber usually corresponds to the partisan complexion of the Commons. Both had a Conservative majority for about the first 30 years and both usually had a Liberal majority after 1900.

As for amendments, Kunz and MacKay calculated that before 1960 the Senate made amendments to about 15 or 20 percent of the bills coming from the Commons.[53] This figure fell to between five percent and 10 percent over the past 50 years. It must be said that in many cases such amendments were introduced in the Senate by the Cabinet itself, reflecting its second thoughts on the matter after a bill had been approved by the Commons, and most of the others were of a technical nature. To reinforce this point, it made little difference to the number of amendments whether or not the majority in both chambers belonged to the same party. Most of the technical amendments to government bills that are moved in the Senate are accepted by the Commons, but this is partly because they have been cleared in informal discussions beforehand.[54]

On the other hand, partisanship is most striking when we consider Senate vetoes of Commons legislation. In almost all such cases, a Liberal majority in the Senate has obstructed a Conservative majority in the Commons, or vice versa. According to MacKay, of approximately 4200 public bills passed by the Commons between 1867 and 1960, about 100 failed to pass the Senate, although many of these were withdrawn voluntarily by the government. Kunz found 18 vetoes out of 1918 bills between 1926 and 1963. Rather than concentrate on total numbers, we have put a list of the 15 most controversial Senate vetoes on this text's website. MacKay argues that in these and other cases the Senate has never defeated the real will of the people when clearly expressed;[55] if it objects to a provision in a bill, the Senate will often accept it with "observations," pointing out its concerns to which the Commons may or may not respond.

Brian Mulroney had considerable difficulty with the Senate, when, between 1984 and 1991, a Liberal majority in that chamber coincided with a Conservative majority in the Commons. The Senate delayed many government bills, and it repeatedly passed amendments to them, only retreating at the last minute.[56] The Senate also tried to alter the Meech Lake Accord, and its amendments had to be overridden by the Commons after the expiry of the 180-day limit on constitutional amendments. Then, in mid-1988, at John Turner's direction, the Liberal majority in the Senate held up the Canada–U.S. Free Trade Agreement until the electorate had a chance to express its will on such an important measure. After the 1988 election, the Senate bowed to the popular will and passed the agreement, but later dug in its heels on other bills, especially the Goods and Services Tax (GST).

It is unlikely that the GST would have passed if Mulroney had not invoked an obscure clause in the 1867 Constitution Act, section 26, which allowed him to appoint eight additional senators (two for each of the four senatorial regions) to tip the balance in favour of the Conservatives.[57] After the GST was approved in an atmosphere of great bitterness, the Senate went ahead and defeated the government's compromise abortion bill (on a tie vote). This became the first measure in 30 years that the Senate actually defeated, but it was a peculiar case in that the government allowed a "free vote," and some Cabinet ministers were probably secretly relieved that the Senate had exercised such a rare veto. The Mulroney era was also exceptional because, engaged on a neoliberal ideological agenda, the House of Commons acted in a more conservative manner than the Senate, which suddenly saw itself as protecting the little people.

By the time the Liberals came to power in 1993, the Conservatives had established a clear majority in the Senate, so positions were reversed, and the Liberals began to pay for their intransigence of a few years earlier. On a rather nonpartisan note, though, the Senate responded to demands from the academic community to veto a bill that would have merged the Social Sciences and Humanities Research Council with the Canada Council. The Conservative majority in the Senate was particularly incensed about the Liberal bill related to the privatization of Toronto Pearson Airport, and the bill was defeated on a tie vote. The PC-controlled Senate then stalled the Liberals' redistribution bill to the point of abandonment, which was also the fate of pro-labour amendments to the Canada Labour Code. The Senate defeated the Newfoundland and Labrador constitutional amendment with respect to removing denominational schools, until it was overridden after 180 days.

Even after the Liberals regained a majority in the Senate, the second chamber remained a more active place than normal, as it amended the government's own Canada Wheat Board bill. But it then did the government a favour by defeating a private members' bill (dealing with profiteering from crime) that had slipped unnoticed through the Commons.[58] The Senate declined to pass a number of bills that Jean Chrétien wanted adopted before he left office; indeed, it is common for many bills to be abandoned by the Senate at the end of a parliamentary session, some deliberately and some by neglect.

Stephen Harper formed a government in 2006 in the unusual situation of holding a minority of seats in both the Commons and the Senate. Although the Conservatives began by being vastly outnumbered, the upper chamber functioned quite cooperatively with the government, such as with reasonable amendments to the Federal Accountability Act. On the other hand,

The *historical-institutional approach* can most usefully be applied to the study of the House of Commons and Senate, considering that they are two of the key institutions of government in Canada that have existed since the beginning. They also confirm the claim that fundamental rules and procedures do not change much once they are established—even though there has been no end of reform recommendations, especially with respect to the Senate, as we will see below. As key institutions of the state, the House of Commons and Senate are also relevant to the *state-based approach*. Even though they are meant to represent the various interests in society, it could be said that the Senate does not always pay attention to wider societal forces, and rigid party discipline in the House of Commons ensures that if the government wants a certain outcome, it will pursue its own objectives and subordinate what it regards as special interests to its conception of the public interest.

the Senate insisted on keeping an ethics officer of its own, and it did not cooperate with Harper's efforts to reform the upper house. In May 2010, when the Conservatives had a near majority in the Senate, but not in the Commons, the upper chamber defeated an NDP private member's bill on climate change that had managed to pass through the Commons. While some of the *elected* parliamentarians protested, the Senate argued that it was not significant to defeat a private member's bill.

Andrew Heard argues that a modern convention has developed such that the Senate can make purely technical amendments or others that it knows will be acceptable to the Commons and to the government. Although it should not act to frustrate the general thrust of Commons legislation put before it, the Senate can on rare occasions make substantive amendments "when the government has no clear support from the majority of Canadians to implement a policy that adversely affects some individuals or groups." If legislation is re-passed by the Commons, however, the Senate should give way.[59]

SENATE REFORM

Given the limited value of the Senate as it traditionally operated, its reform has always been high on the political agenda. Indeed, several hundred proposals for Senate reform have been made over the years. They relate to the Senate's functions and structure, the selection process, the term of office, its powers, and just about everything else. One option, of course, is abolition. This is the official policy of the CCF/NDP because of the undemocratic nature of the Senate and its traditional links to the business community. Colin Campbell also recommended abolition because of the Senate's illegitimate defence of corporate interests and the impossibility of making the institution more effective and more democratic without interfering with the will of the House of Commons. The contrary argument is that the Senate does some useful work, is less linked to corporate interests than in the past, and could be reformed to become even more valuable.

Many reformers have advocated reactivating the Senate's role of representing regional and provincial interests at the federal level because the existing mechanisms of "intrastate federalism" have been flawed. The Trudeau government first attempted to make the Senate a House of the Federation in 1978, with half its members selected by the provinces. However, the Supreme Court held that such a change to the structure of the Senate required provincial approval of a constitutional amendment.[60] In the 1987 Meech Lake Accord, Prime Minister Mulroney promised to appoint senators from lists provided by the provinces, but by the time the Accord died three years later, and this interim measure with it, Mulroney had appointed only a handful of senators from provincial lists.

Meanwhile, Alberta began pushing its **Triple-E Senate** proposal based on the model of the U.S. Senate: senators would be *elected*, the Senate would have additional powers to make it *effective*, and each province would have an *equal* number of representatives in the chamber.[61] Triple-E advocates were not entirely clear on what powers they saw as necessary to make the Senate "effective," nor worried that an elected Senate would feel justified in obstructing the will of the House of Commons. But since they argued that laws currently emanating from the Commons were designed in the interests of central Canada, they were not overly concerned about deadlock between their revamped Senate and the lower house. Altering the structure and powers of the Senate, however, would require a constitutional amendment, an accomplishment that would not be easily achieved. Even if it were, some kind of deadlock-breaking mechanism would have to be provided between two popularly elected chambers.

The government of Alberta felt so strongly about an elected Senate that it held a "senatorial election" in 1989 when a vacancy occurred during the period in which Mulroney asked for a list of provincial nominees. When the Reform Party candidate won the province-wide contest (coinciding with municipal elections), Premier Don Getty forwarded his name to the prime minister, and Mulroney reluctantly gave in. Senate reform was then a prominent part of the 1992 Charlottetown Accord, with changes approximating Triple-E, but when the accord went down to popular defeat, the Senate remained unreformed. Alberta held another senatorial election in 1998, but Prime Minister Chrétien slyly filled a vacancy from that province a month before the election, appointing a former Tory, who sat as an Independent. Alberta held a third senatorial election in 2004 and a fourth in 2012, resulting in a list of "senators-in-waiting." While some reformers advocate equal provincial representation in the Senate, others would like to make it more proportional to population and add seats for the Western provinces.[62]

To some extent, the Senate is changing through informal means. For example, Paul Martin appointed younger and often female senators from a wider diversity of professional backgrounds who were usually prepared to put in more effort than the male corporate lawyers who were previously dominant. In recent years, senators have taken more of their own initiatives and made many useful and objective responses to those of the government, as it aimed to become the "think tank of the Canadian government." In 2014, Liberal leader Justin Trudeau announced that all Liberal senators were being removed from the Liberal caucus and that they would sit as independent senators (though this came as a surprise to the senators themselves, who later developed their own party caucus). Trudeau stated that partisan ties interfere with the senate's functions.

Because so much of its committee work is both impressive and ignored, the Senate has begun to televise some of its committee hearings, as well as making them available on social media platforms, although not the proceedings of the Chamber as a whole.[63] As mentioned, the benefit of appointed senators, at their best, is that a premium can be put on expertise, experience, and continuity, as well as gender and minority representation. But because the appointment process will always dog its accomplishments, the Trudeau government has set up an independent appointments committee (akin to that involved in recommending the appointment of judges) that would take the partisanship and favouritism out of the prime minister's hands.

The Harper Proposals

Stephen Harper came to office from the Triple-E Alberta tradition and was determined, at least, to have senators elected for a specific term.[64] Because of the rigidity of the constitutional amending formula, he did not expect to achieve his objective in that direction, but because that formula is slightly ambiguous, he claimed that he could obtain this "E" through ordinary legislation. Harper introduced a total of three bills during his time as prime minister, with the first attempting to impose an eight-year limit on the length of a Senator's tenure and the second incorporating a means of election which would guide the choice of appointment. Both bills made slow progress and neither passed, owing heavily to concerns the bills were unconstitutional. In the meantime, Harper continued to make appointments of his own choosing, including some from Alberta's list of "elected" senators-in-waiting. After he achieved a majority in both chambers in June 2011, Harper introduced Bill C-7 which provided for nine-year senatorial terms for which he claimed he did not need a provincially approved constitutional amendment. The same bill outlined a more detailed plan for the provinces to hold consultative senatorial elections, by which the PM would be guided in making such appointments. Nevertheless, the questions of whether the constitution permits these changes remained.

Harper ultimately asked the Supreme Court of Canada to advise on the proposed changes. The decision, reached in 2014, was that Ottawa could not unilaterally change the Senate or introduce elections or term limits. Such changes, it stated, require following the necessary constitutional amending formula, which would include consent of seven provinces comprising 50 percent or more of the population. Abolition of the Senate, the court determined, would require unanimity of the provinces along with the federal parliament.

The unpopularity of the Senate reached a high point in recent years, with scandals involving illegitimate expense claims for various senators, the most notable being Conservative senators Mike Duffy, Patrick Brazeau, Pamela Wallin, and (former) Liberal senator Mac Harb. The Senate voted to suspend the former three, while Harb decided to retire. Prime Minister Stephen Harper, unable to implement his desired reforms, chose to simply stop appointing Senators and asked that provincial premiers come forward with a proposal for reform. Whether the prime minister can indefinitely chose to not appoint senators remained a matter before the courts at the time of the 2015 election, though it is less relevant since the Trudeau government intends to continue with appointments.

CONCLUSION

This chapter demonstrates that, apart from MPs who double as Cabinet ministers, the role of the House of Commons in the policymaking process is not impressive and that of the Senate even less so. However, both chambers do have significant functions: in representing varied interests, debating public issues, keeping the government honest, and educating the electorate. The prime minister and Cabinet can win almost every "battle" with Parliament, but may still lose the next electoral "war" if the opposition has alerted the public to their faults via the media. Concentrating the responsibility for public policy in the hands of the prime minister and Cabinet has advantages, but these could still be achieved if better use were made of the talent in the House of Commons and that evident in the Senate. Individual MPs also have important constituency responsibilities.

This chapter is primarily connected to Chapter 21 on the Executive, especially considering that the prime minister and Cabinet ministers are members of Parliament and need to retain the confidence of the House of Commons. It is also linked to chapters on parties and elections because MPs owe their office to election, devote much of their efforts to being re-elected, and perform in a very partisan manner. Although partisanship overwhelms most of its operations, the socioeconomic representation of parliamentarians is of considerable importance, and links this chapter to Part 2 of the book.

DISCUSSION QUESTIONS

1. If Parliament does not play a significant part in the policymaking process, what are its basic functions?

2. What are the advantages and disadvantages of rigid party discipline in the House of Commons?

3. Should the concept of "confidence" be limited to nonconfidence votes, the speech from the throne, and the budget, or applied more broadly?

4. What other aspects of the House of Commons, if any, should be reformed?

5. How does minority government affect the significance of the House of Commons in the policymaking process?

6. Does the Senate do enough to justify its existence, or should it be abolished?

7. What are the pros and cons of the Triple-E Senate? How else could the Senate be reformed?

MindTap®   FOR MORE INFO GO TO http://www.nelson.com/student

NOTES

1. C.E.S. Franks, *The Parliament of Canada* (Toronto: University of Toronto Press, 1987), p. 5. John Stewart, *The Canadian House of Commons: Procedure and Reform* (Montreal: McGill-Queen's University Press, 1977) lists essentially the same functions: "first, to support a government; second, to prevent clandestine governing; third, to test the government's administrative policies and legislative proposals; fourth, to constrain the ministers; and fifth, to educate the electorate," p. 30.
2. Franks, *The Parliament of Canada*, p. 216.
3. Chowdhry, Affan. "Record number of visible minority MPs elected to Commons", *The Globe and Mail*, Oct. 20, 2015, available at: http://www.theglobeandmail.com/news/politics/record-number-of-visible -minority-mps-elected-to-commons/article26892245/.
4. Franks, *The Parliament of Canada*, p. 73; David C. Docherty, *Mr. Smith Goes to Ottawa: Life in the House of Commons* (Vancouver: UBC Press, 1997), Ch. 2; John Porter, *The Vertical Mosaic* (Toronto: University of Toronto Press, 1965), p. 402.
5. Jeffrey Simpson, *The Friendly Dictatorship* (Toronto: McClelland and Stewart, 2001), pp. 36–45; and David C. Docherty, *Legislatures* (Vancouver: UBC Press, 2005).
6. Éric Grenier, "How routine MP speeches are becoming more and more partisan," *The Globe and Mail*, September 24, 2012; Kelly Blidook, "The changing use of Standing Order 31 statements," *Canadian Parliamentary Review* 36 (4) (2013), pp. 25–29.
7. Franks, *The Parliament of Canada*, p. 142.
8. Stewart, *The Canadian House of Commons*, pp. 29–30.
9. Eugene Forsey and Graham Eglington, "Twenty-Five Fairy Tales about Parliamentary Government," in Paul Fox and Graham White, eds., *Politics: Canada*, 7th ed. (Toronto: McGraw-Hill Ryerson, 1991), argue that this is a mistaken belief; Docherty, *Mr. Smith Goes to Ottawa*, Ch. 6; and Simpson, *The Friendly Dictatorship*, pp. 45–53.
10. Sometimes the concept of a "shadow cabinet" is used by opposition leaders, but if the party becomes the government, there is no guarantee that "shadow critics" will be given the corresponding Cabinet post.
11. Franks, *The Parliament of Canada*, pp. 6, 29, 96, 268; Michael M. Atkinson and David C. Docherty, "Parliament and Political Success in Canada," in Michael Whittington and Glen Williams, *Canadian Politics in the 21st Century*, 7th ed. (Toronto: Thomson Nelson, 2008).
12. Andrew Heard, *Canadian Constitutional Conventions* (Toronto: Oxford University Press, 1991), p. 80.
13. Franks, *The Parliament of Canada*, pp. 110–14. Donald Savoie confirms the contention that in Canada, almost every MP wants to be a minister, in *Governing from the Centre: The Concentration of Political Power in Canada* (Toronto: University of Toronto Press, 1999), p. 83.
14. Heard, *Canadian Constitutional Conventions*, p. 83.
15. Meanwhile, Liberal leader Stéphane Dion removed Joe Comuzzi from that party's caucus for supporting the 2007 Conservative budget. Conversely, Bill Casey was dismissed from the Conservative caucus for voting against the 2007 Budget. Harper gave the House of Commons an opportunity to revisit the issue of same-sex marriage in a free vote in December 2006, but the majority voted against reopening the issue.
16. Paul Thomas, "Parliamentary Reform through Political Parties," in John Courtney, ed., *The Canadian House of Commons: Essays in Honour of Norman Ward* (Calgary: University of Calgary Press, 1985); and Paul Thomas, "The Role of National Party Caucuses," in Peter Aucoin, ed., *Party Government and Regional Representation in Canada* (Toronto: University of Toronto Press, 1985). Savoie, *Governing from the Centre*, pp. 91–93, quotes MPs as referring to caucus as "bitching sessions."
17. Kelly Blidook, *Constituency Influence in Parliament: Countering the Centre* (Vancouver: UBC Press, 2012); Thomas, "The Role of the National Party Caucuses"; and Atkinson and Docherty, "Parliament and Political Success in Canada," p. 20.
18. The Speaker allowed a private member's bill that would make contributions to Registered Educational Savings Plans tax deductible and it was passed with the combined strength of the opposition parties, even though it was considered a money bill. The government later found a procedural way to have it quashed. See documents on House of Commons website: *Private Members' Business: Practical Guide*, 9th ed. (Ottawa: Parliament of Canada, 2008), retrieved on April 27, 2009, available at http://www .parl.gc.ca/information/about/process/house/PMB_PracticalGuide/PractGuide_4PMB-e.htm.

19. The government's resort to closure on every stage of the bill was seen as the work of Trade and Commerce Minister C.D. Howe, who was obsessed with getting the construction of the pipeline started.

20. Jessica J. Richardson, "Modernization of Royal Assent in Canada," in *Canadian Parliamentary Review* (Summer 2004).

21. For a compilation of the rules, see the most recent edition of *Standing Orders of the House of Commons*, available at http://www.parl.gc.ca/information/about/process/house/standingorders/toc-e.htm. For a discussion of the Speaker, see "The Impartiality of the Speakership: A Round Table," *Canadian Parliamentary Review* (Summer 2004).

22. Martin Westmacott, "Whips and Party Cohesion," *Canadian Parliamentary Review* (Autumn 1988).

23. Terry Moore and James Robertson, "An Introduction to Parliamentary Privilege," in *Canadian Parliamentary Review* (Autumn 2001).

24. Docherty, *Legislatures*, pp. 165–66; Atkinson and Docherty, "Parliament and Political Success in Canada," p. 21; Jonathan Malloy, "Reconciling Expectations and Reality in House of Commons Committees: The Case of the 1989 GST Inquiry," *Canadian Public Administration* (November 1996); House of Commons Canada, *Committees: Practical Guide*, 9th ed. (Ottawa: Parliament of Canada, 2008), cited on April 27, 2008, available at http://www.parl.gc.ca/information/about/process/house/CommitteesPracticalGuide/CmtesPG2008__cover-e.htm.

25. Jack Stilborn, "Parliamentary Review of Estimates: Initiatives and Prospects," *Canadian Parliamentary Review* (Winter 2006–07); John A. Chenier, Michael Dewing, and Jack Stillborn, "Does Parliament Care? Parliamentary Committees and the Estimates," in G. Bruce Doern, ed., *How Ottawa Spends 2005–2006* (Montreal: McGill-Queen's University Press, 2005); and *Strengthening Parliamentary Scrutiny of Estimates and Supply*, Report of the Standing Committee on Government Operations and Estimates (June 2012), available at http://www.parl.gc.ca/HousePublications/Publication.aspx?DocId=5690996&Language=E&Mode=1&Parl=41&Ses=1.

26. Gomery Report, *Restoring Accountability*, Ch. 4, pp. 75–80, and Ch. 6, pp. 117–19; Jonathan Malloy, "The Standing Committee on Public Accounts," in *Restoring Accountability: Research Studies*, Volume 1.

27. Heather MacIvor, *Parameters of Power: Canada's Political Institutions*, 5th ed. (Toronto: Nelson Education, 2010), p. 224.

28. Grace Skogstad, "Interest Groups, Representation and Conflict Management in the Standing Committees of the House of Commons," *Canadian Journal of Political Science* (December 1985); and David M. McInnes, *Taking It to the Hill: The Complete Guide to Appearing Before (and Surviving) Parliamentary Committees* (Ottawa: University of Ottawa Press, 1999).

29. C.E.S. Franks, "Parliamentarians and the New Code of Ethics," *Canadian Parliamentary Review* (Spring 2005).

30. Docherty, Mr. Smith Goes to Ottawa, Ch. 5.

31. Docherty estimates that constituency work takes up 35 percent of the average MP's time and recommends that more resources at the local level would free up MPs for policy and legislative research. *Legislatures*, pp. 89–90.

32. Docherty, *Mr. Smith Goes to Ottawa*; for American examples, see Richard F. Fenno, *Home Style: House Members in their Districts* (Boston: Little Brown, 1978); Richard E. Neustadt, *Presidential Power and the Modern Presidents: the Politics of Leadership from Roosevelt to Reagan* (New York: The Free Press, 1990).

33. Gary Levy, "A Parliamentary Budget Officer for Canada," *Canadian Parliamentary Review* (Summer 2008); Jeffrey Graham Bell, "Agents of Parliament: A New Branch of Government?" *Canadian Parliamentary Review* (Spring 2006).

34. Eugene Forsey, "The Problem of 'Minority Government' in Canada," *Canadian Journal of Economics and Political Science* (February 1964); Peter Dobell, "What Could Canadians Expect from a Minority Government?" (Montreal: Institute for Research on Public Policy, 2000); and Paul E.J. Thomas, "Measuring the Effectiveness of a Minority Parliament," *Canadian Parliamentary Review* (Spring 2007).

35. Peter H. Russell, *Two Cheers for Minority Government: The Evolution of Canadian Parliamentary Democracy* (Toronto: Emond Montgomery, 2008).

36. Atkinson and Docherty, "Parliament and Political Success in Canada," pp. 8–9.

37. According to Franks, the Trudeau minority was actually defeated on 18 of 81 votes between 1972 and 1974 but chose only to resign on the defeat of the 1974 budget; the Pearson government had suffered

two other defeats without much fanfare. Franks, *The Parliament of Canada*, p. 139. Andrew Heard discusses another controversial vote in May 2005 in "Just What is a Vote of Confidence? The Curious Case of May 20, 2005," *Canadian Journal of Political Science* (June 2007); Bruce Doern, "The Martin Liberals (and the Harper Conservatives): The Politics of Governing Precariously," in *How Ottawa Spends 2005–2006*; Jonathan Malloy, "The Drama of Parliament under Minority Government," in G. Bruce Doern and Christopher Stoney, eds., *How Ottawa Spends 2010–2011* (Montreal: McGill-Queen's University Press, 2010).

38. Peter H. Russell and Lorne Sossin, eds., *Parliamentary Democracy in Crisis* (Toronto: University of Toronto Press, 2009); Peter Aucoin, Mark D. Jarvis, and Lori Turnbull, *Democratizing the Constitution: Reforming Responsible Government* (Toronto: Emond Montgomery, 2011).

39. Franks, *The Parliament of Canada*, p. 132; and John Stewart, "Commons Procedure in the Trudeau Era," in John Courtney, ed., *The Canadian House of Commons: Essays in Honour of Norman Ward* (Calgary: University of Calgary Press, 1985).

40. One of the more controversial aspects of television was the rule that the camera could focus only on the person recognized by the Speaker, rather than show what was going on elsewhere in the chamber.

41. *Report of the Special Committee on Reform of the House of Commons* (Ottawa: House of Commons, 1985).

42. Franks, *The Parliament of Canada*, pp. 9, 261. See also Thomas S. Axworthy, "Parliamentary Reform—Everything Old is New Again," Institute for Research on Public Policy, *Policy Options*, June 2008; Centre for the Study of Democracy, http://www.queensu.ca/csd/.

43. Quoted in R.A. MacKay, *The Unreformed Senate of Canada*, rev. ed. (Toronto: McClelland and Stewart, 1967), pp. 47–48.

44. MacKay, *The Unreformed Senate*, pp. 91–95; and F.A. Kunz, *The Modern Senate of Canada 1925–1963: A Re-appraisal* (Toronto: University of Toronto Press, 1965), pp. 337–47. Andrew Heard argues that a constitutional convention is emerging that the Senate may not insist on altering the financial provisions of money bills. *Canadian Constitutional Conventions*, p. 94.

45. MacKay, *The Unreformed Senate*, Ch. 9; and Kunz, *The Modern Senate of Canada*, Ch. 2; both discuss socioeconomic backgrounds up to 1960 and 1963, respectively.

46. When Paul Martin appointed Dr. Lillian Dyck to the Senate, she sat as a New Democrat, but the NDP were reluctant to acknowledge her and she joined the Liberals instead!

47. Kunz, *The Modern Senate of Canada*, discusses this issue on pp. 53–56. The case was officially referred to as *Edwards v. Att. Gen. of Can.*, [1930] AC 124.

48. Campbell, *The Canadian Senate: A Lobby from Within* (Toronto: Macmillan, 1978), pp. 10–11; and John McMenemy, "The Senate as an Instrument of Business and Party," in Paul Fox and Graham White, eds., *Politics: Canada*, 7th ed. (Toronto: McGraw-Hill Ryerson, 1991), p. 455.

49. MacKay, *The Unreformed Senate*, p. 110; and Kunz, *The Modern Senate of Canada*, p. 186.

50. Campbell, *The Canadian Senate: A Lobby from Within*; and Jeffrey J. MacLeod and Howard Chodos, "The Senate Committee Study on Canada's Health Care System," *Canadian Parliamentary Review* (Spring 2003).

51. Paul Salembier and Peter Bernhardt, "Understanding the Regulation Making Process," *Canadian Parliamentary Review* (Spring 2002).

52. MacKay, *The Unreformed Senate*, writes that it is an "institutional survival of a pre-democratic age" (p. 10) and that "in a democratic age an appointed upper house labours under the handicap that it has no political foundation" (p. 62).

53. MacKay, *The Unreformed Senate*, p. 87; and Kunz, *The Modern Senate of Canada*, pp. 116–17.

54. See Parliament of Canada, *Bills Introduced in the House of Commons and Amended by the Senate, 1960 to Date*"; available at http://www.parl.gc.ca/ParlInfo/Compilations/HouseOfCommons/Legislation/HOCBillsAmandedBySenate.aspx?Language=E.

55. MacKay, *The Unreformed Senate*, pp. 96–112.

56. See the justification offered by Senator Lorna Marsden in "Doing Its Thing—Providing 'Sober Second Thought': The Canadian Senate, 1984–1990," in Fox and White, *Politics: Canada*.

57. In 1873 Alexander Mackenzie had asked the British government to summon additional senators but was refused on the ground that it was not necessary at the time.

58. The Senate also made a small amendment to the Liberals' Youth Criminal Justice Act in 2002.

59. Heard, *Canadian Constitutional Conventions*, p. 95.

60. Reference *Re Legislative Authority of Parliament to Alter or Replace the Senate*, [1980] 1 S.C.R. 54.

61. See, for example, Peter McCormick, "Canada Needs a Triple-E Senate," in Fox and White, eds., *Politics: Canada*; H. McConnell, "The Case for a 'Triple-E' Senate," *Queen's Quarterly* (Autumn 1988); and Simpson, *The Friendly Dictatorship*, pp. 18–29.

62. Special Senate Committee on Senate Reform, "Report on the Motion to Amend the Constitution of Canada (western regional representation in the Senate)" (Ottawa, October 2006).

63. For a fine account of the Senate in recent times, see Serge Joyal, ed., *Protecting Canadian Democracy: The Senate You Never Knew* (Montreal: McGill-Queen's University Press, 2003).

64. Jennifer Smith, ed., *The Democratic Dilemma: Reforming the Canadian Senate* (Montreal and Kingston: McGill-Queen's University Press), 2009.

FURTHER READING

HOUSE OF COMMONS

Atkinson, Michael M., and David C. Docherty. "Parliament and Political Success in Canada," in Michael Whittington and Glen Williams. *Canadian Politics in the 21st Century*, 7th ed. Toronto: Thomson Nelson, 2008.

Aucoin, Peter, Mark D. Jarvis, and Lori Turnbull. *Democratizing the Constitution: Reforming Responsible Government*. Toronto: Emond Montgomery, 2011.

Bejermi, John. *Canadian Parliamentary Handbook*. Ottawa: Borealis Press, annual.

Blidook, Kelly. *Constituency Influence in Parliament: Countering the Centre*. Vancouver: UBC Press, 2012.

Docherty, David C. *Legislatures*. Vancouver: UBC Press, 2005.

———. *Mr. Smith Goes to Ottawa: Life in the House of Commons*. Vancouver: UBC Press, 1997.

Franks, C.E.S. *The Parliament of Canada*. Toronto: University of Toronto Press, 1987.

Heard, Andrew. *Canadian Constitutional Conventions*. Toronto: Oxford University Press, 1991.

Malloy, Jonathan. "The Drama of Parliament under Minority Government," in G. Bruce Doern and Christopher Stoney, eds. *How Ottawa Spends 2010–2011: Recession, Realignment, and the New Deficit Era*. Montreal and Kingston: McGill-Queen's University Press, 2010.

Russell, Peter H. *Two Cheers for Minority Government: The Evolution of Canadian Parliamentary Democracy*. Toronto: Emond Montgomery, 2008.

Smith, David E. *The People's House of Commons: Theories of Democracy in Contention*. Toronto: University of Toronto Press, 2006.

SENATE

Campbell, Colin. *The Canadian Senate: A Lobby from Within*. Toronto: Macmillan, 1978.

Joyal, Serge, ed., *Protecting Canadian Democracy: The Senate You Never Knew*. Montreal: McGill-Queen's University Press, 2003.

Kunz, F.A. *The Modern Senate of Canada 1925–1963: A Re-appraisal*. Toronto: University of Toronto Press, 1965.

Mackay, R.A. *The Unreformed Senate of Canada*, rev. ed. Toronto: McClelland and Stewart, 1967.

Smith, David E. *The Canadian Senate in Bicameral Perspective*. Toronto: University of Toronto Press, 2004.

Smith, Jennifer, ed. *The Democratic Dilemma: Reforming the Canadian Senate*. Montreal and Kingston: McGill-Queen's University Press, 2009.

© Mark Spowart/Alamy Stock Photo

CHAPTER 24

The Judiciary

It remains unclear how many ways Canada's newest Prime Minister, Justin Trudeau, will differ from the previous Conservative government on matters of Canada's judiciary. The Harper government took a hard line on crime that included changing the procedure for appointing judges and giving them less discretion in deciding on sentences. It also foreshadowed a larger inmate population and considerable increases in the costs of administering justice at the provincial level. Four recent appointees to the Supreme Court of Canada have been respectfully interviewed by a House of Commons committee before officially taking office. The Supreme Court decided that jurors can be challenged for racial bias when an accused person is a member of a group subject to widespread prejudice, told lower court judges to find alternatives to putting offenders in prison, and denied Quebec the right to make a unilateral declaration of independence. The Federal Court of Canada has quashed decisions of the Immigration and Refugee Board, overruled the government on security cases, and upheld a major public servants' pay equity claim. Women's and minority ethnocultural groups have criticized the general dominance of white male judges across the country, and Aboriginals have demanded a parallel Aboriginal justice system. The public is troubled by residual patronage appointments to the bench and cutbacks to legal aid plans.

Canadian political science was traditionally interested in the judiciary or court system primarily in terms of its interpretation of the federal–provincial division of powers. Now that the Charter of Rights and Freedoms has catapulted the courts into the middle of many heated political issues, political scientists are giving this fourth branch of government much more attention. Chapter 19 considered the role of the courts in interpreting the Charter of Rights and Freedoms and included a wider discussion of the role of judges in the policymaking process. This chapter examines the judiciary as an institution of government, discussing the function of adjudication, categories of laws, the structure of the courts, the Supreme Court of Canada, and the appointment, retirement, removal, and independence of judges.

THE FUNCTION OF ADJUDICATION

The judiciary has always been associated with the rule adjudication function in the political system, although other institutions may perform part of this function, too. Adjudication can be defined as interpreting the law in cases of dispute, of settling disputes by applying the law to them, or of making a judgment based on the law. Peter Russell defines the term as follows: "providing authoritative settlements in disputes about the law."[1]

Judges engage in the authoritative resolution of legal disputes, but many legal disputes are resolved without going to court or before going through the entire judicial process. Such an "out-of-court" settlement, especially one between individuals or between governments, is likely to be some sort of personal or political compromise. It is only when an accommodation satisfactory to both sides cannot be reached that the formal adjudicatory process is pursued to the bitter end.

The function of the judiciary therefore is to render formal, impartial, authoritative judgments in the case of legal disputes between two parties that cannot be settled otherwise. It is a process that generally relies on the adversarial system, with lawyers representing each side. The judge, clothed with the coercive powers of the state, acts as an independent referee and decides which of the disputants is legally right. As a result, the process usually culminates in the designation of a winner and a loser, rather than in the achievement of some middle ground acceptable to both sides.

Other governmental structures also engage in rule adjudication, especially a great variety of administrative tribunals, as discussed in Chapter 22, and the distinction between them and real courts is often subtle. Moreover, the judiciary also has certain non-adjudicative functions. Because of their prestige and impartiality, for example, judges have frequently been appointed to head royal commissions or other commissions of inquiry. The nature of many such commissions, such as the Gomery Inquiry, has unfortunately been more political than judicial, and observers often feel that this is an inappropriate use of judicial personnel, especially given backlogs in their regular adjudicative work.

Apart from the civil law system in Quebec, Canadian federal, provincial, and territorial legal systems operate in the tradition of the English **common law**. The basis of that system is the accumulation over the centuries of judicial precedents, both in England and more recently in Canada. Thus, in a typical court case, the two sides seek to find precedents—previous court decisions—favouring their respective points of view. The judge (and sometimes the jury) has to decide which precedents most closely resemble the case currently before the court. The principle that precedents are binding on successive decisions is called **stare decisis**.

If the law were always comprehensive and crystal clear, and if the situations to which it applied were always simple and straightforward, rule adjudication would be fairly routine, and the judiciary would not have much discretion in performing this function. The real world is more complex, though, and the law may not be clear on all points or provide for every conceivable situation. Moreover, judges can usually avoid a precedent they dislike by "distinguishing" it— that is, deciding that the facts in the case before them are sufficiently different from the facts of the precedent case that to follow the latter would be inappropriate.[2] Russell refers to the "inescapable generality of the law" such that, although judges theoretically settle disputes according to pre-existing law, they actually shape and develop the law in the very process of settling disputes about it. They "put flesh on the bare skeleton of the law and shape its substance."[3]

The judiciary and the function of judicial interpretation were included in the chart of the policymaking process in Chapter 20. Rather than occurring subsequent to policymaking, where it once was placed, rule adjudication can now be considered as part of the policymaking process. Unlike Americans, Canadian observers did not give much recognition to the concept of judicial involvement in this process until recently. But Russell argues that this Canadian approach "wrongly assumes that all important public policies are expressed in statutes passed by legislatures ... and overlooks the extent to which [such] policies ... are shaped through the process of being applied in particular cases by judges and administrators."[4] He cites such examples as the large element of discretion previously left to judges in the sentencing process, the decision of the Canadian courts to give little weight to the Canadian Bill of Rights, and the increasing judicial

The nine justices of the Supreme Court, in 2015, included (Chief Justice) Beverly McLachlin, Rosalie Abella, Marshall Rothstein (retired 2015), Thomas Cromwell, Michael Moldaver, Andromache Karakatsanis, Richard Wagner, Clément Gascon, and Suzanne Côté.

supervision of the operation of administrative agencies. In addition, judicial interpretation of antimonopoly laws "decisively shaped industrial policy by making it nearly impossible to convict corporations for monopolistic practices."[5] In the course of adjudicating disputes, therefore, the courts are inherently involved in policymaking.

One step beyond **judicial discretion** is the explicit power of **judicial review**. Rather than merely interpreting laws with discretion, judicial review is the power of the courts to declare them invalid, refuting the principle of the **supremacy of parliament**. The original Constitution Act of 1867 did not contain any such provision, although the courts soon appropriated this power in one respect. Chapter 18 detailed the extent to which the courts invalidated federal and provincial legislation as violations of the division of powers between the two levels of government. In rendering federal or provincial legislation void if either encroached on the jurisdiction of the other level of government, the decisions of the courts had a significant effect on the shape of Canadian federalism. The court's power of judicial review was greatly enhanced with the adoption of the Canadian **Charter of Rights and Freedoms** in 1982, and the effects of the first 30 years of that review were discussed in Chapter 19, where the debate over judicial versus legislative supremacy is extensively examined. Peter McCormick writes in this connection: "We should recognize that judges have always had power, have always affected our society by the decisions they make.... The Charter has simply made a longstanding reality more immediately visible and directed us belatedly to an assessment of the implications of judicial power."[6]

Access to and Costs of Justice

Many people, even in the middle class, cannot afford to hire a lawyer to defend them in court, yet the objective of the judicial process must be the search for truth and the obtaining of justice, goals that have traditionally rested on the adversarial system. To give those without the financial resources a fairer chance to achieve justice, legal aid programs financed jointly by the federal and provincial governments have been established. These vary from one province to another, cover only certain kinds of legal work, and have been subject to severe funding cutbacks in recent years so that they are less adequate than ever. In fact, a recent report by the Canadian Bar Association notes an overall 20 percent decrease from 1994 levels calls on the federal government to restore legal aid funding to the level it was in 1994.[7] Community legal clinics serve a similar function to legal aid, and other proposals have been suggested to improve the prospects of less affluent persons in obtaining a fair hearing.[8]

Very few ordinary people can afford to take a case all the way to the Supreme Court of Canada and the **Court Challenges Program** designed to help finance Charter challenges has twice been eliminated by Conservative governments. Increasingly, people are trying to defend themselves without legal counsel, a generally regrettable development. Chief Justice Beverley McLachlin has repeatedly raised the issue of Canadians being routinely denied their basic legal rights because of the unaffordability of the justice system, and Governor General David Johnston, a former dean of law, somewhat similarly criticized the legal profession for a general lack of concern about client welfare.

A related means of reducing the costs of the administration of justice as a whole are the practices of plea-bargaining and pre-trial conferences. Plea bargaining involves discussions between defence and Crown attorneys with the aim of achieving agreement on charges to be pursued, typically by having the accused plead guilty to one charge and the Crown agree to drop other charges. This practice is routine at the provincial or territorial court level and avoids a lengthy, costly trial. In the higher trial courts it is common for the judge to hold a pre-trial conference with the lawyers for each side. Such conferences can result in a negotiated settlement or at least a time-saving clarification of the issues involved. Pre-trial conferences have also proved to be useful at the level of family and small-claims courts. Although plea-bargaining and pre-trial conferences must not be allowed to subvert justice, they are valuable devices to cut costs for everyone involved (including the public) and to reduce the workload of the often congested court system.

CATEGORIES OF LAWS

The law can be defined as "society's system of binding rules."[9] Laws are commonly divided into different categories, primarily "civil" and "criminal." A **civil law** regulates relationships between two private parties, such as individuals or corporations, and if private agreement cannot be reached in the case of dispute, one party may take the other to court. Most aspects of civil law in Canada are within provincial jurisdiction, largely because of the provincial power over property and civil rights. Civil cases often involve disputes over commercial contracts or property, and such cases are normally resolved by the court's ordering one party to pay damages to the other. Civil cases are decided on the basis of the "balance of probabilities" of the merits of each side.

Criminal law, on the other hand, is primarily a federal responsibility; it is thus more or less uniform throughout the country and has been consolidated in the **Criminal Code**. In this case, the commission of a crime, such as murder, sexual assault, or theft, is considered to be a wrong against society as a whole, and the state takes the initiative to bring the suspect to justice by means of the police and Crown attorneys. In criminal cases, judges may impose fines or prison sentences if the accused is found guilty, such guilt having been proven "beyond a reasonable doubt."

One of the peculiarities of Canadian federalism is that although criminal law is within federal jurisdiction, it is usually the provincial attorneys general and their agents, the Crown attorneys, who are responsible for initiating proceedings against the person who is charged. This situation has come about because the provinces have jurisdiction over the administration of justice. Sometimes a case contains both civil and criminal elements, such as a drunk driver who does damage to another person's car. The state pursues the violation of the Criminal Code, but the victim's insurance company would have to take the initiative to sue for property damage.

Instead of the division between civil and criminal law, a distinction is sometimes made between public and private law. Private law is essentially the same as civil law described above—that is, law that centres on private interests. Beyond the contracts and property mentioned, however, private law includes torts, wills, company law, and family law. Public law, primarily involving the public interest or the government, goes beyond criminal law to include constitutional law, administrative law, and taxation law. Constitutional law has traditionally involved questions about federal or provincial jurisdiction, and governments themselves have often been the parties to a constitutional case. With the adoption of the Charter of Rights and Freedoms, however, a whole new aspect of constitutional law in Canada has emerged involving the relationship between government and citizens. Administrative law concerns the operation of government departments and agencies, and as government activity expanded over the years, this branch of law also increased in significance.

By giving the provinces jurisdiction over property and civil rights, the Fathers of Confederation allowed Quebec to retain its distinctive private or civil law system based on the French Napoleonic Code. A new edition of the **Code Civil du Québec** came into force in 1994. The private law system in the other provinces and territories is based on the English common law tradition. The theoretical distinction between the two systems in terms of form is that while the common law consists of a hodgepodge of judicial precedents, the Code Civil is a single, comprehensive document. As Gall puts it, "in a common law system, the courts extract existing principles of law from decisions of previous cases, while in the civil law system, the courts look to the civil code to determine a given principle, and they then apply the facts of an instant case to that principle."[10] The state has far greater ability to assert its authority and power through the written code than in the common law tradition, where the law is written in more general terms and is susceptible to interpretation and application by judges and juries. There are also certain differences in substance, but although much attention is given to this distinction in Canadian legal and political life, the actual difference between the two systems is probably not as great as is often assumed. Lawyers and judges in the civil law system cannot help but pay some attention to precedents within that system and cannot avoid being influenced by the common law system surrounding them.[11]

STRUCTURE OF THE COURTS

Because the provinces that formed Confederation in 1867 already possessed a court system, and because the Judicial Committee of the Privy Council continued to function as a court of appeal for the whole British Empire, it was not necessary to devote much attention to the judiciary in the Constitution Act, 1867. The new federal government was allowed to establish a general court of appeal and any additional courts, but the provinces were otherwise given responsibility for the administration of justice, which included the establishment of a provincial court system. McCormick describes the logic of the Canadian court structure as follows:

- First: Identify the more routine cases and those that involve less serious possible outcomes and assign them to an accessible high-volume, low-delay court, preferably one that sits in many different centres (provincial courts).
- Second: Assign the less routine and more serious cases to a lower-volume court that can devote more time and more focused attention to each individual case (superior trial courts).
- Third: Establish a court of appeal to correct simple errors and to promote uniformity in the application of the law within each province (provincial courts of appeal).
- Fourth: Establish a "general court of appeal" to promote uniformity in the application of the law within the country as a whole and to provide judicial leadership (Supreme Court of Canada).
- Fifth: Create a system of federal courts for cases directly involving the federal government as a party or raising issues concerning the administrative law applied by federal departments (Federal Court of Canada).[12]

As shown in Figure 24.1, the court systems within each province developed into a reasonably uniform three-level hierarchy. At the top are two "superior" courts—the superior trial court and the court of appeal, although they go by different names from province to province.

FIGURE 24.1   THE COURT STRUCTURE IN CANADA

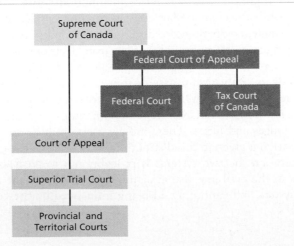

At the bottom are provincial courts. Most provinces originally set up district or county courts between these two levels, but over the 1975–95 period they abolished this intermediate tier and integrated it with their superior courts.[13] Each of the territories has a similar court structure.

Because of the assumption that provinces could not be trusted to make worthy appointments to superior, district, and county courts, the Fathers of Confederation provided that the judges of these courts would be appointed by the governor general, conventionally meaning the federal Cabinet or minister of justice. Such judges were also paid by the federal government. Thus, in another peculiarity of Canadian federalism, each province determines how many superior court judges it needs, but they are appointed and paid by Ottawa.[14] Since these courts were provided for in section 96 of the 1867 document, they are often called "section 96 courts," and their judges, "section 96 judges." Below the level of section 96 courts, each province established various "provincial courts" to which provincial Cabinets appoint the judges. A brief discussion of each level of the judicial hierarchy has been placed on this book's website, so let us emphasize the provincial and territorial courts of appeal at the top of the provincial court hierarchy and the courts established by the federal government.

Provincial and Territorial Courts of Appeal

Provincial and territorial courts of appeal hear criminal, civil, and other appeals, some of which have already been appealed from a lower court to a section 96 trial court. Although some of its judgments are appealed to the Supreme Court of Canada, in most cases the decision of the provincial or territorial court of appeal is final, which adds to the significance of this level of court.[15] The basic function of an appeal court is to correct errors or injustices that one side claims were made in a lower court, but an appeal court is primarily interested in legal rather than factual issues. The second function of the appeal court is to render an opinion in a reference case—that is, on a constitutional issue referred to it by the provincial Cabinet. Russell thus speaks of the "law-making" role of appeal courts because their legal interpretations have a "creative legislative dimension."[16]

BOX 24.1   FUNCTIONS OF THE FEDERAL COURT OF CANADA

- Cases involving admiralty law, and copyright, trademark, and patent disputes
- Citizenship and immigration appeals
- Appeals from other federal administrative tribunals (e.g., CRTC)
- Civil cases involving the federal government
- Cases involving bills of exchange, promissory notes, aeronautics, and inter-provincial works and undertakings
- Appeals from boards of referees under the Employment Insurance Act
- Prerogative writs (e.g., injunctions) applying to agencies of the federal government
- Appeals regarding the Access to Information and Privacy Acts
- Issuance of Canadian Security Intelligence Service warrants

Decisions of the court of appeal are binding on all courts below it and are "strongly persuasive" for trial courts in other provinces and territories. Courts of appeal normally sit in banks of three judges, but the size of these panels can be increased to five for very important cases. Each side of a case submits a brief or "factum" in advance that summarizes its arguments, and lawyers then engage in oral argument.

The Federal Court of Canada

The **Federal Court of Canada** was established in 1971 to replace the Exchequer Court created in 1875. It was intended to relieve the Supreme Court of hearing routine appeals from certain federal administrative agencies and **regulatory tribunals** and to develop a more unified and cohesive body of federal administrative law.[17] Although it is not well known to the public, the Federal Court has significant powers over the operation of the federal government. The Federal Court of Appeal consists of a chief justice and 12 other judges who sit in panels of at least three members. The Federal Court, formerly known as the trial division, contains the chief justice and 32 other full-time and assorted part-time judges. Between its two divisions, the Federal Court has the functions listed in Box 24.1.

The work of the Federal Court is dominated by cases involving the Immigration and Refugee Protection Act and the Immigration and Refugee Board. It has also seen a growth in Aboriginal cases dealing with monetary and constitutional issues, land entitlements, and natural resources. Of great interest to political science, the Federal Court also hears appeals regarding the Access to Information and Privacy Acts and decides on requests for warrants from the Canadian Security Intelligence Service to plant bugs, open mail, and engage in other surreptitious activities. Several Canadians accused of terrorism have recently (and often successfully) taken their cases to the Federal Court.

The Tax Court of Canada is a judicialized version of its predecessor, the Tax Review Board. It provides an easily accessible and independent tribunal for the disposition of tax disputes between citizens and the federal government. It deals primarily with matters arising under the Income Tax Act, the Employment Insurance Act, and the Excise Tax Act. Headed by a chief judge, it consists of 26 other full-time and assorted part-time judges, who hear cases across the country. Some of its decisions are appealable to the Federal Court of Appeal.

THE SUPREME COURT OF CANADA

The Supreme Court of Canada sits at the apex of the Canadian court system. About 85 percent of its work consists of hearing appeals from the provincial and territorial courts of appeal in civil and criminal cases,[18] but it also receives cases from the Federal Court of Appeal in administrative law matters. Besides hearing actual appeal cases from lower courts, the Supreme Court can be asked by the federal Cabinet to consider an important question of law, in what are called **reference cases**. Such cases are usually of a constitutional nature and have always been taken seriously, even though occasional doubt has been expressed as to whether they carry the same weight as an actual case. Box 24.2 lists selected reference cases.

BOX 24.2 SELECTED LEADING REFERENCE CASES

- *Anti-Inflation Act Reference, 1976*: A Trudeau government reference regarding the constitutionality of its own program of wage and price controls
- *Senate Reference, 1981*: A case clarifying the power of the federal government to reform the Senate without provincial consent
- *Patriation Reference, 1981*: A case that combined three provincial reference cases concerning Prime Minister Trudeau's intention to ask the British Parliament to enact the Constitution Act, 1982 without provincial consent
- *Quebec Veto Reference, 1982*: A Quebec reference case clarifying whether that province had a right to veto constitutional amendments
- *Milgaard Reference, 1992*: A federal request to reopen the David Milgaard case because of suspicions of a miscarriage of justice
- *Goods and Services Tax Reference, 1992*: An Alberta reference of the federal law imposing the Goods and Services Tax
- *Quebec Education Act Reference, 1993*: A Quebec reference regarding the constitutionality of changing the basis of the province's education system from religious to linguistic
- *Quebec Secession Reference, 1998*: A federal reference regarding the constitutionality of a unilateral Quebec declaration of independence
- *Firearms Act Reference, 2000*: An Alberta reference challenging the constitutionality of the federal firearms registration scheme
- *Same-Sex Marriage Reference, 2004*: A federal reference seeking approval of a proposed federal law on this question
- *Securities Act Reference, 2011*: A federal reference (following Alberta and Quebec references) regarding the constitutionality of the federal proposal for a national securities regulatory agency
- *Senate Reform Reference, 2014*: A federal reference regarding the constitutionality of various means of reforming the Senate.

The part of the Supreme Court's work of most interest to political science involves constitutional law, whether in terms of the division of powers between federal and provincial governments or interpretations of the Charter of Rights and Freedoms. Although the Supreme Court hears fewer cases than any lower court—it issues about 75 judgments per year—it is interested almost exclusively in questions of law.[19] Thus, of all courts, it is the most heavily engaged in a "law-making" role, and its decisions are binding on all lower courts across the country.

Until 1949, the Supreme Court was a seriously deficient institution. First, its decisions could be appealed to Canada's pre-1949 final court of appeal, the **Judicial Committee of the Privy Council (JCPC)** located in London, and it was bound by JCPC precedents. But even more humiliating, appeals could also go directly to that Empire court from provincial appeal courts, completely bypassing the Supreme Court of Canada. Before 1949, 253 cases went to the JCPC from the Supreme Court of Canada and 414 went there straight from provincial appeal courts.[20] This weakness in authority was enhanced by the relatively poor quality of judges appointed to the Supreme Court in that earlier period, apart from such individuals as Lyman Duff and Ivan Rand.[21]

Canada could have cut off appeals to the Judicial Committee after obtaining complete independence in 1931, and pressure mounted to do so after the unpopular "New Deal" decisions of 1935 that were mentioned in Chapter 18. But the Second World War intervened, and it was unclear whether the provinces would have to be involved in this decision because their appeals could already go directly to the JCPC. If so, there was some question of whether the provinces would agree to it, since they had been so well served by the Judicial Committee over the years. In 1947 it was determined that Ottawa could unilaterally curtail all such appeals, and it promptly did so. The Supreme Court of Canada has not been formally bound by Judicial Committee decisions since 1949 and has explicitly overruled them on occasion.

Until 1974, the Supreme Court had little discretion in deciding which cases it heard, but since then it has basically been in control of its own agenda. Today, only three categories of cases have an automatic right of appeal to the Supreme Court: provincial reference cases, and criminal cases where an acquittal has been set aside in the court of appeal or where a judge in a court of appeal dissented on a question of law. Applications for leave (that is, permission) to appeal discretionary cases are normally handled in writing by a panel of three Supreme Court judges, but sometimes the panel hears the applications live, giving lawyers 15 minutes to make their case, via two-way satellite television if they choose. These panels annually hear over 500 applications for leave to appeal, accepting between 65 and 80: those that involve a question of public importance or an important issue of law. Although the panels give no reasons for agreeing or refusing to hear an appeal, it can be assumed that they agree with the lower court decision if they refuse the appeal. Such discretion considerably enhances the stature of the institution. Figure 24.2 outlines the Supreme Court appeal process.

Although an increasingly important institution of government, the Supreme Court rests primarily on the **Supreme Court Act** rather than being embedded in any constitutional act as such.[22] The Supreme Court Act now provides for a nine-member court (six from 1875 to 1927 and seven from 1927 to 1949). Three of the nine must come from Quebec, with its distinctive civil law system, while convention dictates that of the other six, three normally come from Ontario, two from the West, and one from Atlantic Canada. The act requires that at least five

FIGURE 24.2 SUPREME COURT APPEAL PROCESS

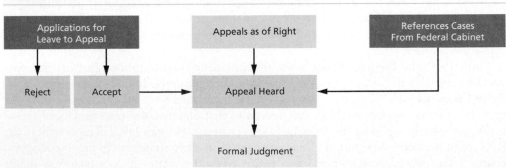

judges constitute a quorum, with the result that civil law cases from Quebec can be heard by a five-member panel, including a majority (three) from the civil law system. The position of Chief Justice normally alternates between francophone and anglophone members, simultaneous interpretation is available, and Supreme Court judges are now expected to be at least functionally bilingual. Among other provisions of the Supreme Court Act are those that lay out the grounds for appeal and reference cases and those that stipulate that judges hold office during good behaviour until the age of 75. One of the merits of the Meech Lake and Charlottetown Accords would have been to "constitutionalize" the Supreme Court in order to give it a firmer foundation and to clarify how it could be changed.

The Court holds three sessions of about two months each per year and adjourns in between to write up its decisions. Justices usually wear black silk robes at sittings of the Court, but have ceremonial robes of bright scarlet trimmed with Canadian white mink for special occasions. As much as possible, the Court tries to hear cases with a full complement of nine. Judges study the lower court proceedings and judgments in advance, along with the written arguments of the lawyers for each side. In preparing for the case, as well as in writing the first draft of decisions, each Supreme Court judge is assisted by three outstanding new law school graduates called law clerks. They help the busy judges search for and sift through precedents and other relevant material, including academic articles on the issues involved. The Court usually hears two cases per day, and oral arguments for each case normally last only two hours, during which time the judges often ask trenchant questions. In some instances the Court also grants "intervener status" to provincial governments and interest groups that are concerned about a case but not directly a party to it. Figure 24.3 shows the areas of law involved in the appeals heard in 2014. Public law cases, especially criminal and constitutional, now clearly predominate over private law disputes on the Supreme Court docket.

Once the arguments are completed, the judges usually "reserve judgment" and meet in private conference to discuss the case. Starting with the most recent appointee, each gives his or her tentative decision, and, if there is a consensus, the Chief Justice asks one member to draft the judgment. The Court tries to come to a unanimous decision, which it achieves

FIGURE 24.3   APPEALS HEARD IN 2014: BY TYPE

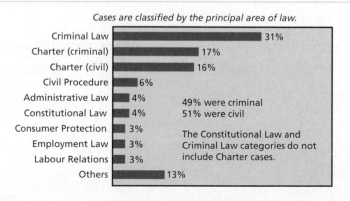

Cases are classified by the principal area of law.

Criminal Law	31%
Charter (criminal)	17%
Charter (civil)	16%
Civil Procedure	6%
Administrative Law	4%
Constitutional Law	4%
Consumer Protection	3%
Employment Law	3%
Labour Relations	3%
Others	13%

49% were criminal
51% were civil

The Constitutional Law and Criminal Law categories do not include Charter cases.

Source: Supreme Court of Canada. Statistics 2004 to 2014, http://www.scc-csc.gc.ca/case-dossier/stat/cat3-eng .aspx. Reproduced with the permission of the Supreme Court of Canada, 2015.

CHAPTER 24   **The Judiciary**

in about 75 percent of cases,[23] but even so, not all the judges may come to the common decision by the same route. If it is a split decision, two or more judges are asked to prepare statements of their point of view. These drafts are then circulated among all the judges on the case and evoke comments before being revised. Judges sometimes compete to write certain judgments, as well as lobby one another for support.[24] This is a crucial point, in which outcomes depend upon the process and the individual judges. Emmett MacFarlane has recently argued that personal and institutional factors weigh heavily, as may the views of the public and media, alongside judges' own socialized perceptions of what their roles are or should be.[25]

So much effort is put into the process of preparing their opinions that a decision is typically not issued until about six months after the Court hears the case, and it has occasionally taken over a year for all members of the Court to make up their minds, write their opinion, or concur with a colleague. When it comes to citing other cases as a basis for their decisions, the Supreme Court of Canada most frequently mentions its own decisions, followed by those of the Ontario Court of Appeal; in the 1984–94 period, about 15 percent of its citations were to English courts and seven percent to U.S. courts.[26] Decisions are usually released in written form by depositing them with the Registrar, but the Court can pronounce formal judgments in the courtroom. Recent membership in the Supreme Court can be seen in Table 24.1.

The structure of Canadian courts is thus an essentially integrated, vertical court system rather than two parallel systems of federal and provincial/territorial courts. With the exception of some federal matters that must be initiated in the Federal Court of Canada, both the provincial/territorial court systems and the Supreme Court of Canada hear cases dealing with federal, provincial, and territorial laws. The judicial system is further integrated with provincial and territorial governments prosecuting federal crimes and with the federal Cabinet appointing judges to section 96 courts within the provinces and territories. Some aspects of the federal–provincial/territorial judicial integration could be improved, such as in the areas of Young Offenders and family law, and federal–provincial conflict has occasionally arisen over provincial attempts to enhance the powers of provincial courts and administrative tribunals at the expense of section 96 courts. However, most authorities argue strenuously in favour of maintaining such an integrated system.

TABLE 24.1   RECENT MEMBERSHIP IN THE SUPREME COURT OF CANADA

APPOINTMENT	NAME	RETIREMENT (DEATH)
1989 (MULRONEY)	BEVERLEY MCLACHLIN CJ*	
1990 (MULRONEY)	WILLIAM STEVENSON	(1992)
1991 (MULRONEY)	FRANK IACOBUCCI	2004
1992 (MULRONEY)	JOHN C. MAJOR	2005
1997 (CHRÉTIEN)	MICHEL BASTARACHE	2008

(Continued)

APPOINTMENT	NAME	RETIREMENT (DEATH)
1998 (CHRÉTIEN)	IAN BINNIE	2011
1999 (CHRÉTIEN)	LOUISE ARBOUR	2004
2000 (CHRÉTIEN)	LOUIS LEBEL	2014
2002 (CHRÉTIEN)	MARIE DESCHAMPS	2012
2003 (CHRÉTIEN)	MORRIS FISH	2013
2004 (MARTIN)	ROSALIE ABELLA	
2004 (MARTIN)	LOUISE CHARRON	2011
2006 (HARPER)	MARSHALL ROTHSTEIN	2015
2008 (HARPER)	THOMAS CROMWELL	
2011 (HARPER)	MICHAEL MOLDAVER	
2011 (HARPER)	ANDROMACHE KARAKATSANIS	
2012 (HARPER)	RICHARD WAGNER	
2014 (HARPER)	CLÉMENT GASCON	
2014 (HARPER)	SUZANNE CÔTÉ	
2015 (HARPER)	RUSSELL BROWN	

NOTE: *CJ = CHIEF JUSTICE

CRITICAL APPROACHES

Being an increasingly important institution in the structure of government, the courts are an appropriate subject of the *historical-institutional approach*. As with most institutions, the judiciary deals in rules that do not change much over time. But in this case, the judicial principle of precedents being binding virtually ensures a continuity of decisions. It is undoubtedly more difficult to change the "rules" in the judicial process than in any of the other institutions of government. Similarly, the *state-based approach* sees the judiciary as an integral part of the state apparatus. Indeed, the courts are more isolated from public opinion than any other branch of government, and when Cabinets appoint judges, they look "for someone very much like themselves."[27]

THE APPOINTMENT OF JUDGES

As has already been established, Supreme and Federal Court of Canada judges, as well as judges of provincial and territorial superior courts are appointed by the federal Cabinet, while provincial court judges are appointed by provincial cabinets. There are approximately 1000 judges in each category. All of the first group must be qualified lawyers of at least ten years' standing, as must provincial court judges in Ontario and Quebec. Elsewhere, provincial court judges have to be members of the bar for a minimum of five years.

In a high proportion of cases over the years Canadian cabinets at both federal and provincial levels have used judicial appointments to reward faithful party supporters, often defeated candidates.[28] Legal expertise was also taken into account in some cases, but it was rarely the primary criterion. The prospect of a judgeship accounts in part for the active involvement of lawyers in many party organizations, while the promise of government legal business explains another part. **Political patronage** raises three main problems in this area: unsuitable individuals are appointed because of their partisan connections; well-qualified candidates are overlooked because of their lack of service to the party in power; and partisan judges may favour their former political colleagues.[29] This patronage system of appointing judges is still alive, although it is not as blatant as it once was.

At the federal level, Pierre Trudeau as minister of justice in 1967 instituted an informal practice of submitting names of potential judicial appointments to the National Committee on the Judiciary of the Canadian Bar Association. To his credit, the next justice minister, John Turner, appointed several prominent judges of non-Liberal backgrounds. Trudeau sullied his own government's record in this field with the appointment of six high-profile Liberal partisans in 1984, including the minister of justice himself and another minister who was not even assessed by the CBA committee. After an even more partisan record of judicial appointments during its first term,[30] the Mulroney government established a somewhat more satisfactory appointment system in 1988 for all "federal" judges except those on the Supreme Court of Canada, and modified it slightly in 1991.

An independent **Commissioner for Federal Judicial Affairs** maintains a record of those interested in federal judicial appointments. When a vacancy occurs, this official submits such names to a committee set up in each province or territory, which includes a section 96 judge; one nominee of each provincial or territorial law society, the provincial or territorial branch of the CBA, and the provincial or territorial attorney general; and three nominees of the federal minister of justice. This committee used to rank each candidate as "highly recommended," "recommended," or "not able to recommend," and the minister made the final decision, not being restricted to the highly recommended names.[31] Given its law-and-order-orientation, the Harper government changed the procedures by adding a representative from the police community to the judicial advisory committees and abandoned the distinction between "highly recommended" and "recommended." These changes were severely criticized, even by the Chief Justice of Canada. Many observers feared that besides entrenching greater partisanship into judicial appointments, the move would add an ideological ingredient—right-wing judges who would be hard on crime—which might compromise the principle of judicial independence.[32]

The minister may also consult senior members of the judiciary and the bar and the provincial and territorial attorney general, but it is possible to skip over the names high on the list to find ones lower down with partisan connections. Greene and colleagues found that even in the late 1990s a large proportion of appeal court judges had been candidates, party activists, or at least party members.[33] Similarly, Forcese and Freeman calculate that between 40 percent and 50 percent of federal judicial appointees in 2003 had made donations to the Liberal party, which is "broadly suggestive of a deeper political involvement."[34] Despite increasing pressure to remove political patronage from this whole system, the actions of the Harper government were no improvement. Moreover, according to a *Globe and Mail* study, in a three-and-a-half-year period, while the Conservatives appointed three Aboriginal judges in the north, 98 out of 100 judges in the south were white.[35]

The prime minister chooses the chief justice in each province, almost always from the existing bench, as well as new members of the Supreme Court of Canada. Patronage has not been a problem on the Supreme Court since the appointment of Finance Minister Douglas Abbott in 1954.[36] Prime ministers consulted widely before making such appointments, and managed to overcome their penchant for partisanship in this one area. The Supreme Court of Canada is usually composed of seven judges with experience on provincial appeal courts, one from the Federal Court, and one without judicial experience, representing the "practising bar."[37]

At the provincial court level, each province's attorney general usually consults with the local judicial council or equivalent in making such appointments. For example, a central nonpartisan nominating commission, half of them non-lawyers, was established in Ontario in 1988, originally headed by political scientist Peter Russell. It advertises widely, encourages women and minority candidates to apply, screens judicial applicants on their merits, and interviews them extensively, giving the government limited leeway. The result is one of least partisan and most representative judiciaries in the country.[38]

Another controversial aspect of judicial appointments concerns the Supreme Court of Canada alone. Because this Court must adjudicate federal–provincial disputes, concern has been expressed in some quarters that all of its members are federally appointed. In theory, once appointed, judges act with total impartiality, and their independence is protected in various ways. Nevertheless, it may not appear as if justice has been done. As early as 1971,

Beverley McLachlin, Chief Justice of Canada.

federal–provincial agreement was achieved on provincial consultation in the appointment of Supreme Court judges, but this agreement was never implemented. Later, the Meech Lake and Charlottetown Accords provided for Ottawa to make Supreme Court of Canada appointments from lists provided by the provinces, but this too was ultimately abandoned. The 1992 document also proposed federal and provincial consultation with Aboriginal peoples in the appointment process.[39] While some mechanism for federal–provincial consultation in this area may eventually be adopted, to begin to regard Supreme Court judges as provincial representatives would do great disservice to the principle of judicial independence.

If a proper geographic balance is characteristic of Canadian judges, what can be said of their other socioeconomic characteristics? Partly as a consequence of geography, judicial appointments have also balanced francophone and anglophone origins at both federal and provincial court levels, especially in recent years as provinces have made more French-language court services available. Those of other origins have generally been excluded, but such names as Laskin (Jewish), Sopinka (Ukrainian), Iacobucci (Italian), and Karakatsanis (Greek) have appeared on the Supreme Court of Canada and increasingly on lower courts as well. Thus, the most serious aspects of judicial underrepresentation relate to women and the working class. In this connection, Paul Weiler writes:

> It is very natural that well-to-do families of the founding races and religions in Canada, especially those with a background of professional and/or public involvement, will produce the sons who will get the right kind of education, and thus the entrée into the kind of practice or position which produces a likely candidate for the Court.[40]

Just as in the case of ethnocultural minorities, however, more female and working-class law school graduates are becoming available for judicial appointments, and governments have at least begun to recognize the necessity of appointing greater numbers of female judges. The Supreme Court finally saw its first woman member in 1982, and from 2004 to 2012, it had a total of four women out of nine. Such female judges have sometimes used their position to point out the male bias in legislatures, judiciaries, and laws.[41] Ian Greene calculates that women now make up about one-quarter of all judges in Canada.[42] However, the appointment of female judges has dropped off under the Harper government, and studies indicate that it has appointed only three non-white judges out of about 200 appointments to the superior courts in the provinces since 2008. The government has also appointed many more prosecutors than defence counsel to the bench.

As noted in Chapter 4, Aboriginal Canadians have serious misgivings about the Canadian judicial system, feeling that it discriminates against them at every turn. While an increase in the number of Aboriginal judges might improve this situation, the establishment of a parallel justice system that would reflect their own distinctive concepts of guilt and punishment is often proposed. Although it seems unlikely that a separate Aboriginal justice system will be created in the near future, the regular courts increasingly recognize traditional Aboriginal concepts in relevant cases: sentencing circles (including a judge, police, elders, peers, family, and victims), elder sentencing panels, and community mediation processes.[43]

CRITICAL APPROACHES

When *class analysts* examine the judiciary, they talk about a "class system" of justice. Even Peter Russell admits that "as long as judges are recruited entirely from the ranks of successful lawyers ... the bourgeois orientation of the Canadian judiciary is unavoidable. This may very well mean that when class issues are clearly at stake in adjudication, the Canadian judiciary is not impartial."[44] McCormick adds that "to make the courts more representative of women, of Canadians other than French and English, of visible minorities, and so on perhaps simply disguises, and may well reinforce, the extent to which they continue to be unrepresentative on a class basis."[45]

The pluralist approach, however, argued that the judiciary adds a relatively independent point of authoritative decision making to the political system and counterbalances the other institutions of government. In Russell's words, "to liberals who are distrustful of an excessive concentration of power in the hands of any group or bureaucrats, the political pluralism fostered by a judiciary enjoying a high degree of independence is fundamental to maintaining political liberty."[46] To some extent, the independent judiciary remains the most likely obstacle to the dominance of the prime minister.

Finally, the *rational choice approach* emphasizes the discretion available to judges and the scope for them to choose lines of interpretation that are in their own self-interest. Thus, judges are not merely interpreting the law when they make decisions, but thinking of what is politically feasible and beneficial to themselves or their office.[47] Several relevant examples were cited in Chapter 19. A *political behaviour approach* to the courts might examine the influence of party affiliation on the decisions of judges. Although this topic has not garnered much attention in Canada, and maybe not as much as it should have, it has been prominent in the U.S., where the Supreme Court judges have well known party affiliations and very predictable voting patterns.

Given the significant law-making potential of higher-level judges, another dimension of the appointment process is a consideration of candidates' views on other issues. Chapter 19 noted that the decisions rendered by the Supreme Court of Canada depended to some extent on the makeup of the panel considering the case. That being so, those who appoint judges are able to take into account the predilections of candidates with respect to being hawks or doves on criminal matters or Charter enthusiasts as opposed to legislative deferentialists.[48] This issue prompts some authorities to recommend public hearings in a House of Commons committee to fathom the views of judicial nominees or at least to add an element of transparency to the process.[49]

Jacob Ziegel proposed the establishment of a Supreme Court nominating commission whenever a vacancy arises. This nine-member body, representing a variety of constituencies, would present the prime minister with a shortlist of candidates from which the federal government would have to pick one.[50] In 2005, Irwin Cotler, justice minister to Paul Martin, proposed a formalized procedure for choosing Supreme Court judges, which was then used toward the end of the year to replace retiring Justice John Major.[51] The minister of justice conducted widespread consultations from which an initial list of six candidates was developed. An advisory committee of nine people was established, including a representative from each recognized party in the House of Commons. This committee provided an unranked shortlist of three, from which the minister of justice was to make a recommendation to the prime minister, but at this point the process was suspended because of the 2006 federal election campaign. The new Harper government allowed the process to continue, selected one of the three, and then insisted that the nominee be subject to a televised interview by an informal Commons committee before being officially appointed by the prime minister. Members of the committee were instructed to use characteristic Canadian reserve in questioning the appointee, and Marshall Rothstein convinced the committee that he would do a good job.

Ostensibly because of the need to make a timely appointment in the context of the 2008 election call, the government appointed Mr. Justice Thomas Cromwell without any parliamentary involvement, although no one objected to his appointment. But in 2011, with two simultaneous vacancies on the Supreme Court from Ontario, a panel of five MPs representing all parties assessed a list of qualified candidates that had been compiled by the minister of Justice after extensive consultations. The committee provided the government with an unranked shortlist of six (because of the two vacancies) and Michael Moldaver and Andromache Karakatsanis were gently interviewed by a Commons committee before their formal appointment. A similar procedure was used in the appointment of Richard Wagner in 2012.

Bado/Artizans

SUPREME COURT: THE SELECTION PROCESS HITS A WALL.

DO YOU HAVE ONE IN BLUE?

artizans.com

Conservatives hope for a judge who will wear their party's colour.

After the retirement of Morris Fish, Marc Nadon was appointed to the Supreme Court following the same procedure as his immediate predecessors. While controversial for several reasons, primary among them was that he had served 20 years on the Federal Court, dealing with federal legal cases and becoming an expert in maritime law. Yet the Supreme Court Act states a judge representing Quebec must come from a Quebec court or be a lawyer practicing in Quebec.

Nadon's selection was challenged by the government of Quebec as well as by a Toronto lawyer. The Harper government amended the Supreme

Court Act and also asked the other eight judges on the Supreme Court to rule on whether or not the appointment was legal. In the meantime, Nadon was not allowed to take his seat. The Supreme Court ruled 6–1 that Nadon was not qualified because he was neither a Quebec judge nor a current practicing Quebec lawyer. It also ruled that the Supreme Court Act could not be amended by Parliament alone. An amendment to the composition (and eligibility requirements) of the Supreme Court constituted a formal constitutional amendment which required the unanimous consent of provincial legislatures.

In June 2014, the government filled the vacant Quebec spot on the Supreme Court of Canada with Clément Gascon. Although it did not follow the recent practice of parliamentary participation in the appointment, the government did consult the government of Quebec and various legal authorities in that province. In December 2014, the government filled the new Quebec vacancy with Suzanne Côté, whose appointment brought the female cohort on the Court back to four. She was appointed from the practicing bar without any judicial experience, and without any parliamentary involvement. Russell Brown was also appointed without any parliamentary screening.

RETIREMENT, REMOVAL, AND INDEPENDENCE OF JUDGES

Whatever the process involved in making judicial appointments, and whatever biases exist in the composition of the courts, judges are expected to abide by the principle of **judicial independence** or impartiality once they are on the bench. They are supposed to adjudicate without fear or favour with respect to private or political interests, and especially without any incentive to give preference to the government side where it is involved.

The independence of judges is primarily based on security of tenure, and it is difficult for the government to remove them before their scheduled date of retirement. Judges on the Supreme and Federal Courts of Canada and provincial superior courts have a mandatory retirement age of 75 years, and provincial court judges of 65 or 70. The general rule for all federally appointed judges and most provincial court judges is that they serve on "good behaviour"—that is, they do not serve at the pleasure of the government and cannot be removed unless they have been guilty of misbehaviour. Although the meaning of these terms has never been definitively established, judges are certainly removable for serious criminal acts and possibly for reasons of infirmity or incapacity, failure to execute their duties, or bringing the judicial system into disrepute.

The process of removing a judge varies with the level of the position, and the degree of difficulty increases with the judge's rank in the hierarchy. Except in Ontario, where legislation is required, provincial court judges can be removed by an order in council of the provincial cabinet but only after an inquiry has been conducted by one of the judge's peers or by the provincial judicial council. It is even more difficult to remove judges of the provincial superior courts and the federal courts. In that situation, the Canadian Judicial Council conducts an inquiry and reports to the minister of justice, after which the passage of a joint address of both houses of Parliament is required.

The **Canadian Judicial Council**, created in 1971, consists of all the chief justices and associate chief justices of courts staffed by federally appointed judges, and is chaired by the

Chief Justice of the Supreme Court of Canada. Like the provincial judicial councils, its primary purpose is to deal with complaints raised against individual judges, but it also has a role in the continuing education of judges, provides a forum for developing consensus among its members, and makes representations to government with respect to judicial salaries and benefits.

Although a number of judges have been reprimanded by judicial councils, the issue of judicial removal of superior court judges has rarely arisen. On the other hand, several provincial court judges have been removed over the years, a practice that is increasingly common as the public becomes less tolerant of their faults. In 2001, the Supreme Court upheld the removal of Judge Richard Therrien from the Court of Quebec on the grounds that when he was appointed a judge he failed to disclose to the authorities that he had been sentenced to imprisonment for one year for unlawfully giving assistance to the FLQ. But only four judges at the old county and district level were removed from office, and not a single superior court judge. Such proceedings were initiated in several cases, but judges either died or resigned during the removal process. For example, Jean Bienvenue of the Quebec Superior Court eventually resigned in 1997 after the Canadian Judicial Council asked the federal Parliament to remove him for having made outrageous sexist and racist comments from the bench.[52] Two years later, Robert Flahiff of the same court lost his position when he was sentenced to three years in jail after being found guilty of laundering $1.7 million in drug money when he was a practising lawyer. Two recent cases involved judges on the Ontario Superior Court, and when the Council recommended removal of Mr. Justice Cosgrove, he resigned.[53]

Besides security of tenure, judicial independence involves financial, administrative, and political independence, and judges are increasingly in control of the administration of the court system.[54] Salaries and pensions are fixed in such a way that judges cannot be individually or collectively intimidated by government threats to reduce them, although some judges challenged freezes or reductions in their salaries as part of provincial government restraint programs. The Supreme Court ruled that each province should create a salary commission to determine judges' remuneration.[55] Provinces proceeded to set up compensation commissions that based their decisions on the grounds that the high incomes of leading lawyers in private practice necessitated substantial judicial salaries. In a 2005 case, however, the Supreme Court clarified the 1997 decision and dismissed pay complaints by judges in several provinces.[56] Nevertheless, judges at all levels never cease asking for increases in pay.

Judges must also be able to function without political pressure—from Cabinet ministers, legislators, bureaucrats, or other judges—whether in public or in private. At both federal and provincial levels, cases have occurred of Cabinet ministers contacting judges, but however innocent their questions might seem, this must not be done.[57] Greene and colleagues report that judges increasingly feel their independence is threatened by certain interest groups, "political correctness," media criticism, political criticism, and even demonstrations.

It is sometimes thought that the prospect of promotion from one court to another might bias a judge's decisions, but no evidence has been found to justify this fear. Judges are rarely promoted from "provincial" to "federal" courts, but, as mentioned, 70 percent of appeal court judges have previous judicial experience.[58] In 1988 it was also felt (by fellow judges) that to deny judges a vote in federal elections was not necessary to guarantee their independence. On the other hand, judges are not supposed to make public speeches that could compromise their impartiality. For example, when Tom Berger of the BC Supreme Court publicly criticized the

1982 Constitution Act for its omission of Quebec and virtual neglect of Aboriginals, his actions were investigated by the Canadian Judicial Council. Although its recommendation was not to dismiss him, he resigned to protest the process employed.[59] Supreme Court judges are giving more public speeches and interviews than previously, but these attempts to engage in a dialogue with the public sometimes lead to criticism. Mr. Justice Bastarache made public comments that were also vetted by the Judicial Council, for example, and was warned that "it is clearly preferable for judges to exercise restraint when speaking publicly."

CONCLUSION

Rule adjudication remains the basic function of the judiciary, one that is becoming increasingly important in the political system. Judges also engage in pre-trial mediation of one kind or another and are occasionally called on to head commissions of inquiry. This chapter has shown, however, that many aspects of the legal system are highly political. The Supreme Court of Canada and the Federal Court of Canada are involved on almost a daily basis in deciding controversial political cases.

This chapter is primarily linked to those on federalism and the Charter of Rights and Freedoms. But the judiciary is also connected to all of the other institutions of government discussed in this part of the book.

DISCUSSION QUESTIONS

1. Should all vestiges of patronage be removed from the appointment of judges, or have existing reforms in this area gone far enough?

2. Should the provinces be involved in the appointment of provincial superior court judges? Of judges of the Supreme Court of Canada? If so, how?

3. How can justice be ensured for women involved in the courts?

4. How can justice be ensured for the working class?

5. Should Canada establish a parallel Aboriginal justice system?

MindTap®   FOR MORE INFO GO TO http://www.nelson.com/student

NOTES

1. Peter Russell, *The Judiciary in Canada: The Third Branch of Government* (Toronto: McGraw-Hill Ryerson, 1987), p. 5.
2. Ian Greene, Carl Baar, Peter McCormick, George Szablowski, and Martin Thomas, *Final Appeal: Decision-Making in Canadian Courts of Appeal* (Toronto: James Lorimer & Co., 1998), p. 201.
3. Russell, *The Judiciary in Canada*, p. 5.

4. Peter Russell, "The Effect of a Charter of Rights on the Policy-Making Role of the Canadian Courts," *Canadian Public Administration* (Spring 1982), p. 2.

5. Ibid., p. 12.

6. Peter McCormick, *Canada's Courts* (Toronto: James Lorimer & Company Ltd., Publishers, 1994), p. 3.

7. Canadian Bar Association, 2013. "Reaching Equal Justice: An Invitation to Envision and Act." http://www.cba.org/cba/equaljustice/secure_pdf/Equal-Justice-Report-eng.pdf.

8. Ian Greene, *The Courts* (Vancouver: UBC Press, 2006), p. 72.

9. Russell, *The Judiciary in Canada*, p. 6.

10. Gerald L. Gall, *The Canadian Legal System*, 4th ed. (Toronto: Carswell, 1995), p. 30.

11. Greene et al., *Final Appeal*, pp. 32 and 85.

12. McCormick, *Canada's Courts*, p. 23. Reproduced with permission.

13. Gall outlines this integration on pp. 157–59 of the third edition of *The Canadian Legal System*. See also Peter Russell, ed., *Canada's Trial Courts: Two Tiers or One?* Toronto: University of Toronto Press, 2007.

14. Occasional federal–provincial disputes have occurred over this point. See Russell, *The Judiciary in Canada*, pp. 122–23.

15. Greene et al., *Final Appeal*, p. x; and McCormick, *Canada's Courts*, p. 56.

16. Russell, *The Judiciary in Canada*, p. 290.

17. Russell, *The Judiciary in Canada*, p. 313.

18. Greene et al., *Final Appeal*, p. 149.

19. Statistics Canada, *Statistics 1998–2008 Bulletin of Proceedings: Special Edition*, available at http://www.scc-csc.gc.ca/stat/pdf/doc-eng.pdf.

20. Greene et al., *Final Appeal*, p. 141.

21. James G. Snell and Frederick Vaughan, *The Supreme Court of Canada: History of the Institution* (Toronto: Osgoode Society, 1985); and Russell, *The Judiciary in Canada, p. 337.*

22. Peter Russell, "Constitutional Reform of the Judicial Branch: Symbolic vs. Operational Considerations," *Canadian Journal of Political Science* (June 1984). See also Emmett Macfarlane, "Administration at the Supreme Court of Canada: Challenges and Change in the Charter era," *Canadian Public Administration* (March 2009).

23. Supreme Court of Canada, *Bulletin of Proceedings: Special Edition, Statistics 2000 to 2010* (50 out of 65 in 2010).

24. Ellen Anderson, *Judging Bertha Wilson: Law As Large As Life* (Toronto: University of Toronto Press, 2002); see also Matthew E. Wetstein and C.L. Ostberg, "Strategic Leadership and Political Chance on the Canadian Supreme Court: Analyzing the Transition to Chief Justice," *Canadian Journal of Political Science* (September 2005).

25. Emmett Macfarlane, *Governing from the Bench: The Supreme Court of Canada and the Judicial Role* (Vancouver: UBC Press, 2013).

26. Greene et al., *Final Appeal*, pp. 151–56.

27. Russell, *The Judiciary in Canada*, p. 107; and Olsen, *The State Elite*, p. 46.

28. Carl Baar quotes an oft-repeated maxim that "to become a judge in the United States, you must be elected; to become a judge in Canada, you must be defeated," in "The Structure and Personnel of the Canadian Judiciary," in Paul Fox and Graham White, eds., *Politics: Canada*, 7th ed. (Toronto: McGraw-Hill Ryerson, 1991), p. 513. See also Craig Forcese and Aaron Freeman, *The Laws of Government: The Legal Foundations of Canadian Democracy* (Toronto: Irwin Law, 2005), Ch. 4.

29. Andrew Heard, *Canadian Constitutional Conventions* (Toronto: Oxford University Press, 1991), p. 135.

30. A study of the first-term record of the Mulroney government revealed that 48 percent of all judges appointed were known Conservative supporters, compared with seven percent who supported opposition parties. Peter Russell and Jacob Ziegel, "Federal Judicial Appointments: An Appraisal of the First Mulroney Government's Appointments and the New Judiciary Advisory Committees," *University of Toronto Law Journal* 41 (1991).

31. Lori Hausegger, Troy Riddell, Matthew Hennigar, and Emmanuelle Richez, "Exploring the Links between Party and Appointment: Canadian Federal Judicial Appointments from 1989 to 2003," *Canadian Journal of Political Science* (September 2010).

32. Heather MacIvor, *Parameters of Power: Canada's Political Institutions*, 5th ed. (Toronto: Nelson Education, 2010), p. 333–34.

33. Greene et al., *Final Appeal*, p. 36.

34. Forcese and Freeman, *The Laws of Government: The Legal Foundations of Canadian Democracy*, pp. 265–69.

35. *The Globe and Mail*, April 18, 2012.

36. Two or three subsequent appointments had marginal partisan pasts, including Julien Chouinard and Michel Bastarache. See MacIvor, *Parameters of Power: Canada's Political Institutions*, p. 354.

37. Greene et al., *Final Appeal*, p. 101.

38. McCormick, *Canada's Courts*, p. 112.

39. On the question of Aboriginal cases, see Larry Chartrand, et al., "Reconciliation and Transformation in Practice: Aboriginal Judicial Appointments to the Supreme Court," *Canadian Public Administration* (March 2008).

40. Dennis Olsen, *The State Elite* (Toronto: McClelland and Stewart, 1980), p. 47. See also Russell, *The Judiciary in Canada*, pp. 164–65; and Greene et al., *Final Appeal*, p. 42.

41. Bertha Wilson said that men didn't understand abortion in the Morgentaler case, but Peter McCormick, *Canada's Courts*, p. 115, discounts the distinctiveness of the judgments of women or visible minorities.

42. Greene, *The Courts*, p. 60.

43. R.G. Green, *Justice in Aboriginal Communities: Sentencing Alternatives* (Saskatoon: Purich Publishing, 1998).

44. Russell, *The Judiciary in Canada*, p. 165; Greene et al., *Final Appeal*, p. 42, also admit that judges are elitist but are not overly concerned either.

45. McCormick, *Canada's Courts*, p. 115.

46. Russell, *The Judiciary in Canada*, p. 24.

47. Vuk Radmilovic, "Strategic Legitimacy Cultivation at the Supreme Court of Canada: Quebec Secession Reference and Beyond," *Canadian Journal of Political Science* (Winter 2010); Rafael Gely and Pablo Spiller, "A Rational Choice Theory of Supreme Court Statutory Decisions with Applications to the 'State Farm' and 'Grove City Cases,'" *Journal of Law, Economics, & Organization* (Autumn 1990).

48. McCormick, *Canada's Courts*, p. 165. C.L. Ostberg and Matthew E. Wetstein, *Attitudinal Decision Making in The Supreme Court of Canada* (Vancouver: UBC Press, 2007); Donald R. Songer and Susan W. Johnson, "Judicial Decision Making In the Supreme Court of Canada: Updating the Personal Attribute Model," *Canadian Journal of Political Science* (December 2007); and Donald R. Songer and Julia Siripurapu, "The Unanimous Decisions of the Supreme Court of Canada as a Test of the Attitudinal Model," *Canadian Journal of Political Science* (March 2009).

49. F.L. Morton and H. Patrick Glenn debate this subject in Mark Charlton and Paul Barker, eds., *Crosscurrents: Contemporary Political Issues*, 3rd ed. (Scarborough: ITP Nelson, 1998), Ch. 15.

50. Joseph S. Ziegel, *Merit Selection and Democratization of Appointments to the Supreme Court of Canada* (Montreal: Institute for Research on Public Policy, 1999). An aborted attempt at parliamentary review occurred in 2004, see MacIvor, *Parameters of Power*, pp. 339–40.

51. Department of Justice Canada, *Speaking Notes for the Minister of Justice and Attorney General of Canada, Vic Towes, Q.C., Ad Hoc Committee to Review a Nominee for the Supreme Court of Canada* (February 27, 2006); available at http://www.justice.gc.ca/eng/news-nouv/spe-disc/2006/doc_31772.html, retrieved on April 28, 2009.

52. Another famous case concerned Leo Landreville of the Supreme Court of Ontario. See Gall, *The Canadian Legal System*, pp. 231, 238–39; Russell, *The Judiciary in Canada*, pp. 176–79; and Greene, *The Courts*, pp. 94–103.

53. Canadian Judicial Council website; MacIvor, *Parameters of Power*, p. 358.

54. The classic statement on this question was made by Mr. Justice LeDain in *Valente v. the Queen*, [1985] 2 S.C.R. 673; see also Perry S. Millar and Carl Baar, *Judicial Administration in Canada* (Montreal: McGill-Queen's University Press, 1981); Peter McCormick, "New Questions about an Old Concept: The Supreme Court of Canada's Judicial Independence Decisions," *Canadian Journal of Political Science* (December 2004); and Greene, *The Courts*, pp. 88–93.

55. *Manitoba Provincial Judges Association v. Manitoba (Minister of Justice)*, [1997] 3 S.C.R. 3; *Reference re Remuneration of Judges of the Provincial Court of PEI*; and *Reference re the Independence and Impartiality of Judges of the Provincial Court of PEI*, [1998] 1 S.C.R. 3.

56. *Provincial Court Judges' Assn. of New Brunswick v. New Brunswick (Minister of Justice)*, [2005] 2 S.C.R. 286. See also MacIvor, *Parameters of Power*, pp. 347–49.
57. See Heard, *Canadian Constitutional Conventions*, p. 128; Russell, *The Judiciary in Canada*, pp. 78–81, especially regarding the "Judges Affair"; and Greene, *The Courts*, p. 77.
58. According to Russell and Ziegel, "Federal Judicial Appointments," former party ties count in promotions.
59. Heard, *Canadian Constitutional Conventions*, p. 131; Russell, *The Canadian Judiciary*, pp. 85–89; Gall, *The Canadian Legal System*, pp. 236–38; McCormick, *Canada's Courts*, pp. 130–31; and Greene, *The Courts*, pp. 95–96.

FURTHER READING

Gall, Gerald. *The Canadian Legal System*, 4th ed. Toronto: Carswell, 1995.

Green, R.G. *Justice in Aboriginal Communities: Sentencing Alternatives*. Saskatoon: Purich Publishing, 1998.

Greene, Ian. *The Courts*. Vancouver: UBC Press, 2006.

———, Carl Baar, Peter McCormick, George Szablowski, and Martin Thomas. *Final Appeal: Decision-Making in Canadian Courts of Appeal*. Toronto: James Lorimer & Co., 1998.

Hausegger, Lori, Troy Riddell, Matthew Hennigar, and Emmanuelle Richez. "Exploring the Links between Party and Appointment: Canadian Federal Judicial Appointments from 1989 to 2003," *Canadian Journal of Political Science* (September 2010).

Heard, Andrew. *Canadian Constitutional Conventions*. Toronto: Oxford University Press, 1991.

Macfarlane, Emmett. 2013. *Governing from the Bench: The Supreme Court of Canada and the Judicial Role*. Vancouver: UBC Press.

MacIvor, Heather. *Parameters of Power: Canada's Political Institutions*, 5th ed. Toronto: Nelson Education, 2010.

Russell, Peter. *The Judiciary in Canada: The Third Branch of Government*. Toronto: McGraw-Hill Ryerson, 1987.

Constitution Act, 1867 (excerpts)

VI. DISTRIBUTION OF LEGISLATIVE POWERS

Powers of the Parliament

91. It shall be lawful for the Queen, by and with the Advice and Consent of the Senate and House of Commons, to make Laws for the Peace, Order, and good Government of Canada, in relation to all Matters not coming within the Classes of Subjects by this Act assigned exclusively to the Legislatures of the Provinces; and for greater Certainty, but not so as to restrict the Generality of the foregoing Terms of this Section, it is hereby declared that (notwithstanding anything in this Act) the exclusive Legislative Authority of the Parliament of Canada extends to all Matters coming within the Classes of Subjects next hereinafter enumerated; that is to say,—

Legislative Authority of Parliament of Canada

1   *The amendment from time to time of the Constitution of Canada, except as regards matters coming within the classes of subjects by this Act assigned exclusively to the Legislatures of the provinces, or as regards rights or privileges by this or any other Constitutional Act granted or secured to the Legislature or the Government of a province, or to any class of persons with respect to schools or as regards the use of the English or the French language or as regards the requirements that there shall be a session of the Parliament of Canada at least once each year, and that no House of Commons shall continue for more than five years from the day of the return of the Writs for choosing the House: Provided, however, that a House of Commons may in time of real of apprehended war, invasion or insurrection be continued by the Parliament of Canada if such continuation is not opposed by the votes of more than one-third of the members of such House.*

[Note: Class 1 was added by the British North America Act (No. 2), 1949 and repealed by the Constitution Act, 1982.]

1A. The Public Debt and Property.

2. The Regulation of Trade and Commerce.

2A. Unemployment insurance.

3. The raising of Money by any Mode or System of Taxation.

4. The borrowing of Money on the Public Credit.

5. Postal Service.

6. The Census and Statistics.

7. Militia, Military and Naval Service, and Defence.

8. The fixing of and providing for the Salaries and Allowances of Civil and other Officers of the Government of Canada.

9. Beacons, Buoys, Lighthouses, and Sable Island.

10. Navigation and Shipping.

11. Quarantine and the Establishment and Maintenance of Marine Hospitals.

12. Sea Coast and Inland Fisheries.

13. Ferries between a Province and any British or Foreign Country or between Two Provinces.

14. Currency and Coinage.

15. Banking, Incorporation of Banks, and the Issue of Paper Money.

16. Savings Banks.

17. Weights and Measures.

18. Bills of Exchange and Promissory Notes.

19. Interest.

20. Legal Tender.

21. Bankruptcy and Insolvency.

22. Patents of Invention and Discovery.

23. Copyrights.

24. Indians, and Lands reserved for the Indians.

25. Naturalization and Aliens.

26. Marriage and Divorce.

27. The Criminal Law, except the Constitution of Courts of Criminal Jurisdiction, but including the Procedure in Criminal Matters.

28. The Establishment, Maintenance, and Management of Penitentiaries.

29. Such Classes of Subjects as are expressly excepted in the Enumeration of the Classes of Subjects by this Act assigned exclusively to the Legislatures of the Provinces.

And any Matter coming within any of the Classes of Subjects enumerated in this Section shall not be deemed to come within the Class of Matters of a local or private Nature comprised in the Enumeration of the Classes of Subjects by this Act assigned exclusively to the Legislatures of the Provinces.

Exclusive Powers of Provincial Legislatures

92. In each Province the Legislature may exclusively make Laws in relation to Matters coming within the Classes of Subjects next hereinafter enumerated; that is to say,—

1   *The Amendment from Time to Time, notwithstanding anything in this Act, of the Constitution of the Province, except as regards the Office of the Lieutenant Governor.*

[Note: Class 1 was repealed by the *Constitution Act, 1982*. The subject is now provided for in section 45 of that Act, and see also sections 38 and 41 to 43 of the same Act.]

2. Direct Taxation within the Province in order to the raising of a Revenue for Provincial Purposes.

3. The borrowing of Money on the sole Credit of the Province.

4. The Establishment and Tenure of Provincial Offices and the Appointment and Payment of Provincial Officers.

5. The Management and Sale of the Public Lands belonging to the Province and of the Timber and Wood thereon.

6. The Establishment, Maintenance, and Management of Public and Reformatory Prisons in and for the Province.

7. The Establishment, Maintenance, and Management of Hospitals, Asylums, Charities, and Eleemosynary Institutions in and for the Province, other than Marine Hospitals.

8. Municipal Institutions in the Province.

9. Shop, Saloon, Tavern, Auctioneer, and other Licences in order to the raising of a Revenue for Provincial, Local, or Municipal Purposes.

10. Local Works and Undertakings other than such as are of the following Classes:—

    (a) Lines of Steam or other Ships, Railways, Canals, Telegraphs, and other Works and Undertakings connecting the Province with any other or others of the Provinces, or extending beyond the Limits of the Province;

    (b) Lines of Steam Ships between the Province and any British or Foreign Country;

    (c) Such Works as, although wholly situate within the Province, are before or after their Execution declared by the Parliament of Canada to be for the general Advantage of Canada or for the Advantage of Two or more of the Provinces.

11. The Incorporation of Companies with Provincial Objects.

12. The Solemnization of Marriage in the Province.

13. Property and Civil Rights in the Province.

14. The Administration of Justice in the Province, including the Constitution, Maintenance, and Organization of Provincial Courts,

both of Civil and of Criminal Jurisdiction, and including Procedure in Civil Matters in those Courts.

15. The Imposition of Punishment by Fine, Penalty, or Imprisonment for enforcing any Law of the Province made in relation to any Matter coming within any of the Classes of Subjects enumerated in this Section.

16. Generally all Matters of a merely local or private Nature in the Province.

Non-Renewable Natural Resources, Forestry Resources and Electrical Energy

Laws respecting non-renewal resources, forestry resources and electrical energy

92A. (1) In each province, the legislature may exclusively make laws in relation to

(a) exploration for non-renewable natural resources in the province;

(b) development, conservation and management of non-renewable natural resources and forestry resources in the province, including laws in relation to the rate of primary production therefrom; and

(c) development, conservation and management of sites and facilities in the province for the generation and production of electrical energy.

Export from province of resources

(2) In each province, the legislature may make laws in relation to the export from the province to another part of Canada of the primary production from non-renewable natural resources and forestry resources in the province and the production from facilities in the province for the generation of electrical energy, but such laws may not authorize or provide for discrimination in prices or in supplies exported to another part of Canada.

Authority of Parliament

(3) Nothing in subsection (2) derogates from the authority of Parliament to enact laws in relation to the matters referred to in that subsection and, where such a law of Parliament and a law of a province conflict, the law of Parliament prevails to the extent of the conflict.

Taxation of resources

(4) In each province, the legislature may make laws in relation to the raising of money by any mode or system of taxation in respect of

(a) non-renewable natural resources and forestry resources in the province and the primary production therefrom, and

(b) sites and facilities in the province for the generation of electrical energy and the production therefrom, whether or not such production is exported in whole or in part from the province, but such laws may not authorize or provide for taxation that differentiates between production exported to another part of Canada and production not exported from the province.

(5) The expression "primary production" has the meaning assigned by the Sixth Schedule. "Primary production"

(6) Nothing in subsections (1) to (5) derogates from any powers or rights that a legislature or government of a province had immediately before the coming into force of this section. Existing powers or rights

Education

93. In and for each Province the Legislature may exclusively make Laws in relation to Education, subject and according to the following Provisions:— Legislation respecting Education

(1) Nothing in any such Law shall prejudicially affect any Right or Privilege with respect to Denominational Schools which any Class of Persons have by Law in the Province at the Union:

(2) All the Powers, Privileges, and Duties at the Union by Law conferred and imposed in Upper Canada on the Separate Schools and School Trustees of the Queen's Roman Catholic Subjects shall be and the same are hereby extended to the Dissentient Schools of the Queen's Protestant and Roman Catholic Subjects in Quebec:

(3) Where in any Province a System of Separate or Dissentient Schools exists by Law at the Union or is thereafter established by the Legislature of the Province, an Appeal shall lie to the Governor General in Council from any Act or Decision of any Provincial Authority affecting any Right or Privilege of the Protestant or Roman Catholic Minority of the Queen's Subjects in relation to Education:

(4) In case any such Provincial Law as from Time to Time seems to the Governor General in Council requisite for the due Execution of the Provisions of this Section is not made, or in case any Decision of the Governor General in Council on any appeal under this Section is not duly executed by the proper Provincial Authority in that Behalf, then and in every such Case, and as far only as the Circumstances of each Case require, the Parliament of Canada may make remedial Laws for the due Execution of the Provisions of this Section and of any Decision of the Governor General in Council under this Section.

Uniformity of Laws in Ontario, Nova Scotia and New Brunswick

94. Notwithstanding anything in this Act, the Parliament of Canada may make Provision for the Uniformity of all or any of the Laws relative to Property and Civil Rights in Ontario, Nova Scotia, and New Brunswick, and of the Procedure of all or any of the Courts in Those Legislation for Uniformity of Laws in Three Provinces

Three Provinces, and from and after the passing of any Act in that Behalf the Power of the Parliament of Canada to make Laws in relation to any Matter comprised in any such Act shall, notwithstanding anything in this Act, be unrestricted; but any Act of the Parliament of Canada making Provision for such Uniformity shall not have effect in any Province unless and until it is adopted and enacted as Law by the Legislature thereof.

Old Age Pensions

Legislation respecting old age pensions and supplementary benefits

94A. The Parliament of Canada may make laws in relation to old age pensions and supplementary benefits, including survivors' and disability benefits irrespective of age, but no such law shall affect the operation of any law present or future of a provincial legislature in relation to any such matter.

Agriculture and Immigration

Concurrent Powers of Legislation respecting Agriculture, etc.

95. In each Province the Legislature may make Laws in relation to Agriculture in the Province, and to Immigration into the Province; and it is hereby declared that the Parliament of Canada may from Time to Time make Laws in relation to Agriculture in all or any of the Provinces, and to Immigration into all or any of the Provinces; and any Law of the Legislature of a Province relative to Agriculture or to Immigration shall have effect in and for the Province as long and as far only as it is not repugnant to any Act of the Parliament of Canada.

VII. JUDICATURE

Appointment of Judges

96. The Governor General shall appoint the Judges of the Superior, District, and County Courts in each Province, except those of the Courts of Probate in Nova Scotia and New Brunswick.

Selection of Judges in Ontario, etc.

97. Until the Laws relative to Property and Civil Rights in Ontario, Nova Scotia, and New Brunswick, and the Procedure of the Courts in those Provinces, are made uniform, the Judges of the Courts of those Provinces appointed by the Governor General shall be selected from the respective Bars of those Provinces.

98. The Judges of the Courts of Quebec shall be selected from the Bar of that Province.

99. *The Judges of the Supreme Courts shall hold Office during good Behaviour, but shall be removable by the Governor General on Address of the Senate and the House of Commons.*

99. (1) Subject to subsection two of this section, the Judges of the Superior Courts shall hold office during good behaviour, but shall be removable by the Governor General on Address of the Senate and House of Commons.

(2) A Judge of a Superior Court, whether appointed before or after the coming into force of this section, shall cease to hold office upon attaining the age of seventy-five years, or upon the coming into force of this section if at that time he has already attained that age.

[Note: Section 99 (in italics) was repealed and the new section substituted by the *Constitution Act, 1960.*]

100. The Salaries, Allowances, and Pensions of the Judges of the Superior, District, and County Courts (except the Courts of Probate in Nova Scotia and New Brunswick), and of the Admiralty Courts in Cases where the Judges thereof are for the Time being paid by Salary, shall be fixed and provided by the Parliament of Canada.

101. The Parliament of Canada may, notwithstanding anything in this Act, from Time to Time provide for the Constitution, Maintenance, and Organization of a General Court of Appeal for Canada, and for the Establishment of any additional Courts for the better Administration of the Laws of Canada.

Tenure of office of Judges

Termination at age 75

Salaries, etc., of Judges

General Court of Appeal, etc.

IX. MISCELLANEOUS PROVISIONS

General

132. The Parliament and Government of Canada shall have all Powers necessary or proper for performing the Obligations of Canada or of any Province thereof, as Part of the British Empire, towards Foreign Countries, arising under Treaties between the Empire and such Foreign Countries.

133. Either the English or the French Language may be used by any Person in the Debates of the Houses of the Parliament of Canada and of the Houses of the Legislature of Quebec; and both those Languages shall be used in the respective Records and Journals of those Houses; and either of those Languages may be used by any Person or in any Pleading or Process in or issuing from any Court of Canada established under this Act, and in or from all or any of the Courts of Quebec.

Treaty Obligations

Use of English and French Languages

The Acts of the Parliament of Canada and of the Legislature of Quebec shall be printed and published in both those Languages.

Constitution Act, 1982, Schedule B

PART I. CANADIAN CHARTER OF RIGHTS AND FREEDOMS

Whereas Canada is founded upon principles that recognize the supremacy of God and the rule of law:

Guarantee of Rights and Freedoms

1. The Canadian Charter of Rights and Freedoms guarantees the rights and freedoms set out in it subject only to such reasonable limits prescribed by law as can be demonstrably justified in a free and democratic society.

Rights and freedoms in Canada

Fundamental Freedoms

2. Everyone has the following fundamental freedoms:
   (a) freedom of conscience and religion;
   (b) freedom of thought, belief, opinion and expression, including freedom of the press and other media of communication;
   (c) freedom of peaceful assembly; and
   (d) freedom of association.

Fundamental freedoms

Democratic Rights

3. Every citizen of Canada has the right to vote in an election of members of the House of Commons or of a legislative assembly and to be qualified for membership therein.

Democratic rights of citizens

	4. (1) No House of Commons and no legislative assembly shall continue for longer than five years from the date fixed for the return of the writs at a general election of its members.

Maximum duration of legislative bodies

4. (1) No House of Commons and no legislative assembly shall continue for longer than five years from the date fixed for the return of the writs at a general election of its members.

Continuation in special circumstances

(2) In time of real or apprehended war, invasion or insurrection, a House of Commons may be continued by Parliament and a legislative assembly may be continued by the legislature beyond five years if such continuation is not opposed by the votes of more than one-third of the members of the House of Commons or the legislative assembly, as the case may be.

Annual sitting of legislative bodies

5. There shall be a sitting of Parliament and of each legislature at least once every twelve months.

Mobility Rights

Mobility of citizens

6. (1) Every citizen of Canada has the right to enter, remain in and leave Canada.

Rights to move and gain livelihood

(2) Every citizen of Canada and every person who has the status of a permanent -resident of Canada has the right

    (a) to move to and take up residence in any province; and

    (b) to pursue the gaining of a livelihood in any province

Limitation

(3) The rights specified in subsection (2) are subject to

    (a) any laws or practices of general application in force in a province other than those that discriminate among persons primarily on the basis of province of present or previous residence; and

    (b) any laws providing for reasonable residency requirements as a qualification for the receipt of publicly provided social services.

Affirmative action programs

(4) Subsections (2) and (3) do not preclude any law, program or activity that has as its object the amelioration in a province of conditions of individuals in that province who are socially or economically disadvantaged if the rate of employment in that province is below the rate of employment in Canada.

Legal Rights

Life, liberty and security of person

7. Everyone has the right to life, liberty and security of the person and the right not to be deprived thereof except in accordance with the principles of fundamental justice.

8. Everyone has the right to be secure against unreasonable search or seizure.

Search or seizure

9. Everyone has the right not to be arbitrarily detained or imprisoned.

10. Everyone has the right on arrest or detention
    (a) to be informed promptly of the reasons therefor;
    (b) to retain and instruct counsel without delay and to be informed of that right; and
    (c) to have the validity of the detention determined by way of habeas corpus and to be released if the detention is not lawful.

11. Any person charged with an offence has the right
    (a) to be informed without unreasonable delay of the specific offence;
    (b) to be tried within a reasonable time;
    (c) not to be compelled to be a witness in proceedings against that person in respect of the offence;
    (d) to be presumed innocent until proven guilty according to law in a fair and public hearing by an independent and impartial tribunal;
    (e) not to be denied reasonable bail without just cause;
    (f) except in the case of an offence under military law tried before a military tribunal, to the benefit of trial by jury where the maximum punishment for the offence is imprisonment for five years or a more severe punishment;
    (g) or was criminal according to the general principles of law recognized by the community of nations; not to be found guilty on account of any act or omission unless, at the time of the act or omission, it constituted an offence under Canadian or international law
    (h) if finally acquitted of the offence, not to be tried for it again and, if finally found guilty and punished for the offence, not to be tried or punished for it again; and
    (i) if found guilty of the offence and if the punishment for the offence has been varied between the time of commission and the time of sentencing, to the benefit of the lesser punishment.

12. Everyone has the right not to be subjected to any cruel and unusual treatment or punishment.

13. A witness who testifies in any proceedings has the right not to have any incriminating evidence so given used to incriminate that witness in any other proceedings, except in a prosecution for perjury or for the giving of contradictory evidence.

14. A party or witness in any proceedings who does not understand or speak the language in which the proceedings are conducted or who is deaf has the right to the assistance of an interpreter.

Equality Rights

15. (1) Every individual is equal before and under the law and has the right to the equal protection and equal benefit of the law without discrimination and, in particular, without discrimination based on race, national or ethnic origin, colour, religion, sex, age or mental or physical disability.

(2) Subsection (1) does not preclude any law, program or activity that has as its object the amelioration of conditions of disadvantaged individuals or groups including those that are disadvantaged because of race, national or ethnic origin, colour, religion, sex, age or mental or physical disability.

Official Languages of Canada

Official languages of Canada

Official languages of New Brunswick

Advancement of status and use

Proceedings of Parliament

Proceedings of New Brunswick legislature

Parliamentary statutes and records

New Brunswick statutes and records

Proceedings in courts established by Parliament

Proceedings in New Brunswick courts

Communications by public with fellow institutions

16. (1) English and French are the official languages of Canada and have equality of status and equal rights and privileges as to their use in all institutions of the Parliament and government of Canada.

   (2) English and French are the official languages of New Brunswick and have equality of status and equal rights and privileges as to their use in all institutions of the legislature and government of New Brunswick.

   (3) Nothing in this Charter limits the authority of Parliament or a legislature to advance the equality of status or use of English and French.

17. (1) Everyone has the right to use English or French in any debates and other proceedings of Parliament.

   (2) Everyone has the right to use English or French in any debates and other proceedings of the legislature of New Brunswick.

18. (1) The statutes, records and journals of Parliament shall be printed and published in English and French and both language versions are equally authoritative.

   (2) The statutes, records and journals of the legislature of New Brunswick shall be printed and published in English and French and both language versions are equally authoritative.

19. (1) Either English or French may be used by any person in, or in any pleading in or process issuing from, any court established by Parliament.

   (2) Either English or French may be used by any person in, or in any pleading in or process issuing from, any court of New Brunswick.

20. (1) Any member of the public in Canada has the right to communicate with, and to receive available services from, any head or central office of an institution of the Parliament or government of Canada in English or French, and has the same right with respect to any other office of any such institution where

   (a) there is a significant demand for communications with and services from that office in such language; or

   (b) to the nature of the office, it is reasonable that communications with and services from that office be available in both English and French

(2) Any member of the public in New Brunswick has the right to communicate with, and to receive available services from, any office of an institution of the legislature or government of New Brunswick in English or French.

Communications by public with New Brunswick's institutions

21. Nothing in sections 16 to 20 abrogates or derogates from any right, privilege or obligation with respect to the English and French languages, or either of them, that exists or is continued by virtue of any other provision of the Constitution of Canada.

Continuation of existing constitutional provisions

22. Nothing in sections 16 to 20 abrogates or derogates from any legal or customary right or privilege acquired or enjoyed either before or after the coming into force of this Charter with respect to any language that is not English or French.

Rights and privileges preserved

Minority Language Educational Rights

23. (1) Citizens of Canada
    (a) whose first language learned and still understood is that of the English or French linguistic minority population of the province in which they reside, or
    (b) who have received their primary school instruction in Canada in English or French and reside in a province where the language in which they received that instruction is the language of the English or French linguistic minority population of the province, have the right to have their children receive primary and secondary school instruction in that language in that province.

Language of instruction

(2) Citizens of Canada of whom any child has received or is receiving primary or secondary school instruction in English or French in Canada, have the right to have all their children receive primary and secondary school instruction in the same language.

Continuity of language instruction

(3) The right of citizens of Canada under subsections (1) and (2) to have their children receive primary and secondary school instruction in the language of the English or French linguistic minority population of a province
    (a) applies wherever in the province the number of children of citizens who have such a right is sufficient to warrant the provision to them out of public funds of minority language instruction; and
    (b) includes, where the number of those children so warrants, the right to have them receive that instruction in minority language educational facilities provided out of public funds.

Application where numbers warrant

Enforcement

Enforcement of guaranteed rights and freedoms

24. (1) Anyone whose rights or freedoms, as guaranteed by this Charter, have been infringed or denied may apply to a court of competent jurisdiction to obtain such remedy as the court considers appropriate and just in the circumstances.

Exclusion of evidence bringing administration of justice into disrepute

(2) Where, in proceedings under subsection (1), a court concludes that evidence was obtained in a manner that infringed or denied any rights or freedoms guaranteed by this Charter, the evidence shall be excluded if it is established that, having regard to all the circumstances, the admission of it in the proceedings would bring the administration of justice into disrepute.

General

Aboriginal rights and freedoms not affected by charter

25. The guarantee in this Charter of certain rights and freedoms shall not be construed so as to abrogate or derogate from any aboriginal, treaty or other rights or freedoms that pertain to the aboriginal peoples of Canada including

    (a) any rights or freedoms that have been recognized by the Royal Proclamation of October 7, 1763;

Other rights and freedoms not affected by charter

    (b) *any rights or freedoms that may be acquired by the aboriginal peoples of Canada by way of land claims settlement;* and

    (c) any rights or freedoms that now exist by way of land claims agreements or may be so acquired.

[Note: Paragraph 25(b) (in italics) was repealed and the new paragraph substituted by the *Constitution Amendment Proclamation, 1983.*]

Multicultural heritage

26. The guarantee in this Charter of certain rights and freedoms shall not be construed as denying the existence of any other rights or freedoms that exist in Canada.

Rights guaranteed equally to both sexes

27. This Charter shall be interpreted in a manner consistent with the preservation and enhancement of the multicultural heritage of Canadians.

Rights respecting certain schools preserved

28. Notwithstanding anything in this Charter, the rights and freedoms referred to in it are guaranteed equally to male and female persons.

29. Nothing in this Charter abrogates or derogates from any rights or privileges guaranteed by or under the Constitution of Canada in respect of denominational, separate or dissentient schools.

Application to territories and territorial authorities

30. A reference in this Charter to a Province or to the legislative assembly or legislature of a province shall be deemed to include a reference to the Yukon Territory and the Northwest Territories, or to the appropriate legislative authority thereof, as the case may be.

Legislative powers not extended

31. Nothing in this Charter extends the legislative powers of any body or authority.

Application of Charter

32. (1) This Charter applies
    (a) to the Parliament and government of Canada in respect of all matters within the authority of Parliament including all matters relating to the Yukon Territory and Northwest Territories; and
    (b) to the legislature and government of each province in respect of all matters within the authority of the legislature of each province.
    (2) Notwithstanding subsection (1), section 15 shall not have effect until three years after this section comes into force.

33. (1) Parliament or the legislature of a province may expressly declare in an Act of Parliament or of the legislature, as the case may be, that the Act or a provision thereof shall operate notwithstanding a provision included in section 2 or sections 7 to 15 of this Charter.
    (2) An Act or a provision of an Act in respect of which a declaration made under this section is in effect shall have such operation as it would have but for the provision of this Charter referred to in the declaration.
    (3) A declaration made under subsection (1) shall cease to have effect five years after it comes into force or on such earlier date as may be specified in the declaration.
    (4) Parliament or the legislature of a province may re-enact a declaration made under subsection (1).
    (5) Subsection (3) applies in respect of a re-enactment made under subsection (4).

Application of Charter

Exception

Exception where express declaration

Operation of exception

Five year limitation

Re-enactment

Citation

34. This Part may be cited as the Canadian Charter of Rights and Freedoms.

PART II. RIGHTS OF THE ABORIGINAL PEOPLES OF CANADA

Recognition of existing aboriginal and treaty rights

35. (1) The existing aboriginal and treaty rights of the aboriginal peoples of Canada are hereby recognized and affirmed.
    (2) In this Act, "aboriginal peoples of Canada" includes the Indian,

Definition of "aboriginal peoples of Canada"

Inuit and Métis peoples of Canada.

(3) For greater certainty, in subsection (1) "treaty rights" includes rights that now exist by way of land claims agreements or may be so acquired.

Aboriginal and
treaty rights are
guaranteed
equally to both
sexes

(4) Notwithstanding any other provision of this Act, the aboriginal and treaty rights referred to in subsection (1) are guaranteed equally to male and female persons.

35.1 The government of Canada and the provincial governments are committed to the principle that, before any amendment is made to Class 24 of section 91 of the "*Constitution Act, 1867*", to section 25 of this Act or to this Part,

(a) a constitutional conference that includes in its agenda an item relating to the proposed amendment, composed of the Prime Minister of Canada and the first ministers of the provinces, will be convened by the Prime Minister of Canada; and

(b) the Prime Minister of Canada will invite representatives of the aboriginal peoples of Canada to participate in the discussions on that item.

PART III. EQUALIZATION AND REGIONAL DISPARITIES

36. (1) Without altering the legislative authority of Parliament or of the provincial legislatures, or the rights of any of them with respect to the exercise of their legislative authority, Parliament and the legislatures, together with the government of Canada and the provincial governments, are committed to

(a) promoting equal opportunities for the well-being of Canadians;

(b) furthering economic development to reduce disparity in opportunities; and

(c) providing essential public services of reasonable quality to all Canadians.

(2) Parliament and the government of Canada are committed to the principle of making equalization payments to ensure that provincial governments have sufficient revenues to provide reasonably comparable levels of public services at reasonably comparable levels of taxation.

PART IV. CONSTITUTIONAL CONFERENCE

37. (1) A constitutional conference composed of the Prime Minister of Canada and the first ministers of the provinces shall be convened by the Prime Minister of Canada within one year after this Part comes into force.

(2) The conference convened under subsection (1) shall have included in its agenda an item respecting constitutional matters that directly affect the aboriginal peoples of Canada, including the identification and definition of the rights of those peoples to be included in the Constitution of Canada, and the Prime Minister of Canada shall invite representatives of those peoples to participate in the discussions on that item.

(3) The Prime Minister of Canada shall invite elected representatives of the governments of the Yukon Territory and the Northwest Territories to participate in the discussions on any item on the agenda of the conference convened under subsection (1) that, in the opinion of the Prime Minister, directly affects the Yukon Territory and the Northwest Territories.

PART V. PROCEDURE FOR AMENDING CONSTITUTION OF CANADA

38. (1) An amendment to the Constitution of Canada may be made by proclamation issued by the Governor General under the Great Seal of Canada where so authorized by
    (a) resolutions of the Senate and House of Commons; and
    (b) resolutions of the legislative assemblies of at least two-thirds of the provinces that have, in the aggregate, according to the then latest general census, at least fifty per cent of the population of all the provinces.

(2) An amendment made under subsection (1) that derogates from the legislative powers, the proprietary rights or any other rights or privileges of the legislature or government of a province shall require a resolution supported by a majority of the members of each of the Senate, the House of Commons and the legislative assemblies required under subsection (1).

Expression of dissent	(3) An amendment referred to in subsection (2) shall not have effect in a province the legislative assembly of which has expressed its dissent thereto by resolution supported by a majority of its members prior to the issue of the proclamation to which the amendment relates unless that legislative assembly, subsequently, by resolution supported by a majority of its members, revokes its dissent and authorizes the amendment.
Revocation of proclamation	(4) A resolution of dissent made for the purposes of subsection (3) may be revoked at any time before or after the issue of the proclamation to which it relates.
Restriction on proclamation	39. (1) A proclamation shall not be issued under subsection 38(1) before the expiration of one year from the adoption of the resolution initiating the amendment procedure thereunder, unless the legislative assembly of each province has previously adopted a resolution of assent or dissent.
Idem	(2) A proclamation shall not be issued under subsection 38(1) after the expiration of three years from the adoption of the resolution initiating the amendment procedure thereunder.
Compensation	40. Where an amendment is made under subsection 38(1) that transfers provincial legislative powers relating to education or other cultural matters from provincial legislatures to Parliament, Canada shall provide reasonable compensation to any province to which the amendment does not apply.
Amendment by unanimous consent	41. An amendment to the Constitution of Canada in relation to the following matters may be made by proclamation issued by the Governor General under the Great Seal of Canada only where authorized by resolutions of the Senate and House of Commons and of the legislative assembly of each province:

    (a) the office of the Queen, the Governor General and the Lieutenant Governor of a province;

    (b) the right of a province to a number of members in the House of Commons not less than the number of Senators by which the province is entitled to be represented at the time this Part comes into force;

    (c) subject to section 43, the use of the English or the French language;

    (d) the composition of the Supreme Court of Canada; and

    (e) an amendment to this Part.

Amendment by general procedure	42. (1) An amendment to the Constitution of Canada in relation to the following matters may be made only in accordance with subsection 38(1):

    (a) the principle of proportionate representation of the provinces in the House of Commons prescribed by the Constitution of Canada;

    (b) the powers of the Senate and the method of selecting Senators;

(c) the number of members by which a province is entitled to be represented in the Senate and the residence qualifications of Senators;

(d) subject to paragraph 41(d), the Supreme Court of Canada;

(e) the extension of existing provinces into the territories; and

(f) notwithstanding any other law or practice, the establishment of new provinces.

(2) Subsections 38(2) to (4) do not apply in respect of amendments in relation to matters referred to in subsection (1).

Exception

43. An amendment to the Constitution of Canada in relation to any provision that applies to one or more, but not all, provinces, including

Amendment of provisions relating to some but not all provinces

(a) any alteration to boundaries between provinces, and

(b) any amendment to any provision that relates to the use of the English or the French language within a province, may be made by proclamation issued by the Governor General under the Great Seal of Canada only where so authorized by resolutions of the Senate and House of Commons and of the legislative assembly of each province to which the amendment applies.

44. Subject to sections 41 and 42, Parliament may exclusively make laws amending the Constitution of Canada in relation to the executive government of Canada or the Senate and House of Commons.

Amendment by Parliament

45. Subject to section 41, the legislature of each province may exclusively make laws amending the constitution of the province.

Amendments by provincial legislatures

46. (1) The procedures for amendment under sections 38, 41, 42 and 43 may be initiated either by the Senate or the House of Commons or by the legislative assembly of a province.

Initiation of amendment procedures

(2) A resolution of assent made for the purposes of this Part may be revoked at any time before the issue of a proclamation authorized by it.

Revocation of authorization

47. (1) An amendment to the Constitution of Canada made by proclamation under section 38, 41, 42 or 43 may be made without a resolution of the Senate authorizing the issue of the proclamation if, within one hundred and eighty days after the adoption by the House of Commons of a resolution authorizing its issue, the Senate has not adopted such a resolution and if, at any time after the expiration of that period, the House of Commons again adopts the resolution.

Amendments without senate resolution

(2) Any period when Parliament is prorogued or dissolved shall not be counted in computing the one hundred and eighty day period referred to in subsection (1).

Computation of period

48. The Queen's Privy Council for Canada shall advise the Governor General to issue a proclamation under this Part forthwith on the adoption of the resolutions required for an amendment made by proclamation under this Part.

Advice to issue proclamation

49. A constitutional conference composed of the Prime Minister of Canada and the first ministers of the provinces shall be convened by the Prime Minister of Canada within fifteen years after this Part comes into force to review the provisions of this Part.

PART VI. AMENDMENT TO THE CONSTITUTION ACT, 1867

50. [See section 92A of the Constitution Act, 1867]
51. The said Act is further amended by adding thereto the following Schedule:

"THE SIXTH SCHEDULE"

1. For the purposes of Section 92A of this Act,
   (a) production from a non-renewable natural resource is primary production therefrom if
      (i) it is in the form in which it exists upon its recovery or severance from its natural state, or
      (ii) it is a product resulting from processing or refining the resource, and is not a manufactured product or a product resulting from refining crude oil, refining upgraded heavy crude oil, refining gases or liquids derived from coal or refining a synthetic equivalent of crude oil; and
   (b) production from a forestry resource is primary production therefrom if it consists of sawlogs, poles, lumber, wood chips, sawdust or any other primary wood product, or wood pulp, and is not a product manufactured from wood.

PART VII. GENERAL

52. (1) The Constitution of Canada is the supreme law of Canada, and any law that is inconsistent with the provisions of the Constitution is, to the extent of the inconsistency, of no force or effect.
    (2) The Constitution of Canada includes

    (a) the *Canada Act* 1982, including this Act;
    (b) the Acts and orders referred to in the schedule; and
    (c) any amendment to any Act or order referred to in paragraph (a) or (b).

(3) Amendments to the Constitution of Canada shall be made only in accordance with the authority contained in the Constitution of Canada.

Amendments to Constitution of Canada

53. (1) The enactments referred to in Column I of the schedule are hereby repealed or amended to the extent indicated in Column II thereof and, unless repealed, shall continue as law in Canada under the names set out in Column III thereof.

Repeals and new names

(2) Every enactment, except the Canada Act 1982, that refers to an enactment referred to in the schedule by the name in Column I thereof is hereby amended by substituting for that name the corresponding name in Column III thereof, and any British North America Act not referred to in the schedule may be cited as the Constitution Act followed by the year and number, if any, of its enactment.

Consequential amendments

54. Part IV is repealed on the day that is one year after this Part comes into force and this section may be repealed and this Act renumbered, consequentially upon the repeal of Part IV and this section, by proclamation issued by the Governor General under the Great Seal of Canada.

Repeal and consequential amendments

54. 1 Part IV.1 and this section are repealed on April 18, 1987.

[Note: Added by the Constitution Amendment Proclamation, 1983.]

55. A French version of the portions of the Constitution of Canada referred to in the schedule shall be prepared by the Minister of Justice of Canada as expeditiously as possible and, when any portion thereof sufficient to warrant action being taken has been so prepared, it shall be put forward for enactment by proclamation issued by the Governor General under the Great Seal of Canada pursuant to the procedure then applicable to an amendment of the same provisions of the Constitution of Canada.

French version of Constitution of Canada

56. Where any portion of the Constitution of Canada has been or is enacted in English and French or where a French version of any portion of the Constitution is enacted pursuant to section 55, the English and French versions of that portion of the Constitution are equally authoritative.

English and French versions of certain constitutional texts

57. The English and French versions of this Act are equally authoritative.

English and French versions of this Act

58. Subject to section 59, this Act shall come into force on a day to be fixed by proclamation issued by the Queen or the Governor General under the Great Seal of Canada.

59. (1) Paragraph 23(1)(a) shall come into force in respect of Quebec on a day to be fixed by proclamation issued by the Queen or the Governor General under the Great Seal of Canada.

Commencement

(2) A proclamation under subsection (1) shall be issued only where authorized by the legislative assembly or government of Quebec.

Commencement
of paragraph
23(1) (A) in
respect of
Quebec
Authorization of
Quebec

Repeal of this
section

Short title and
citations

(3) This section may be repealed on the day paragraph 23(1)(a) comes into force in respect of Quebec and this Act amended and renumbered, consequentially upon the repeal of this section, by proclamation issued by the Queen or the Governor General under the Great Seal of Canada.

60. This Act may be cited as the Constitution Act, 1982, and the Constitution Acts 1867 to 1975 (No. 2) and this Act may be cited together as the *Constitution Acts*, 1867 to 1982.

61. A reference to the "*Constitution Acts*, 1867 to 1982" shall be deemed to include a reference to the "*Constitutional Amendment Proclamation*, 1983."

GLOSSARY

Aboriginal self-government. A demand by Aboriginal groups that they be able to govern themselves. Aboriginals also want recognition that the right is inherent (in their having been here first), and not a gift of the current occupants of their land. (pp. 75, 409)

Aboriginal title. The Aboriginal claim to land on the basis of traditional occupancy and use rather than treaty, as recognized in the 1973 Calder case and defined in the 1997 Delgamuukw case. (p. 75)

Absent mandate. The notion that governments come to power without a clear-cut policy mandate. (p. 353)

Access to Information Act. The 1983 act that gave citizens, journalists, and others the right to gain access to government documents, with certain exceptions, and established the office of Information Commissioner. (p. 563)

Act of Union. The 1840 act that united the colonies of Upper and Lower Canada into the colony of Canada, partly designed to assimilate the French. (pp. 24, 97)

Administrative agencies. Government agencies established to administer a politically sensitive area of public policy and that operate at arm's length from the Cabinet. (p. 558)

Advocacy advertising. Advertising that advocates a political point of view rather than trying to sell a good or service. (pp. 260, 379)

Advocacy, interest, or pressure group. Any group seeking to influence government policy without contesting elections; organizations whose members act together to influence public policy in order to promote their common interest. (pp. 7, 365)

Affirmative action. A law or program that gives preference to individuals with certain characteristics in the hiring or promotion process. (pp. 146, 468, 553)

Agenda-setting. Determining the principal items on the political agenda of the state, usually associated with the mass media. (pp. 8, 262, 308, 366)

Agreement on Internal Trade. A federal–provincial agreement signed in 1995 in which provinces promised to remove preferences for local individuals and companies and other barriers to the free movement of goods, services, and people across provincial borders. (p. 439)

Assembly of First Nations. The largest advocacy group representing status Indians, who now prefer to be called First Nations peoples. (pp. 83, 369)

Asymmetrical federalism. An approach to federal–provincial relations in which Ottawa is open to treating provinces differently from each other. (pp. 112, 422)

Atlantic Canada Opportunities Agency (ACOA). The federal agency that seeks to reduce regional economic disparities in the Atlantic region primarily through grants and loans to private firms. (p. 60)

Auditor General. The official of Parliament whose staff audits the expenditures of government departments and who provides periodic reports on instances of funds being unlawfully or unwisely spent. (pp. 562, 587)

Authority. A type of power based on legitimacy; the subject regards the decision-maker as having a right to make a decision. (p. 4)

Auto Pact. The 1965 bilateral Canada–U.S. agreement under which automobiles and auto parts flowed across the border duty free as long as the value of purchases equalled that of production in each country. (p. 217)

Backbenchers. Members of Parliament on the government side who sit on the backbenches and are not in the Cabinet, or those similarly distant from important posts in opposition parties. (p. 570)

Bandwagon effect. The notion that, if and when they know which party or candidate is going to win the election, voters will move en masse in that direction. (p. 275)

Bill 22. The 1974 language law passed by Quebec that sought to enhance the status of the French language in that province and, among other things, required that immigrant children go to French-language schools unless they could already speak English. (p. 104)

Bill 101. The 1977 Quebec language law that sought to make French the official language of Quebec and put restrictions on the use of English in the courts, schools, and private sector. For example, all commercial signs had to be in French only. (pp. 105, 459)

Block grant. A federal–provincial grant that is given for a specific purpose, such as postsecondary education, but does not contain rigid conditions or standards. (p. 432)

Bourgeoisie. A Marxist term referring to those who own the means of production, otherwise known as the corporate elite. (p. 159)

British North America (BNA) Act, 1867. The act of the British Parliament that created Canada by combining Ontario, Quebec, Nova Scotia, and New Brunswick and that also provided some of the essential elements of the new country's Constitution; renamed the Constitution Act, 1867, in 1982. (pp. 25, 394, 423)

Broker or brokerage. A kind of party system in which political parties try to appeal to many different interests and "broker" compromises among them, rather than having any distinct ideology. (p. 316)

Budget. The annual financial statement of the government usually issued in the early spring by the minister of finance that introduces tax changes and gives an overview of government spending for the next fiscal year. (pp. 527, 573)

Business Council of Canada (BCC). The most powerful peak business pressure group in Canada, representing the 150 largest firms in the country, formerly known as the Canadian Council of Chief Executives (CCCE). (pp. 165, 365)

Cabinet government. A system of government in which the major political decisions are made by the Cabinet as a whole, as opposed to one in which the prime minister acts with considerable autonomy. (p. 517)

Cabinet secrecy. A convention that Cabinet and Cabinet committee meetings are held behind closed doors and that all documents and discussions relating thereto are strictly confidential. (p. 528)

Cabinet solidarity. A convention that all Cabinet ministers publicly support whatever decisions the Cabinet has taken, whatever their personal views. (p. 527)

Canada Act. The 1982 act passed by Britain that terminated all British authority over Canada and under which Canada passed the Constitution Act, 1982, with a domestic constitutional amending formula. (p. 396)

Canada Clause. The clause in the 1992 Charlottetown Accord that attempted to define the fundamental characteristics of Canada. (pp. 248, 409)

Canada Council for the Arts. The government agency established in 1957 as the Canada Council to provide financial support to all aspects of the artistic community. (p. 228)

Canada Elections Act. The act that governs all aspects of federal elections. (p. 291)

Canada Health Act. The 1984 act that re-imposed conditions on federal block grants to the provinces for health programs, especially to prevent extra-billing or other moves toward a profit-oriented, two-tier health system. (p. 433)

Canada Health and Social Transfer (CHST). The annual federal block grant to the provinces that replaced the Canada Assistance Plan and Established Program Funding (health insurance and postsecondary education) after 1996–97, later split into two parts. (pp. 177, 433)

Canada–U.S. Free Trade Agreement. The agreement signed by Canada and the United States that came into effect in 1989 and that gradually eliminated tariffs between the two countries and otherwise prohibited governments from interfering in the private marketplace. (pp. 218, 313)

Canadian Bill of Rights. An act of the Canadian Parliament passed in 1960 that outlined the basic civil liberties of Canadians but whose defects caused judicial confusion and limited the bill's effectiveness. (p. 456)

Canadian Broadcasting Corporation (CBC). The large, national Crown corporation (including its French equivalent, Radio-Canada) with radio and television arms whose mandate is to promote meaningful communication among all parts of the country. (pp. 46, 224, 264)

Canadian Federation of Students. The largest advocacy group for post-secondary students in Canada. (p. 365)

Canadian Judicial Council. An agency composed of the federal and provincial chief justices that disciplines federally appointed judges and otherwise provides leadership and coordination among federal and provincial judicial systems. (p. 629)

Canadian Labour Congress (CLC). The largest labour advocacy group in Canada; the political voice of about three million union members. (pp. 171, 369)

Canadian Radio-television and Telecommunications Commission (CRTC). The regulatory agency established to police the communications industry, including radio, television, telephones, and telecommunications. (pp. 46, 225, 264, 559)

Canadian Wheat Board. A federal Crown corporation established to help grain farmers market their product in an aggressive way and to provide equitable returns to producers. (pp. 57, 187, 320, 558)

Central agencies. Government agencies, such as the PMO, the PCO, the Treasury Board Secretariat, and the Department of Finance, that have certain coordinating functions across the whole federal public service and that prevent individual departments from acting with too much autonomy. (p. 533)

Charlottetown Accord. The constitutional agreement of 1992 that responded to Quebec's demands for distinct society status, Aboriginal demands for self-government, and the West's demand for a Triple-E Senate that was approved by federal, provincial, territorial, and Aboriginal leaders, but then turned down in a national referendum. (pp. 79, 108, 313, 409, 439)

Charter of Rights and Freedoms. That part of the Constitution Act, 1982, that guaranteed fundamental freedoms and rights (legal, democratic, linguistic, mobility, egalitarian, and limited Aboriginal) to individual Canadian citizens. (pp. 32, 106, 128, 147, 313, 397, 457, 516, 563, 570, 613)

Chief electoral officer. The independent and impartial official who is in charge of the operation of the whole electoral system. (p. 287)

Civil law. A branch of the law dealing with relations between private parties, such as individuals and corporations, which do not involve government. (p. 614)

Civil liberties. Liberties or freedoms, including the fundamental freedoms of speech, press, religion, and assembly, that citizens enjoy and that cannot be infringed or encroached upon by government. (p. 453)

Clarity Act. The Act sponsored by Prime Minister Chrétien in 2000 that fleshed out the Supreme Court decision on Quebec separation and requires federal government approval for the question asked. (pp. 108, 414)

Class-based parties. Political parties that appeal to a single socioeconomic class or ideology; when all parties do so, they constitute a class-based party system. (p. 317)

Class-consciousness. An awareness of the social class to which one belongs, which is notoriously lacking in the case of most working-class Canadians. (pp. 160, 351)

Cleavages. Deep divisions in society (based on ethnicity, region, religion, etc.) which have important implications for the political system. (pp. 8, 39, 183)

Clerk of the Privy Council and Secretary to the Cabinet. The head of the Privy Council Office and head of the federal public service; the chief nonpartisan adviser to the prime minister and Cabinet. (p. 534)

Clientele relationship. The intimate and mutually advantageous relationship that sometimes develops between a government department or agency and the advocacy group with which it most frequently interacts. (pp. 376, 555)

Closure. A rule in the House of Commons in which a Cabinet minister introduces a motion to cut off debate. (p. 581)

Code Civil du Québec. The unique system of civil law used in Quebec and based on the Napoleonic Code. (p. 615)

Coercion. Power based on authorized physical force (including police, armed forces, jails, etc.) on which government has a near monopoly. Also used by class analysts as a term for what government does (at the behest of the corporate elite) when the state cannot otherwise get the public to accept its decisions. (pp. 4, 159)

Collective responsibility. A convention holding that all Cabinet ministers are collectively responsible for government policy. (p. 527)

Collectivism. An ideology holding that the public interest is enhanced by substantial collective action, normally via government, as opposed to individualism, which minimizes the role of government. (pp. 242, 319)

Colonialism. Domination or control by one state over a dependent territory or people. (pp. 35, 69)

Commissioner for Federal Judicial Affairs. The official in charge of coordinating the process for the appointment of those judges who fall under the federal minister of Justice. (p. 624)

Common law. The basis of the British and Canadian legal systems, apart from the civil law system in Quebec, which consists of the accumulation of judicial precedents and seeks out the previous decisions in cases most closely resembling the one at hand. (p. 612)

Comprehensive claims. Aboriginal land claims based on Aboriginal title—that is, traditional use and occupancy—rather than on treaties or other legal documents. (p. 76)

Concurrent powers. Powers officially shared by the federal and provincial governments, which in the Constitution Act, 1867, were agriculture, immigration, and, later, old age pensions. (p. 423)

Conditional grant. A federal grant to the provinces, usually in support of a subject within provincial jurisdiction, to which Ottawa attaches conditions or standards before the province receives the money. (p. 430)

Confederation Settlement. The deal made among the Fathers of Confederation that entailed setting up a new federal system of government with a division of powers, a division of financial powers, federal controls over the provinces, provincial representation in federal institutions, and certain cultural guarantees. (p. 423)

Conscription crises. Two political crises in Canada, one in each world war, in which the population and government were divided, largely on French–English lines, over the necessity of compulsory military service. (pp. 99, 312)

Conservatism. A political ideology generally characterized by a belief in individualism and a minimum of government intervention in the economy and society, as well as by tradition, elitism, and opposition to change. (p. 318)

Constitution. The whole body of rules and principles according to which the state is governed that, in the Canadian case, consists of a conglomeration of documents and conventions. (pp. 35, 393)

Constitution Act, 1867. The new name (changed in 1982) for the British North America Act, 1867. (pp. 25, 97, 189, 394, 423, 515, 571)

Constitution Act, 1982. A major amendment to the Canadian Constitution that added a Charter of Rights and Freedoms, an amending formula, clauses on equalization and Aboriginal rights, and a change to the division of powers with respect to natural resources. (pp. 35, 106, 396, 426, 457)

Constitutional Act of 1791. The British law that divided Canada into two separate colonies, Upper and Lower Canada, each with a governor, executive and legislative councils, and an assembly. (pp. 22, 97)

Constitutional amending formula. The process for amending the Constitution, consisting of five different parts. (p. 399)

Constitutional conventions. Unwritten rules of constitutional behaviour that are considered to be binding by and upon those who operate the Constitution, but that are not enforceable by the courts. (p. 398)

Constitutional monarchy. The official designation of the Canadian form of government, characterized by a monarch who is head of state but who rules according to the Constitution, which confides almost all governmental power into other hands. (pp. 35, 507)

Cooperative federalism. A variant of Canadian federalism, in place in the post-1945 period, in which neither level of government is subordinate to the other and in which there is an extensive degree of interaction between them. (p. 437)

Core–periphery system. A geographical term referring to population distribution in which the bulk of the people live in the core, heartland, or metropolis of the country (or province), which has political and economic domination over those living in the distant, sparsely settled periphery or hinterland. (pp. 48, 185)

Corporate elite. A synonym for "big business" or the bourgeoisie—that is, the collection of individuals who own or manage the largest corporations in the country. (p. 163)

Council of the Federation. An organization created by Quebec premier Jean Charest—an institutionalizing of the annual premiers' conference—that encourages the provinces to work together in interprovincial and especially federal–provincial relations. (p. 441)

Court Challenges Program. A program established after the adoption of the Charter of Rights and Freedoms in which the federal government helped finance those (especially francophone minorities and women) who challenged laws on the basis of the Charter, on the assumption that the costs involved would otherwise be prohibitive. (pp. 147, 379, 477, 614)

Criminal Code. A federal document that codifies most of the criminal law in the country. (p. 615)

Criminal law. That branch of the law dealing with wrongs committed against others that are considered to be offensive to society as a whole, for which the state takes the initiative to investigate, and for which perpetrators can be fined or jailed. (pp. 429, 615)

Crow rate. A subsidized rail freight rate for Western goods, named after the Crow's Nest Pass, which was established in 1897, reduced in the 1970s, and eliminated in 1995. (p. 54)

Crown. The collectivity of executive powers exercised by or in the name of the monarch. (pp. 36, 507)

Crown corporation. A corporation owned by the government that assumes a structure similar to that of a private company and that operates semi-independently of the Cabinet. (p. 556)

Cultural hegemony. The dominant values, beliefs, assumptions, and expectations of society, as established historically by political, economic, religious, media, or other elites. (pp. 8, 258)

Declaratory power. The power in section 92(10)(c) of the Constitution Act, 1867, under which Ottawa can declare any local work or undertaking to be for the general advantage of Canada and thereby place it under federal jurisdiction. (p. 425)

Deference to authority. A value considered to be part of the Canadian political culture in which citizens are respectful of government authority and accept its word and orders with little question. (p. 245)

Democracy. A political system characterized by popular sovereignty, political equality, political freedom, and majority rule. (pp. 36, 237)

Democratic rights. A section of the Charter of Rights and Freedoms that, among other things, guarantees the vote to every Canadian citizen. (p. 461)

Department. A kind of government organization headed by a minister who is politically accountable for its operations and a deputy minister who is in charge of its hierarchical administrative apparatus. (p. 546)

Department of Finance. The government department that has overall responsibility for the government's finances and its role in the economy and that has a powerful influence on all government policy. (pp. 536, 551)

Departmental Cabinet. A Cabinet characterized by ministers and departments that operate with substantial autonomy from the prime minister, other ministers, departments, and central agencies. (p. 528)

Dependency ratio. The proportion of the population dependent on others for financing government programs, usually referring to those under the age of 15 and over the age of 65, and expressed as a percentage of those of working age. (p. 197)

Deputy minister. The public servant who heads each government department, manages the department, and advises the minister. (p. 548)

Deregulation. A government policy that removes previous regulations, especially those affecting the corporate sector. (p. 500)

Direct taxes. A category of taxation that can be used by either level of government to extract money from the very person or corporation that is intended to pay it. (p. 424)

Disallowance. A power given to the federal government in the Constitution Act, 1867, but now long obsolete, under which the prime minister and Cabinet can disallow any provincial law. (p. 425)

Dispute-settlement mechanism. A clause in the Canada–U.S. Free Trade Agreement designed to settle such trade disputes as might arise under the treaty by means of binational panels. (p. 218)

Dissolution of Parliament. The ending of a Parliament, usually after four to five years, by calling an election, an act normally in the hands of the prime minister but that formally requires the approval of the governor general. (pp. 287, 511, 574)

Distinct society. A controversial description of Quebec, found in the Meech Lake Accord and slightly modified in the Charlottetown Accord, claiming that Quebec constituted, within Canada, a distinct society. (pp. 107, 406)

Division. A formal standing, roll-call vote in the House of Commons in which members' names are recorded in Hansard. (p. 585)

Division of powers. The distribution of legislative powers between the federal and provincial governments, largely contained in sections 91 and 92 of the Constitution Act, 1867. (pp. 31, 102, 409, 423)

Durham Report. The 1839 report by Lord Durham that recommended the union of Upper and Lower Canada and the granting of responsible government to the colony of Canada. (p. 23)

Egalitarianism. As opposed to elitism, the philosophy or practice of providing everyone with an equal amount of power and/or of treating everyone more or less equally. (pp. 246, 319)

Elite accommodation. The notion that public policies emerge from the interaction of various elites (small groups of people with a disproportionate amount of power) in society, who, sharing many socioeconomic characteristics and values, find it relatively easy to come to agreement. (pp. 12, 377)

Embedded state. The notion that the operations of the state are so extensive that they are connected to virtually every aspect of society, and that government therefore cannot act independently of societal forces. (p. 11)

Emergency doctrine. A constitutional doctrine invented by the Judicial Committee of the Privy Council that in times of national emergency the Peace, Order and Good Government clause of the 1867 Constitution Act became an emergency clause, allowing the federal government to exercise extensive temporary powers. (p. 427)

Employment equity. A policy that seeks to guarantee fairness in hiring, promotion, or remuneration, regardless of gender, ethnicity, and so on, and that may incorporate affirmative action. (pp. 128, 146, 553)

Enumerated powers. The powers of the provincial governments explicitly listed in section 92 of the Constitution Act, 1867. (p. 423)

Equality rights. A section of the Charter of Rights and Freedoms that prohibits governments from discriminating against certain categories of people. (pp. 155, 465)

Equalization payments. A large annual cash payment made by the federal government to have-not provinces to help them provide a satisfactory level of public services. (pp. 59, 434)

Estimates. The annual spending plans of government departments and agencies for the following fiscal year. (pp. 554, 573)

Evangelicalism. A term referring to the active political participation of fundamentalist Christian (usually Protestant) groups who espouse socially conservative views on such issues as abortion and homosexuality. (p. 194)

Executive federalism. A variant of cooperative federalism characterized by extensive federal–provincial interaction at the level of first ministers, departmental ministers, and deputy ministers, such as the process that produced the Meech Lake Accord. (p. 437)

Executive power. The power of the executive branch of government to administer public policies and enforce laws. (p. 5)

Exempt staff. Partisan staff hired by the prime minister and Cabinet ministers who are not subject to the rules and regulations of the regular public service appointment process. (p. 549)

Extra-parliamentary party. That part of a political party beyond its members of Parliament—that is, party members, local and national executives, and party headquarters. (p. 322)

Extraterritoriality. The ability of a state to pass laws having authority beyond its borders, especially related to the United States telling Canadian branches of U.S.-based transnational corporations with whom they can trade. (p. 213)

Federal Accountability Act. The wide-ranging Act sponsored by Stephen Harper in 2006 that dealt with party finance, lobbying, government appointments, ethics, the Auditor General, and other subjects, all designed to make the entire operation of government more accountable. (pp. 288, 384, 536, 549, 590)

Federal Court of Canada. A court established by the federal government dealing with cases involving that level of government and other specialized subjects within federal jurisdiction. (pp. 563, 618)

Federal–provincial conferences. Periodic meetings of federal and provincial officials, especially first ministers or departmental ministers, characteristic of executive federalism, often making decisions that legislatures are not allowed to change. (p. 437)

Federalism. A system of government characterized by two levels of authority (federal and provincial) and a division of powers between them, such that neither is subordinate to the other. (pp. 31, 421)

Federation of Canadian Municipalities. The organization to which all Canadian municipalities belong that functions as an advocacy group for that level of government; although not always taken seriously by federal and provincial governments, it is sometimes granted official status in the policy process. (p. 188)

Feminist. A person who believes in removing barriers to the full equality of men and women. (p. 143)

Feminization of poverty. The notion that a high proportion of people living below the poverty line are women, usually sole-parent women with children. (pp. 149, 172)

Filibuster. An organized attempt by the opposition in the House of Commons to prolong debate and delay adoption of government measures. (p. 581)

First ministers' conference. A federal–provincial conference consisting of the prime minister and provincial premiers (and sometimes territorial and Aboriginal leaders). (p. 437)

First-past-the-post. The kind of electoral system used in Canada in which the candidate with the most votes wins, regardless if it is over 50 percent; synonymous with single-member plurality system (SMP). (p. 290)

Fiscal imbalance. A claim made by some provincial governments, especially Quebec, that the federal government has greater revenues than the provinces and that the provinces have insufficient revenues to finance their responsibilities. (p. 444)

Foreign Investment Review Agency (FIRA). The agency established in the early 1970s to screen foreign investment in Canada and approve of foreign takeovers of Canadian firms; discontinued by the Mulroney government. (p. 214)

Franchise. The right to vote. (p. 290)

Francophonie. The international organization of French-speaking countries. (p. 106)

Free vote. A vote in the House of Commons (or Senate) in which members are not required to abide by the party line. (p. 578)

Front de Libération du Québec (FLQ). The terrorist wing of the Quebec separatist movement in the 1960s and 1970s. (p. 104)

Fundamental freedoms. Political freedoms—of speech, religion, press, assembly, association, and so on—that governments are not supposed to encroach on and that are guaranteed by the Charter of Rights and Freedoms. (p. 458)

Gerrymandering. An attempt to design constituency boundaries in the interests of the government party of the day in order to maximize the number of that party's seats and minimize the seats won by the opposition. (p. 285)

Globalization. The modern phenomenon characterized by nation states declining in stature and power as they give way to the demands of transnational corporations via comprehensive free trade agreements, by massive diffusion of technological change, and by worldwide corporate competition or megamergers. (pp. 49, 169, 203, 489)

Gomery Inquiry and Report. The report written by Judge John Gomery in 2005–06 who was appointed by Paul Martin to investigate the sponsorship scandal in Quebec under Jean Chrétien. (pp. 109, 384, 549)

Government. (1) The set of institutions that make and enforce collective, public decisions for a society, and (2) the group of people—the prime minister and Cabinet—and their supporters in Parliament who are currently charged to make such decisions. (pp. 5, 493, 515, 570)

Government bill. A bill introduced by a Cabinet minister on behalf of the government (prime minister and Cabinet), the kind of bill dominating discussion in the House of Commons. (p. 580)

Gray Report. The government report authored by Herb Gray in 1972 expressing concern about the extent of foreign investment in Canada and recommending a screening agency. (p. 213)

Historical approach. An approach to the study of politics that emphasizes the historical evolution of various aspects of the political system and the difficulty of reversing original arrangements. (p. 10)

Historical-Institutional approach. An approach to the study of politics that combines the historical and institutional approaches. (p. 10)

Horizontal management. The increasing involvement of a wide range of bureaucratic interests in the development of government policy. (p. 550)

Horse-race effect. The notion that election campaigns have degenerated into a "horse race" where everyone, especially the media, is concerned with which party is ahead, not with how parties would tackle serious public issues. (p. 276)

House leader. The person appointed by each party in the House of Commons to deal with counterparts in other parties with respect to scheduling Commons business. (p. 585)

Identity. How one defines oneself; which of one's characteristics one emphasizes, such as ethnicity, gender, location, religion, class, sexual orientation, etc. (pp. 8, 39, 183)

Ideological parties. Political parties that appeal to a single socioeconomic class or ideology; when all parties do so, they constitute a class-based party system. (p. 317)

Immigration Act (now the Immigration and Refugee Protection Act). The law that regulates the immigration process and determines the qualifications, categories, and, to some extent, the origins of immigrants. (p. 123)

Implied bill of rights. The notion that even before the enactment of the Canadian Bill of Rights or the Charter of Rights and Freedoms, the Constitution, especially in its preamble, contained an implied bill that protected civil liberties to some extent. (p. 455)

Indian Act. The act that has governed almost all aspects of First Nation life in Canada since the 1870s, giving extensive authority to government bureaucrats and minimal discretion to First Nations themselves. (p. 72)

Indirect taxes. A category of taxation, especially a tariff or customs duty, restricted to the federal government, in which the party that pays the tax is assumed to pass it along to some other customer. (p. 424)

Individualism. An ideology that individuals should have maximum freedom or liberty to do as they please, especially in economic terms, and that governments should not get involved in taxation, regulation, redistribution, or ownership. (pp. 242, 319)

Information Commissioner. The official of Parliament who encourages government to operate on a more open and transparent basis and makes judgments in cases where departments withhold information under the Access to Information Act. (p. 563)

Initiative. A populist device whereby a sufficient number of signatures on a petition can require the government to take some action or at least call a referendum on some issue. (p. 249)

Institutional approach. An approach to the study of politics that focuses on formal government institutions and how they affect other aspects of the political system. (p. 10)

Institutionalized Cabinet. A Cabinet characterized by collective ministerial decision-making and strong central agencies that support collective Cabinet operations. (p. 528)

Institutionalized group. A kind of advocacy group characterized by permanence, resources, government acceptance, and well-developed links with the authorities. (p. 370)

Interest group. See Advocacy, interest, or pressure group. (pp. 7, 365)

Iron law of oligarchy. A theory about political parties that they almost always come to be controlled by a small group of permanent professional politicians and officials who are in charge of policy, finance, and strategy. (p. 328)

Issue-oriented group. A kind of advocacy group that springs up around an issue and disappears once that issue has been resolved. (p. 370)

James Bay and Northern Quebec Agreement. The deal signed in 1975 by the government of Quebec and its northern Aboriginal residents that gave the latter land, cash, and hunting rights in return for surrendering land for the James Bay hydroelectric project. (p. 76)

Japanese Redress Agreement. The deal signed by the Mulroney government in 1988 to compensate Japanese Canadians for their internment and the confiscation of their property during the Second World War. (p. 128)

Joint committee. A parliamentary committee containing members from both the House of Commons and the Senate. (p. 588)

Judicial Committee of the Privy Council (JCPC). A committee of the British Parliament that functioned as Canada's final court of appeal until 1949. (pp. 35, 397, 426, 619)

Judicial discretion. The leeway inevitably bestowed on the courts when they interpret laws, even when they do not, or have no power to, overturn them. (pp. 454, 613)

Judicial independence. The constitutional principle that the courts should function independently of the rest of the government apparatus—that is, the politicians and bureaucrats—with implications for security of tenure and remuneration. (pp. 28, 629)

Judicial power. The power of the courts to interpret the law in case of conflict. (p. 5)

Judicial review. The power of the courts to overturn legislation or an action of the executive branch of government. (pp. 28, 454, 613)

Kent Royal Commission on Newspapers. The Royal Commission established in 1980 to investigate the newspaper industry after a rash of takeovers and closures in the 1970s. (p. 264)

Keynesian economics. An economic theory first enunciated by John Maynard Keynes that to promote general economic stability, government should counterbalance the private sector, spending (running deficit budgets) in periods of unemployment when the private sector doesn't spend, and taxing (running a budget surplus) in periods of inflation when the private sector is spending too much. (pp. 175, 320, 438, 488)

King–Byng dispute. The dispute in 1926 between Prime Minister Mackenzie King and Governor General Lord Byng over King's request for a dissolution of Parliament, which Byng denied. (p. 511)

Leader of the Opposition. The leader of the main opposition party in the House of Commons, normally the party with the second-largest number of seats. (p. 574)

Leadership review. A clause in the constitutions of some political parties that allows party members to review the leader's performance and to vote on whether they want a leadership convention. (p. 325)

Left. That part of the ideological spectrum that believes in equality in society and the intervention of government via such collectivist measures as taxation, regulation, redistribution, and public ownership to effect such equality. (p. 319)

Legal rights. The rights of a person suspected or accused of committing a crime, now listed in the Charter of Rights and Freedoms. (p. 462)

Legislative power. The power of the legislative branch of government to create laws and public policies. (p. 5)

Liberalism. An ideology based on a belief in the rationality of the individual and on maximizing individual freedom, liberty, and self-fulfillment. Before 1900 this was assumed to entail a minimal role for government, but post-1900 liberalism usually advocated a larger role for the state and therefore was placed on the centre-left of the spectrum. (p. 318)

Limited identities. The notion that while the overall Canadian national identity is elusive, Canadian society is made up of all sorts of more limited identities or subcultures—regional, ethnic, linguistic, and so on. (p. 249)

Lobbying. Any organized attempt to influence the authorities, now often performed by professional lobbying firms. (p. 365)

Lobbying Act. The law, originally passed in 1989 as the Lobbyists' Registration Act, that sought to have lobbyists register with a government agency and submit certain information about what they were doing to influence government. (p. 384)

Majority government. A situation in which the party in power has over 50 percent of the seats in the House of Commons. (pp. 28, 521, 592)

Majority rule. An element in the definition of democracy that in any decision-making setting involving a difference of opinion, the larger number should carry the day. (p. 241)

Marxist approach. An approach to the study of politics, based on the writings of Karl Marx, which emphasizes the conflict between the bourgeoisie and proletariat and the role of classes in shaping the nature of politics and government. (p. 13)

Massey Royal Commission. A 1951 Royal Commission that expressed concern about the future prospects of Canadian culture and recommended ways to promote and protect it. (p. 228)

Meech Lake Accord. The 1987 package of constitutional amendments intended to bring Quebec back into the constitutional fold. (pp. 107, 313, 406, 439)

Memorandum to Cabinet (MC). The formal written document that a minister submits to Cabinet seeking to initiate or change a government policy. (p. 532)

Merit system. A system of hiring or promoting public servants on the basis of their merits (education, training, experience, etc.) rather than on party preference or other considerations. (p. 552)

Ministerial responsibility. The principle that Cabinet ministers are individually responsible to the House of Commons for everything that happens in their department. (pp. 517, 547)

Minority government. A situation in which the government party has less than 50 percent of the seats in the House of Commons. (pp. 28, 521, 593)

Minority-language education rights. Rights established by the 1982 Charter of Rights and Freedoms whereby French-speaking Canadians have the right to send their children to French-language schools, wherever their numbers warrant, applying to English-speaking Canadians as well. (pp. 106, 469)

Mobility rights. A category of rights in the Charter of Rights and Freedoms guaranteeing the freedom to move from one province to another and seek employment there. (p. 462)

Multiculturalism. A policy of encouraging minority ethnocultural groups to maintain their customs and traditions, often with public financial assistance. (p. 127)

Multilateralism. The historic cornerstone of Canadian foreign policy, based on acting with other similarly minded governments and through international organizations rather than unilaterally. (p. 205)

Multi-party system. Typically European in nature, a party system characterized by many parties, without any one having a majority in the legislature. (p. 314)

National Action Committee on the Status of Women (NAC). Before its recent decline, the largest and most vocal women's advocacy group. (p. 148)

National Citizens Coalition. A right-wing advocacy group once headed by Stephen Harper that challenged limitations on third-party advertising during election campaigns. (pp. 302, 379)

National Energy Board. A regulatory agency that makes decisions relating to exports of electricity and petroleum. (pp. 84, 222, 320, 559)

National Energy Program (NEP). A 1980 initiative associated with Pierre Trudeau and designed to skim off more petroleum tax revenue for Ottawa, keep the price of petroleum below world levels, encourage conservation, and Canadianize the industry, which met with great opposition in Western Canada. (pp. 56, 222, 313, 438)

National Policy. A broad nation-building policy of John A. Macdonald unveiled in 1879 that included tariff protection for central Canadian manufacturing, massive immigration, and the construction of a national transportation system. (pp. 54, 122, 213)

Neoconservatism. An ideological term characterizing parties or politicians in the 1980s and after, who advocated reducing the role of government through privatization, deregulation, deficit cutting, and elimination of social programs. Sometimes distinguished from neoliberalism in advocating a continuing role for government to promote certain traditional social values. (pp. 321, 489)

Neoliberalism. An ideological term, generally similar to neoconservatism, characterizing parties or politicians who advocate the government's withdrawal from the economy to allow it to operate on the pre-1900 capitalist principles of laissez-faire. (pp. 169, 321, 489)

New middle class. A term from class analysis describing salaried professionals, such as teachers, public servants, nurses, and so on. (pp. 102, 160)

New Public Management (NPM). A movement within public administration after 1990 that involved downsizing government, encouraging technological change, finding new ways to provide public services, and forming partnerships with private-sector agencies. (p. 496)

News management. A variety of techniques used by politicians and governments to ensure positive media coverage. (p. 272)

Nomination. The act of becoming a candidate in an election, normally entailing being selected to represent a party at a nomination meeting and then completing official nomination forms. (pp. 289, 346)

Nonconfidence motion. A periodic motion in the House of Commons, moved by the opposition, inviting the House to demonstrate its lack of confidence in the government; if successful, such a motion would require the Cabinet's resignation or the calling of an election. (p. 594)

North American Free Trade Agreement (NAFTA). The 1994 extension of the Canada–U.S. Free Trade Agreement to Mexico. (p. 219)

Notwithstanding clause. Section 33 of the Charter of Rights and Freedoms, which allows federal or provincial governments to pass laws that violate certain sections of the Charter. (pp. 106, 147, 405, 472, 570)

Nunavut. The eastern half of the Northwest Territories, which was established as a separate Inuit territory in 1999. (pp. 52, 82)

Oakes test. The strategy outlined in the Oakes case for interpreting the reasonable limits clause of the Charter of Rights and Freedoms. (p. 458)

Official Languages Act. A law passed in 1969 giving citizens the right to deal with head offices as well as certain local offices of the federal government in either official language, and necessitating the hiring and promotion of francophone public servants. (pp. 103, 552)

One-party dominance. A party system characterized by the dominance of a single party, usually related to Conservative Party dominance before 1900 and Liberal Party dominance since. (p. 310)

Open federalism. The approach to federal–provincial relations adopted by Stephen Harper based on flexibility, decentralization, and increased federal–provincial transfers. (p. 441)

Opposition. Those members of Parliament who do not support the government of the day. (p. 570)

Opposition days. Twenty-two days per session set aside in the House of Commons for the opposition to determine the topic of debate and for the government to respond. (p. 574)

Order in Council. A formal, legal decision made by the prime minister and Cabinet (Governor in Council), including regulations and appointments. (p. 515)

Pacific scandal. A party finance scandal involving John A. Macdonald's Conservative Party and a group of businessmen who sought the contract to build the Canadian Pacific Railway. (p. 298)

Padlock Law. An infamous law passed by Premier Maurice Duplessis in Quebec in the late 1930s that allowed him to place a padlock on any building that was being used for purposes of opposing the government. (p. 455)

Parliament. Theoretically, the Queen, the House of Commons, and the Senate functioning collectively, such as in the approval of legislation, but often used to refer to the Commons alone or sometimes the Commons and Senate. (p. 570)

Parliamentary Budget Officer. An officer created under the Federal Accountability Act who serves MPs by providing independent estimates of government revenues and expenditures. (pp. 560, 593)

Parliamentary party. That wing of a political party made up of its elected members—that is, its MPs or its parliamentary caucus. (p. 322)

Parliamentary press gallery. Those members of the media who are registered to sit in the press gallery in the House of Commons and who report on its proceedings or on government in general. (pp. 271, 576)

Parliamentary privileges. Historic privileges that adhere to members of Parliament, the most important residual one being the freedom from prosecution for anything said in the Commons chamber. (p. 586)

Parliamentary secretaries. Government MPs who have been given additional responsibilities to assist a Cabinet minister. (p. 527)

Party caucus. The whole body of MPs of any party, who hold a regular weekly closed meeting, together with such senators as choose to attend, to discuss parliamentary strategy and policy. (pp. 322, 579)

Party discipline. The convention that all MPs within any party vote together on every occasion, as predetermined in the party caucus meeting, ordered by the prime minister in the case of the government party, and enforced by the party whip. (p. 576)

Party identity. A psychological attachment to a single political party that is relatively stable over time. (p. 352)

Party whip. An official of each party in the House of Commons whose function is to enforce party discipline, in part by relying on the incentives of drawing up speaking lists, committee assignments, office allocations, and official parliamentary travel plans. (p. 585)

Pay equity. An element of employment equity programs designed to ensure that all employees are paid equally for work of equal value and are not discriminated against on the basis of gender or other factors. (pp. 145, 552)

Peace, Order and Good Government clause (POGG). The opening words of section 91 of the Constitution Act, 1867, describing the residual powers of the federal government (as well as the essence of the Canadian political culture), but often misinterpreted by the courts as an emergency power only. (p. 426)

Per-vote subsidy. An annual payment made to a political party between 2004 and 2015 of approximately $2 for each vote received in the preceding federal election, designed to compensate for the loss of corporate and union contributions. (pp. 300, 338)

Persons case. The decision by the Judicial Committee of the Privy Council that determined women were persons for the purposes of appointment to the Senate. (pp. 141, 598)

Petite bourgeoisie. A Marxist term to describe self-employed professionals, affluent farmers, and those operating small businesses. (p. 160)

Pipeline debate. The heated House of Commons debate in the mid-1950s regarding the construction of the Trans-Canada Pipeline in which the Liberals treated Parliament in a particularly arrogant way. (pp. 312, 581)

Pluralist approach. An approach to the study of politics that focuses on the interaction of groups in the political system which operate on a reasonably equitable basis. (p. 13)

Policy community. The notion that government policy is made in a series of discrete and specialized clusters of government departments and agencies, advocacy groups, politicians, corporations, and interested individuals. (pp. 11, 374, 495)

Policy instruments. The devices chosen by the government to effect public policy that are commonly categorized according to the degree of intervention, intrusiveness, or coerciveness they represent. (p. 497)

Policy network. The inner core of the policy community that is directly involved in the development and implementation of a government policy. (p. 374)

Political behaviour approach. An approach to the study of politics that focuses on the behaviour of various actors in the political system, especially individuals and groups. (p. 14)

Political culture. The sum total of the politically relevant values, attitudes, beliefs, and orientations in any political system that constitute the context for government policymaking. (p. 235)

Political economy approach. An approach to the study of politics that focuses on the relationship between the state and the economy. (p. 12)

Political efficacy. The feeling that one has political influence and that one's political participation can make an impact. (p. 356)

Political equality. An element in the definition of democracy that entails the principle of "one person–one vote"—every citizen has a vote and each counts equally. (p. 239)

Political freedom. An element in the definition of democracy that entails freedom of speech, press, assembly, association, and so on, such that people can organize and advocate in order to influence election results and public policy. (p. 239)

Political participation. Those voluntary activities by citizens that are intended to influence the selection of government leaders or the decisions they make. (p. 356)

Political party. An organized group that makes nominations and contests elections in the hope of influencing the personnel and policy of government. (pp. 7, 307)

Political patronage. Making appointments to public offices or awarding government contracts on a partisan basis. (pp. 308, 551, 624)

Political psychology approach. An approach to the study of politics that focuses on the role of personality and seeks to understand why people think the way they do. (p. 14)

Political socialization. The process whereby individuals acquire their political values, attitudes, beliefs, and orientations. (p. 258)

Politics. The activity in which conflicting interests struggle for advantage or dominance in the making and execution of public policies. (p. 6)

Popular sovereignty. An element in the definition of democracy that entails periodically allowing the public at large to exert its will—to have the final say—normally through general elections. (p. 238)

Popular vote. The percentage of all votes cast won by a candidate or party, regardless of who was elected. (p. 292)

Poverty line. An amount of income such that anyone who received less would be living in poverty. (p. 172)

Power. The ability of one actor to impose its will on another to get its own way, or to do or get what it wants, usually considered to be the essence of politics and government. (p. 4)

Prerogative powers. That small residual of powers of the Crown—the Queen or governor general—that remain from the era of an all-powerful monarch and that the Crown can still exercise at its own discretion. (p. 510)

Pressure group. See Advocacy, interest, or pressure group. (pp. 7, 365)

Prime ministerial government. The notion that the prime minister is now so pre-eminent that the label "Cabinet government" no longer accurately describes how decisions are made in the political executive. (p. 517)

Prime Minister's Office (PMO). The office that supports and advises the prime minister in partisan terms. (p. 534)

Private bill. A bill introduced in Parliament that only affects a specific individual, company, organization, or group. (p. 580)

Private member's bill. A public bill introduced in the House of Commons or Senate by a member who is not in the Cabinet. (p. 576)

Private sector. The profit-oriented, nongovernmental part of the economy. (pp. 3, 496)

Privatization. Transferring a government program, agency, or Crown corporation to the private sector, such as by selling shares in a Crown corporation to the public at large or to a private firm. (p. 558)

Privy Council Office (PCO). The office that supports and advises the prime minister, Cabinet, and Cabinet committees in nonpartisan terms on such matters as overall government policy, the machinery of government, and senior bureaucratic appointments. (p. 534)

Proletariat. A Marxist term referring to those who sell their labour for an undervalued price to the bourgeoisie; the working class. (p. 159)

Province-building. The converse of "nation-building," the notion of developing strong provincial governments, especially after 1960 or so, whether through provincial bureaucracies, Crown corporations, or central planning agencies, and their capacity to intervene in the process of industrial development. (p. 440)

Public Accounts Committee. See Standing Committee on Public Accounts. (pp. 562, 587)

Public bill. A bill introduced in Parliament dealing with public policy and that affects society in general. (p. 579)

Public opinion. The sum total of opinions held by members of the public on any subject. (p. 273)

Public ownership. A policy instrument involving government purchase ("nationalization") of a private corporation or the creation of a Crown corporation. (p. 501)

Public policy. A course of action or inaction chosen by public authorities to address a given problem or interrelated set of problems. (p. 491)

Public policy purpose. The point of creating a Crown corporation or other government program or agency—that is, to achieve the objectives of a public policy or to serve some public interest. (pp. 45, 558)

Public–private partnership (P3). An administrative arrangement involving the government and one or more private firms, as an alternative to government acting alone, usually in the construction of some major structure—hospital, highway, bridge, etc. (pp. 44, 558)

Public sector. That part of the economy operated or financed by government. (pp. 3, 496)

Public Service Commission. The central personnel agency of government designed to police the merit system and ensure that partisanship is kept out of the regular public service. (p. 551)

Quasi-judicial. Court-like functions, powers, and procedures often possessed by regulatory tribunals (e.g., CRTC licence-issuing powers). (p. 559)

Quasi-legislative. Functions and powers of regulatory agencies to make law-like regulations (e.g., CRTC Canadian-content regulations). (p. 559)

Quebec Act. The British law passed in 1774 that provided for a system of government for the colony of Quebec (Canada) and that provided certain privileges to the French-speaking, Roman Catholic majority. (pp. 22, 97)

Question Period. The daily 45-minute period in the House of Commons in which opposition members spar with the prime minister and Cabinet ministers. (p. 574)

Quiet Revolution. The dramatic change of values, attitudes, and behaviour of French-Canadian Quebeckers, a new collective self-confidence, a new brand of nationalism, and an enormous expansion of the role of the provincial state that characterized Quebec in the 1960s. (pp. 101, 399, 438)

Rational choice approach. An approach to the study of politics that focuses on the behaviour of individual actors in the political system, based on a rational search to maximize their utility. (p. 14)

Reasonable limits clause. Section 1 of the Charter of Rights and Freedoms, which allows the courts to find that even though a law violates a Charter right, it is a reasonable limit on such and is therefore allowed to stand. (p. 458)

Recall. A populist device in which a certain proportion of the electorate signing a petition could cause an elected member of a legislature to resign. (p. 249)

Red Tories. A minority faction within the Canadian Progressive Conservative Party with collectivist leanings akin to many British and European conservatives, stressing order, tradition, stability, and a paternalistic concern for the condition of the working class. (p. 320)

Redistribution. The process of reallocating seats in the House of Commons among the provinces after each decennial census and then redrawing constituency boundaries within each province. (p. 284)

Reference cases. Cases referred to the courts by provincial or federal cabinets in order to obtain a ruling on their constitutionality. (p. 618)

Referendum. A populist device in which certain public policy proposals are submitted directly to the electorate. (pp. 106, 248, 278, 409)

Regional economic development programs. Government programs designed to improve employment prospects in have-not parts of the country, usually by means of giving loans or grants to companies to establish or expand operations in such areas. (p. 60)

Regulations. The detailed rules drafted by the bureaucracy under the authority of laws passed by Parliament that are too voluminous and technical to put into the legislation itself. (pp. 494, 516, 544, 588, 562)

Regulatory tribunals. Government agencies established to regulate an area of public policy, such as transportation or communications, which operate at arm's length from the Cabinet and often have quasi-legislative and/or quasi-judicial powers. (pp. 559, 618)

Representative bureaucracy. A public service that reflects the composition of the population, with the most usual concerns being gender, ethnicity, and region. (p. 552)

Representative government. A form of government including an assembly elected by the citizens, but one that does not necessarily incorporate the principle of responsible government. (p. 23)

Reservation. An obsolete power of the federally appointed lieutenant governor of each province to refrain from giving royal assent to provincial legislation and instead to send it to the federal Cabinet for its consideration. (p. 424)

Residual powers. Those powers not explicitly given to the provinces in the Constitution Act, 1867, that were assigned to the federal government under the opening words of section 91. (p. 423)

Responsible government. A form of government in which the political executive must retain the confidence of the elected legislature or assembly and must resign or call an election if and when it is defeated on a vote of nonconfidence. (pp. 23, 576)

Right. That part of the ideological spectrum that cherishes individualism and believes in leaving the private sector to operate with minimal government intervention. (p. 319)

Rowell–Sirois Commission. The Royal Commission appointed in 1937 to examine federal–provincial relations and whose 1940 report eventually led to many changes in the federal–provincial financial relationship. (p. 431)

Royal commission. An elaborate investigation set up by the Cabinet to research a significant policy problem, to listen to and educate the public, and to make recommendations to the government. (pp. 379, 498, 560)

Royal Commission on Aboriginal Peoples. The Royal Commission appointed in the wake of the defeat of the Meech Lake Accord and the Oka standoff to provide a blueprint for addressing the long-standing needs of the Aboriginal community. (p. 80)

Royal Commission on Bilingualism and Biculturalism. The Royal Commission established in reaction to the Quiet Revolution in Quebec in the 1960s that recommended official bilingualism as a way of keeping the country together. (p. 102)

Royal Commission on Electoral Reform and Party Financing. The Royal Commission established in the wake of the controversial 1988 federal election, with the objective of enhancing the democratic character of Canadian elections. (pp. 302, 344)

Royal Commission on the Status of Women. The Royal Commission that reported in 1970 and helped to inspire the women's movement in its demands for policy changes over the following decades. (p. 143)

Royal Proclamation of 1763. The British policy enunciated after Britain won Quebec from France that in a large area called Indian Territory the purchase or settlement of land was forbidden without a treaty between the Crown and the Indian people concerned. (pp. 20, 70)

Rule of law. The constitutional principle that all government action must be based on law and that governments and government officials must obey the law. (pp. 36, 454)

Rural alienation. The widespread feeling among people living in rural areas that their concerns are of little interest to the majority of urban-based politicians and policymakers. (p. 187)

Safe seats. Constituencies that a single party can be assured of winning election after election, the small number of which results in a high turnover rate in the Canadian House of Commons. (pp. 352, 572)

Sexual orientation. One's sexual preference, usually either heterosexual or homosexual, a ground on which governments and courts now prohibit discrimination. (pp. 153, 467)

Shared-cost programs. Government programs whose cost is shared by the federal and provincial governments. (p. 432)

Single-member-plurality (SMP). The kind of electoral system used in Canada in which the candidate with the most votes wins, regardless if it is over 50 percent; synonymous with first-past-the-post system. (p. 290)

Social cleavages approach. An approach to the study of politics that focuses on the various divisions within society, such as regional, ethnic, and religious. (p. 12)

Social democracy. A leftist political ideology that emphasizes the principle of equality and usually prescribes a large role for government to intervene in society and the economy via taxation, regulation, redistribution, and public ownership. (p. 318)

Social movements. An informal network of organizations and individuals who on the basis of a collective identity and shared values engage in political struggle intended to expand the boundaries of the existing system, such as the women's and environmental movements. (pp. 8, 365)

Social safety net. The conglomeration of social programs developed over the years by federal and provincial governments, individually and jointly, and designed to help those who could not otherwise care for their own basic needs or those of their family. (p. 174)

Social Union Framework Agreement (SUFA). An overall framework of federal–provincial relations, agreed to by the federal government and all provinces except Quebec in 1999, that sought to clarify where and how either level of government could act unilaterally or engage in joint programs. (p. 440)

Sovereignty. Ultimate control or independence, whether in terms of Canadian national sovereignty vis-à-vis other countries or of Quebec sovereignty vis-à-vis the federal government. (p. 107)

Sovereignty-association. The Parti Québécois proposal in which Quebec would be sovereign while maintaining an economic association with the rest of Canada. (pp. 106, 404)

Speaker. The presiding officer of the House of Commons. (p. 583)

Special committee. A committee of the House of Commons appointed for a special, temporary purpose, such as to investigate a problem before the government has prepared legislation on the subject. (p. 587)

Specific claims. Aboriginal land claims arising from the alleged nonfulfillment of Indian treaties and other lawful obligations, as opposed to those based on traditional occupancy and use. (p. 76)

Speech from the throne. The document prepared by the prime minister and Cabinet and read by the governor general at the opening of each session of Parliament outlining the government's legislative proposals for the session to follow. (pp. 516, 573)

Spending power. The unofficial power of the federal government to spend money on any subject, including those within provincial jurisdiction, and even to attach conditions to such grants to the provinces. (pp. 432, 499)

Spin doctors. Party officials and ministerial aides who talk to the media and try to influence media coverage by putting the best face on an event from their party's point of view. (pp. 272, 345)

Split-run magazines. American magazines directed at Canadians by adding a minimal amount of Canadian editorial material and a maximum number of Canadian advertisements. (p. 226)

Spoils system. Hiring public servants on the basis of political partisanship. (p. 551)

Stakeholders. Those individuals, groups, corporations, or other organizations who have a stake in any issue; the principal players involved in any policy community. (pp. 496, 532)

Standing committee. A committee of the House of Commons set up semi-permanently and often parallel to a government department. (p. 587)

Standing Committee on Public Accounts. The House of Commons committee that examines the Auditor General's Report and criticizes government officials for illegal or unwise expenditures. (p. 587)

Standing Joint Committee on Scrutiny of Regulations. The joint parliamentary committee appointed to wade through the voluminous regulations issued by government departments under the authority of legislation and that has the power to recommend rescinding such regulations. (pp. 495, 562, 588)

Standing Orders. The written rules of the House of Commons. (p. 584)

Staples theory. The notion that Canadian economic development has gone through a series of stages based on the exploitation and export of one natural resource or another without the development of a secondary or tertiary sector. (p. 48)

Stare decisis. The legal principle that judicial precedents are binding on similar subsequent cases, which forms the basis of the common law system. (p. 612)

State-based approach. An approach to the study of politics that emphasizes the dominance of state authorities in the political system and their autonomy of action from the rest of society. (p. 11)

State of emergency. A policy instrument that involves the greatest degree of intrusion and coercion on the part of the state, now based on the Emergencies Act rather than the War Measures Act. (p. 501)

Status Indians. Those Aboriginal Canadians registered with the federal government according to the terms of the Indian Act who have not had their status removed for any reason, or those who have regained it. (p. 72)

Statute of Westminster. The 1931 British law that declared Canada and the other Dominions to be fully independent. (pp. 34, 395)

Subcultures. Clusters of people who share basic political values and attitudes based on common regional, ethnic, class, or other characteristics. (p. 249)

Supremacy of Parliament. The principle that no other organ of government can overrule Parliament or its laws, a principle modified to some extent in 1982 with an expanded power of judicial review incorporated in the Charter of Rights and Freedoms. (pp. 27, 570, 613)

Supreme Court Act. The 1875 law of the Canadian Parliament that provided for the Supreme Court of Canada and that serves as a legal base for the institution in the absence of further constitutional entrenchment. (pp. 396, 620)

Tariff. A federal tax placed on imports that raises revenue for Ottawa and protects domestic manufacturers by making imported goods more expensive to buy. (p. 54)

Tax expenditures. A policy instrument that provides a tax credit or tax deduction if taxpayers spend money in a desired way. (p. 498)

Taxation agreements. Federal–provincial agreements, especially with respect to personal and corporate income taxes since 1945, under which Ottawa collects the taxes if provinces use a similar base for calculating their portion of the tax. (p. 431)

Terrorism. An act intended to cause death or serious bodily harm to civilians with the purpose of intimidating a population or compelling a government to do or abstain from doing any act. (pp. 207, 465)

Third-party advertising. Advertising by advocacy groups, as opposed to political parties, during an election campaign. (pp. 301, 379)

Three-party system. A party system characterized by three main parties, all with approximately similar levels of support, as in Canada during the 1980s. (p. 313)

Trade and Commerce clause. Subsection 2 of section 91 of the Constitution Act, 1867, which was intended to provide a broad base for federal jurisdiction in this field but which was whittled away by judicial interpretation. (p. 429)

Transnational corporations. Corporations operating simultaneously in many countries throughout the world that often take orders from company headquarters and that individual states find difficult to control. (p. 206)

Treasury Board. A Cabinet committee whose primary responsibility is to restrain government spending. (p. 533)

Treasury Board Secretariat. The government department that advises the Treasury Board in its deliberations, that functions as a restraining influence on departmental spending, and has general authority over the operations of the public service. (pp. 536, 551)

Treaty power. Section 132 of the Constitution Act, 1867, which speaks of Empire treaties and was intended to provide the federal government with a broad power to sign and implement treaties, but whose scope was limited by judicial interpretation. (p. 429)

Triple-E Senate. A proposal for Senate reform in which each province would have an equal number of senators, who would be elected and who would be given effective powers. (pp. 409, 604)

Two-party system. A type of party system in which two main parties are of approximately equal strength and alternate in office, as in Canada between 1896 and 1921. (p. 310)

Two-plus or two-and-a-half party system. A type of party system in which two main parties are of approximately equal strength and alternate in office, but which are accompanied by one or more minor parties of significant strength, as in Canada between 1921 and 1980. (p. 310)

Union Government. The coalition government from 1917 to the end of the First World War made up of Conservatives and English-speaking Liberals whose aim was to maintain national unity while enforcing conscription and conducting the war in a vigorous manner. (pp. 99, 310)

Victoria Charter. The 1971 package of constitutional amendments including an amending formula, a charter of rights, and provisions designed to respond to demands emanating from the Quiet Revolution in Quebec. (p. 403)

Visible minorities. Members of minority ethnocultural groups, other than Aboriginals, whose skin colour is not white. (p. 119)

Voluntary sector. The non-profit sector of the economy, as opposed to the public sector (government) and the profit-oriented private sector. (pp. 3, 374, 496)

Voters' list. The list of eligible voters now called the National Register of Electors and maintained on a permanent basis. (p. 288)

Wage and price controls. A controversial proposal put forward by the Conservatives in the 1974 election campaign to put a cap on wage and price increases to reduce inflationary pressures. (p. 320)

War Measures Act. The law invoked during both world wars and during the 1970 FLQ crisis under which the federal Cabinet was given emergency powers to deal with a crisis; later replaced by the Emergencies Act. (pp. 104, 501)

Welfare state. The characterization of most Western democracies from about 1950 to 1985 in which governments functioned as provider and protector of individual security and well-being through the implementation of a wide array of social programs and income transfers to individuals. (p. 174, 320, 432, 489)

Western alienation. The feeling shared by many Western Canadians that their interests are not taken seriously in the national policymaking process. (p. 62, 250)

Westminster model. The model of government developed in Britain in which the political executive is given extensive power to provide effective leadership. (p. 27, 569)

White Paper on Indians. The 1969 Trudeau–Chrétien policy proposal to do away with the Indian Act and fully integrate Aboriginals into Canadian society. (p. 74)

Women's movement. The collection of women's groups that mushroomed across the country starting about 1970 and demanding complete equality for women. (p. 143)

World Trade Organization (WTO). An international organization to which Canada and most other countries belong that has the power to disallow national policies and practices that it deems discriminatory against companies from other states. (p. 205)

INDEX

Note: The letters B, F, P, and T following page numbers refer to boxes, figures, pictures, and tables, respectively. Bold page numbers refer to defined terms.

Canadian Association of Petroleum Producers, 365, 380
Canadian Association of Retired Persons, 200
Canadian Association of University Teachers, 365
Canadian Bankers Association, 374
Canadian Bar Association (CBA), 369, 377, 381, 614
Canadian Bill of Rights, 454, **456,** 457, 613
Canadian Broadcasting Corporation (CBC), **46, 224**–25, **264,** 265, 276, 340, 495, 501
Canadian Business magazine, 163
Canadian Cattlemen's Association, 369
Canadian Centre for Policy Alternatives (CCPA), 261, 372, 555
Canadian Chamber of Commerce (CCC), 368, 373, 378, 381
Canadian Citizenship Act, 35
Canadian Civil Liberties Association, 370
Canadian Conference of Catholic Bishops, 369
Canadian Constitution, **35**
  amendments to the Constitution Act, 1867, 395
  British statutes and orders in council, 395–96
  Charter of Rights, 401–2
  components of, 394–98
  Constitution Act, 1867, 394–95, 395B
  Constitution Act, 1982, 396–97
  constitutional conventions, 398
  judicial decisions, 397–98
  organic Canadian statutes, 396
Canadian Construction Association, 376
Canadian Council of Chief Executives (CCCE) **165, 365,** 368

Canadian Council of Churches, 369
Canadian Council on Social Development (CCSD), 173, 174B, 187, 369, 370, 377
Canadian Criminal Code, 462
Canadian Democracy and Corporate Accountability Commission, 165
Canadian Election Survey, 269
Canadian Ethnocultural Council, 129
Canadian Federation of Agriculture (CFA), 376, 377
Canadian Federation of Independent Business (CFIB), 368
Canadian Federation of Students (CFS), **365,** 372, 380, 381
Canadian Firearms Registry, 558
Canadian Food Inspection Agency, 559–60
Canadian Generic Pharmaceutical Association, 379
Canadian Heritage department, 495
Canadian Human Rights Act, 396
Canadian Human Rights Commission, 128, 151, 553
Canadian International Council, 261
Canadian Islamic Congress, 195
Canadian Jewish Congress, 369
Canadian Judicial Council, **629,** 630, 631
Canadian Labour Congress (CLC), **171,** 223B, 260, 369, 372, 373, 379, 381
Canadian Manufacturers and Exporters (CME), 368
Canadian Medical Association (CMA), 260, 369, 373, 376, 377, 379, 381
Canadian Multiculturalism Act, 128
Canadian National, 501
Canadian Nuclear Association, 379
Canadian Nuclear Safety Commission, 214, 558

Canadian Pacific Railway (CPR), 44
Canadian Pensioners Concerned, 200
Canadian Poverty Fact Book, 172
Canadian Radio-television and Telecommunications Commission (CRTC), **46, 225, 264,** 265, 266, 495, 500, 516, **559**
Canadian Reform Conservative Alliance. *See* Canadian Alliance
Canadian Security Intelligence Service (CSIS), 560, 600, 618
The Canadian Senate: A Lobby from Within (Campbell), 599
Canadian Shield, 50
Canadian sovereignty, 32–35
Canadian Tax Foundation, 374, 555
Canadian Television Fund, 225
Canadian television stations, 266
Canadian Tire, 331
Canadian Tobacco Manufacturers' Council, 376, 601
Canadian Transportation Agency, 45, 214–15, 495, 559
Canadian Wheat Board, **57, 187, 320, 558**
candidate advertising, **343**
candidates, 338, 341
canvass organizer, 348
"cap and trade" system, 166
capital punishment, 277
carbon tax, 166
Carter v. Canada, 463
Cartier, George-Étienne, 523
Carty, Ken, 309, 331
Casgrain, Thérèse, 139
"catch-all" parties, 308
categories of laws, 614–15
Catholic Women's League, 260
caucus meetings, 579
caution, 247–48
CBC News Network, 270, **320**
CBC radio, 227
CBC/Radio-Canada, 264, 265
CBC-TV, 266
CCF/NDP, 176, 194, 319, 320
C.D. Howe Institute, 261, 555

census metropolitan areas (CMAs), 185

central agencies, **533**–36, 550–51
  Department of Finance, 536
  Prime Minister's Office (PMO), 534
  Privy Council Office, 534–36
  Treasury Board Secretariat (TBS), 536

chain ownership of newspaper, 263T

Charest, Jean, 108, 112, 144, 194, 414, 441

Charkaoui case, 465B

Charlottetown Accord, 393, 399, 408–**9, 439,** 604
  Aboriginal self-government, 409B
  Canada clause, 409B
  division of powers, 409B
  main provisions of, 409B
  results of the national referendum on, 410T
  Triple-E Senate, 409B

Charlottetown Accord (1992), **108,** 112, 148, 248, **313**
  Aboriginal provisions, **79**
  Referendum, 249

Charlottetown Conference (1864), 25

Charter of Rights and Freedoms (1982), **32, 106, 128, 147,** 164, 187, 229, 235, 238, 249, 286, **313,** 379, **397,** 401–2, **457**–71, **516, 563, 570, 613**
  application of, 471–72
  Cabinet, 516
  civil liberties and, 453
  courts *vs.* legislatures, 474T
  criticism from right and left, 475–77
  decisions, 468B
  defining and protecting rights and freedoms, 454
  democratic rights, 461–62
  dialogue between legislatures and courts, 477
  enforcement, 470
  en route to the charter, 455–57
  equality rights, 465–68
  franchise, 291

freedom of association, 171
fundamental freedoms, 458–61
gender equality, 246
general provisions, 470–71
implications of constitutionalizing, 473–77
increased role of courts, 249
legal rights, 462–65
minority-language education rights, 469
mobility rights, 462
notwithstanding clause, 240, 472
official languages of Canada, 469
other provisions, 470–71
preamble, 237
reasonable limits clause, 458
terrorism and, 465B–466B

Charter of the French Language (*Charte de la langue française*), 105

Charting the Consequences: The Impact of Charter Rights on Canadian Law and Politics, 476

checks and balances of the U.S. system, 29, 29F

chief electoral officer, **287**

chief executive officers (CEOs), 163

child care, 446

childhood development, early, 446

child poverty, 172

Child Tax Benefit, 440

China, 204, 215–16

Chinese Immigration Act of 1923, 124

Chong, Michael, 528, 579, 596

Chrétien, Jean, 106, 145, 155, 261, 289, 315, 326, 339, 343, 347, 405, 445, 489, 519–20, 523, 530, 578, 602

Chrétien government, 277, 381
  Aboriginal issues, 79–83
  "constitutional federalism," 403–4
  ethical problems, 299–300
  Iraq, 209
  Kyoto, 445
  lobbying under the, 383–86

Chrétien Liberals, 108, 164, 177, 411

Christian Sabbath, 459

CHT, 442

CHUM stations, 265

Churchill Falls hydroelectric project, 57

cities, federalism and, 446–47

Citizens' Forum on Canada's Future, 408

Citizenship Act, 396, 508

"citizens plus," 74, 88

civil law, **614**

civil liberties, **453**
  violations of, 456

Civil Service Act, 552

Civil Service Amendment Act, 552

Civil Service Commission, 552. *See also* Public Service Commission

"civil society," **3,** 142, 365

civil union, 155

Clarity Act, **108, 414,** 440, 519, 582

Clark, Christy, 152

Clark, Joe, 192, 313, 321, 408, 531, 599

Clarke, John, 177–78

Clarkson, Adrienne, 145, 513

Clarkson, Stephen, 223

class analysis
  collectivist values, 251B
  divisions in Canada, 161–62
  elections, 301B
  on environment, 223B
  on media, 272B
  middle, 166–68
  objective, 161
  poor, 172–73
  subjective, 161
  theoretical considerations, 159–61
  upper, 163–66
  working, 168–71

class approach, **13**
  to advocacy groups, 371B

class-based parties, **317**–18

class cleavage, 316

class-consciousness, **160,** 317, **351**

classical federalism, 436

class subcultures, 251

economy, 48–53, 223, 353–54
"e-democracy," 249
egalitarianism, 246, **319**
Egan case, 153
election campaign, 337, 345–46
  issues in, 353–54
election platform, 308, 339–40
Elections Act, 341
election strategy, 339
Electoral Boundaries
    Readjustment Act, 285–86
"electoralist" parties, 308
electoral map, 284–86
electoral participation, 356–58
electoral system, 292–97
  conduct, 283
  controversies about the 2011,
    291
  controversies about the 2015,
    291
  election day, 289–90
  election officials, 287–88
  financing, 298–302
  theoretical considerations,
    283–84
elite accommodation, **12,** 251B,
    377
Elizabeth II, 416, 509
embedded state, **11**
Emergencies Act, 272, 396, 501
emergency doctrine, **427**
emergency federalism, 436–37
Emerson, David, 189
empirical beliefs, 3
employment, 49F, 423T
Employment and Social Insurance
    Act, 175
employment equity, **146, 553**
Employment Equity Act, 119,
    128, 146, 553
employment equity groups
  public service by, 553T
"Employment Insurance" (EI), 60,
    130, 170–71, 173
Employment Insurance Act, 429,
    618
enforcement, 470
"enfranchisement" in Indian Act,
    72
English as a second language, 108
English common law, **612**
enumerated powers, **423**

environment, 166, 221–22, 322
  as a case study, 502–4
  federalism in the 21st century
    and, 445
"environmental protection," 445
"equality of cause," 139
"equality of opportunity," 320
equality rights, **155, 465**–68
equalization payments, **59,** 433,
    434, 443–44
equal pay legislation, 141
Erasmus, Georges, 77
Established Programs Financing
    Act, 432
Estimates, **573**–74
Estimates of Health Canada, 587
Estimates system, 554, **554**
ethnic cleavages, 114
ethnic groups, 120T
ethnic/linguistic conflicts, 98–99
ethnic subcultures, 250–51
ethnocultural issues, 129–33
ethnocultural minorities, 119–21
European countries overfishing,
    204
European Union, 204, 217
evangelical Christians, 192, 194,
    260
evangelicalism, **194**
"evil empires," 245
exceptional financial crisis, 146
Exchequer Court, 618
Excise Tax Act, 618
executive federalism, **437**
executive power, **5**
exempt staff, **549**
exhortation, 498
expression, freedom of, 459–60
extinguishment clause in treaties,
    71
extra-parliamentary party
    organization, **322**
extraterritoriality, **213**

Facebook, 269
Fairclough, Ellen, 141
Fair Rail for Grain Farmers Act,
    54–55
"false consciousness," 161
"false majority," 292
family, 258
Family Allowances Act, 141, 175

Farm Credit Canada, 501
farmers, 187, 311
Fathers of Confederation, 29, 423,
    615, 617
Federal Accountability Act, **288,**
    300, **384, 536, 549,** 565,
    582, **590,** 602
federal controls, 435–36
Federal Court Act, 396
Federal Court of Canada, 131,
    563, 611, **618**
  functions of, 617B
Federal Economic Development
    Initiative in Northern
    Ontario (FedNor), 60
Federal Election Finance Law, 299
federal government, 26
federalism, **421**
  in the 21st century, 441–48
  during 1867–1945, 436–37
  during 1945–2000, 437–40
  asymmetrical, **422,** 440
  Canadian and American,
    29–32
  classical, 436
  collaborative, 441
  competitive, 438
  Confederation Settlement,
    423–25, 424B
  cooperative, **437**
  definition, **31**
  division of powers, 426–30
  emergency, 436–37
  evolution
  evolution of, 426–36
  executive, **437**
  federal, provincial/territorial,
    and municipal
    employment, 2012, 423T
  federal controls, 435–36
  federal–provincial finance,
    430–35, 434T
  intrastate, 425
  open, **441**
  phases of, 436–48
  symmetrical, 422
federalism in the 21st century
  Aboriginals, 445–46
  bringing in the cities, 446–47
  child care and early childhood
    development, 446
  the environment, 445

prime ministerial government, **517**

prime ministerial tenure and style, 522–36, 522T

central agencies, 533–36

composition of the Cabinet, 523–27, 526T

operation of the Cabinet, 527–33

prime ministers (1867–1921), 309

prime ministers (1921–1957), 311

prime ministers (1957–1993), 312

prime ministers (1993–), 314

prime ministers, ranked by tenure, 522T

Prime Minister's Office (PMO), 328, 529, **534**, 551

Prince Edward Island, 25, 44, 52, 59

Priorities and Planning (P&P) Committee, 529, 531–32

priority setting, policymaking process, 492F, 493

Privacy Commissioner, 563

private bills, **580**

private discrimination, prohibitions against, 454

private law, 615

private members' bills, **576**

private sector, **3, 496**

privatization, 497, **558**

privatized Crown corporations, **501**

Privy Council, 510, 515

Accountable Government: A Guide for Ministers, 518

Judicial Committee of, 598, 600, **616**

Privy Council Office (PCO), 186, 496, 517–18, 520, 529, 531, **534**–36, 548–51, 554

Machinery of Government section of, 520

Pro-Canada Network, 379

professional pollsters, 274

"programmatic" parties, 308

Progressive Conservative Party, 62, 320

prohibitions against private discrimination, 454

"proletarianized" process, 167

proletariat, **159**

proportionality of the electoral system, 292–97

proportional representation, 296

Pross, Paul, 13

prostitution, 148

Protect Our Economy, 340

"Protestant ethic," 245

province-building, 440B

provinces

autonomous, 421

and the Canada–U.S. and North American Free Trade Agreements, 313

civil liberties violation and, 457

electoral maps, 461

and external relations, 447

gross domestic product per capita, 58T

growth in health and social transfers to, 443F

jurisdiction, 447, 615

municipal governments, 188

own-source revenue, 435

political-legal-constitutional basis of, 42

population of, 47T

powers, 447, 615

public government departments and, 554–55

representation in Cabinet, 525

representation in House of Commons, 284–85, 285T, 571

role in the immigration process, 130

taxation powers, 442

provincial courts of appeal, 617–18

provincial government, 26

Provincial Nominee Program, 131

provincial/territorial subcultures, 250

public

mass media and, 269–71

perceptions of media, 269

Public Accounts Committee, **562**

public bills, **579**

public expenditures, 499, 499T

public health insurance system, 174, 175, 244

"public interest" group, 370

public issue, 3

public law, 615

public opinion, **273**–74

polling firms, 274

public opinion polls, 273–78

impact on authorities, 277–78

importance of, 275–76

measuring, 273–75

public ownership, **501**

public policy

defined, **491**

formulating, 308

purpose, **558**

public policy purpose, **45**

public–private partnerships (P3), **44, 558**

public sector, **3, 496**

public service by employment equity groups, 553T

Public Service Commission (PSC), 550, **551**. *See also* Civil Service Commission

Public Service Employment Act, 558

Public Service Modernization Act, 551

publishing, U.S. influences on, 227

Pyrcz, Greg, 9

Q, 227

"qualified persons," 141

quasi-federalism, 436

quasi-judicial decisions, **559**

quasi-legislative rules and regulations, **559**

Quebec

Bélanger–Campeau Committee report, 408

Bill 101, **459, 469**

as British colony, 99

distinct characteristics, 111–14

economy, 50

ethnic subcultures, 250–51

federalism in the 21st century and, 447–48

identity, 190

nationalism, 100

newcomers, 129

party support, 109

Quebec Act (1774), **22, 97**

Quiet Revolution in, 393, **399**, 402, **438**

seats and votes won by parties, 350–51

social program cutbacks, 320
social safety net, **174**–78
Social Sciences and Humanities
    Research Council of Canada
    (SSHRCC), 228, 560, 602
social spending, 177, 177B
social structures, 137
Social Union Framework
    Agreement (SUFA), **440**
Société des acadiens et
    acadiennes du Nouveau-
    Brunswick, 111
Société franco-manitobaine, 111
sociodemographic bases of party
    support, 349–52
softwood lumber dispute, 219
"solidary benefits," 323
Sona, Michael, 291
sound recordings, U.S. influences
    on, 227
Southam Inc., 464
Southam newspaper chain, 263,
    276
sovereignty, **107,** 352
sovereignty-association, **106, 404**
Spadina Expressway, 370
Sparrow case, 78
Speaker, **583**–84
special committees, **587**
specific claims, **76**
Specific Claims Tribunal Act, 86
"spectators," 358
"spectrum scarcity," 266
speeches, 586
speech from the throne, **516, 573**
spending power, **432, 499**
spin doctors, **272, 345**
"sponsorship scandal," 108, 109,
    261, 351
Sports Illustrated, 226
spousal assault, 149
Spouses' Allowance, 196
stakeholders, **496, 532**
Standing Committee on Finance,
    378, 587
Standing Committee on
    Government Operations and
    Estimates, 587
Standing Committee on Health,
    587
Standing Committee on Public
    Accounts, **587**

standing committees, **587**
Standing Joint Committee on
    Scrutiny of Regulations, **588**
Standing Joint Committee on the
    Scrutiny of Regulations,
    495, 562, 600
Standing Orders, 78, 581, **584**
Stanfield, Robert, 289, 313
staples theory, **48**
"star" candidate recruiting, 347
stare decisis, **612**
Stasiulis, Daiva, 132
state, changing role of, 487–91,
    491T
state-based analysis and
    approaches
    on bureaucratic power, 545B
    the Constitution and
        constitutional change,
        411
    the electorate, 355B
    on federalism, 440B
    on House of Commons, 603B
    on judicial process, 623B
    on media, 272B–273B
    on policymaking process,
        496B
    on political executive, 530B
    on school systems, 272B–273B
    on Senate, 603B
    the study of politics, **11**–12
    women's issues, 142B
    on working class divisions,
        174B
Statement of Reconciliation, 81
state of emergency, 501, **501**
state-owned corporations, 508.
    See also Crown corporations
state-owned lands, 508. *See also*
    Crown lands
Statistics Canada, 558, 560
Status Indians, 72
Status of Women, 143
Statute of Westminster (1931),
    34, 395, 399
"statutory appropriations," 554
Steelworkers, 223
Stevens, Sinclair, 289
St. Laurent, Louis, 310, 312, 315
Stop Spadina group, 370
Stowe, Emily, Dr., 138
strategic voting, 297B, 354–55

*The Structure of Canadian
    Government* (Mallory), 10
subcultures, **249**–51. *See also
    specific subcultures*
    class, 251
    ethnic, 250–51
    provincial/territorial, 250
    regional, 250
"sub-government," 374
subjective class, 161
Succession to the Throne Act,
    416
Suez Crisis, 35
suicide rate, 74
Sun News Network, 266
Sun newspapers, 266
"supraconstitution," 223
supremacy of Parliament, **27,
    570, 613**
Supreme Court Act, **396,** 416,
    620–21, 628–29
Supreme Court of Canada, 106,
    145, 151, 276, 413, 458, 460,
    467, 605, 618–23,
    622T–623T
    appeal process, 620F
    appeals heard, 621F
    Chaoulli case, 442, 463
    compared to JCPC, 427B–428B,
        619
    composition of, 629
    decisions based on Charter,
        171, 190, 404
    decisions related to labour, 171
    Patriation Reference case, 404
    Quebec Secession case, 422
    recent membership in,
        622T–623T
    reference cases, 618, 619B
    rulings on Aboriginals, 85
    Sioui case, 78
*Survey of the Contemporary Indians
    of Canada* (1966), 74
Suzuki, David, 247
symbolic response, 497–98
"symmetrical federalism," 422

Taras, David, 267
tariff policy, **54**
Task Force on Canadian Unity,
    107, 296
taxation, 56, 500–501, 501T

unions
   largest, in Canada, 170T
   middle class, 167
unitary government, 31
"United Alternative," 314
United Auto Workers, 222
United Church of Canada, 369
United Empire Loyalists, 237
   migration to Canada, 22
United Food and Commercial
   Workers, 223
United Nations, 205, 209, 210,
   380, 520
   peacekeeping, 211
   and Sandra Lovelace case, 77
   Universal Declaration on
      Human Rights, 456
United Nations Right-to-Food
   Envoy, 178
United States
   Canada susceptible to influence
      from, 203, 249
   economic influences, 211–17
   influences in defence, foreign,
      and border policies,
      208–11
   influences on Canadian
      culture, 224–28
United Steelworkers of America,
   222
Universal Declaration on Human
   Rights, 456
"universalism," 244
unpaid work, in the home, 147
unwritten constitution, 393
upper class, 163–66
   political subculture, 251
urban, defined, 184
urban Aboriginals, 68, 84
urban Canadian values, 188
urbanization, 186
urban populations, visible
   minorities, 121
urban/rural location, 184–89
USA Today, 227
U.S. Ballistic Missile Defence
   system, 578
U.S. imports of Canadian energy,
   222
U.S. laws extended to Canadian
   branch plants, 213

U.S public television stations,
   224

values, 352
   distinguishing between
      Canadian and American,
      241–48
   other statements of basic, 248
Veterans Affairs Canada, 376
Veterans' Ombudsman, 558
VIA Rail, 44, 495
Victoria Charter, 399, **403–4**
videos, U.S. influences, 226–27
Vietnam War, 210
Vimy Ridge monument, 33P
violence, 148–49
   historical incidents of, 358
violent strikes, 168
visible minorities, **119–21**
Viterra, foreign takeover, 216,
   216B
"voluntary cession," 70
voluntary group, 358
voluntary sector, **3, 374, 496**
Voluntary Sector Initiative, 496
voter choice, 349–55
voters level of information, 357
voters' list, 288–89
voter turnout rate, 356, 356F, 357
voting, 585–86
   economic, 354
   strategic, 354–55

W5, 267
wage and price controls, **320**
Wagner, Richard, 628
Wallin, Pamela, 605
Wall Street Journal, 262
War Measures Act, **104,** 240,
   272, 436–37, 456, 457,
   501
"war on terrorism," 272
"war room," 338
Wartime Taxation Agreements,
   437
watchdog agencies, 563–64
   auditor general, 564
   Information Commissioner,
      563
Watergate scandal in the United
   States, 298

Weber, Max, 4
Weiler, Paul, 626
welfare benefits, 173
welfare liberals, 319–20
welfare state, **174,** 312, **320, 432,**
   489
Wells, Clyde, 191, 407
west coast salmon, 221
Western alienation, **62, 250**
Western and Atlantic Accords,
   439
Western Climate Initiative,
   447
Western Economic Diversification
   Canada (WD), 60
Western industrialized
   democracies, 489
Westminster model of
   government, **27, 569**
White, Graham, 521
White Paper on Indians (1969),
   74
White Papers, 494, 529
Whitney, J.P., 99
Whittington, Michael, 523
Why We Act Like Canadians
   (Berton), 247
Williams, Danny, 59, 444
Wilson, Bertha, 145
Winnipeg General Strike, 168,
   240, 317, 358, 599
Wiseman, Nelson, 250
women
   constitutional equality, 246
   elected to House of Commons,
      140T, 141F
   employment issues, 145–47
   nominated candidates, 347
   as party leaders, 144
   representation in politics and
      government, 143–45
   voters, 152
women's centres, 150–51
women's franchise, 140T
women's groups, 150–51
Women's Legal Education and
   Action Fund (LEAF), 7
women's movement, **143–51**
Women's Program, 143
women's rights, 138–42
Woodsworth, J.S., 311